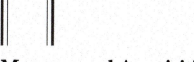

Mergers and Acquisitions

Get started with your **Connected eBook**

Redeem your code below to access the **ebook** with search, highlighting, and note-taking capabilities; **case briefing** and **outlining** tools to support efficient learning; and more.

1. Go to www.casebookconnect.com
2. Enter your access code in the box and click **Register**
3. Follow the steps to complete your registration and verify your email address

ACCESS CODE:
Scratch off with care.

If you have already registered at CasebookConnect.com, simply log into your account and redeem additional access codes from your Dashboard.

Is this a used book? Access code already redeemed? Purchase a digital version at **CasebookConnect.com/catalog**.

If you purchased a digital bundle with additional components, your additional access codes will appear below.

"I liked being able to search quickly while in class."

"Being able to highlight and easily create case briefs was a fantastic resource and time saver for me!"

"I loved it! I was able to study on the go and create a more effective outline."

For technical support, please visit https://support.aspenpublishing.com

10051631-0003

ASPEN CASEBOOK SERIES

Mergers and Acquisitions: Cases, Materials, and Problems

Fifth Edition

Therese H. Maynard
Leonard Cohen Chair for Law and Business
Founder, Transactional Lawyering Institute
Loyola Law School, Loyola Marymount University, Los Angeles

To contact Customer Service, e-mail customer.service@aspenpublishing.com, call 1-800-950-5259, or mail correspondence to:

>   Aspen Publishing
>   Attn: Order Department
>   PO Box 990
>   Frederick, MD 21705

Printed in the United States of America.

2 3 4 5 6 7 8 9 0

ISBN 978-1-5438-1973-1

Library of Congress Cataloging-in-Publication Data

Names: Maynard, Therese H., author.
Title: Mergers and acquisitions : cases, materials, and problems / Therese
  H. Maynard (Leonard Cohen Chair for Law and Business, Founder,
  Transactional Lawyering Institute, Loyola Law School, Loyola Marymount
  University, Los Angeles).
Description: Fifth edition. | Frederick, MD: Aspen Publishing, [2021] | Series:
  Aspen casebook series | Includes bibliographical references and index. |
  Summary: "This is a casebook for use in upper-level mergers and
  acquisitions law course"—Provided by publisher.
Identifiers: LCCN 2020053080 (print) | LCCN 2020053081 (ebook) |
  ISBN 9781543819731 (hardcover) | ISBN 9781543831177 (ebook)
Subjects: LCSH: Consolidation and merger of corporations—United States. |
  LCGFT: Casebooks (Law)
Classification: LCC KF1477 .M329 2021 (print) | LCC KF1477 (ebook) |
  DDC 346.73/06626—dc23
LC record available at https://lccn.loc.gov/2020053080
LC ebook record available at https://lccn.loc.gov/2020053081

About Aspen Publishing

Aspen Publishing is a leading provider of educational content and digital learning solutions to law schools in the U.S. and around the world. Aspen provides best-in-class solutions for legal education through authoritative textbooks, written by renowned authors, and breakthrough products such as Connected eBooks, Connected Quizzing, and PracticePerfect.

The Aspen Casebook Series (famously known among law faculty and students as the "red and black" casebooks) encompasses hundreds of highly regarded textbooks in more than eighty disciplines, from large enrollment courses, such as Torts and Contracts to emerging electives such as Sustainability and the Law of Policing. Study aids such as the *Examples & Explanations* and the *Emanuel Law Outlines* series, both highly popular collections, help law students master complex subject matter.

Major products, programs, and initiatives include:

- **Connected eBooks** are enhanced digital textbooks and study aids that come with a suite of online content and learning tools designed to maximize student success. Designed in collaboration with hundreds of faculty and students, the Connected eBook is a significant leap forward in the legal education learning tools available to students.

- **Connected Quizzing** is an easy-to-use formative assessment tool that tests law students' understanding and provides timely feedback to improve learning outcomes. Delivered through CasebookConnect.com, the learning platform already used by students to access their Aspen casebooks, Connected Quizzing is simple to implement and integrates seamlessly with law school course curricula.

- **PracticePerfect** is a visually engaging, interactive study aid to explain commonly encountered legal doctrines through easy-to-understand animated videos, illustrative examples, and numerous practice questions. Developed by a team of experts, PracticePerfect is the ideal study companion for today's law students.

- The **Aspen Learning Library** enables law schools to provide their students with access to the most popular study aids on the market across all of their courses. Available through an annual subscription, the online library consists of study aids in e-book, audio, and video formats with full text search, note-taking, and highlighting capabilities.

- Aspen's **Digital Bookshelf** is an institutional-level online education bookshelf, consolidating everything students and professors need to ensure success. This program ensures that every student has access to affordable course materials from day one.

- **Leading Edge** is a community centered on thinking differently about legal education and putting those thoughts into actionable strategies. At the core of the program is the Leading Edge Conference, an annual gathering of legal education thought leaders looking to pool ideas and identify promising directions of exploration.

To my Mom and Dad, Anne and Bill Huber,
for always believing in me

and

to my four daughters, who are the source of all inspiration
in my life — Catherine, Hayley Del, Annie, and Remington

Summary of Contents

Contents

|| 2 ||

Corporate Formalities: The Mechanics of Structuring Acquisition Transactions   61

▐ 3 ▐

Scope of Successor Liability: Transferring the Assets (and Liabilities) of Target Co. to Bidder Co.   241

|| 4 ||

Selected Federal Securities Law Provisions that Apply to Negotiated Business Combinations   279

|| 5 ||

Negotiating and Documenting the Transaction   321

❚ 6 ❚

Federal Regulation of Stock Purchases: Tender Offers and the Williams Act   415

❚ 7 ❚

Fiduciary Duty Law: The Responsibilities of Boards of Directors, Senior Executive Officers, and Controlling Shareholders   489

|| 8 ||

Tax, Accounting, and Antitrust Considerations Related to Mergers and Acquisition Transactions

Preface

While the fourth edition of this casebook was written as the global economy was continuing to recover from the Great Recession, this fifth edition was written as the world grapples with the economic uncertainty resulting from the onset of the COVID-19 pandemic. Notwithstanding all of the economic hardship suffered over the past decade, these global events have only served to further intensify interest in, and attention on, the topic of this book: the *law of mergers and acquisitions*. While in the past, this subject may not have been offered on a regular basis, law schools today are facing increasing pressure to provide comprehensive treatment of this important area of modern corporate transactional law practice. Recognizing the increasing importance of this subject within the modern law school curriculum, this casebook is designed to meet the needs of the upper-division law student who seeks to master the basic principles that form the framework of the ever-evolving body of law related to mergers and acquisitions (M&A).

Toward that end, the fifth edition of this casebook continues to be organized based on the fundamental precept that the law student who takes this course is curious about this subject, but generally has limited familiarity with the business world of mergers and acquisitions. Therefore, the fifth edition carries forward the essential goal of the earlier editions, which is to introduce the topics traditionally covered in the study of M&A law in terms that are accessible to the uninitiated law student, and further, to stimulate the student's curiosity in this subject by demystifying what is often an intimidating and overwhelmingly jargon-laden body of law. As such, this fifth edition continues to eschew string citations to the ever-growing body of literature in the area of M&A law, in favor of a more accessible style that breaks the law of mergers and acquisitions down into manageable chunks. In both the selection and editing of the cases and other materials to be included in this edition, the guiding principle has been to present the material in a manner that will enable the law student to master the fundamental principles of M&A law and to appreciate the public policies that underlie this legal framework.

The other, closely related objective of my casebook is to present the relevant legal and business principles of M&A transactions in a manner that will allow law students to hit the ground running when they graduate and enter the practice of business law, which I presume will include representing business interests in M&A deal-making. To this end, the fifth edition continues to be designed so that the law student will appreciate the inherent dynamics of M&A

transactions and will be able to become an effective junior member of a law firm whose practice includes representing clients in planning and structuring their M&A transactions. As part of this effort, this casebook endeavors to instill in the law student a sense of what it takes to be a good business lawyer in the modern practice of corporate law in a transactional setting.[1]

A big part of the modern practice of business law involves analyzing statutes and advising business clients about how to structure their business and financial affairs in order to comply with the mandate of the relevant statute(s). As was the case when I wrote the earlier editions, I (regrettably) continue to believe that, for many law students today, their law school education does not provide them with rigorous and systematic exposure to statutory analysis. This casebook attempts to address this void, primarily by requiring students to analyze problems in light of the relevant state and/or federal statutes. In particular, the problems in Chapter 2, which I consider to be the very heart of the casebook, require the students to work through the terms of various statutes in order to understand what must be done in order to validly consummate the transaction and also to understand why the law imposes these requirements. In so doing, the law student will develop a busines and legal context for understanding the materials to be covered in *all* of the remaining chapters, as well as a perspective that allows the student to better appreciate how to *integrate* all of these materials as part of planning an M&A transaction.

Along these same lines, another common complaint (made, most often in my experience, by experienced lawyers who work with recent law school graduates) is that students fail to appreciate the important role that statutes play in the modern practice of business law. The most common complaint is that today's law students tend to view statutes as prescriptive, whose literal terms are to be mechanically complied with—almost like following the steps in a recipe. As a result, students often fail to appreciate that literal or strict compliance with statutory requirements may yield a harsh or anomalous result. In these cases, students are ill equipped to analyze the proper course in order to avoid inequitable results. As was the case with prior editions, the problems and other materials in this fifth edition of my casebook are designed to fill this gap. Most importantly, I require my students to buy or have access to a statutory supplement that includes relevant provisions of the Delaware and California corporations codes as well as the ABA's Model Business Corporation Act (along with selected provisions of the federal securities laws that are relevant to M&A transactions). Like the earlier editions, the fifth edition includes numerous problems that require the students to work through the various requirements imposed by these statutes. In the process, students analyze the differences (if any) in the results obtained under these statutes. Where there are differences, the materials in the casebook are designed to promote class discussion that explores the public policy premise(s) that lead the legislature (or other state or federal regulators, as the case may be) to opt for a particular statutory treatment.

---

[1] As for my understanding of the qualities that I consider important to being a good business lawyer, *see* Therese Maynard, *Teaching Professionalism: The Lawyer as a Professional*, 34 Georgia Law Review 895, 909-920 (2000).

For all of these reasons, the fifth edition continues to be reflective of the modern practice of M&A law, both from a transactional perspective as well as from the litigator's perspective. Like many other areas of business law, M&A law comes from the courts, legislatures, regulatory agencies, and the continuing evolution of deal-making practices in our modern business world. While the book includes many cases, the fifth edition of this casebook continues to be designed for use in conjunction with a supplemental text that includes the relevant statutes and regulations. The cases included in the casebook then serve to illustrate how the judges endeavor to interpret (and apply) the statutes and regulations to further shape our understanding of M&A law.

In addition to a heavy emphasis on the use of problems to illustrate the planning of modern M&A transactions, this fifth edition also incorporates a heavy emphasis on the following themes in its presentation of the law of mergers and acquisitions. First, unlike the focus of many other casebooks dealing with mergers and acquisitions, the fifth edition of this casebook continues to emphasize the role of the lawyer as transaction planner. Second, as part of this focus on transaction planning, my casebook emphasizes the increasing importance of fiduciary duty law over the past thirty-five years and its all-important role in guiding the transaction planner in structuring M&A deals. Starting with the problems in Chapter 2 and continuing throughout the remaining chapters as part of our analysis of the role of fiduciary duty law in M&A deals, this casebook is constantly asking the law student to consider the corporate governance implications of M&A transactions. Most notably, the fifth edition asks the students to critically assess the relative balance of power among the shareholders, the board of directors, and the senior executive officers—most importantly, the role of the modern chief executive officer—a balance that has been sorely tested in the years since the first edition was published. Indeed, Chapter 7 of the fifth edition (dealing with fiduciary duty obligations) has been updated to address Delaware case law developments in recent years and the public policy implications resulting from the Great Recession as well as the economic and social repercussions of the ongoing global pandemic (as of this writing in Fall 2020).

Finally, and most importantly, these corporate governance themes are presented in the context of M&A activity that occurs on *both* Wall Street *and* on Main Street. That is to say, this book emphasizes not only the type of high-profile M&A transactions that the law student is likely to read about on the front pages of the WALL STREET JOURNAL, but also provides comprehensive treatment of the sale of a closely held business, the type of transaction that continues to form the basis for the M&A practice of many of today's transactional lawyers. This approach is reflected in the two "Deal Stories" that are first introduced in Chapter 1 and then referred to throughout the materials in the remaining chapters. In this fifth edition, I have revised Chapter 1 to provide real-world updates to the two "Deal Stories" that continue to be the focus of the casebook—AT&T's acquisition of DirecTV and Google's acquisition of Nest Labs—two M&A deals that originally grabbed headlines in the financial press and (based on events that have transpired since the last edition) are deals that continue to be of interest to the investing public.

As was the case with the earlier editions, the general convention followed in this edition is to omit case and statute citations from the principal cases as well as quoted excerpts from other materials. In addition, most footnotes have been omitted without indication in the original case or other text, but those footnotes that remain do retain their original numbering.

November 2020

Therese H. Maynard
Loyola Law School
Los Angeles, California

Acknowledgments

I am indebted to many persons for helping me give birth to this labor of love. This project never would have been conceived without many generations of my students who impressed on me the need to write a casebook that facilitated the law student's ability to understand and master the law of mergers and acquisitions. To those many students of mine at Loyola Law School-Los Angeles who suffered through various iterations of teaching materials as I worked my way through various drafts of this casebook to produce the first edition and also to those who suffered through the various ideas that I experimented with in writing the subsequent editions (including this fifth edition), I am eternally grateful for your patience, understanding, and feedback. This project is truly the better for having the benefit of your suggestions and guidance over the years.

This book was inspired not only by my students and others in the legal academy, but also by the many fine business lawyers who practice in the area of M&A law. While there are many who gave me the benefit of their sage counsel over the years, there are several who were instrumental in guiding me toward the goal of educating the law student to be prepared to hit the ground running on graduating law school and embarking on the practice of M&A law. I am particularly grateful to Greg Noell, Mark Bonenfant, Keith Bishop, Jennifer Campbell, Shannon Treviño, and most importantly, my husband, Philip Maynard, who is the best corporate lawyer I know.

Over the years, many research assistants have made valuable contributions to the development and refinement of this casebook, which I consider to still be a "work-in-progress." I want to express particular thanks to Alex Shukman, Ann Carey Camacho, Gregory Ezor, Arif Sikora, April Ho, and Clint Stiffler for their invaluable help in writing the first and second editions. With respect to the third edition, I am grateful for the research and editorial contributions of Sean Montgomery, and I also want to thank Matthew Giovanucci for his insightful comments in preparing the fourth edition. And, finally, with respect to the fifth edition, words can never express my appreciation and gratitude for the extraordinary efforts of my research assistant, Lauren Saylor, whose thoughtful editorial contributions to this edition were incredibly valuable.

As I finalize this fifth edition of my casebook, I want to acknowledge the unwavering support of my editors at Aspen Publishers, Darren Kelly and Paul Sobel, who have worked with me on prior editions as well. Over the years, their editorial advice and thoughtful feedback has enriched the process of writing this casebook and I truly value them as colleagues.

I also want to gratefully acknowledge the permission of the following publishers, authors, and periodicals to reprint excerpts from their publications:

Afsharipour, Afra, *Transforming the Allocation of Deal Risk Through Reverse Termination Fees.* Vanderbilt Law Review, Vol. 63 (2010). Vanderbilt University Law School. Reprinted with permission from the author.

American Bar Association's Committee on Corporate Laws, ABA Section of Business Law, *Changes in the MBCA.* Business Law, Vol. 65 (2010). Copyright © 2010 by the American Bar Association. Reprinted with permission. All rights reserved.

Bainbridge, Stephen M., *Exclusive Merger Agreements and Lock-Ups in Negotiated Corporate Acquisitions.* Minnesota Law Review, Vol. 75 (1990). University of Minnesota Law School. Reprinted with permission from the author.

Bainbridge, Stephen M., *Unocal at 20: Director Primacy in Corporate Takeovers.* Delaware Journal of Corporate Law, Vol. 31 (2006). Widener University Delaware Law School. Reprinted with permission from the author.

Bishop, Gregory, *Changed Circumstances or Buyer's Remorse?* Business Law Today, Vol. 11, No. 4 (March/April 2002). Copyright ©2002 by the American Bar Association. Reprinted with permission. All rights reserved.

Bishop, Keith Paul, *The War Between the States—Delaware's Supreme Court Ignores California's "Outreach" Statute.* Insights, Vol. 19 (July 2005). Wolters Kluwer Law & Business. Copyright © 2005.

Blomberg, Jeffrey, *Private Equity Transactions: Understanding Some Fundamental Principles.* Business Law Today, Vol. 17, No. 3 (January/February 2008). Copyright © 2008 by the American Bar Association. Reprinted with permission. All rights reserved.

Boch, Brian R., et. al., *Poison Pills During the COVID-19 Pandemic.* Jenner & Block newsletter dated May 11, 2020. Copyright © 2020.

Boczko, Ian and John L. Robinson, *The Maturing Market for Representation and Warranty Insurance.* Wachtell, Lipton, Rosen & Katz (April 5, 2018). Reprinted with permission.

Byrd, Francis H., *Dual Class Share Structures: The Next Campaign.* Harvard Law School Forum on Corporate Governance and Financial Regulation (September 16, 2012). Reprinted with permission from the author.

Campbell, Rutherford B., Jr., *Fair Value at Fair Price in Corporate Acquisitions.* North Carolina Law Review, Vol. 78 (1999). University of North Carolina School of Law. Copyright © 1999.

Campbell, Rutherford B., Jr., *The Impact of Modern Finance Theory in Acquisition Cases.* Syracuse Law Review, Vol. 53 (2003). Syracuse University College of Law. Copyright © 2003.

Cole, Thomas A. and Jack B. Jacobs, *Financial Advisor Conflicts in M&A Transactions.* Sidley Perspectives on M&A and Corporate Governance (Sidley Austin LLP law firm memo dated February 2016). Reprinted by permission.

Cowles, Julia, Julie Ryan, and Charles Ortmeyer, *Selected 2011 Developments in Corporate Law.* 2012 Annual Review, State Bar of California, Business Law News. Reprinted with permission from the authors.

Ferrillo, Paul and Joseph T. Verdesca, *M&A Representations and Warranties Insurance: Tips for Buyers and Sellers.* Harvard Law School Forum on

Corporate Governance and Financial Regulation (May 1, 2013). Reprinted with permission from the authors.

Gilson, Ronald J., *Unocal Fifteen Years Later (and What We Can Do About It)*. Delaware Journal of Corporate Law, Vol. 26 (2001). Delaware Law School. Reprinted with permission.

Grant, M. Duncan and Phillip T. Mellett, *Delaware Supreme Court Upholds Caremark Standard for Director Oversight Liability; Clarifies Duty of Good Faith*. Originally published in Pepper Hamilton LLP law firm memo, dated November 21, 2006. Reprinted with permission from the authors.

Hamilton, Robert and Richard Booth, BUSINESS BASICS FOR LAW STUDENTS (4th edition). Wolters Kluwer Law & Business. Copyright © 2006.

Johnston, Andrew M., et. al., *Section 251(h) of the DGCL: Year in Review*. Insights, Vol. 28, No. 9 (September 2014). Wolters Kluwer Law & Business. Copyright © 2014.

Kirkland & Ellis LLP, *M&A Update: Break-Up Fees—Picking Your Number*, law firm memo dated September 6, 2012. Reprinted with permission.

Klein, Spencer D. and Michael G. O'Bryan, *Recent Cases Remind M&A Participants of When Disclosure of Merger Negotiations is Required*. Morrison & Foerster LLP law firm memo dated July 14, 2010. Reprinted with permission from the authors.

Kotler, Meredith E. and Marlie McDonald, *Chancery Court Rejects Disclosure-Only Settlement, Suggests in Future Such Settlements Will Be Approved Only in Narrow Circumstances*. Cleary Gottlieb Steen & Hamilton LLP law firm memo dated January 25, 2016. Reprinted with permission.

Lehot, Louis, et. al., *The Return of the Poison Pill—Lessons Learned in 2010 From the Selectica and Barnes & Noble Cases*. Insights, Vol. 24 (December 2010). Wolters Kluwer Law & Business. Copyright © 2010.

Mirvis, Theodore and Paul K. Rowe, *Settlement of Del Monte Buyout Litigation Highlights Risks Where Target Advisors Seek a Buyer-Financing Role*. Wachtell, Lipton, Rosen, & Katz LLP law firm memo dated October 7, 2011. Reprinted with permission from the authors.

Mirvis, Theodore N., et. al., *Buyout and Deal Protections Enjoined Due to Conflicted Advisor to Clients*. Wachtell, Lipton, Rosen, & Katz LLP law firm memo dated February 15, 2011. Reprinted with authors' permission.

Mirvis, Theodore N., et. al., *Delaware Supreme Court Rejects Claims Against Directors Challenging Sale Process*. Wachtell, Lipton, Rosen, & Katz LLP law firm memo dated March 26, 2009. Reprinted with author's permission.

Neimeth, Clifford E., *Pending DGCL Section 251 Amendment Should Lead to Increase in Negotiated Tender Offers*. Greenberg Taurig LLP law firm memo dated May 29, 2013. Reprinted with permission from the author.

Nixon Peabody, *2012 MAC Survey*. Nixon Peabody LLP, Attorneys at Law. Copyright © 2012. Reprinted with permission.

Pell, Owen and Paul Carberry, *Delaware Court Interprets Material Adverse Effect Clause to Bar Hexion and Apollo from Abandoning Huntsman Deal*. White & Case LLP law firm memo, October 2008). Reprinted with permission.

Ropes and Gray, LLP *Amendments to Delaware General Corporation Law Will Affect Appraisal Actions*, law firm memo dated June 20, 2016. Reprinted with permission.

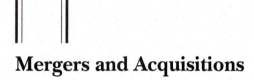

Mergers and Acquisitions

|| 1 ||

Introduction to Business Acquisitions

A.   *What Business Activity Is Covered by M&A Law?*

Mergers and acquisitions (M&A) law is *not* a discrete body of law. Rather, M&A law refers to a particular kind of business activity whereby one business decides to take control of — that is, to purchase, to acquire — the income-producing operations of some other business entity. Hence, M&A is largely about combining previously independent, freestanding businesses into one business organization.

For reasons that are described in more detail in Chapter 2 regarding *interspecies mergers*, this casebook will generally assume that the two businesses that decide to combine together are organized as corporations, although business combinations involving other types of business entities, such as combining two limited liability companies (LLCs), are also possible. In order to keep things simple and allow us to master the basic principles, our study of M&A law will generally be limited to business combinations involving corporations organized under modern state corporation codes.

In the terminology of these modern corporation codes, the companies that plan to combine are usually referred to as the *constituent corporations*. As we shall see, typically one of these constituent corporations plans to acquire control over the business operations of the other when the transaction is consummated. In our study of these transactions, we will usually refer to the acquiring corporation as the Bidder Company (Bidder Co. or Bidder), and the corporation to be acquired will generally be referred to as the Target Company (Target Co. or Target).

M&A is an important recurring part of the business world. Although each deal is unique, there are certain kinds of business combinations that are staples in the daily work of lawyers who practice M&A law. In order to give you a sense of the range of the deals that we will analyze in our study of M&A law, as well as a sense of the problems that M&A lawyers are asked to address in their daily practice, the next section tells the story of two deals that attracted attention in the financial press.

As we go through the materials in the following chapters, we will return to analyze the various legal issues raised by these acquisition transactions. These two stories are important because, for the most part, they include facts that raise the legal issues that we will study in the remaining chapters. These stories provide a real-world anchor in which to address the more abstract principles and legal rules that are the core focus of this casebook. These stories also reflect the time frame that is inherent in doing any M&A deal. The reason that this time frame has grown to be the convention in M&A deals will only become apparent as we address the topics in the remaining chapters. The legal rules and doctrines we will study have clearly shaped the process of—and timetable for—doing the deals that are described in these two stories, a point that can truly be appreciated only at the end of our study of M&A law.

B.   *Two Different Stories—Two Different Deals*

1.   The Story of AT&T's Acquisition of DirecTV

As early as May 1, 2014, the financial press was reporting that telecommunications "titan AT&T has reportedly reached out to satellite giant DirecTV about a possible merger that would reshape the TV business at a time of rapid change in the industry." Sam Gustin, *AT&T Mulls $40 Billion Merger with DirecTV*, TIME, INC., May 1, 2014, *available at:* http://time.com/83735/att-mulls-40-bn-merger-with -DirecTV. In the first part of 2014, DirecTV stock was trading in the mid-to-high $70s on the Nasdaq Stock Market, yielding the company a market capitalization of approximately $40 billion, given that there were then approximately 502 million outstanding shares of DirecTV common stock. Rumors circulating at the time indicated that DirecTV would be open to being acquired and that talks between the two companies had intensified since the announcement a few months earlier (in February 2014) that Comcast Corp. intended to acquire Time Warner Cable Inc. in a deal valued at $45 billion.

As of May 7, "people familiar" with the parties' negotiations said that DirecTV was "working with advisers including Goldman Sachs Group Inc." as part of its efforts to evaluate a deal with AT&T, while at the same time, DirecTV's chief executive officer (CEO), Mike White, noted on a conference call with analysts that recent media reports regarding possible transactions involving DirecTV were not "based on official sources of information" and that he would have no further comment (nor take questions) on these reports, indicating that "we don't view it as productive to speculate about alternative business combinations which may or may not occur." As of the date that these comments were made, DirecTV shares were trading at $88 a share. Thomas Gryta and Dana Cimilluca, *DirecTV Working with Goldman, Advisers on Possible AT&T Deal*, WALL STREET JOURNAL, May 7, 2014, *available at:* http://www.wsj.com/news/articles/ SB10001424052702304655304579548162578579216. As is customary in this kind of Wall Street deal-making, the pending acquisition proposal was given the code name "Project Star." *See* Rebecca Bennett, *AT&T Announces Deal to*

Acquire DirecTV, May 18, 2014, Fox59, *available at:* http://fox59.com/2014/05/18/att-announces-deal-to-acquire-DirecTV.

A few days later, the W*all Street Journal* reported that AT&T was close to striking a deal to acquire DirecTV at a price reported to be "in the low to mid-nineties per share" in a deal "that would involve a mix of cash and AT&T stock." Dana Cimillucca, Shalini Ramachandran, and Thomas Gryta, *available at: AT&T Could Strike $50 Billion Deal for DirecTV*, WALL STREET JOURNAL, May 12, 2014, *available at:* http://www.wsj.com/articles/SB10001424052702303851804 579558232282287084. This same W*all Street Journal* article reported that AT&T was "expected to pay for any deal mainly with stock," which would have "the benefit of limiting its borrowings and thus helping protect its credit rating. But the more stock it issues, the greater its dividend obligations. . . ." However, it was also noted that a takeover of DirecTV would have the benefit of boosting "the flow of cash that AT&T could use to pay its dividend." *Id.* These rumors of a takeover of DirecTV by AT&T "have sent DirecTV shares up about 12 percent this month [May 2014]." David Gelles, *AT&T Courts Satellite TV with an Eye on Growth*, NEW YORK TIMES, May 12, 2014, *available at:* http://dealbook.nytimes.com/2014/05/12/att-said-to-be-in-talks-for-DirecTV/.

At the time of these ongoing negotiations, AT&T's annual dividend stood at $1.84 a share, creating an annual dividend payment of "about $9.7 billion last year—and Wall Street is worried about the company's ability to keep it going." Thomas Gryta, *AT&T Could Bolster Its Dividend with DirecTV Deal*, WALL STREET JOURNAL, May 16, 2014, *availalable at:* http://www.wsj.com/articles/SB1000142 4052702304908304579565981072591464. For its part, "AT&T has insisted that the dividend is sacred and that it would shed assets to fund" payment of the dividend if it should become necessary. *Id.* AT&T's response with respect to its dividend policy came as no surprise because the $1.84 dividend was widely regarded as a "big reason for investors to buy AT&T stock." *Id.* Without a doubt, AT&T's dividend policy definitely played a prominent role in the parties' discussions as to the right mix of cash and AT&T stock to be used to fund its acquisition of DirecTV. AT&T contemplated taking on debt in order to finance the cash component of the purchase price, but taking on too much debt would likely put AT&T's credit rating at risk. *Id.* As others pointed out, though, "AT&T, which is currently worth $185 billion, can definitely afford the deal." Sam Gustin, *AT&T Aiming at Comcast with Planned $50 Billion DirecTV Merger*, TIME, INC., May 13, 2014, *available at:* http://time.com/97045/att-DirecTV-merger-talks.

Following these May 12 press accounts of ongoing talks between AT&T and DirecTV, it was reported that "the two sides [were] actively working toward an announcement" and that "Mike White, DirecTV's chief executive, is not expected to step down if the deal goes through." Sydney Ember, *AT&T Pursues DirecTV*, NEW YORK TIMES, May 13, 2014, *available at:* http://dealbook.nytimes.com/2014/05/13/morning-agenda-att-courts-DirecTV. On Sunday, May 18, 2014, several news outlets reported that the boards of AT&T and DirecTV were scheduled to meet that day "to approve a combination of the two companies," with a deal expected to be announced as early as that Sunday afternoon. Thomas Gryta, Shalini Ramachandran, and Dana Cimillucca, *AT&T, DirecTV to Meet Sunday to Approve Deal to Merge*, WALL STREET JOURNAL, May 18, 2014, *available at:* http://www.wsj.com/articles/SB10001424052702304908304 579568590603893048. And that Sunday evening, the two companies issued a joint press release announcing that AT&T and DirecTV "have entered into a definitive agreement under which AT&T will acquire DirecTV in a stock-and-cash transaction for $95 a share." The $95 a share purchase price was made up of $28.50 per share in cash and $66.50 per share in AT&T stock. "In the stock portion of the deal, [DirecTV shareholders] will receive 1.905 AT&T shares if AT&T's stock price is below $34.90 at closing or 1.724 AT&T shares if its stock price is above $38.58. If AT&T's stock price at closing is between $34.90 and $38.58, DirecTV shareholders will receive between 1.724 share and 1.905 shares of AT&T stock, equal to $66.50 in value." Roger Yu, *AT&T Buys DirecTV for $48.5 Billion*, USA TODAY, May 19, 2014, *available at:* http://www.usatoday .com/story/news/usanow/2014/05/18/att-buys-DirecTV/9247795. Based on this exchange ratio, the deal was worth $48.5 billion — "about 30% higher than where DirecTV shares were trading before word of a potential deal began to emerge" and will leave existing shareholders of DirecTV owning "15 to 16 per-cent of the combined company after closing, which is expected [to occur] in a year's time." Michael J. de la Merced and David Gelles, *AT&T to Buy DirecTV for $48.5 Billion in Move to Expand Clout*, NEW YORK TIMES, May 18, 2014, *available at:* http://dealbook.nytimes.com/2014/05/18/att-to-buy-DirecTV-for-48-5-billion. In order to finance the cash portion of the purchase price, AT&T planned to use its cash resources on hand along with the sale of some of its non-core assets and some borrowing. The terms of the deal were unanimously approved by the boards of directors of both companies.

What was the business justification for the parties' decision to combine together? According to the parties' joint press release,

> The transaction combines complementary strengths to create a unique new competitor with unprecedented capabilities in mobility, video and broadband services.
>
> DIRECTV is the premier pay TV provider in the United States and Latin America, with a high-quality customer base, the best selection of programming, the best technology for delivering and viewing high-quality video on any device and the best customer satisfaction among major U.S. cable and satellite TV provid-ers. AT&T has a best-in-class nationwide mobile network and a high-speed broad-band network that will cover 70 million customer locations with the broadband expansion enabled by this transaction.
>
> The combined company will be a content distribution leader across mobile, video and broadband platforms. This distribution scale will position the company to better meet consumers' future viewing and programming preferences, whether traditional pay TV, on-demand video services like Netflix or Hulu streamed over a broadband connection (mobile or fixed) or a combination of viewing preferences on any screen.
>
> The transaction enables the combined company to offer consumers bundles that include video, high-speed broadband and mobile services using all of its sales channels—AT&T's 2,300 retail stores and thousands of authorized dealers and agents of both companies nationwide.
>
> "This is a unique opportunity that will redefine the video entertainment industry and create a company able to offer new bundles and deliver content to consumers across multiple screens—mobile devices, TVs, laptops, cars and even airplanes. At the same time, it creates immediate and long-term value for our shareholders," said Randall Stephenson, AT&T Chairman and CEO. "DIRECTV is the best option for us because they have the premier brand in pay TV, the best

content relationships, and a fast-growing Latin American business. DIRECTV is a great fit with AT&T and together we'll be able to enhance innovation and provide customers new competitive choices for what they want in mobile, video and broadband services. We look forward to welcoming DIRECTV's talented people to the AT&T family."

"This compelling and complementary combination will bring significant benefits to all consumers, shareholders and DIRECTV employees," said Mike White, president and CEO of DIRECTV. "U.S. consumers will have access to a more competitive bundle; shareholders will benefit from the enhanced value of the combined company; and employees will have the advantage of being part of a stronger, more competitive company, well positioned to meet the evolving video and broadband needs of the 21st century marketplace."

DIRECTV has premier content, particularly live sports programming. It has the exclusive pay TV rights to NFL SUNDAY TICKET that provides every out-of-market game, every Sunday afternoon, on TV, laptops and mobile devices. The new AT&T will be better positioned to develop unique content offerings for consumers through, among other initiatives, AT&T's joint venture with The Chernin Group. Today, DIRECTV's content ownership includes ROOT SPORTS Networks and minority stakes in the Game Show Network, MLB Network, NHL Network and the Sundance Channel.

DIRECTV will continue to be headquartered in El Segundo, California, after the deal closes. . . .

AT&T expects the deal to be accretive on a free cash flow per share and adjusted EPS [earnings per share] basis within the first 12 months after closing.

The combination provides significant opportunities for operating efficiencies. AT&T expects cost synergies to exceed $1.6 billion on an annual basis by year three after closing. The expected synergies are primarily driven by increased scale in video.

Along with DIRECTV's current strong cash flows, this transaction is expected to support future investment in growth opportunities and shareholder returns.

The combination diversifies AT&T's revenue mix and provides numerous growth opportunities as it dramatically increases video revenues, accelerates broadband growth and significantly expands revenues from outside the United States. Given the structure of this transaction, which includes AT&T stock consideration as part of the deal and the monetization of non-core assets, AT&T expects to continue to maintain the strongest balance sheet in the industry following the transaction close.

The merger is subject to approval by DIRECTV shareholders and review by the U.S. Federal Communications Commission, [antitrust regulators at the] U.S. Department of Justice, a few U.S. states and some Latin American countries. The transaction is expected to close within approximately 12 months.

Joint Press Release, issued May 18, 2014. *See AT&T to Acquire DIRECTV, available at:* http://news.DirecTV.com/2014/05/18/DirecTV-att-merger-press-release.

As summarized by one Wall Street observer, by acquiring DirecTV, the country's biggest satellite television provider, "AT&T would become the country's second-biggest pay TV provider, behind only Comcast," and "AT&T would gain more clout in negotiating with media companies as it increasingly focuses on video offerings." *Deal of the Week: AT&T to Buy DirecTV for $48.5B*, PILLARS OF WALL STREET, May 18, 2014, *available at:* http://pillarsofwallstreet.com/wp-content/uploads/2013/02/5.18.14-ATT-to-Buy-DirecTV-for-48.5B.pdf. For its part, DirecTV, while having the second-largest pay-TV subscriber base in the

United States, nonetheless "lacks a competitive broadband-Internet offering of its own. AT&T is moving ahead with its own broadband plans, but DirecTV's satellite-TV business would be a major prize." Sam Gustin, *AT&T Aiming at Comcast with Planned $50 Billion DirecTV Merger*, TIME, INC., May 13, 2014, *available at:* http://time.com/97045/att-directv-merger-talks.

At a special meeting of DirecTV shareholders held on September 25, 2014, the merger with AT&T was overwhelmingly approved. According to the company's September 25 press release, which was issued following adjournment of the meeting, "more than 99 percent of votes cast were in favor of adoption of the [merger agreement with AT&T], representing 77 percent of all outstanding shares." DirecTV Press Release, issued Sept. 25, 2014, *DirecTV Stockholders Approve Merger with AT&T Inc.*, *available at:* http://www.finances.com/company-news/18251-directv-stockholders-approve-merger-with-att-inc.htm. Although the deal received the requisite approval of DirecTV's shareholders, the deal did not close at the conclusion of the shareholder meeting. Instead, the deal remained "subject to regulatory review and approval including [review and approval from] the U.S. Department of Justice and the U.S. Federal Communications Commission [FCC] for required transfer of licenses as well as approval by certain international regulatory bodies." *Id.* Accordingly, the parties estimated that the transaction would "be completed [sometime] in the first half of 2015." *Id.*

As it turns out, the transaction did not close until July 24, 2015, after it received approval by the FCC, which was the last of the required regulatory approvals that were a condition to AT&T's obligation to close on the transaction with DirecTV. These regulatory approvals presented significant challenges to getting the deal done, as AT&T had already learned in connection with its prior acquisition proposals, most notably it's aborted bid three years earlier to acquire T-Mobile USA, Inc., another wireless phone carrier. In March 2011, AT&T announced its $39 billion offer to acquire T-Mobile. However, that deal had been fiercely opposed by anti-trust regulators, primarily on the grounds that the proposed acquisition "would have cut down on the number of wireless phone service providers." Michael J. de la Merced and David Gelles, *AT&T to Buy DirecTV for $48.5 Billion in Move to Expand Clout*, NEW YORK TIMES, May 18, 2014, *available at:* http://dealbook.nytimes.com/2014/05/18/att-to-buy-DirecTV-for-48-5-billion. Following this failed acquisition effort, AT&T pivoted away from growth by expansion within the wireless phone industry and turned its attention to the satellite TV industry, ultimately settling on the acquisition of DirecTV.

In contrast to the struggle that AT&T faced with its proposed acquisition of T-Mobile, many observers believed that AT&T would face much less hostility from the antitrust authorities in connection with its proposed acquisition of DirecTV because "regulators are likely to look favorably on a deal that creates a bulwark" against the then-pending Comcast deal to acquire Time Warner Cable in a transaction that would merge the two largest cable companies in the United States. *Id.* In an interesting turn of events, when the AT&T–DirecTV deal closed in July 2015, the regulators still had not approved Comcast's acquisition of Time Warner Cable, seemingly fulfilling what many observers predicted in May 2014 (following the public announcement of the AT&T–DirecTV merger), which is that the "proposed AT&T deal [would] complicate the federal government's review of Comcast's bid for Time Warner Cable." Cecilia Kang, *AT&T, DirecTV Announce $49 Billion Merger*, WASHINGTON

POST, May 18, 2014, *available at:* https://www.washingtonpost.com/business/
technology/atandt-DirecTV-announce-48-billion-merger/2014/05/18/
62ffc980-dec1-11e3-810f-764fe508b82d_story.html.*

In addition to obtaining regulatory approvals, another important condition to AT&T's obligation to close on its mega-merger with DirecTV specifically
focused on the NFL Sunday Ticket package. *See* Brian Stelter, *AT&T and DirecTV
Strike $49 Billion Deal*, CNN MONEY, May 18, 2014, *available at:* http://money
.cnn.com/2014/05/18/news/companies/att-DirecTV/index.html. The NFL
Sunday Ticket package allows DirecTV subscribers to watch every NFL game on
Sunday afternoon for a fee, a deal that reportedly "costs DirecTV about $1 bil-
lion a season." Joe Flint, *DirecTV Deal with AT&T Includes NFL Sunday Ticket Exit
Clause*, LA TIMES, May 19, 2014, *available at:* http://www.latimes.com/entertain-
ment/envelope/cotown/la-et-ct-directv-att-nfl-sunday-ticket-20140519-story.
html. In other words, DirecTV pays the NFL approximately $1 billion per sea-
son for the rights to broadcast all of the NFL games to DirecTV's subscribers. As
of the time that the proposed merger was signed, DirecTV's deal with the NFL
was set to expire at the end of the 2014 football season and the parties had been
in talks for several months to renew the contract. A big sticking point in these
negotiations was that the NFL was "looking for more money from DirecTV for
Sunday Ticket," reportedly seeking an "annual price tag of $1.4 billion for next
season [to be followed] by annual increases of 4%." *Id.*

Following the announcement of its deal with AT&T, Mike White, the CEO
of DirecTV "said that he [was] very confident that a deal [with the NFL] would
get done before the end of [2014]. [This prediction was not all that surprising
because] [k]eeping Sunday Ticket is so important to DirecTV's future it is a
condition of the deal with AT&T." *Id.* Or, as it was more formally expressed
by the parties in their public disclosure of the deal, "in the unlikely event
that [DirecTV's] agreement for the 'NFL Sunday Ticket' is not renewed on
substantially the terms discussed between the parties, AT&T may elect not to
consummate the merger." *AT&T to Acquire DIRECTV, available at:* http://news
.DirecTV.com/2014/05/18/DirecTV-att-merger-press-release. At this point,
"locking down the [NFL] deal had become an upmost priority for DirecTV."
Erik Brannon, *DirecTV and NFL Renew, Pulling AT&T Merger One Step Closer*, IHS
TECHNOLOGY, Oct. 2, 2014, *available at:* https://technology.ihs.com/512310/
DirecTV-and-nfl-renew-att-merger-one-step-closer. In October 2014, DirecTV
announced that it had reached an agreement with the NFL so that "DirecTV
will remain the exclusive home to NFL Sunday Ticket for the next eight years in
a deal worth a reported $12 billion." *Id.* With this roadblock removed, the only
significant remaining obstacle to closing on the deal was to obtain regulatory

---

* [By the author: In February 2014, Comcast made a $45 billion bid to acquire Time
Warner Cable, which Time Warner Inc. had divested in 2009. *See A Timeline of Time Warner
Inc.,* July 16, 2014, *available at:* https://www.wsj.com/articles/a-timeline-of-time-warner-inc
-1405522663#. However, notwithstanding the parties' considerable efforts to persuade the
antitrust authorities, this takeover bid failed to obtain regulatory approval, and the parties
abandoned the deal in April 2015. *See* Emily Steel, *Under Regulators' Scrutiny, Comcast and Time
Warner Cable End Deal,* April 24, 2015, *available at:* https://www.nytimes.com/2015/04/25/
business/media/comcast-time-warner-cable-deal.html. Ultimately, Charter Communications
acquired Time Warner Cable in May 2016 for $55 billion.]

approvals, most notably from the antitrust authorities and the FCC, all of which were finally obtained in July 2015, over a year after the original merger agreement had been signed by the parties.

According to the terms of the merger, at closing, DirecTV shareholders were to receive $95.00 per share, comprised of $28.50 per share in cash and $66.50 per share in AT&T stock. At the time of closing on this mega-merger in July 2015, the 30-day average trading price of AT&T's stock (or the "Average Parent Stock Price," as defined in the parties' merger agreement) was $35.148, so the DirecTV shareholders "received 1.892 shares of AT&T stock, in addition to $28.50 in cash, per share of DirecTV." *See* AT&T Press Release, *AT&T Completes Acquisition of DIRECTV*, July 24, 2015, *available at:* http://about.att .com/story/att_completes_acquisition_of_DirecTV.html. In an interesting turn of events, this same press release announced that DirecTV's CEO, Mike White, would retire and was to be replaced by John Stankey, who "will report directly to [Randall] Stephenson," AT&T's chairman and CEO. *Id.* Stankey, a long-time senior executive with AT&T, had previously served as the company's Chief Strategy Officer, where he primarily focused on corporate strategy, M&A, and business development initiatives. With the closing of AT&T's acquisition of DirecTV, Stankey was put in charge of running DirecTV in a new role as CEO of AT&T Entertainment and Internet Services.

Postscript: AT&T's Acquisition of DirecTV.   Since closing on its acquisition of DirecTV in July 2015, AT&T has continued its quest to pivot from a telecommunications giant to a media conglomerate. Most notably, on October 22, 2016, AT&T announced that it had agreed to acquire Time Warner for $85 billion in a mix of cash and AT&T stock. AT&T agreed to pay $107.50 per share of Time Warner stock, with Time Warner shareholders to receive $53.75 in cash at closing together with $53.75 in AT&T common stock. *See* Thomas Gryta, et al., *AT&T Reaches Deal to Buy Time Warner for $85.4 Billion*, Oct. 22, 2016, *available at:* https://www.wsj.com/articles/at-t-reaches-deal-to-buy-time-warner-for-more -than-80-billion-1477157084. AT&T announced that it planned to finance the cash portion of the purchase price (approximately $42.7 billion) with new debt, as well as "cash on hand" (that is, cash already on its balance sheet), and, at closing, the deal would leave the Time Warner shareholders owning approximately 15 percent of AT&T's outstanding shares. *See* Ingrid Lunden and Fitz Tepper, *Confirmed: AT&T Is Buying Time Warner for $85.5B in Cash and Shares*, Oct. 22, 2016, *available at:* https://techcrunch.com/2016/10/22/confirmed -att-is-buying-time-warner-for-85-4b-in-cash-and-shares/. If the deal closes, it would give AT&T control over prominent entertainment and news brands such as HBO, Warner Bros., and CNN. *See* T. C. Scottek, *AT&T to Buy HBO, CNN, and the Rest of Time Warner for More than $80 Billion*, Oct. 22, 2016, *available at:* https://www.theverge.com/2016/10/22/13366904/att-hbo-cnn-time-warner. However, the path to closing faced numerous obstacles, not the least of which was the anticipated regulatory scrutiny of the proposed mega-transaction.

At the time the deal was announced, then-presidential candidate Donald Trump objected to the transaction, asserting that the merger would concentrate "power in the hands of too few." *See* Nathan Reiff, *AT&T and Time Warner Merger Case: What You Need to Know*, *available at:* https://www.investopedia.com/ investing/att-and-time-warner-merger-case-what-you-need-know/ (last updated

Dec. 7, 2018). After Donald Trump was elected U.S. president, his administration commenced its antitrust review of the proposed merger. As part of its scrutiny of the mega-deal, the antitrust regulators at the U.S. Department of Justice (DOJ) demanded that AT&T divest itself of certain Time Warner assets, most notably CNN, as a condition to regulatory approval of the transaction, a request that was strongly resisted by AT&T. *See* Keach Hagey, et al., *Regulators Seek Significant Asset Sales in AT&T Deal for Time Warner,* Nov. 8, 2017, *available at:* https://www.wsj.com/articles/at-t-executive-says-timing-of-time-warner-deal-now-uncertain-1510149720 ("The Justice Department has raised the prospect that the telecom giant would have to divest either the Turner television unit, which includes CNN along with other cable channels, or the satellite DirecTV business, [people familiar with the government's investigation said].") Ultimately, the Trump administration, under the leadership of Makan Delrahim as head of the DOJ's antitrust division, sued in November 2017 to block the proposed merger, on the grounds that the merger "would lead to fewer choices for consumers and higher prices for television and internet services." *See* Edmund Lee and Cecilia Kang, *AT&T Closes Acquisition of Time Warner,* June 14, 2008, *available at:* https://www.nytimes.com/2018/06/14/business/media/att-time-warner-injunction.html. For its part, the two companies vigorously defended the proposed merger, claiming that the business combination would result in the "first U.S. wireless company to compete nationwide with cable companies by providing an online-video bundle akin to a traditional pay-television package." *See* Thomas Gryta, et al., *supra.*

Following a six-week trial in the U.S. District Court in Washington, D.C., Judge Richard Leon (a George W. Bush appointee) ruled in favor of AT&T and Time Warner on June 12, 2018, thereby "giving the companies the green light to complete their merger." *See* Nathan Reiff, *supra.* Three days later, on June 15, 2018, AT&T announced that it had closed on its $85 billion acquisition of Time Warner, giving AT&T control over Warner Bros., HBO, and Turner Broadcasting, among other media properties. As part of the company's June 15, 2018 press release (announcing completion of the deal), Randall Stephenson, chairman and CEO of AT&T, Inc. said that "[t]he content and creative talent at Warner Bros., HBO and Turner are first-rate. Combine all that with AT&T's strengths in direct-to-consumer distribution, and we offer customers a differentiated, high-quality, mobile-first entertainment experience. We're going to bring a fresh approach to how the media and entertainment industry works for consumers, content creators, distributors, and advertisers." *See* AT&T Press Release, *AT&T Completes Acquisition of Time Warner Inc.,* June 15, 2008, *available at:* https://about.att.com/story/att_completes_acquisition_of_time_warner_inc.html. In its press release, Stephenson added that John Stankey would be the CEO of AT&T's media properties (including DirecTV, as well as the Time Warner assets), and that a new name for this business unit would be announced later. In March 2019, John Stankey announced a reorganization of the media business unit, which was since renamed WarnerMedia. *See* Edmund Lee and John Koblin, *AT&T Joins Media War As First Hybrid amid Giants,* March 5, 2019, *available at:* https://www.nytimes.com/2019/03/04/business/media/att-warner-greenblatt.html.

In making its $49 billion purchase of DirecTV in 2015 and the $85 billion deal for Time Warner in 2018, AT&T was pursuing its strategy to pivot the 150-year-old company into the entertainment industry in order to compete with established players in the industry, such as Alphabet and Netflix. Notwithstanding Randall Stephenson's promise (in the press release announcing AT&T's acquisition of DirecTV) that AT&T's acquisition strategy would create "immediate and long-term value for our shareholders," AT&T's share price has been flat under Stephenson's tenure as CEO, hitting "a multi-year low near $27" per share in December 2018. Drew FitzzGerald, et. al., *AT&T Chief Laid Plans for His Exit. That Set Off an Activist Challenge*, Sept. 13, 2019, *available at:* https://www.wsj.com/articles/at-t-chief-laid-plans-for-his-exit-that-set-off-an-activist-challenge-11568414629. By summer 2019, Stephenson had "signaled [that] he [was] prepared to step down as CEO as soon as [2020,] . . ." after serving over 10 years as the company's leader. Shalini Ramachandran and Drew FitzGerald, *AT&T Explores Parting Ways with DirecTV*, Sept. 18, 2019, *available at:* https://www.wsj.com/articles/at-t-explores-parting-ways-with-directv-11568841544. And in August 2019, "AT&T's board met to approve the promotion of John Stankey to a newly created role of president and operating chief, [while continuing to serve as the head of WarnerMedia]," making Stankey the likely successor to Stephenson when he retires. FitzGerald, et al., *supra.*

Shortly after the announcement of Stankey's promotion, Stephenson received an unexpected phone call from Jesse Cohn, a hedge fund manager at Elliot Management Corporation, one of Wall Street's largest activist investors.* During the call, which was "brief but cordial," Cohn offered "a stinging rebuke of [Stephenson's] mission to turn the phone company into a media giant and leave a top lieutenant [Stankey] to finish the job" of executing Stephenson's strategic vision. FitzGerald, et al., *supra.* The next day, Elliott Management revealed (in a letter to AT&T's board) that it had purchased $3.2 billion of AT&T shares, which is less than 3 percent of AT&T's outstanding shares and represents a roughly 1 percent stake. The letter expressed Elliot's displeasure with AT&T's acquisition strategy, share price, and operational underperformance, the expensive acquisitions of DirecTV and Time Warner, and AT&T's change in top-level management. *See* BusinessWire, *Elliott Management Sends Letter to Board of Directors of AT&T*, Sept. 9, 2019, *available at:* https://www.businesswire.com/news/home/20190909005482/en/Elliott-Management-Sends-Letter-Board-Directors-ATT.

The letter outlined Elliott's growing concern that AT&T's leadership was unable to articulate a plan to turn the company into a force in the entertainment industry. A little more than a week later, AT&T addressed Elliot's concerns by undertaking a review of AT&T's portfolio of assets, including DirecTV.

---

* [By the author: What is an "activist investor"? "An activist investor is an individual or group that purchases large numbers of a public company's shares and/or tries to obtain seats on the company's board to effect a significant change within the company. A company can become a target for activist investors if it is mismanaged, has excessive costs, and could be run more profitably as a private company or has another problem that the activist investor believes it can fix to make the company more valuable." Will Kenton, *Investopedia's Guide to Hedge Funds: Activist Shareholder,* June 25, 2020, *available at:* https://www.investopedia.com/terms/a/activist-investor.asp (last updated June 25, 2019); *see also,* Patrick Sarch and Tom Matthews, White & Case LLP, *5 Things You Need to Know About . . . Shareholder Activism,* July 21, 2020, *available at*: https://www.whitecase.com/publications/alert/5-things-you-need-know-about-shareholder-activism. We will examine the role of "activist shareholders" (such as Carl Icahn and Elliott Management) in more detail in Chapters 6 and 7.]

Stephenson's proposed strategies included a "spinoff of DirecTV into a separate public company and a combination of DirecTV's assets with Dish Network Corp." Shalini Ramachandran and Drew FitzGerald, *AT&T Explores Parting Ways with DirecTV,* Sept. 18, 2019, *available at:* https://www.wsj.com/articles/at-t-explores-parting-ways-with-directv-11568841544. However, "parting ways with DirecTV" represented a marked departure from Stephenson's bold plan to "diversify beyond the wireless phone business and tap into a growing media industry." *Id.* Despite Elliot's harsh critique and the fact that millions of customers were "cutting the cord" and abandoning their cable providers, Stephenson's heir apparent, John Stankey, defended AT&T's decision to maintain DirecTV within the company's asset portfolio. *See* Joe Flint, *AT&T Operating Chief Defends Media Strategy Built Around Streaming, DirecTV,* Sept. 24, 2019, *available at:* https://www.wsj.com/articles/at-t-operating-chief-defends-media-strategy-built-around-streaming-directv-11569355738.

Not surprisingly, AT&T soon entered into talks with Elliot "to resolve the activist investor's campaign for change." Corrie Driebusch, Drew FitzGerald, and Dana Cimilluca, *AT&T in Talks to Resolve Elliott Management's Activist Campaign* Oct. 17, 2019, *available at:* https://www.wsj.com/articles/at-t-in-talks-to-resolve-elliott-managements-activist-campaign-11571347183?mod=searchresults&page=1&pos=16&mod=article_inline&mod=article_inline. These talks resulted in the parties reaching a truce just a few days ahead of AT&T's unveiling of its new streaming service, HBO Max, which was the by-product of AT&T's acquisition of Time Warner, as well AT&T's response to the mass exodus of "cord cutters." The agreement reached by the parties ultimately ended Elliot's activist campaign and helped AT&T avoid a costly proxy fight, as Elliott had indicated that it was considering mounting a proxy campaign to elect its own nominees to the AT&T board at the next shareholders' meeting. *See* Driebusch, et al., *AT&T in Talks to Resolve Elliott Management's Activist Campaign, supra.* As part of the "truce," both parties agreed to a revamped acquisition strategy that would "forgo big takeovers in the coming years to focus on improving [AT&T's] bottom line." Drew FitzGerald and Corrie Driebusch, *AT&T Reaches Truce with Activist as TV Defections Worsen,* Oct. 28, 2019, *available at:* https://www.wsj.com/articles/at-ts-profit-revenue-fall-on-tv-defections-11572261496?mod=article_inline. In addition, AT&T promised to review its portfolio, pay down the debt burden taken on as part of the Time Warner acquisition, commit to stock buybacks, add two board members who were Elliott nominees, and that Stephenson would remain CEO through 2020. *Id.*

After reaching this "truce" with Elliot, AT&T commenced a search process to find Stephenson's successor. The search process was overseen by a committee consisting of independent directors, who considered both internal and external candidates. In April 2020, AT&T announced that Stephenson would no longer stay on as CEO until the end of the year, and instead planned to retire at the end of June 2020, handing leadership over to John Stankey. *See* Drew FitzGerald, *AT&T's Randall Stephenson to Retire as CEO,* April 24, 2020, *available at:* https://www.wsj.com/articles/at-t-ceo-randall-stephenson-to-retire-coo-john-stankey-to-take-over-as-ceo-11587738567. In connection with this announcement, Elliott issued a statement that said it had been "engaged with the company throughout the search process. . . . We look forward to working with John as he begins his term as CEO." Drew FitzGerald, *AT&T's Randall*

Stephenson to Retire as CEO; April 24, 2020, *available at:* https://www.wsj.com/ articles/at-t-ceo-randall-stephenson-to-retire-coo-john-stankey-to-take-over-as -ceo-11587738567. This change in leadership was announced at AT&T's annual meeting on April 24, 2020, which was held online because of the coronavirus pandemic. *Id.* On July 1, 2020, Stankey assumed the position of CEO and joined AT&T's board, with Stephenson "staying on as executive chairman of the board until January [2021], when AT&T is expected to elect an independent chairman." *Id.*

With this transition in CEOs, Stankey was left to lead the telecommunications company into the new world of entertainment and media in an effort to fulfill Stephenson's bold strategic vision for AT&T, which dated all the way back to the company's acquisition of DirecTV. *Query:* With the benefit of hindsight, do you think that AT&T's acquisition of DirecTV turned out to be a good deal for AT&T and its shareholders?

2.   The Story of Google's Acquisition of Nest Labs

On January 13, 2014, Google, Inc. issued a press release announcing that it had entered into an agreement to acquire Nest Labs, Inc. (Nest or Nest Labs) for $3.2 billion in cash. As part of its announcement, Larry Page, Google's CEO, said that "Nest's founders, Tony Fadell and Matt Rogers, have built a tremendous team that we are excited to welcome into the Google family. They're already delivering amazing products you can buy right now—thermostats that save energy and smoke/CO alarms that can help keep your family safe. We are excited to bring great experiences to more homes in more countries and fulfill their dreams!" Google Press Release, *Google to Acquire Nest,* Jan. 13, 2014, *available at:* http://investor.google.com/release/2014/0113.html. For his part, Tony Fadell, CEO of Nest, said, "We're thrilled to join Google. With their support, Nest will be even better placed to build simple, thoughtful devices that make life easier at home, and that have a positive impact on the world." *Id.* But the story of this business combination has a most interesting background.

Tony Fadell, widely considered to be one of the "fathers of the iPod," left Apple in November 2008, after working for seven years as part of Apple's iPod Group, although he was to remain as a consultant to Apple. Tom Krazit, *Report: Tony Fadell, iPod Chief, to Leave Apple Post,* CNET, Nov. 4, 2008, *available at:* http://www.cnet.com/news/report-tony-fadell-ipod-chief-to-leave-apple -post. As "the inaugural member of the of the iPod engineering team," Fadell was widely credited "as the man behind the idea of a handheld music player combined with a digital music store." *Id.* Both Tony Fadell and his wife, who also announced her resignation as Apple's vice-president of human resources, indicated that they were "reducing their roles within the company [Apple] as they devote more time to their young family." Mike Ricciuti, *Apple's iPod Chief to Step Down,* CNET, Nov. 4, 2008, *available at:* http://www.cnet.com/news/ apples-ipod-chief-to-step-down.

But, as is often the case with entrepreneurs such as Tony Fadell, it wasn't long before he came out of retirement with a new product—the "first 'learning thermostat' in the world." Katie Fehrenbacher, *Introducing a Thermostat Steve*

Jobs Would Love: Nest, GIGAOM, Oct. 24, 2011, *available at:* http://gigaom.com/
2011/10/24/introducing-a-thermostat-steve-jobs-would-love-nest. The idea for
this type of new thermostat grew out of Fadell's frustration, as he was designing a "green home" for his family in Lake Tahoe, California, with the "lack of
options for a thermostat" for the home — the existing products "were expensive, not smart, ugly and basically 'crap' says Fadell. And like all good entrepreneurs he thought to himself: there's got to be a better way." *Id.* With his
next move unknown at the time that he left Apple, Fadell, in true entrepreneur
fashion, operated "in stealth mode," not re-emerging on the Silicon Valley landscape until October 2011. Daniel Terdiman, *iPod Creator's Next Quest: Making
Thermostats Sexy*, CNET, Oct. 24, 2011, *available at:* http://cnet.com/news/
ipod-creators-next-quest-making-thermostats-sexy.

Although the Nest learning thermostat was not introduced to the market
until the fall of 2011, it turns out that Tony Fadell, together with Matt Rogers,
founded the company, Nest Labs, Inc., in 2009. Tony Fadell and Matt Rogers,
Nest's vice-president of engineering and who was also an "early iPod and iPhone
team member" at Apple, came together in 2009 to start Nest Labs with "the
intention of upending an industry that sells 10 million thermostats a year, but
which Rogers [claims] hasn't really innovated in decades." *Id.* Together, they
"bootstrapped the company to build a prototype" and then used the prototype
to raise additional funding to grow the business. Julie Bort, *Nest Co-founder Matt
Rogers: My Friends Told Me I Was Crazy to Leave Apple to Start Nest*, BUSINESS INSIDER,
Jan. 13, 2014, *available at:* http://businessinsider.com/nests-matt-rogers-on
-leaving-apple-2014-1. As of October 2011, Nest, headquartered in Palo Alto,
California, had been "operating for about a year and a half, [had] 100 employees, and [tens of millions of dollars in] funding from Kleiner Perkins [a well-
known Silicon Valley-based venture capital fund], Google Ventures and Al Gore's
investment fund [Generation Capital, among others]." *Id.* As opposed to many
Silicon Valley technology companies that primarily focus on software development, "Nest is capital-intensive because it builds hardware." Claire Cain Miller,
For, Google, a Toehold Into Goods for a Home, NEW YORK TIMES, Jan. 13, 2014, *available
at:* http://nytimes.com/2014/01/14/technology/google-to-buy-nest-labs-for-3
-2-billion.html?ref. In January 2013, the financial press reported that Nest Labs
had raised $80 million, giving the company a valuation of over $800 million,
only to be followed with another round of financing just a year later. In January
2014, it was reported that Nest Labs was "close to completing a deal to raise
upward of $150 million in a new round of financing that values [the company]
at more than $2 billion." Kara Swisher, *Nest Raising Huge New Round from DST,
Valuing Smart Home Startup at Upward of $2 Billion*, RE/CODE, Jan. 2, 2014, *avail-
able at:* http://recode.net/2014/01/02/nest-raising-huge-new-round-from-dst
-valuing-smart-home-startup-at-upwards-of-2-billion.

While other companies, such as Honeywell and Radio Thermostat Company
of America, are targeting a growing consumer market for "smart thermostats,"
Nest's learning thermostat is uniquely designed to create a programmable device
that is "intuitive and simple to use" for any homeowner. Once installed on the
wall of the owner's home, the Nest thermostat "is supposed to learn [the homeowner's] energy consumption behavior and program itself, and then automatically help [the homeowner] save energy in a convenient way. Once installed, the
[Nest] thermostat takes about a week of hardcore learning to recognize the way

[the owner heats or cools the house] and then recommends settings that are slightly more [energy] efficient than what [the homeowner already does]." *Id.* In addition to the thermostat product, Nest's team of engineers and technology advisors (which includes Sebastian Thrun, a Stanford University professor who is a machine learning expert), have "created mobile apps and a website [so that the homeowner is] able to remotely turn up or down the thermostat and [also can] give far more detailed data about home energy use." *Id.*

In a surprising turn of events, shortly after the press reported on January 2, 2014, that Nest Labs was looking to close on another round of financing that valued its business at over $2 billion, Google announced on January 13, 2014, that it had agreed to purchase Nest Labs, Inc., for $3.2 billion in cash. *See* Google Press Release, *Google to Acquire Nest,* Jan. 13, 2014, *available at:* http://investor.google.com/releases/2014/0113.html. "So the $3.2 billion that Google [has agreed to pay] represents a premium price to pay for Nest." Bort, *supra.* While some commentators speculated that "Apple would be a good suitor for Nest, especially given that [founders Tony Fadell and Matt Rogers] both had deep Apple ties," it was Google who made the decisive move. Daniel Terdiman, *Google to Buy Nest for $3.2B in Quest for the 'Conscious Home,'* CNET, Jan. 13, 2014, *available at:* http://cnet.com/news/google-to-buy-nest-for-3-2b-in-quest-for-the-conscious-home.

Why did Google make the decision to acquire Nest Labs? "Google, which dominates much of life on the Internet, has been trying to expand beyond computers and telephones to living rooms, cars and bodies. . . . For Google, gaining visibility into people's habits . . .—whether watching television using Chromecast, taking a walk wearing Google Glass or managing their homes using Nest products—will provide a fuller picture of users. . . . Google has talked for years about connecting home devices, known as the Internet of Things, but has made little traction. Still it has been expanding beyond its search engine roots into hardware, . . . including its development of devices like Google Glass, the Internet-connected eyewear, and Chromecast, for Internet-connected television. . . . It's easy to see how Google products could be integrated into Nest. For instance, Nest users who log in to Google could theoretically someday see their home's temperature . . . and information about a person's home life could [then] be used to target ads." Claire Cain Miller, *For Google, a Toehold into Goods for a Home,* NEW YORK TIMES, Jan. 13, 2014, *available at:* http://www.nytimes.com/2014/01/14/technology/google-to-buy-nest-labs-for-3-2-billion.html?ref. Google's purchase of Nest was "expected to close in the next few months and [was] subject to customary closing conditions including the receipt of regulatory approvals in the US." Shawn Knight, *Google Acquires Nest Labs for $3.2 Billion in Cash,* TECHSPOT, Jan. 13, 2014, *available at:* http://www.techspot.com/news/55314-google-acquires-nest-labs-for-32-billion-in-cash.html.

Given that Nest Labs had "a lot of access to investors and [was] looking at raising money for even higher valuations," why did the company decide to accept Google's offer? According to Tony Fadell, "There was no shortage of funds, but funds are funds and you still have to build the infrastructure. We had been looking at [raising more money], but Google was committed to investing in the business over the long term and they bring more than just money to the game." Liz Gannes, *Nest's Tony Fadell on Why He Sold to Google: "Best of Both Worlds,"* RE/CODE, Jan. 13, 2014, *available at:* http://www.recode.net/2014/1/13/11622282/nest-tony-fadell-on-why-he-sold-to-google-best-of-both-worlds. The

Nest founder admitted to growing increasingly frustrated at having to devote "much of his time to building internal functions such as human resources, legal and distribution, in order to help the company grow." Daisuke Wakabayashi, *In Interview, Nest Founder Extols Google Support*, WALL STREET JOURNAL, Jan. 13, 2014, *available at:* http://blogs.wsj.com/digits/2014/01/13/in-interview-nest-founder-extols-google-support. As part of Google's Internet of Things, Tony Fadell and his team "can focus on products" and rely on Google "to help Nest grow fast and globally." *Id.*

Once the acquisition closes, the parties intend "for Nest to run as a stand-alone business" and that Tony Fadell will continue as CEO of Nest, reporting directly to Larry Page, Google's CEO. Indeed, once the deal was announced, some Silicon Valley observers "were speculating that [Google] spent $3.2 billion just to bring on board Tony Fadell." Dan Gallagher, *Podfather's Nest Filled with Apples*, WALL STREET JOURNAL, Jan. 13, 2014, *available at:* http://blogs.wsj.com/moneybeat/2014/01/13/podfathers-nest-filled-with-apples. And it certainly was not a shabby pay out for Matt Rogers, the other founder of Nest, who "became a very wealthy man with the news that Google bought his company, Nest Labs, for $3.2 billion." Bort, *supra.* And, last, but not least, Google's purchase of Nest Labs "for $3.2 billion is blockbuster territory for the venture capital investors who have backed the Palo Alto, Calif. company since its 2010 founding." Yuliya Chernova, *Google's Nest Deal: 'Fantastic' Return for Investors*, WALL STREET JOURNAL, Jan. 13, 2014, *available at:* http://blogs.wsj.com/venturecapital/2014/01/13/google-to-buy-nest-labs-for-3-2-billion-fantastic-return-for-investors. Although the company has not revealed the total amount of venture capital that it has raised since its inception, Peter Nieh, a partner at Lightspeed Venture Partners (a firm that had invested in Nest), was quoted as saying, "It's a fantastic return." *Id.*

Google publicly disclosed that its acquisition of Nest Labs closed on February 7, 2014, following the decision of the Federal Trade Commission to terminate its review of the deal, "meaning there [were] no antitrust issues that [had] to be dealt with." Randall Suba, *Google Closes $3.2 Bn Nest Labs Deal, Tony Fadell Joins World's Most Innovative Company*, TECH TIMES, Feb. 13, 2014, *available at:* http://www.techtimes.com/articles/3411/20140213/google-closes-3-2-bn-nest-labs-deal-tony-fadell-joins-worlds-most-innovative-company.htm.

Postscript: Google's Acquisition of Nest Labs.   In 2015, a year after Google completed its acquisition of Nest Labs, Google restructured itself into Alphabet Inc., a holding company. By creating Alphabet as a new parent company that would include Google's core search business, as well as eight other independently operated companies spanning "a diverse array of industries, from robotics, to life sciences, to healthcare and anti-aging," Google signaled its intention to evolve into a technology conglomerate. Rakesh Sharma, *Why Google Became Alphabet, available at:* https://www.investopedia.com/articles/investing/081115/why-google-became-alphabet.asp (last updated January 2, 2018).

However, Google assured investors that "[n]ot much will change for investors [as a result of] the reorganization . . . [since] each Google Inc. share [was to] be swapped for an Alphabet Inc. share. Thus, the [reorganization] has minimal consequences in terms of impact to bottom line and company direction." *Id.* Since the 2015 reorganization left Nest Labs as a subsidiary of Alphabet and thus operating independently from Google, the impact of the reorganization on Tony Fadell and his future as the leader of Nest Labs was ultimately quite profound.

In early 2014, following the closing on Google's acquisition of Nest,

> Google's purchase was widely seen both inside and out of Nest as Google investing in hardware to ultimately take on Apple. "I thought Google was genius to buy this company at the price they did," says [Randy] Komisar [the Kleiner Perkins Caufield Byers partner who led that venture capital firm's investment in Nest and served on its board at the time Google offered to buy Nest Labs]. "They got Tony Fadell, they got Matt Rogers, and they got the DNA from Apple hardware. Short of buying Apple, you're not going to get that DNA in one big effective group that was performing. They bought a terrific asset."*
>
> Initially, the acquisition went well—Nest began hiring at impressive rates. "My general impression was that Google was going to be extremely patient and allow them [Tony and Matt] to broaden their reach," says Komisar. "Google was embracing what it took to be the YouTube of hardware."
>
> A bump in the road was the acquisition of Dropcam in June of 2014, which happened at the behest of Google, according to a report in *The Information.* Dropcam was a small company that had attracted loyal customers to its elegant security camera products, and it had a roadmap to ship several other products. But integrating the team proved to be difficult; Fadell's demanding style didn't mesh well with Dropcam CEO Greg Duffy's more laid-back manner. . . . [What's more, Nest] wasn't launching new hardware categories—although the company shipped new generations of each of its products and multiple updates to its app . . ., the failure to launch obvious extensions of existing products like an outdoor camera or enter entirely new markets seemed to indicate that the company had stalled.
>
> [But perhaps the fatal blow to Tony Fadell's tenure with Nest came with the reorganization of Google into Alphabet.] Fadell won't say much about his decision to leave Nest, . . . But Nest was Fadell's baby, and his vision. So how did the switch to Alphabet change things so drastically? . . . The Alphabet restructuring pulled several units out of Google and turned them into separate divisions under a single corporate umbrella. Google itself became the largest and most profitable division of Alphabet. Nest, reporting under a new division called "Other Bets," was the company's other major consumer business, and the dynamics at Nest changed dramatically. . . .
>
> Alphabet money is not like Google money, according to several sources at Nest. Whereas Google was content to float the company, under Alphabet Nest was tightly constrained and asked to demonstrate a level of financial discipline at odds with what the founders had expected when they sold to Google. For a five-year-old hardware startup in a still-unproven market, that meant Fadell's role immediately changed—and that Nest's conversations with their corporate parent went from being focused on growth and investment in technology to what one source called "effectively finance meetings." . . . .

---

* [By the author: Google's acquisition of Nest Labs, calling for Tony Fadell and Matt Rogers to continue to run the business, reflects what M&A market observers often refer to as an "acqui-hire." So, what is an *acqui-hire?* "An acqui-hire basically is a fancy way to say your company is being bought predominantly for the fabulous team you've assembled and not [necessarily] for the product/service you were (trying) to bring to market." Danielle Naftulin, *So You're Being Acqui-hired . . .*, *available at:* https://www.cooleygo.com/acqui-hire-basics/ (last visited August 1, 2020); *see also,* John Coyle and Greg Polsky, *Acqui-hiring,* 63 DUKE L. J. 281 (2013).]

Nilay Patel, *Altering the Deal: Why Tony Fadell Left Nest—and Alphabet,* June 7, 2016, *available at:* https://www.theverge.com/2016/6/7/11874670/nest-founder -tony-fadell-leaving-google-alphabet.

Ultimately, Google's 2015 corporate restructuring represented a substantial departure from Nest Lab's intended business objective in being acquired by Google—obtaining investment capital from Google. As a subsidiary of Alphabet, Nest was no longer receiving direct financial support from Google to help Nest Labs grow and expand globally. Perhaps not surprisingly, the decision to separate Nest Labs from Google led to Fadell's departure in June 2016. *See* Nick Statt and Dieter Bohn, *Google Nest: Why Google Finally Embraced Nest as Its Smart Home Brand,* May 7, 2019, *available at:* https://www.theverge.com/2019/5/7/ 18530609/google-nest-smart-home-brand-merging-hub-max-rebrand-io-2019.

In yet another (rather ironic) turn of events, Nest Labs was reunited with Google in 2018. Facing stiff competition in the form of Alexa, Amazon's voice assistant, Nest Labs was folded into Google Home as part of a strategy to unify all of Google's "smart home efforts." *Id.* And in 2019, "the entire group [was given] a new name: Google Nest . . . [thereby launching] a new product philosophy and—critically—a new set of data privacy policies for Nest customers." *Id.* This rebranding presents its own set of new challenges (including significant "issues related to data privacy and security," *Id.*), which Google and its subsidiary, Google Nest, will now face together. *Query:* With the benefit of hindsight, do you think that Google's acquisition of Nest Labs turned out to be a good deal for Google (now Alphabet) and its shareholders?

3.   Wall Street M&A vs. Main Street M&A

Google's acquisition of Nest Labs, Inc., grabbed headlines in the financial press, both because of the size of the deal (with its $3.2 billion purchase price) and the high profile of the acquiring company (Google, the widely followed Internet of Things firm). It bears emphasizing, however, that many more closely held companies get acquired each year without garnering banner headlines in the financial press. Some of these acquisitions are sizable deals, often involving purchase prices totaling several hundred million dollars, whereas many other deals involve the sale of very small, closely held firms with just a few owners (such as Nest Labs), where the purchase price is much more modest. Such a deal—which is often referred to as *Main Street M&A*—is an important part of the daily practice of M&A law. Indeed, for many practicing lawyers, the purchase and sale of closely held businesses (often family-owned and -managed) are the very lifeblood of their practice. This book will address the planning considerations inherent in both types of deals—high-profile *Wall Street M&A* deals (such as AT&T's acquisition of DirecTV) and the generally much-less-publicized Main Street M&A deals.

If you have not already formed the habit, I would strongly encourage you to read the financial pages (i.e., the business section) of a news source on a daily basis. I make this recommendation for a number of reasons. First, M&A law is about *business* activity, and many law students have no prior exposure to the real-world activity that is the focus of M&A law. In order to fully grasp why the law worries about regulating this set of business transactions, it is important to develop a sense as to what the business side of M&A activity is all about. Reading about current deals in your daily newspaper will help you to understand the rules and legal concepts that we will study in this course. In addition, M&A law, like most other areas of the law, is full of jargon peculiar to this area of business activity. I have found that one of the best ways to acquaint yourself with the lexicon of doing deals is to read about ongoing deals in the daily paper. In this way, you, the law student, will develop a better appreciation and understanding of the range of business activity that is addressed by M&A law.

Equally important, the law student who reads the daily business news will develop a fuller appreciation that doing deals is not stagnant; that the way deals get done continues to evolve as business practices change; and that business practices change as the economic environment for doing deals continues to shift—as we have seen most recently in the dramatic shift from the speculative "dot-com" bubble of the 1990s to the much more difficult environment in the wake of the recent Great Recession of 2008-2009, where deals frequently struggled to get done. As others have observed, "Wall Street is a profoundly cyclical place that has a way of changing just as journalists try to pin it down. A mid-[1990s] bust in the . . . market [gave] way to a tech boom [peaking in the early 2000s, to be] followed eventually by a real estate bubble [that led to the Great Recession of 2008-2009, from which the markets struggled to bounce back]." Yvette Kantrow, *Goodbye to All That, Wall Street,* THE DEAL, Feb. 24, 2012, *available at:* http://www.pipeline.thedeal.com/tdd/ViewArticle.dl?id=10006673193. And this cycle continues as M&A activity bounced back with an upward trend that started in 2013 and culminated in a record volume of M&A deal-making in 2018. Indeed, we are witnessing the continuing evolution of the financial markets as we enter the third decade of the twenty-first century. At the start of 2020, many Wall Street observers were predicting record volumes of M&A activity in that calendar year, only to find these hopes abruptly disappointed due to the outbreak of the COVID-19 pandemic, which brought economic activity (including M&A dealmaking) to a grinding halt in the spring of 2020. *See infra* text at pp. 43-47 for a more detailed discussion of the current state of deal-making in the M&A market (as of Fall 2020).

Thus, deal making in the M&A markets continues to evolve, responding to ever-changing economic conditions and pressures, and M&A lawyers need to be well informed regarding the current business environment in order to be able to provide effective legal counsel. In sum, reading the daily business news will serve to reinforce a fundamental tenet of this casebook: each deal is different since the business incentives and client objectives vary widely from deal to deal. Moreover, the legal advice must be tailored to the business considerations that animate and are specific to the particular deal the M&A lawyer is currently working on.

QUESTIONS

In considering these two very different stories of M&A deals (AT&T's acquisition of publicly traded DirecTV and Google's purchase of privately held Nest Labs), and in reading through the note material that follows, ask yourself the following questions with respect to each of these two deals and consider if there is any variation in your answer as to each deal:

1. Who is the Target? Who is the Bidder?

2. Does this deal present any antitrust concerns? Will this deal require any other regulatory approvals?

3. How will investors in Bidder Co. learn of the proposed acquisition of Target Co.? How will investors in Target Co. learn of the proposed sale of their company?

4. In the case of the AT&T–DirecTV deal, what is the nature of management's concern as to the market's reaction to the public announcement of this proposed transaction? How will management gauge the market's reaction? Why is management worried about the market's reaction to the deal? Why is this concern not found in the press coverage of Google's acquisition of Nest Labs?

5. What is the acquisition consideration? In other words, what is Bidder offering to pay to acquire Target?

6. Why does Bidder want to buy Target? What business objective is to be served by making this acquisition? Is Bidder a strategic or financial buyer?

7. What is the business incentive for Target to engage in this deal? Why is Target willing to let itself be acquired?

NOTES

1. Sale of Venture Capital-Backed Companies.   Google's acquisition of Nest Labs reflects a particular type of M&A deal that has become quite common in the modern world of M&A transactions. Many closely held firms (such as Nest Labs) may seek investment funds from venture capital (VC) or private equity (PE) firms in order to establish and/or grow their business. For these VC investors, the time horizon for use of their capital varies, but it is usually somewhere between three and seven years. This means that when the VC firm invests its capital and buys stock in the start-up company, the VC firm usually considers its *exit strategy* as part of its overall investment decision. The goal of these financial investors is usually to obtain the return of their invested capital along with a certain rate of return on their investment. The VC (or PE) investor's goal, however, often may be at odds with the founding shareholder(s) of the company, who frequently are entrepreneur(s) who closely identify with the business of the company. Often, these entrepreneurs will find themselves unwilling to separate from the company's business. Other entrepreneurs, however, have a very different set of business objectives, often intending only to grow the young business until it is mature enough to be sold off to another (usually more established) business.

Among the exit strategies typically considered by a VC or PE investor is the sale of the business to another company. When the start-up company is acquired, these financial investors will usually get cashed out along with all the other shareholders, including the founding shareholders. Often, though, the acquiring corporation will purchase the start-up company in order to acquire the talent and expertise (human capital) of its founding shareholders and/or managers. In that case, the consideration offered to those founding shareholder(s) and/or manager(s) that the acquiring corporation would like to retain is likely to be different than the consideration offered to the other shareholders, including the financial investors. This disparate treatment of shareholders raises obvious fiduciary duty concerns, which we will examine as we go through the materials in the later chapters.

As of Fall 2020, the M&A markets continue to provide the preferred exit strategy for VC and PE investors to realize their financial objectives. Indeed, following the bursting of the "tech bubble" in the early years of the twenty-first century, venture capitalists and other institutional investors (such as hedge funds) became increasingly reliant on the M&A market as the preferred exit strategy, a trend that only intensified in the wake of the Great Recession of 2008-2009 — particularly in light of the continuing moribund market for initial public offerings (IPOs). "For venture capitalists and other prominent investors in young companies, an initial public offering is supposed to be the big pay-off for years of patience. It's not working out that way [for many investors, especially for backers of new Internet companies]." Scott Thurm and Pei-Wing Tam, *Prominent Investors Miss Web IPO Payoff*, Wall Street Journal, June 19, 2012, at A1. And this trend continues as "many IPO candidates are getting better offers from potential acquirers, including strategic [buyers] and financial firms." Telis Demo and Corrie Driebusch, *Forget IPOs, Firms Want to Get Bought*, Wall Street Journal, Nov. 30, 2015, at C1.

2. Sale of Closely Held Company to Another Closely Held Company. Another common variation of the Main Street M&A deal is where one small business is acquired by another small, closely held business. These transactions will not make the headlines of the *Wall Street Journal* (or even the *Smallville Tribune*), but they are the lifeblood for many corporate lawyers and their small business clients. As an example, an established plumbing business is put up for sale when its founder decides to retire from the business. In its simplest form, we will assume that the founder and manager of the business is the sole shareholder of this thriving business that has added a couple of employees over the years. There are a number of different ways that this founder may go about finding a buyer for his plumbing business. For example, he may offer the business to existing employees or transfer ownership to the next generation of family members. Alternatively, the founder may decide to list the business for sale with a business broker. The broker will actively search for a buyer for the business, usually in exchange for a commission if the broker is successful in finding a buyer and closing on the sale of the business.

Deals involving businesses owned and operated as small, closely held corporations are not usually going to make headlines in the *Wall Street Journal*. However, for the founding shareholder(s), these deals represent an important and defining milestone, often culminating a long career in the business. More to the point in our study of M&A law, exactly the same legal structures are available to both the small Main Street M&A deal as are available to structure the large-scale M&A deal that gets done on Wall Street. Further, the essential sequence of steps necessary to complete any such deal follows a similar chronology, which is described in the next section. However, the dynamics of a deal done on Wall Street will vary considerably from Main Street M&A deals, as we will see when we analyze the problems in Chapter 2.

3. Divestitures vs. Acquisitions.   Very often, management of a company will decide to sell off part of the company's business operations, generally because management has decided that these assets are no longer central (or "core") to the company's business objectives. This type of transaction is generally referred to as a "divestiture" and is largely beyond the scope of this casebook, since this casebook focuses on "acquisitive" transactions. That is, this casebook focuses on the business decision made by one company to acquire another company's business. However, it bears mentioning that when a company decides that certain assets are no longer core to its business model, it will usually undertake steps to *divest* itself of these assets, typically by either selling off the assets or by spinning off the business to its shareholders. As an example, in June 2017, Nestle announced that it was considering a sale of its American candy business, which included such iconic brands as Baby Ruth and Butterfinger, because the "demand for sweets has fallen off in the United States." Michael J. de la Merced, *Nestle Looks to Sell U.S. Candy Business as Americans Eat Fewer Sweets*, June 15, 2017, *available at:* https://www.nytimes.com/2017/06/15/business/ dealbook/nestle-looks-to-sell-us-candy-business-as-americans-eat-fewer-sweets .html?smid=em-share). In 2018, Nestle sold its U.S. confectionery business for $2.8 billion in cash to Ferrero Group, the maker of well-known food brands such as Nutella and Ferrero Roche pralines, claiming that the divestiture of its candy business would allow Nestle to prioritize other "categories [of businesses for] future growth, . . . such as [its] pet care, bottled water, coffee, frozen meal, and infant nutrition." Michael J. de la Merced, *Nestlé Gets Its U.S. Candy Deal Done*, Jan. 16, 2018, *available at:* https://www.nytimes.com/2018/01/16/business/ dealbook/blackrock-fink-social-good.html. With its purchase of Nestlé's confectionery business, Ferrero became the third-largest chocolate confectioncy in the world and continued their expansion into the U.S. market. Zlati Meyer, *Nestle Is Selling Its U.S. Candy Business to Ferrero for About $2.8 Billion*, Jan. 17, 2018, *available at:* https://www.usatoday.com/story/money/2018/01/16/ nestle-selling-its-u-s-candy-business-ferrero-2-9-b/1036675001/. Indeed, a year later, Ferrero purchased the Keebler cookie brands from Kellogg for $1.3 billion in cash. Kellogg sold off its cookie division in an effort to "streamline its portfolio, . . . reduce complexity, [lead to] more targeted investment, and better growth." Connor Smith, *Kellogg Is Getting out of the Cookie Business with Keebler Sale*, April 19, 2019, *available at:* https://www.barrons.com/articles/kellogg-is -getting-out-of-the-cookie-business-with-keebler-sale-51554131727. Both of these transactions, involving well-known food/consumer products, are examples of corporations divesting iconic brands in an effort to innovate and invest in other growing markets. We will briefly examine the mechanics of a "spin-off" transaction as part of our discussion of the problem sets in the next chapter.

4. Strategic vs. Financial Buyers.   Since 2004, the M&A market has seen an explosive growth of private equity firms, which have increasingly become active as deal players in the M&A market in the United States. Indeed, statistics show that by the mid-2000s, buyout (i.e., private equity) firms accounted for more than a quarter of all M&A activity, by deal value, in the United States, and "accounted for 40% of all deals involving public targets in the first quarter [of 2007]." John E. Morris, *Going Private, Mostly*, THE DEAL, May 2007, at 20. This trend continues, as reflected in recent data showing that private equity funds "have plenty of money . . . that they are looking to invest." John Reiss and Gregory Pryor, White & Case, LLP, *Record Breaker: U.S. M&A in 2015*, Feb. 1, 2016 (law firm memo, copy on file with author); *see also*, Bryan K. Mattingly and Keeana Sajadi Boarman, Frost Brown Todd LLC, *M&A Insights for the New World*, May 29, 2020, *available at*: https://frostbrowntodd.com/ma-insights-for-the-new -world/ ("[T]here remains significant dry powder [among private equity firms] that will need to be deployed, . . . and many private equity and other financial buyers may begin to look for more . . . acquisitions as they attempt to grow their existing portfolio companies, . . . much like strategic buyers.").

How do private equity buyers differ from strategic buyers?

> . . . This article provides a brief review of some basic elements of a private equity transaction and some key considerations that distinguish private equity deals from more traditional M&A.
>
> Private equity sponsors (also referred to as financial sponsors) seek to acquire companies that they can grow or improve (or both) with a view toward eventual sale or public offering. In terms of growth, the financial sponsor will usually acquire a platform company in a particular industry and then seek to add additional companies to the platform through acquisition. . . .
>
> Strategic buyers, on the other hand, are companies that are already in the target company's industry or in a similar industry. While strategic buyers use acquisitions for growth, they may have different goals than a financial sponsor. For example, a strategic buyer may not be concerned about an exit strategy for an acquired business because it expects a seamless integration of the target into its own operations.
>
> . . . Private equity investors generally acquire new companies through lever-aged buyouts. The use of leverage distinguishes financial sponsors from strategic buyers engaged in more traditional merger and acquisition transactions. A private equity sponsor needs the assets of the target company as collateral to borrow the funds necessary to acquire the company. Therefore, private equity investors seek target companies that can generate sufficient cash to service the debt that is incurred to acquire them. . . .
>
> In contrast, because strategic buyers often can fund acquisitions from cash on hand, they generally do not need to incur debt and can consummate transactions more quickly. . . .
>
> Private equity investors also are looking for a particular type of seller (references to "seller" refer to the owners/operators of the target company). Since the private equity sponsor will not run the target company's day-to-day operations following the closing, it is imperative that the seller be willing and desirous of continuing to run the company. Ideally, the target must have a founder or principal who will remain with the business . . . to implement its strategy for growth and eventual exit. This is in stark contrast with the desire of strategic buyers who often do not want members of the target's management to continue with the business following the closing. More traditional merger and acquisition transactions usually lead to job eliminations to maximize efficiency. Strategic buyers in the same industry as the target usually have personnel in their organization who can run the target's business.

Jeffrey Blomberg, *Private Equity Transactions: Understanding Some Fundamental Principles*, 17 BUSINESS LAW TODAY 51, 51-52 (Jan./Feb. 2008). As we go through the remaining chapters, we will study transactions involving both financial buyers and strategic bidders, and we will study in more detail the different set of incentives and business considerations that guide these different types of prospective Bidders.

   5. What is an "LBO"? A *leveraged buyout*, or *LBO* as it is more popularly known, employs the extensive use of debt to finance Bidder's purchase of Target and contemplates that the cash flow generated by Target's business and/or the disposition of Target assets will be used to secure and repay the debt that Bidder incurs. Particularly in the current environment of historically low interest rates, debt financing usually has a lower cost of capital than does equity financing. For reasons to be explored in more detail as part of the problem sets in Chapter 2 (where we describe LBOs in more detail), debt financing effectively serves as a "lever," if you will, to increase the returns to the equity investors (i.e., the shareholders), which helps to explain the origin of the term "LBO."

> Usually, the business being purchased becomes the ultimate debtor whose cash flow is expected to discharge the debts incurred in the takeover. This type of acquisition is called . . . a leveraged buyout (if incumbent management and outside financiers end up as the ultimate owners of the business). . . . The decision as to whether such a transaction is feasible may be based on (1) a cash-flow analysis indicating the maximum amount of debt the business can possibly carry [i.e., the amount of interest that the business can pay to its lenders as the cost of the borrowed capital], and (2) estimates of the amounts for which nonessential assets or peripheral lines of business can be sold for. In the most extreme case, most of the business's assets may be sold off to raise funds to reduce the outstanding indebtedness incurred to finance the [original] purchase price [a transaction that is often referred to on Wall Street as a "bust up" bid].

Robert W. Hamilton and Richard A Booth, BUSINESS BASICS FOR LAW STUDENTS 173 (4th ed. 2006). We will examine LBOs in more detail in analyzing the problem sets in Chapter 2.

   6. Payment of a "Premium." In both of the deal stories described at the beginning of this chapter, the Bidder offered to pay a "premium" in order to acquire Target's business. Indeed, M&A transactions are usually characterized by Bidder's payment of a "premium" in order to gain ownership (control) of Target's business. Why? In the case of the sale of Target, Target will no longer remain a freestanding, independent business. Instead, managerial control of Target's business assets and operations will shift to Bidder, as the buyer of Target's business. In the usual case, Target's owners will demand payment of a "premium" to reflect the "true value" (or sometimes referred to as "fair value" or "inherent value") of Target's business in order to entice Target's shareholders to "sell" (that is, to transfer managerial control and/or ownership of Target as a freestanding business) to the Bidder. As we shall see in the problem sets and other materials in Chapter 2, the "true value" of Target's business is typically a matter that is heavily negotiated between the parties, and the parties' assessment of "true value" can vary considerably, such variance often depending on the assumptions that the parties make as to the future financial potential of Target's business. We will explore this issue (and the nature of the assumptions to be made in determining what is a "fair price" to be paid by Bidder in order to acquire Target's business) as part of the valuation materials included at the end of Chapter 2. By way of summary, the following excerpt provides an explanation for the observed phenomenon that Bidders inevitably pay a premium in a takeover transaction—an explanation that is widely accepted by many knowledgeable participants in the M&A market:

> When the common stock of a company is publicly traded on an exchange or in the over-the-counter market, the market price is often considered to be a reliable measure of value. But it is clearly not always so. . . .
>
> Even when a publicly traded stock has a broad market with numerous [daily trading] transactions, it does not necessarily follow that the total value of the business, if it were sold as a single entity, equals the current market price per share multiplied by the total number of shares outstanding [or what is often referred to on Wall Street as the "*market capitalization*" or "*float*" of a publicly traded company]. If this conclusion were correct, valuation of publicly held corporations would be relatively easy, because one could obtain the current value of the entire business simply by adding up the current market values of all outstanding shares. But the premiums typically paid to shareholders in corporate takeovers demonstrate that the value placed on a business by the securities markets is often significantly lower than the amount that a purchaser is willing to pay for the *entire business* (or *all* the outstanding stock). In other words, the market often appears to understate the value of the entire company. This phenomenon has been the subject of considerable speculation.
>
> One plausible explanation for [the payment of a premium in a takeover transaction] . . . is that the trading markets for securities are primarily markets for *investments*, not markets for *controlling interests* in companies. Almost all transactions on public securities markets involve minute fractions of the total outstanding shares of companies, and these transactions individually do not carry with them any meaningful opportunity to affect the company's business policies. If the transactions increase in size so that control of the company may be involved, the purchasers are willing to pay more—usually significantly more—than the prices for smaller blocks of shares that are traded [on the open market] solely as investments. . . . The result is that the market for the whole corporation—the takeover market—. . . is different from the market for investment securities.

Robert Hamilton and Richard Booth, BUSINESS BASICS FOR LAW STUDENTS 172-173 (4th ed. 2006) (*emphasis added*).

At this point, it bears emphasizing that the public announcement of a deal (or, as we shall see in subsequent chapters, even rumors/speculation that a company may be the target of a proposed acquisition) will have a dramatic impact on the trading price of the common stock of the putative Target in the open market. The fundamental reason for this impact on Target's trading price, once the company is "put in play,"* is that the pricing of Target stock in the open

---

* [By the author: What does it mean to "put a company in play"? In Wall Street parlance, this colloquial phrase is generally used to refer to a company that has become (or is rumored to become) the subject of a takeover bid and thus whose stock has become the subject of speculation by traders in the stock markets.]

market shifts from traders pricing Target stock based on what a willing buyer would be willing to pay to a willing seller for a fungible share of Target's common stock — to traders pricing Target's stock based on the assumption Target Co. is being sold — with the trading price being discounted, of course, for the possibility that the deal with Bidder might not close. This shift in perspective among traders in the open market has the inevitable effect of putting upward pressure on the price of Target's stock, as was described in the case of AT&T's acquisition of DirecTV's business.

As another example of this shift in traders' perspective once a company is "put in play," the *Los Angeles Times* reported in August 2011, that shares of the ever popular discount retailer, 99¢ Only Stores, Inc., traded up following reports that the company would receive a new buyout offer. *See* Andrea Chang, *99 Cent Only Stock Jumps on Expectations of New Buyout Offer,* LOS ANGELES TIMES, Aug. 23, 2011, at B3. Earlier in the year, 99¢ Only had received a buyout proposal that "[i]nvestors viewed as too low . . . [and so traders] quickly pushed the stock price [above] the $19.09" price per share that had been offered in March 2011 by the Schiffer/Gold family (the company's controlling shareholder) and Leonard Green and Partners (a buyout/private equity firm). *Id.* Indeed, after the initial buyout proposal was announced in March 2011, "several industry analysts said they expected a higher offer to emerge for the company. . . ." *Id.* Eventually, 99¢ Only Stores was acquired by another buyout fund for $22 per share, representing a 32 percent premium over the company's trading price in March 2011, the day before the company announced the terms of the initial acquisition proposal that it had received from a different private equity firm. *See 99 Cents Only to Be Sold for $1.6 B,* ASSOCIATED PRESS, Oct. 11, 2011, *available at:* http://finance.yahoo.com/news/Retailer-99-Cents-Only-to-be-apf-2517412550 .html. *Query:* Why would the trading price of the company's stock rise above the price offered by the original Bidder?

7. The Problem of "Bidder Overpayment."   We have noted that M&A transactions generally involve the payment of a "premium" to acquire the Target, thus typically generating considerable extra value for Target shareholders. Indeed, "[o]ne important, and undisputed, datum about acquisitive transactions should be noted: acquisitions generate substantial gains to target company shareholders. . . . Without question, the announcement of a [takeover bid or merger agreement] is good news for target shareholders." Roberta Romano, *A Guide to Takeovers: Theory, Evidence & Regulation,* 9 YALE J. ON REG. 119, 122 (1992). With respect to Bidder and its shareholders, there is considerable more controversy as to the benefits achieved through M&A transactions:

> Whether shareholders of acquirers [Bidders] gain from acquisitions, however, is substantially more heavily debated with results from numerous studies finding much more complexity than with respect to target shareholders. Scholars continue to generate extensive empirical research on the effects of acquisitions on acquirer shareholders and on how the interests of acquirer management affect these transactions. While several early studies reported that [Bidder] shareholders benefit from acquisitions, others reported losses to them. A significant body of more recent finance literature finds evidence that many, although clearly not all, acquisitions destroy value for long-term [Bidder] shareholders. This is particularly true in the case of takeovers of publicly traded targets by publicly traded acquirers.

Afra Afsharipour, *A Shareholders' Put Option: Counteracting the Acquirer Over-payment Problem*, 96 MINN. L. REV. 1018, 1028 (2012). In thinking about this issue, consider the following observation made by an experienced M&A lawyer:

> A major merger or acquisition can be a company-defining moment. The right business combination at the right price, with good execution, can reposition the company, accelerate profitable growth and shareholder return, and even change the game for an industry as a whole. But a bad deal—whether the failure is rooted in the concept [i.e., the "logic of the deal," that is, the business justification for the proposed acquisition], the price, or the execution—is probably the fastest legal means of destroying shareholder value.

Ken Smith, *The M&A Buck Stops at the Board*, 41 MERGERS AND ACQUISITIONS 48, 49 (Apr. 2006).

C. The Flow of a Deal: Introducing Timing, Pricing, and Other Structural Considerations

Every acquisition—whether done on Wall Street or Main Street—tends to follow the same timeline. The reason for this convention is that all acquisitions face the same threshold issues, although the way the issues get resolved varies widely depending on a number of variables, not the least of which is the size of the acquisition. As we study the materials in the remaining chapters, we will explore the nature of these threshold issues and the legal rules that must be taken into account in addressing these issues. Since these legal and business issues create a time frame that is fairly typical of any M&A deal, it is worth sketching out the basic steps of any business acquisition, even though the precise reasons for this chronology will not be made clear until we analyze the materials in the remaining chapters.

   With some slight variations that reflect inherent differences between Wall Street and Main Street M&A activity, the essential sequence of an M&A transaction follows a similar pattern that will be referred to as the "flow of a deal." As an illustration of a fairly typical deal flow, this section starts off by describing the process by which AT&T made its offer to acquire DirecTV. The remainder of this section then breaks this timeline down into the various steps involved in a typical acquisition that will culminate in Bidder getting control over Target's business operations.

1. Deal Flow: How Did the AT&T–DirecTV Deal Get Done?

According to the AT&T–DirecTV Joint Proxy Statement (on which this account of the deal flow of AT&T's acquisition of DirecTV is largely based, *see* http://d1lge852tjjqow.cloudfront.net/CIK-0001465112/a6559e3b4-e540-4a7d-813e-c6330e4d4372.pdf), by year end 2009, DirecTV's board had become increasingly aware that the continued growth of its business faced several strategic challenges, most notably the growing consumer demand for broadband services and the concomitant decline in importance of pay television services. In addition, DirecTV's business faced increasing leverage from programmers that had resulted in substantially increasing the cost to DirecTV of obtaining content. Finally, DirecTV's board had also recognized the potential for significant competition resulting from the emerging growth of digital media providers.

Michael White joined DirecTV as its president and CEO in January 2010. Almost immediately, the management team entered into discussions with various potential strategic partners, including both AT&T and Verizon, as well as various content providers and new media companies. However, none of these discussions resulted in any proposal that would help DirecTV to mitigate the strategic challenges (facing its core business) that the board had previously identified.

During 2011, DirecTV's board authorized the company's senior management to contact a competitor in the industry (referred to in the Joint Proxy Statement as "Company A") to discuss a potential business combination. However, these discussions did not result in any offer being made by either party. During 2012 and 2013, the strategic challenges that had previously been identified by DirecTV's board only continued to intensify, leading the DirecTV board to authorize management to evaluate alternatives intended to address these challenges—including the possibility of acquiring a digital media provider.

In January 2013, AT&T's CEO, Randall Stephenson, contacted his counterpart at DirecTV, Michael White, to discuss the possibility of combining DirecTV and AT&T. While the strategic merits of such a combination were intriguing and seemed promising, both Stephenson and White agreed that they should conduct a joint assessment of the regulatory hurdles that such a deal presented *before* entering into any substantive negotiations or commencing any due diligence. In August 2013, advisors representing AT&T and DirecTV met to develop a mutually acceptable regulatory review plan, but these discussions did not bear any fruit. Consequently, in September 2013, AT&T formally advised DirecTV that it did not wish to pursue a potential business combination between the two parties at that time.

In December 2013, White met with the chairman of Company A, and they discussed the merits of a potential business combination. However, they both quickly came to appreciate the significant difficulties they faced in connection with obtaining the necessary regulatory approvals of such a deal between the two companies. So, while the parties suspended any further discussions, they also agreed to resume talks if the regulatory landscape should change.

In February 2014, Comcast and Time Warner Cable, the two leading cable companies in the United States, announced that they would merge. DirecTV's management immediately recognized that this combination, if completed, would further exacerbate the strategic challenges facing DirecTV's business. Following this announcement, DirecTV's board requested that management brief the board as to a possible combination between DirecTV and Company A, including an analysis of the likelihood of obtaining the required regulatory approvals.

In March 2014, both Stephenson and White attended a meeting of a business group in Washington, D.C. Following this meeting, Stephenson suggested that the parties reopen the discussions that had been terminated in September

2013, with an eye toward negotiating a potential transaction. White then advised the DirecTV board of Stephenson's suggestion, and on March 27, 2014, AT&T and DirecTV entered into confidentiality agreements.

On April 1, 2014, the DirecTV board met with representatives of the law firm of Weil, Gotshal & Manges (Weil Gotshal), who was serving as outside counsel for DirecTV. As part of this meeting, the DirecTV board authorized the engagement of Goldman, Sachs & Co. (Goldman Sachs) as financial advisor for DirecTV. Following this board meeting, AT&T's financial and legal advisors commenced their due diligence review of DirecTV.

On April 22, 2014, AT&T submitted to DirecTV a confidential, non-binding proposal to acquire DirecTV, which included the following terms and conditions:

> (1) the acquisition of 100% of the outstanding shares of DirecTV for $85 per share, comprised of $25.50 in cash and the balance in AT&T stock according to a fixed exchange ratio; (2) a requirement that DirecTV extend NFL Sunday Ticket; (3) completion of satisfactory due diligence by AT&T; (4) negotiation and execution of a mutually acceptable definitive merger agreement by the two parties; (5) obtaining AT&T board approval; and (6) obtaining the required state, federal and foreign regulatory approvals.

White then advised all of the individual DirecTV board members of AT&T's proposal.

As part of its regularly scheduled board meeting on April 28-29, 2014, the DirecTV board reviewed the terms of the AT&T merger proposal. At the time of this meeting, the DirecTV board decided to retain Bank of America Merrill Lynch (BofA Merrill Lynch) as an additional financial advisor in connection with any potential strategic transaction. Following detailed presentations by its financial and legal advisors as to the relative merits of AT&T's offer and the potential of consummating a transaction with Company A, including an assessment of the likelihood of obtaining required U.S. regulatory approvals for a transaction with each of AT&T and Company A, the DirecTV board and its advisors discussed at length AT&T's non-binding proposal and other strategic alternatives. Following this discussion, the DirecTV board unanimously decided to authorize management to reject AT&T's preliminary proposal, but also decided to authorize White, the company's CEO, to make a counter offer to AT&T on terms consistent with the board's discussion at this meeting.

Following adjournment of the DirecTV board meeting on April 29, White contacted Stephenson. Consistent with the board's direction, White advised Stephenson that, for the DirecTV board to consider agreeing to a business combination with AT&T, the consideration to DirecTV's shareholders would have to be in the range of the upper $90s per share. The two also discussed other aspects of AT&T's preliminary proposal as part of their conversation.

Stephenson and White held a meeting on May 4, 2014, during which Stephenson advised White that AT&T was willing to increase the price of its offer to a range of $93-$95 per share of DirecTV stock, with the final price to be fixed following negotiation of other terms of the parties' definitive acquisition agreement and completion of AT&T's due diligence process. White then advised Stephenson that a price below $95 per share was not likely to be acceptable to the DirecTV board. The two CEOs also discussed other terms of AT&T's preliminary proposal, most notably the provision relating to NFL Sunday Ticket, which Stephenson emphasized was an important element of the proposed transaction from AT&T's perspective.

On May 5, 2014, Sullivan & Cromwell LLP (Sullivan & Cromwell), counsel for AT&T, delivered a draft merger agreement to Weil Gotshal as counsel for DirecTV. At the same time, AT&T and its financial and legal advisors continued their due diligence review of DirecTV. Lazard Freres & Co., LLC ("Lazard") served as AT&T's financial advisor in connection with the proposed acquisition of DirecTV. Moreover, in light of the proposed AT&T stock component included in the price per share offered by AT&T, DirecTV (together with its legal and financial advisors) commenced their own due diligence review of AT&T.

On May 9, 2014, White held separate meetings with a representative of the NFL Broadcasting Committee and then-NFL Commissioner Roger Goodell. As part of these meetings, White discussed the potential for a business combination with AT&T and the impact any such transaction may have on the NFL Sunday agreement. Also on May 9, Weil Gotshal provided to Sullivan & Cromwell a revised draft of the May 5 merger agreement. Beginning on the evening of May 9 and continuing through May 10, 2014, representatives of AT&T and DirecTV met in person in order to negotiate and resolve remaining issues in connection with the draft merger agreement. These discussions resulted in Sullivan & Cromwell sending a revised draft of the merger agreement to Weil Gotshal and DirecTV on May 11, 2014.

On May 12, 2014, the DirecTV board met by teleconference for the purpose of reviewing the status of negotiations with AT&T and the status of discussions with the NFL, among other things. During the period from May 13 to May 16, 2014, representatives of Weil Gotshal and Sullivan & Cromwell continued to negotiate remaining issues concerning the terms of the parties' proposed merger agreement.

Stephenson telephoned White on May 16, 2014. Based on the outcome of AT&T's due diligence review, Stephenson proposed a price of $93.50 per share, to be comprised of 32 percent cash and the remaining 68 percent to consist of AT&T stock. White immediately responded that he did not believe that this proposal would be acceptable to DirecTV's board of directors. After further discussion, the call ended with no agreement on these issues, but the two CEOs agreed to consider all available options in order to resolve the remaining open issues. Shortly thereafter, Stephenson and White spoke by telephone and they agreed to a price of $95 per share of DirecTV stock, with 30 percent of the purchase price to be paid in cash, and the remaining 70 percent to be paid in AT&T stock. Stephenson and White also reconfirmed that all terms including these were subject to review and approval by their respective boards of directors.

Sullivan & Cromwell provided a revised draft of the merger agreement to Weil Gotshal on the evening of May 16, and the parties continued to discuss the terms of the merger agreement throughout that evening and the next day. The next day, the AT&T board met and unanimously approved the transaction.

On May 18, 2014, the DirecTV board met with senior management of DirecTV, and representatives of Weil Gotshal, Goldman Sachs, and BofA Merrill Lynch (among others) were also in attendance.

At this meeting, the company's legal advisors presented a summary of the material terms of the merger agreement (the final version of which had been previously delivered to the DirecTV board) and reviewed with the DirecTV board the scope of its fiduciary duty obligations in connection with approving the proposed merger with AT&T. The company's legal and financial advisors also summarized the results of the due diligence assessment of AT&T conducted by DirecTV and its advisors. Representatives from both of the company's investment bankers (Goldman Sachs and BofA Merrill Lynch) also made detailed presentations to the DirecTV board of directors in support of their respective conclusions that the terms of AT&T's merger proposal were fair from a financial point of view to the holders of DirecTV common stock. The board also received updated reports from its advisors regarding their assessment of the likelihood of obtaining the required U.S. and foreign regulatory approvals. The board also discussed the concessions that AT&T intended to make, in connection with the terms of the merger agreement, in order to help ensure that the required regulatory approvals are obtained.*

Based on the board's discussions of all of these financial, legal, and strategic presentations, the DirecTV board then unanimously determined that entering into the merger agreement was in the best interests of DirecTV and its stockholders, declared the merger agreement advisable, and recommended that the stockholders adopt the merger agreement. Immediately after this May 18 meeting of the DirecTV board adjourned, DirecTV and AT&T executed the merger agreement that same Sunday afternoon and the parties then promptly issued a joint press release announcing the transaction.

Although the deal seemed to originate with the CEOs of the two companies, both firms retained outside advisors to help with the acquisition process. In particular, these advisors helped negotiate the terms and the structure of the deal, document the transaction, and conduct the required due diligence. As noted above, AT&T relied on Lazard Freres & Co. LLC as its investment banker, and the law firm of Sullivan & Cromwell for legal advice. For its part, DirecTV retained the investment banking firms of Goldman Sachs and BofA Merrill Lynch, and turned to the law firm of Weil Gotshal for legal advice.

After the deal has been approved by the boards of both companies, much legal work remains to be done, no matter what method is used to structure the acquisition. As we will see in the next chapter, there are essentially three methods by which business acquisitions get done. These three consist of statutory mergers, asset purchases, and stock purchases. Much of the focus of the required legal work in this regard consists of ensuring compliance with the corporate formalities required to validly complete a transaction using any of these different methods, including the process for obtaining any required shareholder approvals. We will examine the nature of the requirements imposed by state and federal law in the next chapter, where we analyze in more detail these

---

* [By the author: Executive compensation matters are an important (and recurring) issue in negotiating the terms of any acquisition, including AT&T's acquisition of DirecTV. For reasons to be explained in more detail in later chapters, the DirecTV board delegated responsibility for dealing with these issues to the board's Compensation Committee. We will examine the basis of this decision of the DirecTV board (and its ultimate ratification of the actions taken by the Compensation Committee) as part of Chapter 7, when we will examine in detail the scope of the board's fiduciary duty obligations as part of any M&A transaction.]

different methods for combining corporations. Before we examine this substantive detail, let's conceptually break down the process described above into its essential components, each of which will be examined in more detail as we go through the remaining chapters.

QUESTIONS

1. How did negotiations get started for AT&T's acquisition of DirecTV?

2. Why did the parties enter into confidentiality agreements?

3. When did the parties sign the merger agreement? When did the parties close on the merger agreement?

4. What did the acquisition consideration consist of?

5. What is the goal of the due diligence process? In the case of AT&T's acquisition of DirecTV, why did *both* parties to this transaction undertake a due diligence investigation? What will actually be done during the course of a due diligence process?

6. As a public policy matter, why would the law require that the company's shareholders approve a proposed business combination that was negotiated by the company's management team and approved by the company's board of directors?

7. What regulatory approvals were required as a condition to AT&T's obligation to close on its deal with DirecTV?

D. "Deal Flow": Conceptualizing the Deal-making Process

As we shall see when we analyze the problem sets in Chapter 2, there are differences in the timing as well as certain other aspects of the deal-making process that vary depending on whether the acquisition involves publicly traded companies or privately held companies. Nonetheless, there is a certain convention with respect to the deal-making process that M&A transactions tend to follow—regardless of whether the deal is getting done on Wall Street or Main Street. The legal and business considerations that shape the conventional deal-making process for M&A transactions are the subject matter of the remaining chapters. However, it is helpful to begin our study of M&A law by providing a broad overview of the steps generally involved in any given M&A transaction, which is the topic of the next section.

1. The Start of Negotiations

Deals get started in a variety of different ways. Acquisitions, for example, often get started because a financial advisor (frequently an investment banking firm) will identify a particular business as a potential acquisition candidate.

The potential acquisition candidate may be a client of the investment banking firm who has retained this financial advisor to help the corporate client find a buyer for the company's business. Alternatively, the investment banker may be scouting for potential acquisition candidates for one of its established corporate clients, either at the request of its client or, alternatively, as part of the banker's ongoing professional relationship with that particular corporate client. Yet another way for a deal to get launched is for the Bidder's existing management to contact management of a company that the Bidder itself has identified as a potential acquisition target based on its own internal assessment of the industry and the Bidder's business goals and objectives. In cases where existing management identifies the potential acquisition target, early discussions between Bidder and Target may initially proceed without the assistance of outside advisors. Eventually, though, financial and legal advisors will get involved in the deal-making process.

2. The Role of Financial Advisors

As negotiations are launched in earnest, the assistance of financial and legal advisors becomes important in addressing two threshold issues that are common to all acquisitions: how should the deal be structured, and how much will Bidder pay to acquire Target? In Chapter 2, we will analyze the different types of deal structures available to complete the acquisition. As we shall see, the legal rules that must be satisfied for each type of deal structure will often influence the decision as to which type of structure is most appropriate for a particular deal. In addition, financial advisors will be assisting Bidder in its decision as to how much to pay to acquire Target, which necessarily requires Bidder to value Target's business. On the other side, Target will engage its own set of financial advisors to help it determine whether Bidder is offering a fair price to acquire Target's business. Since Target only gets one chance to sell its business and relinquish control over its income-producing operations, Target has a strong vested interest in making sure that it obtains the best price available. Although Target's management may have a strong sense of what it thinks its business is worth, there are other variables that influence the price that it can obtain for its business, not the least of which is the general condition of the market at the time of sale and the general business environment within Target's specific industry. These variables, as well as the financial well-being of Target's own business, will heavily influence the bargaining process between Bidder and Target as to the purchase price.

Even though Target may have strong convictions as to the true value of its business, there are many variables to be juggled in reaching a consensus with Bidder as to the purchase price. In dealing with the confluence of all these variables in the context of a particular deal, most buyers and sellers—regardless of the size of the deal—understand the need to bring in the expertise of outside advisors. All of which illustrates the fundamental truism that valuation is an art, not a science. And, just as beauty is in the eye of the beholder, judgments as to valuation can vary widely between buyers and sellers. Outside advisors can often provide the experience and expertise that will result in closing the gap between Bidder and Target, thereby facilitating the ability of the parties to reach an agreement as to the terms of the acquisition purchase price and the nature of the consideration to be paid. As part of these negotiations, Bidder may require that Target share information about its business and financial affairs so that Bidder can more accurately determine what it is willing to pay to acquire Target.

Use of Confidentiality Agreements. This exchange of information between Bidder and Target may require the parties to share with each other highly sensitive, confidential, and proprietary information about their businesses. Obviously, each side will be concerned about maintaining the confidentiality of this information. This concern will usually lead to the use of confidentiality agreements to protect against misuse of the business and financial information that Bidder and Target will exchange with each other. Accordingly, early in the deal process, the parties will usually enter into a confidentiality agreement (commonly referred to as a *non-disclosure agreement*, or *NDA*) to assure each other that confidential and proprietary business information shared during the acquisition process will be carefully protected and not used for any purpose other than evaluating the proposed transaction. We will discuss the use of NDAs in detail in Chapter 5.

Who Are the Deal Players? In mega-deals, such as AT&T's acquisition of DirecTV, each side will generally rely on its own Wall Street investment banker, such as the well-known firms of JPMorgan Chase, Goldman Sachs, and Morgan Stanley. In smaller deals involving closely held companies, midsize investment bankers may get involved, firms whose names are not as well known. And, in even smaller deals involving the sale of closely held, often family-owned businesses, no investment banker is used. Instead, the company is listed for sale with a business broker, much in the same way that homeowners list their homes for sale with a real estate broker, who will typically receive a commission when the deal closes. Likewise, the financial advisor will receive a fee for its services as a business broker, which is often framed in terms of a commission to be paid when the deal between Bidder and Target closes. For reasons that we explore in the remaining chapters, M&A transactions are "complex affairs":

> [typically] involving a large number of parties that may—or may not—be prepared to bid higher . . . [Completing an acquisition] may sprawl over weeks and months. The [financial advisors] at the center of these often freewheeling [deals] take on a number of [different] roles: information gatherer and valuation analyst; matchmaker who tries to bring together the right buyer for the right seller; psychologist who can detect subtle shifts in sentiment. He—and they are mostly men—must work discretely, even secretly; he must be seen to be operating evenhandedly, and yet also in the best interests of the client. He must pit bidders against each other [in order] to extract the highest price [for Target Co.]. He must keep the client informed while nudging the [deal-making process] forward, fanning interest at opportune moments, moving [the deal participants forward] from stage to stage. [Finally,] [h]e must be able to close the deal when the time comes.

Vyvyan Tenorio, *Investment Bankers as Auction Stars*, THE DEAL, May 29, 2012, at 6-7. As we shall see in the remaining chapters, the role of the legal advisor often overlaps with that of the financial advisor, with the lawyer sharing important responsibilities for keeping the deal-making process moving forward while also being sensitive to shifts in sentiment among the participants on the deal and simultaneously keeping the client informed.

"Delayed Closing." As with the financial advisor, the lawyer also bears important responsibility for moving the deal from "signing to closing," since virtually all M&A transactions involve a "delayed closing." That is to say, the parties negotiate the transaction and then sign the definitive acquisition agreement reflecting the terms as bargained for by the parties to the transaction. However, the actual transfer of the business typically will not occur until some later date as specified in the parties' acquisition agreement (i.e., the closing date). This is similar to the process involved when a willing seller agrees to sell a parcel of real property to a willing buyer. Once the land sale contract is signed, the parties move into the escrow period, during which time both buyer and seller typically are contractually obligated to complete certain responsibilities before closing the deal. Likewise, in an M&A transaction, the acquisition agreement will typically specify responsibilities that the parties to the transaction must complete before closing on the acquisition. The nature of these obligations is explored in more detail in Chapter 5 as part of a more extensive discussion of the steps involved in documenting and completing an M&A transaction.

Meeting the Client's Business Objectives: Speed, Certainty, and Price. In the situation where Target Co. decides to sell its business (often referred to colloquially as "putting itself on the auction block"), Target's managers will usually retain legal and financial advisors who will be responsible for designing a sale process that allows Target to meet its business objectives, which generally consist of speed, certainty, and price. Let me elaborate. "Speed" refers to the risk that the deal process will disrupt Target's business; that is, Target's management is often concerned that the sale process will disrupt the orderly management of Target's business operations by resulting in the loss of employees (who fear that their jobs may be at risk if the company is sold), the loss of customers, the loss of vendors, and the like. "Certainty" refers to minimizing execution risk; that is, minimizing the risk that Target's deal with Bidder will not close, given that the typical M&A transaction contemplates a delayed closing (as described above). Finally, and probably most important from Target's point of view, is "price," in that Target usually seeks to obtain the best price available for Target's business. For reasons that were described earlier in this chapter, the determination of the best price for Target's business generally focuses on the adequacy of the premium being offered by Bidder.

3.   Use of Non-cash Consideration to Finance the Purchase Price

Often Bidder will seek to acquire Target for non-cash consideration. As we will see when we analyze the diagrams in Appendix A at the end of this book, this will result in a very different treatment of Target Co.'s shareholders after the acquisition is completed. When Bidder issues its stock in exchange for Target's business, Target Co. shareholders will end up owning Bidder Co. stock. This presents a very different investment decision for Target's shareholders. Now they must decide whether they want to invest in Bidder Co., which means that

Target Co. shareholders face a separate and often rather complicated valuation decision of their own. In addition to deciding the amount for which they are willing to sell Target's business, Target's shareholders now must determine what value they place on Bidder's business on a going forward basis. This decision will usually require Bidder to provide to Target's shareholders information about Bidder's business and its plans for the future after acquiring Target's business.

4.   The Due Diligence Process

"Due diligence" is a term of art used to describe the process of information gathering and analysis, which will usually be undertaken by each party to the business acquisition. The focus is on gathering all relevant information necessary for a thorough evaluation of the other company's business and financial affairs. From the perspective of Bidder, the goal of its due diligence investigation of Target is to gain all the information it needs—good and bad—to be sure that it does not overpay to acquire Target, an inherent possibility associated with any M&A transaction. For reasons to be explored in more detail in Chapter 5, Bidder's risk of overpayment is substantially mitigated through adequate due diligence, among other protective provisions, although this risk can never be completely eliminated.

From Target's perspective, the scope of its due diligence will depend in large part on the nature of the acquisition consideration offered by Bidder. In the case of an all-cash deal, Target's primary concern is the adequacy of the price offered. Since Target gets only one chance to sell its business operations, it has a vested interest in making sure that it obtains the largest premium possible—in other words, the best price that it can negotiate. In making this determination, however, Target needs minimal, if any, information about Bidder and its plans for the future since Target shareholders will have no further equity participation in the case of an all-cash purchase price. Rather, Target's concern is typically focused on Bidder's financial ability to pay the all-cash purchase price at the time of closing.

On the other hand, if Bidder is offering to acquire Target in exchange for Bidder's stock, Target's due diligence process will be broader in scope. In this situation, Target shareholders need information about Bidder's plans to integrate Target's assets into Bidder's business operations. This information from Bidder Co. will be an important factor in the Target Co. shareholders' decision about whether to remain independent and continue as the equity owners of Target Co., or alternatively, to combine with Bidder Co. and rely on Bidder Co.'s leadership and business model to maximize their financial return. We will talk at greater length in Chapter 4 about the process for disseminating this information to Target Co. shareholders and the manner in which the federal securities laws regulate this disclosure process in the case of constituent corporation(s) that is/are publicly traded.

5.   Board Approval of an Acquisition

In the case of most acquisitions, approval by the boards of directors of both Bidder and Target will be required in order for the transaction to proceed. Generally speaking, the acquisition proposal does not originate with the company's board. Rather, the CEO, supported by his or her team of senior executive officers, initiates the process and is usually responsible for negotiating the terms of the transaction. Ultimately, the deal will be made binding on the company only if the board approves the terms of the negotiated agreement. In our modern world of corporate governance, and particularly in this post-financial-crisis business environment, there is an interesting tension at work. This tension has always been present, but has been receiving increased attention in light of the recent spate of financial scandals. The origins of this tension stem from the fundamental tenet that the board manages the business affairs of the company; however, it is the company's officers, most importantly the company's CEO, who are responsible for implementing these policy decisions as the agents of the corporation. The board members act collectively (generally by way of a duly noticed board meeting); consequently, no single board member has the individual authority to bind the corporation. Officers, on the other hand, have authority by virtue of their position to bind the company. So, the CEO may enter into contracts that are binding on the company, provided that they are in the ordinary course of business and are not extraordinary.

In the case of an acquisition, there is an interesting threshold question as to whether the CEO has the authority to initiate discussions with another company's CEO about a proposed business combination. If so, at what point is the CEO required to bring these discussions to the attention of the company's board of directors? What level of involvement is the board required to exercise in the process of negotiating the terms of a business acquisition in order to fulfill its fiduciary obligations to the company, as well as any other statutory requirements that may be imposed under the terms of modern corporation codes? The nature of these requirements under state and federal law will be introduced when we analyze the problems in Chapter 2.

As a preliminary matter, it is worth noting that the relative balance of power between the board and the company's CEO is a topic of renewed interest in the wake of the crisis in investor confidence spawned by the numerous financial scandals dating back to the turn of the twenty-first century. In the wake of these scandals, legislators, institutional investors, and other observers have demanded greater oversight of management and greater accountability of officers and directors with respect to management's decision-making process. After all, one of the most important decisions to be made in today's corporate boardrooms is the decision to pursue a business combination. As we go through the problems in Chapter 2, we will examine this question of the board's involvement in the deal-making process in more detail, along with the corporate governance implications triggered by this issue.

6.   Shareholder Approval of an Acquisition

As we will learn when we analyze the problems in the next chapter, state law will often require shareholder approval of the terms of the proposed acquisition in order for the transaction to be validly completed. In those cases where shareholder approval is required, there will be an inevitable delay associated with noticing and conducting a meeting of the shareholders in compliance with the requirements imposed by the law of the state where the company is organized. Further delay may result if the company is publicly traded because the company may be required to prepare and disseminate the disclosure required by the federal proxy rules whenever a publicly traded company solicits a vote by proxy from its shareholders. In Chapter 4, we will examine the nature of the disclosure required under the federal proxy rules of the Securities and Exchange Commission (SEC), along with certain other provisions of the federal securities laws. At this juncture, however, the point to be emphasized is that compliance with these requirements imposed by state and federal law will definitely impact the time frame for completing a proposed acquisition.

7. Regulatory Approval of an Acquisition

Many acquisitions will require approval from federal and/or state regulators in order for the transaction to be validly consummated. This requirement may be imposed contractually (that is, as a condition included in the terms of the parties' acquisition agreement) or alternatively may be imposed by statute. The approval most often required is clearance from antitrust regulators. This casebook will not dwell on the criteria used by the antitrust regulators to decide whether to approve—or clear—an acquisition, thereby allowing the business combination transaction to be completed. I assume that the criteria used by the regulators to decide whether a particular acquisition poses a threat to consumer welfare in violation of the terms of antitrust law is covered as part of a separate course on antitrust law offered in the curriculum of most law schools. Therefore, in Chapter 8, we will mention only a few details of antitrust law that directly and regularly affect M&A activity and of which M&A lawyers need to be aware. For transactions that may present antitrust issues, antitrust counsel typically will be brought in to advise the respective companies. For example, in the failed AT&T–T-Mobile merger (described earlier in this chapter), antitrust counsel likely advised the two companies of the negative stance that antitrust regulators were likely to take if two of the four largest cell phone providers within the United States merged. Sure enough, once the deal was announced, U.S. antitrust regulators filed a lawsuit to block the impending merger, citing the likelihood of decreased competition within the cell phone market and, in turn, higher prices for cell phone services as causes for concern. Michael J. de la Merced, *AT&T Ends $39 Billion Bid for T-Mobile*, DEALBOOK NEW YORK TIMES, Dec. 19, 2011, *available at:* http://dealbook.nytimes.com/2011/12/19/att-withdraws-39-bid-for-t-mobile. In the end, AT&T succumbed to pressure from the antitrust regulators and abandoned its $39 billion bid to acquire T-Mobile, ultimately paying a $4 billion "break-up" fee to Deutsche Telekom, the parent company of T-Mobile. *Id.* We will examine the use of "break-up fees" in more detail in Chapter 7, as part of our discussion of deal protection devices.* *Query:*

---

* [By the author: In April 2020, T-Mobile announced that it had "officially completed a merger with Sprint. The deal, which was [originally] announced in [spring of] 2018, means that the previously *third* and fourth largest wireless companies in the United States have now become the third[-largest such company] – rivaling AT&T and Verizon. . . . The deal had to clear multiple legal hurdles to prove it wouldn't stifle competition – [as] a number of [antitrust authorities and consumer advocates] worried that the consolidation of the industry would lead to higher prices." Andrew Limbong, *T-Mobile Completes Takeover of Rival Company Sprint*, April 1, 2020, *available at*: https://www.npr.org/2020/04/01/825523250/t-mobile-completes-takeover-of-rival-company-sprint#:~:text=Mobile%20carrier%20T%2DMobile%20announced,third%20%E2%80%94%20rivaling%20AT%26T%20and%20Verizon.]

Whose interests are being protected by having antitrust authorities review the terms of these M&A transactions?

In the case of companies operating within regulated industries—such as telecommunications, banking, and aviation—separate approvals may be required from other government regulators (either at the state or federal level) in order to validly complete the transaction. As was the case with antitrust clearance, the requirement for these other regulatory approvals is often imposed contractually or may be required as a matter of law. In the case of regulated industries, government officials intervene to impose some form of regulatory review and approval in order to protect an interest not adequately represented in the process of negotiating and completing a business acquisition, or to promote some other public policy goal that may be undermined by a proposed business combination. The public policy considerations that motivate policymakers at the federal or state level to intervene in the deal-making process through legislative action is not the focus of this class on M&A law. Further, specialized bodies of law—such as labor law, environmental law, pension law, products liability law, telecommunications law, and intellectual property law—may be implicated in the context of a particular M&A deal. In those deals, the M&A lawyer may be required to seek specialized counsel to ensure compliance with the requirements imposed by the terms of these respective laws.

8. Closing on the Acquisition Transaction

As previously mentioned, the parties' agreement will usually fix a date for closing on the acquisition. At this time, Bidder will be obligated to pay the agreed-upon consideration and Target will be obligated to surrender control over its business operations. Until then, Target continues to run the business, much in the same way that the seller continues to be in possession of a house until the close of escrow in a real estate transaction, at which time title and possession of the house are transferred from the seller to the buyer. As in the case of a real estate transaction, there is also the possibility that the deal may never close, even though the parties have a signed acquisition agreement in place. In many cases, the acquisition agreement will include certain conditions that must be satisfied in order for the deal to close. Most notably, the acquisition agreement usually will require that all necessary approvals (including antitrust clearance) be obtained before the closing can occur. If these conditions are not satisfied, the acquisition will not close and Target will remain independent. The nature of these *conditions to closing*, and the consequences that flow from failure to satisfy such conditions, are explored in detail in Chapter 5, as part of our discussion of documenting the transaction.

E. *Business Incentives for M&A Transactions*

The following excerpt provides further insight into the business incentives that generally motivate corporate managers to propose business combinations, which the author (an economist, not an M&A lawyer) generally refers to as "mergers."

Senate Judiciary Committee Hearings on Mergers and Corporate Consolidation in the New Economy, Senate Hearing 105-934 (Serial No. J-105-106 at 38)

June 16, 1998, *Testimony of Dr. Janet Yellen, Chair, Council of Economic Advisers**

Mr. Chairman and members of the Committee, it is a pleasure to be here this morning to talk about some of the economic issues raised by the current merger wave. . . . [Among other things, my testimony] looks at the causes and consequences of mergers. Here there is no simple conclusion. Many, if not most mergers are motivated by the desire to achieve greater operating efficiencies and lower costs. But it is impossible to rule out anticompetitive motives or simple managerial hubris as explanations for mergers. . . .

. . . [L]et me now turn to the causes and consequences of mergers. The main reason managers give for undertaking mergers is to increase efficiency. And studies show that, on average, the combined equity value of the acquired company and the purchasing company rises as a result of the merger. However, an increase in shareholder value can arise for reasons other than greater efficiency—such as increased market power and the resulting ability to increase profits by raising prices. And the separation of ownership from control in the modern corporation means that mergers may serve the interests of managers more than shareholders (e.g., empire building, increased salary associated with running a larger firm). Finally, even if mergers are designed to enhance efficiency, they often don't work and can instead create inefficiencies (some see the merger of the Union Pacific and Southern Pacific railroads in 1995 as a notable example of such an outcome).

There are numerous ways that mergers can contribute to economic efficiency. One is by reducing excess capacity (this justification has been invoked in hospital, defense, and banking mergers). Another is by achieving economies of scale or network externalities (the hub and spoke system that emerged following the deregulation of the airline industry is one example, though it is one that raises questions of increased concentration as well) or economies of scope ("synergy") as in the case of investment/commercial banking, where similar risk management techniques and credit evaluation skills are utilized in a wide variety of financial services. Mergers may also improve management (studies suggest large differences in efficiency among seemingly similar firms like banks).

Most mergers probably are undertaken with the expectation of achieving efficiencies, though the outcomes may sometimes be disappointing and

---

* [By the author: Yellen chaired the Council of Economic Advisors in the Clinton administration from February 1997 through August 1999 and was serving in this position at the time that she provided the accompanying congressional testimony. From 2004-2010, Yellen served as president and CEO of the Federal Reserve Bank of San Francisco and from 2010-2014, she was vice chair of the Federal Reserve Board. President Barack Obama nominated Yellen to succeed Ben Bernanke as chair of the Federal Reserve Board. Following Senate confirmation, she was sworn in on February 3, 2014, making her the first woman to serve as Fed chair, a position that she held until February 3, 2018, when President Trump appointed Jerome Powell to replace her. As of Fall 2020, Yellen has been a Distinguished Fellow in Residence with the Economic Studies Program at the Brookings Institution.]

divorces are not uncommon (such as the unraveling of AT&T's 1991 acquisition of NCR). Studies of bank mergers suggest that, in spite of the potential for improved efficiency, in general, they have not improved the efficiency or profitability of banks.

Mergers can also be undertaken to increase market power and reduce competition. In this event consumers could be harmed through higher prices, lower service, reduced variety, and, in the view of some, a reduced pace of innovation, although some argue that increased market power should raise innovation due to the increased ability to appropriate the benefits of R&D. Mergers can also work to decrease the potential for future competition. There is abundant evidence that, when one compares markets of a given type, such as local banking markets, the degree of concentration in a market is correlated with such measures of economic performance as prices and profits. And there is some evidence that mergers have raised prices, as in the case of the mid-1980s airline mergers. Other things equal, higher concentration leads to worsened performance, which is why the Merger Guidelines, [promulgated by U.S. antitrust regulators] after assessing what the appropriate definition of the market is from a product and geographical perspective, look at the impact of a merger on the level of concentration. However, statistical evidence suggests this is not the main motive for most mergers, perhaps reflecting the presence of antitrust monitoring and enforcement.

Thus far, I have been discussing motives for mergers generally. A natural question is why so many firms are merging now. There is no single reason. The following are some of the prevailing explanations:

1. *Adjusting to falling regulatory barriers.* Mergers have followed the removal of branching restrictions in banking and ownership restrictions in radio. . . . Mergers in the telecommunications industry are also tied to the breakup of AT&T and to the deregulation and market opening steps that followed the Telecommunications Act of 1996.

2. *Technological change.* Innovation can change the size and type of firm that is seen as most profitable. Some mergers today may be motivated by the widely touted, but still nascent, phenomenon of "convergence" in the information technology industry. For instance, as textbook publishers begin to supplement their materials with multimedia software, they may acquire small software companies. . . .

3. *Globalization.* The emergent global economy may demand large scale to participate. A European and American firm may combine to take advantage of the distribution networks that each has on its own continent. . . .

4. *High stock market.* Price-earnings ratios have increased to near-record levels during the current merger wave, and some analysts feel that the market may be overvalued. Such high stock market values may make it seem attractive to fund an acquisition with stock (this is the dominant funding source in the current merger wave). But an overvalued stock market should not necessarily lead to more mergers, because if other firms are also overvalued then there are fewer attractive targets to acquire.

As I mentioned earlier, in evaluating the consequences of mergers we should focus on particular well-defined markets. In this regard, it is important to recognize that mergers do not necessarily increase concentration in any well-defined market. Merging firms may be in different businesses, noncompeting regions, or in supplier-buyer relationships. In banking, for example, national concentration has increased dramatically due to mergers, but concentration measures for local banking deposits have been extremely stable because most mergers have been between banks serving different regions. Even when the merger is among competitors, increasing global competition or domestic entry could be simultaneously reducing concentration. In addition, the entry of new firms or the threat of entry can offset the potentially anticompetitive impact of a merger. And finally, the structural characteristics of markets, and not just the number of firms, influence the nature of competition in a given market. We cannot automatically conclude that markets with 2 or 3 competitors will be less competitive than those with 20 or 30. . . .

F. Historical Perspective and Current Status of M&A Activity

1. Historical Perspective on M&A Activity

Historically, the U.S. economy has been marked by what observers of the financial markets generally agree can be characterized as five different "waves" of merger activity. The following excerpt provides a historical overview that briefly summarizes these "waves" of merger activity, again as seen from the perspective of a well-known economist.

Senate Judiciary Committee Hearings on Mergers and Corporate Consolidation in the New Economy, Senate Hearing 105-934 (Serial No. J-105-106 at 38)
June 16, 1998, *Testimony of Dr. Janet Yellen, Chair, Council of Economic Advisers*

. . . The United States is in the midst of its fifth major merger wave in a hundred years. The previous four merger waves provide background and perspective for assessing today's merger activity.

- *The Great Merger Wave of the 1890s.* The first great merger wave at the turn of the last century [from approximately 1893-1904] was the culmination of the trust movement, when numerous small and midsized firms were consolidated into single dominant firms in a number of industries. Examples include Standard Oil and U.S. Steel. One estimate is that this merger wave encompassed at least 15 percent of all plants and employees in manufacturing at the turn of the century. An estimated 75 percent of merger-related firm disappearances occurred as a result of mergers involving at least five firms, and about a quarter involved ten or more firms at a time. The sharp decline in merger activity during 1903 and 1904 was probably related to the onset of a severe recession and the legal precedent for prohibiting market-dominating mergers under the antitrust laws that was established by the Northern Securities Case.

- *The Roaring Twenties.* The merger movement of the 1920s [from approximately 1919-1929] saw the consolidation of many electric and gas utilities as well as manufacturing and minerals mergers. Some of the most prominent manufacturing mergers (such as the one that produced Bethlehem Steel) created relatively large number-two firms in industries previously dominated by one giant. [The 1929 stock market crash and the ensuing Great Depression ended this wave.]

- *The "Go-Go" Sixties.* The 1960s conglomerate wave [from approximately 1969-1973] represented a deflection of the "urge to merge" away from horizontal (same-industry) mergers, perhaps due to stronger antitrust enforcement. The constant dollar value of mergers in manufacturing and minerals surpassed the prior peak attained in 1899 (though it remained much smaller as a share of the economy). The 1960s boom was also fueled by a strong stock market and financial innovation (such as convertible preferred stocks and debentures). This merger wave ended with a decline in stock prices that was especially severe for companies that had aggressively pursued conglomerate mergers.

- *The Deal Decade of the 1980s.* Unlike other merger booms, this one began in a depressed stock market. With stock prices low relative to the cost of building new capacity, it appeared cheaper to expand by takeover. The 1980s boom [from approximately 1980-1989] was marked by an explosion of hostile takeovers and financial innovation (such as junk bonds and leveraged buyouts). The 1980s wave was unique in the prevalence of cash purchases (as opposed to acquisition through stock). Efforts to dismantle conglomerate firms put together in the previous wave and redeploy their assets more efficiently may have been an important driving force. Finally, the antitrust environment was more permissive and companies were more willing to attempt horizontal mergers.

Qualitatively, the current merger wave [of the late 1990s] appears to be a reversion to pre-1980s form in some ways: It is taking place in a strong stock market, and stock rather than cash is the preferred medium. But many mergers are neither purely horizontal (in general large horizontal mergers would raise antitrust issues) nor purely conglomerate. Rather they represent market extension mergers (companies in the same industry that serve different and currently non-competing markets) or mergers seeking "synergy," in which companies in related markets expect to take advantage of "economies of scope."

By almost any quantitative measure, the current merger boom is substantial. . . . The total value of all deals announced in 1992—a year of especially low activity—was only $150 billion. The value of all deals announced in 1997 ($957 billion) was equivalent to about 12 percent of GDP, and activity so far in 1998 suggests another record year by this measure. . . . The last time merger activity was this large a share of GDP was during the Great Merger Wave at the turn of the last century.

One reason current merger activity is so large relative to the size of the economy is the run up in stock prices in the past few years. When merger activity is expressed relative to the market value of U.S. companies, its level remains lower than it was in the 1980s. . . .

NOTES

1. The "Fifth Wave" of Merger Activity. The "fifth merger wave" that Yellen refers to in her testimony came to an end when the "dot-com bubble" burst in 2000. "Nine of the ten largest [M&A] deals in history all took place in the three-year period 1998-2000, with the tenth in 2006. Most of the 1990s deals were strategic negotiated deals and a major part were [stock-for-stock] deals. . . . The year 2000 started with the announcement of the record-setting $165 billion merger of Time Warner and AOL."* Martin Lipton, *Merger Waves in the 19th, 20th and 21st Centuries,* September 14, 2006, *available at:* https://pdf4pro.com/view/merger -waves-in-the-19th-20th-and-21st-centuries-471e4b.html. This wave of mega-merger activity "ended with the collapse of the Internet stocks" [thereby "bursting the millennium bubble"] and the ensuing financial "scandals, like Enron, which gave rise to the revolution in corporate governance that is continuing today." *Id.*

2. Hostile Takeovers vs. Friendly Acquisitions. In the case of AT&T's deal with DirecTV, the terms of the transaction were fully negotiated by the respective management teams of Bidder and Target and were also approved by each company's board of directors. Such transactions are widely referred to as "friendly" acquisitions, or "fully negotiated" deals. In her testimony, Janet Yellen refers to the M&A market of the 1980s as marked by an explosion of "hostile takeovers." So what is a "hostile takeover"? A takeover is deemed "hostile" when the management of Target Co. is opposed to an unsolicited acquisition proposal made by Bidder Co. As part of the materials in Chapters 6 and 7, we will discuss hostile takeovers in more detail, including how the deal-making process in the context of a hostile takeover fundamentally differs from the fully negotiated transaction reflected in the acquisition of DirecTV by AT&T.

2. Current Status of M&A Activity

By the 1990s, the hostile takeovers that had characterized the deal-making craze of the 1980s had largely disappeared. Indeed, M&A activity all but dried up

---

* [By the author: As part of the fiduciary duty materials in Chapter 7, we will examine the deal making that led to the formation in 1989 of Time Warner Inc., which was then followed by its deal with AOL in 2000, resulting in a "Merger of Equals" that created the company known as AOL Time Warner, which lasted until 2009, when Time Warner divested itself of AOL. *See A Timeline of Time Warner Inc.,* July 16, 2014, *available at:* https://www.wsj.com/ articles/a-timeline-of-time-warner-inc-1405522663#.]

following the collapse of the junk bond market and the ensuing recessionary environment of the early 1990s. The junk bond market had provided much of the financing for the hostile bids of the 1980s. In addition to the demise of the junk bond market, there were other forces that contributed to the decline of hostile takeovers. As we will discuss in detail in Chapter 7, many publicly traded companies have adopted some form of defensive measures that are designed to insulate the company from an unsolicited (i.e., hostile) bid. Probably the most popular of these defensive tactics is what is known as the *poison pill*, which we will analyze in detail in Chapter 7. Another effective barrier to the unwanted bid is the development of antitakeover statutes under state law that operate to further insulate the company from a hostile takeover. We will analyze these state antitakeover statutes (of which Delaware's business combination statute is perhaps the best known) in Chapter 6.

As noted in the preceding excerpt from Janet Yellen's testimony, merger activity increased dramatically by the end of the 1990s, peaking in 2000 — just before the burst of the "dot-com bubble." In 2002, the total volume of M&A transactions stood at 26,531 deals, with a reported dollar value of approximately $1.2 trillion. This level of deal activity stands in stark contrast to the reported volume of 38,744 deals in 2000, with a total dollar value of just under $3.4 trillion. *See* VyVyan Tenorio, *Anatomy of a Cycle: How Big Was It?* THE DEAL, Jan. 2008, at 44. However, by 2004, the pace of M&A activity had rebounded and the M&A market had moved beyond the difficult environment that prevailed throughout 2002 and 2003.

The calendar year 2005 proved to be the best year for M&A activity of the previous five years, ushering in a new cycle of M&A activity of unprecedented proportions. Indeed, new high-water marks for the M&A market were reached in both 2006 and 2007, with a total of 42,921 deals reported in 2007, and a total dollar value of almost $4.5 trillion, eclipsing the previous record set in 2006 of approximately $3.6 trillion in reported total value of M&A deals announced that year. The M&A market of calendar year 2007, however, was characterized by extraordinary volatility.

> The feverish pace of M&A activity continued unabated during the first two quarters of 2007, as mega-LBO transactions dominated the news headlines. The M&A market then seemed to hit a brick wall over the summer with the tightening of financing [credit] markets. The deterioration in [the credit markets] . . . and concerns about aggressive lending terms finally caused investors to pause — quickly slowing deal flow.

Jeff Rosenkranz, et al., *M&A Activity: A Macro Look — 2008*, 12 THE M&A LAWYER 14, 14 (Jan. 2008).

The LBO boom of 2005-2007 came to a screeching halt as the U.S. economy entered the Great Recession of 2008-2009. Indeed, "the first quarter of 2008 featured the biggest quarterly decline, in terms of dollar value of M&A deals announced, of the past six years." Chris O'Leary, *From the Editor: M&A in the Face of Recession*, 12 THE M&A LAWYER 3 (Apr. 2008). The first quarter of 2008 also witnessed the collapse of Bear Stearns, a well-known Wall Street investment banking firm. Amidst the collapse of Bear Stearns and talk of an economic recession, "[m]any would-be acquirers . . . parked themselves on the sidelines, hoping that the credit crisis [that began in summer 2007 and reportedly led to the collapse of Bear Stearns] will finally get under control (though no one really knows what that will take . . .). [Many other would-be Bidders are] waiting until the markets stabilize before agreeing to commit to transactions, even if the [Bidder] has a solid balance sheet and the [T]arget looks attractive. The result is, again, no surprise [to the experienced M&A lawyer]: a great many stalled deals, . . . and a general wariness about how to proceed." *Id.* But that wariness faded as the "market for acquisition financing for leveraged buyouts rebounded strongly in 2010 . . ." Jason Kyrwood, *Industry Insight: Return of the Froth*, THE DEAL, Apr. 25, 2011, at 28.

"During the first half of 2011, the M&A market continued [its] resurgence . . . [However,] M&A activity declined in the second half of 2011, reflecting uncertainties regarding the volatile global [capital markets], . . ." Wachtel, Lipton, Rosen & Katz, *Mergers and Acquisitions — 2012,* Jan. 9, 2012 (law firm memo, copy on file with author). The calendar years 2012 and 2013 continued to see improvements in the global markets for M&A transactions. And, by 2014, there was considerable momentum in the M&A markets, with global M&A activity hitting "$3.5 trillion in 2014, which [was] up 47% from the year before." Dan Primack, *2014 Was a Huge Year for M&A and Private Equity,* FORTUNE, Jan. 5, 2015, *available at:* http://fortune.com/2015/01/05/2014-was-a-huge-year-for -ma-and-private-equity. Indeed, this momentum carried into calendar year 2015. In fact, 2015 proved to be a record year for M&A activity:

> Global M&A volume hit an all-time high of over $5 trillion, surpassing the previous record of $4.6 trillion set in 2007. . . . The "mega-deal" made a big comeback, with a record 69 deals over $10 billion, and 10 deals over $50 billion, . . .
>
> A number of factors provided directors and officers with confidence to pursue large, and frequently transformative, merger transactions in 2015. The economic outlook had become more stable, particularly in the United States. Many companies had trimmed costs in the years following the financial crisis, but still faced challenges generating organic revenue growth. M&A offered a powerful lever for value creation through synergies. In a number of cases, the price of a buyer's stock rose on announcement of an acquisition, as investors rewarded transactions [that offered] strong commercial logic, . . .

Wachtel, Lipton, Rosen & Katz, *Mergers and Acquisitions — 2016,* Feb. 9, 2016 (law firm memo, copy on file with author).

By the fall of 2016, an environment of uncertainty had come to prevail in the global economy, especially in light of the economic insecurity resulting from the June 2016 Brexit vote in Great Britain and the election of Donald Trump as U.S. president in November 2016. Entering 2017, however, this sense of uncertainty gave way to a genuinely robust level of global M&A activity, which reached a total deal volume of $3.6 trillion in 2017. *See* Wachtel, Lipton, Rosen & Katz, *Cross-Border M&A: A Checklist for Successful Acquisitions in the United States,* Jan. 2, 2018 (law firm memo, copy on file with author). Entering into calendar year 2018, the M&A market began to gain momentum, as described more fully in the following excerpt:

> M&A in 2018 began with a bang, with more than $350 billion of deals in January 2018 — a January level not seen since 2000 — and much chatter that M&A volume for the year could hit an all-time record. As it turned out, 2018 was a tale

of two cities, with M&A continuing at a torrid pace during the first half of the year, and falling off markedly during a second half of geopolitical tension and market volatility. Overall, M&A volume for 2018 reached a very robust $4 trillion, but fell short of overtaking deal volume in 2007 and 2015. M&A being lumpy and unpredictable as ever, 2019 has opened with a number of notable deals, . . . somewhat defying gloomy predictions for the year. . . .

Whatever 2019 does bring—in addition to trade tensions and protectionist rhetoric, cyber insecurity, slowdowns in China and a number of other emerging economies, gloom about the interest rate and debt financing pictures in the U.S., geopolitical risks all around the world, and inevitable but as-yet-unknown curve balls from politicians—we expect the pace of [M&A deal activity in] the U.S. to remain strong.

See Wachtel, Lipton, Rosen & Katz, *Cross-Border M&A: 2019 Checklist for Successful Acquisitions in the United States,* Jan. 25, 2019 (law firm memo, copy on file with author); *see also* Nixon Peabody, LLP, *2019 Nixon Peabody MAC Survey* (calendar year "2018 was the third highest year ever for M&A [deal] volume . . .") (law firm memo, copy on file with author). Notwithstanding all of the global economic uncertainty that faced the capital markets at the start of 2019, "M&A activity remained robust in 2019. Total deal volume reached $4 trillion globally, a slight decrease from the $4.1 trillion volume in 2018, but higher than the $3.5 trillion in 2017." *See* Wachtel, Lipton, Rosen & Katz, *Mergers & Acquisitions—2020,* Jan. 14, 2020, *available at:* https://clsbluesky.law.columbia.edu/2020/01/23/wachtell-lipton-discusses-mergers-and-acquisitions-2020/.

Given the robust pace of M&A deal volume over the past few years as the capital markets recovered from the Great Recession, what does the future hold for M&A deal making as we start the third decade of the twenty-first century?

> Some commentators believe that the long-running M&A boom is soon coming to an end. Certain macroeconomic indicators certainly could support this point of view. Trade tensions, fears of a global economic slowdown, periodic dislocations in debt markets and residual uncertainty surrounding Brexit all remain risks as of this writing. In addition, the upcoming U.S. presidential election [in November 2020] and the ever-evolving U.S. political landscape could be a substantial source of uncertainty in 2020. Nonetheless, the U.S. economy remains strong, unemployment and interest rates are low and stock markets continue to perform well. At present, many dealmakers continue to be at least cautiously optimistic that smart M&A creates value,

Wachtel, Lipton, Rosen & Katz, *Mergers & Acquisitions – 2020,* Jan. 14, 2020, at page 14 (law firm memo, copy on file with author). As it turns out, the opportunities that many market observers saw at the start of 2020 were rudely aborted with the "spread of COVID-19 [that] saw market indices [slash] 35% off their value in March [2020] alone, with only a modest recovery in April [2020], [where the indices] still [remained] 20% below previous highs." Morgan Lewis Memo, *M&A in Unprecedented Times,* May 28, 2020, *available at:* https://www.lexology.com/library/detail.aspx?g=ffa1a996-6776-4676-9c1f-396276ce80f3. As of Fall 2020, with the world's economy still in the midst of grappling with the ramifications of the ongoing global pandemic, a climate of uncertainty once again prevails in the capital markets. While some market participants see "the opportunity of a generation" for those "companies with a robust balance sheet", *id.*, others are "preparing for a much less frothy market . . . [that will result in] negative impact on M&A activity." Bryan K. Mattingly and Keeana Sajadi Boarman, Frost Brown Todd LLC, *M&A Insights for the New World,* May 29, 2020, *available at*: https://frostbrowntodd.com/ma-insights-for-the-new-world/. The result once again, as we saw in the years following the Great Recession, was "a general wariness about how to proceed." Chris O'Leary, *supra.*

G.   *Treatment of Fundamental Changes Under Modern Corporation Codes*

1.   Historical Perspective

The law has long recognized that corporations grow and change, both from within and by acquisition. As they grow from within, modern statutes recognize that this process is largely controlled by the company's board of directors, since they are statutorily mandated to manage the business affairs of the corporation without any direct intervention by the shareholders. (*See*, e.g., MBCA §8.01, Delaware §141.) However, when it comes to major organic changes in the nature of the company's business, or alternatively in its financial structure, the law has typically required that the board obtain shareholder approval for these types of "fundamental changes." The board, therefore, cannot implement such fundamental changes unilaterally. So, for example, the board of directors cannot unilaterally amend the company's charter (articles of incorporation) without first obtaining consent from the company's shareholders. In this way, the owners of the corporation—that is, the shareholders—retain some residual control over fundamental changes in the company. Equally important, by requiring the board to persuade shareholders to approve a fundamental change in the company's business affairs, the shareholders retain some direct control over the company's managers and thus can hold management accountable by requiring management to explain and justify the major, organic changes they propose.

Early on, corporate law struggled with the threshold question of which types of organic change in a company's business and/or financial affairs qualified as a *fundamental change* that required shareholder approval, as well as the question of how many shareholders must approve a proposed fundamental change in order for it to be validly consummated. With the promulgation of modern corporation codes, and the development of the view that the modern corporation is entirely a creature of statute, these threshold issues are largely addressed today by the provisions of modern corporation statutes.

2.   Modern Perspective

For the most part, today's corporation statutes allow a business broad freedom to choose to organize itself as a corporation by satisfying the prerequisites imposed by the law of the state where the business chooses to incorporate itself. Delaware is the most popular state for incorporation, with most of the publicly traded corporations choosing to incorporate under Delaware's General Corporation Law (DGCL or Del.). Many small, closely held companies, however, choose to incorporate locally rather than in Delaware. This freedom to choose is important because of the rule of law known as the *internal affairs doctrine.* Under this well-recognized choice of law principle, the law of the state where the business has decided to incorporate will govern the internal affairs of the corporation. Accordingly, under this doctrine, the law of the state where a constituent company is organized will apply to determine the prerequisites that must be satisfied in order for that company to validly consummate a particular method of business combination. Incorporators of a new business may be well advised to take into account the statutory prerequisites for completing an M&A deal in making their decision where to incorporate.

Early on, state corporation codes usually required unanimous shareholder approval for proposed fundamental changes, such as business combinations that were subject to a vote of the shareholders. This view was largely premised on the notion that stock ownership was in the nature of personal property, and therefore, no shareholder should be deprived of his/her/its property interests (here, his/her/its share ownership) without first obtaining his/her/its consent. Not surprisingly, the law quickly recognized the problem of the holdout shareholder and the consequent ability of a minority interest to hold hostage a deal that was otherwise favored by a majority of shareholders. Consequently, all modern statutes have scaled back the shareholder voting requirement to something less than unanimity, with a few imposing some type of supermajority shareholder vote (typically requiring approval by two-thirds or three-fourths of the outstanding shares entitled to vote). As we will see in Chapter 2 when we analyze in detail the statutory prerequisites imposed by modern codes, the dominant approach today, reflected in Delaware's statute, is to further relax the voting requirement to a standard known as the *absolute majority vote* (i.e., requiring approval by a majority of the outstanding shares entitled to vote). By relaxing the voting standard in this manner, Delaware and other modern corporation codes allow the majority of voting shares to overrule the minority of shares who object to a proposed business combination, notwithstanding how strenuous or cogent the objections of the minority may be.

At this point, it is worth emphasizing that the bottom line of modern corporation codes is that minority shareholders may be deprived of their shares (and all the rights, preferences, privileges, and financial interests those shares originally carried) by the simple expedient of convincing a majority of the shares entitled to vote to approve the terms of a business combination as proposed by the company's management. It should come as no surprise that a big part of the study of M&A law, as we shall see in the remaining chapters, involves analyzing the scope and effectiveness of protections offered by state and federal law to prevent abusive treatment of minority shareholders at the hands of the corporate managers who propose a business combination and/or the majority shareholders who approve these management proposals. Although we will examine the nature of these protections in more detail as we go through the next chapter, it is helpful to describe at the outset the general nature of these protections and the public policy concerns that form the basis for a particular set of protective provisions.

H.   An Introduction to Relevant Public Policy Concerns

1.   The Role of Modern Appraisal Rights

As modern corporation statutes were amended to allow the vote of the majority to eliminate the interest of any minority shareholders who objected to a proposed business combination, the state legislatures generally felt compelled to address the plight of this disenfranchised minority interest. The most widely adopted form of statutory relief is the modern right of appraisal made available to those shares who object to—that is, dissent from—certain types of proposed business combinations. The essential nature of this statutory right of appraisal is that it allows the objecting shareholders to compel the corporation to pay them the fair value of their shares in cash. In this way, dissenting shareholders are not locked into continued investment in a corporation that undertakes a fundamental change that they oppose. Instead, these objecting shareholders will receive cash, which they are then free to invest elsewhere as they see fit.

As we go through the problems in the next chapter, we will see that the terms of modern appraisal statutes vary widely. In general, there are four basic issues to consider:

1. *Availability of Appraisal Rights.* What transactions trigger the dissenting shareholder's right to demand payment in cash for his/her/its shares;
2. *Perfecting the Right to an Appraisal.* What procedures must be followed for dissenting shareholders to obtain cash payment from the company for their shares and how burdensome (i.e., time-consuming and costly) these procedures are;
3. *Valuation Issues.* What happens if the dissenting shareholder and the company cannot agree on fair value; and
4. *Exclusivity of the Appraisal Remedy.* Does the modern appraisal provide the *only* remedy the unhappy shareholder may pursue?

These conceptual issues are raised here at the outset so that you can give some critical thought to the adequacy (and effectiveness) of the modern appraisal remedy as you work through the problems in the next chapter and analyze the differing treatment of dissenting shareholders under the modern corporation codes.

2.   The Modern Importance of Fiduciary Duty Law

The other major source of protection for those shareholders who object to a proposed business combination is the law of fiduciary duty. A fundamental premise of modern state corporate law is that the company's senior executive officers (and, more important, its board of directors) owe fiduciary obligations to the company itself. Since management's fiduciary duty obligations run directly to the corporation, as a matter of law, the board does not owe a duty to act as the controlling shareholder directs even though the controlling shareholder may elect the entire board. Instead, the board's duties run directly to the entity itself—that is, to an intangible legal construct that serves the interests of many constituencies, which in the usual case will include, at a minimum, minority shareholders, senior security holders (such as nonvoting preferred stock), debt holders, other business creditors (such as landlords, vendors, etc.), and employees. The relevance of these other interests in the decision-making process of the board as it contemplates a proposed business combination is an important theme of this book.

Duty of Care.   As a matter of law, the board owes a _duty of care_ to the company, obligating the board to manage the company's business affairs in a manner that they reasonably believe to be in the company's best interests. The board's duty of care raises obvious questions as to whose interests are to be considered by the board when deciding what is in the company's "best interests." Although this is a matter of considerable disagreement among scholars of corporate law, it would seem that today, the dominant paradigm of board decision making is the _shareholder primacy model._ Under this approach, the board is required to exercise its decision-making responsibilities to maximize the wealth of the company's shareholders. In the case where there is more than one class of stock outstanding (as where there is an outstanding class of preferred stock), the conventional view is that the board is to maximize the wealth of the residual owners of the company, the common stockholders. This view has been subject to considerable criticism, as we shall explore in Chapter 7 when we analyze the scope of these fiduciary duty obligations in more detail. Moreover, there is increasing pressure in recent years to compel the board to include the interests of "other constituencies" (such as the company's employees, suppliers, etc.) when making decisions about corporate acquisitions, among other things. We will discuss this development in more detail in Chapter 6 when we analyze the recent proliferation of _state antitakeover statutes._

Even more important for the study of M&A law, the process of deciding whether to engage in a business combination tests the very limits of business discretion conferred on modern corporate managers in a manner that is unlike any other business decision routinely made by a company's board of directors. Modern corporate law extends great deference to the board's business decisions with respect to managing the company's business affairs. Thus, the business judgment rule generally presumes that the board acts in the company's best interests in the absence of fraud, illegality, or self-dealing. However, the recent waves of merger activity (most notably the Deal Decade of the 1980s), along with the bursting of the speculative stock market bubble of the 1990s, have led to renewed concern as to what the board must demonstrate in order to obtain the benefit of the protection of the Business Judgment Rule. More specifically, what level of monitoring, oversight, analysis, and deliberation is required in order for the board to demonstrate that it has exercised informed decision making in good faith and in a manner not tainted by any conflict of interest? In the economic downturn of the early 2000s, the courts revisited this question in cases challenging failed business acquisitions. In these cases, very often the shareholders questioned the adequacy of the decision-making process that led the company's managers to propose a particular business combination that ultimately proved to be financially disastrous for the company.

As we shall see in the remaining chapters, the Great Recession of 2008-2009 and its aftermath have only served to intensify investor scrutiny of the role of the CEO and the conduct of the company's board of directors in the context of an M&A transaction. "Reviewing the merits and disadvantages of an M&A transaction constitutes an important area of board decision-making. In terms of the corporate governance environment, these are turbulent times indeed and never before have the actions of the board been subject to such strict scrutiny, given the lessons from the global financial crisis and a fair share of corporate governance scandals. . . ." Uma Kanth Varottil, *Corporate Governance in M&A Transactions: The Indian Story in Global Mergers and Acquisitions*, Luncheon Address, International Bar Association Conference, Mar. 9, 2012 (copy on file with author). As of Fall 2020, in the midst of an economy struggling to cope with the COVID-19 global pandemic, these most certainly continue to be turbulent times. Consequently, today's transaction planners must give renewed consideration as to the conduct required of the board so that it may fulfill its fiduciary duty of care. We will consider this decision-making process in more detail in Chapter 5, as part of our discussion of negotiating and documenting the deal, and again in Chapter 7 when we analyze the scope of management's fiduciary duty obligations.

Duty of Loyalty.   The board's fiduciary obligations also include the separate duty of loyalty, which, like the duty of care, runs directly to the corporation itself. Today, this duty of loyalty requires the board to make business decisions that are not tainted by any conflict of interest—and increasingly, this includes avoiding even the appearance of a conflict of interest. In the wake of recent financial scandals, public policymakers (at both the state and federal level) have focused their attention and investigative resources on the threshold question: who qualifies as a *truly* independent director? Which board members are free of *any* conflict of interest, direct or indirect? In other words, *whom* do we trust to make decisions that are *truly* in the best interests of the company? The fallout from the financial scandals surrounding Enron and others in the early years of the twenty-first century, and the subsequent financial crisis in the banking industry, has resurrected serious corporate governance concerns reminiscent of the post-Watergate era of the 1970s. In the immediate aftermath of Watergate, introspective reform efforts were launched that ultimately led to increasing reliance on the use of outside directors. Specifically, boards were increasingly populated with non-management directors; that is, directors who were not employed either directly (as company officers or managers), or indirectly (such as serving as the company's management consultant or investment banker).

Sarbanes-Oxley Act.   At the dawn of the twenty-first century, in the aftermath of the failures of Enron, Tyco, WorldCom and other financial scandals on a scale not seen since the Great Depression, Congress, the SEC, and other regulators of our financial markets responded by investigating, among other things, the decision-making process of the modern corporate boardroom. Congress's investigation culminated in 2002 with the enactment of a package of far-ranging reform measures commonly referred to as the Sarbanes-Oxley Act, and more affectionately known as "SOX."* The reforms legislated into place by SOX were the product of

> highly publicized hearings, conducted by both houses of Congress in the aftermath of the scandals involving fraud and mismanagement at such major U.S. companies as Enron, Tyco, Adelphia and Worldcom. Hailed as a landmark and comprehensive legislation scheme, SOX was intended to reform corporate governance and behavior, increase the standards of accountability for the accounting profession, and ensure the reliability of financial statements of public companies. [SOX established an] independent accounting oversight board [the PCAOB, Public Company Accounting Oversight Board, which now polices the accounting profession and sets auditing standards], [mandated] auditor independence, strengthened corporate governance and responsibility standards, and [imposed] financial accuracy obligations . . . on senior management. [In adopting SOX], Congress addressed what it perceived to be the corporate governance and auditing shortcomings that had contributed to the scandals culminating in the bankruptcy of Enron.

James M. Lyons, *Representing Independent Directors After Sarbanes-Oxley: The Growing Role of Independent Counsel,* Business Law Today, Jan.-Feb. 2010, at 53. As we examine the materials in later chapters of this casebook, we will refer to several of the reform measures that Congress enacted as part of the SOX legislation.

One of the most important issues addressed in this landmark legislation is the basic question of *who* should decide what is in the company's best interests. As a result of the reform measures introduced by SOX, the SEC (and other market regulators) are addressing the related public policy questions: how much decision-making discretion should be delegated to corporate managers? Which kind of business decisions should be subject to shareholder approval? These same questions are cornerstone issues in our study of M&A law.

Dodd-Frank Act. Many Wall Street observers have questioned the strength and effectiveness of SOX's reforms, and some have faulted SOX for not preventing the most recent financial crisis within the banking industry that ultimately led to the Great Recession of 2008-2009. Not surprisingly, Congress once again responded to this financial crisis by enacting the Dodd-Frank Wall Street Reform and Consumer Protection Act, Pub. L. No. 111-203, 124 Stat. 1376 (2010) ("Dodd-Frank"), which was signed into law by President Obama on July 21, 2010, almost eight years to the day following the enactment of SOX (which was signed into law by President George W. Bush on July 30, 2002). The primary purpose of Dodd-Frank "is to identify and manage threats to the stability of the nation's financial system, such as those that contributed to the economic downturn commencing in 2008. [Among other matters of financial industry regulation, Dodd-Frank addresses consumer protection, derivatives, and hedge fund regulation.] Many [of Dodd-Frank's] provisions require various regulatory bodies to draft, adopt, and implement regulations, and these will have

---

* [By the author: Sarbanes-Oxley Act of 2002, Pub. L. No. 107-204, 116 Stat. 745 (2002). Most of the provisions of this new law are codified in various provisions of the Securities Exchange Act of 1934, 15 U.S.C. §78 (2000).]

a significant effect on the impact [and efficacy of Dodd-Frank's reform measures]." Peter Menard, *The Dodd-Frank Act: A Guide to the Corporate Governance, Executive Compensation, and Disclosure Provisions*, 1 BUSINESS LAW NEWS 1 (State Bar of California, 2011).

In addition, and more important for our study of M&A law, Dodd-Frank "addresses corporate governance and executive compensation matters that will be relevant for most U.S. public companies." Stuart N. Alperin, et al., *Dodd-Frank Act Mandates Say-on-Pay Votes and Other Corporate Governance Changes*, 14 THE M&A LAWYER 7 (July/Aug. 2010). Of the various Dodd-Frank provisions that apply to U.S. public companies, most notable for our purposes are the following provisions, which mandate:

- Shareholder advisory votes on executive compensation — more popularly referred to as "say-on-pay" votes;
- "Clawbacks" of incentive compensation, when public companies are required to restate their financial statements (which go beyond the "clawback" requirements imposed on a company's CEO or CFO by SOX);
- Enhanced independence for board compensation committees and their advisors; and
- Enhanced proxy disclosures as to a number of matters, particularly with respect to disclosure of executive compensation arrangements (including "golden parachute" arrangements of the type we will discuss in Chapter 7, as part of our examination of hostile takeovers).

See Peter Menard, *The Dodd-Frank Act: What Public Companies Should Do Now*, THE CORPORATE COUNSELOR, Winter 2011, at 1; and *see also* Alperin, et al., *supra*. While a comprehensive examination of Dodd-Frank's reform measures is beyond the scope of this casebook, we will address several of Dodd-Frank's executive compensation provisions as part of the materials in Chapters 4 and 7.

The Impact of Modern Fiduciary Duty Law.   During the course of the most recent wave of merger activity in the 1980s and 1990s, the primary legal constraint on managerial discretion was the limitations imposed by the fiduciary obligations of a company's board of directors. The nature of these constraints, as developed primarily by the jurisprudence of the Delaware courts, will be the focus of the materials in Chapter 7. As we shall see, though, when we analyze the problems in Chapter 2, no matter what form the business acquisition takes, fiduciary duty law is implicated at every stage of the board's decision-making process. The problems in the next chapter serve to illustrate the importance of modern fiduciary duty law and to highlight the various pressure points in the deal-making process where fiduciary duty obligations intervene to constrain and guide managerial discretion. Later, in Chapter 7, we will study in more detail the case law that further refines and describes the nature and scope of management's fiduciary obligations in the context of M&A transactions.

The reason for this organizational approach is that you cannot fully appreciate the important constraints imposed by modern fiduciary law until *after* you have finished studying the various state and federal law requirements that regulate M&A activity in the modern financial markets. By introducing principles of fiduciary duty law early in the course, however, you are encouraged to think critically about the terms of these state and federal rules that regulate M&A transactions as we go through each of the topics that build up to Chapter 7, where we will study modern fiduciary duty obligations in considerable detail.

Specifically, you should think critically about whether the legal rules that we will analyze in the next few chapters are sufficient from a public policy perspective to protect the competing interests in M&A transactions. In addition, you should consider whether, as a matter of public policy, these legal rules should be made mandatory, or alternatively, whether business persons should be allowed the freedom to customize the legal rules in order to accommodate their specific business objectives. If you decide that certain legal rules should be made mandatory, then you must consider the justification that supports this legal conclusion. In other words, you need to consider what arguments you would make to persuade the policymakers (whether they be legislators or regulators, and at either the state or federal level) to adopt the legal rule you advocate and to make that rule mandatory (i.e., nonwaivable).

These issues raise large and important questions for which no easy answers exist. These are the public policy issues that now dominate public debate in the wake of the recent financial crisis and the ensuing Great Recession as business leaders, legislators, regulators, and other policymakers consider how best to regulate our modern financial markets. Since the business environment most certainly will only continue to evolve and grow ever more complex, these issues certainly will not go away. Just as assuredly, though, the nature of the legal response that is appropriate is a matter that will require diligent attention so that the legal rules and regulatory environment adequately evolve so as to appropriately accommodate the ever-changing nature of business practices in the world of M&A transactions. The goal of this casebook is to introduce you to the principles that currently guide M&A law and to encourage you to think critically about the adequacy and legitimacy of the current legal framework. This is a large and important task because, after all, that is what you will be called upon to do as a practicing M&A lawyer.

I.　Overview of Different Methods for Structuring Business Acquisitions

Before we launch into our analysis of the substantive detail of M&A law in the next chapter, it is helpful to get a sense of the forest before encountering very many of the trees. This section introduces the three basic methods for one corporation to acquire another: the asset purchase, the stock purchase, and the direct (or statutory) merger. In the process of introducing these basic methods, we will refer to the diagrams that are included in Appendix A. The diagrams are critical for two reasons. First, the diagrams are useful for conceptualizing, and ultimately understanding, the differences in legal consequences of each of the different methods available for structuring a proposed acquisition. Second, the diagrams are crucial to understanding the relationship between Bidder and Target and the financial terms of their acquisition agreement. As we go through the problems and cases in the next chapter, it is important to refer to these diagrams so that you fully appreciate the differences in the mechanics of each type of acquisition transaction.

Finally, the brief overview that follows will serve to highlight the fundamental observation that, as a practical matter, *any* of these three methods can be used today to reach an economic result that is virtually *identical* in each case, although the three different methods have very different legal consequences. In analyzing the problems in the next chapter, we will examine in detail the prerequisites imposed by modern statutes in order to validly consummate each of these three basic methods of business combinations. However, let's begin our study of M&A law by briefly comparing each of the three basic methods for structuring a business acquisition: the merger, the asset purchase, and the stock purchase.

1.   Traditional Form: Direct Merger (Diagram 1)

Under the traditional form of direct merger (or "statutory merger," as it is often called in the M&A literature), the boards of both Bidder Co. and Target Co. initiate a transaction in which, as a practical matter, Bidder will swallow up Target, who will then cease to exist as a separate entity when the transaction is consummated. Hence, the terminology of mergers generally refers to Bidder as the *surviving* corporation and to Target as the *disappearing* corporation.

In order to validly consummate a merger, modern state corporation codes typically require approval of the merger agreement (or the plan of merger as it is sometimes called) by the boards of both constituent corporations. The merger agreement then must be submitted to the shareholders for their approval. Historically, approval required a supermajority vote (most often two-thirds of the outstanding voting stock). Today, however, most states have relaxed the voting standard to an absolute majority of the outstanding shares entitled to vote. The plan of merger is required to set forth certain items. Specifically, the plan of merger must indicate which company is to survive and which company is to disappear, and must identify the nature and amount of the consideration to be exchanged in the merger (generally referred to as the "merger consideration"). In the traditional form of direct merger, the Target Co. shareholders would receive Bidder Co. stock in exchange for their Target shares. When the dust settles and the transaction is consummated, the former Target Co. shareholders end up as shareholders of Bidder Co., the surviving corporation.

Knowing which company is to survive is crucial in the law of mergers because of the rule of successor liability imposed under modern corporation codes. Under this rule, the surviving corporation succeeds by operation of law to all the rights and liabilities of *both* Bidder Co. and Target Co. as the constituent corporations. Briefly stated, the legal significance of this rule of successor liability lies in the transaction cost savings to the parties, which is often quite substantial because the individual assets and liabilities of Target do not have to be separately transferred to Bidder. As a practical matter, this cost savings may be the most efficient way to transfer certain (particularly large and complex) businesses, and often will be the big advantage of the merger over other available forms for structuring a business acquisition. As a final matter, appraisal rights traditionally have been made available (under modern state corporation statutes) to dissenting shareholders of both constituent corporations.

2.   Traditional Form: Asset Purchase for Cash (Diagram 4)

At early common law, the asset purchase was often used in those situations where state law did not permit Bidder to acquire Target using the merger procedures. Most often, this situation would arise where Bidder and Target were incorporated in different jurisdictions, and the law of the state of incorporation of either Bidder or Target did not authorize one or the other to merge with a foreign corporation. As a practical matter, the only option legally available to the determined Bidder was to purchase all of Target's assets directly from the company. Since Target continues to exist, this method of acquisition had the added advantage of allowing Bidder to take on only those debts of Target Co. that Bidder Co. had specifically agreed to assume (in the language of contract law, an *express assumption*).

This rule of successor liability means that Target Co. continues to be obligated on all those claims not specifically transferred to Bidder in the case of an asset acquisition. The direct consequence of this rule is that acquisitions structured as a sale of all of Target's assets will usually contemplate a second step involving the voluntary dissolution and orderly winding up of Target Co.'s business affairs. In dissolution, the proceeds from the sale of Target's assets are used to satisfy the claims of Target Co.'s creditors. Any funds left after paying off Target Co.'s creditors are then distributed in liquidation to Target's shareholders, with priority being given to those shares carrying a liquidation preference (*preferred shares*), as set forth in Target Co.'s articles of incorporation.

In order to validly consummate the sale of all of its assets, most state corporation statutes require that the board of the selling corporation (Target Co.) must approve the transaction. Target's board then must obtain approval from Target's shareholders in order to complete the transaction, on the grounds that the sale of all of the company's assets constitutes a fundamental change for Target Co.

As for Bidder, state corporation codes usually impose no board or shareholder voting requirements, largely on the grounds that this transaction does not involve a fundamental change for Bidder. Once Bidder consummates the transaction with Target, Bidder remains in place, having used its cash resources to acquire the business operations of Target Co. The state corporation statutes generally view this decision to use Bidder's cash resources to acquire Target's assets as a matter left to the business discretion of the board of directors of Bidder Co. Under the traditional view of the corporate norm, this decision is generally entitled to protection under the Business Judgment Rule, and consequently, no vote of Bidder's shareholders is required.

Another advantage that further increased the popularity of the sale of assets method for business acquisitions is that many states deny the right of appraisal to Target's shareholders. These states limit this right of appraisal to merger transactions *only*. Moreover, Bidder Co. shareholders are denied appraisal rights since the transaction does not involve a fundamental change for Bidder Co.

Consequently, the flexibility offered by the sale of assets method often proves quite attractive to Target's management, especially in those situations where Target's management anticipates a large number of shares (albeit less than a majority) to object.

3.   Traditional Form: Stock Purchase for Cash (Diagram 6)

As a final alternative, Bidder can acquire control over Target by the simple expedient of approaching Target shareholders individually and offering to buy Target shares directly from individual shareholders. Unlike the other two methods for acquiring Target, this transaction does not involve Target. Hence, the stock purchase agreement will be entered into directly between Bidder and the individual shareholders of Target. So long as the relevant state corporation statute authorizes Bidder to own shares of another company, and assuming that Bidder's powers are not otherwise limited by an appropriate provision in the company's articles of incorporation, there are usually no other specific statutory prerequisites to be satisfied in order for the parties to validly complete this type of transaction.

Most significantly for purposes of this discussion, Target's board is not required to approve the transaction since Target itself is *not* a party to the transaction. This will prove to be vitally important in those cases where Target's board refuses to make a deal with Bidder. As a practical matter, the only alternative left to the Bidder who remained determined to acquire control over Target (notwithstanding the failure of Target's management to negotiate with Bidder) would be for Bidder to buy Target shares directly from Target shareholders. By structuring the transaction this way, Bidder eliminates any need to obtain approval from Target's board in order to complete the acquisition. In certain situations, this will prove to be a major advantage over the alternative methods of acquiring Target—that is, the statutory merger or the purchase of all of Target's assets—both of which require approval by Target's board in order to be validly consummated. This is probably the key distinguishing feature of using the stock purchase to acquire control of Target. Here, no vote of either Target's board or its shareholders is required. Rather, Target shareholders simply express their objections to Bidder's proposal to acquire Target—that is, their dissent—by refusing to tender their shares. By holding on to their shares in Target, they effectively reject the contract offer made by Bidder. If enough Target shareholders refuse to sell to Bidder, then generally the acquisition fails. Recognizing this possibility, Bidder typically would condition its obligation to purchase Target shares (i.e., to close on the stock purchase agreement) on Bidder's ability to get a sufficient number of Target shareholders to accept Bidder's offer. As a general proposition, Bidder usually would require that enough Target shareholders accept (by tendering their shares to Bidder) in order to give Bidder control over Target, even if it owns less than 100 percent of Target's outstanding voting shares. In this way, the determined Bidder can acquire effective control over Target, even in the face of strenuous objections from Target's management. This has led to what has come to be known as the *market for corporate control*, a topic that will be introduced in analyzing the problem sets in Chapter 2, and then discussed at greater length later in Chapter 7 as part of our examination of fiduciary duty law.

Hostile Takeovers.   One of the best-known hallmarks of the market for corporate control is the *hostile takeover*. While a detailed examination of the hostile takeover will be undertaken in Chapter 7, when we examine the landmark fiduciary duty cases that were decided by the Delaware Supreme Court in the 1980s, a brief description is in order at this point. The hostile takeover (which came to dominate the "Deal Decade of the 1980s," as pointed out in the testimony of Janet Yellen, *see supra*, at pp. 41-43), typically involves a two-step acquisition. First, the hostile Bidder (often more popularly referred to as a *raider*) makes an unsolicited offer to buy Target shares at a (usually rather substantial) premium over the current trading price in the open market. The raider's (Bidder's) obligation to close on this stock purchase is usually conditioned on the raider's ability to get a sufficient number of shares to obtain voting control of Target. Once the first step is completed, the raider will generally undertake the second step, which involves a back-end merger that eliminates (i.e., "squeezes out") the remaining minority shareholder interest in Target. In Chapter 2, we will study the corporate formalities that must be satisfied in order to validly complete this type of two-step acquisition under modern state corporation statutes. However, it bears emphasizing (at the outset) that these hostile takeovers are also subject to regulation under federal securities laws (which we will study in Chapter 6 as part of our discussion of the Williams Act). In addition, we will examine many of the better-known cases involving hostile takeovers as part of our discussion of fiduciary duty law in Chapter 7.

In the case of a stock purchase, Target remains intact, as does Bidder. By purchasing all of (or at least a controlling interest in) Target stock, this type of acquisition transaction will leave Target's business in place, to be operated as a wholly owned (or at least a controlled) subsidiary of Bidder. Hence, this method of acquisition is often referred to as a *change of control transaction* because there has been a change in ownership of all of—or at least a controlling interest in—Target's stock. Since Target remains in place, all of Target's assets remain available to satisfy the claims of Target's creditors, unlike the rule of successor liability that operates in the case of a merger. For reasons that we explore in Chapter 3 (regarding successor liability and the impact of M&A transactions on third-party creditors), it will often be advantageous to leave Target in place, making this method of structuring an acquisition the preferred approach over the other two methods.

As a final advantage, there are *no* appraisal rights available to the shareholders of *either* Bidder or Target in the case of a stock purchase. From the perspective of Target, those shareholders who object to Bidder's acquisition proposal simply hold on to their shares. Since Target shareholders cannot be deprived of their share ownership without their consent in the case of a stock purchase, the law has never perceived the need to extend appraisal rights to this type of acquisition. As for Bidder shareholders, this transaction does not present a fundamental change; consequently, there generally is no requirement for a shareholder vote and therefore no appraisal rights.

NOTES

1. (Getting Fancy by) Varying the Type of Consideration.   As we shall see when we analyze the problems in the next chapter, modern statutes afford corporate managers considerable flexibility in the type of consideration that Bidder can use to acquire Target. Modern statutes generally provide this flexibility in one of two ways. First, today's state corporation codes generally authorize broad powers for the modern corporation unless the company's articles of incorporation limit the scope of its powers. Thus, modern corporations have all the powers of a natural person (unless specifically limited by a provision in their articles or charter), which includes the power to hold stock in another corporation (domestic or foreign) as well as the power to issue debt in the name of the company on any terms that the board decides are consistent with the company's best interests. *See*, e.g., MBCA §3.03 (describing powers conferred on modern corporations in the absence of a limiting provision in the company's articles of incorporation).

The other way in which modern statutes confer considerable flexibility on corporate managers lies in the specific provisions authorizing corporate acquisitions. Most important, today's merger statutes specify a broad range of consideration that Bidder may use to acquire Target shares, including cash, tangible or intangible property, or stock (or other securities) of Bidder or of some other corporation. In similar fashion, the modern corporation codes have liberalized the nature of the consideration that can be used to acquire substantially all of Target's assets.

By authorizing Bidder to use the shares of some *other* corporation, the law moved beyond two-party mergers (involving only the disappearing company and the surviving company) to authorize three-party mergers. These are more commonly known as *triangular mergers*. This topic is introduced in the next section.

2. An Introduction to Three-Party Transactions.   In the case of a three-party transaction, Bidder will generally create a wholly owned subsidiary for purposes of completing the acquisition. Acting as the incorporator, Bidder organizes a new corporation (referred to as "NewCo" in the diagrams of Appendix A). At the organizational meeting of NewCo's board of directors, all of NewCo's outstanding voting common stock is then issued to Bidder, generally in exchange for the consideration that will be used to acquire Target—which will usually be either Bidder's stock (or other securities) or its cash. As a result, Bidder is the sole shareholder of NewCo, and as such, will appoint the entire board of directors of NewCo, thereby creating a parent-subsidiary relationship between Bidder and NewCo.

After incorporating NewCo, Bidder will then cause NewCo to complete the acquisition of Target. So, for example, in the case of an acquisition structured as a sale of assets, NewCo would acquire all of Target's assets, leaving Target's business operations to be held in a wholly owned subsidiary of Bidder once the transaction is completed. This may prove advantageous in those situations where Bidder desires (for either legal or business reasons) to segregate its assets from those of Target. We will explore these considerations in Chapter 3 when we analyze the rules of successor liability in more detail.

By far, however, the most popular form of a three-party acquisition transaction is the *triangular merger*. Triangular mergers are a fairly recent development in corporate law, having really gained popularity only in the last 35 years
or so. Although the mechanics are too complicated to summarize here, the
major advantage of a three-party (triangular) merger over the well-established
two-party (direct) merger is easy to grasp. By using its wholly owned subsidiary
(NewCo) to merge with Target, Bidder shields its assets from the business debts
of Target. By operating Target as a wholly owned subsidiary, and assuming there
is no reason for Target's creditors to pierce the subsidiary's corporate veil to
reach the assets of the parent company, Bidder will be able to protect its asset
base from the claims of Target's creditors.

Another significant advantage of the triangular merger is that it usually
allows Bidder to eliminate the need to obtain approval from its shareholders
and, generally speaking, will also eliminate any right of appraisal for Bidder's
dissenting shares. This may prove to be advantageous to Bidder by allowing it
to avoid the cost and delay associated with obtaining a vote of its shareholders
and the availability of a dissenting right of appraisal, which may be particularly
helpful in the case of a publicly traded Bidder. For all of these reasons, the triangular merger is probably the most widely used method for structuring business
combinations in today's M&A market.

3. Cross-Border Transactions.   It is often the case that U.S. based companies seek to expand their businesses beyond their own domestic markets by
acquiring companies that are based in other countries. A noteworthy, high-
profile example of such a cross-border transaction is Kraft Foods, Inc.'s 2010
bid for Cadbury plc, a business organized under United Kingdom law, which
was ultimately successful. *See* Dana Climillica and Ilan Brat, *Kraft Wins a Reluctant
Cadbury,* WALL STREET JOURNAL, Jan. 20, 2010, at B1.

Regulation of cross-border transactions (such as Kraft's takeover of
Cadbury) is beyond the scope of this text. However, it is interesting to note
that this acquisition in the *global* M&A market raises all of the same important
corporate governance concerns that are an inherent attribute of *domestic* M&A
transactions, and which are also an important theme of this casebook. As originally structured, 60 percent of Kraft's offer to acquire Cadbury consisted of
Kraft stock, and the balance of Kraft's $16.7 billion bid was to be paid in cash.
However, Warren Buffett, one of Kraft's largest stockholders, publicly objected
to this aspect of the deal. In response to this very public criticism coming from
a well-known and well-regarded investor, Kraft's management (led by its CEO,
Irene Rosenfeld) revised the terms of its offer for Cadbury to include more
cash in its bid and thereby significantly reduce the number of Kraft shares to
be issued as part of the acquisition consideration. The nature of the corporate
governance concerns that are implicated in the structure of Kraft's acquisition
of Cadbury are to be explored further, starting with the problem sets in the next
chapter.

||2||

Corporate Formalities: The Mechanics of Structuring Acquisition Transactions

A. An Introduction to Corporate Law Statutes: The Statutory Scheme of Delaware, Model Act, and California

In this chapter, we sketch out the regulatory framework that applies to the acquisition process. This includes a detailed review of the relevant provisions of state corporate law, focusing primarily on the corporation statutes of Delaware and California, with references to the Model Act as well. The reason we focus on Delaware law is that Delaware is the most popular state for incorporation, particularly for large, publicly traded corporations. Accordingly, Delaware is the most important source of jurisprudence in the area of mergers and acquisitions (M&A) transactions. The reason to study California law, aside from the fact that it is an important commercial state, much like Illinois, New York, and Texas, is that California has adopted a regulatory approach to M&A activity that is very different from any other jurisdiction. Since the regulatory philosophy adopted in California's Corporation Code (CCC, or Calif. Corp. Code) stands in stark contrast to Delaware's statute, the Delaware General Corporation Law (DGCL or Delaware), detailed analysis of the provisions of these two jurisdictions allows for critical examination of the public policy considerations that are relevant to regulating the market for M&A transactions.

On a more practical note, the problems in this chapter require you to work through various provisions of each state's corporation code. In doing these problems, you will be exposed to the kind of statutory analysis that is part of the M&A lawyer's daily work. In addition, these problems will allow you to hone your skills involving statutory analysis, as you will be required to read statutory provisions to understand the meaning of the language of a particular statute and to determine how the various provisions of the statute work together to create a comprehensive regulatory framework. Finally, you will be asked to compare the results obtained under Delaware law with those reached in applying the provisions of the California law and examine the public policy implications of each state's regulatory approach.

In addition, we will introduce the role of the federal securities laws in regulating M&A activity. Although we will not study the relevant provisions of the federal securities law in detail until we get to Chapter 4, the problems are useful for illustrating the interaction between federal and state law. M&A lawyers must understand this interaction in order to structure the M&A transaction in compliance with both.

Since many states have adopted corporation statutes that are based in some measure on the Model Business Corporation Act (MBCA), references will be made throughout the materials in this chapter to the MBCA provision that corresponds to the particular Delaware provision at issue. Analyzing the problem under the relevant MBCA provision first, before turning to the relevant Delaware statute, may be helpful in mastering what is often the much more convoluted provisions of the DGCL. More important, the MBCA has undergone major revisions over the years, resulting in a substantial restructuring (and rewording) of its provisions, with the most recent revisions made in 2016. The statutory language of the MBCA provisions thus reflects a deliberate effort to make the MBCA provisions clearer and easier to understand.

A word of caution, though, is still in order. Notwithstanding these recent efforts to clarify the statutory language of the MBCA, there will still be times when the language of these statutes, including the MBCA, is ambiguous as applied to the facts of a particular problem. Alternatively, the statutory language may be clear enough, but as applied to the facts of a particular case, the result may be unjust or unreasonable. In these cases, as with other statutes that lawyers must grapple with as part of their daily practice, you will be called upon to consider how to interpret the statutory language in order to reach a fair result. As part of this analytical process, you will be required to consider the public policy concerns that underlie the relevant statute's regulatory approach. The problems in this chapter are intended to flesh out important public policy considerations—matters of particular concern today in light of the financial scandals of the 21st century that ultimately led to congressional enactment of the Sarbanes-Oxley Act in 2002, and then later the Dodd-Frank Act in 2010.

1. The Requirement of Board and/or Shareholder Approval Under State Law

In the problems in this chapter, you will be asked to consider the relevant statutory prerequisites (generally referred to as the "corporate formalities") that must be satisfied for the M&A transaction to be validly consummated. As reflected in the cases to be analyzed in this chapter, failure to satisfy the statutory prerequisites imposed by the law of the state where the company is organized may create the basis for a shareholder challenge to the validity of the transaction. Most often, this challenge will be an equitable action, usually seeking to enjoin completion of the transaction unless and until the relevant corporate formalities have been satisfied.

Where the transaction is challenged for failure to satisfy the required formalities imposed by state corporate law, the challenge will often focus on shareholder voting rights and/or the availability of appraisal rights. Accordingly, as part of each problem in this chapter, we will analyze whether the transaction requires approval by the shareholders and whether the transaction triggers a right of appraisal for those shareholders who object to the acquisition. In addition, we will consider the threshold requirement of board authorization of an acquisition and the statutory source of this obligation. One of the valuable contributions of a lawyer as the transaction planner is structuring the acquisition in compliance with all relevant statutory requirements on a cost-effective basis so that the transaction will proceed to close in a timely manner.

As an alternative to an injunctive action, which is generally intended to prevent consummation of an acquisition, the shareholder may bring an action for damages, or for rescission of the acquisition, *after* the transaction has been completed. The equitable action for rescission is generally doomed to fail, as most courts are reluctant to unwind completed transactions in order to restore the parties to the status quo ante, as called for under the remedy of rescission. For that reason, among others, it is incumbent on the shareholder who strongly opposes a proposed acquisition to bring an action prior to consummation of the deal if the shareholder's primary goal is to preserve the independence of the company by preventing completion of the transaction.

If, on the other hand, the shareholder's primary objection concerns the adequacy of the acquisition consideration, the shareholder may bring an action for damages. In these cases, the modern appraisal remedy may prove adequate to address the shareholder's grievances. In cases involving management's breach of fiduciary duty, however, there will be a threshold question as to the adequacy of the appraisal remedy to address the public policy concerns raised by this kind of shareholder complaint. At the end of this chapter, we will explore the scope of the appraisal remedy and examine cases that address the adequacy and the exclusivity of this remedy.

2.   Federal Securities Laws and the Stock Exchange Rules

In addition to a thorough understanding of the relevant default rules of state corporate law, the transaction planner must consider the application of the federal securities laws and the rules of self-regulatory organizations, such as the New York Stock Exchange (NYSE). Although we will discuss the federal securities laws in more detail in later chapters, it is useful at this point to summarize the provisions that are relevant to the process of obtaining (shareholder) approval of the proposed acquisition.

a.   *The Federal Proxy Rules*

In the case of acquisitions involving *reporting companies* under the Securities Exchange Act of 1934 (the 1934 Act), the federal proxy rules will apply. For our purposes, reporting companies fall into one of two categories: (i) companies whose shares are listed for trading on a national exchange (which includes the NYSE); or (ii) companies that meet both of the following criteria—they have a class of equity securities held by 2,000 or more persons (or more than 500 shareholders who are not accredited investors) *and* they have assets totaling greater than $10 million. When management solicits votes from shareholders of a reporting company, the proxy rules of the Securities and Exchange Commission (SEC) require that the company's managers file a proxy statement with the SEC and distribute the proxy statement to the company's shareholders. The goal of the SEC's proxy rules is to provide the shareholders of a publicly traded company with the information they need to make an informed decision on whether to approve the terms of an acquisition negotiated by company managers. Hence, the SEC's proxy rules generally obligate company managers to provide full and adequate disclosure of all material facts about the proposed acquisition. We will analyze the appropriate standard of *materiality* in Chapter 4, as part of a more detailed review of the provisions of the federal securities laws that are relevant in the context of M&A transactions.

b. The Securities Act of 1933

Whenever Bidder Co. proposes to use its stock as the acquisition consideration, Bidder needs to comply with the requirements of the Securities Act of 1933 (the 1933 Act). Briefly summarized, the 1933 Act regulates the distribution (i.e., the issuance) of shares by requiring the issuer (here, Bidder) to register the distribution (i.e., the offer and sale) of Bidder's shares unless an exemption from registration is available. The goal of the registration requirements of the 1933 Act is to protect the purchaser of securities by requiring the issuer to disclose all material facts regarding the proposed offering (issuance) of its securities so that the prospective investor (purchaser) can make an informed investment decision. The issuer may avoid (or reduce) the delay and expense associated with preparing a registration statement by establishing that one of the SEC's exemptions from registration is available. In this way, the 1933 Act regulates the process of capital formation, whereby companies sell their stock (or other securities) to the investing public in order to raise the capital they need to finance their business operations.

In the context of M&A transactions, the 1933 Act applies where Bidder proposes to use its stock as the acquisition consideration. In this situation, the SEC views Bidder's issuance of its stock (or other securities) to acquire Target as a distribution that is subject to the regulatory scheme of the 1933 Act. Thus, the issuer (Bidder Co.) must register or find an exemption in order to use its stock to acquire Target. This registration obligation is imposed on all issuers, whether publicly traded or privately held, who propose to sell their stock. Those rules promulgated by the SEC under the 1933 Act that are most pertinent to M&A transactions are discussed in more detail in Chapter 4.

c. Shareholder Approval Requirements of the NYSE

The NYSE is a secondary trading market where persons who already own outstanding shares of a company and wish to sell them deal with other investors who want to buy shares. Thus, the NYSE is *not* where a company goes to raise new capital by issuing (selling) securities to the public, and therefore the provisions of the 1933 Act generally do not apply to the trading activity that occurs on the floor of the NYSE. Rather, the provisions of the 1934 Act apply to regulate the trading practices of sellers, buyers, broker-dealer firms, and other securities professionals who participate in the trading activity of secondary markets such as the NYSE.

The NYSE and other secondary trading markets, most notably the Nasdaq Stock Market (Nasdaq), are heavily regulated by the SEC. Under provisions of the 1934 Act, the NYSE qualifies as a self-regulatory organization (SRO). As such, it has its own set of operating rules and procedures, and it regulates its membership by way of these rules and procedures. As an SRO, the rules and procedures adopted and enforced by the NYSE are subject to oversight by the SEC. Accordingly, any changes to a particular NYSE rule require approval by the SEC.

Very important for our study of M&A law are those NYSE rules that apply to companies whose securities are listed for trading on the NYSE. To be listed, a company must satisfy certain NYSE criteria as to size and share ownership, known as the *listing standards*. Further, each company must enter into a listing agreement with the NYSE, which obligates the *listed company* to comply with the rules and procedures contained in the NYSE Listed Company Manual. Among the most important of these obligations, at least for our purposes, are the disclosure obligations and the shareholder voting rules that are imposed on all NYSE-listed companies—regardless of the company's state of incorporation. With respect to disclosure requirements, the NYSE obligates listed companies to make information about developments affecting the company publicly available on a timely basis. We will describe how this obligation comes into play in Chapter 4, when we describe the obligation of publicly traded constituent corporations to disclose pending negotiations for mergers or other types of business combinations.

More important for purposes of the topic at hand are the shareholder voting rights imposed by the rules of the NYSE. The shareholder voting requirements that are most relevant are set forth in Rule 312 of the NYSE Listed Company Manual. Generally speaking, this NYSE provision grants to shareholders of NYSE-traded companies voting rights that are more rigorous than those required by most state corporation statutes, such as the Delaware statute.* For purposes of analyzing the problems in this chapter, the relevant portions of NYSE Rule 312 provide:

> Shareholder approval is a prerequisite to listing in [the following] situations:
>   . . . (c) Shareholder approval is required prior to the issuance of common stock, or of securities convertible into or exercisable for common stock, in any transaction or series of related transactions if:
>   (1) the common stock has, or will have upon issuance, voting power equal to or in excess of 20 percent of the voting power outstanding before the issuance of such stock or of securities convertible into or exercisable for common stock; or
>   (2) the number of shares of common stock to be issued is, or will be upon issuance, equal to or in excess of 20 percent of the number of shares of common

---

*[By the author: Nasdaq has similar shareholder voting rules (*see* Nasdaq Stock Market Rule 5635(d)), although this chapter and its problem sets will focus only on the shareholder voting requirements of NYSE Rule 312.]

stock outstanding before the issuance of the common stock or of securities convertible into or exercisable for common stock.

However, shareholder approval will not be required for any such issuance involving:

- Any public offering for cash;
- Any bona fide private financing, if such financing involves a sale of: common stock, for cash, at a price at least as great as each of the book and market value of the issuer's common stock; or securities convertible into or exercisable for common stock, for cash, if the conversion or exercise price is at least as great as each of the book and market value of the issuer's common stock. . . .

Where shareholder approval is a prerequisite to the listing of any additional or new securities of a listed company, the minimum vote which will constitute shareholder approval for listing purposes is defined as approval by a majority of votes cast on a proposal in a proxy bearing on the particular matter.

NEW YORK STOCK EXCHANGE Listed Company Manual, Section 312.00, Shareholder Approval Policy, Sections 312.03 and 312.07.

Recent revisions to Section 6.21 of the MBCA were generally patterned on this NYSE shareholder voting requirement. Like Rule 312, MBCA §6.21 is not confined to merger transactions, but rather is part of the MBCA provisions dealing generally with the issuance of shares. Thus, these MBCA rules on issuance of shares apply to *any* M&A transaction where Bidder proposes to use its own stock as the acquisition consideration. In the case of certain acquisitions, the provisions of MBCA §6.21(f) may require shareholder approval in order for Bidder to validly issue its shares in exchange for consideration other than cash (or cash equivalent, such as a personal check). The operation of the NYSE's shareholder voting rule and the scope of the protection offered by Rule 312 to shareholders of a listed company are best appreciated by analyzing the problem sets in this chapter. In addition, the problem sets will analyze the requirement of a shareholder vote under the terms of MBCA §6.21(f).

From a public policy perspective, why would the NYSE want to impose a shareholder voting rule, especially one that grants more extensive shareholder voting rights than required by most states, such as Delaware's corporation statute? The reason for this type of NYSE rule is pretty basic: the NYSE is a trading market that provides essential *liquidity* to those persons who invest in publicly traded securities. Accordingly, the rules of the NYSE are intended to instill confidence in those investors that the trading market provided by the NYSE is efficient and fair—that trading expenses on the NYSE are minimized and the NYSE's market is free of manipulation and fraud. If investors lose confidence in the NYSE's ability to operate a trading market that is liquid, efficient, and honest, then the entire capital market system suffers.

NOTES

1. How Many Shareholders Must Approve the Acquisition?   In the case of a plain vanilla capital structure consisting of a single class of common stock outstanding, the question of *who* gets to vote is easy to resolve. In these situations, the only really tough questions are *how many* shares must approve the proposed acquisition under the terms of the relevant statute (i.e., absolute majority voting standard vs. some supermajority voting standard vs. some other voting standard), and separately, whether there is any basis for *eliminating* the statutory requirement of shareholder approval. As we will see when we analyze the problems, the statutes vary as to the situations where a shareholder vote is not required and the modern codes likewise vary as to the criteria that must be satisfied in order to eliminate the need to obtain shareholder approval. Later in this chapter, we will examine the *VantagePoint* case, where the company has a more complicated capital structure authorizing more than one class of stock, and we will analyze the more complex question of how many of these outstanding shares must approve the transaction and whether there is a right to vote separately as a class (i.e., right to a class vote).

2. Business Combinations in Which One Party Is Not a Corporation: "Interspecies" Transactions.   Many times, a corporation will decide to acquire a business that is *not* organized as a corporation in what is known as an "interspecies" business combination. For example, a corporation may decide to merge with a business organized as a limited liability company (LLC) in a transaction often referred to as an *interspecies merger*. Until quite recently, this transaction was problematic, as most state corporation codes authorized mergers only between corporations, whether they were foreign or domestic. As we will see, most states have amended their codes to authorize "interspecies" business combinations—that is, to allow a corporation to merge with some other type of business entity such as an LLC. *See, e.g.*, MBCA §11.02(a) and §1.40 (*see* the definitions of "eligible entity," "foreign corporation," and "unincorporated entity," provisions which are typical of the statutory language that provides this kind of flexibility to modern corporations).

3. Are the Modern Corporations Statutes Enabling or Regulatory in Nature?   The dominant view today, particularly in the case of Delaware jurisprudence, is to treat the corporation as (entirely) a creature of statute. Because corporations may engage *only* in business combinations authorized by statute and then *only* if done in compliance with *all* the requirements imposed by the relevant corporation statute, the modern statutes are said to be *enabling*. (Remember, the choice of law principle known as the *internal affairs doctrine* governs the company's ability to enter into a proposed acquisition transaction.)

As we analyze the cases later in this chapter, we will see how this view of modern corporation statutes influences judicial decision making and, in particular, how it influences the manner in which the courts (particularly the Delaware judiciary) go about interpreting the language of a specific corporation statute. The problem sets in this chapter are intended to focus attention on the important public policy question of how to balance responsibility and power between the courts, the legislature, and the parties themselves in structuring transactions, especially with regard to the scope of protection to be extended to minority shareholders, creditors, and other interests that are regularly implicated in any given M&A transaction.

B. Corporate Formalities Required for Statutory Mergers Under Delaware Law and the MBCA

1. General Background — Delaware Law of Direct Mergers

Originally enacted in 1967, section 251 is the basic merger statute in Delaware, which has been amended several times in the last half-century in order to further liberalize the procedures for effecting mergers. These piece-meal amendments have resulted in a rather long and often convoluted statutory provision containing many subparts that address different aspects of the merger process. This note material summarizes certain aspects of Delaware §251(a) but (most certainly) is not a substitute for reading the statutory language itself. The problem sets are intended to help you master the relevant statutory provisions by focusing on discrete issues one at a time. By the end of our analysis of these problem sets, you should have developed a sense of the merger process as a whole, particularly as regulated by Delaware law.

As part of this introduction to the merger process, references to corre-sponding provisions of the MBCA will be included. Chapter 11 contains the basic merger procedures under the MBCA. Significant differences between the MBCA and Delaware law will be noted where appropriate.

Board Approval. Reflecting the enabling nature of modern corporation codes, Delaware §251(a) authorizes the merger of any two domestic corporations. In addition, Delaware §252 authorizes a domestic corporation to merge with a foreign corporation, and further authorizes that either the domestic or the foreign corporation may be designated as the surviving corporation. *See also* MBCA §11.02. Under Delaware §251, the board of directors of each *constituent corporation* that is a Delaware corporation must approve the merger agreement, reflecting the corporate norm that the board manages the business affairs of the corporation. Del. §141(a); *see also* MBCA §11.04 and §8.01. Delaware §251(b) describes the terms that must be set forth in the parties' merger agreement. *See also* MBCA §11.02.

Shareholder Approval. Generally speaking, Delaware §251(c) requires that the merger agreement must be submitted to the shareholders for their approval in order for the merger to become effective. *See also* MBCA §11.04. Until revisions were made in 1967, mergers under Delaware law required the affirmative vote of two-thirds of all outstanding shares. Today, though, Delaware §251(c) has relaxed the voting standard to require approval by "a majority of the outstanding shares entitled to vote thereon," thereby making the statutory merger a more attractive means of accomplishing an acquisition. Prior to 1967, the shareholders of *each* constituent corporation were required to approve the terms of the merger. Subsequent amendments to Delaware §251(c), however, have further liberalized the merger process by eliminating the requirement of a shareholder vote in certain situations. Today, the vote of the surviving corpora-tion shareholders may be eliminated if the three conditions of Delaware §251(f) are satisfied. *See also* MBCA §11.04(h).

Moreover, Delaware §251 requires approval by the vote of only an absolute majority of the outstanding common stock, although the certificate of incorporation of a constituent corporation may require a higher percentage. A provision for such a *supermajority vote* will generally be included at the insistence of those minority shareholders who, but for this type of supermajority voting requirement, would be vulnerable to the will of the majority, who could otherwise use their votes to force a merger onto the corporation. Since this requirement for a supermajority vote must be contained in the company's articles of incorporation (or *certificate of incorporation*, as it is called in Delaware), this type of protection is most likely to be bargained for at the time the shares are purchased from the corporation as part of the minority shareholder's original investment decision. (*See* Delaware §102(b)(4) and MBCA §11.04(e).)

Merger Consideration.   As a result of a series of revisions made to Delaware §251, a broad range of consideration may be used today to effect a merger. *See* Delaware §251(b); and MBCA §11.02(d)(4). "Thus, as far as Delaware law is concerned, virtually any type of consideration is now permissible in a merger." FOLK ON THE DELAWARE GENERAL CORPORATION LAW (2020 ed.) at §251.02[C]. Thus, today, merger consideration may consist of cash or Bidder's stock (or other securities, such as debentures or other types of debt instruments). Where cash is used, Bidder will acquire all of Target's business operations while simultaneously eliminating Target's shareholders from any continuing equity ownership in the combined firm. This liberalization of the modern corporation statutes has led to widespread use of the *cash merger* (sometimes referred to as the *cashout merger*), which is illustrated in Diagram 2 of Appendix A.

The great beauty—or, as I like to think of it, the "magic" of the merger procedure—is that the merger "effects *by operation of law* a transmutation of the stock interest in a constituent corporation" into whatever consideration is specified in the terms of the parties' agreement of merger. *Shields v. Shields*, 498 A.2d 161, 167 (Del. Ch. 1985) (*emphasis added*). As a result, significant transaction costs are avoided by the constituent corporations (and their shareholders). "At the moment a stock for stock merger [becomes] effective, the stock in a constituent corporation (other than the surviving corporation) ceases to exist legally." *Id.* at 168. This conversion occurs by operation of law, without the need for any action on the part of the shareholder and notwithstanding any objections or reservations that any individual (minority) shareholders may have.

Successor Liability.   In the case of a direct merger, the result is clear. The surviving corporation succeeds to *all* the rights and *all* the liabilities of *both* constituent corporations by operation of law once the merger takes effect. *See* Delaware §259; MBCA §11.07.

Abandonment of Merger.   Delaware's §251(d) also allows the board of directors of any constituent corporation to abandon a merger without the approval of the shareholders—even if the plan of merger has already been approved by the shareholders—so long as the merger agreement expressly reserves that power to the board. *See also* MBCA §11.08. If the directors reserve this power, however, Delaware case law makes clear that the board must exercise this power in a manner that is consistent with its fiduciary duties. Accordingly, it may be desirable for the merger agreement to specify the circumstances under which the board may decide to abandon a merger.

In 1983, Delaware §251 was amended to permit a board of directors to amend a merger agreement at any time before it is filed with the Secretary of State's office, provided that the agreement expressly reserves this power to the board. *See also* MBCA §11.02. Although the board may reserve the right to amend the agreement either before or after obtaining shareholder approval of the merger, "any amendment made *after* adoption of the agreement by the stockholders may *not* change the consideration to be received in the merger, change any term of the certificate of incorporation of the surviving corporation, or change the agreement in such a way as to adversely affect any class or series of stock of any constituent corporation." *See* FOLK, *supra* at §251.03[B] (*emphasis added*).

2. Introduction to Dissenter's Right of Appraisal

General Background. As was noted in the materials at the end of Chapter 1, the modern evolution of appraisal rights was intended to address the fundamental tension inherent in any proposed acquisition, whether the deal is done on Main Street or Wall Street. In other words,

> [modern appraisal rights deal] with the tension between the desire of the corporate leadership to be able to enter new fields, acquire new enterprises, and rearrange investor rights, and the desire of investors to adhere to the rights and the risks on the basis of which they invested. Contemporary corporation statutes in the United States attempt to resolve this tension through a combination of two devices. On the one hand, through their approval of an amendment to the articles of incorporation, a merger, share exchange or disposition of assets, the majority may change the nature and shape of the enterprise and the rights of *all* its shareholders. On the other hand, shareholders who object to these [fundamental] changes may withdraw the fair value of their investment in cash through their exercise of appraisal rights.
>
> The traditional accommodation has been sharply criticized from two directions. From the viewpoint of investors who object to the transaction, the appraisal process is criticized for providing little help to the ordinary investor because its technicalities make its use difficult, expensive, and risky. From the viewpoint of the corporate leadership, the appraisal process is criticized because it fails to protect the corporation from demands that are motivated by the hope of a nuisance settlement or by fanciful conceptions of value.

Committee on Corporate Laws, ABA Section of Business Law, *Changes in the MBCA*, 65 BUS. LAW. 1121, 1138 (2010) (*emphasis added*).

Although appraisal rights—as both a matter of Delaware law and the MBCA—are designed to balance the competing interests described in the quoted passage above, there are significant differences in the *availability* of appraisal rights under Delaware law as compared to the MBCA. The problem sets in this chapter are intended to focus your attention on the transactions that will trigger appraisal rights for the "dissenting shareholder"—i.e., the shareholder who objects to a proposed acquisition. As was mentioned in Chapter 1, this is an important threshold issue to be taken into account in planning the structure of an acquisition transaction. However, once it is determined that appraisal rights are available to minority shareholders, there are several other issues that then need to be addressed, namely:

- the *procedures* that must be followed to perfect the right to an appraisal;
- the *valuation* issues that must be addressed in the context of a judicially surprised appraisal proceeding; and
- the *exclusivity* of the appraisal remedy, i.e., whether modern appraisal statutes provide the only remedy to the objecting shareholder.

After we analyze the transactions that trigger appraisal rights as part of our discussion of the various problem sets in the next few sections, we will then turn our attention to the issues described above as part of the appraisal materials included at the end of this chapter.

Scope of Appraisal Rights Under Delaware Law.   The availability and scope of the dissenting shareholder's right of appraisal is set out in Delaware §262; moreover, Delaware case law makes clear that the shareholder's right to an appraisal is "*entirely* a creature of statute." *Kaye v. Pantone, Inc.*, 395 A.2d 369, 375 (Del. Ch. 1978) (*emphasis added*). Delaware §262(b) grants a right of appraisal to the "shares of any class or series of stock of a constituent corporation in a merger" to be effected pursuant to Delaware §251. Although the Delaware statute does not define the term "constituent corporation," it is generally understood to refer to all of the corporations that are merging, whether they survive or disappear in the transaction. *See* FOLK, *supra* at §262.02[A]. Accordingly, under Delaware law, there is *no* right of appraisal in the case of a sale of assets or an amendment to the company's certificate of incorporation (known in other states as the *articles of incorporation*).

Delaware's Market Out Exception.   As do many states, Delaware §262(b)(1) eliminates the right of appraisal as to any shares that are listed on a national exchange (such as the NYSE) or that are traded on the Nasdaq. Even if not so listed, the right of appraisal will still be eliminated as to those shares that meet certain criteria set forth in the Delaware statute, which are intended to show that the shares are so widely held as to imply a liquid and substantial trading market. The premise for this exception—customarily referred to as the *market out exception*—is that the right to be cashed out is not necessary where there is a liquid and accessible trading market for the dissenter's shares. Rather than compel the company to cash out the dissenting shareholder, the theory underlying this exception is that the objecting shareholder should simply sell his or her shares into the open market.

The second part of Delaware §262(b)(1) eliminates the right of appraisal as to shares of the *surviving* corporation, but *only* in those situations where the merger is effected without a vote of the shareholders pursuant to the terms of Delaware §251(f).

The "Exception to the Exception"—Restoring the Right of Appraisal Under Delaware Law.   Even in those cases where the market out exception operates to eliminate the dissenting shareholders' right of appraisal, their right to an appraisal may be restored if the tests of Delaware §262(b)(2) are satisfied. Whether appraisal rights are to be restored under Delaware §262(b)(2)—in what is customarily referred to as the *exception to the exception*—depends largely on the *type* of consideration that the dissenting shareholders are required to accept under the terms of the merger agreement. In a rather convoluted manner of drafting, the Delaware statute provides that where the market out exception is triggered and the dissenting shares are required to take any consideration other than stock (such as bonds, debentures, cash, or property), then an "exception to the (market out) exception" of Delaware §262(b)(1) is triggered, which operates to restore the dissenters' right to an appraisal.

So, while today's merger statute in Delaware authorizes use of a broad range of merger consideration (including cash), Delaware's appraisal statute preserves the right of appraisal—even if the dissenting shares are publicly traded—where the shareholders are required to accept merger consideration that consists of anything other than stock (plus cash for any fractional shares). Delaware §§262(b)(2)(a) and (b) further specify that the stock that the dissenting shareholder is to receive must consist of *either* shares of the surviving corporation *or* stock of some other corporation whose shares are publicly traded.

As a result of this rather convoluted style of drafting, Delaware's appraisal statute frequently is difficult to comprehend in the abstract. The problem sets that follow are intended to help you master the rather backhanded manner in which the Delaware appraisal statute is cobbled together. On another level, the problems will serve—much better than any mere narrative description—to illustrate the *availability* of the dissenter's right of appraisal.

Appraisal Rights Under the MBCA. In contrast to Delaware law, the availability of appraisal rights is framed very differently under the equivalent provisions of the MBCA, which are found in Chapter 13. Recent revisions to Chapter 13 have made significant changes to the scope of appraisal rights available under the MBCA. Many of these changes work to bring the MBCA closer to Delaware law, but some of the modifications to the MBCA represent a dramatic departure from Delaware's approach to appraisal rights.

As a general proposition, the availability of appraisal rights under the MBCA proceeds from

> the premise that judicial appraisal should be provided by statute only when two conditions co-exist. First, the proposed corporate action as approved by the majority will result in a fundamental change in the shares to be affected by the action. Second, uncertainty concerning the fair value of the affected shares may cause reasonable persons to differ about the fairness of the terms of the corporate action. Uncertainty is greatly reduced, however, in the case of publicly-traded shares. This explains both the market exception [under §13.02(b)] . . . and the limits provided to [this] exception.
>
> Appraisal rights in connection with . . . mergers and share exchanges under chapter 11, and dispositions of assets requiring shareholder approval under chapter 12 are provided when these two conditions co-exist. Each of these actions will result in a fundamental change in the shares that a disapproving shareholder may feel was not adequately compensated by the terms approved by the majority.

Committee on Corporate Laws, ABA Section of Business Law, *Changes in the MBCA*, 65 Bus. Law. 1121, 1138 (2010).

MCBA §13.02(a) sets forth the events that will trigger the right of appraisal. More specifically, MBCA §13.02(a) grants appraisal rights more broadly than Delaware law since appraisal rights under the MBCA are *not* limited to merger transactions only. With respect to merger transactions, appraisal rights are available in the case of those mergers that require shareholder approval, although appraisal rights are denied as to any shares of the *surviving* corporation that remain outstanding after the merger is completed. *See* MCBA §13.02(a). In addition, appraisal rights are granted under the MBCA in the case of (i) certain share exchanges effected pursuant to MBCA §11.03 (an acquisition procedure that we will discuss later in this chapter); (ii) certain sales of assets effected pursuant to MBCA §12.02; and (iii) certain amendments to the company's articles of incorporation.

Like Delaware, the MBCA includes a market out exception, which eliminates the right of appraisal in certain cases where the dissenter's shares are publicly traded. *See* MBCA §13.02(b)(1). Under MBCA §13.02(b), however, the appraisal right is *restored*—even if the dissenter's shares are publicly traded—in those situations where the dissenting shareholder is required to accept any consideration other than cash or some other publicly traded security. While expanding the availability of appraisal rights beyond that provided by Delaware law, the MBCA framed its market out exception very differently than Delaware. The manner in which the MBCA's market out exception operates, however, actually results in narrowing the availability of appraisal rights as compared to the Delaware approach. Although this difference in approach is a little difficult to appreciate in the abstract, the problem sets that follow are designed to illustrate the differences in the operation of the market out exception under Delaware §262 as compared to the approach adopted by the MBCA.

3. Perfecting the Statutory Right of Appraisal

Broadly speaking, the procedures set forth in Delaware §262, which are fairly typical of most states' appraisal statutes, require dissenting shareholders to take the following steps in order to perfect their right to an appraisal:

- First, before the shareholders vote on the proposed merger, the objecting shareholders must notify the company of their intent to demand an appraisal. This requirement essentially places the company on notice of the number of shareholders' complaints as to the terms of the proposed merger and the extent to which the company's cash resources may be called upon to fulfill this demand.
- At the time of the shareholder meeting, dissenting shareholders must either abstain or vote against the proposed merger. Within a relatively short period of time following shareholder approval of the proposed merger, dissenting shareholders must notify the company in writing of their intent to demand payment in cash for their shares.
- As a final matter, dissenting shareholders must continue to hold their shares through the effective date of the merger.

In order to appreciate the costs and delay associated with shareholders exercising their statutory right of appraisal, we will briefly examine the mechanics involved in perfecting this right as part of the materials at the end of this chapter. We will also examine the nature of the judicially supervised appraisal proceeding that will be instituted to resolve any disputes between the company and the dissenting shareholder over the valuation of the dissenter's shares.

PROBLEM SET NO. 1—STATUTORY (OR DIRECT) MERGERS UNDER DELAWARE LAW AND THE MBCA

A. Stock for Stock Mergers

1. Merger Consideration Comprising 30 Percent of Bidder's Stock—(Plain Vanilla) Stock for Stock Merger (See Diagram 1—Appendix A).   Target Co., a closely held concern, plans to merge into Bidder Co., another closely held firm. The plan of merger calls for Target shareholders to receive shares of Bidder common stock comprising 30 percent of the voting power of Bidder shares that were outstanding immediately before closing on the proposed merger with Target. In addition, Target and Bidder each have a plain vanilla capital structure, consisting of only one class of voting common stock outstanding. Moreover, Bidder has sufficient authorized and unissued shares to complete the transaction.

   a. Which corporation is to survive?
   b. What action is required by the boards of Bidder and Target:

   (1) Under Delaware law?
   (2) Under the MBCA?

   c. Do the shareholders of Bidder and Target have the right to vote:

   (1) Under Delaware law?
   (2) Under the MBCA?

   d. Do the shareholders of Bidder and Target have the right to dissent:

   (1) Under Delaware law?
   (2) Under the MBCA?

   e. What action would be required (under either Delaware law or the MBCA) if Bidder did *not* have a sufficient number of authorized shares to complete the proposed merger with Target? (*Hint:* Consider the text of Delaware §251(b)(3) and MBCA §11.02(d)(5).)

2.   Assume that AT&T, Inc., a NYSE-listed, Delaware company, and DirecTV, Inc., another NYSE-listed, Delaware company, plan to combine into a single firm, with AT&T designated as the surviving corporation. The plan of merger calls for the DirecTV shareholders to receive shares of AT&T common stock comprising 30 percent of the voting power of AT&T's common stock that was outstanding immediately before the proposed merger with DirecTV.

   a. What action is required of the boards of AT&T and DirecTV in order to complete this type of direct merger?

b. Do the shareholders of AT&T and DirecTV have the right to vote:

  (1) Under Delaware law?
  (2) Under the rules of the NYSE?

c. Do the shareholders of AT&T and/or DirecTV have the right to dissent?

d. What action would be required under Delaware law and/or the federal securities laws if AT&T did *not* have a sufficient number of authorized but unissued common shares to complete the transaction?

e. Assume that AT&T has 1 million common shares outstanding entitled to vote. How many shares must vote in favor of the transaction in order for it to be validly approved under the terms of:

  (1) Delaware law?
  (2) The rules of the NYSE? (*Hint*: Consider the text of NYSE Rule 312, excerpted earlier in the text of this chapter.)
  (3) The MBCA (assuming, for purposes of this question only, that the MBCA applies to determine the voting requirements for AT&T shareholders)? (*Hint*: Consider MBCA §11.4 (e) and §7.25(c).)

f. Will this merger automatically become effective once the requisite shareholder approval is obtained? *See* Delaware §251(c) and §259; and MBCA §11.06 and §11.07.

3. *Merger Consideration Consisting of 15 Percent of Bidder's Stock—Another Plain Vanilla Stock for Stock Direct Merger (See Diagram 1—Appendix A)*. Assume once again that Target plans to merge into Bidder as set out in the facts of Problem 1, except that the shareholders of the privately held Target will receive stock in the privately held Bidder comprising only 15 percent of the voting power of Bidder's stock that was outstanding immediately before the proposed merger is completed.

a. What action is required by the boards of Bidder and Target:

  (1) Under Delaware law?
  (2) Under the MBCA?

b. Do the shareholders of Bidder and Target have the right to vote:

  (1) Under Delaware law?
  (2) Under the MBCA?

c. Do the shareholders of Bidder and Target have the right to dissent:

  (1) Under Delaware law?
  (2) Under the MBCA?

4. Assume that DirecTV, a publicly traded company, plans to merge with AT&T, another publicly traded company, in exchange for shares comprising only 15 percent of the voting power of AT&T's outstanding common stock before the merger is completed.

a. What action is required of the boards of AT&T and DirecTV in order to validly consummate this merger:

   (1) Under Delaware law?
   (2) Under the MBCA?

b. Do the shareholders of AT&T and/or DirecTV have the right to vote:

   (1) Under Delaware law?
   (2) Under the rules of the NYSE?
   (3) Under the MBCA?

c. Do the shareholders of AT&T and/or DirecTV have the right to dissent:

   (1) Under Delaware law?
   (2) Under the MBCA?

B. Cash Mergers: Merger Consideration Consists of All Cash (See Diagram 2 — Appendix A)

1. Target Co., a closely held concern, plans to merge into Bidder Co., another closely held concern. The plan of merger calls for the three shareholders of Target to receive all cash. Target and Bidder each have a plain vanilla capital structure, consisting of only one class of voting common stock outstanding.

a. What action is required by the boards of Bidder and Target:

   (1) Under Delaware law?
   (2) Under the MBCA?

b. Do the shareholders of Bidder and Target have the right to vote:

   (1) Under Delaware law?
   (2) Under the MBCA?

c. Do the shareholders of Bidder and Target have the right to dissent:

   (1) Under Delaware law?
   (2) Under the MBCA?

2. Assume that Nest Labs, Inc., a company incorporated under the MBCA, has decided to merge into Google, Inc., an NYSE-listed, Delaware corporation, in exchange for $3.2 billion in cash.

a. What action is required of the boards of Google and Nest Labs in order to complete this cash merger?
b. Do the shareholders of either Google or Nest Labs have the right to vote on the proposed merger?
c. Do the shareholders of either Google or Nest Labs have the right to dissent?

3. Assume that AT&T, a publicly traded company, plans to acquire DirecTV, another publicly traded company, in an all-cash statutory merger. Further assume that AT&T can fund the $49 billion purchase through its own cash resources (and by borrowing any necessary funds).

  a. What action is required of the boards of AT&T and DirecTV in order to complete this cash merger:

  (1) Under Delaware law?
  (2) Under the MBCA?

  b. Do the shareholders of either AT&T or DirecTV have the right to vote:

  (1) Under Delaware law?
  (2) Under the MBCA?
  (3) Under the rules of the NYSE?

  c. Do the shareholders of either AT&T or DirecTV have the right to dissent:

  (1) Under Delaware law?
  (2) Under the MBCA?

C. *Corporate Formalities Required for Short-Form Mergers—Under Delaware Law and the MBCA*

Generally speaking, the short-form merger procedure operates to allow a parent corporation to absorb a subsidiary without a vote of either the parent or the subsidiary's shareholders, so long as the parent owns at least 90 percent of the subsidiary's stock. *See* Delaware §253; MBCA §11.05. The theory is that the outcome of any vote of the subsidiary's shareholders in this situation is a foregone conclusion. Consequently, there is no need for the law to impose the delay and expense associated with obtaining a vote of the shareholders. Rather, modern corporation statutes allow the parent board to effect this type of merger unilaterally if the parent company's board of directors duly adopts a resolution approving the transaction. Since the law assumes that the parent board controls the subsidiary's board of directors by virtue of its share ownership, no action is required to be taken by the subsidiary's board.

While no vote of the shareholders is required to effect a short-form merger, the parent corporation's dealings with the minority shareholders generally will be controlled by fiduciary duty law and therefore may be subject to the *entire fairness test*. We will analyze the entire fairness standard in more detail later in this chapter as part of our discussion of the landmark decision of the Delaware Supreme Court in *Weinberger v. UOP, Inc.*, 457 A.2d 701 (Del. 1983).

PROBLEM SET NO. 2—SHORT-FORM MERGER

1. Assume that Parent Co. owns 92 percent of the outstanding voting common stock of Target Co. Parent Co. now proposes to acquire the remaining 8 percent of Target Co. common stock that it does not own by cashing out the minority shareholders of Target in a short-form merger in which Parent survives. Target and Parent each have only one class of voting common stock outstanding, and each is closely held. (*See Diagram 3—Appendix A.*)

    a. What action is required by the boards of Parent and Target:

        (1) Under Delaware law?
        (2) Under the MBCA?

    b. Do the shareholders of either Parent or Target have the right to vote:

        (1) Under Delaware law?
        (2) Under the MBCA?

    c. Do the shareholders of Parent and Target have the right to dissent:

        (1) Under Delaware law?
        (2) Under the MBCA?

    d. Assume—for purposes of this question only—that the shares of both Parent and Target are listed for trading on the NYSE. Do the shareholders of either Parent or Target have the right to dissent:

        (1) Under Delaware law?
        (2) Under the MBCA?

    e. Is this short-form merger accomplished on a downstream basis or an upstream basis? (*Hint:* Which corporation is to survive and which is to disappear?)

D.   Corporate Formalities Required for Asset Acquisitions—Under Delaware Law and the MBCA

1.   General Background—Asset Acquisitions

In cases involving the sale of a company's assets, a threshold determination must be made in each case as to whether the company proposes to sell *all* or *substantially all* of its assets, as such a transaction is considered a fundamental change. Delaware §271, in turn, sets forth the corporate formalities that must be observed if an asset sale constitutes a fundamental change. Conversely, the sale of *less* than all or substantially all of the company's assets is not a fundamental change, and therefore does not require shareholder approval. As such, these transactions are committed to the business judgment of the company's board of directors. *See* Delaware §141(a); *see also* MBCA §§12.01, 12.02, and 8.01.

In many cases, the threshold determination of whether the transaction presents the sale of *all* the company's assets will be easy to ascertain. But in many cases where *less* than all of the company's assets are to be disposed, a (typically more complex) determination must be made as to whether the transaction involves the sale of "substantially all" of the company's assets. As we will see later in this chapter when we analyze the leading Delaware cases in this area (*Katz* and *Gimbel*), this determination "does not lend itself to a strict mathematical standard to be applied in every case." *Gimbel*, 316 A.2d at 605.

This threshold determination is of vital importance because the corporate formalities that must be observed in order to validly consummate the sale of "all or substantially all" of a company's assets differs from the formalities that must be observed if a company sells *less than substantially all* of its assets. At common law, the rule was that neither the directors nor the stockholders of a prosperous going concern could sell all or substantially all of the corporation's property if a *single* stockholder objected. *See* Edward P. Welch, et al., FOLK ON THE DELAWARE GENERAL CORPORATION LAW at §271.01 (Fundamentals 2020 ed.). Today, all state corporation statutes (including Delaware §271) recognize that a corporation may sell all or substantially all of the company's assets with the approval of *less* than all of the shareholders, usually based on the vote of an absolute majority of shares entitled to vote. Some states, though, may impose some form of supermajority vote, or alternatively, a supermajority vote may be imposed by private ordering, which is usually done by way of a provision in the company's articles of incorporation.

At common law, there was some confusion as to whether a company could sell all or substantially all of its assets for something other than cash, such as stock in Bidder, the purchaser. Today, Delaware §271, like the statutes of most states, resolves this issue by authorizing the sale of Target's assets in exchange for Bidder's shares or other securities. (*See Diagram 5 — Appendix A.*) By varying the nature of the acquisition consideration, the substantive result of an acquisition structured as a sale of assets can bear a striking resemblance to a merger transaction. The problems to be analyzed in this section illustrate this point.

Since Target Co. is selling its assets, it will be a party to the asset purchase agreement, along with the acquiring corporation, Bidder Co. As such, Delaware §271 requires authorization of the transaction by the board of directors of the selling corporation, which most often will occur at a meeting of Target's board, although it is possible for the board to approve the sale without a meeting if all directors consent in writing. *See* Delaware §141(f) and MBCA §8.21 (regarding the requirements for board action by written consent). The terms of "Delaware §271(a) specifically require the Board of Directors to make a judgment that the terms of an asset sale 'are expedient and for the best interests of the corporation.'" FOLK, *supra*, DELAWARE CORPORATE LAW at §271.04[C].

As to shareholder approval, Delaware §271 specifically requires that the shareholders receive at least 20 days' notice of the meeting to vote on the company's proposed sale of assets. As to the shareholder voting standard, Delaware §271(a) requires approval by a vote of a majority of the outstanding shares entitled to vote, unless the written consent procedures of Delaware §228 are used to dispense with the need for a shareholder meeting.

After the dust settles on a sale of all or substantially all of Target Co.'s assets, the entity is left intact, but the company is very different than before the transaction. Now, Target holds all of the consideration received from the sale of its assets (typically, cash or Bidder's stock), in addition to whatever liabilities were not transferred to the Bidder as part of the sale of Target's assets. At this point, Target has several options. First, it may decide to continue in existence as a holding company, holding the consideration received from Bidder on behalf of Target's shareholders. Alternatively, Target may distribute the consideration received from Bidder to its shareholders, usually in the form of an extraordinary dividend, leaving Target to continue in existence as a bare shell of a company. As a third option, Target may distribute the consideration received from Bidder and dissolve the company (a proceeding known as "voluntary dissolution").

With respect to the first two alternatives, Delaware case law generally assumes that the shareholders, by approving the transaction, have (implicitly) consented to one of these alternatives. Indeed, as described in greater detail in Chapter 4, the federal proxy rules require full and adequate disclosure of all material facts so that Target's shareholders, at least where Target is publicly traded, may make an informed decision as to whether to approve the proposed sale of assets transaction. By extension, Delaware case law has held that Target's proxy statement must adequately inform the shareholders as to matters that are relevant to the decision of whether to approve the proposed sale of assets, including the consequences of the plan of sale and any plan for liquidation of Target Co. following the sale.

Very often, the company's future plans for distribution of the consideration received from Bidder will influence Target shareholders in their decision whether to approve the proposed sale of Target's assets. Thus, complete liquidation of Target is *not* the inevitable legal result of Target's decision to sell all of its assets. Most often, though, Target's proposed sale of all of its assets will contemplate the second step of the voluntary dissolution of Target and the orderly winding up of its business affairs.

For reasons discussed at length in Chapter 3, regarding the rules of successor liability, the sale of assets transaction has a very different impact on the creditors of Target. Since Target Co. remains intact following the sale of all of its assets, the general rule is that Target creditors should bring their claims to Target, which will generally be paid out of the proceeds that Target received from Bidder on the sale of all of its assets. Accordingly, the general rule is that Bidder Co. has no direct liability to the creditors of Target, *unless* the Bidder (expressly or impliedly) assumed such an obligation as part of its agreement to purchase Target's assets. As we will see in Chapter 3, this rule of successor liability creates the potential for opportunistic behavior on the part of Target and/or Bidder, which may work to the (financial) detriment of Target's creditors. In the materials in Chapter 3, we will examine in more detail the protections developed by the courts and state legislatures to protect Target's creditors—both contract (voluntary) creditors and tort (involuntary) creditors—from overreaching on the part of Bidder and/or Target, including the judicially developed doctrine known as *de facto mergers.*

Recent amendments to MBCA Chapter 13 reflect that the typical sale of assets involves a two-step transaction, unlike the direct merger. As was just noted, however, the dissolution of Target Co. following the sale of all (or substantially all) of its assets is not the inevitable result. After the sale of its assets, Target remains in place, holding whatever liabilities were not assumed by Bidder, along with the proceeds from the sale of its assets. As we will explore in more detail in Chapter 3, this leaves Target's owners and managers with several choices, one of which is to dissolve Target. Until quite recently, the MBCA extended appraisal rights to any disposition of assets pursuant to §12.02 that required a shareholder vote. However, MBCA §13.02(a)(3) has been revised to eliminate the shareholder's right to an appraisal if:

(i)   under the terms of the corporate action approved by the shareholders there is to be distributed to shareholders in cash its net assets, in excess of a reasonable amount reserved to meet claims of the type described in §14.06 and 14.07, (A) within one year after the shareholders' approval of the action and (B) in accordance with their respective interests determined at the time of distribution [i.e., in accordance with the stated liquidation rights of the shares, if any]; *and*

(ii)   the disposition of assets is not an interested transaction.*

So, by way of summary, this new exception to the availability of appraisal rights in connection with the sale of assets pursuant to MBCA §12.02 is limited to those situations where liquidation of Target *must* take place within one year of the shareholder vote *and* Target's shareholders are to receive *cash* in accordance with their respective interests (i.e., in accordance with their liquidation preferences as set forth in the company's articles of incorporation), so long as the transaction does *not* present a conflict of interest as defined in MBCA §13.01. The premise for this recent amendment to the MBCA is that in the situation where Target "shareholders are being treated on a proportionate basis in accordance with the corporation's governing documents [i.e., the company's articles of incorporation] in an arms' length transaction (akin to a distribution in dissolution), there is no need for the added protection of appraisal rights." *Changes in the MBCA, supra*, 65 Bus. Law. at 1144.

NOTES

1. Non-Acquisitive Restructurings of a Single Firm: Reorganizations and Recapitalizations. Companies will often decide to change the focus of their business operations, such as where conglomerates decide to strip down and concentrate their business operations within a single industry. In the process, the conglomerate will usually sell off (divest itself of) unwanted assets and business operations. These transactions do not involve combining two previously independent businesses into a single firm. Rather, these divestitures result in separating a single firm into different, freestanding business entities.

---

*[By the author: "Interested transaction" is a defined term in MBCA §13.01(5.1) that essentially refers to a transaction presenting one of two types of conflict of interests.]

Divestitures are not the focus of this class since this course concentrates on business combinations. However, we will discuss a few cases that involve restructurings of a single company, often as an alternative to a business combination. Therefore, it will be useful to understand the mechanics and terminology of these deals. This note briefly summarizes the basic mechanics of divestitures and defines relevant terms customarily used in these deals. However, a more thorough analysis of the rules that regulate these recapitalization transactions is left to other law school courses.

In cases where company management has decided, as a business matter, to eliminate certain operations, management may dispose of those assets (which may even consist of entire divisions or operating subsidiaries) in one of several different ways.

First, the company may decide to sell off certain assets. Where the company disposes of unwanted assets that constitute *less* than substantially *all* of its assets, then the disposition does not involve a fundamental change. As such, the sale of these assets is a matter left to the business judgment of the company's board of directors. In this case, the company will find a buyer (often a leveraged buyout firm of the type described in the note material below) who will then enter into a contract for the purchase and sale of the company's unwanted assets. In the case of a management buyout (MBO), it will often be the managers of a particular division or subsidiary (i.e., the managers who are responsible for the assets to be sold off) who will take the initiative to find a buyout firm that will finance the purchase of the company's unwanted assets.

2. Spin-offs.   Alternatively, the company may dispose of assets that are held in a subsidiary by way of a transaction that is known on Wall Street as a *spin-off*. In the case of a spin-off, the assets and business operations to be disposed will be assembled in a subsidiary corporation; the shares of the subsidiary are then distributed out as a non-cash dividend to the shareholders of the parent company. When the dust settles, the shareholders of the parent company will own the subsidiary while still retaining ownership of their shares in the parent company. Henceforth, the former subsidiary will operate as a freestanding business with no continuing equity ownership or control on the part of the parent company, which likewise continues in place as a separate business entity. This type of reorganization of a single firm's business operations is not the focus of this casebook, although restructurings of this type are very common.

Another type of reorganization, which was quite common in the depressed capital markets of the early 2000s and again in the wake of the Great Recession of 2008-2009, is often referred to as *distressed M&A*. Here, a financially troubled company decides to sell off certain assets or business operations, usually in order to raise cash (and remain financially viable). This type of transaction is often undertaken as a last-ditch effort to remain solvent and avoid filing for bankruptcy. Reorganizations undertaken as part of bankruptcy court proceedings is a specialized area of M&A activity, which is typically covered in most law schools as part of a course on bankruptcy law, and as such, lie outside the scope of M&A law.

3. Recapitalization.   One final type of single-firm restructuring is worth noting. In the case of a *recapitalization*, the company decides to change its capital structure by amending its articles of incorporation. This is considered to be a fundamental change that cannot be implemented unilaterally by board action alone. Rather, any amendment of the company's articles — including an amendment to change the rights, preferences, or privileges of outstanding shares, or alternatively, to increase the number of authorized shares or to create a new class of authorized shares — will require board approval, along with approval by the requisite number of shares entitled to vote. *See, e.g.,* Delaware §242; MCBA §10.03.

Today, most states require that an articles amendment receive approval by an absolute majority of outstanding shares of each class entitled to vote. In addition, many states provide for a right to class voting even if the shares are not otherwise entitled to vote. Under the terms of modern corporation statutes, this right to a class vote will most often be granted in situations where the proposed articles amendment would effect a change in the rights, preferences, and privileges of a class of outstanding shares that otherwise carry no voting rights. *See, e.g.,* Calif. §903. The public policy premise underlying this right to a class vote is that the articles represent a contract between the issuer (the company) and the investor (the shareholder), which cannot be unilaterally amended by the company and thus can be amended only if the company obtains the consent of the requisite number of the holders of those nonvoting shares affected by the terms of the proposed articles amendment.

4. Leveraging the Company's Balance Sheet.   As a final observation with respect to single firm restructurings, many recapitalizations are effected without any vote of the company's shareholders. For example, the company's board of directors may decide to leverage the company's balance sheet by borrowing a large amount of money, often granting a security interest in the company's assets to the lender. So long as there is no limitation on the company's issuance of debt (usually effected by way of a provision in the articles of incorporation), the company's board of directors may implement this decision by issuing, for example, new subordinated debentures (an unsecured form of corporate indebtedness) and then using the proceeds of this debt offering to distribute an extraordinary dividend in cash to the company's shareholders. When the dust settles, the shareholders hold the cash dividend, along with exactly the same shares they had *before* the transaction was completed. In the process, the company becomes highly leveraged, with a much higher debt–equity ratio. Although the shareholders remain as equity owners of the company, the nature of their investment is vastly different than before this type of recapitalization transaction was undertaken. In fact, their shares are usually worth much less than before the transaction. In spite of this typical dilution in value, no shareholder vote, generally speaking, is required to effect this type of *leveraged recapitalization.*

5. Blank Check Preferred Stock.   The widespread use today of *blank check preferred stock* offers yet another example of a recapitalization (in the sense of a substantial change in the company's financial structure) that does *not* require shareholder approval. Where blank check preferred shares are authorized, the rights, preferences, and privileges of these shares are not defined in the company's articles of incorporation or in any amendment approved by the shareholders. Rather, the rights, preferences, and privileges will be established later by the company's board of directors, usually at the time of issuance. As we will see in Chapter 7, blank check preferred stock forms the basis for the distribution of the *poison pill*, a strategy commonly used to block hostile takeovers.

6. An Introduction to Leveraged Buyouts.   Any acquisition can be structured as a *leveraged buyout* (LBO), although quite often, the LBO transaction will take the form of an asset purchase. The essential feature of an LBO is the use of borrowed funds to finance Bidder's acquisition of Target. In a typical scenario, Bidder will be an LBO firm, such as the well-known firm of Kohlberg Kravis & Roberts (KKR). When LBOs first became fashionable in the 1980s, this type of financial buyer would usually team up with Target managers to purchase assets, or even entire divisions, typically from a large conglomerate seeking to divest itself of underperforming businesses. Financial buyers such as KKR would finance the acquisition of these assets using a sliver of equity provided by the investment of its own funds coupled with substantial amounts of borrowed funds that would have to be repaid. This debt financing was usually raised by soliciting money from other investors (often institutional investors) who were looking to be repaid (with interest) out of the income stream generated from the purchased assets.

The leveraged acquisition is designed to allow the financial buyer to purchase the *greatest* amount of income-producing assets with the *least* amount of equity investment on the part of the financial buyer. By borrowing against the assets of Target Co., the typical LBO firm can invest a small amount of its own money (say, 10 percent to 20 percent of the purchase price) and borrow the balance of the purchase price, earning a substantial return on its invested equity after paying the carrying cost of the debt. In the typical case, the borrowed funds would be repaid out of the income stream generated by the assets purchased from Target, which hopefully would grow using the business strategies to be implemented by the new management team installed by the LBO firm. The financial buyer would typically plan to improve the financial performance by cutting costs and introducing new measures to streamline and improve business operations. In addition, the LBO firm typically gives the new management team stock options (or other equity participation) in order to tightly align management's financial interests with those of the new stockholders.

Given the heavy debt load usually taken on by the LBO firm in order to finance the acquisition, there will usually be intense pressure on the (sometimes newly installed) team of managers to streamline the business and increase its profitability in order to generate the revenue needed to finance the cost of the borrowed funds. Many financial buyers believe that the heavy debt burden carried on the company's balance sheet following an LBO exerts a disciplining influence on the managers, who must perform optimally in order to generate the income stream needed to provide the resources to pay the interest and principal on the borrowed capital. Of course, carrying this heavy debt load on its balance sheet also leads to an increased risk of default if the company does not generate the revenue stream required to pay the carrying cost of this debt. This heavy debt load also may serve to impair the company's ability to finance new business projects necessary to grow the company's business. In the jargon of Wall Street, this situation is often referred to as *leveraging the company's balance sheet.*

If things go as planned, the leveraged acquisition will usually be followed by a period of debt reduction, thereby reducing (or even eliminating) the borrowed capital from the company's balance sheet. As a direct result of this type of *leveraging*, the increase in value of the business remaining after paying off the debt would belong to the LBO firm. The ultimate goal of many financial buyers is to sell the cleaned-up company to another buyer within a few years for a substantial gain, or alternatively, to take the company public. In the most successful LBOs, the financial buyer could earn a substantial return on the sliver of equity that it had originally invested.

One of the most well known (indeed almost legendary) LBO deals involved Gibson Greeting Cards. In 1981, Wesray, an investment partnership established by William Simon, former secretary of the treasury in the Ford administration, purchased Gibson Greetings from RCA, a large, well-known conglomerate that was shedding its assets in order to slim down and focus on its core business operations. At that time, RCA, an extremely motivated seller as it was anxious to eliminate underperforming assets, sold Gibson Greetings to Wesray for $80 million. Debt financing provided $79 million of the purchase price, with Wesray investing only $1 million of its own funds. This LBO also involved the equity participation of the existing managers of Gibson Greetings, who held a 20 percent interest in the company's common stock and stayed on to run the company. (This type of deal would come to be known on Wall Street as an MBO.) In 1983, less than two years later,

> Wesray took Gibson Greetings public by selling 30% of the company's [stock] for just over $96 million. The IPO valued the whole company at $330 million. Wesray had earned a $250 million pretax paper profit on its $1 million equity investment. [What's more,] Bill Simon looked like a genius.

Bruce Wasserstein, BIG DEAL, 104-105 (2000). This same experienced M&A advisor went on to comment:

> Some observers wrote off Wesray's success as a fluke, a case of sophisticated investors who outwitted an unusually dense conglomerate. Others attributed Wesray's phenomenal profit to opportune timing. A strong economy, a booming stock market—a confluence of unpredictable events—allowed the partners to cash out quickly.
>
> However, other LBO's proved equally remarkable, and the vitality of this transaction structure soon became widely recognized.

Id.

7. The Era of the "Mega-Buyout."   For a remarkably long period of almost 20 years, there had been no bigger LBO deal than KKR's purchase in 1989 of RJR Nabisco, Inc., the tobacco and food conglomerate, for the eye-popping price of $25.1 billion. *See, e.g.,* https://www.nytimes.com/1988/12/02/business/history-of-the-rjr-nabisco-takeover.html; and https://financescp.net/2019/01/22/all-time-classic-kkrs-first-leveraged-buyout-battle-25bn-the-fall-of-rjr-nabisco-yes-barbarians-are-really-at-the-gate/. This LBO deal—valued in today's dollars at $41.9 billion—was characterized by a "legendary, ego-driven bidding war" that ultimately came to be viewed as representing everything that was "grand and grotesque" about the Wall Street money machine.* But, as the M&A market started to heat up in calendar year 2006, many experienced deal-makers began to speculate that the RJR record might finally be broken. *See* Dennis K. Berman and Henry Sender, *Big Deal: Records Were Made to Be Broken*, WALL STREET JOURNAL, Jan. 9, 2006, at C1. Indeed, the first half of calendar year 2007 proved to be a watershed year for private equity firms as the M&A market witnessed an explosive growth of activity by private equity buyers. The extraordinary pace of activity in the first half of 2007 was fueled in substantial part by the extraordinary liquidity of the credit markets, leading to some of the largest LBO deals on record. For starters, Blackstone Group, led by its CEO, Steven Schwarzman, signed up their LBO of Equity Office Properties Trust for the staggering amount of $39 billion—ranking it as the largest LBO in history—only to be "knocked off its perch" shortly thereafter by yet another private equity firm. *See* Gregg Wirth, *From the Editor: The Biggest LBO of All Time! (This Month's Contender)*, THE M&A LAWYER 2 (Mar. 2007). "The *NEW* largest LBO in history—at least as of this writing—is the proposed $40 billion purchase of TXU," the large Texas utility conglomerate. *Id.* This "mega-deal" is being sponsored by two well-known private equity firms, Texas Pacific Group and KKR. This "mega-deal" for TXU puts LBO master Henry Kravis and his firm back on top of the "private equity mountain—although the competition to remain there is [currently] fierce." *Id.* In fact, the reported list of the top ten largest LBO deals in history looks more like a list of the top deals announced in 2006-2007, a period of watershed activity in the M&A market. Indeed, the *only* deal that appears on this top ten list that was *not* announced since 2005 is the legendary buyout of RJR Nabisco by the iconic KKR firm. *Id.*

The feverish pace of LBO activity that led to the relatively brief "era of the mega-buyout" in the first half of 2007 came to an abrupt halt as the credit markets deteriorated. As the credit markets increasingly seized up over the summer months, many of those mega-buyouts collapsed and deal making in the M&A market generally came to a screeching halt in the last half of 2007 as the economy entered the Great Recession.

PROBLEM SET NO. 3—ASSET ACQUISITIONS UNDER DELAWARE LAW AND THE MBCA

1. Sale of Assets for Cash (See Diagram 4—Appendix A). Target Co. is a bicycle store founded 20 years ago by Lance, who continues to own one-third of the outstanding common stock. The remaining shares are evenly divided between his two grown sons, Abe and Biff. As the company's president, Lance has decided to sell all of Target's assets and transfer certain of the company's liabilities to Bidder Co., another closely held firm, in exchange for cash. Immediately after the transfer, Target will be dissolved and its business affairs liquidated, with

---

*[By the author: All you movie buffs will recall that this is the deal made famous in the movie *Barbarians at the Gate.*]

Target transferring to its shareholders any cash remaining after paying off its creditors.

   a. What action is required to be taken by the boards of Bidder and Target:

     (1) Under Delaware law?
     (2) Under the MBCA?

   b. Do the shareholders of Bidder and Target have the right to vote on the transaction:

     (1) Under Delaware law?
     (2) Under the MBCA?

   c. Do the shareholders of Bidder or Target have the right to dissent:

     (1) Under Delaware law?
     (2) Under the MBCA?

2. Assume that Chef America, Inc., a well-known, privately-held business that made the best-selling frozen sandwiches sold under the label "Hot Pockets," has decided to sell all of its assets to Nestlé, Inc., a multi-national conglomerate whose stock is traded on the NYSE, in exchange for $2 billion in cash. Immediately following this sale, the Merage brothers, Paul and David, as equal owners of all of the outstanding voting common stock of Chef America, plan to dissolve the company and distribute out to themselves (as the sole shareholders) any cash remaining after paying off the company's creditors.

   a. What action is required to be taken by the boards of Chef America and Nestlé:

     (1) Under Delaware law?
     (2) Under the MBCA?

   b. Do the shareholders of Chef America and/or Nestlé have the right to vote on the transaction:

     (1) Under Delaware law?
     (2) Under the rules of the NYSE?
     (3) Under the MBCA?

   c. Do the shareholders of Chef America and/or Nestlé have the right to dissent:

     (1) Under Delaware law?
     (2) Under the MBCA?

3. Sale of Assets in Exchange for 30 Percent of Bidder's Stock (See Diagram 5—Appendix A). Assume that Chef America has agreed to sell all of its assets and transfer certain of its liabilities to Nestlé in exchange for shares of Nestlé common stock comprising 30 percent of the voting power of Nestlé's outstanding stock immediately before the proposed asset purchase. Immediately after the transfer of its assets, Chef America plans to dissolve and liquidate its business affairs, transferring the Nestlé shares to the company's shareholders in exchange for all of Chef America's outstanding stock, which will then be canceled. Assume that Nestlé, Inc., has sufficient authorized and unissued shares to complete the transaction.

    a. What action is required to be taken by the boards of Nestlé and Chef America:

      (1) Under Delaware law?
      (2) Under the MBCA?

    b. Do the shareholders of either Nestlé or Chef America have the right to vote on the transaction:

      (1) Under Delaware law?
      (2) Under the MBCA?
      (3) Under the rules of the NYSE?

    c. Do the shareholders of either Nestlé or Chef America have the right to dissent:

      (1) Under Delaware law?
      (2) Under the MBCA?

    4. Sale of Assets in Exchange for 15 Percent of Bidder's Stock (See Diagram 5—Appendix A).   Assume that the facts are the same as set out in Problem 3, except that Nestlé will complete its acquisition of Chef America by issuing Nestlé shares in an amount equal to 15 percent of the voting power of Nestlé's outstanding common stock immediately before the asset purchase is completed.

    a. What action is required to be taken by the boards of Nestlé and Chef America:

      (1) Under Delaware law?
      (2) Under the MBCA?

    b. Do the shareholders of either Nestlé or Chef America have the right to vote on the transaction:

      (1) Under Delaware law?
      (2) Under the rules of the NYSE?
      (3) Under the MBCA?

    c. Do the shareholders of either Nestlé or Chef America have the right to dissent:

      (1) Under Delaware law?
      (2) Under the MBCA?

2.   What Qualifies as "Sale (or Transfer) of Substantially All the Assets"?

In the problems we just finished analyzing, we assumed that Target was selling *all* of its assets, so it was easy for the transaction planner to conclude that this transaction involved a fundamental change requiring shareholder approval under state corporation law. However, in cases where the company proposes to sell *less* than all of its assets, the lawyer planning the transaction must analyze the proposed sale in order to determine if the proposed disposition of Target's assets falls under Delaware §271. The reason that this is an important threshold question is that if the sale is challenged by the shareholders and the court later determines that the transaction involved a sale of "substantially" all of Target's assets but did not receive shareholder approval, then the court may enjoin the transaction unless and until the requisite shareholder approval is obtained.

The following two decisions are generally viewed as the leading cases under Delaware law regarding the appropriate standard for deciding whether a particular disposition of corporate assets involves the sale of "substantially all" of the company's assets and thus cannot be effected unilaterally by the company's board of directors. The last case in this section, *Hollinger, Inc. v. Hollinger International, Inc.*, is a more recent (and noteworthy) pronouncement by the Delaware Chancery Court regarding this important threshold determination.

Gimbel v. The Signal Companies, Inc.
316 A.2d 599 (Del. Ch. 1974)

QUILLEN, Chancellor:

This action was commenced on December 24, 1973 by plaintiff, a stockholder of the Signal Companies, Inc. ("Signal"). The complaint seeks, among other things, injunctive relief to prevent the consummation of the pending sale by Signal to Burmah Oil Incorporated ("Burmah") of all of the outstanding capital stock of Signal Oil and Gas Company ("Signal Oil"), a wholly-owned subsidiary of Signal. The effective sale price exceeds 480 million dollars. The sale was approved at a special meeting of the Board of Directors of Signal held on December 21, 1973.

The agreement provides that the transaction will be consummated on January 15, 1974 or upon the obtaining of the necessary governmental consents, whichever occurs later, but, in no event, after February 15, 1974 unless mutually agreed. The consents evidently have been obtained. On Monday, December 24, 1973, on the occasion of the plaintiff's application for a temporary restraining order, counsel for Signal and Signal Oil reported to this Court that the parties would not consummate this transaction prior to this Court's decision on the plaintiff's application for a preliminary injunction or January 15, 1974, whichever should occur first.

In light of that representation, no temporary restraining order was entered and the matter was set down for a hearing on plaintiff's application for a preliminary injunction. Affidavits and depositions were submitted. The matter was briefed and a hearing was held on January 4, 1974. By agreement, additional affidavits were filed on January 7th and January 9th. This is the Court's decision on plaintiff's application for a preliminary injunction to prevent the sale of Signal Oil to Burmah pending trial on the merits of plaintiff's contentions. . . .

. . . I regret that time has not permitted needed editing and that this opinion is therefore longer than desirable. In applying the law to the transaction in question, the Court believes it is first desirable to review the standards for a preliminary injunction.

An application for a preliminary injunction "is addressed to the sound discretion of the court. . . ."

In exercising its discretion, the Court must ask itself two familiar questions, which have long constituted the backdrop for evaluating the merits of any plaintiff's plea for a preliminary injunction.

Stated briefly, the first question is: "Has the plaintiff satisfied the Court that there is a reasonable probability of his ultimate success on final hearing?" . . .

The second question can be stated as follows: "Has the plaintiff satisfied the Court that he will suffer irreparable injury if the Court fails to issue the requested preliminary injunction?"

Moreover, this second question of irreparable injury to the plaintiff should injunctive relief be denied has a corollary which requires the Court to consider potential hardship to the defendant. . . .

. . . In order for the plaintiff here to "earn" his preliminary injunction against the sale of Signal Oil to Burmah, the Court must be satisfied, on the present record, that the plaintiff has a reasonable probability of succeeding on the merits of his claim. Further, the Court must also be satisfied that a preliminary injunction is necessary to protect the plaintiff from irreparable injury and that the plaintiff's need for such protection outweighs any harm that the Court can reasonably expect to befall the defendants if the injunction were granted.

Partly because of the enormous amount of money involved in this case, it is easy to discuss the irreparable injury aspect. From the plaintiff's point of view, the imminent threat of the closing of the sale does present a situation where it may be impossible to "unscramble the eggs." While the remedy of rescission is available [citation omitted], it is not difficult to imagine the various obstacles to such a remedy including, tax consequences, accounting practices, business reorganizations, management decisions concerning capital investments, dividends, etc. and a host of other problems which as a practical matter will make rescission very difficult indeed. Moreover, when the plaintiff claims with expert support, a potential damage in the neighborhood of $300,000,000, it is doubtful that any damage claim against the directors can reasonably be a meaningful alternative. In short, if the plaintiff can sustain his legal position, it seems to me that he has established he will suffer irreparable harm if the consummation of the sale is not enjoined.

On the other hand, the harm to Signal of entering an injunction is also massive. Under the contract, if the transaction is delayed by litigation, Burmah has a right to withdraw and the Court has no legal power to prevent such withdrawal.[2] The loss of Signal's legal right to enforce the contract is itself irreparable harm. . . .

---

2. The purchaser has the option not to consummate the transaction if the following condition (paragraph 8.07 of the agreement) has not been met.

"8.07 No suit or action, investigation, inquiry, or request for information by an administrative agency, governmental body of private party, and no legal or administrative proceeding shall have been instituted or threatened which questions or reasonably appears to portend subsequent questioning of the validity or legality of this Agreement or the transactions provided for herein."

In summary on the question of irreparable harm, it appears to me that there is irreparable harm to the losing side on this preliminary injunction application in the event the loser should ultimately prevail on the merits. Thus, in this case, the Court feels that the emphasis in analysis on this application for a preliminary injunction should focus on whether the plaintiff has a reasonable probability of success in this lawsuit. . . .

Turning specifically to the pleadings in this case, the complaint . . . alleges a class action on behalf of all Signal stockholders who, according to the complaint, were entitled to vote upon the proposed sale. . . .

Thus, in my judgment, the factual and legal issues are basically reduced to [the question:] does the sale require authorization by a majority of the outstanding stock of Signal pursuant to 8 Del. C. §271(a)? . . .

I turn . . . to the question of 8 Del. C. §271(a) which requires majority stockholder approval for the sale of "all or substantially all" of the assets of a Delaware corporation. A sale of less than all or substantially all assets is not covered by negative implication from the statute. Folk, The Delaware General Corporation Law, Section 271, p. 400, ftnt. 3; 8 Del. C. §141(a).

It is important to note in the first instance that the statute does not speak of a requirement of shareholder approval simply because an independent, important branch of a corporate business is being sold. The plaintiff cites several non-Delaware cases for the proposition that shareholder approval of such a sale is required. But that is not the language of our statute. Similarly, it is not our law that shareholder approval is required upon every "major" restructuring of the corporation. Again, it is not necessary to go beyond the statute. The statute requires shareholder approval upon the sale of "all or substantially all" of the corporation's assets. That is the sole test to be applied. While it is true that test does not lend itself to a strict mathematical standard to be applied in every case, the qualitative factor can be defined to some degree notwithstanding the limited Delaware authority. But the definition must begin with and ultimately necessarily relate to our statutory language. . . . Professor Folk suggests . . . that "the statute would be inapplicable if the assets sale is 'one made in furtherance of express corporate objects in the ordinary and regular course of the business' ". *Folk, supra,* Section 271, p. 401. . . .

But any "ordinary and regular course of the business" test in this context obviously is not intended to limit the directors to customary daily business activities. Indeed, a question concerning the statute would not arise unless the transaction was somewhat out of the ordinary. While it is true that a transaction in the ordinary course of business does not require shareholder approval, the converse is not true. Every transaction out of normal routine does not necessarily require shareholder approval. The unusual nature of the transaction must strike at the heart of the corporate existence and purpose. . . . It is in this sense that the "unusual transaction" judgment is to be made and the statute's applicability determined. If the sale is of assets quantitatively vital to the operation of the corporation and is out of the ordinary and substantially affects the existence and purpose of the corporation, then it is beyond the power of the board of directors. With these guidelines, I turn to Signal and the transaction in this case.

Signal or its predecessor was incorporated in the oil business in 1922. But, beginning in 1952, Signal diversified its interests. In 1952, Signal acquired a substantial stock interest in American President lines. From 1957 to 1962 Signal was the sole owner of Laura Scudders, a nationwide snack food business. In 1964, Signal acquired Garrett Corporation which is engaged in the aircraft, aerospace, and uranium enrichment business. In 1967, Signal acquired Mack Trucks, Inc., which is engaged in the manufacture and sale of trucks and related equipment. Also in 1968, the oil and gas business was transferred to a separate division and later in 1970 to the Signal Oil subsidiary. Since 1967, Signal has made acquisition of or formed substantial companies none of which are involved or related with the oil and gas industry. As indicated previously, the oil and gas production development of Signal's business is now carried on by Signal Oil, the sale of the stock of which is an issue in this lawsuit.

According to figures published in Signal's last annual report (1972) and the latest quarterly report (September 30, 1973) and certain other internal financial information, the following tables can be constructed:

SIGNAL'S REVENUES (in millions)

	9 Mons. Ended September 30, 1973	December 31, 1972	1971
Truck Manufacturing	$655.9	$712.7	$552.5
Aerospace and Industrial	407.1	478.2	448.0
Oil and Gas	185.8	267.2	314.1
Other	16.4	14.4	14.0

SIGNAL'S PRE-TAX EARNINGS (in millions)

	9 Mons. Ended September 30, 1973	December 31, 1972	1971
Truck Manufacturing	$55.8	$65.5	$36.4
Aerospace and Industrial	20.7	21.5	19.5
Oil and Gas	10.1	12.8	9.9

SIGNAL'S ASSETS (in millions)

	9 Mons. Ended September 30, 1973	December 31, 1972	1971
Truck Manufacturing	$581.4	$506.5	$450.4
Aerospace and Industrial	365.2	351.1	331.5
Oil and Gas	376.2	368.3	369.9
Other	113.1	102.0	121.6

SIGNAL'S NET WORTH (in millions)

	9 Mons. Ended September 30, 1973	December 31, 1972	1971
Truck Manufacturing	$295.0	$269.7	$234.6
Aerospace and Industrial	163.5	152.2	139.6
Oil and Gas	280.5	273.2	254.4
Other	(55.4)	(42.1)	(2.0)

Based on the company's figures, Signal Oil represents only about 26% of the total assets of Signal. While Signal Oil represents 41% of Signal's total net worth, it produces only about 15% of Signal's revenues and earnings. Moreover, the additional tables shown in Signal's brief from the Chitiea affidavit are also interesting in demonstrating the low rate of return which has been realized recently from the oil and gas operations.

PRE-TAX DOLLAR RETURN ON VALUE OF ASSETS

	9 Mons. Ended September 30, 1973	December 31, 1972	1971
Truck Manufacturing	12.8%	12.9%	8.1%
Aerospace and Industrial	7.5%	6.1%	5.9%
Oil and Gas	3.6%	3.5%	2.7%

PRE-TAX DOLLAR RETURN ON NET WORTH

	9 Mons. Ended September 30, 1973	December 31, 1972	1971
Truck Manufacturing	25.1%	24.2%	15.5%
Aerospace and Industrial	16.8%	14.1%	14.0%
Oil and Gas	4.8%	4.7%	3.9%

While it is true, based on the experience of the Signal-Burmah transaction and the record in this lawsuit, that Signal Oil is more valuable than shown by the company's books, even if, as plaintiff suggests in his brief, the $761,000,000 value attached to Signal Oil's properties by the plaintiff's expert Paul V. Keyser, Jr., were substituted as the asset figure, the oil and gas properties would still constitute less than half the value of Signal's total assets. Thus, from a straight quantitative approach, I agree with Signal's position that the sale to Burmah does not constitute a sale of "all or substantially all" of Signal's assets.

In addition, if the character of the transaction is examined, the plaintiff's position is also weak. While it is true that Signal's original purpose was oil and gas and while oil and gas is still listed first in the certificate of incorporation, the simple fact is that Signal is now a conglomerate engaged in the aircraft and aerospace business, the manufacture and sale of trucks and related equipment, and other businesses besides oil and gas. The very nature of its business, as it now in fact exists, contemplates the acquisition and disposal of independent branches of its corporate business. Indeed, given the operations since 1952, it can be said that such acquisitions and dispositions have become part of the ordinary course of business. The facts that the oil and gas business was historically first and that authorization for such operations are listed first in the certificate do not prohibit disposal of such interest. As Director Harold M. Williams testified, business history is not "compelling" and "many companies go down the drain because they try to be historic."

It is perhaps true, as plaintiff has argued, that the advent of multi-business corporations has in one sense emasculated §271 since one business may be sold without shareholder approval when other substantial businesses are retained. But it is one thing for a corporation to evolve over a period of years into a multibusiness corporation, the operations of which include the purchase and sale of whole businesses, and another for a single business corporation by a one transaction revolution to sell the entire means of operating its business in exchange for money or a separate business. In the former situation, the processes of corporate democracy customarily have had the opportunity to restrain or otherwise control over a period of years. Thus, there is a chance for some shareholder participation. The Signal development illustrates the difference. For example, when Signal, itself formerly called Signal Oil and Gas Company, changed its name in 1968, it was for the announced "need for a new name appropriate to the broadly diversified activities of Signal's multi-industry complex."

The situation is also dramatically illustrated financially in this very case. Independent of the contract with Burmah, the affidavit of Signal's Board Chairman shows that over $200,000,000 of Signal Oil's refining and marketing assets have been sold in the past five years. This activity, prior to the sale at issue here, in itself constitutes a major restructuring of the corporate structure.

I conclude that measured quantitatively and qualitatively, the sale of the stock of Signal Oil by Signal to Burmah does not constitute a sale of "all or substantially all" of Signal's assets. . . . Accordingly, insofar as the complaint rests on 8 Del. C. §271(a), in my judgment, it has no reasonable probability of ultimate success.

QUESTIONS

1. What is the focus of the inquiry under the quantitative approach to determining whether a sale of assets falls under Delaware §271? What criteria are to be taken into account under the qualitative approach to analyzing the scope of transactions covered by Delaware §271? Is this analysis consistent with the statutory language of Delaware §271?

2. As a matter of modern corporate governance, does this bifurcated approach make sense from a public policy perspective?

3. Along these lines, consider the court's reference to "the processes of corporate democracy" at work in the evolution of Signal's business. In what way does the change in corporate name effected in 1968 reflect on the "process of corporate democracy"?

Katz v. Bregman
431 A.2d 1274 (Del. Ch. 1981)

. . . Marvel, Chancellor:

The complaint herein seeks the entry of an order preliminarily enjoining the proposed sale of the Canadian assets of Plant Industries, Inc. to Vulcan Industrial Packaging, Ltd., the plaintiff Hyman Katz allegedly being the owner of approximately 170,000 shares of common stock of the defendant Plant Industries, Inc., on whose behalf he has brought this action, suing not only for his own benefit as a stockholder but for the alleged benefit of all other record owners of common stock of the defendant Plant Industries, Inc. . . .

The complaint alleges that during the last six months of 1980 the board of directors of Plant Industries, Inc., under the guidance of the individual defendant Robert B. Bregman, the present chief executive officer of such corporation, embarked on a course of action which resulted in the disposal of several unprofitable subsidiaries of the corporate defendant located in the United States, namely Louisiana Foliage Inc., a horticultural business, Sunaid Food Products, Inc., a Florida packaging business, and Plant Industries (Texas), Inc., a business concerned with the manufacture of woven synthetic cloth. As a result of these sales Plant Industries, Inc. by the end of 1980 had disposed of a significant part of its unprofitable assets.

According to the complaint, Mr. Bregman thereupon proceeded on a course of action designed to dispose of a subsidiary of the corporate defendant known as Plant National (Quebec) Ltd., a business which constitutes Plant Industries, Inc.'s entire business operation in Canada and has allegedly constituted Plant's only income producing facility during the past four years. The professed principal purpose of such proposed sale is to raise needed cash and thus improve Plant's balance sheets. And while interest in purchasing the corporate defendant's Canadian plant was thereafter evinced not only by Vulcan Industrial Packaging, Ltd. but also by Universal Drum Reconditioning Co., which latter corporation originally undertook to match or approximate and recently to top Vulcan's bid, a formal contract was entered into between Plant Industries, Inc. and Vulcan on April 2, 1981 for the purchase and sale of Plant National (Quebec) despite the constantly increasing bids for the same property being made by Universal. . . .

In seeking injunctive relief, as prayed for, plaintiff relies on two principles, one that [is] found in 8 Del. C. §271 to the effect that a decision of a Delaware corporation to sell ". . . all or substantially all of its property and assets . . ." requires not only the approval of such corporation's board of directors but also a resolution adopted by a majority of the outstanding stockholders of the corporation entitled to vote thereon at a meeting duly called upon at least twenty days' notice.

Support for the other principle relied on by plaintiff for the relief sought, namely an alleged breach of fiduciary duty on the part of the board of directors of Plant Industries, Inc., is allegedly found in such board's studied refusal to consider a potentially higher bid for the assets in question which is being advanced by Universal.

Turning to the possible application of 8 Del. C. §271 to the proposed sale of substantial corporate assets of National to Vulcan, it is stated in Gimbel v. Signal Companies, Inc., Del. Ch., 316 A.2d 599 (1974) as follows:

> "If the sale is of assets quantitatively vital to the operation of the corporation and is out of the ordinary and substantially affects the existence and purpose of the corporation then it is beyond the power of the Board of Directors."

According to Plant's 1980 10K form, it appears that at the end of 1980, Plant's Canadian operations represented 51% of Plant's remaining assets. Defendants also concede that National represents 44.9% of Plant's sales' revenues and 52.4% of its pre-tax net operating income. Furthermore, such report by Plant discloses, in rough figures, that while National made a profit in 1978 of $2,900,000, the profit from the United States businesses in that year was only $770,000. In 1979, the Canadian business profit was $3,500,000 while the loss of the United States businesses was $344,000. Furthermore, in 1980, while the Canadian business profit was $5,300,000, the corporate loss in the United States was $4,500,000. And while these figures may be somewhat distorted by the allocation of overhead expenses and taxes, they are significant. In any event, defendants concede that ". . . National accounted for 34.9% of Plant's pre-tax income in 1976, 36.9% in 1977, 42% in 1978, 51% in 1979 and 52.4% in 1980." . . .

. . . I am first of all satisfied that historically the principal business of Plant Industries, Inc. has not been to buy and sell industrial facilities but rather to manufacture steel drums for use in bulk shipping as well as for the storage of petroleum products, chemicals, food, paint, adhesives and cleaning agents, a business which has been profitably performed by National of Quebec. Furthermore, the proposal, after the sale of National, to embark on the manufacture of plastic drums represents a radical departure from Plant's historically successful line of business, namely steel drums. I therefore conclude that the proposed sale of Plant's Canadian operations, which constitute over 51% of Plant's total assets and in which are generated approximately 45% of Plant's 1980 net sales, would, if consummated, constitute a sale of substantially all of Plant's assets. By way of contrast, the proposed sale of Signal Oil in Gimbel v. Signal Companies, Inc., supra, represented only about 26% of the total assets of Signal Companies, Inc. And while Signal Oil represented 41% of Signal Companies, Inc. total net worth, it generated only about 15% of Signal Companies, Inc. revenue and earnings.

I conclude that because the proposed sale of Plant National (Quebec) Ltd. would, if consummated, constitute a sale of substantially all of the assets of Plant Industries, Inc., as presently constituted, that an injunction should issue preventing the consummation of such sale at least until it has been approved by a majority of the outstanding stockholders of Plant Industries, Inc., entitled to vote at a meeting duly called on at least twenty days' notice.

In light of this conclusion it will be unnecessary to consider whether or not the sale here under attack, as proposed to be made, is for such an inadequate consideration, viewed in light of the competing bid of Universal, as to constitute a breach of trust on the part of the directors of Plant Industries, Inc.

QUESTIONS

1. What result would be reached on the facts of these two principal cases under the terms of the safe harbor approach of MBCA §12.02? Would the outcome be different than that reached by the Delaware courts?

2. As a public policy matter, what prompted the MBCA draftsmen to develop the safe harbor standard of MBCA §12.02? Whose interests are protected by the terms of MBCA §12.02—management or shareholders?

3. In what sense, if any, do these facts suggest a viable claim of breach of fiduciary duty on the part of the board of directors of Plant Industries, Inc.?

The following case provides a more recent application (and interpretation) of Delaware Section 271:

Hollinger Inc. v. Hollinger Intl., Inc
858 A.2d 342 (Del. Ch. 2004)
Appeal Denied, 871 A.2d 1128 (Del. 2004)

STRINE, Vice Chancellor. . . .

Hollinger Inc. ("Inc.") seeks a preliminary injunction preventing Hollinger International, Inc. ("International") [a newspaper holding company] from selling the *Telegraph* Group Ltd. to Press Holdings International, an entity controlled by Frederick and David Barclay (the "Barclays"). . . .

The key question addressed in this decision is whether Inc. [the controlling shareholder of International] and the other International stockholders must be provided with the opportunity to vote on the sale of the *Telegraph* Group because that sale involves "substantially all" the assets of International within the meaning of 8 *Del.* C. §271. The sale of the *Telegraph* followed a lengthy auction process whereby International and all of [its] operating assets were widely shopped to potential bidders. As a practical matter, Inc.'s vote would be the only one that matters because . . . [it] . . . controls 68% of the voting power [of International]. The controlling shareholder of Inc. is Lord Conrad Black. [However, Inc. cannot exercise control over International's management as a result of an agreement that was reached earlier in this case in order to settle charges of misconduct brought against Lord Conrad Black, the controlling shareholder of Inc.]

Inc. argues that a preliminary injunction should issue because it is clear that the sale of the *Telegraph* satisfies the quantitative and qualitative test used to determine whether an asset sale involves substantially all of a corporation's assets. . . .

[International, however,] contends that the sale of the *Telegraph* Group does not trigger §271.

In this opinion, I conclude that Inc.'s motion for a . . . preliminary injunction . . . should be denied as . . . its §271 [claim does not] . . . have a reasonable probability of success. . . .

I. FACTUAL BACKGROUND

Because of the subject matter of this motion, it is important to understand what kind of company Hollinger International was, what kind of company it now is, and what kind of company it will become if the *Telegraph* sale is consummated. . . . Put simply, International regularly acquired and disposed of sizable publishing assets.

During the years 1995 to 2000, for example, International engaged in the following large transactions:

- The 1996 and 1997 sales of the company's Australian newspapers for more than $400 million.
- The 1998 acquisition of the *Post-Tribune* in Gary, Indiana and the sale of approximately 80 community newspapers, for gross cash proceeds of approximately $310 million.
- The 1998 acquisitions of *The Financial Post* (now *The National Post*), the *Victoria Times Colonist,* and other Canadian newspapers for a total cost of more than $208 million.
- The 1999 sale of 78 community newspapers in the United States, for more than $500 million.
- The 2000 sale of other United States community newspapers for $215 million.
- The 2000 acquisition of newspapers in and around Chicago, for more than $230 million.
- The 2000 sale of the bulk of the company's Canadian newspaper holdings to CanWest for over $2 billion. . . .

Notably, International sold the bulk of the [company's Canadian newspaper holdings] to CanWest for $2 billion without a stockholder vote (the "CanWest sale"). And Inc.—then controlled by the same person who controls it now . . .—never demanded one. . . .

INTERNATIONAL OPERATING UNITS AFTER THE CANWEST SALE

The CanWest sale left International with the set of operating assets it now controls. These operating assets fall into four basic groups, which I label in a reader-friendly manner as: the Canada Group; the Chicago Group, the Jerusalem Group, and the *Telegraph* Group. . . . The Groups operate with great autonomy and there appear to be negligible, if any, synergies generated by their operation under common ownership.

The Jerusalem Group

The Jerusalem Group owns four newspapers that are all editions of the *Jerusalem Post,* which is the most widely read English-language newspaper published in the Middle East and is considered a high-quality, internationally well-regarded source of news about Israel. . . .

The Jerusalem Group makes only a very small contribution to International's revenues. In 2003, it had revenues of approximately $10.4 million, a figure amounting to only around 1% of International's total revenues, and its EBITDA[6] was nearly $3 million in the red. . . .

The Canada Group

The Canada Group is the last of the Canadian publishing assets of International. It operates through three main businesses: 1) 29 daily and community newspapers in British Columbia and Quebec; 2) dozens of trade magazines, directories and websites in 17 different markets, addressed to various industries . . .; and 3) 17 community newspapers and shopping guides in Alberta. . . .

The Canada Group is expected to generate over $80 million in revenues this year, a figure similar to last year. . . .

The Chicago Group

The Chicago Group is one of the two major operating asset groups that International controls. The Chicago Group owns more than 100 newspapers in the greater Chicago metropolitan area. Its most prominent newspaper is the *Chicago Sun-Times,* a daily tabloid newspaper that might be thought of as the "Second Newspaper in the Second City." That moniker would not be a slight, however, when viewed from a national or even international perspective.

Even though it ranks behind the *Chicago Tribune* in terms of overall circulation and readership, the *Sun-Times* has traditionally been and remains one of the top ten newspapers in the United States in terms of circulation and readership. Even though it is a tabloid, the *Sun-Times* is not an undistinguished paper. Its sports coverage is considered to be excellent, its film critic Roger Ebert is nationally prominent, and its pages include the work of many well-regarded journalists. . . .

Regardless of whether it lags the *Tribune,* the *Sun-Times* has generated very healthy EBITDA for International on a consistent basis during the recent past, producing $40 million in EBITDA in 2003, out of a total of nearly $80 million for the entire Chicago Group. . . .

---

6. [By the author – the text of the court's footnote six was moved by the author to here in the court's opinion.] That is, earnings before interest, taxes, depreciation and amortization. According to the court, EBITDA is "significant because it is a measure of free cash flow that is commonly used by investors in valuating newspaper companies."

The *Sun-Times* is only one aspect of the Chicago Group, however. The Chicago Group also owns a valuable group of community newspapers that are published in the greater Chicago metropolitan area. . . .

These community papers have important economic value to the Chicago Group and to International. Their revenues and EBITDA, taken together, are roughly equal to that of the *Sun-Times*. . . .

In recent years, the Chicago Group as a whole has run neck-and-neck with the *Telegraph* Group in terms of generating EBITDA for International. . . .

The Telegraph Group

The *Telegraph* Group includes the Internet site and various newspapers associated with the *Daily Telegraph,* including the *Sunday Telegraph,* as well as the magazines *The Spectator* and *Apollo.* The *Spectator* is the oldest continually published English-language magazine in the world and has an impressive reputation as a journal of opinion for the British intelligentsia, but it is not an economically significant asset. Rather, the *Telegraph* newspaper is the flagship of the *Telegraph* Group economically.

The *Telegraph* is a London-based newspaper but it is international in importance and readership, with a reputation of the kind that U.S. papers like the *New York Times,* the *Washington Post,* and the *Wall Street Journal* enjoy. It is a high-quality, broadsheet newspaper that is noted for its journalistic excellence, with a conservative, establishment-oriented bent. Its daily circulation of over 900,000 is the largest among English broadsheets but it trails the *London Sunday Times* in Sunday circulation by a sizable margin. Several London tabloids also outsell the *Telegraph* by very large margins. London may be the most competitive newspaper market in the world and that market continues to involve a vigorous struggle for market share that has existed since the early 1990s, when the *Times'* owner, Rupert Murdoch, initiated a price war. . . .

On balance, however, there is no question that the *Telegraph* Group is a profitable and valuable one. In the year 2003, it had over a half billion dollars in revenues and produced over $57 million in EBITDA. . . .

II. LEGAL ANALYSIS . . .

A. THE PRELIMINARY INJUNCTION STANDARD

The standard that a party seeking a preliminary injunction must satisfy is a well-known one. "On a motion for preliminary injunctive relief, the moving party must demonstrate a reasonable probability of success on the merits, that absent injunctive relief irreparable harm will occur, and that the harm the moving party will suffer if the requested relief is denied outweighs the harm the opponents will suffer if relief is granted." The resolution of Inc.'s motion in this case turns largely on the merits of its claims, which I now discuss. . . .

C.   **AS A MATTER OF ECONOMIC SUBSTANCE, DOES THE TELEGRAPH GROUP
     COMPRISE SUBSTANTIALLY ALL OF INTERNATIONAL'S ASSETS?**

I now discuss the major question presented by this motion: whether the
Telegraph Group comprises "substantially all" of International's assets, such that
its sale requires a vote under §271.

1. The Legal Standards to Measure Whether the Telegraph Group
    Comprises Substantially All of International's Assets

Section 271 of the Delaware General Corporation Law authorizes a board
of directors of a Delaware corporation to sell "all or substantially all of its property and assets, including goodwill and corporate franchises" only with the
approval of a stockholder vote. The origins of §271 did not rest primarily in a
desire by the General Assembly to protect stockholders by affording them a vote
on transactions previously not requiring their assent. Rather, §271's predecessors were enacted to address the common law rule that invalidated any attempt
to sell all or substantially all of a corporation's assets without unanimous stockholder approval.[42] . . . According to leading commentators, the addition of the
words "substantially all" was "intended merely to codify the interpretation generally accorded to the language of the pre-1967 statute that the word 'all' meant
'substantially all,' so that the statute could not be evaded by retaining a small
amount of property not vital to the operation of the business."[44]

As I will note, our courts arguably have not always viewed cases involving
the interpretation of §271 through a lens focused by the statute's plain words.
Nonetheless, it remains a fundamental principle of Delaware law that the courts
of this state should apply a statute in accordance with its plain meaning, as the
words that our legislature has used to express its will are the best evidence of its
intent. To analyze whether the vote requirement set forth in §271 applies to a
particular asset sale without anchoring that analysis to the statute's own words
involves an unavoidable risk that normative preferences of the judiciary will
replace those of the General Assembly. . . .

. . . There are various metrics that can be used to determine how important
particular assets are in the scheme of things. Should a court look to the percentage of the corporation's potential value as a sales target to measure the statute's
application? Or measures of income-generating potential, such as contributions
to revenues or operating income? To what extent should the flagship nature of
certain assets be taken into account?

---

42. *See, e.g., Gimbel v. Signal Cos.*, 316 A.2d 599, 605 n. 3 (Del. Ch.) (indicating that this
was the purpose of the predecessor to §271), *aff'd*, 316 A.2d 619 (Del. 1974); 1 R. Franklin
Balotti & Jesse A. Finkelstein, DELAWARE LAW OF CORPORATIONS & BUSINESS ORGANIZATIONS §10.1,
at 10-3 (3d ed. Supp. 2004) (same).

44. Balotti & Finkelstein, §10.1, at 10-4 (quoting *Cottrell v. Pawcatuck Co.*, 128 A.2d
225 (Del.1956)); *see also* . . . Ernest L. Folk, III, THE DELAWARE GENERAL CORPORATION LAW: A
COMMENTARY & ANALYSIS 400 (1967 amendment adding "substantially all" explicitly codified
"general consensus" that the existing statute "applied in that situation as well"). . . .

For all these reasons,

> The Supreme Court has long held that a determination of whether there is a sale of substantially all assets so as to trigger section 271 depends upon the particular qualitative and quantitative characteristics of the transaction at issue. Thus, the transaction must be viewed in terms of its overall effect on the corporation, and there is no necessary qualifying percentage.[51]

In other words,

> Our jurisprudence eschewed a definitional approach to §271 focusing on the interpretation of the words "substantially all," in favor of a contextual approach focusing upon whether a transaction involves the sale "of assets quantitatively vital to the operation of the corporation and is out of the ordinary and substantially affects the existence and purpose of the corporation." *Gimbel v. Signal Cos., Inc.*, Del. Ch., 316 A.2d 599, 606, *aff'd*, Del.Supr., 316 A.2d 619 (1974). This interpretative choice necessarily involved a policy preference for doing equity in specific cases over the value of providing clear guidelines for transactional lawyers structuring transactions for the corporations they advise. *See* 1 David A. Drexler, et al., *Delaware Corporation Law and Practice* §37.03 (1999) ("[*Gimbel*] and its progeny represent a clear-cut rejection of the former conventional view that 'substantially all' in Section 271 meant only significantly more than one-half of the corporation's assets.").[52]

It would be less than candid to fail to acknowledge that the §271 case law provides less than ideal certainty about the application of the statute to particular circumstances. This may result from certain decisions that appear to deviate from the statutory language in a marked way[53] and from others that have dilated perhaps longer than they should in evaluating asset sales that do not seem to come at all close to meeting the statutory trigger for a required stockholder vote. In this latter respect, the seminal §271 decision, *Gimbel v. Signal Cos.*, may have contributed to the lack of clarity. In the heat of an expedited injunction proceeding, the Chancellor examined in some detail whether the sale of assets comprising only 26% and 41% of the Signal Companies' total and net assets was subject to stockholder approval. Although the assets involved the oldest business line of the Signal Companies, the magnitude involved does not seem to approach §271's gray zone.

In the morass of particular percentages in the cases, however, remain the key principles articulated in *Gimbel*, which were firmly rooted in the statutory language of §271 and the statute's history. As has been noted, *Gimbel* set forth a quantitative and qualitative test designed to help determine whether a particular sale of assets involved substantially all of the corporation's assets. That test has been adopted by our Supreme Court as a good metric for determining whether an asset sale triggers the vote requirement of §271.[55] . . .

---

51. *Winston v. Mandor,* 710 A.2d 835, 843 (Del. Ch. 1997) (footnotes omitted).

52. *In re General Motors Class H S'holders Litig.,* 734 A.2d 611, 623 (Del. Ch. 1999).

53. The case of *Katz v. Bregman,* 431 A.2d 1274 (Del. Ch. 1981), in particular, represents a striking one. In that case, a sale of assets constituting 51 percent of asset value, 44.9 percent of sales, and 52.4 percent of pre-tax net operating income was held to be subject to stockholder approval as a sale of "substantially all" the corporation's assets.

55. *Oberly v. Kirby,* 592 A.2d 445, 464 (Del.1991); *see also Thorpe v. CERBCO, Inc.,* 676 A.2d 436, 444 (Del.1996).

The test that *Gimbel* articulated—requiring a stockholder vote if the assets to be sold "are quantitatively vital to the operation of the corporation" and "substantially affect[] the existence and purpose of the corporation"—must therefore be read as an attempt to give practical life to the words "substantially all." It is for that reason that *Gimbel* emphasized that a vote would never be required for a transaction in the ordinary course of business and that the mere fact that an asset sale was out of the ordinary had little bearing on whether a vote was required. . . .

And it is in that sense that I apply the *Gimbel* test in this case.

2. Is the Telegraph Group Quantitatively Vital to the Operations of International?

The first question under the *Gimbel* test is whether the *Telegraph* Group is quantitatively vital to the operations of International. The short answer to that question is no, it is not quantitatively vital within the meaning of *Gimbel*.

Why?

Because it is clear that International will retain economic vitality even after a sale of the *Telegraph* because it is retaining other significant assets, one of which, the Chicago Group, has a strong record of past profitability and expectations of healthy profit growth.

Now, it is of course clear that the *Telegraph* Group is a major quantitative part of International's economic value and an important contributor to its profits. I am even prepared to decide this motion on the assumption that the *Telegraph* Group is the single most valuable asset that International possesses, even more valuable than the Chicago Group. . . .

Let's consider the relative contribution to International's revenues of the *Telegraph* Group and the Chicago Group. When considering this and other factors the reader must bear in mind that the contribution of the Canada Group dropped steeply after the 2000 CanWest sale. Before that sale, the Canada Group was a larger contributor to the economic value of International in many respects than the *Telegraph* and Chicago Groups combined and it was sold without a stockholder vote. Bearing that fact in mind, a look at the revenue picture at International since 2000 reveals the following:

Revenue ($MM)								
Operating Unit	2000	%	2001	%	2002	%	Unaudited 2003	%
Telegraph Group	$562.1	26.8	486.4	42.4	481.5	47.9	519.5	49.0
Chicago Group	401.4	19.2	442.9	38.6	441.8	43.9	450.8	42.5
Canada Group	1,065.2	50.8	197.9	17.3	69.6	6.9	80.5	7.6
Jerusalem Group	67.3	3.2	19.1	1.7	13.2	1.3	10.4	1.0
Other	0.0	0.0	0.0	0.0	0.0	0.0	0.0	0.0
Total	2,096.0	100.0	1,146.3	100.0	1,006.2	100.0	1,061.2	100.0

Put simply, the *Telegraph* Group has accounted for less than half of International's revenues during the last three years and the Chicago Group's contribution has been in the same ballpark.

In book value terms, neither the *Telegraph* Group nor the Chicago Group approach 50% of International's asset value because the company's other operating groups and non-operating assets have value:

Book Value of Assets ($MM)								
Operating Unit	2000	%	2001	%	2002	%	Unaudited 2003	%
Telegraph Group	$542.0	19.8	533.2	25.9	568.3	26.0	629.8	35.7
Chicago Group	613.7	22.4	595.9	29.0	557.9	25.5	537.9	30.5
Canada Group	551.6	20.2	448.7	21.8	214.0	9.8	262.0	14.9
Jerusalem Group	61.2	2.2	69.6	3.4	28.9	1.3	30.1	1.7
Other	968.8	35.4	410.5	19.9	819.1	37.4	302.8	17.2
Total	2,737.2	100.0	2,058.0	100.0	2,188.1	100.0	1,762.6	100.0

In terms of vitality, however, a more important measure is EBITDA contribution, as that factor focuses on the free cash flow that assets generate for the firm, a key component of economic value. As to that important factor, the Chicago Group is arguably more quantitatively nutritious to International than the *Telegraph* Group. Here is the picture considering all of International's operating groups:

EBITDA—All Operating Units ($MM)								
Operating Unit	2000	%	2001	%	2002	%	Unaudited 2003	%
Telegraph Group	$106.7	30.3	50.7	85.3	61.4	54.7	57.4	57.4
Chicago Group	59.8	17.0	47.6	80.1	72.1	64.2	79.5	79.4
Canada Group	190.5	54.1	(21.1)	(2.5)	(0.8)	(0.7)	(3.3)	(3.3)
Jerusalem Group	9.6	2.7	(1.5)	(2.5)	(2.8)	(2.5)	(5.3)	(5.3)
Other	(14.3)	(4.1)	(16.3)	(27.4)	(17.5)	(15.6)	(28.3)	(28.3)
Total	352.3	100.0	59.5	100.0	112.4	100.0	100.0	100.0

The picture that emerges is one of rough equality between the two Groups—with any edge tilting in the Chicago Group's direction. . . .

The evidence therefore reveals that neither the *Telegraph* Group nor the Chicago Group is quantitatively vital in the sense used in the *Gimbel* test. . . . International can continue as a profitable entity without either one of them. International is not a human body and the *Telegraph* and the Chicago Group are not its heart and liver. International is a business. Neither one of the two groups is "vital"—i.e., "necessary to the continuation of [International's] life" or "necessary to [its] continued existence or effectiveness."[72] Rather, a sale of either Group leaves International as a profitable entity, even if it chooses to distribute a good deal of the cash it receives from the *Telegraph* sale to its stockholders through a dividend or share repurchase.

---

72. American Heritage Dictionary 1924 (4th ed. 2000).

3. Does the Telegraph Sale Substantially Affect the Existence and Purpose of International?

The relationship of the qualitative element of the *Gimbel* test to the quantitative element is more than a tad unclear. If the assets to be sold are not quantitatively vital to the corporation's life, it is not altogether apparent how they can "substantially affect the existence and purpose of" the corporation within the meaning of *Gimbel*, suggesting either that the two elements of the test are actually not distinct or that they are redundant. In other words, if quantitative vitality takes into account factors such as the cash-flow generating value of assets and not merely book value, then it necessarily captures qualitative considerations as well. Simply put, the supposedly bifurcated *Gimbel* test . . . may simply involve a look at quantitative and qualitative considerations in order to come up with the answer to the single statutory question, which is whether a sale involves substantially all of a corporation's assets. Rather than endeavor to explore the relationship between these factors, however, I will just dive into my analysis of the qualitative importance of the *Telegraph* Group to International.

Inc.'s demand for a vote places great weight on the qualitative element of *Gimbel*. In its papers, Inc. stresses the journalistic superiority of the *Telegraph* over the *Sun-Times* and the social cachet the *Telegraph* has. If you own the *Telegraph*, Inc. notes, "you can have dinner with the Queen." To sell one of the world's most highly regarded newspapers and leave International owning as its flagship the Second Paper in the Second City is to fundamentally, qualitatively transform International. Moreover, after the *Telegraph* sale, International's name will even ring hollow, as it will own only publications in the U.S., Canada, and Israel, and it will own only one paper of top-flight journalistic reputation, the *Jerusalem Post*, which has only a modest readership compared to the *Telegraph*.

The argument that Inc. makes in its papers misconceives the qualitative element of *Gimbel*. That element is not satisfied if the court merely believes that the economic assets being sold are aesthetically superior to those being retained; rather, the qualitative element of *Gimbel* focuses on economic quality and, at most, on whether the transaction leaves the stockholders with an investment that in economic terms is qualitatively different than the one that they now possess. Even with that focus, it must be remembered that the qualitative element is a gloss on the statutory language "substantially all" and not an attempt to identify qualitatively important transactions but ones that "strike at the heart of the corporate existence."[74]

The *Telegraph* sale does not strike at International's heart or soul, if that corporation can be thought to have either one. When International went public, it did not own the *Telegraph*. During the course of its existence, International has frequently bought and sold a wide variety of publications. . . . Thus, no investor in International would assume that any of its assets were sacrosanct. In the words of *Gimbel*, it "can be said that . . . acquisitions and dispositions [of independent branches of International's business] have become part of the [company's] ordinary course of business."[75]

---

74. *Gimbel*, 316 A.2d at 606.
75. *Id.* at 608.

Even more importantly, investors in public companies do not invest their money because they derive social status from owning shares in a corporation whose controlling manager can have dinner with the Queen. Whatever the social importance of the *Telegraph* in Great Britain, the economic value of that importance to International as an entity is what matters for the *Gimbel* test, not how cool it would be to be the *Telegraph*'s publisher. The expected cash flows from the *Telegraph* Group take that into account, as do the bids that were received for the *Telegraph* Group. The "trophy" nature of the *Telegraph* Group means that there are some buyers—including I discern, the Barclays, who run a private, not public, company—who are willing to pay a higher price than expected cash flows suggest is prudent, in purely economic terms, in order to own the *Telegraph* and to enjoy the prestige and access to the intelligentsia, the literary and social elite, and high government officials that comes with that control.

Although stockholders would expect that International would capitalize on the fact that some potential buyers of the *Telegraph* would be willing to pay money to receive some of the non-economic benefits that came with control of that newspaper, it is not reasonable to assume that they invested with the expectation that International would retain the *Telegraph* Group even if it could receive a price that was attractive in light of the projected future cash flow of that Group. Certainly, given the active involvement of International in the M & A market, there was no reason to invest based on that unusual basis. It may be that there exists somewhere an International stockholder (other than Mrs. Black or perhaps some personal friends of the Blacks) who values the opportunities that Conrad Black had to dine with the Queen and other eminent members of British society because he was the *Telegraph*'s publisher. But the qualitative element of the *Gimbel* test addresses the rational economic expectations of reasonable investors, and not the aberrational sentiments of the peculiar (if not, more likely, the non-existent) persons who invest money to help fulfill the social ambitions of inside managers and to thereby enjoy (through the ownership of common stock) vicariously extraordinary lives themselves.

After the *Telegraph* Sale, International's stockholders will remain investors in a publication company with profitable operating assets, a well-regarded tabloid newspaper of good reputation and large circulation, a prestigious newspaper in Israel, and other valuable assets. While important, the sale of the *Telegraph* does not strike a blow to International's heart.

4. Summary of §271 Analysis

When considered quantitatively and qualitatively, the *Telegraph* sale does not amount to a sale of substantially all of International's assets. This conclusion is consistent with the bulk of our case law under §271. Although by no means wholly consistent, that case law has, by and large, refused to find that a disposition involved substantially all the assets of a corporation when the assets that would remain after the sale were, in themselves, substantial and profitable. As *Gimbel* noted, §271 permits a board to sell "one business . . . without shareholder approval when other substantial businesses are retained." In the cases when asset sales were deemed to involve substantially all of a corporation's assets, the record always revealed great doubt about the viability of the business that would remain, primarily because the remaining operating assets were not profitable. But, "if the portion of the business not sold constitutes a substantial, viable, ongoing component of the corporation, the sale is not subject to Section 271."[78]

To conclude that the sale of the *Telegraph* Group was a sale of substantially all of International's assets would involve a determination that International possesses two operating assets, the sale of either of which would trigger a stockholder vote under §271. That is, because there is no significant distinction between the economic importance of the Chicago and *Telegraph* Groups to International, a conclusion that the *Telegraph* Group was substantially all of International's assets would (impliedly but undeniably) supplant the plain language and intended meaning of the General Assembly with an "approximately half" test.[79] I decline Inc.'s invitation for me to depart so markedly from our legislature's mandate. By any reasonable interpretation, the *Telegraph* sale does not

---

78. 1 R. Franklin Balotti & Jesse A. Finkelstein, DELAWARE LAW OF CORPORATIONS & BUSINESS ORGANIZATIONS §10.2, at 10-7 (3d ed. Supp. 2004).

79. As International points out, the MBCA now includes a safe harbor provision that is intended to provide a "greater measure of certainty than is provided by interpretations of the current case law." MODEL BUS. CORP. ACT §12.02 cmt. 1 (2002). The safe harbor is an objective test involving two factors:

> If a corporation retains a business activity that represented at least 25 percent of total assets at the end of the most recently completed fiscal year, and 25 percent of either income from continuing operations before taxes or revenues from continuing operations for that fiscal year, in each case of the corporation and its subsidiaries on a consolidated basis, the corporation will conclusively be deemed to have retained a significant continuing business activity.

Id. §12.02(a).

Moreover, both the MBCA and the ALI Principles of Corporate Governance usefully turn the "substantially all" inquiry on its head by focusing, as *Gimbel* does in a more oblique way, on what remains after a sale. *See* MODEL BUS. CORP. ACT §12.02 cmt. 1 (2002) (stockholder vote required if asset sale would "leave the corporation without a significant continuing business activity"); PRINCIPLES OF CORP. GOVERNANCE §§1.38(a)(2), 6.01(b) (text requiring stockholder approval when asset sale "would leave the corporation without a significant continuing business"); *id.*§1.38 cmt. 3 (commentary indicating that if a company has two principal operating divisions and one will remain following the asset sale, "there should normally be no doubt concerning the significance of the remaining division, even if the division to be sold represented a majority of the corporation's operating assets"). The MBCA, in particular, recognizes that while the "significant continuing business activity" test differs verbally from the "substantially all" language employed in many state corporation statutes, adoption of the MBCA provision would not entail a substantive change from existing law, because "[i]n practice, . . . courts interpreting these statutes [using the phrase 'substantially all'] have commonly employed a test comparable to that embodied in 12.02(a)." MODEL BUS. CORP. ACT §12.02 cmt. 1 (2002). The commentary specifically cites several Delaware judicial decisions as examples of cases employing such a test. *Id.* These approaches support the conclusion I reach.

Although not binding on me, these interpretative approaches provide a valuable perspective on §271 because they are rooted, as is *Gimbel,* in the intent behind the statute (and statutes like it in other jurisdictions). Indeed, taken together, a reading of §271 that: 1) required a stockholder vote for any sales contract to which a parent was a party that involved a sale by a wholly owned subsidiary that, in economic substance, amounted to a disposition of substantially all the parent's assets; combined with 2) a strict adherence to the words "substantially all" (á la the MBCA), could be viewed as the most faithful way to give life to the

involve substantially all of International's assets as substantial operating (and non-operating) assets will be retained, and International will remain a profitable publishing concern. . . .

IV. CONCLUSION

Inc.'s motion for a preliminary injunction is DENIED. IT IS SO ORDERED.

NOTES

1. The Downfall of Lord Conrad Black. Following the attempted sale of the Telegraph Group to Barclays, Lord Conrad Black, Hollinger International's extravagant CEO, was charged and convicted of defrauding investors. As the trial records revealed, the sale of Hollinger International's various subsidiaries between 1998 and 2001 financed Lord Black's luxurious lifestyle to the tune of over $6 million. Ultimately, Lord Black was sentenced to 6½ years in prison and ordered to pay $125,000 in fines. Five years later, thanks to the Supreme Court's determination in *Skilling v. United States*, 130 S. Ct. 2896 (2010), that the honest services law (which was the law used to convict executive officers such as Enron's CEO, Jeffrey Skilling, of corporate fraud) was unconstitutionally vague, Lord Black was released from prison in May 2012. *See Conrad Black Is Freed*, N.Y. TIMES DEAL BOOK, May 4, 2012.

2. Clarifying Delaware Precedent? In the wake of Vice Chancellor Strine's opinion in *Hollinger*, one set of experienced practitioners made the following observation:

> Section 271 has been a thorn in the sides of practitioners for a long time. Although Delaware rightly prides itself on having the pre-eminent corporate law in the U.S., with an extensive body of judicial decisions offering guidance and, in most cases, a relatively high degree of predictability for lawyers and their clients, the cases under Section 271 leave an uncomfortably wide range of transactions in a "grey area." Vice Chancellor Leo E. Strine, Jr. clearly saw in [the excerpted opinion above in] the *Hollinger* dispute an opportunity to clarify the precedents.

Elliot V. Stein and Ophir Nave, *Hollinger—Round Two: "Substantially All" Means "Substantially All,"* 8 THE M&A LAWYER 7 (Sept. 2004). Do you agree? Do you think then Vice Chancellor Strine's opinion "clarifies the precedents," resulting in a narrowing of the "grey area"?

General Assembly's intended use of §271. That is, §271 would have substantive force but only with regard to transactions that genuinely involved substantially all of the corporation's assets.

E.   Corporate Formalities Required for Stock Acquisitions

1.   General Background

Under the terms of modern state corporation statutes, Bidder Co. has the power to hold and to vote shares of another corporation. *See, e.g.,* MBCA §3.02. This allows Bidder to negotiate directly with Target Co. shareholders for the purchase of their shares in Target. Assuming that Bidder acquires all (or at least a controlling interest in) Target shares, Bidder may then exercise its voting rights to remove the incumbent board of directors and replace them with Bidder's own slate of nominees. Consider the situation where Bidder is lucky enough to purchase all of Target's shares for cash, as reflected in Diagram 6 in Appendix A. After the parties close on their stock purchase agreement and this change of control transaction has been consummated, Target Co. will be left as a wholly-owned subsidiary of Bidder.

Consider, though, the economic result where Bidder issues its shares in exchange for all of the shares of Target (as reflected in Diagram 7 in Appendix A), rather than paying cash to purchase Target shares. This transaction, commonly referred to as a "stock exchange offer," raises some interesting questions. Where do the former Target Co. shareholders end up? What is the economic decision that faces Target shareholders in a stock exchange offer? How does a stock exchange offer differ from the decision Target shareholders face when they receive an all-cash offer from Bidder? Finally, consider the situation that confronts the shareholders of Bidder Co. As a general proposition, does it make any difference to Bidder's shareholders whether Bidder uses its cash or its stock to acquire Target shares?

The next problem set is intended to flesh out the concerns that must be addressed in analyzing these issues. Before we analyze these problems, one further consideration deserves mention—the agency cost problem inherent in modern share ownership. This problem is most acute in the case of those investors who own shares in publicly traded companies. Briefly summarized, the agency cost problem is inherent in the corporate form of business organization because of the separation of ownership from control over the company's business operations. When the owners of a company (the shareholders) delegate managerial authority over the company's business affairs to agents (the board of directors and the company's senior executive officers), the resulting separation of ownership and managerial control creates divergent incentives. For example, corporate managers may be tempted to use their authority to load up on executive perks (such as company jets and club memberships), which allow the corporate managers to reap almost all of the benefits while bearing only a fraction of the costs. This is generally referred to as the *agency cost problem*.

The agency cost problem surfaces in M&A transactions, although it is not unique to this setting. (Indeed, the agency cost problem has been reflected most prominently in the ongoing, highly publicized controversy over the use of stock options as part of the executive compensation for corporate CEOs.) In the case of M&A deals, however, the agency cost problem is central to the legal rules imposed on this method of corporation acquisition. The next problem set is designed to flesh out the nature of the agency cost problem in the case of acquisitions structured as stock purchases and the nature of the law's response to this recurring problem. In addition, the problems are further designed to separate out the nature of the agency cost problem in the context of publicly traded companies versus privately held corporations.

PROBLEM SET NO. 4—STOCK PURCHASES UNDER DELAWARE LAW AND THE MBCA

1. Stock Purchase for Cash (See Diagram 6—Appendix A). Assume that Nest Labs has a single class of voting common stock outstanding. Further assume that all of the outstanding common shares are held of record by the company's two founders, Tony Fadell and Matt Rogers, along with several venture capital funds. All of these shareholders signed a stock purchase agreement with Google, Inc., a NYSE-listed U.S. company. Google has agreed to pay $3.2 billion in cash to the shareholders at the time of closing on the parties' stock purchase agreement.

   a. Who are the parties to the stock purchase agreement?
   b. What board action is required of Nest Labs if the company is organized under Delaware law? Under the MBCA?
   c. What board action is required of Google, Inc. if Google is organized under Delaware law? Under the MBCA?
   d. Do the shareholders of Nest Labs have the right to vote:

      (1) Under Delaware law?
      (2) Under the MBCA?
      (3) Under the rules of the NYSE?

   e. Do the shareholders of Google have the right to vote:

      (1) Under Delaware law?
      (2) Under the MBCA?
      (3) Under the rules of the NYSE?

   f. What options are available to the shareholders of Nest Labs (under either Delaware law or the MBCA) if they object to the terms of Google's offer?
   g. What options are available to the shareholders of Google (under either Delaware law or the MBCA) if they object to Google's proposal to acquire Nest Labs?

2. Stock Purchase—in Exchange for 24 Percent of Bidder's Stock (See Diagram 7—Appendix A). Assume the same facts as described in Problem 1, *except* that the parties' stock purchase agreement calls for Google to pay at closing all of the $3.2 billion purchase price by issuing shares of Google common stock comprising 24 percent of the voting power of Google's outstanding common stock immediately before the issuance is completed.

a. Who are the parties to the stock purchase agreement?

b. What board action is required of Nest Labs if the company is organized under Delaware law? Under the MBCA?

c. What board action is required of Google, Inc. if Google is organized under Delaware law? Under the MBCA?

d. Do the shareholders of Nest Labs have the right to vote:

    (1) Under Delaware law?

    (2) Under the MBCA?

    (3) Under the rules of the NYSE?

e. Do the shareholders of Google have the right to vote:

    (1) Under Delaware law?

    (2) Under the MBCA?

    (3) Under the rules of the NYSE?

f. How does your analysis of these issues change if shares comprising only 14 percent of the voting power of Google's outstanding stock immediately before the issuance are to be used as the acquisition consideration?

NOTES

1. An Introduction to Hostile Takeovers. Where management of Bidder Co. directly negotiates with management of Target Co., and these negotiations result in an acquisition proposal whereby Bidder offers to buy Target shares directly from Target shareholders, and further, Target's board recommends that its shareholders accept Bidder's offer, then this transaction is generally referred to on Wall Street as a *friendly takeover.* However, in those cases where Target's board refuses to negotiate and reach a deal with Bidder, then Bidder may bypass Target's management altogether and take its offer to buy Target shares directly to Target's shareholders. In the jargon of Wall Street, this type of acquisition will be referred to as a *hostile takeover.* The ability of the Bidder to engage in this type of end run around the existing management of Target Co. is the core tool of determined Bidders who seek to wrest control from incumbent managers in the *market for corporate control,* a term of art on Wall Street and in the M&A literature.

According to the market for corporate control, the potential for this type of hostile takeover operates as a disciplining influence on incumbent management, who know that if they underperform and the stock price declines far enough in the trading market, the company may become an attractive candidate for a takeover. In the usual case, prospective Bidders will identify an underperforming Target and make an unsolicited offer directly to Target's shareholders for the purpose of getting control over Target and its business operations. Once in control, Bidder will usually move swiftly to replace incumbent management with a more effective business team.

The market for corporate control, therefore, rests in part on the premise that if incumbent management knows that it is vulnerable to this kind of market pressure, then management will be motivated to perform well to keep control over Target's business—and ultimately, their jobs. One of the major public policy debates growing out of the merger wave of the 1980s focused on the appropriate manner of regulating the market for corporate control. The nature of this public policy debate, vestiges of which linger even today, are explored in detail in Chapter 6, where we discuss federal regulation of takeovers under the terms of the Williams Act, and in Chapter 7, where we analyze the nature of directors' fiduciary duty obligations under state law, the limits of which are most acutely tested in the case of unsolicited (hostile) tender offers.

2. An Introduction to Two-Step Transactions.   As we saw in analyzing Problem Set No. 4 above, very often Bidder Co. will be in a position where it is feasible (as a practical matter) for Bidder to purchase all of the outstanding shares of Target Co., as in the case where Google purchases *all* of the outstanding shares of Nest Labs in a single transaction. As a result, once this stock purchase is consummated, Nest Labs becomes a wholly-owned subsidiary of Google. Very often, though, Bidder will *not* be able to acquire 100 percent of the stock of Target in a single transaction. This problem is particularly acute in those cases where Target Co. is publicly traded and Bidder commences an offer to purchase Target shares for cash, in a transaction that is referred to as a cash "tender offer." We will discuss tender offers in more detail in Chapter 6. At this point, though, it bears emphasizing that Bidder will usually condition its obligation to purchase Target shares for cash from the selling shareholders on its ability to obtain a sufficient number of Target shares to give Bidder a majority of the voting stock of Target. In many cases, this will leave a (perhaps substantial) minority interest in Target, which is now operated as a controlled subsidiary of Bidder Co.

For legal and business reasons that are developed in more detail in later chapters of this casebook, Bidder may then desire to eliminate the outstanding minority shares of the subsidiary by acquiring the remaining shares of Target that the parent company (Bidder) does not own. This second step is often referred to as a *squeeze-out* transaction (i.e., "squeezing out" the minority interest from any continued equity ownership of the subsidiary). Very often, the minority shares will be squeezed out in a second step transaction structured as a cash-out merger. (*See Diagram 12—Appendix A.*) For reasons that are developed in the problem set in the next section, this back-end, second-step, cash-out merger will often be accomplished as a triangular merger (as reflected in Diagram 12 of Appendix A).

3. Delaware Section 251(h): Medium-Form Merger.   In 2013, Delaware enacted §251(h), which authorizes a new form of deal structure that has since come to be referred to as the "intermediate" or "medium-form" merger. This new statute was designed to streamline the *two-step transaction* of the type described in the preceding note. The first step is a cash tender offer for shares of a publicly traded Target Co. followed by a back-end, take-out merger that eliminates any shares not acquired in the front-end tender offer. In Chapter 6, we will study the rules governing tender offers under the federal securities laws. Then, in Chapter 7, we will examine this new form of deal structure—that is, a cash tender offer to be followed by a merger effected pursuant to Delaware §251(h)—as part of our discussion of fiduciary duty law, since many of the conditions imposed by this new statutory provision reflect obligations that the Delaware courts impose as part of its case law development of fiduciary duty law in the context of mergers and going-private transactions.

4. Distinguish the "Bust-up Bid" and the "Merger of Equals."   In the case of certain LBO deals of the type described earlier in this chapter (*see supra*, pp. 84-86), the financial buyer's plan of acquisition often calls for the buyout firm to acquire Target in order to sell off the pieces. This LBO model reflects the financial buyer's determination that, in effect, Target is worth *more* if the pieces are sold off. The proceeds raised from the sale of Target's assets would then be used to reduce the debt that had been borrowed in order to finance the purchase price for Target.

The staff of many LBO firms invest much of their time searching for companies where the trading price reflects that management is underutilizing the present combination of business assets. In these cases, the financial buyer can afford to borrow the funds necessary to pay a premium in order to purchase enough Target Co. shares to give the buyout firm control of Target. In the case of a publicly traded Target Co., this purchase will usually take the form of a tender offer regulated by the federal securities laws, a topic that is addressed in Chapter 6. After obtaining control of Target, the buyout firm would then proceed to dismantle Target by selling off its assets in piecemeal fashion. This type of LBO deal became popular in the 1980s and was widely used to dismantle the large, diversified conglomerates that were established through acquisitions made during the M&A wave of the 1960s. As the dominant business paradigm shifted in the 1980s and 1990s to focus on core business activity, LBO firms and other financial buyers helped accelerate the process of deconglomeration.

In contrast to "bust-up" bids, deals known as "mergers of equals" became quite popular in the M&A market of the 1990s. Perhaps the best known of these *mergers-of-equals* deals is the AOL-Time Warner deal. Billed as two firms combining to be managed under the leadership of *both* companies' CEOs, the deal was deliberately structured to avoid the perception that one firm was acquiring (swallowing up) another company. In very short order, however, critics claimed that this kind of power-sharing arrangement between co-CEOs was doomed to fail. The story of the merger of AOL and Time Warner validates the truth of this observation, as we shall see when we study this deal and its aftermath in Chapter 7. At this point, suffice it to say that the financial return of this combination proved dismal for the shareholders, and as it turns out, the power-sharing arrangement at AOL-Time Warner was doomed almost from the very start.

F.   Corporate Formalities Required for Triangular Mergers Under Delaware Law and the MBCA

1.   General Background on Triangular (Three-Party) Mergers

Until the 1970s, the advantages (and convenience) of the merger was limited to direct mergers of the type studied in Problem Set No. 1 earlier in this chapter. In these transactions, Bidder would swallow up Target by operation of law and Target would cease to exist. However, this usually could be accomplished *only* by the vote of the shareholders of *both* constituent corporations.

Consider, though, the situation where Nestlé, Inc., a large NYSE-listed company, decides to buy Trixie's Delites, Inc., a small, gourmet chocolate manufacturer located in Denver, Colorado, in order to obtain Trixie's secret recipe for a unique white chocolate nut confection. The parties (Nestlé and Trixie, the sole shareholder and CEO of Trixie's Delites) agree to a $1 million purchase price. If the acquisition is structured as a direct merger, then the shareholders of *both* constituent corporations must approve the deal. As for Target, the outcome of this shareholder vote is a foregone conclusion since Trixie is the only shareholder. On the other hand, matters are much more cumbersome for Bidder. The business decision to use Nestlé's resources (either the company's cash or a small number of the company's shares, or a combination of both) to merge with this small company, Trixie's Delites, Inc., must be put to a vote of Nestlé's shareholders, a time-consuming and expensive procedure. Over time, the law came to recognize that there are not sufficient benefits to justify the delay and expense associated with obtaining approval of Nestlé's public shareholders for this kind of small acquisition that does not present a fundamental change for the surviving corporation (Nestlé). However, the merger statute left no other alternative if this method was used to structure Nestlé's acquisition of Trixie's Delites.

It bears emphasizing that, in the context of a direct merger of Minnow (Target) into Whale (Bidder), these transactions are greatly facilitated today by virtue of provisions such as Delaware §251(f), which eliminates the need for Bidder to obtain the approval of its shareholders (assuming that the acquisition of Minnow is truly a *de minimis* transaction for Bidder and thus involves cash consideration or, alternatively, a sufficiently small number of shares of Bidder's stock so that Bidder avoids the need to obtain a vote of its shareholders by virtue of §251(f)). Of course, this transaction continues to constitute a fundamental change for Target and thus will require approval by Target's shareholders.

However, there will often be compelling business reasons for leaving Target in place rather than having it disappear by merging into the surviving corporation, Bidder, as called for by the direct merger. For example, Trixie's Delites, Inc., may have certain valuable rights, such as an established trademark, intellectual property license, or a very attractive lease arrangement, that are nontransferable.* As a result, it may be advantageous to leave the corporation, Trixie's Delites, Inc., in place. In such a case, the direct merger would not be a viable acquisition structure since it would call for the Target (Trixie's Delites) to disappear, merging into the surviving corporation (Nestlé). To address this limitation in the merger procedure, and thereby allow the Bidder to acquire Target and operate it as a wholly-owned subsidiary rather than disappear, the law authorized three-party mergers, also called *triangular mergers*.

In a triangular merger, the merger consideration will be provided by Bidder Co. Pursuant to the terms of their agreement, Target Co. will be merged with a wholly-owned subsidiary of Bidder. In order to consummate this plan of merger, Bidder will incorporate a new, wholly-owned subsidiary (NewCo) that will then merge with Target. The merger agreement will usually provide that Target

---

* [By the author: We will explore these issues in more detail in Chapter 3, where we examine the impact of an acquisition transaction on the creditors of Target Co.]

shareholders will receive Bidder shares—*not* shares of NewCo—in exchange for their Target shares. *See* DGCL §251(b); MBCA §11.02(c). In the case of a *forward* triangular merger, NewCo will be the surviving corporation, and Target Co. will disappear once the merger is consummated. In the case of a *reverse* triangular merger, NewCo will merge into Target, leaving Target Co. as the surviving company once the merger is consummated. "By preserving [Target] in the form of a subsidiary [of Bidder], the parties can [very often] preserve any valuable rights possessed by the acquired corporation without the necessity of transferring any patents, licenses, leases, or other rights of the acquired corporation and can in many cases avoid the necessity of securing the consent of a third party to such a transfer or the payment of sales or other transfer taxes." Marshall L. Small, *Corporate Combinations Under the New California General Corporation Law*, 23 UCLA L. Rev. 1190, 1193 n. 10 (1976).

As originally conceived, the triangular merger eliminated the need to obtain approval from Bidder's shareholders because the subsidiary, NewCo—and *not* Bidder itself—was to be the acquiring corporation. As a constituent corporation, the merger statute would generally require the consent of NewCo's shareholders; however, this approval was a foregone conclusion since Bidder was the sole shareholder of NewCo.

So, for example, Nestlé (the Whale) could acquire the much smaller Trixie's Delites (the Minnow) using the triangular merger procedure, and in the process avoid the requirement of approval of the acquisition by Nestlé's shareholders. Since Nestlé (Bidder) is not a constituent corporation in a triangular merger, no vote of Nestlé's shareholders is required. Over time, transaction planners capitalized on the convenience of the triangular merger, extending it well beyond this rather simplistic Whale-Minnow type of business combination:

> To avoid the cost and delay of obtaining shareholder approval (and to avoid paying [any] dissenters), in recent years the use of triangular mergers has become popular, combining the acquired corporation [Target Co.] with a wholly-owned subsidiary of the acquiring corporation [Bidder Co.]. The use of a wholly-owned subsidiary . . . obviate[s] the need for one of the two shareholder votes—the subsidiary [can] merely obtain the written consent of its parent, and the shareholders of the parent would not get to vote—unless the number of shares issued by the parent was sufficient to require such vote under stock exchange listing requirements applicable to the parent.

Small, *supra*, at 1192-1193.

Triangular mergers have become increasingly popular over the last 40 years or so for essentially the reasons described in the quoted excerpt above. Triangular mergers are a variation on the direct merger, and therefore, are not a separate type or method of merger, unlike the short-form merger. In particular, triangular mergers are authorized under state corporate law by the simple expedient of amending the state's merger statute to expand on the type of consideration that may be used in a merger not only to include stock (or other securities) of the *surviving* corporation, but also to authorize use of stock (or other securities) of *any* corporation. *See, e.g.,* MBCA §11.02(d)(4) and DGCL §251(b)(5). So, in a triangular merger, Bidder (for example, Nestlé) and Target (for example, Trixie) negotiate the terms of the merger agreement but the constituent corporations in the merger consist of NewCo (Nestlé's wholly-owned subsidiary formed for purposes of completing this acquisition) and Target (Trixie). Moreover, since Bidder, the parent corporation, is not a party to the merger, no vote of Bidder's shareholders is required to complete the transaction, assuming that Bidder already has sufficient authorized but unissued shares to complete the transaction. Since the right of appraisal generally follows the right to vote under the provisions of most states' corporation statutes, Bidder shareholders customarily will have no right of appraisal either. "Thus, the triangular merger is a straightforward mechanism to avoid the acquiring [i.e., Bidder] corporation's shareholders having a direct vote, and, for that matter, an appraisal remedy, in an acquisition of another company." James D. Cox and Thomas Lee Hazen, TREATISE ON THE LAW OF CORPORATIONS 638 (5th ed. 2020).

In the abstract, triangular mergers are a little difficult to grasp, although the end result may seem clear enough. Problem Set No. 5 (below) is designed to familiarize you with the mechanics of triangular mergers in general, and more specifically, will distinguish the results obtained in structuring the acquisition as either a *forward* or a *reverse* triangular merger.

2. Valuing Exchanges of Stock — Fixing the Exchange Ratio

In analyzing the various problem sets so far in this chapter, we have learned that difficult valuation decisions must be made as part of any acquisition, regardless of how the deal is structured. From the perspective of Target Co., the board must determine the inherent value of Target's business in order to decide at what price to sell the company. In situations where cash is the acquisition consideration, Bidder Co. faces the same business decision — determining what is a fair price for Target so that Bidder does not pay too much to acquire Target's business. If Bidder pays too great a premium to acquire Target, Bidder's management knows that it will face the ire of its own shareholders, whose equity interest will be diluted. On the other hand, from the perspective of Target, the business decision as to the amount of premium is even more compelling. Target's board faces a similar business valuation decision as Bidder's board — *exactly how much is Target worth?* As we have seen in analyzing the problems in this chapter, the decision as to price is vitally important since the acquisition is a fundamental change for Target. As such, the business decision as to the amount of premium that Target should receive in an all-cash purchase price is vitally important since an all-cash deal will eliminate the existing shareholders of Target from any further equity participation in the business. Consequently, the proposed sale of the company's business to Bidder for an all-cash purchase price presents Target shareholders with their *only* opportunity to receive a premium for their investment in Target's business.

As will be examined in more detail in the materials in the last section of this chapter (analyzing appraisal rights), determining the amount of this premium involves a complex valuation exercise. However, in those deals where Bidder's stock (or other securities) will be used as the acquisition consideration, the valuation decision is even more complicated. In this situation, Target's board faces a separate — but equally important — valuation determination. In addition to valuing Target in order to determine what is fair value for Target's business, the board of Target must also value the securities that Bidder proposes to issue in order to acquire Target to be sure that the exchange is fair to Target. The board of Bidder faces a similarly complex valuation decision whenever Bidder proposes to use its stock as the acquisition consideration, as (once again) it must be sure that it does not pay too much to acquire Target's business.

As we have also seen in analyzing the problems in this chapter, the boards of both Bidder and Target generally will retain financial advisors to assist them in their respective valuation exercises. The ultimate decision-making responsibility, however, belongs to the board. The complexity of these valuation determinations is discussed in the following note material.

Fixing the Terms of the Exchange Ratio in Public Company Deals.   When stock is used as the acquisition consideration, the situation is more complicated for the transaction planner than the all-cash deal. As reflected in the terms of the AT&T–DirecTV merger agreement (contained in Appendix B at the end of this casebook), much of this complexity arises from the need to fix the terms of the *exchange ratio*. The need to fix the exchange ratio is an inherent attribute of any stock for stock transaction—regardless of how the deal gets structured (i.e., direct merger, stock purchase, triangular merger, etc.). By contrast, in an all-cash transaction, the acquisition agreement simply specifies the amount of cash that Bidder is obligated to pay to Target shareholders at closing for each Target share they own. In the case of a stock for stock transaction, however, the acquisition agreement must specify the number of shares of Bidder that Target shareholders are to receive at closing in exchange for *each* of Target's outstanding shares.

As reflected in the description in Chapter 1 of AT&T's acquisition of DirecTV, there is a complicated valuation exercise inherent in the board's determination of the terms of any exchange ratio, a process that is quite complex from the perspective of *both* Bidder and Target. For starters, the board of Bidder must be confident in its determination of the inherent value of Target's business. The same is also true for Target's board with respect to the inherent value of Target's business. As we have seen analyzing the various problems in this chapter, nothing less than a fully informed decision-making process will satisfy the directors' fiduciary obligations to their respective shareholders. Where Bidder proposes to pay the purchase price all in cash, valuation of Target's business is the principal focus of the valuation exercise undertaken by the boards of both Bidder and Target.

Determining Fair Value in a Stock-for-Stock Deal.   However, in cases where Bidder proposes to use its own shares as the acquisition consideration, the situation is far more complex for the boards of both Bidder and Target. Bidder's board needs to be sensitive to the potential for equity dilution of its existing shareholders because of the issuance of its own stock as the acquisition consideration. Therefore, Bidder's board must take care to document its determination as to the value of *both* Bidder Co. *and* Target Co. in order to be sure that Bidder is receiving fair value for the shares that it proposes to issue to acquire Target. As we saw in analyzing the previous problem sets in this chapter, the potential for equity dilution of Bidder's shareholders in these cases is often going to trigger their right to vote on the transaction. In general, the public policy justification for giving Bidder shareholders a voice in this transaction when the amount of new shares to be issued exceeds some particular percentage of Bidder's then-outstanding shares (which is 20 percent under NYSE Rule 312) — even though Bidder is going to survive with all of its outstanding shares in place — reflects the difficulties inherent in valuing the non-cash consideration to be received by Bidder in exchange for this large block of its shares. The potential for substantial disagreement as to the precise value that Bidder is to receive in this exchange justifies the delay and cost associated with imposing the requirement that Bidder's shareholders approve the issuance of Bidder's shares in exchange for non-cash consideration (here, in the form of Target's business). As a matter of corporate governance, the requirement for shareholder approval forces management to explain the basis of its decision to acquire Target, including its valuation determination, thereby allowing Bidder shareholders to hold management accountable for their boardroom decision-making.

From Target's perspective, Target shareholders will generally get a right to vote on the transaction as a matter of corporate governance since it involves a fundamental change for the company. Regardless of whether cash or Bidder's stock serves as the acquisition consideration, Target's board owes a fiduciary duty to Target shareholders to obtain the best price available. In those cases where Target is publicly traded, this fiduciary obligation will require the board to negotiate with Bidder for a premium over the trading price of Target's stock. The amount of the premium is a matter of bargaining between Bidder and Target. In any case, however, the decision of the Target board whether to accept the price offered by Bidder will depend on the board's decision as to the inherent value (i.e., true value) of Target's business. Again, in all cash deals, this is the principal focus of the board's decision-making process.

By contrast, in those cases where Bidder is to acquire Target's business in exchange for shares of Bidder Co., the decision-making process of Target's board is more complicated. In such a case, Target's board must determine the value of Bidder and its prospects for the future. Only by engaging in this difficult valuation exercise — valuing Bidder, a business that Target's board is not as familiar with as it (hopefully) is with its own — can Target's board be sure that it is getting the best deal (i.e. *fair value*) for Target's shareholders under the terms of Bidder's exchange offer. This valuation exercise is at the very heart of negotiating the terms of the exchange ratio in those acquisitions where Bidder's stock is to be used as currency in the acquisition.

Once the exchange ratio is fixed based on the respective valuation determinations made by the boards of both Bidder and Target, the parties usually face another round of negotiations, at least in those cases where Bidder is publicly traded. In these cases, the parties must address the problem of changes in the price of Bidder's stock in the time interval between signing the acquisition agreement and closing on the deal, a period that can be quite lengthy (often many months or more) in the case of acquisitions involving publicly traded companies. For example, in the case of AT&T's acquisition of DirecTV (as described in detail in Chapter 1), the parties signed the acquisition agreement in May 2014, but the deal did not close until September 2015 pending regulatory clearance of the transaction from the FCC and certain antitrust authorities, among others. As a result of this delay in closing, the parties to the proposed transaction must address the inevitable possibility that the price of Bidder's stock will fluctuate during this period and evaluate the impact (if any) that this fluctuation will have on the value of the transaction from the perspective of both Bidder and Target shareholders.

Accordingly, at the time of negotiating a stock-for-stock transaction, the parties must deal with certain issues that arise because of the inevitable delay between the time of signing the acquisition agreement and the time of closing on the parties' agreement. This delay often presents challenges in determining the precise number of shares that Target shareholders will receive at closing since the price of Bidder's stock may change in the time interval between signing and closing. In practice, this leads to the use of one of two basic strategies for dealing with fluctuations in the price of Bidder's stock in the interval between signing and closing on the acquisition.

Use of Fixed Exchange Ratio.   The simplest structure is conventionally known as a *fixed exchange ratio*. Here, the acquisition agreement simply says that at closing, every Target share has the right to receive a fixed number of Bidder shares. In the case of a fixed exchange ratio, the number of Bidder shares to be received by Target shareholders at closing will not vary, regardless of what happens to the price of Bidder's shares in the interval between signing and closing. At the other end of the spectrum, the parties to the transaction may agree that Target shareholders shall receive a certain value at the time of closing, which leads to the use of a *fixed dollar value exchange ratio*. Using this kind of ratio means that at closing, every Target share will be exchanged for Bidder shares with a specified dollar value as of the date of closing. Where this kind of ratio is used, the parties will also have to negotiate and agree as to the *method* to be used to determine the *value* of Bidder's shares.

In practice, the *fixed dollar value exchange ratio* is often quite difficult to draft because the parties may be reluctant to agree to a formula that calls for the value to be determined *solely* by reference to the price of Bidder's stock on the day of closing. One obvious concern with this method of determining the value that Target shares are to receive is that the price of Bidder's stock on that particular date (i.e., the day of closing) is hard to predict and may turn out to be an aberration from the historical price performance of Bidder's stock. Another concern is that this method of determining value (i.e., solely by reference to the price of Bidder's stock on the day of closing) is potentially subject to manipulation. In order to address these concerns regarding use of a fixed dollar value exchange ratio, the parties will typically include a provision in the acquisition agreement that looks to fix the dollar value that Target shares will receive by taking an *average* of the price of Bidder's stock in the trading market over, say, a 10- to 20-day period *prior* to the date of closing on the parties' agreement. Of course, this leads to further negotiations over the number of days to be included in the trading period, and further, how to calculate the average of these trading prices. As a matter of drafting, there are numerous ways for the transaction planner to compute the average trading price of Bidder's stock: that is, whether to volume-weight the average, just take the arithmetic average, or other options.

Use of Fixed Dollar Value Exchange Ratio.   When the parties agree to use a fixed dollar value exchange ratio, or as it is more often called today, a *pure floating exchange ratio*, the impact on Target shareholders is quite different. When a *pure floating exchange ratio* is used, the parties agree at the outset that Target shareholders are to receive a fixed value, say $40 for every Target share outstanding as of the signing of the acquisition agreement—no matter what price Bidder's stock is trading at as of the date of closing. For example, if Bidder's stock is trading at $20 as of closing, then under the terms of this particular floating exchange ratio, Target shareholders would receive *two* shares of Bidder stock for every one share of Target stock. On the other hand, if Bidder's stock is trading at $40 at the time of closing, then Target shareholders will receive only *one* share of Bidder stock in exchange for each of their Target shares. Here, the Target shareholders are assured of receiving a fixed value ($40), no matter how many Bidder shares it takes to provide that value. Hence the name *pure floating exchange ratio.* Moreover, in the case of floating exchange ratios, the price fluctuations in Bidder's stock during the time period between signing and closing on the acquisition agreement are usually of no concern to Target shareholders.

Caps, Floors, and the Use of Collars.   In between these two polar extremes, there are several permutations that result from the use of *collars,* the term of art used to refer to the practice of placing limitations (i.e., an upper and lower limit) on the range within which the price of Bidder's stock may vary for purposes of fixing the terms of the exchange ratio. The collar, which may be used in connection with either the fixed exchange ratio or the fixed dollar value ratio, is, in effect, the floor and the cap on valuation resulting from price fluctuations in the trading of Bidder's stock, and may be expressed in terms of either share price, or alternatively, the number of shares to be issued in the transaction. For example, the terms of the collar may be expressed in our example as a share price of no greater than $40 (known as the *cap*) but no less than $20 (referred to as the *floor*); or alternatively, the collar could be expressed in terms of no more than 1.5 million Bidder shares to be issued, but no fewer than 1.25 million.

When using a collar to fix the terms of the exchange ratio, the parties' agreement will typically provide for a right to terminate the transaction if the price extends beyond the limits imposed by the collar. So, for example, the agreement might provide that in the event that Bidder's stock trading price falls below the lower limit (the floor)—say, $20—then Bidder may, but is not required to, provide additional cash consideration to bring the purchase price up to $20, which is the floor established by the terms of the parties' exchange ratio. In the event that Bidder is unwilling to provide the additional consideration, the acquisition agreement will generally provide that Target has the right to terminate the agreement if Target is unwilling to accept the lower price. This simple example illustrates how the use of a collar to establish a floor and a cap on the terms of the agreed-upon exchange ratio operates to protect the parties against extreme fluctuations in the price of Bidder's stock—both on the upside and the downside.

In addition to the use of collars, the investment banking firm working on any particular deal can engineer further variations on these themes as the economics of any particular business acquisition may demand. And therein lays the creative drafting exercise that routinely faces the M&A lawyer as transaction planner: to reduce to writing, in an understandable fashion, the specific terms of whatever novel exchange ratio the parties may negotiate in the context of a particular acquisition.

QUESTIONS

To be clear on the conceptual differences between these two types of exchange ratios, consider the terms of AT&T's acquisition of DirecTV as set forth in Section 4.1(a) of the parties' Merger Agreement (*see* Appendix B):

1.   What type of exchange ratio did the parties agree to use in this transaction?

2.   Under the terms of the agreed-upon exchange ratio, what risks were the DirecTV shareholders being asked to assume?

3.   Shifting to AT&T's shareholders, what financial risks were they assuming once the parties signed their agreement of merger?

PROBLEM SET NO. 5 — FORWARD AND REVERSE TRIANGULAR MERGERS UNDER DELAWARE LAW AND THE MBCA

1. Forward Triangular Merger — Merger Consideration Consists of 30 Percent of Stock of Bidder Corporation (See Diagram 8 — Appendix A). Following extensive negotiations between representatives of Bidder Co., a NYSE-listed corporation, and Target Co., another NYSE-listed corporation, Bidder forms New Company (NewCo), a wholly-owned subsidiary, for the purpose of acquiring Target. Bidder funds NewCo, the acquisition subsidiary, with the merger consideration in exchange for all of the outstanding voting stock of NewCo. The parties plan to structure the acquisition as a forward triangular (or subsidiary) merger. The terms of the parties' merger agreement call for Target to merge into NewCo, with Target shareholders receiving shares of Bidder common stock comprising 30 percent of the voting power of Bidder's common shares that were outstanding immediately before closing on the proposed merger with Target. Assume further that Bidder has sufficient authorized but unissued common shares to complete the proposed transaction. Since the parties' merger agreement provides for a *forward* triangular merger, once the transaction is consummated, the business of Target Co. will be held in NewCo, to be operated as a wholly-owned subsidiary of Bidder Co.

   a.   Which corporation is to survive? Which corporation is to disappear?
   b.   What action is required by the boards of Bidder, Target, and NewCo:

      (1)   Under Delaware law?
      (2)   Under the MBCA?

   c. Do the shareholders of Bidder, NewCo, and/or Target have the right to vote:

     (1) Under Delaware law?
     (2) Under the rules of the NYSE?
     (3) Under the MBCA?

   d. Assume that an individual shareholder owns 151 shares of Target common stock. Further assume that the parties' merger agreement includes the following provision:

> No fractional shares of Bidder Common Stock shall be issued. Notwithstanding any other provision of this Agreement, each holder of shares of Target Common Stock exchanged pursuant to the Merger who otherwise would have been entitled to receive a fraction of a share of Bidder Common Stock shall receive, in lieu thereof, cash (without interest) in an amount equal to the product of (i) such fractional part of a share of Bidder Common Stock multiplied by (ii) the closing price of Bidder Common Stock on the date of the Effective Time.

     For purposes of this problem, assume that the parties' merger agreement provides that each share of outstanding Target common stock is to be exchanged for 1.4 shares of Bidder common stock, and that the closing price of Bidder's stock on the NYSE as of the date that the merger was consummated ("Effective Time") was $32. How many shares of Bidder common stock will this Target shareholder receive when the merger is consummated?

   e. Do the shareholders of Bidder, NewCo, and/or Target have the right to dissent:

     (1) Under Delaware law?
     (2) Under the MBCA?

   f. What action would be required under either Delaware law or the MBCA if Bidder Co. did not have sufficient authorized but unissued shares to complete the proposed acquisition of Target Co.? (*Hint: See* MBCA §11.07(a)(6); Delaware §§251(c) and (e).)

   g. What is the effect of a *forward* triangular merger? How does this transaction differ from the *direct* merger illustrated in Diagram 1?

   2. Reverse Triangular Merger—Merger Consideration Consists of Cash and 16-18 Percent of Bidder Stock (See Diagram 10—Appendix A). AT&T, a NYSE-listed corporation forms New Company (NewCo), a wholly-owned subsidiary, for the purpose of acquiring DirecTV, a NYSE-listed corporation, in a triangular merger. The parties' merger agreement calls for the transaction to be structured as a reverse triangular merger, with the DirecTV shareholders to receive (in exchange for the cancellation of all of the outstanding shares of DirecTV stock) $95 per share of DirecTV stock, consisting of $28.50 per share of DirecTV stock in cash, together with shares of AT&T's common stock comprising between 16 and 18 percent of the voting power of AT&T's common shares that were outstanding immediately before closing on the proposed transaction with DirecTV. In addition, all of AT&T's stock in NewCo will be converted (by operation of law) into stock of DirecTV when the merger is consummated. So, in the case of a reverse triangular merger, when the dust settles and the transaction is consummated, the business of DirecTV will be operated as a wholly-owned subsidiary of AT&T. In considering the following questions, you will need to refer to Articles I through IV of the AT&T-DirecTV Merger Agreement (*see* Appendix B).

a.   Who are the parties to the merger agreement?
b.   Which company is to disappear, and which is to survive?
c.   What is the effect of a *reverse* triangular merger? How does this deal structure differ from the *forward* triangular merger described above in Problem 1?
d.   How many DirecTV shares are outstanding? (*Hint:* Read Section 5.1(b) of the AT&T-DirecTV merger agreement.)
e.   What is the acquisition consideration? What is (i) the maximum number and (ii) the minimum number of AT&T shares to be issued under the terms of the parties' merger agreement?
f.   How many shares of AT&T stock will the DirecTV shareholders receive for each outstanding share of DirecTV stock, assuming that, at the Effective Time, the Average Parent Stock Price was $35.148 per share?
g.   Assuming that the Average Parent Stock Price was $35.148 per share at the Effective Time, what is the total number of AT&T shares to be issued?
h.   Does AT&T have a sufficient number of authorized but unissued shares to fulfill its obligations under the terms of the parties' merger agreement? (*Hint:* See Section 5.2(b) of the AT&T-DirecTV merger agreement.)
i.   What action would be required under either Delaware law and/or the federal securities laws if AT&T did not have sufficient authorized but unissued shares to complete the proposed acquisition of DirecTV?
j.   What action is required by the boards of AT&T, Inc., DirecTV Corp., and NewCo:

   (1)   Under Delaware law?
   (2)   Under the MBCA?

k.   Do the shareholders of AT&T, Inc., DirecTV Corp., or NewCo have the right to vote:

   (1)   Under Delaware law?
   (2)   Under the rules of the NYSE?
   (3)   Under the MBCA?

l.   Will the merger automatically become effective once the requisite shareholder approvals have been obtained? (*Hint:* Read §1.2 and §1.3 of the AT&T-DirecTV merger agreement and refer to DGCL §251(c) and MBCA §11.06.)

m. In considering Section 4.1 of the AT&T–DirecTV merger agreement in Appendix B, at the Effective Time, what happens to the outstanding shares of:

   (1) DirecTV Corp.?
   (2) NewCo?
   (3) AT&T, Inc.?

n. Assume that an individual shareholder owns 151 shares of DirecTV common stock. How many AT&T shares will this shareholder receive when the merger is consummated? How much cash will this shareholder receive? (*Hint:* Read the provisions of §4.2 of the AT&T-DirecTV Merger Agreement in Appendix B, and further assume that the duly appointed Exchange Agent has been instructed as follows: *Each holder of shares of Company Common Stock who would otherwise be entitled to receive a fractional share of Parent Common Stock shall receive, in lieu thereof, cash (without interest) in an amount equal to the product of (i) such fractional part of a share of Parent Common Stock multiplied by (ii) the Average Parent Stock Price as determined in Section 4.1(a).*) For purposes of this problem, also assume that the Exchange Ratio is fixed at 1.892 shares of AT&T stock per share of DirecTV stock, and that the Average Parent Stock Price at the Effective Time was $35.148.

o. Do the shareholders of AT&T, Inc. and/or DirecTV Corp. have the right to dissent:

   (1) Under Delaware law?
   (2) Under the MBCA?

p. Assume for purposes of this problem only that the merger consideration that was agreed to by the parties resulted in AT&T issuing shares comprising 25 percent of the voting power of AT&T's common shares that were outstanding immediately before closing on the proposed transaction with DirecTV, and there was *no* cash component as part of the purchase price other than payment in cash for any fractional shares. How does this change in the terms of the merger consideration impact your analysis of the *voting rights* of the shareholders of AT&T, DirecTV, and NewCo? In addition, how does this change in the terms of the merger consideration impact your analysis of the availability of *appraisal rights* to the shareholders of AT&T and DirecTV?

3. *Reverse Triangular Merger—Merger Consideration Consists of 4.8 Percent of Bidder's Stock.* Assume that Google, a NYSE-listed company, intends to acquire closely held Nest Labs in a transaction structured as a *reverse* triangular merger. The terms of the parties' merger agreement call for the shareholders of Nest Labs to receive shares of Google's common stock comprising 4.8 percent of the voting power of Google's common shares that were outstanding before the acquisition is completed. Nest Labs has four equal shareholders, consisting of the two founders and two venture capital firms. Assume further that Google has sufficient authorized but unissued shares to complete the proposed transaction and that Google has formed NewCo for the purpose of completing its acquisition of Nest Labs.

a. Who should be made parties to the merger agreement?
b. Which corporation is to survive, and which is to disappear?
c. What is the acquisition consideration?
d. What is the effect of this reverse triangular merger? In other words, when the dust settles and the transaction is consummated, what will happen to the shares of:

(1) Google?
(2) Nest Labs?
(3) NewCo?

e. What action is required by the boards of Google, Nest Labs, and NewCo in order to consummate this acquisition structured as a *reverse* triangular merger:

(1) Under Delaware law?
(2) Under the MBCA?

f. Do the shareholders of Google, Nest Labs, or NewCo have the right to vote:

(1) Under Delaware law?
(2) Under the rules of the NYSE?
(3) Under the MBCA?

g. Do the shareholders of Google or Nest Labs have the right to dissent:

(1) Under Delaware law?
(2) Under the MBCA?

h. Assume that one of the founders does not want to sell his shares of Nest Labs. What advice do you give to this founder as to the options available to him under either the MBCA or Delaware law?

4. Hewlett-Packard's Acquisition of Compaq. On September 3, 2001, Hewlett-Packard Company (HP) announced that it had signed a deal to acquire Compaq Computer Corporation (Compaq) using HP's stock as the acquisition consideration. The parties' agreement described the acquisition as follows: (i) Under the terms of the merger agreement, a wholly-owned subsidiary of HP will merge with and into Compaq, and Compaq will survive the merger as a wholly-owned subsidiary of HP. (ii) As of the signing of the merger agreement, the authorized capital stock of HP consisted of 9,600,000,000 common shares, and there were 1,939,159,231 shares of HP common stock issued and outstanding. (iii) The exchange ratio negotiated by the parties provided that Compaq shareholders would receive 0.6325 share of HP common stock for each Compaq share outstanding. Compaq had 1.8 billion shares outstanding as of the signing of the merger agreement.

a. What type of merger is this? Which company will survive? Which company will disappear?

    b. Do the shareholders of Compaq have the right to vote:

        (1) Under Delaware law?
        (2) Under the MBCA?
        (3) Under the rules of the NYSE?

    c. Do the shareholders of Hewlett-Packard have the right to vote:

        (1) Under Delaware law?
        (2) Under the MBCA?
        (3) Under the rules of the NYSE?

    d. Assume that Hewlett-Packard's management reported the following results with respect to the vote of HP's shareholders on the transaction with Compaq: (i) there were 838,401,376 shares of HP common stock voted for the proposed transaction; (ii) there were 793,094,105 shares voted against the proposed transaction; and (iii) there were 13,950,651 HP common shares that abstained from voting. Did the proposed transaction receive shareholder approval:

        (1) Under Delaware law?
        (2) Under the rules of the NYSE?
        (3) Under the MBCA?

    e. Assume that, as part of the parties' acquisition agreement, Hewlett-Packard represented that "all shares of capital stock of HP which may be issued as contemplated or permitted by this agreement will be, when issued, duly authorized." Does Hewlett-Packard have sufficient authorized and unissued shares to complete the transaction? If not, what must be done in order for Hewlett-Packard to fulfill the commitment it made as part of the parties' agreement:

        (1) Under Delaware law? (*Hint:* You may want to refer to Delaware §242.)
        (2) Under the MBCA? (*Hint:* You may want to refer to MBCA §10.03.)

    f. If HP had been required to amend its certificate of incorporation and assuming that the vote count/tabulation is the same as described above in subpart (d), would the vote be sufficient under Delaware law to approve the proposed amendment to HP's certificate of incorporation?

3. A Recent MBCA Innovation: The Binding Share Exchange

The *binding share exchange,* an innovation of the MBCA that has been adopted in a number of states, is another method that can be used to accomplish essentially the same result as a *reverse triangular merger.* The binding share exchange is authorized under the terms of MBCA §11.03, which has no counterpart under Delaware law. Using this method of corporate combination, Bidder Co. obtains ownership of *all* of Target Co.'s shares in exchange for either cash or shares (or other securities) of Bidder. Like the merger, the plan (or agreement) of share exchange *must* be approved in accordance with the terms of MBCA §11.04, including the requisite shareholder vote. The mechanics of (and the result obtained under) the share exchange procedure are reflected in the following diagram and are best understood by analyzing the problems that follow.

DIAGRAM — SHARE EXCHANGE

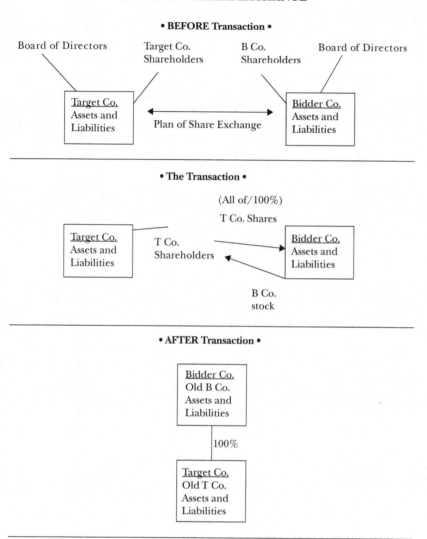

• BEFORE Transaction •

Board of Directors Target Co. Shareholders B Co. Shareholders Board of Directors

Target Co. Assets and Liabilities ⟷ Plan of Share Exchange Bidder Co. Assets and Liabilities

• The Transaction •

(All of/100%)

T Co. Shares

Target Co. Assets and Liabilities   T Co. Shareholders → Bidder Co. Assets and Liabilities

B Co. stock

• AFTER Transaction •

Bidder Co. Old B Co. Assets and Liabilities

100%

Target Co. Old T Co. Assets and Liabilities

PROBLEM SET NO. 6 — MBCA §11.03: THE BINDING (OR COMPULSORY) SHARE EXCHANGE

1. Assume that AT&T, Inc., a NYSE-listed company organized under the MBCA, has agreed to acquire DirecTV, Inc., another NYSE-listed company that is also incorporated under the MBCA, in a compulsory share exchange authorized by MBCA §11.03. The plan of share exchange provides that DirecTV shareholders are to receive shares of AT&T's common stock comprising 23 percent of the voting power of AT&T's common stock that is outstanding immediately before the acquisition is completed. Assume further that AT&T has sufficient authorized but unissued common shares to complete the proposed transaction.

    a. What action is required by the boards of AT&T and DirecTV?

    b. Do the shareholders of either AT&T or DirecTV have the right to vote?

    c. Do the shareholders of either AT&T or DirecTV have the right to dissent?

    d. How does this analysis vary if the parties' plan of share exchange provides that the consideration consists of shares of AT&T common stock comprising only 15 percent of the voting power of AT&T's common stock that is outstanding immediately before the acquisition is consummated?

    e. How does this method of acquisition differ from the *reverse triangular merger* illustrated in Diagram 10 in Appendix A? How does this method of acquisition differ from the *stock exchange offer* illustrated in Diagram 7 in Appendix A? How does this method of acquisition differ from the *direct merger* illustrated in Diagram 1 in Appendix A?

2. Assume that Nest Labs is going to be acquired by Google in a compulsory (or binding) share exchange of the type authorized by MBCA §11.03. Assume that each company has only one class of voting common stock outstanding, and that both companies are incorporated under the provisions of the MBCA. The plan of share exchange calls for the shareholders of Nest Labs to receive $3.2 billion in cash in exchange for all the outstanding shares of Nest Labs common stock.

    a. What action is required by the boards of Nest Labs and Google?

    b. Do the shareholders of either Nest Labs or Google have the right to vote?

    c. Do the shareholders of either Nest Labs or Google have the right to dissent?

G. *De Facto Merger Doctrine: Form vs. Substance Debate*

As we have seen in analyzing the mechanics of triangular mergers, the shareholders of Bidder Co. are denied voting rights under the merger statutes of most states since Bidder is not a party to the transaction. Likewise, there is generally no right of appraisal available to those Bidder shareholders who object to the transaction. The transaction planner's decision to use a three-party merger structure may operate to deny Bidder shareholders protections granted by law in cases where the acquisition is structured as a direct merger.

For similar reasons, the transaction planner may decide to structure an acquisition as a sale of assets rather than a direct merger. If the transaction involves a sale of assets, then Bidder Co., as the buyer of all of Target Co.'s assets, generally does not have to obtain shareholder approval in order to validly consummate the purchase, nor will the right of appraisal be available to those Bidder shareholders who object to the proposed transaction. Generally speaking, the purchase of all of Target's assets does not involve a fundamental change for Bidder, and therefore no shareholder approval is required.

On occasion, however, shareholders may bring an action, claiming that a proposed acquisition has the same substantive result as a merger, even though the acquisition is structured in some other form (such as an asset sale). In these cases, the complaining shareholder will usually invoke the court's equity jurisdiction, asking the court to enjoin a proposed acquisition unless and until the statutory requirements for merger transactions are satisfied, including the requirement of shareholder approval and the satisfaction of any available appraisal rights. By invoking this equitable remedy, the complaining shareholder is asking the court to look through the form of the transaction and to recognize the substance of the transaction as a merger. These cases are known as *de facto mergers*, and this doctrine rests on a principle of equivalency, which simply says that transactions that have the same substantive effect ought to be entitled to the same legal safeguards. In other words, the courts should look through the form of the transaction to ensure that like transactions are treated alike. Of course, there is the threshold question of how the court should go about deciding whether a particular transaction is — in substance — a merger. The cases that follow illustrate the wide disagreement as to the viability of the de facto merger doctrine. Delaware courts, in particular, refuse to recognize the doctrine.

1.   What Is the De Facto Merger Doctrine?

Applestein v. United Board & Carton Corporation
60 N.J. Super. 333, 159 A.2d 146 (Ch. Div. 1960)
Aff'd 33 N.J. 72, 161 A.2d 474 (1960) (per curiam)

. . . KILKENNY, J.S.C.

. . . [The] issue is whether the agreement of July 7, 1959 among United Board and Carton Corporation, hereinafter referred to as [United], Interstate Container Corporation, [Interstate], and Saul L. Epstein, [Epstein], and the transaction set forth in the proxy solicitation statement, [proxy statement], dated September 22, 1959, amount to a merger, entitling dissenting stockholders of United to an appraisal of their stock, and is therefore invalid. . . .

United is [a] New Jersey [corporation primarily engaged] in the manufacture and sale of paper-board, folding boxes, corrugated containers and laminated board, . . . Its present authorized capital stock consists of 400,000 shares, of which 240,000 have already been issued and are held by a great number of stockholders, no one of whom holds in excess of 10% of the outstanding shares. There are 160,000 shares not yet issued. The United stock is publicly held, there being 1,086 shareholders of record as of September 22, 1959, and the stock is traded on the New York Stock Exchange. The book value of each share of stock, as indicated by the proxy statement, is approximately $31.97. The consolidated balance sheet of United and its wholly owned subsidiaries, as of May 31, 1958, shows total assets of $10,121,233, and total liabilities of $2,561,724, and a net total capital of $7,559,509. Its business is managed by the usual staff of officers and a board of directors consisting of seven directors.

Interstate [is a] New York [corporation that] owns several operating subsidiaries . . . engaged primarily in the manufacture and sale of corrugated shipping containers, . . . Interstate has issued and outstanding 1,250 shares, all of which are owned and controlled by a single stockholder, Epstein, . . . The consolidated balance sheet of Interstate and its subsidiaries, as of October 31, 1958, shows that its total assets are $7,956,424, and its total liabilities are $6,318,371, leaving a net total capital of $1,638,053. . . .

United entered into a written agreement with Interstate and Epstein on July 7, 1959. In its language, it is not designated or referred to as a merger agreement, *eo nomine*. In fact, the word "merger" nowhere appears in that agreement. On the contrary, the agreement recites that it is an "exchange of Interstate stock for United Stock." Epstein agrees to assign and deliver to United his 1,250 shares of the common stock of Interstate solely in exchange for 160,000 as yet unissued shares of voting common stock (par value $10) of United. Thus, by this so-called "exchange of stock" United would wholly own Interstate and its subsidiaries, and Epstein would thereupon own a 40% stock interest in United. Dollar-wise, on the basis of the book values of the two corporations hereinabove set forth, a combination of the assets and liabilities of United and Interstate would result in a net total capital of approximately $9,200,000, as against which there would be outstanding 400,000 shares, thereby reducing the present book value of each United share from about $31.97 to about $23, a shrinkage of about 28%. Epstein would contribute, book value-wise, the net total capital of Interstate in the amount of $1,638,053, for which he would receive a 40% interest in $9,200,000, the net total combined capital of United and Interstate, or about $3,680,000. The court is not basing its present decision upon the additional charge made by dissenting stockholders of United that the proposed agreement is basically unfair and inequitable. That is one of the reserved issues. The court recognizes that book values and real values are not necessarily the same thing, and, therefore, apparent inequities appearing from a comparison of the book values might be explained and justified.

The agreement of July 7, 1959 does not contemplate the continued future operation of Interstate, as a subsidiary corporation of United. Rather, it provides that United will take over all the outstanding stock of Interstate, that all of Interstate's "assets and liabilities will be recorded on the books of the Company (United)," and that Interstate will be dissolved. At the time of closing, Epstein has agreed to deliver the resignations of the officers and directors of Interstate and of its subsidiary corporations, so that, in effect, Interstate would have no officers, directors, or stockholders, other than United's. The agreement further stipulates that the by-laws of United shall be amended to increase the number of directors from 7 to 11. It provides for the filling of the additional directorships, it pre-ordains who will be the officers and new directors of United in the combined enterprise, and even governs the salaries to be paid. Epstein would become the president and a director of United and, admittedly, would be in "effective control" of United. As stated in the proxy statement, "The transaction will be accounted for as a 'pooling of interests' of the two corporations."

The stipulation of the parties removed from the court's present consideration not only the issue of the basic equity or fairness of the agreement, but also the legal effect and validity of the pre-determination of directorships, officers, salaries, and other similar terms of the bargain between the parties. The fairness of a merger agreement generally presents a question of a factual nature, ordinarily reserved for final hearing. If the alleged injustice of the project were the sole objection, I would be hesitant to substitute *preliminarily* my judgment for that of a transcendent majority of the stockholders.

In notifying its stockholders of a meeting to be held on October 15, 1959, in its proxy statement United advised the stockholders that "the proposal to approve the issuance of the common stock of the company is being submitted to the vote of the stockholders solely because of the requirements of the New York Stock Exchange; and accordingly stockholders who vote against or who do not vote in favor of the proposal will not [in the opinion of company's counsel] . . . be entitled to any [appraisal] rights . . ." They were also advised that adoption of the proposal would require the affirmative vote of the holders of only a *majority* of the shares present at the meeting in person or by proxy, provided [that the required quorum consisting of] a majority of all shares outstanding and entitled to vote thereon was present at the meeting.

The attorneys for the respective parties herein have conceded in the record that the proposed corporate action would be invalid, if this court determines that it would constitute a merger of United and Interstate, entitling the dissenting stockholders of United to an appraisal of their stock. The notice of the stockholders' meeting and the proxy statement did not indicate that the purpose of the meeting was to effect a *merger,* and failed to give notice to the shareholders of their right to dissent to the plan of merger, if it were one, and claim their appraisal rights under the statute, as inferentially required by R.S. 14:12-3, N.J.S.A. Obviously, the notice of the meeting and proxy statement stressed the contrary, by labeling the proposed corporate action "an exchange of Interstate stock for United stock" rather than a merger, by its emphasis upon the need for a *majority vote* only, instead of the required two-thirds vote for a merger under the statute, and by the express declaration that dissenting stockholders would not be entitled to any rights of appraisal of their stock. . . .

Despite the contrary representations by United to its stockholders in its proxy statement, United's present position is that the proposed corporate action in acquiring and absorbing Interstate is a merger. This is evidenced by its answer to the cross-claim of Interstate and Epstein against it for specific performance of the agreement of July 7, 1959. At the hearing of the motions United's attorney stated in the record that United now contended, in addition to its other asserted defenses, that the fulfillment of the agreement would constitute a merger. In fairness to United's attorney herein, it should be noted that this coincided with an earlier letter opinion furnished privately by him to United's officers substantially to the same effect, which letter he made part of the record, in his affidavit, when a question of good faith was raised.

Needless to say, if United, a New Jersey corporation, had followed that early advice given by its present New Jersey counsel herein and had followed the statutory procedure for corporate mergers, this litigation would have been avoided. Instead, it chose the opposite opinion of New York counsel that the plan would not be a merger, and so indicated to its stockholders in the proxy statement. It now finds itself ready and willing to agree with the plaintiff stockholders that the plan would be a merger of United and Interstate, and relies thereon, *inter alia,* in resisting the cross-claim for specific performance. . . .

The legal contention of Epstein and Interstate, and the four intervening United stockholders . . . is that the transaction constitutes a valid purchase by United of Epstein's shares in Interstate, and thereby the property of Interstate, pursuant to R.S. 14.3-9, N.J.S.A., to be followed by a merger of United, as the parent corporation, with its wholly-owned corporation, Interstate, pursuant to N.J.S.A. 14:12-10. Thus, it is claimed that United's dissenting stockholders have no appraisal rights under these two sections of the statutes, and especially since N.J.S.A. 14:12-10 expressly provides that N.J.S.A. 14:12-6 and R.S. 14:12-7, N.J.S.A., which grant appraisal rights in the usual merger, under R.S. 14:12-1, N.J.S.A., shall not apply to a merger under N.J.S.A. 14:12-10.

When a corporation *sells or exchanges* all, or substantially all of its property and assets, including its good will, as permitted by R.S. 14:3-5, N.J.S.A., the stockholders of the *selling* corporation must approve by a two-thirds vote, and objecting stockholders of the *selling* corporation are given appraisal rights, as provided in N.J.S.A. 14:12-6 in the case of a merger.

But when a corporation *buys* real or personal property, or the stock of another corporation, as permitted under R.S. 14:3-9, N.J.S.A., stockholder approval is not required, and objecting shareholders of the *purchasing* corporation are given no appraisal rights in such a case. Further, the *buying* corporation may pay for such property or stock acquired by it in cash or in the capital stock of the purchasing corporation.

It is true that our present corporation law, R.S. 14:3-5, N.J.S.A., sanctions a corporate *sale* of all or substantially all of the property and assets of the selling corporation, with stockholder approval and appraisal rights in favor of objecting shareholders of the selling corporation. Likewise, our statute, R.S. 14:3-9, N.J.S.A., allows a corporate *purchase* of the property and stock of another corporation to be paid for in cash or the stock of the purchasing corporation. There is no dispute as to the existence of these present statutory devices for the sale and acquisition of corporate property and shares of stock. Hence, if the purchase by United of Interstate and its shares represented a *bona fide* utilization of the corporate power conferred by R.S. 14:3-9, N.J.S.A., and if the intended dissolution of Interstate represented a *bona fide* merger of a parent corporation with a wholly-owned corporation under N.J.S.A. 14:12-10 without more, United's dissenting shareholders would then have no right to an appraisal of their shares.

But when an authorized device, such as that provided for in a sale of [sic] purchase of assets, or a dissolution, is used to bring about a virtual consolidation or merger, minority stockholders may object on the ground that a direct method has been authorized for such a purpose. If consolidation or merger is permitted through a pretended sale of assets or dissolution, minority stockholders may be frozen out of their legal rights of appraisal. If the court is obliged to consider only the device employed, or the mere form of the transaction, a corporate merger in fact can be achieved without any compliance with the statutory requirements for a valid merger, and without any regard for the statutory rights of dissenting shareholders. It would be strange if the powers conferred by our Legislature upon corporations under R.S. 14:3-9, N.J.S.A. for a purchase of the property and shares of another corporation and, under N.J.S.A. 14:12-10, for the merger of a parent corporation with a wholly-owned corporation can effect a corporate merger *de facto*, with all the characteristics and consequences of a merger, without any of the legislative safeguards and rights afforded to a dissenting shareholder in a *de jure* merger under R.S. 14:12-1 et seq., N.J.S.A. If that were so, we obtain the anomalous result of one part of the corporation law rendering nugatory another part of the same law in accomplishing the same result.

[T]he proposed corporate action is more than an "exchange of Interstate stock for United stock," as it is labeled in the agreement of July 7, 1959, and more than a purchase by United of Epstein's Interstate stock and the corporate properties of Interstate, . . . [Indeed,] every factor present in a corporate merger is found in this corporate plan, except, perhaps, a formal designation of the transaction as a "merger." There is proposed: (1) a transfer of all the shares and all the assets of Interstate to United; (2) an assumption by United of Interstate's liabilities; (3) a "pooling of interests" of the two corporations; (4) the absorption of Interstate by United, and the dissolution of Interstate; (5) a joinder of officers and directors from both corporations on an enlarged board of directors; (6) the present executive and operating personnel of Interstate will be retained in the employ of United; and (7) the shareholders of the absorbed corporation, Interstate, as represented by the sole stockholder, Epstein, will surrender his 1,250 shares in Interstate for 160,000 newly issued shares in United, the amalgamated enterprise.

If, in truth and in substance the proposed plan in this case is a "merger," why should the interested parties not frankly and honestly recognize it as such and pursue the statutory procedure under R.S. 14:12-1 et seq., N.J.S.A. for validating the proposal? It is a fundamental maxim of equity that "Equity looks to the substance rather than the form." . . . The courts of equity in New Jersey, and elsewhere, have never hesitated to look behind the form of a particular corporate transaction and find that it constituted a corporate merger, if in fact and in substance it was a merger, regardless of its deceptive outward appearance. . . .

The courts of this State and of other jurisdictions have never hesitated in the past in finding that a particular corporate combination was in fact and in legal effect a merger or a consolidation, even though the transaction might have been otherwise labeled by the parties. This is not a new legal philosophy, but is grounded upon the common sense observation that judges, as well as laymen, have the right, and often the duty, to call a spade a spade, and to follow the long established equitable maxim of looking to the substance rather than the form, whenever justice requires. . . .

Conclusion

This court holds that the corporate combination of United and Interstate, contemplated by their executory contract of July 7, 1959, and explained in United's proxy solicitation statement of September 22, 1959, would be a practical or *de facto* merger, in substance and in legal effect, within the protective purview of N.J.S.A. 14:12-7. Accordingly, the shareholders of United are and were entitled to be notified and advised of their statutory rights of dissent and appraisal. The failure of the corporate officers of United to take these steps and to obtain stockholder approval of the agreement by the statutory two-thirds vote under R.S. 14:12-3, N.J.S.A. at a properly convened meeting of the stockholders would render the proposed corporate action invalid.

Therefore, there will be partial summary judgment on the single, limited issue submitted in accordance with this holding.

NOTES

1. Successor Liability and the De Facto Merger Doctrine. The de facto merger doctrine also arises in another, quite different context. As we'll see in the materials on successor liability in Chapter 3, creditors of Target Co. will often claim that Target's sale of substantially all of its assets is, in substance, a merger. By claiming that the transaction between Bidder and Target is in substance a merger, the creditor of Target is seeking to invoke the rule of successor liability that is part of the law of mergers. If the creditor is successful in showing that the transaction constitutes a de facto merger, then the Target creditor generally will be able to collect from Bidder as the successor in interest to Target. As we will see in Chapter 3, the public policy considerations involved in these cases are very different than the considerations that dominated the court's reasoning in *Applestein*, and accordingly, the courts will often be persuaded to take a different view of the de facto merger doctrine in this context.

2. Attorney Professional Responsibility Rules Under the Sarbanes-Oxley Act. In July 2002, Congress passed the Sarbanes-Oxley Act (more commonly referred to as SOX), enacting a major package of legislative reforms that addressed, among other things, the structure and function of audit committees of 1934 Act reporting companies, the regulation of the accounting profession, and the accountability of CEOs and CFOs. We will examine various aspects of SOX in the remaining chapters as they are relevant to M&A transactions. In connection with the facts of the *Applestein* case, however, it is worth mentioning that, as part of SOX, Congress directed the SEC to adopt regulations intended to strengthen the professional obligations of those attorneys who represent publicly traded companies. The legislative history of SOX makes clear that Congress intended to impose on lawyers some measure of responsibility to take steps in order to prevent financial scandals (such as those that engulfed Enron and Tyco in the early years of the twenty-first century) from occurring in the future.

Pursuant to this legislative mandate, the SEC adopted the attorney professional responsibility rules in January 2003; *see* SEC Release No. 33-8185, Implementation of Standards of Professional Conduct for Attorneys (Jan. 29, 2003). These rules became effective in August 2003; *see* 17 C.F.R. Part 205. Briefly summarized, the key principle to be implemented by the detailed, and somewhat complex, provisions of the SEC's new professional responsibility rules is widely referred to as the "up-the-ladder" rule. Under the SEC's new rules, if a lawyer for a publicly traded company becomes aware of "evidence of a material violation" of the federal securities laws (or a material violation of state law, including evidence of a material breach of fiduciary duty), the lawyer *must* disclose the matter to the company's chief legal officer (CLO) or to the CLO and the company's CEO.* The CLO then *must* conduct an investigation into the matter forming the basis for the "evidence of a material violation" of the federal securities laws. If the attorney who originally reported the violation fails to obtain an appropriate response, then he or she *must* go up the chain—taking the matter all the way "up the ladder" to the company's board of directors, if necessary. The more controversial aspect of the SEC rules as originally proposed—known as the "noisy withdrawal rule"—was not adopted as part of the SEC's newly enacted professional responsibility rules; instead, this rule was reproposed by the SEC and put out for further comment. *See* SEC Release No. 33-8186 (Proposed Rule, Feb. 6, 2003). As of this writing (Fall 2020), no final action has been taken on the proposed "noisy withdrawal rule."

As adopted, the SEC's new rule is clearly designed to implement the congressional mandate of SOX, which had its impetus in the widely held sentiment that corporate advisors, including company counsel, who become aware of misconduct within the corporation should be held accountable. Only time will tell whether these congressional reform measures will evoke the desired result of rehabilitating the corporate governance practices of public companies and restoring investor confidence in our markets. However, it should come as no surprise that Congress reacted to the spate of corporate financial scandals that ushered in the twenty-first century (such as those that engulfed Enron and Tyco) by legislating mandates that hold company managers and their legal advisors responsible for their conduct.

3. California Law. California, in effect, has legislated into place the de facto merger doctrine. The mechanics of the California statute are analyzed in more detail later in this chapter. Suffice it to say, at this point, that California accepts the fundamental premise of the de facto merger doctrine as reflected in the *Applestein* opinion, which says that like transactions should be treated alike.

QUESTIONS

1. What is the public policy premise for the de facto merger doctrine? Where did the court get the authority to decide the case in the way it did?

2. What facts must be present in order to invoke the de facto merger doctrine?

3. What is the professional responsibility of the lawyers advising the parties as to the structure of the acquisition in *Applestein*? What would be the obligation of the transactional lawyers working on this deal under the professional

---

* [By the author: As another alternative, the lawyer may refer the matter to a Qualified Legal Compliance Committee (QLCC). If the lawyer opts to refer the matter to a QLCC, the obligations under the SEC's new rules are very different.]

responsibility rules that were adopted by the SEC pursuant to the congressional mandate of SOX?

4. Even if the court had refused to recognize the de facto merger doctrine in the *Applestein* case, the court hints that plaintiff's lawsuit might still proceed on the basis of other causes of action challenging the validity of the transaction at issue in that case. What other claims does the *Applestein* court hint at, but which it indicates are not presented for decision at this time?

5. As a matter of public policy, does the de facto merger doctrine make sense?

6. As a matter of modern corporate governance, who should decide whether United should issue 40 percent of its stock to acquire the business of Interstate Corp.?

2.   De Facto Merger Doctrine Under Delaware Law

The Delaware courts have flatly rejected the de facto merger doctrine. The basis for this rejection is grounded in the *doctrine of independent legal significance*, the origins of which date back to *Federal United Corp. v. Havender*, 11 A.2d 331 (Del. 1940), a Depression-era case decided by the Delaware Supreme Court. As explained by leading Delaware corporate law practitioners:

> The doctrine of independent legal significance ("ILS") is one of the "bedrock" doctrines of Delaware corporate law. The Delaware Supreme Court has defined ILS as providing that "action taken under one section of that law is legally independent, and its validity is not dependent upon, nor to be tested by the requirements of other unrelated sections under which the same final result might be attained by different means."[2] That is, so long as a transaction is effected in compliance with the requirements of one section of the Delaware General Corporation Law ("DGCL"), Delaware courts will not invalidate it for failing to comply with the requirements of a different section of the DGCL—even if the substance of the transaction is such that it could have been structured under the other section. . . .
>
> [The doctrine of independent legal significance] provides a benefit to Delaware corporations and their counsel by allowing certainty. If corporate lawyers structure a transaction in a certain way, in a way compliant with one section of the DGCL, they can have comfort that the courts will not invalidate the transaction for its failure to comply with a different section.[5]

C. Stephen Bigler & Blake Rohrbacher, *Form or Substance? The Past Present and Future of the Doctrine of Independent Legal Significance*, 63 Bus. Law. 1, 1-2 (Nov.

---

2. *Orzeck v. Englehart*, 195 A.2d 375, 378 (Del. 1963).
5. *See* 1 R. Franklin Balotti & Jesse A. Finkelstein, The Delaware Law of Corporations and Business Organizations §9.4, at 9-9 (3d ed. 2007) ("The doctrine [of independent legal significance] has become a keystone of Delaware corporate law and is continually relied upon by practitioners to assure that transactions can be structured under one section of the General Corporation Law without having to comply with other sections which could lead to the same result.").

2007). The basis for the Delaware courts' development of the doctrine of independent legal significance was further explained by the Court of Chancery as follows:

> . . . As a general matter, those who must shape their conduct to conform to the dictates of statutory law should be able to satisfy such requirements by satisfying the literal demands of the law rather than being required to guess about the nature and extent of some broader or different restriction at the risk of an *ex post facto* determination of error. The utility of a literal approach to statutory construction is particularly apparent in the interpretation of the requirements of our corporation law—where both the statute itself and most transactions governed by it are carefully planned and result from a thoughtful and highly rational process.
>
> Thus, Delaware courts, when called upon to construe the technical and carefully drafted provisions of our statutory corporation law, do so with a sensitivity to the importance of the predictability of that law. That sensitivity causes our law, in that setting, to reflect an enhanced respect for the literal statutory language.
>
> Thus, [the doctrine of independent legal significance] allows Delaware corporations and their counsel to plan transactions secure in the advance knowledge of the legal requirements for, and legal consequences of, those transactions.

Speiser v. Baker, 525 A.2d 1001, 1008 (Del. Ch.), *appeal refused*, 525 A.2d 582 (Del. 1987) (unpublished table decision).

Hariton v. Arco Electronics, Inc.
188 A.2d 123 (Del. 1963)

. . . SOUTHERLAND, Chief Justice.

This case involves a sale of assets under §271 of the corporation law, 8 Del. C. It presents for decision the question presented, but not decided, in Heilbrunn v. Sun Chemical Corporation, Del., 150 A.2d 755. It may be stated as follows:

> A sale of assets is effected under §271 in consideration of shares of stock of the purchasing corporation. The agreement of sale embodies also a plan to dissolve the selling corporation and distribute the shares so received to the stockholders of the seller, so as to accomplish the same result as would be accomplished by a merger of the seller into the purchaser. Is the sale legal?

The facts are these:

The defendant Arco [Electronics, Inc. (Arco)] and Loral Electronics Corporation [(Loral)], a New York corporation, are both engaged, in somewhat different forms, in the electronic equipment business. In the summer of 1961 they negotiated for an amalgamation of the companies. As of October 27, 1961, they entered into a "Reorganization Agreement and Plan." The provisions of this Plan pertinent here are in substance as follows:

1.   Arco agrees to sell all its assets to Loral in consideration (inter alia) of the issuance to it of 283,000 shares of Loral.

2.   Arco agrees to call a stockholders meeting for the purpose of approving the Plan and the voluntary dissolution.
3.   Arco agrees to distribute to its stockholders all the Loral shares received by it as a part of the complete liquidation of Arco.

At the Arco meeting all the stockholders voting (about 80%) approved the Plan. It was thereafter consummated.

Plaintiff, a stockholder who did not vote at the meeting, sued to enjoin the consummation of the Plan on the grounds (1) that it was illegal, and (2) that it was unfair. The second ground was abandoned. Affidavits and documentary evidence were filed, and defendant moved for summary judgment and dismissal of the complaint. The Vice Chancellor granted the motion and plaintiff appeals.

The question before us we have stated above. Plaintiff's argument that the sale is illegal runs as follows:

> The several steps taken here accomplish the same result as a merger of Arco into Loral. In a "true" sale of assets, the stockholder of the seller retains the right to elect whether the selling company shall continue as a holding company. Moreover, the stockholder of the selling company is forced to accept an investment in a new enterprise without the right of appraisal granted under the merger statute. §271 cannot therefore be legally combined with a dissolution proceeding under §275 and a consequent distribution of the purchaser's stock. Such a proceeding is a misuse of the power granted under §271, and a *de facto* merger results.

The foregoing is a brief summary of plaintiff's contention.

Plaintiff's contention that this sale has achieved the same result as a merger is plainly correct. The same contention was made to us in Heilbrunn v. Sun Chemical Corporation, Del., 150 A.2d 755. Accepting it as correct, we noted that this result is made possible by the overlapping scope of the merger statute and section 271 . . . [In our opinion in *Heilbrunn*, we noted] the increased use, in connection with corporate reorganization plans, of §271 instead of the merger statute. Further, we observed that no Delaware case has held such procedure to be improper, and that two cases appear to assume its legality. [See] Finch v. Warrior Cement Corporation, 16 Del. Ch. 44, 141 A. 54, and Argenbright v. Phoenix Finance Co., 21 Del. Ch. 288, 187 A. 124. But we were not required in the *Heilbrunn* case to decide the point.

We now hold that the reorganization here accomplished through §271 and a mandatory plan of dissolution and distribution is legal. This is so because the sale-of-assets statute and the merger statute are independent of each other. They are, so to speak, of equal dignity, and the framers of a reorganization plan may resort to either type of corporate mechanics to achieve the desired end. This is not an anomalous result in our corporation law. As the Vice Chancellor pointed out, the elimination of accrued dividends, though forbidden under a charter amendment (Keller v. Wilson & Co., 21 Del. Ch. 391, 190 A. 115) may be accomplished by a merger. Federal United Corporation v. Havender, 24 Del. Ch. 318, 11 A.2d 331. . . .

Plaintiff concedes, as we read his brief, that if the several steps taken in this case had been taken separately they would have been legal. That is, he concedes that a sale of assets, followed by a separate proceeding to dissolve and distribute, would be legal, even though the same result would follow. This concession exposes the weakness of his contention. To attempt to make any such distinction between sales under §271 would be to create uncertainty in the law and invite litigation.

We are in accord with the Vice Chancellor's ruling, and the judgment below is affirmed.

QUESTIONS

1. How is the proposed business combination between Arco Electronics, Inc. and Loral Electronics Corp. to be structured? What diagram in Appendix A does this proposed transaction between Arco and Loral look like? What is the acquisition consideration?

2. What corporate formalities must be satisfied in order for this acquisition to be validly consummated under Delaware law?

3. How did the Delaware court dispose of plaintiff's claim?

4. How would the transaction at issue in *Hariton* be treated under the terms of the modern MBCA?

NOTES

1.   Before deciding *Hariton,* the Delaware Supreme Court had addressed the applicability of the de facto merger doctrine in the context of asset sales in the well-known case *Heilbrunn v. Sun Chemical Corp.,* 150 A.2d 755 (Del. 1959). The plaintiffs in that case were shareholders of Sun Chemical Corp. and were upset with the terms of the asset purchase agreement that Sun had entered into with Ansbacher-Siegle Corp. This agreement provided, in effect, that Sun Chemical would acquire Ansbacher's assets and assume all of its liabilities in exchange for 225,000 shares of Sun Chemical common stock. Although the court recognized the "overlapping scope of the merger statute and the statute authorizing the sale of all the corporate assets," *Id.* at 757, it rejected the de facto merger doctrine and did not grant the disgruntled plaintiffs appraisal rights. Accordingly, the only source of relief available to the plaintiffs was under fiduciary duty law. How do the facts of *Heilbrunn* differ from those presented in the principal case?

2.   Unlike Delaware law, California has accepted the principle of equivalency that led the common law courts to develop the de facto merger doctrine in the first place. In fact, California has codified the substance of the de facto merger doctrine. In other words, California's statute is predicated on the basic premise that the legal safeguards granted by statute to shareholders of a constituent corporation in the context of a direct merger should be extended to any transaction that has the same effect as a merger. For reasons that are described in more detail later in this chapter, these legal safeguards cannot be avoided by structuring the transaction either as a sale of assets or as a triangular merger.

The operation of California's statute is described at length later in this chapter, along with a more detailed examination of the public policy premise that underlies California's approach.

3.   The Modern Importance of Clear Default Rules

Pasternak v. Glazer
Civil Action No. 15026, 1996 WL 549960 (Del. Ch. Sept. 24, 1996)

. . . JACOBS, Vice Chancellor

On May 31, 1996, the plaintiffs commenced this action challenging a proposed merger (the "Merger") between Zapata Corporation ("Zapata") and Houlihan's Restaurant Group, Inc. ("Houlihan's"). On July 11, 1996, the plaintiffs amended their complaint to allege that the proposed merger is invalid because the June 4, 1996 Agreement and Plan of Merger (the "Merger Agreement") requires approval by only a simple majority of Zapata's shareholders, whereas Article SEVENTH of Zapata's Restated Certificate of Incorporation (the "Supermajority Provision") requires approval by 80% of Zapata's shareholders.

The plaintiffs moved to enjoin the proposed Merger, and a final hearing on their injunction application was held on September 6, 1996. For the reasons next discussed, the application to enjoin the proposed Merger will be granted.

I. FACTS

A.   THE MERGER AGREEMENT

The defendant, Zapata, is a Delaware corporation. Defendant Malcolm Glazer ("Glazer") is the Chairman of Zapata's board of directors, and owns or beneficially controls approximately 35% of Zapata's stock. Glazer also owns or controls 73.3% of the outstanding shares of Houlihan's.

On June 4, 1996, Zapata, Houlihan's and Zapata Acquisition Corp., a wholly owned subsidiary of Zapata specially created to effect the Merger ("Zapata Sub"), entered into the Merger Agreement. Under that Agreement, Houlihan's will merge with and into Zapata Sub, and Houlihan's stockholders will receive shares of Zapata in exchange for their Houlihan's stock.

The Merger Agreement provides that only the approval of a simple majority of Zapata's outstanding shares is required to approve the Merger:

> Section 4.14. Vote Required. The affirmative vote of the holders of a majority of the outstanding shares of [Zapata] Common Stock and Preference Stock, voting together as a class, on the issuance of the shares of [Zapata] Common Stock in the Merger, as required by the NYSE, is the only vote of the holders of any class or series of [Zapata's] capital stock necessary to approve the Merger and the transactions contemplated thereby.

Pl. Cert. Ex. B, at A-23.

The shareholders meeting to vote on the proposed merger was originally scheduled for August 22, 1996, but it has been postponed pending the outcome of this litigation.

B. ARTICLE SEVENTH OF ZAPATA'S RESTATED CERTIFICATE

The charter provision critical to this motion is Article SEVENTH, Subsection (A)(i) of Zapata's Restated Certificate of Incorporation. Article SEVENTH, which was adopted in 1971, states in relevant part as follows:

> . . . the affirmative vote or consent of the holders of 80% of all stock of this corporation entitled to vote in elections of directors, considered for the purposes of this Articles SEVENTH as one class, shall be required:
>
> (i) *for a merger or consolidation with or into any other corporation,* or
> (ii) for any sale or lease of all or any substantial part of the assets of this corporation to any other corporation, person or other entity, or
> (iii) any sale or lease to this corporation or any subsidiary thereof of any assets . . . in exchange for voting securities . . . of this corporation or any subsidiary by any corporation, person or entity. . . .

Pl. Cert. Ex. C, at 31-32 (*emphasis added*). . . .

II. THE PARTIES' CONTENTIONS

The plaintiffs claim that Article SEVENTH unambiguously requires an 80% shareholder approval of the proposed Merger. Specifically, plaintiffs contend that Subsection (A)(i), which governs "a merger or consolidation with or into any other corporation," applies not only to a merger with or into Zapata itself, but also to a merger with or into a wholly owned Zapata subsidiary. That is because, plaintiffs argue, Subsection (A)(i) is broadly worded and contains no language that explicitly limits its application to mergers involving only Zapata itself.[2]

Defendants disagree. They contend that Article SEVENTH is unambiguously inapplicable to mergers with or into a Zapata subsidiary, because Subsection (A)(i) has no language that explicitly encompasses subsidiary merger transactions. Therefore, defendants conclude, Subsection (A)(i), by its own terms and when viewed in the larger context of Article SEVENTH, applies only to a merger where Zapata itself is a constituent corporation.

---

2. In addition to their contract interpretation argument, Plaintiffs claim that the defendants' decision to structure the transaction as a three-party merger (i.e., into a Zapata-owned subsidiary) was specifically intended to circumvent the supermajority voting provision. That, according to plaintiffs, constitutes an inequitable manipulation of the corporate machinery which creates an independent basis to enjoin the Merger. Defendants respond that the current merger structure was contemplated before the supermajority vote issue was even considered. Therefore, defendants say, there is no evidence that the transaction was structured to avoid the Supermajority Provision, or that any inequitable manipulation occurred. Because the Court finds that supermajority approval of the proposed Merger is required by the plain meaning of the Article SEVENTH, Subsection (A)(i), it does not reach the inequitable manipulation claim.

III. Analysis

A. Applicable Principles of Interpretation

Because a certificate of incorporation is a contract between the corporation and its shareholders, it is interpreted according to the rules of contract construction. . . . Accordingly, this Court must give effect to the intent of the contracting parties as evidenced by "the language of the certificate and the circumstances surrounding its creation and adoption." . . .

Except in the case where a charter provision is found ambiguous, this Court must give effect to its clear language. " 'A contract is not rendered ambiguous simply because the parties do not agree upon its proper construction. Rather, . . . [it] is ambiguous only when the provisions in controversy are reasonably or fairly susceptible of different interpretations or may have two or more different meanings.' " In determining whether a charter provision is ambiguous, the intent of the stockholders in enacting the provision is instructive. . . .

Having set forth the applicable principles of construction, I turn to the parties' respective arguments.

B. The Structure and Plain Language of Article Seventh

The defendants contend that this Court must read the Supermajority provision as applying solely to a merger "of this corporation," i.e., a merger involving Zapata itself. Although the defendants concede that these words are not explicitly found in Subsection (A)(i), they argue that that meaning is implicit, because the phrase "this corporation" is found in the paragraph that immediately precedes the enumeration, in the subparts immediately following, of the three categories of transactions requiring supermajority approval.[3] In this Court's view, nothing in Article SEVENTH supports the position that Subsection (A)(i) is or was intended to be so limited.

Unlike the broad language of Subsection (A)(i) (which covers "a merger with or into another corporation"), the language of Subsections (A)(ii) and (A)(iii) explicitly and precisely limits the scope of those two latter Subsections. Thus, Subsection (A)(ii) covers a sale or lease of "all or any substantial part of the assets *of this corporation* to any other corporation, person or other entity . . ." PI. Cert. Ex. C, at 31 (*emphasis added*). Subsection (A)(iii) refers to a sale or lease "to *this corporation or any subsidiary thereof* . . ." *Id.*, at 32 (*emphasis added*). No such language appears in Subsection A(i). If the defendants' argued-for limitation is added to the three Subsections by implication, the explicit limitations in Subsections (A)(ii) and (A)(iii) would become surplusage. An interpretation of a contract that renders one or more terms redundant is not preferred over a construction that gives effect to each of the agreement's terms. See Warner Commun. v. Chris-Craft Industries, Del. Ch., 583 A.2d 962, 971 (1989), aff'd Del. Supr., 567 A.2d 419 (1989).

The use of the phrase "of this corporation" in Subsections (A)(ii) and (A)(iii) demonstrates that had the drafters of Article SEVENTH intended to limit the scope of Subsection A(i) to mergers involving only Zapata, they knew fully

---

3. Specifically, a merger [Subsection (A)(i)], a sale of all or substantially all of Zapata's assets [Subsection (A)(ii)], and a sale of assets of $2 million or more to Zapata or its subsidiary in exchange for voting securities of Zapata or its subsidiary [Subsection (A)(iii)].

well how to accomplish that. The total absence in Subsection A(i) of the limitation expressly contained in Subsections (A)(ii) and (A)(iii), shows that the drafters intended no such limitation. . . .

In contrast to the defendants' interpretation, the plaintiffs' construction of Subsection (A)(i) as encompassing subsidiary mergers requires no implication or importation of any language from other sections of Article SEVENTH. Nor does the plaintiffs' interpretation render any term of that Article redundant. Rather, the plaintiffs' interpretation flows directly from the clear, explicit language requiring a supermajority vote for "any merger with or into any other corporation." . . .

IV. CONCLUSION

For the reasons stated above, the defendants have failed to persuade this Court that their interpretation of Subsection (A)(i) of Article SEVENTH is reasonable or fair, or (as a consequence) that that provision is ambiguous. Clearly and on its face the Supermajority Provision of Article SEVENTH applies to mergers involving a wholly owned subsidiary of Zapata, as well as mergers involving Zapata itself.

To the extent that the Merger Agreement requires only a simple majority stockholder approval of the proposed Merger, it contravenes Article SEVENTH of Zapata's Certificate of Incorporation. On that basis, an injunction prohibiting the consummation of the proposed Merger will issue. Counsel shall submit an implementing form of order.

QUESTIONS

1. How is the proposed business combination between Zapata Corp. and Houlihan's Restaurant Group, Inc. to be structured? What requirements must be satisfied in order to validly consummate this proposed acquisition transaction?
2. Who is suing, and what relief does plaintiff seek?
3. What is the basis for the decision of the Delaware court in this case? In other words, is this a de facto merger case?

H.   California Law

1.   General Background — California's Approach

As we learned from the problems and cases analyzed earlier in this chapter, Delaware law places a premium on the form used to structure an acquisition. Since each method of acquisition carries independent legal significance, transaction planners — that is, Delaware lawyers and their business clients (the corporate managers) — have a great deal of flexibility in deciding how to structure an acquisition under Delaware law. Indeed, Delaware has often been referred to as the leader in corporate law's modern day "race of the lax." *See, e.g.,* Lynn M. LoPucki, *Corporate Charter Competition,* 102 Minn. L. Rev. 2101 (2018); Brian J. Broughman and Darian M. Ibrahim, *Delaware's Familiarity,* 52 San Diego L. Rev.

273 (2015); Brian Cheffins, et al., *The Race to the Bottom Recalculated: Scoring Corporate Law Overtime,* October 10, 2014, *available at*: http://papers.ssrn.com/abstract=2473242. Among the reasons that critics of Delaware law refer to it as the leader in this race of the lax is Delaware's willingness to elevate form over substance, seen perhaps most prominently in Delaware's M&A law.

By contrast, the M&A provisions of California's corporation statute reflect a willingness to look through the form of the transaction to its economic substance. California's approach is designed to ensure that shareholders receive essentially the same legal protections when their corporation is involved in an acquisition that represents a fundamental change in the company's business — regardless of the method that the transaction planner uses to complete the acquisition. In other words, California has legislated into place the basic premise of the judicially developed doctrine of de facto mergers.

Under California law, the same basic methods are available to structure an acquisition: mergers (both direct and triangular), sales of assets, and stock purchases. However, in order to ensure that shareholders receive the protections commonly associated with mergers — namely, shareholder voting rights and the right to an appraisal — California introduces new terminology to the law of M&A by referring to certain types of business combinations as *reorganizations,* a term that is defined in Section 181 of the California statute. The concept of reorganization becomes key to understanding California's statutory scheme and the legal requirements that must be satisfied in planning a business combination under California law. The essential elements of California's statutory scheme are laid out in the following law review excerpt:

> **Marshall L. Small**
> **Corporate Combinations Under the New California**
> **General Corporation Law**
> **23 UCLA L. Rev. 1190 (1976)**

INTRODUCTION

California's new Corporation Law retains the three basic forms of corporate combination with which the bar is familiar: the statutory merger (including the currently popular triangular or reverse triangular merger), the sale of assets, and the stock-for-stock exchange. Shareholder approval requirements, dissenter appraisal rights, and other provisions, however, have been altered in an attempt to achieve two basic objectives:[3] (1) to permit shareholders to vote on a

---

3. The basic purpose of those provisions of the new law dealing with corporate combinations, as explained in the Assembly Select Committee's report, commenting on the new law, is as follows: Report of the Assembly Select Committee on the Revision of the Corporations Code 93-95 (1975) (footnotes omitted).

§1200. Reorganizations-Board Approval.

SOURCE: New. Under the new law, various methods of corporate fusion are treated as different means to the same end for the purpose of codifying the "de facto merger" doctrine. . . .

Report of the Assembly Select Committee on the Revision of the Corporations Code 93-95 1975) (footnotes omitted).

transaction and to provide dissenters with compensation, but only if the transaction will significantly dilute their control of the enterprise or change their rights; and (2) to create a statutory framework under which both the form of the transaction and the entity chosen to be the acquiring or surviving corporation are determined by considerations other than avoidance of stockholders' voting and appraisal rights. Whether this ambitious undertaking has resulted in a promise spoken to the ear but broken to the hope[5] will be left for the reader to judge after analysis of the new law. . . .

II.   Corporate Combinations Under the Revised California Corporations Code

Under the new law, reorganization is defined [in Section 181] as:

(a) A merger pursuant to Chapter 11 . . . other than a short-form merger (a "merger reorganization");

(b) The acquisition by one corporation in exchange in whole or in part for its equity securities (or the equity securities of a corporation which is in control of the acquiring corporation) of shares of another corporation if, immediately after the acquisition, the acquiring corporation has control of such other corporation (an "exchange reorganization"); or

(c) The acquisition by one corporation in exchange in whole or in part for its equity securities (or the equity securities of a corporation which is in control of the acquiring corporation) or for its debt securities (or debt securities of a corporation which is in control of the acquiring corporation) which are not adequately secured and which have a maturity date in excess of five years after the consummation of the reorganization, or both, of all or substantially all of the assets of another corporation (a "sale-of-assets reorganization").

Chapter 12 of the new law applies to all reorganizations. Mergers are additionally regulated by chapter 11. Sale-of-assets and exchange reorganizations are dealt with only in chapter 12. Certain sales of assets for cash or for a form of consideration which was thought not to subject the recipient to the risk of long term investment in the acquiring corporation (herein referred to as "cash equivalent") are not treated as "reorganizations" at all and are dealt with separately in chapter 10. Dissenters' appraisal rights are dealt with in chapter 13. This Part will consider the application of the reorganization provisions generally to mergers, sales of assets and exchanges which qualify as "reorganizations" under the new law's definitions.

A.   Board of Directors' Authorization

Section 1200 of the new law requires that a reorganization be approved by the board of directors of:

(a) Each constituent corporation in a merger reorganization;
(b) The acquiring corporation in an exchange reorganization;

---

5. W. Shakespeare. Macbeth, Act v scene viii, II. 21-22.

(c)   The acquiring corporation and the corporation whose property and assets are acquired in a sale-of-assets reorganization; . . . and

[(e)] The corporation in control of any constituent or acquiring corporation under subdivision (a), (b), or (c) and whose equity securities are issued or transferred in the reorganization (a "parent party").[19]

In effect, section 1200 requires approval of the board of each corporation which is a party to the reorganization. The only board approval not needed is that of the acquired corporation in an exchange reorganization because individual shareholders must decide whether or not to sell their stock in such a reorganization.

Subsections (a), (b) and (c) of section 1200 do not represent a significant change in the law. In the old law, board approval was expressly required for both parties in a merger, but only for the acquired corporation in a sale of assets, and for neither in an exchange. Since all powers of a corporation are generally exercised by its board of directors, however, the acquiring corporation in an exchange or sale-of-assets reorganization was also required to act pursuant to board approval under the old law. In addition, subsection [(e)] merely recognizes existing practice by requiring that the board of the corporation in control approve reorganizations carried out through subsidiaries such as, for example, triangular mergers.

B.   SHAREHOLDERS' AUTHORIZATION

Subsection 1201(a) provides that the principal terms of a reorganization must be approved by the outstanding shares of each class of each corporation where the board of directors is required by section 1200 to approve the reorganization, unless one of two exceptions discussed below applies. A majority vote, or a higher proportion if mandated by the articles or a shareholders' agreement, is required by the shares of each class, regardless of any limitations on the voting power of a class. . . .

The first exception to the requirement of shareholder approval is fairly simple. Preferred shares in the surviving or acquiring corporation or its parent need not assent to the reorganization if the "rights, preferences, privileges, and restrictions granted to or imposed upon" such shares remain unchanged by the reorganization. This exception does not apply if the articles require shareholder approval or if in a merger reorganization the articles of the surviving corporation are amended in a way which would otherwise require the approval of preferred shareholders.[29]

The second exception to the requirement of shareholder consent is more complex. Neither preferred nor common shareholder approval is needed if the corporation, or its shareholders immediately before the reorganization, or

---

19. Control is defined for the purposes of sections 181, 1001 and 1200 as "ownership directly or indirectly of shares possessing more than 50 percent of the total voting power." [*See* §160(b).]

29. *Id.* §1201(c). . . .

both, will own immediately after the reorganization equity securities of the surviving or acquiring corporation or its parent possessing more than five-sixths of the voting power of the surviving or acquiring corporation or its parent. This exception, however, does not apply under two circumstances:

(1) Shareholder approval is needed despite retention of five-sixths of the voting power for the surviving or acquiring corporation or its parent if any amendment which would otherwise require shareholder approval is made to the articles of the surviving corporation in connection with a merger reorganization. [*See* Cal. Corp. Code §1201(c).] In such event, the reorganization must be approved by the "outstanding shares" where the articles expressly provide for such approval or where such approval is required by sections 902 (a) or 903 of the new law. The qualification for contemplated amendments to the articles of the surviving corporation is limited to merger reorganizations for a very simple reason: Of all reorganizations, only mergers permit amendments to the articles as part of the reorganization document. If amendments are contemplated in connection with exchange or sale-of-assets reorganizations,[36] they must be adopted in the usual fashion by amendment of the articles pursuant to chapter 9 with shareholder consent. If shareholder approval were not statutorily required in connection with mergers, however, it could be avoided by inserting amendments to the articles into the merger agreement. Thus, the special qualification for merger reorganizations merely insures voting rights to the shareholders by recognizing the unique method of effecting amendments in mergers.

(2) Under section 1201(d) of the new law the outstanding shares of a class in a disappearing corporation must give their consent to a merger reorganization even though the five-sixths rule applies if the holders of such class receive shares of the surviving corporation that have different rights than those surrendered. . . .[42]

III.   Merger Reorganizations

In addition to the reorganization provisions of chapter 12, merger reorganizations and short-form mergers are regulated by the provisions of chapter 11. Section 1100 states the general proposition that any two or more corporations may be merged into one under chapter 11. Although "corporation" is defined to include only domestic corporations, section 1108 makes clear that mergers are authorized between domestic and foreign corporations and that the surviving corporation may be either domestic or foreign. The new law eliminates as unnecessary the provision of the old law permitting the little used technique of "consolidation" whereby two corporations could agree to be consolidated into a new corporation

---

36. An example of this would be an amendment under section 903(a)(1) of the new law in the case of an increase in authorized shares.

42. Although the new law breaks new ground in many respects, it does not go as far as the proposed addition of section 72-A [the predecessor provision to current Section 11.03] to the Model Business Corporation Act, which would permit a majority of the shareholders of a selling corporation to bind all shareholders in an exchange reorganization and accord dissenters' rights to those who do not approve the transaction. *See* ABA, *Report of Committee on Corporate Laws: Changes in the Model Business Corporation Act*, 30 Bus. Law. 991 (1975). . . .

which would come into being and absorb the existing corporations upon the filing of a consolidation agreement.

A.   THE MERGER AGREEMENT

As explained above, a merger reorganization must be approved by the board of each constituent corporation. Section 1101 requires that the merger agreement also be approved by each board. . . .

The reorganization provisions clearly contemplate that shareholders of a constituent corporation may, in a triangular merger, receive *equity* securities of a parent corporation. These provisions should not be construed to limit the type and source of securities to be issued in a merger to equity securities of a constituent corporation or parent, or to securities of a corporation which is technically in "control" of one of the constituent corporations within the meaning of section 160(b). Section 1101(d) certainly suggests a broader range of alternatives.[56] . . .

B.   SHORT-FORM MERGERS

If a domestic corporation owns all the outstanding shares of a domestic or foreign corporation, the merger of the subsidiary into the parent may, as under the old law, be effected by a resolution adopted by the board of the parent and the filing of a certificate of ownership with the Secretary of State. [*See* Cal. Corp. Code §1110(a).] . . .

C.   DISSENTERS' APPRAISAL RIGHTS

If the approval of outstanding shares of a corporation is required for a merger reorganization under section 1201(a) and (b) . . ., each shareholder of that corporation may require it to pay, in cash, the fair market value of all "dissenting shares." [*See* Cal. Corp. Code §1300(a).] A similar right is accorded to each shareholder of a disappearing corporation in a short-form merger. [*Id.*] Certain shares, including shares listed on a national securities exchange certified by the Commissioner of Corporations to be exempt securities . . . are not "dissenting shares" subject to the appraisal procedures. [*See* Cal. Corp. Code §1300(b)(1). Thus California also includes a "market out exception" for those dissenting shares that are publicly traded, but restores the right of

---

56. One question that was occasionally raised about triangular mergers under the old law was whether a subsidiary's, rather than a parent's, receipt of the assets of the acquired business was adequate consideration to the parent for direct issuance of the parent's securities to the disappearing corporation or its shareholders. Section 409(a) of the new law now establishes that shares may be issued in exchange for property actually received either by the issuing corporation or by a wholly-owned subsidiary. However, under section 409(a), it appears that a parent corporation may not use a *partly-owned* subsidiary to effect a triangular merger involving the direct issuance of the parent's shares to shareholders of the disappearing corporation.

appraisal to these shares if the holders of the shares are required to accept for the shares anything except publicly traded shares and/or cash in lieu of fractional shares.]

IV.   SALE-OF-ASSETS TRANSACTIONS

Unlike statutory mergers under chapter 11, all of which (except for short form mergers) constitute reorganizations under chapter 12, sale-of-assets transactions are divided into two distinct categories, depending upon the types of consideration issued in the transaction. Chapters 12 (reorganizations) and 13 (dissenters' rights) govern "sale-of-assets reorganizations." [*See* Cal. Corp. Code §181 (c).] Such a sale will occur if the acquiring corporation issues any of its equity securities, any equity securities of a corporation which controls the acquiring corporation, any debt securities of the acquiring corporation which are not "adequately secured" and which have a maturity date more than five years after completion of the reorganization, or a combination of equity securities and such debt securities, in exchange for all or substantially all of the property and assets of the selling corporation. If none of these securities is issued as a part of the consideration for transfer of all or substantially all of the assets, then chapters 12 and 13 are inapplicable; instead, the provisions of chapter 10 (sale of assets) apply to the transaction. Chapter 10 governs only sales of assets which are not "sale-of-assets reorganizations" . . . [.]

The original exposure draft of the State Bar Committee on Corporations limited a sale-of-assets reorganization under the new law to one in which the acquiring corporation or its parent issued only equity securities. Since debt securities might be issued in a merger reorganization, after further consideration the Committee extended the provisions of chapters 12 and 13 to sale-of-assets transactions where the consideration issued by the acquiring corporation included debt securities which forced the shareholders of the selling corporation to rely on the long-term prospects of the acquiring corporation for payment. Where the acquiring corporation issues only "adequately secured" long-term debt securities, whose repayment is presumably assured, or short-term debt securities, the drafters concluded that the provisions of chapters 12 and 13 should not apply. . . .

One may question whether a debt security with a maturity date deferred as much as five years is indeed the equivalent of cash, eliminating the investment risk for one who receives the security. Furthermore, the absence of a definition of "adequately secured" in the new law may cause many practitioners to be extremely cautious in concluding that any sale of assets not solely for cash or debt securities of less than five years maturity is anything other than a sale-of-assets reorganization subject to chapters 12 and 13. Where consideration other than cash is given, many practitioners will resolve the matter by using the merger vehicle. In those cases where a limited assumption of liabilities of the selling corporation is desired, they will make sure that some of the securities received constitute equity securities or debt securities with a maturity of more than five years so that the transaction is clearly a sale-of-assets reorganization or else they will consider voluntarily extending to the shareholders of the selling corporation those voting and dissenters' rights to which the shareholders would otherwise be entitled if the transaction were a sale-of-assets reorganization. However, because the new law does attempt to draw a distinction between sales of assets which are reorganizations and those which are for cash or "cash equivalents," and because some sale-of-assets transactions will clearly be for cash, it is useful to consider how the new law treats each type of sale-of-assets transaction.

A. SALES OF ASSETS FOR CASH OR CASH EQUIVALENTS

Chapter 10 of the new law contains provisions substantially similar to those appearing in the old law. Section 1000 continues the rule of section 3900 of the old law that unless the articles otherwise provide, the board of directors may, without shareholder approval, mortgage or hypothecate any part of the corporation's property for the purpose of securing performance of any contract or obligation. . . .

Section 1001 sets forth the general rule that a corporation may sell or otherwise dispose of all of its assets if its board of directors approves the principal terms of the transaction. The principal terms of the transaction must also be approved by the holders of a majority of the outstanding shares entitled to vote unless the transaction is in the usual course of business. . . .

One may question why a shareholder who receives debt securities with a maturity of five years or less should be denied dissenters' rights or, for that matter, why a shareholder who receives only cash should be denied the right to question the fairness of the sale through dissenters' proceedings. Under section 1312(b) of the new law, a shareholder in a *reorganization* transaction may decline to assert dissenters' rights and may attack the fairness of the transaction if one of the parties to the transaction is controlled by or under common control with another party to the reorganization. No similar right to either assert dissenters' rights or attack the fairness of the transaction is expressly extended or denied to a shareholder in a cash or cash equivalent sale.[113] . . .

A proposal to sell "substantially all" the assets of a corporation must be approved by the shareholders, but the new law does not define this term. . . .

B. SALE-OF-ASSETS REORGANIZATIONS

Unlike statutory mergers, which are subject to the detailed procedural provisions of chapter 11, there is no separate chapter in the new law setting forth procedural provisions governing sale-of-assets reorganizations. These transactions are governed by chapter 12 and, to a limited extent, by section 1002, which

---

113. A shareholder in a cash or cash equivalent sale may have the right to attack the fairness of the transaction whether or not there is common control since such a shareholder is not expressly precluded from such an attack. *Id.* §1312(a). This is a dubious result, since, in the absence of common control, it may be better social policy to extend dissenters' rights to aggrieved shareholders in cash or cash equivalent transactions, and, as a quid pro quo, preclude such shareholders from collaterally attacking the transaction under section 1312(a), as in the case of reorganization transactions.

set forth certification provisions to establish compliance with the applicable law for the benefit of third parties.

V. Exchange Reorganizations

As in the case of sale-of-assets reorganizations, no separate chapter in the new law sets forth the procedural provisions governing exchange reorganizations subject to chapter 12. The basic requirements are set forth solely in chapter 12.

An "exchange reorganization" is defined [in California Corporation Code §181(b)] as:

> The acquisition by one corporation in exchange in whole or in part for its equity securities (or the equity securities of a corporation which is in control of the acquiring corporation) of shares of another corporation if, immediately after the acquisition, the acquiring corporation has control of such other corporation. . . .

Section 160(b) provides that control in section 181 means the ownership directly or indirectly of shares possessing more than 50 percent of the voting power.

Although the new law regulates exchange reorganizations in the limited manner described above, no attempt has been made to regulate contested tender offers in the manner undertaken by a growing number of states. [We will consider the modern proliferation of state antitakeover statutes later, in Chapter 6.] Aside from the absence of a takeover bid statute, which absence may be viewed as less than helpful to those defending against tender offers, the new law discloses no marked bias in favor of, or opposition to, hostile tender offers. . . .

PROBLEM SET NO. 7—CALIFORNIA LAW

The following problems are based on problems that we previously analyzed under the terms of Delaware law and the MBCA. For ease of reference, I have noted the problem number where this problem was previously considered in order to facilitate comparison of results obtained applying the reorganization provisions of California law. In analyzing the following problems, you will need to refer to the relevant provisions of the California Corporations Code.

Direct Mergers—California Law

1. Merger—Consideration Consists of 30 Percent of Bidder's Stock (Same as Problem 1 at p. 74).   Target Co., a closely held California corporation, plans to merge into Bidder Co., another closely held California corporation. The plan of merger calls for Target shareholders to receive shares of Bidder common stock comprising 30 percent of the voting power of Bidder's common stock that was outstanding immediately prior to completion of the acquisition. Target and Bidder each have only one class of voting common stock outstanding. Bidder has sufficient authorized and unissued shares to complete the transaction.

    a. What action is required by the boards of Bidder and Target under California law?

    b. Do the shareholders of either Bidder or Target have the right to vote under California law?

    c. Do the shareholders of either Bidder or Target have the right to dissent under California law?

    d. How would this analysis of shareholder voting rights and the availability of the appraisal remedy change if both Bidder Corp. and Target Corp. are publicly traded?

    2. Merger—Consideration Consists of 15 Percent of Bidder's Stock (Same as Problem 3 at p. 75).   Assume that the facts are the same as set out in Problem 1 directly above—*except* that the shareholders of Target will receive shares comprising 15 percent of the voting power of Bidder's common stock that was outstanding immediately prior to the completion of the acquisition.

    a. What action is required by the boards of Bidder and Target under California law?

    b. Do the shareholders of either Bidder or Target have the right to vote under California law?

    c. Do the shareholders of either Bidder or Target have the right to dissent under California law?

    3. Cash Merger—Consideration Consists of All Cash (Same as Problem 1 at p. 76).   Assume that the facts are the same as set out in Problem 1 directly above—*except* that the merger agreement provides that shareholders of Target will receive all *cash* in exchange for their Target shares.

    a. What action is required by the boards of Target and Bidder under California law?

    b. Do the shareholders of either Bidder or Target have the right to vote under California law?

    c. Do the shareholders of either Bidder or Target have the right to dissent under California law?

    d. How would the analysis of shareholder voting rights and the availability of the appraisal remedy change if both Bidder and Target were publicly traded?

Asset Purchases—California Law

    4. Sale of Assets for Cash (Similar to Problem 2 at p. 87).   Nest Labs, Inc., a closely held California corporation, plans to sell all of its assets and transfer certain of its liabilities to Google, Inc., a NYSE-listed California corporation, in exchange for $3.2 billion cash. Immediately following this sale, Nest Labs will dissolve and liquidate itself, with the company distributing out to its shareholders any cash remaining after paying off the company's creditors.

    a. What action is required by the boards of Nest Labs and Google under California law?

    b. Do the shareholders of either Nest Labs or Google have the right to vote under California law?

c. Do the shareholders of either Nest Labs or Google have the right to dissent under California law?

5. Asset Acquisition—Using 30 Percent of Bidder's Stock (Similar to Problem 3 at p. 87). Assume that Nest Labs, a closely held California company, plans to sell all of its assets and transfer certain of its liabilities to Google, Inc., another California company that is publicly traded on the NYSE, in exchange for shares comprising 30 percent of the voting power of Google's common stock that was outstanding immediately prior to the completion of the acquisition. Immediately after the transfer, Nest Labs will dissolve and liquidate itself, with Nest Labs transferring to its shareholders the remaining Google shares in exchange for all of Nest Labs outstanding stock, which will then be canceled in dissolution of the company. Assume further that Google has sufficient authorized and unissued shares to complete the transaction.

a. What action is required by the boards of Nest Labs and Google under California law?
b. Do the shareholders of either Nest Labs or Google have the right to vote under California law?
c. Do the shareholders of either Net Labs or Google have the right to dissent under California law?

6. Asset Acquisition—Using 15 Percent of Bidder's Stock (Similar to Problem 4 at p. 88). Assume that the facts are the same as set out above in Problem 5—*except* that Google plans to complete the acquisition by issuing its stock in an amount equal to 15 percent of the voting power of Google's common stock that was outstanding immediately prior to the completion of the acquisition.

a. What action is required by the boards of Nest Labs and Google under California law?
b. Do the shareholders of either Nest Labs or Google have the right to vote under California law?
c. Do the shareholders of either Nest Labs or Google have the right to dissent under California law?

Stock Purchases—California Law

7. Stock Purchase—for Cash (Same as Problem 1 at p. 110). Assume that the shareholders of Nest Labs, Inc., a California corporation, consist of the two founders and two venture capital investors. Each of the four shareholders owns 25 percent of the outstanding common stock of Nest Labs, which is the only class of stock outstanding. The shareholders have agreed to sell all of their shares of Nest Labs common stock to Google, Inc., a NYSE-listed California corporation. Google has agreed to pay $3.2 billion cash on closing of the parties' stock purchase agreement.

a. Who are the parties to the stock purchase agreement?
b. What action is required by the boards of Net Labs and Google under California law?
c. Do the shareholders of either Nest Labs or Google have the right to vote under California law?

   d. Do the shareholders of either Nest Labs or Google have the right to
      dissent under California law?
   e. What options are available to the shareholders of Nest Labs under
      California law if they object to the terms of Google's offer?
   f. What options are available to the shareholders of Google under
      California law if they object to Google's proposal to acquire Nest Labs?

   **8. Stock Purchase—Using 24 Percent of Bidder's Stock (Same as Problem 2 at
   p. 110; also known as a Stock Exchange Offer).**   Assume the same facts as described
above in Problem 7, *except* that the parties' stock purchase agreement calls for
Google to pay all of the $3.2 billion purchase price by issuing shares of Google
common stock comprising 24 percent of the voting power of Google's common
stock that was outstanding before the transaction is completed.

   a. What action is required by the boards of Nest Labs and Google under
      California law?
   b. Do the shareholders of either Nest Labs or Google have the right to
      vote under California law?
   c. Do the shareholders of either Nest Labs or Google have the right to
      dissent under California law?

   **9. Stock Purchase—Using 14 Percent of Bidder's Stock (Similar to Problem 2(f)
   at p. 111).**   Assume that the facts are the same as set out above in Problem
8—*except* that Google plans to complete its acquisition of Nest Labs by issuing
shares of its common stock in an amount comprising 14 percent of the voting
power of Google's common stock that was outstanding immediately before the
acquisition is completed.

   a. What action is required by the boards of Nest Labs and Google under
      California law?
   b. Do the shareholders of either Nest Labs or Google have the right to
      vote under California law?
   c. Do the shareholders of either Nest Labs or Google have the right to
      dissent under California law?

Triangular Merger Problems—California Law

   **10. Triangular Merger—Consideration Consisting of 25 Percent of Stock of Bidder
   Corporation (Similar to Problem 1 at p. 121).**   AT&T, Inc., a NYSE-listed California
company, forms New Company (NewCo), a wholly-owned California subsidiary,
for the purpose of acquiring DirecTV, Inc, another NYSE-listed California company, in a triangular merger. The parties' merger agreement calls for AT&T to
issue shares of its common stock in an amount equal to 25 percent of the voting
power of AT&T's common stock that was outstanding immediately prior to the
completion of the transaction. Although California law allows for the transaction to be structured either as a *forward* triangular (subsidiary) merger or a
reverse triangular (subsidiary) merger, the parties have decided to use a *reverse*
triangular merger, thereby preserving DirecTV as a wholly-owned subsidiary of
AT&T. Assume further that AT&T has sufficient authorized but unissued voting
common shares to complete the transaction.

a. What action is required by the boards of AT&T, DirecTV, and NewCo under California law?
b. Do the shareholders of either AT&T or DirecTV have the right to vote under California law?
c. Do the shareholders of either AT&T or DirecTV have the right to dissent under California law?

11. Triangular Merger—Consideration Consisting of 15 Percent of Bidder's Stock (Similar to Problem 2 at p. 122).   Assume that the facts are the same as set out above in Problem 10—*except* that the shareholders of DirecTV will receive shares of AT&T common stock comprising 15 percent of the voting power of AT&T's common shares that were outstanding immediately before closing on the proposed transaction with DirecTV.

a. What action is required by the boards of AT&T, DirecTV, and NewCo under California law?
b. Do the shareholders of either AT&T or DirecTV have the right to vote under California law?
c. Do the shareholders of either AT&T or DirecTV have the right to dissent under California law?

12. Triangular Merger—Consideration Consists of Cash. (Similar to Problem 2 at p. 122).   Assume that the facts are the same as set out above in Problem 10—*except* that the terms of the parties' merger agreement call for the DirecTV shareholders to receive *all cash* for their DirecTV shares.

a. What action is required by the boards of AT&T, DirecTV, and NewCo under California law?
b. Do the shareholders of either AT&T or DirecTV have the right to vote under California law?
c. Do the shareholders of either AT&T or DirecTV have the right to dissent under California law?

QUESTIONS

1. From a public policy perspective, which approach do you prefer: California or Delaware? In considering this issue of "form over substance," does it matter whether Target or Bidder is publicly traded?
2. As to dissenters' rights, what do you think of California's approach to the market out exception? How does California's approach differ from that of Delaware or the MBCA?

I.   Is There a Right to Vote as a Class?

In the case of a corporation with multiple classes of outstanding voting stock (i.e., Class A common stock, Class B common stock, and Class C common stock), the issue of whether each class of shares must vote separately to approve a trans-action involving a "fundamental change" may arise. As a threshold matter, we must determine the shareholders' rights by looking to both the provisions of the respective state's corporation code and the corporation's articles of incor-poration. Assuming that a right to a class vote is mandated, what is the effect of class voting? In a class vote, *each class* of shares entitled to vote on such trans-action must approve it by the requisite majority. Thus, shareholder approval votes are not tallied in the aggregate for all outstanding shares, but instead, the requisite approval must be obtained separately within each distinct class.

By way of example, assume that Corporation X has three classes of out-standing shares of voting common stock—Class A (1,000 shares), Class B (500 shares), and Class C (250 shares). Further assume that the voting standard required to effectuate the "fundamental change" under the terms of relevant state law is an absolute majority. If a right to vote as a class is available, then any proposed merger must be approved by at least 501 shares of Class A, 251 shares of Class B, and 126 shares of Class C. Obviously, the right to vote as a class pro-vides an additional layer of protection for each class of shares even if that class represents a minority interest within the corporation.

The following case provides a nice illustration of how the right to vote as a class creates the potential for veto power. The case also reflects on the contin-ued importance of the internal affairs doctrine in determining which corporate laws must be satisfied in order to validly complete corporate transactions such as mergers, sale of assets, and distributions to shareholders, among others.

VantagePoint Venture Partners 1996 v. Examen, Inc.
871 A.2d 1108 (Del. 2005)

HOLLAND, Justice:

This is an expedited appeal from the Court of Chancery following the entry of a final judgment on the pleadings. We have concluded that the judgment must be affirmed.

DELAWARE ACTION

On March 3, 2005, the plaintiff-appellee, Examen, Inc. ("Examen"), filed a Complaint in the Court of Chancery against VantagePoint Venture Partners, Inc. ("VantagePoint"), a Delaware Limited Partnership and an Examen Series A Preferred shareholder, seeking a judicial declaration that pursuant to the con-trolling Delaware law and under the Company's Certificate of Designations of Series A Preferred Stock ("Certificate of Designations"), VantagePoint was not entitled to a class vote of the Series A Preferred Stock on the proposed merger between Examen and a Delaware subsidiary of Reed Elsevier Inc.

CALIFORNIA ACTION

On March 8, 2005, VantagePoint filed an action in the California Superior Court seeking: (1) a declaration that Examen was required to identify whether it was a "quasi-California corporation" under section 2115 of the California Corporations Code;[1] (2) a declaration that Examen was a quasi-California corporation pursuant to California Corporations Code section 2115 and therefore subject to California Corporations Code section 1201(a), and that, as a Series A Preferred shareholder, VantagePoint was entitled to vote its shares as a separate class in connection with the proposed merger; (3) injunctive relief; and (4) damages incurred as the result of alleged violations of California Corporations Code sections 2111(f) and 1201.

DELAWARE ACTION DECIDED

On March 10, 2005, the Court of Chancery granted Examen's request for an expedited hearing on its motion for judgment on the pleadings. On March 21, 2005, the California Superior Court stayed its action pending the ruling of the Court of Chancery. On March 29, 2005, the Court of Chancery ruled that the case was governed by the internal affairs doctrine as explicated by this Court in *McDermott v. Lewis*, 531 A.2d 206 (Del.1987). In applying that doctrine, the Court of Chancery held that Delaware law governed the vote that was required to approve a merger between two Delaware corporate entities.

On April 1, 2005, VantagePoint filed a notice of appeal with this Court. On April 4, 2005, VantagePoint sought to enjoin the merger from closing pending its appeal. On April 5, 2005, this Court denied VantagePoint's request to enjoin the merger from closing, but granted its request for an expedited appeal. . . .

FACTS

Examen was a Delaware corporation engaged in the business of providing web-based legal expense management solutions to a growing list of Fortune 1000 customers throughout the United States. Following consummation of the merger on April 5, 2005, LexisNexis Examen, also a Delaware corporation, became the surviving entity. VantagePoint is a Delaware Limited Partnership

---

1. Section 2115 of the California Corporations Code purportedly applies to corporations that have contacts with the State of California, but are incorporated in other states. *See* Cal. Corp. Code §§171 (defining "foreign corporation"); and Cal. Corp. Code §§2115(a), (b). Section 2115 of the California Corporations Code provides that, irrespective of the state of incorporation, **foreign corporations' articles of incorporation are deemed amended** to comply with California law and are subject to the laws of California if certain criteria are met. *See* Cal. Corp. Code §2115 (*emphasis added*). To qualify under the statute: (1) the average of the property factor, the payroll factor and the sales factor as defined in the California Revenue and Taxation Code must be more than 50 percent during its last full income year; and (2) more than one-half of its outstanding voting securities must be held by persons having addresses in California. *Id.* If a corporation qualifies under this provision, California corporate laws apply "to the exclusion of the law of the jurisdiction where [the company] is incorporated." *Id.* Included among the California corporate law provisions that would govern is California Corporations Code section 1201, which states that the principal terms of a reorganization shall be approved by the outstanding shares of each class of each corporation the approval of whose board is required. *See* Cal. Corp. Code §§2115, 1201 [emphasis in original].

organized and existing under the laws of Delaware. VantagePoint, a major venture capital firm that purchased Examen Series A Preferred Stock in a negotiated transaction, owned eighty-three percent of Examen's outstanding Series A Preferred Stock (909,091 shares) and no shares of Common Stock.

On February 17, 2005, Examen and Reed Elsevier executed the Merger Agreement, which was set to expire on April 15, 2005, if the merger had not closed by that date. Under the Delaware General Corporation Law and Examen's Certificate of Incorporation, including the Certificate of Designations for the Series A Preferred Stock, adoption of the Merger Agreement required the affirmative vote of the holders of a majority of the issued and outstanding shares of the Common Stock and Series A Preferred Stock, *voting together as a single class.* Holders of Series A Preferred Stock had the number of votes equal to the number of shares of Common Stock they would have held if their Preferred Stock was converted. Thus, VantagePoint, which owned 909,091 shares of Series A Preferred Stock and no shares of Common Stock, was entitled to vote based on a converted number of 1,392,727 shares of stock.

There were 9,717,415 total outstanding shares of the Company's capital stock (8,626,826 shares of Common Stock and 1,090,589 shares of Series A Preferred Stock), representing 10,297,608 votes on an as-converted basis. An affirmative vote of at least 5,148,805 shares, constituting a majority of the outstanding voting power on an as-converted basis, was required to approve the merger. If the stockholders were to vote by class, VantagePoint would have controlled 83.4 percent of the Series A Preferred Stock, which would have permitted VantagePoint to block the merger. VantagePoint acknowledges that, if Delaware law applied, it would not have a class vote. . . .

INTERNAL AFFAIRS DOCTRINE

In *CTS Corp. v. Dynamics Corp. of Am.,* the United States Supreme Court stated that it is "an accepted part of the business landscape in this country for States to create corporations, to prescribe their powers, and to define the rights that are acquired by purchasing their shares." [481 U.S. 69, 91 (1987).] In *CTS,* it was also recognized that "[a] State has an interest in promoting stable relationships among parties involved in the corporations it charters, as well as in ensuring that investors in such corporations have an effective voice in corporate affairs." [*Id.*] The internal affairs doctrine is a long-standing choice of law principle which recognizes that only one state should have the authority to regulate a corporation's internal affairs — the state of incorporation.

The internal affairs doctrine developed on the premise that, in order to prevent corporations from being subjected to inconsistent legal standards, the authority to regulate a corporation's internal affairs should not rest with multiple jurisdictions. It is now well established that only the law of the state of incorporation governs and determines issues relating to a corporation's internal affairs. By providing certainty and predictability, the internal affairs doctrine protects the justified expectations of the parties with interests in the corporation.

The internal affairs doctrine applies to those matters that pertain to the relationships among or between the corporation and its officers, directors, and shareholders. . . . Accordingly, the conflicts practice of both state and federal courts has consistently been to apply the law of the state of incorporation to "the entire gamut of internal corporate affairs."[14]

The internal affairs doctrine is not, however, only a conflicts of law principle. Pursuant to the Fourteenth Amendment Due Process Clause, directors and officers of corporations "have a significant right . . . to know what law will be applied to their actions" and "[s]tockholders . . . have a right to know by what standards of accountability they may hold those managing the corporation's business and affairs." *[McDermott, Inc. v. Lewis,* 531 A. 2d at 216.] Under the Commerce Clause, a state "has no interest in regulating the internal affairs of foreign corporations." Therefore, this Court has held that an "application of the internal affairs doctrine is mandated by constitutional principles, except in the 'rarest situations,'" *e.g.,* when "the law of the state of incorporation is inconsistent with a national policy on foreign or interstate commerce."[*Id.*]

CALIFORNIA SECTION 2115

VantagePoint contends that section 2115 of the California Corporations Code is a limited exception to the internal affairs doctrine. Section 2115 is characterized as an outreach statute because it requires certain foreign corporations to conform to a broad range of internal affairs provisions. Section 2115 defines the foreign corporations for which the California statute has an outreach effect as those foreign corporations, half of whose voting securities are held of record by persons with California addresses, that also conduct half of their business in California as measured by a formula weighing assets, sales and payroll factors.

VantagePoint argues that section 2115 "mandates application of certain enumerated provisions of California's corporation law to the internal affairs of 'foreign' corporations if certain narrow factual prerequisites [set forth in section 2115] are met." . . .

In her comprehensive analysis of the internal affairs doctrine, Professor Deborah A. DeMott examined section 2115. As she astutely points out:

> In contrast to the certainty with which the state of incorporation may be determined, the criteria upon which the applicability of section 2115 hinges are not constants. For example, whether half of a corporation's business is derived from California and whether half of its voting securities have record holders with California addresses may well vary from year to year (and indeed throughout any given year). Thus, a corporation might be subject to section 2115 one year but not the next, depending on its situation at the time of filing the annual statement required by section 2108.[23] . . .

STATE LAW OF INCORPORATION GOVERNS INTERNAL AFFAIRS

In *McDermott,* this Court held that the "internal affairs doctrine is a major tenet of Delaware corporation law having important federal constitutional

---

14. *McDermott Inc. v. Lewis,* 531 A.2d [206, 216 (Del. 1987)] (quoting John Kozyris, *Corporate Wars and Choice of Law,* 1985 Duke L.J. 1, 98 (1985)). The internal affairs doctrine does not apply where the rights of third parties external to the corporation are at issue, *e.g.,* contracts and torts. *Id. See also Rogers v. Guaranty Trust of N.Y.,* 288 U.S. 123, 130-31, 53 S.Ct. 295, 77 L.Ed. 652 (1933).

23. Deborah A. DeMott, *Perspectives on Choice of Law for Corporate Internal Affairs,* 48 Law & Contemp. Probs. 161, 166 (1985).

underpinnings." Applying Delaware's well-established choice-of-law rule—the internal affairs doctrine—the Court of Chancery recognized that Delaware courts must apply the law of the state of incorporation to issues involving corporate internal affairs, and that disputes concerning a shareholder's right to vote fall squarely within the purview of the internal affairs doctrine.

Examen is a Delaware corporation. The legal issue in this case—whether a preferred shareholder of a Delaware corporation had the right, under the corporation's Certificate of Designations, to a Series A Preferred Stock class vote on a merger—clearly involves the relationship among a corporation and its shareholders. As the United States Supreme Court held in *CTS*, "[n]o principle of corporation law and practice is more firmly established than a *State's authority* to regulate domestic corporations, including the authority to *define the voting rights of shareholders.*"[34]

In *CTS*, the Supreme Court held that the Commerce Clause "prohibits States from regulating subjects that 'are in their nature national, or admit only of one uniform system, or plan of regulation,'" and acknowledged that the internal affairs of a corporation are subjects that require one uniform system of regulation. In *CTS*, the Supreme Court concluded that "[s]o long as each State regulates voting rights *only in the corporations it has created,* each corporation will be subject to the law of only one State." Accordingly, we hold Delaware's well-established choice of law rules and the federal constitution mandated that Examen's internal affairs, and in particular, VantagePoint's voting rights, be adjudicated exclusively in accordance with the law of its state of incorporation, in this case, the law of Delaware. . . .

CONCLUSION

The judgment of the Court of Chancery is affirmed.

QUESTIONS

1. What is the public policy premise behind §2115? In other words, why did the California legislature decide to adopt §2115?

2. How does Delaware law treat the right to a class vote? How is Delaware's default rule on class voting different from California's statutory provision?

3. How did the Delaware Supreme Court interpret the internal affairs doctrine in deciding this case?

4. The decision of the Delaware Supreme Court in the *VantagePoint* case prompted one experienced California corporate lawyer to make the following observation:

California is a huge state in terms of geography, population and the size of its economy. It is no surprise, therefore, that it serves as headquarters to more public

---

34. *CTS Corp. v. Dynamics Corp. of Am.*, 481 U.S. 69, 89, 107 S.Ct. 1637, 95 L.Ed.2d 67 (1987) (*emphasis added*). *See* Restatement (Second) of Conflict of Laws §304 (1971) (concluding that the law of the incorporating State generally should "determine the right of a shareholder to participate in the administration of the affairs of the corporation").

companies than any other state. One recent study found that California serves as headquarters to more than 1200 public companies while Delaware is headquarters to only 27.[26] These numbers are reversed when the relative numbers of corporations incorporated in the two states but headquartered elsewhere are compared. In this comparison, Delaware accounts for over 3700 corporations while California accounts for only 10.[27] Clearly, California has to a large extent ceded to Delaware (and other states) the ability to charter and thereby govern the corporations that call California home. Viewed in this context, it is not surprising that California would attempt to regain some measure of authority over these corporations through the enactment of outreach statutes such as Section 2115. These data also illustrate why Delaware has a strong interest in knocking out corporate outreach statutes such as Section 2115. If they are allowed to stand, Delaware's ability to compete is reduced by the possible override of headquarters state legislation. On the other hand, if it is ultimately determined that California cannot apply its laws to foreign corporations, it is likely that the exodus of corporations from California will accelerate.

Keith Paul Bishop, *The War Between the States—Delaware's Supreme Court Ignores California's "Outreach" Statute*, 19 INSIGHTS 19 (July 2005). The author of this article (who previously served as California's Commissioner of Corporations) sounds a rather ominous tone in referring to the "exodus of corporations from California." Do you agree with the author's observation? If so, is this troubling as a public policy matter?

J.   Appraisal Rights

1.   Introduction

When the topic of appraisal rights was introduced earlier in this chapter, we identified four issues that generally must be considered in analyzing this topic. The first issue, the availability of appraisal rights, has been thoroughly examined as part of our discussion of the various problem sets earlier in this chapter, where we analyzed each of the different types of acquisition structures. In this section, we will examine the other three issues:

- Procedural requirements in order to perfect dissenters' appraisal rights
- Valuation of dissenters' shares
- Exclusivity of the appraisal remedy

Each of these issues has generated a substantial body of case law and scholarly literature, so no attempt is made here to canvass these other issues in any sort of exhaustive manner. Rather, the materials that follow sketch out the fundamental nature of the public policy concerns presented by each of these issues regarding the scope of the modern appraisal remedy.

---

26. Bebchuk & Cohen, "Firms Decisions Where to Incorporate," 46 J. LAW & ECON. 383, 395 (2003).

27. *Id.* California does slightly better with respect to corporations headquartered in this state. It counts 273 corporations incorporated in the state.

As part of our analysis of the problems earlier in this chapter, we observed a wide disparity as to which transactions involving a fundamental corporate change will trigger the right of appraisal for the dissenting (minority) shareholder. In analyzing these problems, we noted the different public policy considerations that underlie the legislative decision to grant a mandatory right of appraisal without delving into any extended analysis of the scope, purpose, and efficacy of this remedy. Now that we have developed a better sense of the potentially conflicting interests that are implicated whenever a corporation proposes to enter into a transaction resulting in a fundamental change, it is time to turn our attention to the role of appraisal rights as a matter of modern corporate law.

Although this area of law has generated considerable academic commentary, a clear consensus as to the exact purpose to be served by legislatively granting an appraisal remedy for dissenting shares has yet to emerge. The following excerpt offers some perspective on this topic and serves as an excellent overview of the disparate threads of analysis reflected in the various appraisal statutes that we have studied so far in this chapter.

Barry Wertheimer
The Purpose of the Shareholders' Appraisal Remedy
65 Tenn. L. Rev. 661, 662-664 (1998)

At one time, unanimous shareholder approval was required before a corporation could engage in a fundamental corporate transaction. Eventually, corporate statutes were amended to permit such transactions to proceed upon receipt of approval by a majority of shareholders. As a result, individual shareholders no longer had the ability to veto fundamental corporate changes.

There is general agreement that when corporate statutes were amended to allow majority approval of fundamental changes, appraisal rights were granted to shareholders to compensate them for their loss of the power to veto corporate changes. The standard explanation for the existence of the appraisal remedy, therefore, is that it serves as quid pro quo for the loss of shareholders' right to veto fundamental corporate changes.

The other oft-cited justification for the appraisal remedy is that it serves a liquidity rationale. Once shareholders lost the right to veto fundamental changes, it was possible for shareholders to find themselves involuntarily holding an investment in an entity vastly different from the one originally contemplated. For example, if a majority of a corporation's shareholders approved a merger with another entity, a shareholder voting against that transaction would, in the absence of an appraisal remedy, have no choice but to remain a shareholder in the merged entity.[7] The appraisal remedy allows the shareholder a

---

7. This assumes, of course, that the corporation's shares are not publicly traded. If a market exists for the shares of the corporation, the shareholder voting against the merger could sell its shares in the market, rather than be forced to remain an investor in the newly merged corporation. Thus, the liquidity rationale for the appraisal remedy loses force with respect to publicly traded corporations. As a result, a number of states, relying on the liquidity rationale for the appraisal remedy, have created "market exceptions" to their appraisal statutes. . . . These "market exceptions" provide that no appraisal remedy will be available for shareholders of publicly traded corporations. *E.g. Del. Code Ann. tit. 8, 262(b);* . . .

"way out" of an investment involuntarily altered by a fundamental corporation change.

At the time that appraisal rights became part of corporate statutes, merger transactions typically were engaged in by unrelated corporations and structured so that stock in the acquiring corporation was issued to shareholders of the acquired corporation. Cash generally was not used as merger consideration, and the use of a merger or fundamental transaction as a way to eliminate or "cash out" minority shareholders certainly was not contemplated.

Financial practices and legal requirements have changed, however, and today mergers often are used solely to eliminate minority shareholders. This change in the use of fundamental corporate transactions requires a change in thinking about the purpose served by the appraisal remedy. The historic liquidity function of the remedy has diminished, and the remedy now serves a minority shareholder protection rationale, primarily in the context of cash out merger transactions. Although commentators are beginning to recognize that changes in the nature of fundamental transactions have implications for the appraisal remedy,[9] courts and legislators have been more slow to do so.

As you read through the materials that follow and examine the rules that have been adopted as part of the modern appraisal statutes, you should consider the purpose of this remedy and the efficacy of appraisal rights in light of the public policy to be served by this modern remedy.

2. Procedural Requirements to Perfect Appraisal Rights

The steps that the dissenting shareholder generally must follow under the terms of the appraisal statutes of most states were described earlier in this chapter (*see supra*, at pp. 73-74), albeit in a general manner. It bears emphasizing that the law of the particular state must be consulted because local statutes will often modify the nature and timing of these procedural requirements, if only slightly. Compliance with the specific requirements of local statutes is of vital importance, as most courts construe appraisal statutes very strictly. Accordingly, any failure to comply with the procedural requirements of the relevant appraisal statute will usually deprive the dissenting shareholders of their appraisal remedy.

In considering the procedural requirements that dissenting shareholders must satisfy in order to obtain cash payment for their shares, a few observations are in order. There are several affirmative steps that the dissenting shareholder

---

9. Professor Thomson's excellent article in the *Georgetown Law Journal* is the best example. [*See* Robert B. Thompson, *Exit, Liquidity, and Majority Rule: Appraisal's Role in Corporate Law*, 84 Geo. L.J. 1, 3-4, 9-11 (1995); *see also* Daniel R. Fischel, *The Appraisal Remedy in Corporate Law*, 1983 Am. B. Found. Res. J. 875, 877-884; Hideki Kanda & Saul Levmore, *The Appraisal Remedy and the Goals of Corporate Law*, 32 UCLA L. Rev. 429 (1985); Mary Siegel, *Back to the Future: Appraisal Rights in the Twenty-First Century*, 32 Harv. J. on Legis. 79, 93-111 (1995); Melvin Eisenberg, THE STRUCTURE OF THE CORPORATION: A LEGAL ANALYSIS, 77-79 (1976); Bayless Manning, *The Shareholder's Appraisal Remedy: An Essay for Frank Coker*, 72 Yale L.J. 223, 246 (1962).]

typically must satisfy in a timely manner. First, the dissenting shareholder must file — *before* the date of the shareholder vote on the proposed transaction — the shareholder's notice of intent to dissent. Later, and separately, the dissenting shareholder must file the shareholder's written demand for payment, which is to be filed *after* the transaction has received the requisite approval of the shareholders. Modern case law makes clear that these detailed statutory requirements as to the content and timing of these filing obligations must be followed carefully; the dissenting shareholder who fails to do so runs the risk of losing this remedy. *Query:* Why does the law impose these filing obligations on the dissenting shareholder? What purpose is served by imposing a filing obligation *before* the date of the shareholder vote?

Perhaps the best way to appreciate the complexity of modern appraisal procedures is to review the description of the process as contained in a recent proxy filing. Below is an excerpt from the proxy statement of DirecTV, a publicly traded Delaware corporation headquartered in El Segundo, California, seeking shareholder approval to sell its business to AT&T, another well-known, publicly traded Delaware corporation. As part of our analysis of the triangular merger problem set earlier in this chapter (*see* p. 121), we described the basic terms of this transaction (as set forth in the parties' merger agreement contained in Appendix B at the end of this casebook), and also determined that DirecTV was required to obtain shareholder approval of this transaction under Delaware law. For reasons to be explored in detail in Chapter 4, AT&T and DirecTV were required by the federal securities laws to prepare a proxy statement in order to solicit approval of the proposed transaction from DirecTV's shareholders. The complete text of the "Notice of Special Meeting of Stockholders" that accompanied DirecTV's proxy statement is reproduced below. This Notice refers to "Appraisal Rights," which is a particular section of the company's proxy statement; the full text of this section of DirecTV's proxy statement is also reproduced below.

As you read through this excerpt from DirecTV's proxy statement, consider the time and expense involved on the part of the minority shareholder who should decide to assert his/her/its right of appraisal. Although this remedy is available to the DirecTV shareholder objecting to the transaction, consider also the scope of protection this remedy offers to the minority shareholder as a practical matter, particularly in light of the costs imposed on any DirecTV shareholder who asserts this right of appraisal.

DIRECTV
2260 East Imperial Highway
El Segundo, California 90245

MERGER PROPOSED — YOUR
VOTE IS VERY IMPORTANT

August 20, 2014

Dear Stockholders:

We cordially invite you to attend a special meeting of stockholders of DIRECTV, a Delaware corporation, to be held on September 25, 2014, at 10:00 a.m. Eastern time, at the Hilton Hotel New York (in Concourse A on the Concourse level), located at 1335 Avenue of the Americas (Sixth Avenue) at West 53rd Street, New York, New York 10019, which we refer to as the special meeting. As previously announced, on May 18, 2014, DIRECTV entered into a merger agreement providing for the combination of DIRECTV with AT&T Inc., a Delaware corporation. At the special meeting, you will be asked to consider and vote upon a proposal to adopt the merger agreement.

If the merger contemplated by the merger agreement is completed, you will be entitled to receive for each share of DIRECTV common stock an amount equal to $28.50 in cash plus a number of shares of AT&T common stock equal to the exchange ratio set forth in the merger agreement, which we refer to as the exchange ratio. The exchange ratio depends on the volume weighted average of the trading price of AT&T common stock on the New York Stock Exchange, which we refer to as the NYSE, on each of the 30 consecutive NYSE trading days ending on the trading day that is three trading days prior to the date of the merger, which we refer to as the average stock price. If the average stock price is between (or including) $34.903 and $38.577 per share, the exchange ratio shall be the quotient of $66.50 divided by the average stock price. If the average stock price is greater than $38.577, the exchange ratio shall be 1.724. If the average stock price is less than $34.903, the exchange ratio shall be 1.905. AT&T common stock is traded on the NYSE under the trading symbol "T" and we encourage you to obtain quotes for the AT&T common stock, given that part of the merger consideration is payable in shares of AT&T common stock.

The merger cannot be completed unless DIRECTV stockholders holding at least a majority of the shares of DIRECTV common stock outstanding as of the close of business on July 29, 2014, the record date for the special meeting, vote in favor of the adoption of the merger agreement at the special meeting.

Your vote is very important, regardless of the number of shares you own. The merger cannot be completed unless the holders of at least a majority of the outstanding shares of DIRECTV common stock entitled to vote thereon vote to adopt the merger agreement. A failure to vote or an abstention will have the same effect as a vote "AGAINST" the adoption of the merger agreement. . . .

In particular, we urge you to read carefully the section entitled "Risk Factors" of the accompanying proxy statement/prospectus. If you have any questions regarding the accompanying proxy statement/prospectus, you may call MacKenzie Partners, Inc., which we refer to as MacKenzie, DIRECTV's proxy solicitor, by calling toll-free at (800) 322-2885.

We urge you to read carefully and in their entirety the accompanying proxy statement/prospectus, including the Annexes and the documents incorporated by reference.

On behalf of the board of directors of DIRECTV, thank you for your consideration and continued support.

Sincerely,
Michael D. White
*Chairman of the Board, President
and Chief Executive Officer*

NEITHER THE SECURITIES AND EXCHANGE COMMISSION NOR ANY STATE SECURITIES COMMISSION HAS APPROVED OR DISAPPROVED THE MERGER OR OTHER TRANSACTIONS DESCRIBED IN THE ATTACHED PROXY STATEMENT/PROSPECTUS OR THE SECURITIES TO BE ISSUED PURSUANT TO THE MERGER UNDER THE ATTACHED PROXY STATEMENT/PROSPECTUS NOR HAVE THEY DETERMINED IF THE ATTACHED PROXY STATEMENT/PROSPECTUS IS ACCURATE OR ADEQUATE. ANY REPRESENTATION TO THE CONTRARY IS A CRIMINAL OFFENSE.

The accompanying proxy statement/prospectus is dated August 20, 2014 and is first being mailed to DIRECTV stockholders on or about August 20, 2014.

DIRECTV
2260 East Imperial Highway
El Segundo, California 90245

**NOTICE OF SPECIAL
MEETING OF STOCKHOLDERS**

Dear Stockholder:
You are cordially invited to attend a special meeting of DIRECTV stockholders. The special meeting will be held on September 25, 2014, at 10:00 a.m.

Eastern time, at the Hilton Hotel New York (in Concourse A on the Concourse level), located at 1335 Avenue of the Americas (Sixth Avenue) at West 53rd Street, New York, New York 10019, to consider and vote upon the following matters:

1. a proposal to adopt the Agreement and Plan of Merger, dated as of May 18, 2014, as it may be amended from time to time, by and among DIRECTV, a Delaware corporation, AT&T Inc., a Delaware corporation, and Steam Merger, Inc., a Delaware corporation and a wholly owned subsidiary of AT&T Inc. A copy of the merger agreement is attached as **Annex A** to the accompanying proxy statement/prospectus;[1]
2. a proposal to approve, by non-binding, advisory vote, certain compensation arrangements for DIRECTV's named executive officers in connection with the merger contemplated by the merger agreement;[2] and
3. adjournments of the special meeting, if necessary or appropriate, to solicit additional proxies if there are insufficient votes at the time of the special meeting to adopt the merger agreement.

The record date for the special meeting is July 29, 2014. Only stockholders of record as of the close of business on July 29, 2014 are entitled to notice of, and to vote at, the special meeting. All stockholders of record as of that date are cordially invited to attend the special meeting in person.

Your vote is very important, regardless of the number of shares of DIRECTV common stock that you own. The merger cannot be completed unless the merger agreement is adopted by the affirmative vote of the holders

---

1. [By the author] The proxy statement (soliciting shareholder approval of this acquisition transaction) and Annex A thereto (the parties' merger agreement) have been omitted. As a reporting company under the 1934 Act, DirecTV was required to prepare a proxy statement in compliance with the federal proxy rules promulgated by the SEC. In Chapter 4, we will describe the scope of disclosure that DirecTV was required to include in this proxy statement soliciting shareholder approval of the company's proposed transaction with AT&T. In addition, we will consider what information the DirecTV shareholders would need in order to make an informed decision to approve the sale of the company's business to AT&T on the terms negotiated and agreed to by the boards of DirecTV and AT&T. In connection with our discussion of the adequacy of the modern appraisal remedy, it bears emphasizing that the SEC's proxy disclosure rules specifically call for disclosure of certain items regarding the availability and procedural requirements of any appraisal rights granted by state law. *See* Regulation M-A, Item 1004.

2. [By the author] You will recall from Chapter 1 (*see* pp. 52-53) that Congress enacted the Dodd-Frank Act in 2010. Among the many reforms introduced by this legislation, Congress addressed the topic of executive compensation. As part of Dodd-Frank's provisions, Congress mandated what has come to be known as the "say-on-pay" vote, a topic to be addressed in more detail in Chapter 4 as part of our discussion of various aspects of the federal securities laws that relate to M&A transactions. At this point, it bears mentioning that DirecTV was required by the Dodd-Frank Act to solicit shareholder approval of compensation to be paid to the company's senior executives as part of AT&T's proposed acquisition of DirecTV. More specifically, Section 951 of Dodd-Frank (and the SEC rules implementing these provisions of the Dodd-Frank Act) mandate an advisory vote of DirecTV's shareholders with respect to any severance payments (i.e., "golden parachute" compensation) that would be triggered by the acquisition and which payment had not previously been approved by an appropriate "say-on-pay" vote of DirecTV's shareholders.

of at least a majority of the outstanding shares of DIRECTV common stock entitled to vote thereon. Even if you plan to attend the special meeting in person, DIRECTV requests that you complete, sign, date and return, as promptly as possible, the enclosed proxy card in the accompanying prepaid reply envelope or submit your proxy by telephone or the Internet prior to the special meeting to ensure that your shares of DIRECTV common stock will be represented at the special meeting if you are unable to attend. If you hold your shares in "street name" through a bank, brokerage firm or other nominee, you should follow the procedures provided by your bank, brokerage firm or other nominee to vote your shares. If you fail to submit a proxy or to attend the special meeting in person or do not provide your bank, brokerage firm or other nominee with instructions as to how to vote your shares, as applicable, your shares of DIRECTV common stock will not be counted for purposes of determining whether a quorum is present at the special meeting and will have the same effect as a vote "AGAINST" the adoption of the merger agreement.

Your proxy is being solicited by the board of directors of DIRECTV. After careful consideration, our board of directors has unanimously (i) determined that the merger is fair to, and in the best interests of, DIRECTV, (ii) approved the merger and the other transactions contemplated thereby, (iii) adopted, approved and declared advisable the merger agreement, and (iv) resolved to recommend the adoption of the merger agreement to DIRECTV stockholders. **Our board of directors unanimously recommends that you vote "FOR" the adoption of the merger agreement and "FOR" the other proposals described in the accompanying proxy statement/prospectus. The board of directors made its determination after consultation with its legal and financial advisors and after considering a number of factors. In considering the recommendation of the board of directors of DIRECTV, you should be aware that the directors and executive officers of DIRECTV will have interests in the merger that may be different from or in addition to the interests of DIRECTV stockholders generally. See the section entitled "Interests of DIRECTV's Directors and Executive Officers in the Merger" beginning on page 116 of the accompanying proxy statement/prospectus.**[3]

To gain admittance to the special meeting, please detach and retain the admission ticket attached to your proxy card. If your shares of DIRECTV common stock are held through a bank, brokerage firm or other nominee, please bring evidence that you own DIRECTV common stock to the special meeting and we will provide you with an admission ticket. If you received your special meeting materials electronically and wish to attend the meeting, please follow the instructions provided for attendance. A form of government-issued photo ID will be required to enter the special meeting.

Under Delaware law, DIRECTV stockholders who do not vote in favor of the adoption of the merger agreement will have the right to seek appraisal of the fair value of their shares of DIRECTV common stock as determined by the Delaware Court of Chancery if the merger is completed, but only if they submit a written demand for such an appraisal prior to the vote on the adoption

---

3. [By the author] The only portion of the "proxy statement/prospectus" that is reproduced below is the portion titled "Appraisal Rights of DirecTV Shareholders."

of the merger agreement and comply with the other Delaware law procedures explained in the accompanying proxy statement. DIRECTV stockholders who do not vote in favor of the adoption of the merger agreement and who submit a written demand for such an appraisal prior to the vote on the adoption of the merger agreement and comply with the other Delaware law procedures will not receive the merger consideration.

WHETHER OR NOT YOU PLAN TO ATTEND THE SPECIAL MEETING, PLEASE COMPLETE, DATE, SIGN AND RETURN, AS PROMPTLY AS POSSIBLE, THE ENCLOSED PROXY CARD IN THE ACCOMPANYING PREPAID REPLY ENVELOPE, OR SUBMIT YOUR PROXY BY TELEPHONE OR THE INTERNET. IF YOU ATTEND THE SPECIAL MEETING AND VOTE IN PERSON, YOUR VOTE BY BALLOT WILL REVOKE ANY PROXY PREVIOUSLY SUBMITTED.

By Order of the Board of Directors,
Michael Hartman
Corporate Secretary

El Segundo, California
Dated: August 20, 2014

* * *

APPRAISAL RIGHTS OF DIRECTV STOCKHOLDERS

General. If you hold one or more shares of DIRECTV common stock, you are entitled to appraisal rights under Delaware law and have the right to dissent from the merger, have your shares appraised by the Delaware Court of Chancery and receive the "fair value" of such shares (exclusive of any element of value arising from the accomplishment or expectation of the merger) as of completion of the merger in place of the merger consideration, as determined by the court, if you strictly comply with the procedures specified in Section 262 of the DGCL. Any such DIRECTV stockholder awarded "fair value" for their shares by the court would receive payment of that fair value in cash, together with interest, if any, in lieu of the right to receive the merger consideration.

The following discussion is not a full summary of the law pertaining to appraisal rights under the DGCL and is qualified in its entirety by the full text of Section 262 of the DGCL that is attached to this proxy statement/prospectus as **Annex D**.[4] All references in Section 262 of the DGCL and in this summary to a "stockholder" are to the record holder of the shares of DIRECTV common stock. The following discussion does not constitute any legal or other advice, nor does it constitute a recommendation that you exercise your rights to seek appraisal under Section 262 of the DGCL.

Under Section 262 of the DGCL, when a merger is submitted for approval at a meeting of stockholders as in the case of the adoption of the merger agreement, DIRECTV, not less than 20 days prior to the meeting, must notify each

---

4. [By the author] Annex D (containing the full text of Delaware Section 262) has been omitted.

stockholder who was a DIRECTV stockholder on the record date for notice of such meeting and who is entitled to exercise appraisal rights, that appraisal rights are available and include in the notice a copy of Section 262 of the DGCL. This proxy statement/prospectus constitutes the required notice, and the copy of applicable statutory provisions is attached to this proxy statement/prospectus as **Annex D**. A holder of DIRECTV common stock who wishes to exercise appraisal rights or who wishes to preserve the right to do so should review the following discussion and **Annex D** carefully. Failure to strictly comply with the procedures of Section 262 of the DGCL in a timely and proper manner will result in the loss of appraisal rights. A stockholder who loses his, her or its appraisal rights will be entitled to receive the per share merger consideration.

How to Exercise and Perfect Your Appraisal Rights. DIRECTV stockholders wishing to exercise the rights to seek an appraisal of their shares must do ALL of the following:

- you must not vote in favor of the adoption of the merger agreement. Because a proxy that is signed and submitted but does not otherwise contain voting instructions will, unless revoked, be voted in favor of the adoption of the merger agreement, if you vote by proxy and wish to exercise your appraisal rights you must vote against the adoption of the merger agreement or abstain from voting your shares;
- you must deliver to DIRECTV a written demand for appraisal before the vote on the adoption of the merger agreement at the special meeting and all demands for appraisal must be made by you, or in your name, fully and correctly, as your name appears, with respect to shares evidenced by certificates, on your stock certificate, or, with respect to shares held in "street name" through a bank, brokerage firm or other nominee, on the stock ledger, and such demands must reasonably inform DIRECTV of your identity and your intention to demand appraisal of your shares of common stock;
- you must continuously hold the shares from the date of making the demand through the effective time. You will lose your appraisal rights if you transfer the shares before the effective time; and
- you or the surviving company must file a petition in the Delaware Court of Chancery requesting a determination of the fair value of the shares within 120 days after the effective time. The surviving company is under no obligation to file any such petition in the Delaware Court of Chancery and has no intention of doing so. Accordingly, it is the obligation of the DIRECTV stockholders to initiate all necessary action to perfect their appraisal rights in respect of shares of DIRECTV common stock within the time prescribed in Section 262 of the DGCL.

Voting, in person or by proxy, against, abstaining from voting on or failing to vote on the adoption of the merger agreement will not constitute a written demand for appraisal as required by Section 262 of the DGCL. The written demand for appraisal must be in addition to and separate from any proxy or vote.

Who May Exercise Appraisal Rights. Only a holder of record of shares of DIRECTV common stock issued and outstanding immediately prior to the effective time may assert appraisal rights for the shares of stock registered in that holder's name. A demand for appraisal must be executed by or on behalf of the stockholder of record, fully and correctly, as the stockholder's name appears on the stock certificates (or in the stock ledger). The demand must reasonably inform DIRECTV of the identity of the stockholder and that the stockholder intends to demand appraisal of his, her or its common stock. **Beneficial owners who do not also hold their shares of common stock of record may not directly make appraisal demands to DIRECTV. The beneficial holder must, in such cases, have the owner of record, such as a bank, brokerage firm or other nominee, submit the required demand in respect of those shares of common stock of record.** A record owner, such as a bank, brokerage firm or other nominee, who holds shares of DIRECTV common stock as a nominee for others, may exercise his, her or its right of appraisal with respect to the shares of DIRECTV common stock held for one or more beneficial owners, while not exercising this right for other beneficial owners. In that case, the written demand should state the number of shares of DIRECTV common stock as to which appraisal is sought. Where no number of shares of DIRECTV common stock is expressly mentioned, the demand will be presumed to cover all shares of DIRECTV common stock held in the name of the record owner.

IF YOU HOLD YOUR SHARES IN BANK OR BROKERAGE ACCOUNTS OR OTHER NOMINEE FORMS, AND YOU WISH TO EXERCISE APPRAISAL RIGHTS, YOU SHOULD CONSULT WITH YOUR BANK, BROKERAGE FIRM OR OTHER NOMINEE, AS APPLICABLE, TO DETERMINE THE APPROPRIATE PROCEDURES FOR THE BANK, BROKERAGE FIRM OR OTHER NOMINEE TO MAKE A DEMAND FOR APPRAISAL OF THOSE SHARES. IF YOU HAVE A BENEFICIAL INTEREST IN SHARES HELD OF RECORD IN THE NAME OF ANOTHER PERSON, SUCH AS A BANK, BROKERAGE FIRM OR OTHER NOMINEE, YOU MUST ACT PROMPTLY TO CAUSE THE RECORD HOLDER TO FOLLOW PROPERLY AND IN A TIMELY MANNER THE STEPS NECESSARY TO PERFECT YOUR APPRAISAL RIGHTS.

If you own shares of DIRECTV common stock jointly with one or more other persons, as in a joint tenancy or tenancy in common, demand for appraisal must be executed by or for you and all other joint owners. An authorized agent, including an agent for two or more joint owners, may execute the demand for appraisal for a stockholder of record; however, the agent must identify the record owner and expressly disclose the fact that, in exercising the demand, such person is acting as agent for the record owner. If you hold shares of DIRECTV common stock through a broker who in turn holds the shares through a central securities depository nominee such as Cede & Co., a demand for appraisal of such shares must be made by or on behalf of the depository nominee and must identify the depository nominee as record holder.

If you elect to exercise appraisal rights under Section 262 of the DGCL, you should mail or deliver a written demand to:

DIRECTV
2260 East Imperial Highway
El Segundo, California 90245
Attention: Office of the Corporate Secretary

AT&T's Actions After Completion of the Merger. If the merger is completed, the surviving company will give written notice of the effective time within 10 days after the effective time to you if you did not vote in favor of the merger agreement and you made a written demand for appraisal in accordance with Section 262 of the DGCL. At any time within 60 days after the effective time, you have the right to withdraw the demand and to accept the merger consideration in accordance with the merger agreement for your shares of DIRECTV common stock. Within 120 days after the effective time, but not later, either you, provided you have complied with the requirements of Section 262 of the DGCL, or the surviving company may commence an appraisal proceeding by filing a petition in the Delaware Court of Chancery, with a copy served on the surviving company in the case of a petition filed by you, demanding a determination of the value of the shares of DIRECTV common stock held by all dissenting stockholders. The surviving company is under no obligation to file an appraisal petition and has no intention of doing so. If you desire to have your shares appraised, you should initiate any petitions necessary for the perfection of their appraisal rights within the time periods and in the manner prescribed in Section 262 of the DGCL.

Within 120 days after the effective time, provided you have complied with the provisions of Section 262 of the DGCL, you will be entitled to receive from the surviving company, upon written request, a statement setting forth the aggregate number of shares not voted in favor of the adoption of the merger agreement and with respect to which DIRECTV has received demands for appraisal, and the aggregate number of holders of those shares. The surviving company must mail this statement to you within the later of 10 days of receipt of the request or 10 days after expiration of the period for delivery of demands for appraisal. If you are the beneficial owner of shares of stock held in a voting trust or by a nominee on your behalf you may, in your own name, file an appraisal petition or request from the surviving company the statement described in this paragraph.

If a petition for appraisal is duly filed by you or another record holder of DIRECTV common stock who has properly exercised his or her appraisal rights in accordance with the provisions of Section 262 of the DGCL, and a copy of the petition is delivered to the surviving company, the surviving company will then be obligated, within 20 days after receiving service of a copy of the petition, to provide the Chancery Court with a duly verified list containing the names and addresses of all holders who have demanded an appraisal of their shares. The Delaware Court of Chancery will then determine which stockholders are entitled to appraisal rights and may require the stockholders demanding appraisal who hold certificated shares to submit their stock certificates to the Register in Chancery for notation thereon of the pendency of the appraisal proceedings and the Delaware Court of Chancery may dismiss any stockholder who fails to comply with this direction from the proceedings. Where proceedings are not dismissed or the demand for appraisal is not successfully withdrawn, the appraisal proceeding will be conducted as to the shares of DIRECTV common stock owned by such stockholders, in accordance with the rules of the Delaware Court of Chancery, including any rules specifically governing appraisal proceedings. The Delaware Court of Chancery will thereafter determine the fair value of the shares of DIRECTV common stock at the effective time held by dissenting stockholders, exclusive of any element of value arising from the accomplishment or expectation of the merger. Unless the Delaware Court of Chancery in its discretion determines otherwise for good cause shown, interest from the effective time through the date of payment of the judgment will be compounded quarterly and will accrue at 5% over the Federal Reserve discount rate (including any surcharge) as established from time to time during the period between the effective time and the date of payment of the judgment. When the value is determined, the Delaware Court of Chancery will direct the payment of such value, with interest thereon, if any, to the stockholders entitled to receive the same, upon surrender by such stockholders of their stock certificates and book-entry shares.

In determining the fair value, the Delaware Court of Chancery is required to take into account all relevant factors.[5] In *Weinberger v. UOP, Inc.*, the Delaware Supreme Court discussed the factors that could be considered in determining fair value in an appraisal proceeding, stating that "proof of value by any techniques or methods which are generally considered acceptable in the financial community and otherwise admissible in court" should be considered and that "[f]air price obviously requires consideration of all relevant factors involving the value of a company." The Delaware Supreme Court has stated that, in making this determination of fair value, the court must consider market value, asset value, dividends, earnings prospects, the nature of the enterprise and any other factors which could be ascertained as of the date of the merger which throw any light on future prospects of the merged corporation. Section 262 of the DGCL provides that fair value is to be "exclusive of any element of value arising from the accomplishment or expectation of the merger." In *Cede & Co. v. Technicolor, Inc.*, the Delaware Supreme Court stated that such exclusion is a "narrow exclusion [that] does not encompass known elements of value," but which rather applies only to the speculative elements of value arising from such accomplishment or expectation. In *Weinberger*, the Delaware Supreme Court construed Section 262 of the DGCL to mean that "elements of future value, including the nature of the enterprise, which are known or susceptible of proof as of the date of the merger and not the product of speculation, may be considered." In addition, Delaware courts have decided that the statutory appraisal remedy, depending on factual circumstances, may or may not be a dissenter's exclusive remedy. An opinion of an investment banking firm as to the fairness from a financial point of view of the consideration payable in a merger is not an opinion as to, and does not in any manner address, fair value under Section 262

---

5. [By the author] Determining the "fair value" of the dissenter's shares will be the focus of a judicially supervised appraisal proceeding in the event that the dissenting shareholder and the company cannot reach agreement as to fair value. Cases and other materials later in this section explore the difficult factual issues that are inherent in determining what is "fair value," particularly in light of the statutory mandate to ignore "any element of value arising from the accomplishment or expectation of the proposed merger." *See infra*, at pp. 179-230.

of the DGCL. The fair value of their shares as determined under Section 262 of the DGCL could be greater than, the same as, or less than the value of the merger consideration. We do not anticipate offering more than the per share merger consideration to any stockholder exercising appraisal rights and reserve the right to assert, in any appraisal proceeding, that, for purposes of Section 262, the "fair value" of a share of DIRECTV common stock is less than the per share merger consideration.

If no party files a petition for appraisal within 120 days after the effective time, then you will lose the right to an appraisal, and will instead receive the merger consideration described in the merger agreement, without interest thereon, less any withholding taxes.

The Delaware Court of Chancery may determine the costs of the appraisal proceeding and may allocate those costs to the parties as the Delaware Court of Chancery determines to be equitable under the circumstances. However, costs do not include attorneys and expert witness fees. Each dissenting stockholder is responsible for its own attorneys and expert witnesses expenses, although, upon application of a stockholder, the Delaware Court of Chancery may order all or a portion of the expenses incurred by any stockholder in connection with the appraisal proceeding, including reasonable attorneys' fees and the fees and expenses of experts, to be charged pro rata against the value of all shares entitled to appraisal.

If you have duly demanded an appraisal in compliance with Section 262 of the DGCL you may not, after the effective time, vote the DIRECTV shares subject to the demand for any purpose or receive any dividends or other distributions on those shares, except dividends or other distributions payable to holders of record of DIRECTV shares as of a record date prior to the effective time.

If you have not commenced an appraisal proceeding or joined such a proceeding as a named party you may withdraw a demand for appraisal and accept the merger consideration by delivering a written withdrawal of the demand for appraisal to the surviving company, except that any attempt to withdraw made more than 60 days after the effective time will require written approval of the surviving company, and no appraisal proceeding in the Delaware Court of Chancery will be dismissed as to any stockholder without the approval of the Delaware Court of Chancery. Such approval may be conditioned on the terms the Delaware Court of Chancery deems just, provided, however, that this provision will not affect the right of any stockholder who has not commenced an appraisal proceeding or joined such proceeding as a named party to withdraw such stockholder's demand for appraisal and to accept the terms offered in the merger within 60 days. If you fail to perfect, successfully withdraw or lose the appraisal right, your shares will be converted into the right to receive the merger consideration, without interest thereon, less any withholding taxes.

Failure to follow the steps required by Section 262 of the DGCL for perfecting appraisal rights may result in the loss of appraisal rights. In that event, you will be entitled to receive the merger consideration for your shares in accordance with the merger agreement.[6] In view of the complexity of the provisions

---

6. [By the author] Generally speaking, the failure to perfect the right of appraisal will result in the dissenting shares being converted into the right to receive the consideration as set forth under the terms of the merger agreement.

of Section 262 of the DGCL, if you are a DIRECTV stockholder and are considering exercising your appraisal rights under the DGCL, you should consult your own legal advisor.

THE PROCESS OF DEMANDING AND EXERCISING APPRAISAL RIGHTS REQUIRES STRICT COMPLIANCE WITH TECHNICAL PREREQUISITES. IF YOU WISH TO EXERCISE YOUR APPRAISAL RIGHTS, YOU SHOULD CONSULT WITH YOUR OWN LEGAL COUNSEL IN CONNECTION WITH COMPLIANCE UNDER SECTION 262 OF THE DGCL. TO THE EXTENT THERE ARE ANY INCONSISTENCIES BETWEEN THE FOREGOING SUMMARY AND SECTION 262 OF THE DGCL, THE DGCL WILL GOVERN.

QUESTIONS

1. In view of the disclosure contained in DirecTV's proxy statement, do you think lay investors holding shares of DirecTV common stock could competently decide on their own whether to exercise their right of appraisal?

2. Why does the law require shareholders to follow these procedures? What are the competing interests to be balanced in designing the procedures for perfecting the statutorily mandated appraisal remedy? How do the recent reforms adopted by the MBCA address these competing interests? *See, generally,* MBCA Chapter 13, Subchapter B (Procedure for Exercise of Appraisal Rights). More specifically, review the provisions of MBCA §13.24 and consider the following commentary to that section:

> Section 13.24 changes the relative balance [of power] between the corporation and [those] shareholders demanding an appraisal by requiring the corporation to pay in cash within 30 days after the required form [of demand for payment has been submitted by the dissenting shareholder pursuant to MBCA §§13.22 and 13.23] is due the corporation's estimate of the fair value of the stock plus interest.... [Consequently, the dissenting shareholders should have] immediate use of such money. A difference of opinion over the total amount to be paid should not delay payment of the amount that is undisputed. Thus, the corporation must pay its estimate of fair value, plus interest from the effective date of the corporate action, without waiting for the conclusion of the appraisal proceeding.

With respect to the *costs* incurred in bringing an appraisal action, review the provisions of MBCA §13.31 and consider the following commentary to that section:

> Section 13.31(a) provides a general rule that the court costs of the appraisal proceeding should be assessed against the corporation. Nevertheless, the court is authorized to assess these court costs, in whole or in part, against all or some of the shareholders demanding appraisal if it concludes they acted arbitrarily, vexatiously, or not in good faith regarding the rights provided by this chapter. Under section 13.31(b), the court may assess expenses against the corporation or against all or some of the shareholders demanding appraisal for the reasons stated in this subsection. Under section 13.31(c), if the corporation is not

required to pay the expenses incurred by any shareholder demanding appraisal, the court may require all shareholders who benefitted to share in the payment of such expenses. The purpose of all these grants of discretion with respect to expenses is to increase the incentives of both sides to proceed in good faith under this chapter to attempt to resolve their disagreement without the need of a formal judicial appraisal of the value of shares.

3. As a general proposition, management usually tries to structure the transaction to avoid appraisal rights altogether. Why such hostility to the appraisal remedy? Alternatively, management may condition the company's obligation to close on the M&A transaction on receiving no more than a *de minimis* number of demands, typically expressed as a percentage of the company's outstanding shares (e.g., the company's obligation to close is conditioned on no more than 3 percent of the company's outstanding shares exercising the statutory right to an appraisal).

NOTES

1. *Holding Shares in "Street Name."* The preceding excerpt from the AT&T–DirecTV prospectus/proxy statement refers to holding shares in "street name." What is *street name ownership*? In the United States, there are two principal ways of holding stock in a modern corporation: stock certificates or street name accounts. Before the advent of modern technology, shares were held in certificate form, with the company typically issuing a physical (hard copy) share certificate in the name of the investor/shareholder. Today, however, most shareholders of publicly traded U.S. companies hold their shares in street name, which refers to shares of a company that are held electronically in the account of a stockbroker or bank or other custodian. The entity whose name is recorded as the legal owner of the shares is often referred to as the "nominee owner" or "record owner" and the nominee has ownership of these shares, including the right to vote the shares and to receive any dividends distributed with respect to those shares. However, the nominee owner holds these ownership rights on behalf of the true economic owner (i.e., the investor who provided the funds to purchase the shares), also known as the "beneficial owner." So today when an investor buys shares through a brokerage firm, the firm will hold those shares in its name (or in the name of another nominee), but the brokerage firm will keep records showing the investor as the "beneficial owner" of those shares. The investor does not receive a physical stock certificate but instead receives an account statement listing the investor's shareholdings. Today, in the United States, the largest shareholder of most NYSE-listed companies is usually going to be Cede & Co., a nominee of Depository Trust Company. Holding shares in street name has grown be the dominant form of share ownership for publicly-traded companies because it greatly facilitates trading by allowing trading to be done electronically rather than physically delivering a stock certificate.

If Cede & Co. is the street name owner of the shares then, as the registered owner (or record owner), Cede & Co. is entitled to exercise the voting rights

attributable to those shares. Through an elaborate scheme of rule-making promulgated by the SEC and the NYSE, the beneficial owner of the shares is entitled to instruct the registered owner (i.e., Cede & Co.) as to how to vote the
shares held in street name, and Cede & Co. is obliged to vote the shares as
directed. In sending voting materials to beneficial owners of the shares, brokers
have a choice of forwarding a proxy card (which the street name owner returns
directly to the company) or the broker may request that the street name owner
deliver instructions to the broker as to how to vote the shares. Where voting
instructions are sought, brokers must then tabulate the votes and transfer the
votes to a proxy card that is delivered to the company. Inevitably this voting
process can create problems, especially when the instructions are delivered by
the beneficial owner late in the voting process. This potential for "problems"
was illustrated in the high-profile LBO involving Dell, Inc., discussed *infra* at
pg. 208.

   2. Recent Rise in "Appraisal Arbitrage" Activity. Although appraisal rights
have been granted by state corporation statutes (such as Delaware §262) since
the early part of the twentieth century, the conventional view of appraisal is
that it is a remedy used "infrequently" by shareholders. *See* Charles Korsmo and
Minor Meyers, *Reforming Modern Appraisal Litigation*, 41 Del. J. Corp. Law (forthcoming 2016). However, in recent years, Delaware has experienced a substantial
rise in the exercise of the statutory remedy of appraisal rights. As described by
Professors Minor Myers and Charles Korsmo,

>   . . . Delaware is in the midst of a sea-change in appraisal litigation. While
> appraisal may once have been a quiet corner of corporate law, it is now an area
> of active litigation undergoing a period of explosive growth. Furthermore, the
> parties driving that growth are a new group of sophisticated investors [including
> hedge funds and other activist shareholders] who appear to specialize in pursing
> appraisal claims. In short, we have documented the rise of appraisal arbitrage.

Charles Korsmo and Minor Myers, *Appraisal Arbitrage and the Future of Public
Company M&A*, 92 Wash. U. L. Rev. 1551, 1567 (2015) (As documented by
Professors Myers and Korsmo, the value of appraisal claims "in 2013 was nearly
$1.5 billion, [representing] a tenfold increase from 2004 . . ." *Id.* at 1553). What
is *appraisal arbitrage?*

>   Appraisal arbitrage refers to hedge funds and other activist investors acquir-
> ing target shares after an announcement of a public company merger with the
> goal of seeking appraisal rights under state statutory schemes.
>   The appraisal process allows shareholders who are dissatisfied with the con-
> sideration offered by the acquirer to petition a court for an appraisal of their
> shares' "fair value." What makes this attractive to activist investors, particularly
> in an atmosphere of low interest rates [which is the "atmosphere" that has pre-
> vailed since the onset of the Great Recession], is that the "return" on a successful
> appraisal action may yield a higher court-determined price plus interest at a statu-
> tory rate. Given the higher interest rates [prescribed by many modern] appraisal
> statutes, investors can realize quick returns.
>   Critics complain that the increase in appraisal arbitrage may hinder other-
> wise constructive transactions and worry that buyers will offer less in anticipation

of the capital they will lose when appraisal arbitrageurs strike. Proponents argue that appraisal arbitrageurs play an important role as specialists with the ability to hone in on deals and ensure that shareholders receive fair value.

Eli Richlin and Tony Rospert, *The Rise of Appraisal Litigation: Will the Fire Spread?* Autumn 2015, *available at*: www.willamette.com/insights_journal/15/autumn_20151.pdf.

Many commentators believe that appraisal arbitrage is a driving force behind the recent surge in appraisal proceedings. As noted in the preceding excerpt, many commentators also speculate that activist shareholders and hedge funds are incentivized by the interest provisions of Delaware §§262(h)-(i), which allow for "appraisal awards to accrue and compound quarterly interest from the effective time of the merger through the [date of the] appraisal judgment [awarded by the Delaware Chancery Court] at a rate 5 percent over the Federal Reserve discount rate. Interest compounding applies to the entire appraisal award. By extension, even if a court appraises fair value at a price lower than the deal consideration [i.e., merger price], the plaintiff still receives protection by virtue of the interest payments." *Id.* at 5.

3. Recent Amendments to Delaware §262. Given the controversy surrounding the recent emergence of appraisal arbitrage and the public policy concerns raised by the increase in the exercise of the appraisal remedy, it should come as no surprise that critics were soon urging that the Delaware legislature look into these developments. In 2015, legislative reform measures were proposed, but no action was taken at that time. Controversy continued, however, resulting in legislative amendments to Delaware §262 that became effective on August 1, 2016.

    . . . The new legislation amends Section 262(g) to provide that the Court of Chancery must dismiss an appraisal proceeding as to all stockholders who assert appraisal rights unless (a) the total number of shares entitled to appraisal exceeds 1% of the outstanding shares of the class or series eligible for appraisal, or (b) the value of the consideration provided in the merger or consolidation for such total number of shares seeking appraisal exceeds $1 million, or (c) the merger was approved pursuant to Section 253 [i.e., a short-form merger] . . . These provisions thus prevent stockholders from demanding appraisal in cases where the number of their shares or the value of those shares is minimal. This *de minimis* exception applies only to shares that were listed on a national securities exchange immediately before the merger or consolidation.

    Section 262(h) of the DGCL provides that, unless the Court of Chancery determines otherwise for good cause, interest on an appraisal award always accrues from the effective date of the merger through the date of payment of the appraisal award at a rate of 5% over the Federal Reserve discount rate, compounded quarterly. Of course, surviving corporations already have the ability to propose agreements with appraisal petitioners to release all or a portion of the merger consideration and thereby to eliminate the running of statutory interest as to the amount released, but surviving corporations previously could not *require* appraisal petitioners to accept such payments. The legislation now amends Section 262(h) to give the surviving corporation the right to make a voluntary cash payment to stockholders seeking appraisal prior to the Court of Chancery's final judgment regarding fair value, thereby reducing the amount of interest that accrues during the appraisal process. If the surviving corporation makes a prepayment, interest will accrue only on the sum of (i) the difference, if any, between the amount paid and the fair value of the shares as determined by the Court of Chancery and (ii) interest accrued before the prepayment, unless paid at the time of such prepayment. The amount of any prepayment is in the sole discretion of the surviving corporation, and there is no inference that the amount paid by the surviving corporation is equal to, greater than, or less than the fair value of the shares to be appraised.

By providing surviving corporations the absolute right to prepay appraisal amounts and to cut off statutory interest, Delaware may have, at the margins, lessened the incentive for stockholders to bring or prolong appraisal actions [including perhaps lessening the incidence of appraisal arbitrage].

Ropes and Gray LLP, *Amendments to Delaware General Corporation Law Will Affect Appraisal Actions,* June 20, 2016 (law firm memo, copy on file with author).

Indeed, the number of appraisal actions filed in Delaware since 2016 has decreased, with the number of appraisal petitions "declining 21 percent from 2016 to 2017 and 57 percent from 2017 to 2018."Cornerstone Research, *Appraisal Litigation in Delaware: Trends in Petitions and Opinions 2006-2018* (2019); *available at:* https://www.cornerstone.com/publications/reports/appraisal-litigation-delaware-2006-2018.

3. Judicial Determination of Fair Value in an Appraisal Proceeding

In its seminal decision in *Weinberger v. UOP, Inc.,* the Delaware Supreme Court touches on two important issues in considering the modern appraisal remedy: *valuation* of dissenters' shares and the *exclusivity* of the appraisal remedy. Rather than disrupt the flow of the court's analysis by trying to parse the opinion to separate out the court's discussion of these two related issues, the text of this landmark opinion dealing with these two issues is set forth below. In the final section of this chapter, we will consider whether the appraisal proceeding has, in fact, turned out to be the *exclusive remedy* available to the dissenting shareholder as part of our analysis of the Delaware Supreme Court's subsequent decision in *Rabkin v. Philip A. Hunt Chemical Corp.* In the materials that immediately follow the *Weinberger* opinion, we will consider the *valuation* issues that arise from the court's holding.

▌▌ **Weinberger v. UOP, Inc.**
▌▌ **457 A.2d 701 (Del. 1983)**

MOORE, Justice:

This post-trial appeal was reheard en banc from a decision of the Court of Chancery. It was brought by the class action plaintiff below, a former shareholder of UOP, Inc., who challenged the elimination of UOP's minority shareholders by a cash-out merger between UOP and its majority owner, The Signal Companies, Inc. Originally, the defendants in this action were Signal, UOP, certain officers and directors of those companies, and UOP's investment banker, Lehman Brothers Kuhn Loeb, Inc. The present Chancellor held that the terms of the merger were fair to the plaintiff and the other minority shareholders of UOP. Accordingly, he entered judgment in favor of the defendants.

Numerous points were raised by the parties, but we address only the following questions presented by the trial court's opinion:

1. The plaintiff's duty to plead sufficient facts demonstrating the unfairness of the challenged merger;
2. The burden of proof upon the parties where the merger has been approved by the purportedly informed vote of a majority of the minority shareholders;
3. The fairness of the merger in terms of adequacy of the defendants' disclosures to the minority shareholders;
4. The fairness of the merger in terms of adequacy of the price paid for the minority shares and the remedy appropriate to that issue; . . .

. . . In ruling for the defendants, the Chancellor re-stated his earlier conclusion that the plaintiff in a suit challenging a cash-out merger must allege specific acts of fraud, misrepresentation, or other items of misconduct to demonstrate the unfairness of the merger terms to the minority. We approve this rule and affirm it.

The Chancellor also held that even though the ultimate burden of proof is on the majority shareholder to show by a preponderance of the evidence that the transaction is fair, it is first the burden of the plaintiff attacking the merger to demonstrate some basis for invoking the fairness obligation. We agree with that principle. However, where corporate action has been approved by an informed vote of a majority of the minority shareholders, we conclude that the burden entirely shifts to the plaintiff to show that the transaction was unfair to the minority. But in all this, the burden clearly remains on those relying on the vote to show that they completely disclosed all material facts relevant to the transaction.

Here, the record does not support a conclusion that the minority stockholder vote was an informed one. Material information, necessary to acquaint those shareholders with the bargaining positions of Signal and UOP, was withheld under circumstances amounting to a breach of fiduciary duty. We therefore conclude that this merger does not meet the test of fairness, at least as we address that concept, and no burden thus shifted to the plaintiff by reason of the minority shareholder vote. Accordingly, we reverse and remand for further proceedings consistent herewith.

In considering the nature of the remedy available under our law to minority shareholders in a cash-out merger, we believe that it is, and hereafter should be, an appraisal under 8 Del. C. §262 as hereinafter construed. . . . But to give full effect to section 262 within the framework of the General Corporation Law we adopt a more liberal, less rigid and stylized, approach to the valuation process than has heretofore been permitted by our courts. While the present state of these proceedings does not admit the plaintiff to the appraisal remedy per se, the practical effect of the remedy we do grant him will be co-extensive with the liberalized valuation and appraisal methods we herein approve for cases coming after this decision. . . .

Our treatment of these matters has necessarily led us to a reconsideration of the business purpose rule announced in the trilogy of *Singer v. Magnavox Co.*, [380 A.2d 969 (Del 1977)]; *Tanzer v. International General Industries, Inc.*, Del. Supr., 379 A.2d 1121 (1977); and *Roland International Corp. v. Najjar*, Del. Supr., 407 A.2d 1032 (1979). For the reasons hereafter set forth we consider that the business purpose requirement of these cases is no longer the law of Delaware.

I

The facts found by the trial court, pertinent to the issues before us, are supported by the record, and we draw from them as set out in the Chancellor's opinion.

Signal is a diversified, technically based company operating through various subsidiaries. Its stock is publicly traded on the [NYSE, as was the stock of UOP]. . . .

In 1974 Signal sold one of its wholly-owned subsidiaries for $420,000,000 in cash. *See Gimbel v. Signal Companies, Inc.*, Del. Ch., 316 A.2d 599, *aff'd*, Del. Supr., 316 A.2d 619 (1974).* While looking to invest this cash surplus, Signal became interested in UOP as a possible acquisition. Friendly negotiations ensued, and Signal proposed to acquire a controlling interest in UOP at a price of $19 per share. UOP's representatives sought $25 per share [at a time when UOP's stock was trading at a fraction under $14 per share on the NYSE]. In the arm's length bargaining that followed, an understanding was reached [between the parties] whereby Signal agreed to purchase from UOP 1,500,000 shares of UOP's authorized but unissued stock at $21 per share.

This purchase was contingent upon Signal making a successful cash tender offer for 4,300,000 publicly held shares of UOP, also at a price of $21 per share. This combined method of acquisition permitted Signal to acquire [in 1975] 5,800,000 shares of stock, representing 50.5% of UOP's outstanding shares. . . .

. . . [T]he resulting tender offer was greatly oversubscribed. However, Signal limited its total purchase of the tendered shares so that, when coupled with the stock bought from UOP, it had achieved its goal of becoming a 50.5% shareholder of UOP.

Although UOP's board consisted of thirteen directors, Signal nominated and elected only six. . . . [However, when UOP's president retired in 1975,] Signal caused him to be replaced by James V. Crawford, a long-time [Signal] employee . . . Crawford succeeded his predecessor on UOP's board of directors and also was made a director of Signal.

By the end of 1977 Signal basically was unsuccessful in finding other suitable investment candidates for its excess cash, and [decided to consider acquiring the minority interests in UOP] . . .

The trial court found that at the instigation of certain Signal management personnel, including William W. Walkup, its board chairman, and Forrest N. Shumway, its president, a feasibility study was made concerning the possible acquisition of the balance of UOP's outstanding shares. This study was

---

* [By the author: The text of this opinion appears at p. 89.]

performed by two Signal officers, Charles S. Arledge, vice president (director of planning), and Andrew J. Chitiea, senior vice president (chief financial officer). Messrs. Walkup, Shumway, Arledge, and Chitiea were all directors of UOP in addition to their membership on the Signal board.

Arledge and Chitiea concluded that it would be a good investment for Signal to acquire the remaining 49.5% of UOP shares at any price up to $24 each. Their report was discussed between Walkup and Shumway who, along with Arledge, Chitiea and Brewster L. Arms, internal counsel for Signal, constituted Signal's senior management. In particular, they talked about the proper price to be paid if the acquisition was pursued, purportedly keeping in mind that as UOP's majority shareholder, Signal owed a fiduciary responsibility to both its own stockholders as well as to UOP's minority. It was ultimately agreed that a meeting of Signal's Executive Committee would be called to propose that Signal acquire the remaining outstanding stock of UOP through a cash-out merger in the range of $20 to $21 per share.

The Executive Committee meeting was set for February 28, 1978. As a courtesy, UOP's president, Crawford, was invited to attend, although he was not a member of Signal's executive committee. On his arrival, and prior to the meeting, Crawford was asked to meet privately with Walkup and Shumway. He was then told of Signal's plan to acquire full ownership of UOP and was asked for his reaction to the proposed price range of $20 to $21 per share. Crawford said he thought such a price would be "generous," and that it was certainly one which should be submitted to UOP's minority shareholders for their ultimate consideration. He stated, however, that Signal's 100% ownership could cause internal problems at UOP. He believed that employees would have to be given some assurance of their future place in a fully-owned Signal subsidiary. Otherwise, he feared the departure of essential personnel. Also, many of UOP's key employees had stock option incentive programs which would be wiped out by a merger. Crawford therefore urged that some adjustment would have to be made, such as providing a comparable incentive in Signal's shares, if after the merger he was to maintain his quality of personnel and efficiency at UOP.

Thus, Crawford voiced no objection to the $20 to $21 price range, nor did he suggest that Signal should consider paying more than $21 per share for the minority interests. . . .

Thus, it was the consensus that a price of $20 to $21 per share would be fair to both Signal and the minority shareholders of UOP. Signal's executive committee authorized its management "to negotiate" with UOP "for a cash acquisition of the minority ownership in UOP, Inc., with the intention of presenting a proposal to [Signal's] board of directors . . . on March 6, 1978." Immediately after this February 28, 1978 meeting, Signal issued a press release stating:

> The Signal Companies, Inc. and UOP, Inc. are conducting negotiations for the acquisition for cash by Signal of the 49.5 per cent of UOP which it does not presently own, announced Forrest N. Shumway, president and chief executive officer of Signal, and James V. Crawford, UOP president.
>
> Price and other terms of the proposed transaction have not yet been finalized and would be subject to approval of the boards of directors of Signal and UOP, scheduled to meet early next week, the stockholders of UOP and certain federal agencies.

The announcement also referred to the fact that the closing price of UOP's common stock on that day was $14.50 per share.

Two days later, on March 2, 1978, Signal issued a second press release stating that its management would recommend a price in the range of $20 to $21 per share for UOP's 49.5% minority interest. This announcement referred to Signal's earlier statement that "negotiations" were being conducted for the acquisition of the minority shares.

Between Tuesday, February 28, 1978 and Monday, March 6, 1978, a total of four business days, Crawford spoke by telephone with all of UOP's non-Signal, i.e., outside, directors. Also during that period, Crawford retained Lehman Brothers to render a fairness opinion as to the price offered the minority for its stock. He gave two reasons for this choice. First, the time schedule between the announcement and the board meetings was short (by then only three business days) and since Lehman Brothers had been acting as UOP's investment banker for many years, Crawford felt that it would be in the best position to respond on such brief notice. Second, James W. Glanville, a long-time director of UOP and a partner in Lehman Brothers, had acted as a financial advisor to UOP for many years. Crawford believed that Glanville's familiarity with UOP, as a member of its board, would also be of assistance in enabling Lehman Brothers to render a fairness opinion within the existing time constraints.

Crawford telephoned Glanville, who gave his assurance that Lehman Brothers had no conflicts that would prevent it from accepting the task. Glanville's immediate personal reaction was that a price of $20 to $21 would certainly be fair, since it represented almost a 50% premium over UOP's market price. Glanville sought a $250,000 fee for Lehman Brothers' services, but Crawford thought this too much. After further discussions Glanville finally agreed that Lehman Brothers would render its fairness opinion for $150,000.

During this period Crawford also had several telephone contacts with Signal officials. In only one of them, however, was the price of the shares discussed. In a conversation with Walkup, Crawford advised that as a result of his communications with UOP's non-Signal directors, it was his feeling that the price would have to be the top of the proposed range, or $21 per share, if the approval of UOP's outside directors was to be obtained. But again, he did not seek any price higher than $21.

Glanville assembled a three-man Lehman Brothers team to do the work on the fairness opinion. These persons examined relevant documents and information concerning UOP, including its annual reports and its Securities and Exchange Commission filings from 1973 through 1976, as well as its audited financial statements for 1977, its interim reports to shareholders, and its recent and historical market prices and trading volumes. In addition, on Friday, March 3, 1978, two members of the Lehman Brothers team flew to UOP's headquarters in Des Plaines, Illinois, to perform a "due diligence" visit, during the course of which they interviewed Crawford as well as UOP's general counsel, its chief financial officer, and other key executives and personnel.

As a result, the Lehman Brothers team concluded that "the price of either $20 or $21 would be a fair price for the remaining shares of UOP." They telephoned this impression to Glanville, who was spending the weekend in Vermont.

On Monday morning, March 6, 1978, Glanville and the senior member of the Lehman Brothers team flew to Des Plaines to attend the scheduled UOP directors meeting. Glanville looked over the assembled information during the flight. The two had with them the draft of a "fairness opinion letter" in which the price had been left blank. Either during or immediately prior to the directors' meeting, the two-page "fairness opinion letter" was typed in final form and the price of $21 per share was inserted.

On March 6, 1978, both the Signal and UOP boards were convened to consider the proposed merger. Telephone communications were maintained between the two meetings. Walkup, Signal's board chairman, and also a UOP director, attended UOP's meeting with Crawford in order to present Signal's position and answer any questions that UOP's non-Signal directors might have. Arledge and Chitiea, along with Signal's other designees on UOP's board, participated by conference telephone. All of UOP's outside directors attended the meeting either in person or by conference telephone.

First, Signal's board unanimously adopted a resolution authorizing Signal to propose to UOP a cash merger of $21 per share as outlined in a certain merger agreement and other supporting documents. This proposal required that the merger be approved by a majority of UOP's outstanding minority shares voting at the stockholders meeting at which the merger would be considered, and that the minority shares voting in favor of the merger, when coupled with Signal's 50.5% interest would have to comprise at least two-thirds of all UOP shares. Otherwise the proposed merger would be deemed disapproved.

UOP's board then considered the proposal. Copies of the agreement were delivered to the directors in attendance, and other copies had been forwarded earlier to the directors participating by telephone. They also had before them UOP financial data for 1974-1977, UOP's most recent financial statements, market price information, and budget projections for 1978. In addition they had Lehman Brothers' hurriedly prepared fairness opinion letter finding the price of $21 to be fair. Glanville, the Lehman Brothers partner, and UOP director, commented on the information that had gone into preparation of the letter.

Signal also suggests that the Arledge-Chitiea feasibility study, indicating that a price of up to $24 per share would be a "good investment" for Signal, was discussed at the UOP directors' meeting. The Chancellor made no such finding, and our independent review of the record, detailed infra, satisfies us by a preponderance of the evidence that there was no discussion of this document at UOP's board meeting. Furthermore, it is clear beyond peradventure that nothing in that report was ever disclosed to UOP's minority shareholders prior to their approval of the merger.

After consideration of Signal's proposal, Walkup and Crawford left the meeting to permit a free and uninhibited exchange between UOP's non-Signal directors. Upon their return a resolution to accept Signal's offer was then proposed and adopted. While Signal's men on UOP's board participated in various aspects of the meeting, they abstained from voting. However, the minutes show that each of them "if voting would have voted yes."

On March 7, 1978, UOP sent a letter to its shareholders advising them of the action taken by UOP's board with respect to Signal's offer. This document pointed out, among other things, that on February 28, 1978 "both companies had announced negotiations were being conducted."

Despite the swift board action of the two companies, the merger was not submitted to UOP's shareholders until their annual meeting on May 26, 1978.

In the notice of that meeting and proxy statement sent to shareholders in May, UOP's management and board urged that the merger be approved. The proxy statement also advised:

> The price was determined after *discussions* between James V. Crawford, a director of Signal and Chief Executive Officer of UOP, and officers of Signal which took place during meetings on February 28, 1978, and in the course of several subsequent telephone conversations. (*Emphasis added.*)

In the original draft of the proxy statement the word "negotiations" had been used rather than "discussions." However, when the Securities and Exchange Commission sought details of the "negotiations" as part of its review of these materials, the term was deleted and the word "discussions" was substituted. The proxy statement indicated that the vote of UOP's board in approving the merger had been unanimous. It also advised the shareholders that Lehman Brothers had given its opinion that the merger price of $21 per share was fair to UOP's minority. However, it did not disclose the hurried method by which this conclusion was reached.

As of the record date of UOP's annual meeting, there were 11,488,302 shares of UOP common stock outstanding, 5,688,302 of which were owned by the minority. At the meeting only 56%, or 3,208,652, of the minority shares were voted. Of these, 2,953,812, or 51.9% of the total minority, voted for the merger, and 254,840 voted against it. When Signal's stock was added to the minority shares voting in favor, a total of 76.2% of UOP's outstanding shares approved the merger while only 2.2% opposed it.

By its terms the merger became effective on May 26, 1978, and each share of UOP's stock held by the minority was automatically converted into a right to receive $21 cash.

II

A

A primary issue mandating reversal is the preparation by two UOP directors, Arledge and Chitiea, of their feasibility study for the exclusive use and benefit of Signal. This document was of obvious significance to both Signal and UOP. Using UOP data, it described the advantages to Signal of ousting the minority at a price range of $21-$24 per share. Mr. Arledge, one of the authors, outlined the benefits to Signal:[6]

Purpose of the Merger

1) Provides an outstanding investment opportunity for Signal—(Better than any recent acquisition we have seen).
2) Increases Signal's earnings.

---

6. The parentheses indicate certain handwritten comments of Mr. Arledge.

3) Facilitates the flow of resources between Signal and its subsidiaries — (Big factor — works both ways).

4) Provides cost savings potential for Signal and UOP.

5) Improves the percentage of Signal's "operating earnings" as opposed to "holding company earnings."

6) Simplifies the understanding of Signal.

7) Facilitates technological exchange among Signal's subsidiaries.

8) Eliminates potential conflicts of interest.

Having written those words, solely for the use of Signal, it is clear from the record that neither Arledge nor Chitiea shared this report with their fellow directors of UOP. We are satisfied that no one else did either. This conduct hardly meets the fiduciary standards applicable to such a transaction. . . .

. . . The Arledge-Chitiea report speaks for itself in supporting the Chancellor's finding that a price of up to $24 was a "good investment" for Signal. It shows that a return on the investment at $21 would be 15.7% versus 15.5% at $24 per share. This was a difference of only two-tenths of one percent, while it meant over $17,000,000 to the minority. Under such circumstances, paying UOP's minority shareholders $24 would have had relatively little long-term effect on Signal, and the Chancellor's findings concerning the benefit to Signal, even at a price of $24, were obviously correct. *Levitt v. Bouvier,* Del. Supr., 287 A.2d 671, 673 (1972).

Certainly, this was a matter of material significance to UOP and its shareholders. Since the study was prepared by two UOP directors, using UOP information for the exclusive benefit of Signal, and nothing whatever was done to disclose it to the outside UOP directors or the minority shareholders, a question of breach of fiduciary duty arises. This problem occurs because there were common Signal-UOP directors participating, at least to some extent, in the UOP board's decision-making processes without full disclosure of the conflicts they faced.[7]

B

In assessing this situation, the Court of Chancery was required to:

examine what information defendants had and to measure it against what they gave to the minority stockholders, in a context in which "complete candor" is

---

7. Although perfection is not possible, or expected, the result here could have been entirely different if UOP had appointed an independent negotiating committee of its outside directors to deal with Signal at arm's length. *See, e.g., Harriman v. E.I. duPont de Nemours & Co.,* 411 F. Supp. 133 (D. Del. 1975). Since fairness in this context can be equated to conduct by a theoretical, wholly independent, board of directors acting upon the matter before them, it is unfortunate that this course apparently was neither considered nor pursued. *Johnston v. Greene,* Del. Supr., 35 Del. Ch. 479, 121 A.2d 919, 925 (1956). Particularly in a parent-subsidiary context, a showing that the action taken was as though each of the contending parties had in fact exerted its bargaining power against the other at arm's length is strong evidence that the transaction meets the test of fairness. *Getty Oil Co. v. Skelly Oil Co.,* Del. Supr., 267 A.2d 883, 886 (1970); *Puma v. Marriott,* Del. Ch., 283 A.2d 693, 696 (1971).

required. In other words, the limited function of the Court was to determine whether defendants had disclosed all information in their possession germane to the transaction in issue. And by "germane" we mean, for present purposes, information such as a reasonable shareholder would consider important in deciding whether to sell or retain stock. . . . Completeness, not adequacy, is both the norm and the mandate under present circumstances.

Lynch v. Vickers Energy Corp., Del. Supr., 383 A.2d 278, 281 (1977) (*Lynch I*). This is merely stating in another way the long-existing principle of Delaware law that these Signal designated directors on UOP's board still owed UOP and its shareholders an uncompromising duty of loyalty. The classic language of *Guth v. Loft, Inc.*, Del. Supr., 23 Del. Ch. 255, 5 A.2d 503, 510 (1939), requires no embellishment:

> A public policy, existing through the years, and derived from a profound knowledge of human characteristics and motives, has established a rule that demands of a corporate officer or director, peremptorily and inexorably, the most scrupulous observance of his duty, not only affirmatively to protect the interests of the corporation committed to his charge, but also to refrain from doing anything that would work injury to the corporation, or to deprive it of profit or advantage which his skill and ability might properly bring to it, or to enable it to make in the reasonable and lawful exercise of its powers. The rule that requires an undivided and unselfish loyalty to the corporation demands that there shall be no conflict between duty and self-interest.

Given the absence of any attempt to structure this transaction on an arm's length basis, Signal cannot escape the effects of the conflicts it faced, particularly when its designees on UOP's board did not totally abstain from participation in the matter. There is no "safe harbor" for such divided loyalties in Delaware. When directors of a Delaware corporation are on both sides of a transaction, they are required to demonstrate their utmost good faith and the most scrupulous inherent fairness of the bargain. The requirement of fairness is unflinching in its demand that where one stands on both sides of a transaction, he has the burden of establishing its entire fairness, sufficient to pass the test of careful scrutiny by the courts. *Sterling v. Mayflower Hotel Corp.*, Del. Supr., 33 Del. Ch. 293, 93 A.2d 107, 110 (1952); *Bastian v. Bourns, Inc.*, Del. Ch., 256 A.2d 680, 681 (1969), aff'd, Del. Supr., 278 A.2d 467 (1970); *David J. Greene & Co. v. Dunhill International Inc.*, Del. Ch., 249 A.2d 427, 431 (1968).

There is no dilution of this obligation where one holds dual or multiple directorships, as in a parent-subsidiary context. *Levien v. Sinclair Oil Corp.*, Del. Ch., 261 A.2d 911, 915 (1969). Thus, individuals who act in a dual capacity as directors of two corporations, one of whom is parent and the other subsidiary, owe the same duty of good management to both corporations, and in the absence of an independent negotiating structure (*see* note 7, *supra*), or the directors' total abstention from any participation in the matter, this duty is to be exercised in light of what is best for both companies. The record demonstrates that Signal has not met this obligation.

C

The concept of fairness has two basic aspects: fair dealing and fair price. The former embraces questions of when the transaction was timed, how it was initiated, structured, negotiated, disclosed to the directors, and how the approvals of the directors and the stockholders were obtained. The latter aspect of fairness relates to the economic and financial considerations of the proposed merger, including all relevant factors: assets, market value, earnings, future prospects, and any other elements that affect the intrinsic or inherent value of a company's stock. Moore, *The "Interested" Director or Officer Transaction*, 4 Del. J. Corp. L. 674, 676 (1979); Nathan & Shapiro, *Legal Standard of Fairness of Merger Terms Under Delaware Law*, 2 Del. J. Corp. L. 44, 46-47 (1977). *See Tri-Continental Corp. v. Battye*, Del. Supr., 31 Del. Ch. 523, 74 A.2d 71, 72 (1950); 8 Del. C. §262(h). However, the test for fairness is not a bifurcated one as between fair dealing and price. All aspects of the issue must be examined as a whole since the question is one of entire fairness. However, in a nonfraudulent transaction we recognize that price may be the preponderant consideration outweighing other features of the merger. Here, we address the two basic aspects of fairness separately because we find reversible error as to both.

D

Part of fair dealing is the obvious duty of candor required by *Lynch I, supra*. Moreover, one possessing superior knowledge may not mislead any stockholder by use of corporate information to which the latter is not privy. Delaware has long imposed this duty even upon persons who are not corporate officers or directors, but who nonetheless are privy to matters of interest or significance to their company. *Brophy v. Cities Service Co.*, Del. Ch., 31 Del. Ch. 241, 70 A.2d 5, 7 (1949). With the well-established Delaware law on the subject, and the Court of Chancery's findings of fact here, it is inevitable that the obvious conflicts posed by Arledge and Chitiea's preparation of their "feasibility study," derived from UOP information, for the sole use and benefit of Signal, cannot pass muster.

The Arledge-Chitiea report is but one aspect of the element of fair dealing. How did this merger evolve? It is clear that it was entirely initiated by Signal. The serious time constraints under which the principals acted were all set by Signal. It had not found a suitable outlet for its excess cash and considered UOP a desirable investment, particularly since it was now in a position to acquire the whole company for itself. For whatever reasons, and they were only Signal's, the entire transaction was presented to and approved by UOP's board within four business days. Standing alone, this is not necessarily indicative of any lack of fairness by a majority shareholder. It was what occurred, or more properly, what did not occur, during this brief period that makes the time constraints imposed by Signal relevant to the issue of fairness.

The structure of the transaction, again, was Signal's doing. So far as negotiations were concerned, it is clear that they were modest at best. Crawford, Signal's man at UOP, never really talked price with Signal, except to accede to its management's statements on the subject, and to convey to Signal the UOP outside directors' view that as between the $20-$21 range under consideration, it would have to be $21. The latter is not a surprising outcome, but hardly arm's length negotiations. Only the protection of benefits for UOP's key employees and the issue of Lehman Brothers' fee approached any concept of bargaining.

As we have noted, the matter of disclosure to the UOP directors was wholly flawed by the conflicts of interest raised by the Arledge-Chitiea report. All of those conflicts were resolved by Signal in its own favor without divulging any aspect of them to UOP.

This cannot but undermine a conclusion that this merger meets any reasonable test of fairness. The outside UOP directors lacked one material piece of information generated by two of their colleagues, but shared only with Signal. True, the UOP board had the Lehman Brothers' fairness opinion, but that firm has been blamed by the plaintiff for the hurried task it performed, when more properly the responsibility for this lies with Signal. There was no disclosure of the circumstances surrounding the rather cursory preparation of the Lehman Brothers' fairness opinion. Instead, the impression was given UOP's minority that a careful study had been made, when in fact speed was the hallmark, and Mr. Glanville, Lehman's partner in charge of the matter, and also a UOP director, having spent the weekend in Vermont, brought a draft of the "fairness opinion letter" to the UOP directors' meeting on March 6, 1978 with the price left blank. We can only conclude from the record that the rush imposed on Lehman Brothers by Signal's timetable contributed to the difficulties under which this investment banking firm attempted to perform its responsibilities. Yet, none of this was disclosed to UOP's minority.

Finally, the minority stockholders were denied the critical information that Signal considered a price of $24 to be a good investment. Since this would have meant over $17,000,000 more to the minority, we cannot conclude that the shareholder vote was an informed one. Under the circumstances, an approval by a majority of the minority was meaningless. *Lynch I*, 383 A.2d at 279, 281; *Cahall v. Lofland*, Del. Ch., 12 Del. Ch. 299, 114 A. 224 (1921).

Given these particulars and the Delaware law on the subject, the record does not establish that this transaction satisfies any reasonable concept of fair dealing, and the Chancellor's findings in that regard must be reversed.

E

Turning to the matter of price, plaintiff also challenges its fairness. His evidence was that on the date the merger was approved the stock was worth at least $26 per share. In support, he offered the testimony of a chartered investment analyst who used two basic approaches to valuation: a comparative analysis of the premium paid over market in ten other tender offer-merger combinations, and a discounted cash flow analysis.

In this breach of fiduciary duty case, the Chancellor perceived that the approach to valuation was the same as that in an appraisal proceeding. Consistent with precedent, he rejected plaintiff's method of proof and accepted defendants' evidence of value as being in accord with practice under prior case law. This means that the so-called "Delaware block" or weighted average method was employed wherein the elements of value, i.e., assets, market price, earnings, etc., were assigned a particular weight and the resulting amounts added to determine the value per share. This procedure has been in use for decades. *See In re General Realty & Utilities Corp.*, Del. Ch., 29 Del. Ch. 480, 52 A.2d 6, 14-15 (1947). However, to the extent it excludes other generally accepted techniques used in the financial community and the courts, it is now clearly outmoded. It is time we recognize this in appraisal and other stock valuation proceedings and bring our law current on the subject.

While the Chancellor rejected plaintiff's discounted cash flow method of valuing UOP's stock, as not corresponding with "either logic or the existing law" (426 A.2d at 1360), it is significant that this was essentially the focus, i.e., earnings potential of UOP, of Messrs. Arledge and Chitiea in their evaluation of the merger. Accordingly, the standard "Delaware block" or weighted average method of valuation, formerly employed in appraisal and other stock valuation cases, shall no longer exclusively control such proceedings. We believe that a more liberal approach must include proof of value by any techniques or methods which are generally considered acceptable in the financial community and otherwise admissible in court, subject only to our interpretation of 8 Del. C. §262(h), *infra.* This will obviate the very structured and mechanistic procedure that has heretofore governed such matters.

Fair price obviously requires consideration of all relevant factors involving the value of a company. . . . This is not only in accord with the realities of present day affairs, but it is thoroughly consonant with the purpose and intent of our statutory law. Under 8 Del. C. §262(h), the Court of Chancery:

> shall appraise the shares, determining their *fair* value exclusive of any element of value arising from the accomplishment or expectation of the merger, together with a fair rate of interest, if any, to be paid upon the amount determined to be the fair value. In determining such fair value, the Court shall take into account *all relevant factors* . . . (*Emphasis added.*)

See also Bell v. Kirby Lumber Corp., Del. Supr., 413 A.2d 137, 150-51 (1980) (Quillen, J., concurring).

It is significant that section 262 now mandates the determination of "fair" value based upon "all relevant factors." Only the speculative elements of value that may arise from the "accomplishment or expectation" of the merger are excluded. We take this to be a very narrow exception to the appraisal process, designed to eliminate use of pro forma data and projections of a speculative variety relating to the completion of a merger. But elements of future value, including the nature of the enterprise, which are known or susceptible of proof as of the date of the merger and not the product of speculation, may be considered. When the trial court deems it appropriate, fair value also includes any damages, resulting from the taking, which the stockholders sustain as a class. If that was not the case, then the obligation to consider "all relevant factors" in the valuation process would be eroded. . . .

The plaintiff has not sought an appraisal, but rescissory damages of the type contemplated by *Lynch v. Vickers Energy Corp.*, Del. Supr., 429 A.2d 497, 505-06 (1981) (*Lynch II*). In view of the approach to valuation that we announce today, we see no basis in our law for *Lynch II's* exclusive monetary formula for relief. On remand the plaintiff will be permitted to test the fairness of the $21 price by the standards we herein establish, in conformity with the principle applicable to an appraisal—that fair value be determined by taking "into account all relevant factors" [*see* 8 Del. C. §262(h), *supra*]. In our view this includes the elements of rescissory damages if the Chancellor considers them susceptible of proof and a remedy appropriate to all the issues of fairness before him. To the extent that *Lynch II*, 429 A.2d at 505-06, purports to limit the Chancellor's discretion to a single remedial formula for monetary damages in a cash-out merger, it is overruled.

While a plaintiff's monetary remedy ordinarily should be confined to the more liberalized appraisal proceeding herein established, we do not intend any limitation on the historic powers of the Chancellor to grant such other relief as the facts of a particular case may dictate. The appraisal remedy we approve may not be adequate in certain cases, particularly where fraud, misrepresentation, self-dealing, deliberate waste of corporate assets, or gross and palpable overreaching are involved. Under such circumstances, the Chancellor's powers are complete to fashion any form of equitable and monetary relief as may be appropriate, including rescissory damages. Since it is apparent that this long completed transaction is too involved to undo, and in view of the Chancellor's discretion, the award, if any, should be in the form of monetary damages based upon entire fairness standards, *i.e.*, fair dealing and fair price. . . .

III.

Finally, we address the matter of business purpose. The defendants contend that the purpose of this merger was not a proper subject of inquiry by the trial court. The plaintiff says that no valid purpose existed—the entire transaction was a mere subterfuge designed to eliminate the minority. The Chancellor ruled otherwise, but in so doing he clearly circumscribed the thrust and effect of *Singer. Weinberger v. UOP*, 426 A.2d at 1342-43, 1348-50. This has led to the thoroughly sound observation that the business purpose test "may be . . . virtually interpreted out of existence, as it was in *Weinberger*".[9]

The requirement of a business purpose is new to our law of mergers and was a departure from prior case law. *See Stauffer v. Standard Brands, Inc.*, [187 A.2d 78 (Del. 1962)]; *David J. Greene & Co. v. Schenley Industries, Inc.*, [281 A.2d 30 (Del. ch 1971)].

In view of the fairness test which has long been applicable to parent-subsidiary mergers, *Sterling v. Mayflower Hotel Corp.*, Del. Supr., 93 A.2d 107, 109–10 (1952), the expanded appraisal remedy now available to shareholders, and the broad discretion of the Chancellor to fashion such relief as the facts of a given case may dictate, we do not believe that any additional meaningful protection is afforded minority shareholders by the business purpose requirement of the trilogy of *Singer, Tanzer,*[10] *Najjar,*[11] and their progeny. Accordingly, such requirement shall no longer be of any force or effect.

---

9. Weiss, *The Law of Take Out Mergers: A Historical Perspective*, 56 N.Y.U.L.Rev. 624, 671, n. 300 (1981).

10. *Tanzer v. International General Industries, Inc.*, Del. Supr., 379 A.2d 1121, 1124–25 (1977).

11. *Roland International Corp. v. Najjar*, Del. Supr., 407 A.2d 1032, 1036 (1979).

The judgment of the Court of Chancery, finding both the circumstances of the merger and the price paid the minority shareholders to be fair, is reversed. The matter is remanded for further proceedings consistent herewith. Upon remand the plaintiff's post-trial motion to enlarge the class should be granted.
REVERSED AND REMANDED.

QUESTIONS

1. In determining fair value in *Weinberger*, the Delaware Supreme Court interprets §262(h) to exclude any consideration of "pro forma data and projections of a speculative variety relating to the completion of a merger." If the statute mandates consideration of "all relevant factors," why does the Delaware Supreme Court conclude that this information must be excluded?

2. The *Weinberger* case involves a two-step transaction of the type illustrated in Diagram 12 of Appendix A. Following Signal's purchase of 50.1 percent of UOP's stock in 1974, what are the legitimate expectations of the remaining 49.9 percent minority interest in UOP that is publicly traded? In other words, if you were an owner of one of the minority shares of UOP, what could you reasonably expect out of this investment?

3. In *Weinberger*, the Delaware Supreme Court established the entire fairness test, which generally requires the parent to carry the burden of proving both procedural fairness ("fair dealing") and substantive fairness ("fair price") in order for a transaction between the parent and its partially owned subsidiary to withstand judicial scrutiny if challenged by a minority shareholder of the subsidiary. Why did the Delaware Supreme Court decide to impose this obligation on the parent corporation? What public policy supports this result?

4. In fn. 7 of its opinion, the Delaware Supreme Court pointed out that one way in which the parent corporation might avoid, or at least lessen, its burden of proving entire fairness would be to rely on an independent committee of the board of directors of the subsidiary to negotiate the terms of the transaction with representatives of the parent company. What standard will the courts use to review the decision-making process of the committee of the board in this context? In light of the numerous recent financial scandals that ultimately led Congress to enact the Dodd-Frank reform legislation, do you feel confident that an independent board committee will provide adequate protection for the interests of the minority shareholders of the subsidiary?

5. Why did the *Weinberger* court not rely on the principles of Delaware §144 (the cleansing procedures invoked in cases presenting a conflict of interest) to decide this case involving a related party transaction?

6. After *Weinberger*, we know that the entire fairness test requires the controlling shareholder to satisfy a two-pronged test. From a public policy perspective, does this mean that a cash-out merger transaction can satisfy the entire fairness test if the controlling shareholder can establish the fairness of the price, even though the procedures used do not satisfy the "fair dealing" prong of *Weinberger*?

NOTES

1. Importance of the **Weinberger** *Decision.* The significance of the Delaware Supreme Court's *Weinberger* decision lies in the judicial willingness to rely on the appraisal proceeding to efficiently and expeditiously resolve minority shareholder challenges to the terms of a proposed merger transaction. In reaching this decision, the court has sanctioned the use of merger procedures for the sole purpose of eliminating the minority interest, thereby extending considerable flexibility to the board in discharging its statutory responsibility to "manage the company's business affairs." One commentator has summarized the significance of the Delaware Supreme Court's *Weinberger* decision as follows:

> *Weinberger* apparently was intended to revamp the appraisal remedy so that shareholder challenges to merger transactions would be efficiently resolved in an appraisal proceeding, rather than some other form of legal challenge to the transaction.[19] Toward that end, the court in *Weinberger* did three things. First, it eliminated the ability of shareholders to challenge a merger on the ground that it was not undertaken for a valid business purpose.[20] Second, the court stated that the appraisal remedy should ordinarily be the exclusive remedy available to a shareholder objecting to a merger.[21] Finally, and perhaps most importantly, in order to make this now generally exclusive appraisal remedy workable and fair, the court abandoned the inflexible "Delaware block" method of valuation as the exclusive means of establishing fair value. Instead, courts were directed to take a "more liberal approach [that] must include proof of value by any techniques or methods which are generally considered acceptable in the financial community and otherwise admissible in court."

---

19. The most common way to object to a merger transaction, outside of an appraisal proceeding, is to allege that the officers, directors, or shareholders of the corporation breached a fiduciary duty in approving or recommending the transaction. *See, e.g., Smith v. Van Gorkom,* 488 A.2d 858, 872-73 (Del. 1985) (alleging directors breached fiduciary duty by failing to exercise due care in approving cash-out merger). A shareholder making such an allegation might seek injunctive relief, thus preventing the merger from going forward (*see, e.g., Sealy Mattress Co. v. Sealy, Inc.,* 532 A.2d 1324, 1326 (Del. Ch. 1987)), or damages (*see, e.g., Cede & Co. v. Technicolor, Inc.,* No. CIV.A.7129, 1990 Del. Ch. LEXIS 171, at *2-3 (Oct. 19, 1990), rev'd, 684 A.2d 289 (Del. 1996)).

20. See *Weinberger,* 457 A.2d at 715. In 1977, the Delaware Supreme Court had concluded that a majority shareholder could not "cause a merger to be made for the sole purpose of eliminating a minority on a cash-out basis." *Singer v. Magnavox Co.,* 380 A.2d 969, 978-79 (Del. 1977), overruled by *Weinberger v. UOP, Inc.,* 457 A.2d 701 (Del. 1983); cf. *Tanzer v. International General Indus., Inc.,* 379 A.2d 1121, 1123-25 (Del. 1977) (holding that a parent corporation can engage in a cash-out merger of a subsidiary corporation, if the real purpose of the transaction is not to "rid itself of unwanted minority shareholders in the subsidiary," and the transaction satisfies the "entire fairness" test), overruled by *Weinberger v. UOP, Inc.,* 457 A.2d 701 (Del. 1983).

21. See *Weinberger,* 457 A.2d at 714. The court noted that the appraisal remedy may not be adequate in some instances, particularly situations involving "fraud, misrepresentation, self-dealing, deliberate waste of corporate assets, or gross and palpable overreaching," and left open the possibility that litigants may not be limited to the appraisal remedy in those circumstances. *Id.;* see also Model Bus. Corp. Act 13.02(b) (1991) (making the appraisal remedy the exclusive means of challenging corporate action creating an entitlement to appraisal unless such action is unlawful or fraudulent).

Barry M. Wertheimer, *The Shareholders' Appraisal Remedy and How Courts Determine Fair Value*, 47 DUKE L.J. 613, 616-617 (1998). Until *Weinberger,* "Delaware (and many other states) followed the Delaware block method of valuing a [Target] company. This was a mechanistic formula that required a judge to determine separate values of the company—e.g., asset value, market value, and earnings value; to assign a percentage to each of the three methods (so that their sum added up to 100 percent); and then to do a weighted average calculation to come up with the valuation number." Robert B. Thompson, MERGERS AND ACQUISITIONS: LAW AND FINANCE 287 (2010). In the next section, we will examine the range of valuation methods that are now available in the post-*Weinberger* era.

   2. *Business Purpose Test.*   In Part III of its opinion, the *Weinberger* court overruled the business purpose test, which was established in prior Delaware case law. Before *Weinberger,* Delaware cases emphasized two factors when analyzing the proper treatment of "freeze-out" transactions:

> (1) the purpose of the transaction and (2) fairness to the minority shareholders. . . . The utility of the business purpose test appears to be its invitation to the court to review somewhat more widely the overall terms, objectives, and [the controlling shareholder's] motivations surrounding the acquisition. There is little evidence that the business purpose test otherwise provides strong and predictable protection to the minority [shareholders] or [that the test] ensures the majority [shareholders] against unnecessary [judicial] scrutiny of a fair transaction.

James D. Cox and Thomas Lee, Hazen, CORPORATIONS 641 (2d ed. 2003). Against the backdrop of these criticisms, the Delaware Supreme Court abandoned the business purpose test, thereby allowing the minority shareholders' continuing equity interest in the business to be "terminated, albeit at a *fair price,* by the will of the majority [shareholder]." *Id.* at 642 (*emphasis added*). In light of the court's holding in *Weinberger,* the remedy of an appraisal action, with its focus on determining "fair value," takes on heightened importance and also raises the separate question of "whether the appraisal remedy should [form the basis for] the minority's exclusive right to complain" about the fairness of a "freeze-out" transaction. *Id.* The question of the "exclusivity" of the appraisal remedy is to be taken up at the end of this chapter, when we discuss the Delaware Supreme Court's opinion in *Rabkin v. Philip A. Hunt Chemical Corp.*

   3. *Cleansing Procedures of Delaware §144.*   In *Weinberger,* the Delaware Supreme Court recognized that "squeeze-out" (or freeze-out) transactions—whereby the minority shareholder is "cashed out" and thus deprived of the opportunity to share in the future success of the surviving corporation—present an inherent conflict of interest since all of the future gains will accrue to the majority shareholder. This raises the possibility of using modern "cleansing statutes" (such as Delaware §144) to "cleanse" the transaction of the taint of this conflict of interest. In footnote 7 of the *Weinberger* opinion, the court alluded to the possibility of a "cleansing" vote by relying on approval of a proposed "squeeze-out" transaction by "an independent negotiating committee" of the subsidiary's (i.e., UOP's) board of directors; an independent negotiating committee should consist of truly independent outside directors who would then bargain at arm's length with the controlling shareholder/the parent company (i.e., Signal). Use of independent negotiating committees in the post-*Weinberger* era is described in the following note and will be analyzed further as part of the fiduciary duty materials in Chapter 7.

4. Entire Fairness and the Use of Independent Negotiating Committees. In addition to the statutorily mandated appraisal remedy, the *Weinberger* decision also recognizes common law fiduciary duty obligations as a further line of protection for shareholders of Target Co. by imposing an "entire fairness" requirement in connection with freeze-out transactions in order to be sure that the minority interest receives adequate consideration for its interest. In the words of one leading commentator:

> Shareholders of acquired corporations are also protected by fiduciary duty principles. Fiduciary duty claims by disgruntled shareholders of corporations that are acquired in arm's length acquisitions typically are evaluated under the business judgment standard.[28] The standard requires corporate managers to perform their tasks, including the facilitation of acquisitions, in good faith and without any significant conflict and reasonably to investigate the proposed action. If these criteria are met, the ultimate decision of an acquired corporation's managers to pursue a particular acquisition of their company under particular terms violates their fiduciary duty only if that judgment is so bad as to amount to something similar to gross negligence.
>
> On the other hand, an acquisition undertaken in a conflict of interest setting, such as a corporate parent's acquisition through a statutory merger of a public minority's interest in its subsidiary [*i.e.* a "freeze-out" transaction], is evaluated under the intrinsic fairness test.[31] Under the intrinsic fairness test, the decisions of the acquired (subsidiary) corporation's managers and its controlling stockholder (parent) to facilitate or undertake the acquisition are evaluated against a more general concept of fairness. In considering whether the acquisition is fair, courts look at two elements, fair price and fair dealing. . . .
>
> In all cases, whether or not a conflict is present, managers' conduct in acquisitions is measured against some fair price criterion. In cases without a conflict, corporate managers' facilitation of an acquisition of their company at an unfair price will violate their fiduciary duty under the business judgment standard. . . . Cases involving a conflict apply the intrinsic fairness doctrine, and the fair price obligation is even more direct. In these cases, unless managers of the acquired corporation obtain a fair price for the stock of the acquired corporation, the managers risk a determination that the transaction was not intrinsically fair.[33]

---

28. *Smith v. Van Gorkom*, 488 A.2d 858 (Del. 1985), is probably the most famous case applying the business judgment test to acquisitions.

31. *See, e.g., Weinberger v. UOP, Inc.*, 457 A.2d 701, 710 (Del. 1983).

33. Although the fiduciary standard by which managers' conduct is evaluated appropriately changes, depending on whether such managers are acting in a conflict or a non-conflict setting, the constancy of the fair price requirement across all such decisions makes sense. Fundamentally, the fair price requirement is based on the managers' broad obligation to maximize shareholder wealth, and that obligation of managers is ubiquitous. Thus, managers' approval of any acquisition of their company, irrespective of the existence of conflict, always must maximize shareholder wealth in order to meet the managers' fiduciary obligation. In other words, managers must always ensure that shareholders receive a fair price for their shares. . . .

Rutherford B. Campbell, Jr., *Fair Value at Fair Price in Corporate Acquisitions*, 78 N.C. L. Rev. 101, 110-111 (1999).

Following *Weinberger*, the Delaware courts consistently applied the entire fairness standard to review transactions such as the take-out (squeeze-out) merger at issue in *Weinberger*, where the transaction is structured as a long-form merger effectuated pursuant to Delaware section 251. Thus, following *Weinberger*,

> majority shareholders wishing to eliminate minority shareholders [typically used a long-form merger, short-form merger, or a tender offer followed by either a long- or short-form merger]. In light of the general belief that short-form mergers, like long-form mergers, were subject to entire fairness review, controlling shareholders sought in the first step tender offer to acquire as many shares as possible so as to reduce the size of the class of potential challengers to the second step merger. The general belief that entire fairness would apply to all mergers spurred majority shareholders to use independent committees or majority of the minority votes to achieve burden shifting.[66]

Bradley R. Aronstam, et al., *Delaware's Going Private Dilemma: Fostering Protections for Minority Shareholders in the Wake of* Siliconix *and* Unocal Exploration, 58 Bus. Law. 519 (Feb. 2003). Though Delaware case law is (widely) credited with developing protection for minority interests eliminated via a "squeeze-out" merger, more recently the Delaware courts have qualified the scope of the entire fairness standard originally established in *Weinberger*. As we shall see when we discuss "squeeze-out" transactions in more detail as part of the fiduciary duty materials in Chapter 7, Delaware case law has continued to evolve in its delineation of the scope of fiduciary obligations to be imposed on controlling shareholders in connection with these "going private" (aka "squeeze out") transactions. *See Kahn v. M&F Worldwide Corp.*, 88 A.3d 635 (Dec. 2014) at p. 742.

   5. Fairness Opinions.   In the wake of *Weinberger* and its progeny, it became increasingly common for boards of directors (of both Bidders and Targets) to obtain "fairness opinions" from their respective investment bankers, and each board relied on the banker's fairness opinion as one of the factors that it took into account in reaching its determination that the price offered was "fair." However, as *Weinberger* and its progeny make clear, the board of directors cannot abdicate its ultimate responsibility for determining the fair price for Target to the company's bankers. This point is articulated at greater length in the Delaware Supreme Court decision in *Smith v. Van Gorkom*, which we will study as part of our discussion of fiduciary duty law in Chapter 7. In the course of preparing their fairness opinions, the range of valuation methods commonly

---

66. *See* Dennis J. Friedman & Scott A. Kislin, *Going-Private Transactions: Are Special Committees an Endangered Species?* M & A Lawyer, Apr. 2002, at 10. Because entire fairness was believed to apply regardless of the transaction's form, there was no significant benefit to choosing one transactional alternative over another. [By the author: In Chapter 7, we will study how Delaware caselaw regarding "squeeze-out" transactions of the type at issue in *Weinberger* has continued to evolve in the decades since the Delaware Supreme Court handed down its landmark opinion in that case.]

used by the company's investment bankers is described in the materials in the next section.

4. Overview of Methods for Determining Fair Value

As was emphasized in the last section, the Delaware Supreme Court's *Weinberger* decision liberalized the methods available for assessing the *fair value* of the dissenter's shares in the context of an appraisal proceeding. Although it is easy to frame the objective of an appraisal proceeding—to find the "fair value" of the dissenting shares—this is not nearly so easy to accomplish in practice. The following excerpt, from an article that thoroughly examines the procedural and valuation issues that often arise in the context of a modern appraisal proceeding, elaborates on the reasons why the appraisal proceeding reflects that well-established truism: "valuation is an art rather than a science."

Barry M. Wertheimer
The Shareholders' Appraisal Remedy
and How the Courts Determine Fair Value
47 Duke L.J. 613, 626-632 (1998)

The statutory command in an appraisal proceeding is to find the "fair value" of the dissenting shares, or sometimes the "fair market value" or "fair cash value." Fair value is typically defined by statute as "the value of the shares immediately before the effectuation of the corporate action to which the dissenter objects, excluding any appreciation or depreciation in anticipation of the corporate action."[74] Statutes generally provide no further guidance with respect to ascertaining fair value in an appraisal proceeding.[75]

Before *Weinberger*, the traditional means of determining fair value was the Delaware block method of valuation. After *Weinberger* opened up the valuation process to "any techniques or methods which are generally considered acceptable in the financial community," the most prominent method of valuation in Delaware has been the discounted cash flow (DCF) method. This valuation technique operates on the premise that the value of a company is determined by the present value of its projected future cash flows. The DCF method has been described by the Delaware courts as "the preeminent valuation methodology" and "in many situations . . . [theoretically] the single best technique to

---

74. Model Bus. Corp. Act 13.01(3). The Model Act further provides that appreciation or depreciation resulting from the corporate action does not have to be excluded from consideration if it would be fair and equitable to take account of such effects. *See id.* The Delaware statute directs the court to determine fair value of the dissenting shares "exclusive of any element of value arising from the accomplishment or expectation of the merger or consolidation," Del. Code Ann. tit. 8, 262(h) (1991), and goes on to state that in determining fair value, "the Court shall take into account all relevant factors." *Id.*

75. *See* Model Bus. Corp. Act 13.01 cmt. (3) ("The definition of 'fair value' . . . leaves to the parties (and ultimately to the courts) the details by which 'fair value' is to be determined. . . .").

estimate the value of an economic asset."[80] As described by the Delaware Court of Chancery:

> The DCF model entails three basic components: an estimation of net cash flows that the firm will generate and when, over some period; a terminal or residual value equal to the future value, as of the end of the projection period, of the firm's cash flows beyond the projection period; and finally a cost of capital with which to discount to a present value both the projected net cash flows and the estimated terminal or residual value.[81]

The DCF method, although probably the most prominent and frequently used *post-Weinberger* method of appraisal, has not been the exclusive valuation method employed. The Delaware courts have continued to use a variety of valuation techniques, depending on the facts and circumstances of the particular case, including the Delaware block method,[82] valuation based on a comparison to other companies (the "comparable company approach"), valuation based on net asset value, valuation based on earnings and book value, and valuation based on combinations of these techniques.

The valuation technique used by a court is highly dependent on the valuation evidence presented by the parties. "The parties, not the court, establish the record and the court is limited by the record created."[87] Thus, if both parties present evidence of fair value utilizing the DCF method, the court's resolution of the dispute will likely employ a DCF analysis. Similarly, if the parties agree that a net asset value approach is called for, the court typically will adopt such an approach.

There are problems endemic to an appraisal proceeding that cannot be eliminated by the choice of appraisal methodology. Each appraisal technique is but a way of estimating the "fair value" or "true value" or "intrinsic value"

---

80. *Cede & Co. v. Technicolor, Inc.*, No. CIV.A.7129, 1990 Del. Ch. LEXIS 259, at 23 (Oct. 19, 1990) (stating that DCF technique has "become prominent"), *rev'd* on other grounds, 684 A.2d 289 (Del. 1996).

81. *Id.* Dean Samuel C. Thompson, Jr., recognizing the importance of the DCF method in appraisal proceedings (as well as for purposes of fairness opinions, disclosure documents, etc.), has written a "lawyer's guide" explaining the nuts and bolts of this valuation technique. *See generally* Samuel C. Thompson, Jr., *A Lawyer's Guide to Modern Valuation Techniques in Mergers and Acquisitions*, 21 J. Corp. L. 457 (1996).

82. *Weinberger* did not prohibit use of the Delaware block method, and this method has continued to be used in Delaware and elsewhere. *See, e.g., Rosenblatt v. Getty Oil Co.*, 493 A.2d 929, 940 (Del. 1985) (noting that "*Weinberger* did not abolish the block formula, only its exclusivity"); *Gonsalves v. Straight Arrow Publishers, Inc.*, No. CIV.A.8474, 1996 WL 696936, at 4-8 (Del. Ch. Nov. 27, 1996) (noting that *Weinberger* "did not invalidate the Delaware Block Method," and ultimately adopting the valuation calculated by the corporation's expert using that method), *rev'd* on other grounds, 701 A.2d 357 (Del. 1997); *Elk Yarn Mills v. 514 Shares of Common Stock of Elk Yarn Mills*, 742 S.W.2d 638, 640-44 (Tenn. Ct. App. 1987) (applying the Delaware block method); cf. *Oakridge Energy, Inc. v. Clifton*, 937 P.2d 130, 135 (Utah 1997) (suggesting that the appraisal valuation should consider each of three measures of value used in the Delaware block method); *Hernando Bank v. Huff*, 609 F. Supp. 1124, 1126-27 (N.D. Miss. 1985) (considering each of the three Delaware block measures of value, but not employing a weighted average approach), *aff'd*, 796 F.2d 803 (5th Cir. 1986) . . .

87. *Cede & Co. v. Technicolor, Inc.*, No. CIV.A.7129, 1990 Del. Ch. LEXIS 259, at 26 (Oct. 19, 1990), *rev'd* on other grounds, 684 A.2d 289 (Del. 1996).

of a company, and undeniably, "valuation is an art rather than a science."[90] The valuation "answer" given by each of these techniques is very dependent on the assumptions underlying the calculations employed. For example, even though the DCF approach is highly regarded, it relies heavily on a guess as to the future cash flows of the enterprise. This "guess" may be informed by looking at historical data, operating trends, and other relevant factors, but it is still nothing more than a prediction of future events. Once these future cash flows are predicted, they must be discounted to a present value. What discount rate should be employed? Again, there is much room for guesswork and subjectivity.[92] The DCF technique also requires that a terminal value be established and then discounted to a present value; both are further exercises in guesswork and subjectivity.[93]

As a practical matter, this means that both parties to the appraisal proceeding will present expert testimony of valuation. Because of the inherent subjectivity and estimation involved, the parties' experts can compute dramatically different valuations, even if they utilize the same methodology.[94] Of course, each expert is "handsomely paid by one side or the other"[95] such that, "whether consciously or unconsciously, the opinions expressed by the expert witnesses significantly reflect[] the desires of their clients."[96] Thus, the expert retained by

---

90. *In re Appraisal of Shell Oil Co.*, No. CIV.A.8080, 1990 Del. Ch. LEXIS 199, at 16 (Dec. 11, 1990) (quoting testimony of expert witness), *aff'd*, 607 A.2d 1213 (Del. 1992).

92. Factors courts have looked at to determine the discount rate include the firm's cost of equity capital, the risk-free rate of return as reflected in United States treasury bill rates, and the riskiness of the firm's business. *See, e.g., Technicolor,* 1990 Del. Ch. LEXIS 259, at 9093 (using the cost of capital to supply the discount rate); *Neal v. Alabama By-Products Corp.*, No. CIV.A.8282, 1990 WL 109243, at 20 (Del. Ch. Aug. 1, 1990) (accepting capital asset pricing model to determine the discount rate), *aff'd*, 588 A.2d 255 (Del. 1991).

93. These criticisms are not unique to the DCF method. The Delaware block method and other valuation techniques are susceptible to similar criticisms. Under the Delaware block method, it is necessary to determine a company's asset value on a going concern basis. This requires estimation and guesswork. Determining earnings value requires the selection of a price/earnings multiplier, an inherently imprecise and subjective endeavor. After these tasks are accomplished, and a market value is selected, the various valuation factors must be weighted. The selection of the appropriate weight to be accorded each type of valuation is almost wholly arbitrary. *See* [Joel Seligman, *Reappraising the Appraisal Remedy*, 52 GEO. WASH. L. REV. 829, 854-856 (1984)]. As a result, huge discrepancies in the value of companies, as determined by each party's expert, are common under the Delaware block method. *See Francis I. duPont & Co. v. Universal City Studios, Inc.*, 312 A.2d 344, 346 (Del. Ch. 1973) (illustrating how two parties, each employing the Delaware block method, obtained substantially different values: the plaintiff argued for a per share value of $131.89, while the defendant argued for a $52.36 per share value), *aff'd*, 334 A.2d 216 (Del. 1975).

94. For example, differences in future cash flow assumptions can yield very different valuations under the DCF method. For illustrations of the variance in expert valuations, *see Technicolor,* 1990 Del. Ch. LEXIS 259, at 4; *Neal,* 1990 WL 109243, at 7-8; *Cavalier Oil Corp. v. Harnett,* Nos. CIV.A.7959, 7960, 7967, 7968, 1988 Del. Ch. LEXIS 28, at 32-36, 70-72 (Feb. 22, 1988), *aff'd*, 564 A.2d 1137 (Del. 1989). Sometimes the respective experts use different valuation methodologies, which also can lead to significant variance in their valuation conclusions.

95. *In re Appraisal of Shell Oil Co.*, 1990 Del. Ch. LEXIS 199, at 16.

96. *Id., see also Salomon Bros., Inc. v. Interstate Bakeries Corp.*, No. CIV.A.10054, 1992 Del. Ch. LEXIS 100, at 20 (May 1, 1992) ("It appeared to me, both from the experts' reports and their testimony, that their assumptions and choices of multiples were colored by their respective clients' interests.").

the dissenting shareholder invariably concludes that the corporation has a very high fair value, while the corporation's expert determines that the fair value of the corporation is much lower. It is not unusual for the opinions of the experts to differ by a factor of ten. It is, therefore, not surprising that courts have evidenced frustration with this process.

NOTES

1. The Problem of "Dueling Experts."   In the post-*Weinberg* era, the courts are becoming increasingly frustrated (and often overwhelmed) by the technical nature of the financial information introduced into evidence as part of the valuation decision to be made in the context of an appraisal proceeding. Professor Wertheimer has explained the nature of this problem as follows:

> The primary institutional issue in appraisal proceedings involves the court's task of sorting through the testimony of dueling experts to arrive at the fair value of a corporation. The experts' valuation opinions tend to be partisan, and highly divergent. Accordingly, while recognizing that these problems are "to be expected in an adversarial system," courts have expressed frustration with the use of competing experts to resolve appraisal proceedings.
>
> The Delaware courts have gingerly explored two mechanisms to alleviate some of the problems associated with the inevitable battle of partisan experts. Although these mechanisms have some appeal in reducing the courts' task of resolving conflicting expert testimony, they unfortunately import the risk that they will operate to frustrate the achievement of equitable results in appraisal proceedings.
>
> a. Choosing One Party's Valuation. The first mechanism that has been employed in appraisal cases to deal with the "dueling experts" problem is a "rule," adopted in two Delaware Court of Chancery decisions, stating that a court should decide which of the experts' opinions is the more credible, and then accept that expert's model, rather than attempt judicially to create a valuation model composed of the more credible portions of each expert's model. In other words, after each party presents its case, the court should choose the more credible of the two and not attempt to craft a compromise valuation (referred to as a rule requiring a court to "choose one party's valuation"). . . .
>
> b. Court-Appointed Neutral Experts. The second mechanism courts have explored in appraisal cases to address the dueling experts problem is the use of a court-appointed neutral expert. . . .
>
> . . . The use of a neutral expert can, in proper circumstances, be useful to a court conducting an appraisal proceeding. There are, however, two points of caution. First, the use of an additional expert imposes additional costs to the proceeding and probably increases the time involved to reach a final result. It also adds a host of procedural issues associated with the appointment of the expert and how the expert will function in the process. The court must be careful to insure that the benefits of appointing a neutral expert justify the added time and expense and the additional layer of procedure.
>
> The second point of caution involves the potential for excessive reliance by the court on the neutral expert. The court is charged with the statutory responsibility of conducting the appraisal, and should not excessively delegate that responsibility to the neutral expert. . . .

Barry M. Wertheimer, *The Shareholders' Appraisal Remedy and How Courts Determine Fair Value*, 47 DUKE L.J. 613, 696-701 (1998).

    2. Different Methods for Determining "Fair Value." Since the *Weinberger* decision liberalized Delaware's approach to valuation, perhaps the most dominant method for valuing Target's business is to rely on discounted cash flow (DCF). The following excerpt provides a brief overview of this method of valuation, as well as a brief introduction to the other relevant methods of valuation commonly relied on by the parties for determining the value of a company's shares in an appraisal proceeding:

> **Rutherford B. Campbell, Jr.**
> **The Impact of Modern Finance**
> **Theory in Acquisition Cases**
> **53 Syracuse L. Rev. 1, 2-3, 5-6, 9-11, 14-16 (2003)**

    In February of 1983, the Supreme Court of Delaware decided *Weinberger v. UOP, Inc.* The case holds that, in determining the present value of a corporation involved in an acquisition, courts are free to use "any techniques or methods [of valuation] which are generally considered acceptable in the financial community. . . ."

    The rule in Delaware prior to *Weinberger* required courts to determine the present value of a corporation by use of the Delaware block method of valuation exclusively.[3] The Delaware block method, however, is a poor way to determine the present value of a corporation. As a result, even before the *Weinberger* decision, commentators had sharply criticized the methodology, and Delaware courts occasionally had strayed from a rigid application of this mandated valuation method. The *Weinberger* opinion, therefore, offered a welcome opportunity to move away from this tired and unsound valuation methodology. Courts, it seemed, were encouraged to develop a new common law of valuation, one that was informed by sensible, modern finance theory. . . . This section describes the fundamentals of modern present value theory and offers a series of relatively simple rules or concepts about which there is broad agreement among financial economists. [The remainder of this section provides a brief description of other widely used valuation methodologies.]

A. VALUATION BASED ON DISCOUNTED CASH FLOWS

    To the financial economist, present value of an asset, including a company or a partial ownership interest in the company, is determined by projected cash

---

    3. See, e.g., Note, *Valuation of Dissenters' Stock Under Appraisal Statutes*, 79 HARV. L. REV. 1453, 1468-71 (1966) (discussing Delaware's use of the weighted average or Delaware block approach). Under the Delaware Block valuation methodology, up to four factors are considered. *Id.* The factors are earnings value, asset value, market value and dividend value. *Id.* Each value is determined and then weighted to arrive at the final value for the company. *Id.; see also, e.g.,* Steven Rogers, *Note, The Dissenting Shareholder's Appraisal Remedy*, 30 OKLA. L. REV. 629, 632-643 (1977) (discussing the use by courts of the weighted average approach).

flows discounted by an appropriate factor. This approach is broadly agreed upon by financial economists and thus, for example, is the basis for a major portion of modern corporate finance books, such as Professors Brealey and Myers's standard text, *Principles of Corporate Finance.* For an evaluator, including a court, to arrive at a sound estimate of present value, therefore, the evaluator must make a sound estimate of cash flows and determine a sound discount rate.

1. FUTURE—NOT HISTORIC CASH FLOWS

Present value of an asset, including a company or share of stock, is determined by the person's (or the market's) expectations regarding the future value that the asset will generate. A corollary of this is that historical performance is per se irrelevant to present value.

Consider, for example, an apartment building. Assume that last year an apartment generated total cash flows (e.g., revenues less expenses) of $100,000. Due to a dramatic decrease in demand for the apartments in the building (one may assume, for example, that the major employer in the area moved recently), the best estimate of the cash flows from the apartment building for the foreseeable future is $10,000 per year. A rational purchaser determines the price she or he is willing to pay by reference to the future cash flows ($10,000 in this case). It is irrelevant to today's price that last year, in very different conditions from those anticipated in the future, the cash flows from the apartment building were ten times the amount anticipated for next year. . . .

[2.] DISCOUNTING TO REFLECT THE TIME VALUE OF MONEY AND RISK

A stream of payments to be received over a period of time is worth less than the sum of the payments. For example, in our apartment building example above, if one predicts that the apartment building will generate cash flows of $100 per year for ten years and will at that point have no further earning capacity and no salvage, then a rational investor will not pay $1,000 (the sum of the cash flows) for the building.

One reason the investor will not give up $1,000 today for a promise to repay an equal amount of dollars at some future time is because the investor is giving up the use of her or his money for a period of time, which means that the investor must defer consumption or forego a return on the invested sum during the period of time before the investment is repaid. The investor, therefore, demands a return, because money has a "time value." The amount the investor demands as compensation for the time value of money is referred to as the riskless rate of return, since it represents the return demanded for investment that has no risk respecting the future return.

In addition to the riskless rate, the rational investor will demand an additional amount for any risk that is present in an investment. Risk is generally understood as volatility or variability of possible outcomes. Thus, the more volatile an investment or, stated differently, the wider the dispersion of possible outcomes from the investment, the more risk in the investment and the more return an investor demands. The additional return over and above the riskless rate of return that an investor demands for such volatility is referred to as the risk premium.

Financial economists, therefore, will essentially build a discount rate by first determining the appropriate riskless rate of return and then adding to that rate an appropriate risk premium. The first part of this—determining the riskless rate of return—is typically done by reference to government securities, such as treasury bills. It is in the determination of the appropriate risk premium, however, where financial economists begin to disagree with one another.

During the last three decades, the theory of the risk premium that has most dominated the discussion among financial economists has been the capital asset pricing model. Under this theory, the risk premium required for an investment in a particular stock is generally considered to involve only a premium for the systematic or market risk, which is the risk that cannot be eliminated by diversification. The risk premium under the capital asset pricing model is calculated by multiplying the average marketwide risk premium by the company's beta. Beta is a measure of the sensitivity of an individual security to market movements.

The capital asset pricing model is also an integral part of the weighted average cost of capital method for determining a discount rate. Under this method, one first determines the company's cost of equity capital, normally by using the capital asset pricing model. Then, the company's cost of debt is determined, typically by estimating what the company is required to pay for its borrowed money. The cost of the company's equity and its debt are then weighted by the percentages of the company's total capitalization represented by each of the two components, and this weighted average cost of capital is used to discount the company's cash flows before any deduction for interest payments. The result is a present value for the entire stream of earnings or cash flows that are available to service the company's debt and for shareholders. In essence, one ends up with a present value for the company's debt and equity. Finally, in the typical situation in which the issue is the value of the junior equity, the value of the company's debt is subtracted out, which leaves the value of the shareholders' interest in the company.

In more recent times, the capital asset pricing model has been challenged by a number of economists, and alternative theories have been proposed. Nonetheless, the capital asset pricing model continues to have its defenders and continues to draw significant coverage in standard corporate finance treatises. . . .

B. ASSET VALUE

"Asset value" amounts to the market value of the net assets of the company. In this valuation method, therefore, the evaluator calculates the fair market value that the assets of the company would bring in the event of liquidation and subtracts from that figure the liabilities of the company.

A couple of points should be made in order to establish the distinct nature of this methodology. First, asset value is determined by the liquidation value of the assets and not by the going concern value of the assets as presently deployed by the company and its managers. In other words, asset value is essentially an opportunity cost measure of the value of the company's assets and thus amounts to the most valuable alternate use of the assets. It is possible, therefore, that the asset value of a company could exceed the company's going concern value.

The second point is that an asset value methodology does not involve applying any multiple or discount to the net liquidation value of the company's assets. Asset value is merely the amount that the company would bring, if all the assets were sold and all the debts were paid. . . .

C. DEAL VALUE

In this methodology, a company's value is established by reference to the price at which similar companies were acquired. So, for example, if Petroleum Company A were recently acquired at a price of 1.8 times its book value, Petroleum Company B might be valued at 1.8 times its book value. Or, if the acquisition price for Company A were fifteen times its most recently reported earnings, a claim may be made that Company B should be valued at fifteen times its most recent earnings. . . .

D. COMPARATIVE RATIO VALUE

An evaluator using the comparative ratio valuation methodology bases its valuation on certain key ratios derived from comparable companies that are actively traded in the market and that are not being acquired. Significant trading activity in the comparable stock is necessary to ensure that the pricing of the comparable stock is efficient and that data about the comparable stock is readily available.

The ratios from the comparable company are constructed using the market price of the comparable's stock over various financial data from the comparable company. These financial data may include: (a) total revenues, (b) book value, (c) earnings, (d) earnings before deducting certain expenses, such as interest and taxes (EBIT) or interest, taxes, depreciation and amortization (EBITDA). For example, if the present trading price of a computer manufacturer, C Co., is two times its total revenues, then under this methodology one might claim that the fair value of another computer manufacturer, D Co., should be two times D Co.'s total revenues. . . .

E. WEIGHTED AVERAGE VALUE

The old Delaware block method is the most commonly used weighted average valuation technique. There, for example, the evaluator considers up to four separate factors of value and then arrives at a final valuation by weighting each of the factors. The factors typically found in a Delaware block evaluation are: (1) asset value, (2) market value, (3) earnings value, and (4) dividend value. The weights assigned to the factors vary from case to case, and, indeed, not all of the four factors are accorded weight in all cases. Dividend value, for example, is the particular element of value that is omitted from consideration most often. . . .

3. Valuation Methods in Other Contexts. The valuation methods described in the preceding excerpt are not limited to use in the appraisal context. Indeed, it bears emphasizing that these valuation methods are routinely used by investment bankers (and other valuation specialists) as part of the financial advisory services they render in connection with an M&A transaction. "The starting point for both the buyer [i.e., Bidder] and the seller [i.e., Target] in any merger or acquisition transaction is to determine the *value* of the target corporation. For the buyer (i.e., the acquiring corporation), this is a capital budgeting decision similar to any other investment decision, such as the decision to build a new plant. For the seller (i.e., either the target corporation in a sale of assets or its shareholders in a sale of stock), the determination of the target's [intrinsic] value sets the reservation price at which the seller [can be expected to] stop holding and sell [his/hers/it's shares] . . . In many situations it may be appropriate to use multiple techniques in valuing a target." Samuel C. Thompson, *A Lawyer's Guide to Modern Valuation Techniques in Mergers & Acquisitions*, 21 J. Corp. Law 457, 460-462 (1996) (*emphasis added*).

5. How Should the Courts Determine Fair Value in the Modern Appraisal Proceeding?

This next set of Delaware cases focuses on the fundamental question of just exactly *what* it is that the courts are to focus on when determining *fair value* in the context of the modern appraisal remedy. In other words, is the purpose of the appraisal remedy to value the *corporation*? Or, is the goal to value the *shares* of the corporation held by a particular shareholder? Also, how should the court go about determining the relevant elements of value—especially in light of the statutory language in Delaware §262(h) that directs the court to exclude "any element of value arising from the accomplishment or expectation of this merger?"

Cavalier Oil Corp. v. Harnett
564 A.2d 1137 (Del. 1989)

. . . Walsh, Justice:

This is an appeal by Cavalier Oil Corporation ("Cavalier") and a cross-appeal by William J. Harnett ("Harnett") from a final judgment of the Court of Chancery determining the fair value of 1,250 shares of stock owned by Harnett in EPIC Mortgage Servicing, Inc. ("EMSI"), a closely-held Delaware corporation. The appraisal action followed a short form merger, pursuant to 8 Del. C. §253, of EMSI into Cavalier on November 20, 1984.

Harnett rejected Cavalier's offer of $93,950 for his EMSI shares, electing instead to assert his appraisal rights under 8 Del. C. §262. Consolidated appraisal proceedings were tried in the Court of Chancery which, after extensive post-trial briefing, entered judgment fixing the value of Harnett's EMSI stock at $347,000. This appeal and cross-appeal resulted. . . .

We conclude that the Court of Chancery, in both its findings and methodology, correctly applied the standards which govern an appraisal proceeding under Delaware law. Accordingly, we affirm the judgment in all respects. . . .

IV

Cavalier's final claim of error is directed to the Vice Chancellor's refusal to apply a minority discount in valuing Harnett's EMSI stock. Cavalier contends that Harnett's "de minimis" (1.5%) interest in EMSI is one of the "relevant factors" which must be considered under *Weinberger*'s expanded valuation standard. In rejecting a minority or marketability discount, the Vice Chancellor concluded that the objective of a section 262 appraisal is "to value the *corporation* itself, as distinguished from a specific fraction of its *shares* as they may exist in the hands of a particular shareholder" [emphasis in original]. We believe this to be a valid distinction.

A proceeding under Delaware's appraisal statute, 8 Del. C. §262, requires that the Court of Chancery determine the "fair value" of the dissenting stockholders' shares. The fairness concept has been said to implicate two considerations: fair dealing and fair price. *Weinberger v. UOP, Inc.*, 457 A.2d at 711. Since the fairness of the merger process is not in dispute, the Court of Chancery's task here was to value what has been taken from the shareholder: "viz. his proportionate interest in a going concern." *Tri-Continental Corp. v. Battye*, Del. Supr., 74 A.2d 71, 72 (1950). To this end the company must be first valued as an operating entity by application of traditional value factors, weighted as required, but without regard to post-merger events or other possible business combinations. *See Bell v. Kirby Lumber Corp.*, Del. Supr., 413 A.2d 137 (1980). The dissenting shareholder's proportionate interest is determined only after the company as an entity has been valued. In that determination the Court of Chancery is not required to apply further weighting factors at the shareholder level, such as discounts to minority shares for asserted lack of marketability. . . .

The application of a discount to a minority shareholder is contrary to the requirement that the company be viewed as a "going concern." Cavalier's argument, that the only way Harnett would have received value for his 1.5% stock interest was to sell his stock, subject to market treatment of its minority status, misperceives the nature of the appraisal remedy. Where there is no objective market data available, the appraisal process is not intended to reconstruct a *pro forma* sale but to assume that the shareholder was willing to maintain his investment position, however slight, had the merger not occurred. Discounting individual shareholdings injects into the appraisal process speculation on the various factors which may dictate the marketability of minority shareholdings. More important, to fail to accord to a minority shareholder the full proportionate value of his shares imposes a penalty for lack of control, and unfairly enriches the majority shareholders who may reap a windfall from the appraisal process by cashing out a dissenting shareholder, a clearly undesirable result. . . .

The judgment of the Court of Chancery is affirmed in all respects.

QUESTIONS

1. What is the decision to be made in a judicially supervised appraisal proceeding? In considering this question, does it matter whether the dissenting shareholder owns stock in a publicly traded or a privately held company?

2. Why should a minority shareholder get more in an appraisal proceeding than if he/she/it sold his/her/its shares in a secondary, open-market transaction?

NOTES

1. Use of Minority Discounts.   One of the more perplexing questions that a court must decide in determining the *fair value* of the minority's dissenting shares is whether to apply a minority discount in order to reflect that the dissenters' shares are illiquid or otherwise worth less per share than a controlling block of shares in the company. In *Cavalier Oil*, the Delaware Supreme Court rejected the use of a minority discount, focusing instead on valuing the corporation itself and then awarding the dissenter his/her/its proportion of the corporation's value as a going concern by dividing the value of the business by the number of outstanding shares. This approach seems to reflect the view of a majority of courts, although a few have applied a minority discount, largely on the grounds that the purpose of an appraisal proceeding is to value the dissenters' *minority shares* and not to award the dissenter a pro rata share of the value of the corporation *as a whole*. If the statutorily mandated appraisal proceeding must include a minority discount in calculating the fair value of the dissenters' shares, then what behavior on the part of the controlling shareholder is encouraged by framing the default rule in this manner? Consider the following reasoning on this question:

> Courts that have declined to apply a minority discount in the appraisal context have correctly focused on the purpose of the appraisal remedy to justify their conclusion. The primary purpose of the appraisal remedy today is to protect minority shareholders from wrongful conduct. If this purpose is to be fulfilled, the dissenting shareholder must receive a pro rata share of the value of the corporation. . . .
>   . . . Imposing a minority discount in the appraisal process encourages controlling shareholders to take advantage of minority shareholders, and allows them to appropriate a portion of the value of the corporation from the minority shareholders.[146] This problem is exacerbated when the corporation's value as a whole

---

146. It might be argued that if a dissenting shareholder acquired his stock taking advantage of a minority discount, such as by purchasing the stock at a market price, the shareholder should similarly be saddled with a minority discount at the time of exit via an appraisal proceeding. This argument is misguided for several reasons. First, as noted above, if minority shareholders receive less than their pro rata share of the value of the corporation, those engaging in the cash-out merger would necessarily receive more than their pro rata share. This would violate tenets of fundamental fairness and encourage wrongful conduct. Second, shareholders willing to invest their capital and purchase a minority position in a corporation do so with the expectation that if the corporation is acquired or taken private, they will realize

is initially determined by reference to market price. Because market price reflects the value of a small quantity of stock, market price already reflects a minority discount. If a court values a corporation by reference to market price, and then imposes a minority discount, it in effect discounts the stock twice to reflect its minority status, and confers a further windfall on the majority shareholder.

Barry M. Wertheimer, *The Shareholders' Appraisal Remedy and How Courts Determine Fair Value*, 47 DUKE L.J. 613, 643-645 (1998).

    2. Statutory Mandate.   Appraisal statutes commonly mandate that the focus of the appraisal proceeding is to determine *the fair value* of the dissenters' shares as of the date on which the merger closes (i.e., the date of effectiveness of the merger) "exclusive of any element of value arising from the accomplishment or expectation of the merger . . . together with a fair rate of interest. . . ." Delaware §262(h). Or, as expressed in the language of the predecessor provision to MBCA §13.01(4), *fair value* excludes "any appreciation . . . [in the value of dissenting shares] in anticipation of the [acquisition] . . . unless [such] exclusion would be inequitable." MBCA §13.01(3) (1984). Considerable controversy exists as to the meaning of this statutory language, however. Does this statutory language dictate that the courts ignore any control premium in determining fair value? In other words, does this language require the court to exclude the dissenting shares from participating in any of the synergistic gains from the acquisition? If so, how should the court go about measuring those gains? As a broader issue of public policy, how should the gains generated by a merger be divided between Bidder Co. and Target's shareholders since the acquisition involves a change of control of Target? Consider the guidance given on this difficult question of public policy by the Delaware Supreme Court in the case that follows.

Dell, Inc. v. Magnetar Global Event Driven Master Fund Ltd.
177 A.3d 1 (Del. 2017)

VALIHURA, Justice:
    The petitioners left standing in this long-running appraisal saga are former stockholders of Dell Inc. ("Dell" or the "Company") who validly exercised their appraisal rights instead of voting for a buyout led by the Company's founder and CEO, Michael Dell, and affiliates of a private equity firm, Silver Lake Partners ("Silver Lake"). In perfecting their appraisal rights, petitioners acted on their belief that Dell's shares were worth more than the deal price of $13.75 per share — which was already a 37% premium to the Company's ninety-day-average unaffected stock price.

---

their pro rata share of the corporation's value. If such shareholders can be involuntarily removed from their investment through a cash-out merger without receiving a pro rata share of the corporation's value, they will be less willing to make such investments. This would result in an increase in the cost of capital for corporations. Finally, shareholders who are able to acquire corporate stock at a minority discount "pay" for that discount by virtue of their inability to control or influence corporate decision making. They should not have to pay again by virtue of a discount in connection with a forced exit from the corporation.

Our appraisal statute, 8 *Del. C.* §262, allows stockholders who perfect their appraisal rights to receive "fair value" for their shares as of the merger date instead of the merger consideration. The appraisal statute requires the Court of Chancery to assess the "fair value" of such shares and, in doing so, "take into account all relevant factors." The trial court complied: it took into account all the relevant factors presented by the parties in advocating for their view of fair value—including Dell's stock price and deal price—and then arrived at its own determination of fair value.

The problem with the trial court's opinion is not, as the Company argues, that it failed to take into account the stock price and deal price. The trial court *did consider* this market data. It simply decided to give it no weight. But the court nonetheless erred because its reasons for giving that data no weight—and for relying instead exclusively on its own discounted cash flow ("DCF") analysis to reach a fair value calculation of $17.62—do not follow from the court's key factual findings and from relevant, accepted financial principles. . . .

Here, the trial court gave no weight to Dell's stock price because it found its market to be inefficient. But the evidence suggests that the market for Dell's shares was actually efficient and, therefore, likely a possible proxy for fair value. Further, the trial court concluded that several features of management-led buyout ("MBO") transactions render the deal prices resulting from such transactions unreliable. But the trial court's own findings suggest that, even though this was an MBO transaction, these features were largely absent here. Moreover, even if it were not possible to determine the precise amount of that market data's imperfection, as the Court of Chancery concluded, the trial court's decision to rely "exclusively" on its own DCF analysis is based on several assumptions that are not grounded in relevant, accepted financial principles.

We REVERSE, in part, and AFFIRM, in part, and REMAND for these reasons and those that follow. . . .

I.

A. DELL

In June 2012, when the idea of an MBO first arose, Dell was a mature company on the brink of crisis: its stock price had dropped from $18 per share to around $12 per share in just the first half of the year. The advent of new technologies such as tablet computers crippled the traditional PC-maker's outlook. The Company's recent transformation struggled to generate investor optimism about its long- term prospects. And the global economy was still hungover from the financial crisis of 2008.

Other than a brief hiatus from 2004 to his return in 2007, Michael Dell had led Dell as CEO, from the Company's founding in his first-year dorm room at the University of Texas at Austin when he was just nineteen years old, to a Fortune 500 behemoth with global revenues hitting $56.9 billion in the fiscal year ending February 1, 2013. Dell was indisputably one of the world's largest IT companies.

i. *Michael Dell's Return and the Company's Challenges*

Upon his return to the Company in 2007, Mr. Dell perceived three key challenges facing Dell. First, low-margin PC-makers such as Lenovo were muscling into Dell's market share as the performance gap between its higher-end computers and the cheaper alternatives narrowed. Second, starting with the launch of Apple's iPhone in 2007, the impending onslaught of smartphones and tablet computers appeared likely to erode traditional PC sales. Third, cloud-based storage from the likes of Amazon.com threatened the Company's traditional server storage business.

In light of these threats, Mr. Dell believed that, to survive and thrive, the Company should focus on enterprise software and services, which could be accomplished through acquisitions in these spaces. From 2010 through 2012, the Company acquired eleven companies for approximately $14 billion. And Mr. Dell tried to sell the market on this transformation. He regularly shared with equity analysts his view that the Company's enterprise solutions and services divisions would achieve annual sales growth in the double-digits and account for more than half of Dell's profits by 2016.

Yet despite Dell's M&A spurt and Mr. Dell's attempts to persuade Wall Street to buy into the Company's future, the market still "didn't get" Dell, as Mr. Dell lamented. It still viewed the Company as a PC business, and its stock hovered in the mid-teens.

ii. *The Market for Dell's Stock*

Dell's stock traded on the NASDAQ under the ticker symbol DELL. The Company's market capitalization of more than $20 billion ranked it in the top third of the S & P 500. Dell had a deep public float and was actively traded as more than 5% of Dell's shares were traded each week. It was also widely covered by equity analysts, and its share price quickly reflected the market's view on breaking developments. Based on these metrics, the record suggests the market for Dell stock was semi-strong efficient, meaning that the market's digestion and assessment of all publicly available information concerning Dell was quickly impounded into the Company's stock price. For example, on January 14, 2013, Dell's stock jumped 9.8% within a minute of Bloomberg breaking the news of the Company's take-private talks, and the stock closed up 13% from the day prior—on a day the S & P 500 as a whole fell 0.1%.

B. *The Sale Process*

[In August 2012], after [Silver Lake's] Egon Durban [first] proposed the idea of an MBO[,] Mr. Dell enlisted the advice of friend and private equity executive George Roberts of Kohlberg Kravis Roberts & Co. L.P. ("KKR"). [Mr. Dell] received positive feedback, including an indication that KKR might be interested in participating should the Company go that route. Mr. Dell then brought the idea to Dell's Board by calling the Company's lead independent director, Alex Mandl, on Friday, August 14, 2012.

The following Monday, the Board met and created an independent special committee composed of four independent directors (the "Committee") to evaluate possible transactions to acquire the Company proposed by Mr. Dell and/or any other party, as well as to explore possible strategic alternatives. The Board empowered the Committee to hire its own legal and financial advisors, and the Committee selected Debevoise & Plimpton LLP as legal counsel and JP Morgan Chase & Co. as financial advisor. (The Committee eventually hired Evercore Partners ["Evercore"] as a second financial advisor in January 2013.) The Committee also had full and exclusive authority to recommend to the Board a course of action regarding any proposed transaction, and the Board vowed not to recommend that stockholders approve a transaction without receiving a prior favorable recommendation from the Committee.

Dell's earnings for the second quarter of Fiscal 2013, announced the following day, August 21, 2012, underscored the Company's challenges: revenue was down 8% from the prior year, and earnings per share dropped 13%. The Company's revenue fell short of expectations, and its management further revised its EPS [earnings per share] forecast down 20% for Fiscal 2013. Dell management said that the Company was amid a "long-term strategy" expected to "take time" to reap benefits. But one analyst called the Company a "sinking ship" and emphasized that "Dell's turnaround strategy is fundamentally flawed [and] the fundamentals are bad. Dell may have responded too late to save itself." Many analysts also revised their price targets downward.

i. The Pre-Signing Canvass

Mr. Dell [as the owner of 15.4% of Dell's stock] entered into a confidentiality agreement . . . that required him to, among other things, "explore in good faith the possibility of working with any such potential counterparty or financing source if requested by the Committee," a provision designed to prevent his prior involvement with KKR and Silver Lake from deterring other possible bidders.

After consulting with JPMorgan, the Committee decided to limit its initial pre-signing market canvass to KKR and Silver Lake because they were, according to JPMorgan, "among the best qualified potential acquirers," and "there was a low probability of strategic buyer interest in acquiring the Company." Using management forecasts that the Committee still considered "overly optimistic," on October 9, 2012, the day after the Company's stock price closed at $9.66 per share, JPMorgan shared with the Committee that it believed a financial sponsor could pay approximately $14.13 per share . . . At several Committee meetings that fall, JPMorgan and the Company's bankers from Goldman Sachs shared a range of valuations for various transaction scenarios, including Goldman's projections for the Company's future share prices if Dell remained a standalone public Company.

On October 23, 2012, a day on which Dell's stock price was to close at $9.35, both KKR and Silver Lake proposed transactions to the Committee [with both parties indicating interest in an all-cash transaction to be priced in the range of $12 to $13 per share]. [These initial offers were disappointing to the Committee, and so it] . . . asked Mr. Dell to email both firms to encourage them to raise their offers, and he obliged—sending the same email to each in which he offered for Company management to meet with representatives of each firm and solicited their advice on what the Company could do to help improve their proposals. But the Company's third-quarter earnings, released on November 15, 2012, brought more bad news for Dell: revenue dropped 11% from the prior year, and EPS was down 28%. During this period when Dell was trying to sell its long-term vision without success, it kept failing the quarterly tests on which so many market analysts focus . . . The Committee enlisted Boston Consulting Group ("BCG") to formulate independent projections for the Company.

By December 3, 2012, KKR withdrew its proposal as it was unable to "get [its] arms around the risks of the PC business."

For his part, Mr. Dell remained open "to join up with whoever" and was willing to supply as much equity as necessary for a transaction. To restore competition to the process once KKR dropped out, the Committee asked another PE [private equity] heavyweight, Texas Pacific Group ("TPG"), who had recently invested in Dell's down-market rival Lenovo, to explore an acquisition. Though TPG signed a confidentiality agreement, obtained access to the data room, "spent a good deal of resources on it," and its leaders sat through presentations by Dell management, the PE firm reported to the Committee on December 23, 2012, that it decided not to submit a bid as "cash flows attached to the PC business were simply too uncertain, too unpredictable to establish an investment case."

By January 24, 2013, three additional parties had expressed a desire to explore a deal . . . [and all three signed confidentiality agreements] . . .

News that Dell was exploring a strategic transaction had been leaking out since December, and Evercore reasoned that "if there were any people out there who were actively interested, there was a good chance they would have already come forward."

For its part, Silver Lake remained interested in a deal through it all. Over the course of negotiations, the Committee persuaded Silver Lake to raise its offer six times from its initial proposal of $11.22-to-$12.16 per share. It helped that, after the Board resolved to seek $13.75 per share and settle for no less than $13.60 per share, Mr. Dell agreed to accept a lower price to roll over his shares than unaffiliated stockholders were to receive . . . [On] February 4, [Silver Lake made] its "best and final offer" [of $13.65 per share].

The Committee met with its financial advisors on the afternoon of February 4: both Evercore and JPMorgan indicated that they considered $13.65 per share fair to the unaffiliated stockholders from a financial point of view. The Committee recommended that the Board accept Silver Lake's offer, and, aside from Mr. Dell, who was not present, the Board unanimously adopted resolutions approving the transaction. The next morning, February 5, 2013, the Company and three entities affiliated with Silver Lake and Mr. Dell (collectively the "Buyout Group") entered into the merger agreement dated February 5, 2013 (collectively with amendments, the "Merger Agreement"), and they publicly announced the planned transaction.

Mr. Dell signed a voting agreement wherein, he pledged that [he would vote his shares in the same proportion as the public shareholders, including any vote on a "Superior Proposal."] This meant that any outside bidder who persuaded stockholders that its bid was better would have access to Mr. Dell's votes, eliminating one of the key problems other bidders may face when there is a CEO with material voting power.

The transaction contemplated that Mr. Dell would roll over his shares at $13.36 per share and invest up to $500 million in additional equity and that an affiliate of his would invest up to $250 million in additional equity. This transaction structure would give Mr. Dell a 74.9% stake in the Company post-closing, and Silver Lake a 25.1% stake.

The Merger Agreement also provided for a forty-five-day go-shop period ending March 23, 2013; a one-time match right for the Buyout Group available until the stockholder vote; and termination fees of $180 million if the Company agreed to a Superior Proposal as defined in the Merger Agreement that materialized during the go-shop period, or $450 million if the Company agreed to a non-Superior Proposal or to bids produced after the go-shop period.

ii.   The Go-Shop Period

Led by Evercore, the go-shop period began on February 5, 2013. [During the go shop period, Evercore contacted 67 potential buyers, of which 2 developed into serious candidates. The two prospective bidders were the private equity firm Blackstone and Carl Icahn of Icahn Enterprises, L.P. ("Icahn").] . . .

C.   After the Go-Shop . . .

[After conducting due diligence, Blackstone] withdrew from the bidding [process] on April 18, 2013, and cited two key reasons for its decision: "(1) an unprecedented 14 percent market decline in PC volume in the first quarter of 2013, its steepest drop in history, and inconsistent with Management's projections for modest industry growth; and (2) the rapidly eroding financial profile of Dell." . . .

But Icahn remained interested [in bidding for Dell. To that end, Icahn announced in June 2013 that (i) he had purchased 72 million Dell shares; (ii) he opposed the Merger; and (iii) that he had plans to purchase up to 1.1 billion Dell shares at $14 per share in a partial buyout of the public shares.]

On July 17, the day before the [shareholder vote on the Merger,] the Committee's proxy solicitor informed it that the Company's stockholders were unlikely to approve the merger. To avoid defeat, the Committee convened the [Dell shareholders] meeting and adjourned it without holding a vote, affording the Buyout Group time to improve its proposal. . . .

[Following negotiations with the Committee, the Buyout Group (i.e., Silver Lake and Michael Dell) raised its price to $13.75 per share, and Mr. Dell agreed to reduce the value he would receive to $12.51 per share.]

When the Committee met to evaluate the [Buyout Group's] revised proposal on August 2, 2013, both [of the Committee's bankers, Evercore and JPMorgan,] determined the $13.75 per share deal price [was] fair to the unaffiliated [i.e., public] stockholders. Following the Committee's advice, the Board approved the revised transaction (hereinafter, the "Merger") and amended the Merger Agreement to reflect the changed deal terms. A [shareholder] vote was scheduled for September 12, 2013.

ii.   Stockholder Vote

At the special meeting [of Dell shareholders] held September 12, 2013, 57% of all Dell shares approved the Merger (70% of the shares present at the meeting). The Merger closed October 29, 2013, and the shares of non-dissenting Dell stockholders were converted into $13.75 per share in cash. [Although Icahn initially indicated that he would seek appraisal if the Merger were approved, ultimately he withdrew his demand.] However, holders of 38,765,130 shares of Dell common stock demanded appraisal.

D.   The Appraisal Trial

The four-day appraisal trial in October 2015 featured 1,200 exhibits, seventeen depositions, live testimony from seven fact witnesses and five expert witnesses, a 542-paragraph-long pre-trial order, and 369 pages of pre- and post-trial briefing. Petitioners argued that, as demonstrated through their expert's DCF analysis, the fair value of the Company's common stock at the effective time of the Merger was actually $28.61 per share—more than double the deal price of $13.75. If this valuation were correct, the Buyout Group obtained Dell at a $26 billion discount to its actual value. In contrast, Dell maintained that its DCF analysis yielding a $12.68 per share valuation was a more appropriate approximation of fair value, but that, in light of the uncertainties facing the PC industry, fair value could be as high as the deal price (but not greater).

E.   The Court of Chancery's Determination of Fair Value

The Court of Chancery acknowledged that "[t]he consideration that the buyer agrees to provide in the deal and that the seller agrees to accept is one form of market price data, which Delaware courts have long considered in appraisal proceedings." However, the court believed that flaws in Dell's sale process meant that the deal price of $13.75 should not be afforded any weight here since it was "not the best evidence of [the Company's] fair value." Accordingly, the trial court disregarded both Dell's pre-transactional stock price and the deal price entirely.

The Court of Chancery identified three crucial problems with the pre-signing phase of the sale process that contributed to its decision to disregard the market-based indicators of value.

First, the primary bidders were all financial sponsors who used an LBO pricing model to determine their bid prices—meaning that the per-share deal price needed to be low enough to facilitate an IRR [internal rate of return] of approximately 20%. As the court saw it, the prospective PE [private equity] buyers, the Buyout Group, Mr. Dell, and the Committee never focused on determining the intrinsic value of the Company as a going concern.

Second, the trial court believed that Dell's investors were overwhelmingly focused on short-term profit, and that this "investor myopia" created a valuation gap that purportedly distorted the original merger consideration of $13.65. Thus, under the Court of Chancery's logic, the efficient market hypothesis—which teaches that the price of a company's stock reflects all publicly available information as a consensus, per-share valuation—failed when it came to Dell, diminishing the probative value of the stock price. This phenomenon also allegedly depressed the deal price by anchoring deal negotiations at an improperly low starting point.

Third, the trial court concluded that there was no meaningful price competition during the pre-signing phase as, at any given time during the pre-signing phase, there were at most two private equity sponsors competing for the deal, creating little incentive to bid up the deal price. The trial court especially faulted the Committee for declining to reach out to potential strategic bidders, such as HP [Hewlett Packard], during the pre-signing phase, leaving the financial sponsors who were engaged without the incentive "to push their prices upward to pre-empt potential interest from that direction." According to the trial court, large private equity buyers such as those engaged here are notoriously averse to topping each other, and without the specter of a strategic buyer, the Committee lacked "the most powerful tool that a seller can use to extract a portion of the bidder's anticipated surplus"—the "threat of an alternative deal."

Next, the trial court evaluated the post-signing go-shop process, where it identified several additional issues that it believed further contributed to a deal price that fell short of fair value. Though two additional proposals to acquire the Company emerged during the go-shop period, from Blackstone and Icahn, the trial court dismissed their import given that these prospective buyers also operated within the "confines of the LBO model," and that the deal price ultimately increased by just 2% over the original merger consideration of $13.65 per share as a result of this go-shop.

Further, the trial court observed that the deal's structure as an MBO imposed several additional, supposedly insurmountable impediments to Dell's ability to prove at trial that the deal's "structure in fact generated a price that persuasively established the Company's fair value." The trial court emphasized that, to prove a go-shop's worth, it is crucial to show that prospective rival bidders had a "realistic pathway to success" so as to justify the time, expense, and harm to professional relationships that might result from pursuing an offer. Though the trial court recognized that the "relatively open" structure of the Committee's go-shop "raised fewer structural barriers than the norm," the court believed such openness could not obviate the issues imposed by features "endemic to MBO go-shops," which "create a powerful disincentive for any competing bidder—and particularly competing financial bidders—to get involved." These features include a so-called "winner's curse" and the management team's inherent value to the Company.

The concept of a "winner's curse" [according to the trial court] reflects the notion that "incumbent management has the best insight into the Company's value, or at least is perceived to have an informational advantage," so if a financial buyer is willing to outspend management to win a deal, it must be overpaying because it must have overlooked some piece of information that dissuaded management from bidding as much. Further, the trial court inferred that "Mr. Dell's unique value and his affiliation with the Buyout Group were negative factors that inhibited the effectiveness of the go-shop process," despite evidence that suggested that neither Blackstone nor Icahn—nor anyone else, for that matter—believed that Mr. Dell's continued involvement with the Company was essential. Moreover, Mr. Dell appeared willing to work with any viable party.

In light of these apparent flaws in the sale process, both pre- and post-signing, the trial court found that the Company failed to establish that "the sale process offers the most reliable evidence of the Company's value as a going concern." Moreover, the Court of Chancery decided that "[b]ecause it is impossible to quantify the exact degree of the sale process mispricing," it was going to discount the final merger consideration of $13.75 entirely—giving it no weight when determining fair value.

But, given that the trial court deemed it "illogical" to believe that another bidder would not have topped the Buyout Group's offer if the Company were actually worth the $28.61 per share advocated by the petitioners, the Court of Chancery rejected petitioners' DCF and arrived at its "fair value" determination of $17.62 per share through its own DCF analysis, using a mix of the inputs proposed by the petitioners' and the Company's experts and adjustments of its own.

F.   This Appeal

The Company argues that the trial court committed legal error and abused its discretion in failing to assign *any* weight to the deal price. On both fronts, the Company claims that the trial court erred by disregarding Section 262(h)'s requirement that it "take into account all relevant factors" in determining fair value.

The Company articulates three reasons why it believes the trial court committed legal error. First, the Company argues that there is no requirement under Delaware law that the deal price be the "most reliable" or "best" evidence of fair value in order for it to be given any weight. Second, the Company posits that there is no requirement under Delaware law that the Court of Chancery disregard the deal price entirely if it cannot unequivocally quantify the precise amount of sale process mispricing. Third, the Company contends that the trial court erred in fashioning what seems akin to a bright-line rule that the deal prices in MBO transactions are distorted and should be disregarded. Dell states that imposing such a rule would be "inconsistent with the flexible nature of the appraisal inquiry."

Moreover, the Company notes that the trial court's conclusions underpinning its decision to disregard deal price do not follow from the facts as found. In particular, the Company maintains that the trial court lacked a basis for finding that: the market for Dell's stock was inefficient due to the alleged short-term focus of the Company's investor base, yielding a valuation gap between Dell's market value and its intrinsic value; the pre-signing phase lacked "meaningful price competition" because those involved in the sale process were fixated on determining a deal price that would generate the requisite IRR under the LBO model, and there were no strategic bidders involved; banks were reluctant to help finance the deal through debt, limiting the available leverage and therefore capping the deal price; the emergence of "topping bids" underscored the unfairness of the original merger consideration; and features endemic to

MBO go-shops additionally distorted the relevance of the deal price. Thus, the Company argues that the trial court's entire reasoning for assigning no weight to the deal price was based either on flawed premises or on theoretical constructs that lack support in this factual record. . . .

II.

ANALYSIS

We agree with petitioners that the trial court *did consider* all relevant factors presented, including Dell's stock price and deal price. But we reverse because the reasoning behind the trial court's decision to give no weight to any market-based measure of fair value runs counter to its own factual findings. After reviewing our appraisal statute and accompanying jurisprudence, we explore why the facts fail to support the Court of Chancery's reasoning for disregarding, in particular, the deal price. To the extent the trial court can justify giving any weight to its DCF analysis on remand, we conclude that, for the most part, the trial court did not abuse its discretion as to the asserted errors.

A. *The Relevant Legal Framework*

The General Assembly created the appraisal remedy in 1899 after amending the corporate code to allow a corporation to be sold upon the consent of a majority of stockholders instead of unanimous approval as was previously required. Given that a single shareholder could no longer hold up the sale of a company, the General Assembly devised appraisal in service of the notion that "the stockholder is entitled to be paid for that which has been taken from him." Stockholders who viewed the sale price as inadequate could seek "an independent judicial determination of the fair value of their shares" instead of accepting the per-share merger consideration. There is one issue in an appraisal trial: "the value of the dissenting stockholder's stock."

Appraisals are odd. Unlike other cases, where one side loses if the other side fails to persuade the court that the evidence tilts its way, appraisals require the court to determine a number representing the fair value of the shares after considering the trial presentations and submissions of parties who have starkly different objectives: petitioners contend fair value far exceeds the deal price, and the company argues that fair value is the deal price or lower. In reality, the burden "falls on the [trial] judge to determine fair value, using 'all relevant factors.'"

Though the appraisal remedy is "entirely a creature of statute," like most statutes, its specifics have been refined through years of judicial interpretation. Indeed, "fair value" has become a "jurisprudential, rather than purely economic, construct."[85]

---

85. [*DFC Global Corp. v. Muirfield Value Partners,* 172 A.3d 346, 367–68, (Del. 2017)] (citing *Cavalier Oil Corp. v. Harnett,* 564 A.2d 1137, 1144 (Del. 1989)).

Importantly for our purposes here, Section 262 provides that the Court of Chancery "shall determine the fair value of the shares exclusive of any element of value arising from the accomplishment or expectation of the merger or consolidation" plus interest. Equally critical is its requirement that, "[i]n determining such fair value, the Court shall take into account all relevant factors."[87] These provisions explain "what" the Court is valuing, and "how" the court should go about this task.

i. "What" the Court is Valuing

We have explained that the court's ultimate goal in an appraisal proceeding is to determine the "fair or intrinsic value" of each share on the closing date of the merger. To reach this per-share valuation, the court should first envisage the entire pre-merger company as a "going concern," as a standalone entity, and assess its value as such. "[T]he corporation must be viewed as an on-going enterprise, occupying a particular market position in the light of future prospects." The valuation should reflect the "'operative reality' of the company as of the time of the merger."

Because the court strives "to value the *corporation* itself, as distinguished from a specific fraction of its *shares* as they may exist in the hands of a particular shareholder," the court should not apply a minority discount when there is a controlling stockholder. Further, the court should exclude "any synergies or other value expected from the merger giving rise to the appraisal proceeding itself."[93]

Then, once this total standalone value is determined, the court awards each petitioning stockholder his pro rata portion of this total—"his proportionate interest in [the] going concern" plus interest.

ii. "How" the Court Should Approach Valuation

By instructing the court to "take into account all relevant factors" in determining fair value, the statute requires the Court of Chancery to give fair consideration to "proof of value by any techniques or methods which are generally considered acceptable in the financial community and otherwise admissible in court."[95] Given that "[e]very company is different; every merger is different," the appraisal endeavor is "by design, a flexible process."

---

87. [8 Del.C. §262(h).]

93. *Global GT LP v. Golden Telecom, Inc.*, 993 A.2d 497, 507 (Del. Ch. 2010), *aff'd*, 11 A.3d 214 (Del. 2010); *DFC*, 172 A.3d at 368, 2017 WL 3261190, at *16 (The Court should exclude "any value that the selling company's shareholders would receive because a buyer intends to operate the subject company, not as a stand-alone going concern, but as a part of a larger enterprise, from which synergistic gains can be extracted." (quoting *Union Ill. 1995 Inv. LP v. Union Fin. Grp., Ltd*, 847 A.2d 340, 356 (Del. Ch. 2004))). As noted in *DFC*, there are policy reasons for excising the synergistic value: "the specific buyer [should] not end up losing its upside for [the] purchase by having to pay out the expected gains from its own business plans for the company it bought to the petitioners." 172 A.3d at 368, 2017 WL 3261190, at *16. Further, "the broader excision of synergy gains could have also been thought of as a balance to the Court's decision to afford pro rata value to minority stockholders." *Id.*

95. *Weinberger v. UOP*, 457 A.2d 701, 713 (Del. 1983).

This Court has relied on the statutory requirement that the Court of Chancery consider "all relevant factors" to reject requests for the adoption of a presumption that the deal price reflects fair value if certain preconditions are met, such as when the merger is the product of arm's-length negotiation and a robust, non-conflicted market check, and where bidders had full information and few, if any, barriers to bid for the deal. In *Golden Telecom*, we explained that Section 262(h) is "unambiguous[]" in its command that the Court of Chancery undertake an "*independent*" assessment of fair value, and that the statute "vests the Chancellor and Vice Chancellors with significant discretion to consider 'all relevant factors' and determine the going concern value of the underlying company."[99] In *DFC*, we again rejected an invitation to create a presumption in favor of the deal price.[100] Even aside from the statutory command to consider all relevant factors, we doubted our ability to craft the precise preconditions for invoking such a presumption.[101]

As such, "the trial of an appraisal case under the Delaware General Corporation Law presents unique challenges to the judicial factfinder." And this task is complicated by "the clash of contrary, and often antagonistic, expert opinions of value," prompting the trial court to wade through "widely divergent views reflecting partisan positions" in arriving at its determination of a single number for fair value.

In the end, after this analysis of the relevant factors, "[i]n some cases, it may be that a single valuation metric is the most reliable evidence of fair value and that giving weight to another factor will do nothing but distort that best estimate. In other cases, it may be necessary to consider two or more factors." Or, in still others, the court might apportion weight among a variety of methodologies. But, whatever route it chooses, the trial court must justify its methodology (or methodologies) according to the facts of the case and relevant, accepted financial principles.

Given the human element in the appraisal inquiry—where the factfinder is asked to choose between two competing, seemingly plausible valuation perspectives, forge its own, or apportion weight among a variety of methodologies—it is possible that a factfinder, even the same factfinder, could reach different valuation conclusions on the same set of facts if presented differently at trial. There may be no perfect methodology for arriving at fair value for a given set of facts, and the Court of Chancery's conclusions will be upheld if they follow logically from those facts and are grounded in relevant, accepted financial principles. "To be sure, "fair value" does not equal "best value."[108]

---

99. [*Golden Telecom, Inc. v. Global GT LP*, 11 A.3d 214, 217- 218 (Del. 2010).]

100. *DFC*, 172 A.3d at 366–67.

101. *Id.* ("[N]ot only do we see no license in the statute for creating a presumption that the resulting price in such a situation is the 'exclusive,' 'best,' or 'primary' evidence of fair value, we do not share DFC's confidence in our ability to craft, on a general basis, the precise pre-conditions that would be necessary to invoke a presumption of that kind.").

108. [*DFC*, 172 A. 3d at 348-49.]

B.   The Court of Chancery's Reasons for Disregarding
Deal Price do not Follow from the Record

The Company recasts the Court of Chancery's fair value opinion as creating several bright-line rules, including that the court must assign no weight
to the deal price if: (i) it is not the "best" evidence of fair value; (ii) the court
cannot "quantify the exact degree of the sale process mispricing"; or (iii) the
transaction is an MBO. And the Company argues that each such rule is flawed.
Setting aside whether the Court of Chancery's opinion actually purports to
assert these more generalized propositions, we agree with the Company's core
premise that, on this particular record, the trial court erred in not assigning any
mathematical weight to the deal price. In fact, the record as distilled by the trial
court suggests that the deal price deserved heavy, if not dispositive, weight. . . .
     The three central premises that the Court of Chancery relied upon to
assign no weight to the deal price were flawed. First, the court believed that a
"valuation gap" existed between Dell's stock price and the Company's intrinsic
value, and this conclusion—contrary to the efficient market hypothesis—led it
to hypothesize that the bidding over Dell as a company was anchored at an artificially low price that depressed the ultimate deal price below fair value. Second,
the court suggested that the lack of strategic buyers in the sale process—and,
accordingly, the involvement of only private equity bidders—also pushed the
deal price below fair value. Third, the court concluded that several factors
endemic to MBO go-shops further undercut the deal price's credibility. We consider each of these premises in turn and find them untenable in view of the
Court of Chancery's own findings of fact as considered in light of established
principles of corporate finance. Without these premises, the trial court's support for disregarding the deal price collapses. Accordingly, the trial court's reliance on them as a basis for granting no weight to the market-based indicators of
value constituted an abuse of discretion meriting reversal.

i.   The Trial Court Lacked a Valid Basis for Finding
a "Valuation Gap" Between Dell's Market and
Fundamental Values

The Court of Chancery presumed "investor myopia" and hangover from
the Company's "nearly $14 billion investment in its transformation, which had
not yet begun to generate the anticipated results" produced a "valuation gap"
between Dell's fundamental and market prices. That presumption contributed
to the trial court's decision to assign no weight to Dell's stock price or deal price.
The trial court believed that short-sighted analysts and traders impounded an
inadequate—and lowball—assessment of all publicly available information
into Dell's stock price, diminishing its worth as a valuation tool. But the record
shows just the opposite: analysts scrutinized Dell's long-range outlook when
evaluating the Company and setting price targets, and the market was capable
of accounting for Dell's recent mergers and acquisitions and their prospects in
its valuation of the Company.
     Further, the Court of Chancery's analysis ignored the efficient market
hypothesis long endorsed by this Court. It teaches that the price produced by

an efficient market is generally a more reliable assessment of fair value than the view of a single analyst, especially an expert witness who caters her valuation to the litigation imperatives of a well-heeled client.[113] . . .

The record before us provides no rational, factual basis for such a "valuation gap." Indeed, the trial court did not indicate that Dell lacked a vast and diffuse base of public stockholders, that information about the Company was sparse or restricted, that there was not an active trading market for Dell's shares, or that Dell had a controlling stockholder—or that the market for its stock lacked any of the hallmarks of an efficient market. In fact, the record shows that Dell had a deep public float, was covered by over thirty equity analysts in 2012, boasted 145 market makers, was actively traded with over 5% of shares changing hands each week, and lacked a controlling stockholder. As noted in the expert reports, Dell's stock price had a track record of reacting to developments concerning the Company. For example, the stock climbed 13% on the day the Bloomberg first reported on Dell's talks of going private.

Further, the trial court expressly found no evidence that information failed to flow freely or that management purposefully tempered investors' expectations for the Company so that it could eventually take over the Company at a fire-sale price, as in situations where long-term investments actually led to such valuation gaps. In fact, Mr. Dell tried to persuade investors to envision an enterprise solutions and services business enjoying double-digit sales growth and which would more than compensate for any decline in end-user computing. And he pitched this plan for a "prolonged" period, approaching nearly three years.

There is also no evidence in the record that investors were "myopic" or shortsighted. Rather, the record shows analysts understood Dell's long-term plans. But they just weren't buying Mr. Dell's story. . . .

Further, the prospective bidders who later reviewed Dell's confidential information all dropped out due to their considerable discomfort with the future of the PC market. The record simply does not support the Court of Chancery's favoring of management's optimism over the public analysts' and investors' skepticism—especially in the face of management's track record of missing its own projections. (Even Mr. Dell doubted his management team's forecasting abilities and conceded at trial, "We're not very good at forecasting.") And the Court of Chancery does not justify why it chose to do so. In short, the record does not adequately support the Court of Chancery's conclusion that the market for Dell's stock was inefficient and that a valuation gap in the Company's market trading price existed in advance of the lengthy market check, an error that contributed to the trial court's decision to disregard the deal price.

---

113. *See DFC*, 172 A.3d at 370 (also noting that "the relationship between market valuation and fundamental valuation has been strong historically"); *id.* at 373 (describing the price produced by an efficient market as "informative of fair value"); *id.* at 373 n.144, ("In an efficient market you can trust prices, for they impound all available information about the value of each security." (quoting Richard A. Brealey et al., *Principles of Corporate Finance* 214 (2008))). And, even if the market were not precisely efficient, petitioners' own expert has conceded that "[a] market that is not perfectly efficient may still value securities more accurately than appraisers who are forced to work with limited information and whose judgments by nature reflect their own views and biases." Bradford Cornell, *Corporate Valuation* 46 (1993).

ii. The Lack of Strategic Bidders Is Not a Credible Reason for Disregarding the Deal Price

The trial court's complete discounting of the deal price due to financial sponsors' focus on obtaining a desirable IRR and not "fair value" was also error. Although the trial court did not have the benefit of our opinion in *DFC*, we rejected this view there and do so again here given we see "no rational connection" between a buyer's status as a financial sponsor and the question of whether the deal price is a fair price. After all, "all disciplined buyers, both strategic and financial, have internal rates of return that they expect in exchange for taking on the large risk of a merger, or for that matter, any sizeable investment of its capital." . . .

The bankers canvassed the interest of sixty-seven parties, including twenty possible strategic acquirers during the go-shop. The go-shop's forty-five-day window afforded potential bidders enough time to decide whether to continue to explore a transaction by submitting a non-binding indication of interest that qualified as a "Superior Proposal," which accordingly would lower the termination fee from $450 million to $180 million thanks to "Excluded Party" status and give that party months to scrutinize the Company's finances and growth prospects. . . .

The Court of Chancery stressed its view that the lack of competition from a strategic buyer lowered the relevance of the deal price. But its assessment that more bidders—both strategic and financial—should have been involved assumes there was some party interested in proceeding. Nothing in the record indicates that was the case. . . .

And this was not a buyout led by a controlling stockholder. Michael Dell only had approximately 15% of the equity. He pledged his voting power would go to any higher bidder, voting in proportion to other shares.

Other than the Buyout Group, as mentioned, all prospective buyers who reviewed the Company's confidential information retreated for the same reasons that the public markets were purportedly undervaluing Dell—trepidation about the future of the PC industry and the prospects of Dell's long-term turnaround strategy. This consistency confirms that management did not intentionally depress the Company's stock price in order to take advantage of a "trough" that public investors failed to recognize. In fact, the trial court expressly found that, "unlike other situations that this court has confronted, there is no evidence that Mr. Dell or his management team sought to create the valuation disconnect so that they could take advantage of it," and "[t]o the contrary, they tried to convince the market that the Company was worth more." Prospective buyers just did not believe the potential for a turnaround outweighed the risk of further erosion of PC sales and, accordingly, the Company's balance sheet. This coherence in views also makes it hard to take seriously the notion that Dell investors were incapable of accounting for Dell's long-term strategy. And it reinforces the integrity of both Dell's stock price and deal price.

Overall, the weight of evidence shows that Dell's deal price has heavy, if not overriding, probative value. The transaction process exemplifies many of the qualities that Delaware courts have found favor affording substantial, if not exclusive, weight to deal price in the fair value analysis. Even the Court of

Chancery's own summary remarks suggest the deal price deserves weight as the court characterized the sale process as one that "easily would sail through if reviewed under enhanced scrutiny" and observed that "[t]he Committee and its advisors did many praiseworthy things," too numerous to catalog in its opinion, as the trial court noted. Given the objective indicia of the deal price's reliability and our rejection of the notion of a private equity carve out, to the extent that the Court of Chancery chose to disregard Dell's deal price based on the presence of only private equity bidders, its reasoning is not grounded in accepted financial principles, and this assessment weighs in favor of finding an overall abuse of discretion. As explained below, there are other reasons that lead us to this conclusion.

iii. Features of MBOs Which Could Theoretically Undermine the Probative Value of the Deal Price Are Not Present Here . . .

b. The threat of a "winner's curse" does not provide a valid reason for disregarding the deal price based on this record.

The "winner's curse" describes a theory that, in outbidding incumbent management to "win" a deal, a buyer likely overpays for the company because management would presumably have paid more if the company were really worth it. Recognizing this phenomenon, prospective bidders supposedly resist outbidding incumbent management for fear they might later discover the information that prevented management from bidding even higher in the first place. But the likelihood of a winner's curse can be mitigated through a due diligence process where buyers have access to all necessary information. And, here, Dell allowed Blackstone to undertake "extensive due diligence," diminishing the "information asymmetry" that might otherwise facilitate a winner's curse.

Mr. Dell "ultimately spent more time with Blackstone than any of the other participants, including Silver Lake," and the Court of Chancery found that "[t]he record provided no reason to harbor any concern about Mr. Dell's level of cooperation or responsiveness," and "all of the bidders received access to the data they requested." The trial court even concluded that "the Committee appears to have addressed the problem of information asymmetry and the risk of the winner's curse as best they could." Yet in spite of Dell's efforts, the court concluded, the threat of a winner's curse is nonetheless "endemic to MBO go-shops" and imposes a "powerful disincentive for any competing bidder," even though Blackstone and Icahn surfaced with non-binding proposals. But, aside from the theoretical, the Court of Chancery did not point to any bidder who actually shied away from exploring an acquisition out of fear of the winner's curse phenomenon. . . .

c. Management's Inherent Value to the Company

The Court of Chancery also presumed that "Mr. Dell's value to the Company" imposed another impediment to the likelihood of rival bidders succeeding and thus dissuaded them from even trying. But, again, the Court of Chancery's own fact findings contradict and do not rationally support this conclusion. . . .

The Court of Chancery also acknowledged "evidence that Blackstone and Icahn did not regard Mr. Dell as essential to their bids." Blackstone had investigated possible replacements as CEO. And Icahn advised stockholders that he believed "the company would be worth far, far more" without Mr. Dell at the helm. . . .

C. MARKET DATA CONCLUSION

The actual facts concerning Dell's market values—the particularities of its stock market and the sale process—demonstrate that the Court of Chancery's reasons for assigning no weight to the market values are flawed. The apparent efficiency of Dell's pre-signing stock market and the long-term approach of its analysts undermine concerns of a "valuation gap." Competition limited to private equity bidders does not foreclose the sale price reflecting fair value, especially where the special committee instituted and oversaw a robust post-signing go-shop process. And, though the Court of Chancery's theories about MBOs might hold up as applied to other facts, they are not supported by the facts here. This was a case where the supposed prerequisite elements for problematic MBOs did not exist: rival bidders faced minimal structural barriers to a deal; extensive due diligence and cooperation from the Company helped address any information asymmetries that might otherwise imply the possibility of a winner's curse; and, assuming his value, Mr. Dell would have participated with rival bidders.

Taken as a whole, the market-based indicators of value—both Dell's stock price and deal price—have substantial probative value. But here, after examining the sale process, the Court of Chancery summarized that, "[t]aken as a whole, the Company did not establish that the outcome of the sale process offers the *most reliable* evidence of the Company's value as a going concern." These two statements are not incongruous, and the Court of Chancery's statement is not a rational reason for assigning no weight to market data. There is no requirement that a company prove that the sale process is the *most reliable* evidence of its going concern value in order for the resulting deal price to be granted any weight. If, as here, the reasoning behind the decision to assign no weight to market data is flawed, then the ultimate conclusion necessarily crumbles as well—especially in light of the less-than-surefire DCF analyses—as demonstrated below.

In so holding, we are not saying that the market is always the best indicator of value, or that it should always be granted some weight. We only note that, when the evidence of market efficiency, fair play, low barriers to entry, outreach to all logical buyers, and the chance for any topping bidder to have the support of Mr. Dell's own votes is so compelling, then failure to give the resulting price heavy weight because the trial judge believes there was mispricing missed by all the Dell stockholders, analysts, and potential buyers abuses even the wide discretion afforded the Court of Chancery in these difficult cases. And, of course, to give no weight to the prices resulting from the actions of Dell's stockholders and potential buyers presupposes that there is a more plausible basis for determining Dell's value in the form of expert testimony, such as from the petitioners' expert, who argued that his DCF analysis showed the fair value of Dell's stock is $28.61 per share—almost three times higher than the unaffected stock price of $9.97 per share and more than two times higher than the deal price of $13.75 per share.

D. THE DISCOUNTED CASH FLOW ANALYSES

We pause to note that this appraisal case does not present the classic scenario in which there is reason to suspect that market forces cannot be relied upon to ensure fair treatment of the minority. Under those circumstances, a DCF analysis can provide the court with a helpful data point about the price a sale process would have produced had there been a robust sale process involving willing buyers with thorough information and the time to make a bid. When, by contrast, an appraisal is brought in cases like this where a robust sale process of that kind in fact occurred, the Court of Chancery should be chary about imposing the hazards that always come when a law-trained judge is forced to make a point estimate of fair value based on widely divergent partisan expert testimony.

As is common in appraisal proceedings, each party—petitioners and the Company—enlisted highly paid, well-credentialed experts to produce DCF valuations. But their valuations landed galaxies apart—diverging by approximately $28 billion, or 126%. Petitioners' expert arrived at a per-share valuation of $28.61 as of the merger date, and the Company's expert produced a valuation of $12.68 per share. The Court of Chancery recognized that "[t]his is a recurring problem," and even believed the "market data is sufficient to exclude the possibility, advocated by the petitioners' expert, that the Merger undervalued the Company by $23 billion." Thus, the trial court found petitioners' valuation lacks credibility on its face. We agree. Yet, the trial court believed it could reconcile these enormous valuation chasms caused by the over 1,100 variable inputs in the competing DCFs and construct a DCF that more appropriately reflected the fair value of Dell's stock than the market data. And, reconciling the various agreements and divergences among the experts, the trial court determined fair value to be $17.62.

To underscore our concern with the Court of Chancery's decision to give no weight to Dell's stock market price or the deal price and, instead, arrive at a value nearly $7 billion above the transaction price, we consider the trial court's concluding explanation for its reasoning:

> The fair value generated by the DCF methodology comports with the evidence regarding the outcome of the sale process. The sale process functioned imperfectly as a price discovery tool, both during the pre-signing and post-signing phases. Its structure and result are sufficiently credible to exclude an outlier valuation for the Company like the one the petitioners advanced, but sufficient pricing anomalies and disincentives to bid existed to create the possibility that the sale process permitted an undervaluation of several dollars per share. Financial sponsors using an LBO model could not have bid close to $18 per share because of their IRR requirements and the Company's inability to support the necessary

levels of leverage. Assuming the $17.62 figure is right, then a strategic acquirer that perceived the Company's value could have gotten the Company for what was approximately a 25% discount. [But g]iven the massive integration risk inherent in such a deal, it is not entirely surprising that HP did not engage and that no one else came forward. Had the valuation gap approached what the petitioners' expert believed, then the incentives to intervene would have been vastly greater. Because it is impossible to quantify the exact degree of the sale process mispricing, this decision does not give weight to the Final Merger Consideration. It uses the DCF methodology exclusively to derive a fair value of the Company.

What this statement means is that the Court of Chancery's DCF value was the antithesis of any economist's definition of fair market value. The Court of Chancery conceded that its DCF value did not reflect a value deemed attractive to the buyers of Dell's 1,765,369,276 publicly traded shares. Further, it did not reflect the value that private equity buyers (including the biggest players such as KKR, TPG, and Blackstone) put on it, as it was too high for any of them to pay. The trial court also picked a price higher than any strategic would pay because, in economic terms, no strategic believed it could exploit a purported $6.8 billion value gap because the risks and costs of acquiring Dell and integrating it into its company dwarfed any potential for profit and synergy gains if Dell were purchased at the Court of Chancery's determination of fair value. And, of course, as to all buyers, strategic and financial, the Court of Chancery found that a topping bid put them at hazard of overpaying and succumbing to a winner's curse.

When an asset has few, or *no*, buyers at the price selected, that is not a sign that the asset is stronger than believed—it is a sign that it is weaker. This fact should give pause to law-trained judges who might attempt to outguess all of these interested economic players with an actual stake in a company's future. This is especially so here, where the Company worked hard to tell its story over a long time and was the opposite of a standoffish, defensively entrenched target as it approached the sale process free of many deal-protection devices that may prevent selling companies from attracting the highest bid. Dell was a willing seller, ready to pay for credible buyers to do due diligence, and had a CEO and founder who offered his voting power freely to any topping bidder.

Given that we have concluded that the trial court's key reasons for disregarding the market data were erroneous, and given the obvious lack of credibility of the petitioners' DCF model—as well as legitimate questions about the reliability of the projections upon which all of the various DCF analyses are based—these factors suggest strong reliance upon the deal price and far less weight, if any, on the DCF analyses. . . .

III. Fair Value Conclusion

Despite the sound economic and policy reasons supporting the use of the deal price as the fair value award on remand, we will not give in to the temptation to dictate that result. That said, we give the Vice Chancellor the discretion on remand to enter judgment at the deal price if he so chooses, with no further proceedings. If he decides to follow another route, the outcome should adhere to our rulings in this opinion, including our findings with regard to the DCF valuation. If he chooses to weigh a variety of factors in arriving at fair value, he must explain that weighting based on reasoning that is consistent with the record and with relevant, accepted financial principles. . . .

QUESTIONS

1. As used by the Delaware Supreme Court, what does "efficient market" mean?

2. The *Dell* Court observes that an "efficient market" for shares "is likely a possible proxy for fair value." Why?

3. Why was the Chancery Court suspicious that the deal price that was negotiated by the Company and the Buyout Group did not reflect "fair value" (or "intrinsic value" or "real value")?

4. What is the "winner's curse," and why was it of concern in determining "fair value" based on the facts of this case?

5. As noted by the Delaware Supreme Court, Delaware Section 162(h) instructs the court to "determine the fair value of the shares exclusive of any element of value arising from the accomplishment or expectation of the merger" What does this language mean?

6. The Delaware Supreme Court reverses the Chancery Court's determination of "fair value" because the lower court "gave no weight to any market-based measure of fair value." On remand, does this mean that the Chancery Court should give weight to the deal price? Alternatively, does it mean that the lower court should look to the trading price *prior* to the public announcement of the deal? Or, does it mean that the Chancery Court should take *both* into account in determining "fair value"?

7. Does the holding of the Delaware Supreme Court result in creating a (de facto?) presumption that "deal price" is the best evidence of "fair value" in the context of an appraisal proceeding? Does it matter whether the transaction at issue involves an MBO, on the one hand, or a fully-negotiated, arm's-length deal on the other hand?

8. Whose reasoning do you find more persuasive – the Chancery Court or the Supreme Court? Why?

NOTES

1. *On Remand.* On remand, the parties settled, and Dell agreed to pay the dissenting shareholders $13.75 per share in cash plus statutory interest attributable to the $13.75 per share. *See In re Appraisal of Dell Inc.*, 2018 WL 2939448 (Del. Ch., June 11, 2018).

2. *Management-led Buyouts.* Part of what troubled the Chancery Court in considering the pricing of the leveraged buyout of Dell, Inc. was the existence of management participation (most notably by Michael Dell) in this going-private

transaction. This MBO raised conflicts of interest and important issues regarding the scope of fiduciary duty obligations to be imposed on Target's management and (any) controlling shareholder(s). We will examine the conflicts of interest that are an inherent part of a deal such as the management-led Dell buyout when we discuss "going private" transactions in more detail in Chapter 7 as part of our study of fiduciary duty law.

3. "Deal Protection Devices." As part of its description of the sales process at issue in *Dell*, the Delaware Supreme Court describes the use of various "deal protection devices" that were made part of the Merger Agreement between Dell, Inc. and the Buyout Group (Silver Lake and Michael Dell). Notably, the Court describes the use of a "go-shop" period, as well as termination fees. The nature of deal protection provisions in general and the use of specific types of deal protection (such as termination fees and go shop provisions) will be examined in detail as part of the fiduciary duty materials in Chapter 7.

4. The Dell *Appraisal Proceedings: Who Qualifies as a "Dissenting Shareholder"?* The MBO transaction at issue in the principal case spawned another notable decision concerning the exercise of appraisal rights under Del. §262. The factual background for this other important ruling of the Delaware Chancery Court can be briefly summarized as follows:

> As set forth more fully in the facts of the principal case, Michael Dell and his partner, the private equity firm Silver Lake, originally offered to acquire all of the Dell shares not owned by the buying group at a price of $13.65 per share. Almost immediately following public announcement of the terms of this transaction, institutional shareholders such as Southeastern Asset Management and T. Rowe Price & Associates ("T. Rowe") cried foul, objecting that $13.65 was an inadequate offer and claiming that Dell was worth approximately $24 per share. Southeastern also publicly stated that it intended to oppose the proposed transaction, including mounting a proxy fight as well as exercising "any available Delaware statutory appraisal rights."

Ronald Barusch, *Dealpolitik: Is Dell Headed for Record-Breaking Delaware Appraisal Case?*, WALL STREET JOURNAL, Feb. 11, 2013, *available at*: http://blogs.wsj.com/deals/2013/02/11/dealpolitik-is-dell-headed-for-record-breaking-delaware-appraisal-case.

Despite very vocal public opposition to the deal by T. Rowe, the going-private transaction ultimately received the requisite shareholder approval at a special meeting of Dell's stockholders held on September 12, 2013. Thereafter, T. Rowe brought an appraisal action with respect to the Dell shares it held. In its opinion, *In re: Appraisal of Dell, Inc.*, 143 A. 3d 20 (May 11, 2016), the Delaware Court of Chancery decided that T. Rowe was

> not entitled to an appraisal of [its] shares of Dell Inc. in connection with Dell's [going-private] merger, because the record holder had voted the shares at issue in favor of the merger, thus failing to meet the "dissenting stockholder" requirement of Section 262 of Delaware's General Corporation Law. [The court noted that T. Rowe held its Dell shares through custodians (i.e., nominees), and therefore, T. Rowe was the "beneficial owner" of the Dell shares.] The custodians, however, were not record holders of the shares; they were participants of the Depository Trust Company, which held the shares in the name of its nominee, Cede & Co.,

which, for purposes of Delaware law, was the record holder. As the record holder, Cede had the legal right to vote the shares on the Dell merger and to make a written demand for an appraisal of the shares.

The Court noted that, through a "Byzantine" system, Cede was constrained to vote [T. Rowe's] shares in accordance with T. Rowe's instructions [as the beneficial owner of the Dell Shares]. Although [T. Rowe] had publicly opposed the merger, due to [a miscommunication within] its internal voting processes, [T. Rowe] had in fact submitted instructions to vote the [T. Rowe] shares in favor of the merger. . . . [Consequently, T. Rowe had failed to perfect its right to an appraisal of its Dell shares, because Delaware] Section 262 . . . confers appraisal rights upon a stockholder of record who holds shares on the date an appraisal demand is made, continuously holds the shares through the effective date of the merger, submits a demand for appraisal in compliance with the statute, and has not voted in favor of the merger or consented to it in writing. . . . The key consequence for [T. Rowe] is that [its Dell] shares [that were] held of record by Cede & Co., having been voted in favor of the Dell merger, pursuant to T. Rowe's instructions were not entitled to appraisal rights.

Richards Layton & Finger, *In re Appraisal of Dell Inc.: Delaware Court of Chancery Provides Guidance on "Dissenting Stockholder" Requirement*, May 12, 2016, *available at:* http://www.rlf.com/Publications/6463. With respect to the distinction between "record owner" and "beneficial owner," *see supra* note material at pg. 176-177.

5. *Appraisal Proceedings in Delaware After* Dell. In its opinion in *Dell*, the Delaware Supreme Court declined "to create a presumption in favor of [treating] the deal price" as the best evidence of the "fair value" of the company. At the same time, the Delaware Supreme Court "emphasized the probative value of the agreed deal price and de-emphasized the value of alternative valuation methodologies such as discounted cash flow models." Debevoise & Plimpton, *Delaware M&A Appraisal: Where We Stand After* DFC, Dell and Aruba, The Private Equity Report, Spring 2019, vol. 19, no. 1. So what has been the impact of decisions such as *Dell* on the number of appraisal actions filed in Delaware courts?

Not surprisingly, the number of appraisal actions filed in Delaware has declined significantly following the *Dell* and *DFC Global* decisions. In 2018, a total of 26 appraisal petitions were filed in Delaware, a 56% decline from the 60 such petitions filed in 2017 and barely one-third of the 76 appraisal actions filed in 2016.[11] The results of recent appraisal actions that have reached an ultimate award are even more striking. A survey of Delaware appraisals involving public company mergers shows that over the 14-year period ending in December 2016, 68% of appraisal awards were above the deal price. In contrast, of the seven public company appraisal awards in 2017 and 2018, five were below the deal price, one was at the deal price, and one was a modest 2.8% above the deal price.[12]

---

11. Cornerstone Research, *Appraisal Litigation in Delaware: Trends in Petitions and Opinions 2006-2018*, p.4.

12. L. Hamermesh and M. Wachter, *Finding the Right Balance in Appraisal Litigation: Deal Price, Deal Process, and Synergies* (2018), PennLaw: Legal Scholarship Repository. Note that the pre-2016 above-deal price awards include the subsequently reduced *DCF Global* and *Dell* awards. The date in the above text also includes two appraisal awards in 2018 that postdated the Hamermesh and Wachter article.

Going forward, it seems likely that appraisal actions in *strategic* mergers – in which synergies must be factored out of the fair value determination – will be increasingly rare. . . . As a result, we expect future appraisal cases to be largely limited to acquisitions of private and small-cap companies, controlling stockholder transactions (including transactions where a controlling stockholder partners with a private equity firm to take the company private) and deals with significant process flaws.

Debevoise & Plimpton, *supra* at pp. 3-4 (*emphasis added*).

6. Appraisal Rights as Exclusive Remedy

As was noted earlier in this section, *Weinberger* involved a transaction popularly referred to as a "freeze-out" transaction, where the controlling shareholder buys out the minority shareholders' interest, even if the minority shareholder(s) object to being eliminated. Until *Weinberger* was decided, Delaware case law imposed a business purpose requirement, which acted as a limitation on the controlling shareholder's ability to "freeze out" the minority shareholder. Under this business purpose test, a merger could not be effected for the "sole purpose of freezing out minority shareholders." *Singer v. Magnovox*, 380 A.2d 969, 980 (Del. 1977). Subsequent Delaware case law, however, "effectively eviscerated the business purpose test by requiring only that the merger serve some bona fide purpose of the parent corporation [i.e., the controlling shareholder].[22] Because competent transaction planners easily could create a paper trail showing [that] the merger promoted some business interest of the parent, the test was left as mere formalism." Stephen M. Bainbridge, CORPORATE LAW 181 (2d ed. 2009). Recognizing that the business purpose test provided the minority interest with no meaningful protections, the Delaware Supreme Court overruled the business purpose requirement in *Weinberger*. In doing so, the court explained that "a plaintiff's monetary remedy ordinarily should be confined to the more liberalized appraisal proceeding herein established," *Weinberger, supra*, at 714, but at the same time, the court went on to say that "we do not intend any limitation on the historic powers of the Chancellor to grant such other relief as the facts of a particular case may dictate." So the *Weinberger* court recognized that the appraisal remedy "may not be adequate in certain cases, particularly where fraud, misrepresentation, self-dealing, deliberate waste of corporate assets, or gross and palpable overreaching are involved." *Id.*

From this, many commentators concluded that "*Weinberger* appeared to unequivocally leave appraisal as the exclusive remedy in freeze-out mergers. If a minority shareholder thought a merger was unfair, [his/her/its sole] remedy was to bring an appraisal proceeding, which meant there would be no class action and the shareholder would have to perfect [his/her/its] appraisal rights." Bainbridge, *supra*, at 184. As you read the next case, ask yourself whether the appraisal action is, in fact, the shareholder/plaintiff's *exclusive remedy*. Or, did the Delaware Supreme Court "take it all back," *Id.*, —and thus allow shareholders to

---

22. See, e.g., *Tanzer v International General Industries, Inc.*, 379 A2d 1121 (Del. 1977).

bring a class action for money damages—even if these same shareholders had *not* perfected their right to an appraisal remedy?

Rabkin v. Philip A. Hunt Chemical Corp.
498 A.2d 1099 (Del. 1985)

MOORE, Justice.

These consolidated class actions were filed in the Court of Chancery on behalf of the minority stockholders of Philip A. Hunt Chemical Corporation (Hunt), challenging the merger of Hunt with its majority stockholder, Olin Corporation (Olin). For the first time since our decision in *Weinberger v. UOP, Inc.*, Del. Supr., 457 A.2d 701 (1983), we examine the exclusivity of the appraisal remedy in a cash-out merger where questions of procedural unfairness having a reasonable bearing on substantial issues affecting the price being offered are the essential bases of the suit. The Vice Chancellor ordered these cases dismissed on the ground that absent deception *Weinberger* mandated appraisal as the only remedy available to the minority. The plaintiffs sought and were denied leave to amend their complaints. They appeal these rulings.

In our view, the holding in *Weinberger* is broader than the scope accorded it by the trial court. The plaintiffs have charged, and by their proposed amended complaints contend, that the merger does not meet the entire fairness standard required by *Weinberger*. They aver specific acts of unfair dealing constituting breaches of fiduciary duties which if true may have substantially affected the offering price. These allegations, unrelated to judgmental factors of valuation, should survive a motion to dismiss. Accordingly, the decision of the Court of Chancery is reversed, and the matter is remanded with instructions that the plaintiffs be permitted to amend their complaints.

I

The factual background of the merger is critical to the issues before us and will be set forth in substantial detail. On July 5, 1984, Hunt merged into Olin pursuant to a merger agreement that was recommended by the Hunt board of directors. Hunt was a Delaware corporation, while Olin is incorporated in Virginia. On March 1, 1983, Olin bought 63.4% of the outstanding shares of Hunt's common stock from Turner and Newall Industries, Inc. (Turner & Newall) at $25 per share pursuant to a Stock Purchase Agreement (the agreement).

At Turner & Newall's insistence, the agreement also required Olin to pay $25 per share if Olin acquired the remaining Hunt stock within one year thereafter (the one year commitment). It provided:

SUBSEQUENT ACQUISITIONS OF COMMON STOCK

Should [Olin] or an affiliate of [Olin] acquire, through a merger, consolidation, tender offer, or similar transaction, all or substantially all of the remaining outstanding shares of common stock within one year of the closing date [March 1, 1983], [Olin] agrees that the per share consideration to be paid in any such transaction shall, in the opinion of a reputable investment banking firm, be substantially equivalent in value to at least the net purchase price per share paid pursuant to this agreement. . . .

On March 1, 1983, concurrently with the closing of the agreement, the two Hunt directors affiliated with Turner & Newall resigned. They were replaced by John M. Henske, chairman of the board and chief executive officer of Olin, and Ray R. Irani, then president and chief operating officer of Olin. In June 1983, Dr. Irani resigned as a director of both Olin and Hunt. At that time the Hunt board was expanded to nine members, and the resulting vacancies were filled by Richard R. Berry and John W. Johnstone, Jr., executive vice presidents and directors of Olin.

When Olin acquired its 63.4% interest in Hunt, Olin stated in a press release that while it was "considering the acquisition of the remaining public shares of Hunt, it [had] no present intention to do so." Apparently, there were no discussions or negotiations between the boards of Hunt and Olin regarding any purchase of Hunt stock during the one year commitment period.

However, it is clear that Olin always anticipated owning 100% of Hunt. Several Olin interoffice memoranda referred to the eventual merger of the two companies. One document dated September 16, 1983 sent by Peter A. Danna to Johnstone, then a director of both Olin and Hunt, spoke of Olin's long-term strategy which would be relevant "when the rest of Hunt is acquired." Another communication from R.N. Clark to Johnstone and Berry concluded as follows:

> In any event, *until Hunt is all Olin* and we are in the position to have their leadership participate in a centralization decision, any activity to bring Hunt to a new central location must be in abeyance. (*Emphasis added.*)

Finally, on September 19, 1983, Thomas Berardino, then an Olin staff vice-president in Planning and Corporate Development, sent a confidential memorandum to four of the Olin directors, three of whom, Berry, Henske and Johnstone, were also Hunt directors. That document catalogued the "pros and cons of doing a backend of Hunt acquisition this year." Nine "pros" were listed for acquiring Hunt stock prior to March 1, 1984. On the "con" side the following three [sic] considerations were detailed:

- Immediate control will cost approximately $7.3M more in purchase payments than waiting until mid-1984 (e.g. $25 vs 21 ½ share)
- Can recoup $1.2-$1.4M (after tax) of this amount within 12 months through savings noted above
- Since Hunt's performance is currently not covering Olin's goodwill and borrowing costs, additional ownership will increase the dilution of Olin's reported earnings from the current projected 3 cents to 5 cents/share.
- Potential negative reaction of Hunt personnel
- Will be risk whenever Olin buys backend

The Court of Chancery found that it was "apparent that, from the outset, Olin anticipated that it would eventually acquire the minority interest in Hunt." *Rabkin v. Philip A. Hunt Chemical Corp.*, Del. Ch., 480 A.2d 655, 657-58 (1984).

This observation is consistent with the Olin board's authorization, a week before the one year commitment period expired, for its Finance Committee to acquire the rest of Hunt should the Committee conclude on the advice of management that such an acquisition would be appropriate.

On Friday, March 23, 1984, the senior management of Olin met with a representative of the investment banking firm of Morgan, Lewis, Githens & Ahn, Inc. (Morgan Lewis) to discuss the possible acquisition and valuation of the Hunt minority stock. Olin proposed to pay $20 per share and asked Morgan Lewis to render a fairness opinion on that price. Four days later, on Tuesday, March 27, Morgan Lewis delivered its opinion to Olin that $20 per share was fair to the minority. That opinion also contained the following statement:

> We have conducted such investigations as we deemed appropriate including, but not limited to, a review of current financial statements, projections, business activities of Hunt (which information has been supplied to us by Olin) as well as comparative information on other companies. We have not had an appraisal of the assets of Hunt made in connection with our evaluation. We have also regularly monitored the activity of the Hunt stock on the New York Stock Exchange during 1983 and to date. However, we have not met directly with the management of Hunt because of the requirement that Olin maintain total confidentiality prior to you making this merger proposal.

In reaching its conclusion Morgan Lewis evidently gave no consideration to Olin's obligation, including the bases thereof, to pay $25 per share if the stock had been acquired prior to March 1, 1984.

The same day, March 27, 1984, Olin's management presented the Morgan Lewis fairness opinion to the Olin Finance Committee with the recommendation that the remaining Hunt stock be acquired for $20 per share. At that meeting it was stated that management had determined the price based on the following factors: the Morgan Lewis analysis, Hunt's net worth, Hunt's earnings history, including current prospects for 1984, Hunt's failures to achieve the earnings projections set forth in its business plans, and the current and historical market value of Hunt stock from 1982 to 1983. The Finance Committee unanimously voted to acquire the remaining Hunt stock for $20 per share. Later that same evening Henske, Olin's chief executive officer, called Hunt President Alfred Blomquist to inform him that the Finance Committee, acting for Olin's board, had approved Olin's acquisition of the Hunt minority. The following morning, March 28, Olin and Hunt issued a joint press release announcing the cash-out merger.

Later that day the Hunt Board appointed a Special Committee, consisting of the four Hunt outside directors, to review and determine the fairness of Olin's merger proposal. These directors met on April 4, 1984, and retained Merrill Lynch as their financial advisor and the law firm of Shea and Gould as legal counsel. This committee met again on three other occasions. At the May 10, 1984 meeting the Special Committee heard a presentation by the lawyers for several plaintiffs who had filed class actions on behalf of the minority shareholders to enjoin the proposed merger. A representative of Merrill Lynch advised the meeting that $20 per share was fair to the minority from a financial standpoint, but that the range of values for the common stock was probably $19 to $25 per share.

The outside directors subsequently notified the Hunt board that they had unanimously found $20 per share to be fair but not generous. They therefore recommended that Olin consider increasing the price above $20. The next day, May 11, 1984, Olin informed the Hunt Special Committee that it had considered its recommendation but declined to raise the price. The Hunt outside directors then met again on May 14, 1984, by teleconference call, and at a meeting of the Hunt board on May 15, also held by teleconference, the Special Committee announced that it had unanimously found the $20 per share price fair and recommended approval of the merger.

On June 7, 1984, Hunt issued its proxy statement favoring the merger. That document also made clear Olin's intention to vote its 64% of the Hunt shares in favor of the proposal, thereby guaranteeing its passage. There was no requirement of approval by a majority of the minority stockholders.

The proxy statement also described in substantial detail most of the facts related above. Specifically, it disclosed the existence of the one year commitment, the Merrill Lynch conclusion that a fair range for the Hunt common stock was between $19 and $25, and the pendency of these class actions opposing the merger.

II

Taken together, the plaintiffs' complaints challenge the proposed Olin-Hunt merger on the grounds that the price offered was grossly inadequate because Olin unfairly manipulated the timing of the merger to avoid the one year commitment, and that specific language in Olin's Schedule 13D, filed when it purchased the Hunt stock, constituted a price commitment by which Olin failed to abide, contrary to its fiduciary obligations.

The Vice Chancellor granted the defendants' motion to dismiss on the ground that the plaintiffs' complaints failed to state claims upon which relief could be granted. The court's rationale was that absent claims of fraud or deception a minority stockholder's rights in a cash-out merger were limited to an appraisal. *Rabkin v. Philip A. Hunt Chemical Corp.*, Del. Ch., 480 A.2d 655, 660-62 (1984). . . .

A

The issue we address is whether the trial court erred, as a matter of law, in dismissing these claims on the ground that absent deception the plaintiffs' sole remedy under *Weinberger* is an appraisal. The plaintiffs' position is that in cases of procedural unfairness the standard of entire fairness entitles them to relief that is broader than an appraisal. Indeed, the thrust of plaintiffs' contentions is that they eschew an appraisal, since they consider Olin's manipulative conduct a breach of its fiduciary duty to pay the $25 per share guaranteed by the one year commitment. . . .

B

On a motion to dismiss for failure to state a claim it must appear with a reasonable certainty that a plaintiff would not be entitled to the relief sought under any set of facts which could be proven to support the action. . . .

In ordering the complaints dismissed the Vice Chancellor reasoned that:

> Where, . . . there are no allegations of non-disclosures or misrepresentations, *Weinberger* mandates that plaintiffs' entire fairness claims be determined in an appraisal proceeding.

Rabkin, 480 A.2d at 660.

We consider that an erroneous interpretation of *Weinberger*, because it fails to take account of the entire context of the holding.

The Court of Chancery seems to have limited its focus to our statement in *Weinberger* that:

> [T]he provisions of 8 Del. C. §262, as herein construed, respecting the scope of an appraisal and the means for perfecting the same, shall govern the financial remedy available to minority shareholders in a cash-out merger. Thus, we return to the well established principles of *Stauffer v. Standard Brands, Inc.*, Del. Supr., 187 A.2d 78 (1962) and *David J. Greene & Co. v. Schenley Industries, Inc.*, Del. Ch., 281 A.2d 30 (1971), mandating a stockholder's recourse to the basic remedy of an appraisal.

Weinberger, 457 A.2d at 715.

However, *Weinberger* makes clear that appraisal is not necessarily a stockholder's sole remedy. We specifically noted that:

> [W]hile a plaintiff's monetary remedy ordinarily should be confined to the more liberalized appraisal proceeding herein established, we do not intend any limitation on the historic powers of the Chancellor to grant such other relief as the facts of a particular case may dictate. The appraisal remedy we approve may not be adequate in certain cases, particularly where fraud, misrepresentation, self-dealing, deliberate waste of corporate assets, or gross and palpable overreaching are involved. *Cole v. National Cash Credit Association*, Del. Ch., 156 A. 183, 187 (1931).

Id. at 714.

Thus, the trial court's narrow interpretation of *Weinberger* would render meaningless our extensive discussion of fair dealing found in that opinion. In *Weinberger* we defined fair dealing as embracing "questions of when the transaction was timed, how it was initiated, structured, negotiated, disclosed to the directors, and how the approvals of the directors and the stockholders were obtained." 457 A.2d at 711. While this duty of fairness certainly incorporates the principle that a cash-out merger must be free of fraud or misrepresentation, *Weinberger*'s mandate of fair dealing does not turn solely on issues of deception. We particularly noted broader concerns respecting the matter of procedural fairness. *Weinberger*, 457 A.2d at 711, 714. Thus, while "in a nonfraudulent transaction . . . price *may* be the preponderant consideration," *id*. at 711 (*empha-sis added*), it is not necessarily so.[6]

Although the Vice Chancellor correctly understood *Weinberger* as limiting collateral attacks on cash-out mergers, her analysis narrowed the procedural protections which we still intended *Weinberger* to guarantee. Here, plaintiffs are not arguing questions of valuation which are the traditional subjects of an appraisal. Rather, they seek to enforce a contractual right to receive $25 per share, which they claim was unfairly destroyed by Olin's manipulative conduct.

While a plaintiff's mere allegation of "unfair dealing," without more, can-not survive a motion to dismiss, averments containing "specific acts of fraud, misrepresentation, or other items of misconduct" must be carefully examined in accord with our views expressed both here and in *Weinberger. See* 457 A.2d at 703, 711, 714.

III

A

Having outlined the facts and applicable principles, we turn to the details of the Hunt-Olin merger and the plaintiffs' complaints to determine whether the specific acts of misconduct alleged are sufficient to withstand a motion to dismiss.

The Court of Chancery stated that "[t]he gravamen of all the complaints appears to be that the cash-out price is unfair." *Rabkin*, 480 A.2d at 658. However, this conclusion, which seems to be more directed to issues of valuation, is neither supported by the pleadings themselves nor the extensive discussion of unfair dealing found in the trial court's opinion. There is no challenge to any method of valuation or to the components of value upon which Olin's $20 price was based. The plaintiffs want the $25 per share guaranteed by the one year com-mitment, which they claim was unfairly denied them by Olin's manipulations.

According to the Vice Chancellor's analysis, the plaintiffs' complaints alleged three claims—"breach of the fiduciary duty of entire fairness, breach of fiduciary duty under *Schnell v. Chris-Craft Industries,* Del. Supr., 285 A.2d 437 (1971) and promissory estoppel." *Id.* at 659. The entire fairness claim was rejected on the ground that the plaintiffs' exclusive remedy was an appraisal. *Id.* at 660. The *Schnell* analogy was repudiated on the theory that Olin had not impinged on any rights of the minority shareholders by letting the one-year commitment expire before consummating the merger. *Id.* at 661. The court also rejected what it categorized as the promissory estoppel claim on the grounds that the language allegedly forming the promise was too vague to constitute such an undertaking, and that estoppel cannot be predicated upon a promise to do that which the promisor is already obliged to do. *Id.*

---

6. For a thoughtful analysis of this issue of when stockholders have standing to sue after *Weinberger,* see Weiss, *Balancing Interests in Cash-Out Mergers: The Promise of Weinberger v. UOP, Inc.,* 8 Del. J. Corp. L. 1, 54-56 (1983).

B

In *Weinberger* we observed that the timing, structure, negotiation and disclosure of a cash-out merger all had a bearing on the issue of procedural fairness. 457 A.2d at 711. The plaintiffs contend *inter alia* that Olin breached its fiduciary duty of fair dealing by purposely timing the merger, and thereby unfairly manipulating it, to avoid the one year commitment. In support of that contention plaintiffs have averred specific facts indicating that Olin knew it would eventually acquire Hunt, but delayed doing so to avoid paying $25 per share. Significantly, the trial court's opinion seems to accept that point:

> It is apparent that, from the outset, Olin anticipated that it would eventually acquire the minority interest in Hunt. Olin's chief executive officer expected as much when the Agreement was executed and, in evaluating the Agreement, Olin prepared computations based upon the assumption that it would acquire 100% of Hunt.

Rabkin, 480 A.2d at 657-58.

Consistent with this observation are the confidential Berardino memo to the three Olin and Hunt directors, Henske, Johnstone and Berry, about the disadvantages of paying a higher price during the one year commitment; the deposition testimony of Olin's chief executive officer, Mr. Henske, that the one year commitment "meant nothing"; and what could be considered a quick surrender by the Special Committee of Hunt directors in the face of Olin's proposal to squeeze out the minority at $20 per share.[7] While we do not pass on the merits of such questions, Olin's alleged attitude toward the minority, at least as it appears on the face of the complaints and their proposed amendments, coupled with the apparent absence of any meaningful negotiations as to price, all have an air reminiscent of the dealings between Signal and UOP in *Weinberger. See* 457 A.2d at 711. Certainly the Berardino memorandum, although not unusual as an Olin planning document, raises unanswered questions about the recognition by three of its recipients, all Hunt directors, of their undiminished duty of loyalty to Hunt. *See Rosenblatt v. Getty Oil Company*, Del. Supr., 493 A.2d 929, 938-39 (1985). . . . These are issues which an appraisal cannot address, and at this juncture are matters that cannot be resolved by a motion to dismiss.

In our opinion the facts alleged by the plaintiffs regarding Olin's avoidance of the one year commitment support a claim of unfair dealing sufficient to defeat dismissal at this stage of the proceedings. The defendants answer that

---

7. As we noted in *Weinberger*, the use of an independent negotiating committee of outside directors may have significant advantages to the majority stockholder in defending suits of this type. See 457 A.2d at 709-711; 709 n. 7. The efficacy of that procedure was recently indicated by our opinion in *Rosenblatt v. Getty Oil Company*, Del. Supr., 493 A.2d 929, 937-939 (1985). However, we recognize that there can be serious practical problems in the use of such a committee as even *Rosenblatt* demonstrated. See 493 A.2d at 933-936; Herzel & Colling, *Establishing Procedural Fairness in Squeeze-Out Mergers after Weinberger v. UOP*, 39 Business Law. 1525, 1534-37 (1984); Weiss, *Balancing Interests in Cash-Out Mergers: The Promise of Weinberger v. UOP, Inc.*, 8 Del. J. Corp. Law 1, 50-53 (1983). Thus, we do not announce any rule, even in the context of a motion to dismiss, that the absence of such a bargaining structure will preclude dismissal in cases bottomed on claims of unfair dealing.

they had no legal obligation to effect the cash-out merger during the one year period. While that may be so, the principle announced in *Schnell v. Chris-Craft Industries*[8] establishes that inequitable conduct will not be protected merely because it is legal. 285 A.2d at 439. *See also Unocal Corp. v. Mesa Petroleum Co.*, 493 A.2d 946, 955 (1985); *Giuricich v. Emtrol Corp.*, Del. Supr., 449 A.2d 232, 239 (1982); *Lynch v. Vickers Energy Corp.*, Del. Ch., 351 A.2d 570, 575 (1976); *Petty v. Penntech Papers, Inc.*, Del. Ch., 347 A.2d 140, 143 (1975). At the very least the facts alleged import a form of overreaching, and in the context of entire fairness they deserve more considered analysis than can be accorded them on a motion to dismiss.

Similarly, the plaintiffs' pleas arising from the language in Olin's Schedule 13D (referred to by the trial court as the claim for promissory estoppel) should not have been dismissed on the ground that appraisal was the only remedy available to the plaintiffs challenging the entire fairness of the merger.[9]

IV

In conclusion we find that the trial court erred in dismissing the plaintiffs' actions for failure to state a claim upon which relief could be granted. As we read the complaints and the proposed amendments, they assert a conscious intent by Olin, as the majority shareholder of Hunt, to deprive the Hunt minority of the same bargain that Olin made with Hunt's former majority shareholder, Turner and Newall. But for Olin's allegedly unfair manipulation, the plaintiffs contend, this bargain also was due them. In short, the defendants are charged with bad faith which goes beyond issues of "mere inadequacy of price." *Cole v. National Cash Credit Association*, Del. Ch., 156 A. 183, 187-88 (1931). In *Weinberger* we specifically relied upon this aspect of *Cole* in acknowledging the imperfections of an appraisal where circumstances of this sort are present. *See* 457 A.2d at 714.

Necessarily, this will require the Court of Chancery to closely focus upon *Weinberger*'s mandate of entire fairness based on a careful analysis of both the fair price and fair dealing aspects of a transaction. *See* 457 A.2d at 711, 714. We recognize that this can present certain practical problems, since stockholders may invariably claim that the price being offered is the result of unfair dealings. However, we think that plaintiffs will be tempered in this approach by the prospect that an ultimate judgment in defendants' favor may have cost plaintiffs their unperfected appraisal rights. Moreover, our courts are not without a degree of sophistication in such matters. A balance must be struck between sustaining complaints averring faithless acts, which taken as true would constitute breaches of fiduciary duties that are reasonably related to and have a substantial impact upon the price offered, and properly dismissing those allegations questioning

8. The trial court's narrow interpretation of this principle misconceives the thrust of *Schnell*. *See Rabkin*, 480 A.2d at 661.

9. Again, we emphasize that we are not reaching the merits of the plaintiffs' claims. Our holding today is to make clear the scope of *Weinberger* when the Court of Chancery addresses a motion to dismiss a minority stockholder's suit attacking a cash-out merger. However, it is important to bear in mind that *Weinberger* was a case decided after trial on the merits. Here we address those issues solely in a pre-trial context. We neither express nor imply any views as to the outcome of these matters after they have had a fuller exploration at a later stage of the proceedings.

judgmental factors of valuation. *Cole v. National Cash Credit Association,* 156 A. at 187-88. Otherwise, we face the anomalous result that stockholders who are eliminated without appraisal rights can bring class actions, while in other cases a squeezed-out minority is limited to an appraisal, provided there was no deception, regardless of the degree of procedural unfairness employed to take their shares. Without that balance, *Weinberger*'s concern for entire fairness loses all force.

Accordingly, the decision of the Court of Chancery dismissing these consolidated class actions is REVERSED. The matter is REMANDED with directions that the plaintiffs be permitted to file their proposed amendments to the pleadings.

QUESTIONS

1. What is the purpose of the modern appraisal remedy? Is the *sole* purpose to provide the dissatisfied minority shareholder with the opportunity to challenge the price offered by Bidder (i.e., the adequacy of the premium offered)? In other words, in what way does the *mandatory* right to an appraisal serve to hold management accountable for its decision to enter into the proposed transaction?

2. What does "fair dealing" require? Who has the burden to establish fair dealing?

3. Why isn't approval by a majority of outstanding shares sufficient protection against shareholders receiving inadequate acquisition consideration? In other words, if management obtains the requisite shareholder approval, what interests are to be protected by granting the remedy of an appraisal?

4. Delaware §262(c) and MBCA §13.02(a)(5) both allow a corporation's articles to extend the right of appraisal to transactions beyond those described in the statute as a matter of private ordering. Conversely, should the corporation be allowed to amend its articles of incorporation to eliminate the right of appraisal granted by statute, assuming the requisite shareholder approval is obtained for such an article amendment? In considering this issue, does it matter whether the corporation is publicly traded or privately held? *See, Manti Holdings, LLC, et al. v. Authentix Acquisition Company, Inc.,* C.A. No. 2017-0887-SG, 2019 WL 3814453 (Del. Ch. August 14, 2019); John T. Bradley and David A. Rosenfield, Troutman Sanders LLP, *Delaware Court of Chancery Holds that Waiver of Appraisal Rights is Permitted Under Delaware Law,* Aug. 19, 2019, *available at*: https://www.troutman.com/insights/delaware-court-of-chancery-holds-that-waiver-of-appraisal-rights-is-permitted-under-delaware-law.html.

|| 3 ||

Scope of Successor Liability: Transferring the Assets (and Liabilities) of Target Co. to Bidder Co.

In Chapter 2, we analyzed the requirements imposed by state corporate law in connection with each of the different methods for structuring an acquisition. In the process, we examined the substantive differences among the regulatory approaches taken by Delaware, California, and the Model Business Corporation Act (MBCA) as to the requirement of board and/or shareholder approval, as well as the availability of appraisal rights in connection with each of the different methods of effecting an acquisition. In this chapter, we examine the rules of successor liability, another important set of considerations that influence the transaction planner's decision as to the most appropriate method to use to structure a proposed acquisition.

When considering the rules of successor liability, the focus of analysis shifts away from the analysis we conducted in Chapter 2, where we examined who *within* the company should decide whether the company should be acquired. In the process of analyzing the problem sets in Chapter 2, we largely ignored the impact of the proposed transaction on constituencies *outside* the company. In this chapter, we examine the mechanics of transferring ownership of the business of Target (the acquired company) to its new owner, Bidder (the acquiring corporation). As part of our analysis, we will observe how the various forms of business combinations affect constituents *outside* the company. Not surprisingly, the impact of this transfer of ownership on the *creditors* of Target will depend on the method used to complete the acquisition; that is, whether the transaction is structured as a merger, stock purchase, or asset purchase. For reasons that we will analyze later in this chapter, the most problematic form of business combination from a public policy perspective is the acquisition structured as an asset purchase.

A. *Successor Liability in Merger Transactions and Stock Purchases*

1. Introductory Note

In most states, a merger takes effect once the certificate (or articles) of merger are accepted for filing by the secretary of state's office. *See*, e.g., DGCL §251(c); MBCA 11.06. The articles of merger must specify, among other things, the company that is to survive the merger and the company whose shares are to be cancelled (by operation of law) once the merger takes effect. As we learned in Chapter 2, the merger agreement must specify the manner of converting the shares of Target that are to be cancelled. *See*, e.g., MBCA §11.02(c). Once the merger is effective, the holder of any Target shares has no further ownership interest in the business assets of Target and instead will be entitled to receive only the consideration specified in the merger agreement, which may consist of cash or stock (or other securities) of the surviving corporation or stock of some other corporation (or some combination of the foregoing).

As reflected in Diagram 1 in Appendix A, once the merger takes effect, the assets and liabilities of the disappearing corporation, Target, are pooled together with the assets and liabilities of the surviving corporation, Bidder. In effect, once the articles of merger are filed with the secretary of state's office, Bidder succeeds—by operation of law—to *all* of the rights and *all* of the liabilities of Target. No individual transfer of ownership is required. Therein lies the beauty—the magic, if you will—of the merger procedure. Once the merger takes effect, Target disappears in the sense that its separate legal existence is extinguished. At the same time, Target's business operations are transferred by operation of law to the surviving corporation, Bidder. The convenience of the merger procedure lies in the fact that this transfer of control over Target's business takes place by operation of law and without the need for any further action on the part of either Target or Bidder. *See*, e.g., MBCA §11.07. This is known as the *rule of successor liability*, which is part of the statutorily authorized merger procedure.

From the perspective of a creditor of Target, the economic existence of Target continues as part of the surviving corporation, even though Target as a legal entity disappears by operation of law once the *merger* takes effect. Under this rule of successor liability, *all* of the assets of the surviving company are available to satisfy creditors of *both* constituent corporations in a direct merger—that is, the creditors of both Target and Bidder—regardless of whether the third party's claim arises under contract or tort.

By contrast, an acquisition structured as a *stock purchase* leaves the entity, Target, in place. *See* Diagram 7 in Appendix A. Consequently, *all* of Target's assets remain in place to satisfy the claims of Target's creditors, which also remain in place. Even though the ownership of all Target stock has been transferred to Bidder, the assets of Bidder are insulated from liability on the claims of Target's creditors. This is the direct result of the well-established corporate law principle that the corporation is a separate legal entity. As such, the company's owners (the shareholders) are typically shielded from any personal liability on the business debts incurred by the corporation, in the absence of some factual basis that persuades a court to pierce the corporate veil.[1] Particularly in the case of a business operated as a small, closely held corporation, the independent existence of the corporation may get blurred, which may result in the judicial decision to pierce the corporate veil and hold the company's shareholders (and/or managers) personally liable on the business debt. In the case of a publicly traded corporation, however, the existence of the corporation as a separate legal entity that provides the shield of limited liability to its owners (and managers) is of crucial importance, as we shall see in the cases that follow.

Since the corporate entity remains intact after the stock purchase is completed, the assets of Target remain available to satisfy the claims of Target's creditors. On the other hand, whether the assets of Bidder will become subject to the claims of Target's creditors will depend in large part on whether Bidder, as the new controlling shareholder of Target, operates its subsidiary in such a way as to create the basis for liability on a "piercing the corporate veil" cause of action.

2. Commercial Leases

Consider the classic example of a contract creditor: the landlord who has entered into a commercial lease with the tenant, Target Co. This type of contract claim is routinely part of the world of mergers and acquisitions (M&A) transactions because many businesses operate out of some type of office, or storefront, or manufacturing facility, any of which may involve the leasing of commercial space. If Target has entered into a long-term commercial lease with the landlord, the majority view (as you learned in your first-year property and/or contracts courses) is that leases are freely assignable (transferable) unless the lease expressly includes a clause prohibiting assignments (transfers). This default rule is grounded in the strong public policy prevalent throughout the law of real property favoring the free alienability (transferability) of interests in real property. The modern view, however, allows restraints on alienation (i.e., restrictions on the right to assign or otherwise transfer leasehold interests), so long as the terms of the restriction satisfy a standard of reasonableness. This modern view allowing reasonable restraints on alienation has led to widespread use of clauses that allow the landlord to prevent assignment of the tenant's interest under the terms of a commercial lease. In cases where the lease includes a nonassignment clause, the tenant generally will not be able to assign the lease without first obtaining the consent of a third party, usually the landlord. If the tenant, Target, later proposes to enter into a business combination structured as either a merger or a stock purchase, the question arises whether the acquisition qualifies as the type of *transfer* that triggers the nonassignment clause contained in Target's lease with the landlord. The cases that follow address this recurring problem.

---

1. As you learned in your introductory Business Associations or Corporations class, a company's shareholders may be held personally liable for the business debts of their corporation if the plaintiff/creditor establishes a factual basis sufficient to persuade the court to exercise its equity powers and disregard the corporation's shield of limited liability.

3.   Intellectual Property Licensing Agreements

The issue of transferability also arises frequently in the case of licenses of intellectual property rights, such as agreements that grant rights to use patented technology or copyrighted material. Whereas the transfer of rights under commercial leases is usually governed by state law, the analysis of the transfer of rights to intellectual property is further complicated by federal law that protects certain intellectual property rights, particularly patents and copyrights. Accordingly, in an acquisition, the transaction planner must first analyze the threshold question of whether federal or state law applies to determine the transferability of rights to intellectual property.

Although this threshold question can be an issue for any business that licenses intellectual property to, or from, third parties, this issue presents itself most acutely in the case of technology companies. The high-tech company often becomes an attractive acquisition candidate because of its portfolio of intellectual property rights. The portfolio may include intellectual property licensed from third parties ("in-licensed I.P.") as well as licenses of intellectual property to customers and other third parties ("out-licensed I.P."). For many privately held technology companies, the value of the company lies in these license agreements. In these cases, Bidder's willingness to acquire Target is often driven by the ability of Target to transfer its rights under these licensing agreements.

4.   Tort Liability

In the case of tort claims, the same rule of successor liability applies regardless of whether the acquisition is structured as either a merger or a stock purchase. Consequently, the assets of Target will generally be available to satisfy prior tort claims. During the course of its due diligence investigation of Target's financial affairs and business operations, Bidder will generally be able to identify the known, current claims pending against Target, including both contractual and tort claims. Obviously, the information disclosed during the course of Bidder's due diligence investigation as to the number and dollar value of known claimants against Target will affect Bidder's valuation of Target's business and accordingly the purchase price that Bidder is willing to pay to acquire Target. The manner, scope, and dynamics of the due diligence process will be covered in Chapter 5 as part of our discussion of negotiating and preparing the acquisition agreement.

From Bidder's perspective, an area of primary concern in negotiating the terms of the acquisition of Target will usually center on *long-tail* claimants; that is, those claims that may not arise until *long after* the acquisition is completed. Among the most prominent of these long-tail claimants are product liability and environmental claimants. In the case of these types of long-tail claimants, Bidder's primary concern is that, as the successor-in-interest to Target, it will unwittingly absorb liabilities that are not reflected in the purchase price that Bidder paid to acquire Target.

In Chapter 5, where we discuss documenting the acquisition transaction, we will examine strategies that can be used to minimize the potentially disastrous consequences presented by these types of long-tail claims that may surface long after Bidder has closed on its acquisition of Target. As we will see, these strategies typically include the use of due diligence procedures in advance of closing on the acquisition, representation and warranties included in the acquisition agreement itself, and indemnification provisions, all of which are described in more detail in Chapter 5.

Another option that can be used to minimize Bidder's liability exposure to claims of Target's creditors is to structure the acquisition as an asset purchase. By using this method to acquire Target, Bidder can decide which of Target's liabilities it wants to assume expressly, thereby leaving behind all other business debts of Target, whether in tort or in contract. The public policy concerns inherent in using this method of acquisition will be examined later in this chapter. *See Ruiz v. Blentech Corp., infra.*

5. Impact of Nonassignment and Change of Control Clauses

Branmar Theatre Co. v. Branmar, Inc.
264 A.2d 526 (Del. Ch. 1970)

SHORT, Vice Chancellor.

This is an action for a declaratory judgment in which plaintiff seeks to enjoin defendant from cancelling a lease agreement previously executed by the parties. Defendant, by its answer, prays the court to find that it was entitled to treat the lease agreement as terminated because of a violation of a covenant therein prohibiting assignment by the lessee. This is the decision after final hearing.

Plaintiff was incorporated under the laws of Delaware on June 7, 1967. The owners of its outstanding capital stock were the Robert Rappaport family of Cleveland, Ohio. On June 9, 1967 plaintiff and defendant entered into a lease agreement for a motion picture theatre in the Branmar Shopping Center, New Castle County, Delaware. The lease, sixteen pages in length, recites that the lessor is to erect a theatre building in the shopping center. It provides for the payment of rent by the lessee to the lessor of $27,500 per year plus a percentage of gross admissions receipts, plus five per cent of any amounts paid to the lessee by refreshment concessionaires. The percentage of admissions figure is regulated by the type of attractions in the theatre, the minimum being five per cent and the maximum ten. The lease provides for a twenty year term with an option in the lessee to renew for an additional ten years. The lessee is to provide the lessor with a loan of $60,000, payable in installments, to be used for construction. The lessee is to provide, at its cost, whatever fixtures and equipment are necessary to operate the theatre. Paragraph 12 of the lease, the focal point of this lawsuit, provides:

> "Lessee shall not sublet, assign, transfer, or in any manner dispose of the said premises or any part thereof, for all or any part of the term hereby granted, without the prior written consent of the Lessor, such consent shall not be unreasonably withheld."

Joseph Luria, the principal for Branmar Shopping Center testified at trial that he negotiated the lease agreement with Isador Rappaport; that he made inquiries about Rappaport's ability to manage a theatre and satisfied himself that Rappaport had the competence and the important industry connections to successfully operate the theatre. It appears that Rappaport and his son operate a successful theatre in Cleveland, Ohio and have owned and operated theatres elsewhere.

Following execution of the lease the Rappaports were approached by Muriel Schwartz and Reba Schwartz, operators of ten theatres in the Delaware and neighboring Maryland area, with an offer to manage the theatre for the Rappaports who had no other business interests in the Wilmington area. This offer was not accepted but the Schwartzes subsequently agreed with the Rappaports to purchase the lease from plaintiff and have it assigned to them. An assignment was executed by plaintiff to the Schwartzes. Defendant rejected the assignment under the power reserved in Paragraph 12 of the lease. On May 29, 1969 the Schwartzes purchased the outstanding shares of plaintiff from the Rappaports. Upon receipt of notice of the sale defendant advised plaintiff that it considered the sale of the shares to the Schwartzes to be a breach of Paragraph 12 of the lease and the lease to be null and void.

The theatre building is now substantially completed and ready for occupancy. The Schwartzes are ready and willing to perform under the lease agreement. Defendant intends to substitute a new tenant, Sameric Theatres, for the corporate plaintiff, contending that Sameric is a better qualified operator than the Schwartzes.

Defendant argues that the sale of stock was in legal effect an assignment of the lease by the Rappaports to the Schwartzes, was in breach of Paragraph 12 of the lease, and that it was, therefore, justified in terminating plaintiff's leasehold interest. That in the absence of fraud, and none is charged here, transfer of stock of a corporate lessee is ordinarily not a violation of a clause prohibiting assignment is clear from the authorities. . . . Defendant contends, however, that this is not the ordinary case. Here, it says, due to the nature of the motion picture business, the performance required was by the Rappaports personally. But while defendant's negotiations were with a member of the Rappaport family when the lease was executed it chose to let the theatre to a corporation whose stock might foreseeably be transferred by the then stockholders. In the preparation of the lease, a document of sixteen pages, defendant was careful to spell out in detail the rights and duties of the parties. It did not, however, see fit to provide for forfeiture in the event the stockholders sold their shares. Had this been the intent it would have been a simple matter to have so provided. . . .

Conditions and restrictions in a deed or lease which upon a breach work a forfeiture of estate are not favored by the law. . . .

Defendant suggests that since "the Rappaports" could not assign the lease without its consent they should not be permitted to accomplish the same result by transfer of their stock. But the rule that precludes a person from doing indirectly what he cannot do directly has no application to the present case. The attempted assignment was not by the Rappaports but by plaintiff corporation, the sale of stock by its stockholders. Since defendant has failed to show circumstances to justify ignoring the corporation's separate existence reliance upon the cited rule is misplaced.

I find that the sale of stock by the Rappaports to the Schwartzes was not an assignment within the terms of Paragraph 12 of the lease and that the same remains in full force and effect. . . .

QUESTIONS

1. What method was used to structure the acquisition at issue in this case?

2. What is a *change of control* clause? On the facts of this case, who would want to include a change of control clause? In which agreement involved in the facts of this case? Why include such a clause?

PROBLEMS

1. Assume that Target has ten years left on the commercial lease for its primary manufacturing facility. What will happen to Target's rights and liabilities under the lease if Bidder should acquire Target by way of:
   a. A direct merger?
   b. A stock purchase?
   c. A reverse triangular merger?
   d. A forward triangular merger?
   e. A sale of assets?

2. Assume that Target has ten years left on the commercial lease for its primary manufacturing facility. Assume further that this lease includes a nonassignment clause that requires the consent of the landlord in order for Target to assign its remaining interest under the lease. What will happen to Target's rights and obligations under the lease if Bidder should acquire Target by way of:
   a. A direct merger?
   b. A stock purchase?
   c. A reverse triangular merger?
   d. A forward triangular merger?
   e. A sale of assets?

6. Successor Liability in Direct (Statutory) Mergers vs. Triangular Mergers

In this section, we look at the scope of successor liability imposed "by operation of law" under the terms of modern merger statutes such as MBCA §11.07. The following case is notable because it addresses the intersection of federal law on patents *and* state law on the effect of mergers.

PPG Industries, Inc. v. Guardian Industries Corporation
597 F.2d 1090 (6th Cir. 1979)

LIVELY, Circuit Judge.

The question in this case is whether the surviving or resultant corporation in a statutory merger acquires patent license rights of the constituent corporations. The plaintiff, PPG Industries, Inc. (PPG), appeals from a judgment of the district court dismissing its patent infringement action on the ground that the defendant, Guardian Industries, Corp. (Guardian), as licensee of the patents in suit, was not an infringer. . . .

I

Prior to 1964 both PPG and Permaglass, Inc., were engaged in fabrication of glass products, which required that sheets of glass be shaped for particular uses. Independently of each other the two fabricators developed similar processes, which involved "floating glass on a bed of gas, while it was being heated and bent." This process is known in the industry as "gas hearth technology" and "air float technology"; the two terms are interchangeable. After a period of negotiations PPG and Permaglass entered into an agreement on January 1, 1964 whereby each granted rights to the other under "gas hearth system" patents already issued and in the process of prosecution. The purpose of the agreement was set forth in the preamble as follows:

> WHEREAS, PPG is desirous of acquiring from PERMAGLASS a worldwide exclusive license with right to sublicense others under PERMAGLASS Technical Data and PERMAGLASS Patent Rights, subject only to reservation by PERMAGLASS of non-exclusive rights thereunder; and
> WHEREAS, PERMAGLASS is desirous of obtaining a nonexclusive license to use Gas Hearth Systems under PPG Patent Rights, excepting in the Dominion of Canada.

This purpose was accomplished in the two sections of the agreement quoted below:

SECTION 3. GRANT FROM PERMAGLASS TO PPG

> 3.1 Subject to the reservation set forth in Subsection 3.3 below, PERMAGLASS hereby grants to PPG an exclusive license, with right of sub-license, to use PERMAGLASS Technical Data in Gas Hearth Systems throughout the United States of America, its territories and possessions, and all countries of the world foreign thereto.
> 3.2 Subject to the reservation set forth in Subsection 3.3 below, PERMAGLASS hereby grants to PPG an unlimited exclusive license, with right of sublicense, under PERMAGLASS Patent Rights.
> 3.3 The licenses granted to PPG under Subsections 3.1 and 3.2 above shall be subject to the reservation of a non-exclusive, non-transferable, royalty-free, worldwide right and license for the benefit and use of PERMAGLASS.

SECTION 4. GRANT FROM PPG TO PERMAGLASS

> 4.1 PPG hereby grants to PERMAGLASS a non-exclusive, non-transferable, royalty-free right and license to heat, bend, thermally temper and/or anneal glass using Gas Hearth Systems under PPG Patent Rights, excepting in the Dominion of Canada, and to use or sell glass articles produced thereby, but no license,

express or implied, is hereby granted to PERMAGLASS under any claim of any PPG patent expressly covering any coating method, coating composition, or coated article.

Assignability of the agreement and of the license granted to Permaglass and termination of the license granted to Permaglass were covered in the following language:

SECTION 9. ASSIGNABILITY

9.1 This Agreement shall be assignable by PPG to any successor of the entire flat glass business of PPG but shall otherwise be non-assignable except with the consent of PERMAGLASS first obtained in writing.

9.2 This Agreement and the license granted by PPG to PERMAGLASS here-under shall be personal to PERMAGLASS and non-assignable except with the consent of PPG first obtained in writing.

SECTION 11. TERMINATION

11.2 In the event that a majority of the voting stock of PERMAGLASS shall at any time become owned or controlled directly or indirectly by a manufacturer of automobiles or a manufacturer or fabricator of glass other than the present owners, the license granted to PERMAGLASS under Subsection 4.1 shall terminate forthwith.

Eleven patents are involved in this suit. Nine of them originated with Permaglass and were licensed to PPG as exclusive licensee under Section 3.2, *supra*, subject to the non-exclusive, non-transferable reservation to Permaglass set forth in Section 3.3. Two of the patents originated with PPG. Section 4.1 granted a non-exclusive, non-transferable license to Permaglass with respect to the two PPG patents. In Section 9.1 and 9.2 assignability was treated somewhat differently as between the parties, and the Section 11.2 provisions with regard to termination apply only to the license granted to Permaglass.

As of December 1969 Permaglass was merged into Guardian pursuant to applicable statutes of Ohio and Delaware. Guardian was engaged primarily in the business of fabricating and distributing windshields for automobiles and trucks. It had decided to construct a facility to manufacture raw glass and the capacity of that facility would be greater than its own requirements. Permaglass had no glass manufacturing capability and it was contemplated that its operations would utilize a large part of the excess output of the proposed Guardian facility.

The "Agreement of Merger" between Permaglass and Guardian did not refer specifically to the 1964 agreement between PPG and Permaglass. However, among Permaglass' representations in the agreement was the following:

(g) Permaglass is the owner, assignee or licensee of such patents, trademarks, trade names and copyrights as are listed and described in Exhibit "C" attached hereto. None of such patents, trademarks, trade names or copyrights is in litigation and Permaglass has not received any notice of conflict with the asserted rights of third parties relative to the use thereof.

Listed on Exhibit "C" to the merger agreement are the nine patents originally developed by Permaglass and licensed to PPG under the 1964 agreement which is involved in this infringement action.

Shortly after the merger was consummated PPG filed the present action, claiming infringement by Guardian in the use of apparatus and processes described and claimed in eleven patents, which were identified by number and origin. The eleven patents were covered by the terms of the 1964 agreement. PPG asserted that it became the exclusive licensee of the nine patents which originated with Permaglass under the 1964 agreement and that the rights reserved by Permaglass were personal to it and non-transferable and non-assignable. PPG also claimed that Guardian had no rights with respect to the two patents, which had originated with PPG because the license under these patents was personal to Permaglass and non-transferable and non-assignable except with the permission of PPG. In addition it claimed that the license with respect to these two patents had terminated under the provisions of Section 11.2, *supra,* by reason of the merger.

One of the defenses pled by Guardian in its answer was that it was a licensee of the patents in suit. It described the merger with Permaglass and claimed it "had succeeded to all rights, powers, ownerships, etc., of Permaglass, and as Permaglass' successor, defendant is legally entitled to operate in place of Permaglass under the January 1, 1964 agreement between Permaglass and plaintiff, free of any claim of infringement of the patents. . . ."

After holding an evidentiary hearing the district court concluded that the parties to the 1964 agreement did not intend that the rights reserved by Permaglass in its nine patents or the rights assigned to Permaglass in the two PPG patents would not pass to a successor corporation by way of merger. The court held that there had been no assignment or transfer of the rights by Permaglass, but rather that Guardian acquired these rights by operation of law under the merger statutes of Ohio and Delaware. The provisions of the 1964 agreement making the license rights of Permaglass non-assignable and non-transferable were held not to apply because of the "continuity of interest inherent in a statutory merger that distinguishes it from the ordinary assignment or transfer case."

With respect to the termination provision in Section 11.2 of the 1964 agreement, the district court again relied on "the nature of a statutory merger in contrast to an outright sale or acquisition of stock" in holding that a majority of the voting stock of Permaglass did not become owned or controlled by Guardian.

II

Questions with respect to the assignability of a patent license are controlled by federal law. It has long been held by federal courts that agreements granting patent licenses are personal and not assignable unless expressly made so. . . . This has been the rule at least since 1852 when the Supreme Court decided *Troy Iron & Nail v. Corning,* 55 U.S. (14 How.) 193, 14 L. Ed. 383 (1852). . . . The district court recognized this rule in the present case, but concluded that where patent licenses are claimed to pass by operation of law to the resultant or surviving corporation in a statutory merger there has been no assignment or transfer.

There appear to be no reported cases where the precise issue in this case has been decided. At least two treatises contain the statement that rights under a patent license owned by a constituent corporation pass to the consolidated corporation in the case of a consolidation, W. Fletcher, *Cyclopedia of the Law of Corporations* §7089 (revised ed. 1973); and to the new or resultant corporation in the case of a merger, A. Deller, Walker on Patents §409 (2d ed. 1965). . . .

Guardian relies on two classes of cases where rights of a constituent corporation have been held to pass by merger to the resultant corporation even though such rights are not otherwise assignable or transferable. It points out that the courts have consistently held that "shop rights" does pass in a statutory merger. *See e.g., Papazian v. American Steel & Wire Co.,* 155 F. Supp. 111 (N.D. Ohio 1957); *Neon Signal Devices, Inc. v. Alpha-Claude Neon Corp.,* 54 F.2d 793 (W.D. Pa.1931); *Wilson v. J.G. Wilson Corp.,* 241 F. 494 (E.D. Va.1917). A shop right is an implied license, which accrues to an employer in cases where an employee has perfected a patentable device while working for the employer. Though the employee is the owner of the patent he is estopped from claiming infringement by the employer. This estoppel arises from the fact that the patent work has been done on the employer's time and that the employer has furnished materials for the experiments and financial backing to the employee.

The rule that prevents an employee-inventor from claiming infringement against a successor to the entire business and good will of his employer is but one feature of the broad doctrine of estoppel, which underlies the shop right cases. No element of estoppel exists in the present case. The license rights of Permaglass did not arise by implication. They were bargained for at arms length and the agreement, which defines the rights of the parties, provides that Permaglass received non-transferable, non-assignable personal licenses. We do not believe that the express prohibition against assignment and transfer in a written instrument may be held ineffective by analogy to a rule based on estoppel in situations where there is no written contract and the rights of the parties have arisen by implication because of their past relationship.

The other group of cases, which the district court and Guardian found to be analogous, holds that the resultant corporation in a merger succeeds to the rights of the constituent corporations under real estate leases. . . . The most obvious difficulty in drawing an analogy between the lease cases and those concerning patent licenses is that a lease is an interest in real property. As such, it is subject to the deep-rooted policy against restraints on alienation. Applying this policy, courts have construed provisions against assignability in leases strictly and have concluded that they do not prevent the passage of interests by operation of law. . . . There is no similar policy, which is offended by the decision of a patent owner to make a license under his patent personal to the licensee, and non-assignable and non-transferable. In fact the law treats a license as if it contained these restrictions in the absence of express provisions to the contrary.

We conclude that the district court misconceived the intent of the parties to the 1964 agreement. We believe the district court put the burden on the wrong party in stating:

> Because the parties failed to provide that Permaglass' rights under the 1964 license agreement would not pass to the corporation surviving a merger, the Court finds that Guardian succeeded to Permaglass' license pursuant to 8 Del. C. §259, and Ohio Revised Code §§1701.81 and 1701.83.

The agreement provides with respect to the license, which Permaglass granted to PPG that Permaglass reserved "a non-exclusive, non-transferable, royalty-free, world-wide right and license for *the benefit and use of Permaglass*." (*emphasis added*). Similarly, with respect to its own two patents, PPG granted to Permaglass "a non-exclusive, non-transferable, royalty-free right and license. . . ." Further, the agreement provides that both it and the license granted to Permaglass "shall be personal to PERMAGLASS and non-assignable except with the consent of PPG first obtained in writing."

The quoted language from Sections 3, 4, and 9 of the 1964 agreement evinces an intent that only Permaglass was to enjoy the privileges of licensee. If the parties had intended an exception in the event of a merger, it would have been a simple matter to have so provided in the agreement. Guardian contends such an exception is not necessary since it is universally recognized that patent licenses pass from a licensee to the resultant corporation in case of a merger. This does not appear to be the case. In *Packard Instrument Co. v. ANS, Inc.*, 416 F.2d 943 (2d Cir. 1969), a license agreement provided that rights thereunder could not be transferred or assigned "except . . . (b) if the entire ownership and business of ANS is transferred by sale, merger, or consolidation, . . ." 416 F.2d at 944 n. 1. Similarly, the agreement construed in *Freeman v. Seiberling Rubber Co.*, 72 F.2d 124 (6th Cir. 1934), provided that the license was not assignable except with the entire business and goodwill of the licensee. We conclude that if the parties had intended an exception in case of a merger to the provisions against assignment and transfer they would have included it in the agreement. It should be noted also that the district court in *Packard, supra*, held that an assignment had taken place when the licensee was merged into another corporation.

The district court also held that the patent licenses in the present case were not transferred because they passed by operation of law from Permaglass to Guardian. This conclusion is based on the theory of continuity, which underlies a true merger. However, the theory of continuity relates to the fact that there is no dissolution of the constituent corporations and, even though they cease to exist, their essential corporate attributes are vested by operation of law in the surviving or resultant corporation. . . . It does not mean that there is no transfer of particular assets from a constituent corporation to the surviving or resultant one.

The Ohio merger statute provides that following a merger all property of a constituent corporation shall be "deemed to be *transferred* to and vested in the surviving or new corporation without further act or deed, . . ." (*emphasis added*). Ohio Revised Code, [former] §1701.81(A)(4). This indicates that the transfer is by operation of law, not that there is no transfer of assets in a merger situation. The Delaware statute, which was also involved in the Permaglass-Guardian merger, provides that the property of the constituent corporations "shall be vested in the corporation surviving or resulting from such merger or consolidation, . . ." 8 Del. C. s 259(a). The Third Circuit has construed the "shall be vested" language of the Delaware statute as follows:

> In short, the underlying property of the constituent corporations is *transferred* to the resultant corporation upon the carrying out of the consolidation or merger. . . . *Koppers Coal & Transportation Co. v. United States*, 107 F.2d 706, 708 (3d Cir. 1939). (*emphasis added*)

In his opinion in *Koppers*, Judge Biggs disposed of arguments very similar to those of Guardian in the present case, based on the theory of continuity. Terming such arguments "metaphysical" he found them completely at odds with the language of the Delaware statute. *Id.* Finally, on this point, the parties themselves provided in the merger agreement that all property of Permaglass "shall be deemed transferred to and shall vest in Guardian without further act or deed. . . ." A transfer is no less a transfer because it takes place by operation of law rather than by a particular act of the parties. The merger was effected by the parties and the transfer was a result of their act of merging.

Thus, Sections 3, 4, and 9 of the 1964 agreement between PPG and Permaglass show an intent that the licenses held by Permaglass in the eleven patents in suit not be transferable. While this conclusion disposes of the license defense as to all eleven patents, it should be noted that Guardian's claim to licenses under the two patents, which originated with PPG is also defeated by Section 11.2 of the 1964 agreement. This section addresses a different concern from that addressed in Sections 3, 4, and 9. The restrictions on transferability and assignability in those sections prevent the patent licenses from becoming the property of third parties. The termination clause, however, provides that Permaglass' license with respect to the two PPG patents will terminate if the ownership of a majority of the voting stock of Permaglass passes from the 1964 stockholders to designated classes of persons, even though the licenses themselves might never have changed hands.

Apparently PPG was willing for Permaglass to continue as licensee under the nine patents even though ownership of its stock might change. These patents originated with Permaglass and so long as Permaglass continued to use the licenses for its own benefit a mere change in ownership of Permaglass stock would not nullify the licenses. Only a transfer or assignment would cause a termination. However, the agreement provides for termination with respect to the two original PPG patents in the event of an indirect takeover of Permaglass by a change in the ownership of a majority of its stock. The fact that PPG sought and obtained a stricter provision with respect to the two patents which it originally owned in no way indicates an intention to permit transfer of licenses under the other nine in case of a merger. None of the eleven licenses was transferable; but two of them, those involving PPG's own development in the field of gas hearth technology, were not to continue even for the benefit of the licensee if it came under the control of a manufacturer of automobiles or a competitor of PPG in the glass industry "other than the present owners" of Permaglass. A consistency among the provisions of the agreement is discernible when the different origins of the various patents are considered. . . .

QUESTIONS

1. Who are the parties to this acquisition? Who is the Bidder? Who is the Target?

2. What is the structure used to make this acquisition?

3. What is the impact of this acquisition on the creditors of Target?

4. What was the business incentive for Bidder to propose to acquire Target?

5. Who is the plaintiff? What relief does plaintiff seek?

6. What is the issue that the court must decide? Does state or federal law control on this issue?

7. What is the major difference between the reasoning used in the district court's decision and that of the appellate court in this case? Based on this difference, what is the lesson that the transaction planner should take away from reading this case, which will then inform this M&A lawyer in considering how to advise future clients as to the best way to structure future transactions?

8. What was the scope of the representation that Target gave to Bidder in this case? *See* subpart (g) of the acquisition agreement, quoted at p. 249.

9. Based on the reasoning of the appellate court, what result if the parties had structured the transaction as a triangular merger, leaving Permaglass as the surviving corporation? What result if Guardian had purchased all the stock of Permaglass?

NOTES

1. Form Matters.   This case illustrates, once again, that the default rules associated with the different methods for structuring an acquisition *do* influence the choice of structure to be used for a particular deal. It also demonstrates the importance of mastering the default rules so that the transaction planner can responsibly and competently anticipate potential problems and address them in the process of negotiating and documenting the acquisition. Finally, this case illustrates the manner in which the default rules serve to allocate the economic risks associated with completing a particular acquisition, as well as allocating the costs associated with bargaining around the default rule in order to obtain a different economic result that is desired by the parties.

2. Due Diligence.   Consider the provision quoted by the court at p. 249 from the merger agreement entered into by Permaglass and Guardian. Although the language of this representation does not specifically refer to the licenses at issue in the principal case, the language used in this provision clearly seems to anticipate the possibility of an infringement action of the type presented in this case. The language of the representation quoted by the court from the parties' agreement is carefully worded. This wording is likely a direct outgrowth of the *due diligence* process undertaken by the parties prior to signing this merger agreement. As we shall see in Chapter 5, *representations* are a customary provision in the acquisition agreement. One of the most important purposes served by these representations is to allocate business and financial risks between the parties to the agreement. *Query:* What business risk is being allocated to each party by the language of the representation quoted by the court in the principal case? How did the parties learn of this risk inherent in Permaglass's business so that they could negotiate the allocation of this business risk as part of the acquisition agreement?

The next case addresses the impact of a nonassignment clause in the context of a transaction structured as a reverse triangular merger.

Meso Scale Diagnostics, LLC v. Roche Diagnostics GmbH
62 A.3d 62 (Del. Ch. 2013)

Parsons, Vice Chancellor. . . .

I. Background . . .

[In 2007, Roche Industries GmbH ("Roche") acquired BioVeris Corp. ("BioVeris"), a Delaware corporation, in a transaction that was structured as a reverse triangular merger leaving BioVeris as a wholly owned subsidiary of Roche. Earlier, as part of a 2003 transaction, Roche, BioVeris, and the plaintiffs (which included Meso Scale Diagnostics, LLC ("Meso") and several other parties) entered into an agreement that included a provision referred to by the court as the "Global Consent." Roche subsequently acquired BioVeris in a reverse triangular merger in order to gain access to certain intellectual property rights that BioVeris had obtained pursuant to the Global Consent. Plaintiffs/ Meso then sued, claiming, among other things, that the reverse triangular merger constituted an assignment of BioVeris's intellectual property rights in violation of the Global Consent. Specifically, the terms of the Global Consent contained a provision preventing the assignment of BioVeris's intellectual property rights without first obtaining the consent of the other parties to the agreement, which included plaintiff Meso, among others. The language of Section 5.08 of the Global Consent stated:

> Neither this Agreement nor any of the rights, interests or obligations under this Agreement shall be assigned, in whole or in part, *by operation of law or otherwise by any of the parties without the prior written consent of the other parties;* . . . Any purported assignment without such consent shall be void. Subject to the preceding sentences, this Agreement will be binding upon, inure to the benefit of, and be enforceable by, the parties and their respective successors and assigns.

Meso Scale, 62 A.3d at 71-72, n. 53 (*emphasis added*). For its part, Roche contends, among other things, that "as a matter of law, a reverse triangular merger cannot be an assignment by operation of law." *Id.* at 74.]

II. ANALYSIS . . .

3. DID THE BIOVERIS MERGER CONSTITUTE AN ASSIGNMENT "BY OPERATION OF LAW OR OTHERWISE" UNDER SECTION 5.08?

Roche argues that even if this Court concludes that Section 5.08 applies to the assignment of rights, interests, or obligations relating to BioVeris's intellectual property, Roche still is entitled to summary judgment . . . because no assignment by operation of law or otherwise occurred when Roche acquired BioVeris through a reverse triangular merger. Specifically, Roche asserts that BioVeris remained intact as the surviving entity of the merger, and, therefore, BioVeris did not assign anything. Meso, on the other hand, contends that mergers generally, including reverse triangular mergers, can result in assignments by operation of law.

At the motion to dismiss stage, I noted that Section 5.08 does not require Meso's consent for changes in ownership, but prohibits, absent consent from [certain parties to the Global Consent], an assignment of BioVeris's rights and interests *by operation of law or otherwise.* [*See, Meso Scale Diagnostics, LLC v. Roche Diagnostics GmbH,* 2011 WL 1348438 (Del. Ch. April 8, 2011).] I concluded that no Delaware case squarely had addressed whether a reverse triangular merger could ever be viewed as an assignment by operation of law. I further stated that "Plaintiffs plausibly argue that 'by operation of law' was intended to cover mergers that effectively operated like an assignment, even if it might not apply to mergers merely involving changes of control."

To interpret an anti-assignment provision, a court "look[s] to the language of the agreement, read as a whole, in an effort to discern the parties' collective intent."[119] Roche contends that the language "by operation of law or otherwise" makes clear that the parties did not intend Section 5.08 to cover reverse triangular mergers. I find Roche's interpretation of Section 5.08 to be reasonable. Generally, mergers do not result in an assignment by operation of law of assets that began as property of the surviving entity and continued to be such after the merger.

Upon the completion of a merger, Section 259 of the DGCL provides:

> When any merger or consolidation shall have become effective under this chapter, for all purposes of the laws of this State the separate existence of all the constituent corporations, or of all such constituent corporations *except the one into which the other or others of such constituent corporations have been merged,* as the case may be, shall cease and the constituent corporations shall become a new corporation, or be merged into 1 of such corporations . . . the rights, privileges, powers and franchises of each of said corporations, and all property, real, personal and mixed, and all debts due to any of said constituent corporations on whatever account . . . *shall be vested in the corporation surviving or resulting from such merger or consolidation;* and all property, rights, privileges, powers and franchises, and all and every other interest shall be thereafter as effectually the property of the surviving or resulting corporation as they were of the several and respective constituent corporations.[121]

---

119. *Tenneco Automotive Inc. v. El Paso Corp.,* 2002 WL 453930, at *1 (Del. Ch. Mar. 20, 2002).
121. *Id.* §259(a) (emphasis added).

In *Koppers Coal & Transport Co. v. United States*,[122] the United States Court of Appeals for the Third Circuit concluded that "the underlying property of the constituent corporations is transferred to the resultant corporation upon the carrying out of the consolidation or merger as provided by Section 59."[123] Other courts in Delaware have held that Section 259(a) results in the transfer of the *non-surviving corporation's* rights and obligations to the surviving corporation by operation of law.[124] For example, in *DeAscanis v. Brosius–Eliason Co.*,[125] the Delaware Supreme Court associated Section 259 with assignments by operation of law. The language in Section 259, "except the one into which the other or others of such constituent corporations have been merged," however, suggests that the surviving corporation would not have effected any assignment. In sum, Section 259(a) supports Roche's position that a reverse triangular merger generally is not an assignment by operation of law or otherwise, and that, therefore, Section 5.08 was not intended to cover reverse triangular mergers.

I also note that Roche's interpretation is consistent with the reasonable expectations of the parties. Pursuant to the widely accepted "objective theory" of contract interpretation—a framework adopted and followed in Delaware—this Court must interpret a contract in a manner that satisfies the "reasonable expectations of the parties at the time they entered into the contract."[127] The vast majority of commentary discussing reverse triangular mergers indicates that a reverse triangular merger does not constitute an assignment by operation of law as to the surviving entity. For example, this Court has recognized that "it is possible that the only practical effect of the [reverse triangular] merger is the conversion of the property interest of the shareholders of the target corporation."[128] Similarly, in *Lewis v. Ward*,[129] then-Vice Chancellor Strine observed:

> In a triangular merger, the acquiror's stockholders generally do not have the right to vote on the merger, nor are they entitled to appraisal. If a reverse triangular structure is used, the rights and obligations of the target are not transferred, assumed or affected. Because of these and other advantages to using a triangular structure, it is the preferred method of acquisition for a wide range of transactions.[130]

Leading commentators also have noted that a reverse triangular merger does not constitute an assignment by operation of law.[131] Based on the

---

122. 107 F.2d 706 (3d Cir. 1939).

123. *Id.* at 708 (referring to Del. Rev. Code 1935, §2092, a precursor to 8 *Del. C.* §259(a)).

124. *See Heit v. Tenneco, Inc.*, 319 F.Supp. 884, 887 (D. Del. 1970) ("8 *Del. C.* §259 provides that when a merger becomes effective all assets of the merged corporation, including any causes of action which might exist on its behalf, pass by operation to the surviving company.") . . .

125. 533 A.2d 1254, 1987 WL 4628 (Del. 1987) (ORDER).

127. *The Liquor Exchange, Inc. v. Tsaganos*, 2004 WL 2694912, at *2 (Del.Ch. Nov. 16, 2004).

128. *Wells Fargo & Co. v. First Interstate Bancorp*, 1996 WL 32169, at *7 (Del.Ch. Jan. 18, 1996).

129. 2003 WL 22461894 (Del.Ch. Oct. 29, 2003).

130. *Id.* at *4 n. 18.

131. *See, e.g.*, 1 R. Franklin Balotti & Jesse A. Finkelstein, Delaware Law of Corporations and Business Organizations § 9.8 (2013) ("The advantage of this type of merger is that T will become a wholly-owned subsidiary of A without any change in its corporate existence. Thus,

commentary on this subject, I consider it unlikely that the parties would have expected a clause covering assignments by operation of law to have applied to reverse triangular mergers.

Meso disagrees and has advanced [several] theories in support of its interpretation of Section 5.08, *i.e.*, that the anti-assignment clause was intended to cover reverse triangular mergers. Those theories are: (1) the acquisition of BioVeris was nothing more than the assignment of BioVeris's intellectual property rights to Roche . . . and (3) this Court should embrace a California federal court's holding that a reverse triangular merger results in an assignment by operation of law.

First, Meso contends that "the acquisition of BioVeris was nothing more than the assignment of BioVeris's intellectual property rights to Roche" because, as a result of the acquisition, Roche Diagnostics effectively owned the ECL patents. Meso's argument, however, is unavailing because it ignores Delaware's longstanding doctrine of independent legal significance. That doctrine states:

> [A]ction taken in accordance with different sections of [the DGCL] are acts of independent legal significance even though the end result may be the same under different sections. The mere fact that the result of actions taken under one section may be the same as the result of action taken under another section does not require that the legality of the result must be tested by the requirements of the second section.[133]

Indeed, the doctrine of independent legal significance has been applied in situations where deals were structured so as to avoid consent rights. For example, in *Fletcher International, Ltd. v. ION Geophysical Corp.*,[134] this Court noted:

> [T]he fact that one deal structure would have triggered [Plaintiffs] consent rights, and the deal structure in the Share Purchase Agreement did not, does not have any bearing on the propriety of the Share Purchase Agreement or the fact that under that Agreement, [Plaintiff's] consent rights did not apply. This conclusion, for contract law purposes, is analogous to results worked by the "doctrine of independent legal significance" in cases involving similar statutory arguments made under the DGCL.[135]

Here, [the merger subsidiary that was formed by Roche to acquire BioVeris as part of a reverse triangular merger] was merged into BioVeris, with BioVeris as the surviving entity. Under Section 259, the surviving entity continued to

---

the rights and obligations of T, the acquired corporation, are not transferred, assumed or affected. For example, obtaining consents for the transfer of governmental or other licenses may not be necessary, absent a provision to the contrary in the licenses or agreement, since the licenses will continue to be held by the same continuing corporation."); Elaine D. Ziff, *The Effect of Corporate Acquisitions on the Target Company's License Rights*, 57 Bus. Law. 767, 787 (2002) ("One widely-recognized advantage of employing a reverse subsidiary structure is that it purportedly obviates the issue of whether the merger constitutes a transfer of the target company's assets in violation of existing contracts, because the 'surviving company' is the same legal entity as the original contracting party.").

133. *Orzek v. Englehart*, 195 A.2d 375 (Del. 1963).
134. 2011 WL 1167088 (Del.Ch. Mar. 29, 2011).
135. *Id.* at *5 n. 39.

"possess [] all the rights, privileges, powers and franchises" it had before the merger plus those of each of the corporations merged into it. Thus, no assignment by operation of law or otherwise occurred as to BioVeris with respect to what it possessed before the merger. . . .

As a final argument, Meso suggests that this Court should embrace the United States District Court for the Northern District of California's holding in *SQL Solutions, Inc. v. Oracle Corp.*[156] that a reverse triangular merger results in an assignment by operation of law. There the court stated, "an assignment or transfer of rights does occur through a change in the legal form of ownership of a business."[158] The court in *SQL Solutions* applied California law and cited a line of California cases for the proposition that whether "an assignment results merely from a change in the legal form of ownership of a business . . . depends upon whether it affects the interests of the parties protected by the nonassignability of the contract."[159]

I decline to adopt the approach outlined in *SQL Solutions,* however, because doing so would conflict with Delaware's jurisprudence surrounding stock acquisitions, among other things. Under Delaware law, stock purchase transactions, by themselves, do not result in an assignment by operation of law. For example, in the *Baxter Pharmaceutical Products* case,[160] this Court stated, "Delaware corporations may lawfully acquire the securities of other corporations, and a purchase or change of ownership of such securities (again, without more) is not regarded as assigning or delegating the contractual rights or duties of the corporation whose securities are purchased."[161] Similarly, in *Branmar Theatre Co. v. Branmar, Inc.,*[162] the Court held that "in the absence of fraud . . . transfer of stock of a corporate lessee is ordinarily not a violation of a clause prohibiting assignment. . . ."[163]

Delaware courts have refused to hold that a mere change in the legal ownership of a business results in an assignment by operation of law. *SQL Solutions,* on the other hand, noted, "California courts have consistently recognized that an assignment or transfer of rights does occur through a change in the legal form of ownership of a business."[164] The *SQL Solutions* case, however, provides no further explanation for its apparent holding that any change in ownership, including a reverse triangular merger, is an assignment by operation of law.

---

156. 1991 WL 626458 (N.D.Cal. Dec. 18, 1991).

158. *SQL Solutions, Inc. v. Oracle Corp.,* 1991 WL 626458, at *3.

159. *See Trubowitch v. Riverbank Canning Co.,* 30 Cal.2d 335, 344–45, 182 P.2d 182 (1947); *see also People ex rel. Dep't of Pub. Works v. McNamara Corp.,* 28 Cal.App.3d 641, 648, 104 Cal. Rptr. 822 (1972).

160. *Baxter Pharm. Prods., Inc. v. ESI Lederle Inc.,* 1999 WL 160148 (Del.Ch. Mar. 11, 1999).

161. *Id.* at *5 (internal citations omitted) ("The nonassignability clause contains no language that prohibits, directly or by implication, a stock acquisition or change of ownership of any contracting party.").

162. 264 A.2d 526 (Del.Ch.1970).

163. *Id.* at 528.

164. *SQL Solutions, Inc.,* 1991 WL 626458, at *3. It is not entirely clear whether the *SQL* court intended to distinguish between a change in legal ownership and a "change in the legal form of ownership." As I understand it, the *SQL* court intended the latter phrase to include the former.

Both stock acquisitions and reverse triangular mergers involve changes in legal ownership, and the law should reflect parallel results. In order to avoid upsetting Delaware's well-settled law regarding stock acquisitions, I refuse to adopt the approach espoused in *SQL Solutions.*

In sum, Meso could have negotiated for a "change of control provision." They did not. Instead, they negotiated for a term that prohibits "assignments by operation of law or otherwise." Roche has provided a reasonable interpretation of Section 5.08 that is consistent with the general understanding that a reverse triangular merger is not an assignment by operation of law. On the other hand, I find Meso's arguments as to why language that prohibits "assignments by operation of law or otherwise" should be construed to encompass reverse triangular mergers unpersuasive and its related construction of Section 5.08 to be unreasonable.

For the foregoing reasons, I conclude that Section 5.08 was not intended to cover the BioVeris Merger. . . .

QUESTIONS

1. What was the ruling of the district court in *SQL Solutions, Inc. v. Oracle Corp.?* Why did the Delaware court decline to adopt the holding in that case?

2. Based on the court's reasoning in *Meso Scale,* what should the plaintiffs have done in order to avoid the litigation that resulted in this decision?

3. What is the impact of the decision in *Meso Scale* on the federal court's ruling in the *SQL Solutions* case?

NOTE

It also bears emphasizing that Vice Chancellor Parsons' 2013 decision eliminates the uncertainty that resulted from his earlier April 2011 ruling in the *Meso Scale* case, where he indicated that there may be circumstances where a reverse triangular merger could be treated as an assignment for purposes of an nonassignment clause:

> This [2013] ruling is noteworthy because it confirms the view that, until the first *Meso Scale Diagnostics* ruling, practitioners had long taken for granted: a reverse triangular merger does not result in an assignment by operation of law of the acquired corporation's contracts or other assets. The decision should provide comfort to would-be acquirors that they can structure transactions to which the DGCL is applicable in a manner that ensures that consents to assignment do not need to be obtained where there is no change of ownership or control language in the relevant anti-assignment clause. However, the decision also serves as a reminder that, outside of the confines of the DGCL, there remains uncertainty as to the risks associated with anti-assignment clauses — it may be prudent to require that consents be obtained from applicable third parties where a license or other agreement containing such a clause is important to the target's business.

Gibson, Dunn & Crutcher, *Delaware Court of Chancery Confirms That a Reverse Triangular Merger Does Not Result in an Assignment by Operation of Law*, Mar. 1, 2013 (law firm memo, copy on file with author).

B. Successor Liability in Asset Acquisitions

1. Introductory Note

The key characteristic of an asset purchase is that Target remains in place, even though it has sold all (or substantially all) of its assets to Bidder. In many deals, Bidder and Target may negotiate for certain (or even all) of Target's liabilities to be transferred to Bidder as well. This obligation is usually accomplished, as a matter of contract law, by including Bidder's express written assumption of certain designated liabilities of Target as part of the asset purchase agreement entered into by Bidder and Target.

Once the parties close on this asset acquisition, Target remains intact and is generally left holding all of the liabilities that were not expressly assumed by Bidder, along with the consideration paid by Bidder to acquire all or substantially all of Target's assets. As reflected in Diagram 4 in Appendix A, the asset purchase customarily contemplates a two-step transaction in order to distribute the acquisition consideration (usually consisting of either cash or Bidder's stock) into the hands of Target shareholders. To accomplish this, Target will often dissolve following the sale of all of its assets and distribute out the remaining proceeds in liquidation to Target shareholders *after* satisfying the claims of Target's creditors.

Dissolution is another type of fundamental change that requires shareholder approval. *See*, e.g., MBCA §14.02. Often, the board of Target will solicit Target shareholders to approve the dissolution of the company as part of the process of soliciting shareholder approval for the sale of all of Target's assets to Bidder. Indeed, Bidder may insist, as a condition to its obligation to close on the agreement to purchase all of Target's assets, that Target shareholders vote to dissolve Target and distribute the acquisition consideration to Target shareholders in liquidation of the company. *Query:* Why might Bidder insist that Target be contractually obligated to proceed with dissolution of the company following closing on the sale of assets to Bidder, particularly in cases where the acquisition consideration consists entirely of Bidder stock?

At closing on the parties' asset purchase agreement, Bidder will deliver the agreed-upon consideration to Target and, generally speaking, Target will be obligated to transfer ownership of Target's assets to Bidder. This is a more cumbersome procedure than closing an acquisition structured as a merger (regardless whether it is a direct or triangular merger) because Target typically must prepare deeds or bills of sale for each of Target's assets (real and personal). In most cases involving an asset purchase, this method of transferring ownership of Target's business results in substantial transaction costs incurred in connection with preparing the necessary documentation (such as deeds) and the cost and delay associated with making any necessary filings with appropriate state and/ or local authorities.

By contrast, in a merger, this transfer of ownership is effected by operation of law, avoiding the necessity of preparing evidence of transfer of ownership of the individual assets of Target's business. Consequently, in certain types of businesses, the merger may offer significant advantages over other methods of structuring an acquisition since title to *all* assets owned by each constituent corporation is *automatically* vested in the surviving corporation. This transfer takes effect *by operation of law* once the articles of merger are filed with the secretary of state's office. Thus, the only document required to effectuate the transfer of Target's business to Bidder consists of the articles of merger, which will be filed with the secretary of state. Furthermore, in a direct merger, the issue of a second-step dissolution of Target is rendered moot, as Target Co. ceases to exist by operation of law once the merger becomes effective.

2. Dissolution of Target

The second step in an asset acquisition usually involves the orderly winding up and liquidation of Target's business in a voluntary dissolution that has been approved by the shareholders. In most states, voluntary dissolution of a corporation involves the following steps:

1. Gather all of the company's assets.
2. Convert the company's assets to cash.
3. Use the cash to pay off the company's creditors (in their order of priority).
4. Distribute the remaining cash (or other non-cash assets) to the company's shareholders (giving priority to those shares carrying a liquidation preference).

In the case of a dissolution that follows the sale of all of Target's assets, the first two steps have essentially been accomplished by closing on the sale of all of Target's assets to Bidder. At that point, dissolution of Target primarily involves notifying Target Co.'s creditors that Target is winding up its business affairs and providing them with the opportunity to submit their claims to be paid before anything is distributed to Target shareholders in a final, liquidating distribution. The dissolution proceeding extinguishes the separate existence of Target Co. once the articles of dissolution are filed (which, generally speaking, are filed with the secretary of state's office).

In most states, the corporation statute sets forth detailed procedures for Target to use to notify its creditors that Target is winding up its business affairs in a voluntary dissolution of the company. The purpose of these detailed procedural requirements is to protect the legitimate interests of the company's business creditors. It is imperative for directors and shareholders to carefully follow these requirements in the manner prescribed by statute because, in most states, the failure to follow these statutory requirements may result in personal liability to the company's directors and/or shareholders (usually based on the theory that the liquidating distribution to Target shareholders constitutes the unauthorized return of capital). Generally speaking, the detailed notice and other steps prescribed by statutory law for dissolution and winding up are there to protect the rights of creditors against the possibility of opportunistic behavior on the part of Target insiders—a possibility that is inherent in the very process of winding up and dissolving Target. The concern is that Target insiders may be tempted to take advantage of the company's creditors by distributing the proceeds from the sale of all its assets to Target shareholders rather than first applying the acquisition consideration to satisfy the claims of Target creditors. As for contract creditors, these fixed and therefore knowable claims against Target will generally be satisfied in a dissolution proceeding out of the consideration that Bidder paid to acquire all of Target's assets if the statutory procedures for an orderly liquidation are carefully followed.

The traditional approach to voluntary dissolution, followed by most state corporation codes, allows the company to distribute any surplus from a sale of the company's assets to its shareholders after the company has paid off its known creditors. In language that is typical of these modern statutes, MBCA §14.06 provides that Target must notify *all known claimants* in writing of the pending dissolution proceeding. These claimants then have 120 days to present their claims. If a claim is rejected, the statute provides that the claimant must sue on its claim within 90 days of the rejection. Most state statutes then bar claims of Target's creditors who come forward after the expiration of the notice and claims period provided by local law. *See,* e.g., MBCA §14.06 and §14.07. This statutory scheme does not unfairly prejudice *contract creditors* because Target's creditors are no worse off than if Target were still in existence, assuming that Target received fair value for its assets. More specifically, their claims can be satisfied against Target itself, which remains in place, or alternatively, Target's contract creditors will have an opportunity to present their claim for payment as part of the orderly dissolution of Target, and these claims will be paid ahead of any distributions to Target's shareholders.

More problematic, however, are the claims of *involuntary creditors*, particularly those tort claims that do not arise until sometime *after* the dissolution of Target, often referred to as *long-tail* (or contingent) *claims.* As to those tort claims pending at the time of Bidder's acquisition of Target, these are known claims, to be handled in the orderly liquidation of Target Co. in exactly the same manner as the contract claims discussed above.

From a public policy perspective, the most troubling of these long-tail claims in today's M&A market are those product liability claims and environmental claims that arise *long after* Target has sold all of its assets to Bidder and distributed the acquisition consideration to Target shareholders in the process of an orderly winding up and dissolution of Target. As for these long-tail claims, the public policy concerns presented by this two-step method of acquiring Target are reflected in the *Ruiz* case, *infra.*

3.   Contract Creditors

American Paper Recycling Corp. v. IHC Corp.
707 F. Supp. 2d 114 (D. Mass. 2010)

STEARNS, District Judge.

American Paper Recycling Corporation (APR) brought this action in Bristol Superior Court seeking to compel performance by defendants IHC Corporation (IHC)* and MPS/IH, LLC (MPS) of a waste paper sales contract. APR also seeks to enjoin the sale of waste paper by MPS to a competitor, Wilmington Paper Corporation (Wilmington). Defendants removed the case to the federal court on diversity grounds, and then moved to dismiss the Complaint. . . .

BACKGROUND

The following material facts are not in dispute or where disputed are viewed in the light most favorable to the relevant non-moving party. APR is an Illinois corporation engaged in the business of purchasing waste paper and other paper products for recycling. APR is registered as a foreign corporation in Massachusetts and has its principal office in Mansfield, Massachusetts. IHC is a subsidiary of Cinram (U.S.) Holdings, Inc. (Cinram). Cinram is the sole shareholder of IHC. Prior to the events giving rise to this litigation, Ivy (now IHC) was engaged in the business of manufacturing paper packaging for use in the media industry. Ivy operated plants in Terre Haute, Indiana, and Louisville, Kentucky. As a by-product of its manufacturing business, Ivy generated significant quantities of recyclable waste paper. APR paid Ivy an agreed rate based on the volume and quality of the waste paper.

On November 6, 1990, Ivy and APR entered into a Waste Paper Sales Contract (Sales Contract), under which Ivy agreed to sell all of its waste paper to APR. In return, APR provided Ivy with manufacturing equipment on generous terms. The Sales Contract, in relevant part, provided that:

> E. It is mutually agreed that the quantities, classification, price periods during which the Agreement shall be effective, packing, shipping and other provisions shall be as follows:
>   1. Entire accumulation of saleable waste paper stock generated at [Ivy] plants. . . .
>   3. This Agreement shall continue throughout December 31, 2004, and shall be automatically renewed at the same terms unless written cancellation is given by either party 90 days prior to the expiration of this contract period.

Beginning in February of 1991, Ivy and APR executed the first of ten amendments to the Sales Contract dealing with the provision by APR of additional processing equipment and financing to Ivy. In conjunction with several of these amendments, Ivy agreed to extensions of the Sales Contract . . . The final relevant amendment to the Sales Contract occurred on May 1, 2006. Under Amendment #10,

---

* [By the author: After this litigation commenced, the seller, who was known as Ivy Hill Corporation (Ivy) at the time that the original sales contract was signed on Nov. 6, 1990, changed its corporate name to IHC Corporation (IHC).]

APR agreed to finance [a repair project at one of Ivy's plants] and Ivy agreed to an extension of the sales contract. The final version of the Sales Contract, as modified by the series of amendments, was set to expire on December 31, 2020. . . .

On April 9, 2009, pursuant to an Asset Purchase Agreement (APA), Cinram sold substantially all of Ivy's assets to MPS in a cash-and-stock deal.[5] Under the terms of the APA, Cinram received $23,250,000 in cash and 7,750 shares of Series C Preferred Stock in Multi Packaging Solutions, Inc., the parent company of MPS.[6] The APA provided that:

> Buyer hereby purchases and acquires from the Company [Ivy], all of the right, title and interest in and to the Company's Assets, rights, properties and interest in properties of the Company of every kind, nature and description, whether real, personal or mixed, tangible and intangible, whether or not used in, held for usage in or otherwise relating to the Business (other than Excluded assets) . . . .

Additionally, as part of the transaction, MPS agreed to assume substantially all of Ivy's liabilities.

> Assumed Liabilities. On the terms and subject to the conditions contained in this Agreement, simultaneously with the sale, transfer, conveyance and assignment to Buyer of Purchased Assets, Buyer hereby assumes all of the Liabilities of the Company [Ivy] relating to the Business other than the Excluded Liabilities.

APA ¶ 2.1.[7]

The APA then identified certain assets that would not be transferred including cash, pre-paid expenses, insurance policies, pre-paid taxes, corporate documents, bank accounts, certain employee benefit plans, and all real estate owned in fee simple. *See id.* In addition, Schedule 1.2(m) of the APA identified specific assets excluded from the sale, including:

> Waste Paper Sales Contract dated November 6, 1990, as amended, . . . between American Paper Recycling Corporation and [Ivy].

On April 16, 2009, Ray Wheelan, a MPS Vice–President, notified Kenneth Golden, APR's President, that MPS intended to consolidate the recycling business at the [Terre Haute and Louisville plants acquired pursuant to the APA] with MPS's existing contract with Wilmington. Wheelan told Golden that APR's recycling services at these facilities were being terminated effective May 10, 2009. On April 24, 2009, Wheelan wrote to APR warning that "[y]ou need to stop scheduling pick ups at the Terre Haute and Louisville plants effective immediately. All pick ups have been discontinued." APR then filed this lawsuit.

---

5. Prior to its sale to MPS, Ivy had undergone two prior acquisitions. Ivy was first purchased by Time Warner Company, which then sold Ivy to Cinram. In both of these transactions, the Sales Contract was included among the transferred assets. Neither acquisition impacted on APR's ability to continue to purchase Ivy's waste paper.

6. Multi Packaging Solutions, Inc., is a Delaware corporation and the sole owner of a second Delaware corporation, John Henry Holdings, Inc., which in turns owns MPS.

7. The excluded obligations listed at APA ¶ 2.2 are standard exclusions, including tax liabilities, employee benefit plans, environmental contamination, and liabilities covered by existing insurance contracts.

DISCUSSION . . .

THE DE FACTO MERGER EXCEPTION

[In order to hold MPS liable on a breach of contract theory, the federal district court concluded that APR must first establish that the asset purchase constituted a de facto merger between MPS and Ivy Hill (now named IHC).] "Under generally accepted corporate law principles, the purchaser of the assets of another corporation does not assume the debts and liabilities of the transferor. The traditional rule is subject to four generally recognized exceptions: (1) the purchasing corporation expressly or impliedly agrees to assume the selling corporation's liabilities; (2) the transaction is a merger of the two entities; (3) the purchaser is a mere continuation of the seller corporation; and (4) the transaction is a fraudulent attempt to evade the seller's liabilities." *Devine & Devine Food Brokers, Inc. v. Wampler Foods, Inc.*, 313 F.3d 616, 618 (1st Cir. 2002), citing *Dayton v. Peck, Stow & Wilcox Co.*, 739 F.2d 690, 692 (1st Cir. 1984). *See also* 15 W. Fletcher, *Cyclopedia of Law of Private Corporations* § 7122, at 227–243 (1999). Massachusetts law adheres "to traditional corporate law principles that the liabilities of a selling predecessor corporation are not imposed on the successor corporation which purchases its assets unless [one of these four exceptions is met]." *Cargill, Inc. v. Beaver Coal & Oil Co.*, 424 Mass. 356, 359 (1997). . . . In this instance, there is no dispute that the Sales Contract was expressly excluded from the transferred assets. Nor is there any contention that the transaction involved a fraudulent conveyance to MPS. Thus, the first and fourth exceptions do not apply. APR relies instead on the de facto merger and "mere continuation" exceptions.

In determining whether to characterize an asset sale as a de facto merger, courts are to consider whether:

> (1) there is a continuation of the enterprise of the seller corporation so that there is continuity of management, personnel, physical location, assets, and general business operations; whether (2) there is a continuity of shareholders which results from the purchasing corporation paying for the acquired assets with shares of its own stock, this stock ultimately coming to be held by the shareholders of the seller corporation so that they become a constituent part of the purchasing corporation; whether (3) the seller corporation ceases its ordinary business operations, liquidates, and dissolves as soon as legally and practically possible; and whether (4) the purchasing corporation assumes those obligations of the seller ordinarily necessary for the uninterrupted continuation of normal business operations of the seller corporation.

Goguen v. Textron, Inc., 476 F.Supp.2d 5, 12–13 (D. Mass. 2007) (quoting *Cargill*, 424 Mass. at 360), . . . Of the four factors, "no single [one] is necessary or sufficient to establish a de facto merger." *Goguen*, 476 F.Supp.2d at 13 (citing *Cargill*, 424 Mass. at 360). "When a *de facto* merger is alleged, the court must determine 'the substance of the agreement [regardless of] the title put on it by the parties.' " Here, APR argues that none of the four *Cargill* factors emblematic of a de facto merger applies. The court will consider each factor in turn.

CONTINUITY OF THE ENTERPRISE

MPS absorbed the bulk of Ivy's workforce, two of its physical plants, and its core business. However, "[i]n determining whether a de facto merger has occurred, courts pay particular attention to the continuation of management, officers, directors and shareholders." *Cargill*, 424 Mass. at 360. MPS did not retain key members of Ivy's management team, including Ivy's Chief Operating Officer, the Vice President of Finance, the Chief Engineer, the Plant Manager, the Controller, and the IT Director. It had none of the same officers or directors, and as noted below, the exchange involved an arms-length exchange of good and fair consideration, namely a substantial sum of cash and only a nominal interest in the shares of Multi Packaging Solutions, MPS's parent company. MPS discontinued a number of Ivy's previous vendors, including vendors who had supplied the plants with paper, paper board, and corrugate. Finally, MPS chose to exclude the real property at the Louisville plant from the list of purchased assets, and instead chose to lease the property from Ivy–IHC.

Cargill provides an instructive contrast. In that case, not only did the work force remain the same, the key manager stayed in place, and all of the other employees and key people (with one exception) remained the same, "maintaining their same positions and responsibilities." *Cargill*, 424 Mass. at 360. The owner of the former company became a director of the new company and its largest individual shareholder. *Id.* The new company "used the same telephone numbers [as the old company], the same trucks and the same equipment. [The old company's] customer lists and contracts were transferred to [the new company] all of whom were serviced just as they had been. . . ." *Id.* at 361. In short, the new became the old. Similarly, in [*In re Acushet River & New Bradford Proceedings*, 712 F. Supp. 1010 (D. Mass 1989)], the new company continued all of the old company's product lines, the president, vice-president and treasurer of the old company took the same titles and functions in the new company (as well as being made directors), the middle management remained intact, and even the banking and insurance facilities remained the same. "For all the world could tell from outward appearance, [the new company] had simply shortened its name." 712 F. Supp. at 1016. This factor weighs heavily against a de facto merger.

CONTINUITY OF SHAREHOLDERS

The First Circuit, consistent with other courts and learned treatises, has observed that continuity of shareholders is one of the "key requirements" for application of the de facto merger doctrine. *Dayton*, 739 F.2d at 693. Continuity of the shareholders "is found where the purchaser corporation exchanges its own stock as consideration for the seller corporation's assets so that the shareholders of the seller corporation become a constituent part of the purchaser corporation." *Id.* In this case, as consideration for the sale, Cinram received $23,250,000 in cash and 7,750 shares of Series C Preferred Stock in Multi Packaging Solutions. The shares, however, represent less than 3.2 percent of Multi Packaging Solutions' stock. Moreover, as the only Series C stockholder,

Cinram has no voting rights, cannot transfer its shares, and holds the shares subject to a right of unilateral redemption by Multi Packaging Solutions. [While in] *Cargill,* a twelve and one-half percent voting interest was sufficient to tip the balance, this was so because the sale was between two closely-held corporations and left the owner of the predecessor entity with a seat on the successor corporation's board of directors and the largest personal holding of shares of stock. No members of Cinram's board of directors or any of its officers hold a similar position with MPS or were given individual shares of voting stock. This factor weighs decidedly against a de facto merger.

SELLER CORPORATION CEASES ITS FORMER BUSINESS OPERATIONS

A third emblematic factor is the immediate liquidation of the predecessor entity. The rationale underlying this exception is the protection of third parties, for example, consumers harmed by a product defect. "[W]hatever the reach of successor liability under the law of Massachusetts, the doctrine has no applicability where . . . the original manufacturer remains in existence to respond in tort for its alleged negligence and breach of warranty." *Roy v. Bolens Corp.,* 629 F. Supp. 1070, 1073 (D. Mass. 1986). Here, Ivy did not dissolve after the sale and liquidate its assets so as to put them out of the reach of creditors, but remains in existence as IHC. It retained ownership of the real estate where the Louisville plant is located. It collects rents from MPS, and otherwise functions as a commercial landlord with assets, profits, and employees. As in *Roy,* because Ivy "is alive and well and able to respond in damages," *id.,* a finding of a de facto merger is virtually precluded.

ASSUMPTION OF OBLIGATIONS NECESSARY TO CONTINUE NORMAL BUSINESS OPERATIONS

While MPS has continued Ivy's core business, operational changes since acquiring Ivy's manufacturing plants have replaced most of the management. MPS has discontinued or changed vendors, and did not take ownership of Ivy's real property where the Louisville plant is situated. On balance, this factor too weighs against the argument that MPS has simply continued Ivy's business without interruption or notice.

Taking the four factors as a whole, and particularly the "key requirement" of continuity of management, officers, directors, and shareholders, it is clear that no de facto merger occurred.

THE MERE CONTINUATION EXCEPTION

Under the mere continuation exception, "the imposition of liability on the purchaser is justified on the theory that, in substance if not in form, the purchasing corporation is the same company as the selling corporation." *McCarthy v. Litton Indus., Inc.,* 410 Mass. 15, 22, 570 N.E.2d 1008 (1991). Accordingly, "the indices of 'continuation' are, at a minimum: continuity of directors, officers, and stockholders; and the continued existence of only one corporation after the sale of assets." *Goguen,* 476 F. Supp. 2d at 14–15 (citing *McCarthy,* 410 Mass. at 23, 570 N. E. 2d 1008). As the minimum threshold is not met—there is no continuity of directors, officers, or shareholders, or for that matter senior management—this exception has no applicability. . . .

QUESTIONS

1. What is the general rule on transfer of a corporation's liabilities when it sells all of its assets to Bidder?

2. Who is the plaintiff? What relief does the plaintiff seek?

3. What does it take for a creditor of Target to impose liability on Bidder, as the successor-in-interest to Target, in reliance on the de facto merger doctrine?

4. From a public policy perspective, do you think the court reached the right result on the facts of this case? If the plaintiff had prevailed, do you think that would have resulted in a windfall to the plaintiff?

4.   Tort Creditors

Ruiz v. Blentech Corporation
89 F.3d 320 (7th Cir. 1996)

CUDAHY, Circuit Judge.

Felipe Ruiz's case turns on a rather mystifying choice-of-law problem. Ruiz, a citizen of Illinois, suffered an injury in his home state from an allegedly defective product manufactured in California by a California corporation. The manufacturer has dissolved, but another California corporation has followed in its footsteps by purchasing its principal assets and continuing its business. Ruiz seeks to make the successor corporation answer for his tort claims against the manufacturer. Illinois and California have different rules for determining when one corporation is responsible, as a successor, for the tort liabilities of its predecessors. The district court concluded that Illinois' rules, which are less favorable to Ruiz, should apply. As a consequence of this conclusion, it entered summary judgment against him. Ruiz appeals this judgment, arguing that the district court incorrectly resolved the conflict between the rules adopted, respectively, by Illinois and California. We affirm.

I

Felipe Ruiz operated a screw conveyor in a food processing plant in Schiller Park, Illinois. On June 16, 1992, he somehow became entangled in the conveyor's machinery and sustained several grievous injuries, the most severe of which left him paralyzed. He soon filed a lawsuit in an Illinois state court, bringing claims of strict products liability and negligence, among others. The case was removed to the district court on the basis of diversity jurisdiction.

Ruiz eventually directed his case at five defendants, all of whom had some legally significant connection with the screw conveyor. Three of the five had been involved in the sale of the conveyor to Ruiz's employer. These defendants were Weiler and Company, a Wisconsin corporation, Weiler East, a New Jersey corporation, and Dan Schwerdtfeger, an agent for those two companies. Another defendant was Custom Stainless Equipment, the California corporation that had manufactured the conveyor in 1983 and had dissolved in 1986. The last defendant was an entity that Ruiz identified as the successor to Custom Stainless' liabilities in tort. When Custom Stainless dissolved, it sold all of its assets for cash to Blentech, another California corporation. Blentech continued to manufacture Custom Stainless' product lines under its own name, using the same product designs, the same factory, the same management and the same employees. Ruiz contended in the district court that California law defined the relationship between Custom Stainless and Blentech and, therefore, between Blentech and himself. According to Ruiz's interpretation of that law, Blentech's assimilation of Custom Stainless included an assumption of strict liability for any defective products that Custom Stainless had manufactured.

Schwerdtfeger and the two Weilers settled with Ruiz, and Ruiz won a default judgment against the defunct Custom Stainless. The fifth defendant, Blentech, resisted Ruiz's claim by arguing that it did not belong in the case at all. Blentech maintained that its purchase of Custom Stainless' assets had not involved a conveyance of Custom Stainless' tort liabilities, and it made this argument the basis for a motion for summary judgment. The district court held that Illinois law defined the relationship between Custom Stainless, Blentech and Ruiz, and that Illinois law would not permit Ruiz to sustain an action against Blentech. Therefore, the court granted summary judgment to Blentech. *See Ruiz v. Weiler,* 860 F. Supp. 602, 604-06 (N.D. Ill. 1994).

II

Ruiz appeals the entry of summary judgment in Blentech's favor. When considering a summary judgment, our review of matters both factual and legal is *de novo.* Of course there are not issues of fact; Ruiz only contests the district court's legal rulings. He contends that the district court erred by holding that Illinois tort law determined the nature of Blentech's liabilities as a successor to Custom Stainless. He believes that California corporate law should inform this determination and that it prescribes a result favorable to him. He also argues that, even if Illinois law applies, the district court misinterpreted its prescriptions regarding the products liability of successor corporations. . . .

Ruiz's challenge to the summary judgment for Blentech relies on his argument that the choice of state law governing the crucial issues in the case was in error. In a diversity case, of course, state law governs, and the district court determines what state law to apply in accordance with the choice-of-law principles of the state in which it sits. . . . The district court here was bound by the choice-of-law method defined by the Restatement (Second) of Conflicts of Law, which Illinois has adopted. . . .

The Second Restatement method is constructed around the principle that the state with the most significant contacts to an issue provides the law governing that issue. A court therefore conducts a separate choice-of-law analysis for each issue in a case, attempting to determine which state has the most significant contacts with that issue. . . . The Second Restatement enumerates specific factors that identify the state with the most significant contacts to an issue, and the relevant factors differ according to the area of substantive law governing the issue and according to the nature of the issue itself. *See, e.g.*, Restatement (Second) at §§6, 145, 188. To properly apply the Second Restatement method, a court must begin its choice-of-law analysis with a characterization of the issue at hand in terms of substantive law. By prescribing this analytical approach, the Second Restatement follows the principle of *depecage*,[1] which has been long applied in connection with various methods for choice of law. *See* Willis L.M. Reese, *Depecage: A Common Phenomenon in Choice of Law*, 73 Colum. L. Rev. 58 (1973).

With respect to Ruiz's claim against Blentech, the choice-of-law analysis had crucial importance. Only two states have significant contacts with the issues raised. California was the place of the legal relationship between Custom Stainless and Blentech; and Illinois was the place of Ruiz's residence and his injury. The decisive issue in the case was whether Blentech had succeeded to Custom Stainless' liabilities by virtue of its purchase of Custom Stainless' assets and its business. Illinois and California shared a basic rule about corporate successor liability, but California provided an exception to that rule that was not available in Illinois.

Illinois mandates that, as a general rule of corporate law, a corporation that purchases the principal assets of another corporation does not assume the seller's liabilities arising from tort claims or from any other kind of claims. . . . Illinois does recognize four exceptions to this rule. The purchasing corporation assumes the seller's liabilities when: (1) it expressly agrees to assume them; (2) the asset sale amounts to a *de facto* merger; (3) the purchaser is a mere continuation of the seller; (4) the sale is for the fraudulent purpose of escaping liability for the seller's obligations. *Hernandez*, 26 Ill. Dec. at 778-79, 388 N.E.2d at 779-80. California's corporate law establishes the same general rule and the same four exceptions. *Ray v. Alad Corp.*, 19 Cal. 3d 22, 136 Cal. Rptr. 574, 578, 560 P.2d 3, 7 (1977).

California departs from the Illinois rules, however, by adopting a fifth exception. That exception provides that a corporation that purchases a manufacturing business and continues to produce the seller's line of products assumes strict liability in tort for defects in units of the same product line previously manufactured and distributed by the seller. *Ray*, 136 Cal. Rptr. at 582, 560 P.2d at 11. This "products line" exception applies in cases involving tort claims where: (1) the plaintiff lacks an adequate remedy against the seller/manufacturer; (2) the purchaser knows about product risks associated with the line of products that it continues; and (3) the seller transfers good will associated with the product line.

---

1. When roughly translated, depecage refers to the process of cutting something into pieces. Here it refers to the process of cutting up a case into individual issues, each subject to a separate choice-of-law analysis.

The difference between Illinois' and California's rules is decisive here because Ruiz's case against Blentech depends entirely upon whether the "products line" exception applies. Although Ruiz does argue that he can maintain a cause of action against Blentech even without this exception, it is clear that he cannot do so under the basic rule of successor liability, which both Illinois and California share. Blentech did not acquire Custom Stainless' obligations to Ruiz under one of the four standard exceptions to the general rule of successor liability. Blentech has not agreed to assume that obligation. It did expressly agree to assume all of Custom Stainless' tort liabilities arising before the date of the asset sale in 1986, but it emphatically disclaimed all liabilities arising after that date, and Ruiz was not injured until 1992. Neither did Blentech and Custom Stainless combine their corporate identities, either through a *de facto* merger or through some other means. In either Illinois or California, a court will conclude that an asset sale merges two corporations or makes the buyer the continuation of the seller only if it finds an identity of ownership between the two. In effect, the *de facto* merger and continuation exceptions are identical; each exception depends upon an identity of ownership between the seller and purchaser. . . . When Custom Stainless sold its assets to Blentech, Custom Stainless' owners received cash, not stock, and they have not participated in the ownership of Blentech in any way. Finally, Ruiz makes no allegation that the asset sale between Blentech and Custom Stainless was an occasion for fraud; moreover, nothing in the record even remotely supports such an allegation. Thus, Blentech can be liable to Ruiz only if the "products line" exception applies.

The "products line" exception can apply in Illinois courts only through the choice of foreign law. On numerous occasions, Illinois courts have specifically declined to make the "product line" exception part of Illinois law, and they have therefore declined to apply it to tort claims governed by Illinois law. . . . Illinois courts have not, however, specifically decided whether they would apply the "products line" exception to an issue governed by the law of a state which accepted that exception. Our research of Illinois law suggests that the crucial issue in this case is a matter of first impression in Illinois.

As it must, Ruiz's challenge to the district court's decision depends upon the contention that an Illinois court would choose California's "products line" exception as part of the law governing his claim against Blentech. In deciding whether to apply Illinois or California law, the district court considered whether Illinois or California had the most significant contacts with the tort that Ruiz alleged. *Ruiz v. Weiler & Co., Inc.*, 860 F. Supp. 602, 604 (N.D. Ill. 1994). It found that the two states had essentially equal contacts with Ruiz's action, but it concluded that the balance tipped towards Illinois because there is a presumption in favor of applying the laws of the state where the alleged tort occurred. . . . On the basis of this conclusion, the district court applied Illinois law to all of the issues in the case, including both of the issues relevant to Ruiz's claim against Blentech.

Ruiz argues that the district court's choice-of-law analysis was fundamentally flawed because it failed to follow the principles of *depecage*. As we have noted, these principles prescribe that the rules of different states can determine different issues in a single case. In Ruiz's view, the issue of Blentech's assumption of Custom Stainless' tort liabilities is separate and distinct from other issues in the case; and he believes it requires an analysis of significant contacts different from the one that the district court performed. When he applies the principles of *depecage* to this issue, Ruiz concludes that the district court should have determined the legal relationship between Custom Stainless and Blentech according to California law with its "products line" exception.

Ruiz correctly invokes the principle of *depecage* and persuasively criticizes the district court's choice-of-law analysis. The district court threw a single analytical blanket over all of the issues in the case, and this is, of course, a departure from the prescriptions of the Second Restatement. The district court should have conducted one analysis for issues of successor liability and a separate analysis for issues of tort liability. As a matter of corporate law, the issue of successor liability pertains to different significant contacts than does the tort law issue of liability for Ruiz's injury. California clearly has the most significant contacts with a sale of corporate assets by one California corporation to another. Here both corporations have their principal places of business in California. Consequently, California corporate law should determine what liabilities, if any, were conveyed when Custom Stainless sold its business to Blentech. It is equally clear that Illinois has the most significant relationship to an alleged tort befalling one of its citizens within its borders. The district court erred when, ignoring *depecage*, it applied Illinois law to all the issues in the case.

The question we now encounter is whether that error makes any difference here. Ruiz certainly believes that it does. He characterizes California's "product line" exception as a rule of corporate law—a relative of the other four exceptions to the rule determining corporate successor liability. Unlike his argument about the flaws in the district court's choice-of-law analysis, this contention is not so clearly correct. The area of substantive law to which the "product line" exception belongs is a difficult question, and the courts of several states have struggled to decide whether it is a part of corporate law or of tort law.

This struggle has been especially evident in Illinois. As we have noted, Illinois courts have often considered whether to make the "products line" exception a part of Illinois law. In opinions addressing this issue, they have advanced various explanations of the nature of this exception. Consequently, the Illinois precedents contain conflicting characterizations of the exception. Many of these cases insist that there is one and only one way to characterize this rule in terms of substantive law, but these same courts do not agree about what that interpretation would be. . . .

. . . Part of the uncertainty over the nature of the "products line" exception comes from the fact that the exception has a variety of sources each of which articulates a different rationale for the exception and each of which places it within a different realm of substantive law. The way in which the exception is characterized may depend upon the source from which it comes. Michigan law has apparently established the "products line" exception as a means of making it easier to prove that the predecessor and successor corporations have effected a *de facto* merger, although the reasoning behind this conclusion is not entirely clear. *See Turner v. Bituminous Casualty Co.*, 397 Mich. 406, 244 N.W.2d 873, 879-80 (1976). Therefore, in Michigan, the exception seems to be an instrument of corporate law that defines what must pass through an asset sale. In New Jersey, on the other hand, the supreme court has held that the exception has nothing to do with determining whether a *de facto* merger occurred. Instead, the court there held that the exception is an instrument for preserving the system of strict liability for products liability claims by imposing duties on manufacturers. *See Ramirez v. Amsted Indus., Inc.*, 86 N.J. 332, 431 A.2d 811, 819-20 (1981).

For our purposes, California's understanding of the nature of the "products line" exception is what matters. *See* Restatement (Second) at §7(3). At least with respect to this argument, Ruiz does not ask us to generate an abstract version of the exception out of the air and make it a part of Illinois law. In any event, this would be a futile effort because Illinois courts have so emphatically rejected this request when other claimants have made it. . . . Ruiz does, however, ask us to apply a California rule to his case through choice of law. Because the only California rules that we can apply here are the rules of corporate law, we must see whether California characterizes the "products line" exception as a matter of corporate law.

California courts have quite clearly established that the exception is a matter of products liability law, not corporate law. The California Supreme Court derived the exception from its line of cases prescribing strict liability in tort for injuries resulting from defective products. *See Ray*, 136 Cal. Rptr. at 579-80, 560 P.2d at 8-9 (discussing the landmark products liability cases of *Greenman v. Yuba Power Prods., Inc.*, 59 Cal. 2d 57, 27 Cal. Rptr. 697, 377 P.2d 897 (1963) and *Escola v. Coca Cola Bottling Co. of Fresno*, 24 Cal. 2d 453, 150 P.2d 436 (1944)). Moreover, California has limited the application of the exception to cases in which it preserves a plaintiff's ability to collect on a valid strict liability claim. *See Lundell*, 190 Cal. App. 3d at 1556, 236 Cal. Rptr. at 78. In this way, California has established the "products line" exception as a means of advancing the cost-shifting purposes behind its regime of strict liability for injuries caused by defective products. Unlike Michigan, California has not employed the exception generally as a means to limit efforts by corporations to erase corporate identity in the course of asset sales. Instead, California uses the exception to insure that manufacturers generally will bear the costs of defective products.

As we have noted, Ruiz could maintain his case against Blentech only if the "products line" exception applied. Because the exception is a matter of California tort law, not California corporate law, it does not apply to this case. The judgment of the district court is, therefore,

AFFIRMED.

QUESTIONS

1. How would Mr. Ruiz's claim (a product liability claim) be treated if the acquisition of Custom Stainless Equipment Corp. (Target Co.) had been structured as:

    a. A direct merger?
    b. A stock purchase?
    c. A triangular merger? Does it matter to your analysis of this question if the merger is structured as a *reverse* versus a *forward* triangular merger?

2. What happened to the company's assets when Custom Stainless Equipment Corp. was dissolved?

3. In the principal case, Mr. Ruiz did not sue the shareholders of Custom Stainless Equipment to recover from them. Why not?

4. What is the choice of law problem that confronts the court in this case?

5. What is the public policy concern raised by long-tail claimants such as Mr. Ruiz?

6. How should the law address this public policy concern? What is the role of the courts in this area of the law?

7. How can a Bidder in an asset acquisition—or for that matter, in structuring any acquisition, regardless of the method used to complete the transaction—minimize Bidder's risk of unexpected liabilities (such as the claim presented by Mr. Ruiz)?

NOTES

1. Statute of Limitations. The dissolution proceeding allows Target Co. to distribute to its shareholders the assets remaining *after* satisfying the known claims of Target's creditors. What happens to those claims that are not ascertainable at the time that Target commences the statutorily authorized dissolution process? These long-tail claims—such as tort claims that are based on injuries that occur or are discovered (knowable) only after dissolution—present difficult questions of fairness. By distributing out Target's assets in liquidation of the company's business affairs, the shareholders of Target have been able to appropriate for themselves funds that should have been available to satisfy long-tail claimants, such as Mr. Ruiz.

This externality—the opportunity to shift foreseeable risks of Target's business operations to third parties who are not represented in the process of negotiating Bidder's acquisition of Target—is an inherent attribute of this method of acquisition. One obvious solution is to allow long-tail claimants to recover from Target's shareholders the amounts paid as liquidating distributions in the dissolution of Target. Indeed, many state statutes continue to follow the traditional approach and allow those long-tail claimants whose claims mature shortly after payment of the liquidating distribution to Target shareholders to recover directly from the shareholders on their claim. Typically, these state statutes provide that the claim must be brought within two or three years after the dissolution proceeding has concluded, and further provide that each shareholder of Target will be liable only to the extent of the shareholder's personal distribution received in liquidation of Target (or a pro rata share of the claim, whichever is less). Some states have even extended this limitations period to five years, following the lead of prior versions of the MBCA, although the current MBCA provision establishes a limitations period of three years after publication of notice. *See* MBCA §14.07. Although this enhances the possibility of the long-tail claimant recovering for harm suffered, this remedy is not without its costs. The tort victim, such as Mr. Ruiz, is left with the often expensive (and therefore, rather unappealing) prospect of chasing down a diffuse group of shareholders in order to recover for his injuries.

2. Delaware's (Innovative) Procedures for Dissolution. The externalities presented by long-tail claimants in the context of asset acquisitions are a problem that has long vexed public policy makers. On the one hand, business managers (and shareholder investors) need the certainty provided by statutes of limitations, which operate to cut off claims of potential creditors, so that they may proceed confidently to invest in and manage the newly acquired assets and business operations of its predecessor, Target Co. On the other hand, the long-tail claims presented by plaintiffs such as Mr. Ruiz are compelling and present difficult questions of fairness that often result in liability being imposed on Bidder, contrary to the agreement it originally made with the seller, Target.

In 1987, the Delaware legislature responded to this long-standing public policy dilemma by adopting an innovative set of procedures as part of its dissolution provisions. Like the traditional approach followed by most states, Delaware section 281(a) requires Target Co. to use the acquisition proceeds from the sale of all its assets to satisfy all claims known to the corporation at the time of its dissolution. However, the provisions of Delaware sections 280-282 go further and establish two distinct, alternative procedures that allow Delaware corporations to dissolve *and* eliminate potential director and shareholder liability with respect to the amounts distributed in a liquidating distribution. The mandatory default rule of Delaware section 281(b) specifies that the board of directors of the dissolving corporation must adopt a plan of distribution that includes "such provision as will be reasonably likely to be sufficient to provide compensation for claims that have not been made known, or that have not arisen, but that, based on facts known to the corporation, . . . are likely to arise or to become known to the corporation . . . within *ten years* after the date of dissolution." (*emphasis added*). Such claims are not limited to contract creditors but also include long-tail claimants such as product liability claims of the type at issue in *Ruiz*.

> Under section 281(c), directors of a corporation that complies with Section 281(b) in making liquidating distributions will not be liable to creditors whose claims are ultimately unsatisfied. However, because of the lack of notice and other procedural safeguards under the Section 281(b) default procedure, there is no presumption of reasonableness as to the provision made to pay claims and obligations as there is under section 281(a) for directors of a corporation that complies with the provisions of section 280. Thus, compliance with section 281(b)'s "reasonably likely to be sufficient" standard will, in principle, always be litigable and, therefore, may present a risky situation for corporate directors regardless of their good faith and due care. . . . Section 281(c) provides that directors of a dissolved corporation who have complied with section 281(a) or 281(b) cannot be held personally liable to the claimants of the dissolved corporation. This "safe harbor" provided to directors under section 281(c) is a "primary benefit" that flows from compliance with section 281(a) or 281(b).

Edward P. Welch, et al., FOLK ON THE DELAWARE GENERAL CORPORATION LAW §§281.03 and 281.05 (Fundamentals 2020 Edition). Moreover, if the amount provided in the plan of distribution is ultimately found to be insufficient, Delaware section 282(a) still allows claimants to pursue shareholders for amounts received in the liquidating distribution or their pro rata share of the claim, whichever is less, subject to the statute of limitations on the underlying claim itself.

For those shareholders and directors of dissolving corporations who want greater certainty as to their ability to avoid personal liability on long-tail claims, the Delaware legislature adopted an optional safe harbor procedure, which is set forth in section 280(c)(3). It bears emphasizing that compliance with the detailed notice provisions of Delaware §280(a) is required in order to take advantage of this optional safe harbor. As part of the dissolution proceeding conducted pursuant to section 280, Target Co. may petition the court to determine the amount and form of security that is "reasonably likely to be sufficient to provide compensation for claims that have not been made known to the corporation or that have not risen but that, based on facts known to the corporation or successor entity, are likely to arise or to become known to the corporation or successor entity within 5 years after the date of dissolution or such longer period of time as the Court of Chancery may determine not to exceed 10 years after the date of dissolution." Del. §280(c)(3). The Delaware statute also allows the court to appoint a guardian *ad litem* to represent the long-tail claimants. *Id.* Assuming compliance with the court's orders as well as the detailed statutory notice requirements of Delaware §280(a), Target Co. shareholders will not be liable for any claims initiated after the three-year winding-up period established by §278. *See* Del. §282(b). Likewise, Target Co. directors will not be personally liable to any long-tail claimants either. *See* Del. §281(c).

The MBCA has been amended to add a provision that is similar to the innovation of Delaware §280(c)(3). MBCA §14.08 authorizes a safe harbor procedure to protect directors and shareholders of a dissolving corporation against personal liability on long-tail claims (contingent claims that are not barred by publication) by providing security for claims that are reasonably estimated to arise within three years of the effective date of Target's dissolution. This three-year period is considerably shorter than the potential ten-year period provided for in Delaware §280(c)(3), raising anew the public policy dilemma presented by these various long-tail claims.

Notwithstanding the appeal of Delaware's new procedure, there are some practical problems in administering this new safe harbor. Most prominently, the courts have had some difficulty in determining what qualifies as an adequate security arrangement in satisfaction of the terms of Delaware §280(c)(3). *See,* e.g., *In re Rego Co.,* 623 A.2d 92 (Del. Ch. 1992); and *In re Krafft-Murphy Co.,* 82 A.3d 696 (Del. 2013).

‖4‖

Selected Federal Securities Law Provisions that Apply to Negotiated Business Combinations

In Chapter 2, we analyzed the state law provisions that regulate the different methods for structuring an acquisition. In the process, we noted that if either Bidder Co. or Target Co. is publicly traded, then the rules of the New York Stock Exchange (NYSE) apply, or the corresponding provisions of other organized trading markets, such as the Nasdaq Stock Market (Nasdaq). We also noted certain differences in the legal rules that apply depending on the type of consideration used to complete the acquisition of Target Co. (i.e., cash vs. Bidder Co. stock).

As part of our discussion of the problems in Chapter 2, we referred to various aspects of the federal securities laws that may also apply depending on (1) how the transaction is structured; (2) whether the companies involved are publicly traded or privately held; and, (3) whether the acquisition consideration consists of cash or Bidder stock (or, perhaps, a combination of both). Although we noted how a transaction may implicate various provisions of the federal securities laws, we deferred any discussion of these federal rules until after we finished our analysis of the requirements imposed by state law. In this chapter, we take up the various provisions of the federal securities laws that must be considered by the mergers and acquisitions (M&A) lawyer in the context of planning an acquisition transaction.

As a preliminary word of caution, this chapter presents only a cursory overview of the various provisions of the Securities Act of 1933 (1933 Act) and the Securities Exchange Act of 1934 (1934 Act) that must be considered as a threshold matter in planning any business combination. In no way, however, is this a substitute for taking an introductory law school course on securities regulation. Indeed, M&A lawyers must be well informed about the topics covered in this chapter, regardless of whether they represent publicly traded companies or privately held corporations. As we will see in this chapter, however, the provisions of the federal securities laws that get triggered are substantially different depending on whether your client is publicly traded or privately held. So, the modern M&A lawyer, practicing on either Wall Street or Main Street, is typically knowledgeable about *both* corporate and securities laws.

Briefly summarized, this chapter focuses on certain aspects of the 1933 Act and the 1934 Act. Whenever Bidder Co. proposes to use its own stock (or other securities) as the acquisition consideration, Bidder, as the issuer, must comply with the registration requirements of the 1933 Act or find an exemption. This obligation to register the transaction or establish an exemption is imposed on *all* issuers, regardless of whether the company is privately held or publicly traded. On the other hand, whenever Bidder or Target is publicly traded *and* must obtain shareholder approval for a proposed transaction, then the company *must* comply with the federal proxy rules (promulgated pursuant to the 1934 Act) in connection with the company's solicitation of the necessary shareholder votes to approve a proposed acquisition.

Finally, both Bidder and Target must be mindful of the antifraud provisions of the federal securities laws in the context of any communications (oral or written) regarding a proposed acquisition transaction. Most notably, the M&A lawyer must be aware of the implications of Rule 10b-5 in the context of either a negotiated or a hostile acquisition. Although issues surrounding potential liability for Rule 10b-5 violations may surface in a number of different (and often quite novel) ways during the course of negotiating and documenting a particular business combination, M&A lawyers routinely face problems involving potential Rule 10b-5 violations in two contexts when planning an acquisition. The first involves the issue of what triggers the company's duty to disclose ongoing negotiations for a merger or some other type of business combination. The second recurring area of concern under Rule 10b-5 for the transaction planner involves the potential for insider trading in anticipation of a business combination, such as the potential merger of two companies. The possibility of insider trading in the face of a pending merger not only implicates a potential violation of Rule 10b-5, but may lead to liability under §16(b) of the 1934 Act as well, both of which we will briefly consider at the end of this chapter.

A.   Securities Act of 1933: Issuance of Shares (or Other Securities) to Complete the Acquisition

At the risk of oversimplifying the rules covered in the introductory law school course on securities regulation, all of the 1933 Act can be effectively summarized in the following sentence:

> Any time a corporation, regardless whether it is a large, publicly traded or a small, privately held company, proposes to use an instrumentality of interstate commerce in order to issue its stock (or any other securities such as convertible debentures), the corporation (as the issuer of the securities) *must* register the offering *or* find an exemption for the transaction.

In a situation where Bidder offers all cash to acquire Target, the requirements of the 1933 Act do not apply since Bidder does not propose to *issue* (*sell*) any of its *securities* as part of the acquisition transaction. However, if either Bidder or Target is publicly traded, then the federal proxy rules may still apply, regardless of the type of acquisition consideration used in the deal. The requirements imposed by the federal proxy rules are described below.

1.   Registered Transactions

If Bidder Co. issues its stock as the acquisition consideration, then it must either register or find an exemption for this distribution of its securities. Thus, the 1933 Act is transaction oriented; that is, the 1933 Act registers transactions, not securities. This is an important distinction. Since only the transaction in which the issuer sells the security to the investor is registered, this means that any subsequent resale of the security is a *separate transaction*. As such, either the resale must be registered or an exemption must be available to the selling shareholder.

In those cases where the investor seeks to dispose of a security purchased from the issuer in a registered transaction, the provision most often relied on by the seller to exempt this resale is the §4(a)(1) exemption. This workhorse exemption is important because most of the trading activity in the U.S. public markets (such as the trading activity on the NYSE) is exempt under §4(a)(1) as transactions "not involving an issuer, underwriter, or dealer." Consequently, those resales by persons who fall under the statutory definition of an "underwriter" or a "dealer" are not entitled to the §4(a)(1) exemption. The scope of the 1933 Act definitions of these terms is an important component of the study of federal securities regulation.

If the distribution transaction is *registered*, the issuer must file a registration statement (usually using Form S-4 in the context of an M&A transaction) with the Securities and Exchange Commission (SEC), which is subject to review by the staff of the Division of Corporate Finance of the SEC. Once the SEC review process is complete and the SEC declares the registration statement effective, Bidder may issue (i.e., sell) its securities in order to complete its acquisition of Target. Before the SEC will declare the registration effective, however, Target shareholders must have received the *prospectus* (which is typically Part I of the registration statement filed by the issuer with the SEC). The process of preparing and filing the registration statement, as well as completing the SEC's review of the required disclosures contained therein, is obviously time-consuming and expensive. Moreover, in those cases where Bidder proposes to use its stock as the acquisition consideration, the closing date for the transaction will be dependent on the timing of the SEC staff's review of the adequacy and completeness of the registration statement—which adds further delay in completing Bidder's acquisition of Target. Finally, as we will discuss below, certain insiders of Target, referred to as *affiliates* (or *control persons*), may be subject to restrictions on the resale of the stock (or other securities) of Bidder that they receive in the acquisition transaction.

In cases where a publicly traded Bidder Co. proposes to issue additional shares in order to acquire a publicly traded Target Co. (such as AT&T's acquisition of DirecTV using a package of cash *and* shares of AT&T's common stock as the acquisition consideration), the 1933 Act must be satisfied (since AT&T is *issuing* additional authorized but unissued shares of AT&T common stock to complete its acquisition of DirecTV). Historically, there was some confusion as to whether this type of "exchange offer" qualified as a "sale of securities" sufficient to trigger the requirements of the 1933 Act. Today, however, it is clear that this transaction involves a distribution of the issuer's (i.e., AT&T's) securities in exchange for valuable consideration (the surrender of DirecTV shares). Since

DirecTV was publicly traded, this distribution involves a public offering of AT&T stock for which no exemption is available and therefore the transaction must be registered. In certain other types of acquisitions, however, an exemption may be available to eliminate the need to register the issuance of Bidder's stock.

The fundamental premise underlying the issuer's registration obligation under §5, which is the very heart of the 1933 Act, is that prospective investors must be provided with adequate information about the issuer and the terms of the proposed offering. By doing so, the prospective investor can make an informed decision as to whether to purchase the issuer's securities. The prospectus filed by the issuer (generally as Part I of its registration statement) must set forth detailed disclosures, including information about the issuer, its business and financial affairs, and the proposed use of the proceeds received from the offer and sale of the company's stock. The specific items of information that issuers must include in their registration statements are set forth as items of required disclosure; the requirements differ slightly depending on the form of registration statement used by the issuer (known as the *registrant*). The SEC has promulgated a number of different forms of registration statements (e.g., Form S-1, Form S-3, and Form S-4), and detailed instructions for completing these required items of disclosure are set forth in Regulation S-K (also promulgated by the SEC). The form of registration statement most often used in an acquisition transaction is Form S-4, which is used in business combination transactions in which securities (i.e., Bidder's stock) are being used as the acquisition consideration. Indeed, in connection with AT&T's acquisition of DirecTV, the parties prepared a Form S-4 in satisfaction of the registration obligation imposed under §5 of the 1933 Act. The scope of disclosure required under the terms of Form S-4 is described in more detail later in this chapter, as part of our examination of the SEC's federal proxy rules promulgated pursuant to the 1934 Act.

2. Exempt Transactions

Compliance with the registration obligation imposed by §5 of the 1933 Act very often imposes greater costs than the public benefits to be obtained from the issuer's preparation of the detailed disclosures that are required to be part of a registration statement. Congress provided for this possibility by adopting various provisions to exempt the issuer from the §5 registration obligation. These exemptions are set forth in §§3 and 4 of the 1933 Act. For our purposes, the most important of these exemptions are (1) the statutory private placement authorized by §4(a)(2) of the 1933 Act; and (2) the limited offering exemptions made available by the rules of Regulation D, originally promulgated by the SEC in 1982 and further refined by subsequent SEC rulemaking.

The proposed transaction between Google and Nest Labs illustrates the need for some type of exemption from the delay and expense associated with filing a registration statement to satisfy the obligations imposed on the issuer by the 1933 Act. Although the deal involved an all-cash purchase price (and thus no issuance of securities that would trigger the requirements of the 1933 Act), very different considerations are presented if the purchase price were to involve the issuance of Bidder's stock. Assume that, instead of using cash, Google proposed to issue 2 percent of its stock as the acquisition consideration to acquire Nest Labs, and further assume that Nest Labs had four equal shareholders (consisting of the two founders and two venture capital investors). Under this modified set of deal terms, each of the four shareholders of Nest Labs would receive 0.5 percent of Google stock in exchange for all of their shares of Nest Labs stock. The federal proxy rules do not apply to this transaction because (i) Nest Labs is not a 1934 Act reporting company (even though the transaction may be structured so as to grant the Nest Labs shareholders a right to vote); and further, (ii) Google (even though a reporting company) is not required to solicit shareholder approval for the transaction as a matter of state law (assuming, of course, that Google has sufficient authorized but unissued shares). But what about the requirements of the 1933 Act?

Private Placements.   In cases where a Bidder (such as Google) issues shares in an acquisition transaction, the 1933 Act will apply. However, where the terms of the acquisition call for the securities (i.e., Google shares) to be issued to a limited number of investors (such as the four shareholders of Nest Labs), the expense and delay associated with preparing a registration statement will not produce sufficient public benefits to justify these transaction costs. Therefore, the issuer (Google) will try to qualify the issuance of its stock under one of the available exemptions, most often using the *private placement exemption* available under §4(a)(2) of the 1933 Act.

Under the terms of the §4(a)(2) private placement exemption, the issuer must show that the proposed transaction does not involve a public offering of its securities — that is, the issuer must show that it is a nonpublic offering. In *SEC v. Ralston Purina, Inc.*, 346 U.S. 119, 125-126 (1953), the seminal case analyzing whether an offering of the issuer's securities was public or private, the Supreme Court defined a nonpublic offering for purposes of §4(a)(2)[1] as a transaction where the proposed offer and sale of the issuer's securities was limited to those who could "fend for themselves," and thus did need not the protections provided by the 1933 Act. In the context of Google's acquisition of Nest Labs, assuming that Google's stock is to be used as the acquisition consideration, then the Supreme Court's decision in *Ralston Purina* requires the issuer (Google) to establish that all the offerees and purchasers (i.e., the four shareholders of Nest Labs) had "access to the same kind of information that the [1933 Act] would make available in the form of a registration statement." *Id.*

The standards that must be satisfied in order to qualify an offeree as a "self-fending" type have been further developed by subsequent case law in the lower courts, often producing a hodgepodge of confusing (sometimes even conflicting) sets of requirements. The SEC subsequently stepped in to provide a safe harbor in response to pressure (from both the issuer community and the practicing bar) to provide more objective criteria as to what qualifies as a private placement for purposes of §4(a)(2) of the 1933 Act.

---

1. When the Supreme Court decision in *Ralston-Purina* was handed down in 1953, the statutory private placement exemption was found in §4(2) of the 1933 Act. Congressional enactment of the Jumpstart Our Business Startups (JOBS) Act in 2012 resulted in the renumbering of the provisions of §4 of the 1933 Act, and now the statutory private placement exemption is found in §4(a)(2).

Regulation D.   Today, the SEC's safe harbor standard for §4(a)(2) is set forth as Rule 506 of Regulation D. This regulation, originally promulgated in 1982, is composed of Rules 501 through 508 and today the substantive exemptions consist of Rules 504 and 506.[2] Consistent with Supreme Court precedent, there is no dollar limit on the private offering exemption available under Rule 506, so long as the offering is made only to "accredited purchasers" and there are no more than 35 "nonaccredited purchasers" who must also satisfy a Regulation D standard of "financial sophistication." Following the Great Recession, the SEC amended its definition of "accredited investor" pursuant to the legislative mandate contained in section 413 of the Dodd-Frank Act.[3]

The Regulation D requirement of "financial sophistication" has led to a rather substantial body of case law and academic commentary interpreting the standards that the issuer must satisfy to demonstrate the financial sophistication of those investors who do not qualify as accredited purchasers.[4] This is a substantial burden to impose on the issuer because the SEC has interpreted the scope of the Regulation D exemption to mean that a *single* purchaser who fails to satisfy the financial sophistication standard may destroy the basis of the exemption as to the *entire* offering. If the issuer loses the exemption, it will face liability under §12(a)(1) of the 1933 Act, which in effect allows *all* purchasers in the failed offering to rescind the transaction and recover from the issuer the purchase price they paid to acquire shares of issuer's stock.

By contrast, the other substantive exemption, Rule 504, is known as the *limited offering* exemption. Rule 504 was promulgated by the SEC pursuant to §3(b)(1) of the 1933 Act, which delegates rulemaking authority to the SEC to exempt offerings up to $5 million. Following the SEC amendments in 2016, Rule 504 permits offerings of up to $5 million in any 12-month period, with no limitations on the number of purchasers or their qualifications. Accordingly, the small offering exemption of Rule 504 may be helpful in planning the acquisition of small, private companies. However, where Bidder proposes to issue more than $5 million of its securities to acquire Target, the Rule 504 small offering exemption will not be available, and generally the issuer will be forced to rely on the private placement exemption to eliminate the need to file a registration

---

2. In 2016, the SEC amended Regulation D to eliminate Rule 505 and broadened the terms of Rule 504 to fill the void created by reducing the substantive exemptions of Regulation D from three to two.

3. On July 21, 2010, Congress enacted the Dodd-Frank Wall Street Reform and Consumer Protection Act, commonly referred to as the Dodd-Frank Act. *See* Public Law 111-203, 124 Stat. 1376. In the wake of the Great Recession of 2008-2009, Congress enacted the Dodd-Frank Act in order to implement a package of wide-ranging reforms in the regulation of our nation's capital markets.

4. In December 2019, the SEC proposed amendments to expand the definition of "accredited investor." "The proposed amendments are intended to update and improve the definition to identify more effectively the institutional and individual investors with the knowledge and expertise to participate in the private capital markets. Although the proposed amendments would provide issuers with additional tests for accredited investor status, the extent to which they would result in substantial new sources of capital is unclear." Ropes & Gray, LLP, *SEC Proposes Updates to Accredited Investor Definition*, Dec. 30, 2019, *available at:* https://www.ropesgray.com/en/newsroom/alerts/2019/12/SEC-Proposes-Updates-to-Accredited-Investor-Definition. Although the comment period expired in March 2020, no action has been taken by the SEC with respect to the proposed amendments as of Fall 2020.

statement for the transaction. There is no dollar limit on either the statutory private placement under §4(a)(2) or the safe harbor exemption under Rule 506(b), although the offering is limited to 35 non-accredited investors who meet the sophistication standard of Rule 506(b). When it was originally adopted, Regulation D was intended to facilitate capital formation by small businesses; but today, companies of all sizes rely on its exemptions to avoid the burdens of registration under the 1933 Act. And, in the context of M&A transactions, the Rule 506 private offering exemption is used most frequently where the acquisition consideration consists of Bidder's securities.[5]

Use of General Advertising or General Solicitation.   Historically, offerings conducted pursuant to a Regulation D exemption must be done on a nonpublic basis. In one of the more controversial aspects of Regulation D, the SEC has consistently prohibited the use of *any* general advertising or general solicitation ever since its adoption. This prohibition has often proved to be quite troubling for small businesses that do not have the services of financial advisors readily available to them to assist in the process of raising necessary capital. In these situations, small businesses generally have found it to be quite difficult — in some cases, virtually impossible — to recruit investors. In recent years, the SEC has attempted to soften this prohibition through a series of no-action letters that allow broker-dealer firms, in effect, to screen investors. These brokers in turn then match investors up with small business issuers seeking investment capital. More recently, however, the SEC adopted new Rule 506(c), which permits the use of general solicitation in connection with private placements, so long as the issuer takes reasonable steps to verify that *all* of the purchasers qualify as "accredited investors" under the SEC's definition of this term. *See* Keith Bishop, *SEC Enforcement Action Demonstrates That Timing Is Everything,* Jan. 23, 2019, *available at:* https://www.calcorporatelaw.com/sec-enforcement-action-demonstrates-that-timing-is-everything. The SEC adopted Rule 506(c) pursuant to the reforms enacted as part of the Jumpstart Our Business Startups (JOBS) Act.[6] It bears mentioning that the SEC recently implemented several other reform measures that Congress adopted in the JOBS Act, most notably provisions authorizing equity "crowdfunding." Crowdfunding generally refers to the use of the Internet to raise small amounts of money from a large group of investors in exchange for an ownership interest in the new business. The intended goal of these JOBS Act provisions was to stimulate the creation of jobs in the wake of the Great Recession. The primary focus of this important new addition to the federal securities laws is to enhance issuers' ability to raise capital by expanding their ability to reach potential sources of investment capital in order to launch and/or expand start-up businesses. As such, the scope and efficacy of

---

5. The "Section 4(a)(2) exemption and Reg D safe harbors are the most common exemptions used for stock issued as part of a merger or acquisition." Strafford, CLE Webinar, *Securities Law Challenges in Mergers and Acquisitions: Navigating Exemptions for Transfer or Issuance of Securities,* Jan. 30, 2019, *available at:* https://www.straffordpub.com/products/securities-law-challenges-in-mergers-and-acquisitions-navigating-exemptions-for-transfer-or-issuance-of-securities-2019-01-30#.

6. Pub. L. No. 112-106, 126 Stat. 306 (2012).

these JOBS Act reform measures lie outside the scope of our focus on business combination transactions.[7]

Restricted Securities and Rule 144. Shares that are issued by Bidder under any of the Regulation D exemptions, as well as securities that are sold in reliance on the §4(a)(2) private placement exemption, are treated as *restricted securities*. This means that there are significant restrictions on the resale of these shares, even if Bidder's stock is listed for trading on the NYSE or is otherwise publicly traded. The basis for imposing these limitations on resale is rooted in the fundamental tenet of the 1933 Act, which is to register (or exempt) *transactions*—not classes of securities. In order to protect the important 1933 Act concept of registering those *transactions* that qualify as a *distribution,* the SEC historically has imposed rather stringent limitations on the ability of the holder of restricted stock to dispose of these shares. Today, resales of restricted stock are largely governed by SEC's Rule 144.

Until recently, restricted stock could be resold by its owner pursuant to the terms of SEC Rule 144 only after the purchaser held the stock for one year. After satisfying this one-year holding period, owners of restricted stock were permitted to dispose of their shares in open-market transactions, but only in amounts that did not exceed the quantity limitations of Rule 144. After holding the restricted shares for two years, the shares were then freely tradable in open-market transactions without regard to the quantity limitations of Rule 144. Historically, the limitations on resale imposed by the terms of Rule 144 were an important consideration for Target shareholders to take into account in deciding whether to accept Bidder stock as acquisition consideration. If the issuance of Bidder shares was not registered, and therefore Target shareholders received restricted stock of Bidder at closing on the acquisition, it was important for Target shareholders to be aware of the economic risk that they were being asked to assume. Since these former Target shareholders received restricted stock of Bidder, as a practical matter, this meant that they were locked into an investment in Bidder for at least one year before they could rely on the protections of Rule 144 to permit resale of their Bidder shares.

However, effective February 2008, the SEC amended Rule 144 to substantially shorten the holding period imposed by the Rule. *See* Release No. 34-56914

---

7. In March 2020, the SEC issued Release No. 33-10763, in which it proposed amendments to the rules governing exempt offerings under the 1933 Act. "The proposed amendments are intended to address, among other things, gaps and complexities in the current exempt offering framework. Specifically, the proposed amendments (1) discuss the ability of issuers to move from one exemption to another exemption or [to a] registered offering, (2) clarify and establish consistent rules [regarding issuer] communications [including the permitted scope of "general solicitation"], (3) address gaps and inconsistencies in the current rules relating to . . . limits [on the dollar amount of the offering], and (4) harmonize certain differences in the disclosure [provisions of the various exemptions]." Cahill, Gordon & Reindel LLP, *SEC Proposes to Modernize and Harmonize Exempt Offerings Rules,* March 31, 2020, *available at:* https://www.cahill.com/publications/firm-memoranda/2020-03-31-sec-proposes-to-modernize-and-harmonize-exempt-offerings-rules/_res/id=Attachments/index=0/SEC%20Proposes%20To%20Modernize%20and%20Harmonize%20Exempt%20Offerings%20Rules.pdf. As of Fall 2020, no action has been taken by the SEC with regard to this set of proposed reforms.

(Dec. 6, 2007). The amendments to Rule 144 reduced the holding period from one year to six months for resale of restricted securities of reporting companies. Thus, under the amended rules, if the issuer is a reporting company that is current in its filing obligations under the 1934 Act (i.e, the "current public information requirement"), then non-affiliates may sell their restricted securities without any further limitations after satisfying the required six month holding period. Broadly speaking, a "non-affiliate" is a person who is not in "control" of the issuer of the securities, which, for our purposes, refers to the Bidder who uses its shares as the acquisition consideration. It bears emphasizing that the concept of "control" is an important one under the federal securities laws and has been the subject of intense scrutiny both by the courts and the commentators. For purposes of this discussion, executive officers, directors, and 10 percent shareholders of the issuer (i.e., Bidder) are generally to be treated as "affiliates" of the issuer. Furthermore, after one year, the requirement that the issuer meet the "current public information" requirement is eliminated. These reforms have substantially reduced the economic risk associated with the decision to take restricted shares of Bidder's stock under the predecessor provisions of Rule 144 by enhancing the liquidity of Bidder's shares in the hands of the former Target shareholders. *See* Keith F. Higgins, Thomas Holden, & Paul M. Kinsella, *SEC Adopts Amendments to Rules 144 and 145*, 22 INSIGHTS 8 (Jan. 2008).

Registration Rights. Another common way for Target shareholders to address the financial risk inherent in holding restricted stock of Bidder is to bargain for resale registration rights as part of the acquisition agreement. If Bidder is subject to a resale registration obligation, then after closing, Bidder must register the shares that were issued to Target shareholders. On registration, these shares of Bidder's stock will be freely tradable and thereby provide liquidity for the Target shareholders' investment in Bidder.

Resales by Control Persons and Rule 145. A further problem is presented where the resale of Bidder's stock is made by "affiliates" of Target Co., which is a constituent corporation in a merger transaction with Bidder Co., and where the acquisition consideration consists of Bidder's stock. This raises the question of whether these former Target shareholders may freely resell their Bidder shares after the transaction is completed, an issue that has been addressed by the SEC in Rule 145.

As part of the SEC reform measures described above, which became effective in February 2008, the SEC also amended Rule 145. Based on these revisions, securities of Bidder that are held by affiliates of the acquired company (i.e., Target) are now freely tradable, *provided* that these holders are *not* affiliates of Bidder (i.e., the acquiring company). As for those transactions that are effected pursuant to an exemption from registration (such as the private placement exemption under §4(a)(2), or its safe harbor provision, Rule 506), any securities issued in these transactions will result in the issuance of *restricted securities*, and therefore may be resold by an affiliate only pursuant to an effective registration statement or an available exemption, which most often will be Rule 144. *See* Cooley, LLP, *SEC Approves Major Changes to Rule 144 and Rule 145*, Jan. 2008 (law firm memo, copy on file with author). These changes in Rules 144 and 145 should serve to reduce the costs and burdens associated with using Bidder's stock as the acquisition currency.

QUESTIONS

1. Assume that you are counsel to Google in connection with its acquisition of all the stock of Nest Labs for cash. How would you advise Google as to the application of the federal securities law provisions that were described above?

2. How would your analysis of these federal securities law provisions change if Google proposed to acquire Nest Labs by issuing 2 percent of its common stock to the four equal shareholders of Nest Labs in exchange for all of their shares of Nest Labs common stock? If the shares issued to the Nest Labs shareholders are not registered, who has the burden to establish that of all the terms of an exemption have been satisfied?

3. From a public policy perspective, does it make sense to eliminate the need to register Google's stock in connection with its acquisition of Nest Labs? What about the shareholders of Google, the issuer? Do they need to know about the transaction? Does the 1933 Act address the information needs of Google's shareholders?

B.   Scope of Federal Proxy Rules

If shareholder approval is required for a particular acquisition and the company has a class of securities registered under §12 of the 1934 Act ("reporting companies"), then any solicitation of shareholder votes will trigger the provisions of §14 of the 1934 Act and the SEC rules promulgated thereunder (collectively referred to as the "federal proxy rules").

SEC's Proxy Rules.   Section 14(a) of the 1934 Act prohibits solicitation of proxies from shareholders of reporting companies unless made in compliance with the federal proxy rules. The process of soliciting proxies is governed by Regulation 14A, promulgated by the SEC pursuant to the authority delegated to it by Congress under the terms of §14(a) of the 1934 Act. Regulation 14A is a complex set of rules that govern the timing and the process of soliciting shareholder votes to approve an M&A transaction. In addition, the SEC has promulgated Schedule 14A, which sets forth the required items of information that must be included in the proxy statement pursuant to which proxies are solicited. Subject to certain limited exceptions, no solicitation of shareholder votes may be made unless the shareholder being solicited is provided with a written proxy statement that contains the items of information required by Schedule 14A. In the alternative, where Bidder Co. proposes to use its securities as the acquisition consideration and therefore must file a registration statement in order to satisfy the 1933 Act, then Form S-4 is to be used in lieu of Schedule 14A under the proxy rules. Not surprisingly, the information required by Form S-4 and Schedule 14A are very similar, at least insofar as the information required to be disclosed about the proposed acquisition transaction is concerned.

Proxy Statement. Like other required forms of disclosure, proxy statements have developed a conventional form of presentation for the various different types of acquisition transactions. For example, in the case of a proxy statement soliciting shareholder approval of a stock for stock merger in which only the vote of Target shareholders is required, the proxy statement will typically consist of: (1) a cover page that usually takes the form of a short letter to Target shareholders that briefly describes the proposed acquisition; (2) a formal notice of the meeting, which is usually one page; (3) a table of contents that lists the different items of disclosure contained in the proxy statement; and (4) the proxy statement itself. Under the detailed terms of Regulation 14A, and as a result of the SEC's disclosure initiative known as the "plain English rules," the typical proxy statement will consist of the following components (all of which should be referenced in the table of contents):

- A question-and-answer section
- A summary section (usually three to five pages in length) of narrative text and a few pages of financial and stock price information
- A section describing the risk factors related to the proposed transaction and/or the companies involved
- A section containing cautionary statements concerning any forward-looking information (such as sales projections, earnings forecasts, etc.) included in the proxy statement
- A section containing basic information about the details for conducting the shareholder meeting, addressing such things as the vote required, how to vote, how to change or withdraw a vote, and the effect of abstentions
- A section that provides a narrative description of the events and negotiations leading up to the parties' agreement
- A section setting forth the reasons that support the Target board's decision to approve the transaction and recommend shareholder approval as well
- A section detailing the analytical basis for the conclusion of the company's investment banker as to the fairness of the transaction — generally known as the *fairness opinion*
- A section that sets forth any interests that individual officers or directors might have in the transaction, with a particular focus on those interests that present a conflict of interest
- A section that describes the federal income tax consequences to the company and its shareholders
- A section setting forth required financial information disclosures, including pro forma financial information regarding the transaction
- A detailed summary of the terms of the merger agreement, which is a bit of an oxymoron since this "summary" often runs to ten pages or more
- The exhibits, at the very end of the proxy statement, which typically consist of a copy of the merger agreement itself and a copy of the investment banker's fairness opinion

"Say-on-Pay" Votes and "Golden Parachute" Arrangements. Section 951 of the Dodd-Frank Act is popularly referred to as the "say-on-pay requirement." "Say-on-pay" refers to the process by which shareholders of publicly traded companies are asked to give a nonbinding advisory vote on compensation arrangements for the companies' senior executive officers. The Dodd-Frank Act also includes provisions that relate to compensation paid to senior executives as part of an M&A transaction. On January 25, 2011, the SEC adopted its final rules, implementing the congressional mandate of §951 of the Dodd-Frank Act. *See* SEC Release Nos. 33-9178, 34-63768 (Jan. 25, 2011):

> Under the new rules, public companies subject to the federal proxy rules must provide their shareholders with an advisory vote on executive compensation — generally known as a "say-on-pay" vote — at least once every three calendar years, and an advisory vote on the desired frequency of say-on-pay votes at least once every six calendar years.
>
> They must also provide additional proxy statement disclosure regarding the general nature and effect of the "say-on-pay" and frequency votes, including whether the votes are binding. In addition, the Compensation Discussion and Analysis disclosure ("CD&A") must address whether and how the company has responded to the most recent say-on-pay vote, and, to the extent material in determining compensation policies and decisions, include disclosure concerning the results of previous say-on-pay votes.
>
> The "say-on-pay" and frequency votes apply to annual meetings of shareholders at which directors will be elected or special meetings in lieu thereof taking place on or after January 21, 2011. Smaller reporting companies — those with a public float of less than $75 million — are not required to conduct say-on-pay or frequency votes until annual meetings occurring on or after January 21, 2013.

GOLDEN PARACHUTES

> The new rules also require disclosure, in connection with M&A transactions, of "golden parachute" arrangements. "Golden parachutes" are broadly defined to include all agreements and understandings between the target or the acquirer and each named executive officer of the target or the acquirer [i.e., Bidder Co.] that relate to an M&A transaction. Certain types of compensation deemed unrelated to the M&A transaction are excluded from the definition of "golden parachute" payments.
>
> The disclosure requirements apply to solicitation materials for all types of M&A transactions involving a company subject to the SEC's proxy rules (whether involving a tender offer, merger or sale of all or substantially all of a company's assets). Exceptions are provided for third party bidders' tender offer statements in transactions that are not subject to Rule 13e-3, and for foreign private issuers. For an M&A transaction requiring shareholder approval under the SEC's proxy rules, the soliciting company must also include an advisory shareholder vote regarding golden parachute arrangements, known as "say-on-golden parachute" vote.
>
> A company may, but is not required to, address golden parachute arrangements as part of the say-on-pay vote taken at its annual meeting. A company will not be required to include an advisory vote on golden parachutes in a subsequent proxy statement for an M&A transaction if the golden parachute arrangements have already been voted upon in an annual say-on-pay vote and have not been modified to increase total compensation.

These new golden parachute rules are effective for proxy statements and other schedules and forms relating to M&A transactions initially filed on or after April 25, 2011.

Julia Cowles, et al., *Selected 2011 Developments in Corporate Law*, 2012 Annual Review, State Bar of California, Business Law News, 7, 9-10.

As a general proposition,

The theory behind "Say on Pay" is that giving shareholders a periodic referendum on executive compensation will decrease the likelihood that overly generous compensation packages will be paid to senior executives. The vote may also motivate companies to align manager compensation with manager performance more closely, in the belief that shareholders respond most negatively to large compensation packages when stock performance is poor. Additionally, although the vote is non-binding, it might nonetheless powerfully influence the behavior of compensation committees [of publicly traded companies] who may wish to avoid the public opprobrium associated with a negative vote.

Jeffery D. Bauman, 2012 Supplement to Corporations: Law & Policy (7th ed. 2010), at 53.

Fairness Opinions.   Although there is no requirement under the federal proxy rules that a company obtain a fairness opinion, it has become customary for boards of directors to obtain opinions from their investment bankers as to the fairness of the price offered in an M&A transaction. However, almost as soon as it became commonplace to obtain a *fairness opinion*, criticism as to the practice surfaced. First, critics complained that quite often, the fairness opinion was rendered by the very same investment banking firm that brought the deal to the company—and the very same firm that will typically collect a fee when the transaction closes—which, for many commentators, hardly seems to be a completely objective appraiser. While some fairness opinions are written by independent firms that have no connection to the deal, the vast majority of such opinions are written by investment banking firms who stand to make substantial sums of money if the deal closes, thereby creating inherent conflicts of interest that have long troubled many observers of the M&A markets. Critics have raised other concerns as well. "The opinions are loaded with legal disclaimers. [Although the SEC's proxy rules do require disclosure of the fairness opinion obtained by the company as part of its proxy statement, the opinion is] often out of date by the time shareholders vote on the deal. Furthermore, the opinions tend to be so narrowly focused on the specifics of the agreement being evaluated that they do not even address whether directors could have secured a better deal." David Henry, *A Fair Deal—But for Whom?* Business Week, Nov. 24, 2003, at 108.

This same 2003 news article went on to report that Eliot Spitzer, then the attorney general of New York, was expected to investigate Wall Street's practice of preparing fairness opinions, although he had not yet taken any action. Shortly thereafter, however, in November 2004, the National Association of Securities Dealers (NASD) announced that it was requesting comment on whether the NASD should propose a rule that would address conflicts of interest that inevitably arise when its members prepare fairness opinions in M&A transactions. In June 2005, the NASD proposed Rule 2290 to address the procedures used by its members to prepare fairness opinions, as well as its members' practices surrounding the disclosure of fairness opinions. As a self-regulatory organization (SRO), the NASD's rulemaking was subject to SEC approval before the rule could be made effective.[8] This process culminated in final SEC approval of NASD Rule 2290 (now FINRA Rule 5150) in October 2007. FINRA Rule 5150 establishes "(1) certain required disclosures in fairness opinions issued by its members that are disclosed to public shareholders; and (2) certain required procedures in connection with its member firms' fairness opinions practice." Anne L. Benedict, *New FINRA Fairness Opinion Requirements*, 21 INSIGHTS 22 (Dec. 2007).

Specifically, Rule 5150 lists certain disclosures "that must be included in the fairness opinion if, at the time the fairness opinion is issued to the board of directors of a company, the member firm issuing the fairness opinion *knows or has reason to know* that the fairness opinion will be provided or described to the public shareholders of the company. . . ." *Id.* (*emphasis in original*). In its adopting release, the SEC made clear that if stockholder approval of the transaction is required (thereby triggering the preparation of a proxy statement in compliance with the SEC's proxy rules), the member firm will be "deemed to have reason to know that the fairness opinion will be shared with the public." *Id.*, at n. 3. Most notable, at least for our purposes, is that one of the required items of disclosure calls for disclosure of the fact that the compensation that a member firm will receive for rendering a fairness opinion is *contingent* upon successful completion of the M&A transaction. *See* FINRA Rule 5150(a)(1). It bears emphasizing, however, that the rule, as finally adopted, neither requires quantitative disclosure (as to the amount of the banker's fee) nor bans contingent fee arrangements, despite recommendations to the contrary that were submitted by several commentators. Indeed, no less than the likes of "institutional investing heavyweights CALPERS and the AFL-CIO [argued] that a flat prohibition on contingent fee arrangements would be appropriate. . . . [However, securities industry professionals] took the opposite point of view arguing that . . . boards of directors [acting on behalf of the company in making the fee arrangement with the investment banking firm] are quite capable of taking into account any impact that a contingent fee arrangement might have on the [banker's] fairness analysis." Stephen I. Glover & William J. Robers, *The NASD's Proposed Rule Governing Fairness Opinion Practice*, THE M&A LAWYER 22-23 (Sept. 2005).

In the end, the SEC indicated, in its Adopting Release, that it believes "that a descriptive disclosure that alerts shareholders to the existence of a contingent compensation arrangement is sufficient to serve the basic purpose of highlighting for investors that the [member firm] stands to benefit financially from the successful completion of the transaction, and therefore, that a conflict of interests may exist." *See* SEC Release No. 34-56645 (Oct. 11, 2007), 72 FR 59317,

---

8. The Financial Industry Regulatory Authority (FINRA) combined NASD's regulatory functions with the regulatory arm of the NYSE effective as of July 30, 2007. All registered broker-dealers that had been members of NASD automatically became members of FINRA. NASD (and now FINRA) serve as the primary regulator for broker-dealer firms, whose investment banking departments are the key providers of fairness opinions. FINRA combines the regulatory, enforcement, and arbitration functions of the NYSE with those of NASD, and the resulting SRO is now known as FINRA.

59319 (Oct. 19, 2007). *Query:* Do you find the SEC's reasoning on this issue persuasive?

Recent Delaware Case Law Regarding Fairness Opinions. In addition to the disclosure requirements of FINRA Rule 5150, the Delaware judiciary has weighed in on this issue. Delaware case law is clear that

> [d]irectors of Delaware corporations owe to their stockholders a duty of disclosure derived from their ordinary fiduciary duties of care and loyalty. A common disclosure claim [in connection with an M&A transaction] is that the target company's disclosure document . . . was materially misleading or incomplete with respect to the fairness opinion relied on by the target's board in evaluating the transaction. The Delaware courts have decided numerous cases involving claims that disclosure as to some element of a fairness opinion—projections, analysis, assumptions—is defective.

Blake Rohrbacher and John Mark Zeberkiewicz, *Fair Summary: Delaware Framework for Disclosing Fairness Opinions,* 63 BUS. LAW. 881, 881 (2008). As a direct outgrowth of this fiduciary duty obligation, there are legions of Delaware cases addressing disclosure claims relating to investment bankers' fairness opinions in M&A transactions. These cases supplement the disclosures otherwise required under the federal securities laws and provide an additional source of merger-related litigation. While the issues described above regarding fairness opinions continued to be litigated,

> the Court of Chancery has noted that financial disclosures in recent years have been far more robust than they had been in the past—undoubtedly due largely to the court's rulings. In response, plaintiffs have sought new lines of attack, and the Delaware courts have therefore begun to focus not only on the disclosure of underlying financial analyses broadly, but also on specific and discrete issues involving fairness opinions and projections as well as on issues beyond the fairness opinion itself,[1] most notably the financial advisors potential conflicts and incentives.

Blake Rohrbacher and John Mark Zeberkiewicz, *Fair Summary II: An Update on Delaware's Disclosure Regime Regarding Fairness Opinions,* 66 BUS. LAW. 943, 943-944 (Aug. 2011). One can only expect that Delaware case law on this topic will continue to evolve in the coming years. *See, e.g., Chen v. Howard-Anderson,* 87 A.3d 648 (Del. Ch. 2014); and *Vento v. Curry,* 2017 WL 1076725 (Del. Ch. March 22, 2017); *see also* James Langston, *Cleary M&A and Corporate Governance Watch: Assessing Financial Advisor Compensation Disclosure Following* Vento v. Curry, April 10, 2017, *available at:* https://www.clearymawatch.com/ 2017/04/assessing-financial-advisor-compensation-disclosure-following-vento-v-curry/ (The *Vento* case "provides important guidance for principals and

---

1. *Fair Summary, supra* note 1 [63 Bus. Law 881], at 882-883 ("Fairness opinions are typically produced at the request of the target's board (or special committee of the board) by investment bankers who value the target company and come up with a range of values. The bankers then opine on whether the consideration to be received by the target company's stockholders in the business combination is fair. . . ." (footnote omitted)).

[their] financial advisors in evaluating whether disclosure of a financial advisor's transaction-related compensation is required when seeking shareholder approval of an M&A transaction.").

Rule 14a-9. By way of general summary, you can readily see that the preparation of the proxy statement is a labor-intensive, costly, and time-consuming process. Careful attention to detail is required lest any material information be omitted. Liability for false and/or misleading disclosures in the proxy statement is imposed by the terms of Rule 14a-9, which bears a strong family resemblance to the terms of Rule 10b-5. Specifically, liability under Rule 14a-9 extends to materially misleading disclosures contained in a proxy statement filed pursuant to Regulation 14A. In this regard, it is important to emphasize that Schedule 14A establishes only a minimum level of required disclosure. The standard to avoid liability for false and misleading proxy disclosure requires full and adequate disclosure of all material facts, which may require disclosure beyond that mandated by the specific items set forth in Schedule 14A. The relevant standard of materiality is analyzed in detail in the Supreme Court's landmark decision, *Basic Inc. v. Levinson*, set forth below.

C.   Rule 10b-5 and the Timing of Disclosure of Acquisition Negotiations

Basic Incorporated v. Levinson
485 U.S. 224 (1988)

Justice BLACKMUN delivered the opinion of the Court.

This case requires us to apply the materiality requirement of §10(b) of the Securities Exchange Act of 1934, (1934 Act), and the Securities and Exchange Commission's Rule 10b-5, promulgated thereunder, in the context of preliminary corporate merger discussions. . . .

I

Prior to December 20, 1978, Basic Incorporated was a publicly traded company primarily engaged in the business of manufacturing chemical refractories for the steel industry. As early as 1965 or 1966, Combustion Engineering, Inc., a company producing mostly alumina-based refractories, expressed some interest in acquiring Basic, but was deterred from pursuing this inclination seriously because of antitrust concerns it then entertained. . . .

Beginning in September 1976, Combustion representatives had meetings and telephone conversations with Basic officers and directors, including petitioners here, concerning the possibility of a merger. During 1977 and 1978, Basic made three public statements denying that it was engaged in merger negotiations.[4] On December 18, 1978, Basic asked the New York Stock Exchange to suspend trading in its shares and issued a release stating that it had been "approached" by another company concerning a merger. On December 19, Basic's board endorsed Combustion's offer of $46 per share for its common stock, and on the following day publicly announced its approval of Combustion's tender offer for all outstanding shares.

Respondents are former Basic shareholders who sold their stock after Basic's first public statement of October 21, 1977, and before the suspension of trading in December 1978. Respondents brought a class action against Basic and its directors, asserting that the defendants issued three false or misleading public statements and thereby were in violation of §10(b) of the 1934 Act and of Rule 10b-5. Respondents alleged that they were injured by selling Basic shares at artificially depressed prices in a market affected by petitioners' misleading statements and in reliance thereon.

. . . [T]he District Court granted summary judgment for the defendants. It held that, as a matter of law, any misstatements were immaterial: there were no negotiations ongoing at the time of the first statement, and although negotiations were taking place when the second and third statements were issued, those negotiations were not "destined, with reasonable certainty, to become a merger agreement in principle."

The United States Court of Appeals for the Sixth Circuit . . . reversed the District Court's summary judgment, and remanded the case. 786 F.2d 741 (1986). The [Sixth Circuit] reasoned that while petitioners were under no general duty to disclose their discussions with Combustion, any statement the company voluntarily released could not be " 'so incomplete as to mislead.' " In the Court of Appeals' view, Basic's statements that no negotiations were taking place, and that it knew of no corporate developments to account for the heavy trading activity, were misleading. With respect to materiality, the court rejected

---

4. On October 21, 1977, after heavy trading and a new high in Basic stock, the following news item appeared in the Cleveland Plain Dealer:

> "[Basic] President Max Muller said the company knew no reason for the stock's activity and that no negotiations were under way with any company for a merger. He said Flintkote recently denied Wall Street rumors that it would make a tender offer of $25 a share for control of the Cleveland-based maker of refractories for the steel industry." App. 363

On September 25, 1978, in reply to an inquiry from the New York Stock Exchange, Basic issued a release concerning increased activity in its stock and stated that

> "management is unaware of any present or pending company development that would result in the abnormally heavy trading activity and price fluctuation in company shares that have been experienced in the past few days." Id., at 401.

On November 6, 1978, Basic issued to its shareholders a "Nine Months Report 1978." This Report stated:

> "With regard to the stock market activity in the Company's shares we remain unaware of any present or pending developments which would account for the high volume of trading and price fluctuations in recent months." Id., at 403.

the argument that preliminary merger discussions are immaterial as a matter of law, and held that "once a statement is made denying the existence of any discussions, even discussions that might not have been material in absence of the denial are material because they make the statement made untrue." . . .

We granted certiorari to resolve the split, see Part III, *infra*, among the Courts of Appeals as to the standard of materiality applicable to preliminary merger discussions, . . .

II

. . . The Court . . . explicitly has defined a standard of materiality under the securities laws, see *TSC Industries, Inc. v. Northway, Inc.*, 426 U.S. 438 (1976), concluding in the proxy-solicitation context that "[a]n omitted fact is material if there is a substantial likelihood that a reasonable shareholder would consider it important in deciding how to vote." Acknowledging that certain information concerning corporate developments could well be of "dubious significance," the Court was careful not to set too low a standard of materiality; it was concerned that a minimal standard might bring an overabundance of information within its reach, and lead management "simply to bury the shareholders in an avalanche of trivial information—a result that is hardly conducive to informed decision making." It further explained that to fulfill the materiality requirement "there must be a substantial likelihood that the disclosure of the omitted fact would have been viewed by the reasonable investor as having significantly altered the 'total mix' of information made available." We now expressly adopt the *TSC Industries* standard of materiality for the §10(b) and Rule 10b-5 context.

III

The application of this materiality standard to preliminary merger discussions is not self-evident. Where the impact of the corporate development on the target's fortune is certain and clear, the *TSC Industries* materiality definition admits straightforward application. Where, on the other hand, the event is contingent or speculative in nature, it is difficult to ascertain whether the "reasonable investor" would have considered the omitted information significant at the time. Merger negotiations, because of the ever-present possibility that the contemplated transaction will not be effectuated, fall into the latter category.

A

Petitioners urge upon us a Third Circuit test for resolving this difficulty. Under this approach, preliminary merger discussions do not become material until "agreement-in-principle" as to the price and structure of the transaction has been reached between the would-be merger partners. See *Greenfield v. Heublein, Inc.*, 742 F.2d 751, 757 (CA3 1984), cert. denied, 469 U.S. 1215, 105 S. Ct. 1189, 84 L. Ed. 2d 336 (1985). By definition, then, information concerning any negotiations not yet at the agreement-in-principle stage could be withheld or even misrepresented without a violation of Rule 10b-5.

Three rationales have been offered in support of the "agreement-in principle" test. The first derives from the concern expressed in *TSC Industries* that an investor not be overwhelmed by excessively detailed and trivial information, and focuses on the substantial risk that preliminary merger discussions may collapse: because such discussions are inherently tentative, disclosure of their existence itself could mislead investors and foster false optimism. The other two justifications for the agreement-in-principle standard are based on management concerns: because the requirement of "agreement-in-principle" limits the scope of disclosure obligations, it helps preserve the confidentiality of merger discussions where earlier disclosure might prejudice the negotiations; and the test also provides a usable, bright-line rule for determining when disclosure must be made.

None of these policy-based rationales, however, purports to explain why drawing the line at agreement-in-principle reflects the significance of the information upon the investor's decision. The first rationale, and the only one connected to the concerns expressed in *TSC Industries*, stands soundly rejected, even by a Court of Appeals that otherwise has accepted the wisdom of the agreement-in-principle test. "It assumes that investors are nitwits, unable to appreciate—even when told—that mergers are risky propositions up until the closing." *Flamm v. Eberstadt*, 814 F.2d [1169, 1175 (7th Cir.) *cert. denied*, 484 U.S. 853 (1987)]. Disclosure, and not paternalistic withholding of accurate information, is the policy chosen and expressed by Congress. We have recognized time and again, a "fundamental purpose" of the various Securities Acts, "was to substitute a philosophy of full disclosure for the philosophy of *caveat emptor* and thus to achieve a high standard of business ethics in the securities industry." . . .

The second rationale, the importance of secrecy during the early stages of merger discussions, also seems irrelevant to an assessment whether their existence is significant to the trading decision of a reasonable investor. To avoid a "bidding war" over its target, an acquiring firm often will insist that negotiations remain confidential, see, *e.g.*, *In re Carnation Co.*, Exchange Act Release No. 22214, 33 S.E.C. Docket 1025 (1985), and at least one Court of Appeals has stated that "silence pending settlement of the price and structure of a deal is beneficial to most investors, most of the time." *Flamm v. Eberstadt*, 814 F.2d, at 1177.[11]

We need not ascertain, however, whether secrecy necessarily maximizes shareholder wealth—although we note that the proposition is at least disputed as a matter of theory and empirical research—for this case does not concern the *timing* of a disclosure; it concerns only its accuracy and completeness. We face here the narrow question whether information concerning the existence and status of preliminary merger discussions is significant to the reasonable investor's trading decision. Arguments based on the premise that some disclosure

---

11. Reasoning backwards from a goal of economic efficiency, that Court of Appeals stated: "Rule 10b-5 is about *fraud*, after all, and it is not fraudulent to conduct business in a way that makes investors better off. . . . " 814 F.2d, at 1177.

would be "premature" in a sense are more properly considered under the rubric of an issuer's duty to disclose. The "secrecy" rationale is simply inapposite to the definition of materiality.

The final justification offered in support of the agreement-in-principle test seems to be directed solely at the comfort of corporate managers. A bright-line rule indeed is easier to follow than a standard that requires the exercise of judgment in the light of all the circumstances. But ease of application alone is not an excuse for ignoring the purposes of the Securities Acts and Congress' policy decisions. Any approach that designates a single fact or occurrence as always determinative of an inherently fact-specific finding such as materiality, must necessarily be overinclusive or underinclusive. . . . After much study, the Advisory Committee on Corporate Disclosure cautioned the SEC against administratively confining materiality to a rigid formula.[14] Courts also would do well to heed this advice.

We therefore find no valid justification for artificially excluding from the definition of materiality information concerning merger discussions, which would otherwise be considered significant to the trading decision of a reasonable investor, merely because agreement-in-principle as to price and structure has not yet been reached by the parties or their representatives. . . .

C

Even before this Court's decision in *TSC Industries*, the Second Circuit had explained the role of the materiality requirement of Rule 10b-5, with respect to contingent or speculative information or events, in a manner that gave that term meaning that is independent of the other provisions of the Rule. Under such circumstances, materiality "will depend at any given time upon a balancing of both the indicated probability that the event will occur and the anticipated magnitude of the event in light of the totality of the company activity." *SEC v. Texas Gulf Sulphur Co.*, 401 F.2d [833, 849 (2d Cir. 1968) (en banc), *cert. denied sub nom. Coates v. SEC*, 394 U.S. 976 (1969)]. Interestingly, neither the Third Circuit decision adopting the agreement-in-principle test nor petitioners here take issue with this general standard. Rather, they suggest that with respect to preliminary merger discussions, there are good reasons to draw a line at agreement on price and structure.

In a subsequent decision, the late Judge Friendly, writing for a Second Circuit panel, applied the *Texas Gulf Sulphur* probability/magnitude approach in the specific context of preliminary merger negotiations. After acknowledging

---

14. "Although the Committee believes that ideally it would be desirable to have absolute certainty in the application of the materiality concept, it is its view that such a goal is illusory and unrealistic. The materiality concept is judgmental in nature and it is not possible to translate this into a numerical formula. The Committee's advice to the [SEC] is to avoid this quest for certainty and to continue consideration of materiality on a case-by-case basis as disclosure problems are identified." House Committee on Interstate and Foreign Commerce, Report of the Advisory Committee on Corporate Disclosure to the Securities and Exchange [SEC], 95th Cong., 1st Sess., 327 (Comm. Print 1977).

that materiality is something to be determined on the basis of the particular facts of each case, he stated:

> Since a merger in which it is bought out is the most important event that can occur in a small corporation's life, to wit, its death, we think that inside information, as regards a merger of this sort, can become material at an earlier stage than would be the case as regards lesser transactions—and this even though the mortality rate of mergers in such formative stages is doubtless high.

SEC v. Geon Industries, Inc., 531 F.2d 39, 47-48 (1976). We agree with that analysis.

Whether merger discussions in any particular case are material therefore depends on the facts. Generally, in order to assess the probability that the event will occur, a factfinder will need to look to indicia of interest in the transaction at the highest corporate levels. Without attempting to catalog all such possible factors, we note by way of example that board resolutions, instructions to investment bankers, and actual negotiations between principals or their intermediaries may serve as indicia of interest. To assess the magnitude of the transaction to the issuer of the securities allegedly manipulated, a factfinder will need to consider such facts as the size of the two corporate entities and of the potential premiums over market value. No particular event or factor short of closing the transaction need be either necessary or sufficient by itself to render merger discussions material.[17]

As we clarify today, materiality depends on the significance the reasonable investor would place on the withheld or misrepresented information. The fact-specific inquiry we endorse here is consistent with the approach a number of courts have taken in assessing the materiality of merger negotiations. Because the standard of materiality we have adopted differs from that used by both courts below, we remand the case for reconsideration of the question whether a grant of summary judgment is appropriate on this record. . . .

---

17. To be actionable, of course, a statement must also be misleading. Silence, absent a duty to disclose, is not misleading under Rule 10b-5. "No comment" statements are generally the functional equivalent of silence. See *In re Carnation Co.,* Exchange Act Release No. 22214, 33 S.E.C. Docket 1025 (1985). See also New York Stock Exchange Listed Company Manual §202.01, reprinted in 3 CCH Fed. Sec. L. Rep. ¶ 23,515 (1987) (premature public announcement may properly be delayed for valid business purpose and where adequate security can be maintained); American Stock Exchange Company Guide §§401-405, reprinted in 3 CCH Fed. Sec. L. Rep. ¶¶ 23, 124A-23, 124E (1985) (similar provisions). It has been suggested that given current market practices, a "no comment" statement is tantamount to an admission that merger discussions are underway. See *Flamm v. Eberstadt,* 814 F.2d, at 1178. That may well hold true to the extent that issuers adopt a policy of truthfully denying merger rumors when no discussions are underway, and of issuing "no comment" statements when they are in the midst of negotiations. There are, of course, other statement policies firms could adopt; we need not now advise issuers as to what kind of practice to follow, within the range permitted by law. Perhaps more importantly, we think that creating an exception to a regulatory scheme founded on a prodisclosure legislative philosophy, because complying with the regulation might be "bad for business," is a role for Congress, not this Court. See also *id.,* at 1182 (opinion concurring in judgment and concurring in part).

V

In summary:

1. We specifically adopt, for the §10(b) and Rule 10b-5 context, the standard of materiality set forth in *TSC Industries, Inc. v. Northway, Inc.*, 426 U.S., at 449, 96 S. Ct., at 2132.
2. We reject "agreement-in-principle as to price and structure" as the bright-line rule for materiality.
3. We also reject the proposition that "information becomes material by virtue of a public statement denying it."
4. Materiality in the merger context depends on the probability that the transaction will be consummated, and its significance to the issuer of the securities. Materiality depends on the facts and thus is to be determined on a case-by-case basis. . . .

The judgment of the Court of Appeals is vacated, and the case is remanded to that court for further proceedings consistent with this opinion.
It is so ordered. . . .

NOTES

1. NYSE Guidelines.   The policies of the NYSE provide an important source of disclosure obligation for publicly traded companies, as reflected in the following excerpt.

‖ NYSE Listed Company Manual

202.05   TIMELY DISCLOSURE OF MATERIAL NEWS DEVELOPMENTS

A listed company is expected to release quickly to the public any news or information which might reasonably be expected to materially affect the market for its securities. This is one of the most important and fundamental purposes of the listing agreement which the company enters into with the Exchange.

A listed company should also act promptly to dispel unfounded rumors which result in unusual market activity or price variations. . . .

202.01   INTERNAL HANDLING OF CONFIDENTIAL CORPORATE MATTERS

Unusual market activity or a substantial price change has on occasion occurred in a company's securities shortly before the announcement of an important corporate action or development. Such incidents are extremely embarrassing and damaging to both the company and the Exchange since the public may quickly conclude that someone acted on the basis of inside information.

Negotiations leading to mergers and acquisitions, . . . [or] the making of arrangements preparatory to an exchange or tender offer, . . . are the type of developments where the risk of untimely and inadvertent disclosure of corporate plans are most likely to occur. Frequently, these matters require extensive discussion and study by corporate officials before final decisions can be made. Accordingly, extreme care must be used in order to keep the information on a confidential basis.

Where it is possible to confine formal or informal discussions to a small group of the top management of the company or companies involved, and their individual confidential advisors where adequate security can be maintained, premature public announcement may properly be avoided. In this regard, the market action of a company's securities should be closely watched at a time when consideration is being given to important corporate matters. If unusual market activity should arise, the company should be prepared to make an immediate public announcement of the matter.

At some point it usually becomes necessary to involve other persons to conduct preliminary studies or assist in other preparations for contemplated transactions, e.g., business appraisals, tentative financing arrangements, attitude of large outside holders, availability of major blocks of stock, engineering studies and market analyses and surveys. Experience has shown that maintaining security at this point is virtually impossible. Accordingly, fairness requires that the company make an immediate public announcement as soon as disclosures relating to such important matters are made to outsiders.

2. Form 8-K Disclosure Requirements.

2. Form 8-K Disclosure Requirements.   The 1934 Act imposes periodic disclosure obligations on reporting companies. Historically, publicly traded companies generally made disclosure by filing three quarterly reports on Form 10-Q and an annual report on Form 10-K, along with an annual proxy statement. In addition, reporting companies historically have been required to file a current report on Form 8-K, although traditionally the events that would trigger a Form 8-K filing obligation have been limited to a handful of significant events. However, as noted earlier in this casebook, in the wake of the financial scandals involving Enron and WorldCom, Congress enacted the Sarbanes-Oxley Act (SOX). Under Section 409 of the Sarbanes-Oxley Act of 2002, Congress mandated that the SEC move to a "real-time disclosure" model. Proposed even before the provisions of SOX became final, the SEC adopted new Form 8-K rules that became effective in August 2004, and which were later amended in 2006. These new rules "represent the SEC's decision to implement 'real time disclosure' by overlaying enhanced current reporting requirements through Form 8-K [filing obligations] on the traditional periodic reporting system. The new rules are designed to provide investors with greater and more timely disclosure of significant and material corporate events. . . ." Wilmer, Cutler, Pickering, Hall & Dorr, LLP, *Keeping Current with Form 8-K: A Practical Guide,* Dec. 2004, at 2 (law firm memo, copy on file with author).

The SEC's new rules significantly expanded the range of events that must be reported, and further, significantly shortened the time period for filing the Form 8-K disclosure to four business days after a triggering event occurs. The SEC's expanded Form 8-K disclosure requirements accelerate a trend that pre-dates enactment of SOX. Even before the SEC's new Form 8-K rules became effective, "many public companies [had established] practices of communicating with their investors and the market outside of their [periodic] Exchange Act reports through a variety of means, including press releases, analyst calls, discussions with financial press and other media, participation in conferences, and website postings. While less formal than Exchange Act reporting, these communications served to provide material information to the market on a relatively current basis. As a result, investors and analysts now generally expect to receive material information in 'real time.' In addition, stock markets have required and encouraged current disclosure of material developments through press releases by companies with listed securities." *Id.* at 1.

For our purposes, among the most important of the expanded disclosures now required by Form 8-K is Item 1.01, which calls for the company to disclose that it has entered into a "material definitive agreement" not made in the ordinary course of business, the definition of which would include agreements relating to a *material* merger, acquisition, or divestiture. Of course, compliance with this new disclosure obligation still entails the determination that the acquisition agreement at issue is "material," which as we have seen in the principal case is often a complex matter requiring difficult judgment calls to be made. It also bears emphasizing that Form 8-K must be filed within four business days after entering into any such material agreement.

   3. Duty to Disclose.   By itself, Rule 10b-5 does not impose a duty to disclose. Where does this duty come from? The most important source of a duty to disclose for publicly traded companies is the periodic reporting obligations imposed by the terms of the 1934 Act. However, once you speak—whether you are volunteering information in a periodic filing *or* by way of a press release announcing a proposed acquisition *or* in response to an inquiry from a regulator—then Rule 10b-5 requires that you speak truthfully, providing full and adequate disclosure of *all material* facts. This is the very clear message of *Basic Inc. v. Levinson,* a point that was emphasized by the Supreme Court in its opinion in *Matrixx Initiatives, Inc. v. Siracusano,* 131 S. Ct. 1309 (2011). During the course of its opinion, the Supreme Court observed:

> §10(b) and Rule 10b-5(b) do not create an affirmative duty to disclose any and all material information. Disclosure is required under these provisions only when necessary "to make . . . statements made, in the light of the circumstances under which they were made, not misleading." . . . Even with respect to information that a reasonable investor might consider material, companies can control what they have to disclose under these provisions *by controlling what they say to the market.*

Matrixx, 131 S. Ct. at 1321 (*emphasis added*). The Court's express statement that public companies can control what they *must* disclose "by controlling what they say to the market" has led many M&A lawyers to recommend that their clients keep merger negotiations strictly confidential in order to avoid triggering an obligation to disclose ongoing merger negotiations. The importance of this strategy has been highlighted in several recent cases. *See,* e.g., *Thesling v. Bioenvision, Inc.,* 374 F. App'x 141 (2d Cir. 2010); and *Levie v. Sears Roebuck & Co.,* 676 F. Supp. 2d 680, 686-688 (D. Ill. 2009). Notably, the courts have reiterated the following guidelines, which were drawn from the Supreme Court's decision in *Basic, Inc. v. Levinson,* and which (as made clear in the following commentary) are helpful to any public company in considering the scope of its disclosure obligations with respect to ongoing merger negotiations:

- A corporation is not required to disclose a fact merely because a reasonable investor would very much like to know that fact. Disclosure is required only when the corporation is subject to a duty to disclose.
- There are three circumstances in which a duty to disclose arises:
  (1)   when the rules of the SEC affirmatively require disclosure;
  (2)   when a corporation or corporate insider trades on the basis of material, non-public information; and
  (3)   when disclosure is required to make prior statements not misleading.
- No SEC rule requires disclosure of merger negotiations until they ripen into a definitive agreement, in which case a Current Report on Form 8-K is required.
- If, however, a company speaks about mergers or acquisitions or related topics, it must speak truthfully. So it could be materially misleading for a company to deny merger negotiations while negotiations are ongoing. But general statements about a company's business, financial projections, or strategy do not give rise to a duty to disclose merger negotiations that might materially impact its business, projections, or strategy. On the other hand, a statement that the company's business, projections, or strategy will not change could result in a disclosure obligation.
- In the absence of a duty to disclose, silence (or a "no comment" statement) is an acceptable response to questions about merger discussions.

The opinions underscore the fact-specific nature of their conclusions. Decisions regarding when to disclose merger negotiations (or other steps preceding an acquisition) should be made in light of all the relevant circumstances, including other statements [that] the company has made or intends to make and other actions [that] the company may be taking (such as where the company itself is trading in its stock through a repurchase program or otherwise). Disclosure obligations also may arise from other sources, such as stock exchange rules or state law. Finally, we note that there are sometimes tactical reasons for a company to make disclosure even when it has no legal obligation to do so.

Spencer D. Klein & Michael G. O'Bryan, Morrison & Foerster, LLP, *Recent Cases Remind M&A Participants of When Disclosure of Merger Negotiations Is Required,* July 14, 2010, *available at:* https://www.lexology.com/library/detail. aspx?g=1c6fdabf-67a3-43b1-a19d-72c10e361bca.

D.   Insider Trading in Anticipation of Acquisitions

1.   Misappropriation Liability Under Rule 10b-5 and SEC Rule 14e-3

United States v. O'Hagan
521 U.S. 642, 117 S. Ct. 2199 (1997)

Justice GINSBURG delivered the opinion of the Court.

This case concerns the interpretation and enforcement of §10(b) and §14(e) of the Securities Exchange Act of 1934, and rules made by the Securities and Exchange Commission pursuant to these provisions, Rule 10b-5 and Rule 14e-3(a). Two prime questions are presented. The first relates to the misappropriation of material, nonpublic information for securities trading; the second concerns fraudulent practices in the tender setting. In particular, we address and resolve these issues: (1) Is a person who trades in securities for personal profit, using confidential information misappropriated in breach of a fiduciary duty to the source of the information, guilty of violating §10(b) and Rule 10b-5? (2) Did the Commission exceed its rulemaking authority by adopting Rule 14e-3(a), which proscribes trading on undisclosed information in the tender offer setting, even in the absence of a duty to disclose? Our answer to the first question is yes, and to the second question, viewed in the context of this case, no.

I

Respondent James Herman O'Hagan was a partner in the law firm of Dorsey & Whitney in Minneapolis, Minnesota. In July 1988, Grand Metropolitan PLC (Grand Met), a company based in London, England, retained Dorsey & Whitney as local counsel to represent Grand Met regarding a potential tender offer for the common stock of the Pillsbury Company, headquartered in Minneapolis. Both Grand Met and Dorsey & Whitney took precautions to protect the confidentiality of Grand Met's tender offer plans. O'Hagan did no work on the Grand Met representation. Dorsey & Whitney withdrew from representing Grand Met on September 9, 1988. Less than a month later, on October 4, 1988, Grand Met publicly announced its tender offer for Pillsbury stock.

On August 18, 1988, while Dorsey & Whitney was still representing Grand Met, O'Hagan began purchasing call options for Pillsbury stock. Each option gave him the right to purchase 100 shares of Pillsbury stock by a specified date in September 1988. Later in August and in September, O'Hagan made additional purchases of Pillsbury call options. By the end of September, he owned 2,500 unexpired Pillsbury options, apparently more than any other individual investor. O'Hagan also purchased, in September 1988, some 5,000 shares of Pillsbury common stock, at a price just under $39 per share. When Grand Met announced its tender offer in October, the price of Pillsbury stock rose to nearly $60 per share. O'Hagan then sold his Pillsbury call options and common stock, making a profit of more than $4.3 million.

The Securities and Exchange Commission (SEC or Commission) initi-ated an investigation into O'Hagan's transactions, culminating in a 57-count indictment. The indictment alleged that O'Hagan defrauded his law firm and its client, Grand Met, by using for his own trading purposes material, nonpub-lic information regarding Grand Met's planned tender offer.[1] According to the indictment, O'Hagan used the profits he gained through this trading to conceal his previous embezzlement and conversion of unrelated client trust funds.[2] O'Hagan was charged with 20 counts of mail fraud, in violation of 18 U.S.C. §1341; 17 counts of securities fraud, in violation of §10(b) of the Securities Exchange Act of 1934 (Exchange Act), and SEC Rule 10b-5; 17 counts of fraudulent trading in connection with a tender offer, in violation of §14(e) of the Exchange Act, 15 U.S.C. §78n(e), and SEC Rule 14e-3(a); and 3 counts of violating federal money laundering statutes. A jury convicted O'Hagan on all 57 counts, and he was sentenced to a 41-month term of imprisonment.

A divided panel of the Court of Appeals for the Eighth Circuit reversed all of O'Hagan's convictions. 92 F.3d 612 (1996). Liability under §10(b) and Rule 10b-5, the Eighth Circuit held, may not be grounded on the "misappro-priation theory" of securities fraud on which the prosecution relied. *Id.*, at 622. The Court of Appeals also held that Rule 14e-3(a)—which prohibits trading while in possession of material, nonpublic information relating to a tender offer—exceeds the SEC's §14(e) rulemaking authority because the Rule con-tains no breach of fiduciary duty requirement. . . .

Decisions of the Courts of Appeals are in conflict on the propriety of the misappropriation theory under §10(b) and Rule 10b-5, . . . and on the legit-imacy of Rule 14e-3(a) under §14(e). We granted certiorari, 519 U.S. 1087, (1997), and now reverse the Eighth Circuit's judgment.

II

We address first the Court of Appeals' reversal of O'Hagan's convictions under §10(b) and Rule 10b-5. Following the Fourth Circuit's lead, see *United States v. Bryan*, 58 F.3d 933, 943-959 (1995), the Eighth Circuit rejected the

---

1. As evidence that O'Hagan traded on the basis of nonpublic information misappropri-ated from his law firm, the Government relied on a conversation between O'Hagan and the Dorsey & Whitney partner heading the firm's Grand Met representation. That conversation allegedly took place shortly before August 26, 1988. O'Hagan urges that the Government's evidence does not show he traded on the basis of nonpublic information. O'Hagan points to news reports on August 18 and 22, 1988, that Grand Met was interested in acquiring Pillsbury, and to an earlier, August 12, 1988, news report that Grand Met had put up its hotel chain for auction to raise funds for an acquisition. O'Hagan's challenge to the sufficiency of the evidence remains open for consideration on remand.

2. O'Hagan was convicted of theft in state court, sentenced to 30 months' imprison-ment, and fined. *See State v. O'Hagan*, 474 N.W.2d 613, 615, 623 (Minn. App. 1991). The Supreme Court of Minnesota disbarred O'Hagan from the practice of law. *See In re O'Hagan*, 450 N.W.2d 571 (Minn. 1990).

misappropriation theory as a basis for §10(b) liability. We hold . . . that criminal liability under §10(b) may be predicated on the misappropriation theory.[4] . . .

III

We consider next [whether] . . . the [SEC], as the Court of Appeals held, [exceeded] its rulemaking authority under §14(e) when it adopted Rule 14e-3(a) without requiring a showing that the trading at issue entailed a breach of fiduciary duty? We hold that the Commission, in this regard and to the extent relevant to this case, did not exceed its authority.

The governing statutory provision, §14(e) of the Exchange Act, reads in relevant part:

> "It shall be unlawful for any person . . . to engage in any fraudulent, decep-
> tive, or manipulative acts or practices, in connection with any tender offer. . . . The
> [SEC] shall, for the purposes of this subsection, by rules and regulations define,
> and prescribe means reasonably designed to prevent, such acts and practices as are
> fraudulent, deceptive, or manipulative." 15 U.S.C. §78n(e).

Section 14(e)'s first sentence prohibits fraudulent acts in connection with a tender offer. This self-operating proscription was one of several provisions added to the Exchange Act in 1968 by the Williams Act, . . . The section's second sentence delegates definitional and prophylactic rulemaking authority to the Commission. Congress added this rulemaking delegation to §14(e) in 1970 amendments to the Williams Act. . . .

Through §14(e) and other provisions on disclosure in the Williams Act, Congress sought to ensure that shareholders "confronted by a cash tender offer for their stock [would] not be required to respond without adequate informa-tion." *Rondeau v. Mosinee Paper Corp.*, 422 U.S. 49, 58 (1975); . . . As we recognized in *Schreiber v. Burlington Northern, Inc.*, 472 U.S. 1 (1985), Congress designed the Williams Act to make "disclosure, rather than court imposed principles of 'fair-ness' or 'artificiality,' . . . the preferred method of market regulation." . . .

Relying on §14(e)'s rulemaking authorization, the Commission, in 1980, promulgated Rule 14e-3. . . . As characterized by the Commission, Rule 14e-3(a) is a "disclose or abstain from trading" requirement.[15] The Second Circuit concisely described the Rule's thrust:

---

4. Twice before we have been presented with the question whether criminal liability for violation of §10(b) may be based on a misappropriation theory. In *Chiarella v. United States*, 445 U.S. 222, 235-237, 100 S. Ct. 1108, 1118-1119, 63 L. Ed. 2d 348 (1980), the jury had received no misappropriation theory instructions, so we declined to address the ques-tion. See *infra*, at 2211. In *Carpenter v. United States*, 484 U.S. 19, 24, 108 S. Ct. 316, 319-320, 98 L. Ed. 2d 275 (1987), the Court divided evenly on whether, under the circumstances of that case, convictions resting on the misappropriation theory should be affirmed. *See* Aldave, The Misappropriation Theory: *Carpenter* and Its Aftermath, 49 Ohio St. L.J. 373, 375 (1988) (observing that "*Carpenter* was, by any reckoning, an unusual case," for the information there misappropriated belonged not to a company preparing to engage in securities transactions, *e.g.*, a bidder in a corporate acquisition, but to the Wall Street Journal).

15. The Rule thus adopts for the tender offer context a requirement resembling the one Chief Justice Burger would have adopted in *Chiarella* for misappropriators under § 10(b).

One violates Rule 14e-3(a) if he trades on the basis of material nonpublic information concerning a pending tender offer that he knows or has reason to know has been acquired "directly or indirectly" from an insider of the offeror or issuer, or someone working on their behalf. Rule 14e-3(a) is a disclosure provision. It creates a duty in those traders who fall within its ambit to abstain or disclose, *without regard to whether the trader owes a pre-existing fiduciary duty* to respect the confidentiality of the information.

United States v. Chestman, 947 F.2d 551, 557 (1991) (en banc) (*emphasis added*), cert. denied, 503 U.S. 1004 (1992). . . .

In the Eighth Circuit's view, because Rule 14e-3(a) applies whether or not the trading in question breaches a fiduciary duty, the regulation exceeds the SEC's §14(e) rulemaking authority. . . . In support of its holding, the Eighth Circuit relied on the text of §14(e) and our decisions in *Schreiber* and *Chiarella*. See 92 F.3d, at 624-627. . . .

For the meaning of "fraudulent" under §10(b), the Eighth Circuit looked to *Chiarella*. . . . In that case, the Eighth Circuit recounted, this Court held that a failure to disclose information could be "fraudulent" under §10(b) only when there was a duty to speak arising out of "'a fiduciary or other similar relation of trust and confidence.'" *Chiarella*, 445 U.S., at 228, 100 S. Ct., at 1114 (quoting Restatement (Second) of Torts §551(2)(a) (1976)). Just as §10(b) demands a showing of a breach of fiduciary duty, so such a breach is necessary to make out a §14(e) violation, the Eighth Circuit concluded. . . .

We need not resolve in this case whether the Commission's authority under §14(e) to "define . . . such acts and practices as are fraudulent" is broader than the [SEC]'s fraud-defining authority under §10(b), for we agree with the United States that Rule 14e-3(a), as applied to cases of this genre, qualifies under §14(e) as a "means reasonably designed to prevent" fraudulent trading on material, nonpublic information in the tender offer context.[17] A prophylactic measure, because its mission is to prevent, typically encompasses more than the core activity prohibited. . . . We hold, accordingly, that under §14(e), the Commission may prohibit acts not themselves fraudulent under the common law or §10(b), if the prohibition is "reasonably designed to prevent . . . acts and practices [that] are fraudulent." . . .

The United States emphasizes that Rule 14e-3(a) reaches trading in which "a breach of duty is likely but difficult to prove." "Particularly in the context of a tender offer," as the Tenth Circuit recognized, "there is a fairly wide circle of people with confidential information," notably, the attorneys, investment bankers, and accountants involved in structuring the transaction [*SEC v. Peters*,

---

17. We leave for another day, when the issue requires decision, the legitimacy of Rule 14e-3(a) as applied to "warehousing," which the Government describes as "the practice by which bidders leak advance information of a tender offer to allies and encourage them to purchase the target company's stock before the bid is announced." As we observed in *Chiarella*, one of the Commission's purposes in proposing Rule 14e-3(a) was "to bar warehousing under its authority to regulate tender offers." 445 U.S., at 234, 100 S. Ct., at 1117-1118. The Government acknowledges that trading authorized by a principal breaches no fiduciary duty. The instant case, however, does not involve trading authorized by a principal; therefore, we need not here decide whether the Commission's proscription of warehousing falls within its §14(e) authority to define or prevent fraud.

978 F.2d 1162, 1167 (10th Cir. 1992)]. The availability of that information may lead to abuse, for "even a hint of an upcoming tender offer may send the price of the target company's stock soaring." *SEC v. Materia*, 745 F.2d 197, 199 (2d Cir. 1984). Individuals entrusted with nonpublic information, particularly if they have no long-term loyalty to the issuer, may find the temptation to trade on that information hard to resist in view of "the very large short-term profits potentially available [to them]." *Peters*, 978 F.2d, at 1167 . . .

　　"[I]t may be possible to prove circumstantially that a person [traded on the basis of material, nonpublic information], but almost impossible to prove that the trader obtained such information in breach of a fiduciary duty owed either by the trader or by the ultimate insider source of the information." *Ibid.* The example of a "tippee" who trades on information received from an insider illustrates the problem. Under Rule 10b-5, "a tippee assumes a fiduciary duty to the shareholders of a corporation not to trade on material nonpublic information only when the insider has breached his fiduciary duty to the shareholders by disclosing the information to the tippee and the tippee knows or should know that there has been a breach." *Dirks*, 463 U.S., at 660, 103 S. Ct., at 3264. To show that a tippee who traded on nonpublic information about a tender offer had breached a fiduciary duty would require proof not only that the insider source breached a fiduciary duty, but that the tippee knew or should have known of that breach. "Yet, in most cases, the only parties to the [information transfer] will be the insider and the alleged tippee." *Peters*, 978 F.2d, at 1167.

　　In sum, it is a fair assumption that trading on the basis of material, nonpublic information will often involve a breach of a duty of confidentiality to the bidder or target company or their representatives. The SEC, cognizant of the proof problem that could enable sophisticated traders to escape responsibility, placed "disclose or abstain from trading" command within the text of Rule 14e-3(a), which does not require specific proof of a breach of fiduciary duty. That prescription, we are satisfied, applied to this case, is a "means reasonably designed to prevent" fraudulent trading on material, nonpublic information in the tender offer context . . . Therefore, insofar as it serves to prevent the type of misappropriation charged against O'Hagan, Rule 14e-3(a) is a proper exercise of the [SEC]'s prophylactic power under §14(e). . . .

　　The judgment of the Court of Appeals for the Eighth Circuit is reversed, and the case is remanded for further proceedings consistent with this opinion.

　　It is so ordered.

NOTES

　　1. Rule 14e-3: The SEC's Response to Chiarella. The practical impact of the Supreme Court's holding as to the validity of Rule 14e-3 is to prohibit insider trading surrounding tender offers regulated by §14 of the 1934 Act. In its release adopting Rule 14e-3, the SEC explained why it felt compelled to adopt Rule 14e-3 in reaction to the Supreme Court's earlier decision in *Chiarella v. United States*, 445 U.S. 222 (1980):

　　　The *Chiarella* case arose from a series of securities transactions by an employee of a financial printer. On the basis of confidential information obtained in the course of his employment, Mr. Chiarella deducted the identities of various companies that were to be the subject of tender offers that had not yet been publicly announced. Without disclosing the fact of the impending tender offers, Mr. Chiarella purchased target securities and then sold them at a profit immediately after the tender offers were made public.

In the U.S. District Court for the Southern District of New York, Mr. Chiarella was convicted of a criminal violation of Section 10(b) and Rule 10b-5. The U.S. Court of Appeals for the Second Circuit affirmed the conviction and held that he was a "market insider" because of his regular access to market information, and, therefore, was barred from trading on the basis of material, nonpublic information obtained in that capacity.

The Supreme Court reversed the Second Circuit's decision and held "that a duty to disclose under Section 10b does not arise from the mere possession of nonpublic market information." [By adopting Rule 14e-3, the SEC established] a "disclose or abstain from trading" rule under the Williams Act. . . .

The Commission has previously expressed and continues to have serious concerns about trading by persons in possession of material, nonpublic information relating to a tender offer. This practice results in unfair disparities in market information and market disruption.[2] Security holders who purchase from or sell to such persons are effectively denied the benefits of disclosure and the substantive protections of the Williams Act. . . . Moreover, the Williams Act was designed to avert a "stampede effect" in the context of tender offers[3] and the trading on material, nonpublic information and the dissemination of leaks and rumors in connection with such trading tends to promote this detrimental effect.

In view of the continued trading and potential for trading by persons while in possession of material, nonpublic information relating to tender offers and the detrimental impact which such trading has on tender offer practice, shareholder protection and the securities markets, the Commission has determined that Rule 14e-3 is necessary and appropriate in the public interest and for the protection of investors. As adopted, Rule 14e-3 pertains to both the person who receives the information, the tippee, and the person who transmits the information, the tipper.

SEC Release No. 17120 (Sept. 4, 1980) 1980 SEC LEXIS 775.

2. Recent Insider Trading Cases. In an interesting development, the most recent wave of activity in the M&A market, known as the "fifth merger wave," which seemed to peak in mid-2007, also saw "a spike in prosecutions for insider trading," reminiscent of what has been described as the "Deal Decade of the 1980s" (*see* pp. 41-42). In the 1980s, the SEC pursued some of its highest-profile insider trading scandals, including its case against Ivan Boesky, which ultimately led to the prosecution of "junk bond king" Michael Milken and the downfall of his firm, Drexel Burnham. Interestingly enough, four of the five largest M&A transactions announced in 2007 "have been linked to suspicious trading patterns, including proposed deals for TXU Corp., Alcan Inc., First Data Corp., and SLM Corp., . . . [Indeed,] a recent study . . . concluded that 49% of all public M&A transactions displayed evidence of suspicious trading

---

2. Such purchases may result in rapid and unexplained price and volume movements in the subject company's and the bidder's securities.

3. *Rondeau v. Mosinee Paper Co.*, 422 U.S. 49, 58 N.8 (1975).

activity preceding the public deal announcements." Brent Shearer, *Forbidden Fruit*, MERGERS AND ACQUISITIONS 66-67 (Oct. 2007). This phenomenon has not escaped notice by the market regulators, including the SEC, which reports an increase in prosecutions for insider trading. *Id.* at 69.

Even more interesting, recent SEC cases involving charges of insider trading have tended to focus on peripheral deal players, unlike the "Deal Decade." Today, however, "perpetrators [do not] require direct access to the transactions. The network from the deal in question to the ultimate illegal trader can be extensive and convoluted. And deals today involve more advisers, lawyers, and accountants than ever before, meaning that before merger agreements are announced, hundreds of people . . . are kept abreast of the [deal] negotiations." *Id.* at 68. *Query:* What are the (practical) implications of these developments for the lawyer representing either Bidder or Target in an acquisition transaction?

As of Fall 2020, the SEC continues its vigorous prosecution of insider trading violations. Indeed, "[i]nsider trading enforcement remains a cornerstone of the SEC's enforcement program. Over the past 10 years, the SEC has significantly enhanced its insider trading surveillance, detection, and investigative capabilities. Through the adoption of new investigative approaches and the development of new technology, the SEC staff has indicated that it has the ability to connect 'patterns of trading to sources of material nonpublic information' as never before. The implication of this ability is that not only can the SEC use trading data to establish potential relationships among and between traders, but it can use relationship information to deduce whether they have sources of prohibited information who are common to them. According to the SEC, it uses 'data analysis tools to detect suspicious patterns such as improbably successful trading across different securities over time.' And yet, despite these capabilities, people continue to engage in insider trading believing, apparently, that there is little chance their illicit trading will be detected." Daniel M. Hawke, *SEC Data in Insider Trading Investigations*, Aug. 1, 2019, *available at:* https://www.thecorporatecounsel.net/member/Memos/Arnold/08_ 19_SEC.pdf.

2. Tipper-Tippee Liability Under Rule 10b-5

Given the "fairly wide circle of people [who come into possession of] confidential information" in the context of planning an M&A transaction (including a tender offer), the Supreme Court, in its *O'Hagan* opinion, acknowledged that individuals who have been "entrusted with nonpublic information . . . may find the temptation to trade on that information hard to resist. . . ." *O'Hagan, supra,* 117 S. Ct. at 2218. And for many participants in M&A deal making, it is often equally tempting to share with others (i.e., "tip") material nonpublic information that these participants in the capital markets may receive *before* news of the transaction is made public. The following opinion reflects the Supreme Court's most recent pronouncement regarding the scope of "tipper-tippee" liability under Rule 10b-5:

Salman v. United States
137 S.Ct. 420 (2016)

Justice ALITO delivered the opinion of the Court.

Section 10(b) of the Securities Exchange Act of 1934 and the Securities and Exchange Commission's Rule 10b–5 prohibit undisclosed trading on inside corporate information by individuals who are under a duty of trust and confidence that prohibits them from secretly using such information for their personal advantage. Individuals under this duty may face criminal and civil liability for trading on inside information (unless they make appropriate disclosures ahead of time).

These persons also may not tip inside information to others for trading. The tippee acquires the tipper's duty to disclose or abstain from trading if the tippee knows the information was disclosed in breach of the tipper's duty, and the tippee may commit securities fraud by trading in disregard of that knowledge. In *Dirks v. SEC*, 463 U.S. 646 (1983), this Court explained that a tippee's liability for trading on inside information hinges on whether the tipper breached a fiduciary duty by disclosing the information. A tipper breaches such a fiduciary duty, we held, when the tipper discloses the inside information for a personal benefit. And, we went on to say, a jury can infer a personal benefit—and thus a breach of the tipper's duty—where the tipper receives something of value in exchange for the tip or "makes a gift of confidential information to a trading relative or friend." *Id.*, at 664.

Petitioner Bassam Salman challenges his convictions for conspiracy and insider trading. Salman received lucrative trading tips from an extended family member, who had received the information from Salman's brother-in-law. Salman then traded on the information. He argues that he cannot be held liable as a tippee because the tipper (his brother-in-law) did not personally receive money or property in exchange for the tips and thus did not personally benefit from them. The Court of Appeals disagreed, holding that *Dirks* allowed the jury to infer that the tipper here breached a duty because he made a " 'gift of confidential information to a trading relative.' " 792 F. 3d 1087, 1092 (C.A.9 2015) (quoting *Dirks, supra* at 664). Because the Court of Appeals properly applied *Dirks*, we affirm the judgment below.

I

Maher Kara was an investment banker in Citigroup's healthcare investment banking group. He dealt with highly confidential information about mergers and acquisitions involving Citigroup's clients. Maher enjoyed a close relationship with his older brother, Mounir Kara (known as Michael). After Maher started at Citigroup, he began discussing aspects of his job with Michael. At first he relied on Michael's chemistry background to help him grasp scientific concepts relevant to his new job. Then, while their father was battling cancer, the brothers discussed companies that dealt with innovative cancer treatment and pain management techniques. Michael began to trade on the information

Maher shared with him. At first, Maher was unaware of his brother's trading activity, but eventually he began to suspect that it was taking place.

Ultimately, Maher began to assist Michael's trading by sharing inside information with his brother about pending mergers and acquisitions. Maher sometimes used code words to communicate corporate information to his brother. Other times, he shared inside information about deals he was not working on in order to avoid detection. Without his younger brother's knowledge, Michael fed the information to others—including Salman, Michael's friend and Maher's brother-in-law. By the time the authorities caught on, Salman had made over $1.5 million in profits that he split with another relative who executed trades via a brokerage account on Salman's behalf.

Salman was indicted on one count of conspiracy to commit securities fraud, and four counts of securities fraud. Facing charges of their own, both Maher and Michael pleaded guilty and testified at Salman's trial.

The evidence at trial established that Maher and Michael enjoyed a "very close relationship." Maher "love[d] [his] brother very much," Michael was like "a second father to Maher," and Michael was the best man at Maher's wedding to Salman's sister. Maher testified that he shared inside information with his brother to benefit him and with the expectation that his brother would trade on it. While Maher explained that he disclosed the information in large part to appease Michael (who pestered him incessantly for it), he also testified that he tipped his brother to "help him" and to "fulfil[l] whatever needs he had." For instance, Michael once called Maher and told him that "he needed a favor." Maher offered his brother money but Michael asked for information instead. Maher then disclosed an upcoming acquisition. Although he instantly regretted the tip and called his brother back to implore him not to trade, Maher expected his brother to do so anyway.

For his part, Michael told the jury that his brother's tips gave him "timely information that the average person does not have access to" and "access to stocks, options, and what have you, that I can capitalize on, that the average person would never have or dream of." Michael testified that he became friends with Salman when Maher was courting Salman's sister and later began sharing Maher's tips with Salman. As he explained at trial, "any time a major deal came in, [Salman] was the first on my phone list." Michael also testified that he told Salman that the information was coming from Maher.

After a jury trial in the Northern District of California, Salman was convicted on all counts. Salman appealed to the Ninth Circuit. While his appeal was pending, the Second Circuit issued its opinion in *United States v. Newman*, 773 F. 3d 438 (2014), cert. denied, 136 S. Ct. 242, (2015). There, the Second Circuit reversed the convictions of two portfolio managers who traded on inside information. The *Newman* defendants were "several steps removed from the corporate insiders" and the court found that "there was no evidence that either was aware of the source of the inside information." 773 F. 3d, at 443. The court acknowledged that *Dirks* and Second Circuit case law allow a factfinder to infer a personal benefit to the tipper from a gift of confidential information to a trading relative or friend. But the court concluded that, "[t]o the extent" *Dirks* permits "such an inference," the inference "is impermissible in the absence of proof of a meaningfully close personal relationship that generates an exchange that is objective, consequential, and represents at least a potential gain of a pecuniary or similarly valuable nature." 773 F.3d, at 452.[1]

Pointing to *Newman*, Salman argued that his conviction should be reversed. While the evidence established that Maher made a gift of trading information to Michael and that Salman knew it, there was no evidence that Maher received anything of "a pecuniary or similarly valuable nature" in exchange—or that Salman knew of any such benefit. The Ninth Circuit disagreed and affirmed Salman's conviction. The court reasoned that the case was governed by *Dirks*'s holding that a tipper benefits personally by making a gift of confidential information to a trading relative or friend. Indeed, Maher's disclosures to Michael were "precisely the gift of confidential information to a trading relative that *Dirks* envisioned." 792 F.3d, at 1092. To the extent *Newman* went further and required additional gain to the tipper in cases involving gifts of confidential information to family and friends, the Ninth Circuit "decline[d] to follow it."

We granted certiorari to resolve the tension between the Second Circuit's *Newman* decision and the Ninth Circuit's decision in this case.[2]

II

A

In this case, Salman contends that an insider's "gift of confidential information to a trading relative or friend," *Dirks*, 463 U.S. at 664, is not enough to establish securities fraud. Instead, Salman argues, a tipper does not personally benefit unless the tipper's goal in disclosing inside information is to obtain money, property, or something of tangible value. He claims that our insider-trading precedents, and the cases those precedents cite, involve situations in which the insider exploited confidential information for the insider's own "tangible monetary profit." He suggests that his position is reinforced by our

---

1. The Second Circuit also reversed the *Newman* defendants' convictions because the Government introduced no evidence that the defendants knew the information they traded on came from insiders or that the insiders received a personal benefit in exchange for the tips. 773 F.3d, at 453–454. This case does not implicate those issues.

2. *Dirks v. SEC*, 463 U.S. 646, 103 S.Ct. 3255, 77 L.Ed.2d 911 (1983), established the personal-benefit framework in a case brought under the classical theory of insider-trading liability, which applies "when a corporate insider" or his tippee "trades in the securities of [the tipper's] corporation on the basis of material, nonpublic information." *United States v. O'Hagan*, 521 U.S. 642, 651–652, 117 S.Ct. 2199, 138 L.Ed.2d 724 (1997). In such a case, the defendant breaches a duty to, and takes advantage of, the shareholders of his corporation. By contrast, the misappropriation theory holds that a person commits securities fraud "when he misappropriates confidential information for securities trading purposes, in breach of a duty owed to the source of the information" such as an employer or client. *Id.*, at 652, 117 S.Ct. 2199. In such a case, the defendant breaches a duty to, and defrauds, the source of the information, as opposed to the shareholders of his corporation. The Court of Appeals observed that this is a misappropriation case, 792 F.3d, 1087, 1092, n. 4 (C.A.9 2015), while the Government represents that both theories apply on the facts of this case. We need not resolve the question. The parties do not dispute that *Dirks*'s personal-benefit analysis applies in both classical and misappropriation cases, so we will proceed on the assumption that it does.

criminal-fraud precedents outside of the insider-trading context, because those cases confirm that a fraudster must personally obtain money or property. More broadly, Salman urges that defining a gift as a personal benefit renders the insider-trading offense indeterminate and overbroad: indeterminate, because liability may turn on facts such as the closeness of the relationship between tipper and tippee and the tipper's purpose for disclosure; and overbroad, because the Government may avoid having to prove a concrete personal benefit by simply arguing that the tipper meant to give a gift to the tippee. He also argues that we should interpret *Dirks*'s standard narrowly so as to avoid constitutional concerns. Finally, Salman contends that gift situations create especially troubling problems for remote tippees—that is, tippees who receive inside information from another tippee, rather than the tipper—who may have no knowledge of the relationship between the original tipper and tippee and thus may not know why the tipper made the disclosure.

The Government disagrees and argues that a gift of confidential information to anyone, not just a "trading relative or friend," is enough to prove securities fraud. Under the Government's view, a tipper personally benefits whenever the tipper discloses confidential trading information for a noncorporate purpose. Accordingly, a gift to a friend, a family member, or anyone else would support the inference that the tipper exploited the trading value of inside information for personal purposes and thus personally benefited from the disclosure. The Government claims to find support for this reading in *Dirks* and the precedents on which *Dirks* relied.

The Government also argues that Salman's concerns about unlimited and indeterminate liability for remote tippees are significantly alleviated by other statutory elements that prosecutors must satisfy to convict a tippee for insider trading. The Government observes that, in order to establish a defendant's criminal liability as a tippee, it must prove beyond a reasonable doubt that the tipper expected that the information being disclosed would be used in securities trading. The Government also notes that, to establish a defendant's criminal liability as a tippee, it must prove that the tippee knew that the tipper breached a duty—in other words, that the tippee knew that the tipper disclosed the information for a personal benefit and that the tipper expected trading to ensue.

B

We adhere to *Dirks*, which easily resolves the narrow issue presented here.

In *Dirks*, we explained that a tippee is exposed to liability for trading on inside information only if the tippee participates in a breach of the tipper's fiduciary duty. Whether the tipper breached that duty depends "in large part on the purpose of the disclosure" to the tippee. "[T]he test," we explained, "is whether the insider personally will benefit, directly or indirectly, from his disclosure." Thus, the disclosure of confidential information without personal benefit is not enough. In determining whether a tipper derived a personal benefit, we instructed courts to "focus on objective criteria, *i.e.,* whether the insider receives a direct or indirect personal benefit from the disclosure, such as a pecuniary gain or a reputational benefit that will translate into future earnings." This personal benefit can "often" be inferred "from objective facts and circumstances," we explained, such as "a relationship between the insider and the recipient that suggests a *quid pro quo* from the latter, or an intention to benefit the particular recipient." In particular, we held that "[t]he elements of fiduciary duty and exploitation of nonpublic information also exist *when an insider makes a gift of confidential information to a trading relative or friend.*" *Ibid.* (emphasis added). In such cases, "[t]he tip and trade resemble trading by the insider followed by a gift of the profits to the recipient." We then applied this gift-giving principle to resolve *Dirks* itself, finding it dispositive that the tippers "received no monetary or personal benefit" from their tips to Dirks, "*nor was their purpose to make a gift of valuable information to Dirks.*" (emphasis added).

Our discussion of gift giving resolves this case. Maher, the tipper, provided inside information to a close relative, his brother Michael. *Dirks* makes clear that a tipper breaches a fiduciary duty by making a gift of confidential information to "a trading relative," and that rule is sufficient to resolve the case at hand. As Salman's counsel acknowledged at oral argument, Maher would have breached his duty had he personally traded on the information here himself then given the proceeds as a gift to his brother. It is obvious that Maher would personally benefit in that situation. But Maher effectively achieved the same result by disclosing the information to Michael, and allowing him to trade on it. *Dirks* appropriately prohibits that approach, as well. *Dirks* specifies that when a tipper gives inside information to "a trading relative or friend," the jury can infer that the tipper meant to provide the equivalent of a cash gift. In such situations, the tipper benefits personally because giving a gift of trading information is the same thing as trading by the tipper followed by a gift of the proceeds. Here, by disclosing confidential information as a gift to his brother with the expectation that he would trade on it, Maher breached his duty of trust and confidence to Citigroup and its clients—a duty Salman acquired, and breached himself, by trading on the information with full knowledge that it had been improperly disclosed.

To the extent the Second Circuit held that the tipper must also receive something of a "pecuniary or similarly valuable nature" in exchange for a gift to family or friends, *Newman,* 773 F.3d, at 452, we agree with the Ninth Circuit that this requirement is inconsistent with *Dirks.*

C

Salman points out that many insider-trading cases—including several that *Dirks* cited—involved insiders who personally profited through the misuse of trading information. But this observation does not undermine the test *Dirks* articulated and applied. Salman also cites a sampling of our criminal-fraud decisions construing other federal fraud statutes, suggesting that they stand for the proposition that fraud is not consummated unless the defendant obtains money or property. *Sekhar v. United States,* 133 S.Ct. 2720 (2013) (Hobbs Act); *Skilling v. United States,* 561 U.S. 358 (2010) (honest-services mail and wire fraud); *Cleveland v. United States,* 531 U.S. 12 (2000) (wire fraud); *McNally v. United States,* 483 U.S. 350 (1987) (mail fraud). Assuming that these cases are relevant to our construction of § 10(b) (a proposition the Government forcefully disputes), nothing in them undermines the commonsense point we made in *Dirks*. Making a gift of inside information to a relative like Michael is little different from trading on the information, obtaining the profits, and doling them out to the trading relative. The tipper benefits either way. The facts of this case illustrate the point: In one of their tipper-tippee interactions, Michael asked Maher for a favor, declined Maher's offer of money, and instead requested and received lucrative trading information.

We reject Salman's argument that *Dirks*'s gift-giving standard is unconstitutionally vague as applied to this case. *Dirks* created a simple and clear "guiding principle" for determining tippee liability, and Salman has not demonstrated that either § 10(b) itself or the *Dirks* gift-giving standard "leav[e] grave uncertainty about how to estimate the risk posed by a crime" or are plagued by "hopeless indeterminacy." At most, Salman shows that in some factual circumstances assessing liability for gift-giving will be difficult. That alone cannot render "shapeless" a federal criminal prohibition, for even clear rules "produce close cases." We also reject Salman's appeal to the rule of lenity, as he has shown "no grievous ambiguity or uncertainty that would trigger the rule's application." To the contrary, Salman's conduct is in the heartland of *Dirks*'s rule concerning gifts. It remains the case that "[d]etermining whether an insider personally benefits from a particular disclosure, a question of fact, will not always be easy for courts." But there is no need for us to address those difficult cases today, because this case involves "precisely the 'gift of confidential information to a trading relative' that *Dirks* envisioned."

III

Salman's jury was properly instructed that a personal benefit includes "the benefit one would obtain from simply making a gift of confidential information to a trading relative." As the Court of Appeals noted, "the Government presented direct evidence that the disclosure was intended as a gift of market-sensitive information." And, as Salman conceded below, this evidence is sufficient to sustain his conviction under our reading of *Dirks*. . . . Accordingly, the Ninth Circuit's judgment is affirmed.

NOTE

In its opinion in *Salman*, the Supreme Court clearly rejected the holding of the Second Circuit in *United States v. Newman*, which required proof of "an exchange that is objective, consequential, and represents at least a potential gain of a pecuniary or similarly valuable nature" in order to establish the personal benefit to the insider that is necessary to find liability for insider trading under *Dirks v. SEC*. However, the Court in *Salman* "specifically noted that it was not addressing another aspect of the *Newman* decision, which required proof that a tippee know that the insiders had received a personal benefit [in exchange for] the tip. The Court in *Salman* also did not address the Government's argument in that case that a gift to *any* trading person, even if not a friend or relative, would also satisfy the personal benefit requirement. Those issues are important to numerous prosecutions and likely will be addressed in future Supreme Court cases." John Savarese, et. al., Wachtel Lipton, *New Supreme Court Decision on "Personal Benefit" Element of Insider Trading,* (law firm memo dated Dec. 7, 2016, copy on file with author). Thus, the *Salmon* opinion leaves open the vexing question of what level of knowledge must be proven with respect to remote tippees who are more removed from the corporate insider that was Salman on the facts of the principal case.

3. Liability Under §16(b)

> **Texas International Airlines v. National Airlines, Inc.**
> **714 F.2d 533 (5th Cir. 1983)**

JOHNSON, Circuit Judge:

Texas International (TI) appeals the grant of summary judgment for National Airlines (National) holding TI liable to National under section 16(b) of the Securities Exchange Act of 1934 (the Exchange Act) for the "short swing profits" made on the sale of 121,000 shares of National common stock. . . .

On March 14, 1979, during an attempt by TI to gain control of National, TI purchased 121,000 shares of National common stock in open-market brokerage transactions. On March 14, the date of the purchase, TI was a beneficial owner of more than ten percent of National's common stock. On July 28, 1979, within six months of the March 14 purchase, TI and Pan American World Airways, Inc. (Pan Am) entered into a stock purchase agreement whereby TI agreed to sell 790,700 shares of National common stock to Pan Am at $50 per share. The closing was held on July 30, 1979. Under the matching rules of section 16(b) the 790,700 shares sold by TI on July 28, 1979 are deemed to include the 121,000 shares purchased by TI in March.

On September 6, 1978, National and Pan Am had entered into a merger agreement which provided for the merger of National into Pan Am contingent upon certain conditions and, in connection with the merger, for the exchange by Pan Am of not less than $50 in cash for each share of National common stock, other than the shares held by Pan Am. On May 16, 1979, National stockholders approved the merger agreement dated September 6, 1978, as amended. TI, as a National stockholder, stood to receive $50 per share for its National stock if and when the merger closed. For whatever reason, TI decided not to wait until the merger went through to negotiate for the disposition of its holdings to Pan Am. It was not until after the July 28, 1979 sale by TI of its National stock to Pan Am that the National-Pan Am merger was effectuated.

On August 2, 1979, only five days after TI sold its National stock to Pan Am, TI sought declaratory relief that it was not liable to National under section 16(b) for profits realized on the purchase and sale of National common stock. In the alternative, TI sought to reduce its short swing profits by deducting expenses it allegedly incurred in connection with the purchase and sale of its National stock. On September 26, 1979, National counterclaimed, seeking recovery of TI's short swing profits under section 16(b). National moved for summary judgment on November 24, 1980.[6]

On May 11, 1981, the district court granted National's motion in part, finding that TI's purchase and sale of the 121,000 shares of National stock constituted a violation of section 16(b). The district court squarely rejected TI's contention that the control contest situation rendered the transaction at issue "unorthodox" within the meaning of *Kern County Land Co. v. Occidental Petroleum Corp.*, 411 U.S. 582, 93 S. Ct. 1736, 36 L. Ed. 2d 503 (1973). In reaching its conclusion that TI was liable under section 16(b), the district court stated that no court has exempted the type of transaction at issue here—a cash-for-stock transaction—from the automatic application of section 16(b). . . .

TI urges this Court to create an exception to automatic section 16(b) liability in cases where a defendant can prove that, notwithstanding its ownership of over ten percent of the stock of the issuer, the defendant had no access to inside information concerning the issuer. According to TI, the classic example of such a case is a sale of stock in the hostile takeover context. Application of section 16(b) in this type of case, argues TI, does not serve congressional goals—Congress intended short-swing profits to be disgorged only when the particular transaction serves as a vehicle for the realization of these profits based upon access to inside information.

TI's argument is unsupported by the legislative history of section 16(b). Although the abuse Congress sought to curb was speculation by stockholders with inside information, "the only method Congress deemed effective to curb the evils of insider trading was a *flat rule* taking the profits out of a *class of transactions* in which the possibility of abuse was believed to be intolerably great." *Kern County* [*Land Co. v. Occidental Petroleum Corp.*, 411 U.S. 582, 93 S. Ct. 173 (1973)] (*emphasis added*). In explaining the necessity for a "crude rule of thumb" to Congress, Thomas Corcoran, a principal draftsman of the Act, stated: "You have to have a general rule. In particular transactions it might work a hardship, but those transactions that are a hardship represent the sacrifice to the necessity of having a general rule." Hearings on Stock Exchange Practices before the Senate Committee on Banking and Currency, 73d Cong., 2d Sess., 6557 and 6558 (1934). The Supreme Court explained the necessity for the flat rule or "objective approach" of the statute in *Reliance Electric Company v. Emerson Electric Company*, 404 U.S. 418, 92 S. Ct. 596, 599, 30 L. Ed. 2d 575 (1972) *quoting Bershad v. McDonough*, 428 F.2d 693, 696 (7th Cir. 1970):

> In order to achieve its goals, Congress chose a relatively arbitrary rule capable of easy administration. The objective standard of Section 16(b) imposes strict liability upon substantially all transactions occurring within the statutory time period, regardless of the intent of the insider or the existence of actual speculation. This approach maximized the ability of the rule to eradicate speculative abuses by reducing difficulties in proof. Such arbitrary and sweeping coverage was deemed necessary to insure the optimum prophylactic effect. . . .

---

6. By early January 1980, the merger of Pan Am and National had been effectuated. Pan Am became the surviving corporation.

This Court is in agreement with the statements of legislative purpose as expressed . . . by the Supreme Court in *Emerson Electric* and *Kern County*—the mechanical application of section 16(b) to the specified class of transactions is necessary in order to guarantee that the abuse at which the statute is aimed will be effectively curbed.

In *Kern County*, the Supreme Court approved an extremely narrow exception to the objective standard of section 16(b). The Court held that when a transaction is "unorthodox" or "borderline," the courts should adopt a pragmatic approach in imposing section 16(b) liability which considers the opportunity for speculative abuse, i.e., whether the statutory "insider" had or was likely to have access to inside information.

TI engages in an analogy between the hostile and adversary situation that existed between the target company and the putative insider in *Kern County* and the adversary relationship between TI and National in the instant case. Even assuming the alleged parallelism between the adversary situations in the two cases and assuming that TI could prove that it neither had nor was likely to have access to inside information by virtue of its statutory "insider" status, no valid basis for an exception to section 16(b) liability on these facts is perceived. The Supreme Court in *Kern County* inquired into whether the transaction had the potential for abuse of inside information only because the transaction fell under the rubric of "unorthodox" or "borderline."[9] *In Kern County*, Occidental, a shareholder in Kern County Land Company (Old Kern) converted its shares in Old Kern into shares of the acquiring corporation pursuant to a merger. The Supreme Court clearly distinguished the unorthodox transaction—a conversion of securities—before it from the traditional cash-for-stock transaction in the instant case: "traditional cash-for-stock transactions . . . are clearly within the purview of §16(b)." *Kern County*, 411 U.S. at 593.

TI lays frontal attack on the unorthodox transaction test as fundamentally flawed, principally because the form of consideration received—cash or stock—has nothing to do with whether inside information was or might have been used. What this attack fails to consider, however, is the significance of the factor of voluntariness in the Supreme Court's decision. The Court's sole concern was not that cash-for-stock sales present a greater opportunity for abuse of inside information than do stock-for-stock sales. Rather, language in the Supreme Court's opinion indicates that traditional cash-for-stock sales were excluded from the concept of unorthodox transactions because of their voluntary nature. . . . In the instant case, TI voluntarily entered into the stock purchase agreement with Pan Am before the National-Pan Am merger was effectuated. Despite the alleged lack of access to inside information and therefore the possibility of speculative abuse, the volitional character of the exchange is sufficient reason to trigger applicability of the language of section 16(b). For whatever reason, after the National-Pan Am merger had been approved, TI decided to take the initiative for the course of subsequent events into its own hands rather

---

9. The Court, in a nonexhaustive list, enumerated certain transactions which are unorthodox: stock conversions, exchanges pursuant to mergers and other corporate reorganizations, stock reclassifications, and dealings in options, rights, and warrants. *Kern County*, 93 S. Ct. at 1744 n. 24.

than wait for the merger to become accomplished. These circumstances do not warrant the creation of an exception to automatic section 16(b) liability. . . .

This Court finds no valid justification for deviation from the express terms of section 16(b) or the case law interpreting it. The judgment of the district court is affirmed.

AFFIRMED.

QUESTIONS

1. Who has standing to sue for violations of §16(b)?

2. Who is a potential defendant in a §16(b) lawsuit?

3. What is the remedy for §16(b) violations?

4. What is the lesson to be learned from this case? (*Hint:* Is there any planning that could have been done in the principal case so as to avoid a §16(b) violation?)

∥5∥

Negotiating and Documenting the Transaction

In considering the process of negotiating, documenting, and closing on a business acquisition, the parties typically will be required to prepare and sign various documents. While each deal is unique, and the facts of any particular deal may require a wide array of documents not specifically mentioned in this discussion, mergers and acquisitions (M&A) transactions generally follow a certain convention as to the documents required to effect the transaction. In this chapter, we consider the nature and terms of the agreements that are customarily drafted as part of an acquisition transaction, regardless of the method used to structure the deal.

We begin our discussion by considering the use of a letter of intent (LOI) and/or confidentiality agreement early in the deal process. Next, we consider certain mechanisms that are commonly used to close the gap between Bidder and Target in negotiating the terms of the purchase price to be paid by Bidder to acquire Target's business. The devices most commonly used in the acquisition of a privately held company are earn-outs and escrows, both of which are discussed below.

Once the parties have reached consensus on the essential terms of the deal — price and structure — the lawyer turns his or her attention to the preparation of the acquisition agreement, which will generally take the form of either an asset purchase agreement, a stock purchase agreement, or a plan of merger (merger agreement), depending on the deal structure used in the particular acquisition. In Part C of this chapter, we will look at the provisions commonly included in the basic agreement regardless of the method used to structure the acquisition. As part of this discussion, we will examine the dynamic relationship among the key provisions of any acquisition agreement: *representations and warranties, covenants*, and *conditions to closing*. As part of our examination of the process of drafting the acquisition agreement, we will also consider the scope and purpose of the all-important investigative process known as "due diligence" and the role that due diligence plays in determining the scope of the other provisions commonly included in the acquisition agreement. The last component of the acquisition agreement that we will consider is what rights the parties might have after closing on the acquisition, the most important of which are rights of *indemnification*.

A.   Planning Problem: Negotiating and Documenting the Acquisition of a Privately Held Company

A New York–based shoe manufacturer, Galaxy International, Inc., plans to acquire Trekker Marketing Co., which is based in San Diego, California. As proposed, the transaction involves the purchase of all the outstanding capital stock of Trekker in exchange for $35 million of cash, notes, and Galaxy stock, plus the ability for Trekker shareholders to earn up to an additional $7 million if certain performance targets are achieved.

Trekker, a privately held company, was founded ten years ago by two professional skateboarders, Stanley Rockledge and Randy Moses, and started out making high-quality, high-priced skateboards and related accessories. Today, Trekker still makes top-end skateboards, but also makes snowboards, surfboards, and several lines of apparel that are very popular with California skateboarders and surfers. Trekker's irreverent attitude and edgy, bad-boy designs appeal to rebellious teen skaters and boarders, often to the ire of their parents. In 2000, some parents organized a letter-writing campaign to stop a Trekker product promotion that offered a free skateboard to those willing to "relinquish their souls."

As the popularity of skateboarding and snowboarding grew rapidly, so did Trekker's business. The rapid growth sometimes created problems as Trekker experienced product shortages, supply and delivery interruptions, and accompanying lost sales, particularly beyond the southern California market. Nevertheless, Trekker did grow its revenues at a compounded annual growth rate (CAGR) of 12 percent over the last five years, with net income of $4.5 million on revenues of $45 million in its most recently completed fiscal year.

Galaxy, a company traded on the New York Stock Exchange (NYSE), makes several lines of shoes that are popular with the youthful skateboard crowd. By buying Trekker, Galaxy is adding both skateboard hard goods and several top-brand apparel lines to its stable of youth brand products. By moving into skateboarding and related hard goods, Galaxy hopes to gain a competitive advantage over its skate-shoe rivals. Galaxy sees the acquisition of Trekker as a key part of its larger effort to push the edgy sport of skateboarding into the mainstream and grow the business by committing substantial capital resources to expand marketing, production, and distribution capabilities for Trekker product lines.

A sport born of youthful rebellion, skateboarding has grown into an industry that generated $1.4 billion in sales with an estimated target market of about 16 million skateboarders—and skateboard wannabes. Coupling Trekker's popular brands with Galaxy's capital resources and worldwide distribution network of direct and indirect channels, Galaxy intends to take the Trekker irreverence beyond the surf shops and specialty stores and penetrate deep into traditional distribution channels including large department stores such as Macy's, Kohl's, and Target.

Galaxy intends to conduct an offering of its common stock to raise the estimated $30 million needed to close the transaction. Based on its most recent NYSE closing price, Galaxy will be issuing approximately 3 million shares, which is roughly a 6 percent increase in the number of Galaxy's outstanding common shares.

B.   *Negotiating the Transaction*

1.   Initial Negotiations and the Use of a Letter of Intent

In negotiating the terms of a business acquisition, there will often come a point in the process where the parties may wish to commit to paper many of the deal points that they have been discussing. Reasons for doing so are many and quite varied. Sometimes the writing is intended to serve as a discussion outline for future negotiations. In other instances, the writing is intended to memorialize those key terms on which the parties feel they have reached agreement and to identify those items on which no consensus has been reached and on which they will continue to negotiate. Also, a writing may be used when one party faces certain other obligations, often disclosure requirements imposed by the federal securities laws or the rules of the NYSE or other such self-regulatory organizations (SROs), and, before making any disclosures that may be required of the public company, either Bidder or Target (or both) wants the other side to demonstrate its commitment to the transaction by signing some writing.

In these situations, the parties will customarily sign a *letter of intent* (LOI). Generally speaking, this signed writing will expressly provide that the writing is *not* binding on either party. As a result of this almost schizophrenic nature of the LOI, there is a wide divergence of opinion among practicing M&A lawyers as to the usefulness and desirability of entering into such a letter. The potential pitfalls of signing an LOI, even where the writing expressly provides that it is nonbinding, are nicely illustrated in the following case.

Turner Broadcasting System, Inc. v. McDavid
693 S.E.2d 873 (Ga. Ct. App. 2010)

This case involves Turner Broadcasting System, Inc.'s ("Turner") alleged breach of an oral agreement to sell the Atlanta Hawks and Atlanta Thrashers sports teams and the operating rights to Phillips Arena to appellee David McDavid. . . .

. . . [T]he evidence at trial showed that Turner is the former owner of the Hawks and the Thrashers, with operating rights to Philips Arena (the "assets"). In October 2002, Turner publicly announced its interest in selling the assets as part of a "deleveraging program" to reduce its mounting debts. In November 2002, McDavid expressed an interest in buying the assets and entered into negotiations with Turner.

On April 30, 2003, the parties executed a "Letter of Intent," outlining the proposed sale terms and establishing a 45-day exclusive negotiating period. On June 14, 2003, the Letter of Intent expired with no agreement, but the parties continued to negotiate. When McDavid inquired about extending the Letter of Intent, Turner's principal negotiator told him, "Don't worry about it. We're very, very close to a deal. You're our guy." . . .

On July 30, 2003, the parties engaged in a conference call. During the conference call, McDavid's advisors stated that McDavid would agree to Turner's proposed resolution of the tax issue on the condition that it would resolve all the issues and finalize the deal. Turner's CEO, Phil Kent, agreed and announced, "we have a deal." . . .

On or about August 1, 2003, Turner drafted an internal memo to its employees and planned for a press conference to publicly announce the deal with McDavid. In August 2003, Turner consulted with McDavid and his advisor on team management decisions, including the hiring of a general manager and head coach for the Hawks. Turner also obtained McDavid's approval before hiring a trainer, assistants, and scouts.

On or about August 16, 2003, as the drafting process continued, Turner's executive and principal negotiator, James McCaffrey, approached McDavid about a simplified restructure for the transaction, assuring him that the restructure would "not change the deal," that the "deal was done," and that "they were ready to close on the deal that [they] made on July 30th." McDavid agreed to the simplified restructure, and the attorneys circulated revised draft agreements that reflected the restructured terms.

On August 19, 2003, the corporate board of directors of Time Warner, Turner's parent company, approved the sale of the assets to McDavid based upon the restructured terms. However, two of the board members, Ted Turner and Steve Case, opposed the deal, concerned that the assets had been undervalued and had resulted in a "fire sale."

On the day after the Turner board of directors meeting, Ted Turner's son-in-law, Rutherford Seydel, and the son of a member of the Hawks board of directors, Michael Gearon, Jr., approached Turner about purchasing the assets on behalf of their corporation, Atlanta Spirit, LLC. While Turner continued to exchange drafts of the purchase agreement with appellees, it also began negotiations with Atlanta Spirit.

On or about September 12, 2003, McDavid and Turner verbally reached a final agreement on each of the alleged open items for the written agreement and Turner's principal negotiator announced, "[t]he deal is done. Let's get documents we can sign and we'll meet in Atlanta for a press conference and a closing [early next week]." But later that same day, Turner's principal negotiator and its in-house counsel signed an agreement for the sale of the assets to Atlanta Spirit.

On September 15, 2003, as McDavid was preparing to travel to Atlanta for the closing and a press conference to announce the sale, he received a phone call informing him that Turner was "going in another direction" and had sold the assets to Atlanta Spirit. McDavid and his advisors, who had spent months finalizing the McDavid deal, were "stunned," "shocked," "disappointed," and felt "completely broadsided."

McDavid filed suit against Turner, alleging claims of breach of an oral contract to sell the assets, promissory estoppel, fraud, and breach of a confidentiality agreement. Turner denied the existence of any binding agreement, arguing that the parties had not executed a final written purchase agreement and had continued to negotiate the material terms of the transaction. Following an eight-week trial, the jury returned a verdict in favor of McDavid on the breach of oral contract claim and awarded $281 million in damages. Judgment was entered accordingly. . . .

As an initial matter, Georgia law recognizes that oral contracts falling outside the purview of the Statute of Frauds may be binding and enforceable. . . . Even complex or expensive contracts may be oral, as long as the evidence establishes the parties' mutual assent to all essential terms of the contract. . . .

. . . In this case, the determination of whether an oral contract existed, notwithstanding the parties' failure to sign a written agreement, was a question of fact for the jury to decide.

(a)   Parties' Intent to be Bound.

(i) The Parties' Expressions and Conduct.   The parties' objective manifestations of their mutual assent and intent to be bound to the McDavid acquisition deal included testimony that Turner's CEO formally announced, "we have a deal" during the parties' July 30th conference call. On or about August 16, 2003, Turner's principal negotiator, further confirmed the existence of an agreement during discussions pertaining to the deal restructure by stating that the "deal was done," and that "they were ready to close on the deal that [they] made on July 30th." And yet again, on or about September 12, 2003, during the course of another conference call to confirm the parties' final agreement on the terms to be incorporated into the written agreements, Turner's principle negotiator announced, "[t]he deal is done. Let's get documents we can sign and we'll meet in Atlanta for a press conference and a closing [early next week]."

In addition, Turner engaged in conduct from which the jury could conclude that an agreement had been reached. On or about August 1, 2003, Turner drafted an internal memo to its employees and planned for a press conference to publicly announce the deal with McDavid. Furthermore, in August 2003, Turner consulted with McDavid and his advisor on team management decisions, including the hiring of a general manager and head coach for the Hawks. Turner also obtained McDavid's approval before hiring a trainer, assistants, and scouts. There was testimony that according to industry standards, a buyer typically would not be given such formal input on team decisions until after the parties were committed and had formed an agreement. This evidence authorized the jury to conclude that both parties intended to be bound to the McDavid acquisition deal.

(ii) The Letter of Intent.   Turner nevertheless argues that no binding oral agreement could have been reached since the parties' April 30th Letter of Intent expressly provided that "neither party nor any of [their] affiliates [would] be bound unless and until such party (or affiliate) has executed the Definitive Agreements" and that "[n]o such binding agreement shall exist or arise unless and until the parties have negotiated, executed and delivered to each other Definitive Agreements." Undoubtedly, the express terms of the Letter of Intent reflect an intent that the parties would not be bound absent written, signed agreements. Significantly, however, it is undisputed that the terms of the Letter of Intent expired on June 14, 2003, and further

that Turner declined to renew it.[7] The Letter of Intent provided that all of its terms, with the exception of the confidentiality terms, would "automatically terminate and be of no further force and effect at 5:00 p.m. (Atlanta time) on [June 14, 2003,] the date on which the Exclusive Negotiation Period expire[d]." Turner's general counsel affirmed that when the Letter of Intent expired, it "no longer ha[d] any meaning" and the only terms that survived related to confidentiality. The jury therefore was authorized to conclude that upon the expiration of the Letter of Intent, the terms imposing the written agreement requirement also expired and had no effect. And, as recognized by Turner's general counsel, if Turner intended for the writing requirement of the Letter of Intent to remain effective after the expiration date, it could have set forth a survival provision in the same manner that it did for the confidentiality terms. Its failure to do so serves as some evidence contradicting Turner's claim that it maintained an objective manifestation to be bound only by a written agreement.

Turner's general counsel stated that the Letter of Intent was the only place where the parties had expressed their intent to be bound exclusively by executed, written agreements. McDavid and his advisors testified that after the Letter of Intent expired, no one expressed an intention that the parties would be bound only upon the execution of written contracts. When Turner's CEO and principal negotiator made their statements, "we have a deal" and the "deal was done," McDavid and his advisors believed that both parties intended to be bound to the agreement. Although Turner maintains that their intent to be bound only by written agreements never changed, its general counsel conceded that statements such as "we have a deal" may convey otherwise. The parties' failure to communicate an intent to be bound only in writing following the expiration of the Letter of Intent provided some evidence that an oral agreement was not precluded.

(iii) Contemplation of Written Instrument.   It is undisputed that the parties intended to sign written documents that memorialized the terms of their oral agreement. McDavid and his advisors testified that in accordance with the customary deal-making process, the parties first had to reach an oral agreement upon the material terms, and then the lawyers were expected to prepare the written documents that memorialized the parties' agreed upon terms. The evidence further established that the parties' respective lawyers exchanged multiple draft agreements purportedly attempting to ensure that the documents reflected the agreed upon terms. And, while the draft agreements contained a merger clause providing that the written agreement would "supersede all prior agreements, understandings and negotiations, both written and oral," such language could be construed as acknowledging the possibility of an oral agreement, particularly under these circumstances in which the merger clause did not become effective.

McDavid's witnesses further testified that all of the material issues for the written agreements had been resolved by mid-September, when they were planning to travel to Atlanta to formally sign the documents and publicly announce

---

7. After the Letter of Intent expired and McDavid inquired about extending it, Turner's principal negotiator told him that it was unnecessary since they were close to finalizing the deal and assured him, "You're our guy." Based upon this evidence, in addition to Turner's other assurances, the jury was authorized to infer that Turner intended to be bound to the McDavid deal.

the deal. The evidence thus authorized a finding that the only reason for the failure to execute the written agreements was Turner's refusal to proceed with McDavid's deal and its decision to consummate a deal with Atlanta Spirit instead.

While circumstances indicating that the parties intended to prepare a subsequent writing is strong evidence that they did not intend to be bound by a preliminary agreement, contrary evidence bearing upon the parties' intent to be bound and reflecting the existence of a binding oral agreement presents a question of fact for the jury's determination. Moreover, "[a]lthough the parties contemplated the future execution of a written . . . agreement, the jury was authorized to find that a binding oral agreement was in effect, and the failure to sign the written instrument did not affect the validity of the oral agreement." [Citation omitted.] . . .

(b) Agreement Upon All Material Terms. To constitute a binding agreement, the evidence must establish that the parties agreed upon all essential terms.

Again, the evidence on this issue was hotly contested and presented a genuine issue for the jury's determination. While Turner points to evidence that several open issues remained for discussion, that evidence merely conflicted with McDavid's evidence that all the material issues had been resolved. . . .

Despite the conflicts in the evidence, the evidence adduced at trial supports the jury's determination that the parties had reached an agreement on all material terms such that a binding oral agreement had been reached by September 12, 2003 when Turner announced, "[t]he deal is done," before Turner went "in another direction" with Atlanta Spirit. . . .

Judgment affirmed.

QUESTIONS

1. What are the main advantages to entering into an LOI? What are the disadvantages of entering into this kind of written agreement, even if it specifies that it is nonbinding?

2. Would you recommend the use of an LOI in the context of our problem involving Galaxy's proposed acquisition of Trekker? If so, what provisions should be included? Does your recommendation depend on whether you are Bidder's counsel or the lawyer for Target?

3. Consider the LOI included in Appendix D. This is the first draft of an LOI that was prepared, not by lawyers, but rather by senior executives of Bidder (Galaxy International, Inc.) and Target (Trekker Marketing, Inc.), as no lawyers were involved in the early negotiations. This LOI followed a brief but intense period of negotiations between the two sides. In this deal, the lawyers became involved (as is often the case in the real world of M&A deals) when the business clients (i.e., Target's CEO and Bidder's CEO) asked their respective lawyers to review this draft LOI before the parties signed it. As you read through this draft, consider the following:

   a. If you were Target's counsel, what changes would you want to make to this first draft *before* the parties sign this LOI?
   b. From Bidder's perspective, what changes would Bidder's lawyer want to make to this draft LOI *before* agreeing to have Bidder sign it?

c. Of these provisions, which should be made binding? Which provisions should be made expressly nonbinding?

d. Are there any provisions that are *not* contained in this draft that you think should be made part of the LOI? In considering this issue, does it matter whether you are Bidder's lawyer or counsel for Target? (*Hint:* You may want to consult the reading in the next section as part of your analysis of this question.)

2. Use of Non-Disclosure/Confidentiality Agreements

Regardless whether an LOI is signed by the parties, generally speaking, Target Co. (and very often Bidder Co. as well) will insist on the use of a *confidentiality agreement*, or, as it is sometimes called, a *non-disclosure agreement* (NDA). In certain cases, the NDA may be made part of the LOI, in which case Target will want to make clear that this provision of the parties' LOI is binding even if the other provisions of the LOI are specifically made nonbinding. Alternatively, or in lieu of an LOI, the NDA may be the subject of a separate, freestanding written agreement between Bidder and Target.

Why does Target typically insist, fairly early in the bargaining process, that Bidder sign a NDA? In considering this question, you may want to reflect on the following matters, which are typically addressed in any NDA:

- Is Bidder a competitor (or potential competitor) of Target? Why does this make a difference in negotiating the terms of the parties' NDA?
- What is the scope of Bidder's obligation under the terms of the NDA? Does it go beyond a simple non-disclosure obligation? Should there be a prohibition on Bidder's use of confidential information that it receives from Target during the course of the parties' negotiations and the due diligence process?
- Should the NDA include a restriction on the solicitation and/or hiring of Target's employees?
- Should the NDA include any restrictions on Bidder's right to contact or otherwise communicate with Target's customers or vendors?
- How long should the terms of the NDA be binding on the parties?
- Why does Bidder typically insist that Target sign an NDA?

In thinking about how to deal with these issues, which are an inherent part of drafting an NDA for any type of M&A transaction, consider the guidance offered by the Delaware Supreme Court in the following case.

|| **Martin Marietta Materials, Inc. v. Vulcan Materials**
|| **68 A.3d 1208 (Del. 2012)**

JACOBS, Justice:

[Following a trial in this action that was initiated by Martin Marietta Materials, Inc. ("Martin") against Vulcan Materials Company ("Vulcan"),] the

Court of Chancery . . . enjoined Martin, for a four month period, from continuing to prosecute its pending Exchange Offer and Proxy Contest to acquire control of Vulcan. That injunctive relief was granted to remedy Martin's adjudicated violations of two contracts between Martin and Vulcan: a Non-Disclosure Letter Agreement (the "NDA") and a Common Interest, Joint Defense and Confidentiality Agreement (the "JDA").[1]

Martin appealed to this Court from that judgment [and the Delaware Supreme Court affirmed]. . . .

The Facts

A. Background Leading to the Confidentiality Agreements

Vulcan and Martin are the two largest participants in the United States construction aggregates industry. That industry engages in mining certain commodities and processing them into materials used to build and repair roads, buildings and other infrastructure. Vulcan, a New Jersey corporation headquartered in Birmingham, Alabama, is the country's largest aggregates business; and Martin, a North Carolina corporation headquartered in Raleigh, North Carolina, is the country's second-largest.

Since the early 2000s, Vulcan and Martin episodically discussed the possibility of a business combination, but the discussions were unproductive and no significant progress was made. In 2010, Ward Nye, who had served as Martin's Chief Operating Officer since 2006, was appointed Martin's Chief Executive Officer ("CEO"). After that, Nye and Vulcan's CEO, Don James, restarted merger talks. . . .

At the outset Nye was receptive to a combination with Vulcan, in part because he believed the timing was to Martin's advantage. Vulcan's relative strength in markets that had been hard hit by the financial crisis, such as Florida and California, had now become a short-term weakness. As a result, Vulcan's financial and stock price performance were unfavorable compared to Martin's, whose business was less concentrated in those beleaguered geographic regions. To Nye, therefore, a timely merger — before a full economic recovery and before Vulcan's financial results and stock price improved — was in Martin's interest. Moreover, Nye had only recently been installed as Martin's CEO, whereas James, Vulcan's CEO, was nearing retirement age with no clear successor. To Nye, that suggested that a timely merger would also create an opportunity for him to end up as CEO of the combined companies.

Relatedly, although Nye was willing to discuss a possible merger with his Vulcan counterpart, he was not willing to risk being supplanted as CEO. The risk of Nye being displaced would arise if Martin were put "in play" by a leak of its confidential discussions with Vulcan, followed by a hostile takeover bid by Vulcan or a third party. Nye's concern about a hostile deal was not fanciful: recently

---

1. Both agreements expressly provided that they would be construed under Delaware law. Except where otherwise indicated, these two agreements are referred to collectively in this Opinion as the "Confidentiality Agreements."

Martin had engaged in friendly talks with a European company that had turned hostile. The European company's hostile attempt to acquire Martin failed only because the financial crisis "cratered" the bidder's financing.

Understandably, therefore, when Nye first spoke to Vulcan's banker, Goldman Sachs, in April 2010, he stressed that Martin was not for sale, and that Martin was interested in discussing the prospect of a friendly merger, but not a hostile acquisition of Martin by Vulcan. As the Chancellor found, Nye's notes prepared for a conversion [sic] with Vulcan's banker made it clear that "(i) Martin . . . would talk and share information about a *consensual* deal only, and not for purposes of facilitating an *unwanted* acquisition of Martin . . . by Vulcan; and even then only if (ii) absolute confidentiality, even as to the fact of their discussions, was maintained." When James and Nye first met in April 2010, they agreed that their talks must remain completely confidential, and they operated from the "shared premise" that any information exchanged by the companies would be used only to facilitate a friendly deal.

To secure their understanding, Nye and James agreed that their respective companies would enter into confidentiality agreements. That led to the drafting and execution of the two Confidentiality Agreements at issue in this case: the NDA and the JDA.

B. THE NDA

Nye . . . [instructed] Roselyn Bar, Esquire, Martin's General Counsel, . . . to prepare the NDA. In drafting the NDA, . . . [and consistent] with Nye's desire for strict confidentiality, Bar proposed changes . . .

In its final form, the NDA prohibited both the "use" and the "disclosure" of "Evaluation Material," except where expressly allowed. Paragraph 2 permitted either party to *use* the other party's Evaluation Material, but "*solely for the purpose of evaluating a Transaction.*" Paragraph 2 also categorically prohibited either party from *disclosing* Evaluation Material to anyone except the receiving party's representatives. The NDA defined "Evaluation Material" as "any nonpublic information furnished or communicated by the disclosing party" as well as "all analyses, compilations, forecasts, studies, reports, interpretations, financial statements, summaries, notes, data, records or other documents and materials prepared by the receiving party . . . that contain, reflect, are based upon or are generated from any such nonpublic information. . . ." The NDA defined "Transaction" as "a possible business combination transaction . . . between [Martin] and [Vulcan] or one of their respective subsidiaries."

Paragraph 3 of the NDA also prohibited the disclosure of the merger negotiations between Martin and Vulcan, and certain other related information, except for disclosures that were "legally required." Paragraph 3 relevantly provided that:

> Subject to paragraph (4), each party agrees that, without the prior written consent of the other party, it . . . will not disclose to any other person, *other than as legally required*, the fact that any Evaluation Material has been made available

hereunder, that discussions or negotiations have or are taking place concerning a Transaction or any of the terms, conditions or other facts with respect thereto (including the status thereof or that this letter agreement exists).

Paragraph 4 defined specific conditions under which "legally required" disclosure of Evaluation Material (and certain other information covered by Paragraph 3) would be permitted:

> In the event that a party . . . [is] requested or required (by oral questions, interrogatories, requests for information or documents in legal proceedings, subpoena, civil investigative demand or other similar process) to disclose any of the other party's Evaluation Material or any of the facts, the disclosure of which is prohibited under paragraph (3) of this letter agreement, the party requested or required to make the disclosure shall provide the other party with prompt notice of any such request or requirement so that the other party may seek a protective order or other appropriate remedy and/or waive compliance with the provisions of this letter agreement. If, in the absence of . . . the receipt of a waiver by such other party, the party requested or required to make the disclosure . . . should nonetheless, in the opinion of such party's . . . counsel be legally required to make the disclosure, such party . . . may, without liability hereunder, disclose only that portion of the other party's Evaluation Material which such counsel advises is legally required to be disclosed. . . .

As the Chancellor found, "Paragraph (4) establishes the Notice and Vetting Process for disclosing Evaluation Material and Transaction Information that would otherwise be confidential under the NDA in circumstances [where] a party is 'required' to do so in the sense that the party had received an External Demand." The Chancellor further concluded that Ms. Bar's addition of the words "Subject to paragraph (4)" at the beginning of NDA paragraph (3), is "most obviously read as being designed to prevent any reading of ¶ 3 that would permit escape from ¶ 4's narrow definition of legally required and ¶ 4's rigorous Notice and Vetting Process."

Vulcan shared Martin's confidentiality concerns. It therefore agreed to include in the NDA the changes that Ms. Bar proposed . . .

C.   THE JDA

Because the parties were exploring a combination of the two largest companies in their industry, antitrust scrutiny appeared unavoidable. After the NDA was signed, the two companies' inside and outside counsel met to discuss that issue. The discussions implicated nonpublic, privileged information and attorney work-product, leading Martin and Vulcan also to execute the JDA (which was drafted by outside counsel) to govern those exchanges.

The JDA, like the NDA, prohibits and limits the use and the disclosure of information that the JDA describes as "Confidential Materials." The critical prohibitions and limitations are found in JDA Paragraphs 2 and 4. Paragraph 2 prohibits the disclosure of Confidential Materials without "the consent of all Parties who may be entitled to claim any privilege or confidential status with respect to such materials. . . ." JDA Paragraph 4 relevantly provides that "Confidential Materials will be used, consistent with the maintenance of the privileged and confidential status of those materials, solely for purposes of pursuing and completing *the Transaction*." The JDA defines "Transaction" as "a *potential transaction being discussed* by Vulcan and Martin[ ] . . . involving the combination or acquisition of all or certain of their assets or stock. . . ."

D.   MARTIN'S USE AND DISCLOSURE OF VULCAN'S INFORMATION COVERED BY THE NDA AND JDA

After the JDA and the NDA were executed, Vulcan provided to Martin nonpublic information that gave Martin a window into Vulcan's organization, including detailed confidential information about Vulcan's business, revenues, and personnel. . . .

The Court of Chancery found, and Martin does not dispute, that Martin used and disclosed Vulcan's nonpublic information in preparing its Exchange Offer and its Proxy Contest to oust some of Vulcan's board members (collectively, the "hostile takeover bid"). Martin's position is that its use and disclosure of that nonpublic information was not legally prohibited by the Confidentiality Agreements. . . .

It is undisputed that antitrust counsel and other representatives of both companies met on various occasions and exchanged non-public "Confidential Materials" relating to antitrust divestiture risks and synergies. What resulted was a joint antitrust analysis prepared by antitrust counsel for both sides in 2010. Months later, a meeting between Martin's and Vulcan's CFOs and controllers took place on March 8, 2011. The information exchanged at that meeting and the nonpublic information Martin had previously received, caused Martin to revise its estimated merger synergies upwards by as much as $100 million annually, from the $150–$200 million it previously estimated. That synergy jump, plus the fact that Martin's stock price had increased in relation to Vulcan's, led Martin to conclude that it "could offer Vulcan's shareholders a premium in a stock-for-stock exchange, yet still justify the deal to Martin's stockholders" on economic grounds. Martin knew, however, that if it wanted to use all of its projected synergistic gains to justify the transaction, time was of the essence. Not only did current market conditions favor Martin, but also Vulcan already had plans to obtain certain cost savings on its own, independent of any deal with Martin.

Accordingly, as the talks floundered soon after the March 8 meeting, Martin and its bankers began using Vulcan's confidential, nonpublic information to consider alternatives to a friendly deal. By April 2011, Martin's bankers were evaluating the constraints imposed by the NDA upon a non-consensual transaction. At a mid-August 2011 meeting, Martin's board formally authorized management to pursue alternatives to a friendly deal. Four months later, Martin launched its unsolicited Exchange Offer.

As a regulatory matter, an exchange offer carries a line-item requirement under federal securities law to disclose past negotiations. Martin announced its Exchange Offer on December 12, 2011, by sending Vulcan a public "bear hug" letter* and filing a Form S-4 with the United States Securities and Exchange Commission ("SEC"). On January 24, 2012, Martin announced its Proxy Contest and filed a proxy statement in connection therewith.

Both before and after Martin commenced its hostile takeover bid, Martin disclosed Vulcan's nonpublic information, first to third party advisors (investment bankers, lawyers and public relations advisors), and later publicly. Martin did that without Vulcan's prior consent and without adhering to the Notice and Vetting Process mandated by the NDA. Regarding Martin's public relations advisors, the Chancellor found:

> Despite the Confidentiality Agreements, no effort was made to shield these advisors from receiving Evaluation Material or information relating to James' and Nye's negotiations. To the contrary, it is plain that the public relations advisors were given a blow-by-blow of Nye's and [Martin's CFO's] view of the negotiations with Vulcan and access to other Evaluation Material, and they advised Martin['s] . . . management how the process and substance of information sharing and negotiation could be translated into a public communications strategy that would exert pressure on Vulcan to accept an unsolicited bid from Martin . . .

As for its public disclosures, Martin's Form S-4 disclosed not only the history of the negotiations, but also other detailed information that constituted "Evaluation Material" and "Confidential Materials" under the respective Confidentiality Agreements. Those details, as the Court of Chancery found, included:

- Martin's anticipated annual cost synergies of $200 million to $250 million resulting from a merger with Vulcan;
- James' estimates of "achievable synergies" from a merger at different stages of the discussions, "including his belief as of June 2010 that 'a combination of the companies would result in approximately $100 million in synergies,' and not 'synergies at the $175 million to $200 million levels that Mr. Nye believed were achievable'; and James' supposed belief at the time the merger discussions ended, that 'the cost synergies to be achieved in a combination would [not] be greater than $50 million;'"
- "James' view of alternative deal structures designed to minimize tax leakage;"
- "James' conclusion, based on the merger discussions, that the 'potential tax leakage (*i.e.*, taxes arising from the sale or other disposition of certain assets that may be required to obtain regulatory approvals) and the ability to divest overlap[ping] business were significant impediments to a transaction;'" and

---

* [By the author: On Wall Street, a "bear hug letter" typically refers to a Bidder's unsolicited offer to acquire Target at a substantial premium over the market price of Target's shares in an effort to squeeze ("hug") the Target's board of directors into accepting the offer. Bidder will often use a "bear hug letter" when Bidder's board believes that Target's board is likely to resist Bidder's takeover attempt. We will discuss "bear hugs" in more detail as part of our analysis of hostile takeover bids in Chapter 7.]

- "The fact that 'the legal teams did not identify any significant impediments to a business combination transaction' at their antitrust meeting on May 19, 2010."

The disclosures by Martin to the SEC, the Chancellor found, "were . . . a tactical decision influenced by [Martin's] flacks," and "the influence of these public relations advisors is evident in the detailed, argumentative S-4 filed by Martin[ ]." Those disclosures, the trial court found, "exceeded the scope of what was legally required," and involved "selectively using that [Evaluation] Material and portraying it in a way designed to cast Vulcan's management and board in a bad light, to make Martin['s] own offer look attractive, and to put pressure on Vulcan's board to accept a deal on Martin['s] terms."

Lastly, the Chancellor found that after it launched its hostile takeover bid, Martin disclosed Evaluation Material and other confidential information "in push pieces to investors, off the record and on the record communications to the media, and investor conference calls." Those disclosures "include[d] a detailed history of the discussions [and] negotiations that [had taken] place concerning 'the Transaction,' [and] references revealing the 'opinions,' 'analyses' and 'non-public information' of Vulcan" regarding issues such as required antitrust divestitures and synergies.

E. THE COURT OF CHANCERY'S POST-TRIAL DETERMINATIONS

On December 12, 2011, the same day it launched its hostile takeover bid, Martin commenced this Court of Chancery action for a declaration that nothing in the NDA barred Martin from conducting its Exchange Offer and Proxy Contest. Vulcan counterclaimed for a mirror-image determination that Martin breached the NDA, and later amended its counterclaim to add claims that Martin had violated the JDA. Vulcan sought an injunction prohibiting Martin from proceeding with its hostile takeover bid. . . . [After trial, the Chancellor enjoined] Martin from (among other things) proceeding with its Exchange Offer and Proxy Contest for a four month period. Martin then terminated its Exchange Offer and Proxy Contest, and appealed to this Court from the trial court's final order and judgment.

In its Opinion, the Court of Chancery ultimately determined that Martin had breached the NDA and the JDA by impermissibly using and disclosing Evaluation Material under the NDA and Confidential Materials under the JDA. . . .

Specifically, the Court of Chancery found that, although the Confidentiality Agreements did not contain a "standstill" provision, they did bar Martin (and Vulcan) from:

- "Using the broad class of 'evaluation material' defined by the confidentiality agreements except for the consideration of a contractually negotiated business combination transaction between the parties, and not for a combination that was to be effected by hostile, unsolicited activity of one of the parties;"

- "Disclosing either the fact that the parties had merger discussions or any evaluation material shared under the confidentiality agreements unless the party was legally required to disclose because: (i) it had received 'oral questions, interrogatories, requests for information or documents in legal proceedings, subpoena, civil investigative demand or other similar process;' and (ii) its legal counsel had, after giving the other party notice and the chance for it to comment on the extent of disclosure required, limited disclosure to the minimum necessary to satisfy the requirements of law;" and
- "Disclosing information protected from disclosure by the confidentiality agreements through press releases, investor conference calls, and communications with journalists that were in no way required by law." . . .

ANALYSIS . . .

B.   MARTIN'S VIOLATIONS OF THE JDA

The Chancellor determined that Martin, in making its hostile bid, both "used" and "disclosed" Vulcan Confidential Materials in violation of the JDA. That agreement (the trial court found) unambiguously prohibits the use of "Confidential Materials" without Vulcan's consent, except "for purposes of pursuing and completing the Transaction," which the JDA defines as "a potential transaction being discussed by Vulcan and Martin . . . ." The Court of Chancery found as fact that "the only transaction that was 'being discussed' at the time the parties entered into the JDA was a negotiated merger," and that "neither [the] Exchange Offer nor [the] Proxy Contest . . . was 'the' transaction that was 'being discussed' at the time that the JDA was negotiated."

Martin asserts that those determinations are reversibly erroneous, ... First, Martin claims, the court erred in concluding that the only transaction "being discussed" when the parties entered into the JDA was a negotiated merger. Second, Martin advances the related claim that, even if "Transaction" meant a negotiated transaction, Martin committed no contractual breach, because "the JDA expressly allows the use of [protected] information 'for purposes of *pursuing and completing* the Transaction,'" and Martin's hostile bid "ultimately will facilitate . . . a negotiated transaction." . . . [Both of these] claims lack merit. . . .

The trial court properly found that the relevant operative language of the JDA — "a potential transaction being discussed" — is unambiguous, and Martin does not seriously contend otherwise. The only remaining dispute, accordingly, is factual: what transaction was "being discussed?" The *only* transaction being discussed, the trial court found, was a negotiated merger. To say that that finding is not "clearly wrong" would be an understatement: the finding is amply supported by the evidence. Nye told Vulcan that Martin was not for sale. Nye told Vulcan that Martin was interested in discussing the prospect of a merger, not an acquisition, whether by Vulcan or otherwise. And, Nye described the transaction under discussion as a "modified merger of equals."

Equally unpersuasive is Martin's alternative contention that even if "Transaction" means a negotiated merger, Martin did not violate the JDA's use restriction, because the JDA expressly allowed Martin to use Confidential Materials "for purposes of pursuing and completing the Transaction," and Martin's hostile bid "ultimately will facilitate . . . a negotiated transaction." That claim fails because the Chancellor found as fact that the only transaction being discussed would be "friendly" or "negotiated." That finding expressly and categorically excluded Martin's "hostile bid or a business combination . . . effected by a pressure strategy." We uphold the Chancellor's factual finding that the transaction "being discussed" for purposes of the JDA's "use" restriction did not encompass a merger accomplished by means of hostile tactics. Martin's second claim of error, therefore, fails for the same reason as its first. . . .

For these reasons, we uphold the Chancellor's conclusion that Martin used and disclosed Vulcan Confidential Materials in violation of the JDA.

C. MARTIN'S VIOLATIONS OF THE NDA

We next consider Martin's challenges to the Chancellor's determination that Martin violated the disclosure restrictions of the NDA. The Chancellor found as fact that Martin disclosed Vulcan confidential information, including Evaluation Material, in the course of pursuing its hostile bid, and Martin does not contest that finding. Rather, Martin's claim before us is that its disclosure of Vulcan confidential information was permitted by Paragraph 3 of the NDA, and that the Court of Chancery erred in holding otherwise. . . .

. . . [W]e conclude, as a matter of law based upon the NDA's unambiguous terms, that: (i) Paragraph 3, of itself, does not authorize the disclosure of "Evaluation Material," even if such disclosure is otherwise "legally required [pursuant to SEC rules applicable to exchange offers];" (ii) Paragraph 4 is the only NDA provision that authorizes the disclosure of Evaluation Material; (iii) any disclosure under Paragraph 4 is permitted only in response to an External Demand and after complying with the pre-disclosure Notice and Vetting Process mandated by that paragraph; and (iv) because no External Demand was made and Martin never engaged in the Notice and Vetting Process, its disclosure of Vulcan's Evaluation Material violated the disclosure restrictions of the NDA.

The contract provisions that relate to this issue are Paragraphs 2, 3, and 4 of the NDA. Paragraph 2, entitled "Use of Evaluation Material," categorically prohibits the disclosure of a party's Evaluation Material to anyone other than the receiving party's representatives. Paragraph 3, which is entitled "Non-Disclosure of Discussions; Communications," . . . covers only three categories of information: (a) the fact that any Evaluation Material has been made available; (b) the fact that discussions or negotiations concerning a Transaction have been taken or are taking place; and (c) any of the terms, conditions or other facts with respect thereto [*i.e.*, to the negotiations] including the status thereof [*i.e.*, the negotiations] or that the NDA exists. *Not included within those categories is the substance of a party's Evaluation Material*—as distinguished from "the fact that . . . Evaluation Material has been made available."

The omission of Evaluation Material from the coverage of Paragraph 3 is both intentional and logical. Although Paragraph 3 does not expressly prohibit the disclosure of Evaluation Material, it does not need to. Paragraph 2 accomplishes that. Evaluation Material does not fall with Paragraph 3's "legally required" carve-out exception, because that exception can *only* apply to the confidential information specifically identified in Paragraph 3. Moreover—and of critical importance—the permitted disclosure of Evaluation Material is explicitly and separately made the subject of Paragraph 4, which is entitled "Required Disclosure." . . .

Paragraph 4 also mandates a procedural framework within which legally required disclosure of Evaluation Material is permissible. That framework has two elements. The first is that Evaluation Material must be the subject of an External Demand. The second is that a party contemplating disclosure of that information must give pre-disclosure notice of any intended disclosure and (where applicable) engages in a vetting process. . . .

To recapitulate, Paragraphs 2, 3, and 4, both internally and when read together, unambiguously permit a party to the NDA to disclose "legally required" Evaluation Material. But, that may be done *only* if an External Demand for such information has first been made, and *only* if the non-disclosing party is then given prior notice of any intended disclosure and (where applicable) an opportunity to vet the information sought to be disclosed. The Court of Chancery properly so concluded. In our view, that interpretation is compelled by the text of these NDA provisions, their relationship to each other, and by the canon of construction that requires all contract provisions to be harmonized and given effect where possible. That also is the only interpretation that is consistent with the found facts relating to the NDA's overall purpose and import, and the parties' reasons for negotiating the specific language of the disputed NDA provisions.

Martin's contrary argument rests on the premise that Evaluation Material is textually included within the purview of Paragraph 3. Martin claims that the following italicized phrase in Paragraph 3 captures Evaluation Material: "[E]ach party agrees [not to disclose, other than as legally required,] . . . that discussions or negotiations have or are taking place concerning a Transaction or any of the terms, conditions, or *other facts with respect thereto* (including the status thereof or that this letter agreement exists)."

Martin's argued-for interpretation—that "other facts with respect thereto" must be read to cover Evaluation Material—finds no support in the specific language and structure of the NDA. It is also unreasonable. Any doubt about the scope of the phrase "other facts with respect thereto" is put to rest by considering the broader language of which that phrase is but one moving part. The context clarifies that the phrase, "other facts with respect *thereto*," means specific facts indicating that there were "discussions or negotiations . . . concerning a Transaction," including the fact that the NDA even exists. That peripheral species of information differs markedly from the substantive, company-specific internal information that the parties exchanged in order to facilitate their discussions or negotiations (*i.e.,* Evaluation Material).

Evaluation Material is a term that is central to, and defined in, the NDA. That term is specifically referred to by name throughout the agreement. Martin's interpretation of the NDA attempts to shoehorn "Evaluation Material" into language in Paragraph 3 that does not, and is not intended to, include "Evaluation Material." If the drafters of the NDA intended to include Evaluation Material within the category of information disclosable under Paragraph 3, they easily could have done that by referring directly to "Evaluation Material," as they did repeatedly elsewhere in the NDA. . . .

We conclude, for these reasons, that the only reasonable construction of the NDA is that Paragraph 4 alone permitted the disclosure of Evaluation Material, and even then only if triggered by an External Demand and preceded by compliance with Paragraph 4's Notice and Vetting Process. The Court of Chancery found as fact that Martin disclosed Evaluation Material in the course of conducting its hostile bid, without having received an External Demand and without having engaged in the Notice and Vetting Process. Martin has not challenged that finding. We therefore uphold the Court of Chancery's determination that Martin breached the NDA's disclosure restrictions.

D.   THE REMEDY

Lastly, Martin claims that the Court of Chancery reversibly erred in balancing the equities and granting injunctive relief to Vulcan without any evidence that Vulcan was threatened with, or suffered, actual irreparable injury. The injunction prohibited Martin, for a four-month period, from going forward with its Exchange Offer and Proxy Contest, from otherwise taking steps to acquire control of Vulcan shares or assets, and from further violating the NDA and the JDA. As earlier noted, we review this claim for an abuse of discretion.

Martin's claim fails both legally and factually. It fails legally because, as the trial court noted, in Paragraph 9 of the NDA both parties stipulated that "money damages would not be [a] sufficient remedy for *any* breach . . . by either party," and that "the non-breaching party *shall be entitled to equitable relief,* including injunction and specific performance, as a remedy for any such breach." The JDA has a similar provision that obligates the parties to pursue "equitable or injunctive relief"—and *not* monetary damages—in the event of a breach of that agreement.

Our courts have long held that "contractual stipulations as to irreparable harm alone suffice to establish that element for the purpose of issuing . . . injunctive relief." Martin offers no persuasive reason why the parties' stipulation in the NDA that "money damages would not be [a] sufficient remedy for any breach" should not be regarded as a stipulation to irreparable injury, nor why the stipulation that "any breach . . . shall entitle[ ]" the non-breaching party "to equitable relief" should not be given effect in this case. Nor does Martin persuade us that, although the JDA expressly disclaims any right to a money damages remedy, the harm imposed by a breach of that contract is not "irreparable" for injunctive purposes.

Martin's assertions also fail factually, because the Chancellor did make a finding of "actual"—and irreparable—injury. The trial court found, as fact, that "Vulcan is now suffering from exactly the same kind of harm Nye demanded the Confidentiality Agreements shield Martin [ ] from[;]" that Vulcan was injured by Martin's "contractually improper selective revelation of nonpublic Vulcan information[;]" and that Vulcan suffered a loss of "negotiating leverage."

Unable to deny that the trial court so found, Martin shifts ground and asserts that any finding of harm was "speculative" and made "without any support."

To the contrary, the adjudicated harm was not speculative and is supported by ample record evidence. For example, Vulcan's CEO James testified that when Martin revealed publicly the fact of the negotiations, "[i]t put us in play at a time that we would not have wanted to be put into play," because "this industry is in a recession." James also testified that "our employees were very concerned," and that "[o]ur executive team obviously is completely distracted from pursuing our internal strategic plan." That and other non-speculative record evidence solidly supports the Court of Chancery's finding of "actual" irreparable injury.

Martin also attacks the scope of the remedy itself, claiming that the injunction was unreasonable because it would delay Martin's Proxy Contest by one year, rather than four months. In different circumstances that kind of harm might be a legally cognizable factor that a court will take into account in balancing the equities for and against granting an injunction. Here, however, the "delay" is attributable to the NDA's May 3, 2012 expiration date, which—when combined with Vulcan's advance notice bylaw—precluded Martin from disclosing Vulcan confidential information to support its Proxy Contest in time for Vulcan's 2012 annual meeting. Because New Jersey law requires director elections to be held annually, the practical reality was that Martin's first opportunity to disclose that information lawfully to promote a Proxy Contest would not occur until 2013.

Given those facts, the Court of Chancery did not abuse its discretion by holding that the equities favored Vulcan, because "Martin's breaches prevented Vulcan from seeking injunctive relief before the confidential information was made public" and Vulcan "[had] been measured in its request for injunctive relief." The court properly balanced the need to "vindicat[e] Vulcan's reasonable [contractual] expectations" against the "delay" imposed on Martin as a "result of its own conduct." The Chancellor stated that although "an argument can be made that a longer injunction would be justified by the pervasiveness of Martin['s] breaches," an injunction lasting four months was "a responsible period" reflecting the time interval between when Martin launched its Exchange Offer on December 12, 2011, and the NDA's May 3, 2012 expiration date. That this measured form of relief also resulted in delaying Martin for a longer period from seeking to replace the Vulcan board, does not detract from the propriety of the relief the court granted.

CONCLUSION

For the foregoing reasons, the judgment of the Court of Chancery is affirmed.

QUESTIONS

1. Why did the court apply Delaware law in construing the provisions of the NDA at issue in this case?

2. In the context of a breach of an NDA, there is no possibility for suing to enjoin (i.e., prevent) disclosure or misuse of the company's information.

As a result, there is only the possibility of an ex-post remedy. In light of this practical reality, just how valuable are these NDA provisions?

3. Should NDAs include agreed-upon remedies for breach? Is there any language that Vulcan could/should have included in the NDA that would have made it more watertight? In other words, does this case really involve an oversight in drafting the terms of the NDA?

4. In the context of our planning problem (involving Galaxy's acquisition of Trekker's business), would you recommend the use of an NDA? Does your analysis of this issue vary depending on whether you are Trekker's counsel or Galaxy's?

5. In considering the matters that are customarily included in an NDA, what advice would you give Trekker on these issues? What advice would you give to Galaxy on these matters?

C.   *Acquisition Consideration: Business Considerations and Legal Issues*

The key factor in determining whether the parties' negotiations will ultimately result in a deal usually turns on price and price-related considerations. In negotiating the terms of the purchase price in the context of any particular acquisition, there are typically three issues that must be considered as a threshold matter:

1. Will the acquisition consideration consist of cash or Bidder's stock (or some combination of the two)?[1]
2. Once the parties agree on the nature of the acquisition consideration, then they have to reach agreement on the crucial deal point — *how much?*
3. Finally, the parties have to agree on *when* the acquisition consideration is to be paid, which generally will be at closing on the acquisition agreement — *unless* the parties agree that payment of some portion of the purchase price is to be deferred until some time *after* closing.

---

1. As an alternative to using Bidder's stock, Bidder may ask Target to accept Bidder's note or other debt securities of Bidder. This raises a separate set of financing issues (including, most prominently, issues under the federal securities laws, among other things); the complexity thereby created by the use of debt financing generally goes beyond the scope of the introductory materials presented in this chapter. As but one example of the additional legal considerations that counsel must address—where Bidder's debt is to be part of the acquisition consideration—is the threshold issue of whether the debt is a security under federal law and under relevant state blue sky laws. In addition, as a business matter, the parties will have to negotiate the terms of the debt instrument (interest rate, payment schedule, etc.), and further, analyze the impact of these obligations on the company's cash flow and other aspects of its business operations.

With respect to the first issue—use of stock vs. cash as acquisition consideration—this issue was examined in detail in Chapter 2, in particular as part of our analysis of the terms of AT&T's acquisition of DirecTV using a package of AT&T stock and cash. *See* Problem no. 2 at pp. 122-124 of Chapter 2. The remaining two issues will be examined in more detail in this section. It bears emphasizing at the outset, however, that resolution of these issues varies widely from deal to deal, and consequently, is not susceptible to generalizable conclusions. The terms reached in the context of any particular acquisition will generally depend on the relative bargaining power of each side, which can be influenced by a myriad of different factors.

1. Purchase Price: Cash vs. Stock as Acquisition Consideration

If Bidder's stock is to be used as the acquisition consideration, then Bidder will have to comply with the requirements of the Securities Act of 1933 (the "1933 Act"). The obligations imposed on Bidder by the terms of the 1933 Act generally require Bidder to either register the shares or find an exemption from the registration requirement for the issuance of its shares in connection with the acquisition of Target. Detailed examination of the nature of these obligations under the federal securities laws is covered in Chapter 4. Suffice it to say, the delay and cost that results from triggering the requirements of the 1933 Act will often be an important factor in determining whether to use cash or Bidder's securities as the acquisition consideration.

Another important factor that will influence the parties' negotiations regarding the use of cash vs. Bidder's stock as the acquisition consideration is the financial motivations of the parties to the transaction and the business objectives they hope to accomplish by engaging in the proposed transaction. For example, in connection with Google's acquisition of Nest Labs, it is likely that Nest Lab's owners insisted on using cash as the acquisition consideration as the preferred "exit strategy" for the venture capital investors in Nest Labs (*see* Note 1 at pp. 19-20 of Chapter 1). With respect to a family–owned business, such as Chef America (*see* the Asset Purchase Problem Set at pp. 86-88 of Chapter 2), it is most likely that the owners, Paul and David Merage wanted to get out of Chef America's business completely. Their stock in the company constituted an illiquid asset that presumably represented a substantial portion (if not virtually all) of their personal wealth. Assuming that Paul and David were nearing retirement age, they probably faced the pressure of needing to diversify their investment portfolios and the desire to stop working to grow and manage Chef America's business. Therefore, if Nestlé had proposed financing its purchase of Chef America's business using Nestlé's common stock, the Merage brothers likely would have broken off any further discussions with Nestlé. *Query:* Why is this result likely in the context of this particular deal? In other words, why would the business objectives of the Merage brothers *not* be satisfied if Nestlé stock were to be used as the acquisition consideration?

2. Different Mechanisms for Making Purchase Price Adjustments

a. Earn-Outs

Earn-out provisions are a type of pricing formulation most commonly found in agreements for the acquisition of a privately held Target. Simply put, an earn-out is a pricing formulation that allows the financial performance of Target's business on a post-closing basis to directly affect the amount of the purchase price that Bidder will ultimately pay to acquire Target's business. Earn-out provisions may serve several purposes. Typically, earn-out clauses are used to address a big valuation gap in the purchase price expectations of Target's owners versus the price that Bidder is willing to pay to acquire Target's business. An earn-out provision may be used to bridge this valuation gap. In addition, earn-out provisions are often used to provide financial incentives—motivation to "keep their head in the game"—for those selling shareholders who Bidder desires to remain with Target as executives or management after the acquisition closes.

Consequently, an earn-out provision generally will result in a post-closing adjustment to the agreed-upon purchase price. What factors influence the parties' determination to use an earn-out? The decision to use an earn-out may be the product of the stubbornness of the ever-optimistic seller (Target) clinging to, say, a $50 million purchase price, and who cannot understand why Bidder cannot raise its valuation numbers to this $50 million level. On the other hand, the skeptical Bidder insists that it cannot responsibly pay more than $45 million to acquire Target's business. In such a case, Bidder may not believe the rosy forecasts proffered by Target to support its high valuation position. Under these circumstances, the parties might decide to bridge their differing perspectives on the proper valuation of Target's business by resorting to the use of an earn-out. Thus, if the Target executive team can actually achieve the rosy forecasts they have proffered to support Target's high valuation, then Bidder will pay the additional purchase price. As such, the earn-out may be viewed as just another variation on that time-honored expression, "Put your money where your mouth is."

On the facts of the hypothetical scenario described above, where an earn-out is used in order to close the valuation gap between Bidder and Target, the parties might agree to frame the terms of the purchase price as follows: a base price of $45 million to be paid at closing (either in cash or Bidder's stock), subject to an earn-out component that would allow the purchase price to increase by as much as $5 million, with the exact amount of the post-closing price adjustment to be determined by a formula agreed to by the parties. The formula to be used to calculate this post-closing price adjustment may be based on the cumulative pre-tax income, revenue, EBITDA, or other financial metric that is important to the business operations that Bidder acquired from Target over a period of time (say, three years) following the closing on the acquisition agreement. In this hypothetical case, a three-year period is likely to be used in the parties' formula for the earn-out because—as is often the case in the real world—that was the period covered by the seller's (Target's) projections. If these projections are met over the three-year period following closing on the deal, then Target's owners will receive an additional payment of $5 million, thereby allowing the sellers to realize the $50 million purchase price that they (stubbornly) insisted on and thus avoiding a stalemate in the parties' negotiations. On its face, this might seem to be a simple resolution of the parties' differences. In truth, though, this is only the beginning, as the parties then must negotiate the complex terms that make up the formula for a typical earn-out provision.

In the context of our planning problem involving Galaxy's acquisition of Trekker's business, the initial draft of the acquisition agreement (*see* Appendix C) includes an earn-out provision. As you read through the following materials concerning earn-outs, consider whether the principals of Galaxy or Trekker proposed use of an earn-out and what purpose was to be served by including an earn-out provision in their agreement.

Negotiating the Terms of an Earn-Out.   From the perspective of Bidder, drafting an earn-out is a fairly straightforward exercise. For Bidder, the crucial consideration centers on careful drafting of the key accounting terms that will be part of any earn-out provision (such as, in our example, the calculation of *pre-tax income*). However, things may quickly become complicated. The selling shareholders (who may or may not remain with the Target business as managers or executives) will want to maximize pre-tax profit, but the new owner, Bidder, may want to increase sales and marketing expenses, or research and development expenses, which will build future growth but may reduce near-term profitability; and therein lies the risk.

Accordingly, the current owners of Target's business typically will want assurances that Target's business will be run as an isolated business unit (such as a separate subsidiary or division of Bidder) so that the financial revenues generated by Target's business can be measured in a reliable and accurate manner. In addition, and especially in those cases where the existing Target owners/managers are to stay on to run the business after closing, these managers can be expected to demand some measure of autonomy in operating the business during the period covered by the earn-out (which in our simple example above is a three-year post-closing period). Of course, Bidder is likely to resist these demands, insisting that the full value of the acquisition for Bidder can only be realized if Target's business is promptly integrated into Bidder's business operations. Notwithstanding the outcome of the parties' negotiations on this particular issue, there also is likely to be extended negotiations over other details regarding the financial terms of the earn-out (such as the amount of administrative overhead that Bidder—now the parent company—will be able to push down and require Target's business to absorb). Moreover, it is likely that counsel for Bidder will be equally concerned about the possibility for manipulation of business expenses and other items by the managers of Target's business, who Bidder fears may be tempted to act in an opportunistic manner in running the business operations on a post-closing basis in order to satisfy the terms of the parties' earn-out formula, possibly at the expense of the longer term best interests of the business.

Drafting the Formula for the Earn-Out.   From both sides, negotiating and drafting the earn-out formula is likely to become exceedingly complex as each side tries to anticipate what *might* happen to the business *after* closing. Consequently, in the experience of many M&A lawyers, earn-outs frequently prove to be unworkable. Even though there may be an agreement in principle between the parties as to the use of an earn-out, the devil obviously is in the details. Even the simplest of earn-out formulas agreed to in the abstract by the parties quickly devolves into nightmarish drafting sessions as the parties begin focusing on the myriad variables that could affect making, or missing, the earn-out formula, and begin adding adjustments, restrictions, and covenants to address or offset the effect of those variables. For example, if the earn-out is based on achieving a certain amount of pre-tax income, the selling shareholders may seek to limit the new owner's ability to increase expenses, or alternatively, create an adjustment so that increased expenses are not counted against income for purposes of the earn-out formula. Faced with these complexities, it is not uncommon for the parties ultimately to decide to abandon the use of an earn-out, notwithstanding its initial appeal as a creative tool to bridge the valuation gap facing the parties at the outset of their negotiations. Of course, that still leaves a valuation gap to be addressed by the parties.

Even with all these time-consuming negotiating and drafting difficulties, earn-outs are used often in the real world of M&A transactions, particularly in those deals where the valuation differences between the parties are significant. In these cases, as a practical matter, the only way the deal will get done — the only way to close the big gap between the price sought by the optimistic owners of Target and the much lower price offered by the skeptical Bidder — is to use an earn-out to forge a compromise.

Dispute Resolution Mechanisms. One final thing to mention in connection with the use of an earn-out is the perceived need to include some dispute resolution mechanism as part of the acquisition agreement. Although a dispute resolution provision may apply to the agreement as a whole, many lawyers believe that the parties should include a provision that separately and specifically addresses disputes over how to apply the terms of the earn-out formula in order to resolve any differences that may arise between the parties as to the amount of purchase price to be paid on a *post-closing* basis. For example, the parties may agree to appoint a particular accounting firm to resolve issues related to the application of the financial terms of the earn-out formula used in their agreement. Often, though, counsel for seller may resist including such a provision on the grounds that this kind of arbitration provision is an open invitation to the buyer to litigate the terms of the earn-out, which will inevitably result in an arbitration proceeding. In the event of arbitration, Bidder's ultimate concern usually is that the arbitrator is likely to just "split the difference," meaning that Bidder will likely be required to pay half of the maximum amount of the earn-out as set forth under the terms of the parties' acquisition agreement. Depending on the degree of Bidder's apprehension, Bidder may refuse to provide for any specific dispute resolution mechanism, even though it may ultimately agree to the use of an earn-out as part of the acquisition agreement.

While earn-out provisions may provide a useful solution to bridge the valuation gap between Bidder and Target, they can also lead to post-closing controversy that often results in litigation. The next case presents "a cautionary tale relating to the drafting of earn-out provisions in M&A transactions." Shane

C. D'Souza and David P. Badour, McCarthy Tetraut LLP, *Earning Earn-outs*, July 22, 2015, *available at:* https://www.mccarthy.ca/en/insights/blogs/canadian-ma-perspectives/earning-earn-outs-new-decision-affirms-dangers-not-negotiating-objective-measures-and-standards-earn-out-provisions.

Lazard Technology Partners, LLC v. Qinetiq North America Operations, LLC
114 A.3d 193 (Del. 2015)

STRINE, Chief Justice:

This is an appeal in an earn-out dispute arising from a merger. The appellant represents former stockholders of Cyveillance, Inc., a cyber technology company (the "company"), whom we refer to as the "seller" for the sake of clarity. The appellee (the "buyer") paid $40 million up-front to the company and promised to pay up to another $40 million if the company's revenues reached a certain level. Section 5.4 of the merger agreement prohibited the buyer from "tak[ing] any action to divert or defer [revenue] with the intent of reducing or limiting the Earn–Out Payment." When the earn-out period ended, the revenues had not reached the level required to generate an earn-out.

The seller filed suit in the Court of Chancery, arguing that the buyer breached Section 5.4 of the merger agreement. The seller also argued that the buyer violated the merger agreement's implied covenant of good faith and fair dealing by failing to take certain actions that the seller contended would have resulted in the achievement of revenue sufficient to generate an earn-out.

After a trial, extensive briefing, and post-trial oral argument, the Court of Chancery issued a bench decision reviewing the factual circumstances the seller alleged amounted to a breach of Section 5.4 of the merger agreement and the implied covenant. In that decision, the Court of Chancery found that the merger agreement meant what it said, which is that in order for the buyer to breach Section 5.4, it had to have acted with the "intent of reducing or limiting the Earn-out Payment." After reviewing each of the seller's theories as to how the buyer had acted with the requisite intent, the Court of Chancery found that the seller had not proven that any business decision of the buyer was motivated by a desire to avoid an earn-out payment.

Likewise, the Court of Chancery rejected the seller's implied covenant claim. The Court of Chancery held that the merger agreement was complex and required a number of actions, including actions that would occur post-closing. It thus found that the merger agreement's express terms were supplemented by an implied covenant. But as to whether conduct not prohibited under the contract was precluded because it might result in a reduced or no earn-out payment, the Court of Chancery held that, consistent with the language of Section 5.4, the buyer had a duty to refrain from that conduct only if it was taken with the intent to reduce or avoid an earn-out altogether.

On appeal, the seller argues that the Court of Chancery misinterpreted the merger agreement in both respects, and also that its factual conclusions warrant no deference because they were made in a succinct bench ruling. As to the first argument, the seller argues that the Court of Chancery erred because it should have recognized that Section 5.4 precluded any conduct by the buyer that it knew would have the effect of compromising the seller's ability to receive an earn-out. It also claims that the Court of Chancery erred when it held that the implied covenant must be read consistently with Section 5.4 because the specific standard in that contractual term reflected the parties' agreement about how the seller would be protected from post-closing conduct that could jeopardize an earn-out payment.

The seller's arguments are without merit. The Court of Chancery acted properly in giving Section 5.4 its plain meaning.[7] By its unambiguous terms, that term only limited the buyer from taking action intended to reduce or limit an earn-out payment. Intent is a well-understood concept that the Court of Chancery properly applied.[8] The seller seeks to avoid its own contractual bargain by claiming that Section 5.4 used a knowledge standard, preventing the buyer from taking actions simply because it knew those actions would reduce the likelihood that an earn-out would be due. As Section 5.4 is written, it only barred the buyer from taking action specifically motivated by a desire to avoid the earn-out.[9] Contrary to the seller's argument, the Court of Chancery never said that avoiding the earn-out had to the buyer's *sole* intent, but properly held that the buyer's action had to be motivated at least in part by that intention.

Likewise, the seller's argument that it could rely on the implied covenant of good faith and fair dealing to avoid the burden to prove that the buyer intentionally violated Section 5.4 is without merit. Section 5.4 specifically addressed the requirements for an earn-out payment and left the buyer free to conduct its business post-closing in any way it chose so long as it did not act with the intent to reduce or limit the earn-out payment. And as the Court of Chancery found, "[the seller] attempted to negotiate for a range of additional affirmative post-closing obligations, but [the buyer] rejected all of them. . . . Instead of the various affirmative obligations, the agreement provided only that [the buyer] could not take action with the intent of reducing or undermining the earn-out

---

7. *Lorillard Tobacco Co. v. Am. Legacy Found.*, 903 A.2d 728, 739 (Del. 2006) ("When interpreting a contract, the role of a court is to effectuate the parties' intent. In doing so, we are constrained by a combination of the parties' words and the plain meaning of those words where no special meaning is intended."); CORBIN ON CONTRACTS §32.3 (2003) ("The plain, common, or normal meaning of language will be given to the words of a contract. . . .").

8. "Intent" is most often defined and analyzed in the criminal law context. "[T]he modern [criminal law] approach is to define separately the mental states of knowledge and intent ([which is] sometimes referred to as purpose)." Wayne R. LaFave, 1 Subst. Crim. L. Section 5.2 (2d ed. 2014). Most modern codes, including the Model Penal Code, "provide[] that one acts 'purposely' when 'it is his conscious object . . . to cause [] a result.' " *Id.* (quoting Model Penal Code § 2.02(2)(a)(i)); . . .

9. *See Cincinnati SMSA Ltd. P'ship v. Cincinnati Bell Cellular Sys. Co.*, 708 A.2d 989, 992 (Del. 1998) ("Delaware observes the well-established general principle that . . . it is not the proper role of a court to rewrite or supply omitted provisions to a written agreement."); *Rhone–Poulenc Basic Chems. Co. v. Am. Motorists Ins. Co.*, 616 A.2d 1192, 1195–96 (Del. 1992) ("Clear and unambiguous language in [a contract] should be given its ordinary and usual meaning. Absent some ambiguity, Delaware courts will not destroy or twist policy language under the guise of construing it. [W]hen the language of a [contract] is clear and unequivocal, a party will be bound by its plain meaning because creating an ambiguity where none exists could, in effect, create a new contract with rights, liabilities and duties to which the parties had not assented.") (internal citations and quotations omitted).

payment."[11] Accordingly, the Court of Chancery was very generous in assuming that the implied covenant of good faith and fair dealing operated at all as to decisions affecting the earn-out, given the specificity of the merger agreement on that subject, and the negotiating history that showed that the seller had sought objective standards for limiting the buyer's conduct but lost at the bargaining table.[12] Therefore, the Court of Chancery correctly concluded that the implied covenant did not inhibit the buyer's conduct unless the buyer acted with the intent to deprive the seller of an earn-out payment.[13]

Finally, we reject the seller's argument that the Court of Chancery's factual determinations should not be given deference because they were set forth in a bench ruling. That bench ruling dealt with the key factual contentions of the seller and did so clearly. The ruling explained that the Court of Chancery was not persuaded that the buyer had acted with the requisite intent that would allow the seller to prevail on its breach of contract claim.

The Court of Chancery is a busy court charged with giving parties answers to complicated questions in a range of cases, often on an expedited basis. One of the ways in which the judges of that court handle their demanding caseload is by issuing prompt bench decisions on the basis of settled law when they believe they can do so responsibly. That is what the Vice Chancellor did here, and his decision is well grounded in the facts of record and entitled to our deference.

For these reasons, we conclude that the seller's appeal is without merit and that the judgment of dismissal entered for the buyer should be AFFIRMED.

---

11. The affirmative post-closing covenants that the seller sought but did not obtain at the bargaining table included obligations to "act in good faith to maintain existing or greater levels of business, to preserve relationships of customers . . . and cause the Surviving Corporation to have adequate amounts of capital required to achieve the Earn–Out Payments[,] make reasonable commercial efforts to recruit and employ sufficient employees to achieve the Earn–Out Payments[,] market and bid for new contracts consistent with past practice[,] and [] not divert any contracts or business opportunities from the Surviving Corporation to any other entity."

12. *See Nemec v. Shrader*, 991 A.2d 1120, 1125 (Del. 2010) ("The implied covenant of good faith and fair dealing involves a cautious enterprise, inferring contractual terms to handle developments or contractual gaps that the asserting party pleads neither party anticipated. When conducting this analysis, we must assess the parties' reasonable expectations at the time of contracting and not re-write the contract to appease a party who later wishes to rewrite a contract he now believes to have been a bad deal. Parties have a right to enter into good and bad contracts, the law enforces both.") (internal quotations omitted); *Winshall v. Viacom Int'l, Inc.*, 55 A.3d 629, 636–37 (Del. Ch. 2011) ("[T]he implied covenant of good faith and fair dealing should not be applied to give plaintiffs contractual protections that they failed to secure for themselves at the bargaining table. . . . [T]he implied covenant is not a license to rewrite contractual language. . . . Rather, a party may only invoke the protections of the covenant when it is clear from the underlying contract that the contracting parties would have agreed to proscribe the act later complained of had they thought to negotiate with respect to that matter.") (internal citations and quotations omitted), *aff'd*, 76 A.3d 808 (Del. 2013); . . .

13. Because the seller cannot prevail even under the generous assumption the Court of Chancery used in assessing the seller's claim, we need not reach the buyer's well-reasoned argument that Section 5.4 addressed the full range of discretionary conduct relevant to the earn-out calculation, leaving no room for the implied covenant to operate at all.

QUESTIONS

1. What provisions did the seller seek as part of the terms of the earn-out provision included in the parties' merger agreement? Why did the buyer refuse to include these provisions?

2. What is the difference between a knowledge-based prohibition on the buyer's post-closing actions as opposed to an intent-based prohibition? What is the impact of relying on a subjective standard (as opposed to an objective standard) with respect to Bidder's conduct of the business after closing?

NOTES

1. Lessons Learned for Structuring "Earn-Out" Provisions. In a decision that is particularly noteworthy for the brevity of an *en banc* opinion of the Delaware Supreme Court, the decision does offer important lessons for M&A lawyers regarding drafting of an earn-out provision:

> Without finding that there was any ambiguity in the contract as written, the court looked to extrinsic evidence of the negotiations leading up to the final agreement. The Court took careful note of the earn-out language—proposed in negotiations but rejected by the buyer—to interpret the scope of the buyer's duties with regard to operating the business after closing. Buyers and sellers should be cognizant that what they propose and reject in negotiations can be held against them in later disputes regarding the meaning of the subject provisions.

William L. Prickett, et al., Seyfarth Shaw LLP, *Lazard Technology Partners, LLC v Qinetiq North America Operations, LLC: An Earn-Out That Didn't Pay,* July 2015, *available at:* https://www.lexology.com/library/detail.aspx?g=67a4f97f-0618 -4e28-a8f1-67272caa4195.

2. The Inherent Tension in Negotiating the Terms of an M&A Transaction. As reflected in the facts of the *Lazard Technology* case, another consideration that the parties need to keep in mind when negotiating the terms of the earn-out is that the use of an earn-out means that the parties will need to maintain some sort of business relationship *after* closing on the acquisition. In light of this, the parties may have an incentive to avoid contentious and protracted negotiations that might damage, or at least sour, the basis for such a continuing business relationship.

Indeed, the kind of polar disagreement that we have seen reflected in the parties' negotiations over the terms of the earn-out actually reflects a more fundamental tension inherent in the M&A deal making process as a whole: a natural suspicion of the other party, tempered by a business need to trust in the good faith of the other party. As the remaining materials in this chapter make abundantly clear, there is an inherent tension in M&A transactions between profit-maximizing Bidders on the one hand and equally profit-motivated Targets on the other. This tension typically surfaces in rather dramatic fashion in negotiating the specific terms of an earn-out formula. But even in the absence of an earn-out, this inherent tension between Bidder and Target will inevitably spill over to color their negotiations over the wording and terms of the other provisions that are typically made part of the parties' acquisition agreement. While at some level the two parties share a common interest in completing the transaction, their negotiations over the specific terms of the acquisition agreement invariably reflect the parties' divergent interests and desires. Yet the ability to get the deal done — to close on the agreement — depends on the parties' ability to get past these inherent differences and reach an acceptable compromise.

The give-and-take inherent in the deal process for any acquisition is reflected in the remaining materials in this chapter, most notably in Part D (at pp. 351-369), describing a hypothetical dialogue between Bidder's lawyer and Target's lawyer as they negotiate the terms of a specific provision to be made part of the parties' acquisition agreement. The dialogue in this hypothetical bargaining process reflects another important attribute of the good business lawyer when advising clients in an M&A transaction: the vital importance of the lawyer's strong negotiating and drafting skills. These important skills are acquired through experience and the lawyers' continued commitment to communicate effectively and represent their client's interest in a responsible and ethical manner. The remaining materials in this chapter are intended to emphasize this fundamental point about the important role of the good business lawyer in the context of *any* acquisition — whether the deal is done on Wall Street or Main Street.

b.   *Escrows*

In lieu of negotiating an earn-out, the parties may use an *escrow* as the tool of choice to resolve their fundamental differences over valuation. Under this alternative, Bidder will hold back a specified portion of the purchase price at closing. These funds will then be placed in escrow with an independent escrow agent for a specified period of time after closing. The escrow agreement, usually attached as an exhibit to the acquisition agreement and signed and delivered at the closing, will provide specific conditions (or triggers), which, when satisfied, authorize the escrow holder to disburse money to the appropriate party. An escrow, like an earn-out, may serve more than one purpose. An escrow can be used together with an earn-out formula, thereby giving Target's shareholders comfort that the additional purchase price will be paid as soon as the earn-out condition is met.

An escrow fund may also be established to facilitate Bidder's ability to recover on indemnification claims that may arise post-closing. When faced with a requirement by Bidder that a portion of the price be set aside in an escrow to serve as security for possible indemnity claims, Target may respond by insisting that the escrowed funds provide Bidder with its sole remedy for any post-closing claims that may arise. This is explored in more detail later in Part E of this chapter, in connection with the topic of indemnification rights that may be granted to Bidder on a post-closing basis under the terms of the parties' agreement.

c. Post-Closing Purchase Price Adjustments

This final type of purchase price provision, a post-closing purchase price adjustment, is used most often when the parties agree to the essential method for calculating the purchase price but either contemplate considerable delay between signing and closing on their acquisition agreement or certain factors that will affect the calculation cannot be known or finalized until after the closing. For example, the parties may use a purchase price adjustment provision to address the concern that there may be changes in the value of Target between the date of signing the agreement and the date of closing on the acquisition. This is of particular concern in those cases where antitrust review, or the need to obtain some other regulatory approvals, may lead to considerable delay between signing and closing on the parties' acquisition agreement. Likewise, if securities (such as Bidder's stock) must be registered with the SEC or a proxy statement must be filed with the SEC in order to obtain shareholder approval of the proposed transaction, considerable delay may ensue.

In these cases involving the potential for delay, the purchase price adjustment serves to allocate the financial risks associated with the delay. If a purchase price adjustment were not made, then the earnings generated by Target's business between signing and closing will typically accrue to the benefit of Bidder, since most acquisition agreements prohibit Target from making any distributions during the period between signing and closing. Similarly, losses sustained in Target's business would be absorbed by Bidder in the absence of a provision for a post-closing adjustment in the purchase price.

QUESTIONS

In reviewing the planning problem set forth at the beginning of the chapter, consider the following questions in light of the terms of the purchase price that Galaxy agreed to pay to acquire Trekker's business:

1. What is the purchase price? What is the acquisition consideration?

2. What factors do you suppose influenced the parties' determination to use an earn-out in this transaction? Why was an earn-out preferable to an escrow?

3. Why might Trekker not want an escrow? Why might Galaxy want to use an escrow?

4. Did the parties include any dispute resolution mechanism as part of the terms of their earn-out provision?

5. How do the parties treat the potential for existing management of Target to distribute the company's earnings before closing on the agreement?

D. *Negotiating and Drafting the Acquisition Agreement*

1. The Basic Agreement

At this point, it is useful to look at the organizational structure of the merger agreement included in Appendix B and compare it to the structure of the stock purchase agreement included in Appendix D. This stock purchase agreement is fairly typical of the kind of stock purchase agreement that may be used in a deal involving the acquisition of all of the stock of a closely held Target Co. by a single buyer, a publicly traded Bidder Co.

As can be readily discerned from this cursory review of these two different agreements, the basic architecture of any acquisition agreement follows a certain convention regardless of the deal structure. For reasons that are described in more detail in the remaining sections of this chapter, the acquisition agreement will usually include the following provisions, which are customarily ordered in the sequence set forth below:

1. *Introductory provisions*—which typically consist of the names of the parties, recitals, and definitions; often, though, the definitions are made in the very first section of the body of the agreement
2. *Description of the structure of the transaction*—asset, stock, or merger; in an asset acquisition, it is very important for the terms of the agreement to describe exactly what is being sold
3. *Terms of the purchase price* and the payment
4. Target's *representations and warranties*
5. Bidder's *representations and warranties*
6. Target's *pre-closing covenants*
7. Bidder's *pre-closing covenants*
8. *Closing on the transaction:*

    a. When and where
    b. Conditions to Target's obligation to close
    c. Conditions to Bidder's obligation to close
    d. Deliveries at closing

        • By Target (and/or its shareholders)
        • By Bidder

9. *Termination* of the acquisition agreement
10. *Indemnification*

    a. In favor of Bidder
    b. In favor of Target (and/or its selling shareholders)
    c. Time limitations on bringing claims for indemnification under the terms of the agreement
    d. Limitations on indemnification claims (generally involving use of *caps* and *baskets*)

e. Procedural issues with respect to the assertion of claims of indemnification

11. Other post-closing covenants of the parties
12. General ("*Miscellaneous*") provisions

a. *Preparing the First Draft*

The custom among practicing M&A lawyers generally calls for Bidder's lawyer to prepare the initial draft of the acquisition agreement. This is not surprising, given that most of the provisions exist for the protection of the buyer, Bidder; and therefore, the length and complexity of the agreement generally will be driven by the scope of protection that Bidder seeks. Accordingly, the convention has grown up for Bidder's lawyer to prepare the initial draft of the parties' agreement.

The practical wisdom among M&A lawyers is that, if given the chance, the lawyer should *always* seize the opportunity to prepare the initial draft. Most lawyers seize this opportunity to control the draft because they believe that they are in a better negotiating position when their role is evaluating and granting or rejecting requests for changes made by the other party, rather than being the party requesting the changes. In addition, by seizing control of the initial draft, Bidder's lawyers take advantage of the opportunity to slant the agreement to Bidder's advantage, thereby shifting the burden to Target and its lawyer to neutralize these effects through the comment process.

In any acquisition, the purchase price and the terms for the payment of the purchase price (i.e., use cash or Bidder's stock; payment in full at closing or do the parties contemplate deferral of some portion of the purchase price) will be the threshold issue. Typically, the most heavily negotiated section of the acquisition agreement is the set of representations and warranties to be made by Target (and/or its owners) regarding Target's business and financial affairs. Finally, the terms of the indemnification section will usually be another heavily negotiated aspect of the acquisition agreement in a transaction involving the acquisition of a privately held Target, as it is a central tool for allocating and limiting the risks of the transaction.

b. *Circulating the First Draft for Comment*

Historically, the initial draft of the acquisition agreement was typically circulated in print form, leaving Target's lawyer to review and make comments in the margins of the agreement and then generally communicate any limiting language orally or by way of a comment letter that summarized Target's objections to the provisions of Bidder's initial draft. Today, however, initial drafts are usually circulated electronically, typically delivered as e-mail file attachments. This development has resulted in somewhat cannibalizing the conventional practice for circulating and reviewing drafts of acquisition agreements since e-mail delivery allows the recipient to download the entire file. In these cases, rather than making suggestions for changes, either orally or by a comment letter, Target's lawyer now has greater freedom to essentially rewrite the provisions of Bidder's initial draft. Typically, though, Target's lawyer will track any changes made to Bidder's draft by utilizing the "redlining" function available with most word processing programs.

This ability to essentially rewrite the draft agreement as part of the review and comment process raises the separate question of what professional etiquette should be followed when making changes to drafts circulated by the other side. Best practices are in a constant state of evolution, as the commenting lawyers are now empowered to make more substantial and extensive changes to the provisions of the original draft than the prior practice of circulating drafts only in print form may have allowed. Consequently, electronic delivery of drafts may make it more difficult for the initial draftsperson to assert control over the preparation of the document and the process of making revisions to the agreement.

2. Representations and Warranties vs. Covenants vs. Conditions to Closing

a. *Representations and Warranties*

The parties' *representations and warranties* serve several important functions that are interrelated. First, they are disclosure tools; as such, they are an extension of the due diligence review undertaken by the parties as part of the deal process, a process described in more detail later in this chapter. As part of its ongoing diligence process, Bidder is gaining detailed knowledge of Target's business operations and financial well-being. Bidder's understanding of Target's business and financial affairs is then confirmed by a set of representations and warranties[2] made by Target that are Target's way of telling the Bidder, "This is what the company's business is all about, as of this particular moment in time," which is usually the date the acquisition agreement is signed by the parties.

Representations and warranties serve another important purpose in that they are used as risk allocation tools. Most importantly, Target's representations will usually serve as the basis for a *condition to closing* on the acquisition. At the closing—which typically is a date fixed in the agreement for the acquisition of a privately held Target, usually 30 to 60 days after signing the agreement—the truth of Target's representations will be tested again. To clarify, Target's representations in the acquisition agreement regarding the state of its business

---

2. Some practicing M&A lawyers will draw a distinction between *representations* on the one hand, and *warranties* on the other, pointing out that *representations* are usually limited to statements as to existing circumstances or historical facts, whereas "warranties may also cover future situations." James C. Freund, ANATOMY OF A MERGER 153 n. 33 (Law Journal Press 1975). More recently, however, this distinction has faded away into obscurity. *See* Comment to *§3. Representations and Warranties of Seller and Shareholders*, MODEL ASSET PURCHASE AGREEMENT WITH COMMENTARY, prepared by the American Bar Association, Business Law Section, Committee on Negotiated Acquisitions (2001). Consequently, "representations" and "warranties" have become virtually indistinguishable from each other, and the terms are used interchangeably in this discussion.

and financial affairs must be true and accurate not only as of the date that the parties signed the agreement, but also must be true and accurate as of the date of closing on the agreement. This is vitally important to Bidder because it tells Bidder that Target's description of its business and financial affairs, as reflected in its representations and warranties, is true and accurate, not only on the date the parties made their agreement, but continues to remain so as of the date of closing on the agreement. This way, Bidder is assured that there have been no material changes in Target's business and financial affairs in the time period between signing and closing on the agreement. In the event that there has been a material change in Target's business or financial affairs in between signing and closing on the agreement, Bidder will typically be excused from performing on the agreement. As described in more detail later in this section, Target's representations form the basis for Bidder's right to walk away from the deal, thereby relieving Bidder of its obligation under the agreement to pay the purchase price to Target.

Finally, in some acquisitions, most often those involving the acquisition of a privately held Target, the parties' agreement will provide that certain of the representations are to survive closing. In such a case, the representations and warranties will also serve as the basis for contractual liability on a post-closing basis, commonly giving rise to a claim for *indemnification*. Rights of indemnification are discussed in more detail at the end of this chapter.

In summary, the most important purposes served by the parties' representations and warranties in the context of negotiating and documenting any acquisition are disclosure, termination rights, and indemnification rights. The overriding importance served by the representations section of the agreement and its dynamic relationship with other aspects of the acquisition agreement and deal-making process is explored in the remaining materials in this chapter.

Disclosure Schedules.   Generally speaking, the representations will refer to information contained in other documents known as "disclosure schedules." For example, the terms of a particular representation will refer to patents owned by Target Co., but to determine exactly which patents Target owns, the reader must refer to a separate disclosure schedule that lists all of Target's patents. This schedule (listing all the patents) is then incorporated by reference into the terms of Target's representation and warranty. Through the use of these disclosure schedules, Bidder learns about Target's business and financial affairs. Often, these disclosures reveal information that results in the parties changing the terms of their business deal (and, consequently, the terms of their acquisition agreement) in order to reflect the impact of the information revealed during the course of the due diligence process.

Bring-Down.   Second, in the typical acquisition agreement, the representations and warranties will serve as the basis for a closing condition. Since Target's representations and warranties speak as of a particular moment in time — generally the date the acquisition agreement is signed — the parties will customarily include in their agreement a provision known as a "bring-down." The use of a bring-down provision reflects the inevitable delay that typically occurs between the date the parties sign the acquisition agreement and the date of closing on the agreement. In most cases, therefore, the buyer (Bidder Co.) will be allowed to test the accuracy of the representations made by the seller (Target Co. and/ or its shareholders) at the time of *signing* the acquisition agreement, and again at the time of *closing*. If the conditions vary to some degree of *materiality*, this difference will operate to excuse Bidder from performance under the agreement and thereby relieve Bidder of the obligation to pay the purchase price.

This bring-down condition forms the basis for what is known as a "walk-away right." The degree of variance that will trigger Bidder's right to walk away from the deal is usually hotly negotiated by the parties. The terms of this variance are reflected in a clause typically referred to as the "material adverse change" (MAC) clause or the "material adverse effect" (MAE) clause. The importance of materiality qualifiers is specifically addressed later in this chapter in connection with the *IBP* decision.

Basis for Indemnification. Finally, the last contractual purpose generally served by Target's representations and warranties is that these provisions usually provide the basis for Bidder's rights of indemnification *after* closing on the acquisition agreement. The typical agreement for the acquisition of a privately held company will provide that to the extent the representations and warranties were not accurate and the buyer (Bidder) suffers damages following closing as a result of these inaccuracies, Bidder will have a financial remedy based on the parties' contract. The scope and customary terms of Bidder's right of indemnification are described in more detail later in this chapter.

Once again, Target does not want to be financially responsible for just *any* amount (no matter how slight or trivial), so typically this post-closing right of indemnification will also include some form of materiality qualifier. To implement this qualification on the scope of indemnification, the parties will typically negotiate some form of dollar *basket* (or deductible) that must be satisfied before triggering rights of indemnification. The concept of *baskets* (and the related concept of *caps*) is discussed in more detail later in this chapter, as part of a more fulsome discussion of rights of indemnification.

b.   Covenants

By contrast to representations and warranties, a *covenant* does not relate to a particular point in time. Rather, a covenant is the promise of a party to the agreement that relates to the future, obligating the party to do something (or a promise *not* to do something) during the time period between signing and closing on the agreement. As such, covenants typically deal with matters pending the closing on the parties' agreement and therefore usually expire at closing. In certain cases, though, the parties may specify in their agreement that a particular covenant will extend beyond closing on the acquisition. In the vernacular of the M&A lawyer, these provisions are said to "survive closing." A typical example would be Bidder's covenant to register stock that it is issuing to Target as part of the acquisition consideration. Another example would be Target's covenant to proceed with dissolution following closing on the sale of all of the company's assets to Bidder.

To illustrate the difference between a *representation* and a *covenant*, consider the treatment of Target's balance sheet under the terms of a typical acquisition agreement. In most cases, Target Co.'s last balance sheet will be prepared as of a date that *precedes* the date the parties sign the acquisition agreement. In this situation, Target will give Bidder a *representation* to the effect that, from the date that the balance sheet was prepared to the date that the agreement was signed, Target has not taken certain specific actions (most commonly, these would include paying dividends or making significant capital expenditures). Virtually the same terms will appear as a separate provision in the *covenants* portion of the parties' acquisition agreement, where they constitute the seller's promise that Target will not pay a dividend or make a significant capital expenditure in the time period between the date the agreement is signed and the date of closing on the acquisition. *Query:* In considering the stock purchase agreement included in Appendix C, can you find any example(s) of representation(s) that are repeated as covenant(s) in the parties' agreement?

Negative vs. Affirmative Covenants.   The acquisition agreement will typically include both negative and affirmative covenants. The negative covenants restrict the party from taking certain actions, such as the prohibition (described above) against Target paying any dividends between signing and closing of the acquisition agreement. Very often, these negative covenants are phrased in terms of actions that cannot be taken "without the consent of the other party." In these cases, Target may be able to take a particular action—such as making an otherwise prohibited capital expenditure—prior to closing if Target can adequately justify the action and thereby obtain Bidder's consent to the expenditure. As another alternative, Target will often negotiate for a middle ground with respect to these negative covenants by phrasing the covenant in terms of actions that cannot be taken "without the consent of the other party, such consent not to be unreasonably withheld." Why does Target generally find this formulation of the covenant more appealing? Obviously, if Target knows, in advance of signing the acquisition agreement, that it plans to take a certain action *prior* to closing that would otherwise violate the terms of a particular covenant, Target should disclose its plans to Bidder and negotiate an exception to the covenant allowing Target to take such action. *Query:* In considering the terms of the AT&T–DirecTV merger agreement contained in Appendix B, can you find an example of a provision that allows Target to proceed with certain action(s) that would otherwise violate the terms of the parties' merger agreement?

Generally speaking, the burdens imposed by the covenants contained in the typical acquisition agreement will fall on the seller of the business, Target. Occasionally, covenants may impose obligations on Bidder, such as the obligation to list any shares that are to be issued as part of the acquisition consideration. In the usual case of the acquisition of a privately held Target by a large, publicly traded Bidder, it is highly unlikely that Bidder would consent to any type of negative covenant that restricts Bidder in the operation of its business during the time between signing and closing on the acquisition of Target.

☞ c.   Conditions to Closing

The *conditions* section of the parties' agreement creates obligations that must be satisfied by the parties at (or before) the closing on the acquisition.

If these conditions are not satisfied, the deal will not close, and the parties can *walk away* from the transaction. As an example, a typical condition to Bidder's obligation to close on the acquisition and pay the purchase price is the receipt of certain written assurances from Target's auditors. If Target cannot satisfy this *condition* at (or before) the date set for closing, then Bidder can *walk away* from the deal without any recourse on the part of Target. As such, *conditions to closing* give rise to what M&A lawyers customarily refer to as *walk-away rights*.

Bring-Down Condition. Among the most important of the conditions to closing—one typically made as part of any acquisition agreement—is the provision that all representations and warranties made by the other party to the transaction will be true at the closing as if they had been made as of that date. This kind of provision is commonly referred to as the *bring-down condition*. This provision is typically included in order to allocate risks that something might happen in the time period between signing and closing that render the earlier representation untrue. In effect, by including a bring-down, the other side has contracted for the right to refuse to close on the deal. Since one side is usually not willing to let the other side off the hook for just a slight discrepancy in the terms of a representation included in the acquisition agreement, it is not uncommon for the parties to agree to qualify a condition to closing by the express use of a materiality standard. *Materiality qualifiers*—known as MACs and MAEs—are discussed in more detail later in this chapter in connection with the *IBP* decision.

3. Closing: Post-Closing Covenants and Closing Documents

The acquisition agreement will usually contain a description of what happens at closing. This description will vary depending on deal structure (i.e., merger vs. asset purchase vs. stock purchase) and also will vary depending on the nature of the acquisition consideration. For example, in a stock purchase for cash, the stock purchase agreement would typically provide, at a minimum, that Target's shareholders deliver at closing duly endorsed certificates representing the shares to be transferred to Bidder. In exchange, Bidder typically would be required at closing to deliver a specified cash amount to the selling shareholders of Target, usually by way of a bank cashier's check, or perhaps by a wire transfer to certain bank accounts specified by the selling shareholders. This assumes an all-cash purchase price, and that all the conditions to closing have been satisfied so that the parties are obligated to perform under the terms of the acquisition agreement. *Query:* In the case of the stock purchase agreement in Appendix C, involving the acquisition of a privately held company (Trekker) by a publicly traded Bidder (Galaxy), what do the parties contemplate will happen at closing on their agreement?

In addition to the exchange of shares for cash described above, the parties' stock purchase agreement may list other documents that will be exchanged at closing. This obligation often leads to the practice of preparing a *closing checklist* of all the documents that must be prepared for delivery at closing. A representative form of a closing checklist—crafted for purposes of our planning problem involving Galaxy's acquisition of Trekker's business—is included as Appendix F. This checklist serves to illustrate, once again, the high transaction costs associated with transferring ownership of Target's business, a point originally made in the analysis of the problems in Chapter 2.

4. A Mock Negotiation over the Terms of Target's Representations and Warranties

Target's representations and warranties operate in two different time frames. First, they give *pre-closing* walk-away rights to Bidder. Second, they serve as the basis for Bidder's *post-closing* indemnification rights. This raises a predictable tension between the position of Bidder and that of Target during the course of negotiating and documenting the terms of the parties' representations and warranties.

Bidder typically seeks to maximize its protection by obtaining from Target a detailed set of representations and warranties that carefully describe Target's business so that Bidder actually gets the business that it thinks it is buying. Moreover, the level of detail Bidder seeks to obtain in these representations is designed to give Bidder comfort that, if there are *any* discrepancies, Bidder will have one of the two remedies just described: either pre-closing walk-away rights *or* post-closing indemnification rights. From Bidder's perspective, therefore, the goal in these negotiations over the terms of Target's representations is to describe as accurately as possible the business that Bidder is buying, including (but not limited to) the property rights that come with Target's business, the historical performance of Target's business operations, and, finally, that Target's business is free from other third-party claims. In this way, Target's representations and warranties provide Bidder with assurance that it is getting what it agreed to pay for when the parties agreed to the purchase price that Bidder is to pay Target for its business. In addition, Bidder's negotiations seek assurance that Bidder will have an effective remedy—such as a mechanism to adjust the purchase price or to walk away from the deal—*if* the facts represented by Target should later turn out *not* to be true. In summary, the parties' negotiations over the scope of the representations and warranties to be included in their acquisition agreement serve to allocate financial risk between the seller, Target Co., and the buyer, Bidder Co.

Not surprisingly, Target's perspective in these negotiations is dramatically different from that of Bidder. As the seller of an ongoing business, Target is likely to take the position that it is selling the business as a going concern—that is, the business is being sold to Bidder as is, warts and all. Target is usually going to be willing to protect Bidder against fraud on the part of Target as well as against anything truly extraordinary that might arise between the time of signing and closing on the acquisition agreement. In the typical negotiation, therefore, Target will usually try to resist many of the detailed representations and warranties that Bidder is likely to demand from Target.

And so the battle lines get drawn between the parties. Ultimately, where the line falls—in other words, just how much risk Bidder can require Target to absorb on a pre-closing and on a post-closing basis—will ultimately depend on the relative negotiating power of the two parties, which usually depends on which side wants to get the deal done the most.

In this section, I present a hypothetical negotiation between Bidder's lawyer and Target's lawyer that is designed to illustrate how this tension between Bidder and Target influences the negotiating process between the parties and their counsel.[3] Let us assume that the Bidder has presented a first draft of the stock purchase agreement that includes the following financial statements representation:

§3.4 FINANCIAL STATEMENTS

Sellers have delivered to Buyer: (a) audited consolidated balance sheets of the Acquired Companies as at December 31 in each of the years 2001 through 2002, and the related consolidated statements of income, changes in stockholders' equity, and cash flow for each of the fiscal years then ended, (b) an audited consolidated balance sheet of the Acquired Companies as at December 31, 2003 (including the notes thereto, the "Balance Sheet"), and the related consolidated statements of income, changes in stockholders' equity, and cash flow for the fiscal year then ended, together with the report thereon of Ernst & Young, independent certified public accountants, and (c) an unaudited consolidated balance sheet of the Acquired Companies as at April 1, 2004 (the "Interim Balance Sheet") and the related unaudited consolidated statements of income, changes in stockholders' equity, and cash flow for the 3 months then ended, including in each case the notes thereto. Such financial statements and notes fairly present the financial condition and the results of operations, changes in stockholders' equity, and cash flow of the Acquired Companies as at the respective dates of and for the periods referred to in such financial statements, all in accordance with GAAP[, subject, in the case of interim financial statements, to normal recurring year-end adjustments (the effect of which will not, individually or in the aggregate, be materially adverse) and the absence of notes (that, if presented, would not differ materially from those included in the Balance Sheet)]; the financial statements referred to in this Section 3.4 reflect the consistent application of such accounting principles throughout the periods involved[, except as disclosed in the notes to such financial statements]. No financial statements of any Person other than the Acquired Companies are required by GAAP to be included in the consolidated financial statements of the company.[4]

---

3. This section was inspired by various mock negotiation panels presented as part of several professional education programs that I have attended over the years. Most prominently, the continuing education programs sponsored by both Practicing Law Institute (PLI) and the American Bar Association (ABA) provided the basis for the description in the text of a hypothetical bargaining process between Bidder's counsel and Target's lawyer over the terms of just one aspect of the parties' acquisition agreement—the financial statements representation. *See, e.g., Acquiring or Selling Privately Held Company*, 1313 PLI/CORP (June 2002) (David W. Pollack & John F. Seegal, Chairs); and *Negotiating Business Acquisitions* (ABA-CLE Nov. 2003).

4. Section 3.4 of the MODEL STOCK PURCHASE AGREEMENT WITH COMMENTARY, prepared by the Committee on Negotiated Acquisitions of the American Bar Association's Business Law Section (1995). By way of general background, this ABA Model Agreement was deliberately drafted to reflect the form of agreement that Target's lawyer could typically expect to receive as Bidder's initial draft circulated for Target's lawyer to review and comment on.

Why include this particular representation? By including this representation, Bidder seeks Target's assurance as to the integrity of the company's consolidated financial statements. Accordingly, as part of this representation, Target confirms that its financial statements have been prepared in accordance with generally accepted accounting principles (GAAP), and that they fairly present the financial condition of Target and the results of its operations. This representation will usually cover several years of audited financial statements (here, the years 2001-2003), including the most recently concluded fiscal year (2003), and will also typically cover Target's unaudited ("stub period") financial statements relating to some interim period following the end of the most recent fiscal year (here, the stub period is January 1 to April 1, 2004).

To understand why Bidders and Targets haggle so intensely over the terms of the representations and warranties sections of their agreements, consider whether Bidder would ever be willing to forego this type of representation regarding Target's financial statements and therefore agree to *eliminate* this representation *completely* from the terms of the parties' acquisition agreement. For example, Target might try to persuade Bidder that Bidder ought to be able to get the comfort it needs from Target's *audited* financial statements, as prepared by the company's outside, independent auditing firm, and thus dispense with the need for a separate representation from Target itself. Target will try to persuade Bidder that the truthfulness and completeness of Target's financial statements can be assured solely by relying on the accountant's/auditor's certification; that is, by relying on the auditor's opinion with respect to its audit of Target's financials (and for the sake of argument here, we will further assume that the auditing firm was one of the remaining Big Four firms (here, Ernst & Young) and that the auditor issued an unqualified ("clean") opinion on Target's audited financials).

In the face of this kind of argument, one can expect Bidder's counsel to flat out reject Target's request to completely eliminate the financial statement representation based on two different, albeit related, reasons. It bears emphasizing that from Bidder's perspective, this representation serves two purposes. This representation forms the basis for Bidder's financial protection *and* its walk-away rights if Target's statements prove inaccurate.[5] In light of these purposes, Bidder can be expected to argue that the auditor's certification of Target's financials does *not* provide Bidder with sufficient comfort. Why not? Because if Bidder were to rely *only* on the auditor's opinion, Bidder would fail to obtain any walk-away rights if Bidder should learn—before closing—that Target's audited financials are wrong. If Target makes *no* representation in the stock purchase agreement as to the accuracy of its own audited financials—because it has convinced Bidder to rely solely on the auditor's certification—then there will be no condition to closing that allows Bidder the right to walk away from the deal at closing if Bidder learns that Target's audited financials are inaccurate. In other words, if Bidder is persuaded to accept the audited financials in lieu of a representation from Target itself, then Bidder will deprive itself of the ability to test the accuracy of this representation by relying on it as a condition to closing.

---

5. Indeed, as we have previously mentioned in this chapter, the influence of the twofold purposes for these representations and warranties will guide and dominate Bidder's thinking and decision making throughout the parties' negotiation as to specific terms of the parties' representations and warranties. As such, this influence is not limited to the context of the parties' negotiations for the terms of the financial statement representations.

In effect, Bidder would eliminate a potential basis for a right to walk away from the deal. In such a case, the only basis that Bidder might have to refuse to close and thereby walk away from the deal would be some sort of fraud claim, rather than a contractual right to walk away from the deal. Generally speaking, fraud is very tough to establish, and thus Bidder is likely to view the contractual remedy as a far more attractive alternative.

The other reason we can expect Bidder to flat out refuse any request to eliminate the financial statement covenant is that, in fact, Bidder *wants* to impose a measure of responsibility and accountability on Target itself, even as to its *audited* financial statements. Realizing the limitations inherent in the audit process, Bidder's counsel will be quick to point out that the auditor's certification is *not* a guarantee of the accuracy of Target's audited financial statements. Rather, this opinion is simply the auditor's representation—based on its auditing (i.e., accepted testing) procedures and applying GAAP—that these financial statements fairly represent Target's business. However, as the now infamous financial scandals from the early twenty-first century at Adelphia, WorldCom, Tyco, and other companies more than amply demonstrate, the auditor's opinion may be *wrong* even though the auditor may have done nothing wrong during the course of its audit. Rather, the insiders may have "cooked the books"—committed financial fraud—so cleverly that the auditors failed to detect it during the course of their audit of Target. In this extreme case, where Target's financial statements are the product of management's fraud, an auditor would not catch the fraud since generally accepted auditing standards (GAAS) are not designed to detect fraud.

Moreover, in these situations involving financial fraud, there generally would be no basis for Bidder to claim malpractice (professional negligence) against the accounting firm. It is entirely possible that the audit firm could completely fail to detect the fraud and still have conducted the audit non-negligently by strictly following GAAS. Conversely, in those (rather infrequent) cases involving some factual basis for a claim of professional negligence against the auditor, the ability of Bidder to bring this malpractice claim is often hampered in many jurisdictions by privity requirements imposed by local law. These privity requirements limit the ability of a third party (such as Bidder) to bring a cause of action against the auditor based on a defective audit report of Target, a client of the audit firm. In the absence of privity between Bidder and Target's audit firm, Bidder generally will have no claim for negligence against the audit firm. Consequently, Bidder will generally be left with only a fraud claim, a much harder case for Bidder to prevail on (as we all know well from our first-year torts class).

In negotiating with Target's lawyer over whether to exclude any form of financial statement representation, Bidder's lawyer can be expected to engage in this type of reasoning process to conclude that it is not in Bidder's best interests to exclude a financial statement representation from Target itself.[6] As a

---

6. This summary of the respective positions of Bidder Co. and Target Co. in negotiating the exclusion of the financial statement representation only serves to illustrate the tension inherent in virtually all aspects of the parties' negotiations over the terms of the acquisition agreement. The acquisition agreement, the initial draft of which is customarily prepared by Bidder's counsel, will quite predictably contain the usual provisions, all of which are drafted in terms designed to give as much protection as possible to Bidder. Just as predictably, counsel for Target can be expected to object to the breadth of these provisions—and thus the negotiations begin.

result, with respect to negotiating whether to omit any form of a financial statement covenant from their agreement, this issue is most likely to be resolved in favor of Bidder as Bidder is likely to have the more persuasive argument on this point.

Deciding Which Issues* Not *to Negotiate Over.   In the "give-and-take" inherent in negotiating an acquisition, many Targets will decide *not* to spend any time trying to negotiate this financial covenant out of the parties' agreement. Recognizing that it would take considerable effort to convince Bidder to omit a financial statement representation *entirely*, why is the prudent Target (and its lawyer) likely to decide *not* to expend any such effort to negotiate this covenant out of the agreement? As a practical matter, Target's lawyers are likely to advise their client that the very act of trying to disassociate Target and its management from their own audited financial statements would cause such apprehension and nervousness on the part of Bidder (and its lawyer) that the whole effort may ultimately backfire and jeopardize the entire deal. What is the moral of the story? As a negotiating strategy, Bidders and Targets are often well advised *not* to negotiate over every point that the parties could potentially argue about.

Assuming that Bidder has carried the day on this issue, the parties will turn their attention to haggling over the specific terms of Target's financial statement representation and warranty ("rep"). The next section of this hypothetical bargaining process addresses the tension that inevitably results as Target's lawyers seek to limit the scope of the representation demanded by Bidder in the first draft of the acquisition agreement. Target's lawyers can be expected to resist the terms of Bidder's formulation of the financial statement covenant for two principal reasons: first, to curtail the availability of a walk-away right for Bidder at closing; and second, to limit the scope of Bidder's financial remedy on a post-closing basis. In the process of negotiating the terms of the financial statement representation, the general goal of Target's lawyers is to minimize the chance that the deal will "fall out of bed" (fail to close) or otherwise deprive Target of the benefit of the bargain (payment of the full purchase price) that it made with Bidder.

Now that we have concluded that the financial statement covenant will cover *both* audited and unaudited financial statements of Target, let us consider how the negotiations between Bidder and Target might play themselves out as to the specific terms of this representation. The language of the financial statement covenant is typically tied into GAAP, although Bidder may insist on other language. For example, Bidder's first draft of the acquisition agreement may request that Target represent that its "financial statements are true, correct, and complete." How is Target's lawyer likely to respond to this language? Target will probably strongly object to this formulation because, from Target's perspective, the financial statement representation is an essential building block of the parties' acquisition agreement. Many other provisions of the acquisition agreement are keyed to the terms of this financial statement representation. Consequently, the terms of this representation are likely to be quite important to Target as the lawyer for Target anticipates further difficulties down the road in negotiating the terms of *other* representations and warranties in the agreement.[7]

Target, therefore, is likely to respond that the GAAP standard, used to prepare the company's audited financials, is fundamentally inconsistent with a representation that Target's financials are "true, correct, and complete." At this point, Target's counsel may point out that the GAAP standard has many instances requiring the auditor's exercise of professional judgment to make estimates *or* to determine if a standard of materiality has been triggered. Target is likely to contend that these kinds of professional judgments are fundamentally at odds with Target making a representation as to 100 percent accuracy and completeness of its financial statements. Although Bidder often seeks this type of financial statement representation by including it in the first draft of the acquisition agreement, Bidder is likely to be persuaded by Target's reasoning and thus will usually settle for a financial statement covenant that is tied to compliance with GAAP.

The Impact of Sarbanes-Oxley Reforms on Negotiations for a Financial Statement Covenant.   All of this raises the basic question: is there any danger to Bidder in agreeing to eliminate this more aggressive form of financial statement covenant from the acquisition agreement? In the future, we may see Bidders increasingly insist on this more aggressive formulation of the financial statement covenant in order to ensure that Target's financial statements do not contain any surprises giving rise to problems for Bidder (on a post-acquisition basis) in its efforts to comply with the requirements of the Sarbanes-Oxley Act (SOX). Specifically, SOX requires the managers of a publicly traded company to certify that the company's financial statements are a fair representation of the company and its financial affairs. Since Bidder must start making these representations as to Target's business once the acquisition is completed (at least where Bidder is publicly traded), Bidder will naturally worry about the integrity of Target's financial statements. M&A lawyers increasingly report that Bidders are insisting on a financial statement covenant more congruent with the language of the certification that Bidder's officers are required to use under the terms of SOX. If Bidder makes this argument to convince Target to accept the more aggressive form of financial statement representation proposed by the Bidder, Target is likely to respond that SOX compliance is not Target's problem since Target is privately held. Indeed, Target may claim that avoiding this type of SOX-related issue is one of the main reasons that Target decided to sell the business rather than do an initial public offering (IPO), which would force the company to

---

7. As a matter of negotiating strategy, it is worth pointing out that it is vitally important for the lawyer to thoroughly understand all of the terms of the acquisition agreement, and further, to understand how the various provisions work together. In this way, the lawyer can prioritize with the client which terms are most important to the client. Understanding the client's business objectives in doing the deal allows the lawyer to, in effect, horse-trade with opposing counsel. In other words, the lawyer may concede less important points in order to best preserve Target's bargaining position on those points that are of greater importance to Target's lawyer and business client.

comply with all of the many detailed requirements imposed by SOX (including the mandatory officer certification requirements). Moreover, Target will likely suggest that the purchase price that it agreed to accept from Bidder has already been discounted to reflect that Target is avoiding the costs associated with doing an IPO and complying with SOX.

Introduction of a "Materiality Qualifier."   Assuming the parties agree to use a GAAP-based financial statement representation (of the type quoted above—as taken from §3.4 of the ABA's Model Stock Purchase Agreement), Target's lawyer is likely to object to the breadth of this representation unless it is modified to include a provision known as a "materiality qualifier." Target is likely to insist that the financial statement covenant be modified to read that the company's "financial statements fairly present in all *material* respects the financial condition of Target and its results from operation." Target will point out that this language is entirely consistent with the language used in the opinion letter of the company's auditor, which typically reads: "In our [the auditor's] opinion, the [audited] financial statements fairly present, in all *material* respects, the financial condition of Target."[8]

When faced with this kind of requested limitation, Bidder's counsel is likely to object on the grounds that, by including a materiality qualifier in the representation itself, Target is in effect including a *double* materiality qualifier. The basis for this argument is that GAAP's provisions already include a materiality standard that requires the auditor to make certain judgment calls or estimates based on a standard of materiality. By including a separate materiality qualifier in the language of Target's financial statement representation, Target is further limiting the scope of the protection offered to Bidder by this representation. In essence, Bidder claims that Target is "double-dipping" on the materiality qualifier. From Bidder's perspective, the language of this representation is designed to allocate risk between Bidder and Target, and this qualifying language is objectionable because it requires Bidder to absorb more than a "material" measure of financial risk.

A reasonable response by Target's counsel is to agree with Bidder's lawyer that a materiality qualifier may be inappropriate as to the company's *audited* financials but that the materiality qualifier should be left in the representation as to the company's interim, *unaudited* ("stub") financials. Target's lawyer will likely point out that the unaudited, interim financials are not likely to fully comply with GAAP, so a materiality qualifier is appropriate (i.e., as modified, there is no concern of double-dipping on the part of Target). Bidder's lawyer is likely to object on the grounds that Target's concern (regarding the use of *unaudited* interim financial statements) has already been addressed through other provisions in the agreement. For example, Bidder will point out that it has already agreed to several exceptions to GAAP in the preparation of Target's interim financial statements by agreeing, among other things, to the omission

---

8. In order to help clarify the dynamic of this negotiation, in most cases today, the auditor's opinion letter will expressly include a "materiality" qualification. This practice is being adopted so that the auditor's opinion letter better reflects the fact that auditing is not a science of precise measurement, but rather an exercise in professional judgment by the outside auditor.

of footnotes and normal year-end adjustments. From Bidder's perspective, these accommodations should adequately address Target's concerns and therefore eliminate the need for any further qualification to the terms of this representation. Thus, Bidder is likely to object strongly to using a materiality standard to qualify the terms of Target's representation as to its *interim* financials.

Although superficially appealing, Target may dig a little deeper into these exceptions that Bidder has proposed in order to further explicate the nature of Target's concerns if the materiality qualifier is omitted with respect to its unaudited ("stub") financials. For example, the terms of one of the exceptions that Bidder has just pointed to as an accommodation to Target reads:

> The footnotes to Target Co.'s financial statements [which are to be omitted with respect to Target's stub financials] if presented, would not differ materially from the footnotes presented in the last audited financial statements of Target Co.

However, it is often the case that considerable time has elapsed since the date of the Target's last audited financials; consequently, Target is likely to contend that it is quite possible that the footnotes *will differ* considerably from the footnotes that were part of Target's last audited financials. To address this concern, Target is likely to insist that the financial statement covenant be modified to read: "The adjustments to Target's unaudited financials will not individually or in the aggregate be materially adverse." In other words, Target Co. continues to propose using a materiality qualifier to ameliorate its concern over the scope of its representation as to its interim (stub) financials. Why? Target may be concerned about the post-closing risk that Bidder will manipulate the numbers in an opportunistic manner. In other words, Target will point out that Bidder will be responsible for preparing the next set of year-end financial statements for Target's business. Thus, Bidder will decide the footnotes to be made part of the year-end audited financials for Target's business. Target will point out that GAAP is *not* a precise science but rather requires many judgment calls in preparing the company's audited financials, all of which inevitably results in considerable elasticity in reporting the numbers in the company's year-end financials. Unless the limiting language that Target proposes is made part of the terms of Target's representation, then Target will argue that Bidder is left in the enviable position of being able to make year-end adjustments in an opportunistic manner—which works to Bidder's financial advantage and to Target's financial detriment. Consequently, Target's lawyer is likely to insist on this modification to the financial statement covenant, at least with respect to the company's interim (unaudited) financials in order to adequately protect Target's financial interest in getting a fair price for its business. Target's lawyer will also point out that Target's interim unaudited financials may not comply with GAAP in a number of other respects, all of which are unknowable without an audit and which therefore cannot be anticipated at the time of signing and closing on the parties' agreement. Without a materiality qualifier to address the uncertainty inherent in stub financials, Target is likely to insist on obtaining an audit prior to closing to remove this uncertainty, which will delay the closing and incur additional expense to get the deal done.

Bidder's counsel is likely to respond that Target's concern regarding year-end adjustments is a red herring. By insisting on a financial statement representation that omits any materiality qualifier, Bidder merely wants assurance that Target's interim numbers are accurate—subject, of course, to normal year-end GAAP adjustments. This means that if Bidder, in connection with its preparation of audited financials for Target's business on a post-closing basis, proposes to make a year-end adjustment that is *not* normal (or alternatively, *refuses* to make an adjustment that *is* normal), then Target has no grounds for concern under the terms of the representation as Bidder originally drafted it (i.e., without a materiality qualifier). In sum, Bidder is merely asking that Target examine its interim financials to determine the extent to which they are not prepared in accordance with GAAP and provide this information to Bidder by way of a disclosure letter. Bidder is likely to insist that it needs to analyze this information thoroughly in order to be sure that Bidder understands Target's financial statements and thus fully understands exactly what Bidder is buying. Even though they are not audited, these interim financial statements are of crucial importance to Bidder since they reflect the *current* state of affairs as to Target's business. Not surprisingly, Target's stub financials are likely to be an important factor to Bidder in determining the price that it is willing to pay for Target's business. Seen from this perspective, it is likely that Bidder will insist that Target provide a form of financial statement representation that omits *any* use of a materiality qualifier.

And so the negotiations will continue. This kind of back-and-forth between the lawyers for Target and Bidder will persist until they reach some acceptable solution regarding specific terms of the financial statement representation. What form that solution will take depends on many factors, not the least of which is the relative bargaining strength of the parties. This will generally be a function of which party (Bidder or Target) wants (or needs) to get the deal done the most.

In the end, Target will likely provide Bidder with a fairly comprehensive set of representations as to Target's financial statements, both audited and unaudited. The reason for this result is that, from Bidder's perspective, the uncertainty that results if it *cannot* obtain this representation from Target means that Bidder will be required to absorb too great a risk as to the true state of financial affairs currently existing in Target's business. Indeed, Bidder is likely to view Target's unwillingness to provide a fairly comprehensive representation as a red flag that trouble lies ahead. At this point, negotiations over the terms of the all-important financial statement representation may become a "deal-breaker." Unless Target concedes and gives Bidder the scope of protection that Bidder demands, then Bidder is likely to refuse to do the deal (i.e., Bidder is likely to refuse to sign the acquisition agreement because it does not afford Bidder the comfort it needs as to the true state of Target's financial affairs and therefore the deal presents too great a financial risk to Bidder).

Horse Trading Between Bidder and Target.   As part of its willingness to acquiesce to Bidder's demand for a comprehensive financial statement representation, Target's lawyer may then seek to "horse-trade" with Bidder for concessions on the terms of other representations (or, perhaps, the indemnity provisions) contained in the acquisition agreement.[9]

---

9. In order for lawyers to function as effective negotiators and obtain the best result for their business client, it is obvious that they must understand the client's business objectives and the terms that are most important to the client. In addition, the lawyers must be

As an example of the kind of horse trading that may result (and which can only be done effectively if the lawyer is adequately informed as to the client's priorities), let us assume that Target is prepared to provide Bidder with a comprehensive representation of its financial statements, in the form originally demanded by Bidder. Target may then try to use this concession as a bargaining chip to get Bidder to compromise on the terms of some other representation in the agreement, such as the provision regarding specific line items of Target's financial statements. For example, Target may seek to limit the scope of the representation regarding its accounts receivable (§3.8 of the ABA's Model Stock Purchase Agreement) or its inventory (§3.9 of the ABA Agreement).

Regarding these specific line items of Target's balance sheet (e.g., inventory and accounts receivable), Target is likely to object to these provisions on the grounds that these additional representations are essentially redundant to the financial statement covenant that has already been agreed to by the parties and pursuant to which Target has already represented that its balance sheet is accurate. Under the terms of the fairly comprehensive financial statement representation (and the accompanying *bring-down* provision),[10] Target will argue that it has, in effect, already agreed to make an adjustment in the purchase price to reflect any changes in value of the business. In other words, Target has already agreed to make any necessary adjustments to the shareholders' equity (as reflected on the company's balance sheet) to address anything that may arise in the interim between signing and closing on the acquisition agreement. By virtue of agreeing to the terms that Bidder originally sought as part of the financial statement representation, Target has already agreed to take into account (on its balance sheet) any adjustments that may be required due to changes in its inventory or its accounts receivable that may arise after signing the agreement but before closing. Therefore, Target's lawyer is likely to regard Bidder's demand for separate representations as to certain line items of Target's balance sheet as onerous (and inappropriate) and thus unfair to Target because of the protection that Bidder has already been granted by the terms of Target's financial statement representation that the parties just finished negotiating, which now covers *both* audited and unaudited (interim) financials of Target. Given the scope of the financial statement representation that Target has already agreed

---

thoroughly familiar with the terms of the document and understand how the acquisition agreement is put together as an organic whole. Only by thoroughly preparing in this way will the lawyers be able to identify and anticipate those issues that are likely to be the points of serious contention between the parties. The lawyers, together with their business client, can then prioritize these items of potential disagreement so that the lawyers are prepared to deal with them appropriately as they arise during the course of the parties' negotiations. *See generally*, James C. Freund, ANATOMY OF A MERGER: STRATEGIES AND TECHNIQUES FOR NEGOTIATING CORPORATE ACQUISITIONS (Law Journal Seminars-Press 1975); Robert Mnookin, et al., BEYOND WINNING: NEGOTIATING TO CREATE VALUE IN DEALS AND DISPUTES (Harvard University Press 2000); Roger Fisher, William Ury, and Bruce Patton, GETTING TO YES: NEGOTIATING AGREEMENT WITHOUT GIVING IN (Houghton Mifflin Company 1991).

10. In connection with the terms of the financial statement representation just negotiated, it would be entirely appropriate for Bidder to insist on a bring-down of this representation as a condition to closing. Thus, in this context, use of a bring-down condition (of the type described earlier in this chapter, *see supra*, at pp. 356-357) would be a customary term included in the conditions section of the parties' acquisition agreement.

to include in the agreement, coupled with the customary use of a bring-down condition, Target is likely to claim that Bidder is adequately protected.

Bidder, on the other hand, may argue that these supplemental line-item representations are not superfluous. Rather, they are geared specifically toward certain attributes of Target's business that are of particular concern to Bidder. As such, they are intended to give Bidder a clearer understanding of the financial condition of Target's business in areas that Bidder deems important, such as inventory levels or collectability of accounts receivable. From a due diligence perspective, Bidder may have legitimate business reasons for demanding certain line-item representations in order to give Bidder the comfort it needs over and above that provided by Target's balance sheet (financial statements) prepared in accordance with GAAP. In these areas, Bidder may seek the additional comfort it needs as a business matter by demanding specific representations from Target as to certain line item of its balance sheet.

Target may try to avoid including these line-item representations in the acquisition agreement by arguing that Target's obligation is to deliver to Bidder at closing a company that has a certain financial condition as a whole. As such, Target did not contemplate that it would have to take on the burden of digging into all this minutiae as part of the deal it made with Bidder. By insisting on these specific line-item representations, Bidder is forcing Target to go far beyond what is required by GAAP because these line-item representations are in effect allocating (certain economic) risks to Target that are inappropriate. For example, by including a line-item representation as to Target's accounts receivable, Bidder is in effect allocating the risk of the collectability of the company's accounts receivable to the sellers of Target. From Target's perspective, this is tantamount to asking it to guarantee the collection of the company's accounts receivable. In many cases, that is simply going to be a business risk that Target's sellers will be unwilling to take on, believing that this is a risk inherent in operating Target's business and as such goes with the business.

NOTE

Impact of SOX on Acquisition Negotiations.   In July 2002, in response to the financial scandals that engulfed companies such as WorldCom and Tyco at the start of the twenty-first century, Congress enacted SOX. As part of SOX, Congress adopted a far-reaching set of reforms addressing the boardroom practices of directors of publicly traded companies, as well as their senior executive officers, lawyers, auditors, and other financial advisors. While the impact of these federal reform measures is most pronounced in the case of publicly traded corporations, SOX is also having an impact on acquisitions in the M&A market for private companies, such as the kind of deal involved in the hypothetical bargaining described above (between lawyers negotiating the terms of the financial statement covenant to be given by a closely held Target Co. to a publicly traded Bidder Co.). As such, the impact of SOX is being felt beyond the context of public company M&A transactions.

From Bidder's perspective, it is likely that the financial results of Target's business will have to be made part of Bidder's financial statements and thus subject to the requirements of SOX (such as the officer and director certifications required by §303 of SOX) after Bidder closes on the acquisition. Moreover, in the wake of the Great Recession, the current business climate leads to a great deal of skepticism about accepting financial statements at face value and relying on them without any further inquiry or probing, and without the benefit of any additional contractual protections. Many Bidders are simply not willing in today's environment to accept Target's proffer of its financial statements, even though they have been audited by one of the reputable Big Four audit firms. Faced with such a proffer, most Bidders respond by simply rejecting such a proposal and point to numerous high-profile financial/accounting scandals that have occurred over the past couple of decades as the basis for its rejection.

5.   Use of Materiality Qualifier — Herein of MACs and MAEs

To illustrate the use of a *materiality qualifier*, consider the typical provision in Bidder's original draft of the acquisition agreement calling for Target to represent that its business is in compliance with *all laws*. Target is likely to insist that this representation be qualified to limit its scope to refer to *material compliance with all laws*. In this way, Target is informing Bidder that its business is generally in compliance with all laws, without going so far as to represent that it is in 100 percent compliance with *every* provision of federal, state, and local law. Alternatively, the materiality qualifier might be framed slightly differently to provide that Target's business is in *compliance with all material laws*. When the representation is framed in this way, Target is essentially representing that out of the whole universe of laws that might apply to Target's business and focusing only on those that are most relevant to Target's business, Target represents that it is in compliance with all of those laws that really affect the company's business in a meaningful way.

To further illustrate how this materiality qualifier can be used to tailor the scope of Target's representation, consider yet another alternative — a third formulation of the materiality qualifier in the context of this same representation. Target could insist that this representation be framed to read that the company is in *compliance with all laws except as to those laws where the failure to comply would not materially and adversely affect the company's business*. Many M&A lawyers prefer this third formulation of the materiality qualifier. Why? In what way does this provision differ from the prior two formulations of the materiality qualifier? Why is this third alternative an improvement over the other two? In thinking about this question, consider the scope of the representation that Target is making to Bidder under this third formulation of the materiality qualifier.

These different formulations of the materiality qualifier in the context of this particular representation reflect yet another important point about the process of negotiating the terms of the representations to be included in any acquisition agreement. As part of the bargaining process, it is important that the lawyers fully understand the business terms of the parties' deal. In that way, the lawyer for each side will be well informed as to which formulation of the materiality qualifier will be most appropriate for use in the context of that particular transaction.

This point was made in dramatic fashion in a well-known, high-profile M&A case that required the court to construe the use of a *materiality qualifier* as part of a particular representation contained in the parties' acquisition agreement:

In re IBP, Inc. Shareholders Litigation
IBP, Inc. v. Tyson Foods, Inc.
789 A.2d 14 (Del. Ch. 2001)

STRINE, Vice Chancellor.

This post-trial opinion addresses a demand for specific performance of a "Merger Agreement" by IBP, Inc., the nation's number one beef and number two pork distributor. By this action, IBP seeks to compel the "Merger" between itself and Tyson Foods, Inc., the nation's leading chicken distributor, in a transaction in which IBP stockholders will receive their choice of $30 a share in cash or Tyson stock, or a combination of the two.

The IBP-Tyson Merger Agreement resulted from a vigorous auction process that pitted Tyson against the nation's number one pork producer, Smithfield Foods. To say that Tyson was eager to win the auction is to slight its ardent desire to possess IBP. During the bidding process, Tyson was anxious to ensure that it would acquire IBP, and to make sure Smithfield did not. By succeeding, Tyson hoped to create the world's preeminent meat products company—a company that would dominate the meat cases of supermarkets in the United States and eventually throughout the globe.

During the auction process, Tyson was given a great deal of information that suggested that IBP was heading into a trough in the beef business. Even more, Tyson was alerted to serious problems at an IBP subsidiary, DFG, which had been victimized by accounting fraud to the tune of over $30 million in charges to earnings and which was the active subject of an asset impairment study. Not only that, Tyson knew that IBP was projected to fall seriously short of the fiscal year 2000 earnings predicted in projections prepared by IBP's Chief Financial Officer in August, 2000.

By the end of the auction process, Tyson had come to have great doubts about IBP's ability to project its future earnings, the credibility of IBP's management, and thought that the important business unit in which DFG was located—Foodbrands—was broken.

Yet, Tyson's ardor for IBP was such that Tyson raised its bid by a total of $4.00 a share after learning of these problems. Tyson also signed the Merger Agreement, which permitted IBP to recognize unlimited additional liabilities on account of the accounting improprieties at DFG. It did so without demanding any representation that IBP meet its projections for future earnings, or any escrow tied to those projections.

After the Merger Agreement was signed on January 1, 2001, Tyson trumpeted the value of the merger to its stockholders and the financial community, and indicated that it was fully aware of the risks that attended the cyclical nature of IBP's business. In early January, Tyson's stockholders ratified the merger agreement and authorized its management to take whatever action was needed to effectuate it.

During the winter and spring of 2001, Tyson's own business performance was dismal. Meanwhile, IBP was struggling through a poor first quarter. Both companies' problems were due in large measure to a severe winter, which adversely affected livestock supplies and vitality. As these struggles deepened, Tyson's desire to buy IBP weakened.

This cooling of affections first resulted in a slow-down by Tyson in the process of consummating a transaction, a slow-down that was attributed to IBP's on-going efforts to resolve issues that had been raised about its financial statements by the Securities and Exchange Commission ("SEC"). The most important of these issues was how to report the problems at DFG, which Tyson had been aware of at the time it signed the Merger Agreement. Indeed, all the key issues that the SEC raised with IBP were known by Tyson at the time it signed the Merger Agreement. The SEC first raised these issues in a faxed letter on December 29, 2000 to IBP's outside counsel. Neither IBP management nor Tyson learned of the letter until the second week of January, 2001. After learning of the letter, Tyson management put the Merger Agreement to a successful board and stockholder vote.

But the most important reason that Tyson slowed down the Merger process was different: it was having buyer's regret. Tyson wished it had paid less especially in view of its own compromised 2001 performance and IBP's slow 2001 results.

By March, Tyson's founder and controlling stockholder, Don Tyson, no longer wanted to go through with the Merger Agreement. He made the decision to abandon the Merger. His son, John Tyson, Tyson's Chief Executive Officer, and the other Tyson managers followed his instructions. Don Tyson abandoned the Merger because of IBP's and Tyson's poor results in 2001, and not because of DFG or the SEC issues IBP was dealing with. Indeed, Don Tyson told IBP management that he would blow DFG up if he were them.

After the business decision was made to terminate, Tyson's legal team swung into action. They fired off a letter terminating the Agreement at the same time as they filed suit accusing IBP of fraudulently inducing the Merger that Tyson had once so desperately desired.

This expedited litigation ensued, which involved massive amounts of discovery and two weeks of trial.

In this opinion, I address IBP's claim that Tyson had no legal basis to avoid its obligation to consummate the Merger Agreement, as well as Tyson's contrary arguments. The parties' extensive claims are too numerous to summarize adequately, as are the court's rulings.

At bottom, however, I conclude as follows:

- The Merger Agreement and related contracts were valid and enforceable contracts that were not induced by any material misrepresentation or omission;
- The Merger Agreement specifically allocated certain risks to Tyson, including the risk of any losses or financial effects from the accounting improprieties at DFG, and these risks cannot serve as a basis for Tyson to terminate the Agreement;
- None of the non-DFG related issues that the SEC raised constitute a contractually permissible basis for Tyson to walk away from the Merger;

- IBP has not suffered a Material Adverse Effect within the meaning of the Agreement that excused Tyson's failure to close the Merger; and
- Specific performance is the decisively preferable remedy for Tyson's breach, as it is the only method by which to adequately redress the harm threatened to IBP and its stockholders.

I. FACTUAL BACKGROUND

IBP'S KEY MANAGERS

IBP [formerly known as Iowa Beef Packers] was first incorporated in 1960. Its current Chairman of the Board and Chief Executive Officer, Robert Peterson, has been with the company from the beginning. . . .

Peterson is a strong and committed CEO, who loves the business he has helped build and the people who work for it. By the late 1990s, however, Peterson was in his late sixties and cognizant that it would soon be time to turn the reins over to a new CEO. Peterson's heir apparent was IBP's President and Chief Operating Officer, Richard "Dick" Bond. . . .

IBP'S BUSINESS

The traditional business of IBP is being a meat processor that acts as the middleman between ranchers and retail supermarkets and food processors. This is the so-called "fresh meats" business of IBP. . . .

. . . IBP was endeavoring to build up its food processing businesses. These are the businesses that take raw food products and turn them into something canned or packaged for supermarket or restaurant sale. Because these processing activities "add value," they tend to have higher profit margins and generate more stable earnings than middleman meat slaughtering.

To carry out this strategy, IBP had recently made a series of acquisitions, including the purchase of Corporate Food Brands America, Inc. ("CFBA") in February 2000. These purchased entities were being put together within IBP under the larger heading of Foodbrands. . . .

IBP hoped that these processed food investments would provide a vehicle for growth and reduce the year-to-year volatility of IBP's earnings. . . .

Moreover, while Foodbrands was a central part of IBP's strategy for the future, it remained at that time a much smaller contributor to the bottom line than IBP's' fresh meats business. . . .

IBP MANAGEMENT PROPOSES AN LBO

During 1999 and early 2000, IBP's management was frustrated by the stock market's valuation of the company's stock. As earnings-less dot.coms traded at huge multiples to eyeball hits, IBP's stock traded at a relatively small multiple to actual earnings. In response to this problem, Peterson, Bond, and [Larry] Shipley [IBP's chief financial officer] were receptive when the investment bank of Donaldson, Lufkin & Jenrette, Inc. ("DLJ") expressed interest in a leveraged-buyout ("LBO") of the company.

In July, management informed the IBP board that it would like to pursue an LBO seriously. With the help of DLJ, a syndicate of investors who called themselves "Rawhide" was prepared to take the company private if a deal could be negotiated with the IBP board. The board formed a special committee comprised of outside directors, who then selected Wachtell, Lipton, Rosen, & Katz as its legal advisor and J.P. Morgan Securities, Inc. as its financial advisor. . . . [Rawhide eventually abandoned its interest in acquiring IBP.] . . .

PROBLEMS AT DFG FOODS BEGIN TO SURFACE

In 1998, as part of its strategy to grow IBP's higher-margin food processing business, IBP management purchased a specialty hors d'oeuvres, kosher foods, and "airline food" business for $91 million, including assumed debt. IBP bought this business from its managers, including its President, Andrew Zahn. Within IBP, the business became known as DFG Foods, Inc. or "DFG." In late 1999, IBP purchased a competitor of DFG named Wilton Foods, and combined its operations with DFG. Zahn stayed on board after the purchase of DFG and continued to run the business, with a right to certain earn-out payments upon his departure that were tied to the unit's performance.

Although IBP hoped that DFG would become a useful part of its overall strategy to move into higher-margin businesses, as of the year 2000, DFG was an insignificant portion of IBP's overall business. . . .

On September 30, 2000, Andrew Zahn left DFG and took a sizable earn-out payment with him. On October 16, 2000, IBP issued a press release announcing earnings for the third quarter of FY 2000 of $83.9 million and year-to-date earnings of $203 million. Soon after this announcement, Dick Bond learned that there were problems with the integrity of DFG's books and records, and that it was possible that DFG's inventory value was overstated. . . .

When IBP top management learned of the problems at DFG, a full inventory audit was ordered. The audit concluded that DFG's inventory was overvalued by $9 million. On November 7, 2000, IBP therefore announced that it would take a $9 million reduction over pre-tax earnings from the amounts previously reported for third quarter of FY 2000. These amounts were reported to the SEC in IBP's third quarter 10-Q. As of that time, Peterson and Bond were led to believe that the $9 million overstatement was the extent of the problem at DFG, although efforts to get control of DFG's financials continued.

THE AUCTION FOR IBP BEGINS

The rumors about IBP's possible sale had not gone unnoticed among meat industry leaders. Two industry participants had toyed with the idea of making a play for IBP for years.

One was Smithfield Foods, the nation's number one pork processing firm. When combined with IBP, Smithfield would be the number one producer of beef and pork products. . . .

Meanwhile, Tyson Foods had been pondering a deal with IBP for several years. Bob Peterson and Tyson founder and controlling stockholder, Don Tyson, were old industry friends with great respect for one another. . . . Put mildly, Peterson's ardor for a combination with Tyson was much stronger than for a deal with Smithfield. . . .

TYSON MAKES ITS OPENING BID

In early December, the Tyson board of directors met to consider making a bid for IBP. John Tyson's vision for the deal was fundamental: he wanted to dominate the meat case of America's supermarkets and be the "premier protein center-of-the-plate provider" in the world. Tyson/IBP would be number one in beef and chicken, and number two in pork. It would therefore be able to provide supermarkets with nearly all the meat they needed.

Not only that, John Tyson saw the potential to bring Tyson Foods' own experience and unique expertise to bear outside of the poultry realm. . . .

IBP was acknowledged to have a great fresh beefs business with an excellent, long-term track record. While it was beginning to embark on value-added strategies in the beef and pork industry, IBP was by all accounts not as far along in that corporate strategy and could most benefit from Tyson's expertise in that particular area. John Tyson saw the potential for Tyson's expertise to help IBP do in beef and pork what Tyson had done in poultry. His vision of the companies, however, had little to do with DFG specifically, a small subpart of Foodbrands that he knew little, if anything, about.

Tyson's board supported management's recommendation to make a bid. On December 4, 2000, Tyson proposed to acquire IBP in a two-step transaction valued at $26 (half cash, half stock) per share. Tyson trumpeted the fact that its offer was preferable to Smithfield's, in no small measure because Tyson did not face the same degree of anti-trust complications that Smithfield did and could thus deliver on its offer more quickly. . . .

. . . Tyson sent IBP an executed "Confidentiality Agreement," modeled on one signed by Smithfield, which would permit it to have access to non-public, due diligence information about IBP. . . .

. . . The terms of the Confidentiality Agreement also emphasize to an objective reader that the merger negotiation process would not be one during which Tyson could reasonably rely on oral assurances. Instead, if Tyson wished to protect itself, it would have to ensure that any oral promises were converted into contractual representations and warranties. . . . .

THE DUE DILIGENCE PROCESS BEGINS

Tyson did not enter into the due diligence process alone. It retained Millbank, Tweed, Hadley & McCoy as its primary legal advisor, Merrill Lynch & Co. as its primary financial advisor, and Ernst & Young as its accountants.

•   The bidding process was being run by IBP's special committee. . . .

On December 5 and 6, 2000, Tyson's due diligence team reviewed information in the data room at Wachtell, Lipton. Tyson soon learned that the data room did not contain certain information about Foodbrands and the reason why that was so: IBP was reluctant to share competitively sensitive information with Smithfield. The special committee's approach to this sales process was to treat the bidders with parity. As a result, Tyson was told that any information it wanted that was not in the data room could be provided, but that if Tyson received that information, so would Smithfield.

As a result of its due diligence, Tyson flagged certain items including:

- Possible asset impairments at DFG and certain other Foodbrands companies.
- Discrepancies in the way that IBP reported its business segments. . . . .

IBP AND TYSON HOLD A DECEMBER 8, 2000 DUE DILIGENCE MEETING

On December 8, 2000, due diligence teams from Tyson and IBP met in Sioux City, Iowa. The meeting was attended by the top managers from each side. . . .

Tyson came to the meeting expecting the now *de rigeur* PowerPoint presentation. IBP came expecting to answer Tyson's questions. As a result, the meeting became a question and answer session that covered IBP's business, segment by segment.

At least two important issues were discussed at the meeting. I will start with the DFG issue. Going into the December 8, 2000 meeting, the chairwoman of the IBP special committee, Joann Smith, specifically told John Tyson to ask about DFG at the meeting.

According to IBP witnesses, the DFG situation had gotten more serious by December 8. IBP's top management was concerned that the accounting problems at DFG were deeper than they had recognized and that additional charges to earnings might be necessary. The IBP employee-witnesses all remember Peterson saying that the DFG problem had gotten worse by at least $20 million. Peterson himself remembers speaking in angry and vehement terms about Andy Zahn, labeling him as a "thief in the hen house," and the progeny of a female dog who should be hanged on main street in front of a crowd. He also recalls saying that DFG was a "black hole." His colleagues at IBP have far less specific recollections, but do recall Peterson being quite upset.

The Tyson witnesses have a different recollection. They recall being told that DFG was a $9 million problem. Leatherby's notes of the meeting note that there had been a "$9 mm writedown here (guy fired) fudged earnout," that DFG was "not doing well," but that IBP "believe[d] in bus." [Notes taken by Steve Hankins, IBP's CFO] about DFG tersely state: "DFG—At bottom of problem." None of the Tyson witnesses heard Peterson describe Zahn—at that meeting—in such unforgettable terms. They do admit, however, that Peterson appeared agitated and upset by the issue, that the problem was attributed to fraud by Zahn, that Zahn had been the head of the business, that Zahn was now gone, and that IBP was looking into his activities. . . .

I cannot conclude with any certainty exactly what was said at the December 8, 2000 meeting. . . . .

TYSON ASKS FOR ADDITIONAL DUE DILIGENCE REGARDING FOODBRANDS

After the December 8, 2000 meeting, Tyson quickly commenced its tender offer. As due diligence continued, Tyson requested access to additional accounting information involving Foodbrands. IBP management responded with this basic and consistent theme: "if you want to look at it, we have to show it to Smithfield, too. But if you want Smithfield to see it, you can have it."

This line of reasoning was frustrating to certain members of Tyson's due diligence team. Nonetheless, Tyson was never denied access to documents, it was simply told to make a tactical decision. Because Tyson wanted to buy IBP and wanted to compete with Smithfield after doing so, Tyson did not wish Smithfield to see the information. Nor did IBP management, who preferred that Tyson come out on top in the bidding.

Tyson also never chose to narrow its due diligence requests to deal only with the fraud at DFG. It did so even though its own accountants were concerned about the issue and whether IBP had really gotten to the bottom of the problem. . . . Most important, IBP never denied Tyson access and had already told Tyson that there had been fraud at DFG. As a result, it is more probable that Tyson simply wanted to keep Smithfield from having knowledge about a business unit Tyson hoped to soon own. What is certain is that Tyson never demanded access to additional due diligence as a condition to going forward with a merger. . . .

By mid to late December, the IBP special committee was preparing to conduct an auction between Tyson and Smithfield. . . .

On December 21, J.P. Morgan sent Tyson and Smithfield bid instructions which called for them to submit best and final bids, along with proposed merger contracts, by 5:00 p.m. on December 29, 2000. The instructions informed the bidders that the special committee was free to change the rules of the process and that no agreement would be binding until reduced to a signed contract. . . .

TYSON WINS THE AUCTION—TWICE

On December 30, 2000, Smithfield advised the special committee that $30 was its best and final offer. Special committee chair Smith called John Tyson and told him that if Tyson bid $28.50 in cash it would have a deal. John Tyson agreed and Smith said they had a deal. Later, the IBP special committee met to consider the Tyson and Smithfield bids. With the advice of J. P. Morgan, the special committee considered Tyson's $28.50 cash and stock bid to exceed the value of Smithfield's all stock $30 bid. The special committee decided to accept Tyson's bid, subject to negotiation of a definitive merger agreement.

As a courtesy, the special committee and its counsel informed Smithfield that it had lost the auction. On December 31, Smithfield increased its all stock bid to $32.00. With deep chagrin, Smith went back to John Tyson and explained what had happened and the committee's duty to consider the higher bid.* John Tyson was justifiably angry, but understood the realities of the situation.

---

* [By the author: As part of the materials in Chapter 7, we will discuss at length the scope of Target (IBP) Board's fiduciary duty in connection with conducting an auction of the company's business, along with the Board's related "duty to consider the higher bid."]

Tyson Foods went to the well again and drew out another $1.50 a share, increasing its bid to $30 per share. IBP agreed and this time the price stuck.

THE MERGER AGREEMENT NEGOTIATIONS

While the auction was on, the lawyers for IBP's special committee had been negotiating possible merger agreements with Tyson and Smithfield. By December 30, the IBP lawyers were mostly focused on Tyson because it appeared they had prevailed in the auction.

The document that was used as a template for what became the final Merger Agreement was initially prepared by Millbank Tweed, whose team was led by Lawrence Lederman. . . .

TYSON'S BOARD AND SHAREHOLDERS VOTE FOR THE MERGER AGREEMENT

On January 12, 2001, Tyson's board of directors met and ratified management's decision to enter into the Merger Agreement. . . .

The same day the Tyson shareholders meeting was held. The Merger Agreement was put to a vote of the Tyson stockholders. . . . The Tyson's stockholders approved the Merger Agreement and authorized management to consummate the transactions it contemplated.

TYSON GETS NERVOUS AND WANTS TO REPRICE THE DEAL

During February, Tyson Foods became increasingly nervous about the IBP deal and began to stall for time. While Tyson still believed that the deal made strategic sense, it was keen on finding a way to consummate the deal at a lower price. The negotiations with the SEC [over the accounting problems at DMG] were a pressure point that Tyson could use for that purpose and it did.

Tyson's anxiety was heightened by problems it and IBP were experiencing in the first part of 2001. A severe winter had hurt both beef and chicken supplies, with chickens suffering more than cows.

. . . Tyson's performance was way down from previous levels. Eventually, Tyson would have to reduce its earnings estimate for this period, only to find out its reduction was not sufficient. Eventually, Tyson reported a loss of $6 million for the pertinent quarter, compared to a profit of $35.7 million for the prior year's period. . . .

By mid-February, these factors led the Tyson and IBP factions to approach each other warily. IBP sensed that Tyson wanted to renegotiate. Hagen [IBP's General Counsel] prepared for an even worse possibility: that Tyson would walk away and IBP would have to enforce the deal. Bond tried to deal with the problem by being responsive to John Tyson's calls for help in reassuring his father, Don Tyson, that the deal still made sense.

On the Tyson side, its key managers began to slow down the merger implementation process to buy time for John and Don Tyson. While Tyson and IBP continued to do all the merger integration planning that precedes a large combination, Tyson was also bent on using its leverage to extract concessions from IBP. . . .

On March 7, 2001, John Tyson sent all the Tyson employees a memorandum stating that Tyson Foods was still committed to the transaction. But on March 13, 2001, he expressed concern to Bond about IBP's first quarter performance and wanted Bond's best estimates for the rest of the year. . . .

IBP FILED ITS RESTATED FINANCIALS AND TYSON CONTINUES ITS STRATEGY TO PUT PRESSURE ON IBP TO RENEGOTIATE

On March 13, 2001, IBP also formally filed its restatements to the Warranted Financials. The formal restatements were in line with the previous release regarding DFG, as was the $60.4 million DFG "Impairment Charge" took in its year 2000 10-K. None of the other issues covered had any impact on IBP's prospects. Tyson reacted in print in a March 14 press release that indicated that Tyson was pleased IBP had resolved most of its issues with the SEC. The press release also indicated that Tyson was continuing to look at IBP's business and noted its weak first quarter results. Behind the scenes, Tyson's investor relations officer, Louis Gottsponer, was turning up the heat on IBP through comments to analysts. . . .

Sure enough, the next day analysts began reporting that IBP's earnings outlook would possibly lead to a renegotiation of the deal. . . .

TYSON TERMINATES AND SUES IBP

. . . On March 28, 2001, Don Tyson called a meeting of the "old guard" and Tyson's current top management. The agenda's first two items were the state of the economy in general, and the state of Tyson's business. As of that day, Tyson's own performance for the year was very disappointing and it had been forced to admit so publicly only days earlier. Only after discussing the first two items on the agenda did the participants discuss the IBP deal. Don Tyson expressed continued concerns about IBP's current year performance and about mad cow disease. When it came time to make the decision how to proceed, Don Tyson left to caucus with the old guard. The new guard was excluded, including John Tyson. Don Tyson returned to the meeting and announced that Tyson should find a way to withdraw. The problems at DFG apparently played no part in his decision, nor did the comments from the SEC. Indeed, DFG was so unimportant that neither John nor Don Tyson knew about Schedule 5.11 of the Agreement until this litigation was underway.

After the old guard had decided that the Merger should not proceed, Tyson's legal team swung into action. Late on March 29, 2001, [Tyson's General Counsel, Les Baledge] sent a letter stating:

> Tyson Foods . . . will issue a press release today announcing discontinuation of the transactions contemplated by the Agreement and Plan of Merger dated as of January 1, 2001 among IBP, Inc. ("IBP") and Tyson (the "Merger Agreement"). We intend to include this letter with our press release.

On December 29, 2000, the Friday before final competitive negotiations resulting in the Merger Agreement, your counsel received comments from the Securities and Exchange Commission ("SEC") raising important issues concerning IBP's financial statements and reports filed with the SEC. As you know, we learned of the undisclosed SEC comments on January 10, 2001. Ultimately, IBP restated its financials and filings to address the SEC's issues and correct earlier misstatements. Unfortunately, we relied on that misleading information in determining to enter into the Merger Agreement. In addition, the delays and restatements resulting from these matters have created numerous breaches by IBP of representations, warranties, covenants and agreements contained in the Merger Agreement which cannot be cured.

Consequently, whether intended or not, we believe Tyson Foods, Inc. was inappropriately induced to enter into the Merger Agreement. Further, we believe IBP cannot perform under the Merger Agreement. Under these facts, Tyson has a right to rescind or terminate the Merger Agreement and to receive compensation from IBP. We have commenced legal action in Arkansas seeking such relief. We hope to resolve these matters outside litigation in an expeditious and business-like manner. However, our duties dictate that we preserve Tyson's rights and protect the interests of our shareholders.

If our belief is proven wrong and the Merger Agreement is not rescinded, this letter will serve as Tyson's notice, pursuant to sections 11.01 (f) and 12.01 of the Merger Agreement, of termination.

Notably, the letter does not indicate that IBP had suffered a Material Adverse Effect as a result of its first-quarter performance.

But as indicated in the letter, Tyson had sued IBP in Arkansas that evening, shortly before the close of the business day. The next day IBP filed this suit to enforce the Merger Agreement.

II.   The Basic Contentions of the Parties

The parties have each made numerous arguments that bear on the central question of whether Tyson properly terminated the Merger Agreement, which is understandable in view of the high stakes. The plethora of theories and nuanced arguments is somewhat daunting and difficult to summarize. But the fundamental contentions are as follows.

IBP argues that Tyson had no valid reason to terminate the contract on March 29, 2001 and that the Merger Agreement should be specifically enforced. In support of that position, IBP argues that it has not breached any of the contractual representations and warranties. . . .

Tyson argues that its decision to terminate was proper for several reasons. First, Tyson contends that IBP breached its contractual representations regarding the Warranted Financials, as evidenced by the Restatements. Second, Tyson contends that the DFG Impairment Charge as well as IBP's disappointing first quarter 2001 performance are evidence of a Material Adverse Effect, which gave Tyson the right to terminate. . . .

Before turning to the resolution of the parties' various arguments, it is necessary to pause to discuss certain choice of law issues. The parties are in accord that New York law governs the substantive aspects of the contractual and misrepresentation claims before the court. This accord is in keeping with the parties' choice to have New York contract law govern the interpretation of the Merger Agreement. But they part company on certain issues with respect to the precise burden of proof governing these claims.[88] For the sake of clarity, I will outline the approach I take up front.

Under either New York or Delaware law, IBP bears the burden of persuasion to justify its entitlement to specific performance. Under New York law, IBP must show that: (1) the Merger Agreement is a valid contract between the parties; (2) IBP has substantially performed under the contract and is willing and able to perform its remaining obligations; (3) Tyson is able to perform its obligations; and (4) IBP has no adequate remedy at law. . . .

III.   RESOLUTION OF THE PARTIES' MERITS ARGUMENTS

. . ., I first address whether IBP breached a representation and warranty that justified Tyson's termination of the Merger Agreement. . . .

A.   GENERAL PRINCIPLES OF NEW YORK CONTRACT LAW

The Merger Agreement's terms are to be interpreted under New York law. Like Delaware, New York follows traditional contract law principles that give great weight to the parties' objective manifestations of their intent in the written language of their agreement. If a contract's meaning is plain and unambiguous, it will be given effect. . . .

In reading a contract, "the [court's] aim is a practical interpretation of the expressions of the parties to the end that there be a realization of [their] reasonable expectations." . . .

D.   WAS TYSON'S TERMINATION JUSTIFIED BECAUSE IBP HAS
SUFFERED A MATERIAL ADVERSE EFFECT?

Tyson argues that it was . . . permitted to terminate because IBP had breached §5.10 of the Agreement, which is a representation and warranty that IBP had not suffered a material adverse effect since the "Balance Sheet Date" of December 25, 1999, except as set forth in the Warranted Financials or Schedule 5.10 of the Agreement. Under the contract, a material adverse effect (or "MAE") is defined as "any event, occurrence, or development of a state of circumstances or facts which has had or reasonably could be expected to have a Material Adverse Effect" . . . "on the condition (financial or otherwise), business, assets, liabilities or results of operations of [IBP] and [its] Subsidiaries taken as a whole.[146] . . ."

---

88. It is fair to say that this is one of the more tersely argued disputes in the briefs.

146. Agreement §5.10(a) (specific warranty dealing generally with MAE); §5.01 (defining MAE for entire agreement).

Tyson asserts that the decline in IBP's performance in the last quarter of 2000 and the first quarter of 2001 evidences the existence of a Material Adverse Effect. It also contends that the DFG Impairment Charge constitutes a Material Adverse Effect. And taken together, Tyson claims that it is virtually indisputable that the combination of these factors amounts to a Material Adverse Effect.

In addressing these arguments, it is useful to be mindful that Tyson's publicly expressed reasons for terminating the Merger did not include an assertion that IBP had suffered a Material Adverse Effect. The post-hoc nature of Tyson's arguments bear on what it felt the contract meant when contracting, and suggests that a short-term drop in IBP's performance would not be sufficient to cause a MAE. To the extent the facts matter, it is also relevant that Tyson gave no weight to DFG in contracting.

The resolution of Tyson's Material Adverse Effect argument requires the court to engage in an exercise that is quite imprecise. The simplicity of §5.10's words is deceptive, because the application of those words is dauntingly complex. On its face, §5.10 is a capacious clause that puts IBP at risk for a variety of uncontrollable factors that might materially affect its overall business or results of operation as a whole. Although many merger contracts contain specific exclusions from MAE clauses that cover declines in the overall economy or the relevant industry sector, or adverse weather or market conditions, §5.10 is unqualified by such express exclusions.

IBP argues, however, that statements in the Warranted Financials that emphasize the risks IBP faces from swings in livestock supply act as an implicit carve-out, because a Material Adverse Effect under that section cannot include an Effect that is set forth in the Warranted Financials. I agree with Tyson, however, that these disclaimers were far too general to preclude industrywide or general factors from constituting a Material Adverse Effect. Had IBP wished such an exclusion from the broad language of §5.10, IBP should have bargained for it. At the same time, the notion that §5.10 gave Tyson a right to walk away simply because of a downturn in cattle supply is equally untenable. Instead, Tyson would have to show that the event had the required materiality of effect.[148]

The difficulty of addressing that question is considerable, however, because §5.10 is fraught with temporal ambiguity. By its own terms, it refers to any Material Adverse Effect that has occurred to IBP since December 25, 1999 unless that Effect is covered by the Warranted Financials or Schedule 5.10. Moreover, Tyson's right to refuse to close because a Material Adverse Effect has occurred is also qualified by the other express disclosures in the Schedule, by virtue of (i) the language of the Annexes that permits Tyson to refuse to close for breach of a warranty unless that breach results from "actions specifically permitted" by the Agreement; and (ii) the language of the Agreement that makes all disclosure schedules apply to Schedule 5.10 where that is the reasonably apparent intent of the drafters. Taken together, these provisions can be read to require the court to examine whether a MAE has occurred against the December 25,

---

148. *But see Pittsburgh Coke & Chem. Co. v. Bollo*, 421 F. Supp. 908, 930 (E.D.N.Y. 1976) (where Material Adverse Condition ("MAC") clause applied to a company's "financial condition," "business," or "operations," court read that clause narrowly to exclude "technological and economic changes in the aviation industry which undoubtedly affected the business of all who had dealings with that industry").

1999 condition of IBP as adjusted by the specific disclosures of the Warranted Financials and the Agreement itself. This approach makes commercial sense because it establishes a baseline that roughly reflects the status of IBP as Tyson indisputably knew it at the time of signing the Merger Agreement.

But describing this basic contractual approach is somewhat easier than applying it. For example, the original IBP 10-K for FY 1999 revealed the following five-year earnings from operations and earnings per share before extraordinary items:

	1999	1998	1997	1996	1995
Earnings from Operations (in Thousands)	$528,473	$373,735	$226,716	$322,908	$480,096
Net Earnings Per Share	$3.39	$2.21	$1.26	$2.10	$2.96

The picture that is revealed from this data is of a company that is consistently profitable, but subject to strong swings in annual EBIT and net earnings. The averages that emerge from this data are of EBIT of approximately $386 million per year and net earnings of $2.38 per share. If this average is seen as weighting the past too much, a three-year average generates EBIT of $376 million and net earnings of $2.29 per share.

The original Warranted Financials in FY 2000 also emphasize that swings in IBP's performance were a part of its business reality. For example, the trailing last twelve month's earnings from operations as of the end of third quarter of FY 2000 were $462 million, as compared to $528 million for full year 1999, as originally reported. In addition, the third quarter 10-Q showed that IBP's earnings from operations for the first 39 weeks of 2000 were lagging earnings from operations for the comparable period in 1999 by $40 million, after adjusting for the CFBA Charges.

The financial statements also indicate that Foodbrands was hardly a stable source of earnings, and was still much smaller in importance than IBP's fresh meat operations. Not only that, FY 2000 Foodbrands performance was lagging 1999, even accounting for the unusual, disclosed items.

The Rawhide Projections [a set of financial projections prepared by IBP management at the request of the special board committee that was then considering Rawhide's LBO proposal] add another dimension to the meaning of §5.10. These Projections indicated that IBP would not reach the same level of profitability as originally reported *until FY 2004*. In FY 2001, IBP was expected to have earnings from operations of $446 and net profits of $ 1.93 a share, down from what was expected in FY 2000. This diminishment in expectations resulted from concern over an anticipated trough in the cattle cycle that would occur during years 2001 to 2003. Moreover, the performance projected for FY 2001 was a drop even from the reduced FY 2000 earnings that Tyson expected as of the time it signed the Merger Agreement.

These negotiating realities bear on the interpretation of §5.10 and suggest that the contractual language must be read in the larger context in which the parties were transacting. To a short-term speculator, the failure of a company to meet analysts' projected earnings for a quarter could be highly material. Such a failure is less important to an acquiror who seeks to purchase the company as part of a long-term strategy.[151] To such an acquiror, the important thing is whether the company has suffered a Material Adverse Effect in its business or results of operations that is consequential to the company's earnings power over a commercially reasonable period, which one would think would be measured in years rather than months. It is odd to think that a strategic buyer would view a short-term blip in earnings as material, so long as the target's earnings-generating potential is not materially affected by that blip or the blip's cause.[152]

In large measure, the resolution of the parties' arguments turns on a difficult policy question. In what direction does the burden of this sort of uncertainty fall: on an acquiror or on the seller? What little New York authority exists is not particularly helpful, and cuts in both directions. One New York case held a buyer to its bargain even when the seller suffered a very severe shock from an extraordinary event, reasoning that the seller realized that it was buying the stock of a sound company that was, however, susceptible to market swings.[153] Another case held that a Material Adverse Effect was evidenced by a short-term drop in sales, but in a commercial context where such a drop was arguably quite critical.[154] The non–New York authorities cited by the parties provide no firmer guidance.

Practical reasons lead me to conclude that a New York court would incline toward the view that a buyer ought to have to make a strong showing to invoke a Material Adverse Effect exception to its obligation to close. Merger contracts are heavily negotiated and cover a large number of specific risks explicitly. As a result, even where a Material Adverse Effect condition is as broadly written as the one in the Merger Agreement, that provision is best read as a backstop protecting the acquiror from the occurrence of unknown events that substantially threaten the overall earnings potential of the target in a durationally significant

---

151. James C. Freund, *Anatomy of a Merger: Strategies and Techniques for Negotiating Corporate Acquisitions* 246 (Law Journals Seminars-Press 1975) ("[W]hatever the concept of materiality may mean, at the very least it is always relative to the situation.").

152. *Pine State Creamery Co. v. Land-O-Sun Dairies, Inc.*, 201 F.3d 437, 1999 WL 1082539, at *6 (4th Cir. 1999) (*per curiam*) (whether severe losses during a two month period evidenced a MAC was a jury question where there was evidence that the business was seasonal and that such downturns were expected as part of the earnings cycle of the business).

153. *Bear Stearns Co. v. Jardine Strategic Holdings*, No. 31371187, slip. op. (N.Y. Supr. June 17, 1988), *aff'd mem.*, 143 A.D. 2d 1073, 533 N.Y.S. 2d 167 (1988) (Tender offeror who was to purchase 20% of Bear Stearns could not rely on the MAC clause to avoid contract despite $100 million loss suffered by Bear Stearns on Black Monday, October 19, 1987, and the fact that Bear Stearns suffered a $48 million quarterly loss, its first in history. The buyer knew that Bear Stearns was in a volatile cyclical business.).

154. *In Pan Am Corp. v. Delta Air Lines*, 175 B.R. 438, 492-493 (S.D.N.Y. 1994), Pan Am airlines suffered sharp decline in bookings over a three-month period that was shocking to its management. The court held that a MAC had occurred. It did so, however, in a context where the party relying on the MAC clause was providing funding in a work-out situation, making any further deterioration of Pan Am's already compromised condition quite important.

In another New York case, *Katz v. NVF,* 100 A.D. 2d 470, 473 N.Y.S. 2d 786 (1984), two merger partners agreed that one partner has suffered a material adverse change when its full year results showed a *net loss* of over $6.3 million, compared to a $2.1 million profit a year before, and steep operating losses due to plant closure. *Id.* at 788. The *Katz* case thus presents a negative change of much greater magnitude and duration than exists in this case.

manner.[155] A short-term hiccup in earnings should not suffice; rather the Material Adverse Effect should be material when viewed from the longer-term perspective of a reasonable acquiror. In this regard, it is worth noting that IBP never provided Tyson with *quarterly* projections.

When examined from this seller-friendly perspective, the question of whether IBP has suffered a Material Adverse Effect remains a close one. IBP had a very sub-par first quarter. The earnings per share of $.19 it reported exaggerate IBP's success, because part of those earnings were generated from a windfall generated by accounting for its stock option plan, a type of gain that is not likely to recur. On a normalized basis, IBP's first quarter of 2001 earnings from operations ran 64% behind the comparable period in 2000. If IBP had continued to perform on a straight-line basis using its first quarter 2001 performance, it would generate earnings from operations of around $200 million. This sort of annual performance would be consequential to a reasonable acquiror and would deviate materially from the range in which IBP had performed during the recent past.[156]

Tyson says that this impact must also be coupled with the DFG Impairment Charge of $60.4 million. That Charge represents an indication that DFG is likely to generate far less cash flow than IBP had previously anticipated. At the very least, the Charge is worth between $.50 and $.60 cents per IBP share, which is not trivial. It is worth even more, says Tyson, if one realizes that the Rawhide Projections portrayed Foodbrands as the driver of increased profitability in an era of flat fresh meats profits. This deficiency must be considered in view of the overall poor performance of Foodbrands so far in FY 2001. The Rawhide Projections had targeted Foodbrands to earn $137 million in 2001. In a January 30, 2001 presentation to Tyson, Bond had presented an operating plan that hoped to achieve $145 million from Foodbrands. As of the end of the first quarter, Foodbrands had earned only $2 million, and thus needed another $135 million in the succeeding three quarters to reach its Rawhide Projection. IBP's overall trailing last twelve month's earnings had declined from $488 million as of the end of the third quarter of 2000 to $330 million.

As a result of these problems, analysts following IBP issued sharply reduced earnings estimates for FY 2001. Originally, analysts were predicting that IBP would exceed the Rawhide Projections in 2001 by a wide margin. After IBP's poor first quarter, some analysts had reduced their estimate from $2.38 per share to $1.44 a share. *Even accounting for Tyson's attempts to manipulate the analyst community's perception of IBP,* this was a sharp drop.

Tyson contends that the logical inference to be drawn from the record evidence that is available is that IBP will likely have its worst year since 1997, a year which will be well below the company's average performance for all relevant

---

155. A contrary rule will encourage the negotiation of extremely detailed "MAC" clauses with numerous carve-outs or qualifiers. An approach that reads broad clauses as addressing fundamental events that would materially affect the value of a target to a reasonable acquiror eliminates the need for drafting of that sort.

156. *See Raskin v. Birmingham Steel Corp.,* Del. Ch., 1990 WL 193326, at *5, Allen, C. (Dec. 4, 1990) (while "a reported 50% decline in earnings over two consecutive quarters might not be held to be a material adverse development, it is, I believe unlikely to think that might happen").

periods. As important, the company's principal driver of growth is performing at markedly diminished levels, thus compromising the company's future results as it enters what is expected to be a tough few years in the fresh meats business.

IBP has several responses to Tyson's evidence. IBP initially notes that Tyson's arguments are unaccompanied by expert evidence that identifies the diminution in IBP's value or earnings potential as a result of its first quarter performance.[160] The absence of such proof is significant. Even after Hankins [Tyson's CFO] generated extremely pessimistic projections for IBP in order to justify a lower deal price, Merrill Lynch still concluded that a purchase of IBP at $30 per share was still within the range of fairness and a great long-term value for Tyson. The Merrill Lynch analysis casts great doubt on Tyson's assertion that IBP has suffered a Material Adverse Effect.[161]

IBP also emphasizes the cyclical nature of its businesses. It attributes its poor first quarter to an unexpectedly severe winter. This led ranchers to hold livestock back from market, causing a sharp increase in prices that hurt both the fresh meats business and Foodbrands. Once April was concluded, IBP began to perform more in line with its recent year results, because supplies were increasing and Foodbrands was able to begin to make up its winter margins. Bond testified at trial that he expects IBP to meet or exceed the Rawhide Projection of $1.93 a share in 2001, and the company has publicly indicated that it expects earnings of $1.80 to $2.20 a share. Peterson expressed the same view.

IBP also notes that any cyclical fall is subject to cure by the Agreement's termination date, which was May 15, 2001. By May 15, IBP had two weeks of strong earnings that signaled a strong quarter ahead. Moreover, by that time, cattle that had been held back from market were being sold, leading to plentiful supplies that were expected to last for most of the year.

Not only that, IBP notes that not all analyst reporting services had been as pessimistic as Tyson portrays. In March, Morningstar was reporting a mean analyst prediction of $1.70 per share for IBP in 2001. By May, this had grown to a mean of $1.74 a share. Throughout the same period, Morningstar's consensus prediction was an FY 2002 performance of $2.33 range in March, and $2.38 in May. Therefore, according to Morningstar, the analyst community was predicting that IBP would return to historically healthy earnings next year, and that earnings for this year would fall short of the Rawhide Projections by less than $.20 per share.

IBP also argues that the Impairment Charge does not approach materiality as a big picture item. That Charge is a one-time, non-cash charge, and IBP has taken large charges of that kind as recently as 1999. While IBP does not deny that its decision to buy DFG turned out disastrously, it reminds me that DFG is but a tiny fraction of IBP's overall business and that a total shut-down of DFG would likely have little effect on the future results of a combined Tyson/IBP. And as a narrow asset issue, the charge is insignificant to IBP as a whole.

---

160. It has admittedly taken its own payment multiples based on the Rawhide Projections and simply "valued" the effect that way. But IBP never warranted that it would meet those Projections.

161. Tyson's only expert on this subject testified that a MAE would have occurred in his view even if IBP met the Rawhide Projections, because those Projections were more bearish than the analysts. This academic theory is of somewhat dubious practical utility, as it leaves the enforceability of contracts dependent on whether predictions by third-parties come true.

I am confessedly torn about the correct outcome. As Tyson points out, IBP has only pointed to two weeks of truly healthy results in 2001 before the contract termination date of May 15. Even these results are suspect, Tyson contends, due to the fact that IBP expected markedly better results for the second week just days before the actual results come out. In view of IBP's demonstrated incapacity to accurately predict near-term results, Tyson says with some justification that I should be hesitant to give much weight to IBP's assurances that it will perform well for the rest of the year.

In the end, however, Tyson has not persuaded me that IBP has suffered a Material Adverse Effect. By its own arguments, Tyson has evinced more confidence in stock market analysts than I personally harbor. But its embrace of the analysts is illustrative of why I conclude that Tyson has not met its burden.

As of May 2001, analysts were predicting that IBP would earn between $1.50 to around $1.74 per share in 2001. The analysts were also predicting that IBP would earn between $2.33 and $2.42 per share in 2002. These members are based on reported "mean" or "consensus" analyst numbers. Even at the low end of this *consensus* range, IBP's earnings for the next two years would not be out of line with its historical performance during troughs in the beef cycle. As recently as years 1996-1998, IBP went through a period with a three year average earnings of $1.85 per share. At the high end of the analysts' consensus range, IBP's results would exceed this figure by $.21 per year.

This predicted range of performance from the source that Tyson vouches for suggests that no Material Adverse Effect has occurred.[170] Rather, the analyst views support the conclusion that IBP remains what the baseline evidence suggests it was—a consistently but erratically profitable company struggling to implement a strategy that will reduce the cyclicality of its earnings. Although IBP may not be performing as well as it and Tyson had hoped, IBP's business appears to be in sound enough shape to deliver results of operations in line with the company's recent historical performance. Tyson's own investment banker still believes IBP is fairly priced at $30 per share. The fact that Foodbrands is not yet delivering on the promise of even better performance for IBP during beef troughs is unavailing to Tyson, since §5.10 focuses on IBP as a whole and IBP's performance as an entire company is in keeping with its baseline condition.

Therefore, I conclude that Tyson has not demonstrated a breach of §5.10. I admit to reaching this conclusion with less than the optimal amount of confidence. The record evidence is not of the type that permits certainty. . . .

. . . [My conclusion] is that Tyson is in breach of the Merger Agreement because it improperly terminated in late March, 2001. That is, it is in breach of its obligation to close the [merger with IBP] on or before May 15, 2001.[200]

---

170. Again, I emphasize that my conclusion is heavily influenced by my temporal perspective, which recognizes that even good businesses do not invariably perform at consistent levels of profitability. If a different policy decision is the correct one, a contrary conclusion could be reached. That different, more short-term approach will, I fear, make merger agreements more difficult to negotiate and lead to Material Adverse Effect clauses of great prolixity.

200. Throughout the course of this case, IBP has urged upon me another proposition that it believes compels a ruling in its favor. IBP asserts that under New York law, a party cannot refuse to close on a contract in reliance upon a breached contractual representation if that party knew that the representation was false at the time of contracting. Put directly,

IV.   IBP Is Entitled to an Award of Specific Performance

Having determined that the Merger Agreement is a valid and enforceable contract that Tyson had no right to terminate, I now turn to the question of whether the Merger Agreement should be enforced by an order of specific performance. Although Tyson's voluminous post-trial briefs argue the merits fully, its briefs fail to argue that a remedy of specific performance is unwarranted in the event that its position on the merits is rejected.

This gap in the briefing is troubling. A compulsory order will require a merger of two public companies with thousands of employees working at facilities that are important to the communities in which they operate. The impact of a forced merger on constituencies beyond the stockholders and top managers of IBP and Tyson weighs heavily on my mind. The prosperity of IBP and Tyson means a great deal to these constituencies. I therefore approach this remedial issue quite cautiously and mindful of the interests of those who will be affected by my decision.

I start with a fundamental question: is this is a truly unique opportunity that cannot be adequately monetized? If the tables were turned and Tyson was seeking to enforce the contract, a great deal of precedent would indicate that the contract should be specifically enforced. In the more typical situation, an acquiror argues that it cannot be made whole unless it can specifically enforce the acquisition agreement, because the target company is unique and will yield value of an unquantifiable nature, once combined with the acquiring company. In this case, the sell-side of the transaction is able to make the same argument, because the Merger Agreement provides the IBP stockholders with a choice of cash or Tyson stock, or a combination of both. Through this choice, the IBP

IBP says it can win this case even if there was a breach of a representation in the Merger Agreement so long as it can prove that it informed Tyson of facts that demonstrate that the representation was untrue and thus that Tyson did not in fact rely upon the representation in deciding to sign the Merger Agreement. IBP's arguments find some support in some cases applying New York law. *See, e.g., Rogath v. Siebenmann,* 129 F.3d 261, 264-65 (2d Cir. 1997) ("Where the seller discloses up front the inaccuracy of certain of his warranties, it cannot be said that the buyer—absent the express preservation of his rights—believed he was purchasing the seller's promise as to the truth of the warranties."). There is, however, no definitive authority from the New York Court of Appeals to this effect, and the leading case can be read as being at odds with IBP's position. *See CBS v. Ziff-Davis Publishing Co.,* 75 N.Y. 2d 496, 554 N.Y.S. 2d 449, 553 N.E. 2d 997, 1000-01 (1990). Most of IBP's cases also deal with a distinct context, namely situations where a buyer signed the contract on day one, learned that a representation is false from the seller on day three, closed the contract on day five, and sued for damages for breach of warranty on day 10. The public policy reasons for denying relief to the buyer in those circumstances are arguably much different than are implicated by a decision whether to permit a buyer simply to walk away before closing in reliance on a specific contractual representation that it had reason to suspect was untrue as of the time of signing. In any event, my more traditional contract analysis applies settled principles of New York contract law and eliminates any need to delve into these novel issues of another state's law. Likewise, there is no present need to address IBP's other arguments, which are grounded in equitable doctrines such as estoppel, acquiescence, and waiver and ratification. Nor do I address IBP's argument that Tyson breached the Agreement's implied covenant of good faith and fair dealing by terminating for pretextual reasons (i.e., DFG and the Comment Letter) that had no relationship to Tyson's actual motives (i.e., Tyson's alleged desire to renegotiate the deal to a much lower price or terminate because of its own poor performance).

stockholders were offered a chance to share in the upside of what was touted by Tyson as a unique, synergistic combination. This court has not found, and Tyson has not advanced, any compelling reason why sellers in mergers and acquisitions transactions should have less of a right to demand specific performance than buyers, and none has independently come to my mind.

In addition, the determination of a cash damages award will be very difficult in this case. And the amount of any award could be staggeringly large. No doubt the parties would haggle over huge valuation questions, which (Tyson no doubt would argue) must take into account the possibility of a further auction for IBP or other business developments. A damages award can, of course, be shaped; it simply will lack any pretense to precision. An award of specific performance will, I anticipate, entirely eliminate the need for a speculative determination of damages.

Finally, there is no doubt that a remedy of specific performance is practicable. Tyson itself admits that the combination still makes strategic sense. At trial, John Tyson was asked by his own counsel to testify about whether it was fair that Tyson should enter any later auction for IBP hampered by its payment of the Rawhide Termination Fee. This testimony indicates that Tyson Foods is still interested in purchasing IBP, but wants to get its original purchase price back and then buy IBP off the day-old goods table. I consider John Tyson's testimony an admission of the feasibility of specific performance.

Probably the concern that weighs heaviest on my mind is whether specific performance is the right remedy in view of the harsh words that have been said in the course of this litigation. Can these management teams work together? The answer is that I do not know. Peterson and Bond say they can. I am not convinced, although Tyson's top executives continue to respect the managerial acumen of Peterson and Bond, if not that of their financial subordinates.

What persuades me that specific performance is a workable remedy is that Tyson will have the power to decide all the key management questions itself. It can therefore hand-pick its own management team. While this may be unpleasant for the top level IBP managers who might be replaced, it was a possible risk of the Merger from the get-go and a reality of today's M&A market.

The impact on other constituencies of this ruling also seems tolerable. Tyson's own investment banker thinks the transaction makes sense for Tyson, and is still fairly priced at $30 per share. One would think the Tyson constituencies would be better served on the whole by a specific performance remedy, rather than a large damages award that did nothing but cost Tyson a large amount of money.

In view of these factors, I am persuaded that an award of specific performance is appropriate, regardless of what level of showing was required by IBP. That is, there is clear and convincing evidence to support this award. Such an award is decisively preferable to a vague and imprecise damages remedy that cannot adequately remedy the injury to IBP's stockholders. . . .

QUESTIONS

1. Do these facts reflect evidence of "buyer's remorse"? Did the court reach the right result based on these facts? What do you think?

2. What is the standard that the Delaware Chancery Court applied to determine whether these facts give rise to an MAE? Do you think the Court properly framed the relevant standard as a matter of public policy?

3. Who has the burden to establish that an MAE has occurred?

4. In his opinion, then-chancellor Strine focused on the cyclical nature of the meat industry. How did this observation impact his analysis of whether an MAE had occurred on the facts of the *IPB* case?

NOTES

1. Litigation vs. Renegotiation. The use of MAC provisions creates the potential for renegotiating the terms of a deal when one of the parties decides to invoke a MAC provision. Even though the other side may disagree whether the MAC provision has been triggered under the circumstances, renegotiation may often be preferable to the alternative — *litigation*. Moreover, litigation over MACs and MAEs is inherently a fact-intensive proceeding that will turn on both the specific language of the MAC or MAE at issue, as well as the facts of the particular transaction. This is reflected in Vice-Chancellor Strine's detailed (and quite lengthy) opinion in the principal case, *IBP*.

2. What Triggers "Walk-Away Rights"? Be careful not to confuse a purchase price adjustment provision of the type described earlier in this chapter at pp. 342-350 with a "material adverse change" clause of the type at issue in the principal case. Only the MAC gives rise to a walk-away right, which will allow Bidder to walk away from the deal and refuse to close *if* Target's financial results have materially deteriorated in the time period between signing and closing on the acquisition agreement. *Query:* Given this function of a MAC, how broadly do you think courts should construe MACs and MAEs?

3. The Lessons of IBP. What lessons can be learned from the result (and the court's reasoning) in *IBP*? The *IBP* decision led one commentator to offer the following practical guidance:

> Unlike most prior case law interpreting MAC clauses that provides little practical precedential assistance, the *[IBP]* court seems to be sending a clear message. Merger agreements, by their nature, are heavily negotiated documents, and public policy is in favor of making sure the parties honor the spirit of such agreements.
>
> Therefore, any party wishing to terminate a deal on the basis of the broad language of a MAC clause must be able to demonstrate that the "adverse change" is of such a quality and magnitude to overcome a strong presumption in favor of closing the transaction. That will be particularly difficult if the court suspects that the true reason for the termination is buyer's remorse.
>
> The following provides some helpful advice to consider when drafting MAC clauses in purchase or merger agreements. . . .
>
> [Bidder] should specifically address risks of which [Bidder] is aware. Ratios, performance benchmarks and other financial tests (objective criteria) are common methods used to determine thresholds for such specifically identified risks.

Care should be taken, however, to not be "overly" specific (as courts could find that such a high level of specificity rules out other risks not otherwise specified).

[Bidder] should also include potential adverse events not within the seller's control. Courts often find the following events to fall outside the scope of a MAC (unless specifically included):

- events from the announcement or consummation of the transaction;
- business turndowns (generally or industry wide);
- enactment of legislation;
- cancellation of a significant contract; and
- future prospects of the seller.

Therefore, if the buyer wishes such events to trigger the MAC clause, they should be specifically included. After the buyer includes those risks that can be reasonably identified, the most comprehensive, general language should be included to cover unknown risks (both within and outside the seller's control).

Remember the lesson from the *[IBP]* case—courts are not likely to allow a buyer to back out of a transaction due to buyer's remorse. If a buyer is concerned about something specific, it should include that concern in the agreement. The broad language of a general MAC clause should only be triggered by a "durationally significant" event.

The "seller" [Target] should attempt to limit all of the specific carveouts proposed by the buyer [Bidder]—especially those over which it has no control (that is, general or industry economic conditions and adverse effects resulting from the performance of the purchase agreement). The seller should seek to eliminate the remaining specific carve-outs, such as financial benchmarks (over which it *does* have control), or at least negotiate the benchmarks so that the risks of such benchmarks triggering a MAC are low.

The seller will likely encounter heavy resistance to eliminate (or limit) these financial benchmarks. The seller might also propose specific carve-outs that *do not* trigger a MAC. Finally, the seller should attempt to limit the scope of the MAC clause by a qualification requiring "knowledge" of material adverse events.

Gregory Bishop, *Changed Circumstances or Buyer's Remorse?* Business Law Today 49-52 (Mar./Apr. 2002).

4. Subsequent "MAC" Clause Litigation.   Since then-Vice Chancellor Strine handed down his opinion in *IBP*, there have been several subsequent cases further reinforcing the principles enunciated in *IBP*. See, e.g., *Genesco, Inc. v. Finish Line, Inc.*, No. 07-2137-II (Tenn. Ch. Dec. 27, 2007); *United Rentals, Inc. v. Ram Holdings, Inc.*, 937 A.2d 810 (Del. Ch. 2007); and *Hexion Specialty Chemicals, Inc. v. Huntsman Corp.*, 965 A.2d 715 (Del. Ch. 2008). Vice Chancellor Stephen Lamb's decision in *Hexion* is widely regarded as an important development in the law relating to MAC/MAE clauses, which are an important part of acquisition agreements in today's M&A market—both in the context of public company M&A deals as well as in acquisitions of privately held companies. Briefly summarized:

Hexion, a producer of adhesives used in plywood, agreed to purchase Huntsman, the world's largest producer of epoxy additives, in July 2007. Apollo filed suit in June 2008, claiming both that it had no obligation to close the deal as the post-merger entity would be insolvent, and because Huntsman had suffered a MAE. The MAE language in the merger agreement provided that Apollo's obligation to close was conditioned on the absence of "any event, change or development that has had or is reasonably expected to have, individually or in the aggregate" a MAE. "MAE" was in turn defined as "any occurrence . . . that is materially adverse to the financial condition . . . of the Company . . . ," *excluding* changes in "general economic or financial market conditions" or occurrences "affect[ing] the chemical industry generally." . . .

In finding that Huntsman has not suffered a MAE, the Court relied heavily on *In re IBP*, a leading Delaware case (applying New York law) on the interpretation of MAE clauses. Noting that, "absent clear language to the contrary" the party seeking to invoke an MAE clause bears the burden of proving that an MAE has occurred, the Court cited *In re IBP* for the proposition that "a buyer faces a heavy burden when it attempts to invoke a material adverse effect clause in order to avoid its obligation to close," and noted that "Delaware courts have never found a material adverse effect to have occurred in the context of a merger agreement." Elaborating on the oft-cited reasoning from *In re IBP* that "[a] short-term hiccup in earnings should not suffice" to succeed on a MAE claim, the Court explained that "a significant decline in earnings by the target corporation during the period after signing but prior . . . to closing" could constitute a MAE if those poor results can be "expected to persist significantly into the future." . . .

Having found that no MAE had occurred as to Huntsman as a whole, the Court rejected Apollo's claim that (i) a five percent increase in Huntsman's post-closing debt was not material to Apollo's valuation of the transaction and (ii) problems with two Huntsman divisions amounted to a MAE, given that "Huntsman as a whole is not materially impaired by their results." . . .

Hexion is consistent with prior rulings in showing that purchasers face a heavy burden in attempting to use MAE clauses to avoid merger agreements. The case also highlights the importance of carve-outs often used in MAE clauses—as the parties here had excepted general economic or financial market changes, which language figured prominently in the Court's ruling. *Hexion* suggests that parties negotiating MAE clauses seriously consider terms that might (i) shift the burden of proof regarding use of the clause and (ii) provide greater specificity in the types of changes that may constitute a MAE, *including* changes in general market or macroeconomic conditions.

White & Case, LLP, *Delaware Court Interprets Material Adverse Effect Clause to Bar Hexion and Apollo from Abandoning Huntsman Deal*, Oct. 2008, *available at:* https://www.lexology.com/library/detail.aspx?g=5270bc7b-07c9-417d-bcdb-b90edeb21642.

5. "MAC" Clause Surveys. Over the past decade or so, a trend has emerged: several firms and organizations (most notably the ABA Business Law Section's Committee on Mergers and Acquisitions) publish annual surveys of the use and terms of MACs and MAEs. As a general proposition, the purpose of such surveys is to observe and track year to year

. . . . the market's responses to shifts in the myriad economic, geopolitical, and societal forces that shape the manner and environment in which [M&A] transactions occur. With each survey we conduct, we capture a more robust picture of trends in M&A transactions.

Survey results provide . . . vivid insight into the prevailing conditions and concerns surrounding transactions. The tragic events of September 11, 2001 cast an unmistakable shadow over our inaugural survey covering deals during 2001-2002, which notably reflected the growing concern of the potential impact of terrorism on dealmaking. Ensuing years saw the world begin to adjust to a post-9/11 reality, and an increasingly stabilized economy as a consequence. A renewed sense of security helped spur growth during this period, which fostered conditions favorable to targets. The attendant trend toward an increase in MAC exceptions halted, however, once the effects of the credit crisis and the Great Recession began to take hold in 2008 and 2009. Fewer companies found themselves in a position to buy during this time, so those that did wielded greater power in transactional negotiations. We have seen an increase in MAC exceptions in the years since the [Great Recession], indicating that the balance between purchasers [i.e., Bidders] and [Targets] has equalized to some extent. Similar to the last survey we published in 2017, [the] results [from this 2019 survey] indicate an overall acceptance of the concept that MAC clauses should exclude from their reach general business risk. . . .

Material adverse change or material adverse effect clauses, often referred to as MAC or MAE clauses, serve dual purposes. First, a MAC definition is used in qualifications to various representations, warranties, and covenants, establishing a threshold for determining the scope of disclosure or compliance relating to risks associated with the changes in the target's business. For example, a representation may provide that a target has complied with all cybersecurity laws and directives "except as would not have a Material Adverse Effect." Such a MAC qualification would allow, for example, an immaterial breach of a cybersecurity law or directive to have a significantly reduced effect on the consummation of a deal.

As a second function, the MAC clause is used to delineate the circumstances under which a bidder would be permitted to exit a transaction without liability. This right to walk away is frequently referred to as a "MAC out" and generally appears in the conditions precedent to the bidder's obligation to close the deal. A typical MAC-out provision states as a condition that "there shall not have occurred a Material Adverse Change in the Company." The delineated events constituting a MAC are then qualified by a listing of other events, often referred to as "MAC exceptions." MAC exceptions preclude bidders from walking away from a deal or seeking a renegotiation of material terms on the basis that a MAC has taken place. The delineated events constituting a MAC, together with MAC exceptions, allocate carefully calibrated and negotiated deal certainty risk and risk of loss between the bidder and the target that may result from adverse circumstances occurring in the target's business in the sensitive period between deal execution and completion.

MAC clauses are often heavily negotiated between the parties. A target usually attempts to narrow the MAC definitional elements and expand the exceptions in order to shift risk to the bidder. By shifting risk to the bidder, the target bolsters the certainty of the deal's closing and its ability to preserve deal pricing. Bidders, however, strive to shift the risk to the target by expanding MAC elements and reducing the number and scope of the exceptions allowed, thereby reserving for the [Bidder] a greater ability to walk away from the deal or to renegotiate deal terms. While courts generally are reluctant to enforce MAC clauses, in 2018, the Delaware Chancery Court held that a target company's sustained drop in business performance between signing and closing constituted a MAC, and that its breach of representations regarding regulatory compliance would be expected to result in a MAC, allowing the buyer in that case to terminate the merger agreement. [*See Akorn, Inc. v. Fresenius Kabi AG*, No. 2018-0300-JTL, 2018 Del. Ch. LEXIS 325 (Ch. Oct. 1, 2018).] In addition, in recent years, some bidders have successfully invoked MAC provisions in order to re-price a deal.

Nixon Peabody, LLP, *2019 Nixon Peabody MAC Survey, available at:* https://www.nixonpeabody.com/en/ideas/articles/2019/11/19/2019-mac-survey.

PROBLEMS—USE OF MATERIALITY QUALIFIERS

1. For purposes of the following problem, assume that the parties' acquisition agreement contains a materiality qualifier framed as a MAE which is framed in terms substantially the same as the MAE clause at issue in the *IBP* case:

> a MAE is defined as "any event, occurrence or development of a state of circumstances or facts which has had or reasonably could be expected to have a Material Adverse Effect" . . . "on the condition (financial or otherwise), business, assets, liabilities or results of operations of [IBP] and [its] Subsidiaries taken as whole." . . .

As a drafting exercise, consider the following situations and analyze whether the language of this MAE clause would offer your client, Bidder, the right to walk away from the deal. Or, is there a better way to draft/frame the MAC/MAE clause in order to better protect your client's interests?

a. Bidder has agreed to purchase a broadcast station in Texas. In the period between signing and closing on the acquisition agreement, the broadcast station loses half of its subscribers (i.e., viewers and/or listeners), although all of its assets remain in place.

b. Target has two key employees that are critical to Bidder's decision to buy Target's business. Before closing, these two employees either quit, or alternatively, have advised Target's current management that they plan to quit.

2. Bidder Co., a successful, publicly traded pharmaceutical corporation incorporated in Delaware, was looking to expand its business. Target Co., a publicly traded Delaware corporation, was a leading manufacturer of generic drugs. To sell generic drugs, Target must prove to the U.S. Food and Drug Administration ("FDA") that the generic drug is chemically identical to the patented drug and that the generic drug is made using "good manufacturing practices" (as defined by the FDA). After completing its due diligence and finding no major "red flags" regarding Target and its business, Bidder and Target entered into an agreement and plan of merger dated April 24, 2017 (the "Merger Agreement").

As part of the terms of the Merger Agreement, Target made extensive representations about its compliance with applicable regulatory requirements imposed by the FDA (the "Regulatory Compliance Representations"). The parties also agreed to a contractually defined "Outside Date" for closing to occur on April 24, 2018. If the merger closed, then each share of Target common stock would be converted into the right to receive $34 per share in cash. Closing, however, was not a foregone conclusion since the Merger Agreement set forth several conditions to closing.

First, Bidder's obligation to close was conditioned on Target's representations having been true and correct both at signing and at closing, except where "the failure to be true and correct would not individually or in the aggregate reasonably be expected to have a Material Adverse Effect" (the "Bring Down Condition").* If this condition was not met and could not be cured by the Outside Date, then Bidder could terminate the Merger Agreement.

Second, Bidder's obligation to close was conditioned on Target having complied in all material respects with its obligations under the Merger Agreement, including (among other things) that Target commit to use its "commercially reasonable efforts to carry on its business in all material respects in the ordinary course of business" between signing and closing. Once again, if this condition was not met and could not be cured by the Outside Date, then Bidder could terminate the Merger Agreement (the "Covenant Compliance Condition").

Third, Bidder's obligation to close was conditioned on the absence of "any effect, change, event or occurrence that, individually or in the aggregate, has had or would reasonably be expected to have a Material Adverse Effect" (the

---

* The parties' Merger Agreement defines the concept of a "Material Adverse Effect" as follows, although the formatting of this defined term has been modified to enhance the readability of its terms:

"Material Adverse Effect" means any effect, change, event or occurrence that, individually or in the aggregate
(i) would prevent or materially delay, interfere with, impair or hinder the consummation of the [Merger] or the compliance by [Target] with its obligations under this Agreement or
(ii) has a material adverse effect on the business, results of operations or financial condition of [Target] and its Subsidiaries, taken as a whole;
provided, however, that none of the following, and no effect, change, event or occurrence arising out of, or resulting from, the following, shall constitute or be taken into account in determining whether a Material Adverse Effect has occurred, is continuing or would reasonably be expected to occur: any effect, change, event or occurrence
(A) generally affecting (1) the industry in which [Target] and its Subsidiaries operate or (2) the economy, credit or financial or capital markets, in the United States or elsewhere in the world, including changes in interest or exchange rates, monetary policy or inflation, or
(B) to the extent arising out of, resulting from or attributable to . . .
(3) acts of war (whether or not declared), military activity, sabotage, civil disobedience or terrorism, or any escalation or worsening of any such acts of war (whether or not declared), military activity, sabotage, civil disobedience or terrorism,
(4) pandemics, earthquakes, floods, hurricanes, tornados or other natural disasters, weather-related events, force majeure events or other comparable events, . . .
(7) any decline in the market price, or change in trading volume, of the shares of [Target] or
(8) any failure to meet any internal or public projections, forecasts, guidance, estimates, milestones, budgets or internal or published financial or operating predictions of revenue, earnings, cash flow or cash position
(it being understood that the exceptions in clauses . . . [(7) and (8)] shall not prevent or otherwise affect a determination that the underlying cause of any such change, decline or failure referred to therein (if not otherwise falling within any of the exceptions provided by clause (A) and clauses (B)(1) through (8) hereof) is a Material Adverse Effect);
provided further, however, that any effect, change, event or occurrence referred to in clause (A) . . . may be taken into account in determining whether there has been, or would reasonably be expected to be, a Material Adverse Effect to the extent such effect, change, event or occurrence has a disproportionate adverse effect on [Target] and its Subsidiaries, taken as a whole, as compared to other participants in the industry in which [Target] and its Subsidiaries operate (in which case the incremental disproportionate impact or impacts may be taken into account in determining whether there has been, or would reasonably be expected to be, a Material Adverse Effect).

"General MAE Condition). However, the failure to satisfy this condition did not give Bidder a right to terminate but it did give Bidder the right to refuse to close.

After signing the Merger Agreement, Target's business performance fell dramatically. On July 31, 2017, Target publicly announced its financial results for the second quarter of 2017, delivering results that fell substantially below Target's prior-year performance on a year-over-year basis. Further, on the same date that the parties signed the Merger Agreement, Target had reaffirmed (at Bidder's specific request) its full-year guidance to the analyst community for 2017. Needless to say, Target's dismal second quarter of 2017 shocked Bidder.

More specifically, Target announced year-over-year declines in quarterly revenues, operating income and earnings per share of 29%, 84% and 96%, respectively. Bidder consulted with Target about the reasons for the sudden decline, which Target attributed to unexpected entrance of new competitors and the loss of a key customer contract. Target's CEO reassured Bidder that the downturn in second quarter results was temporary, but Target's performance continued to slide through the summer of 2017. Target then revised its forecast downward for the third quarter but fell short of that goal as well. On November 1, 2017, Target announced year-over-year declines in revenues, operating income and earnings per share for the third quarter of 2017 of 29%, 89% and 105%, respectively. Target ascribed the disappointing results for the third quarter primarily to unanticipated supply interruptions and increased competition, among other factors.

In late 2017 and early 2018, Bidder received anonymous letters from whistleblowers alleging flaws in Target's product development and quality control processes that resulted in failures to comply with the FDA's regulatory requirements for data integrity and quality control of Target's manufacturing processes. The letters called into question whether Target's representations in the Merger agreement regarding regulatory compliance were accurate and whether Target had been operating in the ordinary course of business.

Bidder provided the letters to Target. Although Bidder understood that Target would have to investigate the allegations, Bidder informed Target that Bidder also needed to conduct its own investigation into the allegations. Under the Merger Agreement, Bidder had bargained for a right of reasonable access to Target's officers, employees, and information so that Bidder could evaluate Target's contractual compliance and determine whether the conditions to closing were met. Invoking this right, Bidder conducted its own investigation using experienced outside counsel and technical advisors to examine the issues raised by the whistleblower letters.

Bidder's investigation uncovered serious and pervasive flaws in Target's quality control function, including falsification of laboratory data submitted to the FDA regarding a Target product that was on the market. These flaws cast doubt on the accuracy of Target's representations about its regulatory compliance and Bidder grew concerned that the deviation between Target's actual condition and its as-represented condition would reasonably be expected to result in a Material Adverse Effect. During the course of the investigation, tensions escalated between the parties. Matters came to a head following a meeting in March 2018 that Target had with the FDA who was inquiring into Target's data integrity issues. Although Bidder's request to attend this meeting was denied,

Target provided Bidder with a summary of its meeting with the FDA. Bidder became concerned that Target was not fully transparent with the FDA and instead had downplayed its quality control problems and oversold its remedial efforts as part of Target's presentation to the FDA. From Bidder's standpoint, Target was not conducting its operations in the ordinary course of business.

On February 29, 2018, Target announced its results for the final quarter of 2017 and the annual results for 2017. For the fourth quarter of 2017, Target reported year-over-year declines in quarterly revenues, operating income and earnings per share of 34%, 292% and 300%, respectively. These results stood in stark contrast to the performance of Target's business prior to signing the merger agreement with Bidder in April 2017. Over the five-year span that ended in 2016, Target's business grew consistently when measured by revenues, earnings per share and EBITDA. Notably, Target's EBITDA grew each year from 2102 to 2016, but in 2017, EBITDA fell by 55%. Ultimately, over the course of the year following the signing of the merger agreement, Target's EBITDA declined by 86%.

As Target's business performance continued to deteriorate, Bidder became increasingly concerned. In mid-April 2018, Bidder sent Target a letter explaining why the conditions the conditions to Bidder's obligation to close could not be met and identifying contractual bases for terminating the Merger Agreement. Bidder nevertheless offered to extend the Outside Date if Target believed that further investigation would enable Target to resolve its difficulties. Target declined.

On April 22, 2018, Bidder gave notice that it was terminating the Merger Agreement. Bidder asserted that Target's representations regarding regulatory compliance were so incorrect that the deviation would reasonably be expected to result in a Material Adverse Effect. Bidder also cited Target's failure to comply in all material respects with its contractual obligations under the Merger Agreement, including Target's obligation to use commercially reasonable efforts to operate in the ordinary course of business in all material respects. Bidder also cited the section in the Merger Agreement that conditioned Bidder's obligation to close on Target not having suffered a Material Adverse Effect.

Target responded by filing a lawsuit seeking a judicial declaration that Bidder's attempt to terminate the Merger Agreement was invalid and a decree of specific performance compelling Bidder to close on the Merger Agreement. Bidder answered and filed counterclaims, contending it validly terminated the Merger Agreement and was not required to close.

Query: Based on the reasoning of the *IPB* opinion, should Bidder be required to close on the Merger Agreement?

Planning Problem:
Preparing the Stock Purchase Agreement
for Galaxy's Acquisition of Trekker

The first draft of the acquisition agreement for Galaxy's (Bidder's) purchase of Trekker's (Target's) business is set forth in Appendix C. As you read through this draft agreement, please consider the following.

QUESTIONS

1. What are the corporate formalities to be followed if the parties had decided to structure this acquisitions as (i) a direct merger; (ii) a triangular merger; or (iii) a sale of assets? To what extent do these structural considerations influence the advice you would give the parties as to the choice of deal structure for Galaxy's proposed acquisition of Trekker?

2. During the course of conducting its due diligence investigation and before signing the definitive agreement, Galaxy Corp. learns that Trekker's manufacturing plant located in a border town south of San Diego may have problems with its labor force under federal immigration law—a common issue in the context of these types of border plants that are widely used in the garment industry.[11] Alternatively, Galaxy's due diligence review suggests that the plant where Trekker manufactures its skateboards may be subject to liability under relevant environmental laws. How should the parties deal with these issues?

3. Assume that the parties have signed the form of stock purchase agreement included in Appendix C, which includes a representation by the company and certain of the selling shareholders to the effect that there are no undisclosed liabilities. *See* Article 3 of Trekker's Agreement with Galaxy. During the course of its due diligence, Galaxy learns of potential exposure to environmental liability as a result of operations at Trekker's manufacturing plant.

    a. Can Galaxy refuse to complete the transaction? In other words, can Galaxy "walk away" from the deal?
    b. Assume that Galaxy did not discover the potential environmental liability exposure until after closing on the acquisition. What advice can you give Galaxy as to its rights and remedies under the terms of the parties' agreement?

4. What suggestions can you make to Galaxy on structuring the acquisition and/or the purchase price to address the risk of discovering undisclosed liability *after* the closing?

5. In considering the scope of the representations, as well as the conditions to closing included in Galaxy's original draft of the stock purchase agreement delivered to Trekker's lawyer for review and comment (*see* Appendix C), what are the implications of the *IBP* decision for the lawyers engaged to prepare the agreement for Galaxy's proposed acquisition of Trekker?

NOTE

Relationship Between Representations and Due Diligence Process. From Bidder's perspective, the appropriate use of a materiality qualifier requires that

---

11. This type of issue illustrates the fundamental proposition that M&A law is one of the last places in the modern practice of law where counsel truly must be a Renaissance lawyer; or, to frame the proposition in slightly more perjorative terms, the modern M&A lawyer truly must be "a Jack of all trades, Master of none!"

the lawyer negotiating the terms of representations and warranties for Bidder have a thorough understanding of the client's business objectives in proposing to acquire Target's business and a firm grasp of what is really important to Bidder about Target's business. Otherwise, Bidder's counsel runs the risk of agreeing to the use of a materiality qualifier as to a particular representation that will operate to rob Bidder of the full business benefits that Bidder hoped to obtain by purchasing Target. In this regard, Bidder often finds it useful to do its diligence review *before* drafting the terms of the acquisition agreement. After its due diligence investigation is completed, Bidder will have a much better understanding of Target's business and where the difficulties and potential business problems lie; that is, armed with this information, Bidder is in a much better position to negotiate meaningful terms to the representations and warranties to be provided by Target. The difficulty with this strategy is that, in many cases, Target is simply unwilling to share the level of detail sought by most Bidders in the typical thorough diligence review *unless* Target is confident that a deal has been reached with this Bidder. Or, alternatively, the full benefit of the diligence investigation cannot be obtained because the diligence review is proceeding simultaneous with the parties' negotiations over the terms of the acquisition agreement. The due diligence process is discussed in more detail in the next section.

In any case, the *IBP* decision makes clear that the lawyers who wants to negotiate most effectively for a set of representations that will provide meaningful protection to their business client must go beyond the boilerplate representations that are customarily part of any acquisition agreement. To do this, however, the lawyers must have a firm grasp of the business to be acquired and the importance of the proposed transaction for their business client. This is an important task that is time consuming and often left to junior lawyers as part of the diligence review, particularly in the case of large transactions such as the deal involved in the *IBP* decision. To the extent that diligence is delegated to junior members of the acquisition team, the lawyer responsible for organizing the acquisition process must take care to ensure that the relevant information will be filtered out and directed to those members of the acquisition team who most need to know this information as part of the negotiation process. Although many lawyers think of due diligence as drudge work—the equivalent of doing windows and ovens, in housekeeping terms—the importance of adequate and thorough due diligence cannot be overstated. The impact of the diligence review will be felt at many stages in the deal process, not the least of which is in connection with negotiating the terms of the representations and warranties to be included in the parties' acquisition agreement.

E. Indemnification Provisions and Their Relationship to Representations and Warranties

As mentioned earlier in this chapter, one of the other important functions of the *representations* and *warranties* section of the acquisition agreement is that these provisions generally will serve as the basis for the *conditions* that must be satisfied at the time of *closing* on the agreement. This same kind of dynamic interaction surfaces again in considering the relationship between the parties' *representations* and the post-closing rights of *indemnification* typically included in any agreement for the acquisition of a privately held company.

The *indemnification* provisions generally give Bidder the express contractual right to recover from the sellers of Target's business. The terms of a typical indemnification provision will grant Bidder an express right of recovery for *all damages, directly or indirectly, resulting from or caused by Target's breach of one (or more) of the representations it made in the acquisition agreement that Bidder did not discover until after closing on the agreement and taking over Target's business.* By insisting on indemnification provisions as part of the acquisition agreement, Bidder is trying to preserve a contractual right to recover from the seller(s) of Target Co. in order to be sure that Bidder gets the benefit of the bargain that it made when it agreed to buy Target's business. Including this right of indemnification in the parties' contract allows Bidder to tailor the scope of the remedy to address the situation presented by the particular facts of its business transaction with Target. Apart from providing an explicit, contractual, financial remedy to the Bidder, indemnification rights also serve the useful purpose of providing Target with a strong motivational incentive to make full disclosure of all relevant information regarding Target's business and financial affairs in order to avoid the fairly draconian financial remedy granted by the terms of the customary indemnification provision.

Usually, Target will be reluctant to agree to rights of indemnification and can be expected to try to narrow the scope of whatever indemnification rights Bidder demands under the terms of the original draft of the parties' contract. Consequently, the indemnification provisions are usually among the more heavily negotiated sections of the parties' agreement for the acquisition of a privately held Target.

With respect to indemnification rights, Target Co. (and its selling shareholders) often have a fairly persuasive argument to avoid including any such provision in the acquisition agreement. Target will contend that it has already disclosed to Bidder's representatives *all* the risk-bearing attributes relevant to its business and financial affairs during the course of Bidder's extensive due diligence process and the resulting negotiations between the parties over the terms of the representations and warranties that ultimately were made part of their acquisition agreement. Since Target has already advised Bidder of all the risks associated with Target's business, Target is likely to claim that it is unfair for Bidder to demand indemnification rights as well, claiming that such rights are tantamount to an insurance policy. Bidder, on the other hand, has a strong incentive to insist on the post-closing financial remedy of indemnification in order to motivate Target to disclose all material facts regarding its business as part of the terms of its representations and warranties, including any risks associated with the business on a going-forward basis that Target is currently aware of. Therefore, Bidder is likely to reject any suggestion that indemnification rights are unfair by asserting that Bidder is *not* buying the business *as is*; rather, Bidder has agreed to buy the business that Target has described under the terms of its representations and warranties. If it should turn out that any of these representations are inaccurate, Bidder has been deprived of the benefit of the bargain that it made with Target. Not surprisingly, Bidder then wants to be able to pursue a financial remedy against Target.

Target is likely to respond that the business was sold to Bidder based on full disclosure of those risks to the business, and therefore, they have already been factored into the agreed-upon purchase price. Based on that reasoning, no financial remedy should be made available to Bidder on a post-closing basis. For its part, Bidder is likely to argue that it must have a financial remedy in order for Target's representations to have any meaning. In other words, Bidder is likely to insist that in order for Target's representation to have any meaning, Bidder must have a financial remedy against Target in case there is a discrepancy between the terms of Target's representations and what turns out to be the true state of affairs—which Bidder will learn about only *after* closing on the acquisition agreement. Most likely, Target will lose the argument on this point and the agreement will grant rights of indemnification to Bidder. At this point, Target's objective in the negotiations is to limit the scope of indemnification as much as possible.

Use of Baskets. Indemnification provisions typically incorporate a concept known among practicing M&A lawyers as a "basket." The idea of a *basket* is that a certain dollar amount of claims must accumulate (in the basket) before Bidder triggers rights to be indemnified by Target (or, more likely, the sellers of Target). When agreeing to limit its rights of indemnification by use of a basket, Bidder must take into account the use of any materiality qualifiers, which already serve to limit the scope of Target's potential liability for breach of that representation. In these situations, Bidder must be careful that the basket, when coupled with the materiality qualifier, does not undermine the scope of protection that the parties agreed to as a business matter. If Bidder's counsel is not careful, Bidder may inadvertently allow Target to get a break in two different ways. First, Bidder's counsel must be aware that there is already a materiality standard that must be satisfied in order to establish Target's breach of that particular representation. Second, if a basket is to be incorporated into the indemnification provisions, the amount that must accumulate in the basket before triggering Bidder's right to recover from Target needs to take into account the extent to which small, trivial matters have already been addressed (and excluded) as a threshold matter through the operation of the materiality qualifier. In the experience of most M&A lawyers, the negotiations over the terms of indemnification will get intertwined with the negotiations over the terms of the representations whenever the parties introduce the use of a materiality qualifier to limit the scope of Target's representations and thus limit the scope of protection offered to Bidder by the terms of that particular representation.

QUESTIONS

1. Will any of the representations and warranties contained in the AT&T–DirecTV merger agreement (*see* Appendix B) survive closing? Will these provisions provide the basis for any rights of indemnification on a post-closing basis?

2. Will any of the representations and warranties contained in the stock purchase agreement for Galaxy's acquisition of Trekker (*see* Appendix C) survive closing? After closing, who will be obligated if there is a breach of representation? If there is a breach of one of these provisions, what remedies are available?

NOTES

1. Waiver of Breach of Representation. As to those provisions that Bidder knows to be inaccurate at the time of closing but Bidder decided to close on the acquisition anyway, should Bidder be able to recover under the indemnification provisions of the agreement? Or, should we treat Bidder's decision to close on the acquisition as a *waiver* of its right to recover for any breach of representation and warranty? This is a vexing question because in this situation, Bidder presumably had a *walk-away right* that was triggered because of the bring-down condition. This condition to closing typically requires Target to attest to the accuracy of its representations as of the date of closing. Target is likely to disclose the inaccuracy before closing and should be prepared that such disclosure will trigger Bidder's right to walk away and refuse to close on the deal. In this case, Target is likely to feel that Bidder has been adequately protected by its right to walk away, and therefore no post-closing remedy should be available to the Bidder.

2. Post-Closing Risk vs. Pre-Closing Risk. Indemnification addresses post-closing risk allocation, while covenants and conditions address pre-closing risk allocation, which, among other things, includes the risk that the deal will not get completed. From Target's perspective, this is a serious issue because if the deal does not close, then Target (and its selling shareholders) are denied the benefit of the bargain made under the terms of their agreement with Bidder. This is a serious risk because the very process of putting the company up for sale and entering into an agreement with Bidder may leave the company vulnerable. For example, this entire process may have destabilized relationships with key customers, may reduce employee morale (because of the uncertainty about the future), and may have adverse consequences on relationships with vendors and other creditors of the company. The next section of this chapter, as part of the discussion of the due diligence process, describes steps that Target can take to minimize the risk that the deal will not close.

3. Liquidated Damages or Termination Fees. The vast majority of deals involving the acquisition of privately held companies do *not* include break-up fees, termination fees, or liquidated damages provisions. This convention seems to rest on the unspoken assumption of the parties that the deal will proceed to close without any major, unforeseen risks that need to be addressed through break-up fees, unlike the situation presented in a public company deal. It would be unusual to include a break-up fee in a private company M&A acquisition because of the apparent assumption made by the parties that Target (and its owners) is a motivated seller and thus wants to proceed with the transaction.

If, for some reason, Target (and/or its selling shareholders) decided at closing that it did not want to sell Target's business to Bidder, then it would seem most likely that Bidder would have a strong claim for breach of contract against Target and/or its owners. Accordingly, it is generally assumed that there is no need to include any type of break-up fee in the acquisition agreement.[12]

4. Use of Representations and Warranties Insurance.   In the last few years, "Representations and Warranties Insurance," sometimes also referred to as "Transactional Insurance," has become a popular tool in effecting M&A transactions, both here in the United States, as well as on a global basis. What is *reps and warranties* insurance? "Transactional insurance generally shifts responsibility for most seller representations and warranties to one or more third-party insurance underwriters, resulting in a seller generally receiving the benefit of a 'clean exit' in a sale. While fundamentally the same product worldwide, [there are some] differences in Transactional Insurance among the U.S., European and Asian markets." Gabriel Gershowitz, et al., Weil Gotshal and Manges LLP, *Insuring Deals Around the World: Variations of Representations and Warranties Insurance Across the United States, Europe and Asia,* 2016 GLOBAL PRIVATE EQUITY UPDATE, *available at:* https://www.weil.com/~/media/mailings/2016/q3/1600744_global_pe_update_2q2016_v7.pdf?cid=8590507280. The usefulness of this new insurance product is more fully explained in the following blogpost:

> **Paul A. Ferrillo and Joseph T. Verdesca**
> **M&A Representations and Warranties Insurance:**
> **Tips for Buyers and Sellers**
> *available at : https://corpgov.law.harvard.edu/2013/05/01/*
> *ma-representations-and-warranties-insurance-tips-for-*
> *buyers-and-sellers (May 1, 2013).*

No less than two years ago, had one tried to initiate a conversation with a Private Equity Sponsor or an M&A lawyer regarding M&A "reps and warranties" insurance (i.e., insurance designed to expressly provide insurance coverage for the breach of a representation or a warranty contained in a Purchase and Sale Agreement, in addition to or as a replacement for a contractual indemnity), one might have gotten a shrug of the shoulders or a polite response to the effect of "let's try to negotiate around the problem instead." Perhaps because it was misunderstood or perhaps because it had not yet hit its stride in terms of breadth of coverage, reps and warranties insurance was hardly ever used to close deals. Like Harry Potter, it was the poor stepchild often left in the closet.

Today that is no longer the case. One global insurance broker . . . notes that over $4 billion in reps and warranties insurance worldwide was bound [in 2012], of which $1.4 billion thereof was bound in the US and $2.1 billion thereof was

---

12. By contrast, in the context of public company deals, break-up fees are widely used. The reason for this practice is explored in more detail in Chapter 7, where we examine the fiduciary duty constraints imposed on management in negotiating the terms of these break-up fees and Bidder's incentive to include such fees in the acquisition agreement.

bound in the EU. . . . Reps and warranties insurance has become an important tool to close deals that might not otherwise get done. This post is meant to highlight how reps and warranties insurance may be of use . . . in winning bids and finding means of closing deals in today's challenging environment.

WHEN IS REPS AND WARRANTIES INSURANCE BEST USED?

DEAL SIZE

Reps and warranties insurance is best suited to deals of a certain size, range and type. Given the amount of limits that can be purchased in the marketplace for any particular deal, insurance pricing and the size of a typical escrow or indemnity requirement, the "sweet spot" for reps and warranties insurance are deals between $20 million and $1.5 billion. While reps and warranties insurance might have a role to play in larger or smaller deals, it can play a central role in facilitating transactions within this size range. The type of deal is relevant because it is much easier to obtain reps and warranties insurance when the business being acquired is privately owned rather than publicly held. In sum, insurance companies generally prefer to insure transactions where an identifiable seller (rather than a diverse stockholder base) is standing behind the representations of the target business.

SELL-SIDE EXAMPLES

For those finding themselves selling a business or asset, situations that may warrant purchase of a reps and warranties policy for the transaction include the following examples:

- *Minimization of Seller Liability.* A Private Equity or Venture Capital seller near the end of a Fund's life wishes to limit post-closing indemnification liabilities on the sale of a portfolio company in order to safely distribute deal proceeds to the Limited Partners, but the buyer wants a high cap on potential indemnities or a long survival period for the reps at issue. Insurance could be the means to bridge this gap.
- *Removal of Tax Contingency from Negotiations.* A seller [often] restructures itself immediately prior to the closing of a deal for tax purposes. During due diligence, both seller's and buyer's tax advisors agree the deal should be recognized as a tax-free reorganization. In the remote event that the IRS took a different position, the tax consequences to the buyer would be significant. The Seller wishes to retire with the proceeds from the deal, and does not want to provide an indemnity to the buyer for this potential risk. Insurance could serve to remove this risk from the scope of matters needing negotiation between the parties.
- *Minimization of Successor Liability Risk.* In an asset sale transaction where a portion of assets and liabilities remain with the seller, the buyer would have no control over the seller's conduct post-closing and does not want to be subject to potential liabilities related to such excluded assets on a successor

liability theory. If the seller is unwilling or unable to provide an indemnity for such matters, insurance could help the parties past this issue.

BUY-SIDE EXAMPLES

For those wishing to acquire a business or asset, situations that may warrant purchase of a reps and warranties policy for the transaction include the following examples:

- *Bid Enhancement.* A competitive auction process is being held by a seller of prime assets. A potential buyer wishes to distinguish his or her bid from others by arranging and agreeing to look to a reps and warranties insurance policy to take the place of an indemnity from the seller. Such a use of insurance could elevate the likelihood of the buyer winning the auction.
- *Public M&A Indemnity.* In a public M&A acquisition, the buyer could arrange for reps and warranties insurance to provide the indemnity that would not otherwise typically be available in light of the publicly held nature of the target.
- *Distressed M&A Indemnity.* Similarly, in a distressed M&A setting in which the buyer is concerned about the credit risk of the seller post-closing, the use of reps and warranties insurance would enable the buyer to be indemnified for breaches of reps and warranties in the acquisition agreement, while avoiding the seller's credit risk.

WHAT SHOULD THE INSURANCE COVER?

While each policy is unique, a reps and warranties policy generally covers "Loss" from "Claims" made by Buyer for any breach of, or an alleged inaccuracy in any of, the representations and warranties made by the Seller in the Purchase and Sale Agreement ("PSA"). Though a rep and warranty policy can be structured to cover very specific reps or warranties, coverage is generally afforded on a blanket basis for all reps and warranties. The definition of "Loss" in the policy should generally mimic the extent of the Indemnity negotiated in the PSA (which could include things like consequential or special damages). Loss can also include defense costs, fees, and expenses incurred by the Insured (for instance, the Seller) in defense of a Claim brought by a third party (for instance, the Buyer) arising out of alleged breach of a representation or warranty. Note that such policies almost always have a self-insured retention ("deductible") associated with them. The size of the retention can vary considerably from deal to deal, but usually in some fashion equates to the amount of the hold back negotiated.

WHAT SHOULD THE INSURANCE EXCLUDE?

Though the exclusions in a reps and warranties policy are not as numerous as those contained in a traditional directors and officers liability policy, they do exist and should be thoughtfully considered and negotiated. Reps and warranties policies do not cover known issues, such as issues discovered during due diligence or described in disclosure schedules. They also do not cover purchase price, net worth or similar adjustment provisions contained in the PSA. "Sell-Side" reps and warranty policies do not cover claims arising from the adjudicated fraud of the seller. Either buy side or sell side policies might have deal-specific exclusions where the carrier involved simply cannot get comfortable in insuring the particular representation or warranty at issue. Lastly, a rep and warranty policy would also generally not cover any breach of which any member of the deal team involved had actual knowledge prior to the inception of the policy . . .

COST OF COVERAGE

Reps and warranties insurance is priced based on a number of factors, including most prominently the nature of the risk involved, the extent of the due diligence performed by the parties, and the relative size of the deductible. Reps and warranties insurance is currently generally priced as a percentage of the limits of coverage purchased. Nowadays, in the United States, a price range of 2.0% to 3.5% of the coverage limits is typical. Thus, a $20 million reps and warranties insurance policy on a moderately complicated deal might cost approximately $600,000. Who pays this premium is generally a function of the deal, and depends to some extent upon who is deriving the benefit from the insurance. If, for instance, a buyer-side policy is being purchased because a seller doesn't want to deal with putting up an indemnity or hold-back, the premium would generally be the seller's responsibility.

In order to facilitate the due diligence process [to be undertaken by the insurance carrier as part of its underwriting process], many carriers require payment of an up-front underwriting fee. These fees can run from $25,000 to $50,000, and are used by the carrier typically to hire outside counsel to advise it during the underwriting process.

DEDUCTIBLE

Carriers typically determine the policy's deductible according to the transaction value of the deal. In our experience, the current standard deductible ranges from 1% to 3% of the transaction value. The deductible will, however, vary from deal to deal based upon the risk involved. Buy-side policies alternatively tend to use the "hold-back" negotiated between the parties as a deductible.

PROCESS TO GET THE INSURANCE IN PLACE

The reps and warranties insurance market has evolved in response to prior concerns about the amount of time and effort necessary to put a policy in place. The carriers and brokers understand that, as with the deals themselves, the need for the insurance is typically on a very fast track.

Many of the large national insurance brokerages have specialized units that deal with reps and warranties insurance. These units, for the most part, are run not by "insurance people" but by former M&A lawyers who left private practice to become dedicated resources at the brokerages. They are fully familiar with the ins and outs of M&A and private equity transactions, and very little time is needed to get them up to speed. Though not all brokerages provide the same level and depth of resources, the right broker can become quickly integrated into the deal team and, importantly, will serve as an advocate with the insurance carriers.

Within 24 hours, a good broker will have you engaged with one of the handful of carriers that are known to service the reps and warranties insurance area. Be advised that not all carriers are created equally, and your broker should assist in advising as to selection of the best carriers for your purposes (including as to responsiveness, experience in corporate transactions, and reputation for proper claims payment decisions).

The best insurance carriers in this arena will typically provide a price and coverage quote (called a "Non-Binding Indication" or "NBIL") within two or three days of the first conversation. Either in connection with the receipt of the NBIL or in a subsequent phone call, you should expect to receive a list of due diligence requests, and likely a request of the carrier for data room access (both the broker and carrier are accustomed to negotiating and executing a Non-Disclosure Agreement early in the process). The best carriers in this arena are, in our experience, capable of running a very efficient due diligence process and getting up to speed as a quick as possible regarding potential risks associated with the deals (e.g. intellectual property, environmental, etc.).

Within a week of receipt of the NBIL, the carrier, its counsel, the insured, its business people, its deal team members and its counsel (including some-times the private equity sponsor) will typically discuss the due diligence done on the transaction, and answer questions of the insurance carrier to ensure the absence of any risks that might imperil the insurance transaction. Assuming the due diligence call goes well (and there might be follow up diligence calls as well on particular issues), the carrier involved will normally issue a draft insur-ance policy, which is normally then negotiated with the parties (assisted by the broker).

A key issue will be "conforming" the insurance so that it matches what would otherwise have been provided by the PSA in the absence of the insur-ance (or otherwise serves the particular need for which it is being purchased). In negotiating such policy, focus will often be placed on defining the scope of losses included and excluded, the impact of knowledge qualifiers, the term of coverage, operational restrictions, subrogation provisions, and a host of addi-tional issues beyond the scope of this article.

In Summary:

Reps and warranties insurance (1) can be purchased quickly and effi-ciently, and won't delay the deal, (2) can provide real coverage for troublesome aspects of a deal for which alternative solutions may not be readily available, and (3) can serve as a flexible tool to distinguish one's offer in a competitive bidding situation. Teaming up with a well-experienced broker and insurance carrier is essential to making this happen. . . .

Since the preceding description of the market for reps and warranties insurance was published in 2013, the market has only continued to grow. The following article excerpt reflects the continuing interest in relying on reps and warranties insurance as part of the current market for M&A activity.

> **Ian Boczko, John L. Robinson,**
> **and Martin J. E. Arms,**
> **Wachtell Lipton Rosen & Katz**
> **The Maturing Market for Representation**
> **and Warranty Insurance**
> *Available at:* **https://corpgov.law.harvard.edu/2018/04/05/the-maturing-market**
> **-for-representation-and-warranty-insurance/#:~:text=R%26W%20**
> **insurance%2C%20as%20the%20name,the%20time%20of%20the%20purchase**
> **(March 23, 2018)**

While [representation and warranty (R&W)] insurance was viewed historically as a product of limited application, we have seen in recent years a significant expansion of the use and importance of these policies. Today, R&W insurance is generally viewed as an attractive product when deployed in the right circumstances, often providing for a longer period of coverage and higher limits than would be available in a customary seller indemnification arrangement. The increased role of R&W insurance in transactions is evidenced by a steep increase in underwriting: only five years ago, a few hundred R&W insurance policies were being written annually; in 2017, it is estimated that over 1,500 policies were written.

A number of aspects of this growing R&W insurance marketplace are notable and contributed to the dramatic expansion of this product:

1. More than twenty insurance carriers are now writing R&W insurance. At least ten of these carriers are capable of writing primary policies, up from just a handful of carriers even five years ago. The total market capacity for a single R&W insurance placement has likewise increased substantially. It is now relatively straightforward to obtain a R&W insurance program with several hundred million dollars in limits and, based on recent experience, it is possible to obtain a billion dollars or more in limits for a single transaction.

2. The increase in insurance markets writing R&W insurance has led to a competitive marketplace for both policy pricing and terms. Relatedly, policy terms have become somewhat more standardized across the industry.

3. While R&W insurance in the United States was previously used almost exclusively in transactions with private equity sellers, the R&W insurance

market has evolved. Public companies selling divisions or subsidiaries are sometimes expecting buyers to seek protection through R&W insurance; public companies wishing to limit exposure with respect to private acquisitions are sometimes purchasing R&W insurance; and R&W insurance has even been purchased in public company transactions, although this remains a less common approach.

4. Carriers writing R&W insurance have traditionally been hesitant to cover a transaction in which there was no seller indemnity. Rather, the carriers' view was that a seller needed to have some "skin in the game" and that R&W insurance should respond to a claim only in excess of a seller indemnity. More recently, however, carriers have been more receptive to writing R&W insurance in transactions without a seller indemnity. Note, however, that the lack of a seller indemnity may moderately increase policy pricing and result in enhanced carrier due diligence and tighter policy terms and exclusions.

5. As the use of R&W insurance has increased and policies have become more standardized, the time needed to obtain such insurance (primarily, the time that carriers need to underwrite the risk) has decreased. While it is still preferable to have two to three weeks for carrier underwriting and policy negotiation, it is now possible to obtain R&W insurance in less time.

6. While there is not a large amount of publicly available data relating to claims on R&W insurance policies, as the market expands, there has been an increase in claims being made and paid. (This is not to say that every claim is being paid or is being paid in full—and the process can be challenging.) Moreover, the marketplace is sufficiently competitive at present that carriers who develop a poor reputation with respect to claims handling put themselves at risk of losing business to those carriers who conduct themselves more appropriately.

7. Just as new carriers have entered the marketplace, additional brokers are seeking to market R&W insurance. Potential purchasers should be aware of the importance of using experienced and sophisticated brokers when purchasing R&W insurance. Brokers play a more substantial and more substantive role with respect to R&W insurance than they do in some other areas of insurance.

Overall, through the expansion of the R&W insurance market, R&W insurance has become more useful, more accessible and more insured-friendly. Additionally, while it remains crucial to carefully coordinate the R&W insurance process with the broader deal process, the underwriting process for R&W insurance has generally become shorter and smoother. Finally, increasing underwriter familiarity with M&A transactions has also contributed to the growth of other related insurance products, including with respect to regulatory approval risks, break-up fees and certain tax-related risks—areas where we expect continued future expansion.

F. Due Diligence Procedures

The most important objectives of any due diligence investigation (or due diligence review, as many lawyers like to refer to it) are (1) to learn about the business for the purpose of preparing the acquisition agreement and allocating financial and legal risk as to various matters, (2) to discover significant problems and material liabilities that may be an impediment to closing on a particular transaction, and (3) to assist the parties in framing the terms of the representations to be included in the acquisition agreement. In terms of timing, some amount of due diligence review must be done in order for the parties to determine whether to incur the costs of bargaining for the terms of an acquisition. Once the parties determine to proceed with the bargaining process beyond the initial stages, negotiations begin in earnest between Bidder and Target regarding the sharing of sensitive proprietary company information. Assuming appropriate confidentiality agreements are in place, the Bidder will then typically undertake a thorough investigation of Target's business and financial affairs. The information disclosed during the course of this investigation will impact the scope of, and any exclusions to, the terms of the representations to be given by Target to Bidder.

Even the most bare bones of due diligence reviews generally involve a substantial cast of personnel, usually consisting at a minimum of the following: counsel for both Bidder and Target, financial advisors (investment bankers) for both parties, auditors for Target and generally other accounting personnel for both Bidder and Target, and finally, senior management and other internal personnel of both companies. Depending on the nature of Target's business, other experts may be brought into the diligence process. For example, if Target is in the oil and gas industry, petroleum engineers may get involved in the diligence review.

Generally speaking, the diligence process is usually organized by the attorneys, with Bidder's lawyers playing a key role in defining the scope of the investigation. The first draft of the due diligence checklist is typically prepared by Bidder's lawyers with substantial assistance from Bidder's management and the company's investment bankers. A sample checklist is found in Appendix E.

As any experienced M&A lawyer will tell you, there is an ever-present danger that Bidder's diligence procedures may become too routine, thereby impeding the business objectives to be accomplished in the context of any particular investigation. In some situations, the process becomes too mechanical, lacking any careful planning as to the scope of items to be reviewed in order to prioritize those items that are most important to Bidder's decision to purchase Target's business, so as to be sure that these items are carefully reviewed by competent personnel. Alternatively, the investigation may be too superficial, ignoring key operational details, or the investigation may be conducted by personnel too junior and inexperienced to accomplish the purpose of the investigation effectively. For Bidder's part, the failure to conduct adequate due diligence review may be disastrous because it may result in Bidder overpaying to acquire Target. Alternatively, an inadequate diligence review may result in the failure to successfully integrate Target's business operations with Bidder's in order to produce the synergistic gains that Bidder hoped to achieve through the acquisition of Target. In either case, Bidder will often come to regret that it did not undertake a more thorough and systematic due diligence review of Target.

On Target's side, the process is usually coordinated by company counsel who will, like Bidder, assemble a multidisciplinary team to pull together the materials that are responsive to the items on Bidder's due diligence checklist. While the general rule of thumb is that Bidder can never do too much diligence, at the same time, Bidder needs to strike an appropriate balance. Bidder obviously needs to conduct a thorough review of Target's business, and yet avoid an overbroad investigation that may result in undue strain on the negotiation process between the parties. If Bidder conducts an overbroad investigation, it runs the risk that Target may view the process as a time-wasting activity that delays closing while simultaneously imposing costs on Target and disrupting its workforce and business operations. On the other hand, Bidder must conduct that level of diligence that allows it to make an informed decision regarding its plans for Target and its ability to realize on the business and financial synergies that Bidder hopes to obtain by acquiring Target's business.

Due Diligence and the Risk of the Deal **Not** *Closing.* As we have seen in the course of the topics covered in this chapter, there are many risks inherent in the deal process, many of which may lead to the deal *not* closing, even though the acquisition agreement is signed and in place. In addition to the risk that the deal may not close at all, Target also faces the risk that the deal may not close on the financial terms that were originally agreed to by Bidder and Target, usually as the result of a purchase price adjustment that works to the financial detriment of Target. In particular, Target fears that during the course of due diligence and the parties' ongoing negotiations leading up to closing on the transaction, Bidder may learn information that will trigger a right to walk away from the deal. In order to avoid this disastrous result, Target may decide to initiate negotiations to adjust the purchase price to reflect new developments.

How can Target (and its lawyers) mitigate against this type of risk? Essentially, there are two ways: First, at the outset of the parties' negotiation, Target should aggressively negotiate the terms of its representations and the conditions to closing in order to tailor these provisions as narrowly as possible, thereby giving Target the greatest assurance that the deal will close. Second, Target's lawyers can better protect their client from the disastrous consequences of a failed deal by helping the client to prepare itself for the diligence review *before* actually putting Target up for sale. There are two preliminary measures that Target can take to minimize the risk that the acquisition will not close. The first precaution that Target can take is to think carefully through the consequences of its decision to put the company on the auction block. Then, once the decision has been reached to sell the business, Target needs to thoroughly prepare the company for sale. By taking steps to clean up its business and financial affairs *before* putting the company on the auction block, Target will minimize the risk that obstacles will surface later that might give Bidder the right to walk away from the deal, and thus fail to close on the acquisition. These steps would include, at a minimum, preparation of financial statements (i.e., Target either has audited financials already prepared or it has available financial statements that adequately and accurately reflect the company's financial affairs). In addition, Target should have in place a business plan setting forth business and financial objectives that are realistically attainable within the time period covered by the sale process.

Another suggestion that Target lawyers often recommend to their clients is that Target disclose problems early in the process of negotiating the acquisition agreement. In the experience of many M&A lawyers, Target's bargaining leverage will decline steadily as the negotiations proceed. By disclosing problems early, when Target's bargaining power presumably is at its greatest, Target will likely obtain the most optimal resolution of any problems, thereby allowing the deal to proceed to closing. If disclosure is postponed to a later stage in the deal process, Bidder is likely to have the upper hand and either decide to walk away from the deal, or alternatively, to negotiate for a substantial price reduction, both of which work to Target's disadvantage. If Bidder should determine that it is not interested in buying Target, generally it will terminate the deal process. By terminating early in the deal process, the risk to Target is minimized, both in terms of the disruption to its business as well as the out-of-pocket costs incurred in proceeding with this particular Bidder. This advice—to disclose problems early in the negotiating process—often runs contrary to the businessperson's instinct, which usually is to continue marketing the company as the negotiating process begins by continuing to trump the strong points of the company's business. However, in the experience of many M&A lawyers, the strategy of leaving the bad points to be dealt with at the end of the negotiating process often works to Target's disadvantage, especially where Target is serious about doing a deal with this Bidder and thus wants to minimize the risk that the deal will not close.

Use of Due Diligence Checklists.   To illustrate the breadth of business and financial matters typically covered in any thorough due diligence review, consult the checklist in Appendix E. This checklist is fairly representative of the sort that every M&A lawyer uses as the starting point in any given transaction. The lawyer's task then is to tailor this list as appropriate to Target's business and the circumstances of that particular transaction. For example, extensive due diligence as to potential environmental liabilities is usually not warranted in connection with the acquisition of a software development business. Obviously, the same is not true in the case of Bidder's purchase of a local chain of dry-cleaning stores.

In developing the due diligence checklist for any particular acquisition, a threshold issue that must be considered by the transaction planners is the question of how far back in time is Target going to be required to search in order to produce information relevant to the items of information requested by Bidder. Again, resolution of this issue will generally depend on the relative bargaining power of the parties, but it usually ranges from one to three to five years. In some areas, most notably tax matters, the appropriate time period often turns out to be the relevant statute of limitations period.

A quick review of the items contained in the sample due diligence checklist in Appendix E reflects the obvious need for counsel to assemble a multidisciplinary team of personnel in order to fulfill the objectives of a due diligence review. This is true for both Target's lawyers and Bidder's lawyers. In order to assemble the information that is responsive to the items on this checklist, Target's lawyers must contact the key staff members of Target, who gather the information that Bidder requests to review. Typically, all this material is then gathered in one place (generally known as the "data room") and made available for Bidder's inspection. On Bidder's side, counsel will usually be required to assemble a diverse team of experts in order to competently evaluate the information provided by Target.

Impact of Due Diligence on Bidder's Integration Planning. The vital importance of adequate due diligence review to Bidder's strategic planning cannot be overstated. In addition, the due diligence process is also of critical importance to Bidder's ongoing process of planning for the integration of Target's business with Bidder's existing operations. The importance of *integration planning* to the success of any particular M&A strategy is reflected in the planning process undertaken by IBM Corp. in connection with the rapid pace of deal making that this blue-chip company has become known for. For example, from 2000 to 2007, IBM made 69 acquisitions as part of its strategic plan to transform its global business into a leading provider of software and services. As a measure of its success in integrating these acquisitions into IBM's business operations to achieve this transformation, revenue from software and services grew from 54 percent of IBM's total in 2000 to 73 percent in 2007. Given that each acquisition poses its own unique set of integration challenges in order for any particular Bidder to obtain the benefit of the bargain in making the purchase, IBM's track record is quite impressive — regardless of the metric used to measure success. *See* Andrea Orr, *End to End at IBM — Big Blue's Take on Integration,* THE DEAL 58 (Oct. 12, 2007). However, IBM's

> track record is all the more impressive, considering the historically low success rates for transactions in general. . . . And the quantitative results don't account for other key benefits [to be realized from the acquisition,] such as expanding the company's market presence or helping it accelerate internal product development. . . . In the end, what most sets IBM's integration [efforts] apart is its position as part of a comprehensive acquisition process. It's a process where deals are typically championed by line managers going after products their customers want; supported by an experienced corporate development team; and monitored long after closing by top management equipped with tools to measure whether the acquisition is panning out as planned.

Id. at 59-60.

As we enter the third decade of the twenty-first century, integration planning continues to be of vital importance in making sure that the M&A transaction provides Bidder with the anticipated source of value creation for the company and its shareholders. However, time and again, we see evidence of

> one critical, often-overlooked contributory factor to the success of a deal — and steering clear of the pitfalls that bedevil so many [M&A deals] — is post-merger integration ("PMI"), [which is a term that refers to events that arise after the M&A transaction is negotiated and signed by Bidder and Target]. . . . When [Bidder's] management has not structured PMI planning appropriately, resourced it sufficiently, and/or put in place the internal controls needed to monitor [its] implementation, the integration process may well become a company performance issue [after closing on the transaction] — a trend we have repeatedly seen and a leading cause for the lack of success of many [M&A] deals. Alternatively, a

well-structured, well-planned, well-resourced, and well-executed PMI program with appropriate and sufficient internal controls usually delivers superlative integration results. . . . At many companies, management often assumes it will be able to successfully attain value through integration execution, and boards often assume that management can handle the complexities of running a transformational program while management simultaneously runs the business, without the need for board oversight. This shared confidence in outcome has frequently proven to be a fatal flaw. . . . Companies that understand the complexity of PMI and therefore fully prepare for integration, are companies that are more likely to deliver success [on a post-closing basis]. . . . To address the critical PMI issues, [Bidder's] board should be satisfied that the designated PMI leaders establish a detailed, well-thought-through synergy plan both on the cost and growth sides of the business, and that they have a deep, real understanding of the steps needed to implement the plan and achieve its goals. . . . Management should set a timetable for achieving its desired projects and milestones and update the board regularly . . . on their progress. . . . Because M&A activity is a critical part of the growth strategy of many companies, boards should take active oversight of the entire lifespan of a transaction, not just the due diligence [process], but also . . . post-merger integration.

Joel Schlachtenhaufen and Bob Lamm, Deloitte Consulting LLP, *Post-Merger Integration*, July 2017, *available at:* https://www2.deloitte.com/content/dam/ Deloitte/ch/Documents/audit/ch-cbe-july-2017-on-the-boards-agenda.pdf.

The Role of Due Diligence in Preventing Bidder Overpayment.   In August 2011, Hewlett-Packard (HP) announced its plan to acquire Autonomy, Inc. for the eye-popping sum of $11.1 billion, in a deal that HP's management, led by its then-CEO Leo Apotheker, believed would "transform HP from a low-margin producer of printers, PCs, and other hardware into a high-margin, cutting-edge software company." James B. Stewart, *From H.P., a Blunder That Seems to Beat All*, N.Y. TIMES, Nov. 30, 2012, *available at:* http://www.nytimes.com/2012/12/01/business/hps -autonmy-blunder-might-be-one-for-the-record-books.html?pagewanted=all$_ r=0. "Wall Street's reaction to Hewlett-Packard's announcement was swift and harsh," with many analysts claiming that HP's "decision to purchase Autonomy [was] value-destroying." *Id.* Within days of HP's announcement, HP's CEO responded to the wave of criticism regarding HP's "overly expensive acquisition of Autonomy." *Id.* Apotheker was quoted as saying, "We have a pretty rigorous process inside H.P. that we follow for all our acquisitions, which is a [discounted cash flow-based] model. . . . And we try to take a very conservative view." *Id.* Within a year, though, Apotheker was no longer HP's CEO; *and* HP announced that "it was writing down $8.8 billion of its acquisition of Autonomy, in effect admitting that the company" had overpaid by just about a whopping 380 percent. *Id.*

In November 2012, at the time the company announced the write-down, HP attributed more than $5 billion of the write-off to what it called "a willful effort on behalf of certain former Autonomy employees to inflate the underlying financial metrics of the company in order to mislead investors and potential buyers. . . . These representations and lack of disclosure severely impacted HP management's ability to fairly value Autonomy at the time of the deal." *HP Issues Statement Regarding Autonomy Impairment Charge* (press release issued by Hewlett-Packard, Nov. 20, 2012, *available at:* http://www.hp.com/hpinfo/ newsroom/press/2012/121120b.html). The founder of Autonomy, Michael Lynch, promptly denied HP's claims of fraud and non-disclosure "and accused Hewlett-Packard of mismanaging the acquisition." Stewart, *supra. From H.P., a Blunder That Seems to Beat All.* Other observers, however, pointed out that HP's claims of fraud, "while it may offer a face-saving excuse for at least some of HP's huge write-down, shouldn't obscure the fact that the deal was wildly over-priced from the outset, that at least some people at Hewlett-Packard recognized that, and that H.P.'s chairman, Ray Lane, and the board that approved the deal should be held accountable." *Id.* For other knowledgeable observers, however, the more glaring question is: how did HP's financial due diligence process fail to uncover the accounting issues that ultimately contributed to HP's write-down of its acquisition of Autonomy? *See* Ben Worten, et al., *Long Before H-P Deal, Autonomy's Red Flags,* WALL STREET JOURNAL, Nov. 26, 2012, *available at:* http://online.wsj.com/article/SB10001424127887324784404578141462744040072.html ("questions are mounting about how H-P failed to uncover the alleged irregularities ahead of buying Autonomy, particularly as some outside analysts raised concerns about Autonomy's accounting for years.").

‖6‖

Federal Regulation of Stock Purchases: Tender Offers and the Williams Act

We have seen that state law regulates the process of Bidder Co. obtaining control over Target Co.'s business, whether by way of a merger (whether direct or triangular) or by purchasing all of the assets (and agreeing to assume all, or at least some, of the liabilities). Either way, certain procedural safeguards are granted, as a matter of state law, primarily for the protection of Target shareholders in the face of this type of fundamental change in their corporation. However, with respect to the stock purchase, this method of acquisition is largely unregulated by state law.[1] As we observed in analyzing the problems in Chapter 2, the public policy premise that underlies this hands-off approach at the state level is largely based on the notion that no shareholder can be forced (coerced) into selling his/her/its shares by the will of the majority. Rather, each Target shareholder must make the independent decision whether to accept Bidder's offer to buy his/her/its shares and endorse over his/her/its stock certificates to Bidder, thereby surrendering his/her/its equity ownership of Target in exchange for the consideration offered by Bidder.

Consequently, when presented with Bidder's offer to buy Target shares, each Target shareholder must decide whether to accept that offer. At a minimum, the shareholder's decision will depend on whether Bidder is offering "fair value" to acquire Target.[2] The vulnerability of Target shareholders is most acute in those transactions where Bidder offers an all-cash purchase price to acquire Target shares. It is then up to the individual shareholder to bargain

---

1. At the end of this chapter, however, we will describe the recent proliferation of state antitakeover statutes, which do have the effect of regulating this method of acquiring Target Co.

2. It is worth observing that, no matter how fair the offer from Bidder is, at least some Target shareholders can be expected to refuse to sell their shares, either because they think the terms offered are not fair or they just don't want to sell. Instead, they want to remain invested in Target and its business. As we learned in analyzing the scope and availability of the modern appraisal remedy in the materials and problems in Chapter 2, the modern view is that the will of the majority will prevail, notwithstanding the objections of the minority (dissenting) shareholders. Based on this modern view, the Delaware Supreme Court in *Weinberger, supra,* at p. 179, concluded that the controlling shareholder can use the Delaware merger procedure for the sole purpose of cashing out (i.e., eliminating) the minority interest — so long as the transaction satisfies the entire fairness test (i.e., fair price and fair dealing). *Weinberger* thus sets the stage for two-step transactions of the type seen in *Weinberger* and *Rabkin, supra,* at p. 231, involving a stock purchase giving Bidder a controlling interest in

for the best price possible, an exercise that depends heavily on that shareholder's ability to access necessary information about Target's business and financial affairs in order to bargain effectively with Bidder.

In this chapter, we consider the information needs of the individual Target shareholders, an issue that invariably comes up in the case of stock purchases because of the agency cost problem, an inherent attribute of modern share ownership. In the modern corporation, the agency costs of separating ownership from management and control of the business operations of Target inevitably result in an information gap that leaves Target shareholders without access to the information they need to make an informed decision about whether to accept Bidder's offer. Here, the distinction between privately held versus publicly traded corporations becomes important in analyzing this agency cost problem in an acquisition context.

In the closely held corporation, these agency costs are typically addressed as a matter of private ordering at the time the individual invests his/her/its capital to purchase shares of Target Co. At the time of investment in Target, the buyer of these shares (at least if he/she/it is well advised) will bargain for certain rights of control over the business affairs of Target (which may include, among other things, veto rights, election of representative(s) to the board of directors, supermajority quorum or voting requirements, or combinations of these and other types of protections). In the absence of these protections, the investor is at the mercy of the default rules provided by the law of the state where Target is organized, including the fiduciary duty obligations imposed by that jurisdiction. With adequate planning, though, the shareholder of the closely held Target will usually have access to the information needed to make an informed decision whether Bidder's offer constitutes fair value.

By contrast, in those situations where Bidder proposes to issue its stock (or other securities) to acquire Target, this information gap is mitigated (at least somewhat) by the obligations imposed on Bidder by the Securities Act of 1933 ("1933 Act"). As we learned in Chapter 4, Bidder Co. must either register the issuance of its securities in exchange for Target Co. stock or find an exemption for its exchange offer. In the acquisition of a closely held Target, Bidder will often find an exemption for the offering, relying on the statutory private placement exemption or one of the Regulation D exemptions. Either way, the issuer (Bidder Co.) must provide the prospective investor (Target Co. shareholder) sufficient information to allow the Target shareholder to make an informed investment decision whether to accept Bidder's exchange offer by signing the stock purchase agreement. As we saw in analyzing the problems in Chapter 2 involving Google's acquisition of all of the outstanding shares of Nest Labs common stock, this combination of protections offered by state and federal law provided the shareholders of Target (Nest Labs) with the information they needed to make an informed decision about whether to accept Bidder's

---

Target, which is then followed up by a cash-out merger in the back end, thereby eliminating any minority shares of Target that were not acquired in the first step. See Diagram 12 of Appendix A. The protections offered to the minority by way of the appraisal remedy granted as part of the back-end merger were at issue in *Weinberger* and the efficacy of this remedy was discussed at length in Chapter 2.

(Google's) offer to buy all of their shares for cash, or alternatively, for Bidder's (Google's) shares.

More problematic is the situation involving Bidder's offer to buy shares of a *publicly traded* Target for *cash*. Here, the agency costs of separating ownership from control of the business affairs of the modern corporation are most acute. In these cases, Target shareholders first learn of Bidder's offer generally by reading of it in a newspaper of wide circulation (such as the *Wall Street Journal*). It is then up to each Target shareholder—which could be tens of thousands in the case of a very large public company, such as DirecTV—to decide whether to accept Bidder's offer. As passive investors, these public shareholders will usually have little knowledge of the day-to-day business affairs of Target. As a result, they are usually quite vulnerable to the high-pressure sales tactics that characterized the early form of all-cash tender offer, known as the "Saturday night special."

Prior to the adoption of the Williams Act in 1968, Bidder Co. could announce, without any warning to Target Co. or its management, that Bidder was making an all-cash offer to buy Target shares. This tender offer would generally be at a premium over the trading price of Target shares in the open market and usually would be conditioned on obtaining a sufficient number of Target shares to give Bidder control over the company. Additionally, Bidder's offer would typically indicate that those Target shares tendered first would be accepted and all others would be rejected (i.e., first come, first accepted). Such an announcement would generate a stampede effect, as Target shareholders raced to tender their shares into Bidder's offer, lest they run the risk of being left behind and thus lose out on the opportunity to cash out their Target shares at a premium. In the case of the Saturday night special, management of Target would be caught completely off guard, since they had no idea that an unsolicited bid was in the works at Bidder. In the usual case, Target management was left with little time to organize itself in order to erect antitakeover defenses, shop for a better offer, or even notify its stockholders whether Bidder's offer represented fair value. In most of these Saturday night specials, Bidder was an unrelated third party, not an insider of Target, and therefore was not subject to the disclosure obligations imposed by the antifraud rules of the federal securities laws. Equally important, as an unrelated third party, Bidder did not owe any fiduciary duties, as a matter of state law, to Target or its shareholders.

Consequently, one of the principal advantages of the Saturday night special was that it allowed Bidder to announce the all-cash offer to purchase Target shares and then proceed to close quickly on its tender offer, unlike the delay associated with merger procedures that required shareholder approval as a matter of state law. Equally important, at least for Bidder, was that no disclosure was required, either to commence its bid or to complete the all-cash tender offer. The only information Bidder had to disclose (as a matter of contract law) in order to complete the transaction was to set forth the offering price and identify the location where the Target shareholders should tender their stock if they chose to accept Bidder's offer.

However, the advantages of the cash tender offer were substantially eroded, if not eliminated altogether, where the tender offer was made using Bidder's *stock* rather than an all-cash bid for Target. In the case of a *stock exchange offer*, the 1933 Act required Bidder Co. to register the distribution of its shares to Target Co. shareholders in exchange for the surrender of their stock in the publicly traded Target, since no exemption would be available for this issuance of Bidder stock. As we saw in Chapter 4, the issuer's preparation of a registration statement generally resulted in substantial delay in commencing its bid for Target, and the Securities and Exchange Commission's (SEC) review of the Bidder's registration statement once it was filed usually added further delay to the tender offer process.

This all changed when Congress decided to regulate *cash tender offers* by adopting the Williams Act in 1968, which added subsections (d) and (e) to section 13 and subsections (d) and (e) to section 14 of the Securities Exchange Act of 1934 ("1934 Act"). As originally enacted, §13(d) required the filing of a disclosure document with the SEC whenever any person (or group of persons) acquired more than 10 percent of a class of equity security of a company that was registered under the 1934 Act (commonly known as a *reporting company*). As originally adopted, the 10 percent threshold of §13(d), not surprisingly, was tied to the §16 reporting requirements for beneficial owners of more than 10 percent of the equity securities of a reporting company.[3] Later, in 1970, however, Congress amended the statute to reduce the reporting threshold from 10 percent to 5 percent. Today, §13(d) requires anyone who crosses the 5 percent threshold to file a Schedule 13D within ten days[4] after acquiring the securities. The disclosures required by Schedule 13D include, among other things, the name(s) of the buyer(s), the source of funds for the purchase(s) and the price(s) paid, the number of shares owned, the plans for the company if the buyer(s) intend to gain control of the company, and information about any contracts entered into with respect to the acquired securities. The public policy premise for imposing the filing obligations of §13(d) is discussed in *GAF Corp. v. Milstein, infra*, at p. 420.

Whereas §13(d) regulates third-party purchases of Target Co. stock, §13(e) is directed at the issuer's repurchase of its own securities. Congress framed §13(e) as an antifraud provision that delegates broad rulemaking authority to the SEC. Pursuant to this grant of authority, the SEC has adopted Rule 13e-1, which requires issuers that propose to engage in repurchases of their shares during the course of a third party's tender offer to file a disclosure document with the SEC. In addition, where the issuer proposes a self-tender, the SEC adopted Rule 13e-4, which requires the issuer to file Schedule 13E-4. Broadly speaking, Schedule 13E-4 imposes on the issuer disclosure obligations that are substantially similar to those required of a third party (Bidder Co.) when the Bidder commences a tender offer for shares of Target Co.

---

3. We discussed the requirements of §16(b) of the 1934 Act as part of the materials in Chapter 4. *See supra*, pp. 317-320.

4. "Despite the . . . undeniable significance [of Section 13(d)], its meaning remains uncertain. Judges and commentators cannot agree whether the statute mandates filing within ten *business* days or ten *calendar* days. While a seemingly trivial distinction, by last count the timeliness of almost *fifty percent* of Schedule 13D filings hinged on just this issue. [*See* Lucian A. Bebchuk, Alon Bray, Robert J. Jackson, Jr., & Wei Jiang, *Pre-Disclosure Accumulations by Activist Investors: Evidence and Policy*, 39 J. CORP. L 1, 21, tbl. 6 (2013).] And yet, there is no settled answer to a simple question: when must a Schedule 13D be filed?" Samir H. Doshi, Wachtell, Lipton, Rosen, & Katz, June 23, 2019, *available at:* https://corpgov.law.harvard.edu/2019/06/23/the-timing-of-schedule-13d/ (emphasis in original).

In addition, the SEC has promulgated Rule 13e-3, which requires the issuer to file certain disclosures in the case of a going private transaction. In general, a *going private transaction* involves a controlling shareholder who proposes to "take the company private" by purchasing all of the publicly held shares that it does not own. Since the enactment of the Sarbanes-Oxley Act of 2002 ("SOX"), there has been a heightened interest in "taking the (publicly traded) company private" in order to avoid the burden of complying with the enhanced disclosure obligations and other corporate reform measures required by SOX, and the related rules of the SEC, the New York Stock Exchange (NYSE), and other relevant self-regulatory organizations (SROs). We will examine the nature of the SEC's regulation of "going private" transactions later in this chapter, in connection with our discussion of the *SEC v. Carter Hawley Hale Stores, Inc.* case. In addition, as part of the materials in Chapter 7, we will examine the intersection of the disclosure obligations imposed under the federal securities laws and the scope of fiduciary duty obligations imposed under state law with respect to going private transactions.

While §13(d) imposes disclosure obligations in connection with open-market purchases of Target Co.'s stock by a third party, §14(d) imposes disclosure obligations in connection with a *tender offer* by a third party, Bidder Co., for shares of a publicly traded Target. Pursuant to §14(d), the SEC has adopted a substantial set of rules (Regulation 14D), prescribing the requisite procedures for commencing and completing a tender offer, as well as the disclosures required of a third-party Bidder in order to make a valid tender offer for shares of a publicly traded Target Co.

As part of the Williams Act, Congress legislated reforms intended to address the plight of the Target shareholder when confronted with Bidder's launch of the Saturday night special. First, the Williams Act required Bidder to provide detailed disclosures, including, among other things, a description of (1) the source of its funds to finance the cash purchase of Target shares; and (2) Bidder's plans for Target in the event Bidder gains control over Target as a result of its tender offer. The SEC has adopted a detailed set of rules, set forth in Regulation 14D, that expand on the disclosures and procedures required by §14(d) to commence a tender offer.

In addition, Congress legislated other procedural safeguards designed to alleviate the pressures that Target shareholders typically faced when Bidder launched its Saturday night special. These include (1) a minimum period of time (now 20 business days) that the tender offer must remain open (known as the "offering period") (Rule 14e-1); (2) Target shareholders must be given the right to withdraw their shares at any point during the offering period (Rule 14d-7); (3) in the case of a partial bid, if the tender offer is oversubscribed at the end of the offering period, Bidder must purchase the Target shares pro rata from all the tendering shareholders so that all tendering shareholders have the opportunity to cash in their shares (Rule 14d-8); and (4) if the Bidder increases its tender offer price during the offering period, it must pay the increased amount to any shareholder who has previously tendered his/her/its shares into the bid (§14(d)(7) and Rule 14d-10(a)(1)). The general goal of these reforms is to reduce the pressure on the Target shareholder to tender early and thereby afford the Target shareholder the opportunity to make an informed decision as to the merits of Bidder's offer.

As part of the Williams Act, Congress also enacted §14(e), which prohibits material misstatements, omissions, and fraudulent practices in connection with tender offers, regardless of whether Target is a 1934 Act reporting company. Patterned after the broad prohibition of §10(b) of the 1934 Act, §14(e) (and the SEC rules promulgated thereunder) has been held to apply to a bid for shares of a company that is not registered under the 1934 Act, and therefore the third party's tender offer is not subject to the filing and disclosure requirements of §14(d) and Regulation 14D promulgated thereunder. Pursuant to §14(e), the SEC has adopted Rule 14e-2, which requires Target management to file a Schedule 14D-9 with the SEC within ten business days after Bidder commences its tender offer. As part of its obligations under Rule 14e-2, Target management must send a statement to the shareholders recommending either acceptance or rejection of the tender offer, or, alternatively, expressing no opinion toward the offer and the reasons for management's inability to make a recommendation.

The nature and efficacy of all these reforms, which are not without controversy in mergers and acquisitions (M&A) literature, are explored in the materials that follow.

A.   *Disclosure Requirements of §13(d) of the Williams Act*

In addition to describing the scope of the filing obligation imposed under section 13(d), the following case also provides important background regarding the legislative history of the Williams Act and the congressional objectives to be achieved by the enactment of this important addition to the federal securities laws.

outline brief

1.   Filing Obligations Under §13(d)

GAF Corporation v. Milstein
453 F.2d 709 (2d Cir. 1971)

KAUFMAN, Circuit Judge:

This appeal involves the interpretation of section 13(d) of the Securities Exchange Act, hitherto a largely unnoticed provision[2] added in 1968 by the Williams Act. We write, therefore, on a relatively *tabula rasa*, despite the burgeoning field of securities law. Essentially, section 13(d) requires any person, after acquiring more than 10% (now 5%) of a class of registered equity security,

---

2. We are aware of only four other cases which considered the section. Bath Industries, Inc. v. Blot, 305 F. Supp. 526 (E.D. Wis. 1969), aff'd, 427 F.2d 97 (7th Cir. 1970); Ozark Airlines, Inc. v. Cox, 326 F. Supp. 1113 (E.D. Mo. 1971); Sisak v. Wings and Wheels Express, Inc., CCH Fed. Sec. L. Rep. ¶92,991 (S.D.N.Y. Sept. 9, 1970); Grow Chemical Corp. v. Uran, 316 F. Supp. 891 (S.D.N.Y. 1970). *See generally* Comment, Section 13(d) and Disclosure of Corporate Equity Ownership, 119 U. Pa. L. Rev. 853 (1971).

to send to the issuer and the exchanges on which the security is traded and file with the Commission the statement required by the Act. Although the section has not attracted as much comment as section 14(d), also added by the Williams Act and requiring disclosure by persons engaging in tender offers, the section has potential for marked impact on holders, sellers and purchasers of securities.

GAF Corporation filed its complaint in the United States District Court for the Southern District of New York alleging that Morris Milstein, his two sons, Seymour and Paul, and his daughter, Gloria Milstein Flanzer, violated section 13(d) of the Securities Exchange Act first by failing to file the required statements and then by filing false ones. The complaint also alleged violation of section 10(b) based on the same false statements and, in addition, market manipulation of GAF stock. The Milsteins moved for dismissal under Rule 12(b)(6), F. R. Civ. P., on the ground that the complaint failed to state a claim on which relief could be granted or, in the alternative, for summary judgment under Rule 56. Judge Pollack aptly framed the issues involved:

> The ultimate issue presented by the defendants' motion to dismiss the first count is whether, organizing a group of stockholders owning more than 10% of a class of equity securities with a view to seeking control is, without more, a reportable event under Section 13(d) of the Exchange Act; and as to the second count, whether in the absence of a connected purchase or sale of securities, the target corporation claiming violation of Section 10 and Rule 10b(5), has standing to seek an injunction against a control contestant for falsity in a Schedule 13D filing. (Footnote omitted.)

324 F. Supp. 1062, 1064-1065 (S.D.N.Y. 1971). Judge Pollack granted the Milsteins' motion to dismiss under Rule 12(b)(6), and GAF has appealed. We disagree with Judge Pollack's determination that GAF failed to state a claim under section 13(d) and Rule 13d-1 promulgated thereunder, and thus reverse his order in this respect, but we affirm the dismissal of the second claim of the complaint on the ground that GAF, as an issuer, has no standing under section 10(b). . . .

The four Milsteins received 324,166 shares of GAF convertible preferred stock, approximately 10.25% of the preferred shares outstanding, when The Ruberoid Company, in which they had substantial holdings, was merged into GAF in May, 1967. They have not acquired any additional preferred shares since the merger.

The complaint informs us that at some time after July 29, 1968, the effective date of the Williams Act, the Milsteins "formed a conspiracy among themselves and other persons to act as a syndicate or group for the purpose of acquiring, holding, or disposing of securities of GAF with the ultimate aim of seizing control of GAF for their own personal and private purposes." It is necessary for our purposes to examine only a few of the nine overt acts GAF alleged were taken in furtherance of this conspiracy.

The complaint alleged that initially the Milsteins sought senior management and board positions for Seymour Milstein with GAF. When this sinecure was not forthcoming, the Milsteins allegedly caused Circle Floor Co., Inc., a company in their control, to reduce its otherwise substantial purchases from

GAF. It also charged that the Milsteins thereafter undertook a concerted effort to disparage its management and depress the price of GAF common and preferred stock in order to facilitate the acquisition of additional shares. On May 27, 1970, the Milsteins filed a derivative action in the district court, charging the directors, *inter alia*, with waste and spoliation of corporation assets. A companion action was filed in the New York courts. GAF further alleged that these actions were filed only to disparage management, to depress the price of GAF stock and to use discovery devices to gain valuable information for their takeover conspiracy.

In the meantime, the complaint tells us, Paul and Seymour Milstein purchased respectively 62,000 and 64,000 shares of GAF common stock. When GAF contended that the Milsteins were in violation of section 13(d) because they had not filed a Schedule 13D as required by Rule 13d-1, the Milsteins, although disclaiming any legal obligation under section 13(d), filed such a schedule on September 24, 1970. In their 13D statement (appended to the complaint), the Milsteins disclosed their preferred and common holdings and stated they "at some future time [might] determine to attempt to acquire control of GAF. . . ." They also stated that they had "no present intention as to whether or not any additional securities of GAF [might] be acquired by them in the future. . . ." Indeed, within the next two months, commencing with October 2, Paul and Seymour each purchased an additional 41,650 shares of common. The Milsteins thereafter filed a Restated and Amended Schedule 13D on November 10 to reflect these new purchases.

Then, on January 27, 1971, the Milsteins filed a third Schedule 13D, disclosing their intention to wage a proxy contest at the 1971 annual meeting. Although the statement again disclaimed any present intention to acquire additional shares, Paul purchased 28,300 shares of common stock during February, 1971. These last purchases, which brought the Milsteins' total common holdings to 237,600 shares having a value in excess of $2 million and constituting 1.7% of the common shares outstanding, were reflected in a February 23 amendment to the January 27 Schedule 13D.

The last essential datum for our purposes is the proxy contest. On May 10, 1971, it was announced that GAF management had prevailed at the April 16 meeting by a margin of some 2 to 1. . . .

I.

At the time the conspiracy allegedly was formed, section 13(d)(1) in relevant part provided:

> Any person who, after acquiring directly or indirectly the beneficial ownership of any equity security of a class which is registered pursuant to section 12 of this title . . . , is directly or indirectly the beneficial owner of more than 10 per centum [now 5%] of such class shall, within ten days after such acquisition, send to the issuer of the security at its principal executive office, by registered or certified mail, send to each exchange where the security is traded, and file with the Commission, a statement. . . .

This section, however, exempts from its filing requirements any acquisition which, "together with all other acquisitions by the same person of securities of the same class during the preceding twelve months, does not exceed 2 per centum of that class." Section 13(d)(6)(B). Section 13(d)(3), which is crucial to GAF's claim, further provides that "[w]hen two or more persons act as a partnership, limited partnership, syndicate, or other group for the purpose of acquiring, holding, or disposing of securities of an issuer, such syndicate or group shall be deemed a 'person' for the purposes of [section 13(d)]." On the assumption that the facts alleged in the complaint are true, we cannot conclude other than that the four Milsteins constituted a "group" and thus, as a "person," were subject to the provisions of section 13(d). We also are aware of the charge that the Milsteins agreed after July 29, 1968, to hold their GAF preferred shares for the common purpose of acquiring control of GAF. Furthermore, the individuals collectively or as a "group" held more than 10% of the outstanding preferred shares—a registered class of securities. Since the section requires a "person" to file only if he acquires more than 2% of the class of stock in a 12-month period after July 29, 1968,[12] the principal question presented to us is whether the complaint alleges as a matter of law that the Milstein *group* "acquired" the 324,166 shares of preferred stock owned by its members after that date. We conclude that it does and thus that it states a claim under section 13(d).

The statute refers to "acquiring directly or indirectly the beneficial ownership of securities." Thus, at the outset, we are not confronted with the relatively simple concept of legal title, but rather with the amorphous and occasionally obfuscated concepts of indirect and beneficial ownership which pervade the securities acts.

The Act nowhere explicitly defines the concept of "acquisition" as used in section 13(d). Although we are aware of Learned Hand's warning "not to make a fortress out of the dictionary," Cabell v. Markham, 148 F.2d 737, 739 (2d Cir.), aff'd, 326 U.S. 404, 66 S. Ct. 193, 90 L. Ed. 165 (1945), some light, although dim, is shed by Webster's Third International Dictionary. It tells us that "to acquire" means "to come into possession [or] control." If the allegations in the complaint are true, then the group, which must be treated as an entity separate and distinct from its members, could have gained "beneficial control" of the voting rights of the preferred stock[13] only after its formation, which we must assume occurred after the effective date of the Williams Act. Manifestly, according to the complaint, the group when formed acquired a beneficial interest in the individual holdings of its members. We find ourselves in agreement with the statement of the Court of Appeals for the Seventh Circuit in Bath Industries, Inc. v. Blot, 427 F.2d 97, 112 (7th Cir. 1970), that in the context of the Williams Act, where the principal concern is focused on the battle for corporate control, "voting control of stock is the only relevant element of beneficial ownership." Thus, we hardly can agree with Judge Pollack that the language of the statute

---

12. The Milsteins concede that their group would have been required to file if the individual members had acquired additional preferred shares after the effective date of the Williams Act and within a 12-month period which amounted to more than 2% of the outstanding shares.

13. The convertible preferred stock votes share-for-share with the common stock. Each share of preferred is convertible into 1.25 shares of common stock.

compels the conclusion that individual members must acquire shares before the group can be required to file. . . .

The legislative history, as well as the purpose behind section 13(d), bears out our interpretation. Any residual doubt over its soundness is obviated by the following clear statement appearing in both the House and Senate reports accompanying the Williams Act:

> "[Section 13(d)(3)] would prevent a group of persons who seek to pool their voting or other interests in the securities of any issuer from evading the provisions of the statute because no one individual owns more than 10 percent of the securities. *The group would be deemed to have become the beneficial owner, directly or indirectly, of more than 10 percent of a class of securities at the time they agreed to act in concert. Consequently, the group would be required to file the information called for in section 13(d)(1) within 10 days after they agree to act together, whether or not any member of the group had acquired any securities at that time.*" S. Rep. No. 550, 90th Cong., 1st Sess. 8 (1967); H.R. Rep. No. 1711, 90th Cong., 2d Sess. 8-9 (1968), U.S. Code Cong. & Admin. News, p. 2818 (*Emphasis added.*)

Indeed, Professor Loss, one of the foremost scholars of securities law, reached the same interpretation in his treatise, citing this passage. 6 L. Loss, Securities Regulation 3664 (Supp. 1969).

The Senate and House reports and the Act as finally enacted, contrary to appellees' contention,[15] are entirely consistent in our view. This conclusion is buttressed by a consideration of the purpose of the Act. The 1960's on Wall Street may best be remembered for the pyrotechnics of corporate takeovers and the phenomenon of conglomeration. Although individuals seeking control through a proxy contest were required to comply with section 14(a) of the Securities Exchange Act and the proxy rules promulgated by the SEC, and those making stock tender offers were required to comply with the applicable provisions of the Securities Act, before the enactment of the Williams Act there were no provisions regulating cash tender offers or other techniques of securing corporate control. According to the committee reports:

> "The [Williams Act] would correct the current gap in our securities laws by amending the Securities Exchange Act of 1934 to provide for full disclosure in connection with cash tender offers and other techniques for accumulating large blocks of equity securities of publicly held companies." S. Rep. No. 550 at 4; H.R. Rep. No. 1711 at 4, U.S. Code Cong. & Admin. News p. 2814.

Specifically, we were told, "the purpose of section 13(d) is to require disclosure of information by persons who have acquired a substantial interest, or increased their interest in the equity securities of a company by a substantial amount, within a relatively short period of time." S. Rep. No. 550 at 7; H.R. Rep. No. 1711 at 8, U.S. Code Cong. & Admin. News p. 2818. Otherwise, investors cannot

---

15. Appellees in their brief "concede" that the 1968 committee reports are "against" them. Professor Loss, co-counsel for the Milsteins both in this and the lower court, informed us at the argument that the view set forth in his treatise was "a mistake" and that this passage is "diametrically opposed to the text of the statute" and the purpose and intent of the Williams Act.

assess the potential for changes in corporate control and adequately evaluate the company's worth.[16]

That the purpose of section 13(d) is to alert the marketplace to every large, rapid aggregation or accumulation of securities, regardless of technique employed, which might represent a potential shift in corporate control is amply reflected in the enacted provisions. Section 13(d)(1)(C) requires the person filing to disclose any intention to acquire control. If he has such an intention, he must disclose any plans for liquidating the issuer, selling its assets, merging it with another company or changing substantially its business or corporate structure. It is of some interest, moreover, that section 13(d)(6)(D) empowers the Commission to exempt from the filing requirements "any acquisition . . . as not entered into for the purpose of, and not having the effect of, changing or influencing the control of the issuer *or otherwise* as not comprehended within the purpose of [section 13(d)]." (*Emphasis added.*)

The alleged conspiracy on the part of the Milsteins is one clearly intended to be encompassed within the reach of section 13(d). We have before us four shareholders who together own 10.25% of an outstanding class of securities and allegedly agreed to pool their holdings to effect a takeover of GAF. This certainly posed as great a threat to the stability of the corporate structure as the individual shareholder who buys 10.25% of the equity security in one transaction.[17] A shift in the *loci* of corporate power and influence is hardly dependent on an actual transfer of legal title to shares, and the statute and history are clear on this.

In light of the statutory purpose as we view it, we find ourselves in disagreement with the interpretation of *Bath Industries, supra,* that the group owning more than 10%, despite its agreement to seize control, in addition, must agree to acquire more shares before the filing requirement of section 13(d) is triggered. The history and language of section 13(d) make it clear that the statute was primarily concerned with disclosure of *potential changes* in control resulting from new aggregations of stockholdings and was not intended to be restricted to only individual stockholders who made future purchases and whose actions were, therefore, more apparent.[18] *[Citation omitted.]* It hardly can be questioned that a group holding sufficient shares can effect a takeover without purchasing a single additional share of stock. . . .

The Milsteins also caution us against throwing our hook into the water and catching too many fish—namely, hundreds of families and other management groups which control companies with registered securities and whose members collectively own more than 5% of a class of the company's stock. Although this

---

16. The committee reports make it clear that the Act was designed for the benefit of investors and not to tip the balance of regulation either in favor of management or in favor of the person seeking corporate control. *See* S. Rep. No. 550 at 3-4; H.R. Rep. No. 1711 at 4.

17. The appellees correctly argue that section 13(d) was not intended to be retroactive— that is, all persons who held 10% of an outstanding class before July 29, 1968, are not required to file unless they acquire an additional 2% after that date. *Compare* §16(a). But, the Milstein group is not a "person" who held its stock before the effective date of the Williams Act, if the allegations of the complaint are to be accepted. The crucial event under section 13(d) was the formation of the group, which allegedly occurred after the effective date and the purpose of which was to seize control of GAF.

18. Section 13(d)(3) refers to groups formed "for the purpose of acquiring, holding, *or* disposing of securities." *Bath Industries* would read out "holding" and "disposing."

problem is not part of the narrow issue we must decide, we cannot close our eyes to the implications of our decision. Upon examination, however, the argument while superficially appealing proves to be totally without substance. Management groups *per se* are not customarily formed for the purpose of "acquiring, holding, or disposing of securities of [the] issuer" and would not be required to file unless the members conspired to pool their securities interests for one of the stated purposes.[20] . . .

QUESTIONS

1.　Why did Congress impose the §13(d) filing obligation?

2.　Since the Milsteins owned their GAF stock before the Williams Act became effective, what triggered their obligation to file under §13(d)?

3.　If §13(d)(6) exempts acquisitions that in the course of the preceding 12 months do not exceed 2 percent of the class, why did the Milsteins' activity with respect to the common stock of GAF trigger a §13(d) filing obligation?

4.　What does it take to form a "group"?

5.　What is the public policy justification for imposing the disclosure obligation of §13(d) on a group who acquires or holds more than 5 percent of a class of Target's equity securities? Whose interests are to be protected by mandating this disclosure?

6.　What is the regulatory gap that the disclosure obligations imposed under §13(d) of the Williams Act are intended to address?

NOTES

1. Rule 13d-3.　The holding of the principal case has now been codified by the SEC in its Rule 13d-3, reflecting the *GAF* court's "group theory" of beneficial ownership such that will trigger the obligation to file a Schedule 13D.

2. Schedule 13D vs. Schedule 13G Filers.　The SEC's rules permit certain large shareholders to file a more abbreviated form of disclosure on Schedule 13G. In general, Schedule 13G will be filed by "passive shareholders"; that is, shareholders who do not seek to acquire or influence "control" of the issuer and who beneficially own less than 20 percent of the issuer's shares. The SEC's rules also provide that if Schedule 13G filers no longer hold their shares for passive investment purposes (or if their shareholdings exceed 20 percent), then

---

20. The more difficult question, and a question we need not decide on this appeal, is whether management groups which expressly agree to pool their interests to fight a potential takeover are subject to section 13(d). Nor do we intimate any view on whether an insurgent group which has filed under section 13(d) and subsequently is successful in its takeover bid remains subject to the section. In any event, as we have already indicated, the Commission can forestall any untoward effects under the exemptive power conferred upon it by section 13(d)(6)(D).

a Schedule 13D must be filed within ten days. In addition, these passive share-holders must make an annual Schedule 13G filing with the SEC within forty-five days after the end of each calendar year.

3. Stock Parking as a Violation of §13(d).   The "parking of shares" can give rise to a violation of §13(d). In the typical *stock parking* arrangement, one trader will agree to buy shares of a publicly traded company on the open market and to hold these shares for the benefit of another trader, whose identity can then be concealed from other market participants. These arrangements will very often include unwritten agreements on the part of the beneficial owner of the shares to protect the buyer of the shares against losses and to share profits. These arrangements to "park shares" in the account of another trading professional allow the beneficial owner to carve up ownership of the company's stock in order to avoid the disclosure requirements of §13(d), which would otherwise be triggered once the beneficial owner crossed the 5 percent threshold. Parking violations were made famous in the 1980s as a result of the SEC's prosecution of Ivan Boesky; as described in more detail in Chapter 7; this investigation ultimately led to the downfall of Michael Milken and his firm, Drexel Burnham Lambert.

4. The Role of Risk Arbitrageurs.   Ivan Boesky's firm was known as a "risk arbitrageur," which essentially means that his firm specialized in buying shares of a company that was the target of a takeover. As we have seen in earlier chapters (and as we shall see in the takeover cases that we will read later in this chapter and in Chapter 7), the market, or trading, price of Target's shares is usually less than the share price being offered by the Bidder as part of its tender offer for Target's publicly traded shares. The spread (i.e., the difference) between the trading price and the offering price is largely a function of the market's assessment of the probability of Bidder being able to complete the deal and the timing of the closing on the deal, if it is ultimately completed. Traders (such as Ivan Boesky's firm) are essentially making a "Las Vegas-style" bet that there will be a takeover of Target. Of course, from the perspective of risk arbitrage firms, the downside risk is that the deal falls apart, in which case the arbitrage firm loses the opportunity to "cash in" (i.e., tender) its shares to Bidder and receive the offering price. This type of risk arbitrage activity is today, and always has been, an accepted part of M&A activity. As such, risk arbitrageurs serve the legitimate and useful economic function of allowing professional traders to assume much of the financial risk that is inherent in trading shares of companies who are engaged in takeover battles. However, as we shall see in the takeover cases in this chapter as well as in Chapter 7, arbitrage firms are essentially traders with a very short term investment horizon, and therefore, are essentially betting on the success of the takeover bid.

5. Proposals to Reform Section 13(d)'s "10 Day Window."   In March 2011, the law firm of Wachtel, Lipton, Rosen, & Katz submitted a rule-making proposal to the SEC, asking the commission to close the current "ten-day window between crossing the 5 percent disclosure threshold and the initial filing deadline" for a Schedule 13D. The basis for this proposal centered on "[r]ecent maneuvers by activist investors both in the U.S. and abroad that have demonstrated the extent to which current reporting gaps may be exploited, to the detriment of issuers, other investors, and the market as a whole." Wachtell, Lipton, Rosen, & Katz, *Petition for Rulemaking Under Section 13 of the Securities Exchange Act of 1934*, Mar. 7, 2011, *available at:* www .sec.gov/rules/petitions/2011/petn4-624.pdf (Wachtell Lipton Petition). Since this proposal was originally submitted, Wachtell Lipton has expanded on the public policy premise for its proposed reform measures as follows:

> Our [rule-making] petition included the proposal that the disclosure window in the SEC's rules implementing Section 13(d) be reduced from ten days to one business day. This proposal reflects the reality that the mechanics of accumulation that exist today allow blockholders to accumulate massive stakes in the ten-day window, thereby defeating the statutory purpose of alerting the market to creeping threats to control. The trading world has changed around the rule, with the result that the rule no longer does the work for which the statute was enacted. The [Wachtel Lipton Petition] noted numerous situations in which aggressive investors have taken advantage of the legal loophole to build enormously powerful, control-threatening stakes in their ten-day windows, and further highlighted that other sophisticated securities markets have already taken regulatory steps to reduce the risk of undisclosed rapid accumulations . . . [In addition, the Wachtel Lipton Petition] sought to ensure that the [Section 13(d)] reporting rules would continue to operate in a way broadly consistent with the statute's clear purposes* and that loopholes that have arisen by changing market conditions and practices since the statute's adoption over forty years ago could not continue to be exploited by acquirers, to the detriment of the public markets and security holders. The changes suggested by the [Wachtel Lipton Petition] would bring the U.S. blockholder reporting regime broadly in line with those of virtually all other major developed economies.

Adam O. Emmerich, Theodore N. Mirvis, et al., *Fair Markets and Fair Disclosure: Some Thoughts on the Law and Economics of Blockholder Disclosure, and the Use and Abuse of Shareholder Power*, Columbia Law & Economics Working Paper No. 428 (2012), *available at:* http://ssrn.com/abstract=2138945.

Wachtell Lipton's reform proposal has generated considerable controversy. Most notably, Professors Lucian Bebchuk and Robert Jackson, Jr., countered by submitting a letter to the SEC in July 2011, challenging the public policy premise underlying the Wachtell Lipton proposal. *See* Lucian A. Bebchuk and Robert J. Jackson, Jr., *Letter to the Securities and Exchange Commission Regarding Commission Examination of Section 13(d) Rules and Rulemaking Petition Submitted by Wachtell, Lipton, Rosen, and Katz, LLP,* July 11, 2011, *available at:* www.sec.gov/comments/ 4-624/4624 -3.pdf. More specifically, they explain that

> [First, there is] significant empirical evidence indicating that the accumulation and holding of outside blocks in public companies benefits shareholders by making incumbent directors and managers more accountable and thereby reducing agency costs and managerial slack.

---

* [By the author: As set forth in the legislative history, the purpose of Section 13(d) is "to alert the marketplace to every large, rapid aggregation or accumulation of securities," *GAF Corp. v. Milstein*, 453 F.2d 709, 717 (2d Cir. 1971), as well as to provide shareholders with "full disclosure when over 5 percent of their company stock is acquired by an outside group." H.R. Rep. No. 91-1125 (1970).]

Second, we explain that tightening the rules applicable to outside blockholders can be expected to reduce the returns to blockholders and thereby reduce
the incidence and size of outside blocks—and, thus, blockholders' investments in
monitoring and engagement, which in turn could result in increased agency costs
and managerial slack.

Third, we explain that there is currently no empirical evidence to support
[Wachtell Lipton's] assertion that changes in trading technologies and practices
have recently led to a significant increase in pre-disclosure accumulations of ownership stakes by outside blockholders.

Fourth, we explain that, since the passage of Section 13, changes in state
law—including the introduction of poison pills with low-ownership triggers that
impede outside blockholders that are not seeking control—have tilted the playing field against such blockholders.

Finally, we explain that a tightening of the rules [as suggested in Wachtell
Lipton's proposal] cannot be justified on the grounds that such tightening is
needed to protect investors from the possibility that outside blockholders will capture a control premium at other shareholders' expense.

We conclude by recommending that the [SEC] pursue a comprehensive
examination of the rules governing outside blockholders and the empirical questions raised by our analysis. In the meantime, the [SEC] should not adopt new
rules that tighten restrictions on outside blockholders. Existing research and
available empirical evidence provide no basis for concluding that tightening the
rules governing outside blockholders would satisfy the requirement that [SEC]
rulemaking protect investors and promote efficiency—and indeed raise concerns
that such tightening could harm investors and undermine efficiency.

Id.; see also Lucian A. Bebchuk and Robert J. Jackson, Jr., *The Law and Economics
of Blockholder Disclosure,* 2 HARV. BUS. L. REV. 40 (Spring 2012).

In the face of this controversy, the SEC responded in December 2011 by
announcing its plans to undertake a comprehensive review of its beneficial
reporting rules. *See* Chairwoman Mary L. Schapiro, Remarks at the Transatlantic
Corporate Governance Dialogue, U.S. Securities and Exchange Commission,
Washington, D.C., Dec. 15, 2011, www.sec.gov/news/speech/2011/
spch121511mls.htm. In making this announcement, the SEC indicated that

[t]he review process will begin with a concept release and will address
whether the 10-day initial filing requirement for Schedule 13D filings should be
shortened; whether beneficial ownership reporting of cash-settled equity swaps
and other types of derivative instruments should be clarified and strengthened;
and how the presentation of information on Schedule 13D and Schedule 13G can
be improved.

Chairwoman Schapiro [also] noted that under [Section 929R of] the Dodd-
Frank Wall Street Reform and Consumer Protection Act, the SEC has new statutory
authority to shorten the 10-day filing period for initial Schedule 13D filings, as well
as to regulate beneficial ownership reporting of security-based swaps. Specifically,
Congress modified §13(d)(1) of the Exchange Act to read, "within ten days after
such acquisition, or *within such shorter time as the Commission may establish by rule.*"
With this modification, Congress . . . [has] laid the legislative groundwork for
needed reform in this area.

David Katz and Laura McIntosh, *Corporate Governance Update: Section 13(d)
Reporting Requirements Need Updating,* N. Y. LAW J., Mar. 22, 2012, (*emphasis in*

original), *available at:* https://www.wlrk.com/webdocs/wlrknew/WLRKMemos/ WLRK/WLRK.21665.12.pdf.

While no action has been taken by the SEC to address reform of its beneficial reporting rules as of Fall 2020, the controversy surrounding the section 13(d) "10-day window" continues to swirl. In April 2015, "[s]everal public watchdog organizations . . . sent a letter to the leaders of two congressional committees urging that Congress take action to shorten the 10-day filing period applicable to Schedule 13D . . . [which these watchdog organizations now contend is being] exploited by hedge fund activists to hide their share accumulations . . ." Cydney Posner, *Will Congress Shorten the 10-Day Window Applicable to Filing Schedule 13D?*, April 16, 2015, *available at:* http://www.lexology.com/ library/detail.aspx?g=15beac2f-6fbf-44a7-addb-a08c7110fdb6. And legislation (known as the Brokaw Act, S. 2720) was originally introduced in March 2016 by U.S. senators Tammy Baldwin (D-Wisc.) and Jeff Merkley (D-Ore.) to amend Section 13(d). Among other things, the Brokaw Act[5] would reduce the Schedule 13D filing window from ten calendar days to two business days. While "the bill faces significant hurdles in moving through Congress, it nevertheless has considerable support among U.S. Senators, including Elizabeth Warren (D-Mass.) and Bernie Sanders (I-Vt.)." Sidley Austin, LLP, *Proposed Legislation Would Increase 13D and Other Securities Disclosure Requirements for Hedge Funds and Others*, May 31, 2016, *available at:* https://www.sidley.com/en/insights/newsupdates/2016/05/proposed-legislation-would-increase-securities; *see also* Jason N. Ader and Eric Jackson, *Senate Bill Would Limit Shareholder Rights*, N. Y. Times, Mar. 24, 2016, *available at:* http://www.nytimes.com/2016/03/25/business/ dealbook/senate-bill-would-limit-shareholder-rights.html. "The [original] legislation went nowhere, but in the late summer of 2017, Senator Baldwin (D-WI) and Senator David Perdue (R-GA) re-introduced the Brokaw Act,* bipartisan 'legislation [that is intended] to increase transparency and strengthen oversight of predatory activist hedge funds.' The re-introduced legislation would decrease the [section] 13(d) [filing] period from ten days to four days, up from the earlier proposal." Brav, et al., *supra* at 332; *see also*, National Investor Relations Institute, *The Case for 13D Reform*, Sept. 24, 2019, *available at:* https://www.niri. org/NIRI/media/NIRI/Advocacy/NIRI-Case-for-13D-Reform-2019-final.pdf.

2. The Remedy for §13(d) Violations

‖ Rondeau v. Mosinee Paper Corporation
422 U.S. 49, 95 S. Ct. 2069, 45 L. Ed. 2d 12 (1975)

Mr. Chief Justice Burger delivered the opinion of the Court.

---

5. "Sponsoring Senators named [the legislation] after a small town in Wisconsin [Brokaw] that, according to the Act's sponsors, was decimated by the actions of a hedge fund activist in shutting down the local paper mill with a loss of hundreds of jobs." Alon Brav, J. B. Heaton, and Jonathan Zandberg, *Failed Anti-Activist Legislation: The Curious Case of the Brokaw Act*, 11 J. Bus. Entrepreneurship & L. 329 (2018).

* [By the author: *See* the Brokaw Act, S. 1744, 115th Cong. (2017), *available at:* https:// www.congress.gov/bill/115th congress/senatebill/1744/all info.]

I

Respondent Mosinee Paper Corp. is a Wisconsin company engaged in the manufacture and sale of paper, paper products, and plastics. Its principal place of business is located in Mosinee, Wis., and its only class of equity security is common stock which is registered under §12 of the Securities Exchange Act of 1934, 15 U.S.C. §78l. At all times relevant to this litigation there were slightly more than 800,000 shares of such stock outstanding.

In April 1971 petitioner Francis A. Rondeau, a Mosinee businessman, began making large purchases of respondent's common stock in the over-the-counter market. . . . By May 17, 1971, petitioner had acquired 40,413 shares of respondent's stock, which constituted more than 5% of those outstanding. He was therefore required to comply with the disclosure provisions of the Williams Act, by filing a Schedule 13D with respondent and the Securities and Exchange Commission within 10 days. That form would have disclosed, among other things, the number of shares beneficially owned by petitioner, the source of the funds used to purchase them, and petitioner's purpose in making the purchases.

Petitioner did not file a Schedule 13D but continued to purchase substantial blocks of respondent's stock. By July 30, 1971, he had acquired more than 60,000 shares. On that date the chairman of respondent's board of directors informed him by letter that his activity had "given rise to numerous rumors" and "seems to have created some problems under the Federal Securities Laws. . . ." Upon receiving the letter petitioner immediately stopped placing orders for respondent's stock and consulted his attorney. On August 25, 1971, he filed a Schedule 13D which, in addition to the other required disclosures, described the "Purpose of Transaction" as follows:

"Francis A. Rondeau determined during early part of 1971 that the common stock of the Issuer [respondent] was undervalued in the over-the-counter market and represented a good investment vehicle for future income and appreciation. Francis A. Rondeau and his associates presently propose to seek to acquire additional common stock of the Issuer in order to obtain effective control of the Issuer, but such investments as originally determined were and are not necessarily made with this objective in mind. Consideration is currently being given to making a public cash tender offer to the shareholders of the Issuer at a price which will reflect current quoted prices for such stock with some premium added."

Petitioner also stated that, in the event that he did obtain control of respondent, he would consider making changes in management "in an effort to provide a Board of Directors which is more representative of all of the shareholders, particularly those outside of present management. . . ." One month later petitioner amended the form to reflect more accurately the allocation of shares between himself and his companies.

On August 27 respondent sent a letter to its shareholders informing them of the disclosures in petitioner's Schedule 13D.[3] The letter stated that by his

---

3. Respondent simultaneously issued a press release containing the same information. Almost immediately the price of its stock jumped to $19-$21 per share. A few days later it dropped back to the prevailing price of $12.50-$14 per share, where it remained.

"tardy filing" petitioner had "withheld the information to which you [the share-holders] were entitled for more than two months, in violation of federal law." In addition, while agreeing that "recent market prices have not reflected the real value of your Mosinee stock," respondent's management could "see little in Mr. Rondeau's background that would qualify him to offer any meaning full guidance to a Company in the highly technical and competitive paper industry."

Six days later respondent initiated this suit in the United States District Court for the Western District of Wisconsin. . . . It alleged further that share-holders who had "sold shares without the information which defendants were required to disclose lacked information material to their decision whether to sell or hold," and that respondent "was unable to communicate such informa-tion to its stockholders, and to take such actions as their interest required." Respondent prayed for an injunction prohibiting petitioner and his codefen-dants from voting or pledging their stock and from acquiring additional shares, requiring them to divest themselves of stock which they already owned, and for damages. A motion for a preliminary injunction was filed with the complaint but later withdrawn.

After three months of pretrial proceedings petitioner moved for summary judgment. He readily conceded that he had violated the Williams Act, but con-tended that the violation was due to a lack of familiarity with the securities laws and that neither respondent nor its shareholders had been harmed. The District Court agreed. It found no material issues of fact to exist regarding petitioner's lack of willfulness in failing to timely file a Schedule 13D, concluding that he dis-covered his obligation to do so on July 30, 1971, and that there was no basis in the record for disputing his claim that he first considered the possibility of obtaining control of respondent some time after that date. The District Court therefore held that petitioner and his codefendants "did not engage in intentional covert, and conspiratorial conduct in failing to timely file the 13D Schedule." . . .

The Court of Appeals reversed, with one judge dissenting. . . .

II. . .

The Court of Appeals' conclusion that respondent suffered "harm" suf-ficient to require sterilization of petitioner's stock need not long detain us. The purpose of the Williams Act is to insure that public shareholders who are confronted by a cash tender offer for their stock will not be required to respond without adequate information regarding the qualifications and inten-tions of the offering party.[8] By requiring disclosure of information to the target

---

8. The Senate Report describes the dilemma facing such a shareholder as follows:

   "He has many alternatives. He can tender all of his shares immediately and hope they are all purchased. However, if the offer is for less than all the outstanding shares, perhaps only a part of them will be taken. In these instances, he will remain a shareholder in the company, under a new management which he has helped to install without knowing whether it will be good or bad for the company."

corporation as well as the Securities and Exchange Commission, Congress intended to do no more than give incumbent management an opportunity to express and explain its position. The Congress expressly disclaimed an intention to provide a weapon for management to discourage takeover bids or prevent large accumulations of stock which would create the potential for such attempts. Indeed, the Act's draftsmen commented upon the "extreme care" which was taken "to avoid tipping the balance of regulation either in favor of management or in favor of the person making the takeover bid." [Senate Report at 3]. . . .

The short of the matter is that none of the evils to which the Williams Act was directed has occurred or is threatened in this case. Petitioner has not attempted to obtain control of respondent, either by a cash tender offer or any other device. Moreover, he has now filed a proper Schedule 13D, and there has been no suggestion that he will fail to comply with the Act's requirement of reporting any material changes in the information contained therein.[9] On this record there is no likelihood that respondent's shareholders will be disadvantaged should petitioner make a tender offer, or that respondent will be unable to adequately place its case before them should a contest for control develop. Thus, the usual basis for injunctive relief, "that there exists some cognizable danger of recurrent violation," is not present here. United States v. W.T. Grant, 345 U.S. 629, 633 (1953).

Nor are we impressed by respondent's argument that an injunction is necessary to protect the interests of its shareholders who either sold their stock to petitioner at predisclosure prices or would not have invested had they known that a takeover bid was imminent. As observed, the principal object of the Williams Act is to solve the dilemma of shareholders desiring to respond to a cash tender offer, and it is not at all clear that the type of "harm" identified by respondent is redressable under its provisions. In any event, those persons who allegedly sold at an unfairly depressed price have an adequate remedy by way of an action for damages, thus negating the basis for equitable relief.[10]

"The shareholder, as another alternative, may wait to see if a better offer develops, but if he tenders late, he runs the risk that none of his shares will be taken. He may also sell his shares in the market or hold them and hope for the best. Without knowledge of who the bidder is and what he plans to do, the shareholder cannot reach an informed decision."

S. Rep. No. 550, 90th Cong., 1st Sess., 2 (1967) ["Senate Report"]. However, the Report also recognized "that takeover bids should not be discouraged because they serve a useful purpose in providing a check on entrenched but inefficient management." Id., at 3.

9. Because this case involves only the availability of injunctive relief to remedy a §13(d) violation following compliance with the reporting requirements, it does not require us to decide whether or under what circumstances a corporation could obtain a decree enjoining a shareholder who is currently in violation of §13(d) from acquiring further shares, exercising voting rights, or launching a takeover bid, pending compliance with the reporting requirements.

10. The Court was advised by respondent that such a suit is now pending in the District Court and class action certification has been sought. Although we intimate no views regarding the merits of that case, it provides a potential sanction for petitioner's violation of the Williams Act.

Similarly, the fact that the second group of shareholders for whom respondent expresses concern have retained the benefits of their stock and the lack of an imminent contest for control make the possibility of damage to them remote at best. . . .

   Reversed and remanded with directions.

Chromalloy American Corp. v. Sun Chemical Corp.
611 F.2d 240 (8th Cir. 1979)

HENLEY, Circuit Judge.

This case, arising under disclosure provisions of [§13(d) of] the Securities Exchange Act of 1934, requires us to decide whether the district court erred in the partial grant and partial denial of preliminary injunctive relief.

Plaintiff-appellant Chromalloy American Corporation (Chromalloy) appeals the denial of injunctive relief which would compel defendant Sun Chemical Corporation to disclose its proposals for control of Chromalloy, and which would halt the purchase of Chromalloy stock by Sun for ninety days. Defendants-appellees Sun Chemical Corporation (Sun) and Norman E. Alexander cross-appeal from the district court's order that Sun disclose an intention to obtain control of Chromalloy. . . .

In January, 1978 Sun Chemical Corporation began purchasing significant amounts of Chromalloy stock on the New York Stock Exchange. Chromalloy is a diversified corporation with revenues in fiscal year 1978 of nearly $1.4 billion and net earnings of $47 million, while Sun is a considerably smaller corporation with 1978 revenues of $394 million and net earnings of $20 million. Norman E. Alexander is Chief Executive Officer and Chairman of Sun's Board of Directors, and has been instrumental in instigating and furthering the purchase of Chromalloy stock by Sun Chemical Corporation.

By February 5, 1979 Sun had acquired 605,620 shares, or 5.2 percent, of Chromalloy's total outstanding shares. Sun was therefore required to comply with the disclosure provisions of §13(d) of the Securities Exchange Act. Pursuant to the disclosure requirements, Sun on February 5, 1979 filed its first Schedule 13D. Sun stated that its acquisitions were for investment; that it had no present intention of seeking control of Chromalloy; that it presently intended to continue to increase its holdings; that the amount of such increase had not been determined; that Sun had been discussing with certain directors and members of Chromalloy management the possible increase in Sun's holdings; and that Sun might "at any time determine to seek control of Chromalloy." In four subsequent amendments to the Schedule 13D between April, 1979 and late July, 1979 Sun reported its plans to purchase additional stock, its unsuccessful attempt to gain representation on the Chromalloy Board, and its negotiations regarding a "stand-still" agreement whereby Sun would limit its purchases for a period of time as a condition of representation on the Chromalloy Board. In each of the amendments to its Schedule 13D Sun disclaimed any intent to control Chromalloy.

By late July, 1979 Sun's ownership had increased to nearly ten per cent of Chromalloy's outstanding stock. . . .

Under the provisions of the revised SEC regulations, we are confronted with two distinct questions: first, whether the district court erred in finding that Sun has a disclosable purpose to acquire control, and second, whether the district court abused its discretion in refusing to order disclosure of Sun's proposals for corporate changes aside from Sun's control intent.

In assessing Sun's obligation to disclose a control purpose, we look to the definition of "control" appearing in [SEC] Rule 12b-2(f), 17 C.F.R. §240.12b-2(f) (1979), made applicable to Schedule 13D filings by 17 C.F.R. §240.12b-1 (1979).[12] Rule 12b-2(f) provides:

> *Control.* The term "control" (including the terms "controlling", "controlled by" and "under common control with") means the possession, directly or indirectly, of the power to direct or cause the direction of the management and policies of a person, whether through the ownership of voting securities, by contract, or otherwise.

17 C.F.R. §240.12b-2(f) (1979).

. . . Contrary to Sun's first contention, Sun's desire to influence substantially the policies, management and actions of Chromalloy amounts to a purpose to control Chromalloy. There is ample support in the record for the finding of a control purpose. Sun has disclosed its plans to acquire twenty per cent of Chromalloy's stock, its attempts to gain representation on Chromalloy's Board, and its intention to review continually its position with respect to Chromalloy. The district court further found that Sun has prepared an "acquisition model" with Chromalloy as a "target"; that Norman Alexander first learned of the investment opportunities in Chromalloy when a brokerage firm informed him that the thirty-five per cent of common stock held by insiders was not in a solid management block; that Norman Alexander's private memoranda have been concerned from the start with the split on Chromalloy's Board of Directors as a possible avenue to power; and that according to an investment banker, Sun's projected twenty per cent interest in Chromalloy would be a wise business decision only if Sun is attempting to gain control. Taken together, these facts support the finding that Sun proposes to control Chromalloy through a combination of numbers and influence.

As a matter of law, Rule 12b-2(f) contemplates that influence can be an element of control. Control is defined to include "the [*indirect*] power to . . . cause the direction of . . . policies." Disclosure of a control purpose may be required where the securities purchaser has a perceptible desire to influence substantially the issuer's operations. . . .

Moreover, the Securities Exchange Act is remedial legislation and is to be broadly construed in order to give effect to its intent. . . . To protect the

---

12. Although revised Item 4 [of Schedule 13D] does not use the term "control", we assume that any control purpose is still measurable against the definition of control appearing in Rule 12b-2(f).

Cases decided before the revision of Item 4 have considered the definition of "control" in Rule 12b-2(f) to be controlling. *TSC Industries, Inc. v. Northway, Inc.,* 426 U.S. 438, 451 n. 13, 96 S. Ct. 2126, 48 L. Ed. 2d 757 (1976); *Graphic Sciences, Inc. v. International Mogul Mines Ltd.,* 397 F. Supp. 112, 125 & n. 37 (D.D.C. 1974).

investing public through full and fair disclosure of Sun's intentions, the district court was justified in defining control to include working control and substantial influence.

Sun next contends that the district court failed to find a "fixed plan" to acquire control of Chromalloy. This fact is not determinative. Item 4 of Schedule 13D requires disclosure of a purpose to acquire control, even though this intention has not taken shape as a fixed plan. We do not agree with Sun's contention that disclosure of Sun's control purpose will mislead investors by overstating the definiteness of Sun's plans. . . . Item 4 specifically requires disclosure of a purpose to acquire control, regardless of the definiteness or even the existence of any plans to implement this purpose. . . .

In sum, we find no error of law and no abuse of discretion in the district court's order that Sun disclose a purpose to seek control of Chromalloy.

We also perceive no abuse of discretion in the district court's refusal to order disclosures beyond Sun's court-approved Schedule 13D. . . .

In the present case, Sun's long-range hopes for certain corporate changes could prove misleading to investors if disclosed as firm proposals. The district court's findings of fact indicate that Sun has made the following tentative overtures towards corporate changes: Norman Alexander once told Moody's Investor Services that any deal with Chromalloy "would be done with Chromalloy's money or they would get out"; Alexander "hoped" Chromalloy would eventually seek to acquire the assets of Sun; Sun commissioned a study to recommend which divisions of Chromalloy are most feasible to sell off; Alexander expressed the opinion that a profit could be realized if a trim-down of Chromalloy were properly executed; and Alexander offered to "take care of" certain Chromalloy Board members in return for their support. Each of these items involves little more than an unconsummated hope, feasibility study, or opinion, not a firm plan or proposal. We note also that Sun and Alexander have to date been denied a seat on Chromalloy's Board of Directors, and are seemingly not in a position to precipitate any of the hoped-for changes.

The degree of specificity with which future plans must be detailed in Schedule 13D filings presents a difficult question. . . . Thus, within the scope of its discretion, the district court might have required further disclosures of Sun. However, given the arguable danger of overstatement and the rule that parties are not required to disclose plans which are contingent or indefinite, we hold that the district court's order refusing further disclosures involved no abuse of discretion.

The final issue on appeal is whether the district court abused its discretion in refusing Chromalloy's request for a cooling-off period, the mailing of a restated Schedule 13D to Chromalloy shareholders at Sun's expense and the publication of a restated Schedule 13D in the press.

We consider the argument for additional injunctive relief in light of the principles set forth by the Supreme Court in *Rondeau v. Mosinee Paper Corp.*, 422 U.S. 49, 95 S. Ct. 2069, 45 L. Ed. 2d 12 (1975). The Court in *Rondeau* considered the availability of injunctive relief to remedy a §13(d) violation following compliance with the reporting requirements. Recognizing that the injunctive process is designed to deter, not to punish, *id.*, at 61, the Court held that injunctive relief under the Williams Act was subject to traditional equitable limitations.

Relief beyond compliance with the reporting requirements is justified only if the petitioner can show irreparable harm in the absence of such relief. *Id.*[18]

We have concluded that the Schedule 13D approved by the district court adequately discloses Sun's control intention. Given Sun's compliance with §13(d), we do not perceive such ongoing harm to Chromalloy or its present shareholders[19] as would justify a cooling-off period or a stockholder mailing. Shareholders who were misinformed by Sun's original Schedule 13D and amendments have been reapprised by the same form of communication. . . .

There is also no precedent for a cooling-off period. In the closely analogous context of misleading tender offers, courts have held that a misleading tender offer is adequately cured by an amended offer. . . .

The disclosure requirements established by Congress are not intended to provide a weapon for current management to discourage takeover bids or prevent large accumulations of stock. . . . Further injunctive relief, particularly a cooling-off period, would in the present case serve largely as a dilatory tool in the hands of current management, and for this reason was properly denied.

In sum, appellant has failed to sustain the burden of demonstrating abuse of discretion in the district court's denial of further disclosures, a cooling-off period, and a stockholder mailing. Appellees likewise fail to convince us that the district court erred as a matter of law in requiring the disclosure of Sun's control purpose.

Affirmed.

QUESTIONS

1. What is the scope of disclosure required by §13(d)? What is the remedy to be imposed if such disclosure is not made in a timely manner?

2. As a public policy matter, is there a risk to imposing the disclosure obligations required under §13(d)?

3. Is there an implied private right of action for §13(d) violations? If so, who has standing to sue?

4. What is the remedy for a violation of §13(d) —damages or injunctive relief?

---

18. Because this case involves only the availability of injunctive relief *following compliance* with §13(d), we are not required to decide what circumstances might justify a decree enjoining a shareholder who is *currently* in violation of §13(d) from acquiring further shares or exercising voting rights, pending compliance with the reporting requirements. The posture of the case is identical to *Rondeau* in this respect. *Rondeau v. Mosinee Paper Corp., supra,* 422 U.S. at 59 n. 9.

19. We do not reach the issue of harm to former Chromalloy shareholders who may have sold to Sun without attempting to garner a control premium. Chromalloy on appeal has pressed the interests of present shareholders and the public in requesting additional relief, perhaps recognizing that a cooling-off period and additional dissemination of information cannot redress the harm, if any, suffered by past shareholders who have already sold to Sun. These shareholders have an adequate remedy at law through an action for damages. *Rondeau v. Mosinee Paper Corp., supra,* 422 U.S. at 60, 97 S. Ct. 926; *Missouri Portland Cement Co. v. H.K. Porter,* 535 F.2d 388, 395, 399 (8th Cir. 1976).

NOTES

1. Amendments to Schedule 13D. As to any person (or group) that files a Schedule 13D, Rule 13d-2 requires that any "material" change in the information disclosed in a Schedule 13D must be filed "promptly." This can lead to some very practical problems in determining whether an amendment is required by the SEC's rules. Some of these problems are described by an experienced practitioner in the following excerpt:

> In general, information is considered material under U.S. securities laws if there is a substantial likelihood that disclosure of the omitted fact would be viewed by a reasonable investor as significantly altering the total mix of information available. [Consequently, if a person] that already has a Schedule 13D on file decides to purchase additional equity securities of the [Target] or merge with the [Target], such information would be considered material under U.S. securities laws. As to the timeliness of the amendment, no bright line test has been adopted by the SEC in order to determine when a Schedule 13D amendment filing is prompt. The question of whether an amendment is prompt is determined based on all of the facts and circumstances surrounding both prior disclosures by the [Schedule 13D filer] and the market's sensitivity to the particular change of fact [that triggers] the obligation to amend. Given the ability to electronically gather and file information with the SEC, [any person who has filed a Schedule 13D] would be hard pressed to explain why a material amendment to its Schedule 13D was not filed with the SEC within two to four business days after its occurrence. [In addition to raising issues as to what constitutes "timely filing" of amendments,] Schedule 13D's requirement to disclose promptly any "plans or proposals" to acquire additional securities of the [Target] or merge with the [Target] has various ramifications . . . [, not the least of which is that there] is no clear formula to determine whether a "plan or proposal" exists. Instead, U.S. courts have used broadly defined concepts to determine when a "plan or proposal" requires disclosure. . . . Case law suggests that the determination of whether a "plan or proposal" exists is a highly fact-specific inquiry and requires a fact-finding investigation. . . .

Stephen D. Bohrer, *When an Acquisition "Plan or Proposal" Requires a Schedule 13D Amendment*, 19 INSIGHTS 17 (Aug. 2005).

2. Recent Examples of Schedule 13D Disclosures. Below is an excerpt from a Schedule 13D that was filed by Chapman Capital LLC with respect to its investment in Embarcadero Technologies, Inc. (dated Mar. 12, 2007), which provides an example of one of the more outrageous disclosures to be included in a Schedule 13D filing:

Schedule 13D: Embarcadero Technologies, Inc.
Excerpt from Amendment No. 1 to Embarcadero Technologies, Inc., Schedule 13D filed by Chapman Capital LLC, dated March 12, 2007

On March 7, 2007, Mr. Chapman communicated to Mr. Shahbazian that the Board's failure to announce a definitive merger agreement no later than March 30, 2007, would result in the filing by the Reporting Persons [Chapman Capital] of an amended Schedule 13D, which should be expected to include as an exhibit a letter to the Board making public *the results of Chapman Capital's recently accelerated investigation into the Board and management of the Issuer.* Furthermore, in response to certain comments made by Mr. Shahbazian during a conversation later that day, Mr. Chapman conveyed to Mr. Shahbazian Chapman Capital's concern that, according to background checks directed by Chapman Capital, Mr. Shahbazian had been viewed negatively by various shareholders of Niku Corporation, ANDA Networks, Inc. and Walker Interactive, all of which in the past had employed Mr. Shahbazian in the capacity of Chief Financial Officer. *Mr. Shahbazian reacted temperamentally to Mr. Chapman with the eloquent response, "F[***] you!"* Mr. Chapman then forcefully informed Mr. Shahbazian that it was inappropriate and inadvisable for the Chief Financial Officer of a public company to utter such blasphemy to the advisor of a 9.3% ownership stakeholder in the Issuer. [*Emphasis in original.*]

On March 10, 2020, the prominent activist investor Carl Icahn filed a Schedule 13D with respect to the 9.9% stake ("Shares") that he and other investors in his group (the "Reporting Persons") had accumulated in Occidental Petroleum Corp. (referred to in the filing as "Issuer" or "Company"). The excerpt below, from Carl Icahn's Schedule 13D, reflects a more traditional (although no less colorful) approach to the disclosure that is required by Item 4 of Schedule 13D. However, before examining the Schedule 13D excerpt, a brief description of the events that led Carl Icahn to acquire his stake in Occidental is in order.

In April 2019, Chevron Corp., the second-biggest U.S. energy company, announced its proposal to acquire Anadarko Petroleum Corp., an oil and gas driller engaged in hydrocarbon exploration, "in a cash and stock deal valued at $33 billion." Berkeley Lovelace Jr., et al., *Chevron to Buy Anadarko Petroleum in a $33 Billion Cash and Stock Deal*, CNBC, April 19, 2019, *available at:* https://www.cnbc.com/2019/04/12/chevron-to-buy-anadarko-petroleum-in-a-33-billion-cash-and-stock-deal.html. Chevron's bid for Anadarko was quickly matched by Occidental Petroleum, leading to a bidding war between the parties. In its initial bid, Occidental offered to purchase Anadarko for $70 per share, thereby topping Chevron's initial bid of $65 per share. *Id.* Two weeks later, Occidental increased its bid to $76 per share in a cash and stock deal that valued Anadarko at $57 billion. *See* Daniel Faber, *Occidental Petroleum Bids $76 a Share for Anadarko, Trumping Chevron Offer for the Driller,* CNBC, April 24, 2019, *available at:* https://www.cnbc.com/2019/04/24/occidental-petroleum-bids-76-a-share-for-anadarko-trumping-chevron-offer.html. For its part, Anadarko entered into negotiations with Chevron, and Anadarko eventually agreed to sell its business to Chevron for $65 per share. The parties entered into a merger agreement that, among other things, called for payment of a $1 billion termination fee[6] under certain circumstances.

---

6. As part of the materials in Chapter 7, we will discuss the use of termination fees as a customary provision in today's M&A transactions involving publicly traded companies. *See* pp. 664-723 of Chapter 7.

The next step in this bidding war saw Occidental revise its $76 a share offer to increase the cash component of the bid. *See* Tom DiChristopher, *Occidental Revises Bid for Anadarko in Buyout Battle with Chevron, Offers Mostly Cash*, CNBC, May 5, 2019, *available at:* https://www.cnbc.com/2019/05/06/occidental-revises-bid-for-anadarko-in-buyout-battle-with-chevron.html. To finance its revised bid, Occidental agreed to sell certain of Anadarko's assets for $8.8 billion, and also received a $10 billion investment from Warren Buffett's Berkshire Hathaway, Inc., in exchange for preferred stock carrying an 8% annual dividend. *Id.* The divestment and investment would provide Occidental with the necessary cash funds to close on its bid for Anadarko, but would leave Occidental with $38 billion in debt on its balance sheet. On May 9, 2019, Chevron responded to Occidental's revised takeover proposal by withdrawing its bid for Anadarko and instead taking the $1 billion termination fee. *See* Bradley Olson and Christopher Matthews, *Occidental Wins Battle for Anadarko as Chevron Exits Bidding*, May 9, 2019, WALL ST. J., *available at:* https://www.wsj.com/articles/chevron-won-t-increase-offer-for-anadarko-11557405500?mod=article_inline&mod=article_inline.

By increasing the cash component of its bid, and thus reducing the number of shares to be issued, Occidental avoided a shareholder vote to approve its proposed merger with Anadarko and thereby avoided potential shareholder rejection of its proposal to acquire Anadarko. *Id.* "By offering more cash, Occidental will no longer have to seek approval from [its] shareholders to purchase Anadarko. The risk of Occidental shareholders voting down the purchase created uncertainty that Occidental's management [would be able to close on the deal for Anadarko]." DiChristopher, *supra*. However, Occidental's revised bid prompted several investors, including Icahn, to vigorously protest management's decision. In May 2019, it was reported that Icahn had recently taken "a small stake in Occidental, said people familiar with the matter." Olson and Matthews, *supra*.

As Icahn accumulated a growing ownership interest in Occidental, he actively campaigned to fire the incumbent board and take control of the company's board of directors. "Carl Icahn ratcheted up his fight with Occidental Petroleum over its pending purchase of rival Anadarko Petroleum by calling for a special shareholder meeting where he hopes to win board seats. . . . Icahn said he planned to oust and replace four Occidental directors [with his own nominees] . . . ." Adam Jeffery, *Billionaire Carl Icahn Steps up His Fight with Occidental over Anadarko Deal, Wants 4 Board Seats*, Reuters/CNBC, June 27, 2019, *available at:* https://www.cnbc.com/2019/06/27/billionaire-carl-icahn-steps-up-his-fight-with-occidental-over-anadarko-deal-wants-4-board-seats.html?__source=sharebar|email&par=sharebar.

As of the end of 2019, Icahn "held a roughly 2.5% stake [in Occidental]." Cara Lombardo, *Carl Icahn Takes Nearly 10% Stake in Occidental Petroleum as Shares Plunge*, March 11, 2020, Market Watch, *available at:* https://www.marketwatch.com/story/carl-icahn-takes-nearly-10-stake-in-occidental-petroleum-as-shares-plunge-2020-03-11. On March 10, 2020, Icahn filed a Schedule 13D (a portion of which is excerpted here) and disclosed that he had acquired a 9.9% ownership in Occidental, almost quadrupling his stake since the end of 2019. *Id.*

Schedule 13D: Occidental Petroleum Corporation
Excerpt from Occidental Petroleum Corporation Schedule 13D, filed by Carl Icahn and other Reporting Persons, dated March 10, 2020
Available at: **https://fintel.io/doc/sec/921669/000092846420000010/ oxy13d03 122020.htm**

Item 4. Purpose of Transaction

The Reporting Persons acquired their positions in the Shares in the belief that the Shares were undervalued. The Reporting Persons believe the Issuer's merger with Anadarko Petroleum was a terrible transaction and the Issuer's CEO and Board of Directors must be held accountable for the historic loss in stockholder value that has seen the Issuer's share price plummet from almost $70 to $12 in less than a year and which has resulted in the destruction of over $47 billion in stockholder value, which is a decrease of an amazing 83%. It is one of the worst disasters in financial history and we believe the CEO and Board must be held accountable, and the Board must be replaced.

In the near term, critical decisions must be made to ensure OXY's long-term viability, but most importantly, OXY needs a Board that prioritizes stockholder value ahead of their own personal interests. Although Chairman Batchelder is leaving the Board and is not standing for reelection, he alone is not responsible for losing over $47 billion in stockholder value. The whole Board is responsible for allowing this unconscionable deal and we believe the Board cynically gambled stockholder value to prevent stockholders from seeing a possible bid from a well-capitalized, interested acquiror. . . .

The Issuer's CEO and Board unanimously voted to roll the dice and bet the Company by risking stockholder money on a disastrous acquisition. They lost the bet. They have egregiously failed OXY stockholders and should be removed. In other cultures, they would have the dignity to resign, or worse; in the army they would be court-martialed; but here, they will probably award bonuses to themselves because the value of their stock grants collapsed. If we allow them to remain, then corporate democracy is a complete travesty.

The Reporting Persons intend to seek Board representation to represent all stockholders and have notified the Issuer of their intent to nominate directors at the Issuer's 2020 Annual Meeting of Stockholders. We also intend to present stockholder proposals to amend the Issuer's Certificate and Bylaws to improve OXY's restrictive corporate governance that currently serves the incumbent Board of Directors to the detriment of fundamental stockholder rights. In connection with the foregoing, the Reporting Persons have spoken to, and intend to speak with, representatives of the Issuer's Board and management, as well as to other stockholders.

The Reporting Persons are considering all their options . . .

The Reporting Persons may, from time to time and at any time: (i) acquire additional Shares and/or other equity, debt, notes, instruments or other securities of the Issuer and/or its affiliates (collectively, "Securities") in the open market or otherwise; (ii) dispose of any or all of their Securities in the open market or otherwise; or (iii) engage in any hedging or similar transactions with respect to the Securities.

While the company had no immediate comment following the filing of this Schedule 13D, in an unsurprising move, Occidental and Icahn entered into discussions. These talks resulted in the parties reaching a truce by the end of March 2020. As part of a deal that was announced on March 25, 2020, four directors will retire from Occidental's board of directors, to be replaced with two Icahn nominees and two other individuals. *See* Scott Deveau, et al., *Oxy Calls Truce with Carl Icahn, Makes Changes to Its Board*, WORLD OIL, March 26, 2020, *available at:* https://www.worldoil.com/news/2020/3/26/oxy-calls-truce-with-carl-icahn-makes-changes-to-its-board.

Equally important, the deal calls for Occidental's board to create a new committee to explore "inquiries or indications of interest" from prospective buyers for Occidental or its assets. *Id.* However, in an interesting turn of affairs, Occidental's chief executive officer (CEO), Vicki Hollub, "who presided over the Anadarko deal last year, is expected to keep her job — albeit at a much lower salary . . . Ms. Hollub's salary will be slashed by 81% . . . [as the company responds to the] coronavirus pandemic [that] has led to an unprecedented decline in [the] demand for oil [and gas] on a global basis . . ." Rebecca Elliot and Ryan Dezember, *Occidental Petroleum Reaches Truce with Activist Investor Carl Icahn*, WALL ST. J., March 25, 2020, *available at:* https://www.wsj.com/articles/occidental-petroleum-reaches-truce-with-activist-investor-carl-icahn-11585146651.[7]

B. Regulation of Third-Party Tender Offers Under §14(d) of the Williams Act

1. What Is a "Tender Offer"?

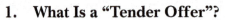

SEC v. Carter Hawley Hale Stores, Inc.
760 F.2d 945 (9th Cir. 1985)

SKOPIL, Circuit Judge:

The issue in this case arises out of an attempt by The Limited ("Limited"), an Ohio corporation, to take over Carter Hawley Hale Stores, Inc. ("CHH"), a publicly-held Los Angeles corporation. The SEC commenced the present action for injunctive relief to restrain CHH from repurchasing its own stock in

---

7. It bears emphasizing that as of March 2020, as the world's economy was reeling from the devastating effects of the coronavirus pandemic, the "entire U.S. oil industry [had] been badly battered . . ., and Occidental [was] among the hardest hit. . . . Occidental's market capitalization . . . plunged below $10 billion, from more than $46 billion at the time of the Anadarko offer [in 2019]." Elliiott and Dezember, *supra.*

an attempt to defeat the Limited takeover attempt without complying with the tender offer regulations. The district court concluded CHH's repurchase program was not a tender offer. The SEC appeals from the district court's denial of its motion for a preliminary injunction. We affirm.

FACTS AND PROCEEDINGS BELOW

On April 4, 1984 Limited commenced a cash tender offer for 20.3 million shares of CHH common stock, representing approximately 55% of the total shares outstanding, at $30 per share. Prior to the announced offer, CHH stock was trading at approximately $23.78 per share (pre-tender offer price). Limited disclosed that if its offer succeeded, it would exchange the remaining CHH shares for a fixed amount of Limited shares in a second-step merger. . . .

While CHH initially took no public position on the offer, it filed an action to enjoin Limited's attempted takeover. *Carter Hawley Hale Stores, Inc. v. The Limited, Inc.*, 587 F. Supp. 246 (C.D. Cal. 1984). CHH's motion for an injunction was denied. *Id.* From April 4, 1984 until April 16, 1984 CHH's incumbent management discussed a response to Limited's offer. During that time 14 million shares, about 40% of CHH's common stock, were traded. The price of CHH stock increased to approximately $29.25 per share. CHH shares became concentrated in the hands of risk arbitrageurs.

On April 16, 1984 CHH responded to Limited's offer. CHH issued a press release announcing its opposition to the offer because it was "inadequate and not in the best interests of CHH or its shareholders." CHH also publicly announced an agreement with General Cinema Corporation ("General Cinema"). . . . Finally, CHH announced a plan to repurchase up to 15 million shares of its own common stock for an amount not to exceed $500 million. . . .

CHH's public announcement stated the actions taken were "to defeat the attempt by Limited to gain voting control of the company and to afford shareholders who wished to sell shares at this time an opportunity to do so." CHH's actions were revealed by press release, a letter from CHH's Chairman to shareholders, and by documents filed with the Securities and Exchange Commission ("SEC") — a Schedule 14D-9 and Rule 13e-1 transaction statement. These disclosures were reported by wire services, national financial newspapers, and newspapers of general circulation. Limited sought a temporary restraining order against CHH's repurchase of its shares. The application was denied. Limited withdrew its motion for a preliminary injunction.

CHH began to repurchase its shares on April 16, 1984. In a one-hour period CHH purchased approximately 244,000 shares at an average price of $25.25 per share. On April 17, 1984 CHH purchased approximately 6.5 million shares in a two-hour trading period at an average price of $25.88 per share. By April 22, 1984 CHH had purchased a total of 15 million shares. It then announced an increase in the number of shares authorized for purchase to 18.5 million.

On April 24, 1984, the same day Limited was permitted to close its offer and start purchasing, CHH terminated its repurchase program having purchased approximately 17.5 million shares, over 50% of the common shares outstanding. On April 25, 1984 Limited revised its offer increasing the offering price to $35.00 per share and eliminating the second-step merger. The market price for CHH then reached a high of $32.00 per share. On May 21, 1984 Limited withdrew its offer. The market price of CHH promptly fell to $20.62 per share, a price below the pre-tender offer price.

On May 2, 1984, two and one-half weeks after the repurchase program was announced and one week after its apparent completion, the SEC filed this action for injunctive relief. The SEC alleged that CHH's repurchase program constituted a tender offer conducted in violation of section 13(e) of the Exchange Act, 15 U.S.C. §78m(e) and Rule 13e-4, 17 C.F.R. §240.13e-4. On May 5, 1984 a temporary restraining order was granted. CHH was temporarily enjoined from further stock repurchases. The district court denied SEC's motion for a preliminary injunction, finding the SEC failed to carry its burden of establishing "the reasonable likelihood of future violations . . . [or] . . . a 'fair chance of success on the merits'. . . ." The court found CHH's repurchase program was not a tender offer because the eight-factor test proposed by the SEC and adopted in *Wellman v. Dickinson*, 475 F. Supp. 783 (S.D.N.Y. 1979), *aff'd on other grounds*, 682 F.2d 355 (2d Cir. 1982), *cert. denied*, 460 U.S. 1069, 103 S. Ct. 1522, 75 L. Ed. 2d 946 (1983), had not been satisfied. The court also refused to adopt, at the urging of the SEC, the alternative test of what constitutes a tender offer as enunciated in *S-G Securities, Inc. v. Fuqua Investment*, 466 F. Supp. 1114 (D. Mass. 1978). On May 9, 1984 the SEC filed an emergency application for an injunction pending appeal to this court. That application was denied.

DISCUSSION

. . . The SEC urges two principal arguments on appeal: (1) the district court erred in concluding that CHH's repurchase program was not a tender offer under the eight-factor *Wellman* test, and (2) the district court erred in declining to apply the definition of a tender offer enunciated in *S-G Securities*, 466 F. Supp. at 1126-27. Resolution of these issues on appeal presents the difficult task of determining whether CHH's repurchase of shares during a third-party tender offer itself constituted a tender offer.

1. THE WILLIAMS ACT

A. Congressional Purposes. The Williams Act amendments to the Exchange Act were enacted in response to the growing use of tender offers to achieve corporate control. Prior to the passage of the Act, shareholders of target companies were often forced to act hastily on offers without the benefit of full disclosure. *See* H.R. Rep. No. 1711, 90th Cong., 2d Sess. (1968), *reprinted in* 1968 U.S. CODE, CONG. & ADMIN. NEWS 2811 (*"House Report 1711"*). The Williams Act was intended to ensure that investors responding to tender offers received full and fair disclosure, analogous to that received in proxy contests. The Act was also designed to provide shareholders an opportunity to examine all relevant facts in an effort to reach a decision without being subject to unwarranted pressure.

This policy is reflected in section 14(d), which governs third-party tender offers, and which prohibits a tender offer unless shareholders are provided with certain procedural and substantive protections including: full disclosure; time in which to make an investment decision; withdrawal rights; and pro rata purchase of shares accepted in the event the offer is oversubscribed.

There are additional congressional concerns underlying the Williams Act. In its effort to protect investors, Congress recognized the need to "avoid favoring either management or the takeover bidder." . . . Congress was also concerned about avoiding undue interference with the free and open market in securities. . . . Each of these congressional concerns is implicated in the determination of whether CHH's issuer repurchase program constituted a tender offer.

B.   *Issuer Repurchases Under Section 13(e).* Issuer repurchases and tender offers are governed in relevant part by section 13(e) of the Williams Act and Rules 13e-1 and 13e-4 promulgated thereunder.

The SEC argues that the district court erred in concluding that issuer repurchases, which had the intent and effect of defeating a third-party tender offer, are authorized by the tender offer rules and regulations. The legislative history of these provisions is unclear. Congress apparently was aware of an intent by the SEC to regulate issuer tender offers to the same extent as third-party offers. At the same time, Congress recognized issuers might engage in "substantial repurchase programs . . . inevitably affect[ing] market performance and price levels." Such repurchase programs might be undertaken for any number of legitimate purposes, including with the intent "to preserve or strengthen . . . control by counteracting tender offer or other takeover attempts. . . ." Congress neither explicitly banned nor authorized such a practice. Congress did grant the SEC authority to adopt appropriate regulations to carry out congressional intent with respect to issuer repurchases. The legislative history of section 13(e) is not helpful in resolving the issues.

There is also little guidance in the SEC Rules promulgated in response to the legislative grant of authority. Rule 13e-1 prohibits an issuer from repurchasing its own stock during a third-party tender offer unless it discloses certain minimal information. The language of Rule 13e-1 is prohibitory rather than permissive. It nonetheless evidences a recognition that not all issuer repurchases during a third-party tender offer are tender offers. In contrast, Rule 13e-4 recognizes that issuers, like third parties, may engage in repurchase activity amounting to a tender offer and subject to the same procedural and substantive safeguards as a third-party tender offer. 17 C.F.R. §240.13e-4 (1984). The regulations do not specify when a repurchase by an issuer amounts to a tender offer governed by Rule 13e-4 rather than 13e-1.[3]

---

3. The procedural and substantive requirements that must be complied with under Rule 13e-4 differ from those under Rule 13e-1. An issuer engaged in a repurchase under Rule 13e-1 is required to file a brief statement with the SEC setting forth the amount of shares purchased; the purpose for which the purchase is made; and the source and amount of funds used in making the repurchase. 17 C.F.R. §240.13e-1 (1984). CHH complied with the requirements of Rule 13e-1.

An issuer engaged in a tender offer under Rule 13e-4 must comply with more burdensome regulations. All the substantive and procedural protections for shareholders come into play under Rule 13e-4 including: full disclosure; time in which to make investment decisions;

We decline to adopt either the broadest construction of Rule 13e-4, to define issuer tender offers as virtually all substantial repurchases during a third-party tender offer, or the broadest construction of Rule 13e-1, to create an exception from the tender offer requirements for issuer repurchases made during a third-party tender offer. Like the district court, we resolve the question of whether CHH's repurchase program was a tender offer by considering the eight-factor test established in *Wellman*.

To serve the purposes of the Williams Act, there is a need for flexibility in fashioning a definition of a tender offer. The *Wellman* factors seem particularly well suited in determining when an issuer repurchase program during a third-party tender offer will itself constitute a tender offer. *Wellman* focuses, *inter alia*, on the manner in which the offer is conducted and whether the offer has the overall effect of pressuring shareholders into selling their stock. Application of the *Wellman* factors to the unique facts and circumstances surrounding issuer repurchases should serve to effect congressional concern for the needs of the shareholder, the need to avoid giving either the target or the offeror any advantage, and the need to maintain a free and open market for securities.

2. APPLICATION OF THE WELLMAN FACTORS

Under the *Wellman* test, the existence of a tender offer is determined by examining the following factors:

(1) Active and widespread solicitation of public shareholders for the shares of an issuer; (2) solicitation made for a substantial percentage of the issuer's stock; (3) offer to purchase made at a premium over the prevailing market price; (4) terms of the offer are firm rather than negotiable; (5) offer contingent on the tender of a fixed number of shares, often subject to a fixed maximum number to be purchased; (6) offer open only for a limited period of time; (7) offeree subjected to pressure to sell his stock; [and (8)] public announcements of a purchasing program concerning the target company precede or accompany rapid accumulation of a large amount of target company's securities.

Not all factors need be present to find a tender offer; rather, they provide some guidance as to the traditional indicia of a tender offer. . . .

The district court concluded CHH's repurchase program was not a tender offer under *Wellman* because only "two of the eight indicia" were present. The SEC claims the district court erred in applying *Wellman* because it gave insufficient weight to the pressure exerted on shareholders; it ignored the existence of a competitive tender offer; and it failed to consider that CHH's offer at the market price was in essence a premium because the price had already risen above pre-tender offer levels.

A. Active and Widespread Solicitation. The evidence was uncontraverted that there was "no direct solicitation of shareholders." No active and widespread

---

withdrawal rights; and requirements for pro rata [acceptance] of shares. 17 C.F.R. §240.13e-4 (1984). CHH did not comply with Rule 13e-4.

solicitation occurred. . . . Nor did the publicity surrounding CHH's repurchase program result in a solicitation. The only public announcements by CHH were those mandated by SEC or Exchange rules. . . .

B. *Solicitation for a Substantial Percentage of Issuer's Shares.* Because there was no active and widespread solicitation, the district court found the repurchase could not have involved a solicitation for a substantial percentage of CHH's shares. It is unclear whether the proper focus of this factor is the solicitation or the percentage of stock solicited. The district court probably erred in concluding that, absent a solicitation under the first *Wellman* factor, the second factor cannot be satisfied, . . . but we need not decide that here. The solicitation and percentage of stock elements of the second factor often will be addressed adequately in an evaluation of the first *Wellman* factor, which is concerned with solicitation, and the eighth *Wellman* factor, which focuses on the amount of securities accumulated. In this case, CHH did not engage in a solicitation under the first *Wellman* factor but did accumulate a large percentage of stock as defined under the eighth *Wellman* factor. An evaluation of the second *Wellman* factor does not alter the probability of finding a tender offer.

C. *Premium Over Prevailing Market Price.* The SEC contends that the open-market purchases made by CHH at market prices were in fact made at a premium not over market price, but over the pre-tender offer price. At the time of CHH's repurchases, the market price for CHH's shares (ranging from $24.00 to $26.00 per share) had risen above the pre-tender offer price (approximately $22.00 per share). Given ordinary market dynamics, the price of a target company's stock will rise following an announced tender offer. Under the SEC's definition of a premium as a price greater than the pre-tender offer price, a premium will always exist when a target company makes open market purchases in response to a tender offer even though the increase in market price is attributable to the action of the third-party offeror and not the target company. The SEC definition not only eliminates consideration of this *Wellman* factor in the context of issuer repurchases during a tender offer, but also underestimates congressional concern for preserving the free and open market. The district court did not err in concluding a premium is determined not by reference to pre-tender offer price, but rather by reference to market price. . . .

D. *Terms of Offer Not Firm.* There is no dispute that CHH engaged in a number of transactions or purchases at many different market prices.

E. *Offer Not Contingent on Tender of Fixed Minimum Number of Shares.* Similarly, while CHH indicated it would purchase up to 15 million shares, CHH's purchases were not contingent on the tender of a fixed minimum number of shares.

F. *Not Open for Only a Limited Time.* CHH's offer to repurchase was not open for only a limited period of time but rather was open "during the pendency of the tender offer of The Limited." The SEC argues that the offer was in fact open for only a limited time, because CHH would only repurchase stock until 15 million shares were acquired. The fact that 15 million shares were acquired in a short period of time does not translate into an issuer-imposed time limitation. The time within which the repurchases were made was a product of ordinary market forces, not the terms of CHH's repurchase program.

G-H.   Shareholder Pressure and Public Announcements Accompanying a Large Accumulation of Stock.   With regard to the seventh *Wellman* factor, following a public announcement, CHH repurchased over the period of seven trading days more than 50% of its outstanding shares. The eighth *Wellman* factor was met.

The district court found that while many shareholders may have felt pressured or compelled to sell their shares, CHH itself did not exert on shareholders the kind of pressure the Williams Act proscribes.

While there certainly was shareholder pressure in this case, it was largely the pressure of the marketplace and not the type of untoward pressure the tender offer regulations were designed to prohibit. . . .

CHH's purchases were made in the open market, at market and not premium prices, without fixed terms and were not contingent upon the tender of a fixed minimum number of shares. CHH's repurchase program had none of the traditional indicia of a tender offer. . . .

The shareholder pressure in this case did not result from any untoward action on the part of CHH. Rather, it resulted from market forces, the third-party offer, and the fear that at the expiration of the offer the price of CHH shares would decrease.

The district court did not abuse its discretion in concluding that under the *Wellman* eight factor test, CHH's repurchase program did not constitute a tender offer.

3. ALTERNATIVE S-G SECURITIES TEST

The SEC finally urges that even if the CHH repurchase program did not constitute a tender offer under the *Wellman* test, the district court erred in refusing to apply the test in *S-G Securities*, 466 F. Supp. at 1114. Under the more liberal *S-G Securities* test, a tender offer is present if there are

> (1) A publicly announced intention by the purchaser to acquire a block of the stock of the target company for purposes of acquiring control thereof, and (2) a subsequent rapid acquisition by the purchaser of large blocks of stock through open market and privately negotiated purchases.

Id. at 1126-27.

There are a number of sound reasons for rejecting the *S-G Securities* test. The test is vague and difficult to apply. It offers little guidance to the issuer as to when his conduct will come within the ambit of Rule 13e-4 as opposed to Rule 13e-1. A determination of the existence of a tender offer under *S-G Securities* is largely subjective and made in hindsight based on an *ex post facto* evaluation of the response in the marketplace to the repurchase program. The SEC's contention that these concerns are irrelevant when the issuer's repurchases are made with the intent to defeat a third-party offer is without merit.

The SEC finds further support for its application of the two-pronged *S-G Securities* test in the overriding legislative intent "to ensure that shareholders . . . are adequately protected from pressure tactics . . . [forcing them to make] . . . ill-considered investment decisions." The *S-G Securities* test does reflect congressional concern for shareholders; however, the same can be said of the *Wellman* test. The legislative intent in the context of open-market repurchases during third-party tender offers is, at best, unclear. The *S-G Securities* test, unlike the *Wellman* test, does little to reflect objectively the multiple congressional concerns underlying the Williams Act, including due regard for the free and open market in securities.

We decline to abandon the *Wellman* test in favor of the vague standard enunciated in *S-G Securities*. The district court did not err in declining to apply the *S-G Securities* test or in finding CHH's repurchases were not a tender offer under *Wellman*.

AFFIRMED.

NOTES

1. Rule 13e-1 vs. Rule 13e-4 Transactions.   Section 13(e) of the Williams Act is essentially an antifraud statute that delegates broad rulemaking authority to the SEC to regulate issuers' repurchases of their own shares. Pursuant to this authority, the SEC has promulgated Rule 13e-1, which requires issuers who propose to engage in repurchases of their shares during the course of a third party's tender offer to file a disclosure document with the SEC. In addition, the SEC has adopted Rule 13e-4, which requires issuers who engage in self-tender offers to file disclosures on Schedule 13E-4 and to otherwise comply with rules that impose procedural safeguards that are very similar to the SEC rules that were described earlier in this chapter with respect to the regulation of third-party tender offers under Section 14(d), such as the proration rules and withdrawal rights.

2. Going Private Transactions: The* Weinberger *Standard of Entire Fairness.
When M&A professionals refer to a "going private transaction," they are usually referring to a transaction involving the squeeze-out of minority shareholders, in which the controlling shareholder acquires all of the shares of Target, a controlled subsidiary, that the majority shareholder (which is usually the parent company, but could be an individual shareholder) does not own. In these transactions, the minority shareholders are eliminated from any further equity participation in the continued growth of Target's business. As we learned in Chapter 2, when we studied the Delaware Supreme Court's landmark decision in *Weinberger*, these squeeze-out transactions are fraught with conflicts of interest, and accordingly, the Delaware Supreme Court imposed an "entire fairness" requirement in connection with freeze-out transactions in order to be sure that the minority shareholders receive adequate consideration for their interest.

As established in *Weinberger*, the concept of entire fairness directs the courts to look at two elements: fair price and fair dealing. Following *Weinberger*, and until quite recently, the Delaware courts consistently applied the entire fairness standard to review squeeze-out transactions of the type that was at issue in *Weinberger*. Indeed, in *Kahn v. Lynch Communication Systems, Inc.*, 638 A.2d 1110 (Del. 1994), the Delaware Supreme Court held that "an approval of [an interested merger] transaction by an independent committee of directors . . . shifts the burden of proof on the issue of fairness from the controlling or dominating shareholder to the challenging shareholder-plaintiff." *Id.* at 1117. The function of a special committee in this setting is to negotiate the price and terms of an interested transaction on behalf of the minority shareholders. In order for the special committee to operate independently for burden-shifting purposes, "[p]articular consideration must be given to evidence of whether the special committee was truly independent, fully informed, and had the freedom to negotiate at arm's length." *Id.* at 1120-1121. Consequently, as was mentioned earlier in the "Notes" material following the *Weinberger* decision (*see supra*, pp. 195-196), most practicing M&A lawyers assumed that the entire fairness standard would apply to any transaction where the controlling shareholder sought to eliminate ("squeeze out") the minority interest—regardless of whether the transaction was structured as a long-form merger, a short-form merger, or a two-step transaction involving a tender offer (i.e., stock purchase) to be followed by either a long-form or a short-form merger. *See* Diagram 12 in Appendix A.

    3. *SEC Regulation of Going Private Transactions: Rule 13e-3.* In 1979, the SEC adopted Rule 13e-3, which regulates going private transactions. As to those going private transactions that are covered by Rule 13e-3, the controlling shareholder will be required to file a Schedule 13E-3 with the SEC. Since the SEC recognizes the significant potential for abuse of the minority interest that is an inherent attribute of going private transactions, the disclosure requirements of Schedule 13E-3 are rather significant. The Schedule 13E-3 must set forth certain information pertaining to the parties to the transaction, the terms of the transaction, the post-transaction plans of the parties, the source of the funds for the transaction, the purpose of the transaction, and a fairly extensive description of the fairness of the transaction. It is generally this requirement—to provide information with respect to the *fairness* of the proposed transaction—that creates the most difficult disclosure issues for those controlling shareholders proposing to take the company private.

    4. *Going Private Transactions: Avoiding Majority Shareholders' Duties Under the* Weinberger *Doctrine.* Since a 2001 decision by the Delaware Supreme Court, Delaware courts have charted a very different path for structuring going private transactions—a path that allows the majority shareholder to avoid the entire fairness doctrine established in *Weinberger* and its progeny. *See Glassman v. Unocal Exploration Corp.*, 777 A.2d 242 (Del. 2001); *In re Pure Resources Shareholders Litigation*, 808 A.2d 421 (Del. Ch. 2002); and *In re Siliconix, Inc. Shareholder Litigation*, No. Civ. A. 18700, 2001 WL 716 787 (Del. Ch. June 19, 2001). So, as a matter of Delaware state law, today there are currently two distinct paths that can be used by transaction planners to take a company private. The first is to structure the transaction as a long-form merger, which will be subject to review under the entire fairness standard set forth in *Weinberger*. The second path is the so-called *Siliconix/Pure Resources* transaction, named after the two cases that spawned this second approach to going private transactions. Under this second approach, the controlling shareholder makes a first-step tender offer, followed by a second-step short-form merger. The reason to structure the transaction using this two-step approach is that the controlling shareholder can avoid review under the entire fairness standard of *Weinberger* if the transaction is structured to satisfy certain conditions.

Given that the Delaware courts have now offered majority shareholders a path to eliminate review of the entire fairness of a going private transaction, this has resulted in an increased emphasis on the scope of disclosures required by SEC Rule 13e-3. And, not surprisingly, the divergent strands of Delaware jurisprudence regarding the scope of fiduciary duty obligations in connection with going private transactions has generated considerable controversy. In Chapter 7, as part of our study of fiduciary duty law, we will examine going private transactions in more detail, with a particular emphasis on the intersection of the controlling shareholder's mandatory fiduciary duty obligations under state law *and* the mandatory disclosure obligations imposed on controlling shareholders under the federal securities laws. *See infra*, p. 733 in Chapter 7.

In another leading case addressing the issue of the definition of "tender offer" in the context of open market purchases of publicly traded shares, the Second Circuit eschewed the *Wellman* test (used by the Ninth Circuit in *Carter Hawley Hale*) in favor of a very different approach.

Hanson Trust PLC v. SCM Corporation *online brief*
774 F.2d 47 (2d Cir. 1985)

MANSFIELD, Circuit Judge:

Hanson Trust PLC, HSCM Industries, Inc., and Hanson Holdings Netherlands B.V. (hereinafter sometimes referred to collectively as "Hanson") appeal from an order of the Southern District of New York, 617 F. Supp. 832 (1985), Shirley Wohl Kram, Judge, granting SCM Corporation's motion for a preliminary injunction restraining them, their officers, agents, employees and any persons acting in concert with them, from acquiring any shares of SCM and from exercising any voting rights with respect to 3.1 million SCM shares acquired by them on September 11, 1985. The injunction was granted on the ground that Hanson's September 11 acquisition of the SCM stock through five private and one open market purchases amounted to a "tender offer" for more than 5% of SCM's outstanding shares, which violated §§14(d)(1) and (6) of the Williams Act, 15 U.S.C. §78n(d)(1) and (6) and rules promulgated by the Securities and Exchange Commission (SEC) thereunder. *See* 17 C.F.R. §§240.14(e)(1) and 240.14d-7. We reverse.

The setting is the familiar one of a fast-moving bidding contest for control of a large public corporation: first, a cash tender offer of $60 per share by Hanson, an outsider, addressed to SCM stockholders; next, a counterproposal by an "insider" group consisting of certain SCM managers and their "White Knight," Merrill Lynch Capital Markets (Merrill), for a "leveraged buyout" at a higher price ($70 per share); then an increase by Hanson of its cash offer to $72 per share, followed by a revised SCM-Merrill leveraged buyout offer of $74 per share with a "crown jewel" irrevocable lock-up option to Merrill designed to discourage Hanson from seeking control by providing that if any other party (in this case Hanson) should acquire more than one-third of SCM's outstanding shares (66-2/3% being needed under N.Y. Bus. L. §903(a)(2) to effectuate a merger) Merrill would have the right to buy SCM's two most profitable businesses (consumer foods and pigments) at prices characterized by some as "bargain basement." The final act in this scenario was the decision of Hanson, having been deterred by the SCM-Merrill option (colloquially described in the market as a "poison pill"), to terminate its cash tender offer and then to make private purchases, amounting to 25% of SCM's outstanding shares, leading SCM to seek and obtain the preliminary injunction from which this appeal is taken. A more detailed history of relevant events follows.

SCM is a New York corporation with its principal place of business in New York City. . . .

On August 21, 1985, Hanson publicly announced its intention to make a cash tender of $60 per share for any and all outstanding SCM shares. Five days later [Hanson] filed the tender offer documents required by §14(d)(1) of the Williams Act and regulations issued thereunder. . . . On August 30, 1985, SCM, having recommended to SCM's stockholders that they not accept Hanson's tender offer, announced a preliminary agreement with Merrill under which a new entity, formed by SCM and Merrill, would acquire all SCM shares at $70 per share in a leveraged buyout sponsored by Merrill. . . . On September 3, Hansen increased its tender offer from $60 to $72 cash per share. However, it expressly reserved the right to terminate its offer if SCM granted to anyone any option to purchase SCM assets on terms that Hansen believed to constitute a "lock-up" device.

The next development in the escalating bidding contest for control of SCM occurred on September 10, 1985, when SCM entered into a new leveraged buyout agreement with its "White Knight," Merrill. The agreement provided for a two-step acquisition of SCM stock by Merrill at $74 per share. The first proposed step was to be the acquisition of approximately 82% of SCM's outstanding stock for cash. Following a merger (which required acquisition of at least $66^2/_3\%$), debentures would be issued for the remaining SCM shares. If any investor or group other than Merrill acquired more than one-third of SCM's outstanding shares, Merrill would have the option to buy SCM's two most profitable businesses, pigments and consumer foods, for $350 and $80 million respectively, prices which Hanson believed to be below their market value.

Hanson, faced with what it considered to be a "poison pill," concluded that even if it increased its cash tender offer to $74 per share it would end up with control of a substantially depleted and damaged company. Accordingly, it announced on the Dow Jones Broad Tape at 12:38 P.M. on September 11 that it was terminating its cash tender offer. A few minutes later, Hanson issued a press release, carried on the Broad Tape, to the effect that "all SCM shares tendered will be promptly returned to the tendering shareholders."

At some time in the late forenoon or early afternoon of September 11 Hanson decided to make cash purchases of a substantial percentage of SCM stock in the open market or through privately negotiated transactions. If Hanson could acquire slightly less than one-third of SCM's outstanding shares it would be able to block the $74 per share SCM-Merrill offer of a leveraged buyout. This might induce the latter to work out an agreement with Hanson, something Hanson had unsuccessfully sought on several occasions since its first cash tender offer.

Within a period of two hours on the afternoon of September 11 Hanson made five privately-negotiated cash purchases of SCM stock and one openmarket purchase, acquiring 3.1 million shares or 25% of SCM's outstanding stock. The price of SCM stock on the NYSE on September 11 ranged from a high of $73.50 per share to a low of $72.50 per share. Hanson's initial private purchase, 387,700 shares from Mutual Shares, was not solicited by Hanson but by a Mutual Shares official, Michael Price, who, in a conversation with Robert Pirie of Rothschild, Inc., Hanson's financial advisor, on the morning of September 11 (before Hanson had decided to make any private cash purchases), had stated that he was interested in selling Mutual's Shares' SCM stock to Hanson. Once Hanson's decision to buy privately had been made, Pirie took Price up on his offer. The parties negotiated a sale at $73.50 per share after Pirie refused Price's asking prices, first of $75 per share and, later, of $74.50 per share. This transaction, but not the identity of the parties, was automatically reported pursuant to NYSE rules on the NYSE ticker at 3:11 P.M. and reported on the Dow Jones Broad Tape at 3:29 P.M.

Pirie then telephoned Ivan Boesky, an arbitrageur who had a few weeks earlier disclosed in a Schedule 13D statement filed with the SEC that he owned approximately 12.7% of SCM's outstanding shares. Pirie negotiated a Hanson purchase of these shares at $73.50 per share after rejecting Boesky's initial demand of $74 per share. At the same time Rothschild purchased for Hanson's account 600,000 SCM shares in the open market at $73.50 per share. An attempt by Pirie next to negotiate the cash purchase of another large block of SCM stock (some 780,000 shares) from Slifka & Company fell through because of the latter's inability to make delivery of the shares on September 12.

Following the NYSE ticker and Broad Tape reports of the first two large anonymous transactions in SCM stock, some professional investors surmised that the buyer might be Hanson. Rothschild then received telephone calls from (1) Mr. Mulhearn of Jamie & Co. offering to sell between 200,000 and 350,000 shares at $73.50 per share, (2) David Gottesman, an arbitrageur at Oppenheimer & Co. offering 89,000 shares at $73.50, and (3) Boyd Jeffries of Jeffries & Co., offering approximately 700,000 to 800,000 shares at $74.00. Pirie purchased the three blocks for Hanson at $73.50 per share. The last of Hanson's cash purchases was completed by 4:35 P.M. on September 11, 1985.

In the early evening of September 11 SCM successfully applied to Judge Kram in the present lawsuit for a restraining order barring Hanson from acquiring more SCM stock. . . .

SCM argued before Judge Kram (and argues here) that Hanson's cash purchases immediately following its termination of its $72 per share tender offer amounted to a *de facto* continuation of Hanson's tender offer, designed to avoid the strictures of §14(d) of the Williams Act, and that unless a preliminary injunction issued SCM and its shareholders would be irreparably injured because Hanson would acquire enough shares to defeat the SCM-Merrill offer. Judge Kram found that the relevant underlying facts (which we have outlined) were not in dispute, and concluded that . . . "SCM has demonstrated a likelihood of success on the merits of its contention that Hanson has engaged in a tender offer which violates Section 14(d) of the Williams Act." The district court, characterizing Hanson's stock purchases as "a deliberate attempt to do an 'end run' around the requirements of the Williams Act," made no finding on the question of whether Hanson had decided to make the purchases of SCM before or after it dropped its tender offer but concluded that even if the decision had been made after it terminated its offer preliminary injunctive relief should issue. From this decision Hanson appeals.

Discussion

. . . Since, as the district court correctly noted, the material relevant facts in the present case are not in dispute, this appeal turns on whether the district court erred as a matter of law in holding that when Hanson terminated its offer and immediately thereafter made private purchases of a substantial share of the target company's outstanding stock, the purchases became a "tender offer" within the meaning of §14(d) of the Williams Act. Absent any express definition of "tender offer" in the Act, the answer requires a brief review of the background and purposes of §14(d). . . .

The typical tender offer, as described in the Congressional debates, hearings and reports on the Williams Act, consisted of a general, publicized bid by an individual or group to buy shares of a publicly-owned company, the shares of which were traded on a national securities exchange, at a price substantially above the current market price. . . . The offer was usually accompanied by newspaper and other publicity, a time limit for tender of shares in response to it, and a provision fixing a quantity limit on the total number of shares of the target company that would be purchased.

Prior to the Williams Act a tender offeror had no obligation to disclose any information to shareholders when making a bid. The Report of the Senate Committee on Banking and Currency ["Senate Report"] aptly described the situation: "by using a cash tender offer the person seeking control can operate in almost complete secrecy. At present, the law does not even require that he disclose his identity, the source of his funds, who his associates are, or what he intends to do if he gains control of the corporation." Senate Report, *supra*, at 2. The average shareholder, pressured by the fact that the tender offer would be available for only a short time and restricted to a limited number of shares, was forced "with severely limited information, [to] decide what course of action he should take." *Id.* "Without knowledge of who the bidder is and what he plans to do, the shareholder cannot reach an informed decision. He is forced to take a chance. For no matter what he does, he does it without adequate information to enable him to decide rationally what is the best possible course of action." *Id.*

The purpose of the Williams Act was, accordingly, to protect the shareholders from that dilemma by insuring "that public shareholders who are confronted by a cash tender offer for their stock will not be required to respond without adequate information." . . .

Although §14(d)(1) clearly applies to "classic" tender offers of the type described above, courts soon recognized that in the case of privately negotiated transactions or solicitations for private purchases of stock many of the conditions leading to the enactment of §14(d) for the most part do not exist. The number and percentage of stockholders are usually far less than those involved in public offers. The solicitation involves less publicity than a public tender offer or none. The solicitees, who are frequently directors, officers or substantial stockholders of the target, are more apt to be sophisticated, inquiring or knowledgeable concerning the target's business, the solicitor's objectives, and the impact of the solicitation on the target's business prospects. In short, the solicitee in the private transaction is less likely to be pressured, confused, or ill-informed regarding the businesses and decisions at stake than solicitees who are the subjects of a public tender offer.

These differences between public and private securities transactions have led most courts to rule that private transactions or open market purchases do not qualify as a "tender offer" requiring the purchaser to meet the pre-filing strictures of §14(d). . . . The borderline between public solicitations and privately negotiated stock purchases is not bright and it is frequently difficult to determine whether transactions falling close to the line or in a type of "no man's land" are "tender offers" or private deals. This has led some to advocate a broader interpretation of the term "tender offer" than that followed by us in *Kennecott Copper Corp. v. Curtiss-Wright Corp.*, [449 F. Supp. 951 (S.D.N.Y.), *aff'd in relevant part*, 584 F.2d 1195, 1206-07 (2d Cir. 1978)], and to adopt the eight-factor "test" of what is a tender offer, which was recommended by the SEC and applied by the district court in *Wellman v. Dickinson*, 475 F. Supp. 783, 823-24 (S.D.N.Y. 1979), *aff'd on other grounds*, 682 F.2d 355 (2d Cir. 1982), *cert. denied*, 460 U.S. 1069, 103 S. Ct. 1522, 75 L. Ed. 2d 946 (1983), and by the Ninth Circuit in *SEC v. Carter Hawley Hale Stores, Inc.* . . .

Although many of [these eight] factors are relevant for purposes of determining whether a given solicitation amounts to a tender offer, the elevation of such a list to a mandatory "litmus test" appears to be both unwise and unnecessary. As even the advocates of the proposed test recognize, in any given case a solicitation may constitute a tender offer even though some of the eight factors are absent or, when many factors are present, the solicitation may nevertheless not amount to a tender offer because the missing factors outweigh those present.

We prefer to be guided by the principle followed by the Supreme Court in deciding what transactions fall within the private offering exemption provided by §4(1) of the Securities Act of 1933, and by ourselves in *Kennecott Copper* in determining whether the Williams Act applies to private transactions. That principle is simply to look to the statutory purpose. . . . [S]ince the purpose of §14(d) is to protect the ill-informed solicitee, the question of whether a solicitation constitutes a "tender offer" within the meaning of §14(d) turns on whether, viewing the transaction in the light of the totality of circumstances, there appears to be a likelihood that unless the pre-acquisition filing strictures of that statute are followed there will be a substantial risk that solicitees will lack information needed to make a carefully considered appraisal of the proposal put before them.

Applying this standard, we are persuaded on the undisputed facts that Hanson's September 11 negotiation of five private purchases and one open market purchase of SCM shares, totaling 25% of SCM's outstanding stock, did not under the circumstances constitute a "tender offer" within the meaning of the Williams Act. Putting aside for the moment the events preceding the

purchases, there can be little doubt that the privately negotiated purchases
would not, standing alone, qualify as a tender offer, for the following reasons:

(1) In a market of 22,800 SCM shareholders the number of SCM sellers here
involved, six in all, was miniscule compared with the numbers involved
in public solicitations of the type against which the Act was directed.

(2) At least five of the sellers were highly sophisticated professionals,
knowledgeable in the market place and well aware of the essential facts
needed to exercise their professional skills and to appraise Hanson's
offer, including its financial condition as well as that of SCM, the likelihood that the purchases might block the SCM-Merrill bid, and the
risk that if Hanson acquired more than 33 $1/_3$%of SCM's stock the
SCM-Merrill lockup of the "crown jewel" might be triggered. . . .

(3) The sellers were not "pressured" to sell their shares by any conduct
that the Williams Act was designed to alleviate, but by the forces of
the market place. Indeed, in the case of Mutual Shares there was no
initial solicitation by Hanson; the offer to sell was initiated by Mr. Price
of Mutual Shares. Although each of the Hanson purchases was made
for $73.50 per share, in most instances this price was the result of pri-
vate negotiations after the sellers sought higher prices and in one case
price protection, demands which were refused. The $73.50 price was
not fixed in advance by Hanson. Moreover, the sellers remained free to
accept the $74 per share tender offer made by the SCM-Merrill group.

(4) There was no active or widespread advance publicity or public solicitation, which is one of the earmarks of a conventional tender offer.
Arbitrageurs might conclude from ticker tape reports of two large
anonymous transactions that Hanson must be the buyer. . . .

(5) The price received by the six sellers, $73.50 per share, unlike that
appearing in most tender offers, can scarcely be dignified with the label
"premium." The stock market price on September 11 ranged from
$72.50 to $73.50 per share. Although risk arbitrageurs sitting on large
holdings might reap sizeable profits from sales to Hanson at $73.50,
depending on their own purchase costs, they stood to gain even more
if the SCM-Merrill offer of $74 should succeed, as it apparently would if
they tendered their shares to it. Indeed, the $73.50 price, being at most
$1 over market or 1.4% higher than the market price, did not meet
the SEC's proposed definition of a premium, which is $2.00 per share
or 5% above market price, whichever is greater. SEC Exchange Act
Release No. 16,385 (11/29/79) [1979-80] Fed. Sec. L. Rep. ¶82,374.

(6) Unlike most tender offers, the purchases were not made contingent
upon Hanson's acquiring a fixed minimum number or percentage
of SCM's outstanding shares. Once an agreement with each individual seller was reached, Hanson was obligated to buy, regardless what
total percentage of stock it might acquire. Indeed, it does not appear
that Hanson had fixed in its mind a firm limit on the amount of SCM
shares it was willing to buy.

(7) Unlike most tender offers, there was no general time limit within
which Hanson would make purchases of SCM stock. Concededly, cash
transactions are normally immediate but, assuming an inability on the

part of a seller and Hanson to agree at once on a price, nothing prevented a resumption of negotiations by each of the parties except the
arbitrageurs' speculation that once Hanson acquired $33^1/_3\%$ or an
amount just short of that figure it would stop buying.

In short, the totality of circumstances that existed on September 11 did not
evidence any likelihood that unless Hanson was required to comply with §14(d)
(1)'s pre-acquisition filing and waiting-period requirements there would be a
substantial risk of ill-considered sales of SCM stock by ill-informed shareholders.

There remains the question whether Hanson's private purchases take on
a different hue, requiring them to be treated as a "*de facto*" continuation of its
earlier tender offer, when considered in the context of Hanson's earlier acknowledged tender offer, the competing offer of SCM-Merrill and Hanson's termination of its tender offer. After reviewing all of the undisputed facts we conclude
that the district court erred in so holding.

In the first place, we find no record support for the contention by SCM that
Hanson's September 11 termination of its outstanding tender offer was false,
fraudulent or ineffective. Hanson's termination notice was clear, unequivocal
and straightforward. Directions were given, and presumably are being followed,
to return all of the tendered shares to the SCM shareholders who tendered
them. Hanson also filed with the SEC a statement pursuant to §14(d)(1) of the
Williams Act terminating its tender offer. . . .

The reason for Hanson's termination of its tender offer is not disputed: in
view of SCM's grant of what Hanson conceived to be a "poison pill" lock-up
option to Merrill, Hanson, if it acquired control of SCM, would have a company
denuded as the result of its sale of its consumer food and pigment businesses to
Merrill at what Hanson believed to be bargain prices. Thus, Hanson's termination of its tender offer was final; there was no tender offer to be "continued." . . .

Nor does the record support SCM's contention that Hanson had decided,
before terminating its tender offer, to engage in cash purchases. Judge Kram
referred only to evidence that "Hanson had *considered* open market purchases
before it announced that the tender offer was dropped" (*emphasis added*) but
made no finding to that effect. Absent evidence or a finding that Hanson had
decided to seek control of SCM through purchases of its stock, no duty of disclosure existed under the federal securities laws. . . .

It may well be that Hanson's private acquisition of 25% of SCM's shares
after termination of Hanson's tender offer was designed to block the SCM-
Merrill leveraged buyout group from acquiring the $66^2/_3\%$ of SCM's stock
needed to effectuate a merger. It may be speculated that such a blocking move
might induce SCM to buy Hanson's 25% at a premium or lead to negotiations
between the parties designed to resolve their differences. But we know of no
provision in the federal securities laws or elsewhere that prohibits such tactics
in "hardball" market battles of the type encountered here. . . .

Thus the full disclosure purposes of the Williams Act as it now stands appear
to have been fully satisfied by Hanson's furnishing to the public, both before
and after termination of its tender offer, all of the essential relevant facts it was
required by law to supply.

SCM further contends, and in this respect it is supported by the SEC as an
amicus, that upon termination of a tender offer the solicitor should be subject

to a waiting or cooling-off period (10 days is suggested) before it may purchase any of the target company's outstanding shares. However, neither the Act nor any SEC rule promulgated thereunder prohibits a former tender offeror from purchasing stock of a target through privately negotiated transactions immediately after a tender offer has been terminated. Indeed, it is significant that the SEC's formal proposal for the adoption of such a rule (Proposed Rule 14e-5) has never been implemented even though the SEC adopted a similar prohibition with respect to an *issuer's* making such purchases within 10 days after termination of a tender offer. *See* Rule 13e-4(f)(6). Thus, the existing law does not support the prohibition urged by SCM and the SEC. We believe it would be unwise for courts judicially to usurp what is a legislative or regulatory function by substituting our judgment for that of Congress or the SEC. . . .

The order of the district court is reversed, the preliminary injunction against Hanson is vacated, and the case is remanded for further proceedings in accordance with this opinion. . . .

NOTE

In 1979, the SEC proposed a rule that would provide objective criteria to determine whether a putative Bidder's activity in Target's stock constituted a "tender offer" that would trigger the requirements of the Williams Act. *See* SEC Release No. 33-6159, Proposed Amendments to Tender Offer Rules, 1979 WL 182307 (Nov. 29, 1979). However, the proposed rule was never adopted, primarily because the SEC could not reach a consensus on precisely what activity constitutes a tender offer. "Needless to say, the SEC's preference for flexibility comes at the cost of sleeplessness for transaction planners, who quite naturally quest for certainty for their client's acquisitions." James D. Cox and Thomas L. Hazen, BUSINESS ORGANIZATIONS LAW (5th ed. 2020) at 706-707.

QUESTIONS

1. What is the *S-G* test for determining whether a buyer's purchases of stock of the publicly traded company constitute a tender offer? How does this approach differ from the eight-factor *Wellman* test? For example, would the court have reached a different result in *Hanson Trust* if the court had applied the *Wellman* test used by the court in the *Carter Hawley Hale* case?
2. Did Hanson's activity constitute a *de facto* continuation of its earlier tender offer for SCM shares? Why did the court decline to impose a "cooling off" period that would prevent Hanson from making any purchases of SCM stock?

2.   Scope of Disclosure Required Under Regulation 14D and Schedule TO

In Chapter 4, we outlined the disclosure requirements imposed by both the federal proxy rules under the 1934 Act and the registration requirements of the 1933 Act (as well as the exemptions from registration promulgated thereunder). In addition to these obligations under the federal securities laws, the acquisition process is also subject to the disclosure requirements of the Williams Act in those transactions that involve a "tender offer" within the meaning of §14(d) of the 1934 Act.

Although not defined in the statute, nor in any SEC rule, the courts generally follow the eight-factor test (described in the two principal cases above) in order to decide whether an acquisition program involves a *tender offer*. If a proposed transaction does constitute a tender offer, then the offeror (i.e., Bidder Co.) must file and distribute the disclosure required by §14(d)(1) of the 1934 Act and the SEC rules promulgated thereunder. The SEC's tender offer rules consist of Regulation 14D and Regulation 14E (governing third-party tender offers), and Rule 13e-4 with respect to issuer self-tenders (i.e., tender offers by a publicly traded issuer for its own equity securities).

The specific disclosure required of Bidder Co. to satisfy this statutory mandate is now set forth in Schedule TO (formerly Schedule 14D-1), and the following excerpt succinctly describes the scope of required disclosure:

> Schedule TO requires certain basic information regarding the bidder and the bid. For example, Schedule TO requires disclosure of the name of the bidder, the name of the target company, and the title of the class securities being sought. . . . But the disclosures demanded of the bidder are more extensive than mere background information. There must be disclosure of the source of funds to be used in connection with the tender offer and the identity and background of the [Bidder]. . . . The tender-offer document must also disclose all contracts, transactions, or negotiations in the preceding three fiscal years between the bidder and the target company, its directors or its officers, the purpose of the tender offer, and the bidder's plans and proposals for the future with regard to the target company. The Schedule TO must divulge the bidder's current interest and holdings of securities of the target company. . . . Schedule TO must identify all persons retained, employed, or compensated in connection with the tender offer. The bidder must also disclose extensive information regarding its financial position if the bidder's financial position is material to an investor's decision regarding whether or not to tender shares in the target company.
>
> Certain prospective information must be disclosed—such as any steps towards compliance with necessary administrative approval for the offer, the possible impact of the antitrust laws, . . . as well as a summary of pending material legal proceedings.

James D. Cox and Thomas L. Hazen, BUSINESS ORGANIZATIONS LAW (5th ed. 2020, West Hornbook Series) at 709-710.

Schedule TO is filed with the SEC on the day that the Bidder commences its tender offer, which is usually intended to acquire a control block of Target's publicly traded common stock, thereby giving the Bidder a majority of Target's outstanding voting common stock. The filing of the Schedule TO is typically accompanied by the publication of Bidder's offer to purchase Target's common stock in a newspaper of wide circulation (such as the *Wall Street Journal*). Target's management is then required under Rule 14d-5 of the SEC's tender offer rules to cooperate in distributing Bidder's tender offer materials to Target's shareholders, which is usually done by either mailing these materials to Target's shareholders (at Bidder's expense), or alternatively, providing the Bidder with a current list of Target's shareholders. In this way, the SEC's tender offer rules are meant to ensure that Target shareholders have sufficient information about the terms of Bidder's offer. In addition, the SEC has promulgated other rules (which were summarized at p. 419 as part of the introduction to this chapter) that are designed to regulate the tender offer process so that Target shareholders have adequate time to evaluate Bidder's offer and are not unfairly pressured into tendering their shares.

Before 1999, a Bidder that proposed to acquire shares of a publicly traded Target in a stock-for-stock exchange offer was required to register the proposed transaction under the 1933 Act *before* Bidder was allowed to commence its exchange offer. By contrast, in the case of an all-cash tender offer to purchase Target's publicly traded common stock, Bidder faced no such delay in commencing its tender offer. In 1999, however, the SEC promulgated Regulation M-A, with the goal of equalizing the regulatory treatment of cash tender offers and stock exchange offers. Under Rule 162 of Regulation M-A, the SEC now permits the Bidder to solicit Target shareholders in a stock-for-stock exchange offer *before* the Bidder's (i.e., the issuer's) registration statement is declared effective by the SEC (in a process that was briefly described in Chapter 4) — so long as the actual exchange of Target's shares for Bidder's securities occurs only *after* the registration statement has become effective pursuant to the SEC's rules promulgated under the 1933 Act. This change in regulatory approach allows Bidder "to distribute [only] one information document that combines the [issuer's] preliminary prospectus [in satisfaction of the 1933 Act, together with Bidder's] tender offer disclosure [as required by the Williams Act]. The deal can then be closed after 20 business days, [which is the] minimum time a tender offer must be kept open. [In addition,] the SEC staff has committed itself to approve effectiveness of the [issuer's/Bidder's] registration statement within this 20-day period." Alan R. Palmiter, Securities Regulation: Examples & Explanations (7th ed. 2017, Wolters Kluwer Law & Business) at 377.

QUESTIONS

1. What information do investors need to know in order to make an informed decision in deciding whether to tender their Target Co. shares into Bidder's public tender offer?

2. Does your analysis of the scope of required disclosure vary depending on whether Bidder is seeking to acquire any and all shares or is instead making a partial tender offer?

3. Does your analysis of investors' information needs depend on whether the tender offer consideration consists of all cash or exclusively shares of Bidder's stock?

3. Rule 14d-10: The Impact of the SEC's Best Price Rule

In 1986, the SEC adopted Rule 14d-10, more popularly known as the Best Price Rule. Consistent with the SEC's mandate of investor protection, the rule requires the tender offeror to pay to all security holders the highest price paid to any security holder during the course of Bidder's tender offer. Although this rule seemed to be relatively straightforward in its terms, by the 1990s, the rule was engulfed in controversy and uncertainty as to its application. The uncertainty largely stemmed from conflicting judicial interpretations as to the scope of Rule 14d-10. "[I]n the early 1990s, some influential courts held that certain compensatory arrangements with officers and other employees of a target who tender shares into a pending tender offer could constitute consideration paid to them by the acquirer.* This led to the virtual demise of the tender offer as an acquisition structure in [friendly, fully negotiated] transactions in which the [Bidder] sought new employment[†] or [other] similar arrangements with [Target's] management." Andrew L. Sommer & Gregory H. Woods, *The Tender Offer Returns: What Does It Mean for Private Equity Buyers?* 7 Debevoise & Plimpton Private Equity Report 1 (Winter/Spring 2007), *available at*: https://www.debevoise.com/insights/publications/2007/04/the-private-equity-report.

At the end of 2006, the SEC adopted amendments to its Best Price Rule that were intended to address the uncertainty regarding Rule 14d-10. The amendments clarify the circumstances in which members of management who tender their Target shares into Bidder's tender offer could also receive new employment agreements or equity-based compensation. "The amended best-price rule now requires that the consideration paid to any security holder 'for securities tendered in the tender offer' be the highest consideration paid to any other security holder 'for securities tendered in the tender offer.' The new phrases are intended to make clear that the rule applies *only* to the consideration paid for securities tendered, not for other arrangements that may be 'integral' to the tender offer[, the test previously applied by a number of courts]. . . . The amendments [also] provide that the best-price rule will *not* prohibit the negotiation, execution, or amendment of an employment compensation, severance, or other employee-benefit arrangement, provided the arrangement is compensation for past or future services or for refraining from performing future services and is not calculated based on the number of securities tendered or to be tendered." *Id.* at 24 (*emphasis added*). As a result of these amendments, most commentators believe that it is much less likely that employment-related compensation will trigger claims that Bidder has violated Rule 14d-10 and will lead to a "return" of the tender offer "as a viable — and in many cases superior — alternative to the single-step [usually structured as a triangular] merger for both

---

* [By the author: *See, e.g., Epstein v. MCA, Inc.,* 50 F.3d 644 (9th Cir. 1995), rev'd on other grounds, *Matsushita Electric Industrial Co. v Epstein,* 516 U.S. 367 (1996) (adopting the "integral element" approach); *see also Lerro v. Quaker Oats Co.,* 84 F.3d 239 (7th Cir. 1996) (adopting the "bright-line" test).]

† [By the author: The "virtual demise of the tender offer" is largely attributable to the devastating financial consequences if a court were to find later that the tender offeror violated Rule 14d-10. "The threat of litigation, . . . [coupled with] the drastic penalties to a [Bidder] for violation of the best price rule (i.e., the mandatory payment of the per share value of the contested [employee compensation] arrangement to all security holders), had a chilling effect on tender offers." Marilyn Mooney, et al., *Amendments to the Best Price Tender Offer Rules,* 20 Insights 5 (December 2006) (*emphasis added*). In other words, the damages to be paid if a court were to determine later that Bidder had violated Rule 14d-10 would require the tender offeror to pay every other shareholder (who had tendered their shares into Bidder's tender offer) the same consideration per share that Bidder had paid to the shareholder that received the highest per-share payment. "Indeed under a worst case scenario, the value of the

strategic" and financial buyers (such as private equity firms). Mark Gordon, *The Return of the Tender Offer*, Wachtell, Lipton, Rosen & Katz, July 23, 2007, *available at:* https://corpgov.law.harvard.edu/wp-content/uploads/2007/07/20070729-return-of-the-tender-offer1.pdf.[8]

> ***Advantages of the Tender Offer.*** So, what are the advantages of the two-step, tender-offer process over the alternative of structuring the acquisition of Target as a single-step, statutory merger? From the perspective of both the Bidder and the Target, the primary advantage of the two-step transaction is the *speed* of the tender-offer process. "Because the minimum number of business days that a tender offer must be kept open is only 20, the [Bidder] can purchase a controlling stake in the [Target] in a relatively short period of time, thereby reducing the probability of a competing bid by another potential buyer. If the [Bidder] acquires enough shares to execute a short-form merger—usually 90% [under state law]—the back-end merger [allowing Bidder to acquire 100% control over Target] can be consummated promptly without filing a proxy or information statement with the SEC or obtaining shareholder approval. A statutory [triangular] merger subject to the SEC's proxy rules generally will take at least three to four months to complete." David Grinberg & Gordon Bava, *A Comeback for Tender Offers?* MERGERS & ACQUISITIONS 73-77 (March 2007). The delay associated with the single-step merger process results from the state-law-mandated requirement that the merger be approved by shareholders at a special meeting following an SEC proxy review process. To be more specific,

>> The obvious reason to employ a tender offer structure is to complete the acquisition as quickly as possible. Both bidder and target companies share this objective. Bidders want to minimize the loss of target company customers, employees and other relationships pending closing, reduce the time during which a competing acquisition proposal may be made, and start integrating the acquired business into its own organization. Target companies want to reduce the time period during which events, such as a material adverse change, might occur and provide a bidder the basis for terminating the transaction or renegotiating the acquisition price, . . . [In addition, in the case of a tender offer, Target shareholders receive the acquisition consideration faster than they would in a statutory merger.]

>> Under SEC rules, a [Bidder] may start a tender offer without pre-clearing [the tender offer] documents with the SEC and purchases of shares in a tender offer may be completed twenty business days after the offer formally begins. If sufficient shares are purchased to permit a [Bidder] to unilaterally complete a "short-form merger" (generally 85% or 90% under state law), the acquisition of 100%

---

richest of these kind of [employment] arrangements (say, for example, [Bidder's payment of a] $4 million [retention bonus to the Target's] CEO), would [then] have to be paid to each other shareholder of [Target]." Sommer & Woods, *supra* at pg. 24 (emphasis added). Obviously, this could lead to potentially crushing liability and eliminate the value of the transaction from Bidder's perspective, thereby "chilling" the willingness of prospective Bidders to structure their acquisitions as a tender offer, even in those situations where the tender offer, for other reasons, may have been the preferred deal structure.]

8. You will recall, from our discussion of the Problem Sets in Chapter 2, that the use of a (typically reverse) triangular merger allows Bidder (in a single-step transaction) to operate the publicly traded Target Co. as a wholly owned subsidiary following closing on the merger agreement and effectiveness of the merger. *See* Diagrams 10 and 11 in Appendix A. However, this same

of the [Target] company may be completed approximately 30 to 40 days after an acquisition agreement is signed assuming no regulatory approvals are required. [In contrast, a] statutory merger requires the filing of preliminary proxy materials with the SEC, the setting of a record date . . . and the calling of a stockholders meeting at which the acquisition is submitted to a shareholder vote. Assuming the SEC does not review the proxy materials, this process is likely to take approximately 40 to 50 days. On the other hand, if the SEC reviews the proxy materials, delays of two to four weeks are possible. Therefore, the preference for tender offers arises from the risk of delay created by the possibility of SEC review.

Peter Golden, et al., *The Return of the Tender Offer,* Fried, Frank, Harris, Shriver & Johnson, LLP, Nov. 20, 2006, *available at:* https://www.friedfrank.com/siteFiles/ Publications/B310EE20F1F930447954D89819E74F38.pdf. Another advantage offered by the tender-offer process is the ability of the Bidder to eliminate appraisal rights in connection with the tender offer, which is an increasingly attractive proposition in the current environment of activist shareholders.[9]

However, the speed (and elimination of appraisal rights) offered by the tender-offer process may not be appropriate for every acquisition. Depending on the facts and circumstances surrounding a proposed acquisition, financing concerns, regulatory considerations, and other factors may favor the traditional single-step merger structure.

[As an example,] in situations where it may take substantially longer to obtain antitrust or other regulatory approvals than to obtain shareholder approval, a single-step merger may be the preferred approach because the transaction will not be subject to third-party topping bid risk [i.e., the risk of a third party bidder coming along and offering a higher price to acquire Target's business] during the period from receipt of shareholder approval until receipt of regulatory approval. In the tender structure, the deal remains exposed to topping risk until the tender offer closes after all [required] regulatory approvals have been obtained.

Mark Gordon, *supra.*

QUESTION

1.   In light of the SEC's amendments to Rule 14d-10, what are the advantages of a cash tender offer, as opposed to the other potential deal structures, such as a reverse triangular merger?

---

result can be achieved in a two-step transaction involving a tender offer (to obtain control of the publicly traded Target), to be followed by a back-end, squeeze-out merger (to eliminate the minority interest and leave Target as a wholly owned subsidiary). *See* Diagram 12 in Appendix A. It also bears mentioning that in 2013, the Delaware legislature amended DGCL §251 to add a new form of deal structure that has come to be known as the "medium form" merger. *See* Del. §251(h). This new form of statutory merger offers further timing and other advantages over the two-step, tender offer process. We will examine the mechanics and statutory requirements of Del. §251(h) in further detail in Chapter 7. *See* Note 2 at p. 756.

   9. You will recall from our analysis of the Stock Purchase Problems in Chapter 2 (*see* Problem Set No. 4 at pp. 110-111), that the shareholder retains the power to decide whether to tender their Target shares into Bidder's pending tender offer. Since each shareholder

4. Tender Offer Conditions: The Importance of Contract Law

Gilbert v. El Paso Company
575 A.2d 1131 (Del. 1988)

Moore, Justice.

... On the afternoon of December 20, 1982, Travis Petty, El Paso's chairman and chief executive officer, received a telephone call from Richard Bressler, the chairman and chief executive officer of Burlington. Bressler confirmed long-circulating rumors of Burlington's interest in acquiring El Paso, and notified Petty that Burlington's board of directors had recently authorized him to initiate a tender offer to gain control of El Paso. The following day, December 21, 1982, Petty received a letter from Bressler confirming that Burlington had launched a tender offer for up to 25,100,000 common shares of El Paso, representing approximately 49.1% of the company's outstanding common stock. The ownership of these shares, when added to the 537,800 already beneficially owned by Burlington, would give Burlington control of over 51.8% of all outstanding El Paso common shares.

The offer stipulated that tendered shares could be withdrawn until January 12, 1983, and that the offer would expire at 12:00 midnight on January 19, 1983. Burlington stated that if the December offer was oversubscribed, any shares tendered before December 30, 1982 would be entitled to proration rights.[7] Significantly, Burlington revealed no future plans to purchase the remaining 49% of El Paso's common shares upon completion of a fully-subscribed December offer. In fact, Burlington specifically cautioned that any future second-step transaction with El Paso's minority shareholders "might be on terms (including the consideration offered per share) the same as, or more or less favorable than, those of the [December] offer." Additionally, Burlington expressly reserved the right to terminate its highly-conditional offer upon the occurrence of any one of a number of specified events.[8] ...

Based in part upon these presentations [by its financial advisor (Merrill Lynch) and its legal advisor (Wachtel Lipton)], the El Paso board unanimously

---

must decide whether to accept Bidder's offer by tendering their stock to Bidder, no appraisal rights are available to those shareholders who tender their Target shares. Instead, if Target Co. shareholders do not approve of the terms offered by Bidder Co., then they just refuse to sell (tender) their shares.

7. We have previously observed that granting such proration rights, in the absence of adequate protections for the company's remaining or back-end shares, has been universally recognized as a "classic coercive measure designed to stampede shareholders into tendering" their shares. *Unocal* [493 A.2d 946, 956 (Del. 1985)]. This stratagem has primarily been criticized by us and has met a timely demise. *See id. See also* 17 C.F.R. §240.14d-8 (1988).

8. Burlington reserved the right to terminate the offer if: (a) any legal action challenging the offer were instituted or threatened; (b) any governmental body took action which might affect or delay the offer; (c) there were substantial and material changes or threatened changes in the business or assets of El Paso; (d) El Paso authorized or proposed to authorize an extraordinary dividend or the creation of new capital stock; (e) El Paso adopted or proposed to adopt any amendments to its articles of incorporation or By-laws; or (f) El Paso and Burlington entered into a definitive agreement or understanding involving a business combination. Not surprisingly, each of these events occurred at some point during the course of this takeover contest.

rejected Burlington's December offer, concluding that it was not in the best interests of the company or its shareholders. The directors were principally concerned with the perceived inadequacy of the $24 offering price, the partial nature of the bid, and the potentially adverse impact upon remaining shareholders if the December offer were successful. The directors also adopted several resolutions, upon the recommendation of legal counsel, designed to impede Burlington's bid. These measures included "golden parachute" employment agreements with El Paso's senior managers; amendments to El Paso's by-laws and Employee Savings and Stock Ownership plans; creation of a new series of preferred stock, with detachable share rights intended to forestall any business combination between El Paso and a 25% or greater shareholder without the approval of 90% of the outstanding preferred shares.[9] . . .

Throughout the weekend of January 8th and 9th, the parties' financial and legal advisors negotiated the essential components of a possible accord between the companies. Central to these negotiations was the amount which Burlington would ultimately invest in El Paso. Despite the apparent urging of El Paso's representatives, Burlington steadfastly refused to increase its frontend offer beyond the minimal amount required under its December offer to gain control of El Paso—approximately $600,000,000. Therefore, in order to reconcile these conflicting points with both companies' desire to augment El Paso's capital structure, the parties agreed in principle to Burlington's acquisition of a majority of El Paso's common stock through a consensual, two-part transaction. Under this proposal, Burlington was granted an option to purchase 4,166,667 treasury shares directly from El Paso for $100,000,000. These funds would then be used to increase El Paso's equity base. Burlington would then terminate the December offer, and would substitute in its place a new offer (the January offer), for a reduced total of 21,000,000 shares at $24 per share,[16] which would then be open to all El Paso shareholders. Notably, in addition to enhancing the equity base of the company, this arrangement satisfied El Paso's objective that all shareholders should benefit from an improved Burlington offer.

As part of this accord, Burlington agreed in principle to El Paso's demand for enhanced procedural safeguards and protections for El Paso's remaining back-end shareholders. Burlington also agreed that Petty and four other El Paso representatives would continue as directors of El Paso ("the Continuing Directors"). Finally, Burlington acknowledged that any contemplated second step for El Paso's remaining minority shares would be subject to the majority approvals of both the Continuing Directors and El Paso's minority (i.e., non-Burlington) shareholders. . . .

Burlington thereafter terminated its December offer, and on the next day, January 11, 1983, instituted the new January offer for 21,000,000 shares at $24

---

9. This novel security, issued as an integral part of a Share Purchase Rights Plan, is generally recognized as the first use and forerunner of the contemporary "poison pill" antitakeover device. *See* M. Johnson, *Takeover: The New Wall Street Warriors* 13, 36-37 (1986).

16. It appears that the number of shares to be purchased by Burlington under the January offer was established after Burlington had agreed to directly invest $100,000,000 in El Paso. The record suggests that the parties worked backwards from Burlington's total investment ceiling of $600,000,000, and determined that the remaining $500,000,000 available for Burlington's acquisition effort could be used to purchase approximately 21,000,000 El Paso shares at $24 per share.

per share. In response to the January offer, 40,246,853 shares were tendered, including most of the shares owned by El Paso's directors. . . .

II.

Plaintiffs primarily challenge two aspects of the settlement agreement between Burlington and El Paso: the substitution of the January offer for the December offer, and the direct purchase by Burlington of 4,166,667 treasury shares from El Paso. Plaintiffs claim, without dispute from the defendants, that those transactions (i) reduced the number of shares that Burlington directly purchased from El Paso's shareholders and (ii) diluted the proration pool initially established under the December offer by allowing *all* shareholders, including those who were not members of the class, to tender into the January offer. . . .

III.

. . . We first address the Court of Chancery's decision in *Gilbert I* dismissing the breach of contract allegations against Burlington. The court noted that "[p]laintiffs' principal complaint is that Burlington breached its contractual obligation to complete its December tender offer." *Gilbert I* [*Gilbert v. El Paso*, 490 A.2d 1050, 1054 (Del. Ch. 1984)]. As characterized, the plaintiffs' breach of contract claim is fundamentally dependent upon their assertion that the class had a recognizable, vested and defendable right to have their shares purchased under the December offer. The plaintiffs' action for contractual breach is contingent upon their presumption that, by tendering their shares into Burlington's highly conditional December offer, the class was vested with certain rights with which neither Burlington nor El Paso could interfere.

It is undisputed that Burlington had conditioned its acceptance of shares tendered into the December offer upon the non-occurrence of a number of specified events, and that *each* of these conditions occurred in the three weeks following the announcement of Burlington's December offer. *See Gilbert I*, 490 A.2d at 1053. It is also well settled that under general contract law an offeror may condition the performance contemplated in his offer upon the occurrence or non-occurrence of specific events. Such conditions may effectively limit the obligation of the promisor to perform. 3A A. Corbin, *Corbin on Contracts* §639 (1960). Under New Jersey law,[26] an offeror has wide latitude over the terms of its offer and is free to engraft any number of conditions or terms upon it. Similarly, in connection with a tender offer, an offeror may specify any number of conditions qualifying its obligation to perform, subject to Securities and Exchange Commission limitations and the requirements established under the Williams

---

26. The December offer provided for performance (the tender of shares) in Newark, New Jersey. The parties agree that New Jersey law controls the plaintiffs' breach of contract claim. The Vice Chancellor correctly found that New Jersey statutory and case law on this issue is consistent with general principles of contract law.

Act. These fundamental principles are clear and are apparently uncontested by the plaintiffs.

Among their ancillary contractual claims, however, plaintiffs argue that Burlington deliberately invoked these conditions solely to acquire El Paso on more advantageous terms, and in so doing, breached its implied covenant of good faith and fair dealing with the class. Although an implied covenant of good faith and honest conduct exists in every contract, such subjective standards cannot override the literal terms of an agreement.

As part of the December offer, Burlington expressly reserved the right to terminate the offer upon the occurrence of a number of objective, factual events over which Burlington exercised no discretion or control. Although an implied covenant of good faith may preclude an offeror from escaping its obligations by deliberately causing the occurrence of a condition precedent, there is no evidence of such activity here. We agree with the Vice Chancellor's finding that an offeror "is free to pursue its economic interests through the application of conditions intended to limit the cost of proceeding." In tendering their shares to Burlington, the class accepted these express limitations and qualifications, and acknowledged that Burlington could be relieved of its promise to perform upon the occurrence of any of the reserved conditions. Thus, Burlington's mere exercise of its contractual right to terminate its tender offer, without more, does not constitute a breach of its implied covenant of good faith and fair dealing.

[In a portion of the Court's opinion that was omitted in this edited excerpt, the Court concluded that the plaintiffs failed to establish that the directors breached their fiduciary duties, relying on *Unocal*'s standard of enhanced judicial scrutiny. *See Unocal Corp. v. Mesa Petroleum, infra,* at p. 521. We will discuss the *Unocal* standard of review at length as part of the fiduciary duty materials in Chapter 7.]

QUESTIONS

1. What were the concerns that the El Paso board had with respect to the terms of Burlington's original bid for El Paso?

2. What were the back-end protections that were included in Burlington's revised January offer? How did these protections address the concerns that the El Paso board had with respect to the terms of Burlington's original offer?

3. What is the basis of the plaintiff's complaint with respect to the revised terms of Burlington's offer?

C.   State Antitakeover Statutes: State Regulation of Stock Purchases

Following enactment of the Williams Act in 1968, and as the market for hostile takeovers subsequently heated up, many states responded by adopting statutes regulating tender offers; indeed, by 1982, thirty-seven states had adopted some form of antitakeover statute. *See* Guhan Subramanian, Steven Herscovici, and Brian Barbetta, *Is Delaware's Anti-Takeover Statute Unconstitutional? Evidence from 1988-2008*, 65 BUS. LAW. 685 (2010). Broadly speaking, the "intent behind [these state antitakeover statutes] is to protect the incumbent management and to preserve the payrolls of local companies that are potential takeover [targets]." Cox & Hazen, BUSINESS ORGANIZATIONS LAW, *supra*, at 719. Or, as Professor Roberta Romano explains in her book, THE GENIUS OF AMERICAN CORPORATE LAW, at 58-59 (1993):

> Like most pork-barrel legislation such as public works ("rivers and harbors") bills, takeover statutes are almost always unanimously approved [when submitted to state legislatures]. The likely explanation for such legislative unanimity is that the benefits and beneficiaries (real or supposed) of such legislation are highly concentrated—many, if not most, of the target company's managers and workers reside within the state—while the costs [imposed by these antitakeover statutes] are borne largely by a loosely organized, geographically dispersed group, of share-holders [—many, if not most, of whom are non-residents].

The terms of the earliest generations of these state antitakeover statutes typically imposed requirements that were more stringent than the requirements imposed by federal law. Concern grew over whether states could regulate the tender offer process in the face of federal legislation or whether the Williams Act had preempted the field. Another challenge to the constitutionality of these state statutes was based on the Commerce Clause. Here, concern focused on whether the state statute imposed an impermissible burden on interstate commerce. The first generation of the state antitakeover statutes to reach the Supreme Court was Illinois's antitakeover statute, which was declared uncon-stitutional in *Edgar v. MITE Corp.*, 457 U.S. 624 (1982). Since this case was decided, state antitakeover statutes have continued to evolve through successive generations, each transition marked by a decision of the U.S. Supreme Court. "Today, [though,] only the second and third generation statutes have survived Constitutional challenge." Cox and Hazen, BUSINESS ORGANIZATIONS LAW, *supra*, at 720. The three generations of state antitakeover statutes are the focus of the following materials.

1. The First Generation—Disclosure and Fairness Statutes

The Illinois antitakeover statute at issue in *Edgar v. MITE Corp.*, *supra*, covered corporations that were incorporated in Illinois, as well as those *non-Illinois* cor-porations that had their principal offices in Illinois (or at least 10 percent of their capital represented within the state), provided further that at least 10 per-cent of the shares sought to be acquired in Bidder's tender offer were held by Illinois residents. In addition, the Illinois statute imposed a mandatory twenty-day waiting period before Bidder's tender offer could commence and allowed for administrative review (by Illinois state officials) as to the fairness of the terms of Bidder's proposed tender offer. Moreover, there was no fixed timetable for completing this review process, which meant this process potentially could extend for an indefinite period of time.

In a very divided opinion, the Supreme Court ruled in 1982 that the Illinois statute was unconstitutional. By a 5-4 majority, the Supreme Court "held that the Illinois statute violated the 'dormant' commerce clause because the statute's burden on out-of-state tender offers outweighed any state interest in disclosure and shareholder protection." Alan R. Palmiter, CORPORATIONS: EXAMPLES AND EXPLANATIONS (8th ed. 2015) at 802. The Illinois statute was also challenged on the grounds that it was preempted by the Williams Act. However, only a plurality of the Court joined in the portion of the *MITE* opinion that found that the Illinois statute was preempted on the grounds that the delays allowed by the Illinois statute frustrated the carefully balanced disclosure scheme adopted by Congress in the Williams Act. In sum, the Court's decision in "*Edgar v. MITE Corp.* was the death knell for first-generation antitakeover statutes," Cox and Hazen, *supra,* at 721, most of which went well "beyond the disclosure philosophy of the Williams Act by giving the state administrator the power to review the merits of the tender offer's terms or the adequacy of the bidder's disclosures" in a manner similar to the terms of the Illinois antitakeover statute. *Id.* at 720.

Following the Supreme Court's decision in *MITE*, states sought to regulate the tender offer process by exploiting the internal affairs doctrine. "The basic thrust of many of these second-generation statutes is to regulate tender offers through state law rules relating to corporate governance . . ." Cox and Hazen, *supra,* at 721. Accordingly, these "second-generation statutes" generally involved amendments to provisions of the state corporation code governing the company's internal affairs. Two types of statutes came to dominate the second-generation statute antitakeover statutes: control share statutes and fair price (or best price) statutes. These statutes are the topic of the next section.

2.   The Second Generation — Control Share and Fair Price Statutes

The *control share statute,* first enacted in Ohio, limited the voting rights of shares held by a control person. Generally speaking, as a prospective Bidder Co. acquires shares of Target Co., it may cross different ownership thresholds; these levels are set forth in the relevant state statute. For example, the Indiana statute at issue in the next case provided that control thresholds are crossed when a person becomes the owner of 20 percent, 33⅓ percent, or 50 percent of the company's voting stock. After crossing a particular threshold, these statutes typically provide that the acquiring shareholder (i.e., Bidder) cannot vote the shares that it just acquired in the absence of a favorable vote by a majority of the company's other shareholders (i.e., a vote of a majority of the "disinterested shares," as defined in the state's statute). Most of these control share statutes define disinterested shares to exclude the shares held by the acquiring shareholder (i.e., Bidder), as well as those held by the management of Target.

By contrast, the *fair price statutes* — or *best price statutes* — typically provide that any Bidder acquiring a "covered corporation" (i.e., a Target Co. covered by the terms of the fair price statute) must pay to *all* shareholders the best price paid to any Target shareholder. Most of these best price statutes allow for waiver of this requirement either by appropriate vote of Target shareholders or by the company's board of directors. Thus, most best price statutes do not present an obstacle to friendly takeovers (i.e., negotiated acquisitions).

The constitutionality of these so-called second-generation statutes was decided by the Supreme Court in the next case.

CTS Corp. v. Dynamics Corp. of America
481 U.S. 69 (1987)

Justice POWELL delivered the opinion of the Court.

I

A

On March 4, 1986, the Governor of Indiana signed . . . the Control Share Acquisitions Chapter (Indiana Act or Act). Beginning on August 1, 1987, the Act will apply to any corporation incorporated in Indiana, unless the corporation amends its articles of incorporation or bylaws to opt out of the Act. Before that date, any Indiana corporation can opt into the Act by resolution of its board of directors. The Act applies only to "issuing public corporations." The term "corporation" includes only businesses incorporated in Indiana. An "issuing public corporation" is defined as:

> a corporation that has:
>   (1) one hundred (100) or more shareholders;
>   (2) its principal place of business, its principal office, or substantial assets within Indiana; and
>   (3) either:
>   (A) more than ten percent (10%) of its shareholders resident in Indiana;
>   (B) more than ten percent (10%) of its shares owned by Indiana residents; or
>   (C) ten thousand (10,000) shareholders resident in Indiana.[1]

The Act focuses on the acquisition of "control shares" in an issuing public corporation. Under the Act, an entity acquires "control shares" whenever it acquires shares that, but for the operation of the Act, would bring its voting power in the corporation to or above any of three thresholds: 20%, 33½%, or 50%. An entity that acquires control shares does not necessarily acquire voting rights. Rather, it gains those rights only "to the extent granted by resolution approved by the shareholders of the issuing public corporation." Section

---

1. §23-1-42-4(a). These thresholds are much higher than the 5% threshold acquisition requirement that brings a tender offer under the coverage of the Williams Act. *See* 15 U.S.C. §78n(d)(1).

23-1-42-9(b) requires a majority vote of all disinterested[2] shareholders holding each class of stock for passage of such a resolution. The practical effect of this requirement is to condition acquisition of control of a corporation on approval of a majority of the pre-existing disinterested shareholders.

The shareholders decide whether to confer rights on the control shares at the next regularly scheduled meeting of the shareholders, or at a specially scheduled meeting. The acquiror can require management of the corporation to hold such a special meeting within 50 days if it files an "acquiring person statement,"[4] requests the meeting, and agrees to pay the expenses of the meeting. If the shareholders do not vote to restore voting rights to the shares, the corporation may redeem the control shares from the acquiror at fair market value, but it is not required to do so. Similarly, if the acquiror does not file an acquiring person statement with the corporation, the corporation may, if its bylaws or articles of incorporation so provide, redeem the shares at any time after 60 days after the acquiror's last acquisition.

B

On March 10, 1986, appellee Dynamics Corporation of America (Dynamics) owned 9.6% of the common stock of appellant CTS Corporation, an Indiana corporation. On that day, six days after the Act went into effect, Dynamics announced a tender offer for another million shares in CTS; purchase of those shares would have brought Dynamics' ownership interest in CTS to 27.5%. . . . On March 27, the board of directors of CTS, an Indiana corporation, elected to be governed by the provisions of the Act.

Four days later, on March 31, Dynamics moved for leave to amend its complaint to allege that the Act is pre-empted by the Williams Act, and violates the Commerce Clause. Dynamics sought a temporary restraining order, a

---

2. "Interested shares" are shares with respect to which the acquiror, an officer, or an inside director of the corporation "may exercise or direct the exercise of the voting power of the corporation in the election of directors." §23-1-42-3. If the record date passes before the acquiror purchases shares pursuant to the tender offer, the purchased shares will not be "interested shares" within the meaning of the Act; although the acquiror may own the shares on the date of the meeting, it will not "exercise . . . the voting power" of the shares.

As a practical matter, the record date usually will pass before shares change hands. Under Securities and Exchange Commission (SEC) regulations, the shares cannot be purchased until 20 business days after the offer commences. 17 CFR §240.14e-1(a) (1986). If the acquiror seeks an early resolution of the issue—as most acquirors will—the meeting required by the Act must be held no more than 50 calendar days after the offer commences, about three weeks after the earliest date on which the shares could be purchased. *See* §23-142-7. The Act requires management to give notice of the meeting "as promptly as reasonably practicable . . . to all shareholders of record as of the record date set for the meeting." §23-1-42-8(a). It seems likely that management of the target corporation would violate this obligation if it delayed setting the record date and sending notice until after 20 business days had passed. Thus, we assume that the record date usually will be set before the date on which federal law first permits purchase of the shares.

4. An "acquiring person statement" is an information statement describing, *inter alia,* the identity of the acquiring person and the terms and extent of the proposed acquisition. *See* §23-1-42-6.

preliminary injunction, and declaratory relief against CTS' use of the Act. On April 9, the District Court ruled that the Williams Act pre-empts the Indiana Act and granted Dynamics' motion for declaratory relief. . . . A week later, on April 17, the District Court issued an opinion accepting Dynamics' claim that the Act violates the Commerce Clause. . . .

On April 23 — [just] 23 days after Dynamics first contested application of the Act in the District Court — the Court of Appeals issued an order affirming the judgment of the District Court. . . .

II

The first question in these cases is whether the Williams Act pre-empts the Indiana Act. As we have stated frequently, absent an explicit indication by Congress of an intent to pre-empt state law, a state statute is pre-empted only

> "where compliance with both federal and state regulations is a physical impossibility . . . ," or where the state "law stands as an obstacle to the accomplishment and execution of the full purposes and objectives of Congress. . . ." *Ray v. Atlantic Richfield Co.*, 435 U.S. 151, 158 (1978).

Because it is entirely possible for entities to comply with both the Williams Act and the Indiana Act, the state statute can be pre-empted only if it frustrates the purposes of the federal law. . . .

B

The Indiana Act differs in major respects from the Illinois statute that the Court considered in *Edgar v. MITE Corp.*, 457 U.S. 624, 102 S. Ct. 2629, 73 L. Ed. 2d 269 (1982). After reviewing the legislative history of the Williams Act, Justice WHITE, joined by Chief Justice BURGER and Justice BLACKMUN (the plurality), concluded that the Williams Act struck a careful balance between the interests of offerors and target companies, and that any state statute that "upset" this balance was pre-empted. . . .

C

As the plurality opinion in *MITE* did not represent the views of a majority of the Court,[6] we are not bound by its reasoning. We need not question that reasoning, however, because we believe the Indiana Act passes muster even

---

6. Justice WHITE's opinion on the pre-emption issue, 457 U.S., at 630-640, 102 S. Ct., at 2634-2640, was joined only by Chief Justice BURGER and by Justice BLACKMUN. Two Justices disagreed with Justice WHITE's conclusion. See *id.*, at 646-647, 102 S. Ct., at 2642-2643 (POWELL, J., concurring in part); *id.*, at 655, 102 S. Ct., at 2647 (STEVENS, J., concurring in part and concurring in judgment). Four Justices did not address the question. See *id.*, at 655, 102 S. Ct., at 2647 (O'CONNOR J., concurring in part); *id.*, at 664, 102 S. Ct., at 2652 (MARSHALL, J., with whom BRENNAN, J., joined, dissenting); *id.*, at 667, 102 S. Ct., at 2653 (REHNQUIST, J., dissenting).

under the broad interpretation of the Williams Act articulated by Justice WHITE in *MITE*. [T]he overriding concern of the *MITE* plurality was that the Illinois statute considered in that case operated to favor management against offerors, to the detriment of shareholders. By contrast, the statute now before the Court protects the independent shareholder against the contending parties. Thus, the Act furthers a basic purpose of the Williams Act, " 'plac[ing] investors on an equal footing with the takeover bidder,' " *Piper v. Chris-Craft Industries, Inc.*, 430 U.S., at 30, 97 S. Ct., at 943 (quoting the Senate Report accompanying the Williams Act, S. Rep. No. 550, 90th Cong., 1st Sess., 4 (1967)).

The Indiana Act operates on the assumption, implicit in the Williams Act, that independent shareholders faced with tender offers often are at a disadvantage. By allowing such shareholders to vote as a group, the Act protects them from the coercive aspects of some tender offers. If, for example, shareholders believe that a successful tender offer will be followed by a purchase of nontendering shares at a depressed price, individual shareholders may tender their shares—even if they doubt the tender offer is in the corporation's best interest—to protect themselves from being forced to sell their shares at a depressed price. As the SEC explains: "The alternative of not accepting the tender offer is virtual assurance that, if the offer is successful, the shares will have to be sold in the lower priced, second step." . . . In such a situation under the Indiana Act, the shareholders as a group, acting in the corporation's best interest, could reject the offer, although individual shareholders might be inclined to accept it. The desire of the Indiana Legislature to protect shareholders of Indiana corporations from this type of coercive offer does not conflict with the Williams Act. Rather, it furthers the federal policy of investor protection. . . .

D

The Court of Appeals based its finding of pre-emption on its view that the practical effect of the Indiana Act is to delay consummation of tender offers until 50 days after the commencement of the offer. As did the Court of Appeals, Dynamics reasons that no rational offeror will purchase shares until it gains assurance that those shares will carry voting rights. Because it is possible that voting rights will not be conferred until a shareholder meeting 50 days after commencement of the offer, Dynamics concludes that the Act imposes a 50-day delay. This, it argues, conflicts with the shorter 20-business-day period established by the SEC as the minimum period for which a tender offer may be held open. We find the alleged conflict illusory.

The Act does not impose an absolute 50-day delay on tender offers, nor does it preclude an offeror from purchasing shares as soon as federal law permits. If the offeror fears an adverse shareholder vote under the Act, it can make a conditional tender offer, offering to accept shares on the condition that the shares receive voting rights within a certain period of time. The Williams Act permits tender offers to be conditioned on the offeror's subsequently obtaining regulatory approval. . . . There is no reason to doubt that this type of conditional tender offer would be legitimate as well.[9]

---

9. Dynamics argues that conditional tender offers are not an adequate alternative because they leave management in place for three extra weeks, with "free rein to take other

Even assuming that the Indiana Act imposes some additional delay, nothing in *MITE* suggested that *any* delay imposed by state regulation, however short, would create a conflict with the Williams Act. The plurality argued only that the offeror should "be free to go forward without *unreasonable* delay." 457 U.S., at 639, (*emphasis added*). In that case, the Court was confronted with the potential for indefinite delay and presented with no persuasive reason why some deadline could not be established. By contrast, the Indiana Act provides that full voting rights will be vested—if this eventually is to occur—within 50 days after commencement of the offer. This period is within the 60-day period Congress established for restitution of withdrawal rights in 15 U.S.C. §78n(d)(5). We cannot say that a delay within that congressionally determined period is unreasonable.

Finally, we note that the Williams Act would pre-empt a variety of state corporate laws of hitherto unquestioned validity if it were construed to pre-empt any state statute that may limit or delay the free exercise of power after a successful tender offer. State corporate laws commonly permit corporations to stagger the terms of their directors. By staggering the terms of directors, and thus having annual elections for only one class of directors each year, corporations may delay the time when a successful offeror gains control of the board of directors. Similarly, state corporation laws commonly provide for cumulative voting. By enabling minority shareholders to assure themselves of representation in each class of directors, cumulative voting provisions can delay further the ability of offerors to gain untrammeled authority over the affairs of the target corporation.

In our view, the possibility that the Indiana Act will delay some tender offers is insufficient to require a conclusion that the Williams Act pre-empts the Act. The longstanding prevalence of state regulation in this area suggests that, if Congress had intended to pre-empt all state laws that delay the acquisition of voting control following a tender offer, it would have said so explicitly. The regulatory conditions that the Act places on tender offers are consistent with the text and the purposes of the Williams Act. Accordingly, we hold that the Williams Act does not pre-empt the Indiana Act.

III

As an alternative basis for its decision, the Court of Appeals held that the Act violates the Commerce Clause of the Federal Constitution. We now address this holding. On its face, the Commerce Clause is nothing more than a grant to Congress of the power "[t]o regulate Commerce . . . among the several States . . . ," Art. I, §8, cl. 3. But it has been settled for more than a century that

---

defensive steps that will diminish the value of tendered shares." Brief for Appellee 37. We reject this contention. In the unlikely event that management were to take actions designed to diminish the value of the corporation's shares, it may incur liability under state law. But this problem does not control our pre-emption analysis. Neither the Act nor any other federal statute can assure that shareholders do not suffer from the mismanagement of corporate officers and directors. Cf. *Cort v. Ash*, 422 U.S. 66, 84, 95 S. Ct. 2080, 2090-2091, 45 L. Ed. 2d 26 (1975).

the Clause prohibits States from taking certain actions respecting interstate commerce even absent congressional action. *See, e.g.,* Cooley v. Board of Wardens, 12 How. 299 (1852). The Court's interpretation of "these great silences of the Constitution," H. P. Hood & Sons, Inc. v. Du Mond, 336 U.S. 525, 535 (1949), has not always been easy to follow. Rather, as the volume and complexity of commerce and regulation have grown in this country, the Court has articulated a variety of tests in an attempt to describe the difference between those regulations that the Commerce Clause permits and those regulations that it prohibits.

A

The principal objects of dormant Commerce Clause scrutiny are statutes that discriminate against interstate commerce. . . . The Indiana Act is not such a statute. It has the same effects on tender offers whether or not the offeror is a domiciliary or resident of Indiana. Thus, it "visits its effects equally upon both interstate and local business," *Lewis v. BT Investment Managers, Inc.,* [447 U.S. 27, at 36 (1980)].

Dynamics nevertheless contends that the statute is discriminatory because it will apply most often to out-of-state entities. This argument rests on the contention that, as a practical matter, most hostile tender offers are launched by offerors outside Indiana. But this argument avails Dynamics little. . . . Because nothing in the Indiana Act imposes a greater burden on out-of-state offerors than it does on similarly situated Indiana offerors, we reject the contention that the Act discriminates against interstate commerce.

B

This Court's recent Commerce Clause cases also have invalidated statutes that may adversely affect interstate commerce by subjecting activities to inconsistent regulations. . . . The Indiana Act poses no such problem. So long as each State regulates voting rights only in the corporations it has created, each corporation will be subject to the law of only one State. No principle of corporation law and practice is more firmly established than a State's authority to regulate domestic corporations, including the authority to define the voting rights of shareholders. . . . Accordingly, we conclude that the Indiana Act does not create an impermissible risk of inconsistent regulation by different States.

C

The Court of Appeals did not find the Act unconstitutional for either of these threshold reasons. Rather, its decision rested on its view of the Act's potential to hinder tender offers. We think the Court of Appeals failed to appreciate the significance for Commerce Clause analysis of the fact that state regulation of corporate governance is regulation of entities whose very existence and attributes are a product of state law. As Chief Justice Marshall explained:

A corporation is an artificial being, invisible, intangible, and existing only in contemplation of law. Being the mere creature of law, it possesses only those properties which the charter of its creation confers upon it, either expressly, or as incidental to its very existence. These are such as are supposed best calculated to effect the object for which it was created. *Trustees of Dartmouth College v. Woodward,* 4 Wheat. 518, 636, 4 L. Ed. 518 (1819).

Every State in this country has enacted laws regulating corporate governance. By prohibiting certain transactions, and regulating others, such laws necessarily affect certain aspects of interstate commerce. This necessarily is true with respect to corporations with shareholders in States other than the State of incorporation. Large corporations that are listed on national exchanges, or even regional exchanges, will have shareholders in many States and shares that are traded frequently. The markets that facilitate this national and international participation in ownership of corporations are essential for providing capital not only for new enterprises but also for established companies that need to expand their businesses. This beneficial free market system depends at its core upon the fact that a corporation—except in the rarest situations—is organized under, and governed by, the law of a single jurisdiction, traditionally the corporate law of the State of its incorporation.

These regulatory laws may affect directly a variety of corporate transactions. Mergers are a typical example. In view of the substantial effect that a merger may have on the shareholders' interests in a corporation, many States require supermajority votes to approve mergers. *See, e.g.,* 2 MBCA §73 (requiring approval of a merger by a majority of all shares, rather than simply a majority of votes cast); RMBCA §11.03 (same). By requiring a greater vote for mergers than is required for other transactions, these laws make it more difficult for corporations to merge. State laws also may provide for "dissenters' rights" under which minority shareholders who disagree with corporate decisions to take particular actions are entitled to sell their shares to the corporation at fair market value. *See, e.g.,* 2 MBCA §§80, 81; RMBCA §13.02. By requiring the corporation to purchase the shares of dissenting shareholders, these laws may inhibit a corporation from engaging in the specified transactions.[12]

---

12. Numerous other common regulations may affect both nonresident and resident shareholders of a corporation. Specified votes may be required for the sale of all of the corporation's assets. *See* 2 MBCA §79; RMBCA §12.02. The election of directors may be staggered over a period of years to prevent abrupt changes in management. *See* 1 MBCA §37; RMBCA §8.06. Various classes of stock may be created with differences in voting rights as to dividends and on liquidation. *See* 1 MBCA §15; RMBCA §6.01 (c). Provisions may be made for cumulative voting. *See* 1 MBCA §33, ¶ 4; RMBCA §7.28; n. 9, *supra.* Corporations may adopt restrictions on payment of dividends to ensure that specified ratios of assets to liabilities are maintained for the benefit of the holders of corporate bonds or notes. *See* 1 MBCA §45 (noting that a corporation's articles of incorporation can restrict payment of dividends); RMBCA §6.40 (same). Where the shares of a corporation are held in States other than that of incorporation, actions taken pursuant to these and similar provisions of state law will affect all shareholders alike wherever they reside or are domiciled.

Nor is it unusual for partnership law to restrict certain transactions. For example, a purchaser of a partnership interest generally can gain a right to control the business only with the consent of other owners. *See* Uniform Partnership Act §27, 6 U.L.A. 353 (1969); Uniform Limited Partnership Act §19 (1916 draft), 6 U.L.A. 603 (1969); Revised Uniform Limited Partnership Act §§702, 704 (1976 draft), 6 U.L.A. 259, 261 (Supp. 1986). These

It thus is an accepted part of the business landscape in this country for States to create corporations, to prescribe their powers, and to define the rights that are acquired by purchasing their shares. A State has an interest in promoting stable relationships among parties involved in the corporations it charters, as well as in ensuring that investors in such corporations have an effective voice in corporate affairs.

There can be no doubt that the Act reflects these concerns. The primary purpose of the Act is to protect the shareholders of Indiana corporations. It does this by affording shareholders, when a takeover offer is made, an opportunity to decide collectively whether the resulting change in voting control of the corporation, as they perceive it, would be desirable. A change of management may have important effects on the shareholders' interests; it is well within the State's role as overseer of corporate governance to offer this opportunity. The autonomy provided by allowing shareholders collectively to determine whether the takeover is advantageous to their interests may be especially beneficial where a hostile tender offer may coerce shareholders into tendering their shares.

Appellee Dynamics responds to this concern by arguing that the prospect of coercive tender offers is illusory, and that tender offers generally should be favored because they reallocate corporate assets into the hands of management who can use them most effectively.[13] See generally Easterbrook & Fischel, The Proper Role of a Target's Management in Responding to a Tender Offer, 94 Harv. L. Rev. 1161 (1981). As [previously] indicated, Indiana's concern with tender offers is not groundless. Indeed, the potentially coercive aspects of tender offers have been recognized by the SEC, *see* SEC Release No. 21079, p. 86, 916, and by a number of scholarly commentators, *see, e.g.,* Bradley & Rosenzweig, Defensive Stock Repurchases, 99 Harv. L. Rev. 1377, 1412-1413 (1986); Macey & McChesney, A Theoretical Analysis of Corporate Greenmail, 95 Yale L.J. 13, 20-22 (1985); Lowenstein, 83 Colum. L. Rev., at 307-309. The Constitution does not require the States to subscribe to any particular economic theory. . . . In our view, the possibility of coercion in some takeover bids offers additional justification for Indiana's decision to promote the autonomy of independent shareholders.

Dynamics argues in any event that the State has "no legitimate interest in protecting the nonresident shareholders." Brief for Appellee 21 (quoting *Edgar v. MITE Corp.,* 457 U.S., at 644). Dynamics relies heavily on the statement by the *MITE* Court that "[i]nsofar as the . . . law burdens out-of-state transactions, there is nothing to be weighed in the balance to sustain the law." 457 U.S., at 644. But that comment was made in reference to an Illinois law that applied as well to out-of-state corporations as to in-state corporations. We agree that Indiana has

---

provisions—in force in the great majority of the States—bear a striking resemblance to the Act at issue in this case.

13. It is appropriate to note when discussing the merits and demerits of tender offers that generalizations usually require qualification. No one doubts that some successful tender offers will provide more effective management or other benefits such as needed diversification. But there is no reason to *assume* that the type of conglomerate corporation that may result from repetitive takeovers necessarily will result in more effective management or otherwise be beneficial to shareholders. The divergent views in the literature—and even now being debated in the Congress—reflect the reality that the type and utility of tender offers vary widely. Of course, in many situations the offer to shareholders is simply a cash price substantially higher than the market price prior to the offer.

no interest in protecting nonresident shareholders *of nonresident corporations.* But this Act applies only to corporations incorporated in Indiana. We reject the contention that Indiana has no interest in providing for the shareholders of its corporations the voting autonomy granted by the Act. Indiana has a substantial interest in preventing the corporate form from becoming a shield for unfair business dealing. Moreover, unlike the Illinois statute invalidated in *MITE,* the Indiana Act applies only to corporations that have a substantial number of shareholders in Indiana. *See* Ind. Code §23-1-42-4(a)(3) (Supp. 1986). Thus, every application of the Indiana Act will affect a substantial number of Indiana residents, whom Indiana indisputably has an interest in protecting.

D

Dynamics' argument that the Act is unconstitutional ultimately rests on its contention that the Act will limit the number of successful tender offers. There is little evidence that this will occur. But even if true, this result would not substantially affect our Commerce Clause analysis. We reiterate that this Act does not prohibit any entity—resident or nonresident—from offering to purchase, or from purchasing, shares in Indiana corporations, or from attempting thereby to gain control. It only provides regulatory procedures designed for the better protection of the corporations' shareholders. . . . The very commodity that is traded in the securities market is one whose characteristics are defined by state law. Similarly, the very commodity that is traded in the "market for corporate control"—the corporation—is one that owes its existence and attributes to state law. Indiana need not define these commodities as other States do; it need only provide that residents and nonresidents have equal access to them. This Indiana has done. Accordingly, even if the Act should decrease the number of successful tender offers for Indiana corporations, this would not offend the Commerce Clause.

IV

On its face, the Indiana Control Share Acquisitions Chapter evenhandedly determines the voting rights of shares of Indiana corporations. The Act does not conflict with the provisions or purposes of the Williams Act. To the limited extent that the Act affects interstate commerce, this is justified by the State's interests in defining the attributes of shares in its corporations and in protecting shareholders. Congress has never questioned the need for state regulation of these matters. Nor do we think such regulation offends the Constitution. Accordingly, we reverse the judgment of the Court of Appeals.

It is so ordered.

Justice SCALIA, concurring in part and concurring in the judgment.

I join Parts I, III-A, and III-B of the Court's opinion. However, having found, as those Parts do, that the Indiana Control Share Acquisitions Chapter neither "discriminates against interstate commerce," *ante,* nor "create[s] an impermissible risk of inconsistent regulation by different States," *ante,* I would conclude without further analysis that it is not invalid under the dormant Commerce Clause. . . .

I also agree with the Court that the Indiana Control Share Acquisitions Chapter is not pre-empted by the Williams Act, but I reach that conclusion without entering into the debate over the purposes of the two statutes. The Williams Act is governed by the antipre-emption provision of the Securities Exchange Act of 1934, 15 U.S.C. §78bb(a), which provides that nothing it contains "shall affect the jurisdiction of the securities commission (or any agency or officer performing like functions) of any State over any security or any person insofar as it does not conflict with the provisions of this chapter or the rules and regulations thereunder." . . .

I do not share the Court's apparent high estimation of the beneficence of the state statute at issue here. But a law can be both economic folly and constitutional. The Indiana Control Share Acquisitions Chapter is at least the latter. I therefore concur in the judgment of the Court.

Justice WHITE, with whom Justice BLACKMUN and Justice STEVENS join as to Part II, dissenting.

The majority today upholds Indiana's Control Share Acquisitions Chapter, a statute which will predictably foreclose completely some tender offers for stock in Indiana corporations. I disagree with the conclusion that the Chapter is neither pre-empted by the Williams Act nor in conflict with the Commerce Clause. The Chapter undermines the policy of the Williams Act by effectively preventing minority shareholders, in some circumstances, from acting in their own best interests by selling their stock. In addition, the Chapter will substantially burden the interstate market in corporate ownership, particularly if other States follow Indiana's lead as many already have done. The Chapter, therefore, directly inhibits interstate commerce, the very economic consequences the Commerce Clause was intended to prevent. The opinion of the Court of Appeals is far more persuasive than that of the majority today, and the judgment of that court should be affirmed. . . .

3.   The Third Generation — Business Combination Statutes

Following the *CTS* decision, the states returned to the laboratory of experimentation resulting in the so-called third generation of state takeover statutes. This third generation of state antitakeover statutes is typified by the terms of Delaware's business combination statute, which is codified at §203 of the Delaware General Corporation Law (DGCL). The terms of this statute prohibit a "business combination" with an "interested stockholder" (defined to be an owner of 15 percent or more of the shares of a company organized under Delaware law) for a period of three years unless either (1) the combination has been approved by the board that was in office *prior to* the interested stockholder's acquisition of its 15 percent stake; (2) the interested stockholder acquired at least 85 percent of the voting stock of the company (exclusive of shares held by officers or directors or certain types of employee stock plans) at the time that it became an interested stockholder; *or* (3) the transaction is approved by the directors *and* by the holders of at least two-thirds of the outstanding stock of the company *not* owned by the interested shareholder. *Query:* Would this Delaware statute (imposing a three-year moratorium on certain business combinations) be constitutional under the test enunciated by the Supreme Court in *CTS?*

The constitutionality of this type of third-generation state antitakeover statute is addressed in the next case, although this issue has yet to reach the Supreme Court.

Amanda Acquisition Corp. v. Universal Foods Corp.
877 F.2d 496 (7th Cir. 1989), *cert. denied,* **493 U.S. 955 (1989)**

EASTERBROOK, Circuit Judge.

States have enacted three generations of takeover statutes in the last 20 years. . . .

Wisconsin has a third-generation takeover statute [that] postpones the kinds of transactions that often follow tender offers (and often are the reason for making the offers in the first place). Unless the target's board agrees to the transaction in advance, the bidder must wait three years after buying the shares to merge with the target or acquire more than 5% of its assets. We must decide whether this is consistent with the Williams Act and Commerce Clause.

I

Amanda Acquisition Corporation is a shell with a single purpose: to acquire Universal Foods Corporation, a diversified firm incorporated in Wisconsin and traded on the New York Stock Exchange. Universal is covered by Wisconsin's anti-takeover law. . . .

In mid-November 1988 Universal's stock was trading for about $25 per share. On December 1 Amanda commenced a tender offer at $30.50, to be effective if at least 75% of the stock should be tendered.[1] This all-cash, all shares offer has been increased by stages to $38.00.[2] Amanda's financing is contingent on a prompt merger with Universal if the offer succeeds, so the offer is conditional on a judicial declaration that the law is invalid. (It is also conditional on Universal's redemption of poison pill stock. For reasons that we discuss below, it is unnecessary to discuss the subject in detail.)

No firm incorporated in Wisconsin and having its headquarters, substantial operations, or 10% of its shares or shareholders there may "engage in a business combination with an interested stockholder . . . for 3 years after the interested stockholder's stock acquisition date unless the board of directors of

---

1. Wisconsin has, in addition to §180.726, a statute modeled on Indiana's, providing that an acquiring firm's shares lose their votes, which may be restored under specified circumstances. Wis. Stat. §180.25(9). That law accounts for the 75% condition, but it is not pertinent to the questions we resolve.

2. Universal contends that an increase after the district court's opinion makes the case moot, or at least requires a remand. It does not. The parties remain locked in combat. Price has no effect on the operation of the Wisconsin law, and as that is the sole issue we shall decide, there is no need to remand for further proceedings.

the [Wisconsin] corporation has approved, before the interested stockholder's stock acquisition date, that business combination or the purchase of stock," Wis. Stat. §180.726(2). An "interested stockholder" is one owning 10% of the voting stock, directly or through associates (anyone acting in concert with it), §180.726(1)(j). A "business combination" is a merger with the bidder or any of its affiliates, sale of more than 5% of the assets to bidder or affiliate, liquidation of the target, or a transaction by which the target guarantees the bidder's or affiliates debts or passes tax benefits to the bidder or affiliate, §180.726(1)(e). The law, in other words, provides for almost hermetic separation of bidder and target for three years after the bidder obtains 10% of the stock—unless the target's board consented before then. No matter how popular the offer, the ban applies: obtaining 85% (even 100%) of the stock held by non-management shareholders won't allow the bidder to engage in a business combination, as it would under Delaware law. . . . Wisconsin firms cannot opt out of the law, as may corporations subject to almost all other state takeover statutes. In Wisconsin it is management's approval in advance, or wait three years. Even when the time is up, the bidder needs the approval of a majority of the remaining investors, without any provision disqualifying shares still held by the managers who resisted the transaction. The district court found that this statute "effectively eliminates hostile leveraged buyouts." As a practical matter, Wisconsin prohibits any offer contingent on a merger between bidder and target, a condition attached to about 90% of contemporary tender offers.

Amanda filed this suit seeking a declaration that this law is preempted by the Williams Act and inconsistent with the Commerce Clause. . . .

II . . .

A

If our views of the wisdom of state law mattered, Wisconsin's takeover statute would not survive. Like our colleagues who decided *MITE* and *CTS*, we believe that antitakeover legislation injures shareholders. . . . Managers frequently realize gains for investors via voluntary combinations (mergers). If gains are to be had, but managers' balk, tender offers are investors' way to go over managers' heads. If managers are not maximizing the firm's value—perhaps because they have missed the possibility of a synergistic combination, perhaps because they are clinging to divisions that could be better run in other hands, perhaps because they are just not the best persons for the job—a bidder that believes it can realize more of the firm's value will make investors a higher offer. Investors tender; the bidder gets control and changes things. . . . The prospect of monitoring by would-be bidders, and an occasional bid at a premium, induces managers to run corporations more efficiently and replaces them if they will not. . . .

Although a takeover-*proof* firm leaves investors at the mercy of incumbent managers (who may be mistaken about the wisdom of their business plan even when they act in the best of faith), a takeover-*resistant* firm may be able to assist its investors. An auction may run up the price, and delay may be essential to an auction. Auctions transfer money from bidders to targets, and diversified investors would not gain from them (their left pocket loses what the right pocket gains); diversified investors would lose from auctions if the lower returns to bidders discourage future bids. But from targets' perspectives, once a bid is on the table an auction may be the best strategy. The full effects of auctions are hard to unravel, sparking scholarly debate.[6] Devices giving managers some ability to orchestrate investors' responses, in order to avoid panic tenders in response to front-end-loaded offers, also could be beneficial, as the Supreme Court emphasized in *CTS*, 481 U.S. at 92-93, 107 S. Ct. at 1651-52. ("Could be" is an important qualifier; even from a perspective limited to targets' shareholders given a bid on the table, it is important to know whether managers use this power to augment bids or to stifle them, and whether courts can tell the two apart.)

. . . Investors who prefer to give managers the discretion to orchestrate responses to bids may do so through "fair-price" clauses in the articles of incorporation and other consensual devices. Other firms may choose different strategies. A law such as Wisconsin's does not add options to firms that would like to give more discretion to their managers; instead it destroys the possibility of divergent choices. Wisconsin's law applies even when the investors prefer to leave their managers under the gun, to allow the market full sway. . . . To put this differently, state laws have bite only when investors, given the choice, would deny managers the power to interfere with tender offers (maybe already *have* denied managers that power). *See also* Roberta Romano, *The Political Economy of Takeover Statutes*, 73 VA. L. REV. 111, 128-31 (1987).

B

Skepticism about the wisdom of a state's law does not lead to the conclusion that the law is beyond the state's power, however. We have not been elected custodians of investors' wealth. States need not treat investors' welfare as their summum bonum. Perhaps they choose to protect managers' welfare instead, or believe that the current economic literature reaches an incorrect conclusion and that despite appearances takeovers injure investors in the long run. Unless a federal statute or the Constitution bars the way, Wisconsin's choice must be respected.

Amanda relies on the Williams Act of 1968, . . . [which] regulates the conduct of tender offers. Amanda believes that Congress created an entitlement for investors to receive the benefit of tender offers, and that because Wisconsin's law makes tender offers unattractive to many potential bidders, it is preempted. . . .

Preemption has not won easy acceptance among the Justices for several reasons. First there is §28(a) of the '34 Act, 15 U.S.C. §78bb(a), which provides

---

6. Compare Lucian Arye Bebchek, *Toward Undistorted Choice and Equal Treatment in Corporate Takeovers*, 98 HARV. L. REV. 1693 (1985), and Ronald J. Gilson, *Seeking Competitive Bids versus Pure Passivity in Tender Offer Defense*, 35 STAN. L. REV. 51 (1982), with Alan Schwartz, *Search Theory and the Tender Offer Auction*, 23 J.L. ECON. & ORG. 229 (1986), and Sanford J. Grossman & Oliver D. Hart, *Takeover Bids, the Free-Rider Problem and the Theory of the Corporation*, 11 BELL J. ECON. 42 (1980). For the most recent round compare Alan Schwartz, *The Fairness of Tender Offer Prices in Utilitarian Theory*, 17 J. LEGAL STUD. 165 (1988), with Lucian Arye Bebchuck, *The Sole Owner Standard for Takeover Policy, id.* at 197, with Schwartz, *The Sole Owner Standard Reviewed, id.* at 231.

that "[n]othing in this chapter shall affect the jurisdiction of the securities commission . . . of any State over any security or any person insofar as it does not conflict with the provisions of this chapter or the rules and regulations thereunder." Although some of the SEC's regulations (particularly the one defining the commencement of an offer) conflict with some state takeover laws, the SEC has not drafted regulations concerning mergers with controlling shareholders, and the Act itself does not address the subject. States have used the leeway afforded by §28(a) to carry out "merit regulation" of securities—"blue sky" laws that allow securities commissioners to forbid sales altogether, in contrast with the federal regimen emphasizing disclosure. So §28(a) allows states to stop some transactions [that] federal law would permit, in pursuit of an approach at odds with a system emphasizing disclosure and investors' choice. Then there is the traditional reluctance of federal courts to infer preemption of "state law in areas traditionally regulated by the States." . . . States have regulated corporate affairs, including mergers and sales of assets, since before the beginning of the nation. . . .

The Williams Act regulates the *process* of tender offers: timing, disclosure, proration if tenders exceed what the bidder is willing to buy, best-price rules. It slows things down, allowing investors to evaluate the offer and management's response. Best-price, proration, and short-tender rules ensure that investors who decide at the end of the offer get the same treatment as those who decide immediately, reducing pressure to leap before looking. After complying with the disclosure and delay requirements, the bidder is free to take the shares. . . .

Any bidder complying with federal law is free to acquire shares of Wisconsin firms on schedule. Delay in completing a second-stage merger may make the target less attractive, and thus depress the price offered or even lead to an absence of bids; it does not, however, alter any of the procedures governed by federal regulation. Indeed Wisconsin's law does not depend in any way on how the acquiring firm came by its stock: open-market purchases, private acquisitions of blocs, and acquisitions via tender offers are treated identically. Wisconsin's law is no different in effect from one saying that for the three years after a person acquires 10% of a firm's stock, a unanimous vote is required to merge. Corporate law once had a generally applicable unanimity rule in major transactions, a rule discarded because giving every investor the power to block every reorganization stopped many desirable changes. (Many investors could use their "hold-up" power to try to engross a larger portion of the gains, creating a complex bargaining problem that often could not be solved.) Wisconsin's more restrained version of unanimity also may block beneficial transactions, but not by tinkering with any of the procedures established in federal law.

Only if the Williams Act gives investors a right to be the beneficiary of offers could Wisconsin's law run afoul of the federal rule. No such entitlement can be mined out of the Williams Act, however. *Schreiber v. Burlington Northern, Inc.,* 472 U.S. 1, 105 S. Ct. 2458, 86 L. Ed. 2d 1 (1985), holds that the cancellation of a pending offer because of machinations between bidder and target does not deprive investors of their due under the Williams Act. The Court treated §14(e) as a disclosure law, so that investors could make informed decisions; it follows that events leading bidders to cease their quest do not conflict with the Williams Act any more than a state law leading a firm not to issue new securities could conflict with the Securities Act of 1933. . . . Investors have no right to receive tender offers. . . .

C. . .

When state law discriminates against interstate commerce expressly—for example, when Wisconsin closes its border to butter from Minnesota—the negative Commerce Clause steps in. The law before us is not of this type: it is neutral between inter-state and intra-state commerce. Amanda therefore presses on us the broader, all-weather, be-reasonable vision of the Constitution. Wisconsin has passed a law that unreasonably injures investors, most of whom live outside of Wisconsin, and therefore it *has* to be unconstitutional, as Amanda sees things. Although *Pike v. Bruce Church, Inc.*, 397 U.S. 137, 90 S. Ct. 844, 25 L. Ed. 2d 174 (1970), sometimes is understood to authorize such general-purpose balancing, a closer examination of the cases may support the conclusion that the Court has looked for discrimination rather than for baleful effects. . . . At all events, although *MITE* employed the balancing process described in *Pike* to deal with a statute that regulated all firms having "contacts" with the state, *CTS* did not even cite that case when dealing with a statute regulating only the affairs of a firm incorporated in the state, and Justice Scalia's concurring opinion questioned its application. The Court took a decidedly confined view of the judicial role: "We are not inclined 'to second-guess the empirical judgments of lawmakers concerning the utility of legislation,' *Kassel v. Consolidated Freightways Corp.*, 450 U.S. [662] at 679 [101 S. Ct. 1309, 1320, 67 L. Ed. 2d 580 (1981)] (Brennan, J., concurring in judgment)." Although the scholars whose writings we cited in Part II.A conclude that laws such as Wisconsin's injure investors, Wisconsin is entitled to give a different answer to this empirical question—or to decide that investors' interests should be sacrificed to protect managers' interests or promote the stability of corporate arrangements. . . .

 . . . Wisconsin, like Indiana, is indifferent to the domicile of the bidder. A putative bidder located in Wisconsin enjoys no privilege over a firm located in New York. So too with investors: all are treated identically, regardless of residence. Doubtless most bidders (and investors) are located outside Wisconsin, but unless the law discriminates according to residence this alone does not matter. . . .

Wisconsin could exceed its powers by subjecting firms to inconsistent regulation. Because §180.726 applies only to a subset of firms incorporated in Wisconsin, however, there is no possibility of inconsistent regulation. Here, too, the Wisconsin law is materially identical to Indiana's. *CTS*, 481 U.S. at 88-89, 107 S. Ct. at 1649-50. This leaves only the argument that Wisconsin's law hinders the flow of interstate trade "too much." *CTS* dispatched this concern by declaring it inapplicable to laws that apply only to the internal affairs of firms incorporated in the regulating state. States may regulate corporate transactions as they choose without having to demonstrate under an unfocused balancing test that the benefits are "enough" to justify the consequences. . . .

AFFIRMED.

QUESTIONS

1. Considering the terms of Delaware's business combination statute, section 203, would it be held constitutional under the reasoning of the Seventh Circuit in *Amanda Acquisition*? *See RP Acquisition v. Staley Continental*, 686 F. Supp. 476 (D. Del. 1988); *BNS v. Koppers*, 683 F. Supp. 454 (D. Del. 1988).

2. Third-generation statutes also include provisions commonly referred to as *stakeholder* or *other constituency* statutes, which generally authorize the board of directors to consider other interests (including those of employees, suppliers, and the local community) as part of its decision-making process. *See,* e.g., 15 Pa. Cons. Stat. Ann. §1715. While not limited to the takeover context, these statutes were widely regarded as having their genesis in the same set of concerns that led states to adopt other forms of takeover statutes. Considering the reasoning of *CTS* and *Amanda Acquisition,* are these other constituency statutes constitutionally valid?

3. As a matter of public policy, do you think state law should regulate the tender offer process? What is the proper role for state law?

NOTES

1. More on Delaware §203.   In 2010, the ABA published a Symposium focusing on Delaware's antitakeover statute. *See* "Symposium," 65 Bus. Law. 685-808 (May 2010). In the lead article, *Is Delaware's Anti-Takeover Statute Constitutional? Evidence from 1988-2008*, the authors presented evidence "that would seem to suggest that the constitutionality of Section 203 is [now] up for grabs," a conclusion that was then challenged in one way or another by the Symposium participants who submitted commentaries that were published as part of the Symposium. In their lead article, the authors summarized their study and its findings as follows:

> Delaware's anti-takeover statute, codified in Section 203 of the Delaware Corporate Code, is by far the most important antitakeover statute in the United States. When it was enacted in 1988, three bidders challenged its constitutionality under the Commerce Clause and the Supremacy Clause of the U.S. Constitution. All three federal district court decisions upheld the constitutionality of Section 203 at the time, relying on evidence indicating that Section 203 gave bidders a "meaningful opportunity for success," but leaving open the possibility that future evidence might change this constitutional conclusion. This Article presents the first systematic empirical evidence since 1988 on whether Section 203 gives bidders a meaningful opportunity for success. The question has become more important in recent years because Section 203's substantive bite has increased, as Exelon's recent hostile bid for NRG illustrates. Using a new sample of all hostile takeover bids against Delaware targets that were announced between 1988 and 2008 and were subject to Section 203 (n=60), we find that no hostile bidder in the past nineteen years has been able to avoid the restrictions imposed by Section 203 by going from less than 15% to more than 85% in its tender offer. At the very least, this finding indicates that the empirical proposition that the federal courts relied

upon to uphold Section 203's constitutionality is no longer valid. While it remains possible that courts would nevertheless uphold Section 203's constitutionality on different grounds, the evidence would seem to suggest that the constitutionality of Section 203 is up for grabs. This Article offers specific changes to the Delaware statute that would preempt the constitutional challenge. If instead Section 203 were to fall on constitutional grounds, as Delaware's prior antitakeover statute did in 1987, it would also have implications for similar anti-takeover statutes in thirty-two other U.S. states, which along with Delaware collectively cover 92% of all U.S. corporations.

Guhan Subramanian, et al., *Is Delaware's Anti-Takeover Statute Unconstitutional? Evidence from 1988-2008*, 65 Bus. Law. 685 (2010).

However, these conclusions were vigorously challenged by the commentary of one of the Symposium participants, a leading Delaware M&A lawyer who offered the following observations:

> The [lead] article comes after twenty-two years of vibrant takeover activity in Delaware. According to SDC Platinum[7] from January 1, 1988, through December 31, 2008, there were 1,101 tender offers for Delaware targets, 145 (or 13%) of which were hostile (i.e., the target's board rejected the offer, but the acquirer persisted) or unsolicited (i.e., the acquirer made an offer without prior negotiations with the target board). In at least 73 of the 145 hostile/unsolicited tender offers, the bidder held less than 15% of the target's stock prior to commencing the tender offer and sought to acquire over 85%. Of those seventy-three, twenty-nine (or 40%) were ultimately completed, while forty-three were withdrawn.[8] Moreover, of the forty-three withdrawn, at least twenty-three of those targets agreed to be acquired in a white-knight type transaction. When laid against the reality that a meaningful number of hostile/unsolicited tender offers can and do result in a takeover, without even reaching the question of how many of the unsuccessful offers were not "beneficial" to stockholders, [the lead article] provide[s] no basis, let alone empirical evidence, to support their argument that the constitutionality of Section 203 is "up for grabs." . . .
>
> In the twenty years following the enactment of Section 203, and giving some credence [to the data presented in the lead article], it appears that defensive measures such as the poison pill and independent directors' willingness to negotiate with unsolicited bidders before a tender offer terminates have affected the number of unsolicited/hostile offers that go to conclusion without board intervention to negotiate an optimal resolution. As we have seen, 33% of the unsolicited/hostile offers in [the] meager sample [contained in the lead article], at least 40% of the broader universe of hostile/unsolicited offers when transactions that turned friendly before expiration of the initial tender are added, and least 71% if one also includes subsequent white-knight transactions, resulted in acquisitions. This supports the premise, appropriately from the perspective of stockholders, that unsolicited offers have a meaningful opportunity to result in successful takeovers and the constitutionality of Section 203 is decidedly not "up for grabs." . . .

---

7. SDC Platinum is a product of Thompson Reuters, which also owns Thompson One, the database [which was used by the authors of the lead article] for their study. SDC Platinum provides data on approximately 672,000 mergers and acquisitions worldwide from 1985 to the present. We did a search of the database on February 1, 2010.

8. SDC reports the outcome of one of the seventy-three hostile/unsolicited tender offers as "unknown."

A. Gilchrist Sparks III and Helen Bowers, *After Twenty-Two Years, Section 203 of the Delaware General Corporation Law Continues to Give Hostile Bidders a Meaningful Opportunity for Success*, 65 BUS. LAW. 761, 761-762, and 769 (2010). *Query:* From a public policy perspective, does Delaware Section 203 make sense? What do you think?

   2. *Fair Price Clauses and Other Charter Provisions.* In his opinion in *Amanda Acquisitions,* Judge Easterbrook referred to fair price clauses that many companies have included in their articles of incorporation. Generally speaking, a *fair price clause* is a provision that is included by amending the articles of incorporation, which we learned in Chapter 2 requires approval by both the company's board of directors and its shareholders. These charter (i.e., articles) amendments are often collectively referred to by M&A professionals as "shark repellents." Among the most common shark repellents are supermajority voting requirements often coupled with a fair price provision. Management will propose to amend the company's articles to modify the default rule otherwise provided as a matter of state law to increase the percentage vote required for shareholder approval of a merger, often increasing the required vote to two-thirds of the outstanding shares, with some amendments raising the bar to as high as 95 percent of the outstanding shares. The reason that this type of articles amendment is referred to as a "shark repellent" is because of the impact that this type of voting requirement will have on prospective Bidders. Generally speaking, this type of charter provision will require Bidder to purchase sufficient shares to assure passage of the back-end take out merger, thereby presumably increasing the cost to Bidder in completing the takeover of Target, as well as creating the possibility of the problem of a shareholder who holds out for a higher price. Very often, the supermajority provision will be subject to a provision that waives the supermajority vote requirement if the price to be paid by Bidder is "fair." As pointed out by Judge Easterbrook in his opinion, all of these shark repellents take the form of "consensual devices," in that they cannot be implemented unilaterally by existing management; instead, all of these charter provisions require shareholder approval. This is to be contrasted with the types of antitakeover measures adopted by the company's board of directors that are the focus of our analysis in the next chapter.

‖7‖

Fiduciary Duty Law: The Responsibilities of Boards of Directors, Senior Executive Officers, and Controlling Shareholders

A. Introduction to the Scope of Fiduciary Duty Obligations

1. Business Judgment Rule: The Duty of Care and the Exercise of Informed Decision Making

In the case of negotiated acquisitions not involving self-dealing or any other form of conflict of interest, *Smith v. Van Gorkom* is the seminal case setting forth the directors' standard of care. In this case, the Delaware Supreme Court is widely credited with giving "teeth" to the more deferential business judgment rule standard of review traditionally invoked by the courts in cases involving what is often described as a naked breach of the duty of care. In analyzing the Delaware Supreme Court's detailed description of the transaction at issue in the *Trans Union* case (as the *Smith v. Van Gorkom* decision is often referred to in the academic literature), consider whether these facts present a "naked breach" of the duty of care. Or, alternatively, does this case involve facts that implicate a breach of the duty of loyalty? If so, how does the Delaware Supreme Court deal with this aspect of the case?

Smith v. Van Gorkom *use corps. brief*
488 A.2d 858 (Del. 1985)

HORSEY, Justice (for the majority):

This appeal from the Court of Chancery involves a class action brought by shareholders of the defendant Trans Union Corporation ("Trans Union" or "the Company"), originally seeking rescission of a cash-out merger of Trans Union into the defendant New T Company ("New T"), a wholly-owned subsidiary of the defendant, Marmon Group, Inc. ("Marmon"). Alternate relief in the form of damages is sought against the defendant members of the Board of Directors of Trans Union, New T, and Jay A. Pritzker and Robert A. Pritzker, owners of Marmon.

Following trial, the former Chancellor granted judgment for the defendant directors by unreported letter opinion dated July 6, 1982. Judgment was based on two findings: (1) that the Board of Directors had acted in an informed manner so as to be entitled to protection of the business judgment rule in approving the cash-out merger; and (2) that the shareholder vote approving the merger should not be set aside because the stockholders had been "fairly informed" by the Board of Directors before voting thereon. The plaintiffs appeal.

Speaking for the majority of the Court, we conclude that both rulings of the Court of Chancery are clearly erroneous. Therefore, we reverse and direct that judgment be entered in favor of the plaintiffs and against the defendant directors for the fair value of the plaintiffs' stockholdings in Trans Union, in accordance with *Weinberger v. UOP, Inc.*, Del. Supr., 457 A.2d 701 (1983). . . .

II.

We turn to the issue of the application of the business judgment rule to the September 20 meeting of the Board, [the meeting at which the Trans Union directors approved the cash-out merger proposal with Pritzker].

The Court of Chancery concluded from the evidence that the Board of Directors' approval of the Pritzker merger proposal fell within the protection of the business judgment rule. The Court found that the Board had given sufficient time and attention to the transaction, since the directors had considered the Pritzker proposal on three different occasions, on September 20, and on October 8, 1980 and finally on January 26, 1981. On that basis, the Court reasoned that the Board had acquired, over the four-month period, sufficient information to reach an informed business judgment on the cashout merger proposal. The [Chancery] Court ruled:

> . . . that given the market value of Trans Union's stock, the business acumen of the members of the board of Trans Union, the substantial premium over market offered by the Pritzkers and the ultimate effect on the merger price provided by the prospect of other bids for the stock in question, that the board of directors of Trans Union did not act recklessly or improvidently in determining on a course of action which they believed to be in the best interest of the stockholders of Trans Union. . . .

The plaintiffs contend that the Court of Chancery erred as a matter of law by exonerating the defendant directors under the business judgment rule without first determining whether the rule's threshold condition of "due care and prudence" was satisfied . . . [The] defendants assert that affirmance is required. We must disagree.

Under Delaware law, the business judgment rule is the offspring of the fundamental principle, codified in 8 Del. C. §141 (a), that the business and affairs of a Delaware corporation are managed by or under its board of directors. In carrying out their managerial roles, directors are charged with an unyielding fiduciary duty to the corporation and its shareholders. The business judgment rule exists to protect and promote the full and free exercise of the managerial power granted to Delaware directors. The rule itself "is a presumption that in making a business decision, the directors of a corporation acted on an informed basis, in good faith and in the honest belief that the action taken was in the best interests of the company." *Aronson [v. Lewis*, 473 A.2d 805, 812 (Del. 1984)]. Thus, the party attacking a board decision as uninformed must rebut the presumption that its business judgment was an informed one.

The determination of whether a business judgment is an informed one turns on whether the directors have informed themselves "prior to making a business decision, of all material information reasonably available to them." *Id.*

Under the business judgment rule there is no protection for directors who have made "an unintelligent or unadvised judgment." [citation omitted] A director's duty to inform himself in preparation for a decision derives from the fiduciary capacity in which he serves the corporation and its stockholders. Since a director is vested with the responsibility for the management of the affairs of the corporation, he must execute that duty with the recognition that he acts on behalf of others. Such obligation does not tolerate faithlessness or self-dealing. But fulfillment of the fiduciary function requires more than the mere absence of bad faith or fraud. Representation of the financial interests of others imposes on a director an affirmative duty to protect those interests and to proceed with a critical eye in assessing information of the type and under the circumstances present here.

Thus, a director's duty to exercise an informed business judgment is in the nature of a duty of care, as distinguished from a duty of loyalty. Here, there were no allegations of fraud, bad faith, or self-dealing, or proof thereof. Hence, it is presumed that the directors reached their business judgment in good faith, and considerations of motive are irrelevant to the issue before us. . . .

We again confirm that . . . the concept of gross negligence is also the proper standard for determining whether a business judgment reached by a board of directors was an informed one.

In the specific context of a proposed merger of domestic corporations, a director has a duty under 8 Del. C. §251 (b), along with his fellow directors, to act in an informed and deliberate manner in determining whether to approve an agreement of merger before submitting the proposal to the stockholders. Certainly in the merger context, a director may not abdicate that duty by leaving to the shareholders alone the decision to approve or disapprove the agreement. Only an agreement of merger satisfying the requirements of 8 Del. C. §251(b) may be submitted to the shareholders under §251(c).

It is against those standards that the conduct of the directors of Trans Union must be tested, as a matter of law and as a matter of fact, regarding their exercise of an informed business judgment in voting to approve the Pritzker merger proposal.

III.

The defendants argue that the determination of whether their decision to accept $55 per share for Trans Union represented an informed business judgment requires consideration, not only of that which they knew and learned on September 20, but also of that which they subsequently learned and did over the following four-month period before the shareholders met to vote on the proposal in February, 1981. . . . Thus, the defendants contend that what the directors did and learned subsequent to September 20 and through January 26, 1981, was properly taken into account by the Trial Court in determining whether the Board's judgment was an informed one. We disagree with this *post hoc* approach.

The issue of whether the directors reached an informed decision to "sell" the Company on September 20, 1980 must be determined only upon the basis of the information then reasonably available to the directors and relevant to their decision to accept the Pritzker merger proposal. This is not to say that the directors were precluded from altering their original plan of action, had they done so in an informed manner. What we do say is that the question of whether the directors reached an informed business judgment in agreeing to sell the Company, pursuant to the terms of the September 20 Agreement presents, in reality, two questions: (A) whether the directors reached an informed business judgment on September 20, 1980; and (B) if they did not, whether the directors' actions taken subsequent to September 20 were adequate to cure any infirmity in their action taken on September 20. We first consider the directors' September 20 action in terms of their reaching an informed business judgment.

On the record before us, we must conclude that the Board of Directors did not reach an informed business judgment on September 20, 1980 in voting to "sell" the Company for $55 per share pursuant to the Pritzker cash-out merger proposal. Our reasons, in summary, are as follows:

> The directors (1) did not adequately inform themselves as to Van Gorkom's role in forcing the "sale" of the Company and in establishing the per share purchase price; (2) were uninformed as to the intrinsic value of the Company; and (3) given these circumstances, at a minimum, were grossly negligent in approving the "sale" of the Company upon two hours' consideration, without prior notice, and without the exigency of a crisis or emergency.

As has been noted, the Board based its September 20 decision to approve the cash-out merger primarily on [the] representations [of Jerome W. Van Gorkom, Trans-Union's CEO and chairman of the company's Board of Directors]. None of the directors, other than Van Gorkom and [Bruce S. Chelberg, President and Chief Operating Officer of Trans-Union], had any prior knowledge that the purpose of the meeting was to propose a cash-out merger of Trans Union. . . .

[Earlier in its opinion, the Delaware Supreme Court noted that, prior to the Board meeting on September 20, Van Gorkom had expressed his willingness "to take $55 per share for his own 75,000 shares. He [had also] vetoed the suggestion of a leveraged buy-out [put forth by several senior executive officers], as involving a potential conflict of interest for [these individuals]. Van Gorkom, a certified public accountant and lawyer, had been an officer of Trans Union for 24 years, its Chief Executive Officer for more than 17 years, and Chairman of its Board for 2 years. It is noteworthy in this connection that he was then approaching 65 years of age and mandatory retirement." [*See Smith v. Van Gorkom, supra,* at 865-866.]] . . .

Without any documents before them concerning the proposed transaction, the members of the Board were required to rely entirely upon Van Gorkom's 20-minute oral presentation of the proposal. No written summary of the terms of the merger was presented; the directors were given no documentation to support the adequacy of $55 price per share for sale of the Company; and the Board had before it nothing more than Van Gorkom's statement of his understanding of the substance of [a merger] agreement which he admittedly had never read, nor which any member of the Board had ever seen. . . .

Under 8 Del. C. §141(e), "directors are fully protected in relying in good faith on reports made by officers." The term "report" has been liberally construed to include reports of informal personal investigations by corporate officers, *Cheff v. Mathes*, Del. Supr., 199 A.2d 548, 556 (1964). However, there is no evidence that any "report," as defined under §141(e), concerning the Pritzker proposal, was presented to the Board on September 20. Van Gorkom's oral presentation of his understanding of the terms of the proposed Merger Agreement, which he had not seen, and [the] brief oral statement [of Donald Romans, Chief Financial Officer of Trans-Union] of his preliminary study regarding the feasibility of a leveraged buy-out of Trans Union do not qualify as §141(e) "reports" for these reasons: The former lacked substance because Van Gorkom was basically uninformed as to the essential provisions of the very document about which he was talking. Romans' statement was irrelevant to the issues before the Board since it did not purport to be a valuation study. At a minimum for a report to enjoy the status conferred by §141(e), it must be pertinent to the subject matter upon which a board is called to act, and otherwise be entitled to good faith, not blind, reliance. Considering all of the surrounding circumstances — hastily calling the meeting without prior notice of its subject matter, the proposed sale of the Company without any prior consideration of the issue or necessity therefor, the urgent time constraints imposed by Pritzker, and the total absence of any documentation whatsoever — the directors were duty bound to make reasonable inquiry of Van Gorkom and Romans, and if they had done so, the inadequacy of that upon which they now claim to have relied would have been apparent.

The defendants rely on the following factors to sustain the Trial Court's finding that the Board's decision was an informed one: (1) the magnitude of the premium or spread between the $55 Pritzker offering price and Trans Union's current market price of $38 per share [based on the trading price of TransUnion's common stock on the NYSE];[5] (2) the amendment of the Agreement as submitted on September 20 to permit the Board to accept any better offer during the "market test" period; (3) the collective experience and expertise of the Board's "inside" and "outside" directors; and (4) their reliance on [the] legal advice [provided by James Brennan, legal counsel for

---

5. [By the author — The text of the Delaware Supreme Court's footnote 5 was moved by the author to here in the Court's opinion.] The common stock of Trans Union was traded on the New York Stock Exchange. Over the five year period from 1975 through 1979, Trans Union's stock had traded within a range of a high of $39½ and a low of $24¼. Its high and low range for 1980 through September 19 (the last trading day before announcement of the merger) was $38¼-$29½.

Trans-Union] that the directors might be sued if they rejected the Pritzker proposal. We discuss each of these grounds *seriatim:*

(1)

A substantial premium may provide one reason to recommend a merger, but in the absence of other sound valuation information, the fact of a premium alone does not provide an adequate basis upon which to assess the fairness of an offering price. Here, the judgment reached as to the adequacy of the premium was based on a comparison between the historically depressed Trans Union market price and the amount of the Pritzker offer. Using market price as a basis for concluding that the premium adequately reflected the true value of the Company was a clearly faulty, indeed fallacious, premise, as the defendants' own evidence demonstrates.

The record is clear that before September 20, Van Gorkom and other members of Trans Union's Board knew that the market had consistently undervalued the worth of Trans Union's stock, despite steady increases in the Company's operating income in the seven years preceding the merger. . . . Van Gorkom testified that he did not believe the market price accurately reflected Trans Union's true worth; and several of the directors testified that, as a general rule, most chief executives think that the market undervalues their companies' stock. Yet, on September 20, Trans Union's Board apparently believed that the market stock price accurately reflected the value of the Company for the purpose of determining the adequacy of the premium for its sale.

In the Proxy Statement, however, the directors reversed their position. There, they stated that, although the earnings prospects for Trans Union were "excellent," they found no basis for believing that this would be reflected in future stock prices. With regard to past trading, the Board stated that the prices at which the Company's common stock had traded in recent years did not reflect the "inherent" value of the Company. But having referred to the "inherent" value of Trans Union, the directors ascribed no number to it. Moreover, nowhere did they disclose that they had no basis on which to fix "inherent" worth beyond an impressionistic reaction to the premium over market and an unsubstantiated belief that the value of the assets was "significantly greater" than book value. By their own admission they could not rely on the stock price as an accurate measure of value. Yet, also by their own admission, the Board members assumed that Trans Union's market price was adequate to serve as a basis upon which to assess the adequacy of the premium for purposes of the September 20 meeting.

The parties do not dispute that a publicly-traded stock price is solely a measure of the value of a minority position and, thus, market price represents only the value of a single share. Nevertheless, on September 20, the Board assessed the adequacy of the premium over market, offered by Pritzker, solely by comparing it with Trans Union's current and historical stock price. *(See supra* note 5 . . .)

Indeed, as of September 20, the Board had no other information on which to base a determination of the intrinsic value of Trans Union as a going concern. As of September 20, the Board had made no evaluation of the Company designed to value the entire enterprise, nor had the Board ever previously considered selling the Company or consenting to a buy-out merger. Thus, the adequacy of a premium is indeterminate unless it is assessed in terms of other competent and sound valuation information that reflects the value of the particular business.

Despite the foregoing facts and circumstances, there was no call by the Board, either on September 20 or thereafter, for any valuation study or documentation of the $55 price per share as a measure of the fair value of the Company in a cash-out context. It is undisputed that the major asset of Trans Union was its cash flow. Yet, at no time did the Board call for a valuation study taking into account that highly significant element of the Company's assets.

We do not imply that an outside valuation study is essential to support an informed business judgment; nor do we state that fairness opinions by independent investment bankers are required as a matter of law. Often insiders familiar with the business of a going concern are in a better position than are outsiders to gather relevant information; and under appropriate circumstances, such directors may be fully protected in relying in good faith upon the valuation reports of their management. *See* 8 Del. C. §141(e). . . .

Here, the record establishes that the Board did not request its Chief Financial Officer, Romans, to make any valuation study or review of the proposal to determine the adequacy of $55 per share for sale of the Company. On the record before us: The Board rested on Romans' elicited response that the $55 figure was within a "fair price range" within the context of a leveraged buyout. No director sought any further information from Romans. No director asked him why he put $55 at the bottom of his range. No director asked Romans for any details as to his study, the reason why it had been undertaken or its depth. No director asked to see the study; and no director asked Romans whether Trans Union's finance department could do a fairness study within the remaining 36-hour[18] period available under the [terms of the] Pritzker offer.

Had the Board, or any member, made an inquiry of Romans, he presumably would have responded as he testified: that his calculations were rough and preliminary; and, that the study was not designed to determine the fair value of the Company, but rather to assess the feasibility of a leveraged buy-out financed by the Company's projected cash flow, making certain assumptions as to the purchaser's borrowing needs. Romans would have presumably also informed the Board of his view, and the widespread view of Senior Management, that the timing of the offer was wrong and the offer inadequate.

The record also establishes that the Board accepted without scrutiny Van Gorkom's representation as to the fairness of the $55 price per share for sale of the Company—a subject that the Board had never previously considered. The Board thereby failed to discover that Van Gorkom had suggested the $55 price to Pritzker and, most crucially, that Van Gorkom had arrived at the $55 figure based on calculations designed solely to determine the feasibility of a leveraged

---

18. Romans' department study was not made available to the Board until circulation of Trans Union's Supplementary Proxy Statement and the Board's meeting of January 26, 1981, on the eve of the shareholder meeting; and, as has been noted, the study has never been produced for inclusion in the record in this case.

buy-out.[19] No questions were raised either as to the tax implications of a cash-out merger or how the price for the one million share option granted Pritzker was calculated.

We do not say that the Board of Directors was not entitled to give some credence to Van Gorkom's representation that $55 was an adequate or fair price. Under §141(e), the directors were entitled to rely upon their chairman's opinion of value and adequacy, provided that such opinion was reached on a sound basis. Here, the issue is whether the directors informed themselves as to all information that was reasonably available to them. Had they done so, they would have learned of the source and derivation of the $55 price and could not reasonably have relied thereupon in good faith.

None of the directors, Management or outside, were investment bankers or financial analysts. Yet the Board did not consider recessing the meeting until a later hour that day (or requesting an extension of Pritzker's Sunday evening deadline) to give it time to elicit more information as to the sufficiency of the offer, either from inside Management (in particular Romans) or from Trans Union's own investment banker, Salomon Brothers, whose Chicago specialist in merger and acquisitions was known to the Board and familiar with Trans Union's affairs.

Thus, the record compels the conclusion that on September 20 the Board lacked valuation information adequate to reach an informed business judgment as to the fairness of $55 per share for sale of the Company.

(2)

This brings us to the post-September 20 "market test" upon which the defendants ultimately rely to confirm the reasonableness of their September 20 decision to accept the Pritzker proposal. In this connection, the directors present a two-part argument: (a) that by making a "market test" of Pritzker's $55 per share offer a condition of their September 20 decision to accept his offer, they cannot be found to have acted impulsively or in an uninformed manner on September 20; and (b) that the adequacy of the $17 premium for sale of the Company was conclusively established over the following 90 to 120 days by the most reliable evidence available—the marketplace. Thus, the defendants impliedly contend that the "market test" eliminated the need for the Board to perform any other form of fairness test either on September 20, or thereafter.

Again, the facts of record do not support the defendants' argument. There is no evidence: (a) that the Merger Agreement was effectively amended to give

---

19. As of September 20 the directors did not know: that Van Gorkom had arrived at the $55 figure alone, and subjectively, as the figure to be used by [Carl Peterson, Trans Union's controller] in creating a feasible structure for a leveraged buy-out by a prospective purchaser; that Van Gorkom had not sought advice, information or assistance from either inside or outside Trans Union directors as to the value of the Company as an entity or the fair price per share for 100% of its stock; that Van Gorkom had not consulted with the Company's investment bankers or other financial analysts; that Van Gorkom had not consulted with or confided in any officer or director of the Company except [Bruce S. Chelberg, president and chief operating officer of Trans Union]; and that Van Gorkom had deliberately chosen to ignore the advice and opinion of the members of his Senior Management group regarding the adequacy of the $55 price.

the Board freedom to put Trans Union up for auction sale to the highest bidder; or (b) that a public auction was in fact permitted to occur. The minutes of the Board meeting make no reference to any of this. Indeed, the record compels the conclusion that the directors had no rational basis for expecting that a market test was attainable, given the terms of the Agreement as executed during the evening of September 20. . . .

The Merger Agreement, specifically identified as that originally presented to the Board on September 20, has never been produced by the defendants, notwithstanding the plaintiffs' several demands for production before as well as during trial. No acceptable explanation of this failure to produce documents has been given to either the Trial Court or this Court. . . .

Van Gorkom states that the Agreement as submitted incorporated the ingredients for a market test by authorizing Trans Union to receive competing offers over the next 90-day period. However, he concedes that the Agreement barred Trans Union from actively soliciting such offers and from furnishing to interested parties any information about the Company other than that already in the public domain. Whether the original Agreement of September 20 went so far as to authorize Trans Union to receive competitive proposals is arguable. . . .

The defendants attempt to downplay the significance of the prohibition against Trans Union's actively soliciting competing offers by arguing that the directors "understood that the entire financial community would know that Trans Union was for sale upon the announcement of the Pritzker offer, and anyone desiring to make a better offer was free to do so." Yet, the press release issued on September 22, with the authorization of the Board, stated that Trans Union had entered into "definitive agreements" with the Pritzkers; and the press release did not even disclose Trans Union's limited right to receive and accept higher offers. Accompanying this press release was a further public announcement that Pritzker had been granted an option to purchase at any time one million shares of Trans Union's capital stock at 75 cents above the then-current price per share.

Thus, notwithstanding what several of the outside directors later claimed to have "thought" occurred at the meeting, the record compels the conclusion that Trans Union's Board had no rational basis to conclude on September 20 or in the days immediately following, that the Board's acceptance of Pritzker's offer was conditioned on (1) a "market test" of the offer; and (2) the Board's right to withdraw from the Pritzker Agreement and accept any higher offer received before the shareholder meeting. . . .

(3)

The directors' unfounded reliance on both the premium and the market test as the basis for accepting the Pritzker proposal undermines the defendants' remaining contention that the Board's collective experience and sophistication was a sufficient basis for finding that it reached its September 20 decision with informed, reasonable deliberation.[21]

---

21. Trans Union's five "inside" directors had backgrounds in law and accounting, 116 years of collective employment by the Company and 68 years of combined experience on its Board. Trans Union's five "outside" directors included four chief executives of major

(4)

Part of the [directors'] defense is based on a claim that the directors relied on legal advice rendered at the September 20 meeting by James Brennan, Esquire, who was present at Van Gorkom's request. Unfortunately, Brennan did not appear and testify at trial even though his firm participated in the defense of this action. There is no contemporaneous evidence of the advice given by Brennan on September 20, only the later deposition and trial testimony of certain directors as to their recollections or understanding of what was said at the meeting. Since counsel did not testify, and the advice attributed to Brennan is hearsay received by the Trial Court over the plaintiffs' objections, we consider it only in the context of the directors' present claims. In fairness to counsel, we make no findings that the advice attributed to him was in fact given. We focus solely on the efficacy of the defendants' claims, made months and years later, in an effort to extricate themselves from liability.

Several defendants testified that Brennan advised them that Delaware law did not require a fairness opinion or an outside valuation of the Company before the Board could act on the Pritzker proposal. If given, the advice was correct. However, that did not end the matter. Unless the directors had before them adequate information regarding the intrinsic value of the Company, upon which a proper exercise of business judgment could be made, mere advice of this type is meaningless; and, given this record of the defendants' failures, it constitutes no defense here.[22]

We conclude that Trans Union's Board was grossly negligent in that it failed to act with informed reasonable deliberation in agreeing to the Pritzker merger proposal on September 20; and we further conclude that the Trial Court erred as a matter of law in failing to address that question before determining whether the directors' later conduct was sufficient to cure its initial error.

A second claim is that counsel advised the Board it would be subject to lawsuits if it rejected the $55 per share offer. It is, of course, a fact of corporate life that today when faced with difficult or sensitive issues, directors often are subject to suit, irrespective of the decisions they make. However, counsel's mere acknowledgement of this circumstance cannot be rationally translated into a justification for a board permitting itself to be stampeded into a patently unadvised act. While suit might result from the rejection of a merger or tender offer, Delaware law makes clear that a board acting within the ambit of the business judgment rule faces no ultimate liability. . . . Thus, we cannot conclude that

---

corporations and an economist who was a former dean of a major school of business and chancellor of a university. The "outside" directors had 78 years of combined experience as chief executive officers of major corporations and 50 years of cumulative experience as directors of Trans Union. Thus, defendants argue that the Board was eminently qualified to reach an informed judgment on the proposed "sale" of Trans Union notwithstanding their lack of any advance notice of the proposal, the shortness of their deliberation, and their determination not to consult with their investment banker or to obtain a fairness opinion.

22. Nonetheless, we are satisfied that in an appropriate factual context a proper exercise of business judgment may include, as one of its aspects, reasonable reliance upon the advice of counsel. This is wholly outside the statutory protections of 8 Del. C. §141(e) involving reliance upon reports of officers, certain experts and books and records of the company.

the mere threat of litigation, acknowledged by counsel, constitutes either legal advice or any valid basis upon which to pursue an uninformed course.

B

We now examine the Board's post-September 20 conduct for the purpose of determining . . . whether it was informed and not grossly negligent . . . [and, therefore,] whether it was sufficient to legally cure the derelictions of September 20. [In this portion of its opinion, the Delaware Supreme Court concluded that the Board's post-September efforts to canvas the market for other potential bidders did not cure the deficiencies surrounding the Board's initial September 20 decision to approve the Pritzker merger.] . . .

V.

The defendants ultimately rely on the stockholder vote of February 10 for exoneration. The defendants contend that the stockholders' "overwhelming" vote approving the Pritzker Merger Agreement had the legal effect of curing any failure of the Board to reach an informed business judgment in its approval of the merger. . . .

On this issue the Trial Court summarily concluded "that the stockholders of Trans Union were fairly informed as to the pending merger. . . ." The Court provided no supportive reasoning nor did the Court make any reference to the evidence of record. . . .

The settled rule in Delaware is that "where a majority of fully informed stockholders ratify action of even interested directors, an attack on the ratified transaction normally must fail." *Gerlach v. Gillam*, Del. Ch., 139 A.2d 591, 593 (1958). The question of whether shareholders have been fully informed such that their vote can be said to ratify director action, "turns on the fairness and completeness of the proxy materials submitted by the management to the . . . shareholders." *Michelson v. Duncan*, [407A.2d 211, 220 (1979)]. . . .

In *Lynch v. Vickers Energy Corp.*, [91 A.2d 278, 281 (Del. 1978)], this Court held that corporate directors owe to their stockholders a fiduciary duty to disclose all facts germane to the transaction at issue in an atmosphere of complete candor. We defined "germane" in the tender offer context as all "information such as a reasonable stockholder would consider important in deciding whether to sell or retain stock." *Accord Weinberger v. UOP, Inc.*, [457 A.2d 701 (Del. 1983)]. . . . In reality, "germane" means material facts.

Applying this standard to the record before us, we find that Trans Union's stockholders were not fully informed of all facts material to their vote on the Pritzker Merger and that the Trial Court's ruling to the contrary is clearly erroneous. We list the material deficiencies in the proxy materials:

> . . . The fact that the Board had no reasonably adequate information indicative of the intrinsic value of the Company, other than a concededly depressed market price, was without question material to the shareholders voting on the merger. . . .

Accordingly, the Board's lack of valuation information should have been disclosed. Instead, the directors cloaked the absence of such information in both the Proxy Statement and the Supplemental Proxy Statement. Through artful drafting, noticeably absent at the September 20 meeting, both documents create the impression that the Board knew the intrinsic worth of the Company . . . Neither in its original proxy statement nor in its supplemental proxy did the Board disclose that it had no information before it, beyond the premium-over-market and the price/earnings ratio, on which to determine the fair value of the Company as a whole. . . . [The Delaware Supreme Court then lists several other disclosure deficiencies contained in the company's proxy disclosures to the Trans Union shareholders.]. . . .

Since we have concluded that Management's [proxy statement disclosures do] not meet the Delaware disclosure standard of "complete candor" under *Lynch v. Vickers, supra,* it is unnecessary for us to address the plaintiffs' legal argument as to the proper construction of §251(c). . . .

. . . The defendants simply failed in their original duty of knowing, sharing, and disclosing information that was material and reasonably available for their discovery. They compounded that failure by their continued lack of candor in the Supplemental Proxy Statement. . . .

The burden must fall on defendants who claim ratification based on shareholder vote to establish that the shareholder approval resulted from a fully informed electorate. On the record before us, it is clear that the Board failed to meet that burden. *Weinberger v. UOP, Inc., supra* at 703; . . .

For the foregoing reasons, we conclude that the director defendants breached their fiduciary duty of candor by their failure to make true and correct disclosures of all information they had, or should have had, material to the transaction submitted for stockholder approval.

VI.

To summarize: we hold that the directors of Trans Union breached their fiduciary duty to their stockholders (1) by their failure to inform themselves of all information reasonably available to them and relevant to their decision to recommend the Pritzker merger; and (2) by their failure to disclose all material information such as a reasonable stockholder would consider important in deciding whether to approve the Pritzker offer.

We hold, therefore, that the Trial Court committed reversible error in applying the business judgment rule in favor of the director defendants in this case.

On remand, the Court of Chancery shall conduct an evidentiary hearing to determine the fair value of the shares represented by the plaintiffs' class, based on the intrinsic value of Trans Union on September 20, 1980. Such valuation shall be made in accordance with *Weinberger v. UOP, Inc., supra* at 712-715. Thereafter, an award of damages may be entered to the extent that the fair value of Trans Union exceeds $55 per share.

REVERSED and REMANDED for proceedings consistent herewith. . . .

QUESTIONS

1. What is a "market check"? What is the usefulness—from either a legal or a business perspective—of conducting a market check?

2. Why was the board's determination that the "premium" that the Pritzkers offered (i.e., the spread between the $55 price offered by the Pritzkers and the then-current trading price of $38 per share) *not* sufficient to establish that the board reached an informed decision as to the adequacy of the offering price? Do you agree with the court's reasoning on this issue?

3. In light of the overwhelming approval of the transaction by the shareholders of Trans Union, why wasn't this shareholder vote sufficient to establish the fairness of the price? Is the court's decision on this issue in *Trans Union* consistent with its decision in *Weinberger*? (*Hint:* You will recall that we read the Delaware Supreme Court's seminal decision in *Weinberger v. UOP, Inc.* in Chapter 2, at p. 179).

NOTES

1. The Dissents in **Trans Union.**   The Delaware Supreme Court was sharply divided, with two justices filing strongly worded dissents. The dissenters emphasized that the majority did not extend the usual measure of deference to the findings of the trial court, nor to the judgment and experience of the company's directors. In his dissent, Justice McNeilly pointed out that the five inside directors, who also served as the company's senior executive officers, "had collectively been employed by [Trans Union] for 116 years and had 68 years of combined experience as directors," whereas the five outside directors, all of whom served as chief executive officers (CEOs) of other companies at least as large as Trans Union, "had 78 years of combined experience as [CEOs], and 53 years cumulative service as Trans Union directors." Based on the experience and qualifications of these ten individuals, Justice McNeilly concluded that

> [d]irectors of this caliber . . . were not taken into this multi-million dollar corporate transaction without being fully informed and aware of [the consequences] as it pertained to the entire corporate panorama of Trans Union. True, even directors such as these, with their business acumen, interest and expertise, can go astray. I do not believe that to be the case here. These men knew Trans Union like the back of their hands and were more than well qualified to make on the spot informed business judgments concerning the affairs of Trans Union including a 100% sale of the corporation. Lest we forget, the corporate world of then and now operates on what is so aptly referred to as "the fast track". These men were at the time an integral part of that world, all professional business men, not intellectual figureheads.

Smith v. Van Gorkum, supra, at 894-95. What do you think? Are you persuaded by the dissent's assertion that these five outside directors "were more than well qualified to make on the spot informed business judgments" concerning the sale of Trans Union to the Pritzkers for $55 per share?

2. *The Fallout from* Trans Union. The *Trans Union* decision clearly sent shock waves through the corporate bar, leading many lawyers to lament the imminent demise of the business judgment rule as they had learned it in law school. To show how time heals all wounds, many practicing mergers and acquisitions (M&A) lawyers today recommend that board members read the facts of the *Trans Union* decision *carefully* before embarking on any M&A transaction. Why this recommendation? A careful read of the boardroom procedures relied on by the directors of Trans Union Corp. (or, more pointedly, the lack thereof) is strongly recommended because it provides a modern case study of how *not* to execute an M&A transaction.

To the extent that boardroom practices of the type reflected in *Smith v. Van Gorkom* represent the norm 30 years ago, it is abundantly clear that these practices fall far short of the decision-making process expected of board members in today's business environment. In light of the fact that business practices have changed dramatically since *Trans Union* was decided, consider (as you read the remaining materials in this chapter) whether any, all, or some combination of the following are required in order for board members to claim the benefit of business judgment rule protection:

a. Consultation with outside financial advisors?
b. Consultation with senior executive officers of the company and/or other personnel within the company?
c. Careful reading of the entire merger agreement?
d. Thorough review of the company's proxy statement soliciting shareholder approval of the transaction?
e. Receipt of a fairness opinion from an independent third party?

In considering how to advise the board as to these procedures, does it matter whether the company is privately held or publicly traded?

3. *Fairness Opinions After* Trans Union. As we saw in Chapter 4, fairness opinions are not required under the federal securities laws or the rules of the Securities and Exchange Commission (SEC) promulgated thereunder, nor are they required under the rules of the New York Stock Exchange (NYSE) or the Nasdaq Stock Market. Moreover, as reflected in the Delaware Supreme Court's opinion in *Trans Union,* fairness opinions are not required in order to validly complete the acquisition as a matter of the state's corporation statute. However, in the wake of the *Trans Union* decision, obtaining a fairness opinion "became standard procedure in corporate transactions" based at least in part on the widely held view that Trans Union's board of directors breached its fiduciary duty of care "by approving a merger without adequate information on the transaction, including whether the offering price reflected [the] company's true value." Donna Block, *Honest Opinion,* THE DEAL, Aug. 31, 2007, *available at:* http://pipeline.thedeal.com/tdd/ViewArticle.dl?id=1188299409205. In the aftermath of the *Trans Union* decision, many experienced observers of M&A transactions came to believe "that relying in good faith on a fairness opinion is one way directors can demonstrate [that they have satisfied their] duty of care." *Id.* You will recall our extended discussion of fairness opinions in Chapter 4, as part of our discussion of the disclosure obligations imposed under the terms of the SEC's proxy rules. There, we noted that the usual process of preparing fairness opinions is hardly the model of an objective and impartial analysis of the financial terms of the merger, in light of the inherent conflicts of interest that arise when fairness "opinions are rendered by [the very same] investment banks that are also advising the merging firms and stand to collect contingency fees if deals go through." *Id.* Given the inherent conflicts of interest, does this call into question the wisdom of relying on fairness opinions to demonstrate whether the board has satisfied its fiduciary duty to bargain on behalf of the company and its shareholders to obtain the best price?

4. *Conflicts of Interest.* Traditionally, the courts (including those in Delaware) have consistently taken a very different approach to deciding cases involving a conflict of interest. These cases implicate the fiduciary duty of loyalty, which has always been scrupulously enforced by the courts. At early common law, cases involving self-dealing transactions (between management and his/her/its corporation, whether in an acquisition context or not) were held to be voidable at the option of the corporation. By the mid-twentieth century, however, the courts were willing to enforce the terms of a self-dealing transaction, so long as the terms of the transaction were fair to the corporation. Today, this standard of fairness is enshrined legislatively in statutes such as Delaware §144. *See Marciano v. Nakash,* 535 A.2d 400 (Del. 1987); *see also* Calif. Corp. Code §310. In the acquisition context, transactions involving a conflict of interest are not automatically voidable. Rather, the modern view is to enforce the terms of the transaction, so long as they meet a more exacting standard of judicial scrutiny known as the "entire fairness test." After the landmark decision of *Weinberger v. UOP, Inc.,* we know that this test involves a probing judicial scrutiny of both substantive fairness ("fair price") and procedural fairness ("fair dealing"). *See* Chapter 2, *supra,* at p. 179.

In addition, modern statutes (such as Del. §144 and Calif. §310) typically provide mechanisms for "cleansing" a proposed transaction that presents a conflict of interest by obtaining approval of either a majority of the disinterested directors *or* a majority of the disinterested shares. We will explore the scope of the obligations required of officers and directors to fulfill this duty of loyalty as part of the materials later in this chapter.

5. *The Doctrine of Shareholder Ratification.* In Part V of its opinion in *Trans Union,* the Delaware Supreme Court addressed the defendant directors' claim that overwhelming shareholder approval of the merger agreement served to exonerate the directors from any personal liability on the grounds that the "legal effect" of the shareholder vote was to cure "any failure of the Board to reach an informed business judgment in its approval of the merger." *Smith v. Van Gorkom,* 488 A.2d at 889. The Delaware Supreme Court rejected this affirmative defense of "shareholder ratification" on the grounds that the record failed to show that *Trans Union* stockholders were "fully informed of all facts material to their vote on the Pritzer Merger" agreement, noting several "material deficiencies in the [company's] proxy materials"—thus proving, once again, the truth of that time-honored maxim: the shareholder vote is only as good as the disclosure that informs the vote.

In reaching this conclusion, the Delaware Supreme Court noted in passing that the "settled rule in Delaware is that where a majority of fully informed stockholders ratify an action of even interested directors, an attack on the ratified transaction must fail." *Id.* at 890. In the wake of *Trans Union*, the doctrine of shareholder ratification followed a tortuous path that resulted in a "distortion" in the doctrine of "shareholder ratification" as that doctrine had "traditionally [been] understood" to operate. Jack B. Jacobs, *Fifty Years of Corporate Law Evolution: A Delaware Judge's Retrospective*, 5 HARV. BUS. L. REV. 156-157 (2015); *see also* J. Travis Laster, *The Effect of Stockholder Approval on Enhanced Scrutiny*, 40 WM. MITCHELL L. REV. 1443, 1491 (2014).

Following *Trans Union*, this "distortion" of the meaning of the shareholder ratification doctrine led to considerable confusion among courts (and practitioners) as to the effect of a fully informed vote of disinterested shareholders in determining the relevant standard of judicial review in the context of a shareholders' challenge to a board's decision. *See, e.g., Gantler v. Stephens*, 965 A.2d 695 (Del. 2009); *Solomon v. Armstrong*, 747 A.2d 1098, 1114-1115 (Del. Ch. 1999), *aff'd*, 746 A.2d 277 (Table) (Del. 2000) (The "legal effect of shareholder ratification, as it relates to alleged breaches of the duty of loyalty, may be one of the most tortured areas of Delaware law."). This confusion (and the resulting uncertainty that it created for M&A lawyers) prevailed until the Delaware Supreme Court handed down its (now landmark) opinion in *Kahn v. M&F Worldwide Corp.*, 88 A.3d 635 (2014). We will examine the Delaware Supreme Court's decision in *MFW* in more detail later in this chapter (at p. 742, as part of our discussion of going-private transactions), and also explore the significance of the holding in *MFW* in the context of planning an M&A transaction so as to avoid scrutiny under the more probing standard of entire fairness and instead obtain the protection of the Business Judgment Rule.

6. *Procedural Fairness and the Business Judgment Rule.*   Following *Trans Union*, academic commentary criticized the Delaware Supreme Court's approach as overly emphasizing the process used by the board to approve an acquisition transaction. *See, e.g.,* Daniel R. Fischel, *The Business Judgment Rule and the* Trans Union *Case,* 40 BUS. LAW. 1437, 1455 (1985) (referring to the case as "one of the worst decisions in the history of corporate law"); Bayless Manning, *Reflections and Practical Tips on Life in the Boardroom After* Van Gorkom, 41 BUS. LAW. 1 (1985) ("The Delaware Supreme Court in *Van Gorkom* exploded a bomb. [Moreover, the] corporate bar generally views the decision as atrocious."). Without a doubt, though, in the years since *Trans Union* was decided, we have seen an increasing focus by the board and its advisors on the *process* undertaken in order to adequately document the board's decision to engage in a particular acquisition. Consequently, notwithstanding criticism regarding the "overproceduralization" of boardroom decision making, it is common practice today to obtain a fairness opinion from an investment banker. In addition to creating more work for investment bankers, the *Trans Union* decision has also led to greater reliance on lawyers to create an adequate "paper trail" for any acquisition decision. Today, it is customary for counsel to get involved early in the acquisition process. By doing so, counsel can advise the constituent corporations to the transaction regarding appropriate board procedures and assist in negotiating and drafting the terms of the acquisition agreement to ensure that the board has fulfilled its fiduciary obligations. Despite the practices that have developed over the more than three decades since *Trans Union* was decided, controversy continues as to whether the increased focus on the procedures used by the board actually increases the probability of good decisions in the modern corporate boardroom. *See, e.g.,* Fred S. McChesney, *A Bird in the Hand and Liability in the Bush: Why* Van Gorkom *Still Rankles, Probably,* 96 N.W.U. L. REV. 631 (2002); Lynn A. Stout, *In Praise of Procedure: An Economic and Behavioral Defense of* Smith v. Van Gorkom *and the Business Judgment Rule,* 96 N.W.U. L. REV. 675 (2002): Usha R. Rodriguez, *Do Conflicts of Interest Require Outside Boards? Yes. BSPs? Maybe,* 74 BUS. LAW. 307 (2019); and Philip C. Thompson, *Capitalism and Pragmatism Govern New Paradigms for Corporate Governance,* 74 BUS. LAW. 367 (2019).

7. *The Legislative Response to the* Trans Union *Decision:* Delaware Section 102(b)(7). The Delaware legislature reacted swiftly and decisively to the tidal wave of criticism over the *Trans Union* decision. In 1986, the Delaware corporation statute was amended to add section 102(b)(7), which authorizes Delaware corporations to include provisions in their certificates (i.e., articles) of incorporation limiting (or even eliminating altogether) directors' personal liability in money damages for conduct constituting a breach of the duty of care, more popularly referred to as "raincoat provisions." Notably, this exculpatory provision does not extend to directors' conduct involving breach of the duty of loyalty, failure to act in good faith, intentional misconduct, intentional violations of the law, receipt of an improper personal benefit, or directors' decisions approving distributions that are illegal under section 174 of the Delaware Corporations Code. In effect, section 102(b)(7) allows existing Delaware corporations to amend their charters to include "raincoat provisions" that exculpate directors from personal liability for money damages for acts of gross negligence amounting to a breach of the duty of care. The public policy premise for this legislative response to the potential for draconian liability to be imposed on directors as a result of *Trans Union* was succinctly summarized in the following legislative history of section 102(b)(7):

> Section 102(b)(7) was added in 1986. Because insurance for directors' liability had become more expensive and sometimes unavailable, a concern developed with respect to the ability of corporations to continue to attract and retain qualified directors. In addition, the insurance crisis threatened desirable entrepreneurial decision making. In response to this problem, the Delaware legislature decided that Delaware corporations should be authorized to include provisions in their certificates of incorporation limiting or eliminating the personal liabilities of directors for breach of the fiduciary duty of care.

Edward P. Welch, et al., FOLK ON THE DELAWARE GENERAL CORPORATION LAW §102.15, at p. 20, n. 22 (Fundamentals, 2020 edition). The scope of protection offered by these exculpatory provisions has been put to the test in recent Delaware cases, most notably the *Disney* litigation involving claims that directors acted in bad faith, and therefore their conduct fell outside the ambit of Delaware §102(b)(7). *See In re The Walt Disney Co. Derivative Litigation,* 907 A.2d 693 (Del. Ch. 2005); *see also In re Cornerstone Therapeutics Inc., S'holder Litig.,* 115 A.3d 1173 (2015).

8. The **Disney** *Litigation.*   In the *Disney* litigation, the plaintiffs brought a shareholder derivative action challenging the controversial hiring and the equally controversial termination of Michael Ovitz as president of the Walt Disney Company. The Disney stockholders claimed that the members of the Disney board did not properly evaluate Ovitz's employment contract, either at the time of his hiring or at the time of his subsequent no-fault termination, which ultimately resulted in the payment of a severance package to Michael Ovitz that was valued at approximately $130 million after only 14 months of employment. At the conclusion of the trial on the plaintiffs' claims, the Delaware Court of Chancery ruled in favor of the Disney directors, confirming that the Disney directors did not violate their fiduciary duties or act in bad faith in connection with the hiring and firing of Michael Ovitz. *See In re Walt Disney Co. Derivative Litigation*, 825 A.2d 275 (Del. Ch. 2003). In August 2006, a unanimous Delaware Supreme Court affirmed the Chancery Court's lengthy, 174-page opinion, upholding all of the legal and factual conclusions set forth in the Chancery Court's "well-crafted" decision. *See In re Walt Disney Co. Derivative Litigation*, 906 A.2d 27, 35 (Del. 2006).

In affirming the Chancery Court's ruling, most commentators believe that the Delaware Supreme Court's opinion provides a ringing endorsement of the business judgment rule and the traditional protections that it affords directors and officers of Delaware corporations in their decision making. *See, e.g.*, Akin Gump Law Firm, *Corporate Governance Alert: Delaware Supreme Court Affirms Disney Decision*, June 26, 2006 ("The post-trial *Disney* decisions are powerful judicial endorsements of the business judgment rule . . . [proving that the] business judgment rule is alive, vigorous and working as it should to protect the business decisions of directors and officers of Delaware corporations.") (law firm memo, copy of file with author). Of course, the protections of the business judgment rule depend on the vigilance of the board members, who continue to be subject to the duty to be informed adequately as to the relevant facts, to discuss and consider the significance of those facts, and to document the board's deliberative process. Although the *Disney* litigation involved board actions concerning executive compensation, its lessons apply with equal vigor in the context of board decision making concerning M&A transactions. The remaining materials in this chapter elaborate in more detail on the scope of the board's fiduciary duty obligations in connection with M&A transactions.

9. Fiduciary Duty Law: Is There a Separate Duty of Good Faith?   One of the more controversial aspects of the *Disney* litigation involves the Delaware Supreme Court's apparent recognition of a separate fiduciary duty of good faith, which the court in *Disney* also recognized is closely connected to the traditional fiduciary duties of care and loyalty that are owed by directors of Delaware corporations. In its 2006 opinion, the Delaware Supreme Court sought to provide much-needed "conceptual guidance to the corporate community" as to the scope of this duty of good faith. However, the Delaware Supreme Court declined to "reach or otherwise address the issue of whether the fiduciary duty to act in good faith is a duty that, like the duties of care and loyalty, can serve as an *independent basis* for imposing liability upon corporate directors and officers."

Disney, 906 A.2d 27, 67 at n. 112 (*emphasis added*). This issue proved to be most vexing to legal advisors to Delaware corporations. In fact, within five months after handing down its decision in the *Disney* litigation, this very issue presented itself to the Delaware Supreme Court in the case of *Stone v. Ritter*, 911 A.2d 362 (Del. 2006).

Stone v. Ritter involved an appeal from the decision of the Delaware Chancery Court dismissing a shareholder derivative action in which the plaintiffs alleged that the directors of AmSouth Bancorporation had failed in good faith to implement sufficient internal controls to guard against violations of federal banking laws and regulations. In upholding the dismissal of the derivative complaint, the Delaware Supreme Court concluded that the directors "discharged their oversight responsibility to establish an information and reporting system" and, further, that this "system was designed to permit the directors to periodically monitor AmSouth's compliance" with federal banking law requirements. *Id.* at 371-372. In reaching this conclusion, the Delaware Supreme Court held that plaintiffs' claim for oversight liability on the part of AmSouth's directors failed to satisfy what has come to be known as "the *Caremark* standard," a standard which was originally established by Chancellor Allen in his well-known opinion in *In re Caremark International Litigation*, 698 A.2d 959 (Del. Ch. 1996). Quoting from Chancellor Allen's decision in *Caremark*, the Delaware Supreme Court concluded that "the lack of good faith that is a necessary condition to liability . . . [can be established] only [by] a sustained or systematic failure of the board to exercise oversight—such as an utter failure to attempt to assure a reasonable information and reporting system exists." *Id.* at 971. The significance of the Delaware Supreme Court's decision in *Stone v. Ritter* has been explained by experienced practitioners as follows:

> It appears that directorial liability for lack of good faith under *Caremark* may be found only in rare circumstances, such as a failure to establish any reporting or information system or controls, or, if such a system or controls exist, a conscious absence of any monitoring or oversight of the system. *Caremark*, therefore, dissuades acts or omissions by a board that preclude the board from obtaining meaningful information about risks or problems requiring its attention.
>
> The Court [in *Stone v. Ritter*] also offered guidance "critical to understanding fiduciary liability under *Caremark*." The Court explained that oversight liability amounts to a breach of the duty of good faith. The failure to exercise good faith does not in and of itself create liability. Instead, "[t]he failure to act in good faith may result in liability because the requirement to act in good faith 'is a subsidiary element,' i.e., a condition 'of the fundamental duty of loyalty.' " "It follows that because a showing of bad faith conduct, in the sense described in *Disney* and *Caremark*, is essential to establish director oversight liability, the fiduciary duty violated by that conduct is the duty of loyalty."
>
> The Court explained that two principles can be derived from its holding. First, although the duty of good faith may be characterized as one of three sets of fiduciary duties, along with the duties of care and loyalty, "the obligation to act in good faith does not establish an independent fiduciary duty that stands on the same footing as the duties of care and loyalty." Second, the duty of loyalty is not limited to cases involving conflicts of interest on the part of directors; it also includes instances in which the fiduciary "fails to act in good faith."

By addressing the concept of good faith for a second time within just a few months after having done so in the *Disney* decision, the Delaware Supreme Court has placed additional focus on an area of the law that had until recently not been well developed. It is potentially a significant issue, because complaints about lack of oversight are categorized as claims for breaches of the duties of loyalty and good faith, and under section 102(b)(7) of the Delaware General Corporation Law, charter provisions are not permitted to immunize directors from personal liability for breaches of the duty of loyalty or for conduct that is not in good faith. That might suggest that an increasing number of derivative claims will assert that directors did not adequately discharge their duties of oversight. Cutting against that possibility, however, is the high standard that the derivative plaintiff must meet to prevail. The Supreme Court quoted a passage from *Caremark*, in which the Court of Chancery stated that a *Caremark* claim remains "possibly the most difficult theory in corporation law upon which a plaintiff might hope to win judgment."

Phillip T. Mellet and M. Duncan Grant, Pepper Hamilton, LLP *Securities Litigation Update: Delaware Supreme Court Upholds Caremark Standard for Director Oversight Liability; Clarifies Duty of Good Faith,* Nov. 21, 2006 (law firm memo, copy on file with author). We will revisit the teachings of *Stone v. Ritter* later in this chapter, as part of our analysis of the more recent Delaware Supreme Court opinion in *Lyondell Chemical Co. v. Ryan.*

10. The Duty of Care and the Exercise of Informed Decision Making. Notwithstanding the continuing controversy regarding the overproceduralization of boardroom decision making, it is clear that the Delaware Supreme Court's call for the exercise of *informed decision making* by truly *independent directors* is now a staple of the advice given by any good business lawyer advising the board of directors of a company considering an acquisition. In the wake of numerous financial scandals of the early years of the twenty-first century, the meaning of "truly independent directors" and the adequacy of the procedures used to establish that the directors have exercised "informed decision making" have been called into question anew. In response to financial scandals that surfaced following the bursting of the speculative "dotcom bubble," Congress enacted the Sarbanes-Oxley Act of 2002 ("SOX"). As was summarized in Chapter 1 (*see supra,* pp. 51-52), this important piece of federal legislation introduced far-reaching reforms addressing, in part, boardroom procedures and practices of publicly traded companies, such as the staffing of board committees and the role of the audit committee. Many of the reforms adopted in SOX represent federal intervention into areas of corporate governance that had previously been the exclusive province of state law, most notably Delaware law. Congress obviously felt compelled to intervene in order to address perceived abuses that led to financial scandals on an unprecedented scale. The efficacy of these federal reform measures in restoring investor confidence in our capital markets is a story that is still unfolding, particularly in the wake of the Great Recession and the economic fallout resulting from the coronavirus pandemic. Moreover, there is the further question of whether these reforms of boardroom procedures and practices will improve the overall quality of boardroom decision making, an issue that continues to be a matter of ongoing controversy.

11. The (Modern) Formulation of the Business Judgment Rule. In an oft-cited opinion, *In re Caremark International Inc. Derivative Litigation,* 698 A.2d 959 (Del. Ch. 1996), then-Chancellor William Allen, a leading Delaware jurist, commented on the traditional formulation of the business judgment rule, as it generally applies to boardroom decision making, by making the following observation:

> [C]ompliance with a director's duty of care can *never* appropriately be judicially determined by reference to the content of the board decision that leads to a *corporate loss,* apart from consideration of the good faith or *rationality of the process* employed. That is, whether a judge or jury considering the matter after the fact, believes a decision substantively wrong, or degrees of wrong extending through "stupid" or "egregious" or "irrational," provides *no ground* for director liability, so long as the court determines that the [decision-making] process employed was either rational or employed in a good faith effort to advance corporate interests. . . . Thus, the business judgment rule is *process oriented* and informed by a deep respect for all *good faith* board decisions.

Id. at 968 (footnotes omitted) (*emphasis added*). In the ensuing years since the Delaware Supreme Court decided *Trans Union,* the Delaware courts have struggled with how to apply the deferential business judgment rule to defensive actions adopted by the board of Target in an effort to resist an unsolicited offer, as well as to board actions in situations involving the sale of the company (such as a merger). The remaining materials in this chapter explore this rather substantial body of case law, a body of case law that is in a constant state of evolution.

2.   Traditional Perspective on Management's Use of Defensive Tactics to Thwart an Unsolicited Offer from Bidder

Before turning to the modern, post-*Trans Union* era of judicial decision making concerning M&A transactions, a brief description of the historical approach of the Delaware courts is in order. In the 1964 case, *Cheff v. Mathes,* 199 A.2d. 548 (Del. 1964), the Delaware Supreme Court was confronted with one of the earliest efforts on the part of Target management to resist an unsolicited offer from an unwanted suitor (i.e., Bidder Co.). In this case, the unwanted suitor (Arnold Maremont and his investment vehicle, Motor Product Corp., collectively referred to as "Maremont") acquired a sizable stake in the putative Target (Holland Furnace Co., a Delaware corporation) through a series of open-market purchases.

Following disclosure of his sizeable stake in Holland's common stock, Maremont demanded to be placed on the Holland board and also informed the Holland board of directors that Maremont believed that Holland's retail sales organization was obsolete. The Holland board was also informed of the results of the investigation by the company's senior executive officers (including Cheff, Holland's CEO and a board member), wherein they concluded that Maremont was likely to liquidate Holland or substantially reorganize the Holland sales force, thereby jeopardizing employees' jobs. According to these same senior executive officers, speculation as to Maremont's intentions with respect to Maremont's large stake in Holland had resulted in, among other things, substantial unrest among Holland's employees. The Holland board ultimately decided to use corporate funds to repurchase the Holland shares owned by Maremont in a transaction that has come to be known today as "greenmail," although at the time it was (somewhat less pejoratively) referred to as a "selective repurchase of the company's stock."

A minority shareholder brought a derivative suit challenging the validity of the Holland board's decision to repurchase Maremont's block of Holland shares at a premium to the then-current trading price of Holland common stock. In addressing plaintiffs' claim that Holland's board of directors breached their fiduciary duties to the corporation, the Delaware Chancery Court held certain Holland directors liable for improper use of corporate funds to purchase Holland shares from Maremont, primarily on the grounds that "the actual purpose behind the purchase [from Maremont] was the desire to perpetuate control" of the incumbent Holland directors, including the company's CEO and board member, Cheff. *Id.* at 553.

On appeal, the Delaware Supreme Court reversed the trial court's decision, reasoning that:

> Under the provisions of 8 Del. C. §160, a corporation is granted statutory power to purchase and sell shares of its own stock. *See Kors v. Carey*, Del. Ch. 158 A.2d 136. Such a right, as embodied in the statute, has long been recognized in this State. The charge here is not one of violation of statute, but the allegation is that the true motives behind such purchases were improperly centered upon perpetuation of control. In an analogous field, courts have sustained the use of proxy funds to inform stockholders of management's views upon the policy questions inherent in an election to a board of directors, but have not sanctioned the use of corporate funds to advance the selfish desires of directors to perpetuate themselves in office. Similarly, if the actions of the board were motivated by a sincere belief that the buying out of the dissident stockholder was necessary to maintain what the board believed to be proper business practices, the board will not be held liable for such decision, even though hindsight indicates the decision was not the wisest course. On the other hand, if the board has acted solely or primarily because of the desire to perpetuate themselves in office, the use of corporate funds for such purposes is improper. . . .
>
> Plaintiffs urge [that the transaction between Holland and Maremont be rescinded on the grounds] that the sale price was unfair in view of the fact that the price was in excess of that prevailing on the open market. However, as conceded by all parties, a substantial block of stock will normally sell at a higher price than that prevailing on the open market, the increment being attributable to a "control premium." Plaintiffs argue that it is inappropriate to require the defendant corporation to pay a control premium, since control is meaningless to an acquisition by a corporation of its own shares. However, it is elementary that a holder of a substantial number of shares would expect to receive the control premium as part of his selling price, and if the corporation desired to obtain the stock, it is unreasonable to expect that the corporation could avoid paying what any other purchaser would be required to pay for the stock. . . .
>
> The question then presented is whether or not defendants satisfied the burden of proof of showing *reasonable grounds to believe a danger to corporate policy and effectiveness existed* by the presence of the Maremont stock ownership. It is

important to remember that the directors satisfy their burden by showing good faith and reasonable investigation; the directors will not be penalized for an honest mistake of judgment, if the judgment appeared reasonable at the time the decision was made. . . .

The [Chancery Court] found that there was no substantial evidence of a liquidation posed by Maremont. This holding overlooks an important contention. The fear of the defendants [i.e., Holland's board members], according to their testimony, was not limited to the possibility of liquidation; it included the alternate possibility of a material change in Holland's sales policies, which the [Holland] board considered vital to its future success. . . .

Accordingly, we are of the opinion that the evidence presented in the [Chancery Court] leads inevitably to the conclusion that [Holland's] board of directors, based upon direct investigation, receipt of professional advice, and personal observations of the contradictory action of Maremont and his explanation of corporate purpose, believed, with justification, that there was a reasonable threat to the continued existence of Holland, or at least existence in its present form, by the plan of Maremont to continue building up his stock holdings. We find no evidence in the record sufficient to justify a contrary conclusion. . . .

Id. at 554-557 (*emphasis added*). The Delaware Supreme Court ultimately concluded that there was no breach of fiduciary duty on the part of the Holland board members, using language that (rather eerily) foreshadows the Delaware Supreme Court's seminal decision in *Unocal Corporation v. Mesa Petroleum Co.*, *infra*, at p. 521.

QUESTIONS

1. What is the standard of review that the Delaware Supreme Court used in *Cheff v. Mathes* to evaluate whether the Holland board breached its fiduciary duties?

2. In what sense do the facts of the principal case give rise to a conflict of interest?

NOTES

1. Business Judgment Rule and Target's Defensive Measures. The traditional approach to the use of defensive tactics is reflected in the early Delaware decision, *Cheff v. Mathes*. To put this decision in some historical context, at the time that the dispute in *Cheff* arose, hostile takeovers as we know them now were then in their infancy. When confronted with the hostilities presented by the facts of *Cheff*, the law of fiduciary duty likewise was in its infancy. At that time, the courts framed management's fiduciary obligations in a two-fold manner, embracing both a duty of care and a duty of loyalty. For the first half of the twentieth century, the scope of the directors' duty of care was defined under the rather deferential standard of the business judgment rule. But with the advent of the 1960s and an unprecedented wave of M&A activity in the capital markets, commentators began to question the efficacy of this traditional framework for analyzing the board's obligations in the face of both the friendly, negotiated acquisition and the more dramatic situation presented by the development of the hostile takeover, which came into prominence in the deal decade of the 1980s. The Delaware courts were not immune to the pressures created by the increasing use of hostile tender offers.

2. Importance of Delaware Law. The remainder of this chapter sketches out the evolution of fiduciary duty law as developed under the jurisprudence of the Delaware courts, the mother lode of case law on this topic. For corporate lawyers, the court of greatest importance is the Delaware Supreme Court, regardless of the state where the lawyer is licensed to practice or the state where the acquisition is to be consummated. Delaware's prominence in this area is quite understandable. It is widely understood that Delaware courts are home to more disputes involving M&A transactions than any other jurisdiction. As such, Delaware case law is usually consulted by lawyers and courts in other states, at least to frame the starting point in analyzing the fiduciary obligations of management in an acquisition transaction. Occasionally, litigation involving M&A activity will arise in jurisdictions other than Delaware, but often these other jurisdictions will refer to the law of Delaware to frame the analysis even if, in the end, the courts of another state decide to adopt an approach that varies from Delaware law. *See, e.g., First Union Corp. v. SunTrust Bank, Inc.,* 2001 WL 1885686 (N.C. Bus. Ct. August 10, 2001); *Hilton Hotels Corp. v. ITT Corp.,* 978 F. Supp. 1342 (D. Nev. 1997).

3. The Fiduciary Duty of Candor

Without a doubt, the reforms introduced by SOX continue a trend set in motion by the Delaware Supreme Court in its opinion in *Van Gorkom,* which emphasized the board's duty to provide the Trans Union shareholders with full and adequate disclosure of all material facts in connection with the solicitation of shareholder approval of the proposed cash-out merger. Over the course of the last 30 years, at both the state and federal level, there has been an increased emphasis on transparency of information about publicly traded companies and their business and financial affairs. Thus, even when the decision is made by a truly independent board — not involving any conflict of interest and otherwise acting in good faith — the board may still be faulted for a failure to fulfill what has come to be known as the fiduciary "duty of candor."

By way of general background, our analysis of the problem sets in Chapter 2 reflect that modern state corporation statutes require that shareholders be provided with notice of shareholders' meetings; but beyond this "cursory notice" requirement, these state "statutes do not specify the information that public shareholders are to receive when management solicits their proxies" in connection with voting on a proposed acquisition. Alan A. Palmiter, CORPORATIONS: EXAMPLES AND EXPLANATIONS 212 (8th ed. 2015). In addition, as part of our study in Chapter 4 of the various provisions of the federal securities laws that are routinely implicated in planning an M&A transaction, we saw that the SEC's proxy rules obligate management to distribute to the shareholders of a publicly traded company a proxy statement that provides full and adequate disclosure of all "material" facts necessary for the shareholders to make an informed decision with respect to an M&A transaction that requires shareholder approval as a matter of state law. In addition to these disclosure obligations required as a matter of federal law, many state courts (most notably the Delaware courts) have promulgated a body of case law that imposes on management what has come to be known as a "duty of candor" (or a "duty of disclosure") that is part of the fiduciary duty obligations of officers and directors. The scope and evolution of this duty of disclosure has been described as follows:

> [In the] seminal Delaware case, *Lynch v. Vickers Energy Corp.*, 383 A.2d 278 (Del. 1977), [the Delaware Supreme Court] imposed on management a "complete candor" duty that explicitly borrows the framework of the federal proxy fraud action [under SEC Rule 14a-9]. Liability is premised on false or misleading information that "a reasonable shareholder would consider important in deciding whether to [vote]." As is true of federal proxy fraud litigation, challenging shareholders need not show [that] the alleged misinformation would have changed the outcome of the shareholder vote; it is enough that the challenged disclosure was material.
>
> In Delaware, shareholders have used the "complete candor" duty (which subsequent courts have labeled a "duty of disclosure") to successfully challenge mergers, reorganizations, and charter amendments. For many shareholder-plaintiffs, Delaware has become preferable to federal court . . . [because, among other reasons,] attorney fees in Delaware are often computed on the basis of class action results, not the less generous federal "lodestar" method. . . .
>
> In an expansion of the duty of disclosure, the Delaware Supreme Court [subsequently] extended the duty of disclosure to include *all* communications to shareholders, not just those seeking shareholder action. *Malone v. Brincat*, 722 A.2d 5 (Del. 1998) [*emphasis added*]. The case, brought as a class action, involved allegation of an ongoing financial fraud made in SEC filings. The court held that directors who knowingly disseminate false information that results in corporate or shareholder harm violate their fiduciary duty and should be held accountable. But given the existence of federal securities fraud liability, the court refused to adopt a "fraud on the market" theory—thus making individual shareholder reliance an element of the action. As a result, *Malone* has not been heavily used.

Alan R. Palmiter, CORPORATIONS: EXAMPLES AND EXPLANATIONS 212-213 (8th ed. 2015).

B. Application of the Williams Act to Defensive Tactics Implemented by a Target

When management of Target Co. seeks to resist the overtures of an unsolicited Bidder, the question arises whether the response of Target's board of directors gives rise to a violation of the provisions of the Williams Act under the federal securities laws. That is the issue presented to the U.S. Supreme Court in the following case.

Schreiber v. Burlington Northern, Inc.
472 U.S. 1, 105 S. Ct. 2458 (1985)

Chief Justice BURGER delivered the opinion of the Court.

We granted certiorari to resolve a conflict in the Circuits over whether misrepresentation or nondisclosure is a necessary element of a violation of §14(e) of the Securities Exchange Act of 1934, 15 U.S.C. §78n(e).

I

On December 21, 1982, Burlington Northern, Inc., made a hostile tender offer for El Paso Gas Co. Through a wholly owned subsidiary, Burlington proposed to purchase 25.1 million El Paso shares at $24 per share. Burlington reserved the right to terminate the offer if any of several specified events occurred. El Paso management initially opposed the takeover, but its shareholders responded favorably, fully subscribing the offer by the December 30, 1982, deadline.

Burlington did not accept those tendered shares; instead, after negotiations with El Paso management, Burlington announced on January 10, 1983, the terms of a new and friendly takeover agreement. Pursuant to the new agreement, Burlington undertook, *inter alia*, to (1) rescind the December tender offer, (2) purchase 4,166,667 shares from El Paso at $24 per share, (3) substitute a new tender offer for only 21 million shares at $24 per share, (4) provide procedural protections against a squeeze-out merger[1] of the remaining El Paso shareholders, and (5) recognize "golden parachute" contracts between El Paso and four of its senior officers. By February 8, more than 40 million shares were tendered in response to Burlington's January offer, and the takeover was completed.

The rescission of the first tender offer caused a diminished payment to those shareholders who had tendered during the first offer. The January offer was greatly oversubscribed and consequently those shareholders who retendered were subject to substantial proration. Petitioner Barbara Schreiber filed suit on behalf of herself and similarly situated shareholders, alleging that Burlington, El Paso, and members of El Paso's board of directors violated §14(e)'s prohibition of "fraudulent, deceptive, or manipulative acts or practices . . . in connection with any tender offer." 15 U.S.C. §78n(e). She claimed that Burlington's

---

1. A "squeeze-out" merger occurs when Corporation A, which holds a controlling interest in Corporation B, uses its control to merge B into itself or into a wholly owned subsidiary. The minority shareholders in Corporation B are, in effect, forced to sell their stock. The procedural protection provided in the agreement between El Paso and Burlington required the approval of non-Burlington members of El Paso's board of directors before a squeeze-out merger could proceed. Burlington eventually purchased all the remaining shares of El Paso for $ 12 cash and one-quarter share of Burlington preferred stock per share. The parties dispute whether this consideration was equal to that paid to those tendering during the January tender offer.

withdrawal of the December tender offer coupled with the substitution of the January tender offer was a "manipulative" distortion of the market for El Paso stock. Schreiber also alleged that Burlington violated §14(e) by failing in the January offer to disclose the "golden parachutes" offered to four of El Paso's managers. She claims that this January nondisclosure was a deceptive act forbidden by §14(e). . . .

II

A

We are asked in this case to interpret §14(e) of the Securities Exchange Act. The starting point is the language of the statute. Section 14(e) provides:

> It shall be unlawful for any person to make any untrue statement of a material fact or omit to state any material fact necessary in order to make the statements made, in the light of the circumstances under which they are made, not misleading, or to engage in any fraudulent, deceptive, or manipulative acts or practices, in connection with any tender offer or request or invitation for tenders, or any solicitation of security holders in opposition to or in favor of any such offer, request, or invitation. The Commission shall, for the purposes of this subsection, by rules and regulations define, and prescribe means reasonably designed to prevent, such acts and practices as are fraudulent, deceptive, or manipulative.

Petitioner relies on a construction of the phrase, "fraudulent, deceptive, or manipulative acts or practices." Petitioner reads the phrase "fraudulent, deceptive, or manipulative acts or practices" to include acts which, although fully disclosed, "artificially" affect the price of the takeover target's stock. Petitioner's interpretation relies on the belief that §14(e) is directed at purposes broader than providing full and true information to investors.

Petitioner's reading of the term "manipulative" conflicts with the normal meaning of the term. We have held in the context of an alleged violation of §10(b) of the Securities Exchange Act:

> Use of the word "manipulative" is especially significant. It is and was virtually a term of art when used in connection with the securities markets. It connotes intentional or willful conduct *designed to deceive or defraud* investors by controlling or artificially affecting the price of securities. *Ernst & Ernst v. Hochfelder,* 425 U.S. 185, 199, 96 S. Ct. 1375, 1384, 47 L. Ed.2d 668 (1976) (*emphasis added*). . . .

She argues, however, that the term "manipulative" takes on a meaning in §14(e) that is different from the meaning it has in §10(b). Petitioner claims that the use of the disjunctive "or" in §14(e) implies that acts need not be deceptive or fraudulent to be manipulative. But Congress used the phrase "manipulative or deceptive" in §10(b) as well, and we have interpreted "manipulative" in that context to require misrepresentation.[6] Moreover, it is a "familiar principle

---

6. *Santa Fe Industries, Inc. v. Green,* 430 U.S. 462 (1977); . . . .

of statutory construction that words grouped in a list should be given related meaning." *Securities Industry Assn. v. Board of Governors, FRS,* 468 U.S. 207, 218, 104 S. Ct. 3003, 3010, 82 L. Ed. 2d 158 (1984). All three species of misconduct, *i.e.,* "fraudulent, deceptive, or manipulative," listed by Congress are directed at failures to disclose. The use of the term "manipulative" provides emphasis and guidance to those who must determine which types of acts are reached by the statute; it does not suggest a deviation from the section's facial and primary concern with disclosure or congressional concern with disclosure which is the core of the Act.

B

Our conclusion that "manipulative" acts under §14(e) require misrepresentation or nondisclosure is buttressed by the purpose and legislative history of the provision. Section 14(e) was originally added to the Securities Exchange Act as part of the Williams Act, 82 Stat. 457. "The purpose of the Williams Act is to insure that public shareholders who are confronted by a cash tender offer for their stock will not be required to respond without adequate information." *Rondeau v. Mosinee Paper Corp.,* 422 U.S. 49, 58, 95 S. Ct. 2069, 2075, 45 L. Ed. 2d 12 (1975).

It is clear that Congress relied primarily on disclosure to implement the purpose of the Williams Act. . . .

The expressed legislative intent was to preserve a neutral setting in which the contenders could fully present their arguments. The Senate sponsor went on to say:

> We have taken extreme care to avoid tipping the scales either in favor of management or in favor of the person making the takeover bids. S. 510 is designed solely to require full and fair disclosure for the benefit of investors. The bill will at the same time provide the offeror and management equal opportunity to present their case. . . .

While legislative history specifically concerning §14(e) is sparse, the House and Senate Reports discuss the role of §14(e). . . . Nowhere in the legislative history is there the slightest suggestion that §14(e) serves any purpose other than disclosure, or that the term "manipulative" should be read as an invitation to the courts to oversee the substantive fairness of tender offers; the quality of any offer is a matter for the marketplace.

To adopt the reading of the term "manipulative" urged by petitioner would not only be unwarranted in light of the legislative purpose but would be at odds with it. Inviting judges to read the term "manipulative" with their own sense of what constitutes "unfair" or "artificial" conduct would inject uncertainty into the tender offer process. An essential piece of information—whether the court would deem the fully disclosed actions of one side or the other to be "manipulative"—would not be available until after the tender offer had closed. This uncertainty would directly contradict the expressed congressional desire to give investors full information. . . .

C

We hold that the term "manipulative" as used in §14(e) requires misrepresentation or nondisclosure. It connotes "conduct designed to deceive or defraud investors by controlling or artificially affecting the price of securities." *Ernst & Ernst v. Hochfelder,* 425 U.S., at 199, 96 S. Ct., at 1384. Without misrepresentation or nondisclosure, §14(e) has not been violated.

Applying that definition to this case, we hold that the actions of respondents were not manipulative. The amended complaint fails to allege that the cancellation of the first tender offer was accompanied by any misrepresentation, nondisclosure, or deception. The District Court correctly found: "All activity of the defendants that could have conceivably affected the price of El Paso shares was done openly." 568 F. Supp., at 203.

Petitioner also alleges that El Paso management and Burlington entered into certain undisclosed and deceptive agreements during the making of the second tender offer. The substance of the allegations is that, in return for certain undisclosed benefits, El Paso managers agreed to support the second tender offer. But both courts noted that petitioner's complaint seeks only redress for injuries related to the cancellation of the first tender offer. Since the deceptive and misleading acts alleged by petitioner all occurred with reference to the making of the second tender offer—when the injuries suffered by petitioner had already been sustained—these acts bear no possible causal relationship to petitioner's alleged injuries. The Court of Appeals dealt correctly with this claim. . . .

The judgment of the Court of Appeals is *Affirmed.*

NOTE

Although the *Schreiber* decision represents yet another example of the Supreme Court's unwillingness to invade areas of the law traditionally committed to the states, that attitude may be changing. By virtue of the well-established choice of law principle known as the internal affairs doctrine, the High Court has adopted a hands-off approach (of the type reflected in *Schreiber)* in a number of other cases, most notably *Santa Fe Indus., Inc. v. Green,* 430 U.S. 462 (1977) (In reversing the court of appeals, the Supreme Court held that a claim for breach of fiduciary duty arising out of a controlling shareholder's decision to cash out the minority shares of a subsidiary in a Delaware short-form merger could not form the basis for a Rule 10b-5 cause of action in the absence of any deception, misrepresentation, or nondisclosure of material facts, emphasizing that the fundamental purpose of the 1934 Act is to implement a " 'philosophy of full disclosure'; once full disclosure has occurred, the fairness of the terms of the transaction is at most a tangential concern of the [1934 Act].").

As you remember from the materials in Chapter 1, Congress adopted SOX in July 2002, enacting a set of reforms that represent a rather substantial intrusion into matters of corporate governance historically relegated to state law. As part of the inevitable process of interpreting and implementing these reforms, the federal courts will necessarily get involved in resolving disputes over the provisions of SOX (such as the SOX-mandated requirements regarding audit committee independence, adequacy of internal financial controls and board monitoring thereof, and officer certification of quarterly SEC filings, among other things). Although the terms of SOX do not prescribe standards for directors' fiduciary obligations, there is growing commentary as to the impact of these reforms on the future development of fiduciary duty law. Will this continue to be an area committed exclusively (or primarily) to state law? What impact will SOX have on the balance between federal and state law in determining the scope of the board's fiduciary obligations to the company and its shareholders? This story continues to unfold, even as of this writing. *See generally*, Marc I. Steinberg, *The Federalization of Corporate Governance – An Evolving Process*, 50 LOYOLA UNIVERSITY CHICAGO LAW JOURNAL 539 (2019). (SOX serves as a rather "poignant reminder to the states – the principal overseers of corporate governance – that laxity toward fiduciary conduct may induce the passage of federal legislation in an effort to remediate state shortcomings, particularly during times of crisis.")

Following the Supreme Court's decision in *Schreiber*, increased importance came to rest on the fiduciary duty obligations of incumbent management (i.e., the directors and senior executive officers) of the company who is the target of an unsolicited takeover bid. As noted above, historically, fiduciary duty obligations have been primarily a matter of state law. The next three sections of this chapter set forth the paradigm cases under Delaware law describing the duties and responsibilities of Target's management in the context of a hostile takeover.

C.   The Dawn of a New Era of Enhanced Scrutiny

Early judicial reliance on the business judgment rule to evaluate Target Co. management's response to an unsolicited tender offer from Bidder Co. was criticized by many commentators for overlooking a fundamental tenet of this method for acquiring Target Co.—that Target Co. is *not* a party to the transaction. The question then becomes: Where does the board get the authority to intervene in a transaction that Target is *not* a party to, particularly in those situations where Target's board takes steps to thwart Bidder's efforts to buy Target shares directly from the company's shareholders? That is the central inquiry in the next case, which forms the foundation for the next 30 years of Delaware jurisprudence on fiduciary duty law in the M&A context.

In order to fully appreciate the teachings of the Delaware courts in its landmark decisions handed down in the 1980s, it is important to place these cases in some historical context. The 1970s ushered in the first of what came to be known as "hostile takeovers." Prior to the 1970s, most investment banking firms had shunned participating in hostile deals as a matter of generally accepted business practice. However, in the 1970s, hostile deals became a respectable business strategy and thus became part of the culture of "doing business" in corporate America. Indeed, hostile deals became an established part of the business landscape once the well-respected blue-chip firm Morgan Stanley abandoned its earlier refusal to participate in hostile deals and decided to act as financial advisor to a "raider" seeking to acquire control of a target company through a hostile bid.

As the hostile bid came to be an accepted practice on Wall Street in the 1980s, this new frontier broadened its horizons with Michael Milken's "discovery" of the junk bond. The willingness of Milken and his firm, Drexel Burnham, to provide financing to non-strategic buyers (such as T. Boone Pickens) led to enormous financing capacity for would-be bidders who came to be known as "corporate raiders." "Junk bonds" are debt instruments that are below investment grade as determined by one of the rating services (such as Moody's or Standard & Poor's), if they are rated at all. Junk bonds (or "high-yield" bonds as they are often (less pejoratively) referred to in today's M&A market) are bonds with a very low credit rating, reflecting the higher yield (i.e., interest rate) because of the significantly higher risk of default associated with junk bonds as compared to investment-grade debt (i.e., debt securities that have received a higher quality rating from Moody's or Standard & Poor's).

In the 1980s, Drexel ushered in a new era of takeover activity by financing takeover deals that came to be known as "boot-strap, bust-up, two-tiered" tender offers. The raider's offer generally would be financed by nothing more than a "highly confident" commitment letter from Drexel; that is to say, the raider would obtain a commitment letter from Drexel in which Drexel would indicate that it was "highly confident" that it could raise the necessary financing on behalf of the raider so that Bidder would have the necessary funding to complete the stock purchase at the time of closing. During the go-go years of the 1980s, junk bonds were sold by Drexel to raise very large amounts of capital, often billions of dollars, for takeover bids by raiders. In these highly leveraged situations, it was anticipated that the cash flow generated by Target's business would provide the source of funds to service the debt, often coupled with the sale of Target's assets in a "busting up" of Target's business.

Raiders often used the disclosure requirements of §13(d) of the Williams Act to their advantage to seek greenmail payments from the putative Target. Raiders would make "toehold" purchases (i.e., accumulating just under 5 percent of Target stock) and threaten to put the company "in play" in order to obtain "greenmail payments" from Target Co. (i.e., the raider gets paid to go away when the company buys back all of the shares of Target that the raider owns). Alternatively, the raider may cross the 5 percent mark and make the required filing under §13(d), thereby putting the company "in play" with the arbitrageurs, who accumulate stock of Target betting that the company will be taken over. The raider then makes money on the spread between the price paid to acquire Target's shares and the premium that will be received when Target gets acquired.

The surge in hostile takeover activity in the 1980s led to the development of takeover defenses, the earliest form of which was litigation, typically brought by Target management and often claiming that the raider was in violation of some aspect of the requirements of the Williams Act (and/or the SEC's rules promulgated thereunder). By bringing this litigation, management of Target bought itself time to mount a further defense in an effort to thwart the raider's takeover bid and thus allow Target to remain independent. This led to a variety of structural defenses, such as providing for staggered terms for the board of directors, eliminating the shareholders' ability to remove directors without cause, and eliminating the shareholders' ability to take action by written consent. Most of these structural defenses required amendments to the company's articles of incorporation, thereby triggering the need to obtain shareholder approval, which was usually forthcoming. However, these structural defenses required advance planning because of the need to obtain shareholder approval, and thus they took time to implement. *Query:* How does the use of staggered boards coupled with a charter provision that permits directors to be removed only for cause work as an antitakeover device?

In the case of an unsolicited offer that takes Target management by surprise, the only real defense that is available in most cases is the negotiated "friendly" deal with a white-knight suitor, or alternatively, the defensive corporate restructuring unilaterally undertaken by Target's management. Thus, in the early years, hostile takeover bids were frequently resisted by Target management leveraging the company's balance sheet and taking on debt to finance the issuer's self-tender and consequent recapitalization of Target's business (*see Carter Hawley Hale, supra,* at p. 442). The M&A market of the 1980s also saw the emergence of the LBO as private equity firms (such as Kohlberg Kravis & Roberts (KKR)) arrived on the scene, willing to provide the beleaguered Target management with a white-knight transaction as an alternative to the raider's hostile takeover bid. By 1988, it is reported that LBOs accounted for over 33 percent of the volume of M&A activity in the United States. Indeed, most observers of the M&A market regard KKR's purchase of RJR Nabisco for $25 billion as the "deal of the decade" in the 1980s, a deal that held the record for the largest LBO transaction for over two decades.

Against this backdrop, Marty Lipton, of the New York law firm Wachtell, Lipton, Rosen, & Katz, invented the "shareholder rights plan," which came to be more popularly known as the "poison pill." The operation of the pill is described by its inventor, *infra,* at p. 550, and its validity was upheld by the Delaware Supreme Court in the watershed year of 1985, in the landmark decision *Moran v. Household International, Inc.* (*see infra,* p. 540). In 1985, the Delaware Supreme Court also decided the seminal cases of *Unocal Corp. v. Mesa Petroleum ;Co.* (*see* below) and *Revlon, Inc. v. MacAndrews & Forbes Holdings, Inc.* (*see infra,* p. 583), which established new ground rules for hostile takeovers.

By 1989, as the deal decade drew to a close, the takeover boom of the 1980s went bust. In 1989, the insider trading scandal hits Wall Street, resulting in the indictment of Michael Milken on insider trading charges (among other counts) and leading to the demise of his employer, Drexel Burnham, with then-U.S. attorney Rudy Guiliani as the federal prosecutor making the headlines in the financial press. Likewise, the junk bond market collapsed as junk bonds turned into real junk and the cash buyout craze came to an abrupt halt as financing for the raiders disappeared once their banker of choice, Drexel Burnham, went under.

With that background in mind, let's review the paradigm fiduciary duty cases that were decided by the Delaware Supreme Court in the watershed year of 1985. Then we will turn our attention to the 1990s and the companion cases of *Time-Warner* (*see infra,* p. 613) and *QVC* (*see infra,* p. 629), which reflect further developments in the market for M&A activity and further refinements by the Delaware courts as to the scope of fiduciary duty obligations imposed on Target's management in the context of an M&A transaction.

Unocal Corporation v. Mesa Petroleum Co.
493 A.2d 946 (Del. 1985)

MOORE, Justice.

We confront an issue of first impression in Delaware—the validity of a corporation's self-tender for its own shares which excludes from participation a stockholder making a hostile tender offer for the company's stock.

The Court of Chancery granted a preliminary injunction to the plaintiffs, Mesa Petroleum Co., Mesa Asset Co., Mesa Partners II, and Mesa Eastern, Inc. (collectively "Mesa")[1], enjoining an exchange offer of the defendant, Unocal Corporation (Unocal), for its own stock. The trial court concluded that a selective exchange offer, excluding Mesa, was legally impermissible. We cannot agree with such a blanket rule. The factual findings of the Vice Chancellor, fully supported by the record, establish that Unocal's board, consisting of a majority of independent directors, acted in good faith, and after reasonable investigation found that Mesa's tender offer was both inadequate and coercive. Under the circumstances the board had both the power and duty to oppose a bid it perceived to be harmful to the corporate enterprise. On this record we are satisfied that the device Unocal adopted is reasonable in relation to the threat posed, and that the board acted in the proper exercise of sound business judgment. We will not substitute our views for those of the board if the latter's decision can be "attributed to any rational business purpose." *Sinclair Oil Corp. v. Levien,* Del. Supr., 280 A.2d 717, 720 (1971). Accordingly, we reverse the decision of the Court of Chancery and order the preliminary injunction vacated.

I.

The factual background of this matter bears a significant relationship to its ultimate outcome.

On April 8, 1985, Mesa, the owner of approximately 13% of Unocal's stock, commenced a two-tier "front loaded" cash tender offer for 64 million shares, or approximately 37%, of Unocal's outstanding stock at a price of $54 per share. The "back-end" was designed to eliminate the remaining publicly held shares by an exchange of securities purportedly worth $54 per share. However, pursuant to an order entered by the United States District Court for the Central District of California on April 26, 1985, Mesa issued a supplemental proxy statement to Unocal's stockholders disclosing that the securities offered in the second-step merger would be highly subordinated, and that Unocal's capitalization would differ significantly from its present structure. Unocal has rather aptly termed such securities "junk bonds."

---

1. T. Boone Pickens, Jr., is President and Chairman of the Board of Mesa Petroleum and President of Mesa Asset and controls the related Mesa entities.

Unocal's board consists of eight independent outside directors and six insiders. It met on April 13, 1985, to consider the Mesa tender offer. Thirteen directors were present, and the meeting lasted nine and one-half hours. The directors were given no agenda or written materials prior to the session. However, detailed presentations were made by legal counsel regarding the board's obligations under both Delaware corporate law and the federal securities laws. The board then received a presentation from Peter Sachs on behalf of Goldman Sachs & Co. (Goldman Sachs) and Dillon, Read & Co. (Dillon Read) discussing the bases for their opinions that the Mesa proposal was wholly inadequate. Mr. Sachs opined that the minimum cash value that could be expected from a sale or orderly liquidation for 100% of Unocal's stock was in excess of $60 per share. In making his presentation, Mr. Sachs showed slides outlining the valuation techniques used by the financial advisors, and others, depicting recent business combinations in the oil and gas industry. The Court of Chancery found that the Sachs presentation was designed to apprise the directors of the scope of the analyses performed rather than the facts and numbers used in reaching the conclusion that Mesa's tender offer price was inadequate.

Mr. Sachs also presented various defensive strategies available to the board if it concluded that Mesa's two-step tender offer was inadequate and should be opposed. One of the devices outlined was a self-tender by Unocal for its own stock with a reasonable price range of $70 to $75 per share. The cost of such a proposal would cause the company to incur $6.1-6.5 billion of additional debt, and a presentation was made informing the board of Unocal's ability to handle it. The directors were told that the primary effect of this obligation would be to reduce exploratory drilling, but that the company would nonetheless remain a viable entity.

The eight outside directors, comprising a clear majority of the thirteen members present, then met separately with Unocal's financial advisors and attorneys. Thereafter, they unanimously agreed to advise the board that it should reject Mesa's tender offer as inadequate, and that Unocal should pursue a self-tender to provide the stockholders with a fairly priced alternative to the Mesa proposal. The board then reconvened and unanimously adopted a resolution rejecting as grossly inadequate Mesa's tender offer. Despite the nine and one-half hour length of the meeting, no formal decision was made on the proposed defensive self-tender.

On April 15, the board met again with four of the directors present by telephone and one member still absent. This session lasted two hours. Unocal's Vice President of Finance and its Assistant General Counsel made a detailed presentation of the proposed terms of the exchange offer. A price range between $70 and $80 per share was considered, and ultimately the directors agreed upon $72. The board was also advised about the debt securities that would be issued, and the necessity of placing restrictive covenants upon certain corporate activities until the obligations were paid. The board's decisions were made in reliance on the advice of its investment bankers, including the terms and conditions upon which the securities were to be issued. Based upon this advice, and the board's own deliberations, the directors unanimously approved the exchange offer. . . . The board resolution also stated that the offer would be subject to other conditions that had been described to the board at the meeting, or which were deemed necessary by Unocal's officers, including the exclusion of Mesa from the proposal (the Mesa exclusion). Any such conditions were required to be in accordance with the "purport and intent" of the offer.

Unocal's exchange offer was commenced on April 17, 1985, and Mesa promptly challenged it by filing this suit in the Court of Chancery. . . . On April 22, 1985, the Unocal board met again and was advised by Goldman Sachs and Dillon Read . . . that they should tender their own Unocal stock into the exchange offer as a mark of their confidence in it.

Another focus of the board was the Mesa exclusion. Legal counsel advised that under Delaware law Mesa could only be excluded for what the directors reasonably believed to be a valid corporate purpose. The directors' discussion centered on the objective of adequately compensating shareholders at the "back-end" of Mesa's proposal, which the latter would finance with "junk bonds". To include Mesa would defeat that goal, because under the proration aspect of the exchange offer (49%) every Mesa share accepted by Unocal would displace one held by another stockholder. Further, if Mesa were permitted to tender to Unocal, the latter would in effect be financing Mesa's own inadequate proposal. . . .

[O]n April 22, 1985, Mesa amended its complaint in this action to challenge the Mesa exclusion. . . .

After the May 8 hearing the Vice Chancellor issued an unreported opinion on May 13, 1985 granting Mesa a preliminary injunction. Specifically, the trial court noted that "[t]he parties basically agree that the directors' duty of care extends to protecting the corporation from perceived harm whether it be from third parties or shareholders." The trial court also concluded . . . that "[a]lthough the facts, . . . do not appear to be sufficient to prove that Mesa's principle objective is to be bought off at a substantial premium, they do justify a reasonable inference to the same effect.". . .

II.

The issues we address involve these fundamental questions: Did the Unocal board have the power and duty to oppose a takeover threat it reasonably perceived to be harmful to the corporate enterprise, and if so, is its action here entitled to the protection of the business judgment rule? . . .

III.

We begin with the basic issue of the power of a board of directors of a Delaware corporation to adopt a defensive measure of this type. Absent such authority, all other questions are moot. Neither issues of fairness nor business judgment are pertinent without the basic underpinning of a board's legal power to act.

The board has a large reservoir of authority upon which to draw. Its duties and responsibilities proceed from the inherent powers conferred by 8 Del. C. §141 (a), respecting management of the corporation's "business and affairs".

Additionally, the powers here being exercised derive from 8 Del. C. §160(a), conferring broad authority upon a corporation to deal in its own stock.[7] From this it is now well established that in the acquisition of its shares a Delaware corporation may deal selectively with its stockholders, provided the directors have not acted out of a sole or primary purpose to entrench themselves in office. . . .

Finally, the board's power to act derives from its fundamental duty and obligation to protect the corporate enterprise, which includes stockholders, from harm reasonably perceived, irrespective of its source. . . . Thus, we are satisfied that in the broad context of corporate governance, including issues of fundamental corporate change, a board of directors is not a passive instrumentality.[8]

Given the foregoing principles, we turn to the standards by which director action is to be measured. In *Pogostin v. Rice*, Del. Supr., 480 A.2d 619 (1984), we held that the business judgment rule, including the standards by which director conduct is judged, is applicable in the context of a takeover. *Id.* at 627. The business judgment rule is a "presumption that in making a business decision the directors of a corporation acted on an informed basis, in good faith and in the honest belief that the action taken was in the best interests of the company." *Aronson v. Lewis*, Del. Supr., 473 A.2d 805, 812 (1984) (citations omitted). A hallmark of the business judgment rule is that a court will not substitute its judgment for that of the board if the latter's decision can be "attributed to any rational business purpose." *Sinclair Oil Corp. v. Levien*, Del. Supr., 280 A.2d 717, 720 (1971).

When a board addresses a pending takeover bid it has an obligation to determine whether the offer is in the best interests of the corporation and its shareholders. In that respect a board's duty is no different from any other responsibility it shoulders, and its decisions should be no less entitled to the respect they otherwise would be accorded in the realm of business judgment.[9] *See also Johnson v. Trueblood*, 629 F.2d 287, 292-293 (3d Cir. 1980). There are, however, certain caveats to a proper exercise of this function. Because of the

---

7. This power under 8 Del. C. §160(a), with certain exceptions not pertinent here, is as follows:

> (a) Every corporation may purchase, redeem, receive, take or otherwise acquire, own and hold, sell, lend, exchange, transfer or otherwise dispose of, pledge, use and otherwise deal in and with its own shares; . . .

8. Even in the traditional areas of fundamental corporate change, i.e., charter, amendments [8 Del. C. §242(b)], mergers [8 Del. C. §§251(b), 252(c), 253(a), and 254(d)], sale of assets [8 Del. C. §271(a)], and dissolution [8 Del. C. §275(a)], director action is a prerequisite to the ultimate disposition of such matters. *See also, Smith v. Van Gorkom*, Del. Supr., 488 A.2d 858, 888 (1985).

9. This is a subject of intense debate among practicing members of the bar and legal scholars. Excellent examples of these contending views are: Block & Miller, *The Responsibilities and Obligations of Corporate Directors in Takeover Contests*, 11 Sec. Reg. L.J. 44 (1983); Easterbrook & Fischel, *Takeover Bids, Defensive Tactics, and Shareholders' Welfare*, 36 Bus. Law. 1733 (1981); Easterbrook & Fischel, *The Proper Role of a Target's Management in Responding to a Tender Offer*, 94 Harv. L. Rev. 1161 (1981). Herzel, Schmidt & Davis, *Why Corporate Directors Have a Right to Resist Tender Offers*, 3 Corp. L. Rev. 107 (1980); Lipton, *Takeover Bids in the Target's Boardroom*, 35 Bus. Law. 101 (1979).

omnipresent specter that a board may be acting primarily in its own interests, rather than those of the corporation and its shareholders, there is an enhanced duty which calls for judicial examination at the threshold before the protections of the business judgment rule may be conferred. This Court has long recognized that:

> We must bear in mind the inherent danger in the purchase of shares with corporate funds to remove a threat to corporate policy when a threat to control is involved. The directors are of necessity confronted with a conflict of interest, and an objective decision is difficult.

Bennett v. Propp, Del. Supr., 187 A.2d 405, 409 (1962). In the face of this inherent conflict directors must show that they had reasonable grounds for believing that a danger to corporate policy and effectiveness existed because of another person's stock ownership. *Cheff v. Mathes*, 199 A.2d at 554-55. However, they satisfy that burden "by showing good faith and reasonable investigation. . . ." *Id.* at 555. Furthermore, such proof is materially enhanced, as here, by the approval of a board comprised of a majority of outside independent directors who have acted in accordance with the foregoing standards. . . .

IV.

A.

In the board's exercise of corporate power to forestall a takeover bid our analysis begins with the basic principle that corporate directors have a fiduciary duty to act in the best interests of the corporation's stockholders. *Guth v. Loft, Inc.*, Del. Supr., 5 A.2d 503, 510 (1939). As we have noted, their duty of care extends to protecting the corporation and its owners from perceived harm whether a threat originates from third parties or other shareholders.[10] But such powers are not absolute. A corporation does not have unbridled discretion to defeat any perceived threat by any Draconian means available.

The restriction placed upon a selective stock repurchase is that the directors may not have acted solely or primarily out of a desire to perpetuate themselves in office. *See Cheff v. Mathes*, 199 A.2d at 556; *Kors v. Carey*, 158 A.2d at 140. Of course, to this is added the further caveat that inequitable action may not be taken under the guise of law. *Schnell v. Chris-Craft Industries, Inc.*, Del. Supr., 285 A.2d 437, 439 (1971). The standard of proof established in *Cheff v. Mathes* . . . is designed to ensure that a defensive measure to thwart or impede a takeover is indeed motivated by a good faith concern for the welfare of the corporation and its stockholders, which in all circumstances must be free of any fraud or

---

10. It has been suggested that a board's response to a takeover threat should be a passive one. Easterbrook & Fischel, *supra*, 36 Bus. Law. at 1750. However, that clearly is not the law of Delaware, and as the proponents of this rule of passivity readily concede, it has not been adopted either by courts or state legislatures. Easterbrook & Fischel, *supra*, 94 Harv. L. Rev. at 1194.

other misconduct. *Cheff v. Mathes*, 199 A.2d at 554-55. However, this does not end the inquiry.

B.

A further aspect is the element of balance. If a defensive measure is to come within the ambit of the business judgment rule, it must be reasonable in relation to the threat posed. This entails an analysis by the directors of the nature of the takeover bid and its effect on the corporate enterprise. Examples of such concerns may include: inadequacy of the price offered, nature and timing of the offer, questions of illegality, the impact on "constituencies" other than shareholders (i.e., creditors, customers, employees, and perhaps even the community generally), the risk of nonconsummation, and the quality of securities being offered in the exchange. *See* Lipton and Brownstein, *Takeover Responses and Directors' Responsibilities: An Update*, p. 7, ABA National Institute on the Dynamics of Corporate Control (December 8, 1983). While not a controlling factor, it also seems to us that a board may reasonably consider the basic stockholder interests at stake, including those of short term speculators, whose actions may have fueled the coercive aspect of the offer at the expense of the long term investor. Here, the threat posed was viewed by the Unocal board as a grossly inadequate two-tier coercive tender offer coupled with the threat of greenmail.

Specifically, the Unocal directors had concluded that the value of Unocal was substantially above the $54 per share offered in cash at the front end. Furthermore, they determined that the subordinated securities to be exchanged in Mesa's announced squeeze out of the remaining shareholders in the "back-end" merger were "junk bonds" worth far less than $54. It is now well recognized that such offers are a classic coercive measure designed to stampede shareholders into tendering at the first tier, even if the price is inadequate, out of fear of what they will receive at the back end of the transaction. Wholly beyond the coercive aspect of an inadequate two-tier tender offer, the threat was posed by a corporate raider with a national reputation as a "greenmailer."[13]

In adopting the selective exchange offer, the board stated that its objective was either to defeat the inadequate Mesa offer or, should the offer still succeed, provide the 49% of its stockholders, who would otherwise be forced to accept "junk bonds," with $72 worth of senior debt. We find that both purposes are valid.

However, such efforts would have been thwarted by Mesa's participation in the exchange offer. First, if Mesa could tender its shares, Unocal would effectively be subsidizing the former's continuing effort to buy Unocal stock at

---

13. The term "greenmail" refers to the practice of buying out a takeover bidder's stock at a premium that is not available to other shareholders in order to prevent the takeover. The Chancery Court noted that "Mesa has made tremendous profits from its takeover activities although in the past few years it has not been successful in acquiring any of the target companies on an unfriendly basis." Moreover, the trial court specifically found that the actions of the Unocal board were taken in good faith to eliminate both the inadequacies of the tender offer and to forestall the payment of "greenmail."

$54 per share. Second, Mesa could not, by definition, fit within the class of shareholders being protected from its own coercive and inadequate tender offer.

Thus, we are satisfied that the selective exchange offer is reasonably related to the threats posed. It is consistent with the principle that "the minority stockholder shall receive the substantial equivalent in value of what he had before." *Sterling v. Mayflower Hotel Corp.*, Del. Supr., 93 A.2d 107, 114 (1952). This concept of fairness, while stated in the merger context, is also relevant in the area of tender offer law. Thus, the board's decision to offer what it determined to be the fair value of the corporation to the 49% of its shareholders, who would otherwise be forced to accept highly subordinated "junk bonds," is reasonable and consistent with the directors' duty to ensure that the minority stockholders receive equal value for their shares.

V.

Mesa contends that it is unlawful, and the trial court agreed, for a corporation to discriminate in this fashion against one shareholder. It argues correctly that no case has ever sanctioned a device that precludes a raider from sharing in a benefit available to all other stockholders. However, as we have noted earlier, the principle of selective stock repurchases by a Delaware corporation is neither unknown nor unauthorized. . . . The only difference is that heretofore the approved transaction was the payment of "greenmail" to a raider or dissident posing a threat to the corporate enterprise. All other stockholders were denied such favored treatment, and given Mesa's past history of greenmail, its claims here are rather ironic.

However, our corporate law is not static. It must grow and develop in response to, indeed in anticipation of, evolving concepts and needs. Merely because the General Corporation Law is silent as to a specific matter does not mean that it is prohibited. In the days when *Cheff, Bennett, Martin* and *Kors* were decided, the tender offer, while not an unknown device, was virtually unused, and little was known of such methods as two-tier "front-end" loaded offers with their coercive effects. Then, the favored attack of a raider was stock acquisition followed by a proxy contest. Various defensive tactics, which provided no benefit whatever to the raider, evolved. Thus, the use of corporate funds by management to counter a proxy battle was approved. . . . Litigation, supported by corporate funds, aimed at the raider has long been a popular device.

More recently, as the sophistication of both raiders and targets has developed, a host of other defensive measures to counter such ever mounting threats has evolved and received judicial sanction. These include defensive charter amendments and other devices bearing some rather exotic, but apt, names: Crown Jewel, White Knight, Pac Man, and Golden Parachute. Each has highly selective features, the object of which is to deter or defeat the raider.

Thus, while the exchange offer is a form of selective treatment, given the nature of the threat posed here the response is neither unlawful nor unreasonable. If the board of directors is disinterested, has acted in good faith and with due care, its decision in the absence of an abuse of discretion will be upheld as a proper exercise of business judgment.

To this Mesa responds that the board is not disinterested, because the directors are receiving a benefit from the tender of their own shares, which because of the Mesa exclusion, does not devolve upon *all* stockholders equally. *See Aronson v. Lewis*, Del. Supr., 473 A.2d 805, 812 (1984). However, Mesa concedes that if the exclusion is valid, then the directors and all other stockholders share the same benefit. The answer of course is that the exclusion is valid, and the directors' participation in the exchange offer does not rise to the level of a disqualifying interest. The excellent discussion in *Johnson v. Trueblood*, [629 F.2d 287, 292-293 (3rd Cir. 1980)], of the use of the business judgment rule in take-over contests also seems pertinent here.

Nor does this become an "interested" director transaction merely because certain board members are large stockholders. As this Court has previously noted, that fact alone does not create a disqualifying "personal pecuniary interest" to defeat the operation of the business judgment rule. *Cheff v. Mathes*, 199 A.2d at 554.

Mesa also argues that the exclusion permits the directors to abdicate the fiduciary duties they owe it. However, that is not so. The board continues to owe Mesa the duties of due care and loyalty. But in the face of the destructive threat Mesa's tender offer was perceived to pose, the board had a supervening duty to protect the corporate enterprise, which includes the other shareholders, from threatened harm.

Mesa contends that the basis of this action is punitive, and solely in response to the exercise of its rights of corporate democracy.[14] Nothing precludes Mesa, as a stockholder, from acting in its own self-interest. . . . However, Mesa, while pursuing its own interests, has acted in a manner which a board consisting of a majority of independent directors has reasonably determined to be contrary to the best interests of Unocal and its other shareholders. In this situation, there is no support in Delaware law for the proposition that, when responding to a perceived harm, a corporation must guarantee a benefit to a stockholder who is deliberately provoking the danger being addressed. There is no obligation of self-sacrifice by a corporation and its shareholders in the face of such a challenge.

Here, the Court of Chancery specifically found that the "directors' decision [to oppose the Mesa tender offer] was made in the good faith belief that the Mesa tender offer is inadequate." Given our standard of review under *Levitt v. Bouvier*, Del. Supr., 287 A.2d 671, 673 (1972), and *Application of Delaware Racing Association*, Del. Supr., 213 A.2d 203, 207 (1965), we are satisfied that Unocal's board has met its burden of proof. *Cheff v. Mathes*, 199 A.2d at 555.

---

14. This seems to be the underlying basis of the trial court's principal reliance on the unreported Chancery decision of *Fisher v. Moltz*, Del. Ch. No. 6068 (1979), published in 5 Del. J. Corp. L. 530 (1980). However, the facts in *Fisher* are thoroughly distinguishable. There, a corporation offered to repurchase the shares of its former employees, except those of the plaintiffs, merely because the latter were then engaged in lawful competition with the company. No threat to the enterprise was posed, and at best it can be said that the exclusion was motivated by pique instead of a rational corporate purpose.

VI.

In conclusion, there was directorial power to oppose the Mesa tender offer, and to undertake a selective stock exchange made in good faith and upon a reasonable investigation pursuant to a clear duty to protect the corporate enterprise. Further, the selective stock repurchase plan chosen by Unocal is reasonable in relation to the threat that the board rationally and reasonably believed was posed by Mesa's inadequate and coercive two-tier tender offer. Under those circumstances the board's action is entitled to be measured by the standards of the business judgment rule. Thus, unless it is shown by a preponderance of the evidence that the directors' decisions were primarily based on perpetuating themselves in office, or some other breach of fiduciary duty such as fraud, overreaching, lack of good faith, or being uninformed, a Court will not substitute its judgment for that of the board.

In this case that protection is not lost merely because Unocal's directors have tendered their shares in the exchange offer. Given the validity of the Mesa exclusion, they are receiving a benefit shared generally by all other stockholders except Mesa. In this circumstance the test of *Aronson v. Lewis*, 473 A.2d at 812, is satisfied. *See also Cheff v. Mathes*, 199 A.2d at 554. If the stockholders are displeased with the action of their elected representatives, the powers of corporate democracy are at their disposal to turn the board out. *Aronson v. Lewis*, Del. Supr., 473 A.2d 805, 811 (1984). *See also* 8 Del. C. §§141(k) and 211(b).

With the Court of Chancery's findings that the exchange offer was based on the board's good faith belief that the Mesa offer was inadequate, that the board's action was informed and taken with due care, that Mesa's prior activities justify a reasonable inference that its principle objective was greenmail, and implicitly, that the substance of the offer itself was reasonable and fair to the corporation and its stockholders if Mesa were included, we cannot say that the Unocal directors have acted in such a manner as to have passed an "unintelligent and unadvised judgment." *Mitchell v. Highland-Western Glass Co.*, Del. Ch., 167 A. 831, 833 (1933). The decision of the Court of Chancery is therefore REVERSED, and the preliminary injunction is VACATED.

QUESTIONS

1. What is the perceived threat posed by the terms of Mesa's offer to acquire Unocal?

2. What is "greenmail"?

3. Given the board's fiduciary duty to manage the business for the benefit of *all* shareholders, why is it permissible for the board to discriminate against one of its own shareholders (here, T. Boone Pickens and his investment vehicle, Mesa)?

4. As a public policy matter, why allow Target's (here, Unocal's) board to get involved when Target (Unocal) itself is not a party to the transaction? What is the "passivity theory"? Why did the Delaware Supreme Court

refused to adopt the "passivity theory"? In thinking about this issue, consider the following perspective by leading scholars advocating the "passivity theory":

> Under existing federal and state law, a corporation's managers can resist and often defeat a premium tender offer without liability to either the corporation's shareholders or the unsuccessful tender offeror. Professors Easterbrook and Fischel argue that resistance by a corporation's managers to premium tender offers, even if it triggers a bidding contest, ultimately decreases shareholder welfare. Shareholders would be better off, the authors claim, were such resistance all but proscribed. The authors consider, but find wanting, a number of potential criticisms of their analysis; they conclude by proposing a rule of managerial passivity. . . .

Frank Easterbrook & Daniel Fischel, *The Proper Role of Target's Management in Responding to a Tender Offer*, 94 Harv. L. Rev. 1161, 1194 (1981).

NOTES

1. The Market for Corporate Control. Those commentators who advocate the passivity theory often rely on the seminal writings of Professor Henry Manne to support their views. In his path-breaking article, *Mergers and the Market for Control,* Professor Manne offered the following introduction to the "market for corporate control":

> [As explained by Professor Manne in this article,] the market for corporate control gives . . . shareholders both power and protection commensurate with their interest in corporate affairs.
>
> A fundamental premise underlying the market for corporate control is the existence of a high positive correlation between corporate managerial efficiency and the market price of shares of that company. As an existing company is poorly managed—in the sense of not making as great a return for the shareholders as could be accomplished under other feasible managements—the market price of the shares declines relative to the values of other companies on the same industry or relative to the market as a whole. . . . The lower the stock price, relative to what it could be with more efficient management, the more attractive the take-over becomes to those who believe that they can manage the company more efficiently. And the potential return from the successful take-over and revitalization of the company can be enormous.
>
> [T]he greatest benefits of the take-over . . . probably inure to those least conscious of it. Apart from the stock market, we have no objective standard of managerial efficiency. Courts, as indicated by the so-called business-judgment rule, are loath to second guess business decisions or remove directors from office. Only the take-over . . . provides some assurance of competitive efficiency among corporate managers and therefore affords strong protection to the interests of vast numbers of small non-controlling shareholders. Compared to this mechanism, the efforts of the SEC and the courts to protect shareholders through the development of a fiduciary duty concept and the shareholder's derivative suit seem small indeed. It is true that sales by dissatisfied shareholders are necessary to trigger the mechanism and that these shareholders may suffer considerable losses. On the other

hand, even greater capital losses are prevented by the existence of a competitive market for corporate control.

Henry Manne, *Mergers and the Market for Corporate Control,* 73 J. POLITICAL ECONOMY 110, 117 (1965). In this article, Professor Manne then goes on to describe the three basic techniques for taking over control of corporations—the proxy fight, the direct purchase of shares, and the merger—and to evaluate the "costs, practical difficulties, and legal consequences" of each of these approaches. The modern sets of legal considerations that regulate each of these "three basic techniques" have been set forth in the materials contained in the prior chapters of the casebook. In this chapter, therefore, we will build on our understanding of the modern rules and regulations for these "three basic techniques" by analyzing the interaction of the relevant legal rules and regulations (as set forth in the prior chapters of this book) with the ongoing evolution of fiduciary duty law.

2. Development of an Intermediate Standard of Judicial Review for Takeover Cases. The Delaware Supreme Court's pronouncement in *Unocal* of a new, intermediate standard of judicial review was not without its critics. On the fifteenth anniversary of the *Unocal* decision, a leading scholar of corporate law observed:

> A natural inclination towards stocktaking accompanies the new millennium. It coincidences [sic] with the fifteenth anniversary of the Delaware Supreme Court's announcement in *Unocal Corp. v. Mesa Petroleum Co.* of a new approach to takeover law provides an appropriate occasion to step back and evaluate a remarkable experiment in corporate law—the Delaware Supreme Court's development of an intermediate standard for evaluating defensive tactics.
>
> This experiment began with, and was surely a response to, an earlier and extremely controversial takeover wave. . . .
>
> . . . I have been quite negative in my assessment of the fifteen-year *Unocal* experiment. However, no cloud is without a silver lining, and in this case the silver lining is substantial even if accidental.
>
> Given the decision to take on the task of distinguishing between good and bad defensive tactics, the manner in which the Delaware courts have carried out that charge is interesting. A fair reading of the supreme court's intermediate standard decisions, buttressed by the chancery court's and especially Chancellor Allen's repeated dicta about the critical role of independent directors in management buyouts, is that independent directors are expected to be the controlling parties in a target company's conduct of its defense. Only when the directors appear to have abdicated their role to management—think of *Van Gorkom, Macmillan,* and *QVC*—will the court intervene.
>
> As I have made clear to this point, I think this is the wrong approach; evaluating target board conduct misses the question of who should be making the decision in the first place. But, it seems to me, there has been at least one beneficial, if unintended, consequence of this focus on director performance. The role the Delaware Supreme Court has assigned independent directors in connection with takeovers is quite different than the role directors assigned to themselves prior to the turbulent 1980s. At least in the takeover arena, independent directors, the Delaware courts have stated pointedly, are not merely advisers to management, who have no stake in whether their advice is followed. In the takeover arena, independent directors must be the *real* decision-makers and courts will

expect them to play a central role in conducting the target's response to a hostile or competing offer.

Ronald J. Gilson, Unocal *Fifteen Years Later (and What We Can Do about It)*, 26 DEL. J. CORP. L. 491, 491-492, 513 (2001) (*emphasis in original*).

Professor Gilson's concern highlights one of the central public policy issues raised by the takeover wave of the 1980s and the ensuing case law that came out of this period: *Who should decide when and on what terms a publicly held company is for sale?* This question goes to the fundamental balance of power between the board of directors (most notably the outside, independent directors), the senior executive officers (most notably, the CEO), and the company's stockholders. The remaining materials in this chapter explore the various considerations implicated in Delaware case law over the past several decades addressing this issue of modern corporate governance, a matter that continues to be of considerable importance in the wake of the Great Recession and the economic turbulence resulting from the coronavirus pandemic beginning in 2020.

3. The SEC's Response: Regulation of Issuer Self-Tenders.   The SEC filed an amicus brief in *Unocal* opposing the discriminatory self-tender undertaken by Target. Following the decision in *Unocal,* the SEC responded by adopting what is known as the "all-holders rule," Rule 13e-4, and Rule 14d-10. *See* Securities Exchange Act Rel. No. 23421 (1986). Under the SEC's all-holders rule, both issuer self-tender offers and third-party tender offers must be open to *all* shareholders and the best price paid by the acquiror to any tendering shareholder must be paid to all other tendering shareholders (the latter aspect of this SEC rule is often referred to as the "best price" rule). The practical effect of this SEC rulemaking is to eliminate the exclusionary self-tender as a viable defensive strategy, thereby nullifying the Delaware Supreme Court decision in *Unocal.* Even though the defensive strategy undertaken in *Unocal* has been consigned to the scrap heap as a result of this SEC rulemaking, the standard of review first enunciated in *Unocal* lives on, spawning a new era of judicial decision making. The continuing evolution of the *Unocal* standard of review is examined in the remaining cases in this chapter.

4. Rise (and Decline) of Merger-Related Litigation.   Without a doubt, litigation challenging M&A transactions rose in the early part of the 21st century. A March 2012 study reports that, with respect to shareholder litigation related to acquisitions of public companies valued at over $100 million that were announced in 2010 and 2011,

> almost every acquisition of that size elicited multiple lawsuits, which were filed shortly after the deal's announcement and often settled before the deal's closing. Only a small fraction of these lawsuits resulted in payments to shareholders; the majority settled for additional disclosures or, less frequently, changes in merger terms, such as deal protection provisions.

Robert Daines & Olga Koumrian, *Recent Developments in Shareholder Litigation Involving Mergers & Acquisitions*, March 2012 Update, Cornerstone Research, *available at*: https://www.cornerstone.com/Publications/Reports/Recent-Developments-in-Shareholder-Litigation-Invo.pdf. And this worrisome (at least for some commentators) trend continued unabated until the Chancery Court issued its opinion in *Trulia*, as described more fully below:

> In 2014, lawsuits were filed in 93 percent of all announced public company transactions valued over $100 million, up from 44 percent in 2007.[1] Unfortunately for defendant companies and directors, many of these lawsuits are not triggered by failures to properly exercise fiduciary duties, . . . and [many of these lawsuits] result in disclosure-only settlement agreements together with plaintiffs' counsel fee awards that are nothing more than a *transaction tax*.[2] . . .
>
> However, Delaware entities may take solace in recent developments in the Delaware Chancery Court that indicate that Delaware courts will closely scrutinize M&A litigation settlements and will reject settlements involving a global release for defendants where the court believes that the shareholder benefits obtained by plaintiffs, even if tangible, do not justify such a release. The court's recent actions may indicate a sea change is beginning that could alter the M&A litigation landscape in the Delaware Chancery Court and potentially elsewhere.
>
> Although courts in Delaware, New York and Texas have in recent years rejected some "disclosure-only" settlements, historically, such settlements have been routinely approved. [However, the Delaware Chancery Court decision in *In re Trulia, Inc. Stockholder Litigation*, C.A. No. 10020-CB (Del. Ch. Jun. 22, 2016), illustrates just] how troubling that court now finds these settlements [and also reflects the Chancery Court's] increasing willingness to break with the tradition of routinely approving [such] "disclosure-only" settlements, . . . The Delaware courts appear focused on ensuring that under the facts of each case the relief obtained by plaintiffs in the settlement provides sufficient value to justify a global release and [the award of attorneys' fees to] plaintiffs' counsel . . .

Nancy B. Bostic and J. Wesley Dorman, Jr., Hutton Andrews Kurth LLP, *Delaware Courts Scrutinize Recent Proposed Settlement Agreements— A Harbinger of Fewer M&A "Transaction Tax" Lawsuits?*, Sept. 10, 2015, *available at*: https://www.natlaw-review.com/article/delaware-courts-scrutinize-recent-proposed-settlement-agreements-harbinger-fewer-ma.

In the *Trulia* case, Chancellor Bouchard "issued a seminal decision that may signal the end of (at least) most disclosure-only settlements" in shareholder lawsuits challenging M&A transactions. Francis G.X, Pileggi, *Chancery Sounds Death Knell for Most Disclosure -Only Settlements*, Delaware Corporate & Commercial Litigation Blog, Jan. 31, 2016, *available at*: http://www.delewarelitigation.com/2016/01/articles/chancery-court-updates/trulia/. Joining a host of critics of "disclosure-only settlements," Chancellor Bouchard rejected a proposed settlement of a lawsuit challenging Zillow, Inc.'s acquisition of Trulia, Inc. in a stock-for-stock transaction:

> After defendants agreed to moot plaintiffs' disclosure claims by supplementing their disclosures before the stockholder vote, the proposed settlement would

---

1. *See* Cornerstone Research, Shareholder Litigation Involving Acquisitions of Public Companies: Review of 2014 M&A Litigation at p. 1, [*available at:* https://www.cornerstone.com/GetAttachment/897c61ef-bfde-46e6-a2b8-5f94906c6ee2/Shareholder-Litigation-Involving-Acquisitions-2014-Rev].

2. Although the majority of resolved M&A litigation in 2014 settled, only eight percent of the settlements resulted in monetary consideration for shareholders as opposed to 79 percent that resulted in only supplemental disclosures. *Id.* at p. 4-5.

have resulted in a fee to plaintiffs' counsel and broad releases for defendants, but no economic benefit to the stockholder class. Although not the first to express distaste for such settlements and the incentives they create, the Chancellor's Opinion is notable for its comprehensive discussion of their problems and firm proposals to avoid such problems going forward, including a clear message that the [Delaware Chancery] Court will no longer hesitate to reject disclosure settlements involving supplemental disclosures of dubious value and overbroad releases, even if unopposed.

As has become commonplace, multiple Trulia stockholders filed lawsuits challenging the proposed merger shortly after it was announced. The actions were consolidated and, after expedited discovery, plaintiffs moved for a preliminary injunction on the grounds that the proxy was false and misleading in certain respects. Before the preliminary injunction motion could be heard by the Court, the parties entered into an agreement-in-principle to settle the [shareholder] litigation for certain supplemental disclosures. The merger was then overwhelmingly approved by the Trulia stockholders. After plaintiffs conducted confirmatory discovery, the parties executed a final settlement agreement containing, in the Court's words, "an extremely broad release" of defendants and a provision that plaintiffs' counsel intended to seek $375,000 in fees, which defendants agreed not to oppose. At the September 16, 2015 hearing to consider the fairness of the proposed settlement, the Court expressed concerns even though no party had objected.

On January 22, 2016, the Court issued its Opinion rejecting the proposed settlement. Before addressing its fairness, the Court discussed "some of the dynamics that have led to the proliferation of disclosure settlements" generally, and noted concerns among academics, practitioners, and other members of the Chancery Court "that these settlements rarely yield genuine benefits for stockholders and threaten the loss of potentially valid claims that have not been investigated with rigor." In particular, the Chancellor pointed to evidence that the supplemental disclosures in such cases rarely change stockholders' vote, and that the broad releases obtained by defendants (often before any meaningful discovery) could preclude viable claims, . . . The Court also discussed the institutional challenges of a law-trained judge evaluating the materiality of disclosures without the benefit of adversarial argument by attorneys assisted by financial advisors.

Based on these considerations, the [Chancery] Court proposed that, in the future, disclosure claims should be adjudicated outside the non-adversarial settlement context, "in at least two ways": First, the materiality of disclosures could be adjudicated in the context of a contested preliminary injunction motion. Second, if defendants chose to moot the disclosure claims by issuing supplemental disclosures before the stockholder vote, their materiality could be addressed in the context of an application by plaintiffs' counsel for a mootness fee award, where defendants would be incentivized to contest materiality in order to avoid paying any fees (unlike in the settlement context, in which the prospect of gaining broad releases incentivizes defendants not to contest materiality). Although in this scenario defendants would not obtain the benefit of any releases, Chancellor Bouchard suggests that any remaining claims in the case may be amenable to dismissal under the familiar standards of *Unocal*, [and its progeny] . . . Alternatively, after "some discovery to probe the merits" of such claims, plaintiffs may stipulate to dismiss their claims without a class-wide release, likely ending the case "as a practical matter."

Otherwise, the Court will be "increasingly vigilant in scrutinizing the 'give' and the 'get'" of disclosure-only settlements. More specifically, the Court says that "practitioners should expect that disclosure settlements are likely to be met with continued disfavor in the future unless [i] the supplemental disclosures address a plainly material misrepresentation or omission, and [ii] the subject matter of the release is narrowly circumscribed to encompass nothing more than disclosure claims and fiduciary duty claims concerning the sale process, if the record shows that such claims have been investigated sufficiently." By "plainly material," the Court said it meant that "it should not be a close call that the supplemental information is material as that term is defined under Delaware law."

Applying this test to the proposed settlement before it, the Chancellor found that none of the supplemental disclosures (all of which related to minutiae regarding the analysis of JPMorgan, Trulia's financial advisor) were material. Accordingly, the Court found these disclosures did not constitute a sufficient "get" to justify the "give" of any releases, . . .

Going forward, one can expect to see fewer cases challenging mergers filed in Delaware, at least involving arms-length mergers between unrelated parties (indeed, recent studies have already shown a marked drop in such suits in the last quarter of 2015). Chancellor Bouchard acknowledged that plaintiffs may simply choose to file such suits elsewhere, but noted that Delaware corporations now have the power to (and many have) enacted a forum selection bylaw to address this concern. . . .

Meredith E. Kotler and Marlie McDonald, Cleary Gottlieb Steen & Hamilton LLP, *Chancery Court Rejects Disclosure-Only Settlement, Suggests in Future Such Settlements Will Be Approved Only in Narrow Circumstances*, Jan. 25, 2016, *available at:* https://www.clearymawatch.com/2016/01/chancery-court-rejects-disclosure-only-settlement-suggests-in-future-such-settlements-will-be-approved-only-in-narrow-circumstances/. The growing use of "forum selection by-laws" is addressed below.

While 2014 is regarded by many commentators as representing the high-water mark, the pace of shareholder lawsuits challenging M&A transactions continued unabated for the first nine months of 2015. As reported in the *Wall Street Journal,* "[o]ver the first nine months of 2015, 78% of [publicly traded] Delaware companies [that were Targets to be acquired in an M&A transaction] faced at least one lawsuit, according to a review of filings by the *Wall Street Journal* involving deals valued at $100 million or more. But since October 1, [2015,] just 34% of mergers have been challenged, after [the Delaware Courts] began aggressively shooting down settlements." Liz Hoffman, *The Judge Who Shoots Down Merger Lawsuits,* WALL STREET JOURNAL, Jan. 10, 2016 at C1, *available at:* https://www.wsj.com/articles/the-judge-who-shoots-down-merger-lawsuits-1452076201. Shortly after this article appeared in the *Wall Street Journal,* Chancellor Bouchard issued his much-anticipated ruling in the *Trulia* case, discussed in the excerpt above. Data for 2016 suggest that the "market" for M&A-related litigation "has been substantially disrupted." Matthew D. Cain and Steven Davidoff Solomon, *Takeover Litigation in 2015,* Jan. 14, 2016, www.ssrn.com/abstract=2715890.

Since 2016, this trend of "substantial disruption" has continued. Without a doubt, *Trulia* has "contributed to a stark change in the M&A litigation landscape. . . . In the years before *Trulia,* shareholders litigated around 90 percent of M&A deals valued over $100 million. In 2016 – the year [that *Trulia* was decided] – that rate declined to just 71 percent. In 2017 and 2018, however, the litigation rate rebounded to 82 percent. At 82 percent, however, [M&A

deal-related] litigation is still below its pre-2015 levels." Cornerstone Research, *Shareholder Litigation Involving Acquisitions of Public Companies: Review of 2018 M&A Litigation,* Sept. 17, 2019, *available at:* https://www.cornerstone.com/Publications/Reports/Shareholder-Litigation-Involving-Acquisitions-of-Public-Companies-Review-of-2018-M-and-A-Litigation-pdf.

    5. Migration of Fiduciary Duty Litigation from Delaware Courts to Other Jurisdictions: Use of Forum Selection Clauses.   Historically, Delaware courts were widely regarded as the principal source of litigation concerning the proper scope of the directors' fiduciary duty obligations in connection with a proposed M&A transaction. However, in recent years, the Delaware courts have seen a migration of such cases to courts of other jurisdictions. This migration of cases has led some to worry about the continued robustness of Delaware case law. Under the internal affairs doctrine, these other courts will often be required to interpret and apply Delaware law to the facts of the pending dispute. Will this migration result in a dilution of the efficacy and coherence of Delaware jurisprudence?

> Delaware's expert courts are seen as an integral part of the state's success in attracting incorporation by public companies. However, the benefit that Delaware companies derive from this expertise depends on whether corporate lawsuits against Delaware companies are brought before the Delaware courts. We report evidence that these suits are increasingly brought outside Delaware. . . . We find . . . [an] increase in litigation rates for all companies in large M&A transactions and for Delaware companies in LBO transactions. We also see trends toward (1) suits being filed outside Delaware in both large M&A and LBO transactions and in cases generating opinions; and (2) suits being filed both in Delaware and elsewhere in large M&A transactions. Overall, Delaware courts are losing market share in lawsuits, and Delaware companies are gaining lawsuits, often filed elsewhere. . . . Our evidence suggests that serious as well as nuisance cases are leaving Delaware. The trends we report potentially present a challenge to Delaware's competitiveness in the market for incorporations.

John Armour, et al., *Is Delaware Losing Its Cases?,* 9 J. EMPIRICAL LEGAL STUDIES 605 (2012). In other papers, these same authors have offered an explanation for this recent migration of cases out of Delaware. *See* John Armour, et al., *Delaware's Balancing Act,* 87 IND. L. J. 1345 (2010); and Brian Cheffins, et al., *Delaware Corporate Litigation and the Fragmentation of the Plaintiff's Bar,* 2012 COLUM. BUS. L. REV. 427 (2012). Needless to say, this migration of M&A related litigation to courts in other states was not lost on the Delaware legislature.

    To address the growing concern regarding the burgeoning practice of plaintiffs' bar bringing shareholder derivative actions challenging M&A deals in multiple jurisdictions, the Delaware legislature amended its corporation statute to add a new section, Section 115, which took effect on August 1, 2015. Section 115 authorizes Delaware corporations to include a provision known as a "forum selection clause" in either the company's certificate of incorporation or its bylaws. This clause allows the Delaware corporation to designate Delaware courts (including the U.S. District Court for the District of Delaware) as the exclusive forum in which "internal corporate claims" may be brought. Section 115 defines "internal corporate claims" as those claims based on violations of current or former officers' or directors' [fiduciary] duties and violations that fall under the jurisdiction of the Delaware Court of Chancery. Internal corporate claims do *not* include federal securities class actions or claims brought by individuals who are not stockholders. . . . Section 115 codifies the Delaware Court of Chancery's holding in *Boilermakers Local 154 Retirement Fund v. Chevron Corp.*, 73 A.3d 934 (Del. Ch. 2013), that the bylaws of a Delaware corporation may provide that certain claims, including claims for breach of fiduciary duty, must be brought in a court in Delaware. Section 115 further provides that "*no* provision of the certificate of incorporation [of a Delaware corporation] or the bylaws may prohibit bringing such claims in the courts of [Delaware]," such as provisions in the certificate of incorporation or bylaws of a Delaware corporation selecting a non-Delaware forum as the sole and exclusive forum in which internal corporate claims may be brought. The [legislative] Amendment [adopting new Section 115] neither authorizes nor prohibits provisions in a Delaware corporation's certificate of incorporation or bylaws that specify a forum other than Delaware as an additional, nonexclusive forum.

Matthew Greenberg, James H.S. Cevine, Christopher Chiff, and Ashleigh K. Reiback, Pepper Hamilton LLP, *Delaware Legislature Prohibits Fee Shifting and Authorizes Exclusive Forum Selection,* July 29, 2015, *available at:* http://www.lexology.com/library/detail.aspx?g=b1959cdc-4513-47db-8647-310abedadc22 (*emphasis added*).

Following the *Boilermakers* decision in 2013, "hundreds of public companies (including many S&P 500 companies) [amended] their bylaws [in order] to adopt [exclusive forum selection] provisions. Companies that have done so have generally faced little, if any, negative feedback from [their] shareholders . . . and courts in other states have broadly agreed to enforce these [forum selection] provisions when invoked. [Legislative enactment of Section 115] is supportive of that trend." Sullivan and Cromwell LLP, *Delaware Legislature Says No to "Loser-Pays" Fee- Shifting Bylaws But Yes to Forum Selection Bylaws for Stock Corporations,* June 12, 2015, *available at:* http://www.lexology.com/library/detail.aspx?g=a56a7c4d-9559-4b1f-9dfc-b1b2a032b3ab); *see also Roberts v. TriQuint Semiconductor, Inc.,* 364 P.3d 328 (Ore. S. Ct., Dec. 10, 2015).

By mandating that internal disputes are to be adjudicated in Delaware courts, Section 115 promotes "forum certainty [which] is advantageous because it fosters predictability for businesses. . . ." Carol W. Sherman, Kelley Drye & Warren LLP, *Delaware House of Representatives Bars Fee-Shifting Provisions But Approves Forum-Selection,* June 22, 2015, *available at:* http://www.lexology.com/library/detail.aspx?g=473da56b-b17d-416f-9a55-f1127a0f4fcd&). Just as important, legislative adoption of Section 115 is intended to address the "migration of cases" to non-Delaware courts, presumably in order "to ensure that [internal corporate claims] will be adjudicated with the benefit of the experience and expediency of the Delaware courts and judges. . . ." Greenberg, et al., *supra.*

Notably, the forum selection clause authorized by Delaware Section 115 does not mention "federal securities class action" lawsuits, leading to considerable controversy as to whether Delaware corporations could amend their certificates of incorporation to designate federal courts as the exclusive forum for litigation of claims arising under the Securities Act of 1933 ("1933 Act"). This controversy was laid to rest by the Delaware Supreme Court's decision in *Sciabacucchi v. Salzberg,* 227 A.3d 102 (Del. 2020), in which the Supreme Court "reversed a Chancery Court decision[*] invalidating federal forum selection provisions contained in the certificates of incorporation of three Delaware corporations – Blue Apron Holdings, Inc., Roku, Inc., and Stitch Fix, Inc. The federal forum provisions required claims by their stockholders under the [1933 Act] to be filed in federal court." Dustin B. Hillsley, et. al., Akerman LLP, *Delaware Supreme Court Validates Cost Saving Federal Forum Selection Provisions in Corporate Charters,* March 25, 2020, *available at*: https://www.akerman.com/en/perspectives/delaware-supreme-court-validates-cost-saving-federal-forum-selection-provisions-in-corporate-charters.html. The Delaware Supreme Court's decision "is significant in light of the U.S. Supreme Court's decision in *Cyan, Inc. v. Beaver County Employees Retirement Fund,* [138 S. Ct. 1061 (2018),] which held that federal and state courts have concurrent jurisdiction over class actions based on 1933 Act claims and that such claims brought in state court were not removable to federal court. In the wake of *Cyan,* many companies have been facing an onslaught of 1933 Act claims in state courts, . . . and have been forced to litigate duplicative claims in both state and federal courts." Skadden, Arps, Slate, Meagher & Flom LLP, *Delaware Supreme Court Upholds Validity of Provisions Designating Federal Courts as Exclusive Forum of 1933 Act Claims,* March 18, 2020, *available at*: https://www.skadden.com/insights/publications/2020/03/delaware-supreme-court-upholds-validity.

In its opinion, the Delaware Supreme Court "rejected the Court of Chancery's reasoning that because 1933 Act claims arise under federal law, they are 'external' matters that may not be regulated by Delaware corporations' charters, noting that while 1933 Act claims are not 'internal affairs,' they are a form of 'intra-corporate litigation,' which Delaware corporations may regulate as to procedure." Roger A. Cooper, et. al., Cleary Gottlieb Steen & Hamilton LLP, *Delaware Supreme Court Green Lights Federal-Forum Charter Provisions,* March 20, 2020, *available at*: https://www.clearymawatch.com/2020/03/delaware-supreme-court-green-lights-federal-forum-charter-provisions/. In the wake of the Delaware Supreme Court's ruling, many experienced M&A lawyers are recommending that Delaware corporations consider amending their certificates of incorporation (pursuant to Delaware Section 102(b)) to include a federal forum provision. These lawyers believe that this type of charter provision "should reduce the burdens and inefficiencies of 1933 Act litigation created by the U.S. Supreme Court's [2018 decision in *Cyan,* which led to a significant increase in securities class action lawsuits] proceeding simultaneously in multiple federal and state courts. A number of questions remain unresolved, however, including whether other state and federal courts will similarly uphold federal-forum provisions, and under what circumstances; [and] whether such courts will reach the same conclusion with respect to federal-forum provisions adopted in a corporation's *bylaws* . . ." *Id.* (emphasis in original).

---

[*] *Sciabacucchi v. Salzberg,* 2018 WL 6719718 (Del. Ch. Dec. 19, 2018).

D. *The "Poison Pill": Addressing the Risk of Selling Target Co. "Too Cheaply"*

In order to set the stage for the competing considerations that are central to the reasoning of the Delaware Supreme Court in connection with its case law addressing the validity of the "poison pill," consider the public policy implications presented by the facts of the following hypothetical involving a proposed change of control transaction:

> . . . Assume an acquiring company buys 25% of the target's stock in a small number of privately negotiated transactions. It then commences a public tender offer for 26% of the company stock at a cash price that the board, in good faith, believes is inadequate. Moreover, the acquiring corporation announces that it may or may not do a second-step merger, but if it does one, the consideration will be junk bonds that will have a value, when issued, in the opinion of its own investment banker, of no more than the cash being offered in the tender offer. In the face of such an offer, the board may have a duty to seek to protect the company's shareholders from the coercive effects of this inadequate offer. Assume, for purposes of the hypothetical, that neither newly amended Section 203, nor any defensive device available to the target specifically, offers protection. Assume that the target's board turns to the market for corporate control to attempt to locate a more fairly priced alternative that would be available to all shareholders. And assume that just as the tender offer is closing, the board locates an all cash deal for all shares at a price materially higher than that offered by the acquiring corporation. Would the board of the target corporation be justified in issuing sufficient shares to the second acquiring corporation to dilute the 51% stockholder down so that it no longer had a practical veto over the merger or sale of assets that the target board had arranged for the benefit of all shares? It is not necessary to now hazard an opinion on that abstraction. . . .

Blasius Industries, Inc. v. Atlas Corp., 564 A.2d 651, 658 fn. 5 (Del. Ch. 1988). Although Chancellor Allen declined to present his views on the hypothetical that he posed in this footnote to his opinion in *Blasius,* the facts of this proposed change of control transaction crystallize the vexing public policy issues that the courts must grapple with in deciding the proper role for Target's board of directors when faced with an unsolicited tender offer from Bidder.

Since the *Unocal* decision, these public policy considerations have surfaced most prominently in connection with the development (and continued evolution) of the poison pill defense, which is the focus of the cases in this section. We begin our consideration of "poison pills" by examining the landmark case of *Moran v. Household International, Inc.*, decided the same year as *Unocal,* a watershed year in the development of modern fiduciary duty law in Delaware.

In order to put these cases into some context, a bit of general background is in order. You will recall that our analysis of the problem sets in Chapter 2 reflected that the stock purchase agreement is a contract entered into between the buyer, Bidder Co., and the selling shareholders of Target Co. in the case of a closely held Target. In the case of a publicly traded Target Co., however, the process for Bidder to make a contract offer to purchase Target's outstanding shares directly from the company's stockholders is regulated by the provisions of the federal securities laws known as the Williams Act, which we studied in Chapter 6. The materials and problems in these two chapters underscore that this deal structure is the *only* method available to Bidder to acquire Target *without* obtaining approval from Target's board of directors. The hypothetical fact pattern that Chancellor Allen posed above highlights the fundamental question presented by the development of the "poison pill" defense: *What is the proper role for Target's board?* With the development of the poison pill, this takeover defense results in giving Target's board a "seat at the negotiating table," a point that is made in the next case in which the Delaware Supreme Court upholds the validity of the "shareholder rights plan," aka the "poison pill."

1.   Delaware Supreme Court Establishes the Validity of the Poison Pill

Moran v. Household International, Inc.
500 A.2d 1346 (Del. 1985)

McNEILLY, Justice:

This case presents to this Court for review the most recent defensive mechanism in the arsenal of corporate takeover weaponry—the Preferred Share Purchase Rights Plan ("Rights Plan" or "Plan"). The validity of this mechanism has attracted national attention. *Amici curiae* briefs have been filed in support of appellants by the Security [sic] and Exchange Commission ("SEC")[1] and the Investment Company Institute. An *amicus curiae* brief has been filed in support of appellees ("Household") by the United Food and Commercial Workers International Union.

In a detailed opinion, the Court of Chancery upheld the Rights Plan as a legitimate exercise of business judgment by Household. *Moran v. Household International, Inc.*, Del. Ch., 490 A.2d 1059 (1985). We agree, and therefore, affirm the judgment below.

I

The facts giving rise to this case have been carefully delineated in the Court of Chancery's opinion. *Id.* at 1064-69. A review of the basic facts is necessary for a complete understanding of the issues.

On August 14, 1984, the Board of Directors of Household International, Inc. adopted the Rights Plan by a fourteen to two vote.[2] The intricacies of the

---

1. The SEC split 3-2 on whether to intervene in this case. The two dissenting Commissioners have publicly disagreed with the other three as to the merits of the Rights Plan. 17 Securities Regulation & Law Report 400; The Wall Street Journal, March 20, 1985, at 6.

2. Household's Board has ten outside directors and six who are members of management. Messrs. Moran (appellant) and Whitehead voted against the Plan. The record reflects that Whitehead voted against the Plan not on its substance but because he thought it was novel and would bring unwanted publicity to Household.

Rights Plan are contained in a 48-page document entitled "Rights Agreement." Basically, the Plan provides that Household common stockholders are entitled to the issuance of one Right per common share under certain triggering conditions. There are two triggering events that can activate the Rights. The first is the announcement of a tender offer for 30 percent of Household's shares ("30% trigger") and the second is the acquisition of 20 percent of Household's shares by any single entity or group ("20% trigger").

If an announcement of a tender offer for 30 percent of Household's shares is made, the Rights are issued and are immediately exercisable to purchase 1/100 share of new preferred stock for $100 and are redeemable by the Board for $.50 per Right. If 20 percent of Household's shares are acquired by anyone, the Rights are issued and become non-redeemable and are exercisable to purchase 1/100 of a share of preferred. If a Right is not exercised for preferred, and thereafter, a merger or consolidation occurs, the Rights holder can exercise each Right to purchase $200 of the common stock of the tender offeror for $100. This "flip-over" provision of the Rights Plan is at the heart of this controversy.

Household is a diversified holding company with its principal subsidiaries engaged in financial services, transportation and merchandising. HFC, National Car Rental and Vons Grocery are three of its wholly-owned entities.

Household did not adopt its Rights Plan during a battle with a corporate raider, but as a preventive mechanism to ward off future advances. The Vice Chancellor found that as early as February 1984, Household's management became concerned about the company's vulnerability as a takeover target and began considering amending its charter to render a takeover more difficult. After considering the matter, Household decided not to pursue a fair price amendment.[3]

In the meantime, appellant Moran, one of Household's own Directors and also Chairman of the Dyson-Kissner-Moran Corporation, ("D-K-M") which is the largest single stockholder of Household, began discussions concerning a possible leveraged buy-out of Household by D-K-M. D-K-M's financial studies showed that Household's stock was significantly undervalued in relation to the company's break-up value. It is uncontradicted that Moran's suggestion of a leveraged buy-out never progressed beyond the discussion stage.

Concerned about Household's vulnerability to a raider in light of the current takeover climate, Household secured the services of Wachtell, Lipton, Rosen and Katz ("Wachtell, Lipton") and Goldman, Sachs & Co. ("Goldman, Sachs") to formulate a takeover policy for recommendation to the Household Board at its August 14 meeting. After a July 31 meeting with a Household Board member and a pre-meeting distribution of material on the potential takeover problem and the proposed Rights Plan, the Board met on August 14, 1984.

Representatives of Wachtell, Lipton and Goldman, Sachs attended the August 14 meeting. The minutes reflect that Mr. Lipton explained to the Board that his recommendation of the Plan was based on his understanding that the

---

3. A fair price amendment to a corporate charter generally requires supermajority approval for certain business combinations and sets minimum price criteria for mergers. *Moran*, 490 A.2d at 1064, n. 1.

Board was concerned about the increasing frequency of "bust-up"[4] takeovers, the increasing takeover activity in the financial service industry, such as Leucadia's attempt to take over Arco, and the possible adverse effect this type of activity could have on employees and others concerned with and vital to the continuing successful operation of Household even in the absence of any actual bust-up takeover attempt. Against this factual background, the Plan was approved.

Thereafter, Moran and the company of which he is Chairman, D-K-M, filed this suit. On the eve of trial, Gretl Golter, the holder of 500 shares of Household, was permitted to intervene as an additional plaintiff. The trial was held, and the Court of Chancery ruled in favor of Household. Appellants now appeal from that ruling to this Court.

II

The primary issue here is the applicability of the business judgment rule as the standard by which the adoption of the Rights Plan should be reviewed. Much of this issue has been decided by our recent decision in *Unocal Corp. v. Mesa Petroleum*, Del. Supr., 493 A.2d 946 (1985). In *Unocal*, we applied the business judgment rule to analyze Unocal's discriminatory self-tender. We explained:

> When a board addresses a pending takeover bid it has an obligation to determine whether the offer is in the best interests of the corporation and its shareholders. In that respect a board's duty is no different from any other responsibility it shoulders, and its decisions should be no less entitled to the respect they otherwise would be accorded in the realm of business judgment.

Id. at 954 (citation and footnote omitted).

Other jurisdictions have also applied the business judgment rule to actions by which target companies have sought to forestall takeover activity they considered undesirable. *See Gearhart Industries, Inc. v. Smith International*, 5th Cir., 741 F.2d 707 (1984) (sale of discounted subordinate debentures containing springing warrants); *Treco, Inc. v. Land of Lincoln Savings and Loan*, 7th Cir., 749 F.2d 374 (1984) (amendment to by-laws); *Panter v. Marshall Field*, 7th Cir., 646 F.2d 271 (1981) (acquisitions to create antitrust problems); *Johnson v. Trueblood*, 3d Cir., 629 F.2d 287 (1980), *cert. denied*, 450 U.S. 999, 101 S. Ct. 1704, 68 L. Ed. 2d 200 (1981) (refusal to tender); *CrouseHinds Co. v. InterNorth, Inc.*, 2d Cir., 634 F.2d 690 (1980) (sale of stock to favored party); *Treadway v. Cane Corp.*, 2d Cir., 638 F.2d 357 (1980) (sale to White Knight); *Enterra Corp. v. SGS Associates*, E.D. Pa., 600 F. Supp. 678 (1985) (standstill agreement); *Buffalo Forge Co. v. Ogden Corp.*, W.D.N.Y., 555 F. Supp. 892, *aff'd*, (2d Cir.) 717 F.2d 757, *cert. denied*, 464 U.S. 1018, 104 S. Ct. 550, 78 L. Ed. 2d 724 (1983) (sale of treasury shares and grant of stock option to White Knight); *Whittaker Corp. v. Edgar*, N.D. Ill., 535 F. Supp. 933 (1982)

---

4. "Bust-up" takeover generally refers to a situation in which one seeks to finance an acquisition by selling off pieces of the acquired company.

(disposal of valuable assets); *Martin Marietta Corp. v. Bendix Corp.*, D. Md., 549 F. Supp. 623 (1982) (Pac-Man defense).

This case is distinguishable from the ones cited, since here we have a defensive mechanism adopted to ward off possible future advances and not a mechanism adopted in reaction to a specific threat. This distinguishing factor does not result in the Directors losing the protection of the business judgment rule. To the contrary, pre-planning for the contingency of a hostile takeover might reduce the risk that, under the pressure of a takeover bid, management will fail to exercise reasonable judgment. Therefore, in reviewing a pre-planned defensive mechanism it seems even more appropriate to apply the business judgment rule. *See Warner Communications v. Murdoch*, D. Del., 581 F. Supp. 1482, 1491 (1984).

Of course, the business judgment rule can only sustain corporate decision making or transactions that are within the power or authority of the Board. Therefore, before the business judgment rule can be applied it must be determined whether the Directors were authorized to adopt the Rights Plan.

III

Appellants vehemently contend that the Board of Directors was unauthorized to adopt the Rights Plan. First, appellants contend that no provision of the Delaware General Corporation Law authorizes the issuance of such Rights. Secondly, appellants, along with the SEC, contend that the Board is unauthorized to usurp stockholders' rights to receive hostile tender offers. Third, appellants and the SEC also contend that the Board is unauthorized to fundamentally restrict stockholders' rights to conduct a proxy contest. We address each of these contentions in turn.

A

While appellants contend that no provision of the Delaware General Corporation Law authorizes the Rights Plan, Household contends that the Rights Plan was issued pursuant to 8 Del. C. §§151 (g) and §157. It explains that the Rights are authorized by §157[7] and the issue of preferred stock underlying

---

7. The power to issue rights to purchase shares is conferred by 8 Del. C. §157 which provides in relevant part:

> Subject to any provisions in the certificate of incorporation, every corporation may create and issue, whether or not in connection with the issue and sale of any shares of stock or other securities of the corporation, rights or options entitling the holders thereof to purchase from the corporation any shares of its capital stock of any class or classes, such rights or options to be evidenced by or in such instrument or instruments as shall be approved by the board of directors.

the Rights is authorized by §151.[8] Appellants respond by making several attacks upon the authority to issue the Rights pursuant to §157.

Appellants begin by contending that §157 cannot authorize the Rights Plan since §157 has never served the purpose of authorizing a takeover defense. Appellants contend that §157 is a corporate financing statute, and that nothing in its legislative history suggests a purpose that has anything to do with corporate control or a takeover defense. Appellants are unable to demonstrate that the legislature, in its adoption of §157, meant to limit the applicability of §157 to only the issuance of Rights for the purposes of corporate financing. Without such affirmative evidence, we decline to impose such a limitation upon the section that the legislature has not. As we noted in *Unocal:*

> [O]ur corporate law is not static. It must grow and develop in response to, indeed in anticipation of, evolving concepts and needs. Merely because the General Corporation Law is silent as to a specific matter does not mean that it is prohibited.

493 A.2d at 957. *See also Cheff v. Mathes,* Del. Supr., 199 A.2d 548 (1964).

Secondly, appellants contend that §157 does not authorize the issuance of sham rights such as the Rights Plan. They contend that the Rights were designed never to be exercised, and that the Plan has no economic value. In addition, they contend the preferred stock made subject to the Rights is also illusory, citing *Telvest, Inc. v. Olson,* Del. Ch., C.A. No. 5798, Brown, V.C. (March 8, 1979).

Appellants' sham contention fails in both regards. As to the Rights, they can and will be exercised upon the happening of a triggering mechanism, as we have observed during the current struggle of Sir James Goldsmith to take control of Crown Zellerbach. *See* Wall Street Journal, July 26, 1985, at 3, 12. As to the preferred shares, we agree with the Court of Chancery that they are distinguishable from sham securities invalidated in *Telvest, supra.* The Household preferred, issuable upon the happening of a triggering event, have superior dividend and liquidation rights.

Third, appellants contend that §157 authorizes the issuance of Rights "entitling holders thereof to purchase from the corporation any shares of *its* capital stock of any class . . ." (*emphasis added*). Therefore, their contention continues,

---

8. Del. C. §151(g) provides in relevant part:

When any corporation desires to issue any shares of stock of any class or of any series of any class of which the voting powers, designations, preferences and relative, participating, optional or other rights, if any, or the qualifications, limitations or restrictions thereof, if any, shall not have been set forth in the certificate of incorporation or in any amendment thereto but shall be provided for in a resolution or resolutions adopted by the board of directors pursuant to authority expressly vested in it by the provisions of the certificate of incorporation or any amendment thereto, a certificate setting forth a copy of such resolution or resolutions and the number of shares of stock of such class or series shall be executed, acknowledged, filed, recorded, and shall become effective, in accordance with §103 of this title.

the plain language of the statute does not authorize Household to issue rights to purchase another's capital stock upon a merger or consolidation.

Household contends, *inter alia*, that the Rights Plan is analogous to "antide-struction" or "anti-dilution" provisions which are customary features of a wide vari-ety of corporate securities. While appellants seem to concede that "anti-destruction" provisions are valid under Delaware corporate law, they seek to distinguish the Rights Plan as not being incidental, as are most "anti-destruction" provisions, to a corporation's statutory power to finance itself. We find no merit to such a distinc-tion. We have already rejected appellants' similar contention that §157 could only be used for financing purposes. We also reject that distinction here.

"Anti-destruction" clauses generally ensure holders of certain securities of the protection of their right of conversion in the event of a merger by giving them the right to convert their securities into whatever securities are to replace the stock of their company. *See Broad v. Rockwell International Corp.*, 5th Cir., 642 F.2d 929, 946, *cert. denied*, 454 U.S. 965, 102 S. Ct. 506, 70 L. Ed. 2d 380 (1981); *Wood v. Coastal States Gas Corp.*, Del. Supr., 401 A.2d 932, 937-39 (1979); *B.S.F. Co. v. Philadelphia National Bank*, Del. Supr., 204 A.2d 746, 750-51 (1964). The fact that the rights here have as their purpose the prevention of coercive two-tier tender offers does not invalidate them. . . .

Having concluded that sufficient authority for the Rights Plan exists in 8 Del. C. §157, we note the inherent powers of the Board conferred by 8 Del. C. §141 (a), concerning the management of the corporation's "business and *affairs*" (*emphasis added*), also provides the Board additional authority upon which to enact the Rights Plan. *Unocal*, 493 A.2d at 953.

B

Appellants contend that the Board is unauthorized to usurp stockholders' rights to receive tender offers by changing Household's fundamental structure. We conclude that the Rights Plan does not prevent stockholders from receiving tender offers, and that the change of Household's structure was less than that which results from the implementation of other defensive mechanisms upheld by various courts.

Appellants' contention that stockholders will lose their right to receive and accept tender offers seems to be premised upon an understanding of the Rights Plan which is illustrated by the SEC *amicus* brief which states: "The Chancery Court's decision seriously understates the impact of this plan. In fact, as we discuss below, the Rights Plan will deter not only two-tier offers, but virtually all hostile tender offers."

The fallacy of that contention is apparent when we look at the recent takeover of Crown Zellerbach, which has a similar Rights Plan, by Sir James Goldsmith. Wall Street Journal, July 26, 1985, at 3, 12. The evidence at trial also evidenced many methods around the Plan ranging from tendering with a condition that the Board redeem the Rights, tendering with a high minimum condition of shares and Rights, tendering and soliciting consents to remove the Board and redeem the Rights, to acquiring 50% of the shares and causing Household to self-tender for the Rights. One could also form a group of up to 19.9% and solicit proxies for consents to remove the Board and redeem the

Rights. These are but a few of the methods by which Household can still be acquired by a hostile tender offer.

In addition, the Rights Plan is not absolute. When the Household Board of Directors is faced with a tender offer and a request to redeem the Rights, they will not be able to arbitrarily reject the offer. They will be held to the same fiduciary standards any other board of directors would be held to in deciding to adopt a defensive mechanism, the same standard as they were held to in originally approving the Rights Plan. *See Unocal,* 493 A.2d at 954-55, 958.

In addition, appellants contend that the deterrence of tender offers will be accomplished by what they label "a fundamental transfer of power from the stockholders to the directors." They contend that this transfer of power, in itself, is unauthorized.

The Rights Plan will result in no more of a structural change than any other defensive mechanism adopted by a board of directors. The Rights Plan does not destroy the assets of the corporation. The implementation of the Plan neither results in any outflow of money from the corporation nor impairs its financial flexibility. It does not dilute earnings per share and does not have any adverse tax consequences for the corporation or its stockholders. The Plan has not adversely affected the market price of Household's stock.

Comparing the Rights Plan with other defensive mechanisms, it does less harm to the value structure of the corporation than do the other mechanisms. Other mechanisms result in increased debt of the corporation. *See Whittaker Corp. v. Edgar, supra* (sale of "prize asset"), *Cheff v. Mathes, supra,* (paying greenmail to eliminate a threat), *Unocal Corp. v. Mesa Petroleum Co., supra,* (discriminatory self-tender).

There is little change in the governance structure as a result of the adoption of the Rights Plan. The Board does not now have unfettered discretion in refusing to redeem the Rights. The Board has no more discretion in refusing to redeem the Rights than it does in enacting any defensive mechanism.

The contention that the Rights Plan alters the structure more than do other defensive mechanisms because it is so effective as to make the corporation completely safe from hostile tender offers is likewise without merit. As explained above, there are numerous methods to successfully launch a hostile tender offer.

C

Appellants' third contention is that the Board was unauthorized to fundamentally restrict stockholders' rights to conduct a proxy contest. Appellants contend that the "20% trigger" effectively prevents any stockholder from first acquiring 20% or more shares before conducting a proxy contest and further, it prevents stockholders from banding together into a group to solicit proxies if, collectively, they own 20% or more of the stock.[12] In addition, at trial, appellants

---

12. Appellants explain that the acquisition of 20% of the shares trigger the Rights, making them non-redeemable, and thereby would prevent even a future friendly offer for the ten-year life of the Rights.

contended that read literally, the Rights Agreement triggers the Rights upon the mere acquisition of the right to vote 20% or more of the shares through a proxy solicitation, and thereby precludes any proxy contest from being waged.[13]

Appellants seem to have conceded this last contention in light of Household's response that the receipt of a proxy does not make the recipient the "beneficial owner" of the shares involved which would trigger the Rights. In essence, the Rights Agreement provides that the Rights are triggered when someone becomes the "beneficial owner" of 20% or more of Household stock. Although a literal reading of the Rights Agreement definition of "beneficial owner" would seem to include those shares which one has the right to vote, it has long been recognized that the relationship between grantor and recipient of a proxy is one of agency, and the agency is revocable by the grantor at any time. Henn, *Corporations* §196, at 518. Therefore, the holder of a proxy is not the "beneficial owner" of the stock. As a result, the mere acquisition of the right to vote 20% of the shares does not trigger the Rights.

The issue, then, is whether the restriction upon individuals or groups from first acquiring 20% of shares before waging a proxy contest fundamentally restricts stockholders' right to conduct a proxy contest. Regarding this issue the Court of Chancery found:

> Thus, while the Rights Plan does deter the formation of proxy efforts of a certain magnitude, it does not limit the voting power of individual shares. On the evidence presented it is highly conjectural to assume that a particular effort to assert shareholder views in the election of directors or revisions of corporate policy will be frustrated by the proxy feature of the Plan. Household's witnesses, Troubh and Higgins described recent corporate takeover battles in which insurgents holding less than 10% stock ownership were able to secure corporate control through a proxy contest or the threat of one.

Moran, 490 A.2d at 1080.

We conclude that there was sufficient evidence at trial to support the Vice Chancellor's finding that the effect upon proxy contests will be minimal. Evidence at trial established that many proxy contests are won with an insurgent ownership of less than 20%, and that very large holdings are no guarantee of success. There was also testimony that the key variable in proxy contest success is the merit of an insurgent's issues, not the size of his holdings.

IV

Having concluded that the adoption of the Rights Plan was within the authority of the Directors, we now look to whether the Directors have met their burden under the business judgment rule.

---

13. The SEC still contends that the mere acquisition of the right to vote 20% of the shares through a proxy solicitation triggers the rights. We do not interpret the Rights Agreement in that manner.

The business judgment rule is a "presumption that in making a business decision the directors of a corporation acted on an informed basis, in good faith and in the honest belief that the action taken was in the best interests of the company." *Aronson v. Lewis*, Del. Supr., 473 A.2d 805, 812 (1984) (citations omitted). Notwithstanding, in *Unocal* we held that when the business judgment rule applies to adoption of a defensive mechanism, the initial burden will lie with the directors. The "directors must show that they had reasonable grounds for believing that a danger to corporate policy and effectiveness existed. . . . [T]hey satisfy that burden 'by showing good faith and reasonable investigation. . . .'" *Unocal*, 493 A.2d at 955 (citing *Cheff v. Mathes*, 199 A.2d at 554-55). In addition, the directors must show that the defensive mechanism was "reasonable in relation to the threat posed." *Unocal*, 493 A.2d at 955. Moreover, that proof is materially enhanced, as we noted in *Unocal*, where, as here, a majority of the board favoring the proposal consisted of outside independent directors who have acted in accordance with the foregoing standards. *Unocal*, 493 A.2d at 955; *Aronson*, 473 A.2d at 815. Then, the burden shifts back to the plaintiffs who have the ultimate burden of persuasion to show a breach of the directors' fiduciary duties. *Unocal*, 493 A.2d at 958.

There are no allegations here of any bad faith on the part of the Directors' action in the adoption of the Rights Plan. There is no allegation that the Directors' action was taken for entrenchment purposes. Household has adequately demonstrated, as explained above, that the adoption of the Rights Plan was in reaction to what it perceived to be the threat in the market place of coercive two-tier tender offers. Appellants do contend, however, that the Board did not exercise informed business judgment in its adoption of the Plan.

Appellants contend that the Household Board was uninformed since they were, *inter alia*, told the Plan would not inhibit a proxy contest, were not told the plan would preclude all hostile acquisitions of Household, and were told that Delaware counsel opined that the plan was within the business judgment of the Board.

As to the first two contentions, as we explained above, the Rights Plan will not have a severe impact upon proxy contests and it will not preclude all hostile acquisitions of Household. Therefore, the Directors were not misinformed or uninformed on these facts.

Appellants contend the Delaware counsel did not express an opinion on the flip-over provision of the Rights, rather only that the Rights would constitute validly issued and outstanding rights to subscribe to the preferred stock of the company.

To determine whether a business judgment reached by a board of directors was an informed one, we determine whether the directors were grossly negligent. *Smith v. Van Gorkom*, Del. Supr., 488 A.2d 858, 873 (1985). Upon a review of this record, we conclude the Directors were not grossly negligent. The information supplied to the Board on August 14 provided the essentials of the Plan. The Directors were given beforehand a notebook which included a three-page summary of the Plan along with articles on the current takeover environment. The extended discussion between the Board and representatives of Wachtell, Lipton and Goldman, Sachs before approval of the Plan reflected a full and candid evaluation of the Plan. Moran's expression of his views at the meeting served to place before the Board a knowledgeable critique of the Plan. The factual happenings here are clearly distinguishable from the actions of the directors of Trans Union Corporation who displayed gross negligence in approving a cash-out merger. *Id.*

In addition, to meet their burden, the Directors must show that the defensive mechanism was "reasonable in relation to the threat posed". The record reflects a concern on the part of the Directors over the increasing frequency in the financial services industry of "boot-strap" and "bust-up" takeovers. The Directors were also concerned that such takeovers may take the form of two-tier offers.[14] In addition, on August 14, the Household Board was aware of Moran's overture on behalf of D-K-M. In sum, the Directors reasonably believed Household was vulnerable to coercive acquisition techniques and adopted a reasonable defensive mechanism to protect itself.

V

In conclusion, the Household Directors receive the benefit of the business judgment rule in their adoption of the Rights Plan.

The Directors adopted the Plan pursuant to statutory authority in 8 Del. C. §§141, 151, 157. We reject appellants' contentions that the Rights Plan strips stockholders of their rights to receive tender offers, and that the Rights Plan fundamentally restricts proxy contests.

The Directors adopted the Plan in the good faith belief that it was necessary to protect Household from coercive acquisition techniques. The Board was informed as to the details of the Plan. In addition, Household has demonstrated that the Plan is reasonable in relation to the threat posed. Appellants, on the other hand, have failed to convince us that the Directors breached any fiduciary duty in their adoption of the Rights Plan.

While we conclude for present purposes that the Household Directors are protected by the business judgment rule, that does not end the matter. The ultimate response to an actual takeover bid must be judged by the Directors' actions at that time, and nothing we say here relieves them of their basic fundamental duties to the corporation and its stockholders. *Unocal,* 493 A.2d at 954-55, 958; *Smith v. Van Gorkom,* 488 A.2d at 872-73; *Aronson,* 473 A.2d at 812-13; *Pogostin v. Rice,* Del. Supr., 480 A.2d 619, 627 (1984). Their use of the Plan will be evaluated when and if the issue arises.

AFFIRMED.

QUESTIONS

1. What is the source of the board's authority to adopt the poison pill?

2. What is the "flip-over" feature of the pill at issue in *Moran?*

---

14. We have discussed the coercive nature of two-tier tender offers in *Unocal,* 493 A.2d at 956, n. 12. We explained in *Unocal* that a discriminatory self-tender was reasonably related to the threat of two-tier tender offers and possible greenmail.

3. What is the basis for the plaintiff's claim that the board's decision to adopt a poison pill usurps the shareholders of their right to receive tender offers? Do you agree with the court's reasoning on this issue?

4. Why does the plaintiff claim that the mere adoption of the poison pill involves a fundamental transfer of power from the company's shareholders to its board of directors?

5. What are the objectives that the board of directors hopes to accomplish by adopting the poison pill? How does the poison pill serve to implement those objectives?

6. Why did the board of directors in *Moran* include a redemption provision as part of the terms of the poison pill that it adopted?

7. What is the standard of review used by the *Moran* court to determine the validity of the board's decision to adopt the poison pill?

NOTES

1. The Validation of the Poison Pill Is a Game-Changing Event.   The validation of the poison pill by the Delaware Supreme Court revolutionized the takeover defense practices of incumbent corporate managers. The development of the shareholder rights plan (aka "the pill") solved many of the problems that were associated with several of the takeover defenses that were widely employed at the time (which was before the *Moran* case was decided). Notably, and as was seen in the *Moran* case, the poison pill could be implemented unilaterally by manage-ment and without obtaining shareholder approval; moreover, adoption of the pill generally had no effect on the company's capital structure, its accounting, or its fundamental value, and yet it provided Target management with a potent tool to ward off the unsolicited Bidder. As such, company managers no lon-ger felt as though they were sitting ducks; instead, the implementation of the poison pill gave the board of directors a seat at the bargaining table by leaving the board in control of the acquisition process. Consequently, the determined Bidder was left to negotiate with Target management, or alternatively, replace the recalcitrant directors, usually by mounting a proxy fight.

2. Introduction to the Terms of a "Shareholder Rights Plan"—Or, What Is a "Poison Pill"?   The primary architect of the poison pill defense is Martin Lipton of the well-known New York law firm of Wachtell, Lipton, Rosen & Katz. The development and efficacy of the pill is described in the firm's own words as follows:

Wachtell, Lipton, Rosen & Katz (1996)
THE SHARE PURCHASE RIGHTS PLAN

Background of the Rights Plan

The basic objectives of the rights plan are to deter abusive takeover tactics by making them unacceptably expensive to the raider and to encourage prospective acquirors to negotiate with the board of directors of the target rather than to attempt a hostile takeover.

The plan includes a "flip-in" feature designed to deter creeping accumulations of a company's stock. The "flip-in" feature is structured to be available from a 10% to a 20% ownership threshold. If triggered, the flip-in feature would give shareholders, other than the holder triggering the flip-in, the right to purchase shares of the company at a discount to market price (thereby diluting the triggering shareholder). The plan also has a "flip-over" feature which provides shareholders protection against a squeeze-out. The flip-over feature would give shareholders the right to purchase shares of the acquiring company at a discount in the event of a freeze-out merger or similar transaction (thereby diluting the acquiring company).

The rights issued pursuant to the plan are redeemable for a nominal amount prior to the acquisition of a large block of the target's shares. Thus, the effect of the plan is to force potential acquirors to deal with the company's board of directors (or conduct a proxy contest to replace directors) before acquiring shares in excess of the threshold levels. This increases the negotiating power of the Board. Part II contains a summary of the terms of our recommended plan.

The rights plan was designed not to interfere, and has not interfered, with the day to day operations of the companies that have adopted it. Prior to its being activated by an acquisition of a large block of the target company's shares, it has no effect on a company's balance sheet or income statement and it has no tax effect on the company or the shareholders. Companies have split their stock without interference from the plan. While the plan requires special care in such transactions, it has not hindered public offerings of common stock or SEC clearance of pooling of interests mergers.

The efficacy of the rights plan has made it a common feature among U.S. corporations. . . . Indeed, in upholding the adoption rights plan as a proportionate response to a tender offer in the . . . *Unitrin* case, the Delaware Supreme Court commented that the rights plan is an "effective takeover device" that has resulted in a "remarkable transformation in the market for corporate control."

Rights plans are also now well established in case law and statutory law. Starting with the Delaware Supreme Court's 1985 decision in the *Household* case, upholding one of the first right's plans to be adopted, the Delaware courts and courts in other jurisdictions, have widely recognized the legality and legitimate uses of a variety of rights plans. In each of the few jurisdictions in which a rights plan has been held invalid under the state's corporation law (because of the discriminatory flip in feature), the state legislature has amended the corporation law to establish clearly the legality of the flip-in feature of the rights plan.

The *Household* case and subsequent case law establish that adoption of a plan does not change the fiduciary standards to be followed by a board of directors in responding to a takeover bid. In the event of a specific takeover bid, the plan and its operation will have to be assessed in light of the response that the board decides is appropriate based on the advice at that time of the company's financial advisors and legal counsel. Much of the case law since *Household* has focused on how the board uses the rights plan in the face of a takeover bid, particularly on the decision whether to redeem the rights in response to a particular takeover bid. Some early Delaware Chancery Court cases suggested that a board would have an obligation to redeem a rights plan following an opportunity to search for alternatives where the bid offered a higher value than or was close in value to the identified alternatives. However, [subsequent] Delaware case law (*e.g.*, the Delaware Supreme Court decisions in *Paramount v. Time, QVC v. Paramount* and *Unitrin v. American General*) supports the view that, where the board has not made a decision to sell the company, the board may "just say no" and refuse to redeem the rights if the board determines in its business judgment that the bid is not in the best interests of the shareholders and would interfere with the company's long-term business plans and strategy.

The Flip-In Plan

The rights plan combines the flip-over with a flip-in that is triggered by an acquisition at the 20% level. The flip-in at a 20% threshold provides protection against takeover abuses involving partial and creeping accumulations. The plan also allows the board of directors to lower the threshold to not less than 10% if appropriate in light of specific circumstances.

If the flip-in is triggered, each holder of rights (other than the raider, whose rights become void) will be able to exercise the rights for common stock of the target having a market value, at the time the raider crosses the 20% threshold, of twice the right's exercise price. This would result in dilution to the raider both economically and in terms of its percentage ownership of the target's shares. The exact level of the dilution would depend on the market value of the target's common stock in relation to the exercise price of the rights.

The rights plan also contains a feature that gives the board of directors the option, after the flip-in is triggered by an acquisition at the 20% level (or such lower threshold down to 10% as has been set by the board) but before there has been a 50% acquisition, to exchange one new share of common stock of the company for each then valid right (which would exclude rights held by the raider that have become void). This provision will have an economically dilutive effect on the acquiror, and provide a corresponding benefit to the remaining rightsholders, that is comparable to the flip-in without requiring shareholders to go through the process and expense of exercising their rights. . . .

The Debate over Rights Plan

Rights plans have been anathema to the efficient market theorists of the Chicago School whose concept of a free market for corporate control is used as a policy justification by the opponents of plans. The evidence, however, does not support their argument that rights plans hurt shareholder values. . . .

Institutional Investor Activists

[In recent] years, institutions such as the College Retirement Equities Fund and the California Public Employees Retirement System, several union pension funds and other shareholder activists have submitted resolutions to several companies each year, generally those with institutions holding a majority of the outstanding shares, requesting rescission of their plans unless submitted to a shareholder vote and approved by a majority of the shares. Although these proposals often receive significant support, only a few proposals have been approved. . . .

Conclusion

Takeover activity continues and the dynamics of takeovers are constantly changing. While the rights plan decreases the potential of hostile takeover activity, it will not, and is not intended to, make a company takeover-proof. The rights plan protects against takeover abuses, it gives all parties an increased period of time in which to make decisions on such a fundamentally important question as a takeover, and it strengthens the ability of the board of directors of a Target to fulfill its fiduciary duties to obtain the best result for the shareholders. We recommend that the Company adopt the rights plan.

TERMS OF RIGHTS PLAN[1]

Issuance: One right to buy 1/100th f a share of a new series of preferred stock as a dividend on each outstanding share of common stock of the company. Until the rights become exercisable, all further issuances of common stock, including common stock issuable upon exercise of outstanding options, would include issuance of rights.

Term: 10 years.

Exercise price: An amount per 1/100th of a share of the preferred stock which approximates the board's view of the long-term value of the company's common stock. Factors to be considered in setting the exercise price include the company's business and prospects, its long-term plans and market conditions. For most companies that have adopted rights plans, the exercise price has been between three and five times current market price. The exercise price is subject to certain anti-dilution adjustments. For illustration only, assume an exercise price of $150 per 1/100th of a share.

Rights detach and become exercisable: The rights are not exercisable and are not transferable apart from the company's common stock until the tenth day after such time as a person or group acquires beneficial ownership of 20% or more of the company's common stock or the tenth business day (or such later time as the board of directors may determine) after a person or group announces its intention to commence or commences a tender or exchange offer the consummation of which would result in beneficial ownership by a person or group of 20% or more of the company' common stock. As soon as practicable after the rights become exercisable, separate right certificates would be issued and the rights would become transferable apart from the company's common stock.

Protection against squeezeout: If, after the rights have been triggered, an acquiring company were to merge or otherwise combine with the company, or the company were to sell 50% or more of its assets or earning power, each right than outstanding would "flip over" and thereby would become a right to buy that number of shares of common stock of the acquiring company which at the time of such transaction would have a market value of two times the exercise price of the rights. Thus, if the acquiring company's common stock at the time

---

1. These terms are as they would be set by a company that uses authorized blank check preferred stock, with terms that make 1/100th of a share of the preferred stock the economic equivalent of one share of common stock, as the security for which the rights are exercisable.

of such transaction were trading at $75 per share and the exercise price at the rights at such time were $150, each right would thereafter be exercisable $150 for four shares (*i.e.,* the number of shares that could be purchased for $300, or two times the exercise price of the rights) of the acquiring company's common stock.

Protection against creeping acquisition/open market purchases: In the event a person or group were to acquire a 20% or greater position in the company, each right then outstanding would "flip in" and become a right to buy that number of shares of common stock of the company which at the time of the 20% acquisition had a market value of two times the exercise price of the rights. The acquiror who triggered the rights would be excluded from the "flip-in" because his rights would have become null and void upon his triggering acquisition. Thus, if the company's common stock at the time of the "flip-in" were trading at $75 per share and the exercise price of the rights at such time were $150, each right would thereafter be exercisable at $150 for four shares of the company's common stock. As described below, the amendment provision of the Rights Agreement provides that the 20% threshold can be lowered to not less than 10%. The board can utilize this provision to provide additional protection against creeping accumulations.

Exchange: At any time after the acquisition by a person or group of affiliated or associated persons of beneficial ownership of 20% or more of the outstanding common stock of the company and before the acquisition by a person or group of 50% or more of the outstanding common stock of the company, the board of directors may exchange the rights (other than rights owned by such person or group, which have become avoid), in whole or in part, at an exchange ratio of one share of the company's common stock (or 1/100th of a share of junior participating preferred stock) per right, subject to adjustment.

Redemption: The rights are redeemable by the company's board of directors at a price of $.01 per right at any time prior to the acquisition by a person or group of beneficial ownership of 20% or more of the company's common stock. The redemption of the rights may be made effective at such time, on such basis, and with such conditions as the board of directors in its sole discretion may establish. Thus, the rights would not interfere with a negotiated merger or a white knight transaction, even after a hostile tender offer has been commenced. The rights may prevent a white knight transaction after a 20% acquisition (unless the exchange feature described above is used to eliminate the rights and the white knight's price is adjusted for the issuance of the additional shares).

Voting: The rights would not have any voting rights.

Terms of preferred stock: The preferred stock issuable upon exercise of the rights would be non-redeemable and rank junior to all other series of the company's preferred stock. The dividend, liquidation and voting rights, and nonredemption features of the preferred stock are designed so that the value of the 1/100th interest in a share of new preferred stock purchasable with each right will approximate the value of the one share of common stock. Each whole share of preferred stock would be entitled to receive a quarterly preferential dividend of $1 per share but would be entitled to receive, in the aggregate, a dividend of 100 times the dividend declared on the common stock. In the event of liquidation, the holders of the new preferred stock would be entitled to receive a preferential liquidation payment of $100 per share but would be entitled to receive, in the aggregate, a liquidation payment equal to 100 times the payment made per share of common stock. Each share of preferred stock would have 100 votes, voting together with the common stock. Finally, in the event of any merger, consolidation or other transaction in which shares of common stock are exchanged for or changed into other stock or securities, cash and/or other property, each share of preferred stock would be entitled to receive 100 times the amount received per share of common stock. The foregoing rights are protected against dilution in the event of additional shares of common stock are issued. Since the "out of the money" rights would not be exercisable immediately, registration of the preferred stock issuable upon exercise of the rights with the Securities and Exchange Commission need not be effective until the rights become exercisable and are "in the money" or are so close to being "in the money" so as to make exercise economically possible. . . .

Miscellaneous: The Rights Agreement provides that the company may not enter into any transaction of the sort which would give rise to the "flip-over" right if in connection therewith there are outstanding securities or there are agreements or arrangements intended to counteract the protective provisions of the rights. The Rights Agreement may be amended from time to time in any manner prior to the acquisition of a 20% position. . . .

3. How Does the Pill Work as a Takeover Defense? The essential features and the basic mechanics of the terms that are typically included as part of most modern shareholder rights plans (aka poison pills) have been briefly summarized as follows:

Stockholder right plans were born in the 1980s in response to the proliferation of corporate raiders making hostile bids for public companies, and were designed to provide public company boards of directors with a "poison pill" with which to defend themselves against hostile takeover bids. Stockholder rights plans allow the target board of directors time and leverage to negotiate for a control premium or other alternatives to hostile bids. Typically, a stockholder rights plan provides rights to all holders of common stock that, if fully activated, will give all stockholders, other than the hostile bidder, the right to buy additional stock at a substantial discount. The rights initially trade together with the common stock, do not have separate certificates and are not exercisable.

A poison pill typically has two triggers that will cause the rights to be distributed separately from the common stock and to become exercisable. The date this occurs is usually called the "distribution date."

One trigger occurs when a potential acquirer launches a tender offer for the purchase of at least a specified percentage of the stock of the target company. Upon this trigger, the rights are distributed and become exercisable. Upon a distribution for this trigger, one right is usually exercisable to purchase the equivalent of one share of common stock at a fixed price (the "exercise price"), which is customarily set at a price representing the hypothetical appreciation of the stock over the duration of the plan. Often, a board seeks the advice of an investment bank on setting the exercise price.

The second trigger occurs when someone actually acquires beneficial ownership of stock over a specified percentage. When this occurs, the holder is usually given some time to divest itself of excess holdings, and if it does not, the rights undergo what is called a "flip-in." On a flip-in, each right other than rights held by the holder that triggered the flip-in becomes exercisable for the number of shares equal to the exercise price divided by one-half the then-current trading price of the stock. For example, if a company's stock is trading at $15 per share at a time when someone triggers a flip-in by acquiring 25 percent of the outstanding shares, and the rights have a $30 per share exercise price, each right, other than those held by the triggering holder, will enable the purchase of 4 common stock equivalents for $30, which is an effective price per share of $7.50. Assuming all the rights are exercised, the holdings of the holder that triggered the rights will decrease from 25 percent to 6.25 percent. Typically, upon a flip-in event, the board can elect to exchange each right for one (or more) common stock equivalents in lieu of permitting the rights to be exercised for cash.

Louis Lehot, et al., *The Return of the Poison Pill—Lessons Learned in 2010 from the* Selectica *and* Barnes & Noble *Cases,* 24 INSIGHTS 23-24 (Dec. 2010).

4. The Poison Pill Is a Very Potent Defense.   With respect to the early generation of flip-over pills, the only case that I am aware of where this type of pill has been triggered is the Crown-Zellerbach situation (as described in the *Moran* opinion), where Sir Jimmy Goldsmith triggered the company's pill, leaving him a substantial shareholder in the company. Once Sir Jimmy Goldsmith acquired 51 percent of the stock of Crown-Zellerbach, the board's power to redeem the pill was terminated. At this point, the controlling shareholder could not undertake a second-step, takeout merger without triggering the devastating consequences of the flip-over rights of the poison pill. The moral of this story was obvious: a poison pill with flip-over rights generally will operate to prevent a second-step merger, but it will not necessarily prevent a change in control of the company. To discourage this type of open-market purchase activity that allowed a prospective bidder to accumulate a sizeable stake in the Target company, the pill evolved to include a "flip-in" feature. The evolution of the flip-in pill is supported by the Delaware Supreme Court's decision in *Unocal,* where the Delaware Supreme Court upheld the discriminatory self-tender. Based on this, the inventor of the pill was emboldened to include a flip-in provision, which depends (as it must to be effective) on a discriminatory feature. While the pill is a potent deterrent to an unsolicited bid and thus encourages Bidders to negotiate with Target management, it bears emphasizing that the pill does not provide Target with an impenetrable defense against the unsolicited takeover. That is, the poison pill does not erect a bulletproof shield that operates to prevent hostile takeovers. Instead, Bidder is encouraged to come to the bargaining table and negotiate with Target management, and the option of "going hostile" usually becomes Bidder's tool of last resort.

5. The Pill Becomes Widely Adopted as a Takeover Defense.   Following the Delaware Supreme Court's ruling in *Moran,* the poison pill became a staple in the arsenal of takeover defenses erected by public companies. Indeed, by "the mid-1990s, poison pills had been widely adopted by public companies in the United States, and were a key structural defense, or 'shark repellent' to hostile corporate raiders. By the end of 1993, approximately 1,375 companies had poison pills in place. Adoptions and extensions of poison pills continued and

by the end of 2001, approximately 2,200 companies had poison pills in force."
Louis Lehot, et al., *supra* at 24.

6. Recent Activist Shareholder Movement Questions the Wisdom of the Pill. The
development of the poison pill defense has not been without its critics. Almost
from its inception, controversy surrounded the wisdom of implementing a pill.
See, e.g., Gregg Jarrell and Michael Ryngaert, Office of the Chief Economist
of the Securities and Exchange Commission, *The Effect of Poison Pills on the
Wealth of Target Shareholders* (Oct. 23, 1986); and the controversy continues; *see,
e.g.,* John C. Coates IV, *The Contestability of Corporate Control: A Critique of the
Scientific Evidence on Takeover Defenses,* 79 Tex. L. Rev. 271 (2000). In the wake
of unprecedented financial scandals involving some of the largest corporations in the United States, the dawn of the twenty-first century saw institutional shareholders once again take to the offensive. Following the collapse of
the tech bubble in 2002 and the end of the dotcom era, hedge funds began
to join other institutional shareholder activists in advocating the dismantling
of many antitakeover measures. These shareholders frequently used the SEC's
shareholder proposal rule (Rule 14a-8 of Regulation 14A, the federal proxy
rules) to bring their reform proposals before the shareholders for a nonbinding vote; one of the more popular proposals that the proponents would put
forth recommended termination of the shareholder rights plan. As these proposals started meeting with success at the ballot box, companies quietly began
dismantling the takeover defenses that had been so carefully erected in the
past, rather than face the prospect of defeat at the ballot box. In the post-SOX
era, these activist shareholders were further emboldened as investors generally grew more skeptical of incumbent management; and, as management's
often quite lavish pay packages came under greater scrutiny, this resulted in
ever greater shareholder disenchantment with incumbent management. So,
not surprisingly:

> The last decade saw major corporate scandals from Enron to WorldCom to
> Tyco, the adoption of the Sarbanes-Oxley Act of 2002 and the rise of organized
> institutional investor voting and corporate governance metrics. Stockholder activ-
> ists and proxy advisory firms [such as Institutional Shareholder Services (ISS) or
> Glass Lewis, two of the most prominent proxy advisory firms operating in today's
> capital markets] rallied against poison pills, arguing that they often resulted in
> the entrenchment of management and the loss of stockholder value. With these
> changes came declines in the annual number of pill adoptions and extensions,
> with annual decreased activity each year. By the end 2007, the number of compa-
> nies with poison pills in place had declined to the levels seen in 1994. By the third
> quarter of 2009, boards of directors of established public companies had largely
> allowed their stockholder rights plans to expire, companies in registration ceased
> adopting stockholder rights plans in the course of going public and less than a
> third of S&P 1,500 companies had a poison pill in place.

Louis Lehot, et al., *The Return of the Poison Pill— Lessons Learned from the* Selectica
and Barnes & Noble *Cases,* 24 INSIGHTS 23, 27 (Dec. 2010). Consequently, by

2011, "only about 900 U.S. publicly traded companies had a [poison pill] in place—a nearly 60% drop over the last ten years." John F. Grossbauer and Pamela L. Millard, *Stockholder Rights, Plans in Negotiated Mergers: Issues of Delaware Law*, 44 SEC. & COMMODITIES REG. 269 (Dec. 2011).

Even more important, the explosive growth of institutional investment in the stock markets has led to a dramatic power shift to shareholders and away from the dominance of management that was prevalent in the 1970s. This shift has resulted in focusing increasing attention on the most basic of corporate tenets: Will this seeming power shift to shareholders (most notably, institutional shareholders, including the explosive growth of hedge funds over the past decade) fundamentally change the long-standing paradigm that directors—not shareholders—manage the business affairs of the modern corporation? This is the question that is currently being hotly debated by the practicing M&A bar, by the regulators, and in the academic literature—a question that as of this writing has no readily discernible answer.

7. *The Influence of Proxy Advisory Firms.* Many of today's institutional investors rely on the advisory services of firms such as ISS to make recommendations to their clients regarding how to vote their shares of publicly traded U.S. corporations. In connection with the annual election of directors, ISS promulgated guidelines recommending that shareholders vote against the entire board of directors of a company if it, among other things, adopts a stockholder rights plan with a term longer than 12 months without prior shareholder approval. ISS adopted other, more specific guidelines with respect to voting recommendations where a company seeks shareholder approval of a poison pill. Taken together,

> . . . [In today's world of corporate governance,] ISS's voting policies create a [powerful] disincentive to adopt a poison pill that does not meet ISS's specifications and that is not submitted for stockholder ratification. Poison pills may be adopted once a particular threat has emerged, and at such a time, the board may be less concerned with ISS voting policies. Because a hostile bidder may emerge without warning and may quickly seek to take control through a hostile tender offer, boards should consider having a "pill-on-the-shelf" that will be ready to be implemented quickly in response to a specific threat. The work involved in drafting and implementing a poison pill is not trivial, and the need to do so "from scratch" in the face of an actual threat can distract the board and its advisors at a time when resources are already under pressure from the threat itself.

Lehot, et al., *supra*. Indeed, as described more fully below, the truth of this observation can be seen in the response of many publicly traded companies to the economic havoc wreaked (in an incredibly short period of time) as the world grappled with the fallout from the coronavirus pandemic in the early part of 2020.

8. *Poison Pills and the Coronavirus Pandemic.* The debate over the continuing wisdom of implementing (or dismantling, as the case may be) a poison pill as a takeover defense continues to rage as we enter the third decade of the 21st century. As noted above, well-known (and influential) proxy advisory firms (such as ISS and Glass Lewis) have intensely scrutinized public companies who have a pill in place. As a result of this scrutiny, by the end of 2019, very few public companies had a poison pill in place. However, in early 2020, with the global onset of the coronavirus pandemic and the resulting decline (not to mention volatility) in stock prices, many companies began

> to once again consider poison pills to protect against unsolicited takeovers or activist attacks during the crisis. For example, between March 15, 2020 and April 30, 2020, 31 US public companies adopted "traditional" poison pills [that is, pills that include the customary "flip in" and "flip over" provisions] . . . In response to the COVID-19 pandemic and renewed interest in poison pills, two of the major proxy advisory firms, ISS and Glass Lewis, released updated guidance for companies considering this defensive mechanism.
>
> ISS reiterated in April 2020 that their current guidance on poison pills is flexible enough to account for "genuine, short-term potential threat situations such as during the current pandemic." As such, ISS noted that it would continue its practice of considering poison pills with a duration less than one year on a case-by-case basis, taking into account factors such as the disclosed rationale for adopting the poison pill and "whether directors appear to have sought to appropriately protect shareholders from abusive bidders without inappropriately entrenching the existing board and management team." ISS stated that it will generally consider both the board's explanation for its adoption of the poison pill, including any imminent threats, . . . In its guidance, ISS also clarified that "a severe stock price decline as a result of the COVID-19 pandemic is likely to be considered valid justification in most cases for adopting a pill of less than one year in duration; however, boards should provide detailed disclosure regarding their choice of duration, or on any decisions to delay or avoid putting plans to a shareholder vote beyond that period."
>
> Glass Lewis stated in their April 2020 guidance that while Glass Lewis remains "generally skeptical" of and "generally opposes" poison pills, it supports poison pills that meet certain conditions, particularly those that are limited in scope to accomplish a particular objective. For example, Glass Lewis noted that it considers companies that are impacted by COVID-19 and the related economic crisis "as reasonable context for adopting a poison pill" as long as the duration of the poison pill is one year or less and the company discloses a "sound rationale" for adoption of the poison pill due to the pandemic. Glass Lewis warned, however, that if a poison pill does not meet its conditions, Glass Lewis will recommend opposing the re-election of all board members who served at the time of the poison pill's adoption.

Brian R. Boch, et al., *Poison Pills during the COVID-19 Pandemic*, Jenner & Block LLP, May 11, 2020, *available at*: https://jenner.com/system/assets/

publications/19916/original/Poison%20Pills%20during%20the%20COVID-19%20Pandemic%20-%20May%202020.pdf?1589206964.

9. Proxy Contests Mounted by Activist Shareholders. Historically, corporate raiders who disagreed with a particular company's business strategy (such as Carl Icahn and T. Boone Pickens) would purchase a controlling interest in the company (typically through a tender offer) and then "squeeze out" the remaining shareholders by engaging in a second-step, back-end merger. The raider, as the new owner of the company, would then implement a different business strategy, which might include "busting up" the company by selling off its assets. Reflecting that business practices of M&A transactions are continually evolving, a very different strategy is often employed today by those investors who disagree with the business strategy of a particular company. Now activist shareholders are purchasing as little as 2 percent or 3 percent of Target's stock and then undertaking a proxy campaign to elect the insurgent shareholders' slate of nominees to Target's board. If an activist shareholder succeeds in electing its nominees to the board, the investor "can often effectively [gain] control of the target [company], without purchasing any additional shares, without payment of a control premium to the existing shareholders and, if the board seats are received in settlement of a proxy contest [as where the activist shareholder reaches an agreement with Target company's management to appoint the investors' nominees to the company's board of directors*] without receiving

---

* As a reflection of how the times have changed — and how the market for M&A activity continues to evolve in our post-Enron world — Carl Icahn has been quoted as saying publicly, "What's changed is the perception. Now, instead of being called a corporate raider, I'm an activist." [This quote was included in the materials submitted by James C. Morphy as part of his presentation at the Twentieth Annual Tulane Corporate Law Institute on April 4, 2008; see p. 21 of his slide presentation, a copy of which is on file with the author.]

Indeed, as an activist investor, Carl Icahn has deployed this very strategy (as described in the accompanying text) on several occasions. One high-profile example was his run at Occidental Petroleum. In April 2019, Occidental Petroleum acquired Anadarko Petroleum for $55 billion, as was described in more detail in Chapter 6 as part of our discussion of the filing obligations mandated by Section 13(d) of the Williams Act. *See supra* at pp. 439-442. Unhappy with the deal terms, Icahn actively campaigned to fire the board that had approved this acquisition and to take control of Occidental's board of directors. As of December 2019, Icahn was reported to have accumulated over a 2% ownership interest and, in March 2020, Icahn disclosed in a Schedule 13D filing that he had acquired a 9.9% interest in Occidental. Eventually, Icahn and Occidental reached a "truce" in which Occidental agreed to place two directors chosen by Icahn on the board, to create "a new board oversight committee that must be informed of any offers to acquire the company or its assets," and to cut salaries by 30% for Occidental's U.S. employees. Rebecca Elliot and Ryan Dezember, *Occidental Petroleum Reaches Truce With Activist Investor Carl Icahn*, WALL STREET JOURNAL, March 25, 2020, *available at*: https://www.wsj.com/articles/occidental-petroleum-reaches-truce-with-activist-investor-carl-icahn-11585146651.

a single vote in an election of directors." Gary D. Gilson and Michelle Torline, *Control for the Taking: Activist Shareholder Election Contests,* 5 BOARDROOM BRIEFING 33 (Summer 2008). In light of the recent market activity of these activist investors, not surprisingly many experienced market participants are revisiting the longstanding debate over the wisdom of implementing (or dismantling, as the case may be) defensive measures such as shareholder rights plans and staggered boards. *See, e.g.,* Martin Lipton, *Shareholder Activism and the "Eclipse" of the Public Corporation: Is the Current Wave of Activism Causing Another Tectonic Shift in the American Corporate World?,* Keynote Address, The 2008 Directors Forum of the University of Minnesota Law School, June 25, 2008; Martin Lipton, Wachtell, Lipton, Rosen & Katz, *Dealing with Activist Hedge Funds and Other Activist Investors,* January 20, 2020, *available at:* https://corpgov.law.harvard.edu/2020/01/20/dealing-with-activist-hedge-funds-and-other-activist-investors-3/; and Lucian Bebchuk, et. al., *Dancing with Activists,* May 30, 2017, *available at:* https://corpgov.law.harvard.edu/2017/05/30/dancing-with-activists/.

10. Fair Price Provisions and Other Charter Amendments. In footnote 3 of the *Moran* opinion, the Delaware Supreme Court describes the fair price provisions that some companies have included in their corporate charter (i.e, in the company's articles of incorporation), or, in the case of Delaware companies, in the company's certificate of incorporation, although these provisions may in some cases be made part of the company's by-laws. Other types of charter provisions—that also operate as antitakeover devices—include staggered terms for the company's board of directors (sometimes referred to as a "classified board"), a provision that a board can be removed only for cause, and limitations on the use of special meetings of the shareholders and the setting of the date for shareholder meetings. Collectively, these various types of charter provisions are often colloquially referred to as "shark repellents," a reference to the fact that these provisions are designed not only to protect the company's shareholders from certain harmful effects that may accompany a change in control of the company, but also to discourage prospective bidders from launching an unsolicited bid seeking control of the company. *Query:* How do these types of charter provisions work to achieve these objectives?

11. The Continuing Evolution of the Pill. Shareholder rights plans (or poison pills, as they are more popularly known) are widely regarded as one of the most effective, if not the most effective, device developed yet to protect the company from an inadequate bid or other type of abusive takeover tactic. Since the invention of the poison pill in 1984, these rights plans have continued to evolve. Although the key features of a rights plan continue to be the flip-in and flip-over provisions, modern versions of the poison pill have added other features designed to address specific concerns or specific types of Bidder tactics. Thus, today, modern variations of rights plans include "dead-hand pills," "no-hand pills," and "chewable pills." The operation of these modern variations and their validity under the evolving standards of modern fiduciary duty law are addressed in the cases in the next section.

2. The Evolution of Delaware's Standard of "Enhanced Scrutiny" and Further Development of the Poison Pill Defense

Unitrin, Inc. v. American General Corp.
651 A.2d 1361 (Del. 1995)

HOLLAND, Justice.

This is an appeal from the Court of Chancery's entry of a preliminary injunction on October 13, 1994, upon plaintiffs' motions in two actions: American General Corporation's ("American General") suit against Unitrin, Inc. ("Unitrin") and its directors . . .

American General, which had publicly announced a proposal to merge with Unitrin for $2.6 billion at $50⅜ per share, and certain Unitrin shareholder plaintiffs, filed suit in the Court of Chancery, *inter alia*, to enjoin Unitrin from repurchasing up to 10 million shares of its own stock (the "Repurchase Program"). On August 26, 1994, the Court of Chancery temporarily restrained Unitrin from making any further repurchases. After expedited discovery, briefing and argument, the Court of Chancery preliminarily enjoined Unitrin from making further repurchases on the ground that the Repurchase Program was a disproportionate response to the threat posed by American General's inadequate all cash for all shares offer, under the standard of this Court's holding in *Unocal Corp. v. Mesa Petroleum Co.*, Del. Supr., 493 A.2d 946 (1985) *("Unocal")*. . . .

This Court has concluded that the Court of Chancery erred in applying the proportionality review *Unocal* requires by focusing upon whether the Repurchase Program was an "unnecessary" defensive response. The Court of Chancery should have directed its enhanced scrutiny: first, upon whether the Repurchase Program the Unitrin Board implemented was draconian, by being either preclusive or coercive and; second, if it was not draconian, upon whether it was within a range of reasonable responses to the threat American General's Offer posed. Consequently, the interlocutory preliminary injunctive judgment of the Court of Chancery is reversed. This matter is remanded for further proceedings in accordance with this opinion. . . .

AMERICAN GENERAL'S OFFER . . .

On July 12, 1994, American General sent a letter to [Richard Vie, Unitrin's Chief Executive Officer] proposing a consensual merger transaction in which it would "purchase all of Unitrin's 51.8 million outstanding shares of common stock for $50⅜ per share, in cash" (the "Offer"). The Offer was conditioned on the development of a merger agreement and regulatory approval. The Offer price represented a 30% premium over the market price of Unitrin's shares. In the Offer, American General stated that it "would consider offering a higher price" if "Unitrin could demonstrate additional value." American General also offered to consider tax-free "[a]lternatives to an all cash transaction."

UNITRIN'S REJECTION

Upon receiving the American General Offer, the Unitrin Board's Executive Committee [consisting of Vie, Jerrold V. Jerome, Chairman of the Board, and Dr. Henry Singleton, Unitrin's largest shareholder, owning in excess of 14% of the outstanding stock but never employed by Unitrin] engaged legal counsel and scheduled a telephonic Board meeting for July 18. At the July 18 special meeting, the Board reviewed the terms of the Offer. The Board was advised that the existing charter and bylaw provisions might not effectively deter all types of takeover strategies. It was suggested that the Board consider adopting a shareholder rights plan and an advance notice provision for shareholder proposals.

The Unitrin Board met next on July 25, 1994 in Los Angeles for seven hours. All directors attended the meeting. The principal purpose of the meeting was to discuss American General's Offer.

Vie reviewed Unitrin's financial condition and its ongoing business strategies. The Board also received a presentation from its investment advisor, Morgan Stanley & Co. ("Morgan Stanley"), regarding the financial adequacy of American General's proposal. Morgan Stanley expressed its opinion that the Offer was financially inadequate. Legal counsel expressed concern that the combination of Unitrin and American General would raise antitrust complications due to the resultant decrease in competition in the home service insurance markets.

The Unitrin Board unanimously concluded that the American General merger proposal was not in the best interests of Unitrin's shareholders and voted to reject the Offer. The Board then received advice from its legal and financial advisors about a number of possible defensive measures it might adopt, including a shareholder rights plan ("poison pill") and an advance notice bylaw provision for shareholder proposals. Because the Board apparently thought that American General intended to keep its Offer private, the Board did not implement any defensive measures at that time.

AMERICAN GENERAL'S PUBLICITY
UNITRIN'S INITIAL RESPONSES

On August 2, 1994, American General issued a press release announcing its Offer to Unitrin's Board to purchase all of Unitrin's stock for $50^3/_8$ per share. The press release also noted that the Board had rejected American General's Offer. After that public announcement, the trading volume and market price of Unitrin's stock increased.

At its regularly scheduled meeting on August 3, the Unitrin Board discussed the effects of American General's press release. The Board noted that the market reaction to the announcement suggested that speculative traders or arbitrageurs were acquiring Unitrin stock. The Board determined that American General's public announcement constituted a hostile act designed to coerce the sale of Unitrin at an inadequate price. The Board unanimously approved the poison pill and the proposed advance notice bylaw that it had considered previously. . . .

Beginning on August 2 and continuing through August 12, 1994, Unitrin issued a series of press releases to inform its shareholders and the public market [that, among other things,] . . . the Unitrin Board believed Unitrin's stock was worth more than the $50⅜ American General offered; . . . that the Board felt that the price of American General's Offer did not reflect Unitrin's long term business prospects as an independent company; and . . . that the [Unitrin] Board had adopted a shareholder rights plan (poison pill) to guard against undesirable takeover efforts.

UNITRIN'S REPURCHASE PROGRAM

The Unitrin Board met again on August 11, 1994. The minutes of that meeting indicate that its principal purpose was to consider the Repurchase Program. At the Board's request, Morgan Stanley had prepared written materials to distribute to each of the directors. Morgan Stanley gave a presentation in which alternative means of implementing the Repurchase Program were explained. Morgan Stanley recommended that the Board implement an open market stock repurchase. The Board voted to authorize the Repurchase Program for up to ten million shares of its outstanding stock [i.e., that is, to buy back up to 20 percent of Unitrin's outstanding shares].

On August 12, Unitrin publicly announced the Repurchase Program. The Unitrin Board expressed its belief that "Unitrin's stock is undervalued in the market and that the expanded program will tend to increase the value of the shares that remain outstanding." The announcement also stated that the director stockholders were not participating in the Repurchase Program, and that the repurchases "will increase the percentage ownership of those stockholders who choose not to sell."

Unitrin's August 12 press release also stated that the directors owned 23% of Unitrin's stock, that the Repurchase Program would cause that percentage to increase, and that Unitrin's certificate of incorporation included a supermajority voting provision. . . .

UNOCAL IS PROPER REVIEW STANDARD . . .

The Court of Chancery held that all of the Unitrin Board's defensive actions merited judicial scrutiny according to *Unocal.* The record supports the Court of Chancery's determination that the Board perceived American General's Offer as a threat and adopted the Repurchase Program, along with the poison pill and advance notice bylaw, as defensive measures in response to that threat. Therefore, the Court of Chancery properly concluded the facts before it required an application of *Unocal* and its progeny. . . .

AMERICAN GENERAL THREAT
REASONABLENESS BURDEN SUSTAINED . . .

The first aspect of the *Unocal* burden, the reasonableness test, required the Unitrin Board to demonstrate that, after a reasonable investigation, it determined in good faith, that American General's Offer presented a threat to Unitrin that warranted a defensive response. This Court has held that the presence of a majority of outside independent directors will materially enhance such evidence. . . . An "outside" director has been defined as a non-employee and non-management director, (*e.g.*, Unitrin argues, five members of its seven-person Board). . . . Independence "means that a director's decision is based on the corporate merits of the subject before the board rather than extraneous considerations or influences."

The Unitrin Board identified two dangers it perceived the American General Offer posed: inadequate price and antitrust complications. The Court of Chancery characterized the Board's concern that American General's proposed transaction could never be consummated because it may violate antitrust laws and state insurance regulations as a "makeweight excuse" for the defensive measure. It determined, however, that the Board reasonably believed that the American General Offer was inadequate and also reasonably concluded that the Offer was a threat to Unitrin's uninformed stockholders.

The Court of Chancery [therefore] held that the Board's evidence satisfied the first aspect or reasonableness test under *Unocal.*

PROPORTIONALITY BURDEN
CHANCERY APPROVES POISON PILL . . .

With regard to the second aspect or proportionality test of the initial *Unocal* burden, the Court of Chancery analyzed each stage of the Unitrin Board's defensive responses separately. Although the Court of Chancery characterized Unitrin's antitrust concerns as "makeweight," it acknowledged that the directors of a Delaware corporation have the prerogative to determine that the market undervalues its stock and to protect its stockholders from offers that do not reflect the long term value of the corporation under its present management plan. The Court of Chancery concluded that Unitrin's Board believed in good faith that the American General Offer was inadequate and properly employed a poison pill as a proportionate defensive response to protect its stockholders from a "low ball" bid. [No appeal was taken from this ruling.] . . .

PROPORTIONALITY BURDEN
CHANCERY ENJOINS REPURCHASE PROGRAM

The Court of Chancery did not view either its conclusion that American General's Offer constituted a threat, or its conclusion that the poison pill was a reasonable response to that threat, as requiring it, *a fortiori*, to conclude that the Repurchase Program was also an appropriate response. The Court of Chancery then made two factual findings: first, the Repurchase Program went beyond what was "necessary" to protect the Unitrin stockholders from a "low ball" negotiating strategy; and second, it was designed to keep the decision to combine with American General within the control of the members of the Unitrin Board, as stockholders, under virtually all circumstances. Consequently, the Court of Chancery held that the Unitrin Board failed to demonstrate that the Repurchase Program met the second aspect or proportionality requirement of the initial burden *Unocal* ascribes to a board of directors. . . .

The Court of Chancery concluded that, although the Unitrin Board had properly perceived American General's inadequate Offer as a threat and had properly responded to that threat by adopting a "poison pill," the additional defensive response of adopting the Repurchase Program was unnecessary and disproportionate to the threat the Offer posed. Accordingly, it concluded that the plaintiffs had "established with reasonable probability that the [Unitrin Board] violated its duties under *Unocal* [by authorizing the Repurchase Program]" because the Board had not sustained its burden of demonstrating that the Repurchase Program was a proportionate response to American General's Offer. Therefore, the Court of Chancery held that the plaintiffs proved a likelihood of success on that issue and granted the motion to preliminarily enjoin the Repurchase Program.[18]

PROXY CONTEST
SUPERMAJORITY VOTE
REPURCHASE PROGRAM

Before the Repurchase Program began, Unitrin's directors collectively held approximately 23% of Unitrin's outstanding shares. Unitrin's certificate of incorporation already included a "shark-repellent"[19] provision barring any business combination with a more-than-15% stockholder unless approved by a majority of continuing directors or by a 75% stockholder vote ("Supermajority Vote"). Unitrin's shareholder directors announced publicly that they would not participate in the Repurchase Program and that this would result in a percentage increase of ownership for them, as well as for any other shareholder who did not participate.

The Court of Chancery found that by not participating in the Repurchase Program, the Board "expected to create a 28% voting block to support the Board's decision to reject [a future] offer by American General." From this underlying factual finding, the Court of Chancery concluded that American General might be "chilled" in its pursuit of Unitrin:

> Increasing the board members' percentage of stock ownership, combined with the supermajority merger provision, does more than protect uninformed stockholders from an inadequate offer, it chills any unsolicited acquiror from making an offer. . . .

---

18. We note that the directors' failure to carry their initial burden under *Unocal* does not, *ipso facto*, invalidate the board's actions. Instead, once the Court of Chancery finds the business judgment rule does not apply, the burden remains on the directors to prove "entire fairness." *See Cede & Co. v. Technicolor, Inc.*, Del. Supr., 634 A.2d 345, 361 (1993); . . .

19. A "shark-repellent" is a provision in a company's by-laws or articles of incorporation that is intended to deter a bidder's interest in that company as a target for a takeover. . . .

TAKEOVER STRATEGY
TENDER OFFER/PROXY CONTEST

We begin our examination of Unitrin's Repurchase Program mindful of the special import of protecting the shareholder's [voting] franchise within *Unocal's* requirement that a defensive response be reasonable and proportionate. . . .

The record reflects that the Court of Chancery's decision to enjoin the Repurchase Program is attributable to a continuing misunderstanding, i.e., that in conjunction with the longstanding Supermajority Vote provision in the Unitrin charter, the Repurchase Program would operate to provide the director shareholders with a "veto" to preclude a successful proxy contest by American General. The origins of that misunderstanding are three premises that are each without [factual support in the record]. Two of those premises are objective misconceptions and the other is subjective. . . .

The subjective premise was the Court of Chancery's *sua sponte* determination that Unitrin's outside directors, who are also substantial stockholders, would not vote like other stockholders in a proxy contest, *i.e.*, in their own best economic interests. At American General's Offer price, the outside directors held Unitrin shares worth more than $450 million. Consequently, Unitrin argues the stockholder directors had the same interest as other Unitrin stockholders generally, when voting in a proxy contest, to wit: the maximization of the value of their investments.

In rejecting Unitrin's argument, the Court of Chancery stated that the stockholder directors would be "subconsciously" motivated in a proxy contest to vote against otherwise excellent offers which did not include a "price parameter" to compensate them for the loss of the "prestige and perquisites" of membership on Unitrin's Board. The Court of Chancery's subjective determination that the *stockholder directors* of Unitrin would reject an "excellent offer," unless it compensated them for giving up the "prestige and perquisites" of directorship, appears to be subjective and without record support. It cannot be presumed . . . [but instead] . . . must be the subject of proof that the Unitrin directors' objective in [implementing] the Repurchase Program was to forego the opportunity to sell their stock at a premium. . . .

WITHOUT REPURCHASE PROGRAM
ACTUAL VOTING POWER EXCEEDS 25%

The first objective premise relied upon by the Court of Chancery, unsupported by the record, is that the shareholder directors needed to implement the Repurchase Program to attain voting power in a proxy contest equal to 25%. The Court of Chancery properly calculated that if the Repurchase Program was completed, Unitrin's shareholder directors would increase their absolute voting power to 25%. It then calculated the odds of American General marshalling enough votes to defeat the Board and its supporters.

The Court of Chancery and all parties agree that proxy contests do not generate 100% shareholder participation. The shareholder plaintiffs argue that 80-85% may be a usual turnout. Therefore, *without* the Repurchase Program, the director shareholders' absolute voting power of 23% would already constitute *actual voting power greater than* 25% in a proxy contest with normal shareholder participation below 100%.

SUPERMAJORITY VOTE
NO REALISTIC DETERRENT

The second objective premise relied upon by the Court of Chancery, unsupported by the record, is that American General's ability to succeed in a proxy contest depended on the Repurchase Program being enjoined because of the Supermajority Vote provision in Unitrin's charter. Without the approval of a target's board, the danger of activating a poison pill renders it irrational for bidders to pursue stock acquisitions above the triggering level.[30] Instead, "bidders intent on working around a poison pill must launch and win proxy contests to elect new directors who are willing to redeem the target's poison pill." Joseph A. Grundfest, *Just Vote No: A Minimalist Strategy for Dealing with Barbarians Inside the Gates*, 45 Stan. L. Rev. 857, 859 (1993).

As American General acknowledges, a less than 15% stockholder bidder need not proceed with acquiring shares to the extent that it would ever implicate the Supermajority Vote provision. In fact, it would be illogical for American General or any other bidder to acquire more than 15% of Unitrin's stock because that would not only trigger the poison pill, but also the constraints of 8 Del. C. §203. If American General were to initiate a proxy contest *before* acquiring 15% of Unitrin's stock, it would need to amass only 45.1% of the votes assuming a 90% voter turnout. If it commenced a tender offer at an attractive price contemporaneously with its proxy contest, it could seek to acquire 50.1% of the outstanding voting stock.

The record reflects that institutional investors own 42% of Unitrin's shares. Twenty institutions own 33% of Unitrin's shares. It is generally accepted that proxy contests have re-emerged with renewed significance as a method of acquiring corporate control because "the growth in institutional investment has reduced the dispersion of share ownership." Lucian A. Bebchuk & Marcel Kahan, *A Framework for Analyzing Legal Policy Towards Proxy Contests*, 78 Cal. L. Rev. 1071, 1134 (1990)....

The assumptions and conclusions American General sets forth in this appeal . . . are particularly probative with regard to the effect of the institutional holdings in Unitrin's stock. American General's two predicate assumptions are a 90% stockholder turnout in a proxy contest and a bidder with 14.9% holdings, i.e., the maximum the bidder could own to avoid triggering the poison

---

30. "The . . . flip-in and flip-over features [of a poison pill] stop individual shareholders or shareholder groups from accumulating large amounts of the target company's stock. No potential acquiror or other shareholder will risk triggering a [poison pill] by accumulating more than the threshold level of shares because of the threat of massive discriminatory dilution. The trigger level therefore effectively sets a ceiling on the amount of stock that any shareholder can accumulate before launching a proxy contest." Randall S. Thomas, *Judicial Review of Defensive Tactics in Proxy Contests: When is Using a Rights Plan Right?* 46 Vand. L. Rev. 503, 512 (1993).

pill and the Supermajority Vote provision. American General also calculated the votes available to the Board or the bidder with and without the Repurchase Program[.] . . .

[Based on American General's calculations, in order] to prevail in a proxy contest with a 90% turnout, the percentage of additional shareholder votes a 14.9% shareholder bidder needs to prevail is 30.2% [in an election] for directors and 35.2% in a subsequent [shareholder vote on a] merger. The record reflects that institutional investors held 42% of Unitrin's stock and 20 institutions held 33% of the stock. . . .

The key variable in a proxy contest would be the merit of American General's issues, not the size of its stockholdings. If American General presented an attractive price as the cornerstone of a proxy contest, it could prevail, irrespective of whether the shareholder directors' absolute voting power was 23% or 28%. . . .

Consequently, a proxy contest apparently remained a viable alternative for American General to pursue notwithstanding Unitrin's poison pill, Supermajority Vote provision, and a fully implemented Repurchase Program.

SUBSTANTIVE COERCION
AMERICAN GENERAL'S THREAT

This Court has recognized "the prerogative of a board of directors to resist a third party's unsolicited acquisition proposal or offer." *Paramount Communications, Inc. v. QVC Network, Inc.*, Del. Supr., 637 A.2d 34, 43 n. 13 (1994). The Unitrin Board did not have unlimited discretion to defeat the threat it perceived from the American General Offer by any draconian means available. *See Unocal*, 493 A.2d at 955. Pursuant to the *Unocal* proportionality test, the nature of the threat associated with a particular hostile offer sets the parameters for the range of permissible defensive tactics. Accordingly, the purpose of enhanced judicial scrutiny is to determine whether the Board acted reasonably in "relation to the threat which a particular bid allegedly poses to stockholder interests." *Mills Acquisition Co. v. Macmillan, Inc.*, Del. Supr., 559 A.2d 1261, 1288 (1989).

"The obvious requisite to determining the reasonableness of a defensive action is a clear identification of the nature of the threat." *Paramount Communications, Inc. v. Time, Inc.*, Del. Supr., 571 A.2d 1140, 1154 (1990). Courts, commentators and litigators have attempted to catalogue the threats posed by hostile tender offers. *Id.* at 1153. Commentators have categorized three types of threats:

> (i) *opportunity loss* . . . [where] a hostile offer might deprive target shareholders of the opportunity to select a superior alternative offered by target management [or, we would add, offered by another bidder]; (ii) *structural coercion*, . . . the risk that disparate treatment of non-tendering shareholders might distort shareholders' tender decisions; and (iii) *substantive coercion*, . . . the risk that shareholders will mistakenly accept an underpriced offer because they disbelieve management's representations of intrinsic value.

Id. at 1153 n. 17 (*quoting* Ronald J. Gilson & Reinier Kraakman, *Delaware's Intermediate Standard for Defensive Tactics: Is There Substance to Proportionality Review?*, 44 Bus. Law. 247, 267 (1989)).

This Court has held that the "inadequate value" of an all cash for all shares offer is a "legally cognizable threat." *Paramount Communications, Inc. v. Time, Inc.,* 571 A.2d at 1153. . . .

The record reflects that the Unitrin Board perceived the threat from American General's Offer to be a form of substantive coercion. The Board noted that Unitrin's stock price had moved up, on higher than normal trading volume, to a level slightly below the price in American General's Offer. The Board also noted that some Unitrin shareholders had publicly expressed interest in selling at or near the price in the Offer. The Board determined that Unitrin's stock was undervalued by the market at current levels and that the Board considered Unitrin's stock to be a good long-term investment. The Board also discussed the speculative and unsettled market conditions for Unitrin stock caused by American General's public disclosure. The Board concluded that a Repurchase Program would provide additional liquidity to those stockholders who wished to realize short-term gain, and would provide enhanced value to those stock-holders who wished to maintain a long-term investment. Accordingly, the Board voted to authorize the Repurchase Program for up to ten million shares of its outstanding stock on the open market. . . .

The record appears to support Unitrin's argument that the Board's justification for adopting the Repurchase Program was its reasonably perceived risk of substantive coercion, *i.e.,* that Unitrin's shareholders might accept American General's inadequate Offer because of "ignorance or mistaken belief regarding the Board's assessment of the long-term value of Unitrin's stock. *See Shamrock Holdings, Inc. v. Polaroid Corp.*, Del. Ch., 559 A.2d 278, 290 (1989). . . .

RANGE OF REASONABLENESS
PROPER PROPORTIONALITY BURDEN . . .

The Court of Chancery applied an incorrect legal standard when it ruled that the Unitrin decision to authorize the Repurchase Program was disproportionate because it was "unnecessary." The Court of Chancery stated:

> Given that the Board had already implemented the poison pill and the advance notice provision, the repurchase program was unnecessary to protect Unitrin from an inadequate bid.

In *QVC*, this Court recently elaborated upon the judicial function in applying enhanced scrutiny, citing *Unocal* as authority, albeit in the context of a sale of control and the target board's consideration of one of several reasonable alternatives. That teaching is nevertheless applicable here:

> a court applying enhanced judicial scrutiny should be deciding whether the directors made *a reasonable* decision, not *a perfect* decision. If a board selected one of several reasonable alternatives, a court should not second guess that choice even though it might have decided otherwise or subsequent events may have cast

doubt on the board's determination. Thus, courts will not substitute their business judgment for that of the directors, but will determine if the directors' decision was, on balance, within a range of reasonableness. *See Unocal*, 493 A.2d at 955-56; *Macmillan*, 559 A.2d at 1288; *Nixon*, 626 A.2d at 1378.

Paramount Communications, Inc. v. QVC Network, Inc., Del. Supr., 637 A.2d 34, 45-46 (1994) (*emphasis in original*). The Court of Chancery did not determine whether the Unitrin Board's decision to implement the Repurchase Program fell within a "range of reasonableness."

The record reflects that the Unitrin Board's adoption of the Repurchase Program was an apparent recognition on its part that all shareholders are not alike. This court has stated that distinctions of shareholders are neither inappropriate nor irrelevant for a board of directors to make, *e.g.,* distinctions between long-term shareholders and short-term profit-takers, such as arbitrageurs, and their stockholding objectives. In *Unocal* itself, we expressly acknowledged that "a board may reasonably consider the basic stockholder interests at stake, including those of short-term speculators, whose actions may have fueled the coercive aspect of the offer at the expense of the long term investor." *Unocal*, 493 A.2d at 955-56.

The Court of Chancery's determination that the Unitrin Board's adoption of the Repurchase Program was unnecessary constituted a substitution of its business judgment for that of the Board, contrary to this Court's "range of reasonableness" holding in *Paramount Communications, Inc. v. QVC Network, Inc.*, 637 A.2d at 45-46. . . .

DRACONIAN DEFENSES
COERCIVE OR PRECLUSIVE
RANGE OF REASONABLENESS

In assessing a challenge to defensive actions by a target corporation's board of directors in a takeover context, this Court has held that the Court of Chancery should evaluate the board's overall response, including the justification for each contested defensive measure, and the results achieved thereby. Where all of the target board's defensive actions are inextricably related, the principles *of Unocal* require that such actions be scrutinized collectively as a unitary response to the perceived threat. Thus, the Unitrin Board's adoption of the Repurchase Program, in addition to the poison pill, must withstand *Unocal's* proportionality review. *Id.*

In *Unocal*, the progenitor of the proportionality test, this Court stated that the board of directors' "duty of care extends to protecting the corporation and its [stockholders] from perceived harm whether a threat originates from third parties or other shareholders." *Unocal*, 493 A.2d at 955. We then noted that "such powers are not absolute." *Id.* Specifically, this Court held that the board "does not have unbridled discretion to defeat any perceived threat by any Draconian means available." *Id.* Immediately following those observations in *Unocal*, when exemplifying the parameters of a board's authority in adopting a restrictive stock repurchase, this Court held that "the directors may not have acted *solely* or *primarily* out of a desire to perpetuate themselves in office" (preclusion of the stockholders' corporate franchise right to vote) and, further, that the stock repurchase plan must not be inequitable. *Unocal*, 493 A.2d at 955 (*emphasis added*).

An examination of the cases applying *Unocal* reveals a direct correlation between finidings of proportionality or disproportionality and the judicial determination of whether a defensive response was draconian because it was ether coercive or preclusive in character. . . .

. . . In the modern takeover lexicon, it is now clear that since *Unocal*, this Court has consistently recognized that defensive measures which are either preclusive or coercive are included within the . . . definition of draconian.

If a defensive measure is not draconian, however, because it is not either coercive or preclusive, the *Unocal* proportionality test requires the focus of enhanced judicial scrutiny to shift to "the range of reasonableness." Proper and proportionate defensive responses are intended and permitted to thwart perceived threats. When a corporation is not for sale, the board of directors is the defender of the metaphorical medieval corporate bastion and the protector of the corporation's shareholders. The fact that a defensive action must not be coercive or preclusive does not prevent a board from responding defensively before a bidder is at the corporate bastion's gate.[38]

The *ratio decidendi* for the "range of reasonableness" standard is a need of the board of directors for latitude in discharging its fiduciary duties to the corporation and its shareholders when defending against perceived threats. The concomitant requirement is for judicial restraint. Consequently, if the board of directors' defensive response is not draconian (preclusive or coercive) and is within a "range of reasonableness," a court must not substitute its judgment for the board's. *Paramount Communications, Inc. v. QVC Network, Inc.*, 637 A.2d at 45-46.

THIS CASE
REPURCHASE PROGRAM
PROPORTIONATE WITH POISON PILL

In this case, the initial focus of enhanced judicial scrutiny for proportionality requires a determination regarding the defensive responses by the Unitrin Board to American General's offer. We begin, therefore, by ascertaining whether the Repurchase Program, as an addition to the poison pill, was draconian by being either coercive or preclusive.

A limited nondiscriminatory self-tender, like some other defensive measures, may thwart a current hostile bid, but is not inherently coercive. Moreover, it does not necessarily preclude future bids or proxy contests by stockholders who decline to participate in the repurchase. A selective repurchase of shares

---

38. This Court's choice of the term draconian in *Unocal* was a recognition that the law affords boards of directors substantial latitude in defending the perimeter of the corporate bastion against perceived threats. . . . Stated more directly, depending upon the circumstances, the board may respond to a reasonably perceived threat by adopting individually or sometimes in combination: advance notice by-laws, supermajority voting provisions, shareholder rights plans, repurchase programs, etc.

in a public corporation on the market, such as Unitrin's Repurchase Program, generally does not discriminate because all shareholders can voluntarily realize the same benefit by selling. Here, there is no showing on this record that the Repurchase Program was coercive.

We have already determined that the record in this case appears to reflect that a proxy contest remained a viable (if more problematic) alternative for American General even if the Repurchase Program were to be completed in its entirety. Nevertheless, the Court of Chancery must determine whether Unitrin's Repurchase Program would only inhibit American General's ability to wage a proxy fight and institute a merger or whether it was, in fact, preclusive[39] because American General's success would either be mathematically impossible or realistically unattainable. If the Court of Chancery concludes that the Unitrin Repurchase Program was not draconian because it was not preclusive, one question will remain to be answered in its proportionality review: whether the Repurchase Program was within a range of reasonableness?

The Court of Chancery found that the Unitrin Board reasonably believed that American General's Offer was inadequate and that the adoption of a poison pill was a proportionate defensive response. Upon remand, in applying the correct legal standard to the factual circumstances of this case, the Court of Chancery may conclude that the implementation of the limited Repurchase Program was also within a range of reasonable additional defensive responses available to the Unitrin Board. In considering whether the Repurchase Program was within a range of reasonableness the Court of Chancery should take into consideration whether: (1) it is a statutorily authorized form of business decision which a board of directors may routinely make in a non-takeover context; (2) as a defensive response to American General's Offer it was limited and corresponded in degree or magnitude to the degree or magnitude of the threat, (*i.e.*, assuming the threat was relatively "mild," was the response relatively "mild?"); (3) with the Repurchase Program, the Unitrin Board properly recognized that all shareholders are not alike, and provided immediate liquidity to those shareholders who wanted it. . . .

REMAND TO CHANCERY

In this case, the Court of Chancery erred by substituting its judgment, that the Repurchase Program was unnecessary, for that of the Board. The Unitrin Board had the power and the duty, upon reasonable investigation, to protect Unitrin's shareholders from what it perceived to be the threat from American General's inadequate all-cash for all-shares Offer. *Unocal*, 493 A.2d at 958. The adoption of the poison pill *and* the limited Repurchase Program was not coercive and the Repurchase Program may not be preclusive. Although each made a takeover more difficult, individually and collectively, if they were not coercive

---

39. The record in this case, when properly understood, appears to reflect that the Repurchase Program's effect on a proxy contest would not be preclusive. *Accord Moran v. Household Int'l, Inc.*, Del. Supr., 500 A.2d 1346, 1355 (1985). If the stockholders of Unitrin are "displeased with the action of their elected representatives, the powers of corporate democracy" remain available as a viable alternative to turn the Board out in a proxy contest. *Unocal*, 493 A.2d at 959.

or preclusive the Court of Chancery must determine whether they were within the range of reasonable defensive measures available to the Board. *Accord Cheff v. Mathes,* Del. Supr., 199 A.2d 548, 554-56 (1964).

If the Court of Chancery concludes that individually and collectively the poison pill and the Repurchase Program were proportionate to the threat the Board believed American General posed, the Unitrin Board's adoption of the Repurchase Program and the poison pill is entitled to review under the traditional business judgment rule. The burden will then shift "back to the plaintiffs who have the ultimate burden of persuasion [in a preliminary injunction proceeding] to show a breach of the directors' fiduciary duties." *Moran v. Household Int'l, Inc.,* Del. Supr., 500 A.2d 1346, 1356 (1985) *(citing Unocal,* 493 A.2d at 958). In order to rebut the protection of the business judgment rule, the burden on the plaintiffs will be to demonstrate, "by a preponderance of the evidence that the directors' decisions were *primarily* based on [(1)] perpetuating themselves in office or [(2)] some other breach of fiduciary duty such as fraud, overreaching, lack of good faith, or [(3)] being uninformed." *Unocal,* 493 A.2d at 958 *(emphasis added)*. . . .

QUESTIONS

1. Why does the court decide to apply *Unocal* as the proper standard of judicial review to the decisions made by the Unitrin board of directors?

2. Do you agree with the Delaware Supreme Court's decision as to the proper application of *Unocal*'s intermediate standard of review on the facts of this case?

3. Why does the Delaware Supreme Court remand this case to the Court of Chancery? What is supposed to happen on remand?

4. What does the court's reasoning with respect to "coerciveness" and "preclusiveness" add to our understanding of the two-pronged scrutiny under *Unocal*'s intermediate standard of review?

As the Delaware Supreme Court continued to refine the application of *Unocal*'s enhanced scrutiny standard of judicial review to the issue of takeover defenses, corporate lawyers (and their business clients) likewise continued to tinker with the provisions of the poison pill to address new concerns (i.e., "threats") as the capital markets continued to evolve. The next generation of shareholder rights plans includes dead-hand pills, no-hand pills, and chewable pills, as previously mentioned. The validity of one of these variations – known as the "slow-hand" pill – is at issue in the next case.

Quickturn Design Systems, Inc. v. Shapiro
721 A.2d 1281 (Del. 1998)

HOLLAND, Justice:
This is an expedited appeal from a final judgment entered by the Court of Chancery. The dispute arises out of an ongoing effort by Mentor Graphics

Corporation ("Mentor"), a hostile bidder, to acquire Quickturn Design Systems, Inc. ("Quickturn"), the target company. The plaintiffs-appellees are Mentor and an unaffiliated stockholder of Quickturn. The named defendants-appellants are Quickturn and its directors.

In response to Mentor's tender offer and proxy contest to replace the Quickturn board of directors, as part of Mentor's effort to acquire Quickturn, the Quickturn board enacted two defensive measures. First, it amended the Quickturn shareholder rights plan ("Rights Plan") by adopting a "no hand" feature of limited duration (the "Delayed Redemption Provision" or "DRP"). Second, the Quickturn board amended the corporation's by-laws to delay the holding of any special stockholders meeting requested by stockholders for 90 to 100 days after the validity of the request is determined (the "Amendment" or "By-Law Amendment").

Mentor filed actions for declarative and injunctive relief in the Court of Chancery challenging the legality of both defensive responses by Quickturn's board. The Court of Chancery conducted a trial on the merits. It determined that the By-Law Amendment is valid. It also concluded, however, that the DRP is invalid on fiduciary duty grounds.

In this appeal, Quickturn argues that the Court of Chancery erred in finding that Quickturn's directors breached their fiduciary duty by adopting the Delayed Redemption Provision. We have concluded that, as a matter of Delaware law, the Delayed Redemption Provision was invalid. Therefore, on that alternative basis, the judgment of the Court of Chancery is affirmed. . . .

QUICKTURN'S DEFENSIVE MEASURES

At the August 21 board meeting, the Quickturn board adopted two defensive measures in response to Mentor's hostile takeover bid. First, the board amended Article II, §2.3 of Quickturn's by-laws, which permitted stockholders holding 10% or more of Quickturn's stock to call a special stockholders meeting. The By-Law Amendment provides that if any such special meeting is requested by shareholders, the corporation (Quickturn) would fix the record date for, and determine the time and place of, that special meeting, which must take place not less than 90 days nor more than 100 days after the receipt and determination of the validity of the shareholders' request.

Second, the board amended Quickturn's shareholder Rights Plan by eliminating its "dead hand" feature and replacing it with the Deferred Redemption Provision, under which no newly elected board could redeem the Rights Plan for six months after taking office, if the purpose or effect of the redemption would be to facilitate a transaction with an "Interested Person" (one who proposed, nominated or financially supported the election of the new directors to the board).[15] Mentor would be an Interested Person.

---

15. . . . An "Interested Person" is defined under the amended Rights Plan as "any Person who (i) is or will become an Acquiring Person if such Transaction were to be consummated or an Affiliate or Associate of such a Person, and (ii) is, or directly or indirectly proposed, nominated or financially supported, a director of [Quickturn] in office at the time of consideration of such Transaction who was elected at an annual or special meeting of stockholders."

The effect of the By-Law Amendment would be to delay a shareholder called special meeting for at least three months. The effect of the DRP would be to delay the ability of a newly-elected, Mentor-nominated board to redeem the Rights Plan or "poison pill" for six months, in any transaction with an Interested Person. Thus, the combined effect of the two defensive measures would be to delay any acquisition of Quickturn by Mentor for at least nine months. . . .

QUICKTURN'S DELAYED REDEMPTION PROVISION

At the time Mentor commenced its bid, Quickturn had in place a Rights Plan that contained a so-called "dead hand" provision. That provision had a limited "continuing director" feature that became operative only if an insurgent that owned more than 15% of Quickturn's common stock successfully waged a proxy contest to replace a majority of the board. In that event, only the "continuing directors" (those directors in office at the time the poison pill was adopted) could redeem the rights.

During the same August 21, 1998 meeting at which it amended the special meeting by-law, the Quickturn board also amended the Rights Plan to eliminate its "continuing director" feature, and to substitute a "no hand" or "delayed redemption provision" into its Rights Plan. The Delayed Redemption Provision provides that, if a majority of the directors are replaced by stockholder action, the newly elected board cannot redeem the rights for six months if the purpose or effect of the redemption would be to facilitate a transaction with an "Interested Person."

It is undisputed that the DRP would prevent Mentor's slate, if elected as the new board majority, from redeeming the Rights Plan for six months following their election, because a redemption would be "reasonably likely to have the purpose or effect of facilitating a Transaction" with Mentor, a party that "directly or indirectly proposed, nominated or financially supported" the election of the new board. Consequently, by adopting the DRP, the Quickturn board built into the process a six month delay period in addition to the 90 to 100 day delay mandated by the By-Law Amendment. . . .

DELAYED REDEMPTION PROVISION VIOLATES FUNDAMENTAL DELAWARE LAW

In this appeal, Mentor argues that the judgment of the Court of Chancery should be affirmed because the Delayed Redemption Provision is invalid as a matter of Delaware law. According to Mentor, the Delayed Redemption Provision, like the "dead hand" feature in the Rights Plan that was held to be invalid in *Toll Brothers*,[29] will impermissibly deprive any newly elected board of both its statutory authority to manage the corporation under 8 Del. C. §141(a) and its concomitant fiduciary duty pursuant to that statutory mandate. We agree.

---

29. *Carmody v. Toll Brothers, Inc.*, Del. Ch., C.A. No. 15983, Jacobs, V.C. 1998 WL 418896 (July 24, 1998) ("*Toll Brothers*"). . . .

Our analysis of the Delayed Redemption Provision in the Quickturn Rights Plan is guided by the prior precedents of this Court with regard to a board of directors authority to adopt a Rights Plan or "poison pill." In *Moran*, this Court held that the "inherent powers of the Board conferred by 8 Del. C. §141(a) concerning the management of the corporation's 'business and affairs' provides the Board additional authority upon which to enact the Rights Plan." Consequently, this Court upheld the adoption of the Rights Plan in *Moran* as a legitimate exercise of business judgment by the board of directors. In doing so, however, this Court also held "the rights plan is not absolute":

> When the Household Board of Directors is faced with a tender offer and a request to redeem the Rights [Plan], they will not be able to arbitrarily reject the offer. They will be held to the same fiduciary standards any other board of directors would be held to in deciding to adopt a defensive mechanism, the same standards as they were held to in originally approving the Rights Plan.[33]

In *Moran*, this Court held that the "ultimate response to an actual takeover bid must be judged by the Directors' actions at the time and nothing we say relieves them of their fundamental duties to the corporation and its shareholders." Consequently, we concluded that the use of the Rights Plan would be evaluated when and if the issue arises.

One of the most basic tenets of Delaware corporate law is that the board of directors has the ultimate responsibility for managing the business and affairs of a corporation. Section 141(a) requires that any limitation on the board's authority be set out in the certificate of incorporation. The Quickturn certificate of incorporation contains no provision purporting to limit the authority of the board in any way. The Delayed Redemption Provision, however, would prevent a newly elected board of directors from *completely* discharging its fundamental management duties to the corporation and its stockholders for six months. While the Delayed Redemption Provision limits the board of directors' authority in only one respect, the suspension of the Rights Plan, it nonetheless restricts the board's power in an area of fundamental importance to the shareholders—negotiating a possible sale of the corporation. Therefore, we hold that the Delayed Redemption Provision is invalid under Section 141(a), which confers upon any newly elected board of directors *full* power to manage and direct the business and affairs of a Delaware corporation.

In discharging the statutory mandate of Section 141(a), the directors have a fiduciary duty to the corporation and its shareholders. This unremitting obligation extends equally to board conduct in a contest for corporate control. The Delayed Redemption Provision prevents a newly elected board of directors from completely discharging its fiduciary duties to protect fully the interests of Quickturn and its stockholders.

This Court has recently observed that "although the fiduciary duty of a Delaware director is unremitting, the exact course of conduct that must be charted to properly discharge that responsibility will change in' the specific

---

33. [*Moran v. Household Intl., Inc.*, 500 A.2d 1346, 1354 (Del. 1985)]; *see also Unocal Corp. v. Mesa Petroleum Co.*, 493 A.2d at 954-55, 958.

context of the action the director is taking with regard to either the corporation or its shareholders."[42] This Court has held "[t]o the extent that a contract, or a provision thereof, purports to require a board to act *or not act* in such a fashion as to limit the exercise of fiduciary duties, it is invalid and unenforceable."[43] The Delayed Redemption Provision "tends to limit in a substantial way the freedom of [newly elected] directors' decisions on matters of management policy."[44] Therefore, "it violates the duty of each [newly elected] director to exercise his own best judgment on matters coming before the board."[45]

In this case, the Quickturn board was confronted by a determined bidder that sought to acquire the company at a price the Quickturn board concluded was inadequate. Such situations are common in corporate takeover efforts. In *Revlon*, this Court held that no defensive measure can be sustained when it represents a breach of the directors' fiduciary duty. *A fortiori*, no defensive measure can be sustained which would require a new board of directors to breach its fiduciary duty. In that regard, we note Mentor has properly acknowledged that in the event its slate of directors is elected, those newly elected directors will be required to discharge their unremitting fiduciary duty to manage the corporation for the benefit of Quickturn and its stockholders.

CONCLUSION

The Delayed Redemption Provision would prevent a new Quickturn board of directors from managing the corporation by redeeming the Rights Plan to facilitate a transaction that would serve the stockholders' best interests, even under circumstances where the board would be required to do so because of its fiduciary duty to the Quickturn stockholders. Because the Delayed Redemption Provision impermissibly circumscribes the board's statutory power under Section 141 (a) and the directors' ability to fulfill their concomitant fiduciary duties, we hold that the Delayed Redemption Provision is invalid. On that alternative basis, the judgment of the Court of Chancery is AFFIRMED.

NOTES

1. What Is an Advance Notice Bylaw Provision?   In its opinion in *Quickturn*, the Delaware Supreme Court addressed the validity of an "advance notice bylaw" provision, which is a type of "shark repellant" that a company includes in "its bylaws or its articles of incorporation that is intended to deter a bidder's interest in that company as a target for a takeover [bid] . . ." *Unitrin, supra* at 1377 n. 19. "Advance notice bylaws provide public companies with notice of shareholder director nominations or proposals in advance of an annual

---

42. *Malone v. Brincat*, Del. Supr., 722 A.2d 5 (1998).
43. *See Paramount Communications, Inc. v. QVC Network, Inc.*, 637 A.2d at 51 (*emphasis added*). . . .
44. *Abercrombie v. Davies*, Del. Ch., 123 A.2d 893, 899 (1956), *rev'd on other grounds*, Del. Supr., 130 A.2d 338 (1957).
45. *Id.*

or special meeting, as well as establish a deadline for a shareholder to submit such nominations or proposals to public companies. By obtaining information regarding shareholder proponents [such as activist investors] and shareholder director nominations or proposals in advance of a shareholders meeting, boards can consider and appropriately respond to shareholder nominations and proposals." Kevin Douglas, et al., Bass, Berry & Sims PLC *Revisiting Advance Notice Bylaw Provisions and Proxy Access*, August 12, 2019, *available at:* https://www .bassberrysecuritieslawexchange.com/advance-notice-provisions-proxy-access/#:~:text=Advance%20notice%20bylaws%20provide%20public,or%20 proposals%20to%20public%20companies. Although the focus on advance notice bylaws as a useful shark repellent seems to have waned in recent years, nonetheless these provisions continue to be viewed as "an important aspect of a public company's preparedness for shareholder activism." *Id.*

2. *Recent Poison Pill Cases.*   In 2010, the Delaware Supreme Court decided an important (and well-known) case involving the enforceability of poison pills, *Versata Enterprises, Inc., v. Selectica, Inc.*, 5 A.3d 586 (Del. 2010), involving the use of a poison pill to protect the company's net operating losses (NOLs). Later that same year, the Delaware Chancery Court decided another important case regarding the enforceability of a poison pill. *See Yucaipa American Alliance Fund II, L.P. v. Riggo, et al.*, 1 A.3d 310 (Del. Ch. 2010) (involving the validity of a poison pill adopted as a defense to a hostile takeover bid). These two recent cases (and their implications) are described in the excerpt below.

> **Louis Lehot, Kevin Rooney, John Tishler,
> and Camille Formosa**
> **The Return of the Poison Pill: Lessons Learned From
> the *Selectica* and *Barnes & Noble* Cases,**
> **24 Insights 27 (December 2010)**

RECENT DEVELOPMENTS . . .

SELECTICA

In December 2008, Versata Enterprises, Inc. intentionally triggered an NOL poison pill adopted by Selectica, Inc., marking the first intentional triggering of a modern poison pill. In response to share accumulations earlier in 2008 by Versata, a direct competitor of Selectica, Selectica's board reduced the trigger threshold of its existing rights plan from 15 percent to 4.99 percent. Stockholders owning more than five percent at the time of this action, including Versata, were grandfathered in under the poison pill, subject to a trigger threshold of half a percent above their then-current ownership. Versata's intentional triggering of the poison pill in turn triggered a 10-day period during which the board of directors could negotiate and, if beneficial, waive the triggering acquisition, thereby avoiding the dilutive effects of the pill. Selectica declined to grant a waiver and instead decided to exercise the exchange feature in its poison pill, thereby avoiding potential threats to use of its NOLs presented by a flip-in. Selectica then instated a new poison pill, again with a 4.99 percent threshold. In the ensuing litigation, the Delaware Chancery Court determined that the poison pill was not preclusive, that the Selectica directors had showed that they had reasonable grounds for believing that a danger to corporate policy and effectiveness existed because of another person's stock ownership and had acted reasonably in relation to the threat posed by Versata. The court upheld each of the initial poison pill, the adopted replacement poison pill and the exchange. The Delaware Supreme Court affirmed the lower court's decision on October 4, 2010.

BARNES & NOBLE

In November of 2009, following failed discussions regarding company strategy and policies between investor Ronald Burkle and Barnes & Noble's founder and largest stockholder, Leonard Riggio, Yucaipa, and several other investment funds affiliated with Burkle increased their 8 percent ownership stock in Barnes & Noble to 17.8 percent and indicated in a Schedule 13D filing the possibility of Yucaipa acquiring Barnes & Noble. In response to the rapid accumulation of shares by Yucaipa, the board of directors of Barnes & Noble adopted a stockholder rights plan. The rights plan had a 20 percent trigger, but grandfathered Riggio's significantly higher stake from triggering the plan, which, together with family members, equaled almost 30 percent. In the ensuing lawsuit brought by Burkle, the Delaware Court of Chancery applied the *Unocal* standard and upheld the Barnes & Noble rights plan as a reasonable and proportionate response to the threat posed by Yucaipa. On November 17, 2010, the stockholders of Barnes & Noble overwhelmingly approved the poison pill at the 20 percent threshold.

[THE IMPLICATIONS OF *SELECTICA* AND *BARNES & NOBLE*]

BOARD DECISION-MAKING PROCESS

In *Selectica* and *Barnes & Noble*, the courts painstakingly reviewed the board's decision-making processes that resulted in the determination that an identifiable threat to a legitimate corporate purpose warranted the adoption of a poison pill, including the involvement of independent and interested directors in the decision-making process and the board's reliance on outside experts. Despite ultimately upholding the decisions of the Barnes & Noble board, the court faulted the board and its advisors for failing to exclude Riggio from the boardroom when discussing Riggio's motivations and interests and for the selection of outside experts to advise the board (certain of the advisors selected had previously advised Riggio on business and personal matters). The court in *Selectica* affirmed the board's determination that the NOLs had potential value, despite noted skepticism, because the board reasonably relied on outside experts to analyze the potential value of the NOLs and the potential threat that an ownership change presented to the NOL asset. These decisions reiterate the importance of independent directors, outside advisors that are free of relationships with interested directors and thorough documentation of the board process.

TRIGGERING THRESHOLD

In determining the reasonableness of the triggering threshold, courts have generally focused on whether it is so low that it would preclude a holder from undertaking and winning a proxy contest. Traditionally, the triggering threshold for poison pills has hovered between 10 percent and 20 percent. Delaware's anti-takeover statute has a 15 percent threshold percentage and, . . . ISS policy has a minimum 20 percent trigger under its guidelines. Allowing accumulations up to a larger trigger make it easier for a bidder to win a proxy contest.

The Selectica pill's triggering threshold was 4.99 percent due to Internal Revenue Service regulations with respect to NOLs, which provide that if a five percent stockholder increases its ownership by more than 50 percent, an "ownership change" is triggered and a company's ability to use its NOLs following an "ownership change" is limited. The *Selectica* court examined evidence from proxy solicitors and others as to the feasibility of running a proxy contest against a company of Selectica's size from a 4.99 percent ownership position. The court found that there was evidence that bidders had succeeded in winning proxy contests from that position, and hence the threshold was not preclusive. The court made this determination without reviewing whether running a proxy contest was possible in Versata's particular circumstances. Despite a range of acceptable thresholds from 10 percent to 20 percent, a threshold as low as 4.99 percent will be upheld, provided it meets the *Unocal/Unitrin* test. The new 2011 ISS guidelines regarding NOL poison pills acknowledge the general five percent threshold for NOL poison pills.

In the *Barnes & Noble* case the threshold was 20 percent—in line with ISS guidelines. However, Burkle initially argued that the 20 percent trigger was preclusive, since Riggio, who was adverse to Burkle, already held 30 percent of the outstanding shares. The court found that, due to the make-up of the stockholders other than Riggio and the activity of proxy advisory firms, Burkle's fund Yucaipa could win a proxy contest (as it turned out, Burkle lost the proxy contest in September 2010).

These cases demonstrate the importance of the board keeping a record to show that the poison pill will not prevent someone from winning a proxy contest. . . .

DELAYED TRIGGER

Many poison pills include a window of time, commonly 10 days, after a stockholder purchases above the triggering threshold and before the activation of the rights occurs. The window gives the board fiduciary flexibility to ensure the pill wasn't triggered inadvertently, or to negotiate with the triggering stockholder and potentially amend the rights plan or redeem the rights. However, the existence of a delay in triggering can create pressure for the board to amend the plan rather than allow the draconian result of allowing the rights to activate. Boards should carefully weigh the benefits and detriments of the delayed trigger for a particular company's situation.

EXCHANGE FEATURE

As discussed above, poison pills typically permit the board to exchange the rights for common stock equivalents upon a flip-in event. The exchange is most commonly one share of common stock or common stock equivalent for each right, but some poison pills provide for an exchange that equates to a cashless exercise of the flip-in option. That is, each holder of the right receives the net number of shares it would receive if it sold shares to pay the exercise price. For Selectica, the dilution that would have been caused by the flip-in posed potential threats to the company's use of its NOLs, which was the very corporate asset the poison pill was designed to protect. To avoid the threat, Selectica chose to use the exchange feature in its poison pill, exchanging each right for one share of common stock. The exchange feature may avoid the need to register under the Securities Act of 1933 the sale of securities upon exercise of the rights and it may also avoid a situation where receipt of the exercise price would put unwanted cash on the company's balance sheet.

CONCLUSION

[In today's world of turbulent economic conditions,] unsolicited deal activity [will often] cause many companies to reconsider the [usefulness of a] poison pill. Whether a company is renewing or restoring a poison pill or putting one in place for the first time, it can expect that:

- a poison pill adopted in good faith by independent directors advised by outside experts with the intention of maximizing shareholder value is a valid defensive measure;
- Delaware courts will review carefully the board's decision making and record keeping processes in the context of a challenged poison pill;
- poison pills will be an available tool for protecting a company's NOLs; and
- design features will have a significant effect on the poison pill's effectiveness at achieving its desired goals.

NOTE

In the wake of the global economic crisis brought on by the coronavirus pandemic in early 2020, the poison pill (including the NOL pill) is enjoying something of a revival in popularity. As observed by a pair of experienced M&A lawyers,

[As of this writing in March 2020, the] financial markets have experienced unprecedented volatility as heightened concerns about the ongoing coronavirus (COVID-19) pandemic take hold and its impact on the global macroeconomic landscape remains unknown. From its record high, the S&P 500 has plunged as much as 30%, and companies in sectors disproportionately impacted by

COVID-19 . . . have experienced stock price declines of more than 70% from their 52-week highs.

As companies continue to see their market capitalizations adversely impacted by the volatility in the financial markets—perhaps to a point where their market valuation does not reflect the company's intrinsic value and ability to persevere through the current crisis—some may want to consider adopting a "poison pill" (more technically known as a shareholder rights plan), whether it be a traditional takeover-defense poison pill or a net operating loss (NOL) poison pill intended to protect and preserve NOLs from being limited by Section 382 of the Internal Revenue Code (IRC).

Even those companies that may not be at the point where they believe the benefits of adopting a poison pill outweigh some of the countervailing considerations, this may be the time to have a "shelf" poison pill and related documents prepared and internally vetted so a poison pill can be adopted and publicly announced on very short notice.

Keith E. Gottfried and Shawn M. Donahue, *As COVID-19 Disrupts Financial Markets, Is It Time to Consider a Poison Pill?*, Morgan, Lewis & Bockius LLP, March 18, 2020, *available at:* https://www.morganlewis.com/pubs/as-covid-19-disrupts-financial-markets-is-it-time-to-consider-a-poison-pill; *see also* Matthew J. Gardella, et al., Mintz, Levin, Cohn, Ferris, Glovsky, and Popeo, P.C., *COVID-19 and Poison Pills: The Right Prescription?*, April 30, 2020, *available at:* https://www.mintz.com/insights-center/viewpoints/2871/2020-04-30-covid-19-and-poison-pills-right-prescription ("The pace of adoption of new Rights Plans has continued at an elevated level in April 2020. Further, while there is no way to estimate how many companies instead put 'pills on the shelf' during this period, there is strong anecdotal evidence that many more companies took that action, so overall defensive activity in the last two months has been high and may continue to be for some time.").

E.   The Board's Decision to Sell the Company: The Duty to "Auction" the Firm

Revlon, Inc. v. MacAndrews & Forbes Holdings, Inc.
506 A.2d 173 (Del. 1985)

MOORE, Justice:

In this battle for corporate control of Revlon, Inc. (Revlon), the Court of Chancery enjoined certain transactions designed to thwart the efforts of Pantry Pride, Inc. (Pantry Pride) to acquire Revlon.[1] The defendants are Revlon, its

---

1. The nominal plaintiff, MacAndrews & Forbes Holdings, Inc., is the controlling stockholder of Pantry Pride. For all practical purposes their interests in this litigation are virtually identical, and we hereafter will refer to Pantry Pride as the plaintiff.

board of directors, and Forstmann Little & Co. and the latter's affiliated limited partnership (collectively, Forstmann). The injunction barred consummation of an option granted Forstmann to purchase certain Revlon assets (the lock-up option), a promise by Revlon to deal exclusively with Forstmann in the face of a takeover (the no-shop provision), and the payment of a $25 million cancellation fee to Forstmann if the transaction was aborted. The Court of Chancery found that the Revlon directors had breached their duty of care by entering into the foregoing transactions and effectively ending an active auction for the company. The trial court ruled that such arrangements are not illegal *per se* under Delaware law, but that their use under the circumstances here was impermissible. We agree. *See MacAndrews & Forbes Holdings, Inc. v. Revlon, Inc.*, Del. Ch., 501 A.2d 1239 (1985). Thus, we granted this expedited interlocutory appeal to consider for the first time the validity of such defensive measures in the face of an active bidding contest for corporate control. Additionally, we address for the first time the extent to which a corporation may consider the impact of a takeover threat on constituencies other than shareholders. *See Unocal Corp. v. Mesa Petroleum Co.*, Del. Supr., 493 A.2d 946, 955 (1985).

In our view, lock-ups and related agreements are permitted under Delaware law where their adoption is untainted by director interest or other breaches of fiduciary duty. The actions taken by the Revlon directors, however, did not meet this standard. Moreover, while concern for various corporate constituencies is proper when addressing a takeover threat, that principle is limited by the requirement that there be some rationally related benefit accruing to the stockholders. We find no such benefit here.

Thus, under all the circumstances we must agree with the Court of Chancery that the enjoined Revlon defensive measures were inconsistent with the directors' duties to the stockholders. Accordingly, we affirm.

I.

The somewhat complex maneuvers of the parties necessitate a rather detailed examination of the facts. The prelude to this controversy began in June 1985, when Ronald O. Perelman, chairman of the board and chief executive officer of Pantry Pride, met with his counterpart at Revlon, Michel C. Bergerac, to discuss a friendly acquisition of Revlon by Pantry Pride. Perelman suggested a price in the range of $40-50 per share, but the meeting ended with Bergerac dismissing those figures as considerably below Revlon's intrinsic value. All subsequent Pantry Pride overtures were rebuffed, perhaps in part based on Mr. Bergerac's strong personal antipathy to Mr. Perelman.

Thus, on August 14, Pantry Pride's board authorized Perelman to acquire Revlon, either through negotiation in the $42-$43 per share range, or by making a hostile tender offer at $45. Perelman then met with Bergerac and outlined Pantry Pride's alternate approaches. Bergerac remained adamantly opposed to such schemes and conditioned any further discussions of the matter on Pantry Pride executing a standstill agreement prohibiting it from acquiring Revlon without the latter's prior approval.

On August 19, the Revlon board met specially to consider the impending threat of a hostile bid by Pantry Pride.[3] At the meeting, Lazard Freres, Revlon's investment banker, advised the directors that $45 per share was a grossly inadequate price for the company. Felix Rohatyn and William Loomis of Lazard Freres explained to the board that Pantry Pride's financial strategy for acquiring Revlon would be through "junk bond" financing followed by a break-up of Revlon and the disposition of its assets. With proper timing, according to the experts, such transactions could produce a return to Pantry Pride of $60 to $70 per share, while a sale of the company as a whole would be in the "mid 50" dollar range. Martin Lipton, special counsel for Revlon, recommended two defensive measures: first, that the company repurchase up to 5 million of its nearly 30 million outstanding shares; and second, that it adopt a Note Purchase Rights Plan. Under this plan, each Revlon shareholder would receive as a dividend one Note Purchase Right (the Rights) for each share of common stock, with the Rights entitling the holder to exchange one common share for a $65 principal Revlon note at 12% interest with a one-year maturity. The Rights would become effective whenever anyone acquired beneficial ownership of 20% or more of Revlon's shares, unless the purchaser acquired all the company's stock for cash at $65 or more per share. In addition, the Rights would not be available to the acquiror, and prior to the 20% triggering event the Revlon board could redeem the rights for 10 cents each. Both proposals were unanimously adopted.

Pantry Pride made its first hostile move on August 23 with a cash tender offer for any and all shares of Revlon at $47.50 per common share and $26.67 per preferred share, subject to (1) Pantry Pride's obtaining financing for the purchase, and (2) the Rights being redeemed, rescinded or voided.

The Revlon board met again on August 26. The directors advised the stockholders to reject the offer. Further defensive measures also were planned. On August 29, Revlon commenced its own offer for up to 10 million shares, exchanging for each share of common stock tendered one Senior Subordinated Note (the Notes) of $47.50 principal at 11.75% interest, due 1995, and one-tenth of a share of $9.00 Cumulative Convertible Exchangeable Preferred Stock valued at $100 per share. Lazard Freres opined that the notes would trade at their face value on a fully distributed basis.[4] Revlon stockholders tendered 87 percent of the outstanding shares (approximately 33 million), and the company accepted the full 10 million shares on a pro rata basis. The new Notes contained covenants which limited Revlon's ability to incur additional debt, sell assets, or pay dividends unless otherwise approved by the "independent" (non-management) members of the board.

---

3. There were 14 directors on the Revlon board. Six of them held senior management positions with the company, and two others held significant blocks of its stock. Four of the remaining six directors were associated at some point with entities that had various business relationships with Revlon. On the basis of this limited record, however, we cannot conclude that this board is entitled to certain presumptions that generally attach to the decisions of a board whose majority consists of truly outside independent directors.

4. Like bonds, the Notes actually were issued in denominations of $ 1,000 and integral multiples thereof. A separate certificate was issued in a total principal amount equal to the remaining sum to which a stockholder was entitled. Likewise, in the esoteric parlance of bond dealers, a Note trading at par ($ 1,000) would be quoted on the market at 100.

At this point, both the Rights and the Note covenants stymied Pantry Pride's attempted takeover. The next move came on September 16, when Pantry Pride announced a new tender offer at $42 per share, conditioned upon receiving at least 90% of the outstanding stock. Pantry Pride also indicated that it would consider buying less than 90%, and at an increased price, if Revlon removed the impeding Rights. While this offer was lower on its face than the earlier $47.50 proposal, Revlon's investment banker, Lazard Freres, described the two bids as essentially equal in view of the completed exchange offer.

The Revlon board held a regularly scheduled meeting on September 24. The directors rejected the latest Pantry Pride offer and authorized management to negotiate with other parties interested in acquiring Revlon. Pantry Pride remained determined in its efforts and continued to make cash bids for the company, offering $50 per share on September 27, and raising its bid to $53 on October 1, and then to $56.25 on October 7.

In the meantime, Revlon's negotiations with Forstmann and the investment group Adler & Shaykin had produced results. The Revlon directors met on October 3 to consider Pantry Pride's $53 bid and to examine possible alternatives to the offer. Both Forstmann and Adler & Shaykin made certain proposals to the board. As a result, the directors unanimously agreed to a leveraged buyout by Forstmann. The terms of this accord were as follows: each stockholder would get $56 cash per share; management would purchase stock in the new company by the exercise of their Revlon "golden parachutes";[5] Forstmann would assume Revlon's $475 million debt incurred by the issuance of the Notes; and Revlon would redeem the Rights and waive the Notes covenants for Forstmann or in connection with any other offer superior to Forstmann's. The board did not actually remove the covenants at the October 3 meeting, because Forstmann then lacked a firm commitment on its financing, but accepted the Forstmann capital structure, and indicated that the outside directors would waive the covenants in due course. Part of Forstmann's plan was to sell Revlon's Norcliff Thayer and Reheis divisions to American Home Products for $335 million. Before the merger, Revlon was to sell its cosmetics and fragrance division to Adler & Shaykin for $905 million. These transactions would facilitate the purchase by Forstmann or any other acquiror of Revlon.

When the merger, and thus the waiver of the Notes covenants, was announced, the market value of these securities began to fall. The Notes, which originally traded near par, around 100, dropped to 87.50 by October 8. One director later reported (at the October 12 meeting) a "deluge" of telephone calls from irate noteholders, and on October 10 the Wall Street Journal reported threats of litigation by these creditors.

Pantry Pride countered with a new proposal on October 7, raising its $53 offer to $56.25, subject to nullification of the Rights, a waiver of the Notes covenants, and the election of three Pantry Pride directors to the Revlon board. On October 9, representatives of Pantry Pride, Forstmann and Revlon conferred in an attempt to negotiate the fate of Revlon, but could not reach agreement.

---

5. In the takeover context "golden parachutes" generally are understood to be termination agreements providing substantial bonuses and other benefits for managers and certain directors upon a change in control of a company.

At this meeting Pantry Pride announced that it would engage in fractional bidding and top any Forstmann offer by a slightly higher one. It is also significant that Forstmann, to Pantry Pride's exclusion, had been made privy to certain Revlon financial data. Thus, the parties were not negotiating on equal terms.

Again privately armed with Revlon data, Forstmann met on October 11 with Revlon's special counsel and investment banker. On October 12, Forstmann made a new $57.25 per share offer, based on several conditions.[6] The principal demand was a lock-up option to purchase Revlon's Vision Care and National Health Laboratories divisions for $525 million, some $100-$175 million below the value ascribed to them by Lazard Freres, if another acquiror got 40% of Revlon's shares. Revlon also was required to accept a no-shop provision. The Rights and Notes covenants had to be removed as in the October 3 agreement. There would be a $25 million cancellation fee to be placed in escrow, and released to Forstmann if the new agreement terminated or if another acquiror got more than 19.9% of Revlon's stock. Finally, there would be no participation by Revlon management in the merger. In return, Forstmann agreed to support the par value of the Notes, which had faltered in the market, by an exchange of new notes. Forstmann also demanded immediate acceptance of its offer, or it would be withdrawn. The board unanimously approved Forstmann's proposal because: (1) it was for a higher price than the Pantry Pride bid, (2) it protected the noteholders, and (3) Forstmann's financing was firmly in place.[7] The board further agreed to redeem the rights and waive the covenants on the preferred stock in response to any offer above $57 cash per share. The covenants were waived, contingent upon receipt of an investment banking opinion that the Notes would trade near par value once the offer was consummated.

Pantry Pride, which had initially sought injunctive relief from the Rights plan on August 22, filed an amended complaint on October 14 challenging the lock-up, the cancellation fee, and the exercise of the Rights and the Notes covenants. Pantry Pride also sought a temporary restraining order to prevent Revlon from placing any assets in escrow or transferring them to Forstmann. Moreover, on October 22, Pantry Pride again raised its bid, with a cash offer of $58 per share conditioned upon nullification of the Rights, waiver of the covenants, and an injunction of the Forstmann lock-up.

On October 15, the Court of Chancery prohibited the further transfer of assets, and eight days later enjoined the lock-up, no-shop, and cancellation fee provisions of the agreement. The trial court concluded that the Revlon directors had breached their duty of loyalty by making concessions to Forstmann, out of concern for their liability to the noteholders, rather than maximizing the

---

6. Forstmann's $57.25 offer ostensibly is worth $1 more than Pantry Pride's $56.25 bid. However, the Pantry Pride offer was immediate, while the Forstmann proposal must be discounted for the time value of money because of the delay in approving the merger and consummating the transaction. The exact difference between the two bids was an unsettled point of contention even at oral argument.

7. Actually, at this time about $400 million of Forstmann's funding was still subject to two investment banks using their "best efforts" to organize a syndicate to provide the balance. Pantry Pride's entire financing was not firmly committed at this point either, although Pantry Pride represented in an October 11 letter to Lazard Freres that its investment banker, Drexel Burnham Lambert, was highly confident of its ability to raise the balance of $350 million. Drexel Burnham had a firm commitment for this sum by October 18.

sale price of the company for the stockholders' benefit. *MacAndrews & Forbes Holdings, Inc. v. Revlon, Inc.,* 501 A.2d at 1249-50.

II.

To obtain a preliminary injunction, a plaintiff must demonstrate both a reasonable probability of success on the merits and some irreparable harm which will occur absent the injunction. . . . Additionally, the Court shall balance the conveniences of and possible injuries to the parties.

A

We turn first to Pantry Pride's probability of success on the merits. The ultimate responsibility for managing the business and affairs of a corporation falls on its board of directors. In discharging this function the directors owe fiduciary duties of care and loyalty to the corporation and its shareholders. *Guth v. Loft, Inc.,* 23 Del. Supr. 255, 5 A.2d 503, 510 (1939); *Aronson v. Lewis,* Del. Supr., 473 A.2d 805, 811 (1984). These principles apply with equal force when a board approves a corporate merger pursuant to 8 Del. C. §251(b); *Smith v. Van Gorkom,* Del. Supr., 488 A.2d 858, 873 (1985); and of course they are the bedrock of our law regarding corporate takeover issues. . . . While the business judgment rule may be applicable to the actions of corporate directors responding to takeover threats, the principles upon which it is founded—care, loyalty and independence—must first be satisfied.

If the business judgment rule applies, there is a "presumption that in making a business decision the directors of a corporation acted on an informed basis, in good faith and in the honest belief that the action taken was in the best interests of the company." *Aronson v. Lewis,* 473 A.2d at 812. However, when a board implements anti-takeover measures there arises "the omnipresent specter that a board may be acting primarily in its own interests, rather than those of the corporation and its shareholders. . ." *Unocal Corp. v. Mesa Petroleum Co.,* 493 A.2d at 954. This potential for conflict places upon the directors the burden of proving that they had reasonable grounds for believing there was a danger to corporate policy and effectiveness, a burden satisfied by a showing of good faith and reasonable investigation. In addition, the directors must analyze the nature of the takeover and its effect on the corporation in order to ensure balance—that the responsive action taken is reasonable in relation to the threat posed. *Id.*

B

The first relevant defensive measure adopted by the Revlon board was the Rights Plan, which would be considered a "poison pill" in the current language of corporate takeovers—a plan by which shareholders receive the right to be bought out by the corporation at a substantial premium on the occurrence of a stated triggering event. *See generally Moran v. Household International, Inc.,* Del.

Supr., 500 A.2d 1346 (1985). By 8 Del. C. §§141 and 122(13), the board clearly had the power to adopt the measure. *See Moran v. Household International, Inc.,* 500 A.2d at 1351. Thus, the focus becomes one of reasonableness and purpose.

The Revlon board approved the Rights Plan in the face of an impending hostile takeover bid by Pantry Pride at $45 per share, a price which Revlon reasonably concluded was grossly inadequate. Lazard Freres had so advised the directors, and had also informed them that Pantry Pride was a small, highly leveraged company bent on a "bust-up" takeover by using "junk bond" financing to buy Revlon cheaply, sell the acquired assets to pay the debts incurred, and retain the profit for itself.[12] In adopting the Plan, the board protected the shareholders from a hostile takeover at a price below the company's intrinsic value, while retaining sufficient flexibility to address any proposal deemed to be in the stockholders' best interests.

To that extent the board acted in good faith and upon reasonable investigation. Under the circumstances it cannot be said that the Rights Plan as employed was unreasonable, considering the threat posed. Indeed, the Plan was a factor in causing Pantry Pride to raise its bids from a low of $42 to an eventual high of $58. At the time of its adoption the Rights Plan afforded a measure of protection consistent with the directors' fiduciary duty in facing a takeover threat perceived as detrimental to corporate interests. *Unocal,* 493 A.2d at 954-55. Far from being a "show-stopper," as the plaintiffs had contended in *Moran,* the measure spurred the bidding to new heights, a proper result of its implementation. *See Moran,* 500 A.2d at 1354, 1356-67.

Although we consider adoption of the Plan to have been valid under the circumstances, its continued usefulness was rendered moot by the directors' actions on October 3 and October 12. At the October 3 meeting the board redeemed the Rights conditioned upon consummation of a merger with Forstmann, but further acknowledged that they would also be redeemed to facilitate any more favorable offer. On October 12, the board unanimously passed a resolution redeeming the Rights in connection with any cash proposal of $57.25 or more per share. Because all the pertinent offers eventually equaled or surpassed that amount, the Rights clearly were no longer any impediment in the contest for Revlon. This mooted any question of their propriety under *Moran* or *Unocal.*

C

The second defensive measure adopted by Revlon to thwart a Pantry Pride takeover was the company's own exchange offer for 10 million of its shares. The directors' general broad powers to manage the business and affairs of the corporation are augmented by the specific authority conferred under 8 Del. C. §160(a), permitting the company to deal in its own stock. *Unocal,* 493 A.2d at 953-54. However, when exercising that power in an effort to forestall a hostile

---

12. As we noted in *Moran,* a "bust-up" takeover generally refers to a situation in which one seeks to finance an acquisition by selling off pieces of the acquired company, presumably at a substantial profit. *See Moran,* 500 A.2d at 1349, n. 4.

takeover, the board's actions are strictly held to the fiduciary standards outlined in *Unocal*. These standards require the directors to determine the best interests of the corporation and its stockholders, and impose an enhanced duty to abjure any action that is motivated by considerations other than a good faith concern for such interests. *Unocal*, 493 A.2d at 954-55.

The Revlon directors concluded that Pantry Pride's $47.50 offer was grossly inadequate. In that regard the board acted in good faith, and on an informed basis, with reasonable grounds to believe that there existed a harmful threat to the corporate enterprise. The adoption of a defensive measure, reasonable in relation to the threat posed, was proper and fully accorded with the powers, duties, and responsibilities conferred upon directors under our law. *Unocal*, 493 A.2d at 954.

D

However, when Pantry Pride increased its offer to $50 per share, and then to $53, it became apparent to all that the break-up of the company was inevitable. The Revlon board's authorization permitting management to negotiate a merger or buyout with a third party was a recognition that the company was for sale. The duty of the board had thus changed from the preservation of Revlon as a corporate entity to the maximization of the company's value at a sale for the stockholders' benefit. This significantly altered the board's responsibilities under the *Unocal* standards. It no longer faced threats to corporate policy and effectiveness, or to the stockholders' interests, from a grossly inadequate bid. The whole question of defensive measures became moot. The directors' role changed from defenders of the corporate bastion to auctioneers charged with getting the best price for the stockholders at a sale of the company.

III.

This brings us to the lock-up with Forstmann and its emphasis on shoring up the sagging market value of the Notes in the face of threatened litigation by their holders. Such a focus was inconsistent with the changed concept of the directors' responsibilities at this stage of the developments. The impending waiver of the Notes covenants had caused the value of the Notes to fall, and the board was aware of the noteholders' ire as well as their subsequent threats of suit. The directors thus made support of the Notes an integral part of the company's dealings with Forstmann, even though their primary responsibility at this stage was to the equity owners.

The original threat posed by Pantry Pride—the break-up of the company—had become a reality which even the directors embraced. Selective dealing to fend off a hostile but determined bidder was no longer a proper objective. Instead, obtaining the highest price for the benefit of the stockholders should have been the central theme guiding director action. Thus, the Revlon board could not make the requisite showing of good faith by preferring the noteholders and ignoring its duty of loyalty to the shareholders. The rights of the former already were fixed by contract. The noteholders required no further protection, and when the Revlon board entered into an auction-ending lock-up agreement with Forstmann on the basis of impermissible considerations at the expense of the shareholders, the directors breached their primary duty of loyalty.

The Revlon board argued that it acted in good faith in protecting the note-holders because *Unocal* permits consideration of other corporate constituencies. Although such considerations may be permissible, there are fundamental limitations upon that prerogative. A board may have regard for various constituencies in discharging its responsibilities, provided there are rationally related benefits accruing to the stockholders. *Unocal*, 493 A.2d at 955. However, such concern for non-stockholder interests is inappropriate when an auction among active bidders is in progress, and the object no longer is to protect or maintain the corporate enterprise but to sell it to the highest bidder.

Revlon also contended that by *Gilbert v. El Paso Co.*, Del. Ch., 490 A.2d 1050, 1054-55 (1984), it had contractual and good faith obligations to consider the noteholders. However, any such duties are limited to the principle that one may not interfere with contractual relationships by improper actions. Here, the rights of the noteholders were fixed by agreement, and there is nothing of substance to suggest that any of those terms were violated. The Notes covenants specifically contemplated a waiver to permit sale of the company at a fair price. The Notes were accepted by the holders on that basis, including the risk of an adverse market effect stemming from a waiver. Thus, nothing remained for Revlon to legitimately protect, and no rationally related benefit thereby accrued to the stockholders. Under such circumstances we must conclude that the merger agreement with Forstmann was unreasonable in relation to the threat posed.

A lock-up is not *per se* illegal under Delaware law. . . . Such options can entice other bidders to enter a contest for control of the corporation, creating an auction for the company and maximizing shareholder profit. Current economic conditions in the takeover market are such that a "white knight" like Forstmann might only enter the bidding for the target company if it receives some form of compensation to cover the risks and costs involved. . . . However, while those lock-ups which draw bidders into the battle benefit shareholders, similar measures which end an active auction and foreclose further bidding operate to the shareholders' detriment. . . .

The Forstmann option had a destructive effect on the auction process. Forstmann had already been drawn into the contest on a preferred basis, so the result of the lock-up was not to foster bidding, but to destroy it. The board's stated reasons for approving the transactions were: (1) better financing, (2) noteholder protection, and (3) higher price. As the Court of Chancery found, and we agree, any distinctions between the rival bidders' methods of financing the proposal were nominal at best, and such a consideration has little or no significance in a cash offer for any and all shares. The principal object, contrary to the board's duty of care, appears to have been protection of the noteholders over the shareholders' interests.

While Forstmann's $57.25 offer was objectively higher than Pantry Pride's $56.25 bid, the margin of superiority is less when the Forstmann price is adjusted for the time value of money. In reality, the Revlon board ended the auction in return for very little actual improvement in the final bid. The principal benefit went to the directors, who avoided personal liability to a class of creditors to whom the board owed no further duty under the circumstances. Thus, when a board ends an intense bidding contest on an insubstantial basis, and where a significant by-product of that action is to protect the directors against a perceived threat of personal liability for consequences stemming from the adoption of previous defensive measures, the action cannot withstand the enhanced scrutiny which *Unocal* requires of director conduct. *See Unocal,* 493 A.2d at 954-55.

In addition to the lock-up option, the Court of Chancery enjoined the no-shop provision as part of the attempt to foreclose further bidding by Pantry Pride. *MacAndrews & Forbes Holdings, Inc. v. Revlon, Inc.,* 501 A.2d at 1251. The no-shop provision, like the lock-up option, while not *per se* illegal, is impermissible under the *Unocal* standards when a board's primary duty becomes that of an auctioneer responsible for selling the company to the highest bidder. The agreement to negotiate only with Forstmann ended rather than intensified the board's involvement in the bidding contest.

It is ironic that the parties even considered a no-shop agreement when Revlon had dealt preferentially, and almost exclusively, with Forstmann throughout the contest. After the directors authorized management to negotiate with other parties, Forstmann was given every negotiating advantage that Pantry Pride had been denied: cooperation from management, access to financial data, and the exclusive opportunity to present merger proposals directly to the board of directors. Favoritism for a white knight to the total exclusion of a hostile bidder might be justifiable when the latter's offer adversely affects shareholder interests, but when bidders make relatively similar offers, or dissolution of the company becomes inevitable, the directors cannot fulfill their enhanced *Unocal* duties by playing favorites with the contending factions. Market forces must be allowed to operate freely to bring the target's shareholders the best price available for their equity.[16] Thus, as the trial court ruled, the shareholders' interests necessitated that the board remain free to negotiate in the fulfillment of that duty.

The court below similarly enjoined the payment of the cancellation fee, pending a resolution of the merits, because the fee was part of the overall plan to thwart Pantry Pride's efforts. We find no abuse of discretion in that ruling.

IV.

Having concluded that Pantry Pride has shown a reasonable probability of success on the merits, we address the issue of irreparable harm. The Court of Chancery ruled that unless the lock-up and other aspects of the agreement were enjoined, Pantry Pride's opportunity to bid for Revlon was lost. The court also held that the need for both bidders to compete in the marketplace outweighed any injury to Forstmann. Given the complexity of the proposed transaction

---

16. By this we do not embrace the "passivity" thesis rejected in *Unocal. See* 493 A.2d at 954-55, nn. 8-10. The directors' role remains an active one, changed only in the respect that they are charged with the duty of selling the company at the highest price attainable for the stockholders' benefit.

between Revlon and Forstmann, the obstacles to Pantry Pride obtaining a meaningful legal remedy are immense. We are satisfied that the plaintiff has shown the need for an injunction to protect it from irreparable harm, which need outweighs any harm to the defendants.

V.

In conclusion, the Revlon board was confronted with a situation not uncommon in the current wave of corporate takeovers. A hostile and determined bidder sought the company at a price the board was convinced was inadequate. The initial defensive tactics worked to the benefit of the shareholders, and thus the board was able to sustain its *Unocal* burdens in justifying those measures. However, in granting an asset option lock-up to Forstmann, we must conclude that under all the circumstances the directors allowed considerations other than the maximization of shareholder profit to affect their judgment, and followed a course that ended the auction for Revlon, absent court intervention, to the ultimate detriment of its shareholders. No such defensive measure can be sustained when it represents a breach of the directors' fundamental duty of care. *See Smith v. Van Gorkom*, Del. Supr., 488 A.2d 858, 874 (1985). In that context the board's action is not entitled to the deference accorded it by the business judgment rule. The measures were properly enjoined. The decision of the Court of Chancery, therefore, is AFFIRMED.

QUESTIONS

1. What were the conditions of Pantry Pride's original tender offer?

2. What were the terms of the poison pill (i.e., the Note Purchase Rights Plan) adopted by the Revlon board?

3. In light of the facts involved in *Revlon*, why did Revlon management propose to engage in a self-tender (i.e., issuer repurchase of its shares)? What did management hope to accomplish through this repurchase of Revlon shares?

4. Did the Revlon board satisfy the *Unocal* standard when they decided to adopt the pill? Did the pill work in the way the board intended? In other words, did the pill serve its stated business objective?

5. Why was the board's decision to approve the repurchase of $10 million of its shares protected by the *Unocal* standard? Why was this board decision subject to judicial review under the *Unocal* standard rather than the more protective, traditional business judgment rule standard of review?

6. This decision of the Delaware Supreme Court coined a new expression in the growing lexicon related to M&A defensive strategies: the "*Revlon* mode," or as it sometimes is referred to, the "auction mode." When did the company (Revlon) enter the auction mode? What is the board's responsibility once the company enters the *Revlon* mode? Once the company enters the

Revlon mode, is the board's responsibility (as described by the *Revlon* decision) consistent with the Delaware court's steadfast refusal to adopt the passivity theory?

7. What is a "no-shop" clause?

8. What is a "crown jewel lock-up" option? Why did the granting of this option end up working as a "showstopper" — that is to say, operate to end the competitive bidding process in *Revlon*?

9. What is "change of control" compensation (aka "golden parachutes")? (*Hint*: Refer to footnote 5 of the *Revlon* opinion.) What are the arguments in favor of these executive compensation packages that take effect on a change of control of Target Co.? Who might oppose this form of executive compensation and why?

10. According to *Revlon*, are all lock-up options *per se* invalid? If not, then under what circumstances can Target's board of directors grant a valid and enforceable lock-up option?

11. As a public policy matter, what are the competing interests to be balanced in deciding whether to invalidate or enforce a lock-up option?

12. Who should decide whether a particular lock-up option is valid?

13. According to *Revlon*, what is the relevance of the interests of "other constituencies" in deciding how Target's board should respond to an unsolicited takeover bid?

14. What is the nature of the Delaware Supreme Court's public policy concern regarding the "preclusive effect" of granting a "lock-up" option to a "white knight" Bidder?

15. What was the Revlon board's stated reason(s) for approving the revised Forstman LBO at its meeting on October 12? In invalidating this decision of the Revlon board, is the Delaware Supreme Court substituting its business judgment for that of the Revlon board?

NOTES

1. What Qualifies as Appropriate Auction Procedures?   The holding in *Revlon* makes clear that the fiduciary obligations of the board of directors of Target Co. are especially significant when the company is for sale. In those cases where management decides to put the company up for sale (to put the company "on the auction block," so to speak), *Revlon* requires that Target's board of directors must take reasonable steps to maximize shareholder value, and further, must take care to place the interests of the company and all of its stockholders ahead of (what may often be) the divergent personal interests of the directors and/or senior executive officers. Subsequent Delaware cases also make clear that there is no definitive set of procedures — "no single blueprint" — that the board is required to follow in order to demonstrate that Target's board has fulfilled its duties under *Revlon*. Thus, *Revlon* "does not require, for example, that before every corporate merger agreement can be validly entered into, the constituent corporations must be 'shopped' or, more radically, an auction process undertaken, even though the merger may be regarded as a sale of the company." *City Capital Associates v. Interco, Inc.*, 551 A.2d 787, 802 (Del. Ch. 1988). Rather, post-*Revlon* case law reflects that directors' duties in the context of the sale of Target are very fact specific, and further reflects that the board has fairly broad latitude to fashion the direction and structure of the sale ("auction") process.

Although Delaware courts confer broad discretion on the board, the courts also make clear that the board of directors cannot enter into a definitive merger agreement without obtaining information about other potential transactions. "There must be a reasonable basis for the board . . . to conclude that the transaction involved is in the best interests of the shareholders. This involves having information about possible alternatives. The essence of rational choice is an assessment of costs and benefits and the consideration of alternatives." *Id.* Several recent cases underscore that Target's board of directors (and their legal and financial advisors) must take care that the board's decisions in connection with the sale of the company are custom-tailored to the factual setting of Target's particular situation, which is vitally important in light of the willingness of the Delaware courts to scrutinize the sale process carefully to determine compliance with the board's duties under *Revlon. See, e.g., In re Toys "R" Us, Inc. Shareholder Litigation*, 877 A.2d 975 (Del. Ch. 2005); *In re Netsmart Technologies, Inc. Shareholder Litigation*, 924 A.2d 171 (Del. Ch. 2007); *In re Lear Corporation Shareholder Litigation*, 926 A.2d 94 (Del. Ch. 2007); and *In re Topps Company Shareholders Litigation*, 926 A. 2d 58 (Del. Ch. 2007). We will examine one of these cases (*Topps*) in more detail later in this section, as part of our discussion of the validity of various types of deal protection measures under Delaware law.

2. What Are Lock-Up Options?   The court in *Revlon* referred to the use of *lock-up options*. What is a "lock-up option"?

> When confronted by two or more opposing [i.e., competing] bids for control, target management sometimes enters into an arrangement with one of the bidders that has the effect of conferring on that bidder a strategic advantage in the contest for control vis-a-vis the other bidders. These arrangements can take several forms, such as an option by the preferred bidder to acquire significant target assets at a favorable price (called a "lock-up option"), an agreement not to seek other bidders (called a "no shop clause"), the payment of a significant fee if that bidder's offer does not result in the bidder obtaining control (called a "termination fee," "hello fee," or "goodbye fee"), . . .

James D. Cox and Thomas Lee Hazen, CORPORATIONS §23.07 at 661 (2nd ed. 2003). We will explore the use of lock-up options, and the validity of this and other forms of deal protection measures, as part of our discussion of the fiduciary duty cases in the next section of this chapter.

3. Use of "Termination" Fees.   In public company deals, similar to the provisions found in an agreement for the acquisition of a private company, the parties' agreement will typically provide that the deal will terminate if the Target shareholders vote it down, if Bidder shareholders vote it down (in those cases where Bidder share-holders get the right to vote on the deal), if a nonappealable order or injunction is entered prohibiting the consummation of the transaction, or if there are breaches of certain representations and warranties or, alternatively, the occurrence of a "material adverse change." The occurrence of one of these events (i.e., conditions to closing) will typically trigger payment of a termination (or "break-up") fee (usually in cash) in the amount specified in the agreement.

4. Use of "Break-up" Fees.   In the context of an acquisition of a publicly traded Target Co., the parties' agreement will usually provide for payment of a break-up fee that is triggered in the event that Target jilts Bidder Co., usually in favor of some other acquiror. Bidder typically will insist on a break-up fee as part of the parties' definitive agreement for the acquisition of a publicly held Target out of concern that Bidder may otherwise turn out to be a stalking horse. In other words, Bidder is concerned that when its proposal to acquire Target is publicly announced, some other third-party bidder will come forward offer-ing Target and its shareholders a better offer. In this case, Bidder wants to be compensated for its expenses and lost opportunity in the event that this kind of "topping bid" comes along (i.e., a third party's superior offer is often called a "topping bid"). In negotiating the terms of a break-up fee to be paid in the event that Target walks away from the deal with Bidder, there are several issues that must be addressed, most important of which are:

   a. What triggers a break-up fee?
   b. How large can the break-up fee be?
   c. When in the deal process will the break-up fee become payable?

Break-up fees can be used in connection with any of the different methods for structuring an acquisition (mergers, direct or triangular, as well as two-step acquisitions involving a front-end tender offer followed by a back-end merger). How these terms get fixed will vary from deal to deal, but in the end, the Target board's discretion in negotiating these terms is limited by its fiduciary duty obli-gations to Target and its shareholders. The manner in which fiduciary duty law constrains management's discretion in this important area is examined in the materials later in this chapter regarding the use of "deal protection devices," such as termination fees and break-up fees.

5. Use of "No-Shop" Clauses.   Under the terms of a *no-shop* provision, the board of Target promises Bidder that to the extent that Target is currently engaged in ongoing discussions with a competing third-party bidder, any fur-ther discussions with this third party will cease as soon as an agreement with Bidder is signed. In addition, a no-shop clause will typically provide that Target's board will not do anything to initiate discussions in the future with a competing bidder, nor will Target do anything to assist (or facilitate) another bidder in proposing a competing transaction. Of course, Bidder and Target will usually engage in extensive negotiations as to what qualifies as a "competing transac-tion." For example, will a proposed sale of assets trigger the no-shop provision, or will Target's board be allowed to proceed with the sale without violating the terms of the no-shop clause?

From Bidder's perspective, the goal of the no-shop provision is not only to prevent Target from sharing information with another prospective bidder, but also to eliminate the ability of Target's board to extend any assistance to a third party in an effort to encourage or facilitate a competing offer. Of course, what qualifies as "facilitation" or "encouragement" will also be heavily negotiated by the parties. Bidder's objective in these negotiations usually is to create as many obstacles as possible in order to minimize the likelihood that Target will receive a competing offer that will jeopardize Bidder's ability to close on its proposed transaction with Target. At the same time, Target's board is under considerable pressure in these negotiations with Bidder over the terms of a no-shop clause to reserve for itself enough flexibility so that Target's board can fulfill its fiduciary obligations to Target shareholders. If the terms of the no-shop clause (or other form of deal protection device) are so draconian as to eliminate (or unreasonably limit) the board's freedom to take those actions necessary to fulfill the fiduciary duty obligations that they owe to Target Co. shareholders, then Bidder runs the risk that the deal protection device will be declared invalid and therefore unenforceable on the grounds that the provision violates the board's fiduciary duties. As a result, there is an inherent tension in negotiating the terms of any deal protection measure, including a no-shop clause.

6. Use of Golden Parachutes. In footnote 5 of its *Revlon* opinion, the Delaware Supreme Court refers to the "golden parachute" agreements that were in place for certain Revlon executives; these arrangements may also be referred to (somewhat less pejoratively) as "management retention agreements," "severance agreements," "change of control agreements," or occasionally, "evergreen employment agreements." Generally speaking, this type of agreement involves an employment contract between a company and one of its executives that calls for the payment of benefits (in often a quite generous amount) if there is a change in control (i.e., ownership) of the company (in what is known as a "single trigger"); or alternatively, such payment may be required if there is a change of control *and* the executive's continued employment is either actually or "constructively" terminated (in what is known as a "double trigger"). "Constructive termination" is customarily a defined term in the employment contract that, in its typical form, allows the executive to resign following a change in the control of the company that results in the executive being demoted, relocated, or experiencing other changes in the terms of his employment that the executive negotiated as part of his employment contract—such changes being viewed as an attempt to force the executive out. It is important to bear in mind that these payments are to be made to the executive only *after* an event constituting a change in control of the company. As such, these compensation arrangements have the effect of keeping the executive in office until the change of control event occurs, all of which has led some observers to refer to these arrangements as management retention contracts. In the words of one leading M&A lawyer, golden parachute agreements generally do not operate as "a takeover defense because they do not cost the buyer enough to be a significant economic deterrent. In fact, they may be an important factor in helping to mitigate the natural inclination [of the company's managers] to resist" a hostile takeover effort by an unsolicited suitor. *See* David A. Katz, Wachtell, Lipton, Rosen, & Katz, *Glossary of M&A Terms*, 15TH ANNUAL NATIONAL INSTITUTE ON NEGOTIATING BUSINESS

ACQUISITIONS, Nov. 2010 at 24. *Query:* In what way do these executive compensation plans work "to mitigate [managers'] natural inclination to resist" hostile bids? Is there any advantage to the company by including change of control provisions in their contracts with senior executives?

Notwithstanding the suggested benefits that golden parachutes may provide to Target Co. in the event of an unsolicited bid, by the mid-1980s, there was growing criticism of what many perceived to be the quite generous (even lavish) payments that were paid to a handful of Target's senior executives in the event of a change of control. The large size of these headline-grabbing golden parachute payments angered many and eventually led Congress to adopt Section 280G of the Internal Revenue Code of 1986 in an effort to discourage use of golden parachutes. In a rather complex set of provisions, Congress sought to impose punitive treatment on "excess parachute payments," which are defined to be payments in excess of three years of compensation for an executive. In general, the company will lose the deduction for the amount of "excess parachute payments" and, in addition, the employee will be subject to a 20 percent excise tax on receipt of such payments.

Another more recent development that may also have an impact on the use of golden parachutes is the executive pay reforms adopted by Congress as part of the Dodd-Frank Act. You will recall from the materials in Chapter 1 discussing the provisions of the Dodd-Frank Act (*see supra,* pp. 52-53), that Congress mandated a shareholder vote with respect to golden parachute payments in a change of control transaction. And, again, in Chapter 2 (at p. 167), we saw that DirecTV was required by the Dodd-Frank Act (as part of the company's proxy solicitation materials,) to obtain shareholder approval of the compensation to be paid to the company's senior executives as part of AT&T's proposed acquisition of DirecTV. More specifically, Dodd-Frank (and the SEC rules implementing these provisions of the Dodd-Frank Act) mandated an advisory vote of DirecTV's shareholders with respect to any severance payments (i.e., golden parachute compensation) that would be triggered by the acquisition and which payment had not previously been approved by an appropriate "say-on-pay" vote of DirecTV's shareholders. *See* Chapter 4, at p. 290.

City Capital Associates v. Interco, Inc.
551 A.2d 787 (Del. Ch. 1988)

ALLEN, Chancellor.

This case, before the court on an application for a preliminary injunction, involves the question whether the directors of Interco Corporation are breaching their fiduciary duties to the stockholders of that company in failing to now redeem certain stock rights originally distributed as part of a defense against unsolicited attempts to take control of the company. In electing to leave Interco's "poison pill" in effect, the board of Interco seeks to defeat a tender offer for all of the shares of Interco for $74 per share cash, extended by plaintiff Cardinal Acquisition Corporation [which is wholly owned by City Capital Associates (CCA), a Delaware limited partnership]. The $74 offer is for all shares and the offeror expresses an intent to do a back-end merger at the same price promptly if its offer is accepted. Thus, plaintiffs' offer must be regarded as noncoercive.

As an alternative to the current tender offer, the board is endeavoring to implement a major restructuring of Interco that was formulated only recently. The board has grounds to conclude that the alternative restructuring transaction may have a value to shareholders of at least $76 per share. The restructuring does not involve a Company self-tender, a merger or other corporate action requiring shareholder action or approval.

It is significant that the question of the board's responsibility to redeem or not to redeem the stock rights in this instance arises at what I will call the endstage of this takeover contest. That is, the negotiating leverage that a poison pill confers upon this company's board will, it is clear, not be further utilized by the board to increase the options available to shareholders or to improve the terms of those options. Rather, at this stage of this contest, the pill now serves the principal purpose of "protecting the restructuring"—that is, precluding the shareholders from choosing an alternative to the restructuring that the board finds less valuable to shareholders.

Accordingly, this case involves a further judicial effort to pick out the contours of a director's fiduciary duty to the corporation and its shareholders when the board has deployed the recently innovated and powerful antitakeover device of flip-in or flip-over stock rights. That inquiry is, of course, necessarily a highly particularized one.

In *Moran v. Household International, Inc.*, Del. Supr., 500 A.2d 1346 (1985), our Supreme Court acknowledged that a board of directors of a Delaware corporation has legal power to issue corporate securities that serve principally not to raise capital for the firm, but to create a powerful financial disincentive to accumulate shares of the firm's stock . . . In upholding the board's power under Sections 157 and 141 of our corporation law to issue such securities or rights, the court, however, noted that:

> When the Household Board of Directors is faced with a tender offer and a request to redeem rights, they will not be able to arbitrarily reject the offer. They will be held to the same fiduciary standards any other board of directors would be held to in deciding to adopt a defensive mechanism, the same standard they were held to in originally approving the Rights Plan. *See Unocal*, 493 A.2d at 954-55, 958.

Moran v. Household International, Inc., Del. Supr., 500 A.2d at 1354. Thus, the Supreme Court in *Moran* has directed us specifically to its decision in *Unocal Corp. v. Mesa Petroleum Co.*, Del. Supr., 493 A.2d 946 (1985) as supplying the appropriate legal framework for evaluation of the principal question posed by this case.[1]

---

1. In saying that *Unocal* supplies the framework for decision of this aspect of the case, I reject plaintiffs' argument that the board bears a burden to demonstrate the entire fairness of its decision to keep the pill in place while its recapitalization is effectuated. *Ivanhoe Partners v. Newmont Mining Corp.*, Del. Supr., 535 A.2d 1334, 1341 (1987). While the recapitalization does represent a transaction in which the 14 person board (and most intensely, its seven inside members) has an interest—in the sense referred to in *Unocal*—it does not represent a self-dealing transaction in the sense necessary to place upon the board the heavy burden of the intrinsic fairness test. *See Weinberger v. U.O.P., Inc.*, Del. Supr., 457 A.2d 701 (1983); *Sinclair Oil Corp. v. Levien*, Del. Supr., 280 A.2d 717 (1971).

In addition to seeking an order requiring the Interco board to now redeem the Company's outstanding stock rights, plaintiffs seek an order restraining any steps to implement the Company's alternative restructuring transaction.

For the reasons that follow, I hold that the board's determination to leave the stock rights in effect is a defensive step that, in the circumstances of this offer and at this stage of the contest for control of Interco, cannot be justified as reasonable in relationship to a threat to the corporation or its shareholders posed by the offer; that the restructuring itself does represent a reasonable response to the perception that the offering price is "inadequate"; and that the board, in proceeding as it has done, has not breached any duties derivable from the Supreme Court's opinion in *Revlon v. MacAndrews & Forbes Holdings, Inc.,* Del. Supr., 506 A.2d 173 (1986).

I turn first to a description of the general background facts. . . .

I.

INTERCO INCORPORATED

Interco is a diversified Delaware holding company that comprises 21 subsidiary corporations in four major business areas: furniture and home furnishings, footwear, apparel and general retail merchandising. Its principal offices are located in St. Louis, Missouri. The Company's nationally recognized brand names include London Fog raincoats; Ethan Allen, Lane and Broyhill furniture; Converse All Star athletic shoes and Le Tigre and Christian Dior sportswear. . . .

. . . Owing to the lack of integration between its operating divisions, the Company is, in management's opinion, particularly vulnerable to a highly leveraged "bust-up" takeover of the kind that has become prevalent in recent years. To combat this perceived danger, the Company adopted a common stock rights plan, or poison pill, in late 1985, which included a "flip-in" provision.

The board of directors of Interco is comprised of 14 members, seven of whom are officers of the Company or its subsidiaries.

THE RALES BROTHERS' ACCUMULATION OF INTERCO STOCK; THE INTERCO BOARD'S RESPONSE

In May, 1988, Steven and Mitchell Rales began acquiring Interco stock through CCA. The stock had been trading in the low 40's during that period. Alerted to the unusual trading activity taking place in the Company's stock, the Interco board met on July 11, 1988, to consider the implications of that news. At that meeting, the board redeemed the rights issued pursuant to the 1985 rights plan and adopted a new rights plan that contemplated both "flip-in" and "flip-over" rights.

In broad outline, the "flip-in" provision contained in the rights plan adopted on July 11 provides that, if a person reaches a threshold shareholding of 30% of Interco's outstanding common stock, rights will be exercisable entitling each holder of a right to purchase from the Company that number of shares per right as, at the triggering time, have a market value of twice the exercise price of each right.[3] The "flip-over" feature of the rights plan provides that, in the event of a merger of the Company or the acquisition of 50% or more of the Company's assets or earning power, the rights may be exercised to acquire common stock of the acquiring company having a value of twice the exercise price of the right. The exercise price of each right is $160. The redemption price is $.01 per share.

On July 15, 1988, soon after the adoption of the new rights plan, a press release was issued announcing that the Chairman of the Company's board, Mr. Harvey Saligman, intended to recommend a major restructuring of Interco to the board at its next meeting.

On July 27, 1988, the Rales brothers filed a Schedule 13D with [the SEC] disclosing that, as of July 11, they owned, directly or indirectly, 3,140,300 shares, or 8.7% of Interco's common stock. On that day, CCA offered to acquire the Company by merger for a price of $64 per share in cash, conditioned upon the availability of financing. On August 8, before the Interco board had responded to this offer, CCA increased its offering price to $70 per share, still contingent upon receipt of the necessary financing.

At the Interco board's regularly scheduled meeting on August 8, Wasserstein Perella, Interco's investment banker, informed the board that, in its view, the $70 CCA offer was inadequate and not in the best interests of the Company and its shareholders. This opinion was based on a series of analyses, including discounted cash flow, comparable transaction analysis, and an analysis of premiums paid over existing stock prices for selected tender offers during early 1988. Wasserstein Perella also performed an analysis based upon selling certain Interco businesses and retaining and operating others. This analysis generated a "reference range" for the Company of $68-$80 per share. Based on all of these analyses, Wasserstein Perella concluded the offer was inadequate. The board then resolved to reject the proposal. Also at that meeting, the board voted to decrease the threshold percentage needed to trigger the flip-in provision of the rights plan from 30% to 15% and elected to explore a restructuring plan for the Company.

THE INITIAL TENDER OFFER FOR INTERCO STOCK

On August 15, the Rales brothers announced a public tender offer for all of the outstanding stock of Interco at $70 cash per share. The offer was conditioned upon (1) receipt of financing, (2) the tender of sufficient shares to give the offeror a total holding of at least 75% of the Company's common stock on a

---

3. Rights, however, will not be exercisable in the event that an acquiror who holds 20% or less of Interco's common stock acquires not less than 80% of its outstanding stock in a single transaction.

fully diluted basis at the close of the offer, (3) the redemption of the rights plan, and (4) a determination as to the inapplicability of 8 Del. C. §203.[4]

The board met to consider the tender offer at a special meeting a week later on August 22. Wasserstein Perella had engaged in further studies since the meeting two weeks earlier. It was prepared to give a further view about Interco's value. Now the studies showed a "reference range" for the whole Company of $74-$87. The so-called reference ranges do not purport to be a range of fair value; but just what they purport to be is (deliberately, one imagines) rather unclear.

In all events, after hearing the banker's opinion, the Interco board resolved to recommend against the tender offer. In rejecting the offer, the board also declined to redeem the rights plan or to render 8 Del. C. §203 inapplicable to the offer. Finally, the board refused to disclose confidential information requested by CCA in connection with its tender offer unless and until CCA indicated a willingness to enter into a confidentiality and standstill agreement with the Company.[5]

The remainder of the meeting was devoted to an exploration of strategic alternatives to the CCA proposal. Wasserstein Perella presented the board with a detailed valuation of each operating component of the Company. The board adopted a resolution empowering management ". . . to explore all appropriate alternatives to the CCA offer, including, without limitation, the recapitalization, restructuring or other reorganization of the company, the sale of assets of the company in addition to the Apparel Manufacturing Group, and other extraordinary transactions, to maximize the value of the company to the stockholders. . . ."

On August 23, 1988, a letter was sent to CCA informing it that Interco intended to explore alternatives to the offer and planned to make confidential information available to third parties in connection with that endeavor. Interco informed CCA that it would not disclose information to it absent compliance with a confidentiality agreement and a standstill agreement. (*See* fn. 5). Interco's proposal was met with an August 26, 1988 counterproposal by CCA suggesting an alternative confidentiality agreement—without standstill provisions.

Apart from the exchange of letters, there were no communications between CCA and Interco between the time the $70 offer was made on August 22 and a later, higher offer at $72 per share was made on September 10. . . .

[O]n September 10, the Rales brothers did amend their offer, increasing the price offered to $72 per share. The Interco board did not consider that offer until September 19 when its investment banker was ready to report on a proposed restructuring. At that meeting, the board rejected the $72 offer on grounds of financial inadequacy and adopted the restructuring proposal.

---

4. CCA sued Interco in the federal district court for a determination that Section 203 [Delaware's antitakeover statute] was an invalid enactment under the federal Constitution. It was unsuccessful in that attempt. *See City Capital Associates LP v. Interco Incorporated,* 696 F. Supp. 1551 (D. Del. 1988).

5. The standstill agreement would commit CCA not to make any tender offer for three years unless asked to do so by the Company; it apparently does not have an out should CCA seek to make an offer for all shares at a price higher than an offer endorsed by the board.

THE PROPOSED RESTRUCTURING

Under the terms of the restructuring designed by Wasserstein Perella, Interco would sell assets that generate approximately one-half of its gross sales and would borrow $2.025 billion. It would make very substantial distributions to shareholders, by means of a dividend, amounting to a stated aggregate value of $66 per share. The $66 amount would consist of (1) a $25 dividend payable November 7 to shareholders of record on October 13, consisting of $14 in cash and $11 in face amount of senior subordinated debentures, and (2) a second dividend, payable no earlier than November 29, which was declared on October 19, of (a) $24.15 in cash, (b) $6.80 principal amount of subordinated discount debentures, (c) $5.44 principal amount of junior subordinated debentures, (d) convertible preferred stock with a liquidation value of $4.76, and (e) a remaining equity interest or stub that Wasserstein Perella estimates (based on projected earnings of the then remaining businesses) will trade at a price of at least $10 per share. Thus, the total value of the restructuring to shareholders would, in the opinion of Wasserstein Perella, be at least $76 per share on a fully distributed basis.

The board had agreed to a compensation arrangement with Wasserstein Perella that gives that firm substantial contingency pay if its restructuring is successfully completed. Thus, Wasserstein Perella has a rather straightforward and conventional conflict of interest when it opines that the inherently disputable value of its restructuring is greater than the all cash alternative offered by plaintiffs. The market has not, for whatever reason, thought the prospects of the Company quite so bright. It has, in recent weeks consistently valued Interco stock at about $70 a share. [. . . , which is the] value at which Drexel Burnham has valued the restructuring in this litigation. Steps have now been taken to effectuate the restructuring. On September 15, the Company announced its plans to sell the Ethan Allen furniture division, which is said by the plaintiffs to be the Company's "crown jewel." Ethan Allen, the Company maintains, has a unique marketing approach which is not conductive to integration of that business with Interco's other furniture businesses, Lane and Broyhill. Moreover, the Company says that Ethan Allen is not a suitable candidate for the cost cutting measures which must be undertaken in connection with the proposed restructuring. . . .

THE PRESENT CCA OFFER AND THE INTERCO BOARD'S REACTION

In its third supplemental Offer to Purchase dated October 18, 1988, CCA raised its bid to $74. Like the preceding bid, the proposal is an all cash offer for all shares with a contemplated back-end merger for the same consideration.

At its October 19, 1988 board meeting, the board rejected the $74 offer as inadequate and agreed to recommend that shareholders reject the offer. The board based its rejection both on its apparent view that the price was inadequate and on its belief that the proposed restructuring will yield shareholder value of at least $76 per share.

II.

This case was filed on July 27, 1988. Following extensive discovery, it was presented on plaintiffs' application for a preliminary injunction on October 24, 1988. As indicated above, the relief now sought has two principal elements. First, CCA seeks an order requiring the Interco board to redeem the defensive stock rights and effectively give the Interco shareholders the opportunity to choose as a practical matter. Second, it seeks an order restraining further steps to implement the restructuring, including any steps to sell Ethan Allen.

In order to justify that relief, plaintiffs offer several theories. First, it is their position that this case involves an interested board which has acted to entrench itself at the expense of the stockholders of the Company. Second, because they assert that the board comprises interested directors, plaintiffs also assert that the proposed restructuring transaction involves self-dealing, and that the board is therefore obligated, under *Weinberger v. U.O.P., Inc.,* Del. Supr., 457 A.2d 701 (1983), to establish the entire fairness of the restructuring and its refusal to rescind the stock rights, which plaintiffs assert it cannot do. Third, plaintiffs urge that under the approach first adopted by the Delaware Supreme Court in *Unocal,* the board's action is said *not* to be reasonable in relation to any threat posed by the plaintiffs because, they say, their noncoercive, all cash offer does not pose a threat. Fourth and last, plaintiffs claim that the proposed restructuring does not importantly differ from a sale of the Company, and that under *Revlon v. MacAndrews & Forbes Holdings, Inc.,* Del. Supr., 506 A.2d 173 (1986), the Interco directors have a duty to obtain the highest available price for the Company's stockholders in the market, which the directors have not done.

Interco answers that only the *Unocal* standard applies in this case. Defendants urge that the *Weinberger* entire fairness test is inapposite because there has been no self-dealing. *(See* n. 1, *supra.)* Similarly, defendants claim that no *Revlon* duties have arisen because the restructuring does not amount to a sale of the Company and the Company is not, in fact, for sale. Defendants state that the Interco board is proceeding in good faith to protect the best interests of the Company's stockholders. The board believes that CCA's offer is inadequate, and therefore constitutes a threat to the Company's stockholders; it is their position that the restructuring and the poison pill are, therefore, reasonable reactions to the threat posed. Moreover, defendants assert that leaving the pill in place to protect the restructuring is reasonable because the restructuring will achieve better value for stockholders than will be garnered by shareholders' acceptance of the plaintiffs' inadequate offer. . . .

III.

The pending motion purports to seek a preliminary injunction. The test for the issuance of such a provisional remedy is well established. It is necessary for the applicant to demonstrate both a reasonable probability of ultimate success on the claims asserted and, most importantly, the threat of an injury that will occur before trial which is not remediable by an award of damages or the later shaping of equitable relief. Beyond that, it is essential for the court to consider the offsetting equities, if any, including the interests of the public and other innocent third parties, as well as defendants. . . .

It is appropriate, therefore, before subjecting the board's decision not to redeem the pill to the form of analysis mandated by *Unocal*, to identify what relevant facts are not contested or contestable, and what relevant facts may appropriately be assumed against the party prevailing on this point. They are as follows:

First. The value of the Interco restructuring is inherently a debatable proposition, most importantly (but not solely) because the future value of the stub share is unknowable with reasonable certainty.

Second. The board of Interco believes in good faith that the restructuring has a value of "at least" $76 per share.

Third. The City Capital offer is for $74 per share cash.

Fourth. The board of Interco has acted prudently to inform itself of the value of the Company.

Fifth. The board believes in good faith that the City Capital offer is for a price that is "inadequate."

Sixth. City Capital cannot, as a practical matter, close its tender offer while the rights exist; to do so would be to self-inflict an enormous financial injury that no reasonable buyer would do.

Seventh. Shareholders of Interco have differing liquidity preferences and different expectations about likely future economic events.

Eighth. A reasonable shareholder could prefer the restructuring to the sale of his stock for $74 in cash now, but a reasonable shareholder could prefer the reverse.

Ninth. The City Capital tender offer is in no respect coercive. It is for all shares, not for only a portion of shares. It contemplates a prompt follow-up merger, if it succeeds, not an indefinite term as a minority shareholder. It proposes identical consideration in a follow-up merger, not securities or less money.

Tenth. While the existence of the stock rights has conferred time on the board to consider the City Capital proposals and to arrange the restructuring, the utility of those rights as a defensive technique has, given the time lines for the restructuring and the board's actions to date, now been effectively exhausted except in one respect: the effect of those rights continues to "protect the restructuring."

These facts are sufficient to address the question whether the board's action in electing to leave the defensive stock rights plan in place qualifies for the deference embodied in the business judgment rule.

IV.

I turn then to the analysis contemplated by *Unocal*, the most innovative and promising case in our recent corporation law. That case, of course, recognized that in defending against unsolicited takeovers, there is an "omnipresent specter that a board may be acting primarily in its own interest." 493 A.2d at 954. That fact distinguishes takeover defense measures from other acts of a board which, when subject to judicial review, are customarily upheld once the court

finds the board acted in good faith and after an appropriate investigation. *E.g.,
Aronson v. Lewis*, Del. Supr., 473 A.2d 805 (1984). *Unocal* recognizes that human
nature may incline *even one acting in subjective good faith* to rationalize as right
that which is merely personally beneficial. Thus, it created a new intermediate
form of judicial review to be employed when a transaction is neither self-dealing
nor wholly disinterested. That test has been helpfully referred to as the "proportionality test."[8]

The test is easy to state. Where it is employed, it requires a threshold examination "before the protections of the business judgment rule may be conferred."
493 A.2d 954. That threshold requirement is in two parts. First, directors claiming the protections of the rule "must show that they had reasonable grounds
for believing that a danger to corporate policy and effectiveness existed." The
second element of the test is the element of balance. "If a defensive measure is
to come within the ambit of the business judgment rule, it must be reasonable
in relationship to the threat posed." 493 A.2d 955.

Delaware courts have employed the *Unocal* precedent cautiously.[9] The promise of that innovation is the promise of a more realistic, flexible and, ultimately,
more responsible corporation law. The danger that it poses is, of course, that
courts—in exercising some element of substantive judgment—will too readily
seek to assert the primacy of their own view on a question upon which reasonable, completely disinterested minds might differ. Thus, inartfully applied, the
Unocal form of analysis could permit an unraveling of the well-made fabric of
the business judgment rule in this important context. Accordingly, whenever, as
in this case, this court is required to apply the *Unocal* form of review, it should
do so cautiously, with a clear appreciation for the risks and special responsibility
this approach entails.

A.

Turning to the first element of the *Unocal* form of analysis, it is appropriate to note that, in the special case of a tender offer for all shares, the threat
posed, if any, is not importantly to corporate policies (as may well be the case in
a stock buy-back case such as *Cheff v. Mathes*, Del. Supr., 199 A.2d 548 (1964) or
a partial tender offer case such as *Unocal* itself), but rather the threat, if any, is
most directly to shareholder interests. Broadly speaking, threats to shareholders
in that context may be of two types: threats to the voluntariness of the choice

8. *See* Gilson & Kraakman, *Delaware's Intermediate Standard for Defensive Tactics: Is There
Substance to the Proportionality Review?*, John M. Olin Program in Law & Economics, Stanford
Law School (Working Paper No. 45, August, 1988), 44 Bus. Law. [247] (forthcoming February,
1989). Professors Gilson and Kraakman offer a helpful structure for reviewing problems of
this type and conclude with a perceptive observation concerning the beneficial impact upon
corporate culture that the *Unocal* test might come to have.

9. Only two cases have found defensive steps disproportionate to a threat posed by a
takeover attempt. *See AC Acquisitions Corp. v. Anderson, Clayton & Co.*, Del. Ch., 519 A.2d 103
(1986); *Robert M. Bass Group, Inc. v. Evans*, Del. Ch., C.A. No. 9953, Jacobs, V.C. (July 14,
1988) [1988 WL 73744].

offered by the offer, and threats to the substantive, economic interest represented by the stockholding.

1.   Threats to voluntariness.

It is now universally acknowledged that the structure of an offer can render
mandatory in substance that which is voluntary in form. The so-called "front-
end" loaded partial offer—already a largely vanished breed—is the most
extreme example of this phenomenon. An offer may, however, be structured
to have a coercive effect on a rational shareholder in any number of different
ways. Whenever a tender offer is so structured, a board may, or perhaps should,
perceive a threat to a stockholder's interest in exercising choice to remain a
stockholder in the firm. The threat posed by structurally coercive offers is typically amplified by an offering price that the target board responsibly concludes
is substantially below a fair price.[10]

Each of the cases in which our Supreme Court has addressed a defensive
corporate measure under the *Unocal* test involved the sharp and palpable threat
to shareholders posed by a coercive offer. *See Unocal Corp. v. Mesa Petroleum Co.,*
Del. Supr., 493 A.2d 946 (1985); *Moran v. Household International, Inc.,* Del. Supr.,
500 A.2d 1346 (1985); *Ivanhoe Partners v. Newmont Mining Corp.,* Del. Supr., 535
A.2d 1334 (1987).

2.   Threats from "inadequate" but noncoercive offers.

The second broad classification of threats to shareholder interests that
might be posed by a tender offer for all shares relates to the "fairness" or
"adequacy" of the price. It would not be surprising or unreasonable to claim
that where an offer is not coercive or deceptive (and, therefore, what is in
issue is essentially whether the consideration it offers is attractive or not), a
board—even though it may expend corporate funds to arrange alternatives
or to inform shareholders of its view of fair value—is not authorized to take
preclusive action. By preclusive action I mean action that, as a practical matter,
withdraws from the shareholders the option to choose between the offer and
the status quo or some other board sponsored alternative.

Our law, however, has not adopted that view and experience has demonstrated the wisdom of that choice. We have held that a board is not required
simply by reason of the existence of a noncoercive offer to redeem outstanding
poison pill rights. [Citations to cases omitted.] The reason is simple. Even where
an offer is noncoercive, it may represent a "threat" to shareholder interests in
the special sense that an active negotiator with power, in effect, to refuse the
proposal may be able to extract a higher or otherwise more valuable proposal,
or may be able to arrange an alternative transaction or a modified business plan
that will present a more valuable option to shareholders. . . . Our cases, however,
also indicate that in the setting of a noncoercive offer, absent unusual facts,

---

10. A different form of threat relating to the voluntariness of the shareholder's choice
would arise in a structurally noncoercive offer that contained false or misleading material
information.

there may come a time when a board's fiduciary duty will require it to redeem the rights and to permit the shareholders to choose.

B.

In this instance, there is no threat of shareholder coercion. The threat is to shareholders' economic interests posed by an offer the board has concluded is "inadequate." If this determination is made in good faith (as I assume it is here), it alone will justify leaving a poison pill in place, even in the setting of a noncoercive offer, for a period while the board exercises its good faith business judgment to take such steps as it deems appropriate to protect and advance shareholder interests in light of the significant development that such an offer doubtless is. That action may entail negotiation on behalf of shareholders with the offeror, the institution of a *Revlon*-style auction for the Company, a recapitalization or restructuring designed as an alternative to the offer, or other action.[13]

Once that period has closed, and it is apparent that the board does not intend to institute a *Revlon*-style auction,[14] or to negotiate for an increase in the unwanted offer, and that it has taken such time as it required in good faith to arrange an alternative value-maximizing transaction, then, in most instances, the legitimate role of the poison pill in the context of a noncoercive offer will have been fully satisfied.[15] The only function then left for the pill at this end-stage is to preclude the shareholders from exercising a judgment about their own interests that differs from the judgment of the directors, who will have some interest in the question. What then is the "threat" in this instance that might justify such a result? Stating that "threat" at this stage of the process most specifically, it is this: *Wasserstein Perella may be correct in their respective valuations of the offer and the restructuring but a majority of the Interco shareholders may not accept that fact and may be injured as a consequence.* [emphasis in original]

C.

Perhaps there is a case in which it is appropriate for a board of directors to in effect permanently foreclose their shareholders from accepting a noncoercive offer for their stock by utilization of the recent innovation of "poison pill" rights. If such a case might exist by reason of some special circumstance, a

---

13. I leave aside the rare but occasionally encountered instance in which the board elects to do nothing at all with respect to an any and all tender offer.

14. If a board elects to conduct an auction of a company, the deployment or continuation of a poison pill will serve as a method to permit the board to act as an effective auctioneer.

15. The role of a poison pill in an auction setting may presumably be affected by provisions in the bid documents. For example, should a disinterested board or committee agree in good faith to a provision requiring that a pill remain in place following bidding (which they might do in order to elicit bidders), such a commitment would presumably validly bind the corporation.

review of the facts here show[s] this not to be it. The "threat" here, when viewed with particularity, is far too mild to justify such a step in this instance.

Even assuming Wasserstein Perella is correct that when received (and following a period in which full distribution can occur), each of the debt securities to be issued in the restructuring will trade at par, that the preferred stock will trade at its liquidation value, and that the stub will trade initially at $10 a share, the difference in the values of these two offers is only 3%, and the lower offer is all cash and sooner. Thus, the threat, at this stage of the contest, cannot be regarded as very great even on the assumption that Wasserstein Perella is correct.

More importantly, it is incontestable that the Wasserstein Perella value is itself a highly debatable proposition. Their prediction of the likely trading range of the stub share represents one obviously educated guess. Here, the projections used in that process were especially prepared for use in the restructuring. Plaintiffs claim they are rosy to a fault, citing, for example, a $75 million cost reduction from remaining operations once the restructuring is fully implemented. This cost reduction itself is $2 per share; 20% of the predicted value of the stub. The Drexel Burnham analysis, which offers no greater claim to correctness, estimates the stub will trade at between $4.53 and $5.45. Moreover, Drexel opines that the whole package of restructure consideration has a value between $68.28 and $70.37 a share, which, for whatever reason, is quite consistent with the stock market price of a share of Interco stock during recent weeks.

The point here is not that, in exercising some restrained substantive review of the board's decision to leave the pill in place, the court finds Drexel's opinion more persuasive than Wasserstein Perella's. I make no such judgment. What is apparent—indeed inarguable—is that one could do so. More importantly, without access to Drexel Burnham's particular analysis, a shareholder could prefer a $74 cash payment now to the complex future consideration offered through the restructuring. The defendants understand this; it is evident.

The information statement sent to Interco shareholders to inform them of the terms of the restructuring accurately states and repeats the admonition:

> There can be no assurances as to actual trading values of [the stub shares]. . . .
>
> It should be noted that the value of securities, including newly-issued securities and equity securities in highly leveraged companies, are subject to uncertainties and contingencies, all of which are difficult to predict and therefore any valuation [of them] may not necessarily be indicative of the price at which such securities will actually trade.

October 1, 1988 Interco Information Statement, at 3.

Yet, recognizing the relative closeness of the values and the impossibility of knowing what the stub share will trade at, the board, having arranged a value maximizing restructuring, elected to preclude shareholder choice. It did so not to buy time in order to negotiate or arrange possible alternatives, but asserting in effect a right and duty to save shareholders from the consequences of the choice they might make, if permitted to choose.

Without wishing to cast any shadow upon the subjective motivation of the individual defendants, I conclude that reasonable minds not affected by an inherent, entrenched interest in the matter, could not reasonably differ with respect to the conclusion that the CCA $74 cash offer did not represent a threat to shareholder interests sufficient in the circumstances to justify, in effect, fore-closing shareholders from electing to accept that offer.

Our corporation law exists, not as an isolated body of rules and principles, but rather in a historical setting and as a part of a larger body of law premised upon shared values. To acknowledge that directors may employ the recent inno-vation of "poison pills" to deprive shareholders of the ability effectively to choose to accept a noncoercive offer, after the board has had a reasonable opportunity to explore or create alternatives, or attempt to negotiate on the shareholders' behalf, would, it seems to me, be so inconsistent with widely shared notions of appropriate corporate governance as to threaten to diminish the legitimacy and authority of our corporation law.

I thus conclude that the board's decision not to redeem the rights follow-ing the amendment of the offer to $74 per share cannot be justified in the way *Unocal* requires. This determination does not rest upon disputed facts and I conclude that affirmative relief is therefore permissible at this stage. . . .

VII.

Having concluded, under the *Unocal* analysis, that—putting aside the ques-tion of the poison pill—the restructuring appears at this stage to be a reason-able response to the CCA offer that is perceived as inadequate, it is necessary to address briefly CCA's argument that the implementation of that restructur-ing in this setting constitutes a violation of the board's fiduciary duty under *Revlon v. MacAndrews & Forbes Holdings, Inc.*, Del. Supr., 506 A.2d 173 (1986). That argument, in essence, is that the restructuring—which involves the sale of assets generating about one-half of Interco's sales; massive borrowings; and the distribution to shareholders of cash and debt securities (excluding the preferred stock) per share equal to approximately 85% of the market value of Interco's stock[19]—in effect involves the breakup and sale of the Company as it has existed. This argument contends that such a transaction, even if not in form a sale, necessarily involves a duty recognized in *Revlon* to sell the Company, through an auction, only for the best available price.

To this assertion, the defendants reply that Interco is not for sale and, in any event, the board intends to force upon the stockholders the best available transaction anyway. In authorizing management to discuss the terms on which the Company might be sold (which the board did), the board was only fulfilling its obligation to be informed; it has never made a determination that it was in the best interests of the shareholders to sell the Company. Thus, it is said that the teaching of *Revlon*, even if it is presumed to reach every sale of a Company, is not implicated here.

I agree that the board of Interco has no duty, in the circumstances as they now appear, to conduct an auction sale of the Company. I do not think this

---

19. That is, the value (using Wasserstein Perella numbers) of the distribution of cash and debt is approximately $60 and the market price of the stock is approximately $70.

question, however, is answered by merely referring to a board resolve to try to keep the Company independent.

The contours of a board's duties in the face of a takeover attempt are not, stated generally, different from the duties the board always bears: to act in an informed manner and in the good faith pursuit of corporate interests and only for that purpose. . . .

Revlon should not, in my opinion, be interpreted as representing a sharp turn in our law. It does not require, for example, that before every corporate merger agreement can validly be entered into, the constituent corporations must be "shopped" or, more radically, an auction process undertaken, even though a merger may be regarded as a sale of the Company. But mergers or recapitalizations or other important corporate transactions may be authorized by a board only advisedly. There must be a reasonable basis for the board of directors involved to conclude that the transaction involved is in the best interest of the shareholders. This involves having information about possible alternatives. The essence of rational choice is an assessment of costs and benefits and the consideration of alternatives.

Indeed, the central obligation of a board (*assuming it acts in good faith*—an assumption that would not hold for *Revlon*) is to act in an informed manner. When the transaction is so fundamental as the restructuring here (or a sale or merger of the Company), the obligation to be informed would seem to require that reliable information about the value of alternative transactions be explored. . . .

When, as in *Revlon*, two bidders are actively contesting for control of a company, the most reliable source of information as to what may be the best available transaction will come out of an open contest or auction. . . .

When the transaction is a defensive recapitalization, a board may not proceed, consistently with its duty to be informed, without appropriately considering relevant information relating to alternatives.[21] But if a board does probe prudently to ascertain possible alternative values, and thus is in a position to act advisedly, I do not understand the *Revlon* holding as requiring it to turn to an auction alternative, if it has arrived at a good faith, informed determination that a recapitalization or other form of transaction is more beneficial to shareholders. Should the board produce a reactive recapitalization, any steps it may take to implement it in the face of an offer for all stock may, as here, be judicially tested not under *Revlon*, but under the *Unocal* form of judicial review.

Here, given the significance of the restructuring and its character as an alternative to an all cash tender offer, the requirement to inform oneself of possible alternatives may be seen as demanding. It appears, however, that defendants have appropriately informed themselves. . . .

---

21. A delicate question is how far a board must go to satisfy its obligation to inform itself, with respect to the question whether the bidder would pay more. Must it disclose information? Must it negotiate? Surely it need not enter into negotiations if it has not reached a decision to sell the Company, but its duty to shareholders may not permit the board to simply ignore the offeror. This issue may come down to the reasonableness of the terms of a confidentiality and standstill agreement. These agreements which always play an important role for a period in cases of this kind rarely get litigated.

Accordingly, I can detect no basis to conclude that the board did not proceed prudently and in good faith to pursue the restructuring as an alternative to the CCA offer. I do not read *Revlon* as requiring it to follow any different course.

QUESTIONS

1. Why does Chancellor Allen treat CCA's offer as "non-coercive"?

2. What is the procedural posture of this case? What relief does the plaintiff (Bidder/CCA) seek?

3. What are the terms of the flip-in feature of the poison pill adopted by the Interco board?

4. In deciding to apply *Unocal* to the actions taken by the Interco board, why did Chancellor Allen reject the use of the "entire fairness" standard of judicial review?

5. Why does Chancellor Allen conclude that Interco is not in the *Revlon* mode?

6. How does Chancellor Allen apply the two-pronged *Unocal* standard to the actions taken by the Interco board? What is the nature of Chancellor Allen's concern regarding the preclusive effect of the decision of the Interco board not to redeem the pill? How does this concern fit into the two-pronged *Unocal* standard of review? (*Hint:* You may want to reconsider your analysis of this question after you read the next set of Delaware Supreme Court decisions, and again after we analyze Chancellor Chandler's opinion in *Airgas, Inc. v. Air Products, Inc.* at the end of this chapter.)

NOTES

1. The Delaware Supreme Court's Response to **Interco.** Following Chancellor Allen's decision in the principal case, the Rales brothers decided not to proceed with a takeover bid for Interco. Accordingly, the Delaware Supreme Court was not presented with the opportunity to review the Chancery Court's *Unocal* analysis as to the validity of the decision of the Interco board of directors to implement a poison pill defense (*see* Part IV of Chancellor Allen's opinion). Nonetheless, the Delaware Supreme Court broadly hinted at how it might have decided such an appeal from the Chancery Court's poison pill ruling as part of the Court's opinion in the next case. In *Paramount Communications, Inc. v. Time, Inc., infra,* the Delaware Supreme Court made the following (rather pointed) observations as to the reasoning used by Chancellor Allen with regard to the application of the *Unocal* analysis to a poison pill defense:

> . . . [T]he Court of Chancery has [previously] suggested that an all-cash, all-shares offer, falling within a range of values that a shareholder might reasonably prefer, *cannot* constitute a legally recognized "threat" to shareholder interests sufficient to withstand a *Unocal* analysis. *See* . . . [*e.g., City Capital Associates v. Interco. Inc.,* 551 A.2d 787 (Del. Ch. 1988)]. In those cases, the Court of Chancery determined that whatever threat existed related only to the shareholders and only to price and not to the corporation.

From those decisions by our Court of Chancery, Paramount and the individual plaintiffs extrapolate a rule of law that an all-cash, all-shares offer with values reasonably in the range of acceptable price *cannot* pose any objective threat to a corporation or its shareholders. Thus, Paramount would have us hold that *only* if the value of Paramount's offer were determined to be clearly inferior to the value created by management's plan to merge with Warner could the offer be viewed — objectively — as a threat.

Implicit in the plaintiffs' argument is the view that a hostile tender offer can pose only two types of threats: the threat of coercion that results from a two-tier offer promising unequal treatment for nontendering shareholders; and the threat of inadequate value from an all-shares, all-cash offer at a price below what a target board in good faith deems to be the present value of its shares. *See, e.g., Interco*, 551 A.2d at 797; *see also BNS, Inc. v. Koppers*, D. Del., 683 F. Supp. 458 (1988). Since Paramount's offer was all cash, the only conceivable "threat," plaintiffs argue, was inadequate value. We disapprove of such a narrow and rigid construction of *Unocal*, . . .

Plaintiffs' position represents a fundamental misconception of our standard of review under *Unocal* principally because it would involve the court in substituting its judgment as to what is a "better" deal for that of a corporation's board of directors. To the extent that the Court of Chancery has recently done so in certain of its opinions, we hereby reject such approach as not in keeping with a proper *Unocal* analysis. *See, e.g., Interco*, 551 A.2d 787, and its progeny; . . .

Paramount Communications, Inc. v. Time Inc., 571 A.2d 1140, 1152-1153 (Del. 1989) (*emphasis added*). We will revisit this tension between the perspective of Chancellor Allen and the subsequent, more critical perspective of the Delaware Supreme Court (with respect to the *Unocal* analysis of the poison pill defense in Chancellor Allen's well-known *Interco* opinion) later in this chapter when we examine Chancellor Chandler's 2011 decision in *Air Products and Chemicals, Inc. v. Airgas, Inc.*

2. The Era of the "Merger of Equals."   With the collapse of the junk bond market, the most viable players left at the dawn of the 1990s were the strategic buyers. The prevailing sentiment at the time frowned on the use of borrowed capital and leveraging the company's balance sheet. In this market, stock for stock deals became the order of the day, a trend that was further encouraged as the stock market rebounded in the 1990s into a robust bull market, thereby making stock a favored form of acquisition currency. "Merger of equals" became the new buzzword, thereby allowing for even bigger strategic deals, which were often accompanied by lower premiums. It was in this climate that the Delaware Supreme Court decided the following case (which is widely referred to as the *Time-Warner* decision), and, as we shall see in the subsequent *QVC* case (*see infra*, p. 629), the Time-Warner deal became the harbinger of things to come.

Paramount Communications, Inc. v. Time, Inc.
571 A.2d 1140 (Del. 1989)

HORSEY, Justice:
Paramount Communications, Inc. ("Paramount") and two other groups of plaintiffs ("Shareholder Plaintiffs"), shareholders of Time Incorporated ("Time"), a Delaware corporation, separately filed suits in the Delaware Court of

Chancery seeking a preliminary injunction to halt Time's tender offer for 51% of Warner Communication, Inc.'s ("Warner") outstanding shares at $70 cash per share. The court below consolidated the cases and, following the development of an extensive record, after discovery and an evidentiary hearing, denied plaintiffs' motion. In a 50-page unreported opinion and order entered July 14, 1989, the Chancellor refused to enjoin Time's consummation of its tender offer, concluding that the plaintiffs were unlikely to prevail on the merits. . . .

The principal ground for reversal, asserted by all plaintiffs, is that Paramount's June 7, 1989 uninvited all-cash, all-shares, "fully negotiable" (though conditional) tender offer for Time triggered duties under *Unocal Corp. v. Mesa Petroleum Co.*, Del. Supr., 493 A.2d 946 (1985), and that Time's board of directors, in responding to Paramount's offer, breached those duties. As a consequence, plaintiffs argue that in our review of the Time board's decision of June 16, 1989 to enter into a revised merger agreement with Warner, Time is not entitled to the benefit and protection of the business judgment rule.

Shareholder Plaintiffs also assert a claim based on *Revlon v. MacAndrews & Forbes Holdings, Inc.*, Del. Supr., 506 A.2d 173 (1986). They argue that the original Time-Warner merger agreement of March 4, 1989 resulted in a change of control which effectively put Time up for sale, thereby triggering *Revlon* duties. Those plaintiffs argue that Time's board breached its *Revlon* duties by failing, in the face of the change of control, to maximize shareholder value in the immediate term.

Applying our standard of review, we affirm the Chancellor's ultimate finding and conclusion under *Unocal*. We find that Paramount's tender offer was reasonably perceived by Time's board to pose a threat to Time and that the Time board's "response" to that threat was, under the circumstances, reasonable and proportionate. Applying *Unocal*, we reject the argument that the only corporate threat posed by an all-shares, all-cash tender offer is the possibility of inadequate value.

We also find that Time's board did not by entering into its initial merger agreement with Warner come under a *Revlon* duty either to auction the company or to maximize short-term shareholder value, notwithstanding the unequal share exchange. Therefore, the Time board's original plan of merger with Warner was subject only to a business judgment rule analysis. *See Smith v. Van Gorkom*, Del. Supr., 488 A.2d 858, 873-74 (1985).

I

Time is a Delaware corporation with its principal offices in New York City. Time's traditional business is publication of magazines and books; however, Time also provides pay television programming through its Home Box Office, Inc. and Cinemax subsidiaries. In addition, Time owns and operates cable television franchises through its subsidiary, American Television and Communication Corporation. During the relevant time period, Time's board consisted of sixteen directors. Twelve of the directors were "outside," nonemployee directors. Four of the directors were also officers of the company. . . .

As early as 1983 and 1984, Time's executive board began considering expanding Time's operations into the entertainment industry. . . .

The board's consensus was that a merger of Time and Warner was feasible, but only if Time controlled the board of the resulting corporation and thereby preserved a management committed to Time's journalistic integrity. To accomplish this goal, the board stressed the importance of carefully defining in advance the corporate governance provisions that would control the resulting entity. Some board members expressed concern over whether such a business combination would place Time *"in play."* The board discussed the wisdom of adopting further defensive measures to lessen such a possibility.[5] . . .

From the outset, Time's board favored an all-cash or cash and securities acquisition of Warner as the basis for consolidation. Bruce Wasserstein, Time's financial advisor, also favored an outright purchase of Warner. However, Steve Ross, Warner's CEO, was adamant that a business combination was only practicable on a stock-for-stock basis. Warner insisted on a stock swap in order to preserve its shareholders' equity in the resulting corporation. Time's officers, on the other hand, made it abundantly clear that Time would be the acquiring corporation and that Time would control the resulting board. Time refused to permit itself to be cast as the "acquired" company.

Eventually Time acquiesced in Warner's insistence on a stock-for-stock deal, but talks broke down over corporate governance issues. . . . Time's board refused to compromise on its position on corporate governance. Time, and particularly its outside directors, viewed the corporate-governance provisions as critical for preserving the "Time Culture" through a pro-Time management at the top. . . .

Warner and Time resumed negotiations in January 1989. The catalyst for the resumption of talks was a private dinner between Steve Ross and Time outside director, Michael Dingman. Dingman was able to convince Ross that the transitional nature of the proposed co-CEO arrangement did not reflect a lack of confidence in Ross. Ross agreed that this course was best for the company and a meeting between Ross and Munro resulted. Ross agreed to retire in five years and let Nicholas succeed him. Negotiations resumed and many of the details of the original stock-for-stock exchange agreement remained intact. In addition, Time's senior management agreed to long-term contracts.

Time insider directors Levin and Nicholas met with Warner's financial advisors to decide upon a stock exchange ratio. Time's board had recognized the potential need to pay a premium in the stock ratio in exchange for dictating the governing arrangement of the new Time-Warner. Levin and outside director Finkelstein were the primary proponents of paying a premium to protect the "Time Culture." The board discussed premium rates of 10%, 15% and 20%. Wasserstein also suggested paying a premium for Warner due to Warner's rapid growth rate. The market exchange ratio of Time stock for Warner stock was .38 in favor of Warner. Warner's financial advisors informed its board that any exchange rate over .400 was a fair deal and any exchange rate over .450 was "one hell of a deal." The parties ultimately agreed upon an exchange rate favoring

---

5. Time had in place a panoply of defensive devices, including a staggered board, a "poison pill" preferred stock rights plan triggered by an acquisition of 15% of the company, a fifty-day notice period for shareholder motions, and restrictions on shareholders' ability to call a meeting or act by consent.

Warner of .465. On that basis, Warner stockholders would have owned approximately 62% of the common stock of Time-Warner.

On March 3, 1989, Time's board, with all but one director in attendance, met and unanimously approved the stock-for-stock merger with Warner. Warner's board likewise approved the merger. The agreement called for Warner to be merged into a wholly-owned Time subsidiary with Warner becoming the surviving corporation. The common stock of Warner would then be converted into common stock of Time at the agreed upon ratio. Thereafter, the name of Time would be changed to Time-Warner, Inc.

The rules of the New York Stock Exchange required that Time's issuance of shares to effectuate the merger be approved by a vote of Time's stockholders. The Delaware General Corporation Law required approval of the merger by a majority of the Warner stockholders. Delaware law did not require any vote by Time stockholders. The Chancellor concluded that the agreement was the product of "an arms-length negotiation between two parties seeking individual advantage through mutual action."

The resulting company would have a 24-member board, with 12 members representing each corporation. The company would have co-CEO's, at first Ross [CEO of Warner] and Munro [CEO of Time], then Ross and Nicholas [an executive of Time], and finally, after Ross' retirement, by Nicholas alone. The board would create an editorial committee with a majority of members representing Time. A similar entertainment committee would be controlled by Warner board members. A two-thirds supermajority vote was required to alter CEO successions but an earlier proposal to have supermajority protection for the editorial committee was abandoned. . . .

At its March 3, 1989 meeting, Time's board adopted several defensive tactics. Time entered an automatic share exchange agreement with Warner. Time would receive 17,292,747 shares of Warner's outstanding common stock (9.4%) and Warner would receive 7,080,016 shares of Time's outstanding common stock (11.1%). Either party could trigger the exchange. Time sought out and paid for "confidence" letters from various banks with which it did business. In these letters, the banks promised not to finance any third-party attempt to acquire Time. Time argues these agreements served only to preserve the confidential relationship between itself and the banks. The Chancellor found these agreements to be inconsequential and futile attempts to "dry up" money for a hostile takeover. Time also agreed to a "no-shop" clause, preventing Time from considering any other consolidation proposal, thus relinquishing its power to consider other proposals, regardless of their merits. Time did so at Warner's insistence. Warner did not want to be left "on the auction block" for an unfriendly suitor, if Time were to withdraw from the deal.

Time's board simultaneously established a special committee of outside directors, Finkelstein, Kearns, and Opel, to oversee the merger. The committee's assignment was to resolve any impediments that might arise in the course of working out the details of the merger and its consummation.

Time representatives lauded the lack of debt to the United States Senate and to the President of the United States. Public reaction to the announcement of the merger was positive. Time-Warner would be a media colossus with international scope. The board scheduled the stockholder vote for June 23; and a May 1 record date was set. On May 24, 1989, Time sent out extensive proxy statements to the stockholders regarding the approval vote on the merger. In the meantime, with the merger proceeding without impediment, the special committee had concluded, shortly after its creation, that it was not necessary either to retain independent consultants, legal or financial, or even to meet. Time's board was unanimously in favor of the proposed merger with Warner; and, by the end of May, the Time-Warner merger appeared to be an accomplished fact.

On June 7, 1989, these wishful assumptions were shattered by Paramount's surprising announcement of its all-cash offer to purchase all outstanding shares of Time for $175 per share. The following day, June 8, the trading price of Time's stock rose from $126 to $170 per share. Paramount's offer was said to be "fully negotiable."[8]

Time found Paramount's "fully negotiable" offer to be in fact subject to at least three conditions. First, Time had to terminate its merger agreement and stock exchange agreement with Warner, and remove certain other of its defensive devices, including the redemption of Time's shareholder rights. Second, Paramount had to obtain the required cable franchise transfers from Time in a fashion acceptable to Paramount in its sole discretion. Finally, the offer depended upon a judicial determination that section 203 of the General Corporate Law of Delaware (The Delaware Anti-Takeover Statute) was inapplicable to any Time-Paramount merger. While Paramount's board had been privately advised that it could take months, perhaps over a year, to forge and consummate the deal, Paramount's board publicly proclaimed its ability to close the offer by July 5, 1989. Paramount executives later conceded that none of its directors believed that July 5th was a realistic date to close the transaction.

On June 8, 1989, Time formally responded to Paramount's offer. Time's chairman and CEO, J. Richard Munro, sent an aggressively worded letter to Paramount's CEO, Martin Davis. Munro's letter attacked Davis' personal integrity and called Paramount's offer "smoke and mirrors." Time's nonmanagement directors were not shown the letter before it was sent. However, at a board meeting that same day, all members endorsed management's response as well as the letter's content.

Over the following eight days [in June], Time's board met three times to discuss Paramount's $175 offer. The board viewed Paramount's offer as inadequate and concluded that its proposed merger with Warner was the better course of action. Therefore, the board declined to open any negotiations with Paramount and held steady its course toward a merger with Warner.

In June, Time's board of directors met several times. During the course of their June meetings, Time's outside directors met frequently without management, officers or directors being present. At the request of the outside directors, corporate counsel was present during the board meetings and, from time to time, the management directors were asked to leave the board sessions. During the course of these meetings, Time's financial advisors informed the board that, on an auction basis, Time's per share value was materially higher than Warner's

---

8. Subsequently, it was established that Paramount's board had decided as early as March 1989 to move to acquire Time. However, Paramount management intentionally delayed publicizing its proposal until Time had mailed to its stockholders its Time-Warner merger proposal along with the required proxy statements.

$175 per share offer. After this advice, the board concluded that Paramount's $175 offer was inadequate.

At these June meetings, certain Time directors expressed their concern that Time stockholders would not comprehend the long-term benefits of the Warner merger. Large quantities of Time shares were held by institutional investors. The board feared that even though there appeared to be wide support for the Warner transaction, Paramount's cash premium would be a tempting prospect to these investors. In mid-June, Time sought permission from the New York Stock Exchange to alter its rules and allow the TimeWarner merger to proceed without stockholder approval. Time did so at Warner's insistence. The New York Stock Exchange rejected Time's request on June 15; and on that day, the value of Time stock reached $182 per share.

The following day, June 16, Time's board met to take up Paramount's offer. The board's prevailing belief was that Paramount's bid posed a threat to Time's control of its own destiny and retention of the "Time Culture." Even after Time's financial advisors made another presentation of Paramount and its business attributes, Time's board maintained its position that a combination with Warner offered greater potential for Time [and thus decided to reject Paramount's offer]. Warner provided Time a much desired production capability and an established international marketing chain. Time's advisors suggested various options, including defensive measures. . . .

At the same meeting, Time's board decided to recast its consolidation with Warner into an outright cash and securities acquisition of Warner by Time; and Time so informed Warner. Time accordingly restructured its proposal to acquire Warner as follows: Time would make an immediate all-cash offer for 51% of Warner's outstanding stock at $70 per share. The remaining 49% would be purchased at some later date for a mixture of cash and securities worth $70 per share. To provide the funds required for its outright acquisition of Warner, Time would assume 7-10 billion dollars worth of debt, thus eliminating one of the principal transaction-related benefits of the original merger agreement.

Warner agreed. . . .

On June 23, 1989, Paramount raised its all-cash offer to buy Time's outstanding stock to $200 per share. Paramount still professed that all aspects of the offer were negotiable. Time's board met on June 26, 1989 and formally rejected Paramount's $200 per share second offer. The board reiterated its belief that, despite the $25 increase, the offer was still inadequate. The Time board maintained that the Warner transaction offered a greater long-term value for the stockholders and, unlike Paramount's offer, did not pose a threat to Time's survival and its "culture." Paramount then filed this action in the Court of Chancery.

II

The Shareholder Plaintiffs first assert a *Revlon* claim. They contend that the March 4 Time-Warner agreement effectively put Time up for sale, triggering *Revlon* duties, requiring Time's board to enhance short-term shareholder value and to treat all other interested acquirors on an equal basis. The Shareholder Plaintiffs base this argument on two facts: (i) the ultimate Time-Warner exchange ratio of .465 favoring Warner, resulting in Warner shareholders' receipt of 62% of the combined company; and (ii) the subjective intent of Time's directors as evidenced in their statements that the market might perceive the Time-Warner merger as putting Time up "for sale" and their adoption of various defensive measures.

The Shareholder Plaintiffs further contend that Time's directors, in structuring the original merger transaction to be "takeover-proof," triggered *Revlon* duties by foreclosing their shareholders from any prospect of obtaining a control premium. In short, plaintiffs argue that Time's board's decision to merge with Warner imposed a fiduciary duty to maximize immediate share value and not erect unreasonable barriers to further bids. Therefore, they argue, the Chancellor erred in finding: that Paramount's bid for Time did not place Time "for sale"; that Time's transaction with Warner did not result in any transfer of control; and that the combined Time-Warner was not so large as to preclude the possibility of the stockholders of Time-Warner receiving a future control premium.

Paramount asserts only a *Unocal* claim in which the shareholder plaintiffs join. Paramount contends that the Chancellor, in applying the first part of the *Unocal* test, erred in finding that Time's board had reasonable grounds to believe that Paramount posed both a legally cognizable threat to Time shareholders and a danger to Time's corporate policy and effectiveness. Paramount also contests the court's finding that Time's board made a reasonable and objective investigation of Paramount's offer so as to be informed before rejecting it. Paramount further claims that the court erred in applying *Unocal's* second part in finding Time's response to be "reasonable." Paramount points primarily to the preclusive effect of the revised agreement which denied Time shareholders the opportunity both to vote on the agreement and to respond to Paramount's tender offer. Paramount argues that the underlying motivation of Time's board in adopting these defensive measures was management's desire to perpetuate itself in office.

The Court of Chancery posed the pivotal question presented by this case to be: Under what circumstances must a board of directors abandon an in place plan of corporate development in order to provide its shareholders with the option to elect and realize an immediate control premium? As applied to this case, the question becomes: Did Time's board, having developed a strategic plan of global expansion to be launched through a business combination with Warner, come under a fiduciary duty to jettison its plan and put the corporation's future in the hands of its shareholders?

While we affirm the result reached by the Chancellor, we think it unwise to place undue emphasis upon long-term versus short-term corporate strategy. Two key predicates underpin our analysis. First, Delaware law imposes on a board of directors the duty to manage the business and affairs of the corporation. 8 Del. C. §141 (a). This broad mandate includes a conferred authority to set a corporate course of action, including time frame, designed to enhance corporate profitability. Thus, the question of "long-term" versus "short-term" values is largely irrelevant because directors, generally, are obliged to chart a course for a corporation which is in its best interests without regard to a fixed investment horizon. Second, absent a limited set of circumstances as defined under *Revlon*, a board of directors, while always required to act in an informed manner, is not under any *per se* duty to maximize shareholder value in the short term, even in the context of a takeover.[12] In our view, the pivotal question presented by this case is: "Did Time, by entering into the proposed merger with Warner, put itself up for sale?" A resolution of that issue through application of *Revlon* has a significant bearing upon the resolution of the derivative *Unocal* issue.

A.

We first take up plaintiffs' principal *Revlon* argument, summarized above. In rejecting this argument, the Chancellor found the original Time-Warner merger agreement not to constitute a "change of control" and concluded that the transaction did not trigger *Revlon* duties. The Chancellor's conclusion is premised on a finding that "[b]efore the merger agreement was signed, control of the corporation existed in a fluid aggregation of unaffiliated shareholders representing a voting majority—in other words, in the market." The Chancellor's findings of fact are supported by the record and his conclusion is correct as a matter of law. However, we premise our rejection of plaintiffs' *Revlon* claim on different grounds, namely, the absence of any substantial evidence to conclude that Time's board, in negotiating with Warner, made the dissolution or break-up of the corporate entity inevitable, as was the case in *Revlon*.

Under Delaware law there are, generally speaking and without excluding other possibilities, two circumstances which may implicate *Revlon* duties. The first, and clearer one, is when a corporation initiates an active bidding process seeking to sell itself or to effect a business reorganization involving a clear break-up of the company. *See, e.g., Mills Acquisition Co. v. Macmillan, Inc*, Del. Supr., 559 A.2d 1261 (1988). However, *Revlon* duties may also be triggered where, in response to a bidder's offer, a target abandons its long-term strategy and seeks an alternative transaction involving the breakup of the company. Thus, in *Revlon*, when the board responded to Pantry Pride's offer by contemplating a "bust-up" sale of assets in a leveraged acquisition, we imposed upon the board a duty to maximize immediate shareholder value and an obligation to auction the company fairly. If, however, the board's reaction to a hostile tender offer is found to constitute only a defensive response and not an abandonment of the corporation's continued existence, *Revlon* duties are not triggered, though *Unocal* duties attach.[14]

---

12. Thus, we endorse the Chancellor's conclusion that it is not a breach of faith for directors to determine that the present stock market price of shares is not representative of true value or that there may indeed be several market values for any corporation's stock. We have so held in another context. *See Van Gorkom*, 488 A.2d at 876.

14. Within the auction process, any action taken by the board must be reasonably related to the threat posed or reasonable in relation to the advantage sought, *See Mills Acquisition Co. v. Macmillian, Inc.*, Del. Supr., 559 A.2d 1261, 1288 (1988). Thus, a *Unocal* analysis may be appropriate when a corporation is in a *Revlon* situation and *Revlon* duties may be triggered by a defensive action taken in response to a hostile offer. Since *Revlon*, we have stated that differing treatment of various bidders is not actionable when such action reasonably relates to achieving the best price available for the stockholders. *Macmillian*, 559 A.2d at 1286-87.

The plaintiffs insist that even though the original Time-Warner agreement may not have worked "an objective change of control," the transaction made a "sale" of Time inevitable. Plaintiffs rely on the subjective intent of Time's board of directors and principally upon certain board members' expressions of concern that the Warner transaction *might* be viewed as effectively putting Time up for sale. Plaintiffs argue that the use of a lock-up agreement, a no-shop clause, and so-called "dry-up" agreements prevented shareholders from obtaining a control premium in the immediate future and thus violated *Revlon*.

We agree with the Chancellor that such evidence is entirely insufficient to invoke *Revlon* duties; and we decline to extend *Revlon's* application to corporate transactions simply because they might be construed as putting a corporation either "in play" or "up for sale." . . . The adoption of structural safety devices alone does not trigger *Revlon*. . . .

Finally, we do not find in Time's recasting of its merger agreement with Warner from a share exchange to a share purchase a basis to conclude that Time had either abandoned its strategic plan or made a sale of Time inevitable. The Chancellor found that although the merged Time-Warner company would be large (with a value approaching approximately $30 billion), recent takeover cases have proven that acquisition of the combined company might nonetheless be possible. . . .

B.

We turn now to plaintiffs' *Unocal* claim. We begin by noting, as did the Chancellor, that our decision does not require us to pass on the wisdom of the board's decision to enter into the original Time-Warner agreement. That is not a court's task. Our task is simply to review the record to determine whether there is sufficient evidence to support the Chancellor's conclusion that the initial Time-Warner agreement was the product of a proper exercise of business judgment.

We have purposely detailed the evidence of the Time board's deliberative approach, beginning in 1983-84, to expand itself. Time's decision in 1988 to combine with Warner was made only after what could be fairly characterized as an exhaustive appraisal of Time's future as a corporation. After concluding in 1983-84 that the corporation must expand to survive, and beyond journalism into entertainment, the board combed the field of available entertainment companies. By 1987 Time had focused upon Warner; by late July 1988 Time's board was convinced that Warner would provide the best "fit" for Time to achieve its strategic objectives. The record attests to the zealousness of Time's executives, fully supported by their directors, in seeing to the preservation of Time's "culture," i.e., its perceived editorial integrity in journalism. We find ample evidence in the record to support the Chancellor's conclusion that the Time board's decision to expand the business of the company through its March 3 merger with Warner was entitled to the protection of the business judgment rule.

The Chancellor reached a different conclusion in addressing the Time-Warner transaction as revised three months later. He found that the revised agreement was defense-motivated and designed to avoid the potentially disruptive effect that Paramount's offer would have had on consummation of the proposed merger were it put to a shareholder vote. Thus, the court declined to apply the traditional business judgment rule to the revised transaction and instead analyzed the Time board's June 16 decision under *Unocal*. The court ruled that *Unocal* applied to all director actions taken, following receipt of Paramount's hostile tender offer, that were reasonably determined to be defensive. Clearly that was a correct ruling and no party disputes that ruling.

In *Unocal*, we held that before the business judgment rule is applied to a board's adoption of a defensive measure, the burden will lie with the board to prove (a) reasonable grounds for believing that a danger to corporate policy and effectiveness existed; and (b) that the defensive measure adopted was reasonable in relation to the threat posed. *Unocal*, 493 A.2d 946. Directors satisfy the first part of the *Unocal* test by demonstrating good faith and reasonable investigation. We have repeatedly stated that the refusal to entertain an offer may comport with a valid exercise of a board's business judgment. . . .

Unocal involved a two-tier, highly coercive tender offer. In such a case, the threat is obvious: shareholders may be compelled to tender to avoid being treated adversely in the second stage of the transaction. In subsequent cases, the Court of Chancery has suggested that an all-cash, all-shares offer, falling within a range of values that a shareholder might reasonably prefer, cannot constitute a legally recognized "threat" to shareholder interests sufficient to withstand a *Unocal* analysis. . . . [*See City Capital Associates v. Interco, Inc.*, 551 A.2d 787 (Del. Ch. 1988).] . . .

From those decisions by our Court of Chancery, Paramount and the individual plaintiffs extrapolate a rule of law that an all-cash, all-shares offer with values reasonably in the range of acceptable price cannot pose any objective threat to a corporation or its shareholders. Thus, Paramount would have us hold that only if the value of Paramount's offer were determined to be clearly inferior to the value created by management's plan to merge with Warner could the offer be viewed—objectively—as a threat.

Implicit in the plaintiffs' argument is the view that a hostile tender offer can pose only two types of threats: the threat of coercion that results from a two-tier offer promising unequal treatment for nontendering shareholders; and the threat of inadequate value from an all-shares, all-cash offer at a price below what a target board in good faith deems to be the present value of its shares. Since Paramount's offer was all-cash, the only conceivable "threat," plaintiffs argue, was inadequate value. We disapprove of such a narrow and rigid construction of *Unocal*, for the reasons which follow.

Plaintiffs' position represents a fundamental misconception of our standard of review under *Unocal* principally because it would involve the court in substituting its judgment as to what is a "better" deal for that of a corporation's board of directors. To the extent that the Court of Chancery has recently done so in certain of its opinions, we hereby reject such approach as not in keeping with a proper *Unocal* analysis. *See, e.g.,* [*City Capital Associates v. Interco., Inc.*, 551 A.2d 787, 797 (Del. Ch. 1988)] and its progeny, . . .

The usefulness of *Unocal* as an analytical tool is precisely its flexibility in the face of a variety of fact scenarios. *Unocal* is not intended as an abstract standard; neither is it a structured and mechanistic procedure of appraisal. Thus, we have said that directors may consider, when evaluating the threat posed by a takeover bid, the "inadequacy of the price offered, nature and timing of the offer, questions of illegality, the impact on 'constituencies' other than share-holders . . . the risk of nonconsummation, and the quality of securities being offered in the exchange." 493 A.2d at 955. The open-ended analysis mandated by *Unocal* is not intended to lead to a simple mathematical exercise: that is, of comparing the discounted value of Time-Warner's expected trading price at some future date with Paramount's offer and determining which is the higher. Indeed, in our view, precepts underlying the business judgment rule militate against a court's engaging in the process of attempting to appraise and evaluate the relative merits of a long-term versus a short-term investment goal for share-holders. To engage in such an exercise is a distortion of the *Unocal* process and, in particular, the application of the second part of *Unocal's* test, discussed below.

In this case, the Time board reasonably determined that inadequate value was not the only legally cognizable threat that Paramount's all-cash, all-shares offer could present. Time's board concluded that Paramount's eleventh hour offer posed other threats. One concern was that Time shareholders might elect to tender into Paramount's cash offer in ignorance or a mistaken belief of the strategic benefit which a business combination with Warner might produce. Moreover, Time viewed the conditions attached to Paramount's offer as intro-ducing a degree of uncertainty that skewed a comparative analysis. Further, the timing of Paramount's offer to follow issuance of Time's proxy notice was viewed as arguably designed to upset, if not confuse, the Time stockholders' vote. Given this record evidence, we cannot conclude that the Time board's decision of June 6 that Paramount's offer posed a threat to corporate policy and effectiveness was lacking in good faith or dominated by motives of either entrenchment or self-interest.

Paramount also contends that the Time board had not duly investigated Paramount's offer. Therefore, Paramount argues, Time was unable to make an informed decision that the offer posed a threat to Time's corporate policy. Although the Chancellor did not address this issue directly, his findings of fact do detail Time's exploration of the available entertainment companies, includ-ing Paramount, before determining that Warner provided the best strategic "fit." In addition, the court found that Time's board rejected Paramount's offer because Paramount did not serve Time's objectives or meet Time's needs. Thus, the record does, in our judgment, demonstrate that Time's board was ade-quately informed of the potential benefits of a transaction with Paramount. We agree with the Chancellor that the Time board's lengthy pre-June investigation of potential merger candidates, including Paramount, mooted any obligation on Time's part to halt its merger process with Warner to reconsider Paramount. Time's board was under no obligation to negotiate with Paramount. Time's fail-ure to negotiate cannot be fairly found to have been uninformed. The evidence supporting this finding is materially enhanced by the fact that twelve of Time's sixteen board members were outside independent directors. *Unocal,* 493 A.2d at 955; *Moran v. Household Intern., Inc.,* Del. Supr., 500 A.2d 1346, 1356 (1985).

We turn to the second part of the *Unocal* analysis. The obvious requisite to determining the reasonableness of a defensive action is a clear identification of the nature of the threat. As the Chancellor correctly noted, this "requires an evaluation of the importance of the corporate objective threatened; alter-native methods of protecting that objective; impacts of the 'defensive' action, and other relevant factors." It is not until both parts of the *Unocal* inquiry have been satisfied that the business judgment rule attaches to defensive actions of a board of directors. *Unocal*, 493 A.2d at 954.[18] As applied to the facts of this case, the question is whether the record evidence supports the Court of Chancery's conclusion that the restructuring of the Time-Warner transaction, including the adoption of several preclusive defensive measures, was a *reasonable response* in relation to a perceived threat.

Paramount argues that, assuming its tender offer posed a threat, Time's response was unreasonable in precluding Time's shareholders from accepting the tender offer or receiving a control premium in the immediately foreseeable future. Once again, the contention stems, we believe, from a fundamental misunderstanding of where the power of corporate governance lies. Delaware law confers the management of the corporate enterprise to the stockholders' duly elected board representatives. 8 Del. C. §141(a). The fiduciary duty to manage a corporate enterprise includes the selection of a time frame for achievement of corporate goals. That duty may not be delegated to the stockholders. *Van Gorkom*, 488 A.2d at 873. Directors are not obliged to abandon a deliberately conceived corporate plan for a short-term shareholder profit unless there is clearly no basis to sustain the corporate strategy. *See, e.g., Revlon*, 506 A.2d 173.

Although the Chancellor blurred somewhat the discrete analyses required under *Unocal*, he did conclude that Time's board reasonably perceived Paramount's offer to be a significant threat to the planned Time-Warner merger and that Time's response was not "overly broad." We have found that even in light of a valid threat, management actions that are coercive in nature or force upon shareholders a management-sponsored alternative to a hostile offer may be struck down as unreasonable and nonproportionate responses.

Here, on the record facts, the Chancellor found that Time's responsive action to Paramount's tender offer was not aimed at "cramming down" on its shareholders a management-sponsored alternative, but rather had as its goal the carrying forward of a pre-existing transaction in an altered form. Thus, the response was reasonably related to the threat. The Chancellor noted that the revised agreement and its accompanying safety devices did not preclude Paramount from making an offer for the combined Time-Warner company or from changing the conditions of its offer so as not to make the offer dependent upon the nullification of the Time-Warner agreement. Thus, the response was proportionate. We affirm the Chancellor's rulings as clearly supported by the record. Finally, we note that although Time was required, as a result of Paramount's hostile offer, to incur a heavy debt to finance its acquisition of Warner, that fact alone does not render the board's decision unreasonable so long as the directors could reasonably perceive the debt load not to be so injurious to the corporation as to jeopardize its well-being.

---

18. Some commentators have criticized *Unocal* by arguing that once the board's deliberative process has been analyzed and found not to be wanting in objectivity, good faith or deliberateness, the so-called "enhanced" business judgment rule has been satisfied and no further inquiry is undertaken. *See generally* Johnson & Siegel, *Corporate Mergers: Redefining the Role of Target Directors*, 136 U. Pa. L. Rev. 315 (1987). We reject such views.

C.

Conclusion

Applying the test for grant or denial of preliminary injunctive relief, we find plaintiffs failed to establish a reasonable likelihood of ultimate success on the merits. Therefore, we affirm.

QUESTIONS

1. With the benefit of hindsight, do you think that the Time-Warner merger proved to be a good deal for the Time shareholders? This inevitably leads to the vexing question that commentators are still grappling with in the wake of the Time-Warner business combination—indeed, that we have grappled with throughout our study of M&A law—*Who should decide the fate of the company: Time's board of directors or Time's shareholders?*

2. According to the Delaware Supreme Court, what triggers the *Revlon* duties? In other words, how does the legal advisor to the company determine when the company is in the *Revlon* mode?

3. In light of the numerous financial scandals that have marked the dawn of the twenty-first century, does reliance on independent outside directors continue to be as compelling as it was for the Delaware Supreme Court in its *Time-Warner* decision? In the wake of the Great Recession, do you find the Delaware Supreme Court's reasoning on this issue persuasive as a matter of public policy?

4. What are the public policy concerns that the Delaware Supreme Court identified in connection with the decision of Time's board to take on debt (i.e., leverage the company's balance sheet) in order to finance the acquisition of Warner on a cash basis?

5. What standard of review applies to the decision of Time's board of directors to restructure the transaction from a single-step, reverse triangular merger into a two-step acquisition? How does the Delaware Supreme Court apply that standard of review to determine whether Time's board of directors has fulfilled its fiduciary duty obligations?

NOTES

1. *The Aftermath of the* **Time-Warner** *Decision.* Following the Delaware Supreme Court's decision, the trading price of Time shares fell to $93 per share, a far cry from the lofty cash offer of $200 per share that Paramount offered Time's shareholders, leading to considerable criticisms of the Court's decision. As succinctly described by one leading commentator: "In [*Time-Warner*], the Delaware court let incumbent directors block an any-and-all tender offer paying a 100 percent premium. So preposterous was its opinion that it quickly became

the target of massive ridicule." J. Mark Ramseyer, BUSINESS ORGANIZATIONS 375 (2012).

2. The "Just Say No" Defense.   The *Time-Warner* decision gave rise to what is popularly referred to as the "just say no" defense. "[M]any commentators concluded that [the *Time-Warner* decision] validated the 'just say no' defense, pursuant to which the target's board simply refuses to allow the firm to be acquired, backing up that refusal by a poison pill or other takeover defenses." Stephen M. Bainbridge, MERGERS & ACQUISITIONS 227 (2nd ed. 2009). It is important to note that at least one court had previously rejected this defense, at least implicitly. You will recall that Chancellor Allen's opinion in *City Capital Associates, supra*, at p. 598, "at least implicitly rejected the 'just say no' defense. . . . Chancellor Allen indicated that 'in most instances' the use of takeover defenses was only legitimate in connection with attempts by the board to negotiate with [the] unsolicited bidder or to assemble an alternative transaction. *City Capital Assoc. Ltd. Partnership v. Interco Inc.*, 551 A.2d 787, 798 (Del. Ch. 1988). In other words, the [Target] Board cannot simply just say no." Bainbridge, *supra*, at 227 n. 83. However, in its *Time-Warner* opinion, the Delaware Supreme Court rejected the view "that an all-cash, all-shares offer, falling within a range of values that a shareholder might reasonably prefer, *cannot* constitute a legally recognized 'threat' to shareholder interests sufficient to withstand scrutiny under the first prong of *Unocal's* intermediate standard of judicial scrutiny." *Time-Warner, supra* at 1152 (*emphasis added*). *Query*: Should the Target board be able to "just say no" to an unsolicited Bidder?

3. Long-Term vs. Short-Term Perspective.   In recent years, there has been considerable public controversy over excessive executive compensation, particularly with respect to the continued use of change of control compensation (i.e., golden parachutes) in connection with M&A transactions involving publicly traded companies. The important public policy issues that are presented by this modern controversy, especially with respect to management's incentives to manage the company's business affairs in order to maximize gain in the short run or the long run, were recently highlighted by then-Chancellor Strine:

> During the last quarter century, the compensation of top executives, particularly CEOs, has grown enormously. There is a heated argument about why that is the case and whether, on balance, that increase is largely attributable to demands by the institutional investor community that the takeover market operate with great vibrancy, that underperforming management be replaced, that executive compensation take the form of stock options, and that top executives engage in measures (such as job cutting and outsourcing) that they may find distasteful but which increase corporate bottom lines. Arguably, these pressures to manage to an avaricious market, greatly decreased job security, and a change in the public

perception of CEOs of public companies from being community leaders running important societal institutions into being ruthless sharpies willing to do whatever it takes to increase the corporation's stock price, have led CEOs to seek much greater compensation. Ironically, some say, the one corporate constituency that has little to complain about executive compensation are stockholders, whose returns have largely tracked the increases in CEO pay, while returns to ordinary corporate workers in the form of wages and returns to society in the form of increases in median family income have stagnated.

Leo E. Strine, Jr., *One Fundamental Corporate Governance Question We Face: Can Corporations Be Managed for the Long Term Unless Their Power Electorates Also Act and Think Long Term?* 66 Bus. Law. 1, 19-20 (2010). In a more recent paper, former Chief Justice Strine once again raises this fundamental question of how corporations can be managed to promote long-term growth if the company's officers and directors are not adequately incentivized to manage the business with the long term in mind. *See, e.g.,* Leo E. Strine, *Toward Fair and Sustainable Capitalism,* August 2020, *available at:* https://rooseveltinstitute.org/wp-content/uploads/2020/08/RI_TowardFairandSustainableCapitalism_WorkingPaper_202008.pdf.

As an observer of the U.S. capital markets, and more specifically, a student of the M&A markets, what do you think of this important public policy question posed by Chancellor Strine: "[S]hould we expect [the managers of modern] corporations to chart a sound long-term course of economic growth, if the so-called investors who determine the fate of their managers do not themselves act or think with the long term in mind?" Strine, *supra,* 66 Bus. Law. at 1-2. This tension in our system of corporate governance that Chancellor Strine describes surfaces most acutely in M&A transactions as policy makers, including the Delaware judiciary, face the fundamental question: *who should decide when and on what terms the corporation should be sold?*

4. The Director Primacy Model of Corporate Governance. In *Unocal,* the Delaware Supreme Court firmly rejected the "passivity theory"; that is to say, the board of Target is not a "passive instrumentality" when faced with an unsolicited takeover bid. Instead, as subsequent Delaware cases have made clear, the board of Target is to serve as "the defender of the metaphorical medieval corporate bastion and the protector of the corporation's shareholders." *Unitrin, Inc., v. Am. Gen. Corp.,* 651 A.2d 1361, 1388 (Del. 1995). Thus, *Unocal* and its progeny have led some scholars to suggest that modern U.S. corporate law follows a model of "director primacy" to address one of the most fundamental questions that scholars of modern corporate governance struggle with:

Who decides whether a transaction is beneficial for the corporation? Although questions of this sort pervade corporate governance, few transactions present it so starkly as does an unsolicited tender offer. Are such transactions mere "transfers of stock by stockholders to a third party" that do not "implicate the internal affairs of the target company"?[1] Or, as with most aspects of corporate governance, does the target company's board of directors have a gatekeeping function?

In statutory acquisitions, such as mergers or asset sales, the target's board of directors' gatekeeping function is established by statute. If the board rejects a proposed transaction, the shareholders are neither invited to, nor entitled to, pass on the merits of that decision.[3] Only if the target's board of directors approves the transaction are the shareholders invited to ratify that decision.[4]

In nonstatutory acquisitions, such as tender offers, the answer is more complicated. A tender offer enables the bidders to go directly to the shareholders of the target corporation, bypassing the board of directors.[5] When the hostile tender offer emerged in the 1970s as an important acquirer tool, lawyers and investment bankers working for target boards responded by developing defensive tactics designed to impede such offers.[6] Takeover defenses reasserted the target board's primacy by extending the board's gatekeeping function to the nonstatutory acquisition setting.

The Delaware Supreme Court came down in favor of a target board gatekeeping function in *Unocal Corp. v. Mesa Petroleum Co.*[7] . . .

[*Unocal* and its progeny make clear that] control [in the sense of authority to manage the business affairs of a corporation] is vested not in the hands of the firm's so-called owners, the shareholders, who exercise virtually no control over either day-to-day operations or long-term policy, but in the hands of the board of directors and their subordinate professional managers. On the other hand, the separation of ownership and control in modern public corporations obviously implicates important accountability concerns, which corporate law must also address. . . .

[In order to answer the fundamental question of who should decide when and on what terms the company should be sold, one must first consider some basic principles:] What is the nature of the corporation? What is the nature of the shareholders' relationship to the corporation? What is the proper role and function of the board of directors? And so on.[24]

Stephen M Bainbridge, Unocal *at 20: Director Primacy in Corporate Takeovers,* 31 DEL. J. CORP. LAW 769, 771-775 (2006). Professor Bainbridge has written extensively on the "director primacy model," strongly advocating

---

1. Edgar v. MITE Corp., 457 U.S. 624, 645 (1982).

3. *See* Jennifer J. Johnson & Mary Siegel, *Corporate Mergers: Redefining the Role of Target Directors,* 136 U. PA. L. REV. 315, 321-322 (1987) (explaining corporate law vests the decision to reject a merger in the unilateral discretion of the target corporation's board of directors).

4. *See, e.g.,* 3 MODEL BUS. CORP. ACT ANN. §11.04(b) (3d ed. Supp. 2000-2002) (providing that "*after* adopting the plan of merger . . . the board of directors must submit the plan to the shareholders for their approval") (*emphasis added*).

5. *See* Roberta Romano, *Competition for Corporate Charters and the Lesson of Takeover Statutes,* 61 FORDHAM L. REV. 843, 844 (1993) (explaining "takeovers . . . , in contrast to mergers, are achieved by tender offers to the shareholders, and thus bypass incumbent management's approval").

6. *See generally,* PATRICK A. GAUGHAN, MERGERS, ACQUISITIONS, AND CORPORATE RESTRUCTURINGS 167-234 (3d ed. 2002) (tracing the development of takeover defenses).

7. 493 A.2d 946 (Del. 1985).

24. The analysis in this [article] draws heavily on my recent work on director primacy. *See, e.g.,* Stephen M Bainbridge, *Director Primacy: The Means and Ends of Corporate Governance,* 97 NW. U. L. REV. 547 (2003) [hereinafter Bainbridge, *Director Primacy*]; Stephen M. Bainbridge, *The Board of Directors as Nexus of Contracts,* 88 IOWA L. REV. 1 (2002) [hereinafter Bainbridge,

that the power and right to exercise decisionmaking fiat is vested neither in the shareholders nor the managers, but in the board of directors. According to this director primacy model, the board of directors is not a mere agent of the shareholders, but rather is a sort of Platonic guardian serving as the nexus of the various contracts making up the corporation. As a positive theory of corporate governance, the director primacy model strongly emphasizes the role of fiat—i.e., the centralized decisionmaking authority possessed by the board of directors. As a normative theory of corporate governance, director primacy claims that resolving the resulting tension between authority and accountability is the central problem of corporate law. The substantial virtues of fiat can be realized only by preserving the board's decisionmaking authority from being trumped by either shareholders or courts. Achieving an appropriate balance between authority and accountability is a daunting but necessary task. Ultimately, authority and accountability cannot be reconciled. At some point, greater accountability necessarily makes the decisionmaking process less efficient, while highly efficient decisionmaking structures necessarily reduce accountability. In general, that tension is resolved in favor of authority. Because only shareholders are entitled to elect directors, boards of public corporations are insulated from pressure by nonshareholder corporate constituencies, such as employees or creditors. At the same time, the diffuse nature of U.S. stockownership and regulatory impediments to investor activism insulate directors from shareholder pressure. Accordingly, the board has virtually unconstrained freedom to exercise business judgment. . . . Hence the term "director primacy," which reflects the board's sovereignty.

Stephen M. Bainbridge, *Director Primacy: The Means and the Ends of Corporate Governance*, 97 N.W. U. L. Rev. 547, 605 (2003). *Query:* In considering the decisions in *Time-Warner* and *QVC* (which follows), does the Delaware Supreme Court seem to be adopting the director primacy model?

Paramount Communications, Inc. v. QVC Network, Inc.
637 A.2d 34 (Del. 1994)

Veasey, Chief Justice.

In this appeal we review an order of the Court of Chancery dated November 24, 1993 (the "November 24 Order"), preliminarily enjoining certain defensive measures designed to facilitate a so-called strategic alliance between Viacom Inc. ("Viacom") and Paramount Communications Inc. ("Paramount") approved by the board of directors of Paramount (the "Paramount Board" or the "Paramount directors") and to thwart an unsolicited, more valuable, tender offer by QVC Network Inc. ("QVC"). In affirming, we hold that the sale of control in this case, which is at the heart of the proposed strategic alliance, implicates enhanced judicial scrutiny of the conduct of the Paramount Board under

---

Board as Nexus]. . . . For a constructive critique of my director primacy model, *see* Wayne O. Hanewicz, *Director Primacy*, Omnicare, *and the Function of Corporate Law*, 71 Tenn L. Rev. 511 (2004). For an instructive application of the model to shareholder voting, see Harry G. Hutchison, *Director Primacy and Corporate Governance: Shareholder Voting Rights Captured by the Accountability/Authority Paradigm*, 36 Loy. U. Chi. L.J. 111 (2005).

Unocal Corp. v. Mesa Petroleum Co., Del. Supr., 493 A.2d 946 (1985), and *Revlon, Inc. v. MacAndrews & Forbes Holdings, Inc.*, Del. Supr., 506 A.2d 173 (1986). We further hold that the conduct of the Paramount Board was not reasonable as to process or result.

. . . This action arises out of a proposed acquisition of Paramount by Viacom through a tender offer followed by a second-step merger (the "Paramount-Viacom transaction"), and a competing unsolicited tender offer by QVC. The Court of Chancery granted a preliminary injunction. . . .

The Court of Chancery found that the Paramount directors violated their fiduciary duties by favoring the Paramount-Viacom transaction over the more valuable unsolicited offer of QVC. The Court of Chancery preliminarily enjoined Paramount and the individual defendants (the "Paramount defendants") from amending or modifying Paramount's stockholder rights agreement (the "Rights Agreement"), including the redemption of the Rights, or taking other action to facilitate the consummation of the pending tender offer by Viacom or any proposed second-step merger, including the Merger Agreement between Paramount and Viacom dated September 12, 1993 (the "Original Merger Agreement"), as amended on October 24, 1993 (the "Amended Merger Agreement"). Viacom and the Paramount defendants were enjoined from taking any action to exercise any provision of the Stock Option Agreement between Paramount and Viacom dated September 12, 1993 (the "Stock Option Agreement"), as amended on October 24, 1993. The Court of Chancery did not grant preliminary injunctive relief as to the termination fee provided for the benefit of Viacom in Section 8.05 of the Original Merger Agreement and the Amended Merger Agreement (the "Termination Fee").

Under the circumstances of this case, the pending sale of control implicated in the Paramount-Viacom transaction required the Paramount Board to act on an informed basis to secure the best value reasonably available to the stockholders. Since we agree with the Court of Chancery that the Paramount directors violated their fiduciary duties, we have AFFIRMED the entry of the order of the Vice Chancellor granting the preliminary injunction and have REMANDED these proceedings to the Court of Chancery for proceedings consistent herewith.

We also have attached an Addendum to this opinion addressing serious deposition misconduct by counsel who appeared on behalf of a Paramount director at the time that director's deposition was taken by a lawyer representing QVC.[2]

I. FACTS

. . . Paramount is a Delaware corporation with its principal offices in New York City. Approximately 118 million shares of Paramount's common

---

2. It is important to put the Addendum in perspective. This Court notes and has noted its appreciation of the outstanding judicial workmanship of the Vice Chancellor and the professionalism of counsel in this matter in handling this expedited litigation with the expertise and skill which characterize Delaware proceedings of this nature. The misconduct noted in the Addendum is an aberration which is not to be tolerated in any Delaware proceeding. [Addendum omitted]

stock are outstanding and traded on the New York Stock Exchange. The majority of Paramount's stock is publicly held by numerous unaffiliated investors. Paramount owns and operates a diverse group of entertainment businesses, including motion picture and television studios, book publishers, professional sports teams, and amusement parks.

There are 15 persons serving on the Paramount Board. Four directors are officer-employees of Paramount: Martin S. Davis ("Davis"), Paramount's Chairman and Chief Executive Officer since 1983; Donald Oresman ("Oresman"), Executive Vice-President, Chief Administrative Officer, and General Counsel; Stanley R. Jaffe, President and Chief Operating Officer; and Ronald L. Nelson, Executive Vice President and Chief Financial Officer. Paramount's 11 outside directors are distinguished and experienced business persons who are present or former senior executives of public corporations or financial institutions.

Viacom is a Delaware corporation with its headquarters in Massachusetts. Viacom is controlled by Sumner M. Redstone ("Redstone"), its Chairman and Chief Executive Officer, who owns indirectly approximately 85.2 percent of Viacom's voting Class A stock and approximately 69.2 percent of Viacom's nonvoting Class B stock through National Amusements, Inc. ("NAI"), an entity 91.7 percent owned by Redstone. Viacom has a wide range of entertainment operations, including a number of well-known cable television channels such as MTV, Nickelodeon, Showtime, and The Movie Channel. Viacom's equity coinvestors in the Paramount-Viacom transaction include NYNEX Corporation and Blockbuster Entertainment Corporation.

QVC is a Delaware corporation with its headquarters in West Chester, Pennsylvania. QVC has several large stockholders, including Liberty Media Corporation, Comcast Corporation, Advance Publications, Inc., and Cox Enterprises Inc. Barry Diller ("Diller"), the Chairman and Chief Executive Officer of QVC, is also a substantial stockholder. QVC sells a variety of merchandise through a televised shopping channel. . . .

Beginning in the late 1980s, Paramount investigated the possibility of acquiring or merging with other companies in the entertainment, media, or communications industry. Paramount considered such transactions to be desirable, and perhaps necessary, in order to keep pace with competitors in the rapidly evolving field of entertainment and communications. Consistent with its goal of strategic expansion, Paramount made a tender offer for Time Inc. in 1989, but was ultimately unsuccessful. *See Paramount Communications, Inc. v. Time Inc.*, Del. Supr., 571 A.2d 1140 (1990) *("Time-Warner")*.

Although Paramount had considered a possible combination of Paramount and Viacom as early as 1990, recent efforts to explore such a transaction began at a dinner meeting between Redstone and Davis on April 20, 1993. Robert Greenhill ("Greenhill"), Chairman of Smith Barney Shearson Inc. ("Smith Barney"), attended and helped facilitate this meeting. After several more meetings between Redstone and Davis, serious negotiations began taking place in early July.

It was tentatively agreed that Davis would be the chief executive officer and Redstone would be the controlling stockholder of the combined company, but the parties could not reach agreement on the merger price and the terms of a stock option to be granted to Viacom. With respect to price, Viacom offered a package of cash and stock (primarily Viacom Class B nonvoting stock) with a market value of approximately $61 per share, but Paramount wanted at least $70 per share.

Shortly after negotiations broke down in July 1993, two notable events occurred. First, Davis apparently learned of QVC's potential interest in Paramount, and told Diller over lunch on July 21, 1993, that Paramount was not for sale. Second, the market value of Viacom's Class B nonvoting stock increased from $46.875 on July 6 to $57.25 on August 20. QVC claims (and Viacom disputes) that this price increase was caused by open market purchases of such stock by Redstone or entities controlled by him.

On August 20, 1993, discussions between Paramount and Viacom resumed when Greenhill arranged another meeting between Davis and Redstone. . . .

On September 12, 1993, the Paramount Board met again and unanimously approved the Original Merger Agreement whereby Paramount would merge with and into Viacom. The terms of the merger provided that each share of Paramount common stock would be converted into 0.10 shares of Viacom Class A voting stock, 0.90 shares of Viacom Class B nonvoting stock, and $9.10 in cash [for a total of $69.14 per share of paramount common stock]. In addition, the Paramount Board agreed to amend its "poison pill" Rights Agreement to exempt the proposed merger with Viacom. The Original Merger Agreement also contained several provisions designed to make it more difficult for a potential competing bid to succeed. We focus, as did the Court of Chancery, on three of these defensive provisions: a "no-shop" provision (the "No-Shop Provision"), the Termination Fee, and the Stock Option Agreement.

First, under the No-Shop Provision, the Paramount Board agreed that Paramount would not solicit, encourage, discuss, negotiate, or endorse any competing transaction unless: (a) a third party "makes an unsolicited written, bona fide proposal, which is not subject to any material contingencies relating to financing"; and (b) the Paramount Board determines that discussions or negotiations with the third party are necessary for the Paramount Board to comply with its fiduciary duties.

Second, under the Termination Fee provision, Viacom would receive a $100 million termination fee if: (a) Paramount terminated the Original Merger Agreement because of a competing transaction; (b) Paramount's stockholders did not approve the merger; or (c) the Paramount Board recommended a competing transaction.

The third and most significant deterrent device was the Stock Option Agreement, which granted to Viacom an option to purchase approximately 19.9 percent (23,699,000 shares) of Paramount's outstanding common stock at $69.14 per share if any of the triggering events for the Termination Fee occurred. In addition to the customary terms that are normally associated with a stock option, the Stock Option Agreement contained two provisions that were both unusual and highly beneficial to Viacom: (a) Viacom was permitted to pay for the shares with a senior subordinated note of questionable marketability instead of cash, thereby avoiding the need to raise the $1.6 billion purchase price (the "Note Feature"); and (b) Viacom could elect to require Paramount to pay Viacom in cash a sum equal to the difference between the purchase price and the market price of Paramount's stock (the "Put Feature"). Because the Stock Option Agreement was not "capped" to limit its maximum dollar value, it had the potential to reach (and in this case did reach) unreasonable levels.

After the execution of the Original Merger Agreement and the Stock Option Agreement on September 12, 1993, Paramount and Viacom announced their proposed merger. In a number of public statements, the parties indicated that the pending transaction was a virtual certainty. Redstone described it as a "marriage" that would "never be torn asunder" and stated that only a "nuclear attack" could break the deal. Redstone also called Diller and John Malone of Tele-Communications Inc., a major stockholder of QVC, to dissuade them from making a competing bid.

Despite these attempts to discourage a competing bid, Diller sent a letter to Davis on September 20, 1993, proposing a merger in which QVC would acquire Paramount for approximately $80 per share, consisting of 0.893 shares of QVC common stock and $30 in cash. QVC also expressed its eagerness to meet with Paramount to negotiate the details of a transaction. When the Paramount Board met on September 27, it was advised by Davis that the Original Merger Agreement prohibited Paramount from having discussions with QVC (or anyone else) unless certain conditions were satisfied. In particular, QVC had to supply evidence that its proposal was not subject to financing contingencies. The Paramount Board was also provided information from Lazard describing QVC and its proposal.

On October 5, 1993, QVC provided Paramount with evidence of QVC's financing. The Paramount Board then held another meeting on October 11, and decided to authorize management to meet with QVC. . . .

On October 21, 1993, QVC filed this action and publicly announced an $80 cash tender offer for 51 percent of Paramount's outstanding shares (the "QVC tender offer"). Each remaining share of Paramount common stock would be converted into 1.42857 shares of QVC common stock in a second-step merger. The tender offer was conditioned on, among other things, the invalidation of the Stock Option Agreement, which was worth over $200 million by that point.[5] QVC contends that it had to commence a tender offer because of the slow pace of the merger discussions and the need to begin seeking clearance under federal antitrust laws.

Confronted by QVC's hostile bid, which on its face offered over $10 per share more than the consideration provided by the Original Merger Agreement, Viacom realized that it would need to raise its bid in order to remain competitive. Within hours after QVC's tender offer was announced, Viacom entered into discussions with Paramount concerning a revised transaction. These discussions led to serious negotiations concerning a comprehensive amendment to the original Paramount Viacom transaction. In effect, the opportunity for a "new deal" with Viacom was at hand for the Paramount Board. With the QVC hostile bid offering greater value to the Paramount stockholders, the Paramount Board had considerable leverage with Viacom.

At a special meeting on October 24, 1993, the Paramount Board approved the Amended Merger Agreement and an amendment to the Stock Option Agreement. The Amended Merger Agreement was, however, essentially the

---

5. By November 15, 1993, the value of the Stock Option Agreement had increased to nearly $500 million based on the $90 QVC bid.

same as the Original Merger Agreement, except that it included a few new provisions. One provision related to an $80 per share cash tender offer by Viacom for 51 percent of Paramount's stock, and another changed the merger consideration so that each share of Paramount would be converted into 0.20408 shares of Viacom Class A voting stock, 1.08317 shares of Viacom Class B nonvoting stock, and 0.20408 shares of a new series of Viacom convertible preferred stock. The Amended Merger Agreement also added a provision giving Paramount the right not to amend its Rights Agreement to exempt Viacom if the Paramount Board determined that such an amendment would be inconsistent with its fiduciary duties because another offer constituted a "better alternative." Finally, the Paramount Board was given the power to terminate the Amended Merger Agreement if it withdrew its recommendation of the Viacom transaction or recommended a competing transaction.

Although the Amended Merger Agreement offered more consideration to the Paramount stockholders and somewhat more flexibility to the Paramount Board than did the Original Merger Agreement, the defensive measures designed to make a competing bid more difficult were not removed or modified. In particular, there is no evidence in record that Paramount sought to use its newly-acquired leverage to eliminate or modify the No-Shop Provision, the Termination Fee, or the Stock Option Agreement when the subject of amending the Original Merger Agreement was on the table.

Viacom's tender offer commenced on October 25, 1993, and QVC's tender offer was formally launched on October 27, 1993. Diller sent a letter to the Paramount Board on October 28 requesting an opportunity to negotiate with Paramount, and Oresman responded the following day by agreeing to meet. The meeting, held on November 1, was not very fruitful, however, after QVC's proposed guidelines for a "fair bidding process" were rejected by Paramount on the ground that "auction procedures" were inappropriate and contrary to Paramount's contractual obligations to Viacom.

On November 6, 1993, Viacom unilaterally raised its tender offer price to $85 per share in cash and offered a comparable increase in the value of the securities being proposed in the second-step merger. At a telephonic meeting held later that day, the Paramount Board agreed to recommend Viacom's higher bid to Paramount's stockholders.

QVC responded to Viacom's higher bid on November 12 by increasing its tender offer to $90 per share and by increasing the securities for its secondstep merger by a similar amount. In response to QVC's latest offer, the Paramount Board scheduled a meeting for November 15, 1993. Prior to the meeting, Oresman sent the members of the Paramount Board a document summarizing the "conditions and uncertainties" of QVC's offer. One director testified that this document gave him a very negative impression of the QVC bid.

At its meeting on November 15, 1993, the Paramount Board determined that the new QVC offer was not in the best interests of the stockholders. The purported basis for this conclusion was that QVC's bid was excessively conditional. The Paramount Board did not communicate with QVC regarding the status of the conditions because it believed that the No-Shop Provision prevented such communication in the absence of firm financing. Several Paramount directors also testified that they believed the Viacom transaction would be more advantageous to Paramount's future business prospects than a QVC transaction.[7] Although a number of materials were distributed to the Paramount Board describing the Viacom and QVC transactions, the only quantitative analysis of the consideration to be received by the stockholders under each proposal was based on then-current market prices of the securities involved, not on the anticipated value of such securities at the time when the stockholders would receive them.

The preliminary injunction hearing in this case took place on November 16, 1993. On November 19, Diller wrote to the Paramount Board to inform it that QVC had obtained financing commitments for its tender offer and that there was no antitrust obstacle to the offer. On November 24, 1993, the Court of Chancery issued its decision granting a preliminary injunction in favor of QVC and the plaintiff stockholders. This appeal followed.

II. APPLICABLE PRINCIPLES OF ESTABLISHED DELAWARE LAW

The General Corporation Law of the State of Delaware (the "General Corporation Law") and the decisions of this Court have repeatedly recognized the fundamental principle that the management of the business and affairs of a Delaware corporation is entrusted to its directors, who are the duly elected and authorized representatives of the stockholders. 8 Del. C. §141(a). Under normal circumstances, neither the courts nor the stockholders should interfere with the managerial decisions of the directors. The business judgment rule embodies the deference to which such decisions are entitled.

Nevertheless, there are rare situations which mandate that a court take a more direct and active role in overseeing the decisions made and actions taken by directors. In these situations, a court subjects the directors' conduct to enhanced scrutiny to ensure that it is reasonable.[9] The decisions of this Court have clearly established the circumstances where such enhanced scrutiny will be applied. *E.g., Unocal*, 493 A.2d 946; *Moran v. Household Int'l, Inc.*, Del. Supr., 500 A.2d 1346 (1985); *Revlon*, 506 A.2d 173; *Mills Acquisition Co. v. Macmillan, Inc.*, Del. Supr., 559 A.2d 1261 (1989); *Gilbert v. El Paso Co.*, Del. Supr., 575 A.2d 1131 (1990). The case at bar implicates two such circumstances: (1) the approval of a transaction resulting in a sale of control, and (2) the adoption of defensive measures in response to a threat to corporate control.

---

7. This belief may have been based on a report prepared by Booz-Allen and distributed to the Paramount Board at its October 24 meeting. The report, which relied on public information regarding QVC, concluded that the synergies of a Paramount-Viacom merger were significantly superior to those of a Paramount-QVC merger. QVC has labeled the Booz-Allen report as a "joke."

9. Where actual self-interest is present and affects a majority of the directors approving a transaction, a court will apply even more exacting scrutiny to determine whether the transaction is entirely fair to the stockholders. *E.g., Weinberger v. UOP, Inc.*, Del. Supr., 457 A.2d 701, 710-11 (1983); *Nixon v. Blackwell*, Del. Supr., 626 A.2d 1366, 1376 (1993).

A. THE SIGNIFICANCE OF A SALE OR CHANGE OF CONTROL

When a majority of a corporation's voting shares are acquired by a single person or entity, or by a cohesive group acting together, there is a significant diminution in the voting power of those who thereby become minority stockholders. Under the statutory framework of the General Corporation Law, many of the most fundamental corporate changes can be implemented only if they are approved by a majority vote of the stockholders. Such actions include elections of directors, amendments to the certificate of incorporation, mergers, consolidations, sales of all or substantially all of the assets of the corporation, and dissolution. 8 Del. C. §§211, 242, 251-258, 263, 271, 275. Because of the overriding importance of voting rights, this Court and the Court of Chancery have consistently acted to protect stockholders from unwarranted interference with such rights.

In the absence of devices protecting the minority stockholders, stockholder votes are likely to become mere formalities where there is a majority stockholder. For example, minority stockholders can be deprived of a continuing equity interest in their corporation by means of a cash-out merger. *Weinberger,* 457 A.2d at 703. Absent effective protective provisions, minority stockholders must rely for protection solely on the fiduciary duties owed to them by the directors and the majority stockholder, since the minority stockholders have lost the power to influence corporate direction through the ballot. The acquisition of majority status and the consequent privilege of exerting the powers of majority ownership come at a price. That price is usually a control premium which recognizes not only the value of a control block of shares, but also compensates the minority stockholders for their resulting loss of voting power.

In the case before us, the public stockholders (in the aggregate) currently own a majority of Paramount's voting stock. Control of the corporation is not vested in a single person, entity, or group, but vested in the fluid aggregation of unaffiliated stockholders. In the event the Paramount-Viacom transaction is consummated, the public stockholders will receive cash and a minority equity voting position in the surviving corporation. Following such consummation, there will be a controlling stockholder who will have the voting power to: (a) elect directors; (b) cause a break-up of the corporation; (c) merge it with another company; (d) cash-out the public stockholders; (e) amend the certificate of incorporation; (f) sell all or substantially all of the corporate assets; or (g) otherwise alter materially the nature of the corporation and the public stockholders' interests. Irrespective of the present Paramount Board's vision of a long-term strategic alliance with Viacom, the proposed sale of control would provide the new controlling stockholder with the power to alter that vision.

Because of the intended sale of control, the Paramount-Viacom transaction has economic consequences of considerable significance to the Paramount stockholders. Once control has shifted, the current Paramount stockholders will have no leverage in the future to demand another control premium. As a result, the Paramount stockholders are entitled to receive, and should receive, a control premium and/or protective devices of significant value. There being no such protective provisions in the Viacom-Paramount transaction, the Paramount directors had an obligation to take the maximum advantage of the current opportunity to realize for the stockholders the best value reasonably available.

B. THE OBLIGATIONS OF DIRECTORS IN A SALE OR CHANGE OF CONTROL TRANSACTION

The consequences of a sale of control impose special obligations on the directors of a corporation. In particular, they have the obligation of acting reasonably to seek the transaction offering the best value reasonably available to the stockholders. The courts will apply enhanced scrutiny to ensure that the directors have acted reasonably. . . .

In the sale of control context, the directors must focus on one primary objective—to secure the transaction offering the best value reasonably available for the stockholders—and they must exercise their fiduciary duties to further that end. The decisions of this Court have consistently emphasized this goal. *Revlon*, 506 A.2d at 182 ("The duty of the board . . . [is] the maximization of the company's value at a sale for the stockholders' benefit."); *Macmillan*, 559 A.2d at 1288 ("[I]n a sale of corporate control the responsibility of the directors is to get the highest value reasonably attainable for the shareholders."). . . .

In pursuing this objective, the directors must be especially diligent. . . . In particular, this Court has stressed the importance of the board being adequately informed in negotiating a sale of control. . . . This requirement is consistent with the general principle that "directors have a duty to inform themselves, prior to making a business decision, of all material information reasonably available to them." *Aronson*, 473 A.2d at 812. *See also Cede & Co. v. Technicolor, Inc.*, Del. Supr., 634 A.2d 345, 367 (1993); *Smith v. Van Gorkom*, Del. Supr., 488 A.2d 858, 872 (1985). Moreover, the role of outside, independent directors becomes particularly important because of the magnitude of a sale of control transaction and the possibility, in certain cases, that management may not necessarily be impartial.

Barkan [*Barkan v. Amsted Indus., Inc.*, 567 A.2d 1279 (Del. 1989)] teaches some of the methods by which a board can fulfill its obligation to seek the best value reasonably available to the stockholders. . . . These methods are designed to determine the existence and viability of possible alternatives. They include conducting an auction, canvassing the market, etc. Delaware law recognizes that there is "no single blueprint" that directors must follow. . . .

In determining which alternative provides the best value for the stockholders, a board of directors is not limited to considering only the amount of cash involved, and is not required to ignore totally its view of the future value of a strategic alliance. *See Macmillan*, 559 A.2d at 1282 n. 29. Instead, the directors should analyze the entire situation and evaluate in a disciplined manner the consideration being offered. Where stock or other non-cash consideration is involved, the board should try to quantify its value, if feasible, to achieve an objective comparison of the alternatives. . . . While the assessment of these factors may be complex, the board's goal is straightforward: Having informed themselves of all material information reasonably available, the directors must decide which alternative is most likely to offer the best value reasonably available to the stockholders.

C. ENHANCED JUDICIAL SCRUTINY OF A SALE OR CHANGE OF CONTROL TRANSACTION

Board action in the circumstances presented here is subject to enhanced scrutiny. Such scrutiny is mandated by: (a) the threatened diminution of the current stockholders' voting power; (b) the fact that an asset belonging to public stockholders (a control premium) is being sold and may never be available again; and (c) the traditional concern of Delaware courts for actions which impair or impede stockholder voting rights . . . In *MacMillan,* this Court held:

> When *Revlon* duties devolve upon directors, this Court will continue to exact an enhanced judicial scrutiny at the threshold, as in *Unocal,* before the normal presumptions of the business judgment rule will apply.[15]

559 A.2d at 1288. The *Macmillan* decision articulates a specific two-part test for analyzing board action where competing bidders are not treated equally:[16]

> In the face of disparate treatment, the trial court must first examine whether the directors properly perceived that shareholder interests were enhanced. In any event the board's action must be reasonable in relation to the advantage sought to be achieved, or conversely, to the threat which a particular bid allegedly poses to stockholder interests.

Id. . . .

The key features of an enhanced scrutiny test are: (a) a judicial determination regarding the adequacy of the decisionmaking process employed by the directors, including the information on which the directors based their decision; and (b) a judicial examination of the reasonableness of the directors' action in light of the circumstances then existing. The directors have the burden of proving that they were adequately informed and acted reasonably.

Although an enhanced scrutiny test involves a review of the reasonableness of the substantive merits of a board's actions,[17] a court should not ignore the

---

15. Because the Paramount Board acted unreasonably as to process and result in this sale of control situation, the business judgment rule did not become operative.

16. Before this test is invoked, "the plaintiff must show, and the trial court must find, that the directors of the target company treated one or more of the respective bidders on unequal terms." *Macmillian,* 559 A.2d at 1288.

17. It is to be remembered that, in cases where the traditional business judgment rule is applicable and the board acted with due care, in good faith, and in the honest belief that they are acting in the best interests of the stockholders (which is not this case), the Court gives great deference to the substance of the directors' decision and will not invalidate the decision, will not examine its reasonableness, and "will not substitute our views for those of the board if the latter's decision can be 'attributed to any rational business purpose.' " *Unocal,*

complexity of the directors' task in a sale of control. There are many business and financial considerations implicated in investigating and selecting the best value reasonably available. The board of directors is the corporate decisionmaking body best equipped to make these judgments. Accordingly, a court applying enhanced judicial scrutiny should be deciding whether the directors made *a reasonable* decision, not *a perfect* decision. If a board selected one of several reasonable alternatives, a court should not second-guess that choice even though it might have decided otherwise or subsequent events may have cast doubt on the board's determination. Thus, courts will not substitute their business judgment for that of the directors, but will determine if the directors' decision was, on balance, within a range of reasonableness. *See Unocal*, 493 A.2d at 955-56; *Macmillan*, 559 A.2d at 1288; *Nixon*, 626 A.2d at 1378.

D.   REVLON AND TIME-WARNER DISTINGUISHED

The Paramount defendants and Viacom assert that the fiduciary obligations and the enhanced judicial scrutiny discussed above are not implicated in this case in the absence of a "break-up" of the corporation, and that the order granting the preliminary injunction should be reversed. This argument is based on their erroneous interpretation of our decisions in *Revlon* and *Time-Warner*.

In *Revlon*, we reviewed the actions of the board of directors of Revlon, Inc. ("Revlon"), which had rebuffed the overtures of Pantry Pride, Inc. and had instead entered into an agreement with Forstmann Little & Co. ("Forstmann") providing for the acquisition of 100 percent of Revlon's outstanding stock by Forstmann and the subsequent break-up of Revlon. Based on the facts and circumstances present in *Revlon*, we held that "[t]he directors' role changed from defenders of the corporate bastion to auctioneers charged with getting the best price for the stockholders at a sale of the company." We further held that "when a board ends an intense bidding contest on an insubstantial basis, . . . [that] action cannot withstand the enhanced scrutiny which *Unocal* requires of director conduct."

It is true that one of the circumstances bearing on these holdings was the fact that "the break-up of the company . . . had become a reality which even the directors embraced." It does not follow, however, that a "break-up" must be present and "inevitable" before directors are subject to enhanced judicial scrutiny and are required to pursue a transaction that is calculated to produce the best value reasonably available to the stockholders. In fact, we stated in *Revlon* that "when bidders make relatively similar offers, or dissolution of the company becomes inevitable, the directors cannot fulfill their enhanced *Unocal* duties by playing favorites with the contending factions." *Revlon* thus does not hold that an inevitable dissolution or "breakup" is necessary.

---

493 A.2d at 949 (*quoting Sinclair Oil Corp. v. Levien*, Del.Supr., 280 A.2d 717, 720 (1971)). *See Aronson*, 473 A.2d at 812.

The decisions of this Court following *Revlon* reinforced the applicability of enhanced scrutiny and the directors' obligation to seek the best value reasonably available for the stockholders where there is a pending sale of control, regardless of whether or not there is to be a break-up of the corporation. In *Macmillan*, this Court held:

> We stated in *Revlon*, and again here, that *in a sale of corporate control* the responsibility of the directors is to get the highest value reasonably attainable for the shareholders.

559 A.2d at 1288 (*emphasis added*). . . .

Although *Macmillan* and *Barkan* are clear in holding that a change of control imposes on directors the obligation to obtain the best value reasonably available to the stockholders, the Paramount defendants have interpreted our decision in *Time-Warner* as requiring a corporate break-up in order for that obligation to apply. The facts in *Time-Warner*, however, were quite different from the facts of this case, and refute Paramount's position here. In *Time-Warner*, the Chancellor held that there was no change of control in the original stock-for-stock merger between Time and Warner because Time would be owned by a fluid aggregation of unaffiliated stockholders both before and after the merger. . . . Moreover, the transaction actually consummated in *Time-Warner* was not a merger, as originally planned, but a sale of Warner's stock to Time.

In our affirmance of the Court of Chancery's well-reasoned decision, this Court held that "The Chancellor's findings of fact are supported by the record and *his conclusion is correct as a matter of law.*" 571 A.2d at 1150 (*emphasis added*). Nevertheless, the Paramount defendants here have argued that a break-up is a requirement and have focused on the following language in our *Time-Warner* decision:

> However, we premise our rejection of plaintiffs' *Revlon* claim on different grounds, namely, the absence of any substantial evidence to conclude that Time's board, in negotiating with Warner, made the dissolution or break-up of the corporate entity inevitable, as was the case in *Revlon*.
>
> Under Delaware law there are, generally speaking and *without excluding other possibilities*, two circumstances which may implicate *Revlon* duties. The first, and clearer one, is when a corporation *initiates an active bidding process seeking to sell itself* or to effect a business reorganization involving a clear breakup of the company. However, *Revlon* duties may also be triggered where, in response to a bidder's offer, a target abandons its long-term strategy and seeks an alternative transaction involving the breakup of the company.

Id. at 1150 (*emphasis added*) (citation and footnote omitted).

The Paramount defendants have misread the holding of *Time-Warner*. Contrary to their argument, our decision in *Time-Warner* expressly states that the two general scenarios discussed in the above-quoted paragraph are not the *only* instances where "*Revlon* duties" may be implicated. The Paramount defendants' argument totally ignores the phrase "without excluding other possibilities." Moreover, the instant case is clearly within the first general scenario set forth in *Time-Warner*. The Paramount Board, albeit unintentionally, had "initiate[d] an active bidding process seeking to sell itself" by agreeing to sell control of the corporation to Viacom in circumstances where another potential acquiror (QVC) was equally interested in being a bidder.

The Paramount defendants' position that *both* a change of control *and* a break-up are *required* must be rejected. Such a holding would unduly restrict the application *of Revlon*, is inconsistent with this Court's decisions in *Barkan* and *Macmillan*, and has no basis in policy. There are few events that have a more significant impact on the stockholders than a sale of control or a corporate break-up. Each event represents a fundamental (and perhaps irrevocable) change in the nature of the corporate enterprise from a practical standpoint. It is the significance of *each* of these events that justifies: (a) focusing on the directors' obligation to seek the best value reasonably available to the stockholders; and (b) requiring a close scrutiny of board action which could be contrary to the stockholders' interests.

Accordingly, when a corporation undertakes a transaction which will cause: (a) a change in corporate control; or (b) a break-up of the corporate entity, the directors' obligation is to seek the best value reasonably available to the stockholders. This obligation arises because the effect of the Viacom-Paramount transaction, if consummated, is to shift control of Paramount from the public stockholders to a controlling stockholder, Viacom. Neither *Time-Warner* nor any other decision of this Court holds that a "break-up" of the company is essential to give rise to this obligation where there is a sale of control.

III. BREACH OF FIDUCIARY DUTIES BY PARAMOUNT BOARD

We now turn to duties of the Paramount Board under the facts of this case and our conclusions as to the breaches of those duties which warrant injunctive relief.

A. THE SPECIFIC OBLIGATIONS OF THE PARAMOUNT BOARD

Under the facts of this case, the Paramount directors had the obligation: (a) to be diligent and vigilant in examining critically the Paramount-Viacom transaction and the QVC tender offers; (b) to act in good faith; (c) to obtain, and act with due care on, all material information reasonably available, including information necessary to compare the two offers to determine which of these transactions, or an alternative course of action, would provide the best value reasonably available to the stockholders; and (d) to negotiate actively and in good faith with both Viacom and QVC to that end.

Having decided to sell control of the corporation, the Paramount directors were required to evaluate critically whether or not all material aspects of the Paramount-Viacom transaction (separately and in the aggregate) were reasonable and in the best interests of the Paramount stockholders in light of current circumstances, including: the change of control premium, the Stock Option Agreement, the Termination Fee, the coercive nature of both the Viacom and

QVC tender offers,[18] the No-Shop Provision, and the proposed disparate use of the Rights Agreement as to the Viacom and QVC tender offers, respectively.

These obligations necessarily implicated various issues, including the questions of whether or not those provisions and other aspects of the Paramount-Viacom transaction (separately and in the aggregate): (a) adversely affected the value provided to the Paramount stockholders; (b) inhibited or encouraged alternative bids; (c) were enforceable contractual obligations in light of the directors' fiduciary duties; and (d) in the end would advance or retard the Paramount directors' obligation to secure for the Paramount stockholders the best value reasonably available under the circumstances.

The Paramount defendants contend that they were precluded by certain contractual provisions, including the No-Shop Provision, from negotiating with QVC or seeking alternatives. Such provisions, whether or not they are presumptively valid in the abstract, may not validly define or limit the directors' fiduciary duties under Delaware law or prevent the Paramount directors from carrying out their fiduciary duties under Delaware law. To the extent such provisions are inconsistent with those duties, they are invalid and unenforceable. *See Revlon,* 506 A.2d at 184-85.

Since the Paramount directors had already decided to sell control, they had an obligation to continue their search for the best value reasonably available to the stockholders. This continuing obligation included the responsibility, at the October 24 board meeting and thereafter, to evaluate critically both the QVC tender offers and the Paramount-Viacom transaction to determine if: (a) the QVC tender offer was, or would continue to be, conditional; (b) the QVC tender offer could be improved; (c) the Viacom tender offer or other aspects of the Paramount-Viacom transaction could be improved; (d) each of the respective offers would be reasonably likely to come to closure, and under what circumstances; (e) other material information was reasonably available for consideration by the Paramount directors; (f) there were viable and realistic alternative courses of action; and (g) the timing constraints could be managed so the directors could consider these matters carefully and deliberately.

B.   THE BREACHES OF FIDUCIARY DUTY BY THE PARAMOUNT BOARD

The Paramount directors made the decision on September 12, 1993, that, in their judgment, a strategic merger with Viacom on the economic terms of the Original Merger Agreement was in the best interests of Paramount and its stockholders. Those terms provided a modest change of control premium to the stockholders. The directors also decided at that time that it was appropriate to agree to certain defensive measures (the Stock Option Agreement, the Termination Fee, and the No-Shop Provision) insisted upon by Viacom as part of

---

18. Both the Viacom and the QVC tender offers were for 51 percent cash and a "back-end" of various securities, the value of each of which depended on the fluctuating value of Viacom and QVC stock at any given time. Thus, both tender offers were two-tiered, front-end loaded, and coercive. Such coercive offers are inherently problematic and should be expected to receive particularly careful analysis by a target board. *See Unocal,* 493 A. 2d at 956.

that economic transaction. Those defensive measures, coupled with the sale of control and subsequent disparate treatment of competing bidders, implicated the judicial scrutiny of *Unocal, Revlon, Macmillan,* and their progeny. We conclude that the Paramount directors' process was not reasonable, and the result achieved for the stockholders was not reasonable under the circumstances.

When entering into the Original Merger Agreement, and thereafter, the Paramount Board clearly gave insufficient attention to the potential consequences of the defensive measures demanded by Viacom. The Stock Option Agreement had a number of unusual and potentially "draconian"[19] provisions, including the Note Feature and the Put Feature. Furthermore, the Termination Fee, whether or not unreasonable by itself, clearly made Paramount less attractive to other bidders, when coupled with the Stock Option Agreement. Finally, the No-Shop Provision inhibited the Paramount Board's ability to negotiate with other potential bidders, particularly QVC which had already expressed an interest in Paramount.[20]

Throughout the applicable time period, and especially from the first QVC merger proposal on September 20 through the Paramount Board meeting on November 15, QVC's interest in Paramount provided the *opportunity* for the Paramount Board to seek significantly higher value for the Paramount stockholders than that being offered by Viacom. QVC persistently demonstrated its intention to meet and exceed the Viacom offers, and frequently expressed its willingness to negotiate possible further increases.

The Paramount directors had the opportunity in the October 23-24 time frame, when the Original Merger Agreement was renegotiated, to take appropriate action to modify the improper defensive measures as well as to improve the economic terms of the Paramount-Viacom transaction. Under the circumstances existing at that time, it should have been clear to the Paramount Board that the Stock Option Agreement, coupled with the Termination Fee and the No-Shop Clause, were impeding the realization of the best value reasonably available to the Paramount stockholders. Nevertheless, the Paramount Board made no effort to eliminate or modify these counterproductive devices, and instead continued to cling to its vision of a strategic alliance with Viacom.

---

19. The Vice Chancellor so characterized the Stock Option Agreement. Court of Chancery Opinion, 635 A.2d 1245, 1272. We express no opinion whether a stock option agreement of essentially this magnitude, but with a reasonable "cap" and without the Note and Put Features, would be valid or invalid under other circumstances. *See Hecco Ventures v. Sea-Land Corp.,* Del. Ch., C.A. No. 8486, 1986 WL 5840, Jacobs, V.C. (May 19, 1986) (21.7 percent stock option); *In re Vitalink Communications Corp. Shareholders Litig.,* Del. Ch., C.A. No. 12085, Chandler, V.C. (May 16, 1990) (19.9 percent stock option).

20. We express no opinion whether certain aspects of the No-Shop Provision here could be valid in another context. Whether or not it could validly have operated here at an early stage solely to prevent Paramount from actively "shopping" the company, it could not prevent the Paramount directors from carrying out their fiduciary duties in considering unsolicited bids or in negotiating for the best value reasonably available to the stockholders. *Macmillan,* 559 A.2d at 1287. As we said in *Barkan:* "Where a board has no reasonable basis upon which to judge the adequacy of a contemplated transaction, a no-shop restriction gives rise to the inference that the board seeks to forestall competing bids." 567 A.2d at 1288. *See also Revlon,* 506 A.2d at 184 (holding that "[t]he no-shop provision, like the lock-up option, while not *per se* illegal, is impermissible under the *Unocal* standards when a board's primary duty becomes that of an auctioneer responsible for selling the company to the highest bidder").

Moreover, based on advice from the Paramount management, the Paramount directors considered the QVC offer to be "conditional" and asserted that they were precluded by the No-Shop Provision from seeking more information from, or negotiating with, QVC.

By November 12, 1993, the value of the revised QVC offer on its face exceeded that of the Viacom offer by over $1 billion at then current values. This significant disparity of value cannot be justified on the basis of the directors' vision of future strategy, primarily because the change of control would supplant the authority of the current Paramount Board to continue to hold and implement their strategic vision in any meaningful way. Moreover, their uninformed process had deprived their strategic vision of much of its credibility.

When the Paramount directors met on November 15 to consider QVC's increased tender offer, they remained prisoners of their own misconceptions and missed opportunities to eliminate the restrictions they had imposed on themselves. Yet, it was not "too late" to reconsider negotiating with QVC. The circumstances existing on November 15 made it clear that the defensive measures, taken as a whole, were problematic: (a) the No-Shop Provision could not define or limit their fiduciary duties; (b) the Stock Option Agreement had become "draconian"; and (c) the Termination Fee, in context with all the circumstances, was similarly deterring the realization of possibly higher bids. Nevertheless, the Paramount directors remained paralyzed by their uninformed belief that the QVC offer was "illusory." This final opportunity to negotiate on the stockholders' behalf and to fulfill their obligation to seek the best value reasonably available was thereby squandered.

IV.   VIACOM'S CLAIM OF VESTED CONTRACT RIGHTS

Viacom argues that it had certain "vested" contract rights with respect to the No-Shop Provision and the Stock Option Agreement. In effect, Viacom's argument is that the Paramount directors could enter into an agreement in violation of their fiduciary duties and then render Paramount, and ultimately its stockholders, liable for failing to carry out an agreement in violation of those duties. Viacom's protestations about vested rights are without merit. This Court has found that those defensive measures were improperly designed to deter potential bidders, and that such measures do not meet the reasonableness test to which they must be subjected. They are consequently invalid and unenforceable under the facts of this case.

The No-Shop Provision could not validly define or limit the fiduciary duties of the Paramount directors. To the extent that a contract, or a provision thereof, purports to require a board to act or not act in such a fashion as to limit the exercise of fiduciary duties, it is invalid and unenforceable. Despite the arguments of Paramount and Viacom to the contrary, the Paramount directors could not contract away their fiduciary obligations. Since the No-Shop Provision was invalid, Viacom never had any vested contract rights in the provision.

As discussed previously, the Stock Option Agreement contained several "draconian" aspects, including the Note Feature and the Put Feature. While we have held that lock-up options are not *per se* illegal, *see Revlon*, 506 A.2d at 183, no options with similar features have ever been upheld by this Court. Under the circumstances of this case, the Stock Option Agreement clearly is invalid. Accordingly, Viacom never had any vested contract rights in that Agreement.

Viacom, a sophisticated party with experienced legal and financial advisors, knew of (and in fact demanded) the unreasonable features of the Stock Option Agreement. It cannot be now heard to argue that it obtained vested contract rights by negotiating and obtaining contractual provisions from a board acting in violation of its fiduciary duties. As the Nebraska Supreme Court said in rejecting a similar argument in *ConAgra, Inc. v. Cargill, Inc.*, 222 Neb. 136, 382 N.W.2d 576, 587-88 (1986), "To so hold, it would seem, would be to get the shareholders coming and going." Likewise, we reject Viacom's arguments and hold that its fate must rise or fall, and in this instance fall, with the determination that the actions of the Paramount Board were invalid.

V. CONCLUSION

The realization of the best value reasonably available to the stockholders became the Paramount directors' primary obligation under these facts in light of the change of control. That obligation was not satisfied, and the Paramount Board's process was deficient. The directors' initial hope and expectation for a strategic alliance with Viacom was allowed to dominate their decisionmaking process to the point where the arsenal of defensive measures established at the outset was perpetuated (not modified or eliminated) when the situation was dramatically altered. QVC's unsolicited bid presented the opportunity for significantly greater value for the stockholders and enhanced negotiating leverage for the directors. Rather than seizing those opportunities, the Paramount directors chose to wall themselves off from material information which was reasonably available and to hide behind the defensive measures as a rationalization for refusing to negotiate with QVC or seeking other alternatives. Their view of the strategic alliance likewise became an empty rationalization as the opportunities for higher value for the stockholders continued to develop. . . .

For the reasons set forth herein, the November 24, 1993, Order of the Court of Chancery has been AFFIRMED, . . .

QUESTIONS

1. Why does the proposed transaction between Paramount and Viacom constitute a change of control? Why is it legally significant that this transaction involves a change of control?

2. How does the Delaware Supreme Court reconcile the reasoning of its decision in *Time-Warner* with the result that it reaches in this case and the reasoning that it uses to support this result? In light of the Court's holding in this case, was there a sale of control in *Time-Warner*?

3. What happened to the duties imposed on the board under *Revlon*? After *QVC*, what triggers the board's duties under *Revlon*? In other words, based on the result reached in this case, when is the company in *Revlon* mode?

4. What standard of judicial review should apply to the original decision of the Paramount board to merge with Viacom? Business judgement rule? *Unocal?* *Revlon?* Entire fairness?

NOTES

1. Dual-Class Stock Structure. The facts of this case reflect another type of shark repellent (i.e., a charter provision that operates as an antitakeover device). Viacom is a publicly traded, Delaware-based company that has two classes of stock outstanding: Class A shares and Class B shares. As described in the case, Sumner Redstone, Viacom's chairman and CEO, controlled approximately 85 percent of the company's voting Class A shares and approximately 70 percent of the company's non-voting Class B stock at the time. *Query:* How does this capital structure operate as an antitakeover device? It is worth noting that this type of dual-class structure is not without some controversy. *See, generally,* Stephen Bainbridge, *The Short Life and Resurrection of SEC Rule 19c-4,* 69 Wash. U. L.Q. 565 (1991); and George W. Dent, *Dual Class Capitalization: A Reply to Professor Seligman,* 54 Geo. Wash. L. Rev. 725 (1986). In fact, during the go-go years of M&A activity in the 1980s, the SEC adopted a one-share/one-vote rule (Rule 19c-4), which was immediately challenged in the courts as exceeding the SEC's authority to regulate stock exchange practices and an encroachment on the province of state corporate law. The rule was ultimately invalidated in *Business Roundtable v. SEC,* 905 F. 2d 406 (D.C. Cir. 1990), although, in the end, the SEC's view prevailed. Under considerable pressure from the SEC, among others, the NYSE voluntarily agreed to adopt a one-share/one-vote standard similar to Rule 19c-4. *See* NYSE Listed Company Manual §313.10. However, the NYSE's provision includes a "grandfather clause" for companies with a dual-class voting structure in place at the time the company lists its shares for trading with the NYSE. As a result, many companies have taken advantage of this grandfather clause by going public with a dual-class voting structure in place at the time of the company's initial public offering (IPO), as was the case with Google's IPO back in 2004, as just one high-profile example.

2. Recent Criticism of the Dual-Class Capital Structure. In 2004, Google went public with a dual-class capital structure in place that gave co-founders Larry Page and Sergey Brin two-thirds of the voting power. "While Google had to overcome opposition [from investment bankers and prospective investors] at the time, [Mark] Zuckerberg [faced] less resistance [at the time Facebook, Inc. went public in 2011]." Jeff Green and Ari Levy, *Zuckerberg Grip Becomes New Normal in Silicon Valley,* May 7, 2012, *available at:* http://bloomberg.com/news/print/2012-05-07/zuckerberg-stock-grip-becomes-new-normal-in-silicon-valley-tech.html. While other technology companies (such as Groupon, Inc., Zillow, Inc., and LinkedIn Corp.) have since gone public with dual-class capital structures in place, arguments over the merits of these capital structures have been "heating up":

> as institutional investors have complained about the increasing number of IPO companies (Facebook, Groupon, Zynga being the most notable) who have gone public as dual class stock companies[, thereby] limiting the rights and influence of shareholders and turning them into economic bystanders. . . .

Institutional investors raise the point that dual class shares limit their ability to press boards and managements to make corrections or changes through the use of the shareholder vote. Those limits, investors allege, create an economic imbalance between management insiders, who usually hold the high voting rights shares and ordinary shareholders whose voting rights are essentially proscribed. Thus insulated, the board and management may engage in (or ignore) value destroying behavior—i.e., News Corp in the phone-hacking scandal or company insiders whose proposed transactions may appear, to some investors, to lack value for all shareholders and could be seen as questionable.

Companies with dual class structures argue that the insulation provides boards and management with an ability to plan and execute for the long-term, lessening the harsh power of quarterly earnings analysis and the short-term challenge of "making the numbers." Dual class stock schemes also create a permanent level of protection against hostile takeovers by short-term holders. The advocates for the use of dual structures state that institutions with concerns about stock performance or shareholder rights can simply sell the stock and walk away.

Both sides cite studies defending their points of view. Governance advocates claim that companies with dual class structures trade at a discount to their non-dual class peers and create less value for ordinary shareholders in the long-term. Dual class companies point to their stock performance refuting the charge they underperform or are perceived by the market as discounted.

In reality institutional investors—the mutual fund complexes, the large public pension funds and the institutional asset managers—with their large pools of indexed capital—are limited in the nature of the responses they can undertake. Simply selling the stock, the "Wall Street Walk" is not a viable option.

Divestment is a difficult process especially for the public pension funds that would need to manage the cost of financial and legal opinions, and lost opportunity cost to the fund's equity portfolios.

So the question, from the governance advocate perspective, is what to do about this trend? Well the answer may be, as posited by some investor[s], to force changes in regulation via Congress, the SEC, the stock exchanges or at the index creators, the Russell Indexes.

What are the prospects for those changes?. . . No matter the results of the upcoming November [2016] election, the House and Senate are likely to remain divided regardless of which party controls the White House so the legislation mandating such a change is doubtful. [Consequently], the [controversy surrounding] dual class structures is one we will be hearing more about in the [future].

Francis H. Byrd, *Dual Class Share Structures: The Next Campaign*, Harvard Law School Forum on Corporate Governance & Financial Regulation, Sept. 16, 2012, *available at*: https://corpgov.law.harvard.edu/2012/09/16/dual-class-share-structures-the-next-campaign/. And, indeed, in Fall 2020 as we once again approach the November election, the controversy surrounding the use of dual class share structures continues to swirl. *See, e.g.,* Lucian Bebchuk and Kobi Kastiel, *The Untenable Case for Perpetual Dual-Class Stock*, Harvard Law School Forum on Corporate Governance & Financial Regulation, April 24, 2017, *available at*: https://corpgov.law.harvard.edu/2017/04/24/the-untenable-case-for-perpetual-dual-class-stock/; and Kosmas Papadopoulos, Institutional Shareholder Services, Inc., *Dual-Class Shares: Governance Risks and Company Performance,* June 28, 2019, *available at*: https://corpgov.law.harvard.edu/2019/06/28/dual-class-shares-governance-risks-and-company-performance/.

In the next case, the Delaware Supreme Court provides important insight into and guidance about what triggers *Revlon* duties, and the court also provides important guidance about what a board *must* do in order to satisfy its *Revlon* duties.

Lyondell Chemical Co. v. Ryan
970 A.2d 235 (Del. 2009)

BERGER, Justice.

We accepted this interlocutory appeal to consider a claim that directors failed to act in good faith in conducting the sale of their company. The Court of Chancery decided that "unexplained inaction" permits a reasonable inference that the directors may have consciously disregarded their fiduciary duties. The trial court expressed concern about the speed with which the transaction was consummated; the directors' failure to negotiate better terms; and their failure to seek potentially superior deals. But the record establishes that the directors were disinterested and independent; that they were generally aware of the company's value and its prospects; and that they considered the offer, under the time constraints imposed by the buyer, with the assistance of financial and legal advisors. At most, this record creates a triable issue of fact on the question of whether the directors exercised due care. There is no evidence, however, from which to infer that the directors knowingly ignored their responsibilities, thereby breaching their duty of loyalty. Accordingly, the directors are entitled to the entry of summary judgment.

FACTUAL AND PROCEDURAL BACKGROUND

Before the merger at issue, Lyondell Chemical Company ("Lyondell") was the third largest independent, publicly traded chemical company in North America. Dan Smith ("Smith") was Lyondell's Chairman and CEO. Lyondell's other ten directors were independent and many were, or had been, CEOs of other large, publicly traded companies. Basell AF ("Basell") is a privately held Luxembourg company owned by Leonard Blavatnik ("Blavatnik") through his ownership of Access Industries. Basell is in the business of polyolefin technology, production and marketing.

In April 2006, Blavatnik told Smith that Basell was interested in acquiring Lyondell. A few months later, Basell sent a letter to Lyondell's board offering $26.50-$28.50 per share. Lyondell determined that the price was inadequate and that it was not interested in selling. During the next year, Lyondell prospered and no potential acquirors expressed interest in the company. In May 2007, an Access affiliate filed a Schedule 13D with the Securities and Exchange Commission disclosing its right to acquire an 8.3% block of Lyondell stock owned by Occidental Petroleum Corporation. The Schedule 13D also disclosed Blavatnik's interest in possible transactions with Lyondell.

In response to the Schedule 13D, the Lyondell board immediately convened a special meeting. The board recognized that the 13D signaled to the market that the company was "in play,"[3] but the directors decided to take a "wait and see" approach. A few days later, Apollo Management, L.P. contacted Smith to suggest a management-led LBO, but Smith rejected that proposal. In late June 2007, Basell announced that it had entered into a $9.6 billion merger agreement with Huntsman Corporation ("Huntsman"), a specialty chemical company. Basell apparently reconsidered, however, after Hexion Specialty Chemicals, Inc. made a topping bid for Huntsman. Faced with competition for Huntsman, Blavatnik returned his attention to Lyondell.

On July 9, 2007, Blavatnik met with Smith to discuss an all-cash deal at $40 per share. Smith responded that $40 was too low, and Blavatnik raised his offer to $44-$45 per share. Smith told Blavatnik that he would present the proposal to the board, but that he thought the board would reject it. Smith advised Blavatnik to give Lyondell his best offer, since Lyondell really was not on the market. The meeting ended at that point, but Blavatnik asked Smith to call him later in the day. When Smith called, Blavatnik offered to pay $48 per share. Under Blavatnik's proposal, Basell would require no financing contingency, but Lyondell would have to agree to a $400 million break-up fee and sign a merger agreement by July 16, 2007.

Smith called a special meeting of the Lyondell board on July 10, 2007 to review and consider Basell's offer. The meeting lasted slightly less than one hour, during which time the board reviewed valuation material that had been prepared by Lyondell management for presentation at the regular board meeting, which was scheduled for the following day. The board also discussed the Basell offer, the status of the Huntsman merger, and the likelihood that another party might be interested in Lyondell. The board instructed Smith to obtain a written offer from Basell and more details about Basell's financing.

Blavatnik agreed to the board's request, but also made an additional demand. Basell had until July 11 to make a higher bid for Huntsman, so Blavatnik asked Smith to find out whether the Lyondell board would provide a firm indication of interest in his proposal by the end of that day. The Lyondell board met on July 11, again for less than one hour, to consider the Basell proposal and how it compared to the benefits of remaining independent. The board decided that it was interested, authorized the retention of Deutsche Bank Securities, Inc. ("Deutsche Bank") as its financial advisor, and instructed Smith to negotiate with Blavatnik.

Basell then announced that it would not raise its offer for Huntsman, and Huntsman terminated the Basell merger agreement. From July 12-July 15 the parties negotiated the terms of a Lyondell merger agreement; Basell conducted due diligence; Deutsche Bank prepared a "fairness" opinion; and Lyondell conducted its regularly scheduled board meeting. The Lyondell board discussed the Basell proposal again on July 12, and later instructed Smith to try to negotiate better terms. Specifically, the board wanted a higher price, a go-shop provision,[4] and a reduced break-up fee. As the trial court noted,

---

3. On the day that the 13D was made public, Lyondell's stock went from $33 to $37 per share.

4. A "go-shop" provision allows the seller to seek other buyers for a specified period after the agreement is signed.

Blavatnik was "incredulous." He had offered his best price, which was a substantial premium, and the deal had to be concluded on his schedule. As a sign of good faith, however, Blavatnik agreed to reduce the break-up fee from $400 million to $385 million.

On July 16, 2007, the board met to consider the Basell merger agreement. Lyondell's management, as well as its financial and legal advisers, presented reports analyzing the merits of the deal. The advisors explained that, notwithstanding the no-shop provision in the merger agreement, Lyondell would be able to consider any superior proposals that might be made because of the "fiduciary out" provision. In addition, Deutsche Bank reviewed valuation models derived from "bullish" and more conservative financial projections. Several of those valuations yielded a range that did not even reach $48 per share, and Deutsche Bank opined that the proposed merger price was fair. Indeed, the bank's managing director described the merger price as "an absolute home run." Deutsche Bank also identified other possible acquirors and explained why it believed no other entity would top Basell's offer. After considering the presentations, the Lyondell board voted to approve the merger and recommend it to the stockholders. At a special stockholders' meeting held on November 20, 2007, the merger was approved by more than 99% of the voted shares. . . .

DISCUSSION

The class action complaint challenging this $13 billion cash merger alleges that the Lyondell directors breached their "fiduciary duties of care, loyalty and candor . . . and . . . put their personal interests ahead of the interests of the Lyondell shareholders." Specifically, the complaint alleges that: 1) the merger price was grossly insufficient; 2) the directors were motivated to approve the merger for their own self-interest;[5] 3) the process by which the merger was negotiated was flawed; 4) the directors agreed to unreasonable deal protection provisions; and 5) the preliminary proxy statement omitted numerous material facts. The trial court rejected all claims except those directed at the process by which the directors sold the company and the deal protection provisions in the merger agreement.

The remaining claims are but two aspects of a single claim, under *Revlon v. MacAndrews & Forbes Holdings, Inc.*, that the directors failed to obtain the best available price in selling the company. As the trial court correctly noted, *Revlon* did not create any new fiduciary duties. It simply held that the "board must perform its fiduciary duties in the service of a specific objective: maximizing the sale price of the enterprise."[7] The trial court reviewed the record, and found that Ryan might be able to prevail at trial on a claim that the Lyondell directors breached their duty of care. But Lyondell's charter includes an exculpatory provision, pursuant to 8 *Del. C.* §102(b)(7), protecting the directors

---

5. The directors' alleged financial interest is the fact that they would receive cash for their stock options.

7. *Malpiede v. Townson*, 780 A.2d 1075, 1083 (Del. 2001).

from personal liability for breaches of the duty of care. Thus, this case turns on whether any arguable shortcomings on the part of the Lyondell directors also implicate their duty of loyalty, a breach of which is not exculpated. Because the trial court determined that the board was independent and was not motivated by self-interest or ill will, the sole issue is whether the directors are entitled to summary judgment on the claim that they breached their duty of loyalty by failing to act in good faith.

This Court examined "good faith"[8] in two recent decisions. *In In re Walt Disney Co. Deriv. Litig.*,[9] the Court discussed the range of conduct that might be characterized as bad faith, and concluded that bad faith encompasses not only an intent to harm but also intentional dereliction of duty:

> [A]t least three different categories of fiduciary behavior are candidates for the "bad faith" pejorative label. The first category involves so-called "subjective bad faith," that is, fiduciary conduct motivated by an actual intent to do harm. . . . [S]uch conduct constitutes classic, quintessential bad faith. . . .
>
> The second category of conduct, which is at the opposite end of the spectrum, involves lack of due care — that is, fiduciary action taken solely by reason of gross negligence and without any malevolent intent. . . . [W]e address the issue of whether gross negligence (including failure to inform one's self of available material facts), without more, can also constitute bad faith. The answer is clearly no. . . .
>
> That leaves the third category of fiduciary conduct, which falls in between the first two categories. . . . This third category is what the Chancellor's definition of bad faith — intentional dereliction of duty, a conscious disregard for one's responsibilities — is intended to capture. The question is whether such misconduct is properly treated as a non-exculpable, nonindemnifiable violation of the fiduciary duty to act in good faith. In our view, it must be. . . .

The *Disney* decision expressly disavowed any attempt to provide a comprehensive or exclusive definition of "bad faith."

A few months later, in *Stone v. Ritter*,[11] this Court addressed the concept of bad faith in the context of an "oversight" claim. We adopted the standard articulated ten years earlier, in *In re Caremark Int'l Deriv. Litig.*:[12]

> [W]here a claim of directorial liability for corporate loss is predicated upon ignorance of liability creating activities within the corporation . . . only a sustained or systematic failure of the board to exercise oversight — such as an utter failure to attempt to assure a reasonable information and reporting system exists — will establish the lack of good faith that is a necessary condition to liability.

---

8. Our corporate decisions tend to use the terms "bad faith" and "failure to act in good faith" interchangeably, although in a different context we noted that, "[t]he two concepts-bad faith and conduct not in good faith are not necessarily identical." 25 *Massachusetts Avenue Property LLC v. Liberty Property Limited Partnership*, Del.Supr., No. 188, 2008, Order at p. 5 (November 25, 2008). For purposes of this appeal, we draw no distinction between the terms.

9. 906 A.2d 27, [at 64-66] (Del. 2006).

11. 911 A.2d 362 (Del. 2006).

12. 698 A.2d 959, 971 (Del. Ch. 1996).

The *Stone* Court explained that the *Caremark* standard is fully consistent with the *Disney* definition of bad faith. *Stone* also clarified any possible ambiguity about the directors' mental state, holding that "imposition of liability requires a showing that the directors knew that they were not discharging their fiduciary obligations."[13]

The Court of Chancery recognized these legal principles, but it denied summary judgment in order to obtain a more complete record before deciding whether the directors had acted in bad faith. Under other circumstances, deferring a decision to expand the record would be appropriate. Here, however, the trial court reviewed the existing record under a mistaken view of the applicable law. Three factors contributed to that mistake. First, the trial court imposed *Revlon* duties on the Lyondell directors before they either had decided to sell, or before the sale had become inevitable. Second, the court read *Revlon* and its progeny as creating a set of requirements that must be satisfied during the sale process. Third, the trial court equated an arguably imperfect attempt to carry out *Revlon* duties with a knowing disregard of one's duties that constitutes bad faith.

. . . The Court of Chancery identified several undisputed facts that would support the entry of judgment in favor of the Lyondell directors: the directors were "active, sophisticated, and generally aware of the value of the Company and the conditions of the markets in which the Company operated." They had reason to believe that no other bidders would emerge, given the price Basell had offered and the limited universe of companies that might be interested in acquiring Lyondell's unique assets. Smith negotiated the price up from $40 to $48 per share—a price that Deutsche Bank opined was fair. Finally, no other acquiror expressed interest during the four months between the merger announcement and the stockholder vote.

Other facts, however, led the trial court to "question the adequacy of the Board's knowledge and efforts. . . ." After the Schedule 13D was filed in May, the directors apparently took no action to prepare for a possible acquisition proposal. The merger was negotiated and finalized in less than one week, during which time the directors met for a total of only seven hours to consider the matter. The directors did not seriously press Blavatnik for a better price, nor did they conduct even a limited market check. Moreover, although the deal protections were not unusual or preclusive, the trial court was troubled by "the Board's decision to grant considerable protection to a deal that may not have been adequately vetted under *Revlon*."

The trial court found the directors' failure to act during the two months after the filing of the Basell Schedule 13D critical to its analysis of their good faith. The court pointedly referred to the directors' "two months of slothful indifference despite *knowing* that the Company was in play," and the fact that they "languidly awaited overtures from potential suitors. . . ." In the end, the trial court found that it was this "failing" that warranted denial of their motion for summary judgment . . .

The problem with the trial court's analysis is that *Revlon* duties do not arise simply because a company is "in play."[23] The duty to seek the best available price

---

13. *Stone*, 911 A.2d at 370.

23. *Paramount Communications, Inc. v. Time, Inc.*, 571 A.2d 1140, 1151 (Del. 1989).

applies only when a company embarks on a transaction—on its own initiative or in response to an unsolicited offer—that will result in a change of control. Basell's Schedule 13D did put the Lyondell directors, and the market in general, on notice that Basell was interested in acquiring Lyondell. The directors responded by promptly holding a special meeting to consider whether Lyondell should take any action. The directors decided that they would neither put the company up for sale nor institute defensive measures to fend off a possible hostile offer. Instead, they decided to take a "wait and see" approach. That decision was an entirely appropriate exercise of the directors' business judgment. The time for action under *Revlon* did not begin until July 10, 2007, when the directors began negotiating the sale of Lyondell.

The Court of Chancery focused on the directors' two months of inaction, when it should have focused on the one week during which they considered Basell's offer. During that one week, the directors met several times; their CEO tried to negotiate better terms; they evaluated Lyondell's value, the price offered and the likelihood of obtaining a better price; and then the directors approved the merger. The trial court acknowledged that the directors' conduct during those seven days might not demonstrate anything more than lack of due care.[25] But the court remained skeptical about the directors' good faith—at least on the present record. That lingering concern was based on the trial court's synthesis of the *Revlon* line of cases, which led it to the erroneous conclusion that directors must follow one of several courses of action to satisfy their *Revlon* duties.

There is only one *Revlon* duty—to "[get] the best price for the stockholders at a sale of the company."[26] No court can tell directors exactly how to accomplish that goal, because they will be facing a unique combination of circumstances, many of which will be outside their control. As we noted in *Barkan v. Amsted Industries, Inc.*, "there is no single blueprint that a board must follow to fulfill its duties."[27] That said, our courts have highlighted both the positive and negative aspects of various boards' conduct under *Revlon*.[28] The trial court drew several principles from those cases: directors must "engage actively in the sale process," and they must confirm that they have obtained the best available price either by conducting an auction, by conducting a market check, or by demonstrating "an impeccable knowledge of the market."

The Lyondell directors did not conduct an auction or a market check, and they did not satisfy the trial court that they had the "impeccable" market knowledge that the court believed was necessary to excuse their failure to pursue one of the first two alternatives. As a result, the Court of Chancery was unable to conclude that the directors had met their burden under *Revlon*. In evaluating the

---

25. [*Ryan v. Lyondell Chemical Co.*, WL 4174038 at *4 (Del. Ch. 2008).]

26. *Revlon*, 506 A.2d at 182.

27. 567 A.2d 1279, 1286 (Del. 1989).

28. *See, e.g.: Barkan v. Amsted Industries, Inc.*, 567 A.2d at 1287 (Directors need not conduct a market check if they have reliable basis for belief that price offered is best possible.); *Paramount Communications, Inc. v. QVC Network, Inc.*, 637 A.2d 34, 49 (Del. 1994) (No-shop provision impermissibly interfered with directors' ability to negotiate with another known bidder); *In re Netsmart Technologies, Inc., Shareholders Litig.*, 924 A.2d 171, 199 (Del. Ch. 2007) (Plaintiff likely to succeed on claim based on board's failure to consider strategic buyers.)

totality of the circumstances, even on this limited record, we would be inclined to hold otherwise. But we would not question the trial court's decision to seek additional evidence if the issue were whether the directors had exercised due care. Where, as here, the issue is whether the directors failed to act in good faith, the analysis is very different, and the existing record mandates the entry of judgment in favor of the directors.

As discussed above, bad faith will be found if a "fiduciary intentionally fails to act in the face of a known duty to act, demonstrating a conscious disregard for his duties."[31] The trial court decided that the *Revlon* sale process must follow one of three courses, and that the Lyondell directors did not discharge that "known set of [*Revlon*] 'duties.' " But, as noted, there are no legally prescribed steps that directors must follow to satisfy their *Revlon* duties. Thus, the directors' failure to take any specific steps during the sale process could not have demonstrated a conscious disregard of their duties. More importantly, there is a vast difference between an inadequate or flawed effort to carry out fiduciary duties and a conscious disregard for those duties.

Directors' decisions must be reasonable, not perfect.[33] "In the transactional context, [an] extreme set of facts [is] required to sustain a disloyalty claim premised on the notion that disinterested directors were intentionally disregarding their duties."[34] The trial court denied summary judgment because the Lyondell directors' "unexplained inaction" prevented the court from determining that they had acted in good faith. But, if the directors failed to do all that they should have under the circumstances, they breached their duty of care. Only if they knowingly and completely failed to undertake their responsibilities would they breach their duty of loyalty. The trial court approached the record from the wrong perspective. Instead of questioning whether disinterested, independent directors did everything that they (arguably) should have done to obtain the best sale price, the inquiry should have been whether those directors utterly failed to attempt to obtain the best sale price.

Viewing the record in this manner leads to only one possible conclusion. The Lyondell directors met several times to consider Basell's premium offer. They were generally aware of the value of their company and they knew the chemical company market. The directors solicited and followed the advice of their financial and legal advisors. They attempted to negotiate a higher offer even though all the evidence indicates that Basell had offered a "blowout" price. Finally, they approved the merger agreement, because "it was simply too good not to pass along [to the stockholders] for their consideration." We assume, as we must on summary judgment, that the Lyondell directors did absolutely nothing to prepare for Basell's offer, and that they did not even consider conducting a market check before agreeing to the merger. Even so, this record clearly establishes that the Lyondell directors did not breach their duty of loyalty by failing to act in good faith. In concluding otherwise, the Court of Chancery reversibly erred.

---

31. *Disney* at 67.
33. *Paramount Communications, Inc. v. QVC Network, Inc.*, 637 A.2d at 45.
34. *In re Lear Corp. S'holder Litig.*, 2008 WL 4053221 at *11 (Del.Ch.).

CONCLUSION

Based on the foregoing, the decision of the Court of Chancery is reversed and this matter is remanded for entry of judgment in favor of the Lyondell directors. Jurisdiction is not retained.

NOTES

1. The Implications of Lyondell for Future M&A Transactions. The legal significance of the Delaware Supreme Court's decision in *Lyondell* has been the subject of considerable commentary. In the words of one leading M&A law firm:

> In an important decision, the Delaware Supreme Court [in *Lyondell*] has firmly rejected post-merger stockholder claims that directors failed to act in good faith in selling the company, even if it were assumed that they did nothing to prepare for an impending offer and did not even consider conducting a market check before entering into a merger agreement (at a substantial premium to market) containing a no-shop provision and a 3.2% break-up fee. The *en banc* decision, authored by Justice Berger, is a sweeping rejection of attempts to impose personal liability on directors for their actions in responding to acquisition proposals, and reaffirms the board's wide discretion in managing a sale process. . . .
>
> The key to the Supreme Court's opinion was its unremitting focus on the effect of the charter exculpation provision [*see* Del. §102(b)(7)] foreclosing liability for duty of care claims, leaving only the possibility of duty of loyalty claims based on a failure to act in good faith—which requires a court to find a "conscious disregard" of "known duties." [*See Stone v. Ritter*, 911 A.2d 362 (Del. 2006); and *In re Caremark International Derivative Litigation*, 698 A.2d 959 (Del. Ch. 1996).] The Court made clear that hindsight debate about whether directors should have done something more or differently will not suffice to create a possibility of post-transaction personal liability . . . .
>
> The Supreme Court's opinion is a powerful statement that courts appreciate the complex decisions directors must make in selling the company, and will not allow post hoc process attacks to be deemed indicative of bad faith. Stockholders can still seek a preliminary injunction against a merger. But disinterested, independent directors will not face the threat of personal monetary liability unless truly egregious circumstances are shown in which the directors consciously disregard their known duties by utterly failing to attempt to obtain the best available sale price.
>
> In this fundamental sense, the Supreme Court's decision [in *Lyondell*] fully implements Delaware's legislative policy, reflected in Section 102(b)(7), of protecting directors from personal liability for what are essentially duty of care claims, whether pleaded in that form or not. The need for the legislation was itself created by the Court's 1985 decision in *Smith v. Van Gorkom*, imposing person liability on directors for failing to devote sufficient care to approval of an arms-length, premium-to-market merger agreement subject to an open stockholder vote. *Lyondell* shows that the legislative response to *Van Gorkom* has worked as intended: the Delaware courts will not permit plaintiffs to plead around it.

Theodore N. Mirvis, et al., Wachtell, Lipton, Rosen, & Katz, *Delaware Supreme Court Rejects Claims against Directors Challenging Sale Process*, Mar. 26, 2009, *available at:*

https://www.wlrk.com/webdocs/wlrknew/AttorneyPubs/WLRK.16565.09.pdf.
Query: What do you think—did the Delaware Supreme Court reached the correct result in *Lyondell?* Is the decision in *Lyondell* consistent with the result and
reasoning of the Delaware Supreme Court's decision in *Smith v. Van Gorkom?* Is
the decision in *Lyondell* consistent with the standards established in *Revlon* and
its progeny?

   2. The RBC *Case: The Role of the Investment Banker in an M&A Transaction.*
As we saw in the case in Chapter 1 describing AT&T's acquisition of DirecTV,
the investment banker will typically take the lead in advising Target Co. with
regard to the best process for selling the company. In addition, in Chapter 4, we
saw that the investment banker will typically be retained by the publicly traded
Target to provide the board of directors with a "fairness opinion," in which the
banker opines as to the adequacy of the consideration being offered by the
Bidder. We observed that, in preparing the fairness opinion, the investment
banker faces inherent conflicts of interest, most notably that the banker's compensation is usually contingent on successful completion of the M&A transaction. *See supra,* pp. 291-294.
   In the case of *RBC Capital Markets, LLC v Jervis,* 129 A. 3d 816 (Del. 2015),
the Delaware Supreme Court addressed this potential for investment bankers'
conflict of interest. More important for our purposes, in the course of its opinion, the Delaware Supreme Court offered important guidance as to the proper
role of the investment banker when serving as financial advisor to Target Co.
in connection with advising the board of directors regarding the process for
selling Target's business. For purposes of focusing on the banker's conflict of
interest that was at issue in the *RBC* case, the facts of this rather complicated
case are briefly summarized in the following excerpt:

> **Edward B. Micheletti**
> **Delaware Supreme Court Provides Guidance on**
> **Aiding-and-Abetting Liability for Financial Advisors**
> **Skadden, Arps, Slate, Meagher & Flom LLP, Insights (May 19, 2016)**
> *Available at:* **https://www.skadden.com/insights/publications/2016/05/**
> **delaware-supreme-court-provides-guidance-on-aiding**

[Factual] Background

   On March 28, 2011, Rural/Metro Corporation (Rural) entered into a
merger agreement with Warburg Pincus LLC, a private equity firm, to sell Rural
for $17.25 per share. Stockholder plaintiffs brought class claims for breach of
fiduciary duty against the board, alleging that the sale process was not reasonable under *Revlon,* and that the proxy statement issued in connection with the
merger was materially misleading. The plaintiffs included claims against Rural's
financial advisors—RBC Capital Markets, LLC (RBC) and Moelis, LLC—for
aiding and abetting the board's breaches of fiduciary duty.

Days before trial, Moelis and the board agreed to pay $5 million and $6.6 million, respectively, to settle the claims against them. The case proceeded to trial, with claims pending against RBC alone. In March 2014, the Court of Chancery issued its post-trial opinion, finding RBC liable for aiding and abetting the board's breaches of the duty of care. *In re Rural/Metro Corp. Stockholders Litig.*, 88 A.3d 54, 63 (Del. Ch. 2014).

In his opinion, Vice Chancellor J. Travis Laster found that in December 2010 the board formed a special committee to explore strategic alternatives, including the possible acquisition of a business owned by its chief competitor, Emergency Medical Services [Corporation] (EMS). The court went on to find, however, that the board had not expressly authorized the special committee to initiate a sale process at that time. Nevertheless, the court found that the special committee proceeded as if Rural was for sale and interviewed several financial advisors, ultimately selecting RBC to serve as its primary financial advisor. According to the court, RBC pitched the board on the efficacy of coordinating the timing of the Rural sale with the sale of EMS but did not disclose its plan to use the Rural engagement as an "angle" to provide financing to potential bidders for EMS.

The court held that RBC's desire to obtain financing work for the EMS acquisition also drove it to favor certain bidders in the Rural sale process. Specifically, the court found that RBC's "two-track" auction process enabled it to prioritize EMS bidders so they would include RBC in their financing trees.* The court also explained that RBC continued to drive this dual track process despite receiving negative feedback about its timing and design [from other prospective buyers interested in acquiring Rural's business]. The vice chancellor found that this "faulty design prevented the emergence of the type of competitive dynamic among multiple bidders that is necessary for reliable price discovery," as many of the large private equity firms were "sidelined" because of the EMS process, and the timing was not right for the logical strategic bidders. As a result, Warburg (which had withdrawn from the EMS process) was able to price its offers aggressively.

The court also found that in the last days before the merger was approved, RBC unsuccessfully lobbied Warburg to provide "stapled financing" for the Rural acquisition. The court held that during this time, RBC purposely manipulated its fairness analysis in order to make the Warburg offer look more attractive. Moelis and RBC provided written financial analyses [as part of RBC's fairness opinion to the Rural board], and RBC orally opined that the merger was fair to the Rural stockholders at $17.25 per share, or roughly $437 million equity value. According to the court, the board had never before received any valuation for the company and received these analyses just three hours before the [Rural] board met to consider the [proposed] transaction [with Warburg]. Nevertheless, the board approved the merger, and it closed in June 2011 following approval by Rural's stockholders.

The Court of Chancery concluded that the board's actions beginning in December 2010 were subject to enhanced scrutiny under *Revlon*, and that the

---

* [By the author: In the lexicon of investment bankers, the term "financing tree" refers to the efforts of investment banking firms to "run multiple teams competing to offer [financing services] to different bidders [seeking to acquire] strong LBO targets..." Ross Pooley, Latham & Watkins, LLP, *Acquisition Financing Trends: The New Battlefield*, April 16, 2010, *available at:* http://www.lexology.com/library/detail.aspx?g=ea950586-8a1e41c4-871c0567161d5600.]

plaintiffs had proven the board's decisions in the sale process were outside the range of reasonableness. The vice chancellor further held that the proxy statement Rural issued in connection with the transaction was materially misleading as to several issues, including RBC's financial analysis and its undisclosed conflicts of interest arising from its use of the Rural deal as an "angle" to obtain business from an EMS transaction. Finally, the court held that RBC was liable for aiding and abetting the board's breaches of fiduciary duty. . . .

[DELAWARE] SUPREME COURT'S OPINION . . .

[In a unanimous opinion, the Delaware Supreme Court affirmed all of the holdings of the Court of Chancery.]

[With respect to the board's] breaches of fiduciary duty, the Supreme Court affirmed the Court of Chancery's conclusion that under *Revlon*, the board's overall course of conduct in the sale process was outside the range of reasonableness ["by failing to take reasonable steps to attain the best value reasonably available to the stockholders"]. In support of that conclusion, the Supreme Court pointed to the board's lack of awareness regarding RBC's conflicts and the "two-track" bidding process. Because the board was ill-informed, it "took no steps to address or mitigate RBC's conflicts." In addition, the Supreme Court agreed that the board was not adequately informed as to Rural's stand-alone value, which, based on the evidence adduced at trial, exceeded what Warburg or another private equity buyer would have paid. Finally, the Supreme Court affirmed the Court of Chancery's holding that the proxy statement was materially misleading, because it did not accurately represent the valuation analysis RBC conducted and did not disclose RBC's "unquestionably material" conflicts of interest. . . .

In that portion of the *RBC* opinion set forth below, the Delaware Supreme Court analyzes the claim against RBC for aiding-and-abetting the Rural board's breaches of fiduciary duty during a sale of control transaction that invoked the board's *Revlon* duties.

▌▌ RBC Capital Markets, LLC v Jervis,
129 A.3d 816 (Del. 2015)

VALIHURA, Justice . . .

C.   RBC AIDED AND ABETTED THE BOARD'S BREACHES . . .

3.   DISCUSSION

In *Malpiede v. Townson*, this Court described the elements of aiding and abetting breaches of fiduciary duty as: (i) the existence of a fiduciary relationship,

(ii) a breach of the fiduciary's duty, (iii) knowing participation in that breach by the defendants, and (iv) damages proximately caused by the breach.[164] The first two elements are established . . . [by virtue of the Court's ruling that Rural's board of directors had breached their fiduciary duties].

As to the third element, this Court, in *Malpiede*, observed that "[a] third party may be liable for aiding and abetting a breach of a corporate fiduciary's duty to the stockholders if the third party 'knowingly participates' in the breach."[165] We stated further that "[k]nowing participation in a board's fiduciary breach requires that the third party act with the knowledge that the conduct advocated or assisted constitutes such a breach."[166] As an example, this Court has said that "a bidder may be liable to the target's stockholders if the bidder attempts to create or exploit conflicts of interest in the board."[167] The trial court, in a lengthy analysis of aiding and abetting law and tort law, held that if a "[i]f the third party knows that the board is breaching its duty of care and participates in the breach by misleading the board or creating the informational vacuum, then the third party can be liable for aiding and abetting."[168] We affirm this narrow holding.

It is the aider and abettor that must act with *scienter*. The aider and abettor must act "knowingly, intentionally, or with reckless indifference . . . [;]"[169] that is, with an "illicit state of mind."[170] To establish *scienter*, the plaintiff must demonstrate that the aider and abettor had "actual or constructive knowledge that their conduct was legally improper."[171] Accordingly, the question of whether a defendant acted with *scienter* is a factual determination. The trial court found that, "[o]n the facts of this case, RBC acted with the necessary degree of *scienter* and can be held liable for aiding and abetting."[173] The evidence supports this finding.

---

164. *Malpiede [v. Townson*, 780 A.2d 1075], 1096 [(Del. 2001)] (quoting *Penn Mart Realty Co. v. Becker*, 298 A.2d 349, 351 (Del. Ch.1972)). . . In *Malpiede*, we "express[ed] no view on the question whether a third party may 'knowingly participate' in or give substantial assistance to a board's grossly negligent conduct or whether a third party may be liable for aiding and abetting only if the board's breach is intentional." *Malpiede*, 780 A.2d at 1097 n.78 (citations omitted).

165. *Malpiede*, 780 A.2d at 1096 (quoting [*Gilbert v. El Paso Co.*, Del. Ch., 490 A.2d 1050, 1057 (1984)], (citations omitted). *See also* [*Mills Acquisition Co. v. MacMillan, Inc.*, 559 A.2d 1261, 1284 n.33 (Del. 1989)] (noting that "it is bedrock law that the conduct of one who knowingly joins with a fiduciary, including corporate officials, in a breach of a fiduciary obligation, is equally culpable").

166. *Malpiede*, 780 A.2d at 1097 (citations omitted).

167. *Id.* (citing *Gilbert*, 490 A.2d at 1058 ("[A]lthough an offeror may attempt to obtain the lowest possible price for stock through arm's-length negotiations with the target's board, it may not knowingly participate in the target board's breach of fiduciary duty by extracting terms which require the opposite party to prefer its interests at the expense of its shareholders.") (citations omitted).

168. [*In re Rural Metro Corp. Stockholders Litig.*, 88 A.3d 54, 97 (Del. Ch. 2014) (*Rural I*).]

169. *Metro Commc'n Corp. BVI v. Advanced Mobilecomm Techs. Inc.*, 854 A.2d 121, 143 (Del. Ch.2004) (quoting *DRR, L.L.C. v. Sears, Roebuck & Co.*, 949 F.Supp. 1132, 1137 (D.Del.1996)). . . .

170. *In re Oracle Corp.*, 867 A.2d 904, 931 (Del. Ch.2004).

171. *Wood v. Baum*, 953 A.2d 136, 141 (Del.2008) (citing *Malpiede, 780 A.2d 1075*); . . .

173. *Rural I*, 88 A.3d at 97.

RBC knowingly induced the breach by exploiting its own conflicted interests to the detriment of Rural and by creating an informational vacuum. RBC's knowing participation included its failure to disclose its interest in obtaining a financing role in the EMS transaction and how it planned to use its engagement as Rural's advisor to capture buy-side financing work from bidders for EMS; its knowledge that the Board and Special Committee were uninformed about Rural's value; and its failure to disclose to the Board its interest in providing the winning bidder in the Rural process with buy-side financing and its eleventh-hour attempts to secure that role while simultaneously leading the negotiations on price. RBC's desire for Warburg's business also manifested itself in its financial analysis, provided by RBC the day the Board approved the merger. RBC's illicit manipulation of the Board's deliberative processes for self-interested purposes was enabled, in part, by the Board's own lack of oversight, affording RBC "the opportunity to indulge in the misconduct which occurred."[175] The Board was unaware of RBC's modifications to the valuation analysis, back-channel communications with Warburg, and eleventh-hour attempt to capture at least a portion of the acquirer's buy-side financing business. RBC made no effort to advise the Rural directors about these contextually shaping points. The result was a poorly-timed sale at a price that was not the product of appropriate efforts to obtain the best value reasonably available and, as the trial court found, a failure to recognize that Rural's stand-alone value exceeded the sale price.

RBC's failure to fully disclose its conflicts and ulterior motives to the Board, in turn, led to a lack of disclosure in the Proxy Statement. The Proxy Statement included materially misleading information that RBC presented to the Board in its financial presentation and omitted information about RBC's conflicts.

The manifest intentionality of RBC's conduct—as evidenced by the bankers' own internal communications—is demonstrative of the advisor's knowledge of the reality that the Board was proceeding on the basis of fragmentary and misleading information. Propelled by its own improper motives, RBC misled the Rural directors into breaching their duty of care, thereby aiding and abetting the Board's breach of its fiduciary obligations. . . .

IV. CONCLUSION

For the foregoing reasons, the Final Order and Judgment of the Court of Chancery is hereby AFFIRMED.

NOTES

1. "Staple Financing" and the Investment Banker's Conflict of Interest. In the course of its opinion, the Delaware Supreme Court in *RBC* referred to "staple financing." On Wall Street, *staple financing* is generally understood to refer to an arrangement made between investment bankers and prospective Bidders

---

175. *Mills*, 559 A.2d at 1279.

whereby the banking firm representing the *seller;* i.e., Target Co., agrees to provide *buy-side financing* in order to allow the prospective Bidder Co. to complete its proposed acquisition of Target. Of course, very often these staple financing arrangements further provide that the (rather substantial) fees to be paid to the investment banking firm are contingent on the closing of the proposed acquisition. The name *staple financing* refers to the fact that the financing details (i.e., the principal amount of the loan, any fees, and any loan covenants) are typically "stapled" to the back of the acquisition term sheet.

Many participants in the M&A market believe that the use of staple financing arrangements provides certain benefits in the context of an acquisition. Since Bidder's financing is already in place, Target is often able to generate more timely bids. In addition, since staple financing is in reality a form of pre-approved loan, Bidders can avoid the last-minute, often frenzied scramble to secure financing for the proposed acquisition, thereby expediting the deal-making process. However, this financing arrangement does put the investment banker on both sides of the transaction — that is, the banker is providing financial advisory services to Target (for a fee) and is also lending money to Bidder (also for a fee). This has led some market participants to harbor concerns about the conflicts of interest that are inherent in a staple financing arrangement.

One such "staple financing" arrangement was challenged as part of the leveraged buyout (LBO) transaction that was at issue in *In re Del Monte Foods Co. Shareholders Litigation*, 25 A.3d 813 (Del. Ch. 2011). Briefly summarized, Vice Chancellor Laster

> found that after the Del Monte board called off a process of exploring a potential sale [of the company] in early 2010, [Del Monte's] investment bankers continued to meet with several of the [prospective] bidders — without the approval or knowledge of Del Monte — ultimately yielding a new joint bid from two buyout firms late in 2010. While still representing the [Del Monte] board and before the parties had reached agreement on price, Del Monte's bankers sought and received permission to provide buy-side financing, which [in turn] required [Del Monte] to retain another investment advisor to render an unconflicted fairness opinion. Del Monte reached a high-premium deal with a "go-shop" provision and deal protection devices including a termination fee and matching rights. The original bankers were then tasked with running Del Monte's go-shop process (which yielded no further offers), although the Court noted [that the bankers] stood to earn a substantial fee from financing the pending acquisition [as a result of the "staple financing" arrangement entered into with the two buyout firms.]
>
> Vice Chancellor Laster was troubled by the investment bank's effort to combine two bidders without consulting the board and in apparent contravention of a "no teaming" provision [that was part of the] confidentiality agreements entered into in connection with the original [deal-making] process. While the Court noted that "the blame for what took place appears at this preliminary stage to lie with [the banker], the buck stops with the Board" because "Delaware law requires that a board take an active and direct role in the sale process." [*Del Monte, supra,* at 835.] The Court also faulted [Del Monte's] board for agreeing to allow the competing bidders to work together and [also for allowing] the bankers to provide buy-side financing (even while overseeing the go-shop period) without "making any effort to obtain a benefit for Del Monte and its stockholders." . . . [Vice Chancellor Laster] warned that "investment banks representing sellers [should] not create

the appearance that they desire buy-side work" but instead focus on assisting the target board in fulfilling its fiduciary duties.

In response to these process deficiencies, the Court enjoined the vote on the transaction and the enforcement of the deal protection devices for twenty days, holding that without such relief, "the Del Monte stockholders will be deprived forever of the opportunity to receive a pre-vote topping bid in a process free of taint from [these] improper activities." [*Id.* at 838.] The Court also expressly held open the possibility of a damages remedy against the lead bidder for "colluding" with the bankers.

[Vice Chancellor Laster's decision in *Del Monte*] serves as an important reminder to all participants in M&A transactions that the terms of confidentiality agreements should be properly respected, that bankers should receive and follow clear instructions from [Target] boards, and that bankers should ensure that any conflicts of interest are disclosed in advance, [and] with specificity, to the [Target's] board of directors. . . . [Equally important, Target] boards should pay close attention to how a sales process is managed to avoid findings of favoritism. The [Target] board should lead any sales process and actively supervise [its bankers].

Theodore N. Mirvis, *et al.*, Wachtell, Lipton, Rosen, & Katz, *Buyout and Deal Protections Enjoined Due to Conflicted Advisor*, Feb. 15, 2011, *available at:* https://corpgov.law.harvard.edu/2011/02/16/buyout-and-deal-protections-enjoined-due-to-conflicted-advisor/; and Theodore N. Mirvis and Paul K. Rowe, Wachtell, Lipton, Rosen, & Katz, *Settlement of* Del Monte *Buyout Litigation Highlights Risks Where Target Advisors Seek a Buyer-Financing Role*, October 21, 2011, *available at:* https://corpgov.law.harvard.edu/2011/10/21/del-monte-settlement-highlights-risk-of-conflicts-in-buyout-financing/.

2. Investment Banker as Gatekeeper? What is the proper role of the investment banker in an M&A transaction? In its opinion, the Court of Chancery stated that, as the financial advisor to the board, RBC had obligations to act as a "gatekeeper" and thus to prevent the Rural board from breaching its fiduciary duties. For its part, in a much-discussed footnote (footnote 191), the Delaware Supreme Court took great pains to distance itself from the Chancery Court's observations—even though it otherwise affirmed the trial court's decision:

In affirming the principal legal holdings of the trial court, we do not adopt the Court of Chancery's description of the role of a financial advisor in M&A transactions. In particular, the trial court observed that "[d]irectors are not expected to have the expertise to determine a corporation's value for themselves, or to have the time or ability to design and carryout a sale process. Financial advisors provide these expert services. In doing so, they function as gatekeepers." *Rural I,* 88 A.3d at 88 (citations omitted). Although this language was *dictum,* it merits mention here. The trial court's description does not adequately take into account the fact that the role of a financial advisor is primarily contractual in nature, is typically negotiated between sophisticated parties, and can vary based upon a myriad of factors. Rational and sophisticated parties dealing at arm's-length shape their own contractual arrangements and it is for the board, in managing the business and affairs of the corporation, to determine what services, and on what terms, it will hire a financial advisor to perform in assisting the board in carrying out its oversight function. The engagement letter typically defines the parameters of the financial advisor's relationship and responsibilities with its client. Here, the Engagement Letter expressly permitted RBC to explore staple financing. But, this permissive language was general in nature and disclosed none of the conflicts that ultimately emerged. As became evident in the instant matter, the conflicted banker has an informational advantage when it comes to knowledge of its real or potential conflicts. *See* William W. Bratton & Michael L. Wachter, *Bankers and Chancellors*, 93 TEX. L. REV. 1, 36 (2014) ("The basic requirements of disclosure and consent make eminent sense in the banker-client context. The conflicted banker has an informational advantage. Contracting between the bank and the client respecting the bank's conflict cannot be expected to succeed until the informational asymmetry has been ameliorated. Disclosure evens the field: the client board has choices in the matter . . . and needs to make a considered decision regarding the seriousness of the conflict."). The banker is under an obligation not to act in a manner that is contrary to the interests of the board of directors, thereby undermining the very advice that it knows the directors will be relying upon in their decision making processes. Adhering to the trial court's amorphous "gatekeeper" language would inappropriately expand our narrow holding here by suggesting that any failure by a financial advisor to prevent directors from breaching their duty of care gives rise to an aiding and abetting claim against the advisor.

RBC Capital Markets, supra, 129 A. 3d at 865 n. 191.

3. Lessons to be Learned From RBC.   The Delaware Supreme Court's decision in *RBC* "has received considerable attention and has generated [numerous] 'lessons learned' lists directed at both financial advisors and the corporations and boards that they advise." Thomas A. Cole and Jack B. Jacobs, Sidley Austin LLP, *Financial Advisor Conflicts in M&A Transactions*, SIDLEY PERSPECTIVES ON M&A AND CORPORATE GOVERNANCE, Feb. 16, 2016, *available at:* https://www.sidley.com/-/media/update-pdfs/2016/02/mn3141_perspectives_newsletter_0216_v8.pdf?la=en. With respect to the investment banking community, these authors offer the following lessons to be learned from the *RBC* opinion:

> As a result of [*RBC*], investment banks and other financial advisors [now] expect to be asked about conflicts at the outset of engagements [with their corporate clients]. They are now prepared to generate reports about business relationships with potential counterparties and to update those reports as needed during the pendency of the advisory relationship. Boards should not overreact to disclosures that their bankers engage in financing or other business with potential counterparties. That is routine [and nothing in the court's reasoning in *RBC*] relates to those kind of plain-vanilla conflicts.
>
> It is critical, however, that banker reports about business relationships be supplemented with due diligence (consistent with confidentiality obligations) about (1) relationships of individual members of their deal team with potential counterparties, (2) "pitches" that the banks may have made in the recent past pertaining to the target. . . and (3) concurrent pitches that the bank may be making not directly related to, but nevertheless material to, the target (i.e., the [*RBC*]-type situation). Disclosures along those lines will not necessarily be disqualifying, but should prompt consideration of whether to take steps to adequately "cabin" the conflict . . . , such as retaining a second bank. In those circumstances, the role of

the second bank and the structure of its compensation must be carefully considered for it to have the desired "cleansing" effect.

Cole and Jacobs, *supra* at 4. With respect to boards of directors, these same experienced M&A lawyers offer the following recommendations based on the teachings of the Delaware Supreme Court's opinion in *RBC*:

> A board's efforts to identify and evaluate banker conflicts should be clearly documented in board meeting minutes, including all relevant facts and diligence efforts that guided the board's business judgement. The minutes should be purely factual and avoid advocacy. In [*RBC*], Vice Chancellor Laster criticized the discussion of a potential banker conflict in the minutes of a key target board meeting as being partially inaccurate and having the "the feel of a document drafted in anticipation of litigation." More than ever before, the minutes of board proceedings are being scrutinized, making contemporaneous and accurate drafting important. As Chief Justice Strine advised in an article in the Summer 2015 issue of THE BUSINESS LAWYER entitled *Documenting the Deal: How Quality Control and Candor Can Improve Boardroom Decision-making and Reduce the Litigation Target Zone*, [70 BUS. LAW 69] "[minutes of a board meeting] documenting an M&A [decision making] process should be comprehensive and timely produced. This, in turn, raises the questions of (1) how much of what is captured in the board minutes should be included in the proxy statement and (2) will an expectation of such publication have a chilling effect on the robustness of the underlying disclosure to the board?"

Id.; see also Wachtell, Lipton, Rosen & Katz, *The Delaware Courts and the Investment Banks*, Oct. 29, 2015, *available at:* https://corpgov.law.harvard.edu/2015/10/30/the-delaware-courts-and-the-investment-banks/; and Wilson, Sonsini, Goodrich & Rosati, *Delaware Supreme Court Issues Long-Awaited Decision in* Rural/Metro *Affirming Liability against Financial Advisor*, WSGR ALERT, Dec. 2, 2015, *available at:* https://www.jdsupra.com/legalnews/delaware-supreme-court-issues-long-32454/. *Query:* What is the role of counsel for Target in connection with negotiating the terms of Target's engagement letter to retain an investment banker to serve as Target's financial advisor on a prospective M&A transaction?

F.   Board Approval of Acquisition Agreements and the Use of "Deal Protection Devices"

Deal protection measures come in various forms, including no-shop clauses, lock-up options, and termination fees (also referred to as *break-up fees*). Generally speaking, the essence of these deal protection measures is to allow Bidder Co. to prevent the Target Co. board from taking any steps that would encourage a competing bidder to come forward with a superior offer for Target. With the rise of strategic mergers in the M&A market of the 1990s, the use of deal protection measures took on increasing importance. This leads to an inherent tension because the board of Target owes a fiduciary duty to the company's shareholders; the board's fiduciary obligations may constrain the board's ability to agree to limit its conduct in the manner that Bidder demands under the terms of whatever deal protection device Bidder proposes to include in the parties' acquisition agreement. At the same time, the dilemma from Bidder's perspective is that Target may terminate the fully negotiated transaction in the event that a better offer should appear—what is known as a *topping bid*. This leads to the very real concern that Bidder may invest considerable resources in negotiating a deal, incurring expenses to perform the necessary due diligence, retaining and paying legal and financial advisors—only to see the deal evaporate once a topping bid appears later. So not surprisingly, Bidder will generally seek some form of protection to guard against this disappointment.

In the case of a publicly traded Target, the use of deal protection devices is an important element of modern M&A deals in that these devices allow Bidder to address the inherent risk that the deal will not close (i.e., the risk of non-consummation). In the case of M&A transactions, there are a number of reasons that a fully negotiated transaction may not close, not the least of which is that Target shareholders may decide not to approve the transaction. Other recurring risks of non-consummation are summarized in the following excerpt:

> . . . [Deal protection measures, including lock-ups and termination fees] developed as a response to the substantial risk that the parties entering a negotiated merger agreement will not consummate the merger. This risk is inherent in the negotiated acquisition process. A two to four month delay typically transpires between the signing of the merger agreement and the closing[3], which provides ample opportunity for intervening events to hinder the merger. Changes in the business environment occasionally may lead the target board to renege. Competition is an even greater risk. Another party may approach the target board with an alternative, presumably higher-priced, acquisition proposal; indeed, target management might initiate negotiations with a second party before presenting the initial bid to the shareholders. Alternatively, a competing bidder may directly present its proposal to target shareholders by making a tender offer for their shares.
>
> The substantial risk of nonconsummation is especially important to the prospective acquirer, which incurs substantial up-front costs in making the initial offer. Depending on the circumstances, the initial bidder may incur significant search costs to identify an appropriate target. Once an appropriate target is identified, preparation of the offer typically requires the services of outside legal, accounting, and financial advisers. If the bidder will pay all or part of the purchase price from sources other than cash reserves, a likely scenario, the bidder also incurs commitment and other financing fees. Finally, the bidder may pass up other acquisition opportunities while negotiating with the target. Although the bidder will recover these up-front costs if the parties consummate the merger, the emergence of a competing bid may eliminate or reduce the bidder's expected return on its sunk costs[.]

Stephen M. Bainbridge, *Exclusive Merger Agreements and Lock-Ups in Negotiated Corporate Acquisitions*, 75 MINN. L. REV. 239, 241-243 (1990). Today, Bidders

---

3. This delay period is necessitated by, among other things, the need to obtain shareholder, and perhaps also regulatory, approval, prepare and file a detailed proxy statement, register and list any securities to be issued in connection with the acquisition, and take other necessary steps. Although the delay between signing the merger agreement and closing the transaction can be reduced by efficient execution of those steps, it cannot be eliminated in light of various statutory time limits. *See, e.g.*, 17 C.F.R. §240.14a-6(a) (1990) (proxy statement may not be mailed until at least 10 days after the preliminary statement is filed with the Securities and Exchange Commission (SEC)); DEL. CODE ANN., tit. 8, §251(c) (1988) (requiring at least 20 days notice before shareholder meeting may be held). . . .

address this inherent risk of non-consummation by seeking to include deal protection provisions as part of the acquisition agreement, which are (broadly speaking) designed to "discourage[] the target board from reneging on the . . . agreement or, at the least, reimburse[] the . . . bidder's up-front costs if the parties do not consummate the merger." *Id.*

In an early (non-Delaware) case, *Jewel Companies, Inc. v. Pay Less Drug Stores Northwest, Inc.*, 741 F.2d. 1555 (9th Cir. 1984), the court struggled with the (rather metaphysical) question of the "legal effect" of "a merger agreement [including any deal protection provisions] entered into by the boards of two corporations . . . *prior* to shareholder approval." *Id.* at 1560 (*emphasis added*). The Ninth Circuit concluded that the merger provisions of the California Corporations Code "contemplate[] that the boards of two corporations seeking [to merge] . . . may enter into a *binding* merger agreement governing the conduct of the parties pending submission of the agreement to the shareholders for approval." *Id.* at 1561 (*emphasis added*). Although the merger transaction could not be validly consummated without obtaining the necessary shareholder approval, the Ninth Circuit concluded that:

> In light of California's statutory scheme preserving the board's traditional management function in the case of corporate control transactions, we see no reason to conclude that the drafters of the Corporate Code intended to deprive a corporate board of the authority to agree to refrain from negotiating or accepting competing offers until the shareholders have considered an initial offer [a provision that is widely referred to today as a "no-shop" clause]. . . .
>
> We do, of course, recognize that a board may not lawfully divest itself of its fiduciary obligations in a contract . . . However, to permit a board of directors to decide that a proposed merger transaction is in the best interests of its shareholders at a given point in time, and to agree to refrain from entering into competing contracts until the shareholders consider the proposal, does not conflict in any way with the board's fiduciary obligation . . .
>
> . . . While the board can bind itself to exert its best efforts to consummate the merger under California law,[11] it can only bind the corporation temporarily, and in limited areas,[12] pending shareholder approval. The shareholders retain the ultimate control over the corporation's assets. They remain free to accept or reject the merger proposal presented by the board, to respond to a merger proposal or tender offer made by another firm subsequent to the board's execution of exclusive merger agreement, or to hold out for a better offer. Given the benefits that may accrue to shareholders from an exclusive merger agreement, we fail to see how such an agreement would compromise their legal rights. . . .
>
> We therefore hold that the district court erred in ruling that a merger agreement between boards of directors is of no legal effect prior to shareholder

---

11. It is not necessary for us to delineate the full scope of a board's "best efforts" obligation. The term does, however, include at a minimum a duty to act in good faith toward the party to whom it owes a "best efforts" obligation.

12. The board can bind the corporation temporarily with provisions like those included in the Jewel-Pay Less agreement, which essentially require the board of the target firm to refrain from entering any contract outside the ordinary course of business or from altering the corporation's capital structure. Such provisions are intended, essentially, to preserve the status quo until the shareholders consider the offer.

approval. To the contrary, we hold that under California law a corporate board of directors may lawfully bind itself in a merger agreement to forbear from negotiating or accepting competing offers until the shareholders have had an opportunity to consider the initial proposal.[13]

Jewel Companies, Inc., supra at 1562-1564.

Since this case was decided by the Ninth Circuit in 1984, it has become accepted practice in fully negotiated M&A transactions to include deal protection devices as part of the terms of the acquisition agreement. A no-shop clause (sometimes referred to as a "no-talk" clause) of the type at issue in *Jewel Companies* is now commonly used.

QUESTIONS

1. Can the parties' acquisition agreement delineate the entire scope of the board's fiduciary duty? For example, can the terms of a no-shop clause included in the parties' agreement prescribe precisely what steps Target's board must undertake in order for it to conclude that a third-party competing Bidder is offering a superior proposal? Or, is there some residual layer of fiduciary duty law that survives notwithstanding the parties' efforts to define contractually the scope of the board's fiduciary duty to the company and its shareholders?

2. Should the courts treat a no-shop/no-talk clause differently when it is made a binding provision in a letter of intent signed by the parties, as opposed to including such a provision in the definitive agreement to be signed by both Bidder and Target? Is there a public policy justification for treating a no-shop clause that is fairly stringent in its terms as valid in a letter of intent but invalid when made part of the parties' definitive merger agreement?

In the case of a publicly traded Target Co., it is accepted practice today for Bidder Co. to seek payment of a termination fee by Target in the event that Target decides to terminate the original deal with Bidder in order to accept a competing bid offering superior terms. The validity of termination fees, another form of deal protection, is the subject of the next case.

Brazen v. Bell Atlantic Corporation
695 A.2d 43 (Del. 1997)

VEASEY, Chief Justice:

In this appeal, the issues facing the Court surround the question of whether a two-tiered $550 million termination fee in a merger agreement is

---

13. We do not decide the question whether upon the unsolicited receipt of a more favorable offer after signing a merger agreement, the board still must recommend to its shareholders that they approve the initial proposal.

a valid liquidated damages provision or whether the termination fee was an invalid penalty and tended improperly to coerce stockholders into voting for the merger.

Although there are judgmental aspects involved in the traditional liquidated damages analysis applicable here, we do not apply the business judgment rule as such. We hold that the termination fee should be analyzed as a liquidated damages provision because the merger agreement specifically so provided. Under the appropriate test for liquidated damages, the provisions at issue here were reasonable in the context of this case. We further find that the fee was not a penalty and was not coercive. Accordingly, we affirm the judgment of the Court of Chancery, but upon an analysis that differs somewhat from the rationale of that Court.

FACTS

In 1995, defendant below-appellee, Bell Atlantic Corporation, and NYNEX Corporation entered into merger negotiations. In January 1996, NYNEX circulated an initial draft merger agreement that included a termination fee provision. Both parties to the agreement determined that the merger should be a stock-for-stock transaction and be treated as a merger of equals. Thus, to the extent possible, the provisions of the merger agreement, including the termination fee, were to be reciprocal.

Representatives of Bell Atlantic and NYNEX agreed that a two-tiered $550 million termination fee was reasonable for compensating either party for damages incurred if the merger did not take place because of certain enumerated events. The termination fee was divided into two parts. First, either party would be required to pay $200 million if there were both a competing acquisition offer for that party and either (a) a failure to obtain stockholder approval, or (b) a termination of the agreement. Second, if a competing transaction were consummated within eighteen months of termination of the merger agreement, the consummating party would be required to pay an additional $350 million to its disappointed merger partner.

In the negotiations where such a fee was discussed, the parties took into account the losses each would have suffered as a result of having focused attention solely on the merger to the exclusion of other significant opportunities for mergers and acquisitions in the telecommunications industry. The parties concluded that, with the recent passage of the national Telecommunications Act of 1996, the entire competitive landscape had been transformed for the regional Bell operating companies, creating a flurry of business combinations. The parties further concluded that the prospect of missing out on alternative transactions due to the pendency of the merger was very real. The "lost opportunity" cost issue loomed large. The negotiators also considered as factors in determining the size of the termination fee (a) the size of termination fees in other merger agreements found reasonable by Delaware courts, and (b) the lengthy period during which the parties would be subject to restrictive covenants under the merger agreement while regulatory approvals were sought.

Bell Atlantic and NYNEX decided that $550 million, which represented about 2% of Bell Atlantic's approximately $28 billion market capitalization, would serve as a "reasonable proxy" for the opportunity cost and other losses associated with the termination of the merger. In addition, senior management advised Bell Atlantic's board of directors that the termination fee was at a level consistent with percentages approved by Delaware courts in earlier transactions, and that the likelihood of a higher offer emerging for either Bell Atlantic or NYNEX was very low. . . .

In addition, section 9.2(e) of the merger agreement states,

> NYNEX and Bell Atlantic agree that the agreements contained in Sections 9.2(b) and (c) above are an integral part of the transactions contemplated by this Agreement and constitute liquidated damages and not a penalty. If one Party fails to promptly pay to the other any fee due under such Sections 9.2(b) and (c), the defaulting Party shall pay the costs and expenses (including legal fees and expenses) in connection with any action, including the filing of any lawsuit or other legal action, taken to collect payment, together with interest on the amount of any unpaid fee at the publicly announced prime rate of Citibank, N.A. from the date such fee was required to be paid.

Finally, section 9.2(a), also pertinent to this appeal, states,

> In the event of termination of this Agreement as provided in Section 9.1 hereof, and subject to the provisions of Section 10.1 hereof, this Agreement shall forthwith become void and there shall be no liability on the part of any of the Parties except (i) as set forth in this Section 9.2 . . . and (ii) nothing herein shall relieve any Party from liability for any willful breach hereof.

Plaintiff below-appellant, Lionel L. Brazen, a Bell Atlantic stockholder, filed a class action against Bell Atlantic and its directors for declaratory and injunctive relief. Plaintiff alleged that the termination fee was not a valid liquidated damages clause because it failed to reflect an estimate of actual expenses incurred in preparation for the merger. Plaintiffs alleged that the $550 million payment was "an unconscionably high termination or 'lockup' fee," employed "to restrict and impair the exercise of the fiduciary duty of the Bell Atlantic board and coerce the shareholders to vote to approve the proposed merger. . . ."

The parties filed cross-motions for summary judgment. Bell Atlantic sought a declaration that the decision to include and structure the termination fee was a valid exercise of business judgment. The Court of Chancery denied the relief sought by plaintiff after concluding that the termination fee structure and terms were protected by the business judgment rule and that plaintiff failed to rebut its presumptions. . . .

TERMINATION FEE AS LIQUIDATED DAMAGES

The Court of Chancery determined that the proper method for analyzing the termination fee in this merger agreement was to employ the business judgment rule rather than the test accepted by Delaware courts for analyzing the validity of liquidated damages provisions. In arriving at this determination, the Court of Chancery concluded that a liquidated damages analysis was not appropriate in this case because, notwithstanding section 9.2(e) of the merger agreement, which states that the $550 million fee constitutes liquidated damages,

> the event which triggers payment of the fees is not a breach but a termination. Liquidated damages, by definition, are damages paid in the event of a breach. . . . In addition, the Merger Agreement clearly provides that nothing in the Agreement (including the payment of termination fees) "shall relieve any Party from liability for any willful breach hereof." Accordingly, the Boards' decision to include these termination fees, which are triggered by a *termination* of the Merger Agreement and payment of which will not hinder either party's ability to recover damages from a breach, is protected by the business judgment rule and the fees will not be struck down unless plaintiff demonstrates that their inclusion was the result of disloyal or grossly negligent acts.[8]

Plaintiff argued below and argues again here that the proper analysis for determining the validity of the termination fee in section 9.2(c) of the merger agreement is to analyze it as a liquidated damages clause employing a test different from the business judgment rule. We agree.

The express language in section 9.2(e) of the agreement unambiguously states that the termination fee provisions "constitute liquidated damages and not a penalty."[9] The Court of Chancery correctly found that liquidated damages, by definition, are damages paid in the event of a breach of a contract. While a breach of the merger agreement is not the only event that would trigger payment of the termination fee, the express language of section 9.2(c) states that a party's breach of section 7.2 (which provides that the parties are required to take all action necessary to convene a stockholders' meeting and use all commercially reasonable efforts to secure proxies to be voted in favor of the merger), coupled with other events, may trigger a party's obligation to pay the termination fee.

Thus, we find no compelling justification for treating the termination fee in this agreement as anything but a liquidated damages provision, in light of the express intent of the parties to have it so treated.

ANALYZING THE VALIDITY OF LIQUIDATED DAMAGES

In *Lee Builders v. Wells,* a case involving a liquidated damages provision equal to 5% of the purchase price in a contract for the sale of land, the Court of Chancery articulated the following two-prong test for analyzing the validity of the amount of liquidated damages: "Where the damages are uncertain

---

8. Slip op. at 8-10 (quoting Merger Agreement §9.2(a)(ii)). . . .

9. At oral argument in this Court, counsel for Bell Atlantic explained that the liquidated damages language was "boilerplate" terminology for termination fees in merger transactions such as this one. So be it, but in our view, the drafters of corporate documents bear the responsibility for the selection of appropriate and clear language. *See Kaiser v. Matheson*, Del. Supr., 681 A.2d 392, 398-99 (1996). Accordingly, the parties to this merger cannot disown their own language.

and the amount agreed upon is reasonable, such an agreement will not be disturbed."[12]

Plaintiff argues that the termination fee, if properly analyzed as liquidated damages, fails the *Lee Builders* test because both portions of the fee are punitive rather than compensatory, having nothing to do with actual damages but instead being designed to punish Bell Atlantic stockholders and the subsequent third-party acquirer if Bell Atlantic were ultimately to agree to merge with another entity. We find, however, that the termination fee safely passes both prongs of the *Lee Builders* test.

To be a valid liquidated damages provision under the first prong of the test, the damages that would result from a breach of the merger agreement must be uncertain or incapable of accurate calculation. Plaintiff does not attack the fee on this ground. Given the volatility and uncertainty in the telecommunications industry due to enactment of the Telecommunications Act of 1996 and the fast pace of technological change, one is led ineluctably to the conclusion that advance calculation of actual damages in this case approaches near impossibility.

Plaintiff contends, however, that the $550 million fee violates the second prong of the *Lee Builders* test, i.e., that it is not a reasonable forecast of actual damages, but rather a penalty intended to punish the stockholders of Bell Atlantic for not approving the merger. Plaintiff's attack is without force.

Two factors are relevant to a determination of whether the amount fixed as liquidated damages is reasonable. The first factor is the anticipated loss by either party should the merger not occur. The second factor is the difficulty of calculating that loss: the greater the difficulty, the easier it is to show that the amount fixed was reasonable. In fact, where the level of uncertainty surrounding a given transaction is high, "[e]xperience has shown that . . . the award of a court or jury is no more likely to be exact compensation than is the advance estimate of the parties themselves."[14] Thus, to fail the second prong of *Lee Builders*, the amount at issue must be unconscionable or not rationally related to any measure of damages a party might conceivably sustain.

Here, in the face of significant uncertainty, Bell Atlantic and NYNEX negotiated a fee amount and a fee structure that take into account the following: (a) the lost opportunity costs associated with a contract to deal exclusively with each other; (b) the expenses incurred during the course of negotiating the transaction; (c) the likelihood of a higher bid emerging for the acquisition of either party; and (d) the size of termination fees in other merger transactions. The parties then settled on the $550 million fee as reasonable given these factors. Moreover, the $550 million fee represents 2% of Bell Atlantic's market capitalization of $28 billion. This percentage falls well within the range of

---

12. *Lee Builders v. Wells*, Del. Ch., 103 A.2d 918, 919 (1954); *accord Wilmington Housing Authority v. Pan Builders, Inc.*, D. Del., 665 F. Supp. 351, 354, (1987); RESTATEMENT (SECOND) OF CONTRACTS §356 (1981).

14. 5 Arthur L. Corbin, Corbin on Contracts §1060, at 348 (1964).

termination fees upheld as reasonable by the courts of this State.[17] We hold that it is within a range of reasonableness and is not a penalty.

This is not strictly a business judgment rule case. If it were, the Court would not be applying a reasonableness test. . . .

Since we are applying the liquidated damages rubric, and not the business judgment rule, it is appropriate to apply a reasonableness test, which in some respects is analogous to some of the heightened scrutiny processes employed by our courts in certain other contexts. Even then, courts will not substitute their business judgment for that of the directors, but will examine the decision to assure that it is, "on balance, within a range of reasonableness."[20] Is the liquidated damages provision here within the range of reasonableness? We believe that it is, given the undisputed record showing the size of the transaction, the analysis of the parties concerning lost opportunity costs, other expenses and the arms-length negotiations.

Plaintiff further argues that the termination fee provision was coercive. Plaintiff contends that (a) the stockholders never had an option to consider the merger agreement without the fee, and (b) regardless of what the stockholders thought of the merits of the transaction, the stockholders knew that if they voted against the transaction, they might well be imposing a $550 million penalty on their company. Plaintiff contends that the termination fee was so enormous that it "influenced" the vote. Finally, plaintiff argues that the fee provision was meant to be coercive because the drafters deliberately crafted the termination fees to make them applicable when Bell Atlantic's stockholders decline to approve the transaction as opposed to a termination resulting from causes other than the non-approval of the Bell Atlantic stockholders. We find plaintiff's arguments unpersuasive.

First, the Court of Chancery properly found that the termination fee was not egregiously large. Second, the mere fact that the stockholders knew that voting to disapprove the merger may result in activation of the termination fee does not by itself constitute stockholder coercion. Third, we find no authority

---

17. *See, e.g., Kysor,* 674 A.2d at 897 (where the Superior Court held that a termination fee of 2.8% of Kysor's offer was reasonable); *Roberts v. General Instrument Corp.,* Del. Ch., C.A. No. 11639, slip op. at 21, Allen, C., 1990 WL 118356 (Aug. 13, 1990) (breakup fee of 2% described as "limited"); *Lewis v. Leaseway Transp. Corp.,* Del. Ch., C.A. No. 8720, slip op. at 6, Chandler, V.C., 1990 WL 67383 (May 16, 1990) (dismissing challenge to a transaction which included a breakup fee and related expenses of approximately 3% of transaction value); *Braunschweiger v. American Home Shield Corp.,* Del. Ch., C.A. No. 10755, slip op. at 19-20, Allen, C., 1989 WL 128571 (Oct. 26, 1989) (2.3% breakup fee found not to be onerous).

20. *QVC,* 637 A.2d at 45. It is to be noted that, in *QVC,* the termination fee of $100 million, which was 1.2% of the original merger agreement, was upheld by the Vice Chancellor because it "represents a fair liquidated amount to cover Viacom's expenses should the Paramount-Viacom merger not be consummated." *QVC Network, Inc. v. Paramount Communications, Inc.,* Del. Ch., 635 A.2d 1245, 1271 (1993), *aff'd on other grounds, Paramount Communications, Inc. v. QVC Network, Inc.,* Del. Supr., 637 A.2d at 50 n. 22 and accompanying text (termination fee considered in context with other measures in that case was problematic, but termination fee, standing alone, was not considered by Supreme Court since there was no cross-appeal to present the issue). *See also In re J.P. Stevens & Co., Inc. Shareholders Litigation,* Del. Ch., 542 A.2d 770, 783 (1988), *interlocutory appeal refused,* Del. Supr., 1988 WL 35145, 1988 DEL. LEXIS 103 (Apr. 12, 1988) (reasonable termination fee negotiated in good faith upheld as conventional and not product of disloyal action).

to support plaintiff's proposition that a fee is coercive because it can be triggered upon stockholder disapproval of the merger agreement, but not upon the occurrence of other events resulting in termination of the agreement.

In *Williams v. Geier,* this Court enunciated the test for stockholder coercion. Wrongful coercion that nullifies a stockholder vote may exist "where the board or some other party takes actions which have the effect of causing the stockholders to vote in favor of the proposed transaction for some reason other than the merits of that transaction."[21] But we also stated in *Williams v. Geier* that "[i]n the final analysis . . . the determination of whether a particular stockholder vote has been robbed of its effectiveness by impermissible coercion depends on the facts of the case."

In this case, the proxy materials sent to stockholders described very clearly the terms of the termination fee. Since the termination fee was a valid, enforceable part of the merger agreement, disclosure of the fee provision to stockholders was proper and necessary. Plaintiff has not produced any evidence to show that the stockholders were forced into voting for the merger for reasons other than the merits of the transaction. To the contrary, it appears that the reciprocal termination fee provisions, drafted to protect both Bell Atlantic and NYNEX in the event the merger was not consummated, were an integral part of the merits of the transaction. Thus, we agree with the finding of the Court of Chancery that, although the termination fee provision may have influenced the stockholder vote, there were "no structurally or situationally coercive factors" that made an otherwise valid fee provision impermissibly coercive in this setting.

CONCLUSION

Because we find that actual damages in this case do not lend themselves to reasonably exact calculation, and because we further find that the $550 million termination fee was a reasonable forecast of damages and that the fee was neither coercive nor unconscionable, we hold that the fee is a valid liquidated damages provision in this merger agreement.

In light of the foregoing, we affirm, albeit on somewhat different grounds, the judgment of the Court of Chancery.

QUESTIONS

1. What standard should courts use to review the validity of any termination fee included as part of an acquisition agreement (such as the merger agreement before the court in *Brazen*)? Why not review this contract provision under the traditional formulation of the business judgment rule?

2. How does the liquidated damages analysis used by the *Brazen* court differ from the application of the business judgment rule standard of review

---

21. *Williams v. Geier* Del. Supr., 671 A.2d 1368, 1382-83 (1996) (citations omitted).

to these facts? In other words, would you get a different result had the Delaware court analyzed the validity of the termination fee under the business judgment rule?

3.   In what way is the termination fee at issue in *Brazen* "coercive"? Why is its "coerciveness" (or lack thereof) legally significant?

4.   What is the source of the board's authority to bind the company to a no-shop clause or a termination fee as part of the acquisition agreement, even though the consummation of the transaction itself is conditioned on obtaining shareholder approval of the transaction?

5.   With respect to determining the *amount* of "termination fees," how does the analysis of this issue vary under *Unocal*'s two-pronged test versus the analysis required to determine the validity of a liquidated damages clause? Would the court have reached a different outcome if the court had applied the traditional business judgment rule standard of review to assess the validity of the amount of the termination fee in *Brazen*?

NOTES

1. Use of Termination Fees in Fully Negotiated Transactions.   As illustrated in the facts of *Brazen*, termination fees generally refer to a provision in the parties' acquisition agreement that requires Target to pay a pre-agreed amount to Bidder in the event that Target terminates the deal. In the case of a publicly traded Target Co., it is accepted practice today for Bidder Co. to seek payment of a termination fee by Target in the event that Target decides to terminate the original deal with Bidder in order to accept a competing bid offering superior terms. What other events might trigger payment of a termination fee? This can vary (and is subject to negotiation between the parties), but common examples include: failing to close the deal by a specified date; failing to submit the transaction to Target shareholders for their approval; and, finally, deciding to enter into a transaction with a competing Bidder. *Query:* What is the termination fee provision that was made part of the merger agreement between AT&T and DirecTV?

2. Fixing the Amount of the Termination Fee.   In light of the fact that termination fees are routinely sought by Bidders in order to protect the deal that they entered into with their Targets, the next logical question is what should be the *amount* of the fee to be paid in the event that Target jilts Bidder in favor of accepting a "topping bid." In other words, when is the amount of the fee "too much"? The following excerpt offers helpful guidelines in considering this recurring issue:

> During the course of negotiations of every public company deal, inevitably the conversation will turn to the amount of the breakup fee payable by a target company to a buyer if the deal is terminated under certain circumstances. Because U.S. corporate law generally requires a target company to retain the ability to consider post-signing superior proposals, a breakup fee is an important element of the

suite of deal protection devices . . . that an initial buyer [seeks in order] to protect its position as the favored suitor. Speaking broadly, a breakup fee will increase the cost to a topping bidder as it will also need to cover the expense of the fee payable to the first buyer. However, with respect to deal protection terms in general, as well as the amount of breakup fees in particular, courts have indicated that they cannot be so tight or so large as to be preclusive of a true superior proposal. Starting from this somewhat ambiguous principle, the negotiations therefore turn to the appropriate amount for the breakup fee given the particular circumstances of the deal at hand.

Unquestionably, precedent often informs the discussion, and there is a significant amount of statistical data to back up a general proposition that fees "usually" fall in the 3% to 4% range. A variety of studies has shown that median termination fees as a percentage of transaction or equity value consistently fell between 3.2% and 3.4% over the course of the last four years. Fees measured by enterprise value have been similarly stable between 3.1% and 3.3% over the same period. Studies have also shown that, as deal size goes up, fees, measured on a percentage basis, tend to go down. This inverse correlation between deal and fee size is probably a function of the optics resulting from the absolute, rather than relative (percentage), amount of the fees in megadeals. As then VC Strine admonished in the *Toys "R" Us* decision, [*In re Toys "R" Us, Inc. Shareholder Litigation*, 877 A.2d 975 (Del. Ch. 2005)], regardless of historical precedent for accepted ranges, when dealmakers are working with very large numbers they can run afoul of the "preclusive differences between termination fees starting with a 'b' rather than an 'm.' "

While the statistical data have some baseline value, not least because of their consistency over long periods of time, dealmakers should be cognizant that the Delaware courts have resisted providing a bright line or range test for reasonableness of breakup fees. In a relatively consistent set of rulings, Delaware courts have upheld breakup fees falling within the statistically supported 3% to 4% range . . . That said, the Delaware courts have regularly taken the position that acceptability of a breakup fee is a highly fact specific inquiry, [and] not a function of consistency with statistical ranges. . . .

Beyond the simple question of the percentage of the breakup fee, parties will often discuss the appropriate denominator for the exercise—specifically whether it is measured as a percentage of equity value or of enterprise value. As to this question, the Delaware courts generally have taken a similar fact-specific approach. The court has avoided stating that one metric is appropriate to all situations. . . .

Despite the surface appeal of relying on statistical and court precedent, dealmakers must resist the temptation to rely solely on these data. The amount of a breakup fee is not a matter that can be viewed in isolation from other factors such as the other deal protection devices (including any separate expense reimbursements), the circumstances in which the fee is payable and the history of the sale process. Historical ranges may have value as one reference point for a discussion, but a more nuanced, fact-specific and tailored approach to setting a breakup fee is required for each deal.

Kirkland & Ellis, LLP, *M&A Update: Break-Up Fees—Picking Your Number*, Sept. 11, 2012, *available at*: https://corpgov.law.harvard.edu/2012/09/11/breakup-fees-picking-your-number/.

3. The Use of Lock-up Options: Another Form of Deal Protection.   While termination fees are a common form of deal protection sought by Bidder to address the inherent risk of non-consummation, another type of deal protection involves the use of "lock-up options":

> Three types of lockups[2] can be distinguished. Stock lockups give the acquirer [Bidder] a call option on a specified number of shares of the target at a specified strike price. Asset lockups give the acquirer a call option on certain assets of the target at a specified price. Breakup fees give the acquirer a cash payment from the target if a specified event occurs. An acquirer's rights under each type of lockup are "triggered" by specified events that vary but usually make completion of the original deal unlikely or impossible.[16] More than one type of lockup may be included in a deal, and in mergers both parties may obtain one or more lockups.[17] . . .

John C. Coates IV and Guhan Subramanian, *A Buy-Side Model of M&A Lock-Ups: Theory and Evidence*, 53 STANFORD L. REV. 307, 314 (2000).

4. Use of "Shareholder Lock-ups." In M&A deals where the publicly traded Target has a controlling shareholder, "it is legal, advisable, and hence common for a bidder to obtain a binding agreement [often called a "voting agreement"] from the controlling shareholder [obligating the shareholder] to vote for (or tender into) the deal, and to oppose other bids. Unlike merger agreements, such shareholder lockups are not generally subject to approval by other shareholders or regulators, or other significant conditions, so that shareholder lockups greatly if not completely reduce the odds of competing bids." Coates and Subramanian, *supra*, at 314-315 n. 18. If a shareholder lockup is used in connection with a fully negotiated merger, the merger agreement will often contain a "fiduciary out" clause, of the type discussed below.

5. Use of "Reverse" Termination Fees. With the advent of the private equity boom of 2005-2007, the M&A markets saw increasing use of a new form of deal protection device—what came to be known as the "reverse" termination fee. The origins and expansion of the reverse termination fee are described in the following excerpt:

---

2. The very word "lockup" can be controversial in the M&A context, since it implies the agreement is designed to ensure that an M&A transaction is completed. Many "lockups" do not provide complete insurance of that sort, and would be illegal if they did. [In this article, we] follow industry practice in using "lockup" to mean a term in an agreement related to an M&A transaction involving a public company target that provides value to the bidder in the event that the transaction is not consummated due to specified conditions ("trigger events"). "Lockup" thus includes asset options, stock options, breakup fees, and expense reimbursement.

16. Standard trigger events include an agreement for a business combination with a third party, rejection of the first bidder's deal by target shareholders after a bust-up bid, or acquisition of a block of target stock by a third party. Some lockups contain "dual triggers," which extend the life of the lockup if other events occur. Fees payable upon events unrelated to bust-up risk (such as regulatory denials) are sometimes called "breakup" fees, but raise distinct practical and policy issues.

17. In hostile deals, lockups are by definition not available.

Acquisition agreements are peppered with various provisions designed to mitigate, allocate, or address the ramifications of deal risk.[1] The potential for deal risk is particularly pronounced in acquisition transactions involving public companies, which generally entail a significant interim period between the date of the signing of the acquisition agreement and the date of the completion of the transaction.[2] . . .

Perhaps the most obvious deal risk is of one party abandoning the transaction. One of the primary ways of dealing with this risk is through termination fee provisions. Typically, acquisition agreements provide for a standard termination fee ("STF") to be paid by the [Target] in the event that [Target] does not complete the transaction due to specific triggers. These triggers commonly involve situations where a third-party bidder for [Target] emerges. In an increasing number of transactions, acquisition agreements provide for a reverse termination fee ("RTF")—that is, a payment [made] by the [Bidder] in the event the [Bidder] cannot or does not complete the acquisition as specified in the agreement.[4]

. . . RTFs came under focus following the private equity[16] acquisition boom of 2005-2007.[7] While RTFs were seldom used prior to 2005, in an unprecedented manner, private equity buyers used RTF provisions to either renegotiate pending deals or to abandon deals altogether.[8] While the private equity RTF structure ultimately proved problematic for public company sellers, it may have paved a way for innovation in strategic deals entered into during the economic crisis.[9] . . .

---

1. Deal risk includes all the factors that could prevent or delay the closing of an announced acquisition transaction. For an overview of deal risks in business combinations, see Robert T. Miller, *The Economics of Deal Risk: Allocating Risk Through MAC Clauses in Business Combination Agreements,* 50 Wm. & Mary L. Rev. 2007, 2015-34 (2009), and Albert H. Choi & George G. Triantis, *Strategic Vagueness in Contract Design: The Case of Corporate Acquisitions,* 119 Yale L.J. 848, 851-54 (2010).

2. *See* Lou R. Kling, Eileen Nugent Simon & Michael Goldman, *Summary of Acquisition Agreements* 51 U. Miami L. Rev. 779, 781 (1997) (explaining corporate and regulatory reasons for delay between signing and closing, including stockholder approval by [Target's] and/or [Bidder's] shareholders, antitrust filings under the Hart-Scott-Rodino Antitrust Improvements Act of 1976 or other needed regulatory approvals, and time needed to line up financing, if necessary). Various corporate and regulatory requirements may mean that acquisition transactions can take months to complete. In transactions with a significant regulatory component, the time between signing and closing can take over six months. *See* Miller, *supra* note 1, at 2029 (discussing possible time frames for transactions).

4. RTFs are also referred to as "reverse breakup fees," "bidder termination fees," and "acquirer termination fees."

16. [By the author – the text of this footnote 16 was moved to here in this law review article.] The term "private equity" as used in this Article refers to privately held partnerships, which acquire and "take private" publicly held companies, primarily using a leveraged financing structure. *See* Brian Cheffins & John Armour, *The Eclipse of Private Equity* 33 Del. J. Corp. L. 1, 9 (2008) (using similar terminology).

7. According to practitioner surveys, in 2005-2006, over sixty percent of all private equity buyouts had reverse termination fees. Franci J. Blassberg & Kyle A. Pasewark, *Trendwatch: Deal Terms,* Debevoise & Plimpton Private Equity Rep., Winter 2006, at 11; Doug Warner & Alison Hampton, Weil, Gotshal & Manges, LLP, Survey of Sponsor-Backed Going Private Transactions 15 (2006).

8. For an excellent account of the rise of RTFs in private equity deals and their contribution to the demise of some of these deals, see generally Steven M. Davidoff, *The Failure of Private Equity,* 82 S. Cal. L. Rev. 481, 482-87 (2008).

9. Strategic acquisition transactions are deals where the buyer and seller are both operating companies and agree to the transaction in order to achieve operating synergies, market power or empire building.

An analysis of RTF provisions is particularly timely. In part due to the [onset of the Great Recession and the ensuing difficult economic environment], the payment of such fees and their role as an exclusive remedy in acquisition agreements have recently been at the center of debate among parties in broken deals and the subject of heated litigation in the Delaware courts.[10] . . .

The RTF structure also raises important questions regarding the appropriate level of review of a board of director's decision to enter an acquisition agreement with an RTF. The ability of shareholders for either the [Bidder] or the [Target] to bring RTF-related fiduciary duty and disclosure claims against boards is a matter of considerable importance. . . .

In general. . . . both [Bidders] and [Targets] . . . have been less than forthcoming with the shareholders in public disclosure about the role of the RTF in the transaction. [Targets] have touted that they entered into a "definitive agreement" to be acquired, focusing on the value of the transaction and the premium to be received by the company's stockholders, but rarely including much relevant information from which one could decipher whether the agreement included an RTF. In fact, even experienced practitioners have noted that, while acquisition agreements are presented to the [Target's] shareholders and the public as a committed agreement by the [Bidder] to complete the acquisition, one can determine if the agreement actually gives the [Bidder] an option to pay the fee and walk away from the transaction without further liabilities "only by carefully parsing the [reverse termination fee] and remedies provisions of the merger agreement. . . ." [Bidders] have been similarly circumspect in their disclosure about RTF provisions in acquisition transactions.

The lack of effective disclosure could lead to potential liability for disclosure violations under state and federal law relating to the [Bidder's] or [Target's] public statements about the transaction.[240] In an economic environment filled with uncertainty, courts have been heavily focused on shareholder disclosure in connection with acquisition transactions. . . .

RTFs may also implicate board fiduciary duties for both the [Bidder] and [Target] boards. A failed transaction resulting in the payment of a high RTF may potentially create significant cash flow problems for a [Bidder]. Furthermore, a [Bidder] board could arguably use an RTF provision as a form of takeover defense to prevent a hostile acquisition of the [Bidder] by another third-party bidder. When used in this manner, the RTF is analogous to the Customer Assurance Program ("CAP") used by PeopleSoft to deter the hostile bid from Oracle in their heated 2005 acquisition.[243] The CAP, which required a significant contractual rebate to PeopleSoft customers in the event an acquirer discontinued new sales of the PeopleSoft product line or "materially reduce[d] support services" for the company's products, has been described as a "perfect defense" that would cost a potential acquirer hundreds of million, if not billions, of dollars. Like the CAP, the RTF has two important features. First, it is a contract term embedded in an acquisition agreement that cannot be easily renegotiated and used as a bargaining chip against a third-party hostile bidder

---

10. *See, e.g.,* United Rentals, Inc., v. RAM Holdings, Inc., 937 A.2d 810, 822 (Del. Ch. 2007) (discussing a party's payment of reverse break-up fees as its exclusive remedy).

240. Disclosure-related litigation has been identified by Delaware practitioners and scholars as an emerging battle ground in fiduciary duty litigations. *See* Lloyd L. Drury III, *Private Equity and the Heightened Fiduciary Duty of Disclosure,* 6 N.Y.U. J. L. & Bus. 33, 35 (2009).

243. For a more detailed description of the Customer Assurance Program used by PeopleSoft, *see* David Millstone & Guhan Subramanian, *Oracle v. PeopleSoft: A Case Study,* 12 Harv. Negot. L. Rev. 1, 12 (2007).

for the buyer in exchange for a higher price. Second, although the size of the RTF is dependent on arm's length bargaining between the [Bidder] and the [Target] in the initial acquisition agreement, when used as a poison pill, both the [Bidder] and the [Target] would clearly prefer a higher RTF amount.

The Delaware courts have yet to address directly RTF provisions in acquisition agreements, and there is much uncertainty regarding the nature of such review. In general, the Delaware courts are extremely reluctant to question the substantive decisions of boards, particularly [Bidder] boards, to enter into acquisition transaction.[246] In fact, in a recent decision arising out of a shareholder derivative claim against the board of directors of Dow Chemical regarding its acquisition of Rohm & Haas, the court appeared unwilling not only to question the decision to enter into the transaction, but also to question substantive buy-side decisions, including how to structure the transaction and what terms to include in an acquisition agreement.[247] However, given the growing complexities of RTF provisions, one can certainly envision RTF arrangements that would implicate board fiduciary duties.

Afra Afsharipour, *Transforming the Allocation of Deal Risk through Reverse Termination Fees*, 63 VAND. L. REV. 1161 (2010).

6. Use of "Fiduciary Out" Clauses. The term *fiduciary out* is customarily used to refer to a provision in an acquisition agreement that allows the board of Target to terminate the agreement if Target's board, usually on the advice of counsel, concludes that its fiduciary duties require the board to accept an offer from a competing bidder, most often because the competing bid offers superior terms. The importance of fiduciary out provisions is discussed in the next case.

Omnicare, Inc. v. NCS Healthcare, Inc.
818 A.2d 914 (Del. 2003)

HOLLAND, Justice, for the majority:

NCS Healthcare, Inc. ("NCS"), a Delaware corporation, was the object of competing acquisition bids, one by Genesis Health Ventures, Inc. ("Genesis"), a Pennsylvania corporation, and the other by Omnicare, Inc. ("Omnicare"), a Delaware corporation. . . .

---

246. *See, e.g.,* Ash v. McCall, No. 17132, 2000 WL 1370341 (Del. Ch. Sept. 15, 2000). In *Ash v. McCall,* the Delaware Court of Chancery dismissed the plaintiff's allegations that the board had breached its duties and committed waste by failing to detect accounting irregularities at the selling company during its due diligence investigation. The *Ash* court refused to second-guess the good faith business judgment of a board which approved an acquisition based on expert advice and a thorough board process. *Id.* at *8.

247. *See In Re Dow Chem. Derivative Litig.,* Cons. No. 4339, 2010 WL 66769, at *9 (Del. Ch., Jan. 11, 2010) ("[S]ubstantive second-guessing of the merits of a business decision . . . is precisely the kind of inquiry that the business judgment rule prohibits.").

THE PARTIES

The defendant, NCS, is a Delaware corporation [and] . . . a leading independent provider of pharmacy services to long-term care institutions including skilled nursing facilities, assisted living facilities and other institutional healthcare facilities. NCS common stock consists of Class A shares and Class B shares. The Class B shares are entitled to ten votes per share and the Class A shares are entitled to one vote per share. The shares are virtually identical in every other respect.

The defendant Jon H. Outcalt is Chairman of the NCS board of directors. Outcalt owns 202,063 shares of NCS Class A common stock and 3,476,086 shares of Class B common stock. The defendant Kevin B. Shaw is President, CEO and a director of NCS. At the time the merger agreement at issue in this dispute was executed with Genesis, Shaw owned 28,905 shares of NCS Class A common stock and 1,141,134 shares of Class B common stock. [Collectively, Shaw and Outcalt own over 65 percent of the voting power of NCS stock.]

The NCS board has two other members, defendants Boake A. Sells and Richard L. Osborne. Sells is a graduate of the Harvard Business School. He was Chairman and CEO at Revco Drugstores in Cleveland, Ohio from 1987 to 1992, . . . Osborne is a full-time professor at the Weatherhead School of Management at Case Western Reserve University. . . .

The defendant Genesis is a Pennsylvania corporation with its principal place of business in Kennett Square, Pennsylvania. It is a leading provider of healthcare and support services to the elderly. The defendant Geneva Sub, Inc., a wholly owned subsidiary of Genesis, is a Delaware corporation formed by Genesis to acquire NCS. . . .

Omnicare is a Delaware corporation with its principal place of business in Covington, Kentucky. Omnicare is in the institutional pharmacy business, with annual sales in excess of $2.1 billion during its last fiscal year. Omnicare purchased 1000 shares of NCS Class A common stock on July 30, 2002. . . .

FACTUAL BACKGROUND . . .

NCS SEEKS RESTRUCTURING ALTERNATIVES

Beginning in late 1999, changes in the timing and level of reimbursements by government and third-party providers adversely affected market conditions in the health care industry. As a result, NCS began to experience greater difficulty in collecting accounts receivables, which led to a precipitous decline in the market value of its stock. NCS common shares that traded above $20 in January 1999 were worth as little as $5 at the end of that year. By early 2001, NCS was in default on approximately $350 million in debt, including $206 million in senior bank debt and $102 million of its 5¾% Convertible Subordinated Debentures (the "Notes"). After these defaults, NCS common stock traded in a range of $0.09 to $0.50 per share until days before the announcement of the transaction at issue in this case.

NCS began to explore strategic alternatives that might address the problems it was confronting. As part of this effort, in February 2000, NCS retained UBS Warburg, L.L.C. to identify potential acquirers and possible equity investors. UBS Warburg contacted over fifty different entities to solicit their interest in a variety of transactions with NCS. UBS Warburg had marginal success in its efforts. By October 2000, NCS had only received one non-binding indication of interest valued at $190 million, substantially less than the face value of NCS's senior debt. This proposal was reduced by 20% after the offeror conducted its due diligence review.

NCS FINANCIAL DETERIORATION

In December 2000, NCS terminated its relationship with UBS Warburg and retained Brown, Gibbons, Lang & Company as its exclusive financial advisor. During this period, NCS's financial condition continued to deteriorate. In April 2001, NCS received a formal notice of default and acceleration from the trustee for holders of the Notes. As NCS's financial condition worsened, the Noteholders formed a committee to represent their financial interests (the "Ad Hoc Committee"). At about that time, NCS began discussions with various investor groups regarding a restructuring in a "prepackaged" bankruptcy. NCS did not receive any proposal that it believed provided adequate consideration for its stakeholders. At that time, full recovery for NCS's creditors was a remote prospect, and any recovery for NCS stockholders seemed impossible.

OMNICARE'S INITIAL NEGOTIATIONS

In the summer of 2001, NCS invited Omnicare, Inc. to begin discussions with Brown Gibbons regarding a possible transaction. On July 20, Joel Gemunder, Omnicare's President and CEO, sent Shaw a written proposal to acquire NCS in a bankruptcy sale under Section 363 of the Bankruptcy Code. This proposal was for $225 million subject to satisfactory completion of due diligence. NCS asked Omnicare to execute a confidentiality agreement so that more detailed discussions could take place.[3]

In August 2001, Omnicare increased its bid to $270 million, but still proposed to structure the deal as an asset sale in bankruptcy. Even at $270 million, Omnicare's proposal was substantially lower than the face value of NCS's outstanding debt. It would have provided only a small recovery for Omnicare's Noteholders and no recovery for its stockholders. In October 2001, NCS sent Glen Pollack of Brown Gibbons to meet with Omnicare's financial advisor,

---

3. Discovery had revealed that, at the same time, Omnicare was attempting to lure away NCS's customers through what it characterized as the "NCS Blitz." The "NCS Blitz" was an effort by Omnicare to target NCS's customers. Omnicare has engaged in an "NCS Blitz" a number of times, most recently while NCS and Omnicare were in discussions in July and August 2001.

Merrill Lynch, to discuss Omnicare's interest in NCS. Omnicare responded that it was not interested in any transaction other than an asset sale in bankruptcy.

There was no further contact between Omnicare and NCS between November 2001 and January 2002. Instead, Omnicare began secret discussions with Judy K. Mencher, a representative of the Ad Hoc Committee. In these discussions, Omnicare continued to pursue a transaction structured as a sale of assets in bankruptcy. In February 2002, the Ad Hoc Committee notified the NCS board that Omnicare had proposed an asset sale in bankruptcy for $313,750,000. [Omnicare's offer was for an amount that was lower than the face value of NCS's outstanding debt and provided for no recovery for NCS shareholders.]

NCS INDEPENDENT BOARD COMMITTEE

In January 2002, Genesis was contacted by members of the Ad Hoc Committee concerning a possible transaction with NCS. Genesis executed NCS's standard confidentiality agreement and began a due diligence review. Genesis had recently emerged from bankruptcy because, like NCS, it was suffering from dwindling government reimbursements.

Genesis previously lost a bidding war to Omnicare in a different transaction. This led to bitter feelings between the principals of both companies. More importantly, this bitter experience for Genesis led to its insistence on exclusivity agreements and lock-ups in any potential transaction with NCS.

NCS FINANCIAL IMPROVEMENT

NCS's operating performance was improving by early 2002. As NCS's performance improved, the NCS directors began to believe that it might be possible for NCS to enter into a transaction that would provide some recovery for NCS stockholders' equity. In March 2002, NCS decided to form an independent committee of board members who were neither NCS employees nor major NCS stockholders (the "Independent Committee"). The NCS board thought this was necessary because, due to NCS's precarious financial condition, it felt that fiduciary duties were owed to the enterprise as a whole rather than solely to NCS stockholders.

Sells and Osborne were selected as the members of the committee, and given authority to consider and negotiate possible transactions for NCS. The entire four member NCS board, however, retained authority to approve any transaction. The Independent Committee retained the same legal and financial counsel as the NCS board.

The Independent Committee met for the first time on May 14, 2002. At that meeting Pollack suggested that NCS seek a "stalking-horse merger partner" to obtain the highest possible value in any transaction. The Independent Committee agreed with the suggestion.

GENESIS INITIAL PROPOSAL

Two days later, on May 16, 2002, [representatives of Brown Gibbons, and Boake Sells met with representatives of Genesis]. At that meeting, Genesis made it clear that if it were going to engage in any negotiations with NCS, it would not do so as a "stalking horse." . . . Thus, Genesis "wanted a degree of certainty that to the extent [it] w[as] willing to pursue a negotiated merger agreement . . . , [it] would be able to consummate the transaction [it] negotiated and executed."

In June 2002, Genesis proposed a transaction that would take place outside the bankruptcy context. . . . As discussions continued, the terms proposed by Genesis continued to improve. On June 25, the economic terms of the Genesis proposal included repayment of the NCS senior debt in full, full assumption of trade credit obligations, an exchange offer or direct purchase of the NCS Notes providing NCS Noteholders with a combination of cash and Genesis common stock equal to the par value of the NCS Notes (not including accrued interest), and $20 million in value for the NCS common stock. Structurally, the Genesis proposal continued to include consents from a significant majority of the Noteholders as well as support agreements from stockholders owning a majority of the NCS voting power.

GENESIS EXCLUSIVITY AGREEMENT

NCS's financial advisors and legal counsel met again with Genesis and its legal counsel on June 26, 2002, to discuss a number of transaction-related issues. At this meeting, Pollack asked Genesis to increase its offer to NCS stockholders. Genesis agreed to consider this request. Thereafter, Pollack and Hager had further conversations. Genesis agreed to offer a total of $24 million in consideration for the NCS common stock, or an additional $4 million, in the form of Genesis common stock.

At the June 26 meeting, Genesis's representatives demanded that, before any further negotiations take place, NCS agree to enter into an exclusivity agreement with it. As Hager from Genesis explained it: "[I]f they wished us to continue to try to move this process to a definitive agreement, that they would need to do it on an exclusive basis with us. We were going to, and already had incurred significant expense, but we would incur additional expenses . . . , both internal and external, to bring this transaction to a definitive signing. We wanted them to work with us on an exclusive basis for a short period of time to see if we could reach agreement." On June 27, 2002, Genesis's legal counsel delivered a draft form of exclusivity agreement for review and consideration by NCS's legal counsel.

The Independent Committee met on July 3, 2002, to consider the proposed exclusivity agreement. Pollack presented a summary of the terms of a possible Genesis merger, which had continued to improve. . . .

NCS director Sells testified, Pollack told the Independent Committee at a July 3, 2002 meeting that Genesis wanted the Exclusivity Agreement to be the first step towards a completely locked up transaction that would preclude a higher bid from Omnicare . . . .

After NCS executed the exclusivity agreement, Genesis provided NCS with a draft merger agreement, a draft Noteholders' support agreement, and draft voting agreements for Outcalt and Shaw, who together held a majority of the voting power of the NCS common stock. Genesis and NCS negotiated the terms of the merger agreement over the next three weeks. During those negotiations, the Independent Committee and the Ad Hoc Committee persuaded Genesis to improve the terms of its merger.

The parties were still negotiating by July 19, and the exclusivity period was automatically extended to July 26. At that point, NCS and Genesis were close to executing a merger agreement and related voting agreements. Genesis proposed a short extension of the exclusivity agreement so a deal could be finalized. On the morning of July 26, 2002, the Independent Committee authorized an extension of the exclusivity period through July 31.

OMNICARE PROPOSES NEGOTIATIONS

By late July 2002, Omnicare came to believe that NCS was negotiating a transaction, possibly with Genesis or another of Omnicare's competitors, that would potentially present a competitive threat to Omnicare. Omnicare also came to believe, in light of a run-up in the price of NCS common stock, that whatever transaction NCS was negotiating probably included a payment for its stock. Thus, the Omnicare board of directors met on the morning of July 26 and, on the recommendation of its management, authorized a proposal to acquire NCS that did not involve a sale of assets in bankruptcy.

On the afternoon of July 26, 2002, Omnicare faxed to NCS a letter outlining a proposed acquisition. The letter suggested a transaction in which Omnicare would retire NCS's senior and subordinated debt at par plus accrued interest, and pay the NCS stockholders $3 cash for their shares. Omnicare's proposal, however, was expressly conditioned on negotiating a merger agreement, obtaining certain third party consents, and completing its due diligence.

Mencher [a member of the ad hoc committee of noteholders] saw the July 26 Omnicare letter and realized that, while its economic terms were attractive, the "due diligence" condition substantially undercut its strength. In an effort to get a better proposal from Omnicare, Mencher telephoned Gemunder [Omnicare's CEO] and told him that Omnicare was unlikely to succeed in its bid unless it dropped the "due diligence outs." She explained this was the only way a bid at the last minute would be able to succeed. Gemunder considered Mencher's warning "very real," and followed up with his advisors. They, however, insisted that he retain the due diligence condition "to protect [him] from doing something foolish." Taking this advice to heart, Gemunder decided not to drop the due diligence condition.

Late in the afternoon of July 26, 2002, NCS representatives received voice-mail messages from Omnicare asking to discuss the letter. The exclusivity agreement prevented NCS from returning those calls. In relevant part, that agreement precluded NCS from "engag[ing] or participat[ing] in any discussions or negotiations with respect to a Competing Transaction or a proposal for one." The July 26 letter from Omnicare met the definition of a "Competing Transaction."

Despite the exclusivity agreement, the Independent Committee met to consider a response to Omnicare. It concluded that discussions with Omnicare about its July 26 letter presented an unacceptable risk that Genesis would abandon merger discussions. The Independent Committee believed that, given Omnicare's past bankruptcy proposals and unwillingness to consider a merger, as well as its decision to negotiate exclusively with the Ad Hoc Committee, the risk of losing the Genesis proposal was too substantial. Nevertheless, the Independent Committee instructed Pollack to use Omnicare's letter to negotiate for improved terms with Genesis.

GENESIS MERGER AGREEMENT AND VOTING AGREEMENTS

Genesis responded to the NCS request to improve its offer as a result of the Omnicare fax the next day. On July 27, Genesis proposed substantially improved terms. First, it proposed to retire the Notes in accordance with the terms of the indenture, thus eliminating the need for Noteholders to consent to the transaction. This change involved paying all accrued interest plus a small redemption premium. Second, Genesis increased the exchange ratio for NCS common stock to one-tenth of a Genesis common share for each NCS common share, an 80% increase. Third, it agreed to lower the proposed termination fee in the merger agreement from $10 million to $6 million. In return for these concessions, Genesis stipulated that the transaction had to be approved by midnight the next day, July 28, or else Genesis would terminate discussions and withdraw its offer.

The Independent Committee and the NCS board both scheduled meetings for July 28. The committee met first. Although that meeting lasted less than an hour, the Court of Chancery determined the minutes reflect that the directors were fully informed of all material facts relating to the proposed transaction. After concluding that Genesis was sincere in establishing the midnight deadline, the committee voted unanimously to recommend the transaction to the full board.

The full board met thereafter. After receiving similar reports and advice from its legal and financial advisors, the board concluded that "balancing the potential loss of the Genesis deal against the uncertainty of Omnicare's letter, results in the conclusion that the only reasonable alternative for the Board of Directors is to approve the Genesis transaction." The board first voted to authorize the voting agreements with Outcalt and Shaw, for purposes of Section 203 of the Delaware General Corporation Law ("DGCL"). The board was advised by its legal counsel that "under the terms of the merger agreement and because NCS shareholders representing in excess of 50% of the outstanding voting power would be *required* by Genesis to enter into stockholder voting agreements contemporaneously with the signing of the merger agreement, and would agree to vote their shares in favor of the merger agreement, shareholder approval of the merger would be assured even if the NCS Board were to withdraw or change its recommendation. *These facts would prevent NCS from engaging in any alternative or superior transaction in the future.*" (*emphasis added*).

After listening to a *summary* of the merger terms, the board then resolved that the merger agreement and the transactions contemplated thereby were advisable and fair and in the best interests of all the NCS stakeholders. The NCS board further resolved to recommend the transactions to the stockholders for their approval and adoption. A definitive merger agreement between NCS and Genesis and the stockholder voting agreements were executed later that day. The Court of Chancery held that it was not *a per se* breach of fiduciary duty that the NCS board never read the NCS/Genesis merger agreement word for word.[4]

NCS/GENESIS MERGER AGREEMENT

Among other things, the NCS/Genesis merger agreement provided the following:

- NCS stockholders would receive 1 share of Genesis common stock in exchange for every 10 shares of NCS common stock held;
- NCS stockholders could exercise appraisal rights under 8 Del. C. §262;
- NCS would redeem NCS's Notes in accordance with their terms;
- NCS would submit the merger agreement to NCS stockholders regardless of whether the NCS board continued to recommend the merger;
- NCS would not enter into discussions with third parties concerning an alternative acquisition of NCS, or provide non-public information to such parties, unless (1) the third party provided an unsolicited, *bonafide* written proposal documenting the terms of the acquisition; (2) the NCS board believed in good faith that the proposal was or was likely to result in an acquisition on terms superior to those contemplated by the NCS/Genesis merger agreement; and (3) before providing non-public information to that third party, the third party would execute a confidentiality agreement at least as restrictive as the one in place between NCS and Genesis; and
- If the merger agreement were to be terminated, under certain circumstances NCS would be required to pay Genesis a $6 million termination fee and/or Genesis's documented expenses, up to $5 million.

VOTING AGREEMENTS

Outcalt and Shaw, in their capacity as NCS stockholders, entered into voting agreements with Genesis. NCS was also required to be a party to the voting agreements by Genesis. Those agreements provided, among other things, that :

- Outcalt and Shaw were acting in their capacity as NCS stockholders in executing the agreements, not in their capacity as NCS directors or officers;
- Neither Outcalt nor Shaw would transfer their shares prior to the stockholder vote on the merger agreement;

---

4. *See, e.g., Smith v. Van Gorkom*, 488 A.2d 858, 883 n. 25 (Del. 1985).

- Outcalt and Shaw agreed to vote all of their shares in favor of the merger agreement; and
- Outcalt and Shaw granted to Genesis an irrevocable proxy to vote their shares in favor of the merger agreement.
- The voting agreement was specifically enforceable by Genesis.

The merger agreement further provided that if either Outcalt or Shaw breached the terms of the voting agreements, Genesis would be entitled to terminate the merger agreement and potentially receive a $6 million termination fee from NCS. Such a breach was impossible since Section 6 provided that the voting agreements were specifically enforceable by Genesis.

OMNICARE'S SUPERIOR PROPOSAL

On July 29, 2002, hours after the NCS/Genesis transaction was executed, Omnicare faxed a letter to NCS restating its conditional proposal and attaching a draft merger agreement. Later that morning, Omnicare issued a press release publicly disclosing the proposal.

On August 1, 2002, Omnicare filed a lawsuit attempting to enjoin the NCS/ Genesis merger, and announced that it intended to launch a tender offer for NCS's shares at a price of $3.50 per share. On August 8, 2002, Omnicare began its tender offer. By letter dated that same day, Omnicare expressed a desire to discuss the terms of the offer with NCS. Omnicare's letter continued to condition its proposal on satisfactory completion of a due diligence investigation of NCS.

On August 8, 2002, and again on August 19, 2002, the NCS Independent Committee and full board of directors met separately to consider the Omnicare tender offer in light of the Genesis merger agreement. NCS's outside legal counsel and NCS's financial advisor attended both meetings. The board was unable to determine that Omnicare's expressions of interest were likely to lead to a "Superior Proposal," as the term was defined in the NCS/Genesis merger agreement. On September 10, 2002, NCS requested and received a waiver from Genesis allowing NCS to enter into discussions with Omnicare without first having to determine that Omnicare's proposal was a "Superior Proposal."

On October 6, 2002, Omnicare irrevocably committed itself to a transaction with NCS. Pursuant to the terms of its proposal, Omnicare agreed to acquire all the outstanding NCS Class A and Class B shares at a price of $3.50 per share in cash. As a result of this irrevocable offer, on October 21, 2002, the NCS board withdrew its recommendation that the stockholders vote in favor of the NCS/ Genesis merger agreement. NCS's financial advisor withdrew its fairness opinion of the NCS/Genesis merger agreement as well.

GENESIS REJECTION IMPOSSIBLE

The Genesis merger agreement permits the NCS directors to furnish nonpublic information to, or enter into discussions with, "any Person in connection with an unsolicited bona fide written Acquisition Proposal by such person" that the board deems likely to constitute a "Superior Proposal." That provision has absolutely no effect on the Genesis merger agreement. Even if the NCS board "changes, withdraws or modifies" its recommendation, as it did, it must still submit the merger to a stockholder vote.

A subsequent filing with the Securities and Exchange Commission ("SEC") states: "the NCS independent committee and the NCS board of directors have determined to withdraw their recommendations of the Genesis merger agreement and recommend that the NCS stockholders vote against the approval and adoption of the Genesis merger." In that same SEC filing, however, the NCS board explained why the success of the Genesis merger had already been predetermined [by virtue of the voting agreements entered into by Outcalt and Shaw, obligating them to vote their NCS shares in favor of the merger]. . . . This litigation was commenced to prevent the consummation of the inferior Genesis transaction.

LEGAL ANALYSIS

BUSINESS JUDGMENT OR ENHANCED SCRUTINY . . .

The prior decisions of this Court have identified the circumstances where board action must be subjected to enhanced judicial scrutiny before the presumptive protection of the business judgment rule can be invoked. One of those circumstances was described in *Unocal:* when a board adopts defensive measures in response to a hostile takeover proposal that the board reasonably determines is a threat to corporate policy and effectiveness. In *Moran v. Household,* we explained why a *Unocal* analysis also was applied to the adoption of a stockholder's rights plan, even in the absence of an immediate threat. Other circumstances requiring enhanced judicial scrutiny give rise to what are known as *Revlon* duties, such as when the board enters into a merger transaction that will cause a change in corporate control, initiates an active bidding process seeking to sell the corporation, or makes a break-up of the corporate entity inevitable.[17]

MERGER DECISION REVIEW STANDARD . . .

The Court of Chancery concluded that, because the stock-for-stock merger between Genesis and NCS did not result in a change of control, the NCS directors' duties under *Revlon* were not triggered by the decision to merge with Genesis. The Court of Chancery also recognized, however, that *Revlon* duties are imposed "when a corporation initiates an active bidding process seeking to sell itself." The Court of Chancery then concluded, alternatively, that *Revlon* duties had not been triggered because NCS did not start an active bidding process,

---

17. *Paramount Communications Inc. v. QVC Network Inc.* [637 A.2d 34, 47 (Del. 1993)]; *Revlon, Inc. v. MacAndrews & Forbes Holdings, Inc.,* 506 A.2d 173, 182 (Del. 1986).

and the NCS board "abandoned" its efforts to sell the company when it entered into an exclusivity agreement with Genesis.

After concluding that the *Revlon* standard of enhanced judicial review was completely inapplicable, the Court of Chancery then held that it would examine the decision of the NCS board of directors to approve the Genesis merger pursuant to the business judgment rule standard. After completing its business judgment rule review, the Court of Chancery held that the NCS board of directors had not breached their duty of care by entering into the exclusivity and merger agreements with Genesis. The Court of Chancery also held, however, that "even applying the more exacting *Revlon* standard, the directors acted in conformity with their fiduciary duties in seeking to achieve the highest and best transaction that was reasonably available to [the stockholders]." . . .

The Court of Chancery's decision to review the NCS board's decision to merge with Genesis under the business judgment rule rather than the enhanced scrutiny standard of *Revlon* is not outcome determinative for the purposes of deciding this appeal. We have assumed arguendo that the business judgment rule applied to the decision by the NCS board to merge with Genesis.[23] We have also assumed arguendo that the NCS board exercised due care when it: abandoned the Independent Committee's recommendation to pursue a stalking horse strategy, without even trying to implement it; executed an exclusivity agreement with Genesis; acceded to Genesis' twenty-four hour ultimatum for making a final merger decision; and executed a merger agreement that was summarized but never completely read by the NCS board of directors.[24]

DEAL PROTECTION DEVICES REQUIRE ENHANCED SCRUTINY

The dispositive issues in this appeal involve the defensive devices that protected the Genesis merger agreement. The Delaware corporation statute provides that the board's management decision to enter into and recommend a merger transaction can become final only when ownership action is taken by a vote of the stockholders. Thus, the Delaware corporation law expressly provides for a balance of power between boards and stockholders which makes merger transactions a shared enterprise and ownership decision. Consequently, a board of directors' decision to adopt defensive devices to protect a merger agreement may implicate the stockholders' right to effectively vote contrary to the initial recommendation of the board in favor of the transaction.[25] . . .

It is well established that conflicts of interest arise when a board acts to prevent stockholders from effectively exercising their to vote contrary to the will of the board. The "omnipresent specter" of conflict may be present whenever a board adopts defensive devices to protect a merger agreement. The stockholders' ability to effectively reject a merger agreement is likely to bear an inversely

---

23. *Paramount Communications, Inc. v. Time Inc.*, 571 A.2d 1140, 1152 (Del. 1989).
24. *But see Smith v. Van Gorkom*, 488 A.2d 858 (Del. 1985).
25. *See MM Companies v. Liquid Audio, Inc.*, 813 A.2d Co., 1118, 1120 (Del. 2003).

proportionate relationship to the structural and economic devices that the board has approved to protect the transaction.

In *Paramount v. Time*, the original merger agreement between Time and Warner did not constitute a "change of control." The plaintiffs in *Paramount v. Time* argued that, although the original Time and Warner merger agreement did not involve a change of control, the use of a lock-up, no-shop clause, and "dry-up" provisions violated the Time board's *Revlon* duties. This Court held that "[t]he adoption of structural safety devices alone does not trigger *Revlon*. Rather, as the Chancellor stated, *such devices are properly subject to a* Unocal *analysis*."

In footnote 15 of *Paramount v. Time*, we stated that legality of the structural safety devices adopted to protect the original merger agreement between Time and Warner were not a central issue on appeal. That is because the issue on appeal involved the "Time's board [decision] to recast its consolidation with Warner into an outright cash and securities acquisition of Warner by Time." Nevertheless, we determined that there was substantial evidence on the record to support the conclusions reached by the Chancellor in applying a *Unocal* analysis to each of the structural devices contained in the original merger agreement between Time and Warner.

There are inherent conflicts between a board's interest in protecting a merger transaction it has approved, the stockholders' statutory right to make the final decision to either approve or not approve a merger, and the board's continuing responsibility to effectively exercise its fiduciary duties at all times after the merger agreement is executed. These competing considerations require a threshold determination that board-approved defensive devices protecting a merger transaction are within the limitations of its statutory authority and consistent with the directors' fiduciary duties. Accordingly, in *Paramount v. Time*, we held that the business judgment rule applied to the Time board's original decision to merge with Warner. We further held, however, that defensive devices adopted by the board to protect the original merger transaction must withstand enhanced judicial scrutiny under the *Unocal* standard of review, even when that merger transaction does not result in a change of control.[34]

ENHANCED SCRUTINY GENERALLY

In *Paramount v. QVC*, this Court identified the key features of an enhanced judicial scrutiny test. The first feature is a "judicial determination regarding the adequacy of the decision making process employed by the directors, including the information on which the directors based their decision." The second feature is "a judicial examination of the reasonableness of the directors' action in light of the circumstances then existing." We also held that "the directors have the burden of proving that they were adequately informed and acted reasonably." . . .

---

34. *Id.* at 1151-55; *Unocal Corp. v. Mesa Petroleum Co.*, 493 A.2d 946 (Del. 1985); *see In re Santa Fe Pacific Corp. Shareholder Litigation*, 669 A.2d 59 (Del. 1995).

A board's decision to protect its decision to enter a merger agreement with defensive devices against uninvited competing transactions that may emerge is analogous to a board's decision to protect against dangers to corporate policy and effectiveness when it adopts defensive measures in a hostile takeover contest. In applying *Unocal's* enhanced judicial scrutiny in assessing a challenge to defensive actions taken by a target corporation's board of directors in a takeover context, this Court held that the board "does not have unbridled discretion to defeat perceived threats by any Draconian means available".[46] Similarly, just as a board's statutory power with regard to a merger decision is not absolute, a board does not have unbridled discretion to defeat any perceived threat to a merger by protecting it with any draconian means available.

Since *Unocal,* "this Court has consistently recognized that defensive measures which are either preclusive or coercive are included within the common law definition of draconian."[47] In applying enhanced judicial scrutiny to defensive actions under *Unocal,* a court must "evaluate the board's overall response, including the justification for each contested defensive measure, and the results achieved thereby." If a "board's defensive actions are inextricably related, the principles of *Unocal* require that such actions be scrutinized collectively as a unitary response to the perceived threat."

Therefore, in applying enhanced judicial scrutiny to defensive devices designed to protect a merger agreement, a court must first determine that those measures are not preclusive or coercive *before* its focus shifts to the "range of reasonableness" in making a proportionality determination. If the trial court determines that the defensive devices protecting a merger are not preclusive or coercive, the proportionality paradigm of *Unocal* is applicable. The board must demonstrate that it has reasonable grounds for believing that a danger to the corporation and its stockholders exists if the merger transaction is not consummated. That burden is satisfied "by showing good faith and reasonable investigation." Such proof is materially enhanced if it is approved by a board comprised of a majority of outside directors or by an independent committee.

When the focus of judicial scrutiny shifts to the range of reasonableness, *Unocal* requires that any defensive devices must be proportionate to the perceived threat to the corporation and its stockholders if the merger transaction is not consummated. Defensive devices taken to protect a merger agreement executed by a board of directors are intended to give that agreement an advantage over any subsequent transactions that materialize before the merger is approved by the stockholders and consummated. This is analogous to the favored treatment that a board of directors may properly give to encourage an initial bidder when it discharges its fiduciary duties under *Revlon.* . . .

The latitude a board will have in either maintaining or using the defensive devices it has adopted to protect the merger it approved will vary according to the degree of benefit or detriment to the stockholders' interests that is presented by the value or terms of the subsequent competing transaction. . . .

---

46. *Unocal Corp. v. Mesa Petroleum Co.,* 493 A.2d. at 955.
47. *Unitrin, Inc. v. Am. Gen. Corp.,* 651 A.2d at 1387.

DEAL PROTECTION DEVICES

Defensive devices, as that term is used in this opinion, is a synonym for what are frequently referred to as "deal protection devices." Both terms are used interchangeably to describe any measure or combination of measures that are intended to protect the consummation of a merger transaction. Defensive devices can be economic, structural, or both.

Deal protection devices need not all be in the merger agreement itself. In this case, for example, the Section 251(c) provision in the merger agreement was combined with the separate voting agreements to provide a structural defense for the Genesis merger agreement against any subsequent superior transaction. Genesis made the NCS board's defense of its transaction absolute by insisting on the omission of any effective fiduciary out clause in the NCS merger agreement.

Genesis argues that stockholder voting agreements cannot be construed as deal protection devices taken by a board of directors because stockholders are entitled to vote in their own interest. Genesis cites *Williams v. Geier*[57] and *Stroud v. Grace*[58] for the proposition that voting agreements are not subject to the *Unocal* standard of review. Neither of those cases, however, holds that the operative effect of a voting agreement must be disregarded *per se* when a *Unocal* analysis is applied to a comprehensive and combined merger defense plan.

In this case, the stockholder voting agreements were inextricably intertwined with the defensive aspects of the Genesis merger agreement. In fact, the voting agreements with Shaw and Outcalt were the linchpin of Genesis' proposed tripartite defense. Therefore, Genesis made the execution of those voting agreements a non-negotiable condition precedent to its execution of the merger agreement. In the case before us, the Court of Chancery held that the acts which locked-up the Genesis transaction were the Section 251(c) provision and "the execution of the *voting agreement* by Outcalt and Shaw."

With the assurance that Outcalt and Shaw would irrevocably agree to exercise their majority voting power in favor of its transaction, Genesis insisted that the merger agreement reflect the other two aspects of its concerted defense, i.e., the inclusion of a Section 251(c) provision and the omission of any effective fiduciary out clause. Those dual aspects of the merger agreement would not have provided Genesis with a complete defense in the absence of the voting agreements with Shaw and Outcalt.

THESE DEAL PROTECTION DEVICES UNENFORCEABLE

In this case, the Court of Chancery correctly held that the NCS directors' decision to adopt defensive devices to *completely* "lock up" the Genesis merger mandated "special scrutiny" under the two-part test set forth in *Unocal*. That conclusion is consistent with our holding in *Paramount v. Time* that "safety devices" adopted to protect a transaction that did not result in a change of control are

---

57. *Williams v. Geier*, 671 A.2d 1368 (Del. 1996).
58. *Stroud v. Grace*, 606 A.2d 75 (Del. 1992).

subject to enhanced judicial scrutiny under a *Unocal* analysis. The record does not, however, support the Court of Chancery's conclusion that the defensive devices adopted by the NCS board to protect the Genesis merger were reasonable and proportionate to the threat that NCS perceived from the potential loss of the Genesis transaction.

Pursuant to the judicial scrutiny required under *Unocal's* two-stage analysis, the NCS directors must first demonstrate "that they had reasonable grounds for believing that a danger to corporate policy and effectiveness existed. . . ." To satisfy that burden, the NCS directors are required to show they acted in good faith after conducting a reasonable investigation. The threat identified by the NCS board was the possibility of losing the Genesis offer and being left with no comparable alternative transaction.

The second stage of the *Unocal* test requires the NCS directors to demonstrate that their defensive response was "reasonable in relation to the threat posed." This inquiry involves a two-step analysis. The NCS directors must first establish that the merger deal protection devices adopted in response to the threat were not "coercive" or "preclusive," and then demonstrate that their response was within a "range of reasonable responses" to the threat perceived. In *Unitrin*, we stated:

- A response is "coercive" if it is aimed at forcing upon stockholders a management-sponsored alternative to a hostile offer.
- A response is "preclusive" if it deprives stockholders of the right to receive all tender offers or precludes a bidder from seeking control by fundamentally restricting proxy contests or otherwise.

This aspect of the *Unocal* standard provides for a disjunctive analysis. If defensive measures are either preclusive or coercive they are draconian and impermissible. In this case, the deal protection devices of the NCS board were *both* preclusive and coercive.

This Court enunciated the standard for determining stockholder coercion in the case of *Williams v. Geier.* A stockholder vote may be nullified by wrongful coercion "where the board or some other party takes actions which have the effect of causing the stockholders to vote in favor of the proposed transaction for some reason other than the merits of that transaction." In *Brazen v. Bell Atlantic Corporation,* [695 A.2d 43 (Del. 1997)], we applied that test for stockholder coercion and held "that although the termination fee provision may have influenced the stockholder vote, there were 'no structurally or situationally coercive factors' that made an otherwise valid fee provision impermissibly coercive" under the facts presented.

In *Brazen,* we concluded "the determination of whether a particular stockholder vote has been robbed of its effectiveness by impermissible coercion depends on the facts of the case." In this case, the Court of Chancery did not expressly address the issue of "coercion" in its *Unocal* analysis. It did find as a fact, however, that NCS's public stockholders (who owned 80% of NCS and overwhelmingly supported Omnicare's offer) will be forced to accept the Genesis merger because of the structural defenses approved by the NCS board. Consequently, the record reflects that any stockholder vote would have been robbed of its effectiveness by the impermissible coercion that predetermined the outcome of the merger without regard to the merits of the Genesis transaction at the time the vote was scheduled to be taken. Deal protection devices that result in such coercion cannot withstand *Unocal's* enhanced judicial scrutiny standard of review because they are not within the range of reasonableness.

Although the minority stockholders were not forced to vote for the Genesis merger, they were required to accept it because it was *a fait accompli.* The record reflects that the defensive devices employed by the NCS board are preclusive and coercive in the sense that they accomplished *a fait accompli.* In this case, despite the fact that the NCS board has withdrawn its recommendation for the Genesis transaction and recommended its rejection by the stockholders, the deal protection devices approved by the NCS board operated in concert to have a preclusive and coercive effect. Those tripartite defensive measures — the Section 251(c) provision, the voting agreements, and the absence of an effective fiduciary out clause — made it "mathematically impossible" and "realistically unattainable" for the Omnicare transaction or any other proposal to succeed, no matter how superior the proposal.[72]

The deal protection devices adopted by the NCS board were designed to coerce the consummation of the Genesis merger and preclude the consideration of any superior transaction. The NCS directors' defensive devices are not within a reasonable range of responses to the perceived threat of losing the Genesis offer because they are preclusive and coercive. Accordingly, we hold that those deal protection devices are unenforceable.

EFFECTIVE FIDUCIARY OUT REQUIRED

The defensive measures that protected the merger transaction are unenforceable not only because they are preclusive and coercive but, alternatively, they are unenforceable because they are invalid as they operate in this case. Given the specifically enforceable irrevocable voting agreements, the provision in the merger agreement requiring the board to submit the transaction for a stockholder vote and the omission of a fiduciary out clause in the merger agreement completely prevented the board from discharging its fiduciary responsibilities to the minority stockholders when Omnicare presented its superior transaction. "To the extent that a [merger] contract, or a provision thereof, purports to require a board to act or not act in such a fashion as to limit the exercise of fiduciary duties, it is invalid and unenforceable."[74]

In *QVC,* this Court recognized that "[w]hen a majority of a corporation's voting shares are acquired by a single person or entity, or by *a cohesive group acting together* [as in this case], there is a significant diminution in the voting power of those who thereby become minority stockholders." Therefore, we acknowledged that "[i]n the absence of devices protecting the minority stockholders, stockholder votes are likely to become mere formalities," where a cohesive

---

72. *See Unitrin, Inc. v. Am. Gen. Corp.,* 651 A.2d at 1388-89; *see also Carmody v. Toll Bros., Inc.,* 723 A.2d 1180, 1195 (Del. Ch. 1998) (citations omitted).

74. *Paramount Communications Inc. v. QVC Network Inc.,* 637 A.2d 34, 51 (Del. 1993) (citation omitted)....

group acting together to exercise majority voting powers have already decided the outcome. Consequently, we concluded that since the minority stockholders lost the power to influence corporate direction through the ballot, "minority stockholders must rely for protection solely on the fiduciary duties owed to them by the directors."

Under the circumstances presented in this case, where a cohesive group of stockholders with majority voting power was irrevocably committed to the merger transaction, "[e]ffective representation of the financial interests of the minority shareholders imposed upon the [NCS board] an affirmative responsibility to protect those minority shareholders' interests."[79] The NCS board could not abdicate its fiduciary duties to the minority by leaving it to the stockholders alone to approve or disapprove the merger agreement because two stockholders had already combined to establish a majority of the voting power that made the outcome of the stockholder vote a foregone conclusion.

The Court of Chancery noted that Section 251(c) of the Delaware General Corporation Law now permits boards to agree to submit a merger agreement for a stockholder vote, even if the Board later withdraws its support for that agreement and recommends that the stockholders reject it.[80] The Court of Chancery also noted that stockholder voting agreements are permitted by Delaware law. In refusing to certify this interlocutory appeal, the Court of Chancery stated "it is simply nonsensical to say that a board of directors abdicates its duties to manage the 'business and affairs' of a corporation under Section 141 (a) of the DGCL by agreeing to the inclusion in a merger agreement of a term authorized by §251(c) of the same statute."

Taking action that is otherwise legally possible, however, does not *ipso facto* comport with the fiduciary responsibilities of directors in all circumstances. . . .

Genesis admits that when the NCS board agreed to its merger conditions, the NCS board was seeking to assure that the NCS creditors were paid in full and that the NCS stockholders received the highest value available for their stock. In fact, Genesis defends its "bulletproof" merger agreement on that basis. We hold that the NCS board did not have authority to accede to the Genesis demand for an absolute "lock-up."

The directors of a Delaware corporation have a continuing obligation to discharge their fiduciary responsibilities, as future circumstances develop, after a merger agreement is announced. Genesis anticipated the likelihood of a superior offer after its merger agreement was announced and demanded defensive measures from the NCS board that *completely* protected its transaction.[84] Instead of agreeing to the absolute defense of the Genesis merger from a superior offer,

---

79. *McMullin v. Beran*, 765 A.2d 910, 920 (Del. 2000).

80. Section 251(c) was amended in 1998 to allow for the inclusion in a merger agreement of a term requiring that the agreement be put to a vote of stockholders whether or not their directors continue to recommend the transaction. Before this amendment, Section 251 was interpreted as precluding a stockholder vote if the board of directors, after approving the merger agreement but before the stockholder vote, decided no longer to recommend it. *See Smith v. Van Gorkom*, 488 A.2d 858, 887-88 (Del. 1985).

84. The marked improvements in NCS's financial situation during the negotiations with Genesis strongly suggests that the NCS board should have been alert to the prospect of competing offers or, as eventually occurred, a bidding contest.

however, the NCS board was required to negotiate a fiduciary out clause to protect the NCS stockholders if the Genesis transaction became an inferior offer. By acceding to Genesis' ultimatum for complete protection *in futuro*, the NCS board disabled itself from exercising its own fiduciary obligations at a time when the board's own judgment is most important, i.e. receipt of a subsequent superior offer.

Any board has authority to give the proponent of a recommended merger agreement reasonable structural and economic defenses, incentives, and fair compensation if the transaction is not completed. To the extent that defensive measures are economic and reasonable, they may become an increased cost to the proponent of any subsequent transaction. Just as defensive measures cannot be draconian, however, they cannot limit or circumscribe the directors' fiduciary duties. Notwithstanding the corporation's insolvent condition, the NCS board had no authority to execute a merger agreement that subsequently prevented it from effectively discharging its ongoing fiduciary responsibilities.

The stockholders of a Delaware corporation are entitled to rely upon the board to discharge its fiduciary duties at all times. The fiduciary duties of a director are unremitting and must be effectively discharged in the specific context of the actions that are required with regard to the corporation or its stockholders as circumstances change. The stockholders with majority voting power, Shaw and Outcalt, had an absolute right to sell or exchange their shares with a third party at any price. This right was not only known to the other directors of NCS, it became an integral part of the Genesis agreement. In its answering brief, Genesis candidly states that its offer "came with a condition—Genesis would not be a stalking horse and would not agree to a transaction to which NCS's controlling shareholders were not committed."

The NCS board was required to contract for an effective fiduciary out clause to exercise its continuing fiduciary responsibilities to the minority stockholders. The issues in this appeal do not involve the general validity of either stockholder voting agreements or the authority of directors to insert a Section 251(c) provision in a merger agreement. In this case, the NCS board combined those two otherwise valid actions and caused them to operate in concert as an absolute lock up, in the absence of an effective fiduciary out clause in the Genesis merger agreement.

In the context of this preclusive and coercive lock up case, the protection of Genesis' contractual expectations must yield to the supervening responsibility of the directors to discharge their fiduciary duties on a continuing basis. The merger agreement and voting agreements, as they were combined to operate in concert in this case, are inconsistent with the NCS directors' fiduciary duties. To that extent, we hold that they are invalid and unenforceable. . . .

VEASEY, Chief Justice, with whom STEELE, Justice, joins dissenting.

. . . Fiduciary duty cases are inherently fact-intensive and, therefore, unique. This case is unique in two important respects. First, the peculiar facts presented render this case an unlikely candidate for substantial repetition. Second, this is a rare 3-2 split decision of the Supreme Court.[90] . . .

---

90. Split decisions by this Court, especially in the field of corporation law, are few and far between. One example is our decision in *Smith v. Van Gorkom*, 488 A.2d 858 (Del.1985),

The process by which this merger agreement came about involved a joint decision by the controlling stockholders and the board of directors to secure what appeared to be the only value-enhancing transaction available for a company on the brink of bankruptcy. The Majority adopts a new rule of law that imposes a prohibition on the NCS board's ability to act in concert with controlling stockholders to lock up this merger. The Majority reaches this conclusion by analyzing the challenged deal protection measures as isolated board actions. The Majority concludes that the board owed a duty to the NCS minority stockholders to refrain from acceding to the Genesis demand for an irrevocable lock-up notwithstanding the compelling circumstances confronting the board and the board's disinterested, informed, good faith exercise of its business judgment.

Because we believe this Court must respect the reasoned judgment of the board of directors and give effect to the wishes of the controlling stockholders, we respectfully disagree with the Majority's reasoning that results in a holding that the confluence of board and stockholder action constitutes a breach of fiduciary duty. The essential fact that must always be remembered is that this agreement and the voting commitments of Outcalt and Shaw concluded a lengthy search and intense negotiation process in the context of insolvency and creditor pressure where no other viable bid had emerged. Accordingly, we endorse the Vice Chancellor's well-reasoned analysis that the NCS board's action before the hostile bid emerged was within the bounds of its fiduciary duties under these facts.

We share with the Majority and the independent NCS board of directors the motivation to serve carefully and in good faith the best interests of the corporate enterprise and, thereby, the stockholders of NCS. It is now known, of course, after the case is over, that the stockholders of NCS will receive substantially more by tendering their shares into the topping bid of Omnicare than they would have received in the Genesis merger, as a result of the post-agreement Omnicare bid and the injunctive relief ordered by the Majority of this Court. Our jurisprudence cannot, however, be seen as turning on such ex post felicitous results. Rather, the NCS board's good faith decision must be subject to a real-time review of the board action before the NCS-Genesis merger agreement was entered into.

AN ANALYSIS OF THE PROCESS LEADING TO THE LOCK-UP REFLECTS A QUINTESSENTIAL, DISINTERESTED AND INFORMED BOARD DECISION REACHED IN GOOD FAITH

The Majority has adopted the Vice Chancellor's findings and has assumed arguendo that the NCS board fulfilled its duties of care, loyalty, and good faith

---

where only three Justices supported reversing the Court of Chancery's decision. As Justice Holland and David Skeel recently noted, while our decision making process fosters consensus, dissenting opinions "illustrate that principled differences of opinion about the law [are] . . . never compromised for the sake of unanimity." Randy J. Holland & David A. Skeel, Jr., *Deciding Cases Without Controversy*, 5 Del. L. Rev. 115, 118 (2002).

by entering into the Genesis merger agreement. Indeed, this conclusion is indisputable on this record. The problem is that the Majority has removed from their proper context the contractual merger protection provisions. The lock-ups here cannot be reviewed in a vacuum. A court should review the entire bidding process to determine whether the independent board's actions permitted the directors to inform themselves of their available options and whether they acted in good faith.

Going into negotiations with Genesis, the NCS directors knew that, up until that time, NCS had found only one potential bidder, Omnicare. Omnicare had refused to buy NCS except at a fire sale price through an asset sale in bankruptcy. Omnicare's best proposal at that stage would not have paid off all creditors and would have provided nothing for stockholders. The Noteholders, represented by the Ad Hoc Committee, were willing to oblige Omnicare and force NCS into bankruptcy if Omnicare would pay in full the NCS debt. Through the NCS board's efforts, Genesis expressed interest that became increasingly attractive. Negotiations with Genesis led to an offer paying creditors off and conferring on NCS stockholders $24 million—an amount infinitely superior to the prior Omnicare proposals.

But there was, understandably, a sine qua non. In exchange for offering the NCS stockholders a return on their equity and creditor payment, Genesis demanded certainty that the merger would close. If the NCS board would not have acceded to the Section 251(c) provision, if Outcalt and Shaw had not agreed to the voting agreements and if NCS had insisted on a fiduciary out, there would have been no Genesis deal! Thus, the only value-enhancing transaction available would have disappeared. NCS knew that Omnicare had spoiled a Genesis acquisition in the past, and it is not disputed by the Majority that the NCS directors made a reasoned decision to accept as real the Genesis threat to walk away.

When Omnicare submitted its conditional eleventh-hour bid, the NCS board had to weigh the economic terms of the proposal against the uncertainty of completing a deal with Omnicare. Importantly, because Omnicare's bid was conditioned on its satisfactorily completing its due diligence review of NCS, the NCS board saw this as a crippling condition, as did the Ad Hoc Committee. As a matter of business judgment, the risk of negotiating with Omnicare and losing Genesis at that point outweighed the possible benefits. The lock-up was indisputably a sine qua non to any deal with Genesis.

A lock-up permits a target board and a bidder to "exchange certainties." Certainty itself has value. The acquirer may pay a higher price for the target if the acquirer is assured consummation of the transaction. The target company also benefits from the certainty of completing a transaction with a bidder because losing an acquirer creates the perception that a target is damaged goods, thus reducing its value.

While the present case does not involve an attempt to hold on to only one interested bidder, the NCS board was equally concerned about "exchanging certainties" with Genesis. If the creditors decided to force NCS into bankruptcy, which could have happened at any time as NCS was unable to service its obligations, the stockholders would have received nothing. The NCS board also did not know if the NCS business prospects would have declined again, leaving NCS less attractive to other bidders, including Omnicare, which could have changed its mind and again insisted on an asset sale in bankruptcy.

Situations will arise where business realities demand a lock-up so that wealth-enhancing transactions may go forward. Accordingly, any bright-line rule prohibiting lock-ups could, in circumstances such as these, chill otherwise permissible conduct.

OUR JURISPRUDENCE DOES NOT COMPEL THIS COURT TO INVALIDATE THE JOINT ACTION OF THE BOARD AND THE CONTROLLING STOCKHOLDERS

The Majority invalidates the NCS board's action by announcing a new rule that represents an extension of our jurisprudence. That new rule can be narrowly stated as follows: A merger agreement entered into after a market search, before any prospect of a topping bid has emerged, which locks up stockholder approval and does not contain a "fiduciary out" provision, is per se invalid when a later significant topping bid emerges. As we have noted, this bright-line, per se rule would apply regardless of (1) the circumstances leading up to the agreement and (2) the fact that stockholders who control voting power had irrevocably committed themselves, *as stockholders,* to vote for the merger. Narrowly stated, this new rule is a judicially-created "third rail" that now becomes one of the given "rules of the game," to be taken into account by the negotiators and drafters of merger agreements. In our view, this new rule is an unwise extension of existing precedent.

Although it is debatable whether *Unocal* applies—and we believe that the better rule in this situation is that the business judgment rule should apply[102]—we will, nevertheless, assume arguendo—as the Vice Chancellor did—that *Unocal* applies. Therefore, under *Unocal* the NCS directors had the burden of going forward with the evidence to show that there was a threat to corporate policy and effectiveness and that their actions were reasonable in response to that threat. The Vice Chancellor correctly found that they reasonably perceived the threat that NCS did not have a viable offer from Omnicare—or anyone else—to pay off its creditors, cure its insolvency and provide some payment to stockholders.

---

102. The basis for the *Unocal* doctrine is the "omnipresent specter" of the board's self-interest to entrench itself in office. *Unocal Corp. v. Mesa Petroleum Co.,* 493 A.2d 946, 954 (Del. 1985). NCS was not plagued with a specter of self-interest. Unlike the *Unocal* situation, a hostile offer did not arise here until *after* the market search and the locked-up deal with Genesis. The *Unocal* doctrine applies to unilateral board actions that are defensive and reactive in nature. Thus, a *Unocal* analysis was necessary in *Paramount Communications v. Time Inc.* because Time and Warner restructured their original transaction from a merger to an acquisition *in response* to the Paramount bid. 571 A.2d 1140, 1148 (Del. 1989). In *Time,* the original Time-Warner stock-for-stock merger, which this Court held was entitled to the presumption of the business judgment rule, was jettisoned by the parties in the face of Paramount's topping bid. *Id.* at 1152. The merger was replaced with a new transaction which was an all cash tender offer by Time to acquire 51% of the Warner stock. It was the revised agreement, not the original merger agreement, that was found to be "defense-motivated" and subject to *Unocal. Id.*

The NCS board's actions—as the Vice Chancellor correctly held [in ruling that the NCS directors satisfied *Unocal*]—were reasonable in relation to the threat because the Genesis deal was the "only game in town," the NCS directors got the best deal they could from Genesis and—but-for the emergence of Genesis on the scene—there would have been no viable deal. . . .

In our view, the Majority misapplies the *Unitrin* concept of "coercive and preclusive" measures to preempt a proper proportionality balancing. Thus, the Majority asserts that "in applying *enhanced judicial scrutiny* to *defensive devices* designed to protect a merger agreement, . . . a court must . . . determine that those measures are not preclusive or coercive. . . ." Here, the deal protection measures were not adopted unilaterally by the board to fend off an existing hostile offer that threatened the corporate policy and effectiveness of NCS.[105] They were adopted because Genesis—the "only game in town"—would not save NCS, its creditors and its stockholders without these provisions.

The very measures the Majority cites as "coercive" were approved by Shaw and Outcalt through the lens of their independent assessment of the merits of the transaction. The proper inquiry in this case is whether the NCS board had taken actions that "have the effect of causing the stockholders to vote in favor of the proposed transaction for some reason other than the merits of that transaction."[109] Like the termination fee upheld as a valid liquidated damages clause against a claim of coercion in *Brazen v. Bell Atlantic Corp.*, the deal protection measures at issue here were "an integral part of the merits of the transaction" as the NCS board struggled to secure—and did secure—the only deal available.

Outcalt and Shaw were fully informed stockholders. As the NCS controlling stockholders, they made an informed choice to commit their voting power to the merger. The minority stockholders were deemed to know that when controlling stockholders have 65% of the vote they can approve a merger without the need for the minority votes. Moreover, to the extent a minority stockholder may have felt "coerced" to vote for the merger, which was already a *fait accompli*, it was a meaningless coercion—or no coercion at all—because the controlling votes, those of Outcalt and Shaw, were already "cast." Although the fact that the controlling votes were committed to the merger "precluded" an overriding vote against the merger by the Class A stockholders, the pejorative "preclusive" label applicable in a *Unitrin* fact situation has no application here. Therefore, there was no meaningful minority stockholder voting decision to coerce.

---

105. The Majority states that our decisions in *Williams v. Geier* and *Stroud v. Grace* do not hold that "the operative effect of a voting agreement must be disregarded *per se* when a *Unocal* analysis is applied to a comprehensive and combined merger defense plan." *Majority Opinion* at 934. In *Stroud v. Grace*, however, we noted that "The record clearly indicates, and [plaintiff] . . . concedes, that over 50% of the outstanding shares of . . . [the corporation] are under the direct control of [the defendants]. . . . These directors controlled the corporation in fact and law. *This obviates any threat contemplated by* Unocal. . . ." 606 A.2d 75, 83 (Del. 1992) (*emphasis supplied*). According to *Stroud*, then, Shaw's and Outcalt's decision to enter into the voting agreements should not be subject to a *Unocal* analysis because they controlled the corporation "in fact and law." *Id.* Far from a breach of duty, the joint action of the stockholders and directors here represents "the highest and best form of corporate democracy." *Williams v. Geier,* 671 A.2d 1368, 1381 (Del. 1996).

109. *Geier,* 671 A.2d at 1382-83 (citations omitted).

In applying *Unocal* scrutiny, we believe the Majority incorrectly preempted the proportionality inquiry. In our view, the proportionality inquiry must account for the reality that the contractual measures protecting this merger agreement were necessary to obtain the Genesis deal. The Majority has not demonstrated that the director action was a disproportionate response to the threat posed. Indeed, it is clear to us that the board action to negotiate the best deal reasonably available with the only viable merger partner (Genesis) who could satisfy the creditors and benefit the stockholders, was reasonable in relation to the threat, by any practical yardstick.

AN ABSOLUTE LOCK-UP IS NOT A PER SE VIOLATION OF FIDUCIARY DUTY

We respectfully disagree with the Majority's conclusion that the NCS board breached its fiduciary duties to the Class A stockholders by failing to negotiate a "fiduciary out" in the Genesis merger agreement. What is the practical import of a "fiduciary out?" It is a contractual provision, articulated in a manner to be negotiated, that would permit the board of the corporation being acquired to exit without breaching the merger agreement in the event of a superior offer.

In this case, Genesis made it abundantly clear early on that it was willing to negotiate a deal with NCS but only on the condition that it would not be a "stalking horse." Thus, it wanted to be certain that a third party could not use its deal with NCS as a floor against which to begin a bidding war. As a result of this negotiating position, a "fiduciary out" was not acceptable to Genesis. The Majority Opinion holds that such a negotiating position, if implemented in the agreement, is invalid per se where there is an absolute lock-up. We know of no authority in our jurisprudence supporting this new rule, and we believe it is unwise and unwarranted.

The Majority relies on our decision in *QVC* to assert that the board's fiduciary duties prevent the directors from negotiating a merger agreement without providing an escape provision. Reliance on *QVC* for this proposition, however, confuses our statement of a board's responsibilities when the directors confront a superior transaction and turn away from it to lock up a less valuable deal with the very different situation here, where the board committed itself to the *only* value-enhancing transaction available. The decision in *QVC* is an extension of prior decisions in *Revlon* and *Mills* that prevent a board from ignoring a bidder who is willing to match and exceed the favored bidder's offer. The Majority's application of "continuing fiduciary duties" here is a further extension of this concept and thus permits, wrongly in our view, a court to second-guess the risk and return analysis the board must make to weigh the value of the only viable transaction against the prospect of an offer that has not materialized.

The Majority also mistakenly relies on our decision in *QVC* to support the notion that the NCS board should have retained a fiduciary out to save the minority stockholder from Shaw's and Outcalt's voting agreements. Our reasoning in *QVC*, which recognizes that minority stockholders must rely for protection on the fiduciary duties owed to them by directors, does not create a *special* duty to protect the minority stockholders from the consequences of a controlling stockholder's ultimate decision unless the controlling stockholder stands on both sides of the transaction, which is certainly not the case here. Indeed, the discussion of a minority stockholders' lack of voting power in *QVC* notes the importance of enhanced scrutiny in change of control transactions *precisely because* the minority stockholders' interest in the *newly merged entity* thereafter will hinge on the course set by the controlling stockholder. In *QVC*, Sumner Redstone owned 85% of the voting stock of Viacom, the surviving corporation. Unlike the stockholders who are confronted with a transaction that will relegate them to a minority status in the corporation, the Class A stockholders of NCS purchased stock knowing that the Charter provided Class B stockholders voting control.

Conclusion

It is regrettable that the Court is split in this important case. One hopes that the Majority rule announced here—though clearly erroneous in our view—will be interpreted narrowly and will be seen as *sui generis*. By deterring bidders from engaging in negotiations like those present here and requiring that there must always be a fiduciary out, the universe of potential bidders who could reasonably be expected to benefit stockholders could shrink or disappear. Nevertheless, if the holding is confined to these unique facts, negotiators may be able to navigate around this new hazard.

Accordingly, we respectfully dissent.

STEELE, Justice, dissenting. . . .

In my view, the Vice Chancellor's unimpeachable factual findings preclude further judicial scrutiny of the NCS board's business judgment that the hotly negotiated terms of its merger agreement were necessary in order to save the company from financial collapse, repay creditors and provide some benefits to NCS stockholders. . . .

In my opinion, Delaware law mandates deference under the business judgment rule to a board of directors' decision that is free from self-interest, made with due care and in good faith. . . .

Importantly, *Smith v. Van Gorkom*, correctly casts the focus on any court review of board action challenged for alleged breach of the fiduciary duty of care "only upon the basis of the information then reasonably available to the directors and relevant to their decision. . . ." Though criticized particularly for the imposition of personal liability on directors for a breach of the duty of care, *Van Gorkom* still stands for the importance of recognizing the limited circumstances for court intervention and the importance of focusing on the timing of the decision attacked. . . .

I believe that the absence of a suggestion of self-interest or lack of care compels a court to defer to what is a business judgment that a court is not qualified to second guess. However, I recognize that another judge might prefer to view the reasonableness of the board's action through the *Unocal* prism before deferring. Some flexible, readily discernible standard of review must be applied no matter what it may be called. Here, one deferring or one applying *Unocal* scrutiny would reach the same conclusion. When a board agrees rationally, in good faith, without conflict and with reasonable care to include provisions in a contract to preserve a deal in the absence of a better one, their business judgment should not be second-guessed in order to invalidate or declare unenforceable an otherwise valid merger agreement. The fact that majority stockholders free of conflicts have a choice and every incentive to get the best available deal and then make a rational judgment to do so as well neither unfairly impinges upon minority shareholder choice or the concept of a shareholder "democracy" nor has it any independent significance bearing on the reasonableness of the board's separate and distinct exercise of judgment. . . .

Therefore, I respectfully dissent.

QUESTIONS

1. Why would Genesis insist on an exclusivity agreement? What is required under the terms of this exclusivity agreement?

2. What is a "force the vote" provision? Why is that provision considered a "deal protection" measure?

3. Does *Revlon* apply? In other words, did Omnicare enter the *Revlon* mode?

4. What is the analytical approach used by the Delaware Supreme Court to decide the validity of the deal protection devices used here? Is it the same (consistent with) the analytical approach used in prior takeover cases involving breach of fiduciary duty claims? For example, is the reasoning used in *Omnicare* consistent with the court's analytical approach in *Brazen*?

5. What standard of review would the dissent apply to these facts?

6. How does the combination of deal protection devices that were at issue in *Omnicare* differ from the use of a dual capital structure of the type in place at Google, Inc.? *See supra*, at pp. 646-647.

7. Generally speaking, Delaware case law does not draw a distinction between directors of privately held and publicly held companies in defining the scope of directors' duties to the corporation. Well-established Delaware case law makes it clear that the same fiduciary duties of due care, good faith, and loyalty are applicable to all companies incorporated in Delaware. However, is there any reason to distinguish acquisitions of private companies from those involving public companies? Based on the reasoning in *Omnicare*, do you think the Delaware courts would reach the same result in the case of an acquisition of a privately held Target in which a majority of the voting shares were locked up (i.e., committed to vote in favor of the proposed transaction with Bidder) at the time the acquisition agreement was signed? Is there any principled way to validate the kind of lock-up arrangement involved in *Omnicare* in the context of the acquisition of a privately held Target in order to reach a different result than *Omnicare*? Does it affect your analysis if Target has only two shareholders who each own 50 percent of Target's outstanding stock, as opposed to a privately held company involving 30-40 shareholders, many of whom are also employees of Target Co.?

8. Delaware §203 applied to the facts involved in *Omnicare,* and thus board approval was required for the proposed transaction. Does the application of Delaware §203 present a principled basis on which to distinguish public company deals from those involving private company targets?

9. Can the written consent procedure available under Delaware law (*see* DGCL §228) be used to avoid the result in *Omnicare?* Is a written consent distinguishable from a voting agreement of the type used in *Omnicare?* (*Hint:* a "sign-and-consent" shareholder approval structure in a merger transaction typically requires that Target's shareholders provide "written consent" (pursuant to DGCL §228) approving the merger transaction shortly *after* the signing of the merger agreement.)

10. Does the court in *Omnicare* suggest that the coerciveness and/or preclusiveness analysis must be done before analyzing the validity of a deal protection measure under the two-pronged *Unocal* standard? In other words, how does the court's concern about the preclusiveness and/or coerciveness of a particular defensive measure fit into the *Unocal* standard of intermediate scrutiny?

11. After *Omnicare,* can controlling shareholders do whatever they want with their shares (i.e., vote their shares as they see fit)? Does this type of property-based theory of share ownership continue to hold true under Delaware law after the *Omnicare* decision?

12. What is a "fiduciary out"? Why does the Delaware Supreme Court require use of a fiduciary out? Does *Omnicare* stand for the proposition that *all* acquisition agreements (or perhaps just those involving publicly traded targets) *must* include a fiduciary out?

NOTES

1. "Force the Vote" Provision. As a result of provisions that were originally made part of Delaware §251(c), and which are now codified in Delaware §146,* the board is no longer required to recommend the merger to the company's shareholders; all that is now required is that the board initially conclude that it is advisable to submit the merger to Target shareholders. Under what is commonly referred to as a "force the vote" provision, many merger agreements now include a provision that requires a merger transaction be submitted to

---

* [By the author: "Section 146 was added to the [Delaware GCL] in 2003. Under this section, directors may authorize the corporation to agree with another person to submit a matter to the stockholders, but the directors reserve the ability to change their recommendation of the matter. Prior to the 2003 amendment, a rule similar to that set forth in section 146 was codified at section 251(c) and applied to mergers and consolidations. Section 146 was enacted to clarify that the rule previously set forth in section 251(c) applies to *any* matter submitted to stockholders." Edward R. Welch, et al., FOLK ON THE DELAWARE GENERAL CORPORATION LAW §146.01 (FUNDAMENTALS 2020 ed.) (*emphasis added*).]

a vote of Target's shareholders even in those cases where Target's board has withdrawn its recommendation. Although rare, there have been instances (such as *Omnicare*) where Target's board has withdrawn its recommendation but still proceeded to submit the transaction to a vote of the company's shareholders. In general, most proxy statements will include a section setting forth the basis for the board's recommendation that shareholders approve a transaction and that the board recommends that shareholders vote to approve the transaction.

2. Sharply Divided Opinion.   The *Omnicare* decision was the result of a rather unusual 3-2 split of the Delaware Supreme Court, with two very sharply worded dissents being filed by Chief Justice Veasey and Justice Steele. This split, which is highly unusual for the Delaware Supreme Court (a court that is widely regarded as striving to reach its decisions on a unanimous basis) has led many observers to speculate whether this decision will be further refined or modified by the Delaware court in the near future, which was the hope clearly expressed by the both of the dissents. The authors of the two dissents (Chief Justice Veasey and then-Justice Steele) have since retired from the bench, leading some observers to speculate "that if *Omnicare* were to get back to the Supreme Court it would either be overruled or limited to . . . its particular facts." *Deal Protection: The Latest Developments in an Economic Tsunami,* THE DEAL LAWYER, Webcast Transcript, May 12, 2009, *available at:* http://www.deallawyers.com/Member/Programs/Webcast/2009/05_12/transcript.htm.

3. The Fall-Out from Omnicare.   Since the Delaware Supreme Court decided *Omnicare* over a decade ago, controversy has surrounded its decision, with criticism coming from both practicing M&A lawyers and academic lawyers. Although the decision remains controversial, with many experienced observers opining that the Delaware Supreme Court will eventually overturn its ruling, *Omnicare* "remains the common law of Delaware with respect to the precise facts in that case — a fully locked-up deal that was a *fait accompli.*" *M&A Deal Protections: The Latest Developments and Techniques,* THE DEAL LAWYER, *Webcast Transcript,* Sept. 18, 2012, *available at:* http://www.deallawyers.com/member/Programs/Webcast/2012/09_18/transcript.html. While *Omnicare* remains the law of the land, the Delaware Chancery courts have nonetheless "sought to narrow the reach of *Omnicare*" by distinguishing the facts at issue in subsequent cases in order "to find *Omnicare* inapplicable. . . . In the wake of *Omnicare*, a variety of deal structures have emerged to avoid replicating the facts [of *Omnicare*] where the [prospective M&A] deal involves a controller [i.e., controlling shareholder] or a majority selling block [of Target shares]." *Id.* As a general proposition, the strategy to avoid "replicating" *Omnicare* centers on "the fact that there are three legs to it": the force-the-vote provision, the shareholder voting agreements and the failure to include a fiduciary out clause. So, the strategy is to "kick-out any of one of those [three] legs [in order to] distinguish *Omnicare.*" *Id.* One commonly accepted strategy "is to not have a voting agreement that gets you to the level of a *fait accompli.* What level is that? That's up for debate when it's not a majority [of the shares]. But how close can you get to a majority is one issue that gets debated. And it tends to be . . . [very] fact specific." *Id.*

4. **Omnicare** *and the* **Revlon** *Mode.*   It bears emphasizing that the Delaware Supreme Court in *Omnicare* applied *Unocal* as the appropriate standard of judicial review, not *Revlon.*

> The directors' *Revlon* obligations were not triggered because the NCS-Genesis merger agreement did not involve a sale of control. The deal was a stock-for-stock combination. Genesis was a public, listed company that had no controller or control group. So, in the *Paramount v. Time* sense, stockholders of NCS were going to receive shares that traded in a fluid, changing and changeable market. [For many commentators, this has left] a bit of fuzziness after *Omnicare*, as a result of the dissent in this 3-2 decision and the criticism surrounding the appropriateness of using *Unocal* and *Unitrin* [*Unitrin, Inc. v. American General Corp.*, 651 A.2d 1361 (Del. 1995)] as the judicial review standard to assess the validity of deal protections in a friendly merger transaction. This may be more of an academic point with no meaningful distinction, but there's still a question . . . of whether deal protections in transactions where *Revlon* applies should be reviewed under the *Revlon* standard or whether, in all contexts, deal protections should be reviewed under the *Unocal* and *Unitrin* standard. In any case, [it would seem that] after *Omnicare* . . . heightened scrutiny is the prevailing judicial review standard for [analyzing the validity of] deal protection [devices].

THE DEAL LAWYER, *Webcast Transcript, supra. Query:* What do you think? What should be the standard of review in determining the validity of deal protection measures in the context of an M&A transaction involving a change of control? *Revlon? Unocal?* Business Judgment Rule?

5. The Deal-Making Process in M&A Transactions Continues to Evolve.   Starting with our description of the "flow of a deal" in Chapter 1, which details the deal-making process typically involved in an M&A transaction, we have observed that the life cycle of an M&A transaction continues to evolve, responding to ever-changing market conditions. In addition, starting with the problem sets in Chapter 2, we have seen how the legal constraints imposed on M&A transactions—as a matter of both state and federal law—have contributed to the further evolution of the deal-making process. Most notably, since the tumultuous period of the mid-1980s, when the Delaware Supreme Court decided the seminal cases of *Unocal, Moran,* and *Revlon,* "deal-makers have devised various tactics and sale methods in response [to these landmark Delaware decisions and their progeny] . . . Similar to Delaware's takeover jurisprudence, corporate sale methods are not formed in a vacuum, but are products of the periods in which they are developed." Christina M. Sautter, *Shopping During Extended Store Hours: From No Shops to Go Shops,* 73 BROOK. L. REV. 525, 526 (2008). The next two Delaware cases move us into a new era of M&A deal making. These cases also offer the opportunity to further reflect on how the Delaware courts are continually refining their takeover jurisprudence in order to address the fiduciary duty concerns presented by the facts of this new deal-making trend broadly referred to as "going-private" deals.

In re The Topps Company Shareholders Litigation
926 A.2d 58 (Del. Ch. 2007)

STRINE, Vice Chancellor.

I.   INTRODUCTION

The Topps Company, Inc. is familiar to all sports-loving Americans. Topps makes baseball and other cards (think Pokemon), this is Topps's so-called "Entertainment Business." It also distributes Bazooka bubble gum and other old-style confections, this is Topps's "Confectionary Business." Arthur Shorin, the son of Joseph Shorin, one of the founders of Topps and the inspiration for "Bazooka Joe," is Topps's current Chairman and Chief Executive Officer. Shorin has served in those positions since 1980 and has worked for Topps for more than half a century, though he owns only about 7% of Topps's equity. Shorin's son-in-law, Scott Silverstein, is his second-in-command, serving as Topps's President and Chief Operating Officer.

Despite its household name, Topps is not a large public company. Its market capitalization is less than a half billion dollars and its financial performance has, as a general matter, flagged over the past five years.

In 2005, Topps was threatened with a proxy contest. It settled that dispute by a promise to explore strategic options, including a sale of its Confectionary Business. Topps tried to auction off its Confectionary Business, but a serious buyer never came forward. Insurgents reemerged the next year, in a year when Shorin was among the three directors up for re-election to Topps's classified board. With the ballots about to be counted, and defeat a near certainty for the management nominees, Shorin cut a face-saving deal, which expanded the board to ten and involved his re-election along with the election of all of the insurgent nominees.

Before that happened, former Disney CEO and current private equity investor Michael Eisner ["Eisner"] had called Shorin and offered to be "helpful." Shorin understood Eisner to be proposing a going private transaction.

Once the insurgents were seated, an "Ad Hoc Committee" was formed of two insurgent directors and two "Incumbent Directors" to evaluate Topps's strategic direction. Almost immediately, the insurgent directors and the incumbent directors began to split on substantive and, it is fair to say, stylistic grounds. The insurgents then became "Dissident Directors."

In particular, the Ad Hoc Committee divided on the issue of whether and how Topps should be sold. The Dissident Directors waxed and waned on the advisability of a sale, but insisted that if a sale was to occur, it should involve a public auction process. The Incumbent Directors were also ambivalent about a sale, but were resistant to the idea that Topps should again begin an auction process, having already failed once in trying to auction its Confectionary Business.

From the time the insurgents were seated, Eisner was on the scene, expressing an interest in making a bid. Two other financial buyers also made a pass. But Topps's public message was that it was not for sale.

Eventually, the other bidders dropped out after making disappointingly low value expressions of interest. Eisner was told by a key Incumbent Director that the Incumbent Directors might embrace a bid of $10 per share. Eisner later bid $9.24 in a proposal that envisioned his retention of existing management, including Shorin's son-in-law. Eisner was willing to tolerate a post-signing Go Shop process, but not a pre-signing auction.

The Ad Hoc Committee split 2-2 over whether to negotiate with Eisner. Although offered the opportunity to participate in the negotiation process, the apparent leader of the Dissidents refused, favoring a public auction. One of the Incumbent Directors who was an independent director took up the negotiating oar, and reached agreement with Eisner on a merger at $9.75 per share. The "Merger Agreement" gave Topps the chance to shop the bid for 40 days after signing, and the right to accept a "Superior Proposal" after that, subject only to Eisner's receipt of a termination fee and his match right.

The Topps board approved the Merger Agreement in a divided vote, with the Incumbent Directors all favoring the Merger, and the Dissidents all dissenting. Because of the dysfunctional relations on the Ad Hoc Committee, that Committee was displaced from dealing with the Go Shop process by an Executive Committee comprised entirely of Incumbent Directors.

Shortly before the Merger Agreement was approved, Topps's chief competitor in the sports cards business, plaintiff The Upper Deck Company, expressed a willingness to make a bid. That likely came as no surprise to Topps since Upper Deck had indicated its interest in Topps nearly a year and half earlier. In fact, Upper Deck had expressed an unrequited ardor for a friendly deal with Topps since 1999, and Shorin knew that. But Topps signed the Merger Agreement with Eisner without responding to Upper Deck's overture. Shortly after the Merger was approved, Topps's investment banker began the Go Shop process, contacting more than 100 potential strategic and financial bidders, including Upper Deck, who was the only serious bidder to emerge.

Suffice it to say that Upper Deck did not move with the clarity and assiduousness one would ideally expect from a competitive rival seeking to make a topping bid. Suffice it also to say that Topps's own reaction to Upper Deck's interest was less than welcoming. Instead of an aggressive bidder and a hungry seller tangling in a diligent, expedited way over key due diligence and deal term issues, the story that emerges from the record is of a slow-moving bidder unwilling to acknowledge Topps's legitimate proprietary concerns about turning over sensitive information to its main competitor and a seller happy to have a bid from an industry rival go away, even if that bid promised the Topps's stockholders better value.

By the end of the Go Shop period, Upper Deck had expressed a willingness to pay $10.75 per share in a friendly merger, subject to its receipt of additional due diligence and other conditions. Although having the option freely to continue negotiations to induce an even more favorable topping bid by finding that Upper Deck's interest was likely to result in a Superior Proposal, the Topps board, with one Dissident Director dissenting, one abstaining, and one absent, voted not to make such a finding.

After the end of the Go Shop period, Upper Deck made another unsolicited overture, expressing a willingness to buy Topps for $10.75 without a financing contingency and with a strong come hell or high water promise to deal with manageable (indeed, mostly cosmetic) antitrust issues. The bid, however, limited Topps to a remedy for failing to close limited to a reverse break-up fee in the same amount ($12 million) Eisner secured as the only recourse against him. Without ever seriously articulating why Upper Deck's proposal for addressing the antitrust issue was inadequate and without proposing a specific higher reverse break-up fee, the Topps Incumbent Directors have thus far refused to treat Upper Deck as having presented a Superior Proposal, a prerequisite to putting the onus on Eisner to match that price or step aside.

In fact, Topps went public with a disclosure about Upper Deck's bid, but in a form that did not accurately represent that expression of interest and disparaged Upper Deck's seriousness. Topps did that knowing that it had required Upper Deck to agree to a contractual standstill (the "Standstill Agreement") prohibiting Upper Deck from making public any information about its discussions with Topps or proceeding with a tender offer for Topps shares without permission from the Topps board.

The Topps board has refused Upper Deck's request for relief from the Standstill Agreement in order to allow Upper Deck to make a tender offer and to tell its side of events. A vote on the Eisner Merger is scheduled to occur within a couple of weeks.

A group of "Stockholder Plaintiffs" and Upper Deck (collectively, the "moving parties") have moved for a preliminary injunction. They contend that the upcoming Merger vote will be tainted by Topps's failure to disclose material facts about the process that led to the Merger Agreement and about Topps's subsequent dealings with Upper Deck. Even more, they argue that Topps is denying its stockholders the chance to decide for themselves whether to forsake the lower-priced Eisner Merger in favor of the chance to accept a tender offer from Upper Deck at a higher price. Regardless of whether the Topps board prefers the Eisner Merger as lower risk, the moving parties contend that the principles animating *Revlon, Inc. v. MacAndrews & Forbes Holdings, Inc.* prevent the board from denying the stockholders the chance to make a mature, uncoerced decision for themselves.

In this decision, I conclude that a preliminary injunction against the procession of the Eisner Merger vote should issue until such time as: (1) the Topps board discloses several material facts not contained in the corporation's "Proxy Statement," including facts regarding Eisner's assurances that he would retain existing management after the Merger; and (2) Upper Deck is released from the standstill for purposes of: (a) publicly commenting on its negotiations with Topps; and (b) making a non-coercive tender offer on conditions as favorable or more favorable than those it has offered to the Topps board.

The moving parties have established a reasonable probability of success that the Topps board is breaching its fiduciary duties by misusing the Standstill in order to prevent Upper Deck from communicating with the Topps stockholders and presenting a bid that the Topps stockholders could find materially more favorable than the Eisner Merger. Likewise, the moving parties have shown a likelihood of success on their claim that the Proxy Statement is materially misleading in its current form.

The injunction that issues is warranted to ensure that the Topps stockholders are not irreparably injured by the loss of an opportunity to make an informed decision and to avail themselves of a higher-priced offer that they might find more attractive. . . .

III.   FACTUAL BACKGROUND

A.   THE EISNER MERGER AGREEMENT

Eisner proposes to acquire Topps through a private equity firm he controls, The Tornante Company, LLC, in an alliance with another private equity group, Madison Dearborn Capital Partners, LLC. For simplicity's sake, I refer to Eisner and his private equity partners simply as "Eisner."

Eisner and Topps executed the Merger Agreement on March 5, 2006, under which Eisner will acquire Topps for $9.75 per share or a total purchase price of about $385 million. The Merger Agreement is not conditioned on Eisner's ability to finance the transaction, and contains a representation that Eisner has the ability to obtain such financing. But the only remedy against Eisner if he breaches his duties and fails to consummate the Merger is his responsibility to pay a $12 million reverse break-up fee.

The "Go Shop" provision in the Merger Agreement works like this. For a period of forty days after the execution of the Merger Agreement, Topps was authorized to solicit alternative bids and to freely discuss a potential transaction with any buyer that might come along. Upon the expiration of the "Go Shop Period," Topps was required to cease all talks with any potential bidders unless the bidder had already submitted a "Superior Proposal," or the Topps board determined that the bidder was an "Excluded Party," which was defined as a potential bidder that the board considered reasonably likely to make a Superior Proposal. If the bidder had submitted a Superior Proposal or was an Excluded Party, Topps was permitted to continue talks with them after the expiration of the Go Shop Period.

The Merger Agreement defined a Superior Proposal as a proposal to acquire at least 60% of Topps that would provide more value to Topps stockholders than the Eisner Merger. The method in which the 60% measure was to be calculated, however, is not precisely defined in the Merger Agreement, but was sought by Eisner in order to require any topping bidder to make an offer for all of Topps, not just one of its Businesses.

Topps was also permitted to consider unsolicited bids after the expiration of the 40-day Go Shop period if the unsolicited bid constituted a Superior Proposal or was reasonably likely to lead to one. Topps could terminate the Merger Agreement in order to accept a Superior Proposal, subject only to Eisner's right to match any other offer to acquire Topps.

The Eisner Merger Agreement contains a two-tier termination fee provision. If Topps terminated the Eisner Merger Agreement in order to accept a Superior Proposal during the Go Shop Period, Eisner was entitled to an $8 million termination fee (plus a $3.5 million expense reimbursement), in total, or approximately 3.0% of the transaction value. If Topps terminates the Merger Agreement after the expiration of the Go Shop Period, Eisner is entitled to a $12 million termination fee (plus a $4.5 million expense reimbursement), or approximately 4.6% of the total deal value.

The Eisner Merger Agreement is subject to a number of closing conditions, such as consent to the transaction by regulatory authorities and the parties to certain of Topps's material contracts, such as its licenses with Major League Baseball and other sports leagues.

In connection with the Eisner Merger Agreement, Shorin and Eisner entered into a letter agreement pursuant to which Shorin agreed to retire within sixty days after the consummation of the Merger and to surrender $2.8 million to which he would otherwise be entitled under his existing employment agreement in the event of a change of control of Topps. Shorin would remain a consultant to Topps for several years with sizable' benefits, consistent with his existing employment agreement. . . .

IV. THE ESSENCE OF THE REVLON CLAIMS

The *Revlon* arguments advanced by the Stockholder Plaintiffs and Upper Deck differ a bit in their focus. I begin with the Stockholder Plaintiffs' *Revlon* arguments, which are premised on the notion that the Incumbent Directors who constitute a majority of the Topps board have been motivated by a desire to ensure that Topps remains under the control of someone friendly to the Shorin family and who will continue Shorin family members in the top leadership position. Since Shorin was forced into a face-saving settlement adding the Dissidents to the board, Shorin has known that time was running out on him. Therefore, he was motivated to find a buyer who was friendly to him and would guarantee that Shorin and Silverstein, his son-in-law, would continue to play leading roles at Topps. If Shorin didn't strike a deal to that effect before the 2007 annual meeting, he faced the prospect of having a new board majority oust him and his son-in-law from their managerial positions, and being relegated to a mere 7% stockholder of the company his father and uncles started, and that he has personally managed as CEO for more than a quarter century. According to the Stockholder Plaintiffs, Eisner was the answer to Shorin's dilemma, as he promised to be "helpful" by taking Topps private and retaining Silverstein as CEO.

To the supposed end of helping Shorin meet his personal objectives, the Topps board majority resisted the Dissidents' desire for a public auction of Topps, and signed up a deal with Eisner without any effort to shop the company beforehand. Not only that, the Stockholder Plaintiffs contend that defendant Greenberg capped the price that could be extracted from Eisner by making an ill-advised and unauthorized decision to mention to Eisner that a $10 per share bid was likely to command the support of the non-Dissident directors.

The Stockholder Plaintiffs also complain that the deal protection measures in the Merger Agreement precluded any effective post-signing market check. Although the Stockholder Plaintiffs admit the Merger Agreement contained a Go Shop provision allowing Topps to shop the company for forty days, the Stockholder Plaintiffs contend that that time period was too short and that the break-up fee and match right provided to Eisner were, in combination, too bid-chilling. Therefore, although Topps approached over 100 financial and strategic bidders to solicit their interest, the Stockholder Plaintiffs say that effort was bound to fail from the get-go, especially given the market's justifiable suspicions that Shorin and the board majority wanted to do a deal with Eisner to preserve the Shorin family's managerial influence.

It is at this stage that the arguments of the Stockholder Plaintiffs and Upper Deck intersect. Although Upper Deck does not stress the failure of Topps to seek out a bid from it before signing up a deal with Eisner, it does contend that the Topps board's lack of responsiveness to its expression of interest in presenting a bid at $10.75 per share evidences the entrenchment motivations highlighted by the Stockholder Plaintiffs.

Upper Deck contends that the Topps board unjustifiably delayed its access to, and the scope of, due diligence materials. Upper Deck argues that the Topps board manufactured pretextual excuses not to decide before the end of the Go Shop Period that Upper Deck had presented a proposal reasonably likely to result in a Superior Proposal. By that decision, the Topps board gave up its ability freely to continue discussions with Upper Deck.

When Upper Deck refused to lose heart and continued to press ahead by making a formal unsolicited bid at $10.75 per share, Upper Deck says it met with further resistance, in the form of withheld due diligence and unsubstantiated concerns about Upper Deck's ability and commitment to closing a deal. Finally, Upper Deck found itself publicly criticized by the Topps board for having failed to act as a diligent, serious bidder.

When it met those obstacles, Upper Deck asked to be released from the Standstill so that it could: (1) present a tender offer directly to the Topps stockholders; and (2) present its own version of events to the Topps stockholders to correct the misstatements allegedly made by Topps about Upper Deck. But Topps refused, despite its undisputed right under the Eisner Merger Agreement to grant such a relief if the board believed its fiduciary duties so required.

According to Upper Deck (and the Stockholder Plaintiffs), by this pattern of behavior, the Topps board majority has clearly abandoned any pretense of trying to secure the highest price reasonably available. Instead of using the Standstill Agreement for a proper value-maximizing purpose, the Topps board majority is using that Agreement to leave the Topps stockholders with only one viable alternative, Eisner's bid, based on a skewed informational base. Unless injunctive relief issues to prevent the Merger vote, Upper Deck (and the Stockholder Plaintiffs) contend that the Topps stockholders face irreparable injury because they will vote on the Merger in ignorance of Upper Deck's version of events and, even more important, without the chance to accept a tender offer from Upper Deck at a price higher than Eisner's offer.

These are in essence, the key *Revlon* arguments made by the Stockholder Plaintiffs and Upper Deck in support of their application for a preliminary injunction.

V. RESOLUTION OF THE REVLON CLAIMS AND DECISION ON THE SCOPE OF THE INJUNCTION

Upper Deck and the Stockholder Plaintiffs have moved for a preliminary injunction seeking to (1) stop the shareholder vote on the Eisner Merger; (2) require Topps to correct material misstatements in the Proxy Statement; and

(3) prevent Topps from using the Standstill Agreement to preclude Upper Deck from publicly discussing its bid for Topps or from making a non-coercive tender offer directly to the Topps stockholders. In the previous sections, I addressed the moving parties' disclosure claims and identified the additional and corrective disclosures that are required before the Eisner Merger vote may proceed.*
The only task remaining therefore is to determine whether the moving parties' *Revlon* claims warrant the broader injunctive relief sought.

The legal standard governing the resolution of that question is well settled. In order to warrant injunctive relief, the moving parties must prove that (1) they are likely to succeed on the merits of their *Revlon* claims; (2) they will suffer imminent irreparable harm if an injunction is not granted; and (3) the balance of the equities weighs in favor of issuing the injunction. I turn to those issues now, dividing the analysis in two parts. First, I address the decisions of the Topps board leading up to the signing of the Merger Agreement with Eisner. I then turn to the Topps board's dealings with Upper Deck after the Merger Agreement was executed.

The Stockholder Plaintiffs have largely taken the lead on the first time period. They argue that the Incumbent Directors unreasonably resisted the desire of the Dissident Directors to conduct a full auction before signing the Merger Agreement, that Greenberg capped the price Eisner could be asked to pay by mentioning that a $10 per share price would likely command support from the Incumbent Directors, that the Incumbent Directors unfairly restricted the Dissident Director's ability to participate in the Merger negotiation and consideration process, and that the Incumbent Directors foreclosed a reasonable possibility of obtaining a better bid during the Go Shop Period by restricting that time period and granting Eisner excessive deal protections. For its part, Upper Deck echoes these arguments, and supplements them with a contention that Upper Deck had made its desire to make a bid known in 2005, before Eisner ever made a formal bid, and was turned away.

Although these arguments are not without color, they are not vibrant enough to convince me that they would sustain a finding of breach of fiduciary duty after trial. . . .

The market knew that Topps, which had no poison pill in place, had compromised a proxy fight in 2006, with the insurgents clearly prevailing. . . . [O]ne must assume that Upper Deck is run by adults. As Topps's leading competitor, it knew the stress the Dissident Directors would be exerting on Shorin to increase shareholder value. If Upper Deck wanted to make a strong move at that time, it could have contacted Shorin directly . . . , written a bear hug letter, or made some other serious expression of interest, as it had several years earlier. The fact that it did not, inclines me toward the view that the defendants are likely correct in arguing that Upper Deck was focused on acquiring and then digesting

---

* [By the author: The complaint alleged a number of disclosure deficiencies in the Proxy Statement soliciting shareholder approval of the Eisner merger. In a portion of the opinion that has been omitted, the court considered a number of "problems with the Proxy Statement." Most importantly, the court agreed with plaintiffs' assertion that the Proxy Statement did not communicate all material facts regarding Eisner's assurances during the course of the merger negotiations that his bid is "friendly to [Topps' incumbent] management and [that his bid] depends on their retention."]

another company, Fleer, during 2005 and 2006, and therefore did not make an aggressive run at (a clearly reluctant) Topps in those years.

Given these circumstances, the belief of the Incumbent Directors on the Ad Hoc Committee, and the full board, that another failed auction could damage Topps, strikes me, on this record, as a reasonable one. . . .

Likewise, I am not convinced that the Incumbent Directors treated the Dissident Directors in a manner that adversely affected the ability of the board to obtain the highest value. The Dissident Directors were full of ideas—ideas that diverged widely. Their views of Topps's value do not suggest that the Topps board's approach was off the mark. . . .

In the end, I perceive no unreasonable flaw in the approach that the Topps board took to negotiating the Merger Agreement with Eisner. I see no evidence that another bidder who expressed a serious interest to get in the game during 2006 was fended off. There is no suggestion by even the Stockholder Plaintiffs that the two other private equity firms who discussed making a bid with Topps were inappropriately treated.

Most important, I do not believe that the substantive terms of the Merger Agreement suggest an unreasonable approach to value maximization. The Topps board did not accept Eisner's $9.24 bid. They got him up to $9.75 per share—not their desired goal but a respectable price, especially given Topps's actual earnings history and the precarious nature of its business.

Critical, of course, to my determination is that the Topps board recognized that they had not done a pre-signing market check. Therefore, they secured a 40-day Go Shop Period and the right to continue discussions with any bidder arising during that time who was deemed by the board likely to make a Superior Proposal. Furthermore, the advantage given to Eisner over later arriving bidders is difficult to see as unreasonable. He was given a match right, a useful deal protection for him, but one that has frequently been overcome in other real-world situations. Likewise, the termination fee and expense reimbursement he was to receive if Topps terminated and accepted another deal—an eventuality more likely to occur after the Go Shop Period expired than during it—was around 4.3% of the total deal value. Although this is a bit high in percentage terms, it includes Eisner's expenses, and therefore can be explained by the relatively small size of the deal. At 42 cents a share, the termination fee (including expenses) is not of the magnitude that I believe was likely to have deterred a bidder with an interest in materially outbidding Eisner. In fact, Upper Deck's expression of interest seems to prove that point—the termination fee is not even one of the factors it stresses.

Although a target might desire a longer Go Shop Period or a lower break fee, the deal protections the Topps board agreed to in the Merger Agreement seem to have left reasonable room for an effective post-signing market check. For 40 days, the Topps board could shop like Paris Hilton. Even after the Go Shop Period expired, the Topps board could entertain an unsolicited bid, and, subject to Eisner's match right, accept a Superior Proposal. The 40-day Go Shop Period and this later right work together, as they allowed interested bidders to talk to Topps and obtain information during the Go Shop Period with the knowledge that if they needed more time to decide whether to make a bid, they could lob in an unsolicited Superior Proposal after the Period expired and resume the process.

In finding that this approach to value maximization was likely a reasonable one, I also take into account the potential utility of having the proverbial bird in hand. Although it is true that having signed up with Eisner at $9.75 likely prevented Topps from securing another deal at $10, the $9.75 bird in hand might be thought useful in creating circumstances where other bidders would feel more comfortable paying something like Upper Deck now says it is willing to bid. Because a credible buying group—comprised not only of Eisner, an experienced buyer of businesses for Disney, but also the experienced private equity firm, Madison Dearborn—had promised to pay $9.75, other bidders could take some confidence in that and have some form of "sucker's insurance" for considering a bid higher than that. Human beings, for better or worse, like cover. We tend to feel better about being wrong, if we can say others made the same mistake. Stated more positively, recognizing our own limitations, we often, quite rationally, take comfort when someone whose acumen and judgment we respect validates our inclinations. A credible, committed first buyer serves that role.

In this regard, Topps's decision to enter into the Merger Agreement with Eisner despite its having received an unsolicited indication of interest from Upper Deck a few days before the signing was also likely not an unreasonable one. This is perhaps a closer call, but the suggestion of Dissident Director Brog to respond to Upper Deck only after inking the Eisner deal bolsters this conclusion. Although the facts on this point are less than clear, as discussed, Topps appears to have had rational reason to be suspicious of Upper Deck's sincerity. Upper Deck had made proposals before, but had often appeared flaky. Moreover, Upper Deck was only expressing an interest in the Entertainment Business, not the whole company at that point. A sale of the Entertainment Business would have left Topps with a floundering Confectionary Business that it had already tried to sell once, without success. Signing up a sure thing with Eisner forced Upper Deck to get serious about the whole company, and set a price floor that Upper Deck knew it had to beat by a material amount.

For all these reasons, I cannot buttress the issuance of an injunction on the alleged unreasonableness of the Topps's board decision to sign up the Merger Agreement. I now turn to the more troubling claims raised, which are about the board's conduct after the Merger Agreement was consummated.

The parties have presented competing versions of the events surrounding Topps's discussions with Upper Deck during the Go Shop Period, beginning with a fight over who was the first to contact the other and when the parties began discussing the Standstill Agreement, which was not executed until the start of the third week of the Go Shop Period. Neither party emerges from these arguments in an entirely positive light. Regardless of whose version of events is correct, the Topps board was hardly as receptive as one would expect in a situation where it received an unsolicited overture from a competitor who had long expressed interest in buying Topps in a friendly deal and who, given the likely synergies involved in a combination of the two businesses, might, if serious about doing a deal, be able to pay a materially higher price than a financial buyer like Eisner. . . .

At the same time, Upper Deck hardly moved with the speed expected of an interested buyer that has a limited time in which to secure a deal. Rather, Upper Deck initially acted in a manner that created rational questions about its seriousness and whether it was simply looking to poke around in Topps's files. To that point, Upper Deck failed to acknowledge Topps's legitimate concerns about entering into serious discussions with its only baseball card competitor. Upper Deck overreached when it asked for a provision in the Standstill Agreement obligating Topps to turn over to it the same information it provided to Eisner and the other bidders. Upper Deck was not the same as the other bidders and Topps had good reason to be skeptical of Upper Deck's intentions. Topps had to balance its concerns about the possibility that Upper Deck might use the Go Shop process as a pretext for gaining access to Topps's proprietary information with the possibility that Upper Deck might be willing to make higher bid than Eisner. There is a colorable argument that in the weeks that followed, Topps did not balance those concerns properly and rather relied on Upper Deck's status as a competitor as a pretext to keep Upper Deck at bay in order to preserve its friendly deal with Eisner. At the same time, Upper Deck's contention that it was delayed in submitting an actual bid for Topps by due diligence gamesmanship is undermined by the fact that Upper Deck claims (hotly disputed by Topps) to have made a blind, unsolicited bid for Topps at $11 a share in 2005. If it was able to make a blind bid then, why not in 2007?

In any event, I need not obsess over the behavior of the parties during the Go Shop Period. Upper Deck did finally make a formal bid for Topps at $10.75 per share two days before the close of the Go Shop. The Topps board had a fiduciary obligation to consider that bid in good faith and to determine whether it was a Superior Proposal or reasonably likely to lead to one. That is especially the case because the Topps board was duty bound to pursue the highest price reasonably attainable, given that they were recommending that the stockholders sell their shares to Eisner for cash.[26]

Because of the final-hour nature of the bid, the Topps board had to determine whether to treat Upper Deck as an Excluded Party under the Merger Agreement so that it could continue negotiations with it after the close of the Go Shop Period. The Topps board's decision not to do so strikes me as highly questionable. In reaching that conclusion, I recognize that Topps had legitimate concerns about Upper Deck's bid. Although there was no financing contingency in the proposal, Topps had reason for concern because Upper Deck has proposed to limit its liability under its proposed deal to $12 million in the event it was not able to close the transaction. Underlying Topps's skepticism of the seriousness of Upper Deck's proposal was perhaps the suspicion that Upper Deck was willing to pay $12 million simply to blow up Topps's deal with Eisner. Topps had to consider the possibility that Upper Deck was afraid that Eisner, by leveraging his reputation in the entertainment community, might be able to turn Topps into a stronger competitor than it had previously been.

Moreover, Upper Deck's initial proposal arguably did not address Topps's concerns that Upper Deck's proposal raised antitrust concerns. In its initial unsolicited overture to Topps before the Eisner deal was signed, Upper Deck acknowledged that there might be some antitrust issues associated with a merger of the two firms. Yet, in its initial bid, Upper Deck proposed placing virtually all of the antitrust risk on Topps. True, Topps had been down this road

---

26. [*Revlon, Inc. v. MacAndrews and Forbes Holdings, Inc.*, 506 A. 2d 173, 184 *n.* 16 (Del. 1986).]

itself before, and won, but the lack of any more substantial antitrust assurance in Upper Deck's initial bid arguably gave Upper Deck too easy an out in the event that regulators raised even a minor objection because of the optics of the transaction.

That said, Upper Deck was offering a substantially higher price, and rather than responding to Upper Deck's proposal by raising these legitimate concerns, the Topps board chose to tie its hands by failing to declare Upper Deck an Excluded Party in a situation where it would have cost Topps nothing to do so. Eisner would have had no contractual basis to complain about a Topps board decision to treat Upper Deck as an Excluded Party in light of Upper Deck's 10% higher bid price.

Upper Deck's first bid may not have been a Superior Proposal. But Topps had no reason to believe that the terms of Upper Deck's bid were non-negotiable, and it would have been reasonable for the Topps directors to have believed that their financing and antitrust concerns were manageable ones that could and, indeed, should have been capable of reasonable resolution in subsequent negotiating rounds. Topps could have gone back to Upper Deck with a proposal to increase the reverse termination fee and could have proposed a reasonable provision to deal with the antitrust concerns. By declaring Upper Deck an Excluded Party, the Topps board would have preserved maximum flexibility to negotiate freely with Upper Deck. The downside of such a declaration is hard to perceive.

The only advantage I can perceive from the decision not to continue talking with Upper Deck was if that decision was intended to signal Topps's insistence on a better bid that satisfied its concerns. But the behavior of the Topps's Incumbent Directors and their advisors, as revealed in this record, does not suggest such a motivation. The decision of Brog to abstain from the vote on that issue is an oddment, I admit, which lends support to the decision, but is consistent with the Dissident Directors' enigmatic behavior and possibly a refusal by Brog to vote on the issue, given his exclusion from the sale process. The reason I remain troubled by the decision is that the behavior of the Topps Incumbent Directors after this point inspires no confidence that their prior actions were motivated by a desire to advance the interests of Topps stockholders.

Upper Deck came back a month later with an improved unsolicited bid. That bid again offered a price materially higher than Eisner's: $10.75 per share. That bid also was, again, not any more financially contingent than Eisner's bid; there was no financial contingency, but Topps's remedy was limited to a $12 million reverse break-up fee. This time, to address Topps's antitrust concerns, Upper Deck offered a strong "come hell or high water" provision offering to divest key licenses if required by antitrust regulators, as well as an opinion by a respected antitrust expert addressing Topps's still unspecified antitrust concerns.

Although the Topps Incumbent Directors did obtain a waiver from Eisner to enter discussions with Upper Deck about this bid, they did not pursue the potential for higher value with the diligence and genuineness expected of directors seeking to get the best value for stockholders. Topps made no reasonable counter-offer on the antitrust issue and failed to identify why the transaction proposed a genuine antitrust concern. Instead, Topps insisted that Upper Deck agree to accept any condition, however extreme, proposed by antitrust regulators, and Topps never acknowledged its own past antitrust victories. Although Topps felt free to negotiate price with Eisner when he was promising to pay a materially lower price, cap his liability at $12 million, and condition his deal on approval by Topps licensors (which Upper Deck did not), it never made reasonable suggestions to Upper Deck about a higher reverse break-up fee, anti-trust issues, or price. Furthermore, although it did a deal with Eisner with only very limited remedial recourse if he breached, largely one senses, because of the reputational damage Eisner would suffer if he failed to close, the Topps board never seems to have taken into account the reputational damage Upper Deck would suffer if it did the same, despite its knowledge that Upper Deck has acquired other businesses in the past (remember Fleer?) and may therefore wish to continue to do so.

This behavior is consistent with a record that indicates that Shorin was never enthusiastic about the idea of having his family company end up in the hands of an upstart rival. That possible motivation is one that I do not approach in the same reductivist manner as the moving parties. Quite frankly, neither of the moving parties has made the case that Shorin and Silverstein are not skilled, competent, hard-working executives. More important, it is often the case that founders (and sons of founders) believe that their businesses stand for something more than their stock price. Founders therefore often care how their family legacy—in the form of a corporate culture that treats workers and con-sumers well, or a commitment to product quality—will fare if the corporation is placed under new stewardship.

The record before me clearly evidences Shorin's diffidence toward Upper Deck and his comparatively much greater enthusiasm for doing a deal with Eisner. Eisner's deal is premised on continuity of management and involvement of the Shorin family in the firm's business going forward. Upper Deck is in the same business line and does not need Shorin or his top managers.

Although Shorin and the other defendants claim that they truly desire to get the highest value and want nothing more than to get a topping bid from Upper Deck that they can accept, their behavior belies those protestations. In reaching that conclusion, I rely not only on the defendants' apparent failure to undertake diligent good faith efforts at bargaining with Upper Deck, I also rely on the misrepresentations of fact about Upper Deck's offer that are contained in Topps's public statements.

This raises the related issue of how the defendants have used the Standstill. Standstills serve legitimate purposes. When a corporation is running a sale pro-cess, it is responsible, if not mandated, for the board to ensure that confiden-tial information is not misused by bidders and advisors whose interests are not aligned with the corporation, to establish rules of the game that promote an orderly auction, and to give the corporation leverage to extract concessions from the parties who seek to make a bid.

But standstills are also subject to abuse. Parties like Eisner often, as was done here, insist on a standstill as a deal protection. Furthermore, a standstill can be used by a target improperly to favor one bidder over another, not for reasons con-sistent with stockholder interest, but because managers prefer one bidder for their own motives.

In this case, the Topps board reserved the right to waive the Standstill if its fiduciary duties required. That was an important thing to do, given that there was no shopping process before signing with Eisner.

The fiduciary out here also highlights a reality. Although the Standstill is a contract, the Topps board is bound to use its contractual power under that contract only for proper purposes. On this record, I am convinced that Upper Deck has shown a reasonable probability of success on its claim that the Topps board is misusing the Standstill. As I have indicated, I cannot read the record as indicating that the Topps board is using the Standstill to extract reasonable concessions from Upper Deck in order to unlock higher value. The Topps board's negotiating posture and factual misrepresentations are more redolent of pretext, than of a sincere desire to comply with their *Revlon* duties.

Frustrated with its attempt to negotiate with Topps, Upper Deck asked for a release from the Standstill to make a tender offer on the terms it offered to Topps and to communicate with Topps's stockholders. The Topps board refused. That refusal not only keeps the stockholders from having the chance to accept a potentially more attractive higher priced deal, it keeps them in the dark about Upper Deck's version of important events, and it keeps Upper Deck from obtaining antitrust clearance, because it cannot begin the process without either a signed merger agreement or a formal tender offer.

Because the Topps board is recommending that the stockholders cash out, its decision to foreclose its stockholders from receiving an offer from Upper Deck seems likely, after trial, to be found a breach of fiduciary duty. If Upper Deck makes a tender at $10.75 per share on the conditions it has outlined, the Topps stockholders will still be free to reject that offer if the Topps board convinces them it is too conditional. Indeed, Upper Deck is not even asking for some sort of prior restraint preventing the Topps board from implementing a rights plan in the event of a tender offer (although Upper Deck has indicated that will begin round two of this litigation if Topps does). What Upper Deck is asking for is release from the prior restraint on it, a prior restraint that prevents Topps's stockholders from choosing another higher-priced deal. Given that the Topps board has decided to sell the company, and is not using the Standstill Agreement for any apparent legitimate purpose, its refusal to release Upper Deck justifies an injunction. Otherwise, the Topps stockholders may be foreclosed from ever considering Upper Deck's offer, a result that, under our precedent, threatens irreparable injury.[29]

Similarly, Topps went public with statements disparaging Upper Deck's bid and its seriousness but continues to use the Standstill to prevent Upper Deck from telling its own side of the story. The Topps board seeks to have the Topps stockholders accept Eisner's bid without hearing the full story. That is not a proper use of a standstill by a fiduciary given the circumstances presented here. Rather, it threatens the Topps stockholders with making an important decision on an uninformed basis, a threat that justifies injunctive relief.

As this reasoning recognizes, one danger of an injunction based on the Topps board's refusal to waive the Standstill is that it will reduce the board's leverage to bargain with Upper Deck. Because this record suggests no genuine desire by the board to use the Standstill for that purpose, that danger is minimal.

---

29. *E.g., MacAndrews & Forbes Holdings, Inc. v. Revlon, Inc.*, 501 A.2d 1239, 1251 (Del. Ch. 1985), *aff'd*, 506 A.2d 173 (Del. 1986).

To address it, however, the injunction I will issue will not allow Upper Deck to go backwards as it were. The Merger vote will be enjoined until after Topps has granted Upper Deck a waiver of the Standstill to: (1) make an all shares, non-coercive tender offer of $10.75 cash or more per share, on conditions as to financing and antitrust no less favorable to Topps than contained in Upper Deck's most recent offer; and (2) communicate with Topps stockholders about its version of relevant events. The parties shall settle the order in good faith so as to avoid any timing inequities to either Eisner or Upper Deck, and therefore to the Topps stockholders. The injunction will not permit Upper Deck any relief from its obligations not to misuse Topps's confidential information. . . .

The other danger of an injunction of this kind is premised on a fear that stockholders will make an erroneous decision. In this regard, it is notable that nothing in this decision purports to compel the Topps board to enter a merger agreement with Upper Deck that it believes to be unduly conditional. What this decision does conclude is that, on this record, there is no reasonable basis for permitting the Topps board to deny its stockholders the chance to consider for themselves whether to prefer Upper Deck's higher-priced deal, taking into account its unique risks, over Eisner's lower-priced deal, which has its own risks. If the Topps board sees the Upper Deck tender offer and believes it should not be accepted, it can tell the stockholders why. It can even consider the use of a rights plan to prevent the tender offer's procession, if it can square use of such a plan with its obligations under *Revlon* and *Unocal*. But it cannot at this point avoid an injunction on the unsubstantiated premise that the Topps stockholders will be unable, after the provision of full information, rationally to decide for themselves between two competing, non-coercive offers.

Consistent with this reasoning, the vote on the Eisner Merger will also be enjoined until Topps issues corrective disclosures addressing the problems identified earlier in this decision.

VI.   CONCLUSION

For all these reasons, the moving parties' motion for a preliminary injunction is GRANTED.

QUESTIONS

1.   Why is Topps in the *Revlon* mode?

2.   What is a "go-shop clause"? As a negotiating strategy, what does Chancellor Strine suggest are the advantages of relying on a go-shop clause rather than engaging in a full auction process before signing the merger agreement with Bidder (here, Michael Eisner and his private equity partners)?

3.   What is the nature of the problem that Chancellor Strine identifies regarding the behavior of the Topps board of directors during the postsigning go-shop period?

4. Is the decision (and the court's reasoning) in the *Topps* case consistent with the result reached in *Omnicare* and the reasoning of the Delaware Supreme Court's opinion in that case?

NOTES

1. Go-Shop Clauses.   What is a go-shop clause? These provisions represent an important recent development in the evolution of M&A transactions. As explained by one experienced M&A practitioner:

> A new trend is emerging on the mergers and acquisitions landscape. While M&A deals frequently include no-shop clauses that prevent boards from soliciting higher offers, some companies are now negotiating provisions that allow for the opposite result. These provisions are aptly named go-shop clauses. . . .
>
> The no-shop clause prohibits the target company from soliciting bids from other buyers. However, in order to ensure the board of directors of the target company is not in breach of its fiduciary duties, no-shop clauses generally allow the board to respond to superior unsolicited bids. In such cases, the target company usually gives the original buyer the opportunity to match the bid. If the original bidder does not match the superior bid, merger agreements generally provide for break [up] fees to be paid to the original buyer.
>
> A go-shop clause allows the target board to actively shop for additional buyers that will pay a higher price after the board has agreed to deal with an initial buyer. In concept, this provides the opportunity for the target company to obtain better value for its shareholders by using the initial bid as a floor price in the market. Go-shop clauses developed, in part, from the skepticism shareholders have for management-led buyouts. They are meant to reassure shareholders that the target company's board is fulfilling its fiduciary duties and getting the best deal possible. Go-shop clauses have the benefit of promoting greater transparency and openness by allowing the target board to actively seek offers, as opposed to restricting the company to only reacting to unsolicited competing offers.

Blair Horn, *No Shop vs. Go Shop: New Trends in Mergers and Acquisitions*, MERGERS & ACQUISITIONS 55 (May 2007). *Query:* What are the business motivations that might prompt the parties to include a no-shop clause as part of the acquisition agreement? Notwithstanding the advantages described above regarding a go-shop clause, who might object to the use of such a clause?

2. The Use of Go-Shops.   In Chapter 2, we described the private equity boom of 2005-2007. *See supra*, pp. 85-86. During this period, financial buyers, such as Eisner in the *Topps* case, used "an important new deal-making technology" that emerged in this period: the go-shop clause. *See* Guhan Subramanian, *Go-Shops vs. No-Shops in Private Equity Deals: Evidence and Implications*, 63 BUS. LAW. 729, 730 (2008). The emerging importance of the go-shop clause in the M&A deal-making process has been described by Professor Subramanian as follows:

> The "go-shop" clause has emerged as an important new deal-making technology during the private equity boom of 2005-2007. Under the so-called *Revlon*

duty, the seller's board of directors must obtain the highest possible price in the sale of the company. Traditionally, the board would satisfy its *Revlon* duty by canvassing the market (through investment bankers), identifying serious bidders, holding a formal or informal auction among them, and signing a deal with the winning bidder. The merger agreement would typically include a "no-shop" clause, which would prevent the target from talking to potential "deal jumpers," unless the target board's fiduciary duty required it to do so (a "fiduciary out"). The go-shop clause turns this traditional approach on its head: rather than canvassing the marketplace first, the seller negotiates with a single bidder, announces the deal, and then has thirty to fifty days to "go shop" to find a higher bidder. At the highest level, then, the traditional route involves a market canvass followed by exclusivity with the winning bidder; while the go-shop route in its pure form involves . . . exclusivity with a bidder followed by a market canvass.

Id. at 729. Based on the empirical evidence collected and analyzed by Professor Subramanian involving all going-private deals between January 2006 and August 2007 that included a private equity buyer, Professor Subramanian reached the following conclusions:

that go-shop provisions, appropriately structured, can satisfy target board's *Revlon* duties . . . and that private equity firms are not stealing companies from the public shareholders at low-ball prices through go-shops, as some commentators suggest; . . . rather, the go-shop process includes a full price from the first bidder, which is meaningfully shopped post-signing . . . While the evidence presented [in this article] suggests no reason for categorical skepticism of go-shops, the data does indicate some reason to be wary in the specific context of management buyouts ("MBOs") . . . Taken as a whole, these findings have implications for how sell-side boards should structure a meaningful go-shop process, and where the Delaware courts should focus their attention in determining whether a particular go-shop satisfies the selling board's *Revlon* duties. To date, practitioners and courts have focused on the length of the go-shop window and the magnitude of the breakup fee in assessing the viability of the go-shop process. The analysis presented here suggests additional features that boards should negotiate for and courts should look for, particularly in the context of MBOs: bifurcated breakup fees, no contractual match right or (even better) no ability to participate in the post-signing auction, a contractual commitment for the initial bidder to sell in to any higher offer that emerges during the go-shop period, and ex ante inducement fees for subsequent bidders, among other deal features. This proposal tracks the Delaware courts' general approach to conflict [of interest] transactions, which begins with substantive fairness review[9] but gives up fairness review if appropriate procedural protections are in place.[10]

Id. at 730-731. *See also* Kirkland & Ellis, LLP, *M&A Update: Test-Driving a Hybrid Go-Shop*, Oct. 28, 2010, *available at:* https://www.kirkland.com/siteFiles/Publications/MAUpdate_102810.pdf ("With the return of private equity deal-making beginning in 2009, it has quickly become apparent that the predilection

---

9. *See Weinberger v. UOP, Inc.*, 457 A.2d 701, 710-11 (Del. 1983); *Kahn v. Lynch Commc'ns Sys., Inc.*, 638 A.2d 1110, 1115 (Del. 1994).

10. *See* Faith Stevelman, *Going Private at the Intersection of the Market and the Law*, 62 BUS. LAW. 777, 783 (2007).

towards go-shops . . . is undiminished."); and Sacha Jamal, et al., Weil Gotshal & Manges, LLP, *Private Equity Alert: The Latest Tips You Must Know Before You Go-Shop*, Oct. 2010, *available at*: https://www.weil.com/~/media/files/pdfs/Private_Equity_Alert_Oct_2010_.pdf.

G.   *Management Buyouts: The Duty of Loyalty and Conflicts of Interest*

For many observers of recent M&A market activity, the deal at issue in the *Topps* case typifies the type of management buyout (MBO) that came to dominate the private equity boom period that prevailed during 2005-2007. During this period, private equity buyers (such as Michael Eisner and his buyout firm) took advantage of the cheap financing that was available because of the then-prevailing low interest rates. Using substantial amounts of borrowed capital, these financial buyers would then team up with Target's management to propose acquiring Target Co. As then-chancellor Strine pointed out in his *Topps* decision, these MBO deals are fraught with conflicts of interest that will, at a minimum, result in the Delaware courts carefully scrutinizing the sale process and its participants. The next case involves a deal where the board of directors decided to undertake a "going private recapitalization" as an alternative to an acquisition. *Query:* Do the facts of the deal at issue in the next case, *Gantler v. Stephens*, present the same concerns that Chancellor Strine emphasized in his opinion in the *Topps* case? Does the Delaware Supreme Court rely on the same standard of review as did the court in *Topps*?

| **Gantler v. Stephens**
| 965 A.2d 695 (Del. 2009)

JACOBS, Justice.
   The plaintiffs in this breach of fiduciary duty action, who are certain shareholders of First Niles Financial, Inc. ("First Niles" or the "Company"), appeal from the dismissal of their complaint by the Court of Chancery. The complaint alleges that the defendants, who are officers and directors of First Niles, violated their fiduciary duties by rejecting a valuable opportunity to sell the Company, deciding instead to reclassify the Company's shares in order to benefit themselves, and by disseminating a materially misleading proxy statement to induce shareholder approval. We conclude that the complaint pleads sufficient facts to overcome the business judgment presumption, and to state substantive fiduciary duty and disclosure claims. We therefore reverse the Court of Chancery's judgment of dismissal and remand the case for further proceedings consistent with this Opinion.

FACTUAL AND PROCEDURAL BACKGROUND

A.   THE PARTIES

First Niles, a Delaware corporation headquartered in Niles, Ohio, is a holding company whose sole business is to own and operate the Home Federal Savings and Loan Association of Niles ("Home Federal" or the "Bank"). The Bank is a federally chartered stock savings association that operates a single branch in Niles, Ohio.

The plaintiffs (Leonard T. Gantler and his wife, Patricia A. Cetrone; John and Patricia Gernat; and Paul and Marsha Mitchell) collectively own 121,715 First Niles shares. Plaintiff Gantler was a First Niles director from April 2003 until April 2006.

Defendant William L. Stephens is the Chairman of the Board, President and CEO of both First Niles and the Bank, and has been employed by the Bank since 1969. Defendant P. James Kramer, a director of First Niles and the Bank since 1994, is president of William Kramer & Son, a heating and air conditioning company in Niles that provides heating and air conditioning services to the Bank. Defendant William S. Eddy has been a director of First Niles and the Bank since 2002. Defendant Daniel E. Csontos has been a director of First Niles and the Bank since April 2006. Csontos has also been a full-time employee, serving as compliance officer and corporate secretary of both institutions since 1996 and 2003, respectively. Defendant Robert I. Shaker, who became a director of First Niles and the Bank in January of 2006 after former director Ralph A. Zuzolo passed away, is a principal of a law firm in Niles, Ohio. Defendant Lawrence Safarek is the Treasurer and Vice President of both First Niles and the Bank.

Until his death in August of 2005, Mr. Zuzolo (who is not a party) was a director and corporate board secretary of First Niles and the Bank. Zuzolo was also both a principal in the law firm of Zuzolo, Zuzolo & Zuzolo, and the CEO and sole owner of American Title Services, Inc., a real estate title company in Niles, Ohio. Zuzolo's law firm frequently provided legal services to the Bank, and American Title provided title services for nearly all of the Bank's real estate closings.

B.   EXPLORING A POTENTIAL SALE OF FIRST NILES

In late 2003, First Niles was operating in a depressed local economy, with little to no growth in the Bank's assets and anticipated low growth for the future. At that time Stephens, who was Chairman, President, CEO and founder of First Niles and the Bank, was beyond retirement age and there was no heir apparent among the Company's officers. The acquisition market for banks like Home Federal was brisk, however, and First Niles was thought to be an excellent acquisition for another financial institution. Accordingly, the First Niles Board sought advice on strategic opportunities available to the Company, and in August 2004, decided that First Niles should put itself up for sale (the "Sales Process").

After authorizing the sale of the Company, the First Niles Board specially retained an investment bank, Keefe, Bruyette & Woods (the "Financial Advisor"), and a law firm, Silver, Freedman & Taft ("Legal Counsel"). At the next Board meeting in September 2004, Management advocated abandoning the Sales Process in favor of a proposal to "privatize" the Company. Under Management's proposal, First Niles would delist its shares from the NASDAQ SmallCap Market, convert the Bank from a federally chartered to a state chartered bank, and reincorporate in Maryland. The Board did not act on that proposal, and the Sales Process continued.

In December 2004, three potential purchasers—Farmers National Banc Corp. ("Farmers"), Cortland Bancorp ("Cortland"), and First Place Financial Corp. ("First Place")—sent bid letters to Stephens. Farmers stated in its bid letter that it had no plans to retain the First Niles Board, and the Board did not further pursue the Farmers' offer. In its bid letter, Cortland offered $18 per First Niles share, 49% in cash and 51% in stock, representing a 3.4% premium over the current First Niles share price. Cortland also indicated that it would terminate all the incumbent Board members, but would consider them for future service on Cortland's board. First Place's bid letter, which made no representation regarding the continued retention of the First Niles Board, proposed a stock-for-stock transaction valued at $18 to $18.50 per First Niles Share, representing a 3.4% to 6.3% premium.

The Board considered these bids at its next regularly scheduled meeting in December 2004. At that meeting the Financial Advisor opined that all three bids were within the range suggested by its financial models, and that accepting the stock-based offers would be superior to retaining First Niles shares. The Board took no action at that time. Thereafter, at that same meeting, Stephens also discussed in further detail Management's proposed privatization.

On January 18, 2005, the Board directed the Financial Advisor and Management to conduct due diligence in connection with a possible transaction with First Place or Cortland. The Financial Advisor met with Stephens and Safarek, and all three reviewed Cortland's due diligence request. Stephens and Safarek agreed to provide the materials Cortland requested and scheduled a due diligence session for February 6. Cortland failed to receive the materials it requested, canceled the February 6 meeting, and demanded the submission of those materials by February 8. The due diligence materials were never furnished, and Cortland withdrew its bid for First Niles on February 10. Management did not inform the Board of these due diligence events until after Cortland had withdrawn its bid.

First Place made its due diligence request on February 7, 2005, and asked for a due diligence review session the following week. Initially, Stephens did not provide the requested materials to First Place and resisted setting a date for a due diligence session. After Cortland withdrew its bid, however, Stephens agreed to schedule a due diligence session.

First Place began its due diligence review on February 13, 2005, and submitted a revised offer to First Niles on March 4. As compared to its original offer, First Place's revised offer had an improved exchange ratio. Because of a decline in First Place's stock value, the revised offer represented a lower implied price per share ($17.25 per First Niles share), but since First Niles' stock price had also declined, the revised offer still represented an 11% premium over market price. The Financial Advisor opined that First Place's revised offer was within an acceptable range, and that it exceeded the mean and median comparable multiples for previous acquisitions involving similar banks.

On March 7, 2005, at the next regularly scheduled Board meeting, Stephens informed the directors of First Place's revised offer. Although the Financial Advisor suggested that First Place might again increase the exchange ratio, the Board did not discuss the offer. Stephens proposed that the Board delay considering the offer until the next regularly scheduled Board meeting. After the Financial Advisor told him that First Place would likely not wait two weeks for a response, Stephens scheduled a special Board meeting for March 9 to discuss the First Place offer.

On March 8, First Place increased the exchange ratio of its offer to provide an implied value of $17.37 per First Niles share. At the March 9 special Board meeting, Stephens distributed a memorandum from the Financial Advisor describing First Place's revised offer in positive terms. Without any discussion or deliberation, however, the Board voted 4 to 1 to reject that offer, with only Gantler voting to accept it. After the vote, Stephens discussed Management's privatization plan and instructed Legal Counsel to further investigate that plan.

C.   THE RECLASSIFICATION PROPOSAL

Five weeks later, on April 18, 2005, Stephens circulated to the Board members a document describing a proposed privatization of First Niles ("Privatization Proposal"). That Proposal recommended reclassifying the shares of holders of 300 or fewer shares of First Niles common stock into a new issue of Series A Preferred Stock on a one-to-one basis (the "Reclassification"). The Series A Preferred Stock would pay higher dividends and have the same liquidation rights as the common stock, but the Preferred holders would lose all voting rights except in the event of a proposed sale of the Company. The Privatization Proposal claimed that the Reclassification was the best method to privatize the Company because it allowed maximum flexibility for future capital management activities, such as open market purchases and negotiated buy-backs. Moreover, First Niles could achieve the Reclassification without having to buy back shares in a fair market appraisal.

On April 20, 2005, the Board appointed Zuzolo to chair a special committee to investigate issues relating to the Reclassification, specifically: (1) reincorporating in a state other than Delaware, (2) changing the Bank's charter from a federal to a state charter, (3) deregistering from NASDAQ, and (4) delisting. However, Zuzolo passed away before any other directors were appointed to the special committee.

On December 5, 2005, Powell Goldstein, First Niles' outside counsel specially retained for the Privatization ("Outside Counsel"), orally presented the Reclassification proposal to the Board. The Board was not furnished any written materials. After the presentation, the Board voted 3 to 1 to direct Outside Counsel to proceed with the Reclassification program. Gantler cast the only dissenting vote.

Thereafter, the makeup of the Board changed. Shaker replaced Zuzolo in January of 2006, and Csontos [a full-time employee of First Niles, who also served as the company's compliance officer and corporate secretary] replaced

Gantler in April of 2006. From that point on, the Board consisted of Stephens, Kramer, Eddy, Shaker and Csontos.

On June 5, 2006, the Board determined, based on the advice of Management and First Niles' general counsel, that the Reclassification was fair both to the First Niles shareholders who would receive newly issued Series A Preferred Stock, and to those shareholders who would continue to hold First Niles common stock. On June 19, the Board voted unanimously to amend the Company's certificate of incorporation to reclassify the shares held by owners of 300 or fewer shares of common stock into shares of Series A Preferred Stock that would have the features and terms described in the Privatization Proposal.

D.   THE RECLASSIFICATION PROXY AND THE SHAREHOLDER VOTE

On June 29, 2006, the Board submitted a preliminary proxy to the United States Securities and Exchange Commission ("SEC"). An amended version of the preliminary proxy was filed on August 10. Plaintiffs initiated this lawsuit after the amended filing, claiming that the preliminary proxy was materially false and misleading in various respects. On November 16, 2006, the Board, after correcting some of the alleged deficiencies, disseminated a definitive proxy statement ("Reclassification Proxy" or "Proxy") to the First Niles shareholders. On November 20, the plaintiffs filed an amended complaint, alleging (inter alia) that the Reclassification Proxy contained material misstatements and omissions.

In the Reclassification Proxy, the Board represented that the proposed Reclassification would allow First Niles to "save significant legal, accounting and administrative expenses" relating to public disclosure and reporting requirements under the Exchange Act. The Proxy also disclosed the benefits of deregistration as including annual savings of $142,500 by reducing the number of common shareholders, $81,000 by avoiding Sarbanes-Oxley related compliance costs, and $174,000 by avoiding a one-time consulting fee to design a system to improve the Company's internal control structure. The negative features and estimated costs of the transaction included $75,000 in Reclassification-related expenses, reduced liquidity for both the to-be-reclassified preferred and common shares, and the loss of certain investor protections under the federal securities laws.

The Reclassification Proxy also disclosed alternative transactions that the Board had considered, including a cash-out merger, a reverse stock-split, an issue [sic] tender offer, expense reduction and a business combination. The Proxy stated that each of the directors and officers of First Niles had "a conflict of interest with respect to [the Reclassification] because he or she is in a position to structure it in such a way that benefits his or her interests differently from the interests of unaffiliated shareholders." The Proxy further disclosed that the Company had received one firm merger offer, and that "[a]fter careful deliberations, the board determined in its business judgment the proposal was not in the best interests of the Company or our shareholders and rejected the proposal."

The Company's shareholders approved the Reclassification on December 14, 2006. Taking judicial notice of the Company's Rule 13e-3 Transaction

Statement,[5] the trial court concluded that of the 1,384,533 shares outstanding and eligible to vote, 793,092 shares (or 57.3%) were voted in favor and 11,060 shares abstained. Of the unaffiliated shares, however, the proposal passed by a bare 50.28% majority vote[.]

E. PROCEDURAL HISTORY

The amended complaint asserts [several] claims. Count I alleges that the defendants breached their fiduciary duties to the First Niles shareholders by rejecting the First Place merger offer and abandoning the Sales Process.

ANALYSIS . . .

I. THE COURT OF CHANCERY ERRONEOUSLY DISMISSED COUNT I OF THE COMPLAINT

Count I of the complaint alleges that the defendants breached their duties of loyalty and care as directors and officers of First Niles by abandoning the Sales Process. Specifically, plaintiffs claim that the defendants improperly: (1) sabotaged the due diligence aspect of the Sales Process, (2) rejected the First Place offer, and (3) terminated the Sales Process, all for the purpose of retaining the benefits of continued incumbency.

In his opinion, the Vice Chancellor concluded that *Unocal* did not apply, because the complaint did not allege any "defensive" action by the Board. . . . [On appeal, the Delaware Supreme Court agreed with the Chancellor's decision that *Unocal* did not apply, observing that the board's decision to reject "an acquisition offer, without more, is not a defensive action under *Unocal*." The Delaware Supreme Court then proceeded to consider the ruling of the Chancery Court, holding the plaintiff had failed to rebut the business judgment rule.]

. . . Because the Board had "initiated the Sales Process on its own accord, seemingly as a market check as part of an exploration of strategic alternatives[,]" that supported the Board's stated business purpose — to reduce corporate expense associated with federal securities law compliance. The Vice Chancellor also concluded that the complaint failed to plead facts sufficient to infer disloyalty, and that given the Board's extensive discussions with, and receipt of reports from, the Financial Advisor, and given the involvement of specially retained Outside Counsel, the alleged facts were insufficient to establish a violation of the duty of care. The court therefore concluded that the challenged conduct was entitled to business judgment protection, which required the dismissal of Count I. . . .

---

5. Rules promulgated under the Exchange Act require the filing of a Rule 13e-3 transaction statement for any transaction that may result in a company reclassifying any of its securities. *See* 17 C.F.R. §240.13e–3 (2008) ("Going Private Transactions by Certain Issuers or Their Affiliates").

B.   THE COURT OF CHANCERY MISAPPLIED THE
BUSINESS JUDGMENT STANDARD

The plaintiffs next claim that the legal sufficiency of Count I should have been reviewed under the entire fairness standard. That claim is assessed within the framework of the business judgment standard, which is "a presumption that in making a business decision the directors of a corporation acted on an informed basis, in good faith and in the honest belief that the action taken was in the best interests of the company."

Procedurally, the plaintiffs have the burden to plead facts sufficient to rebut that presumption. On a motion to dismiss, the pled facts must support a reasonable inference that in making the challenged decision, the board of directors breached either its duty of loyalty or its duty of care. If the plaintiff fails to satisfy that burden, "a court will not substitute its judgment for that of the board if the . . . decision can be 'attributed to any rational business purpose.' "[27]

We first consider the sufficiency of Count I as against the Director Defendants. That Count alleges that those defendants (together with non-party director Zuzolo) improperly rejected a value-maximizing bid from First Place and terminated the Sales Process. Plaintiffs allege that the defendants rejected the First Place bid to preserve personal benefits, including retaining their positions and pay as directors, as well as valuable outside business opportunities. The complaint further alleges that the Board failed to deliberate before deciding to reject the First Place bid and to terminate the Sales Process. Indeed, plaintiffs emphasize, the Board retained the Financial Advisor to advise it on the Sales Process, yet repeatedly disregarded the Financial Advisor's advice.

A board's decision not to pursue a merger opportunity is normally reviewed within the traditional business judgment framework. In that context the board is entitled to a strong presumption in its favor, because implicit in the board's statutory authority to propose a merger, is also the power to decline to do so.[29]

Our analysis of whether the Board's termination of the Sales Process merits the business judgment presumption is two pronged. First, did the Board reach its decision in the good faith pursuit of a legitimate corporate interest? Second, did the Board do so advisedly? For the Board's decision here to be entitled to the business judgment presumption, both questions must be answered affirmatively.

We consider first whether Count I alleges a cognizable claim that the Board breached its duty of loyalty. In *TW Services v. SWT Acquisition Corporation*, the Court of Chancery recognized that a board's decision to decline a merger is often rooted in distinctively corporate concerns, such as enhancing the corporation's long term share value, or "a plausible concern that the level of debt likely to be borne by [the target company] following any merger would be

---

27. *Unocal v. Mesa Petroleum Co.*, 493 A.2d 946, 954 (Del. 1985) (quoting *Sinclair Oil Corp. v. Levien*, 280 A.2d 717, 720 (Del. 1971)).

29. *See* 8 *Del. C.* §251 for the grant of authority to enter into a merger; *see also* [*TW Servs., Inc. v. SWT Acquisition Corp.*, 1989 WL 20290, at *10–11 [(Del. Ch. March 2, 1989)]; *see generally Kahn v. MSB Bancorp, Inc.*, 1998 WL 409355 (Del. Ch. July 16, 1998), *af'd*, 734 A.2d 158 (Table) (Del. 1999) (describing a board's power under Section 251 and reviewing a decision not to negotiate a merger under the business judgment standard).

detrimental to the long term function of th[at] [c]ompany." A good faith pursuit of legitimate concerns of this kind will satisfy the first prong of the analysis.

Here, the plaintiffs allege that the Director Defendants had a disqualifying self-interest because they were financially motivated to maintain the status quo. A claim of this kind must be viewed with caution, because to argue that directors have an entrenchment motive solely because they could lose their positions following an acquisition is, to an extent, tautological. By its very nature, a board decision to reject a merger proposal could always enable a plaintiff to assert that a majority of the directors had an entrenchment motive. For that reason, the plaintiffs must plead, in addition to a motive to retain corporate control, other facts sufficient to state a cognizable claim that the Director Defendants acted disloyally.[32]

The plaintiffs have done that here. At the time the Sales Process was terminated, the Board members were Stephens, Kramer, Eddy, Zuzolo and Gantler. Only Gantler voted to accept the First Place merger bid. The pled facts are sufficient to establish disloyalty of at least three (*i.e.*, a majority) of the remaining directors, which suffices to rebut the business judgment presumption. First, the Reclassification Proxy itself admits that the Company's directors and officers had "a conflict of interest with respect to [the Reclassification] because he or she is in a position to structure it in a way that benefits his or her interests differently from the interest of the unaffiliated stockholders." Second, a director-specific analysis establishes (for Rule 12(b)(6) purposes) that a majority of the Board was conflicted.

Stephens: Aside from Stephens losing his long held positions as President, Chairman and CEO of First Niles and the Bank, the plaintiffs have alleged specific conduct from which a duty of loyalty violation can reasonably be inferred. Stephens never responded to Cortland's due diligence request. The Financial Advisor noted that Stephens' failure to respond had caused Cortland to withdraw its bid. Even after Cortland had offered First Niles an extension, Stephens did not furnish the necessary due diligence materials, nor did he inform the Board of these due diligence problems until after Cortland withdrew. Cortland had also explicitly stated in its bid letter that the incumbent Board would be terminated if Cortland acquired First Niles. From these alleged facts it may reasonably be inferred that what motivated Stephens' unexplained failure to respond promptly to Cortland's due diligence request was his personal financial interest, as opposed to the interests of the shareholders. That same inference can be drawn from Stephens' response to the First Place bid: Count I alleges that Stephens attempted to "sabotage" the First Place due diligence request in a manner similar to what occurred with Cortland.

---

32. *See Pogostin v. Rice*, 480 A.2d 619, 627 (Del. 1984), *overruled on other grounds by Brehm v. Eisner*, 746 A.2d 244 (Del. 2000) ("plaintiffs have failed to plead any facts supporting their claim[s] that the . . . board rejected the . . . offer solely to retain control. Rather, plaintiffs seek to establish a motive or primary purpose to retain control only by showing that the . . . board opposed a tender offer. Acceptance of such an argument would condemn any board, which successfully avoided a takeover, regardless of whether that board properly determined that it was acting in the best interests of the shareholders.").

Thus, the pled facts provide a sufficient basis to conclude, for purposes of a Rule 12(b)(6) motion to dismiss, that Stephens acted disloyally.

Kramer: Director Kramer's alleged circumstances establish a similar disqualifying conflict. Kramer was the President of William Kramer & Son, a heating and air conditioning company in Niles that provided heating and air conditioning services to the Bank. It is reasonable to infer that Kramer feared that if the Company were sold his firm would lose the Bank as a client. The loss of such a major client would be economically significant, because the complaint alleges that Kramer was a man of comparatively modest means, and that his company had few major assets and was completely leveraged. Because Kramer would suffer significant injury to his personal business interest if the Sales Process went forward, those pled facts are sufficient to support a reasonable inference that Kramer disloyally voted to terminate the Sales Process and support the Privatization Proposal.

Zuzolo: As earlier noted, Director Zuzolo was a principal in a small law firm in Niles that frequently provided legal services to First Niles and the Bank. Zuzolo was also the sole owner of a real estate title company that provided title services in nearly all of Home Federal's real estate transactions. Because Zuzolo, like Kramer, had a strong personal interest in having the Sales Process not go forward, the same reasonable inferences that flow from Kramer's personal business interest can be drawn in Zuzolo's case.

In summary, the plaintiffs have alleged facts sufficient to establish, for purposes of a motion to dismiss, that a majority of the First Niles Board acted disloyally. Because a cognizable claim of disloyalty rebuts the business judgment presumption, we need not reach the separate question of whether, in deciding to terminate the Sales Process, the Director Defendants acted advisedly (*i.e.*, with due care). Because the claim of disloyalty was subject to entire fairness review, the Court of Chancery erred in dismissing Count I as to the Director Defendants on the basis of the business judgment presumption.

In dismissing Count I as to the Officer Defendants, the Court of Chancery similarly erred. The Court of Chancery has held, and the parties do not dispute, that corporate officers owe fiduciary duties that are identical to those owed by corporate directors. That issue — whether or not officers owe fiduciary duties identical to those of directors — has been characterized as a matter of first impression for this Court. In the past, we have implied that officers of Delaware corporations, like directors, owe fiduciary duties of care and loyalty, and that the fiduciary duties of officers are the same as those of directors.[36] We now explicitly so hold.[37] The only question presented here is whether the complaint alleges sufficiently detailed acts of wrongdoing by Stephens and Safarek to state a claim that they breached their fiduciary duties as officers. We conclude that it does.

---

36. That officers and directors of Delaware corporations have identical fiduciary duties has long been an articulated principle of Delaware law. *See, e.g., Guth v. Loft, Inc.*, 5 A.2d 503, 510 (Del. 1939) (discussing the duty of loyalty applicable to officers and directors); *Cede & Co. v. Technicolor, Inc.*, 634 A.2d 345, 361 (Del. 1993) (same).

37. That does not mean, however, that the consequences of a fiduciary breach by directors or officers, respectively, would necessarily be the same. Under 8 *Del. C.* §102(b)(7), a corporation may adopt a provision in its certificate of incorporation exculpating its directors

Stephens and Safarek were responsible for preparing the due diligence materials for the three firms that expressed an interest in acquiring First Niles. The alleged facts that make it reasonable to infer that Stephens violated his duty of loyalty as a director, also establish his violation of that same duty as an officer. It also is reasonably inferable that Safarek aided and abetted Stephens' separate loyalty breach. Safarek, as First Niles' Vice President and Treasurer, depended upon Stephen's continued good will to retain his job and the benefits that it generated. Because Safarek was in no position to act independently of Stephens, it may be inferred that by assisting Stephens to "sabotage" the due diligence process, Safarek also breached his duty of loyalty.

The Court of Chancery found otherwise. Having characterized Safarek's actions as causing "a delay of a matter of days, or at most a couple of weeks," the Vice Chancellor observed that he could not see how that "conceivably could be a breach of Safarek's fiduciary duties." This analysis is inappropriate on a motion to dismiss. The complaint alleges that Safarek never responded to Cortland's due diligence requests and that as a result, Cortland withdrew a competitive bid for First Niles. Those facts support a reasonable inference that Safarek and Stephens attempted to sabotage the Cortland and First Place due diligence process. On a motion to dismiss, the Court of Chancery was not free to disregard that reasonable inference, or to discount it by weighing it against other, perhaps contrary, inferences that might also be drawn. By dismissing Count I as applied to Stephens and Safarek as officers of First Niles, the trial court erred. . . .

NOTES

1. The Scope of Fiduciary Duty Obligations of Officers. Until the decision in *Gantler*, Delaware case law was unclear regarding the contours of the fiduciary duty obligations of company officers, especially in the context of pending M&A transactions. The *Gantler* opinion establishes that the fiduciary duties owed by officers are the *same* as those owed by directors. "It is important to note that, unlike directors, officers are not protected by Delaware's exculpatory statute. [*See* Delaware §102(b)(7).] Whether that distinction could have significant implications for directors who also serve as officers remains to be seen." Hunton Williams, LLP, *Corporate Law Update: Delaware Supreme Court Addresses M&A Process, Officers' Duties and Stockholder Ratification*, Feb. 2009 (law firm memo, copy on file with author).

2. "Going-Private" Transactions. In the next section, we will explore in more detail the conflicts of interest that are inherent in the case of a "going-private" transaction of the type that was at issue in the *Gantler* case. Since the enactment of the Sarbanes-Oxley Act (SOX), the reform legislation adopted by Congress in 2002, going private transactions have been on the rise, as many

---

from monetary liability for an adjudicated breach of their duty of care. Although legislatively possible, there currently is no statutory provision authorizing comparable exculpation of corporate officers.

public companies seek to avoid the costs associated with the reforms imposed by SOX on publicly traded companies.

> The number of . . . going private transactions is increasing . . . The driving forces behind the . . . increase in going private transactions include . . . [t]he regulatory costs and burdens associated with being a public company[, which in turn,] often contribute to the determination by a board of directors and management of public companies, particularly smaller cap public companies, to consider going private. The disclosure, compliance and corporate governance requirements of a public company results in increased costs, both in terms of hard dollars and management time, not to mention the increased risk of personal liability to both directors and officers. Whether it is debating proper amounts of disclosure, increasing internal controls, revamping audit committees or rebalancing risks, the costs for a public company have increased considerably since the enactment of the Sarbanes Oxley Act and the related stock exchange requirements.

Michael Weisser and Lindsay Germano, Weil, Gotshal, & Manges, LLP, *Private Equity Alert: Going . . . Going . . . Going . . . Gone Private*, Aug. 2006 (law firm memo, copy on file with author). Given the increasing prevalence of going private transactions, it is important to understand the framework of state and federal regulation of these transactions, which is the focus of the materials in the next section.

H. "Going-Private" Transactions: "Squeeze-Outs" of Minority Interests and the Scope of Fiduciary Duty Obligations

In this section, we "bring it all home" (so to speak) by returning to study in more detail the modern regulatory and judicial framework of the "freeze-out" transaction that we first encountered in Chapter 2 as part of our analysis of the Delaware Supreme Court's opinion in *Weinberger v. UOP, Inc., supra*, at p. 179. As you will recall, a freeze-out of the type at issue in *Weinberger* is a transaction in which a controlling shareholder buys out the interest held by the minority shareholders in a publicly traded corporation. The consideration usually consists of cash or shares of the controlling shareholder (i.e., parent corporation). Freeze-out transactions may also be referred to as "going private" transactions, "squeeze-outs," "parent-subsidiary mergers," "minority buyouts," or "cash-out mergers." As was noted at the end of the last section, the number of going private transactions has been on the rise since the enactment of SOX by Congress in 2002.

The increase in squeeze-outs since 2002 is widely viewed as an effort by many public companies to avoid the additional burdens that resulted from the reform measures that SOX imposed on public companies. As a result of the rise in freeze-out transactions, increasing pressure has been placed on Delaware case law with respect to delineating the proper scope of fiduciary duty obligations that must be satisfied in order to validly consummate the elimination of the minority interest in a publicly traded corporation by the controlling share-holder. In addition, increasing importance has been placed on the disclosure obligations imposed on these squeeze-out transactions by SEC rulemaking. Both of these topics are analyzed in detail in this section.

The spike in freeze-out transactions following the enactment of SOX is reminiscent of the early 1940s and late 1960s when the level of freeze-out activity likewise increased markedly. *See* Guhan Subramanian, *Fixing Freeze-outs*, 115 YALE L.J. 2, 9 n. 29 (2005). In 1979, the SEC responded to this development in the trading markets by promulgating Rule 13e-3, which was briefly described in Chapter 6 (*see* pp. 449-451) as part of our examination of the SEC's rules governing issuer self-tenders and open-market purchases of the issuer's own stock.

In Rule 13e-3, the SEC imposed significant disclosure obligations on market participants engaged in a so-called Rule 13e-3 transaction, which is a defined term under the rule. *See* SEC Rule 13e-3(a)(3), 17 C.F.R. §240.13e-3 (2012). The definition of a Rule 13e-3 transaction has two components—a structural standard and a results standard—both of which must be satisfied. Structurally, a transaction will be subject to the rule if it meets any of the following three criteria:

- A *purchase* of any equity security by the issuer of such security or by an *affiliate* of such issuer (i.e., a controlling shareholder);
- A *tender offer* for or request or invitation for tenders of any equity security made by the issuer of such class of securities or by an affiliate of such issuer; or
- A *solicitation subject to Regulation 14A of any proxy, consent, or authorization of, or a distribution subject to Regulation 14C of information statements* to, any equity security holder by the issuer of the class of securities or by an affiliate of such issuer, in connection with: a merger, consolidation, reclassification, recapitalization, reorganization, or similar corporate transaction of an issuer or between an issuer (or its subsidiaries) and its affiliate; a sale of substantially all the assets of an issuer to its affiliate or group of affiliates; or a reverse stock split of any class of equity securities of the issuer involving the purchase of fractional interests.

In addition to satisfying this structural standard, the transaction must produce one of the following effects (i.e., the results standard) in order to trigger the disclosure obligations of Rule 13e-3:

- Cause any class of equity securities of the issuer that is subject to section 12(g) or section 15(d) of the Securities Exchange Act to be held of record by *less than* 300 persons; or
- Cause any class of equity securities of the issuer that is either listed on a national securities exchange or authorized to be quoted in an inter-dealer quotation system of a registered national securities association *to be neither listed on any national securities exchange nor authorized to be quoted on an inter-dealer quotation system* of any registered national securities association.

In adopting Rule 13e-3, it is clear that the SEC was worried about protecting minority shareholders:

> . . . The nature of and methods utilized in effecting going private transactions present an opportunity for overreaching of unaffiliated security holders by an issuer or its affiliates [i.e., controlling shareholder(s)]. This is due, in part, to the lack of arm's length bargaining and the inability of unaffiliated security holders [i.e., minority shareholders] to influence corporate decisions to enter into such transactions. Additionally, such transactions have a coercive effect in that [minority shareholders] confronted by a going private transaction are faced with the prospects of an illiquid market, termination of the protections under the federal securities laws and further efforts by the proponent to eliminate their equity interest. Because of the potential for harm to [the minority interest], particularly small investors, and the need for full and timely disclosure, the Commission continues to believe that Rule 13e-3 is necessary and appropriate for the public interest and the protection of investors.

SEC Release No. 34-17719 (Apr. 13, 1981).

While the disclosure obligations of Rule 13e-3 are considerable, for our purposes, the most important item of disclosure—unique to Rule 13e-3 going-private transactions—obligates the directors in a going-private transaction to disclose their view regarding the "fairness" of the terms of the proposed squeeze-out transaction. This disclosure requirement stands in stark contrast to the usual and customary premise underlying the SEC's disclosure philosophy, which (as we saw in the materials in Chapter 4) is to require full disclosure of all material facts in order to let the shareholders evaluate the merits of a proposed transaction. Here, in a marked departure to its usual approach, the SEC specifically requires Target's directors to express their view as to the merits (i.e., the fairness) of a proposed freeze-out transaction. *Query:* Given the potential conflict of interest that is inherent in these transactions, how much protection does the SEC's disclosure requirement provide to the minority shareholders?

1.   Going-Private Transactions: Delaware Case Law Developments

While the SEC focused on the perceived potential for abuse of minority shareholders presented by going-private transactions—by using its rulemaking authority to adopt enhanced disclosures—at the same time the Delaware courts were addressing these transactions. In the wake of the landmark Delaware Supreme Court opinion in *Weinberger* in Chapter 2 *(see supra,* p. 179), Delaware case law evolved to establish certain procedural protections for the benefit of minority shareholders. The Delaware case law developments over the past several decades with respect to freeze-outs are summarized in the following excerpt, which also provides a general background that is important to a thorough understanding of the competing interests that are inherently involved in freeze-out transactions.

Guhan Subramanian
Fixing Freezeouts
115 Yale L.J. 2 (2005)

B.   DEVELOPMENT OF PROCEDURAL PROTECTION [IN FREEZEOUT MERGERS]

The seminal case on freezeouts in the modern era is *Weinberger v. UOP*, [which was] handed down by the Delaware Supreme Court in 1983. . . .

While *Weinberger* did several notable things, [for present purposes,] its most important contribution was the identification of the procedural protections that minority shareholders should receive in freezeout mergers. The Court began by noting that entire fairness [standard of judicial] review required both "fair dealing" and "fair price," and clarified what each of these entailed. . . .

But in the midst of its litany of criticisms of [the controlling shareholder Signal's process for freezing out the minority interest], the *Weinberger* court paused to provide crucial guidance for transactional lawyers. In a much-noticed footnote [footnote 7], the court stated:

> Although perfection is not possible, or expected, the result here could have been entirely different if UOP [the subsidiary] had appointed an independent negotiating committee of its outside directors to deal with Signal [the controlling shareholder of UOP] at arm's length. Since fairness in this context can be equated to conduct by a theoretical, wholly independent, board of directors acting upon the matter before them, it is unfortunate that this course apparently was neither considered nor pursued. Particularly in a parent-subsidiary context, a showing that the action taken was as though each of the contending parties had in fact exerted its bargaining power against the other at arm's length is strong evidence that the transaction meets the test of fairness.

Transactional lawyers took the hint: An SC [i.e., special committee] of independent directors quickly became standard practice in freezeout mergers.[47]

Two opposing concerns developed in response to the *Weinberger* SC mechanism. The first, voiced primarily by judges and academics, is that an SC can never be truly independent from the controlling shareholder because the controller is an "800-pound gorilla"[48] who inevitably will dominate the independent directors.[49] Among those who hold this view, some (generally academics)

---

47. *See* Donald J. Wolfe, Jr., & Janine M. Salomone, *Pure Resources, Printcafe and the Pugnacious Special Committee*, M&A Law., May 2003, at 10, 10 ("Since [Weinberger], the use of special negotiating committees has become commonplace. . . .").

48. *See* Leo E. Strine, Jr., *The Inexcapably Empirical Foundation of the Common Law of Corporations*, 27 DEL. J. CORP. L. 499, 509 (2002) ("[T]his strain of thought was premised on the notion that when an 800-pound gorilla wants the rest of the bananas, little chimpanzees, like independent directors and minority stockholders, cannot be expected to stand in the way, even if the gorilla putatively gives them veto power.").

49. *See, e.g., Kahn v. Tremont Corp.*, 694 A.2d 422, 428 (Del. 1997) ("Entire fairness remains applicable even when an independent committee is utilized because the underlying factors which raise the specter of impropriety can never be completely eradicated and still require careful judicial scrutiny."); William T. Allen, et al., *Function over Form: A Reassessment of Standards of Review in Delaware Corporation Law*, 56 BUS. LAW. 1287, 1308 (2001) (noting that outside directors "are not hermetically sealed off from the inside directors").

conclude that SCs should not warrant significant deference from the courts as suggested by *Weinberger*, while others (generally judges) conclude that, even if soft ties exist between the controller and the SC, at least some judicial deference to an SC process is warranted because courts are not well-positioned to assess questions of value.

The second concern, diametrically opposite from the first and voiced primarily by practitioners, is that SCs are too independent from the controller. As described by Charles Nathan, global co-chair of the mergers and acquisitions group at Latham & Watkins: "There are a number of times the committee turns down perfectly fine deals, or drags things out for months, because they can't get their act together. And it's a very, very frustrating experience." Under this view, the *Weinberger* SC roadmap actually works to the detriment of minority shareholders by allowing independent directors with imperfect incentives to veto [value-creating] transactions. . . .

[All of this raises the fundamental question of what] level of deference should courts afford to a freezeout merger that was approved by an SC of independent directors? Footnote 7 of *Weinberger* was vague on this critical question. In the absence of guidance, judges on the Delaware Chancery Court divided in their approaches to this fundamental question [in the cases that were decided] in the late 1980s and early 1990s. In *In re Trans World Airlines, Inc. Shareholders Litigation*, for example, Chancellor Bill Allen held that SC approval changed the standard of [judicial] review for a freeze-out merger from entire fairness to highly deferential business judgment review.[53] In contrast, . . . [in] *Rabkin v. Olin Corp.*,[55] . . . [Vice Chancellor Bill Chandler] held that SC approval only shifted the burden on entire fairness review from the defendant to the plaintiff. . . .

One could argue that while an SC may be captured by the controller, the minority shareholders cannot be, and therefore greater judicial deference should be afforded to approval by a majority of the minority shareholders (a "MOM condition"). Whatever appeal this argument may have as a matter of logic, the Delaware courts have rejected it, choosing instead to afford only minimal deference to MOM conditions. The seminal case on this point is *Rosenblatt v. Getty Oil Co.*, [493 A.2d 929 (Del. 1985),] handed down by the Delaware Supreme Court just two years after *Weinberger*. . . .

. . . In [*Rosenblatt*], the Delaware Supreme Court [ultimately concluded that approval by a majority of] the minority shareholders shifted the burden on entire fairness to the plaintiff but did not shift the standard of [judicial] review [from entire fairness] to [the] business judgment [rule]. . . .

[Accordingly,] one puzzling (if unintended) [practical] consequence of [the evolution of Delaware case law since *Weinberger* was decided on 1983 is] that either SC approval or a MOM condition shifts the burden on entire fairness review, but the combination of the two procedural protections provides no further benefit to the controlling shareholder in terms of [establishing the relevant standard of judicial review of the merger freeze-out transaction]. . . .

---

53. Civ. A. No. 9844, 1988 WL 111271, at *7 (Del. Ch. Oct. 21, 1988), abrogated by *Kahn v. Lynch Commc'n Sys.*, 638 A.2d 1110 (Del. 1994).

55. C.A. No. 7547, 1990 WL 47648, at *6 (Del. Ch. Apr. 17, 1990), *aff'd*, 586 A.2d 1202 (Del. 1990).

To summarize, while *Weinberger* provides the procedural roadmap for freezeout transactions, . . . [subsequent decisions of the Delaware courts establish that approval by *both* an independent SC *and* by a majority of the minority] combination does not eliminate [the transaction from judicial scrutiny under the] entire fairness [standard of] review. From a transactional lawyer's perspective, merger-freezeout doctrine . . . [thus] represents the worst of all possible worlds: a fully empowered SC and a feisty negotiation with the controller, to be followed nevertheless with entire fairness review by the court, even if [a majority of disinterested] minority shareholders have approved the deal. Of course, the potential beneficiaries of this approach are the minority shareholders, who should gain from both the procedural protections that *Weinberger* encourages and the judicial scrutiny that [is mandated by Delaware case law, all of which serves to illustrate the Delaware Supreme Court's unwillingness to relinquish entire fairness review, regardless of the procedural protections that the controller provides in the case of a merger freeze-out.]. . . .

C. DISRUPTIVE TECHNOLOGY: THE TENDER OFFER FREEZEOUT

A statutory merger is not the only way to execute a freezeout [of the minority interest in a controlled subsidiary] . . . Another method that began to appear in the 1990s was a freezeout via [a] tender offer. In this route, the controlling shareholder would begin, or announce its intention to begin, a tender offer [to be made] directly to the minority shareholders. The target [company] would [then] form an SC of independent directors to assess the transaction, negotiate with the controller, and issue a Schedule 14D-9 recommendation to the minority (*e.g.*, approve, reject, neutral, or unable to take a position). If the controller gained sufficient shares in its tender offer to get to 90% voting control of the target, it would then execute a short-form merger, which does not require a shareholder vote, in order to eliminate the remaining (nontendering) minority shareholders. Because 90% is the critical threshold in a tender offer freezeout, the controller would typically condition its offer on getting to 90% control (a "90% condition"). . . .

Historically, [M&A lawyers] assumed that tender offer freezeouts would also be subject to entire fairness review, because they achieved the same end result as merger freezeouts, namely, the elimination of the minority shareholders. As a result there was no obvious benefit to be gained from a tender offer freezeout, and the merger form continued to dominate in practice. This calculus began to change in the mid-1990s with the Delaware Supreme Court's decision in *Solomon v. Pathe Communications Corp.* [672 A.2d 35 (Del. 1996)]. The *Solomon* court affirmed a chancery court holding that a tender offer by a controlling shareholder to the minority was not subject to entire fairness review. The court reasoned that a tender offer was a deal between the controlling shareholder and minority shareholders, which involved no conflict of interest. . . .

[Five years after the *Solomon* decision, the Delaware Supreme Court decided] *In re Siliconix Inc. Shareholders Litigation.*[84] *Siliconix* involved Vishay

---

84. No. Civ. A 18700, 2001 WL 716787 (Del. Ch. June 19, 2001).

Intertechnology's freezeout of the minority shareholders in Siliconix. Vishay, which owned 80.4% of Siliconix, announced a tender offer for the minority shares . . . With Vishay's encouragement, Siliconix appointed an SC of two independent directors to negotiate with Vishay. The SC hired legal and financial advisors and concluded that the offer price was inadequate. After three months of negotiations, Vishay switched from a cash tender offer to a stock exchange offer . . . Minority shareholders brought suit alleging that [Vishay's exchange offer] . . . was unfair. Citing *Solomon*, among other cases, the Delaware Chancery Court [in its *Siliconix* decision in 2001] declined to apply entire fairness review to the tender offer freezeout: "Because . . . there were no disclosure violations and the tender [offer] is not coercive, Vishay was not obligated to offer a fair price in its tender [offer]." [*Id.* at *6.] . . .

Just one month after *Siliconix*, the Delaware Supreme Court [decided] *Glassman v. Unocal Exploration Corp.*,[90] [in which] the parent company Unocal Corporation (Unocal) owned 96% of its subsidiary Unocal Exploration Corporation (UXC). Unocal decided to freeze out the minority shareholders, and UXC appointed an SC of three directors to negotiate the terms of the deal. The parties negotiated an exchange ratio of 0.54 Unocal shares for each UXC share, and, because Unocal held more than 90% of UXC, the freezeout was executed as a short-form merger under section 253 of the Delaware corporate code.

Minority shareholders brought suit alleging that the transaction was unfair. The Delaware Chancery Court declined to apply entire fairness [standard of judicial] review and dismissed the claim. The Delaware Supreme Court affirmed, holding that "absent fraud or illegality, appraisal is the exclusive remedy available to a minority shareholder who objects to a short-form merger." [*Glassman*, 777 A. 2d at 248.] The court reasoned that section 253 was intended to provide a streamlined process for accomplishing a merger, which is squarely at odds with the procedural apparatus that the fair process prong of entire fairness [standard of judicial review] requires: "If . . . the corporate fiduciary sets up negotiating committees, hires independent financial and legal experts, etc., then it will have lost the very benefit provided by the statute—a simple, fast and inexpensive process for accomplishing a merger." [*Id.* at 247-248.]

Thus, with [the decisions in *Glassman* and *Siliconix*,] practitioners now had a blueprint for avoiding entire fairness review in a freezeout transaction. Under *Siliconix*, a tender offer to the minority would be exempt from entire fairness review, and if the controller got to 90% voting control, the back-end short-form merger would also be exempt under *Glassman*. Practitioners, academics, and judges quickly noted the disparity in judicial treatment between tender offer freezeouts and merger freezeouts. . . . The result was dramatically different standards of review for two functionally identical transactional forms. . . .

To summarize, [prior to the Delaware Supreme Court's decision in 2014 in the *MFW* case set forth below,] Delaware law [provided] a controlling shareholder two transactional forms for a freezeout [of the minority interest]: the statutory merger route and the tender offer route. These two forms appear similar at the outset. In each case the process begins when the controller

---

90. 777 A.2d 242 (Del. 2001).

informs the target board of its intention to freeze out the minority, and the target board responds by establishing an SC of independent directors. But at this point the similarity disappears. While the SC in a merger freezeout has veto power over the transaction and in theory can negotiate indefinitely, the SC in a tender offer freezeout cannot veto the transaction and has only ten days to issue its [Schedule] 14D-9 recommendation [as required by the SEC's tender offer rules] to the minority. The difference continues in the standard of judicial review imposed: entire fairness review for merger freezeouts compared to business judgment review for tender offer freezeouts. . . .

NOTES

1. Use of a "Top Up Option."   In the wake of the *Siliconix/Glassman* decisions that were described in the preceding excerpt, it became rather commonplace for Bidders who chose to use the tender offer freeze-out path to eliminate the unwanted minority interest to use a "top up option" as part of the squeeze-out transaction. In those situations where the controlling shareholder did not already own more than 90 percent of Target's stock, Bidder would condition its obligation to close on the first step (i.e., the front-end tender offer) on receiving at least 90 percent of Target's outstanding stock. This would then allow Bidder to proceed promptly with the back-end, squeeze-out merger structured as a short-form merger *and* avoid the entire fairness obligations in the squeeze-out as a result of the court's holding in *Glassman*. To deal with the possibility that Bidder may not be able to convince enough Target shareholders to tender their shares in order to obtain 90 percent ownership, Bidder would include a "top up option" as part of the deal structure. The top up option

> provided that, if the acquirer (i.e., Bidder) received a certain number of shares of stock in the front-end tender [offer], the target corporation would issue to the acquirer that number of additional shares to enable it to own 90 percent of each class of voting stock and [thus] to consummate a short-form merger [pursuant to] Section 253 . . . of the DCGL. While the top-up structure has been recognized as valid by the Delaware courts,[2] and it has in recent years become a common feature in the M&A landscape, it is not available in every situation. That is, whether a top-up option is available depends upon the number of authorized and unissued shares of the target corporation. Since the number of shares needed to increase the acquirer's stake by even a single percentage point is often massive, the top-up option, even if available, is frequently limited, since the acquirer must first obtain a supermajority of the shares (and often in the range of 80 to 85 percent) before it can exercise the top-up option.

William J. Haubert, et al., *Corporate Governance: Significant Proposed Amendments to the General Corporation Law of the State of Delaware,* 27 INSIGHTS 26 (June 2013). As we shall see later in this chapter, as part of our discussion of the enactment of Delaware Section 251(h) at pp. 756-761, this new subsection allows the parties to dispense with the need for the top up option. *Id.* at 28.

---

2. *Olson v. ev3. Inc.,* C.A. No. 5583-VCL (Del. Ch. Feb. 21, 2011).

2. Chancellor Strine's Suggestion of a "Unified Standard." In an important opinion, *In re Cox Communications Shareholders Litigation*, 879 A.2d 604 (Del. Ch. 2005), then-Vice Chancellor Leo Strine set forth his recommendation for a "unified standard" of judicial review of "going-private" transactions, thereby addressing (in dicta) "the peculiar situation where different transaction structures having the same functional result (taking a company private) are challenged by plaintiffs [i.e., shareholders] and reviewed under divergent standards." Christopher J. Hewitt and A. Guthrie Paterson, *Going Private Transactions: Delaware Revisits Negotiated Mergers and Tender Offers Involving Controlling Stockholders*, Jones Day Commentary, July 2006 (law firm memo, copy on file with author). As proposed by Vice Chancellor Strine, "the reform would be to invoke the business judgment rule standard of review when a going-private merger with a controlling shareholder was effected using a process that mirrored *both* elements of an arms-length merger: (1) approval by disinterested directors; and (2) approval by disinterested stockholders." *Cox Communications, supra* at 606. This proposed reform was intended to level the playing field for determining whether to use a long-form merger or a tender offer. As suggested by then-Vice Chancellor Strine, the reform of "our common law in this manner also honors our law's traditions, by respecting the informed business judgment of disinterested directors and stockholders." *Id.* at 607.

3. Standard of Judicial Review in Merger Freeze-outs. Given that Delaware case law provided transaction planners with two deal structures to allow a controlling shareholder to "squeeze out" the minority interest—each involving very different standards of judicial review for what are functionally equivalent transactions—the obvious question becomes: what should be the proper scope of judicial review with respect to *merger freeze-out* transactions? In thinking about this question, what are the competing interests that must (should) be taken into account? Consider the following assessment of the competing interests offered by experienced M&A lawyers:

> Determination of the appropriate approach to [judicial] review [of] controlling stockholder/minority buyout transactions—i.e., where a controlling stockholder acquires the "minority" shares that it does not already own—requires resolution of the tension between deference to business judgment and protection against self-dealing and coercion [provided by the entire fairness standard of review]. Delaware courts, along with legal practitioners and academics have been fascinated with this tension in the context of minority buyouts, and the debate continues. . . .
>
> Delaware courts have sought to create a framework for analyzing controlling stockholder buyout transactions that balance traditional deference for business judgment with the need to discourage self-dealing by the controlling stockholder. The courts' efforts have given rise to two different analytical frameworks: (1) the heightened "entire fairness" review of transactions pursuant to negotiated merger agreements; and (2) deferential business judgment review where the controlling stockholder pursues the buyout of the unaffiliated or "minority" shares through a unilateral tender offer (i.e., outside the context of a negotiated agreement with the target's board).

Suneela Kim, et al., *Examining Data Points in Minority Buy-outs: A Practitioners' Report*, 36 DEL. J. CORP. LAW 939, 940-946 (2011). This "tension" in the Delaware case law with respect to what should be the proper scope of judicial review of "minority buyouts" structured as "*merger* freeze-outs" was ultimately addressed by the Delaware Supreme Court in the following important decision.

Kahn v. M & F Worldwide Corp.
88 A.3d 635 (Del. 2014)

HOLLAND, Justice:

This is an appeal from a final judgment entered by the Court of Chancery in a proceeding that arises from a 2011 acquisition by MacAndrews & Forbes Holdings, Inc. ("M & F" or "MacAndrews & Forbes")—a 43% stockholder in M & F Worldwide Corp. ("MFW")—of the remaining common stock of MFW (the "Merger"). From the outset, M & F's proposal to take MFW private was made contingent upon two stockholder-protective procedural conditions. First, M & F required the Merger to be negotiated and approved by a special commit-tee of independent MFW directors (the "Special Committee"). Second, M & F required that the Merger be approved by a majority of stockholders unaffiliated with M & F. The Merger closed in December 2011, after it was approved by a vote of 65.4% of MFW's minority stockholders.

The Appellants initially sought to enjoin the transaction. They withdrew their request for injunctive relief after taking expedited discovery, including several depositions. The Appellants then sought post-closing relief against M&F, Ronald O. Perelman, and MFW's directors (including the members of the Special Committee) for breach of fiduciary duty. Again, the Appellants were provided with extensive discovery. The Defendants then moved for summary judgment, which the Court of Chancery granted.

COURT OF CHANCERY DECISION

The Court of Chancery found that the case presented a "novel question of law," specifically, "what standard of review should apply to a going private merger conditioned upfront by the controlling stockholder on approval by both a properly empowered, independent committee and an informed, unco-erced majority-of-the-minority vote." The Court of Chancery held that business judgment review, rather than entire fairness, should be applied to a very limited category of controller mergers. That category consisted of mergers where the controller voluntarily relinquishes its control—such that the negotiation and approval process replicate those that characterize a third-party merger.

The Court of Chancery held that, rather than entire fairness, the business judgment standard of review should apply "if, *but only if:* (i) the controller condi-tions the transaction on the approval of both a Special Committee and a major-ity of the minority stockholders; (ii) the Special Committee is independent; (iii) the Special Committee is empowered to freely select its own advisors and to say no definitively; (iv) the Special Committee acts with care; (v) the minority vote is informed; and (vi) there is no coercion of the minority."[2]

---

2. Emphasis by the Court of Chancery.

The Court of Chancery found that those prerequisites were satisfied and that the Appellants had failed to raise any genuine issue of material fact indicating the contrary. The court then reviewed the Merger under the business judgment standard and granted summary judgment for the Defendants. . . .

FACTS

MFW AND M & F

MFW is a holding company incorporated in Delaware. Before the Merger that is the subject of this dispute, MFW was 43.4% owned by MacAndrews & Forbes, which in turn is entirely owned by Ronald O. Perelman. MFW had four business segments. Three were owned through a holding company, Harland Clarke Holding Corporation ("HCHC"). . . .

The MFW board had thirteen members. They were: Ronald Perelman, Barry Schwartz, William Bevins, Bruce Slovin, Charles Dawson, Stephen Taub, John Keane, Theo Folz, Philip Beekman, Martha Byorum, Viet Dinh, Paul Meister, and Carl Webb. Perelman, Schwartz, and Bevins were officers of both MFW and MacAndrews & Forbes. Perelman was the Chairman of MFW and the Chairman and CEO of MacAndrews & Forbes; Schwartz was the President and CEO of MFW and the Vice Chairman and Chief Administrative Officer of MacAndrews & Forbes; and Bevins was a Vice President at MacAndrews & Forbes.

THE TAKING MFW PRIVATE PROPOSAL

In May 2011, Perelman began to explore the possibility of taking MFW private. At that time, MFW's stock price traded in the $20 to $24 per share range. MacAndrews & Forbes engaged a bank, Moelis & Company, to advise it. After preparing valuations based on projections that had been supplied to lenders by MFW in April and May 2011, Moelis valued MFW at between $10 and $32 a share.

On June 10, 2011, MFW's shares closed on the New York Stock Exchange at $16.96. The next business day, June 13, 2011, Schwartz sent a letter proposal ("Proposal") to the MFW board to buy the remaining MFW shares for $24 in cash. The Proposal stated, in relevant part:

> The proposed transaction would be subject to the approval of the Board of Directors of the Company [*i.e.,* MFW] and the negotiation and execution of mutually acceptable definitive transaction documents. It is our expectation that the Board of Directors will appoint a special committee of independent directors to consider our proposal and make a recommendation to the Board of Directors. *We will not move forward with the transaction unless it is approved by such a special committee. In addition, the transaction will be subject to a non-waivable condition requiring the approval of a majority of the shares of the Company not owned by M & F or its affiliates. . . .*[3]

---

3. Emphasis added.

. . . In considering this proposal, you should know that in our capacity as a stockholder of the Company we are interested only in acquiring the shares of the Company not already owned by us and that in such capacity we have no interest in selling any of the shares owned by us in the Company nor would we expect, in our capacity as a stockholder, to vote in favor of any alternative sale, merger or similar transaction involving the Company. If the special committee does not recommend or the public stockholders of the Company do not approve the proposed transaction, such determination would not adversely affect our future relationship with the Company and we would intend to remain as a long-term stockholder. . . .

In connection with this proposal, we have engaged Moelis & Company as our financial advisor and Skadden, Arps, Slate, Meagher & Flom LLP as our legal advisor, and we encourage the special committee to retain its own legal and financial advisors to assist it in its review.

MacAndrews & Forbes filed this letter with the U.S. Securities and Exchange Commission ("SEC") and issued a press release disclosing substantially the same information.

THE SPECIAL COMMITTEE IS FORMED

The MFW board met the following day to consider the Proposal. At the meeting, Schwartz presented the offer on behalf of MacAndrews & Forbes. Subsequently, Schwartz and Bevins, as the two directors present who were also directors of MacAndrews & Forbes, recused themselves from the meeting, as did Dawson, the CEO of [one of the business units owned by MFW], who had previously expressed support for the proposed offer.

The independent directors then invited counsel from Willkie Farr & Gallagher—a law firm that had recently represented a Special Committee of MFW's independent directors in a potential acquisition of a subsidiary of MacAndrews & Forbes—to join the meeting. The independent directors decided to form the Special Committee, and resolved further that:

> [T]he Special Committee is empowered to: (i) make such investigation of the Proposal as the Special Committee deems appropriate; (ii) evaluate the terms of the Proposal; (iii) negotiate with Holdings [*i.e.*, MacAndrews & Forbes] and its representatives any element of the Proposal; (iv) negotiate the terms of any definitive agreement with respect to the Proposal (it being understood that the execution thereof shall be subject to the approval of the Board); (v) report to the Board its recommendations and conclusions with respect to the Proposal, including a determination and *recommendation as to whether the Proposal is fair and in the best interests of the stockholders of the Company other than Holdings* and its affiliates and should be approved by the Board; and (vi) determine to elect not to pursue the Proposal. . . .[4]

---

4. Emphasis added.

. . . [T]he Board shall not approve the Proposal without a prior favorable recommendation of the Special Committee. . . .

. . . [T]he Special Committee [is] empowered to retain and employ legal counsel, a financial advisor, and such other agents as the Special Committee shall deem necessary or desirable in connection with these matters. . . .

The Special Committee consisted of Byorum, Dinh, Meister (the chair), Slovin, and Webb. The following day, Slovin recused himself because, although the MFW board had determined that he qualified as an independent director under the rules of the New York Stock Exchange, he had "some current relationships that could raise questions about his independence for purposes of serving on the Special Committee."

ANALYSIS

WHAT SHOULD BE THE REVIEW STANDARD?

Where a transaction involving self-dealing by a controlling stockholder is challenged, the applicable standard of judicial review is "entire fairness," with the defendants having the burden of persuasion. In other words, the defendants bear the ultimate burden of proving that the transaction with the controlling stockholder was entirely fair to the minority stockholders. In *Kahn v. Lynch Communication Systems, Inc.,*[6] however, this Court held that in "entire fairness" cases, the defendants may shift the burden of persuasion to the plaintiff if either (1) they show that the transaction was approved by a well-functioning committee of independent directors; **or** (2) they show that the transaction was approved by an informed vote of a majority of the minority stockholders.

This appeal presents a question of first impression: what should be the standard of review for a merger between a controlling stockholder and its sub-sidiary, where the merger is conditioned *ab initio* upon the approval of **both** an independent, adequately-empowered Special Committee that fulfills its duty of care, and the uncoerced, informed vote of a majority of the minority stockholders. The question has never been put directly to this Court.

Almost two decades ago, in *Kahn v. Lynch,* we held that the approval by *either* a Special Committee *or* the majority of the noncontrolling stockholders of a merger with a buying controlling stockholder would shift the burden of proof under the entire fairness standard from the defendant to the plaintiff.[8] *Lynch* did not involve a merger conditioned by the controlling stockholder on both procedural protections. The Appellants submit, nonetheless, that statements in *Lynch* and its progeny could be (and were) read to suggest that even if both pro-cedural protections were used, the standard of review would remain entire fair-ness. However, in *Lynch* . . . and [again in] *Kahn v. Tremont*, the controller did not give up its voting power by agreeing to a non-waivable majority-of-the-minority

---

6. *Kahn v. Lynch Comc'n Sys., Inc., 638 A.2d 1110 (Del. 1994).*

8. *Kahn v. Lynch Commc'n Sys. (Lynch I)*, 638 A.2d 1110, 1117 (Del. 1994).

condition.[9] That is the vital distinction between those cases and this one. The question is what the legal consequence of that distinction should be in these circumstances.

The Court of Chancery held that the consequence should be that the business judgment standard of review will govern going private mergers with a controlling stockholder that are conditioned *ab initio* upon (1) the approval of an independent and fully-empowered Special Committee that fulfills its duty of care and (2) the uncoerced, informed vote of the majority of the minority stockholders.

The Court of Chancery rested its holding upon the premise that the common law equitable rule that best protects minority investors is one that encourages controlling stockholders to accord the minority both procedural protections. A transactional structure subject to both conditions differs fundamentally from a merger having only one of those protections, in that:

> By giving controlling stockholders the opportunity to have a going private transaction reviewed under the business judgment rule, a strong incentive is created to give minority stockholders much broader access to the transactional structure that is most likely to effectively protect their interests. . . . That structure, it is important to note, is critically different than a structure that uses only *one* of the procedural protections. The "or" structure does not replicate the protections of a third-party merger under the DGCL approval process, because it only requires that one, and not both, of the statutory requirements of director and stockholder approval be accomplished by impartial decisionmakers. The "both" structure, by contrast, replicates the arm's-length merger steps of the DGCL by "requir[ing] two independent approvals, which it is fair to say serve independent integrity-enforcing functions."[10]

Before the Court of Chancery, the Appellants acknowledged that "this transactional structure is the optimal one for minority shareholders." Before us, however, they argue that neither procedural protection is adequate to protect minority stockholders, because "possible ineptitude and timidity of directors" may undermine the special committee protection, and because majority-of-the-minority votes may be unduly influenced by arbitrageurs that have an institutional bias to approve virtually any transaction that offers a market premium, however insubstantial it may be. Therefore, the Appellants claim, these protections, even when combined, are not sufficient to justify "abandon[ing]" the entire fairness standard of review.

With regard to the Special Committee procedural protection, the Appellants' assertions regarding the MFW directors' inability to discharge their duties are not supported either by the record or by well-established principles of Delaware law. As the Court of Chancery correctly observed:

> Although it is possible that there are independent directors who have little regard for their duties or for being perceived by their company's stockholders (and the

---

9. *Id.*; . . .*Kahn v. Tremont Corp.*, 694 A.2d 422, 428 (Del. 1997).

10. *In re MFW Shareholders Litigation*, 67 A.3d 496, 528 (Del. Ch. 2013) (citing *In re Cox Commc'ns, Inc. S'holders Litig.*, 879 A.2d 604, 618 (Del. Ch. 2005)).

larger network of institutional investors) as being effective at protecting public stockholders, the court thinks they are likely to be exceptional, and certainly our Supreme Court's jurisprudence does not embrace such a skeptical view.

Regarding the majority-of-the-minority vote procedural protection, as the Court of Chancery noted, "plaintiffs themselves do not argue that minority stockholders will vote against a going private transaction because of fear of retribution." Instead, as the Court of Chancery summarized, the Appellants' argued as follows:

> [Plaintiffs] just believe that most investors like a premium and will tend to vote for a deal that delivers one and that many long-term investors will sell out when they can obtain most of the premium without waiting for the ultimate vote. But that argument is not one that suggests that the voting decision is not voluntary, it is simply an editorial about the motives of investors and does not contradict the premise that a majority-of-the-minority condition gives minority investors a free and voluntary opportunity to decide what is fair for themselves.

BUSINESS JUDGMENT REVIEW STANDARD ADOPTED

We hold that business judgment is the standard of review that should govern mergers between a controlling stockholder and its corporate subsidiary, where the merger is conditioned *ab initio* upon both the approval of an independent, adequately-empowered Special Committee that fulfills its duty of care; and the uncoerced, informed vote of a majority of the minority stockholders. We so conclude for several reasons.

First, entire fairness is the highest standard of review in corporate law. It is applied in the controller merger context as a substitute for the dual statutory protections of disinterested board and stockholder approval, because both protections are potentially undermined by the influence of the controller. However, as this case establishes, that undermining influence does not exist in every controlled merger setting, regardless of the circumstances. The simultaneous deployment of the procedural protections employed here create a countervailing, offsetting influence of equal — if not greater — force. That is, where the controller irrevocably and publicly disables itself from using its control to dictate the outcome of the negotiations and the shareholder vote, the controlled merger then acquires the shareholder-protective characteristics of third-party, arm's-length mergers, which are reviewed under the business judgment standard.

Second, the dual procedural protection merger structure optimally protects the minority stockholders in controller buyouts. As the Court of Chancery explained:

> [W]hen these two protections are established up-front, a potent tool to extract good value for the minority is established. From inception, the controlling stockholder knows that it cannot bypass the special committee's ability to say no. And, the controlling stockholder knows it cannot dangle a majority-of-the-minority vote before the special committee late in the process as a deal-closer rather than having to make a price move.

Third, and as the Court of Chancery reasoned, applying the business judgment standard to the dual protection merger structure:

> . . . is consistent with the central tradition of Delaware law, which defers to the informed decisions of impartial directors, especially when those decisions have been approved by the disinterested stockholders on full information and without coercion. Not only that, the adoption of this rule will be of benefit to minority stockholders because it will provide a strong incentive for controlling stockholders to accord minority investors the transactional structure that respected scholars believe will provide them the best protection, a structure where stockholders get the benefits of independent, empowered negotiating agents to **bargain for the best price and say no** if the agents believe the deal is not advisable for any proper reason, plus the critical ability to determine for themselves whether to accept any deal that their negotiating agents recommend to them. A transactional structure with both these protections [in place] is fundamentally different from one with only one protection.[11]

Fourth, the underlying purposes of the dual protection merger structure utilized here and the entire fairness standard of review both converge and are fulfilled at the same critical point: **price**. Following *Weinberger v. UOP, Inc.*, this Court has consistently held that, although entire fairness review comprises the dual components of fair dealing and fair price, in a non-fraudulent transaction "price may be the preponderant consideration outweighing other features of the merger."[12] The dual protection merger structure requires two price-related pretrial determinations: first, that a fair price was achieved by an empowered, independent committee that acted with care; and, second, that a fully-informed, uncoerced majority of the minority stockholders voted in favor of the price that was recommended by the independent committee.

THE NEW STANDARD SUMMARIZED

To summarize our holding, in controller buyouts, the business judgment standard of review will be applied *if and only if:* (i) the controller conditions the procession of the transaction on the approval of both a Special Committee and a majority of the minority stockholders; (ii) the Special Committee is independent; (iii) the Special Committee is empowered to freely select its own advisors and to say no definitively; (iv) the Special Committee meets its duty of care in negotiating a fair price; (v) the vote of the minority is informed; and (vi) there is no coercion of the minority.[14]

---

11. Emphasis added.

12. *Weinberger v. UOP, Inc.*, 457 A.2d 701, 711 (Del.1983).

14. The Verified Consolidated Class Action Complaint would have survived a motion to dismiss under this new standard. First, the complaint alleged that Perelman's offer "value[d] the company at just four times" MFW's profits per share and "five times 2010 pre-tax cash flow," and that these ratios were "well below" those calculated for recent similar transactions. Second, the complaint alleged that the final Merger price was two dollars per share *lower* than the trading price only about two months earlier. Third, the complaint alleged particularized

If a plaintiff that can plead a reasonably conceivable set of facts showing that any or all of those enumerated conditions did not exist, that complaint would state a claim for relief that would entitle the plaintiff to proceed and conduct discovery. If, after discovery, triable issues of fact remain about whether either or both of the dual procedural protections were established, or if established were effective, the case will proceed to a trial in which the court will conduct an entire fairness review.

This approach is consistent with *Weinberger, Lynch* and their progeny. A controller that employs and/or establishes only one of these dual procedural protections would continue to receive burden-shifting within the entire fairness standard of review framework. Stated differently, unless *both* procedural protections for the minority stockholders are established *prior to trial*, the ultimate judicial scrutiny of controller buyouts will continue to be the entire fairness standard of review.

Having articulated the circumstances that will enable a controlled merger to be reviewed under the business judgment standard, we next address whether those circumstances have been established as a matter of undisputed fact and law in this case.

DUAL PROTECTION INQUIRY

To reiterate, in this case, the controlling stockholder conditioned its offer upon the MFW Board agreeing, *ab initio*, to both procedural protections, *i.e.*, approval by a Special Committee and by a majority of the minority stockholders. For the combination of an effective committee process and majority-of-the-minority vote to qualify (jointly) for business judgment review, each of these protections must be effective singly to warrant a burden shift.

We begin by reviewing the record relating to the independence, mandate, and process of the Special Committee. In *Kahn v. Tremont Corp.*, this Court held that "[t]o obtain the benefit of burden shifting, the controlling stockholder must do more than establish a perfunctory special committee of outside directors."[18]

Rather, the special committee must "function in a manner which indicates that the controlling stockholder did not dictate the terms of the transaction and that the committee exercised real bargaining power 'at an arms-length.'"[19] As we have previously noted, deciding whether an independent committee was effective in negotiating a price is a process so fact-intensive and inextricably intertwined with the merits of an entire fairness review (fair dealing and fair

---

facts indicating that MFW's share price was depressed at the times of Perelman's offer and the Merger announcement due to short-term factors such as MFW's acquisition of other entities and Standard & Poor's downgrading of the United States' creditworthiness. Fourth, the complaint alleged that commentators viewed both Perelman's initial $24 per share offer and the final $25 per share Merger price as being surprisingly low. These allegations about the sufficiency of the price call into question the adequacy of the Special Committee's negotiations, thereby necessitating discovery on all of the new prerequisites to the application of the business judgment rule.

18. *Kahn v. Tremont Corp.*, 694 A.2d 422, 429 (Del.1997) (citation omitted). *See Emerald Partners v. Berlin*, 726 A.2d 1215, 1222–23 (Del.1999) (describing that the special committee must exert "real bargaining power" in order for defendants to obtain a burden shift); . . .

19. *Kahn v. Tremont Corp.*, 694 A.2d at 429 (citation omitted).

price) that a pretrial determination of burden shifting is often impossible.[20] Here, however, the Defendants have successfully established a record of independent committee effectiveness and process that warranted a grant of summary judgment entitling them to a burden shift prior to trial.

We next analyze the efficacy of the majority-of-the-minority vote, and we conclude that it was fully informed and not coerced. That is, the Defendants also established a pretrial majority-of-the-minority vote record that constitutes an independent and alternative basis for shifting the burden of persuasion to the Plaintiffs.

THE SPECIAL COMMITTEE WAS INDEPENDENT

The Appellants do not challenge the independence of the Special Committee's Chairman, Meister. They claim, however, that the three other Special Committee members—Webb, Dinh, and Byorum—were beholden to Perelman because of their prior business and/or social dealings with Perelman or Perelman-related entities. . . .

To evaluate the parties' competing positions on the issue of director independence, the Court of Chancery applied well-established Delaware legal principles. To show that a director is not independent, a plaintiff must demonstrate that the director is "beholden" to the controlling party "or so under [the controller's] influence that [the director's] discretion would be sterilized."[27] Bare allegations that directors are friendly with, travel in the same social circles as, or have past business relationships with the proponent of a transaction or the person they are investigating are not enough to rebut the presumption of independence. . . .

The Court of Chancery found that to the extent the Appellants claimed the Special Committee members, Webb, Dinh, and Byorum, were beholden to Perelman based on prior economic relationships with him, the Appellants never developed or proffered evidence showing the materiality of those relationships. . . .

The record supports the Court of Chancery's holding that none of the Appellants' claims relating to Webb, Dinh or Byorum raised a triable issue of material fact concerning their individual independence or the Special Committee's collective independence.

THE SPECIAL COMMITTEE WAS EMPOWERED

It is undisputed that the Special Committee was empowered to hire its own legal and financial advisors, and it retained Willkie Farr & Gallagher LLP as its legal advisor. After interviewing four potential financial advisors, the Special Committee engaged Evercore Partners ("Evercore"). The qualifications and independence of Evercore and Willkie Farr & Gallagher LLP are not contested.

---

20. *Ams. Mining Corp. v. Theriault*, 51 A.3d 1213 (Del. 2012).
27. *Rales v. Blasband*, 634 A.2d 927, 936 (Del. 1993) (citing *Aronson v. Lewis*, 473 A.2d 805, 815 (Del. 1984)).

Among the powers given the Special Committee in the board resolution was the authority to "report to the Board its recommendations and conclusions with respect to the [Merger], including a determination and recommendation as to whether the Proposal is fair and in the best interests of the stockholders. . . ." The Court of Chancery also found that it was "undisputed that the [S]pecial [C]ommittee was empowered not simply to 'evaluate' the offer, like some special committees with weak mandates, but to negotiate with [M & F] over the terms of its offer to buy out the noncontrolling stockholders. This negotiating power was accompanied by the clear authority to say no definitively to [M & F]" and to "make that decision stick." MacAndrews & Forbes promised that it would not proceed with any going private proposal that did not have the support of the Special Committee. Therefore, the Court of Chancery concluded, "the MFW committee did not have to fear that if it bargained too hard, MacAndrews & Forbes could bypass the committee and make a tender offer directly to the minority stockholders."

The Court of Chancery acknowledged that even though the Special Committee had the authority to negotiate and "say no," it did not have the authority, as a practical matter, to sell MFW to other buyers. MacAndrews & Forbes stated in its announcement that it was not interested in selling its 43% stake. Moreover, under Delaware law, MacAndrews & Forbes had no duty to sell its block, which was large enough, again as a practical matter, to preclude any other buyer from succeeding unless MacAndrews & Forbes decided to become a seller. Absent such a decision, it was unlikely that any potentially interested party would incur the costs and risks of exploring a purchase of MFW.

Nevertheless, the Court of Chancery found, "this did not mean that the MFW Special Committee did not have the leeway to get advice from its financial advisor about the strategic options available to MFW, including the potential interest that other buyers might have *if MacAndrews & Forbes was willing to sell.*"[36] The undisputed record shows that the Special Committee, with the help of its financial advisor, did consider whether there were other buyers who might be interested in purchasing MFW, and whether there were other strategic options, such as asset divestitures, that might generate more value for minority stockholders than a sale of their stock to MacAndrews & Forbes.

THE SPECIAL COMMITTEE EXERCISED DUE CARE

The Special Committee insisted from the outset that MacAndrews (including any "dual" employees who worked for both MFW and MacAndrews) be screened off from the Special Committee's process, to ensure that the process replicated arm's-length negotiations with a third party. In order to carefully evaluate M & F's offer, the Special Committee held a total of eight meetings during the summer of 2011.

From the outset of their work, the Special Committee and Evercore had projections that had been prepared by MFW's business segments in April and May 2011. Early in the process, Evercore and the Special Committee asked MFW management to produce new projections that reflected management's most

---

36. Emphasis added.

up-to-date, and presumably most accurate, thinking. Consistent with the Special Committee's determination to conduct its analysis free of any MacAndrews influence, MacAndrews—including "dual" MFW/MacAndrews executives who normally vetted MFW projections—were excluded from the process of preparing the updated financial projections. . . .

The updated projections, which formed the basis for Evercore's valuation analyses, reflected MFW's deteriorating results, ...

On August 10, Evercore produced a range of valuations for MFW, based on the updated projections, of $15 to $45 per share. Evercore valued MFW using a variety of accepted methods, including a discounted cash flow ("DCF") model. Those valuations generated a range of fair value of $22 to $38 per share, and a premiums paid analysis resulted in a value range of $22 to $45. MacAndrews & Forbes's $24 offer fell within the range of values produced by each of Evercore's valuation techniques.

Although the $24 Proposal fell within the range of Evercore's fair values, the Special Committee directed Evercore to conduct additional analyses and explore strategic alternatives that might generate more value for MFW's stockholders than might a sale to MacAndrews. The Special Committee also investigated the possibility of other buyers, *e.g.,* private equity buyers, that might be interested in purchasing MFW. In addition, the Special Committee considered whether other strategic options, such as asset divestitures, could achieve superior value for MFW's stockholders. Mr. Meister testified, "The Committee made it very clear to Evercore that we were interested in any and all possible avenues of increasing value to the stockholders, including meaningful expressions of interest for meaningful pieces of the business."

The Appellants insist that the Special Committee had "no right to solicit alternative bids, conduct any sort of market check, or even consider alternative transactions." But the Special Committee did just that, even though MacAndrews' stated unwillingness to sell its MFW stake meant that the Special Committee did not have the practical ability to market MFW to other buyers. The Court of Chancery properly concluded that despite the Special Committee's inability to solicit alternative bids, it *could* seek Evercore's advice about strategic alternatives, including *values that might be available if MacAndrews was willing to sell.*

Although the MFW Special Committee considered options besides the M & F Proposal, the Committee's analysis of those alternatives proved they were unlikely to achieve added value for MFW's stockholders. The Court of Chancery summarized the performance of the Special Committee as follows:

> [t]he special committee did consider, with the help of its financial advisor, whether there were other buyers who might be interested in purchasing MFW, and whether there were other strategic options, such as asset divestitures, that might generate more value for minority stockholders than a sale of their stock to MacAndrews & Forbes.

On August 18, 2011, the Special Committee rejected the $24 a share Proposal, and countered at $30 per share. The Special Committee characterized the $30 counteroffer as a negotiating position. The Special Committee recognized that $30 per share was a very aggressive counteroffer and, not surprisingly, was prepared to accept less.

On September 9, 2011, MacAndrews & Forbes rejected the $30 per share counteroffer. Its representative, Barry Schwartz, told the Special Committee Chair, Paul Meister, that the $24 per share Proposal was now far less favorable to MacAndrews & Forbes—but more attractive to the minority—than when it was first made, because of continued declines in MFW's businesses. Nonetheless, MacAndrews & Forbes would stand behind its $24 offer. Meister responded that he would not recommend the $24 per share Proposal to the Special Committee. Later, after having discussions with Perelman, Schwartz conveyed MacAndrews's "best and final" offer of $25 a share.

At a Special Committee meeting the next day, Evercore opined that the $25 per share *price was fair* based on generally accepted valuation methodologies, including DCF and comparable companies analyses. At its eighth and final meeting on September 10, 2011, the Special Committee, although empowered to say "no," instead unanimously approved and agreed to recommend the Merger at a price of $25 per share.

Influencing the Special Committee's assessment and acceptance of M & F's $25 a share price were developments in both MFW's business and the broader United States economy during the summer of 2011 . . . all of which created [considerable] financing uncertainties.

In scrutinizing the Special Committee's execution of its broad mandate, the Court of Chancery determined there was no "evidence indicating that the independent members of the special committee did not meet their duty of care. . . ." To the contrary, the Court of Chancery found, the Special Committee "met frequently and was presented with a rich body of financial information relevant to whether and at what *price* a going private transaction was advisable." The Court of Chancery ruled that "the plaintiffs d[id] not make any attempt to show that the MFW Special Committee failed to meet its duty of care. . . ." Based on the undisputed record, the Court of Chancery held that, "there is no triable issue of fact regarding whether the [S]pecial [C]ommittee fulfilled its duty of care." In the context of a controlling stockholder merger, a pretrial determination that the *price* was negotiated by an empowered independent committee that acted with care would shift the burden of persuasion to the plaintiffs under the entire fairness standard of review.[37]

MAJORITY OF MINORITY STOCKHOLDER VOTE

We now consider the second procedural protection invoked by M&F—the majority-of-the-minority stockholder vote.[38] Consistent with the second condition imposed by M & F at the outset, the Merger was then put before MFW's stockholders for a vote. On November 18, 2011, the stockholders were provided with a proxy statement, which contained the history of the Special Committee's

---

37. *Kahn v. Lynch Commc'n Sys. (Lynch I)*, 638 A.2d 1110, 1117 (Del.1994).

38. The MFW board discussed the Special Committee's recommendation to accept the $25 a share offer. The three directors affiliated with MacAndrews & Forbes, Perelman, Schwartz, and Bevins, and the CEOs of [business units owned by MFW] and Mafco, Dawson and Taub, recused themselves from the discussions. The remaining eight directors voted unanimously to recommend the $25 a share offer to the stockholders.

work and recommended that they vote in favor of the transaction at a price of $25 per share.

The proxy statement disclosed, among other things, that the Special Committee had countered M & F's initial $24 per share offer at $30 per share, but only was able to achieve a final offer of $25 per share. The proxy statement disclosed that the MFW business divisions had discussed with Evercore whether the initial projections Evercore received reflected management's latest thinking. It also disclosed that the updated projections were lower. The proxy statement also included the five separate price ranges for the value of MFW's stock that Evercore had generated with its different valuation analyses.

Knowing the proxy statement's disclosures of the background of the Special Committee's work, of Evercore's valuation ranges, and of the analyses supporting Evercore's *fairness opinion,* MFW's stockholders—representing more than 65% of the minority shares—approved the Merger. In the controlling stockholder merger context, it is settled Delaware law that an uncoerced, informed majority-of-the-minority vote, without any other procedural protection, is itself sufficient to shift the burden of persuasion to the plaintiff under the entire fairness standard of review.[39] The Court of Chancery found that "the plaintiffs themselves do not dispute that the majority-of-the-minority vote was fully informed and uncoerced, because they fail to allege any failure of disclosure or any act of coercion."

BOTH PROCEDURAL PROTECTIONS ESTABLISHED

Based on a highly extensive record,[40] the Court of Chancery concluded that the procedural protections upon which the Merger was conditioned—approval by an independent and empowered Special Committee and by a uncoerced informed majority of MFW's minority stockholders—had *both* been undisputedly established *prior to trial.* We agree and conclude the Defendants' motion for summary judgment was properly granted on all of those issues.

BUSINESS JUDGMENT REVIEW PROPERLY APPLIED

We have determined that the business judgment rule standard of review applies to this controlling stockholder buyout. Under that standard, the claims against the Defendants must be dismissed unless no rational person could have believed that the merger was favorable to MFW's minority stockholders. In this

---

39. *Rosenblatt v. Getty Oil Co.,* 493 A.2d 929, 937 (Del. 1985).

40. The Appellants received more than 100,000 pages of documents, and deposed all four Special Committee members, their financial advisors, and senior executives of MacAndrews and MFW. After eighteen months of discovery, the Court of Chancery found that the Appellants offered no evidence to create a triable issue of fact with regard to: (1) the Special Committee's independence; (2) the Special Committee's power to retain independent advisors and to say no definitively; (3) the Special Committee's due care in approving the Merger; (4) whether the majority-of-the-minority vote was fully informed; and (5) whether the minority vote was uncoerced.

case, it cannot be credibly argued (let alone concluded) that no rational person would find the Merger favorable to MFW's minority stockholders.

CONCLUSION

For the above-stated reasons, the judgment of the Court of Chancery is affirmed.

NOTES

1. Convergence to a Unified Standard of Judicial Review? As has been observed by one experienced practitioner:

> *MFW* lays out a path . . . for controlling stockholders buyouts to follow in the context of negotiated mergers. The Court held that, notwithstanding prior precedents that had been read by many practitioners and academics to the contrary, a merger agreement for a controlling stockholder buyout will be subject to deferential business judgment review when the transaction arises from an offer by the controlling stockholder that, from the outset, commits both to proceed only on terms negotiated with and approved by an independent special committee *and* to inclusion in the merger agreement of an unwaivable condition that approval by a majority of the shares held by the "minority" shall have been obtained. Before *MFW*, the only pathway to dismissal pre-trial of challenges to a controlling stockholder buyout was for the parties to follow the . . . [tender offer freeze-out by commencing a] unilateral tender offer [which required the existence of an independent special committee process at the target board *and* an unwaiveable conditioning of the tender offer on acceptance by a majority of the minority shareholders]. If, instead, the transaction included the execution of a merger agreement, the transaction would always be subject to heightened "entire fairness" review. . . .
>
> [It has been suggested that, in the wake of *MFW*,] controlling stockholders are more likely to start embracing unwaivable majority-of-the-minority conditions in negotiated mergers if, as a result, the presumption of the business judgment rule will be available. But there is [also] a good chance that some controlling stockholders will prefer to take their chances on "entire fairness" review of a buyout negotiated with a special committee (and without a majority-of-the minority condition), rather than embracing the carrot of the business judgment rule offered in *MFW*, ...

Clearly Gottlieb Steen & Hamilton LLP, *Controlling Stockholder "Going Private" Transactions After* In re MFW: *Reasons to be Wary of the Path to the Business Judgment Rule*, CLEARY M & A AND CORPORATE GOVERNANCE REPORT, June 25, 2013, *available at*: https://www.clearymawatch.com/2013/06/controlling-stockholder-going-private-transactions-after-in-re-mfw-reasons-to-be-wary-of-the-path-to-the-business-judgment-rule/.

2. Post-MFW Developments. Since *MFW* was decided, the Delaware Chancery Court has vigorously enforced all six of the requirements established by the Delaware Supreme Court in order for the freeze-out transaction to qualify for the benefit of business judgment rule protection. For example, in *In re Dell Technologies Class V Stockholders Litigation*, 2020 WL 3096748 (Del. Ch. June 11, 2020), the Chancery Court refused to grant the defendant directors' motion to dismiss the plaintiff-shareholders' complaint alleging that the structure of the transaction with the controlling shareholder (Dell) did not mimic the procedural protections of a third-party, arms-length merger negotiations. Therefore, plaintiffs claim that the freeze-out transaction should be subject to review under the more stringent entire fairness standard of judicial review. In ruling on the motion to dismiss, the Chancery Court held that it was reasonably conceivable that Dell had not complied with all six of *MFW*'s conditions, emphasizing that satisfying the requirements of *MFW* involves more than a cursory "check all the boxes" type of exercise. Instead, the court must be satisfied that the substantive requirements of *MFW* have been satisfied resulting in an atmosphere that is conducive to negotiating an arm's-length transaction in order to obtain the protection provided by the business judgment rule. In another case, *Olenik v. Lodzinski*, C.A. No. 2017-0414-JRS (Del. Ch. Jul. 20, 2017), the Chancery Court concluded that, under the framework established in *MFW*, "a merger transaction with a controlling [shareholder] on both sides was entitled to business judgment review. The decision helpfully outlines the elements of the *MFW* 'roadmap' and clarifies that its '*ab initio*' requirement only requires that the *MFW* elements be in place prior to the commencement of negotiations that, if accepted, would yield an agreement of the parties." Ropes & Gray, LLP, Mergers & Acquisitions Law News: The Ropes Recap at p. 7 (Fall 2018), *available at:* https://www.ropesgray.com/en/newsroom/alerts/2018/11/The-Ropes-Recap-Mergers-Acquisitions-Law-News; *see also Flood v. Symutra Int'l, Inc.*, 195 A. 3d 754 (Del. 2018) (likewise emphasizing that the protections of the business judgment rule will apply *only* where the procedural protections of *MFW* are put in place *prior* to commencement of negotiations between the parties).

3. Legislative Development: Enactment of Delaware Section 251(h). As the Delaware courts struggled to reconcile the conflicting interests in the context of transactions undertaken by controlling shareholders in order to squeeze out the unwanted minority interest (with the resulting divergent standards of judicial review of these freeze-out transactions), the Delaware legislature was also turning its attention more broadly to the two-step deal structure in the context of public company M&A transactions. In what some commentators have described as one "of the most substantial and ground breaking developments in statutory law in Delaware in years," William J. Haubert, et al., *Corporate Governance: Significant Proposed Amendments to the General Corporation Law of the State of Delaware*, 27 Insights 26 (June 2013), the Delaware legislature amended its code in 2013 and added new section §251(h). This new statutory provision has been summarized by an experienced M&A lawyer as follows:

> Recently, amendments to the Delaware General Corporation Law (DGCL) have been introduced by the Delaware State Bar Association (Section on Corporation Law) which, if adopted as proposed, should have a meaningful impact on, and lead to the increased use of, two-step public company acquisition structures (i.e., acquisitions effected by means of a first-step tender offer [whereby Bidder acquires more than 50% of the outstanding stock of the Target to be]

followed by a second-step, or "back-end", merger). [These proposed amendments became effective August 1, 2013.]

The [statutory] amendments (which would apply purely on a permissive basis to target companies listed on a national securities exchange or whose voting stock is held by more than 2,000 holders) [added] new subsection (h) to Section 251 of the DGCL to permit the consummation of a second-step merger following completion of the front-end tender offer without the need to obtain stockholder approval of the [back-end] merger, but only if certain structural and contractual conditions are satisfied. Accordingly, this would eliminate the need for the purchaser to convene a special stockholders' meeting and obtain stockholder approval for a long-form, second-step merger where the purchaser fails to acquire (whether directly in the initial tender offer period, as extended, or subsequently by means of exercising a "top-up" option* . . .) the 90% or more of the target's outstanding voting stock necessary to complete a "short-form" merger under Section 253 of the DGCL.

Specifically, [under] new Section 251(h) of the DGCL, . . . the constituents to a negotiated merger agreement providing for a first-step tender offer could agree that stockholder approval of the back-end merger is not required, so long as:

  i. the merger agreement expressly states that the merger will be effected under Section 251(h) and that the [back-end] merger will be completed promptly after consummation of the tender offer;
 ii. the purchaser commences and completes, in accordance with the terms of the merger agreement, an "any and all" tender offer for such number of outstanding target shares that otherwise would be entitled to vote to adopt the merger agreement (i.e., a majority of the outstanding shares or such higher percentages as may be required by the target's certificate of incorporation) and the purchaser, in fact, owns such requisite percentage of [target's] stock following consummation of the tender offer;
iii. the consideration paid in the second-step merger for shares is the same (both in amount and type) as the consideration paid to tendering stockholders whose shares were accepted for payment and paid for in the front-end tender offer (excluding shares cancelled in the merger or qualifying for disenters' rights);
 iv. following completion of the tender offer the purchaser, in fact, merges with the target; and
  v. at the time the target's directors approve the merger agreement, no party to the agreement is an "interested stockholder" (i.e., a holder of 15% or more of the target's outstanding stock) within the meaning of Section 203 of the DGCL (i.e., Delaware's three-year business combination/moratorium statute).

[This] legislation reflects the recognition that, over the past decade, the use of top-up options to achieve the 90% ownership threshold for a short-form merger under Section 253 of the DGCL has become de rigueur (except where the target lacks sufficient authorized and unissued capital stock "headroom" to effect the top-up grant and exercise). . . .

Moreover, where the tender offer is completed (and the purchaser becomes a majority parent of the target company, but is unable to effect a short-form merger

---

* [By the author: You will recall from note material earlier in this chapter (*see* p. 740) that a top-up option is a stock option granted by Target to Bidder that is designed to help Bidders using a "two-step" deal structure reach the 90 percent ownership threshold necessary to effect a short-form merger on the back end.]

because it does not own at least 90% of the target's stock), the need to prepare a merger proxy statement and convene a special stockholders' meeting to solicit stockholder votes to adopt the merger agreement, is a costly and often protracted formality, often allowing more time for strike-suit plaintiffs to attack the transaction price, process and disclosure.

Although merger agreements for two-step acquisitions require that, following consummation of the tender offer but prior to the effective time of the second-step merger, a formula-percentage of the target's directors (i.e., those who are unaffiliated and not associated with the purchaser) must continue on the target's board as a "special committee" to enforce on behalf of minority stockholders the purchaser's compliance with the merger agreement, the stockholder vote on the merger is, nevertheless, a "done deal" because the parent will simply vote its shares "for" adoption.

[As enacted,] Section 251(h) of the DGCL is an "opt-in" provision. If not elected to be used by the parties, the constituents to the merger agreement can simply continue to use top-up options (if available), . . . and other methods [in order] to expedite completion of the second-step merger [and thereby] acquire the minority shares not tendered and obtain 100% voting and economic control of the target.

"Entire fairness" judicial review does not apply to a parent's squeeze-out merger effected pursuant to Section 253 of the DGCL. In contrast, the decision of target company directors to enter into a merger agreement that utilizes new Section 251(h) and to declare it "advisable" and recommend it for adoption, will remain subject to fulfillment of all relevant fiduciary duties (i.e., care, loyalty and candor). Such duties will not be altered in any way by the enactment of the proposed amendments.

One . . . consequence of new Section 251(h) could be an increase in the percentage of tender offer "holdouts" (due to stockholder apathy) and/or an increase in stockholders seeking to exercise (back-end merger) appraisal rights under Section 262 of the DGCL. Also, the no "interested stockholder" requirement (as it may relate to the bidder at the time the merger agreement is entered into) could give rise to interpretive issues under Section 203 and Section 251(h) of the DGCL to the extent a voting/tender support agreement, arrangement or understanding is deemed to have been reached between the bidder and the stockholder prior to the actual signing thereof. However, this result can be avoided by synchronizing the signing of the support agreement and the merger agreement and, with respect to all pre-signing correspondences and discussions, by paying careful attention to [SEC] Regulation 13D concepts of acquiring "beneficial ownership."

The enactment of new Section 251(h) should make permanent (i.e., non-bridge) financing of two-steps acquisitions easier to obtain because of the increased assurance that the purchaser will acquire 100% economic and voting control of the target immediately following completion of the tender offer and gain direct access to all of the target's assets for collateral.

That said, because the satisfaction of a financing condition (including, under certain circumstances, the funding of a financing commitment) could necessitate an extension of the tender offer period (to the extent less than five business days remain before the stated expiration date), new Section 251(h) could result in changes to the traditional structure, terms and timing of funding of financing commitment letters and the use (and even phraseology) of certain tender offer financing conditions. This would likely have more impact on non-strategic buyers [i.e. financial buyers] (especially in large cap deals) who rely on external debt financing (in addition to limited partner capital commitments and management equity rollovers) and who may need to expedite the marketing and sale of debt securities to help fund the acquisition. As with any new legislation, [however,] the benefits and consequences [of new Section 251(h)] will evolve and, therefore, may not be 100% apparent until [long] after enactment.

Overall, this is a very positive and significant legislative development (much like the [SEC's] adoption of Regulation M-A in 2000 [discussed in Chapter 6 at pp. 458-460] and the SEC's amendment and clarification of the "all-holders/best price" rules in 2006 [discussed in Chapter 6 at pp. 460-463]). The enactment of new Section 251(h) of the DGCL should lead to an increase in the use of the tender offer structure for negotiated mergers and acquisitions of Delaware public companies. By eliminating the purchaser's need to conduct a long-form, second-step merger to take out minority stockholders who did not participate in the front-end tender offer (where "top-up" options, . . . and other methods to achieve 90% ownership either are unavailable or do not mathematically work), 100% voting and economic control can be purchased and sold quickly, which is in the best interests of the target's stockholders and all constituent parties to the merger agreement.

Clifford E. Neimeth, Greenberg Taurig LLP, *Pending DGCL Section 251 Amendment Should Lead to Increase in Negotiated Tender Offers,* May 29, 2013, *available at:* https://www.lexology.com/library/detail.aspx?g=d7f80ce8-fecc-43d0 -9b5e-a625a2c375f3-.

4. Further Refinement of the Delaware Section 251(h) "Medium-Form" Merger. Following effectiveness of Delaware section 251(h) in August 2013, this newly authorized form of deal structure came to be known as a "medium-form" merger and quickly grew in popularity as an attractive deal structure where Target was a publicly traded Delaware corporation. However, it soon became apparent that certain aspects of this new deal structure required clarification. Most notably, as originally adopted, Section 251(h) provided that no party to the merger agreement could be an "interested stockholder" of Target, as that term is used in Section 203 of the DGCL.

. . . [A]s originally drafted, Section 251(h) was intended only to be applicable to true third-party acquisitions (and not, *e.g.,* to squeeze out transactions initiated by controlling or other large stockholders who would roll a large portion of their target stock into surviving company equity). To achieve this goal, Section 251(h) used the definition of "interested stockholder" in Section 203 of the DGCL, and required that the acquiror [i.e., Bidder] not be an interested stockholder at the time the merger agreement is approved by the target board. . . . [T]his particular condition caused concern to some practitioners . . . Specifically, Section 251(h) originally provided that it would be inapplicable if, at the time the target's board approved the merger agreement, another party to the merger agreement was an "interested stockholder," as defined in Section 203 of the DGCL. Section 203, in turn, defines an "interested stockholder" to include the "owner" of 15 percent or more of the target company's outstanding voting stock, with ownership being attributed by way of "agreements, arrangements or understandings" with respect to the voting or disposition of target shares.

Subsequent to adoption of Section 251(h), some concern was raised that, even if a support agreement with a large target stockholder was negotiated indirectly by the acquiror through the target (and not with the stockholder), was not signed prior to target board approval of the merger agreement, and was conditioned upon target board approval of the merger agreement, an argument could be made that an "understanding" with respect to the disposition of the subject shares existed between the [target] stockholder and the acquiror [bidder] prior to target board approval of the merger agreement. As a result, if support agreements with the acquiror (together with whatever target stock the acquiror already held) equaled 15 percent or more of the target's outstanding stock, the acquiror would be an "interested stockholder" and disqualified from using Section 251(h). . . . The 2014 Amendments [to Delaware Section 251(h) have] eliminate[d] this restriction in its entirety.

Although the cross-reference to Section 203's definition of "interested stockholder" as an express condition on the availability of Section 251(h) has been removed, [it bears emphasizing that] the restrictions on business combinations with interested stockholders contained in Section 203 do remain applicable to the same extent they would have been regardless of Section 251(h). Practitioners, as always, should remain mindful of navigating these potential restrictions.

Andrew M. Johnston, et al., *Section 251 (h) of DGLC: Year in Review*, 28 INSIGHTS 13-17 (Sept. 2014). Given the almost immediate popularity of this new deal structure, it should come as no surprise that other jurisdictions were quick to amend their corporate statutes to authorize a deal structure similar to Delaware's new Section 251(h). *See, e.g.*, MBCA §11.04(j); Maryland General Corporation Law §3-106.1; and Texas Business Organizations Code §21.459(c).

5. *What Standard of Judicial Review Applies to Section 251(h) "Medium-Form" Mergers?* With the rise in popularity of Delaware's new "medium-form" merger, it should also come as no surprise that litigation would ensue over deals effected pursuant to Delaware Section 251(h), typically alleging claims that Target's board breached its fiduciary duties in connection with negotiating this two-step transaction. In a case of first impression, *In re Volcano Corp. Shareholder Litigation*, C.A. No. 10485-VCMR (June 30, 2016), the Delaware Chancery Court "concluded that acceptance of a first-step tender offer by a fully informed and uncoerced majority of disinterested stockholders insulates a two-step merger from challenge except on the ground of waste even if a majority of directors were not disinterested and independent." Greg Beauman and Jason M. Halper, *The Ever-Increasing Importance of the Shareholder Vote: Delaware Chancery Court Extends* Corwin *to Two-Step Mergers Under DGCL Sec. 251(h)*, July 6, 2016, *available at:* http://www .lexissecuritiesmosaic.com/net/Blogwatch/Blogwatch.aspx?ID=29031.

> *Volcano* involved a stockholder challenge to a completed two-step tender offer structured under section 251(h) of the DGCL. Section 251(h), adopted in 2013, permits a buyer to promptly consummate a second-step merger without having to call a stockholders meeting or reaching the 90% threshold to consummate a short-form merger if, among other conditions, it acquired the same number of shares in the tender offer that would be required to approve a long-form merger. In this transaction, 89.1% of the outstanding shares were tendered to the buyer. The plaintiffs then filed suit and sought to have the court review the directors' negotiation and approval of the transaction under the *Revlon* enhanced scrutiny standard. . . .
>
> In *Volcano*, the court granted the defendants' motion to dismiss claims challenging a two-step merger. The court concluded that the business judgment rule irrebuttably applies where a majority of disinterested, fully informed, and uncoerced stockholders tender into a two-step merger under section 251(h) of the Delaware General Corporate Law (the "DGCL"). The court's opinion establishes that a tender of shares to the acquirer in a section 251(h) transaction "essentially replicates [the] statutorily required stockholder vote in favor of a merger."

Herbert F. Kozlov, *et.al.*, Reed Smith LLP, *Delaware Chancery Court Confirms: Two Step Merger Initiated as a Tender Offer Enjoys Business Judgment Rule Protection,* July 2016 (law firm memo, copy on file with author). *Query:* Why does the court emphasize that the stockholders' tender of their Target Co. shares in the first step must be "uncoerced" in order for the Section 251(h) transaction to be subject to the business judgment rule standard of judicial review?

I.   The **Corwin** *Doctrine: The Continuing Evolution of Fiduciary Duty Obligations*

In the landmark case of *Smith v. Van Gorkum* (*supra* at p. 489), the director defendants of Trans Union (i.e., Target) relied on the doctrine of "shareholder ratification" to avoid personal liability for breach of their fiduciary duty of care in connection with their negotiation and approval of a proposed merger transaction with the Prtizkers (i.e., Bidder). As you will recall, the Delaware Supreme Court soundly rejected this defense of "shareholder ratification" on the grounds that the record failed to show that the Trans Union stockholders were "fully informed of all facts material to their vote on the Pritzer Merger" agreement, noting several "material deficiencies in the [company's] proxy materials"—thus proving, once again, the truth of that time-honored maxim: the shareholder vote is only as good as the disclosure that informs the vote. *See supra*, at pp. 503-504. In the wake of the Delaware Supreme Court's holding in *Trans Union* considerable confusion existed among the bench and bar as to the legal effect of a fully informed vote of the disinterested shareholders of a proposed merger agreement. This confusion was further confounded by the Delaware Supreme Court's ruling in *Gantler v. Stephens* (*supra*, at p. 723) and lingered until the Delaware Supreme Court's seminal decision in the following case.

| **Corwin v. KKR Fin. Holdings LLC**
| **125 A. 3d 304 (Del. 2015)**
| **Before STRINE, Chief Justice; HOLLAND, VALIHURA, VAUGHN, Justices;**
| **and RENNIE, Judge,*** constituting the Court en Banc.**

STRINE, Chief Justice:
In a well-reasoned opinion, the Court of Chancery held that the business judgment rule is invoked as the appropriate standard of review for a post-closing damages action when a merger that is not subject to the entire fairness standard of review has been approved by a fully informed, uncoerced majority of the disinterested stockholders[1]. For that, and other reasons, the Court of Chancery, dismissed the plaintiffs' complaint. In this decision, we find that the Chancellor

---

* Sitting by designation under Del. Const. Art. IV, §12
1. In re KKR Fin. Holdings LLC S'holder Litig., 101 A.3d 980, 1003 (Del. Ch. 2014).

was correct in finding that the voluntary judgment of the disinterested stock-holders to approve the merger invoked the business judgment rule standard of review and that the plaintiffs' complaint should be dismissed. For sound policy reasons, Delaware corporate law has long been reluctant to second-guess the judgment of a disinterested stockholder majority that determines that a transaction with a party other than a controlling stockholder is in their best interests.

I. The Court of Chancery Properly Held That the Complaint Did Not Plead Facts Supporting an Inference That KKR Was a Controlling Stockholder of Financial Holdings

The plaintiffs filed a challenge in the Court of Chancery to a stock-for-stock merger between KKR & Co. L.P. ("KKR") and KKR Financial Holdings LLC ("Financial Holdings") in which KKR acquired each share of Financial Holdings's stock for 0.51 of a share of KKR stock, a 35% premium to the unaffected market price. [In the Court of Chancery], the plaintiffs' primary argument was that the transaction was presumptively subject to the entire fairness standard of review because Financial Holdings's primary business was financing KKR's leveraged buyout activities, and instead of having employees manage the company's day-to-day operations, Financial Holdings was managed by KKR Financial Advisors, an affiliate of KKR, under a contractual management agreement that could only be terminated by Financial Holdings if it paid a termination fee. As a result, the plaintiffs alleged that KKR was a controlling stockholder of Financial Holdings, which was an LLC, not a corporation. [3]

The defendants filed a motion to dismiss, taking issue with that argument. In a thoughtful and thorough decision, the Chancellor found that the defendants were correct that the plaintiffs' complaint did not plead facts supporting an inference that KKR was Financial Holdings's controlling stockholder. Among other things, the Chancellor noted that KKR owned less than 1% of Financial Holdings's stock, had no right to appoint any directors, and had no contractual right to veto any board action. Although the Chancellor acknowledged the unusual existential circumstances the plaintiffs cited, he noted that those were known at all relevant times by investors, and that Financial Holdings had real assets its independent board controlled and had the option of pursuing any path its directors chose.

In addressing whether KKR was a controlling stockholder, the Chancellor was focused on the reality that in cases where a party that did not have majority control of the entity's voting stock was found to be a controlling stockholder,

---

3. We wish to make a point. We are keenly aware that this case involves a merger between a limited partnership and a limited liability company, albeit both ones whose ownership interests trade on public exchanges. But, it appears that both before the Chancellor, and now before us on appeal, the parties have acted as if this case was no different from one between two corporations whose internal affairs are governed by the Delaware General Corporation Law and related case law. We have respected the parties' approach to arguing this complex case, but felt obliged to note that we recognize that this case involved alternative entities, and that in cases involving those entities, distinctive arguments often arise due to the greater contractual flexibility given to those entities under our statutory law.

the Court of Chancery, consistent with the instructions of this Court, looked for a combination of potent voting power[7] and management control such that the stockholder could be deemed to have effective control of the board without actually owning a majority of stock. Not finding that combination here, the Chancellor noted:

> Plaintiffs' real grievance, as I see it, is that [Financial Holdings] was structured from its inception in a way that limited its value-maximizing options. According to plaintiffs, [Financial Holdings] serves as little more than a public vehicle for financing KKR-sponsored transactions and the terms of the Management Agreement make [Financial Holdings] unattractive as an acquisition target to anyone other than KKR because of [Financial Holdings]'s operational dependence on KKR and because of the significant cost that would be incurred to terminate the Management Agreement. I assume all that is true. But, every contractual obligation of a corporation constrains the corporation's freedom to operate to some degree and, in this particular case, the stockholders cannot claim to be surprised. Every stockholder of [Financial Holdings] knew about the limitations the Management Agreement imposed on [Financial Holdings]'s business when he, she or it acquired shares in [Financial Holdings]. They also knew that the business and affairs of [Financial Holdings] would be managed by a board of directors that would be subject to annual stockholder elections.
>
> At bottom, plaintiffs ask the Court to impose fiduciary obligations on a relatively nominal stockholder, not because of any coercive power that stockholder could wield over the board's ability to independently decide whether or not to approve the merger, but because of preexisting contractual obligations with that stockholder that constrain the business or strategic options available to the corporation. Plaintiffs have cited no legal authority for that novel proposition, and I decline to create such a rule.

After carefully analyzing the pled facts and the relevant precedent, the Chancellor held:

> [T]here are no well-pled facts from which it is reasonable to infer that KKR could prevent the [Financial Holdings] board from freely exercising its independent judgment in considering the proposed merger or, put differently, that KKR had the power to exact retribution by removing the [Financial Holdings] directors from their offices if they did not bend to KKR's will in their consideration of the proposed merger.

Although the plaintiffs reiterate their position on appeal, the Chancellor correctly applied the law and we see no reason to repeat his lucid analysis of this question.

---

7. For example, the Chancellor noted the importance of examining whether an insurgent could win a proxy contest or whether the company could take action without the stockholder's consent.

II. The Court of Chancery Correctly Held That the Fully Informed, Uncoerced Vote of the Disinterested Stockholders Invoked the Business Judgment Rule Standard of Review

On appeal, the plaintiffs further contend that, even if the Chancellor was correct in determining that KKR was not a controlling stockholder, he was wrong to dismiss the complaint because they contend that if the entire fairness standard did not apply, *Revlon*[11] did, and the plaintiffs argue that they pled a *Revlon* claim against the defendant directors. But, as the defendants point out, the plaintiffs did not fairly argue below that *Revlon* applied and even if they did, they ignore the reality that Financial Holdings had in place an exculpatory charter provision, and that the transaction was approved by an independent board majority and by a fully informed, uncoerced stockholder vote.[12] Therefore, the defendants argue, the plaintiffs failed to state a non-exculpated claim for breach of fiduciary duty.

But we need not delve into whether the Court of Chancery's determination that *Revlon* did not apply to the merger is correct for a single reason: it does not matter. Because the Chancellor was correct in determining that the entire fairness standard did not apply to the merger, the Chancellor's analysis of the effect of the uncoerced, informed stockholder vote is outcome-determinative, even if *Revlon* applied to the merger.

As to this point, the Court of Chancery noted, and the defendants point out on appeal, that the plaintiffs did not contest the defendants' argument below that if the merger was not subject to the entire fairness standard, the business judgment standard of review was invoked because the merger was approved by a disinterested stockholder majority. The Chancellor agreed with that argument below, and adhered to precedent supporting the proposition that when a transaction not subject to the entire fairness standard is approved by a fully informed, uncoerced vote of the disinterested stockholders, the business judgment rule applies. Although the Chancellor took note of the possible conflict between his ruling and this Court's decision in *Gantler v. Stephens*, he reached the conclusion that *Gantler* did not alter the effect of legally required stockholder votes on the appropriate standard of review. . . .

---

11. *Revlon v. MacAndrews & Forbes Holdings, Inc.*, 506 A.2d 173 (Del. 1986).

12. The Court of Chancery indicated that the merger was not subject to review under *Revlon* because KKR was a widely held, public company and that Financial Holdings's stockholders would therefore own stock after the merger in a company without a controlling stockholder. *In re KKR Fin. Holdings*, 101 A.3d at 989. On appeal, the plaintiffs argue that that observation was incorrect and that ownership in KKR was not dispersed after the merger because "KKR is a limited partnership *that is controlled by its managing partner,* which is in turn controlled by KKR's founders." The defendants, for their part, stress that the plaintiffs' focus on *Revlon* is a novel one in the course of this case, and that claims such as this should be made in the trial court initially, and not on appeal. Although we do not reach this issue, we note that the defendants are correct in their argument that the plaintiffs should have fairly raised their *Revlon* argument below and did not. Consistent with their failure to argue the point fairly below, the plaintiffs press this argument on appeal without citation to supporting facts pled in the complaint.

. . . [A]s the Chancellor noted, the issue presented in this case was not even squarely before the Court in *Gantler* because it found the relevant proxy statement to be materially misleading. To erase any doubt on the part of practitioners, we embrace the Chancellor's well-reasoned decision, and the precedent it cites to support an interpretation of *Gantler* as a narrow decision focused on defining a specific legal term, "ratification," and not on the question of what standard of review applies if a transaction not subject to the entire fairness standard is approved by an informed, voluntary vote of disinterested stockholders. This view is consistent with well-reasoned Delaware precedent.

Furthermore, although the plaintiffs argue that adhering to the proposition that a fully informed, uncoerced stockholder vote invokes the business judgment rule would impair the operation of *Unocal*[25] and *Revlon*, or expose stockholders to unfair action by directors without protection, the plaintiffs ignore several factors. First, *Unocal* and *Revlon* are primarily designed to give stockholders and the Court of Chancery the tool of injunctive relief to address important M & A decisions in real time, before closing. They were not tools designed with post-closing money damages claims in mind, the standards they articulate do not match the gross negligence standard for director due care liability under *Van Gorkom*,[26] and with the prevalence of exculpatory charter provisions, due care liability is rarely even available.

Second and most important, the doctrine applies only to fully informed, uncoerced stockholder votes, and if troubling facts regarding director behavior were not disclosed that would have been material to a voting stockholder, then the business judgment rule is not invoked.[27] Here, however, all of the objective facts regarding the board's interests, KKR's interests, and the negotiation process, were fully disclosed.

Finally, when a transaction is not subject to the entire fairness standard, the long-standing policy of our law has been to avoid the uncertainties and costs of judicial second-guessing when the disinterested stockholders have had the free and informed chance to decide on the economic merits of a transaction for themselves. There are sound reasons for this policy. When the real parties in interest — the disinterested equity owners — can easily protect themselves at the ballot box by simply voting no, the utility of a litigation-intrusive standard of review promises more costs to stockholders in the form of litigation rents and inhibitions on risk-taking than it promises in terms of benefits to them. The reason for that is tied to the core rationale of the business judgment rule, which is that judges are poorly positioned to evaluate the wisdom of business decisions and there is little utility to having them second-guess the determination of impartial decision-makers with more information (in the case of directors) or an actual economic stake in the outcome (in the case of informed, disinterested stockholders). In circumstances, therefore, where the stockholders have had

---

25. *Unocal Corp. v. Mesa Petroleum Co.*, *493* A.2d 946 (Del. 1985).

26. *Smith v. Van Gorkom*, 488 A.2d 858 (Del. 1985).

27. *See* . . . *In re Rural Metro Corp*,, 88 A.3d 54, 84 n.10 (Del. Ch. 2014) ("Because the Proxy Statement contained materially misleading disclosures and omissions, this case does not provide any opportunity to consider whether a fully informed stockholder vote would lower the standard of review from enhanced scrutiny to the business judgment rule."); . . .

the voluntary choice to accept or reject a transaction, the business judgment rule standard of review is the presumptively correct one and best facilitates wealth creation through the corporate form.

For these reasons, therefore; we affirm the Court of Chancery's judgment, on the basis of its well-reasoned decision.

QUESTIONS

1. In its opinion, the Delaware Supreme Court was careful to point out that the plaintiffs did not allege a *Revlon* cause of action in their complaint, and so a breach of *Revlon* duties was not fairly presented in the Court of Chancery. But, assume that the plaintiffs had properly maintained a *Revlon* claim, and further assume that the facts show that the directors of Financial Holdings (i.e., Target Co.) had not properly determined whether any third parties were interested in bidding. Assuming also that there was full and adequate disclosure of these facts (regarding the sales process) as part of the company's proxy statement soliciting shareholder approval of the transaction, would this result in a violation of *Revlon* duties? If so, how would this *Revlon* violation have affected the court's reasoning in *Corwin*?

2. If the facts show that the board of directors violated their *Revlon* duties, is it nonetheless possible for the company's shareholders to be fully informed of all material facts in a vote sufficient to approve the transaction, and thereby shift the relevant standard of judicial review of the board's decision making process to the business judgment rule?

3. Given the Delaware Supreme Court's reasoning in *Corwin*, are plaintiffs now encouraged to bring their claims under *Revlon* as part of *pre-closing* litigation?

NOTES

1. Impact of **Corwin.** As recognized by a leading M&A lawyer, the significance of the Delaware Supreme Court's decision in *Corwin* cannot be overstated:

> The 2015 decision of the Delaware Supreme Court in *Corwin* is probably the most significant Delaware M&A decision in 15 years. While [the decision in] *MFW* . . . can be seen as [elaborating] on existing doctrine, it is hard to categorize *Corwin* the same way. One can argue that *Corwin* involves a reversal of almost 30 years of Delaware doctrine regarding judicial review of actions by boards of target companies. . . .
>
> Under the *Corwin* doctrine, the Delaware courts will apply the deferential business judgment rule standard of review to decisions of a board of directors of a target company if the relevant M&A transaction is approved by a fully informed, uncoerced vote of disinterested stockholders (other than in a squeeze out [i.e., freeze-out transaction], in which *MFW* applies). [As of winter 2018, the] Delaware courts have already substantially elaborated on *Corwin* . . . by explicitly acknowledging that *Corwin* is a substantial limitation on two iconic Delaware decisions

from the 1980's: *Unocal*, dealing with takeover defenses, and *Revlon*, dealing with directors' responsibilities when selling a target company. . . .

    Corwin represents a profound challenge to the [traditional approach under Delaware caselaw to issues of corporate governance and the scope of target board's fiduciary duty obligations in the context of M&A transactions]. Historically, a key component to the process of holding target boards accountable in M&A transactions has been the combination of searching judicial scrutiny [under *Unocal* and its progeny] and private litigation as the vehicle for that [judicial] scrutiny. By allowing business judgment rule deference, the Delaware courts are now saying that "M&A is not different [from other business decisions made by a company's board of directors] – at least if the stockholders approve." . . . [As such, *Corwin* represents a marked departure from established M&A precedent in which] the Delaware courts historically have scrutinized the conduct of boards of directors to determine whether it met the standards of care, loyalty and good faith expected of boards of directors, [and Delaware courts were] not solely [focused on whether the proposed M&A transaction negotiated by target's board was] . . . in the best interests of [the company's] stockholders. . . . [For now, however, the] guiding principle of *Corwin* stands uneasily next to such decisions as *Airgas*, . . .

Richard Hall, *The Hot Topic in United States M&A* – Corwin, THE LEGAL 500 & THE IN-HOUSE LAWYER (Winter 2018), *available at:* https://www.inhouselawyer.co.uk/legal-briefing/the-hot-topic-in-united-states-ma-corwin/. It bears mentioning that we will examine the *Airgas* case in the next section of this chapter, and we will revisit the issue raised by the author at the end of the excerpt above—namely, can you reconcile the reasoning of these two landmark decisions?

    ***2. Post-*Corwin** *Case Law Developments.* Lest there be any confusion, the holding in *Corwin* did not (and does not) mean the end of M&A deal-related litigation. Instead, the evolution of Delaware case law since *Corwin* reflects the courts' ongoing efforts to develop a coherent theory of what constitutes "coercion of stockholders," as well as of what qualifies as a "fully informed" vote of the shareholders. So, while the holding in *Corwin* is widely regarded as giving rise to a powerful defense in cases involving claims that Target's board breached its fiduciary duties in negotiating and approving M&A transactions, the Delaware courts are still refining the scope of the *Corwin* doctrine and its application to board decision making in the context of M&A transactions. Indeed, there have been cases where the Delaware courts refused to apply *Corwin*. For example, *Chester Cty. Employees' Ret. Fund v. KCG Holdings, Inc.*, No. CV 2017-0421-KSJM, 2019 WL 2564093 (Del. Ch. June 21, 2019), the Court of Chancery denied defendants' motion to dismiss claims challenging an M&A transaction, finding that plaintiffs' allegations of disclosure deficiencies defeated application of the *Corwin* defense. *See* Edward B. Micheletti, et al., Skadden, Arps, Slate, Meagher & Flom LLP, Corwin, MFW *and Beyond: Developing Trends in Delaware Disclosure Law*, INSIGHTS: THE DELAWARE EDITION, Nov. 19, 2019, *available at:* https://www.skadden.com/insights/publications/2019/11/insights-the-delaware-edition/corwin-mfw-and-beyond. On the other hand, in its opinion in *English v. Narang*, No. CV 2018-0221-AGB, 2019 WL 1300855 (Del. Ch. Mar. 20, 2019), *aff'd*, 222 A.3d 581 (Del. 2019), and *aff'd*, 222 A.3d 581 (Del. 2019), "the Court of Chancery applied the *Corwin* doctrine to dismiss a [breach of fiduciary duty] challenge to a merger following what the court ultimately held to be a fully informed stockholder vote." *Id.* Accordingly, as of Fall 2020, we await further developments as the *Corwin* doctrine continues to be refined by the Delaware courts.

J.   The Ongoing Public Policy Debate: What Is the Proper Role for Target's Management?

The following opinion, *Air Products and Chemicals, Inc. v. Airgas, Inc.*, offers a summary of Delaware case law and the continuing controversy surrounding the appropriate balance of the competing interests that are central to any court's analysis of the fiduciary obligations of the board of directors of the modern publicly traded corporation in the context of an M&A transaction. To put the case in historical context, Chancellor William Chandler issued his opinion before the Delaware Supreme Court handed down its opinion in *Corwin*, which raises the fundamental question of whether Chancellor Chandler's interpretation of Delaware precedent will withstand scrutiny in light of the Delaware Supreme Court's reasoning in *Corwin*. Equally important, the issue presented in *Airgas* takes us back to the fundamental inquiry which we first examined in analyzing the problem sets in Chapter 2, and which has been a theme throughout this casebook, namely: who should decide when, and on what terms, a publicly traded company should be sold?

By way of general background, Chancellor Chandler issued this opinion and shortly thereafter the Chancellor announced his retirement from the Delaware judiciary, following eight years serving as Vice Chancellor and fourteen years of service as Chancellor. For many observers of the Delaware judiciary, this opinion was something of a "swan song" for the esteemed Delaware jurist. His decision is seen "as the most important ruling on the [use of a] poison pill since the mid-1990s . . . and also is viewed as something of a coda to [Chancellor] Chandler's quarter-century on the bench. . . . The [*Airgas*] case gave [Chancellor] Chandler the rare opportunity to consider a body of doctrine that has developed largely in his time as a judge [on the Delaware Chancery Court] and he took full advantage with a 153-page opinion [with over 500 footnotes] in which he commented on the caselaw, [and] evaluated the enormous body of scholarship on it . . . ." David Marcus, *A Pill of a Swan Song*, THE DEAL (Feb. 18, 2011).

Air Products and Chemicals, Inc. v. Airgas, Inc.
16 A.3d 48 (Del. Ch. 2011)

CHANDLER, Chancellor.

This case poses the following fundamental question: Can a board of directors, acting in good faith and with a reasonable factual basis for its decision, when faced with a structurally non-coercive, all-cash, fully financed tender offer directed to the stockholders of the corporation, keep a poison pill in place so as to prevent the stockholders from making their own decision about whether they want to tender their shares—even after the incumbent board has lost one election contest, a full year has gone by since the offer was first made public, and the stockholders are fully informed as to the target board's views on the inadequacy of the offer? If so, does that effectively mean that a board can "just say never" to a hostile tender offer?

The answer to the latter question is "no." A board cannot "*just* say no" to a tender offer. Under Delaware law, it must first pass through two prongs of exacting judicial scrutiny by a judge who will evaluate the actions taken by, and the motives of, the board. Only a board of directors found to be acting in good faith, after reasonable investigation and reliance on the advice of outside advisors, which articulates and convinces the Court that a hostile tender offer poses a legitimate threat to the corporate enterprise, may address that perceived threat by blocking the tender offer and forcing the bidder to elect a board majority that supports its bid.

In essence, this case brings to the fore one of the most basic questions animating all of corporate law, which relates to the allocation of power between directors and stockholders. That is, "when, if ever, will a board's duty to 'the corporation and its shareholders' require [the board] to abandon concerns for 'long term' values (and other constituencies) and enter a current share value maximizing mode?"[1] More to the point, in the context of a hostile tender offer, who gets to decide when and if the corporation is for sale?

Since the Shareholder Rights Plan (more commonly known as the "poison pill") was first conceived and throughout the development of Delaware corporate takeover jurisprudence during the twenty-five-plus years that followed, the debate over who ultimately decides whether a tender offer is adequate and should be accepted — the shareholders of the corporation or its board of directors — has raged on. Starting with *Moran v. Household International, Inc.* in 1985, when the Delaware Supreme Court first upheld the adoption of the poison pill as a valid takeover defense, through the hostile takeover years of the 1980s, and in several recent decisions of the Court of Chancery and the Delaware Supreme Court,[3] this fundamental question has engaged practitioners, academics, and members of the judiciary, but it has yet to be confronted head on.

For the reasons much more fully described in the remainder of this Opinion, I conclude that, as Delaware law currently stands, the answer must be that the power to defeat an inadequate hostile tender offer ultimately lies with the board of directors. As such, I find that the Airgas board has met its burden under *Unocal* to articulate a legally cognizable threat (the allegedly inadequate price of Air Products' offer, coupled with the fact that a majority of Airgas's stockholders would likely tender into that inadequate offer) and has taken defensive measures that fall within a range of reasonable responses proportionate to that threat. I thus rule in favor of defendants. Air Products' and the Shareholder Plaintiffs' requests for relief are denied, and all claims asserted against defendants are dismissed with prejudice.

---

1. *TW Servs., Inc. v. SWT Acquisition Corp.*, 1989 WL 20290, at *8 (Del. Ch. Mar. 2, 1989).

3. *See, e.g., Yucaipa Am. Alliance Fund II, L.P. v. Riggio*, 1 A.3d 310, 351 n.229 (Del. Ch. 2010); *eBay Domestic Holdings, Inc. v. Newmark*, 2010 WL 3516473 (Del. Ch. Sept. 9, 2010); *Versata Enters., Inc. v. Selectica, Inc.*, 5 A.3d 586 (Del. 2010).

INTRODUCTION

This is the Court's decision . . . in this long-running takeover battle between Air Products & Chemicals, Inc. ("Air Products") and Airgas, Inc. ("Airgas"). The now very public saga began quietly in mid-October 2009 when John McGlade, President and CEO of Air Products, privately approached Peter McCausland, founder and CEO of Airgas, about a potential acquisition or combination. After McGlade's private advances were rebuffed, Air Products went hostile in February 2010, launching a public tender offer for all outstanding Airgas shares.

Now, over a year since Air Products first announced its all-shares, all-cash tender offer, the terms of that offer (other than price) remain essentially unchanged. After several price bumps and extensions, the offer currently stands at $70 per share and is set to expire today, February 15, 2011—Air Products' stated "best and final" offer. The Airgas board unanimously rejected that offer as being "clearly inadequate." The Airgas board has repeatedly expressed the view that Airgas is worth at least $78 per share in a sale transaction—and at any rate, far more than the $70 per share Air Products is offering.

So, we are at a crossroads. Air Products has made its "best and final" offer—apparently its offer to acquire Airgas has reached an end stage. Meanwhile, the Airgas board believes the offer is clearly inadequate and its value in a sale transaction is at least $78 per share. At this stage, it appears, neither side will budge. Airgas continues to maintain its defenses, blocking the bid and effectively denying shareholders the choice whether to tender their shares. [Plaintiff] Air Products and Shareholder Plaintiffs [i.e., other Airgas shareholders] now ask this Court to order Airgas to redeem its poison pill and other defenses that are stopping Air Products from moving forward with its hostile offer, and to allow Airgas's stockholders to decide for themselves whether they want to tender into Air Products' (inadequate or not) $70 "best and final" offer. . . .

Although I have a hard time believing that inadequate price alone (according to the target's board) in the context of a non-discriminatory, all-cash, all-shares, fully financed offer poses any "threat"—particularly given the wealth of information available to Airgas's stockholders at this point in time—under existing Delaware law, it apparently does. Inadequate price has become a form of "substantive coercion" as that concept has been developed by the Delaware Supreme Court in its takeover jurisprudence. That is, the idea that Airgas's stockholders will disbelieve the board's views on value (or in the case of merger arbitrageurs who may have short-term profit goals in mind, they may simply ignore the board's recommendations), and so they may mistakenly tender into an inadequately priced offer. Substantive coercion has been clearly recognized by our Supreme Court as a valid threat.

. . . Thus, for reasons explained in detail below, I am constrained by Delaware Supreme Court precedent to conclude that defendants have met their burden under *Unocal* to articulate a sufficient threat that justifies the continued maintenance of Airgas's poison pill. That is, assuming defendants have met their burden to articulate a legally cognizable threat (prong 1), Airgas's defenses have been recognized by Delaware law as reasonable responses to the threat posed by an inadequate offer—even an all-shares, all-cash offer (prong 2). . . .

That being said, however, as I understand binding Delaware precedent, I may not substitute my business judgment for that of the Airgas board. The Delaware Supreme Court has recognized inadequate price as a valid threat to corporate policy and effectiveness.[10] The Delaware Supreme Court has also made clear that the "selection of a time frame for achievement of corporate goals . . . may not be delegated to the stockholders."[11] Furthermore, in powerful dictum, the Supreme Court has stated that "[d]irectors are not obliged to abandon a deliberately conceived corporate plan for a short-term shareholder profit unless there is clearly no basis to sustain the corporate strategy."[12] Although I do not read that dictum as eliminating the applicability of heightened _Unocal_ scrutiny to a board's decision to block a non-coercive bid as underpriced, I do read it, along with the actual holding in _Unitrin_, as indicating that a board that has a good faith, reasonable basis to believe a bid is inadequate may block that bid using a poison pill, irrespective of stockholders' desire to accept it.

Here, even using heightened scrutiny, the Airgas board has demonstrated that it has a reasonable basis for sustaining its long term corporate strategy—the Airgas board is independent, and has relied on the advice of three different outside independent financial advisors in concluding that Air Products' offer is inadequate. Air Products' _own three nominees_ who were elected to the Airgas board in September 2010 have joined wholeheartedly in the Airgas board's determination, and when the Airgas board met to consider the $70 "best and final" offer in December 2010, it was one of those Air Products Nominees who said, "We have to protect the pill." Indeed, one of Air Products' _own directors_ conceded at trial that the Airgas board members had acted within their fiduciary duties in their desire to "hold out for the proper price," and that "if an offer was made for Air Products that [he] considered to be unfair to the stockholders of Air Products . . . [he would likewise] use every legal mechanism available" to hold out for the proper price as well. Under Delaware law, the Airgas directors have complied with their fiduciary duties. Thus, as noted above, and for the reasons more fully described in the remainder of this Opinion, [following a weeklong trial,] I am constrained to deny Air Products' and the Shareholder Plaintiffs' requests for [injunctive] relief.

I. FACTS . . .

A. THE PARTIES

Plaintiff Air Products is a Delaware corporation headquartered in Allentown, Pennsylvania that serves technology, energy, industrial and healthcare customers globally. . . . Air Products currently owns approximately 2% of Airgas outstanding common stock.

---

10. _See Unitrin, Inc. v. Am. Gen. Corp.,_ 651 A.2d 1361, 1384 (Del. 1995) ("This Court has held that the 'inadequate value' of an all cash for all shares offer is a 'legally cognizable threat.'") (quoting _Paramount Commc'ns, Inc. v. Time, Inc.,_ 571 A.2d 1140, 1153 (Del. 1990)).

11. _Paramount,_ 571 A.2d at 1154.

12. _Id._

The Shareholder Plaintiffs are Airgas stockholders. . . .

Airgas is a Delaware corporation headquartered in Radnor, Pennsylvania. Founded in 1982 by Chief Executive Officer Peter McCausland, it is a domestic supplier and distributor of industrial, medical and specialty gases and related hardgoods. . . .

Before its September 15, 2010 annual meeting, Airgas was led by a nine-member staggered board of directors, divided into three equal classes with one class (three directors) up for election each year. Other than McCausland, the rest of the board members are independent outside directors ["director defendants"]. . . .

B.   AIRGAS'S ANTI-TAKEOVER DEVICES

As a result of Airgas's classified board structure, it would take two annual meetings to obtain control of the board. In addition to its staggered board, Airgas has three main takeover defenses: (1) a shareholder rights plan ("poison pill") with a 15% triggering threshold, (2) Airgas has not opted out of Delaware General Corporation Law ("DGCL") §203, which prohibits business combinations with any interested stockholder for a period of three years following the time that such stockholder became an interested stockholder, unless certain conditions are met, and (3) Airgas's Certificate of Incorporation includes a supermajority merger approval provision for certain business combinations. Namely, any merger with an "Interested Stockholder" (defined as a stockholder who beneficially owns 20% or more of the voting power of Airgas's outstanding voting stock) requires the approval of 67% or more of the voting power of the then-outstanding stock entitled to vote, unless approved by a majority of the disinterested directors or certain fair price and procedure requirements are met.

Together, these are Airgas's takeover defenses that Air Products and the Shareholder Plaintiffs challenge and seek to have removed or deemed inapplicable to Air Products' hostile tender offer.

C.   AIRGAS'S FIVE-YEAR PLAN

In the regular course of business, Airgas prepares a five-year strategic plan approximately every eighteen months, forecasting the company's financial performance over a five year horizon. . . .

In the summer of 2009, Airgas management was already working on an updated five-year plan. . . .

D.   AIR PRODUCTS PRIVATELY EXPRESSES INTEREST IN AIRGAS

Air Products first became interested in a transaction with Airgas in 2007, but did not pursue a transaction at that time because Airgas's stock price was too high. Then the global recession hit, and in the spring or summer of 2009, Air Products' interest in Airgas was reignited. On September 17, 2009, the Air

Products board of directors authorized [John McGlade, Air Products' CEO, President and Chairman of the board,] to approach McCausland [the CEO of Airgas] and discuss a possible transaction between the two companies. The codename for the project was "Flashback," because Air Products had previously been in the packaged gas business and wanted to "flash back" into it.

On October 15, 2009, McGlade and McCausland met at Airgas's headquarters. At the meeting, McGlade conveyed Air Products' interest in a potential business combination with Airgas and proposed a $60 per share all equity deal. . . .

At its three-day strategic planning retreat from November 5-7, 2009, . . . the full board first learned of Air Products' proposal. In advance of the retreat, the board had received copies of the five-year strategic plan, which served as the basis for the board's consideration of the $60 offer. . . .

After reviewing the numbers, the board's view on the inadequacy of the offer was not even a close call. The board agreed that $60 was "just so far below what we thought fair value was" that it would be harmful to Airgas's stockholders if the board sat down with Air Products. . . . No one on the Airgas board thought it made sense to have any further discussions with Air Products at that point. On November 11, McCausland called McGlade to inform him of the board's decision. . . .

F.   THE $60 TENDER OFFER

On February 11, 2010, Air Products launched its tender offer for all outstanding shares of Airgas common stock $60 per share, all-cash, structurally non-coercive, non-discriminatory, and backed by secured financing. The tender offer is conditioned, among other things, upon the following:

(1)   a majority of the total outstanding shares tendering into the offer;
(2)   the Airgas board redeeming its rights plan or the rights otherwise having been deemed inapplicable to the offer;
(3)   the Airgas board approving the deal under DGCL §203 or DGCL §203 otherwise having been deemed inapplicable to the offer;
(4)   the Airgas board approving the deal under Article VI of Airgas's charter or Article VI otherwise being inapplicable to the offer;
(5)   certain regulatory approvals having been met; and
(6)   the Airgas board not taking certain action (i.e., entering into a third-party agreement or transaction) that would have the effect of impairing Air Products' ability to acquire Airgas. . . .

On February 20, 2010, the Airgas board held another special telephonic meeting to discuss Air Products' tender offer. . . .

In a [Schedule] 14D-9 filed with the SEC on February 22, 2010, Airgas recommended that its shareholders not tender into Air Products' offer because it "grossly undervalues Airgas." . . .

G. THE PROXY CONTEST

On March 13, 2010, Air Products nominated its slate of three independent directors for election at the Airgas 2010 annual meeting. The three Air Products nominees were:

- John P. Clancey;
- Robert L. Lumpkins; and
- Ted B. Miller, Jr. (together, the "Air Products Nominees").

Air Products made clear in its proxy materials that its nominees to the Airgas board were independent and would act in the Airgas stockholders' best interests. Air Products told the Airgas stockholders that "the election of the Air Products Nominees . . . will establish an Airgas Board that is more likely to act in your best interests." Air Products actively promoted the independence of its slate, . . .

Over the next several months leading up to Airgas's 2010 annual meeting, both Air Products and Airgas proceeded to engage in a protracted "high-visibility proxy contest widely covered by the media," during which the parties aggressively made their respective cases to the Airgas stockholders. . . .

H. AIRGAS DELAYS ANNUAL MEETING

In April 2010, the Airgas board . . . pushed back the [annual shareholder] meeting date [to September 15, 2010, in order] to buy itself more time to "provide information to stockholders" before the annual meeting, as well as more time to "demonstrate performance of the company." . . .

I. THE $63.50 OFFER

On July 8, 2010, Air Products raised its offer to $63.50. Other than price, all other material terms of the [tender] offer remained unchanged. . . .

The Airgas board [met] to consider the revised $63.50 offer [and]. . . . on July 21, 2010, Airgas filed an amendment to its [Schedule] 14D-9, rejecting the $63.50 offer as "grossly inadequate" and recommending that Airgas stockholders not tender their shares. In this filing, Airgas set out many of the reasons for its recommendation, including its view that the offer "grossly undervalue[d]" Airgas because it did not reflect the value of Airgas's future prospects and strategic plans. . . .

K. THE $65.50 OFFER

On September 6, 2010, Air Products further increased its offer to $65.50 per share. Again, the rest of the terms and conditions of the February 11, 2010 [tender] offer remained the same. In connection with this increased offer,

Air Products threatened to walk if the Airgas stockholders did not elect the three Air Products Nominees to the Airgas board. . . .

The . . . Airgas board met to consider Air Products' revised offer. . . . [and the] board unanimously rejected the $65.50 offer as inadequate, ...

M. THE ANNUAL MEETING

On September 15, 2010, Airgas's 2010 annual meeting was held. The Airgas stockholders elected all three of the Air Products Nominees to the board . . . .

The evidence at trial also incontrovertibly demonstrated that $65.50 was not as high as Air Products was willing to go. . . .

. . . [B]y December 21, 2010 the new Air Products Nominees seem to . . . fully support the view that Airgas is worth *at least* $78 in a sale transaction [for reasons that will be explained in more detail below].

R. THE $70 "BEST AND FINAL" OFFER

Meanwhile, over at Air Products, the board was considering its position with respect to its outstanding tender offer, and on December 9, 2010, the board met to discuss its options. . . .

. . . [O]n December 9, 2010 . . . Air Products made its "best and final" offer for Airgas, raising its offer price to $70 per share. . . .

The Airgas board, in initially considering the $70 offer, did not really believe that $70 was actually Air Products' "best and final" offer, despite Air Products' public statements saying as much. . . .

Air Products has repeatedly represented, both in publicly available press releases, public filings with the SEC, and submissions to this Court, that $70 per share is its "best and final" offer. The testimony offered by representatives of Air Products . . . regarding the $70 offer provides further evidence to this Court that Air Products' offer is now, as far as this Court is concerned, at its end stage.

. . . Thus, for purposes of my analysis and the context of this litigation, based on the representations made in public filings and under oath to this Court, I treat $70, as a matter of fact, as Air Products' "best and final" offer. . . .

S. THE AIRGAS BOARD UNANIMOUSLY REJECTS THE $70 OFFER

On December 21, the Airgas board met to consider Air Products' "best and final" offer. Management kicked off the meeting by presenting an updated five-year plan to the board. . . .

After considering Airgas's updated five-year plan and the inadequacy opinions of all three of the company's financial advisors, the Airgas board unanimously—including the Air Products Nominees—rejected the $70 offer. Interestingly, the Air Products Nominees were some of the most vocal opponents to the $70 offer. . . .

The next day, December 22, 2010, Airgas filed another amendment to its [Schedule] 14D-9, announcing the board's unanimous rejection of Air Products' $70 offer as "clearly inadequate" and recommending that Airgas stockholders not tender their shares. The board reiterated once more that the value of Airgas in a sale is at least $78 per share. In this filing, Airgas listed numerous reasons for its recommendation, in two pages of easy-to-read bullet points. These reasons included the Airgas board's knowledge and experience in the industry; the board's knowledge of Airgas's financial condition and strategic plans, including current trends in the business and the expected future benefits of . . . substantial capital investments that have yet to be realized; Airgas's historical trading prices and strong position in the industry; the potential benefits of the transaction for Air Products, including synergies and accretion; the board's consideration of views expressed by various stockholders; and the inadequacy opinions of its financial advisors. All three of the outside financial advisors' written inadequacy opinions were attached to the filing. . . .

Once again, the evidence presented . . . was that the Airgas stockholders are a sophisticated group, and that they had an extraordinary amount of information available to them with which to make an informed decision about Air Products' offer. Although a few of the directors expressed the view that they understood the potential benefits . . . and the details of the [company's strategic] five-year plan better than [the company's] stockholders could, the material information underlying management's assumptions has been released to stockholders through SEC filings and is reflected in public analysts' reports as well. . . .

II.   STANDARD OF REVIEW

A.   THE UNOCAL STANDARD

Because of the "omnipresent specter" of entrenchment in takeover situations, it is well-settled that when a poison pill is being maintained as a defensive measure and a board is faced with a request to redeem the rights, the *Unocal* standard of enhanced judicial scrutiny applies. Under that legal framework, to justify its defensive measures, the target board must show (1) that it had "reasonable grounds for believing a danger to corporate policy and effectiveness existed" (i.e., the board must articulate a legally cognizable threat) and (2) that any board action taken in response to that threat is "reasonable in relation to the threat posed."

The first hurdle under *Unocal* is essentially a process-based review. . . .

But the inquiry does not end there; process alone is not sufficient to satisfy the first part of *Unocal* review—"under *Unocal* and *Unitrin* the defendants have the burden of showing the reasonableness of their investigation, the reasonableness of their process and *also of the result that they reached.*"[295] That is, the "process" has to lead to the finding of a threat. . . .

---

295. *Chesapeake Corp. v. Shore,* 771 A.2d 293, 301 n. 8 (Del. Ch. 2000) (internal citation omitted) (*emphasis added*).

Once the board has reasonably perceived a legitimate threat, *Unocal* prong 2 engages the Court in a substantive review of the board's defensive actions: Is the board's action taken in response to that threat proportional to the threat posed? . . . This proportionality review asks first whether the board's actions were "draconian, by being either preclusive or coercive." If the board's response was not draconian, the Court must then determine whether it fell "within a range of reasonable responses to the threat" posed.

B.   *UNOCAL* — NOT THE BUSINESS JUDGMENT RULE — APPLIES HERE

Defendants argue that "*Unocal* does not apply in a situation where the bidder's nominees agree with the incumbent directors after receiving advice from a new investment banker." . . . Thus, they argue, because Airgas has presented overwhelming evidence that the directors—particularly now including the three new Air Products Nominees—are independent and have acted in good faith, the "theoretical specter of disloyalty does not exist" and therefore "*Unocal's* heightened standard of review does not apply here."

That is simply an incorrect statement of the law. . . .

Because the Airgas board is taking defensive action in response to a pending takeover bid, the "theoretical specter of disloyalty" *does* exist—indeed, it is the very reason the Delaware Supreme Court in *Unocal* created an intermediate standard of review applying enhanced scrutiny to board action before directors would be entitled to the protections of the business judgment rule. . . .

The idea that boards may be acting in their own self-interest to perpetuate themselves in office is, in and of itself, the "omnipresent specter" justifying enhanced judicial scrutiny. There is "no doubt that the basis for the omnipresent specter is the interest of incumbent directors, both insiders and outsiders, in retaining the 'powers and perquisites' of board membership." To pass muster under this enhanced scrutiny, those directors bear the burden of proving that they were acting in good faith and have articulated a legally cognizable threat *and* that their actions were reasonable in response to that perceived threat—not simply that they were independent and acting in good faith. . . .

Accordingly, defendants are wrong. The *Unocal* standard of enhanced judicial scrutiny—not the business judgment rule—is the standard of review that applies to a board's defensive actions taken in response to a hostile takeover. This is how Delaware has always interpreted the *Unocal* standard. . . .

C.   A BRIEF POISON PILL PRIMER — *MORAN* AND ITS PROGENY

This case unavoidably highlights what former-Chancellor Allen has called "an anomaly" in our corporation law. The anomaly is that "[p]ublic tender offers are, or rather can be, change in control transactions that are functionally similar to merger transactions with respect to the critical question of control over the corporate enterprise." Both tender offers and mergers are "extraordinary" transactions that "threaten [ ] equivalent impacts upon the corporation and all of its constituencies including existing shareholders." But our corporation law statutorily views the two differently—under DGCL §251, board approval and recommendation is required before stockholders have the opportunity to vote on or even consider a merger proposal, while traditionally the board has been given no statutory role in responding to a public tender offer. The poison pill was born "as an attempt to address the flaw (as some would see it) in the corporation law" giving boards a critical role to play in the merger context but no role to play in tender offers.

These "functionally similar forms of change in control transactions," however, have received disparate legal treatment—on the one hand, a decision not to pursue a merger proposal (or even a decision not to engage in negotiations at all) is reviewed under the deferential business judgment standard, while on the other hand, a decision not to redeem a poison pill in the face of a hostile tender offer is reviewed under "intermediate scrutiny" and must be "reasonable in relation to the threat posed" by such offer.

In *Moran v. Household International, Inc.*, written shortly after the *Unocal* decision in 1985, the Delaware Supreme Court first upheld the legality of the poison pill as a valid takeover defense. Specifically, in *Moran,* the Household board of directors "react[ed] to what it perceived to be the threat in the market place of coercive two-tier tender offers" by adopting a stockholder rights plan that would allow the corporation to protect stockholders by issuing securities as a way to ward off a hostile bidder presenting a structurally coercive offer. . . .

Notably, the pill in *Moran* was considered reasonable in part because the Court found that there were many methods by which potential acquirers could get around the pill. One way around the pill was the "proxy out"—bidders could solicit consents to remove the board and redeem the rights. In fact, the Court did "not view the Rights Plan as much of an impediment on the tender offer process" at all. After all, the board in *Moran* was not classified, and so the entire board was up for reelection annually—meaning that all of the directors could be replaced in one fell swoop and the acquiror could presumably remove any impediments to its tender offer fairly easily after that. . . .

Two scholars at the time penned an article[325] suggesting that there were three types of threats that could be recognized under *Unocal:* (1) structural coercion—"the risk that disparate treatment of non-tendering shareholders might distort shareholders' tender decisions" (i.e., the situation involving a two-tiered offer where the back end gets less than the front end); (2) opportunity loss—the "dilemma that a hostile offer might deprive target shareholders of the opportunity to select a superior alternative offered by target management;" and (3) substantive coercion—"the risk that shareholders will mistakenly accept an underpriced offer because they disbelieve management's representations of intrinsic value." . . .

. . . [With respect to substantive coercion,] Gilson & Kraakman believed that, if used correctly, an effective proportionality test could properly incentivize management, protect stockholders and ultimately increase value for stockholders in the event that management does resist a hostile bid—but only if a real "threat" existed. To demonstrate the existence of such a threat, management

---

325. Ronald Gilson & Reinier Kraakman, *Delaware's Intermediate Standard for Defensive Tactics: Is There Substance to Proportionality Review?* 44 Bus. Law. 247, 258, 267 (1989).

must show (in detail) how its plan is better than the alternative (the hostile deal) for the target's stockholders. Only then, if management met that burden, could it use a pill to block a "substantively coercive," but otherwise [structurally] non-coercive bid.

The test proposed by the professors was taken up, and was more or less adopted, by then-Chancellor Allen in *City Capital Associates v. Interco*.[330] There, the board of Interco had refused to redeem a pill that was in place as a defense against an unsolicited tender offer to purchase all of Interco's shares for $74 per share. The bid was non-coercive (structurally), because the offer was for $74 both on the front and back end, if accepted. As an alternative to the offer, the board of Interco sought to effect a restructuring that it claimed would be worth at least $76 per share.

After pointing out that every case in which the Delaware Supreme Court had, to that point, addressed a defensive corporate measure under *Unocal* involved a structurally coercive offer (i.e. a threat to voluntariness), the Chancellor recognized that "[e]ven where an offer is noncoercive, it may represent a 'threat' to shareholder interests" because a board with the power to refuse the proposal and negotiate actively may be able to obtain higher value from the bidder, or present an alternative transaction of higher value to stockholders. Although he declined to apply the term "substantive coercion" to the threat potentially posed by an "inadequate" but non-coercive offer, Chancellor Allen clearly addressed the concept. . . .

The Chancellor held that the "mild threat" posed by the tender offer (a difference of approximately $2 per share, when the tender offer was for all cash and the value of management's alternative was less certain) did not justify the board's decision to keep the pill in place, effectively precluding stockholders from exercising their own judgment—despite the board's good faith belief that the offer was inadequate and keeping the pill in place was in the best interests of stockholders.

In *Paramount Communications, Inc. v. Time, Inc.*, however, the Delaware Supreme Court explicitly rejected [this] approach to *Unocal* analysis [primarily on the grounds that this approach] "would involve the court in substituting its judgment as to what is a 'better' deal for that of a corporation's board of directors."[335] . . .

As the Supreme Court put it, the case presented them with the following question: "Did Time's board, having developed a [long-term] strategic plan . . . come under a fiduciary duty to jettison its plan and put the corporation's future in the hands of its stockholders?" Key to the Supreme Court's ruling was the underlying pivotal question in their mind regarding the Time board's specific long-term plan—its proposed merger with Warner—and whether by entering into the proposed merger, Time had essentially "put itself up for sale." This was important because, so long as the company is *not* "for sale," then *Revlon* duties do not kick in and the board "is not under any *per se* duty to maximize shareholder value in the short term, even in the context of a

---

330. *City Capital Assocs. Ltd. P'ship v. Interco Inc.*, 551 A.2d 787 (Del. Ch. 1988).
335. *Paramount Commc'ns, Inc. v. Time Inc.*, 571 A.2d 1140, 1153 (Del. 1990).

takeover." The Supreme Court held that the Time board had not abandoned its long-term strategic plans; thus *Revlon* duties were not triggered and *Unocal* alone applied to the board's actions.

In evaluating the Time board's actions under *Unocal*, the Supreme Court embraced the concept of substantive coercion, agreeing with the Time board that its stockholders might have tendered into Paramount's offer "in ignorance or a mistaken belief of the strategic benefit which a business combination with Warner might produce." . . . [T]he Supreme Court held that Time's response was proportionate to the threat of Paramount's offer. Time's defensive actions were not aimed at "cramming down" a management-sponsored alternative to Paramount's offer, but instead, were simply aimed at furthering a pre-existing long-term corporate strategy. This, held the Supreme Court, comported with the board's valid exercise of its fiduciary duties under *Unocal*. . . .

. . . [In its opinion in the *Paramount case*,] the Supreme Court . . . grappled with the following "critical question[:] *when* is a corporation in a *Revlon* mode?" It is not until the board is under *Revlon* that its duty "narrow[s]" to getting the best price reasonably available for stockholders in a sale of the company. The reason the board's duty shifts at that point to maximizing shareholder value is simple: "In such a setting, for the present shareholders, *there is no long run.*"[361] This is not so when the board is under *Unocal*, the company is not for sale, and the board is instead pursuing long run corporate interests. . . .

Thus, it [seems to be the case under Delaware law], . . . that so long as a corporation is not for sale, it is not in *Revlon* mode and is free to pursue its long run goals. In essence, [Delaware case law appears] to support the view that a well-informed board acting in good faith in response to a reasonably perceived threat may, in fact, be able to "just say no" to a hostile tender offer.

The foregoing legal framework describes what I believe to be the current legal regime in Delaware. With that legal superstructure in mind, I now apply the *Unocal* standard to the specific facts of this case.

III.   ANALYSIS

A.   HAS THE AIRGAS BOARD ESTABLISHED THAT IT REASONABLY PERCEIVED THE EXISTENCE OF A LEGALLY COGNIZABLE THREAT?

1.   Process

Under the first prong of *Unocal*, defendants bear the burden of showing that the Airgas board, "after a reasonable investigation . . . determined in good faith, that the [Air Products offer] presented a threat . . . that warranted a defensive response." I focus my analysis on the defendants' actions in response to Air Products' current $70 offer, but I note here that defendants would have cleared

---

361. [*TW Services, Inc. v. SWT Acquisition Corp.*, 1989 WL 20290 (Del. Ch. Mar. 2, 1989)] (*emphasis added*). . . .

the *Unocal* hurdles with greater ease when the relevant inquiry was with respect to the board's response to the $65.50 offer.

In examining defendants' actions under this first prong of *Unocal*, "the presence of a majority of outside independent directors coupled with a showing of reliance on advice by legal and financial advisors, 'constitute[s] a prima facie showing of good faith and reasonable investigation.'" Here, it is undeniable that the Airgas board meets this test.

First, it is currently comprised of a majority of outside independent directors—including the three recently-elected insurgent directors who were nominated to the board by Air Products. Air Products does not dispute the independence of the Air Products Nominees, and the evidence at trial showed that the rest of the Airgas board, other than McCausland [the company's CEO], are outside, independent directors who are not dominated by McCausland.

Second, the Airgas board relied on not one, not two, but three outside independent financial advisors in reaching its conclusion that Air Products' offer is "clearly inadequate." . . . In addition, the Airgas board has relied on the advice of legal counsel, and the three Air Products Nominees have retained their own additional independent legal counsel (Skadden, Arps). In short, the Airgas board's process easily passes the smell test.

2.   What Is the "Threat?"

Although the Airgas board meets the threshold of showing good faith and reasonable investigation, the first part of *Unocal* review requires more than that; it requires the board to show that its good faith and reasonable investigation ultimately gave the board "grounds for concluding that a threat to the corporate enterprise existed."[377] . . . Airgas (and its lawyers) attempted to identify numerous threats posed by Air Products' $70 offer: It is coercive. It is opportunistically timed. . . . It undervalues Airgas—it is a "clearly inadequate" price. The merger arbitrageurs who have bought into Airgas need to be "protected from themselves." The arbs are a "threat" to the minority. The list goes on.

The reality is that the Airgas board discussed essentially none of these alleged "threats" in its board meetings, or in its deliberations on whether to accept or reject Air Products' $70 offer, or in its consideration of whether to keep the pill in place. The board did not discuss "coercion" or the idea that Airgas's stockholders would be "coerced" into tendering. . . . The board did not discuss Air Products' offer in terms of any "danger" that it posed to the corporate enterprise. . . .

Airgas's board members testified that the concepts of coercion, threat, and the decision whether or not to redeem the pill were nonetheless "implicit" in the board's discussions due to their knowledge that a large percentage of Airgas's stock is held by merger arbitrageurs who have short-term interests and would be willing to tender into an inadequate offer. But the only threat that the board discussed—the threat that has been the central issue since the beginning

---

377. *Versata Enters., Inc. v. Selectica, Inc.*, 5 A.3d 586, 599 (Del. 2010).

of this case — is the inadequate price of Air Products' offer. Thus, inadequate price, coupled with the fact that a majority of Airgas's stock is held by merger arbitrageurs who might be willing to tender into such an inadequate offer, is the only real "threat" alleged. In fact, Airgas directors have admitted as much. . . .

In the end, it really is "All About Value." Airgas's directors and Airgas's financial advisors concede that the Airgas stockholder base is sophisticated and well-informed, and that they have all the information necessary to decide whether to tender into Air Products' offer.

a. Structural Coercion

Air Products' offer is not structurally coercive. A structurally coercive offer involves "the risk that disparate treatment of non-tendering shareholders might distort shareholders' tender decisions."[390] *Unocal,* for example, "involved a two-tier, highly coercive tender offer" where stockholders who did not tender into the offer risked getting stuck with junk bonds on the back end. "In such a case, the threat is obvious: shareholders may be compelled to tender *to avoid being treated adversely* in the second stage of the transaction."[392]

Air Products' offer poses no such structural threat. It is for all shares of Airgas, with consideration to be paid in all cash. The offer is backed by secured financing. There is regulatory approval. The front end will get the same consideration as the back end, in the same currency, as quickly as practicable. Air Products is committed to promptly paying $70 in cash for each and every share of Airgas and has no interest in owning less than 100% of Airgas. Air Products would seek to acquire any non-tendering shares "[a]s quick[ly] as the law would allow." It is willing to commit to a subsequent offering period. In light of that, any stockholders who believe that the $70 offer is inadequate simply *would not tender* into the offer — they would risk nothing by not tendering because if a majority of Airgas shares did tender, any non-tendering shares could tender into the subsequent offering period and receive the exact same consideration ($70 per share in cash) as the front end. In short, if there were an antonym in the dictionary for "structural coercion," Air Products' offer might be it. . . .

b. Opportunity Loss

Opportunity loss is the threat that a "hostile offer might deprive target stockholders of the opportunity to select a superior alternative offered by target management or . . . offered by another bidder."[401] . . .

---

390. Ronald Gilson & Reinier Kraakman, *Delaware's Intermediate Standard for Defensive Tactics: Is There Substance to Proportionality Review?* 44 Bus. Law. 247, 258 (1989).

392. *Paramount Commc'ns, Inc. v. Time, Inc.,* 571 A.2d 1140, 1152 (Del. 1990) (*emphasis added*).

401. *Unitrin, Inc. v. Am. Gen. Corp.,* 651 A.2d 1361, 1384 (Del. 1995) (quoting Ronald Gilson & Reinier Kraakman, *Delaware's Intermediate Standard for Defensive Tactics: Is There Substance to Proportionality Review?* 44 Bus. Law. 247, 267 (1989)).

. . . As such, Air Products' offer poses no threat of opportunity loss. The Airgas board has had, at this point, over sixteen months to consider Air Products' offer and to explore "strategic alternatives going forward as a company." After all that time, there is no alternative offer currently on the table, and counsel for defendants represented during the October trial that "we're not asserting that we need more time to explore a specific alternative." The "superior alternative" Airgas is pursuing is simply to "continue[ ] on its current course and execute[ ] its strategic [five-year, long-term] plan."

c. Substantive Coercion

Inadequate price and the concept of substantive coercion are inextricably related. The Delaware Supreme Court has defined substantive coercion, . . . as "the risk that [Airgas's] stockholders might accept [Air Products'] inadequate Offer because of 'ignorance or mistaken belief' regarding the Board's assessment of the long-term value of [Airgas's] stock."[406] In other words, if management advises stockholders, in good faith, that it believes Air Products' hostile offer is inadequate because in its view the future earnings potential of the company is greater than the price offered, Airgas's stockholders might nevertheless reject the board's advice and tender.

In the article that gave rise to the concept of "substantive coercion," Professors Gilson and Kraakman argued that, in order for substantive coercion to exist, two elements are necessary: (1) management must actually expect the value of the company to be greater than the offer—and be correct that the offer is in fact inadequate, and (2) the stockholders must reject management's advice or "*believe* that management will not deliver on its promise."[407] Both elements must be present because "[w]ithout the first element, shareholders who accept a structurally non-coercive offer have not made a mistake. Without the second element, shareholders will believe management and reject underpriced offers."

Defendants' argument involves a slightly different take on this threat, based on the particular composition of Airgas's stockholders (namely, its large "short-term" base). In essence, Airgas's argument is that "the substantial ownership of Airgas stock by these short-term, deal-driven investors poses a threat to the company and its shareholders"—the threat that, because it is likely that the arbs would support the $70 offer, "shareholders will be coerced into tendering into an inadequate offer." The threat of "arbs" is a new facet of substantive coercion, different from the substantive coercion claim recognized in *Paramount*.[410] There, the hostile tender offer was purposely timed to confuse the stockholders. The terms of the offer could cause stockholders to mistakenly tender if they

---

406. *Unitrin, Inc. v. Am. Gen. Corp.*, 651 A.2d 1361, 1385 (Del. 1995).

407. Ronald Gilson & Reinier Kraakman, *Delaware's Intermediate Standard for Defensive Tactics: Is There Substance to Proportionality Review?* 44 Bus. Law. 247, 260 (1989).

410. *Paramount Commc'ns, Inc. v. Time, Inc.*, 571 A.2d 1140 (Del. 1990). Similar concerns about short-term investors were noted in *Paramount*, however: "Large quantities of Time shares were held by institutional investors. The board feared that even though there appeared to be wide support for the Warner transaction, Paramount's cash premium would be a tempting prospect to these investors." *Id.* at 1148.

did not believe or understand (literally) the value of the merger with Warner as compared with the value of Paramount's cash offer. The terms of the offer introduced uncertainty. In contrast, here, defendants' claim is not about "confusion" or "mistakenly tendering" (or even "disbelieving" management) — Air Products' offer has been on the table for over a year, Airgas's stockholders have been barraged with information, and there is no alternative offer to choose that might cause stockholders to be confused about the terms of Air Products' offer. Rather, Airgas's claim is that it needs to maintain its defensive measures to prevent control from being surrendered for an unfair or inadequate price. The argument is premised on the fact that a large percentage (almost half) of Airgas's stockholders are merger arbitrageurs—many of whom bought into the stock when Air Products first announced its interest in acquiring Airgas, at a time when the stock was trading much lower than it is today—who would be willing to tender into an inadequate offer because they stand to make a significant return on their investment even if the offer grossly undervalues Airgas in a sale. "They don't care a thing about the fundamental value of Airgas."[411] In short, the risk is that a majority of Airgas's stockholders will tender into Air Products' offer despite its inadequate price tag, leaving the minority "coerced" into taking $70 as well. The defendants do not appear to have come to grips with the fact that the arbs bought their shares from long-term stockholders who viewed the increased market price generated by Air Products' offer as a good time to sell.

The threat that merger arbs will tender into an inadequately priced offer is only a legitimate threat if the offer is indeed inadequate. "The only way to protect stockholders [from a threat of substantive coercion] is for courts to ensure that the threat is real and that the board asserting the threat is not imagining or exaggerating it."[415] Air Products and Shareholder Plaintiffs attack two main aspects of Airgas's five-year plan — (1) the macroeconomic assumptions relied upon by management, and (2) the fact that Airgas did not consider what would happen if the economy had a "double-dip" recession. . . .

The next question is, if a majority of stockholders *want* to tender into an inadequately priced offer, is that substantive coercion? Is that a threat that justifies continued maintenance of the poison pill? Put differently, is there evidence in the record that Airgas stockholders are so "focused on the short-term" that they would "take a smaller harvest in the swelter of August over a larger one in Indian Summer"? Air Products argues that there is none whatsoever. . . .

But there is at least some evidence in the record suggesting that this risk may be real. Moreover, both Airgas's expert and well as *Air Products' own expert* testified that a large number—if not all—of the arbitrageurs who bought into Airgas's stock at prices significantly below the $70 offer price would be happy to tender their shares at that price regardless of the potential long-term value of the company. Based on the testimony of both expert witnesses, I find sufficient

---

411. [Trial Testimony of McCausland] ("They don't care a thing about the fundamental value of Airgas. I know that. I naively spent a lot of time trying to convince them of the fundamental value of Airgas in the beginning. But I'm quite sure now, given that experience, that they have no interest in the long-term.").

415. *Chesapeake Corp. v. Shore*, 771 A.2d 293, 326 (Del. Ch. 2000).

evidence that a majority of stockholders might be willing to tender their shares regardless of whether the price is adequate or not—thereby ceding control of Airgas to Air Products. This is a clear "risk" under the teachings of *TW Services* and *Paramount* because it would essentially thrust Airgas into *Revlon* mode.

Ultimately, it all seems to come down to the Supreme Court's holdings in *Paramount* and *Unitrin*. In *Unitrin*, the Court held: "[T]he directors of a Delaware corporation have the prerogative to determine that the market undervalues its stock and to protect its stockholders from offers that do not reflect the long-term value of the corporation under its present management plan."[428] When a company is not in *Revlon* mode, a board of directors "is not under any *per se* duty to maximize shareholder value in the short term, even in the context of a take-over."[429] The Supreme Court has unequivocally "endorse[d the] conclusion that it is not a breach of faith for directors to determine that the present stock market price of shares is not representative of true value or that there may indeed be several market values for any corporation's stock."[430] As noted above, based on all of the facts presented to me, I find that the Airgas board acted in good faith and relied on the advice of its financial and legal advisors in coming to the conclusion that Air Products' offer is inadequate. And as the Supreme Court has held, a board that in good faith believes that a hostile offer is inadequate may "properly employ[ ] a poison pill as a proportionate defensive response to protect its stockholders from a 'low ball' bid."

B.   IS THE CONTINUED MAINTENANCE OF AIRGAS'S DEFENSIVE MEASURES PROPORTIONATE TO THE "THREAT" POSED BY AIR PRODUCTS' OFFER?

Turning now to the second part of the *Unocal* test, I must determine whether the Airgas board's defensive measures are a proportionate response to the threat posed by Air Products' offer. Where the defensive measures "are inextricably related, the principles of *Unocal* require that [they] be scrutinized collectively as a unitary response to the perceived threat." Defendants bear the

---

428. *Unitrin*, 651 A.2d 1361, 1376 (citing *Paramount*, 571 A.2d at 1153). Vice Chancellor Strine has pointed out that "[r]easonable minds can and do differ on whether it is appropriate for a board to consider an all cash, all shares tender offer as a threat that permits any response greater than that necessary for the target board to be able to negotiate for or otherwise locate a higher bid and to provide stockholders with the opportunity to rationally consider the views of both management and the prospective acquiror before making the decision to sell their personal property." *In re Gaylord Container Corp. S'holders Litig.*, 753 A.2d 462, 478 n. 56 (Del. Ch. 2000). But the Supreme Court cited disapprovingly to the approach taken in *City Capital Associates v. Interco, Inc.*, 551 A.2d 787 (Del. Ch. 1988), which had suggested that an all-cash, all-shares bid posed a limited threat to stockholders that justified leaving a poison pill in place only for some period of time while the board protects stockholder interests, but "[o]nce that period has closed . . . and [the board] has taken such time as it required in good faith to arrange an alternative value-maximizing transaction, then, in most instances, the legitimate role of the poison pill in the context of a noncoercive offer will have been fully satisfied." The Supreme Court rejected that understanding as "not in keeping with a proper *Unocal* analysis."

429. *Paramount*, 571 A.2d at 1150.

430. *Id.* at 1150 n. 12. . . .

burden of showing that their defenses are not preclusive or coercive, and if neither, that they fall within a "range of reasonableness."

1.   Preclusive or Coercive

A defensive measure is coercive if it is "aimed at 'cramming down' on its shareholders a management-sponsored alternative." Airgas's defensive measures are certainly not coercive in this respect, as Airgas is specifically *not* trying to cram down a management sponsored alternative, but rather, simply wants to maintain the status quo and manage the company for the long term.

A response is preclusive if it "makes a bidder's ability to wage a successful proxy contest and gain control [of the target's board] . . . 'realistically unattainable.'" Air Products and Shareholder Plaintiffs argue that Airgas's defensive measures are preclusive because they render the possibility of an effective proxy contest realistically unattainable. What the argument boils down to, though, is that Airgas's defensive measures make the possibility of Air Products obtaining control of the Airgas board and removing the pill realistically unattainable *in the very near future,* because Airgas has a staggered board in place. Thus, the real issue posed is whether defensive measures are "preclusive" if they make gaining control of the board realistically unattainable in the short term (but still realistically attainable sometime in the future), or if "preclusive" actually means "preclusive"—i.e. forever unattainable. In reality, or perhaps I should say in practice, these two formulations ("preclusive for now" or "preclusive forever") may be one and the same when examining the combination of a staggered board plus a poison pill, because no bidder to my knowledge has ever successfully stuck around for two years and waged two successful proxy contests to gain control of a classified board in order to remove a pill.[436] So does that make the combination of a staggered board and a poison pill preclusive?

This precise question was asked and answered four months ago in *Versata Enterprises, Inc. v. Selectica, Inc.* There, Trilogy (the hostile acquiror) argued that in order for the target's defensive measures not to be preclusive: (1) a successful proxy contest must be realistically attainable, and (2) the successful proxy contest must result in gaining control of the board at the next election. The Delaware Supreme Court rejected this argument, stating that "[i]f that preclusivity argument is correct, then it would apply whenever a corporation has both a classified board and a Rights Plan. . . . *[W]e hold that the combination of a classified board and a Rights Plan do not constitute a preclusive defense.*"[437]

The Supreme Court explained its reasoning as follows:

> Classified boards are authorized by statute and are adopted for a variety of business purposes. Any classified board also operates as an antitakeover defense by preventing an insurgent from obtaining control of the board in one election. More than a decade ago, in *Carmody [v. Toll Brothers, Inc.],* the Court of Chancery noted "because only one third of a classified board would stand for election each

---

436. Indeed, Airgas's own expert testified that no bidder has ever replaced a majority of directors on a staggered board by winning two consecutive annual meeting elections.

437. *Selectica*, 5 A.3d 586, 604 (Del. 2010) (*emphasis added*).

year, a classified board would *delay— but not prevent— a hostile acquiror from obtaining control of the board*, since a determined acquiror could wage a proxy contest and obtain control of two thirds of the target board over a two year period, as opposed to seizing control in a single election."[438]

The Court [in *Versata*] concluded: "The fact that a combination of defensive measures makes it more difficult for an acquirer to obtain control of a board does not make such measures realistically unattainable, i.e., preclusive."[439] . . .

I am thus bound by this clear precedent to proceed on the assumption that Airgas's defensive measures are not preclusive if they delay Air Products from obtaining control of the Airgas board (even if that delay is significant) so long as obtaining control at some point in the future is realistically attainable. I now examine whether the ability to obtain control of Airgas's board in the future is realistically attainable.

Air Products has already run one successful slate of insurgents. Their three independent nominees were elected to the Airgas board in September. Airgas's next annual meeting will be held sometime around September 2011. Accordingly, if Airgas's defensive measures remain in place, Air Products has two options if it wants to continue to pursue Airgas at this time: (1) It can call a special meeting and remove the entire board with a supermajority vote of the outstanding shares, or (2) It can wait until Airgas's 2011 annual meeting to nominate a slate of directors. I will address the viability of each of these options in turn.

a. Call a Special Meeting to Remove the Airgas Board by a 67% Supermajority Vote

Airgas's charter allows for 33% of the outstanding shares to call a special meeting of the stockholders, and to remove the entire board without cause by a vote of 67% of the outstanding shares. . . .

[W]hat seems clear to me, quite honestly, is that a poison pill is assuredly preclusive in the everyday common sense meaning of the word; indeed, its *rasion d'etre* is preclusion—to stop a bid (or *this* bid) from progressing. That is what it is intended to do and that is what the Airgas pill has done successfully for over sixteen months. Whether it is realistic to believe that Air Products can, at some point in the future, achieve a 67% vote necessary to remove the entire Airgas board at a special meeting is (in my opinion) impossible to predict given the host of variables in this setting, but the sheer lack of historical examples where an insurgent has ever achieved such a percentage in a contested control election must mean something. Commentators who have studied actual hostile takeovers for Delaware companies have, at least in part, essentially corroborated this common sense notion that such a victory is not realistically attainable. Nonetheless, while the special meeting may not be a realistically attainable mechanism for circumventing the Airgas defenses, that assessment does not end the analysis under existing precedent.

---

438. *Id.* (quoting *Carmody v. Toll Bros., Inc.,* 723 A.2d 1180. 1186 n.17 (Del. Ch. 1998)).
439. *Id.* . . .

b. Run Another Proxy Contest

Even if Air Products is unable to achieve the 67% supermajority vote of the outstanding shares necessary to remove the board in a special meeting, it would only need a simple majority of the voting stockholders to obtain control of the board at next year's annual meeting. Air Products has stated its unwillingness to wait around for another eight months until Airgas's 2011 annual meeting. There are legitimately articulated reasons for this—Air Products' stockholders, after all, have been carrying the burden of a depressed stock price since the announcement of the offer. But that is a business determination [to be made] by the Air Products board. The reality is that obtaining a simple majority of the voting stock is significantly less burdensome than obtaining a supermajority vote of the outstanding shares, and considering the current composition of Airgas's stockholders (and the fact that, as a result of that shareholder composition, a majority of the voting shares today would likely tender into Air Products' $70 offer), if Air Products and those stockholders choose to stick around, an Air Products victory at the next annual meeting is very realistically attainable.

Air Products certainly realized this. . . . If Air Products is unwilling to wait another eight months to run another slate of nominees, that is a business decision of the Air Products board, but as the Supreme Court has held, waiting until the next annual meeting "delay[s]—but [does] not prevent—[Air Products] from obtaining control of the board."[479] I thus am constrained to conclude that Airgas's defensive measures are not preclusive.[480]

2. Range of Reasonableness

"If a defensive measure is neither coercive nor preclusive, the *Unocal* proportionality test requires the focus of enhanced judicial scrutiny to shift to the range of reasonableness."[481] The reasonableness of a board's response is evaluated in the context of the specific threat identified—the "specific nature of the

---

479. *Selectica*, 5 A.3d at 604. Although the three Air Products Nominees from the September 2010 election all have joined the rest of the Airgas board in its current views on value, if Air Products nominated another slate of directors who were elected, there is no question that it would have "control" of the Airgas board—i.e. it will have nominated and elected the majority of the board members. There is no way to know at this point whether or not those three hypothetical New Air Products Nominees would join the rest of the board in its view, or whether the entire board would then decide to remove its defensive measures. The preclusivity test, though, is whether obtaining control of the board is realistically unattainable, and here I find that it is not. Considering whether some future hypothetical Air-Products-Controlled Airgas board would vote to redeem the pill is not the relevant inquiry.

480. Our law would be more credible if the Supreme Court acknowledged that its later rulings have modified *Moran* and have allowed a board acting in good faith (and with a reasonable basis for believing that a tender offer is inadequate) to remit the bidder to the election process as its only recourse. The tender offer is in fact precluded and the only bypass of the pill is electing a new board. If that is the law, it would be best to be honest and abandon the pretense that preclusive action is *per se* unreasonable.

481. *Selectica*, 5 A.3d at 605 (internal quotations omitted).

threat [ ] 'sets the parameters for the range of permissible defensive tactics' at any given time."[482]

Here, the record demonstrates that Airgas's board, composed of a majority of outside, independent directors, acting in good faith and with numerous outside advisors concluded that Air Products' offer clearly undervalues Airgas in a sale transaction. The board believes in good faith that the offer price is inadequate by no small margin. Thus, the board is responding to a legitimately articulated threat.

This conclusion is bolstered by the fact that the three Air Products Nominees on the Airgas board have now wholeheartedly joined in the board's determination—what is more, they believe it is their fiduciary duty to keep Airgas's defenses in place. And Air Products' *own directors* have testified that (1) they have no reason to believe that the Airgas directors have breached their fiduciary duties, (2) even though plenty of information has been made available to the stockholders, they "agree that Airgas management is in the best position to understand the intrinsic value of the company," and (3) if the shoe were on the other foot, they would act in the same way as Airgas's directors have. . . .

. . . Air Products chose to replace a minority of the Airgas board with three *independent directors* who promised to take a "fresh look." Air Products ran its nominees expressly premised on that independent slate. It could have put up three nominees premised on the slogan of "shareholder choice." It could have run a slate of nominees who would promise to remove the pill if elected. It could have gotten three directors elected who were resolved to fight back against the rest of the Airgas board.

Certainly what occurred here is not what Air Products expected to happen. Air Products ran its slate on the promise that its nominees would "consider without any bias [the Air Products] Offer," and that they would "be willing to be outspoken in the boardroom about their views on these issues." Air Products *got what it wanted.* Its three nominees got elected to the Airgas board and then questioned the directors about their assumptions. (They got answers.) They looked at the numbers themselves. (They were impressed.) They requested outside legal counsel. (They got it.) They requested a third outside financial advisor. (They got it.) And in the end, they *joined in the board's view* that Air Products' offer was inadequate. . . .

The Supreme Court has clearly held that "the 'inadequate value' of an all cash for all shares offer is a 'legally cognizable threat.' "[492] Moreover, "[t]he fiduciary duty to manage a corporate enterprise includes the selection of a time frame for achievement of corporate goals. *That duty may not be delegated to the stockholders.*"[493] The Court continued, "Directors are not obligated to abandon a deliberately conceived corporate plan for a short-term shareholder profit unless there is clearly no basis to sustain the corporate strategy." Based on all of the foregoing factual findings, I cannot conclude that there is "clearly no basis" for the Airgas board's belief in the sustainability of its long-term plan.

---

482. *Id.* at 606 (quoting *Unitrin,* 651 A.2d at 1384).

492. *Unitrin, Inc. v. Am. Gen. Corp.,* 651 A.2d 1361, 1384 (Del. 1995) (quoting *Paramount*).

493. *Paramount Commc'ns, Inc. v. Time, Inc.,* 571 A.2d 1140, 1154 (Del. 1990) (*emphasis added*).

On the contrary, the maintenance of the board's defensive measures must fall within a range of reasonableness here. The board is not "cramming down" a management-sponsored alternative — or *any* company-changing alternative. Instead, the board is simply maintaining the status quo, running the company for the long-term, and consistently showing improved financial results each passing quarter. The board's actions do not *forever* preclude Air Products, or any bidder, from acquiring Airgas or from getting around Airgas's defensive measures if the price is right. In the meantime, the board is preventing a change of control from occurring at an inadequate price. This course of action has been clearly recognized under Delaware law: "directors, when acting deliberately, in an informed way, and in the good faith pursuit of corporate interests, may follow a course designed to achieve long-term value even at the cost of immediate value maximization." . . .

CONCLUSION

Vice Chancellor Strine recently suggested that:

> The passage of time has dulled many to the incredibly powerful and novel device that a so-called poison pill is. That device has no other purpose than to give the board issuing the rights the leverage to prevent transactions it does not favor by diluting the buying proponent's interests.[513]

There is no question that poison pills act as potent anti-takeover drugs with the potential to be abused. Counsel for plaintiffs (both Air Products and Shareholder Plaintiffs) make compelling policy arguments in favor of redeeming the pill in this case — to do otherwise, they say, would essentially make all companies with staggered boards and poison pills "takeover proof." The argument is an excellent sound bite, but it is ultimately not the holding of this fact-specific case, although it does bring us one step closer to that result.

As this case demonstrates, in order to have any effectiveness, pills do not — and can not — have a set expiration date. To be clear, though, this case does not endorse "just say never." What it does endorse is Delaware's long-understood respect for reasonably exercised managerial discretion, so long as boards are found to be acting in good faith and in accordance with their fiduciary duties (after rigorous judicial fact-finding and enhanced scrutiny of their defensive actions). The Airgas board serves as a quintessential example.

Directors of a corporation still owe fiduciary duties to *all stockholders* — this undoubtedly includes short-term as well as long-term holders. At the same time, a board cannot be forced into *Revlon* mode any time a hostile bidder makes a tender offer that is at a premium to market value. The mechanisms in place to get around the poison pill — even a poison pill in combination with a staggered board, which no doubt makes the process prohibitively more difficult — have been in place since 1985, when the Delaware Supreme Court first decided to

---

513. *Hollinger Int'l, Inc. v. Black*, 844 A.2d 1022, 1083 (Del. Ch. 2004).

uphold the pill as a legal defense to an unwanted bid. That is the current state of Delaware law until the Supreme Court changes it.

For the foregoing reasons, Air Products' and the Shareholder Plaintiffs' requests for relief are denied, and all claims asserted against defendants are dismissed with prejudice. . . .

QUESTIONS

1. Why does Chancellor Chandler decide that *Unocal* applies, rather than the more deferential business judgment rule standard of judicial review?

2. According to Chancellor Chandler, where do the public policy concerns regarding "coerciveness and preclusiveness" of shareholder voting fit into the two-pronged *Unocal* standard of review?

3. Was Airgas in the *Revlon* mode?

4. Can the duty of loyalty force Target's board into the *Revlon* mode? In other words, can a fully financed, "any and all shares," all-cash offer by Bidder put Target "in play" (i.e., in the *Revlon* mode)?

5. What are the defensive measures that Airgas had in place that are at issue in this case?

6. How does Chancellor Chandler rule on the validity of these defensive measures?

7. Does the decision Chancellor Chandler reached in *Airgas* mean that boards of directors can "just say no" to a prospective bidder?

8. After considering Chancellor Chandler's review of Delaware jurisprudence and the analytical approach that he ultimately adopted in *Airgas*, what do you think is the appropriate framework for judicial decision making in this area? In other words, we return to the fundamental question that we have grappled with throughout the materials in this casebook: *who should decide whether, and on what terms, a publicly traded company should be sold?* With respect to the sale of a publicly traded company, does the COVID-19 global pandemic (and the ensuing recessionary economy) influence your thinking regarding the relevant public policy concerns that must be taken into account? Does your analysis of this issue change in the case of a sale of a privately held company?

9. As the Supreme Court observed in *CTS Corp. v. Dynamics Corp. of America*, 481 U.S. 69, 88 (1987), "[n]o principle of corporation law and practice is more firmly established that a State's authority to regulate domestic corporations," which has resulted in the design of the modern American system of corporate governance being left to the states. While that may very well have been true from a historical perspective, it is clear that the reforms introduced by the passage of the Sarbanes-Oxley Act (SOX) in July 2002 have sorely tested the continuing vitality of this proposition. In considering the views expressed by Chancellor Chandler in his *Airgas* opinion, should

future development of corporate governance systems be left to the states? If so, what are the relative merits of committing this to the states rather than the federal government? Do the recent financial scandals and the ensuing Great Recession influence your thinking on this issue?

10. How does your assessment of the public policy to be served by providing for judicial review of the board's actions in this area compare with your assessment of the efficacy of the modern appraisal remedy that we studied at the end of Chapter 2 and the court's role in enforcing this statutorily authorized remedy?

11. Is the reasoning used (or the result reached) by Chancellor Chandler consistent with the Delaware Supreme Court's holding in the *Corwin* case (*supra,* at p. 761)?

12. In the text of a footnote that is often referred to by knowledgeable commentators, Chancellor Chandler observes:

> Marty Lipton himself has written that "the pill was neither designed nor intended to be an absolute bar. It was always contemplated that the possibility of a proxy fight to replace the board would result in the board's taking shareholder desires into account, but that the delay and uncertainty as to the outcome of a proxy fight would give the board the negotiating position it needed to achieve the best possible deal for all the shareholders, which in appropriate cases could be the target's continuing as an independent company.... A board cannot say 'never,' but it can say 'no' in order to obtain the best deal for its shareholders." Martin Lipton, *Pills, Polls, and Professors Redux*, 69 U. Chi. L.Rev. 1037, 1054 (2002) (citing Marcel Kahan & Edward Rock, *How I Learned to Stop Worrying and Love the Pill: Adaptive Responses to Takeover Law*, 69 U. CHI. L.REV. 871, 910 (2002) ("[T]he ultimate effect of the pill is akin to 'just say wait.' ")). As it turns out, for companies with a "pill plus staggered board" combination, it might actually be that a target board can "just say wait . . . a very long time" because the Delaware Supreme Court has held that having to wait two years is not preclusive.

Airgas, supra, at p. 126, n. 504. *Query:* Do you agree with Chancellor Chandler's assessment of Delaware case law that a Target Co. board can tell a hostile Bidder to "just wait for a very long time"? Do you think that this assessment reflects sound public policy?

NOTES

1. The "Strange Case" of Delaware Section 203. Because Chancellor Chandler "reluctantly endorsed the Airgas Board's use of the [poison] pill to thwart a hostile bid" from Air Products, the implications of Delaware's antitakeover statute, Section 203, in the context of this hostile deal were not fully considered by Chancellor Chandler in his opinion. "But the maneuverings of the parties in the battle for Airgas" raised the possibility that Delaware Section 203 "might have posed an important obstacle to the Air Products bid had [Chancellor Chandler] ordered Airgas to redeem its pill." David Marcus, *The*

Strange Case of Section 203, THE DEAL, Mar. 2011, *available at:* http://www.thedeal.com/magazine/ID/038635/2011/the-strange-case-of-section-03.php. *Query:* In what way would the terms of Delaware Section 203 present "an obstacle" to Air Products' bid for Airgas? Should Chancellor Chandler have evaluated the terms of Delaware Section 203 as part of the total array of takeover defenses that Airgas had in place? Should the board's decision whether or not to waive application of Delaware Section 203 be subject to a fiduciary duty challenge, much in the way that the decision of the Airgas board not to redeem the pill was subject to a claim of breach of the board's fiduciary duties?

2. The "Linguistic Box" of Delaware Fiduciary Duty Case Law.   One of the leading commentaries on the "linguistic box"* that has resulted from the evolution of judicial standards of review under Delaware case law over the past two decades is an article written by three esteemed (current and former) members of the Delaware judiciary. *See* William T. Allen, Jack B. Jacobs, and Leo E. Strine, *Function over Form: A Reassessment of Standards of Review in Delaware Corporation Law*, 56 BUS. LAW 1287 (2001). In their article, the authors address *Unocal* and its progeny:

> This article focuses on a central aspect of the protean growth in the conceptual vocabulary of the Delaware corporation law since 1985 — judicial standards of review. Our thesis is that certain key Delaware decisions articulated and applied standards of review without adequately taking into account the policy purposes those standards were intended to achieve. Moreover, new standards of review proliferated when a smaller number of functionally-thought-out standards would have provided a more coherent framework. In this Article, we suggest a closer alignment between the standards of judicial review used in Delaware corporate law and the underlying policies that that body of law seeks to achieve. In our view, a rigorous functional evaluation of existing corporate law standards of review will clarify their application, reduce their number, and facilitate the task of corporate advisors and courts. . . .
>
> Our analysis concludes by proposing that the corporation law can function most effectively with three basic standards of judicial review: (i) a gross negligence standard of review for claims that directors are liable for damages caused by their inattention — a standard that would require plaintiff to prove both a breach of the duty and the fact and extent of any damages caused by the breach; (ii) a rehabilitated entire fairness standard to address duty of loyalty claims; and (iii) an intermediate standard of review to govern challenges to director decisions arguably influenced by an entrenchment motive, *e.g.*, the adoption of anti-takeover defense measures or the approval of a change in control.

Id. at 1293. *Query:* Which of the three standards proposed by the authors should be used to analyze the facts of the *Airgas* case? What result would you obtain

---

* [By the author: *See First Union Corporation Suntrust Banks, Inc.*, 2001 WL 1885686 at *18 (N.C. Bus. Ct., August 10, 2001) (Following an extensive review of the development of Delaware fiduciary duty case law over the past twenty years, the North Carolina court observes that the evolution of Delaware law has resulted in "trapping" counsel "in the linguistic box of Delaware [fiduciary duty] law.").]

using that standard of judicial review? Does the Delaware Supreme Court's *Corwin* opinion (which was handed down in 2015, more than a decade after this article was published) influence your thinking on this question?

2. ***Post-Mortem on the Fate of Airgas.***   As it turns out, following Chancellor Chandler's February 2011 decision, the trading price of Airgas stock was usually higher than $78, well above Air Products' "best and final" offer of $70. And, in November 2015, in what Marty Lipton viewed as a "vindication of the Airgas board's [business] judgment. . . . Airgas agreed to be [acquired by] Air Liquide [in a fully negotiated merger transaction at] a price of $143 per share, in cash, nearly 2.4x Air Products' original $60 offer and more than double the final $70 offer, in each case before considering the more than $9 per share of dividends received by Airgas shareholders in the intervening years." Martin Lipton, *et al.*, Wachtell, Lipton, Rosen & Katz, Dec. 17, 2015, *"Just Say No"— The Long-Term Value of the Poison Pill* (law firm memo, copy on file with author).

3. ***Ongoing "Shareholder versus Stakeholder" Controversy.*** In a portion of his opinion in *Airgas* that is not part of the excerpt above, Chancellor Chandler explores ideas that were originally floated back in the "deal decade" of the 1980s by then-Chancellor William Allen in his opinion in *TW Services, Inc. v. SWT Acquisition Corp.*, 1989 WL 20290 (Del. Ch. Mar. 2, 1989). More specifi- cally, in his opinion in *Airgas*, Chancellor Chandler refers to the critical ques- tion of whether circumstances may exist where a board's duty of loyalty to "the corporation and its shareholders" forces it into *Revlon* mode, thereby requiring it to abandon its efforts to promote long-term corporate values in favor of tak- ing steps that maximize current value for the company's shareholders. Neither Chancellor Allen nor Chancellor Chandler directly answers this question. Instead, Chancellor Chandler refers to a famous footnote in Allen's opinion in *TW Services*, in which he muses:

> Questions of this type call upon one to ask, what is our model of corporate gover- nance? "Shareholder democracy" is an appealing phrase, and the notion of share- holders as the ultimate voting constituency of the board has obvious pertinence, but that phrase would not constitute the only element in a well articulated model [of corporate governance in the modern, publicly-traded corporation]. While cor- porate democracy is a pertinent concept, *a corporation is not a New England town meeting; directors, not shareholders, have responsibilities to manage the business and affairs of the corporation*, subject however to a fiduciary obligation.

TW Services, Inc. v. SWT Acquisition Corp., 1989 WL 20290 at *8 n. 14 (Del. Ch. Mar. 2, 1989 (*emphasis added*).

It seems fitting that this chapter – in which we examine the scope of man- agement's fiduciary obligations – should conclude by mentioning the ongoing controversy over "shareholder versus stakeholder" primacy, a long-standing debate that raises many of the same issues that Chancellors Allen and Chandler mused over. In summer 2019, CEOs of over 175 of the largest U.S. corporations signed a "Statement on the Purpose of a Corporation," which was authored by the Business Roundtable, an association of CEOs of the leading companies in the United States. "Since 1978, Business Roundtable has periodically issued

Principles of Corporate Governance. Each version of the document issued since 1997 has endorsed principles of shareholder primacy — that corporations exist principally to serve shareholders [and thus to maximize shareholder wealth]. With today's announcement, the new Statement supersedes previous statements and outlines a modern standard for corporate responsibility." *See* Business Roundtable, *Business Roundtable Redefines the Purpose of a Corporation to Promote an Economy That Serves All Americans*, Aug. 19, 2019, *available at*: https://www.businessroundtable.org/business-roundtable-redefines-the-purpose-of-a-corporation-to-promote-an-economy-that-serves-all-americans.

In this new statement, and in a marked departure from its prior pronouncements, the Business Roundtable committed itself to serve "long-term value creation for all stakeholders." *Id.* As such, the CEOs who signed the new statement committed themselves "to lead their companies for the benefit of all stakeholders – customers, employees, suppliers, communities and shareholders." *Id.* As the American – and indeed the world's – economy continues to grapple (as of Fall 2020) with the crippling effects of the coronavirus pandemic, the resolve of the signatories to fulfill "their commitment to run their companies for the benefit of workers and communities, and not just for shareholders" is being sorely tested. Peter S. Goodman, *A Vow by Big Business Proves Too Hard to Keep*, N. Y. Times, April 14, 2020, *Big Business Pledged Gentler Capitalism. It's Not Happening in a Pandemic.*, N. Y. Times, April 13, 2020, *available at*: https://www.nytimes.com/2020/04/13/business/business-roundtable-coronavirus.html. Needless to say, the modern corporate governance story, and more specifically, issues of accountability on the part of officers and directors for the decisions they make as the managers of the business affairs of the modern publicly traded corporation, is a story that continues to evolve. So stay tuned for further developments in this long-running public policy debate . . .

|8|

Tax, Accounting, and Antitrust Considerations Related to Mergers and Acquisition Transactions

A. Overview of Taxable Transactions vs. Tax-Deferred Reorganizations

The conventional wisdom in the mergers and acquisitions (M&A) field is that tax consequences are the primary driver in the selection of M&A deal structures. Thus, any seasoned tax lawyer is likely to advise that tax considerations are the single most important factor in determining whether an acquisition will be structured as a merger, an asset purchase, or a stock purchase. While many corporate lawyers may dismiss this as a bit of an overstatement, it is undoubtedly true that the tax treatment of a proposed acquisition will be one of the major considerations that influence how the deal will be structured. Under the provisions of §368 of the Internal Revenue Code (IRC), transactions may be structured so as to avoid (defer) immediate tax consequences, and, hence, are generally referred to as *nontaxable* (or *tax-free*) *deals*. However, the criteria used under IRC §368 to classify methods of reorganization is a bit different from the basic types of deal structures authorized under the terms of modern state corporation codes. A brief summary of the provisions of IRC §368 is provided below, although this general overview is certainly no substitute for a law school course that analyzes in detail the requirements that must be satisfied for an acquisition to qualify as a tax-deferred transaction.

The statutory requirements of the IRC, like federal securities laws and state corporation statutes, are subject to further development through the promulgation of regulations and by the courts. One of the most important judicially developed principles is generally known as the *continuity of interest doctrine*. The continuity of interest doctrine is central to the law of tax-deferred transactions. At the risk of oversimplification, a transaction is not likely to qualify for tax-deferred treatment unless the investment interest of the shareholders of Target Co. is carried over as a similar investment in Bidder Co. (or the surviving business), without the opportunity for the shareholder to cash out as a part of the acquisition transaction. This judicially developed requirement is now included in the regulations under §368.

The tax treatment of an acquisition is usually of most concern to Target Co. and its shareholders. The tax liability associated with the recognition of gain (or loss, as the case may be) by either Target Co. or the shareholders of Target may have significant financial consequences for these shareholders, which may heavily influence the attractiveness of Bidder's offer. The tax attributes of an acquisition generally do not loom as large for Bidder Co. From a tax perspective, Bidder is usually most worried about two things: first, determining its tax basis in Target's assets once Bidder acquires Target's business; and second, avoiding liability for any of Target's existing tax problems.

A taxable M&A transaction usually consists of the purchase of stock or assets of Target for consideration — usually consisting of cash or Bidder's debt securities — that precludes the transaction from being able to qualify as a tax-free reorganization under IRC §368. This section first describes the taxable forms of acquisition structures, and then briefly describes the criteria that must be satisfied under §368 for a transaction to qualify as a tax-free acquisition.

1. Taxable Acquisitions

Stock Purchase for Cash. If Bidder Co. purchases Target shares directly from the stockholders for cash, Target shareholders would be required to recognize a gain (or loss) on the sale of their shares. Generally, Target shareholders will qualify for a long-term capital gain or loss if the shares were held as a capital asset for more than one year. On Bidder's side, its tax basis in the shares will usually be equal to the price paid (plus acquisition expenses). In the hands of Bidder, the tax basis of the underlying assets of Target Co. will generally be carried over since the corporate form of the entity (Target Co.) essentially remains untouched. However, Bidder Co. may make an election under IRC §338, which will allow Bidder a step up in its basis in the acquired assets, but at the cost of a tax on the unrealized appreciation in its assets.

Asset Purchase for Cash. If Bidder Co. buys all (or substantially all) of Target's assets for cash, then Target Co. would be subject to a tax at the corporate level *and* generally there would be a second level of tax imposed on Target shareholders when the proceeds of this asset sale are distributed to the shareholders in the liquidation of Target Co. If no second-step dissolution is contemplated, then generally, Target's sale of its assets has no effect on the company's stockholders. In the likely event of a complete liquidation of Target, this liquidating distribution to Target's shareholders will be treated as a sale of Target Co. stock by its shareholders, requiring the shareholders to recognize a capital gain (or loss) at the time of the distribution in the liquidation of Target Co. (assuming that the individual shareholders qualify for capital gain treatment).

2. Tax-Deferred Reorganizations

To qualify as a tax-free acquisition (or, more properly, tax-deferred reorganization), the transaction must conform to the rather technical terms of one of the specific definitions of tax-free reorganization under §368(a). The rather technical requirements of the different types of reorganizations are summarized below. In addition, the transaction must pass muster under the additional gloss imposed by the courts and the applicable regulations on transactions seeking to qualify as tax-free under §368: continuity of interest, continuity of business enterprise, and business purpose.

First, continuity of interest usually means that the shareholders of Target Co. must receive a substantial equity interest in Bidder Co. (the acquiring company), thereby maintaining a continuing ownership interest in Target's business operations. The continuity of business enterprise test usually requires Bidder to continue to operate a historic business of Target Co., or, alternatively, use all (or a significant portion) of Target's historic business assets in its business operations. Finally, the transaction must be entered into for a valid business purpose.

Assuming that these requirements are all satisfied, the transaction must satisfy one of the different types of reorganizations set forth under §368(a), the terms of which are briefly summarized below. Generally speaking, the parties to an acquisition will obtain an opinion of counsel, or a letter ruling from the Internal Revenue Service (IRS), as to the tax-free nature of the transaction.

Statutory Merger — the "A" Reorganization.   An "A" reorganization is an acquisition transaction that is structured as a merger (or consolidation) pursuant to the laws of a particular state. This is the most flexible of the §368(a) reorganization definitions in terms of the allowable type of acquisition consideration because Bidder can pay Target shareholders up to approximately half of the purchase price in cash, property, or debt securities (all of which are collectively referred to in tax parlance as "boot" — that is, non-qualifying (taxable) consideration under the terms of §368(a)) and the remainder of the purchase price can be paid using any class of Bidder's stock (permitting use of voting or nonvoting shares). As for the tax effects, the shareholders of Target Co. must recognize any realized gain to the extent of money plus the fair market value of any other boot (non-qualifying consideration) received. Generally speaking, Bidder recognizes no taxable gain or loss and usually takes a basis in the assets acquired that is equal to the basis of these assets in the hands of Target Co.

Stock for Stock Exchange Offer — the "B" Reorganization.   This transaction is defined as Bidder's acquisition of Target Co. shares directly from the company's shareholders *solely* in exchange for voting stock of Bidder Co. *if,* immediately after the transaction, Bidder has at least 80 percent control of Target Co. The *sole* consideration allowed under this type of reorganization is voting stock of Bidder Co., although voting preferred stock can be used, so long as the voting rights afford the former Target shareholders significant participation in the management of Bidder. For purposes of "B" reorganizations, "control" is defined as requiring Bidder to acquire at least 80 percent of Target's voting stock and at least 80 percent of each other class of Target stock outstanding.

Acquisition of Assets in Exchange for Stock — the "C" Reorganization.   Where Bidder acquires "substantially all" of Target's assets (which usually means that

Bidder must purchase at least 90 percent of the fair market value of Target's net assets and 70 percent of the fair market value of the gross assets held by Target immediately prior to the transaction) *solely* in exchange for Bidder's voting stock, the acquisition qualifies as a tax-deferred "C" reorganization. As is the case with a "B" reorganization, the only form of acquisition consideration allowed is voting stock of Bidder Co. At least 80 percent of the consideration must consist of Bidder's voting stock, although the remainder of the purchase price may be paid in cash, property, or debt securities, provided that the total amount of such non-qualifying consideration *plus* the amount of Target liabilities that Bidder agrees to assume do not constitute more than 20 percent of the total consideration paid by Bidder. Generally speaking, Target Co. must be liquidated immediately following this type of reorganization, thereby distributing the acquisition consideration to its shareholders as part of the orderly dissolution of Target. As for Target's shareholders, there is no taxable gain or loss to the extent that the acquisition consideration consists of Bidder's voting stock. However, Target's shareholders do incur a tax to the extent of the "boot" (nonqualifying consideration) received in the transaction. Bidder Co. usually recognizes no taxable gain or loss and generally takes a tax basis in the acquired assets equal to the basis of these assets in the hands of Target Co. Target Co. generally recognizes no taxable gain or loss, either at the time of closing on the sale of substantially all of its assets to Bidder or at the time of dissolution of Target.

Forward Triangular (Subsidiary) Merger — the "(a)(2)(D)" Reorganization.   In those cases where Target is merged into a subsidiary of Bidder Co. ("NewCo"), with NewCo as the surviving corporation (forward triangular merger), the transaction will qualify as an "(a)(2)(D)" reorganization, so long as it results in NewCo acquiring "substantially all" of Target's assets. To determine if NewCo holds "substantially all" of Target's assets, the same standard must be satisfied as for "C" reorganizations. However, unlike a "C" reorganization, Bidder is not as limited in the type of acquisition consideration that it may use to fund the purchase price. So a forward triangular merger may still qualify as a tax-free reorganization, even though consideration other than Bidder's voting stock is used (such as cash), so long as the form of consideration is authorized by the relevant merger statute. Recall, though, that the transaction still must satisfy the continuity of interest requirement to qualify for tax-deferred treatment under the terms of §368. The tax consequences of this form of reorganization are essentially the same as for an "A" reorganization.

Reverse Triangular (Subsidiary) Merger — the "(a)(2)(E)" Reorganization.   This provision covers those cases where Target Co. is to merge with a subsidiary of Bidder Co. and the merger agreement calls for Target to survive (reverse triangular merger). The transaction will qualify for tax-deferred treatment so long as, *after* the transaction is completed, Target (as the surviving company) continues to own "substantially all" of its assets. In addition, Bidder Co. must exchange its voting stock for an amount of Target Co. stock that constitutes control of Target (using the 80 percent definition of §368(c)), although the remaining consideration may consist of boot. In this way, the transaction is analogous to a "B" reorganization in that Bidder must acquire "control" of Target "solely" in exchange for its voting stock. However, unlike a "B" reorganization, there is greater flexibility in the type of consideration that may be used since Bidder must acquire only 80 percent of Target's stock in exchange for voting stock of Bidder, and the remaining 20 percent of Target's stock can be acquired for other nonqualifying consideration (boot). The tax effects of this type of reorganization are essentially the same as in the case of an "A" reorganization.

B.   Federal Antitrust Law and the Hart-Scott-Rodino Antitrust Improvement Act: An Overview of Hart-Scott-Rodino Requirements

"The Clayton Act is the primary merger control legislation in the [United States] and precludes acquisitions of stock or assets, the effect of which may be substantially to lessen competition. Mergers may also be challenged under the Sherman Act, which prohibits agreements that unreasonably restrain trade, as well as [monopolization], attempted [monopolization] and conspiracy to [monopolize], or the Federal Trade Commission Act (FTC Act), which focuses on unfair methods of competition and unfair or deceptive acts or practices. The Hart-Scott-Rodino Antitrust Improvements Act of 1976 (HSR Act), which governs the premerger notification process in the [United States], is incorporated into the Clayton Act. . . . The FTC and the Antitrust Division of the Department of Justice [DOJ] . . . share jurisdiction for reviewing proposed mergers. . . . Pursuant to the HSR Act, the FTC is authorized to prescribe the regulations and format of notification that are 'necessary and appropriate' to carry out the purposes of the HSR Act." James Fishkin, et al., Dechert LLP, *Merger Control: Law and Practice USA*, August 2020, *available at:* https://www .deallawyers.com/Member/Docs/Firms/Dechert/08_20_USA.pdf. In addition, certain transactions may require approval by the Committee on Foreign Investment in the United States (CFIUS). Generally speaking, CFIUS is authorized to review acquisitions of control of U.S. businesses by non-U.S. persons in order to determine the effect of the proposed transaction on national security interests. "While most reviews are initiated voluntarily by [the parties to the] transaction . . . , [in certain cases,] CFIUS may initiate the review. CFIUS reviews are more likely to occur where target entities involve [defense-related] activities, critical infrastructure or critical technologies, or are located near sensitive US governmental facilities." *Id.*

Most commonly, the HSR Act requires the parties to file notification of their proposed transaction — such as a merger or a stock purchase or an asset acquisition — if the proposed transaction meets specified thresholds involving both a "size-of-person" test and a "size-of-transaction" test and no exemptions are available. These filing thresholds are adjusted annually by the FTC. *See, e.g.,* Andrea Agathoklis Murino, et al., Goodwin Procter LLP, *FTC Announces New Thresholds for 2020* ("Each year, the [FTC] adjusts the reporting thresholds under the [HSR Act] based on changes in gross national prod-uct."), Jan. 28, 2020, *available at:* https://www.goodwinlaw.com/publications/ 2020/01/01_28-ftc-announces-new-thresholds-2020. "An acquisition that is subject to an HSR Act notification may not be completed until the requisite HSR forms have been filed with the agencies and the applicable [statutory] waiting period has expired or has been terminated early. In most transactions, the acquired and the acquiring parties must file separate HSR forms, and the waiting period will not commence until both parties make their filings. In tender offers, the waiting period commences with the filing of the HSR form by the acquirer. . . . The initial waiting period is 30 days (or 15 days, in the case of a cash tender offer . . .). . . . The FTC and the DOJ have con-current jurisdiction over HSR Act notifications. . . . A clearance process exists between the agencies whereby one of the agencies can get 'cleared' to investigate the transaction. Once an agency is cleared, it can contact the parties (and third parties) for information relating to the transaction." Ilene Knable Gotts, *The Merger Control Regime in the U.S.*, Wachtell, Lipton, Rosen & Katz, Sept. 11, 2019, *available at:* https://www.lexology.com/library/detail. aspx?g=9adb940e-346e-4b1e-b148-a941d1681a68&l=8T5CPYN.

During this waiting period, the federal government (either the FTC or the DOJ) can delay the closing of the transaction while it commences an in-depth investigation in order to determine if the acquisition will pose problems under the federal antitrust laws. For our purposes, the essential inquiry under the relevant antitrust laws is whether the proposed acquisition will substantially lessen competition in the United States. The scope of this inquiry is covered in detail in a law school course devoted to the comprehensive study of antitrust law and thus lies outside the scope of this casebook. It bears emphasizing, however, that this potential for antitrust review is one reason that many M&A transactions are frequently not consummated until many months after they are announced, as the parties wait to clear antitrust review in the United States (and perhaps other jurisdictions as well). Indeed, as reflected in the "Deal Story" in Chapter 1, the merger agreement entered into between AT&T and DirecTV was signed on May 18, 2014, but the parties did not close their trans-action until July 24, 2015, when the transaction finally cleared antitrust review. It also bears emphasizing that the failure to comply with the filing require-ments of the HSR Act may result in rather substantial statutory penalties. *See, e.g.,* Sullivan & Cromwell LLP, *ValueAct Pays Record Fine to Resolve Alleged HSR Violations,* July 14, 2016, *available at:* https://www.sullcrom.com/siteFiles/ Publications/SC_Publication_Hart_Scott_Rodino_Act_07_14_2016.pdf ("On Tuesday, July 12, 2016, ValueAct agreed to pay a record fine of $11 million to settle allegations by the DOJ that it had violated the reporting requirements of the [HSR] Act . . ."); and Barry A. Nigro, Jr., *ValueAct Settlement: A Record Fine for HSR Violation,* July 19, 2016, *available at:* https://corpgov.law.harvard. edu/2016/07/19/valueact-settlement-a-record-fine-for-hsr-violation/; *see also* Michele Harrington, et al., Hogan Lovells US LLP, *Third Point to Pay Monetary Penalty to Settle Allegations of HSR Act Violations,* Sept. 4, 2019, *available at:* https://www.hoganlovells.com/~/media/hogan-lovells/pdf/2019/2019_09 _04_acer_alert_third_point_to_pay_monetary_penalty.pdf?la=en. The nature (and implications) of this HSR Act filing obligation are nicely illustrated in the next case.

Heublein, Inc. v. Federal Trade Commission
539 F. Supp. 123 (D. Conn. 1982)

CLARIE, Chief Judge:

I.   FACTUAL BACKGROUND

A.   THE PARTIES

1. Plaintiff Heublein, is a Connecticut corporation having its principal place of business at Farmington, Connecticut. Heublein is engaged in the production and distribution of distilled spirits and wines, the operation and franchising of Kentucky Fried Chicken, H. Salt and Zantigo Mexican-American quick service restaurants, and the production and distribution of other specialty food products.

2. Defendant Federal Trade Commission ("Commission") is an agency of the United States and . . . is one of two federal agencies responsible for administering the premerger notification program established by the Hart-Scott-Rodino Antitrust Improvements Act of 1976 ("H-S-R Act").

3. Defendant James C. Miller, III is Chairman, and defendants David A. Clanton, Michael Pertschuk and Patricia P. Bailey are members of the Federal Trade Commission. Defendant Thomas J. Campbell is Director of the Bureau of Competition of the Federal Trade Commission. The Bureau of Competition is the organizational unit of the Commission responsible for administering the premerger notification program under the H-S-R Act. The Commission has delegated to the Director of the Bureau of Competition the power to permit persons to consummate acquisitions which are subject to the H-S-R Act prior to the expiration of the waiting period prescribed in that Act.

B.   HART-SCOTT-RODINO ACT AND PREMERGER NOTIFICATION REGULATIONS RELEVANT TO THIS CASE

4. Title II of the H-S-R Act, enacted in 1976, added section 7A to the Clayton Act, which established a new premerger notification program governing certain acquisitions of voting securities or assets. The legislative purposes of Title II were to provide the Commission and the Antitrust Division of the United States Department of Justice ("Department"), in advance of an acquisition: (a) information concerning both the nature of the particular transaction and the competitive effects of the acquisition and (b) sufficient time to analyze the competitive effects of the acquisition to determine whether to challenge the acquisition prior to its consummation.

5. If a stock acquisition is subject to the H-S-R Act, both the acquiring and acquired parties must: (a) file with the Commission and the Department a premerger notification form and exhibits, which report the required information concerning their businesses and the details of the particular transaction; and (b) wait a prescribed period before consummating the acquisition, subject to the Commission's authority to extend or reduce that waiting period.

6. After a premerger notification form and exhibits have been filed by an acquiring party with both the Commission and the Department, personnel of those agencies confer and decide which agency will assume responsibility for analyzing those materials to determine whether the particular acquisition is likely to lessen competition or whether additional information or documents are required to make that determination.

7. In the case of an acquisition of voting securities on the open market through a national securities exchange or through private transactions, the waiting period under the Commission's premerger notification rules expires on the thirtieth day after the acquiring party has filed its premerger notification form and exhibits, unless: (a) the waiting period is terminated, by the Commission and the Department, prior to the expiration of the thirty-day period; or (b) prior to the expiration of the thirty-day period, the Commission or the Department (as the case may be) requests additional information or documents from either the acquiring or the acquired party. Such a request for additional information or documents extends the H-S-R waiting period until the twentieth day following the agencies' receipt of such additional information or documents.

8. As amended by the H-S-R Act, section 7A(b)(2) of the Clayton Act expressly authorizes the Commission and the Department to reduce the H-S-R Act waiting period "and allow any person to proceed with any acquisition subject to" the H-S-R Act. The Commission's premerger notification rules expressly provide that "early termination" of the waiting period may be granted either upon written request by a party to the acquisition or sua sponte by the Commission or the Department.

9. A Formal Interpretation of those rules and regulations, issued by the Bureau of Competition on April 10, 1979, identifies the principles governing the Bureau's consideration of "early termination" requests. This Interpretation states that such requests will not be granted unless the Commission has concluded that it will not take any further action within the waiting period and unless the requesting party demonstrates "some special business reason that warrants early termination of the waiting period," such as a "need to complete the transaction before the waiting period would normally expire." . . .

C.   **CINEMA'S REQUEST FOR PERMISSION TO ACQUIRE UP TO 49.9%**
      OF HEUBLEIN'S STOCK

12. General Cinema Corporation ("Cinema") is a Delaware corporation, having its principal place of business in Chestnut Hill, Massachusetts, and is primarily engaged in bottling and marketing carbonated soft drinks and in the exhibition of motion pictures.

13. On February 4, 1982, Cinema filed with the Commission and the Department a premerger notification form and exhibits, in which Cinema sought approval from the Commission and the Department to acquire, through open market and private transactions, up to 49.9% of Heublein's common stock. Upon the filing of Cinema's premerger notification form, it was determined that the Commission, rather than the Department, would assume responsibility for evaluating the competitive effects of Cinema's proposed acquisition of up to 49.9% of Heublein's stock.

14. On February 19, 1982, Heublein filed the premerger notification form and exhibits required to be submitted by parties whose stock may be acquired in a transaction subject to the H-S-R Act.

15. Upon receipt of Cinema's and Heublein's premerger notification filings, the Commission reviewed Cinema's proposed acquisition of up to 49.9% of Heublein's stock and determined to allow Cinema to consummate the acquisition. Under the Commission's premerger notification rules, Cinema's waiting period expired at 11:59 p.m. on March 6, 1982, and, effective at that time, the Commission permitted Cinema to acquire up to 49.9% of Heublein stock.

D. HEUBLEIN'S REQUEST FOR PERMISSION TO ACQUIRE UP TO 49.9% OF CINEMA'S STOCK

16. On March 2, 1982, Heublein filed a premerger notification form and exhibits in which Heublein sought approval to acquire, through open market or private transactions, up to 49.9% of Cinema's common stock. Under the Commission's premerger notification rules, the H-S-R Act waiting period with respect to Heublein's acquisition of up to 49.9% of Cinema's stock will not expire until 11:59 p.m. on April 2, 1981 unless reduced by the Commission pursuant to its authority to grant an "early termination" of the waiting period.

17. By letter dated March 2, 1981, submitted pursuant to section 7A(b)(2) of the Clayton Act, as amended by the H-S-R Act, Heublein requested that the Commission terminate the H-S-R Act waiting period with respect to Heublein's acquisition of up to 49.9% of Cinema's stock as soon as possible, but no later than the expiration of the waiting period with respect to Cinema's acquisition of up to 49.9% of Heublein's stock. As grounds for early termination of its H-S-R Act waiting period, Heublein's letter of March 2, 1982 stated:

(a) That there is no likelihood that Heublein's acquisition of Cinema stock will lessen competition in any line of commerce in any section of the country;
(b) That unless Heublein's waiting period was terminated simultaneously with Cinema's, Cinema would be permitted to acquire up to 49.9% of Heublein's stock, while Heublein would not be permitted to acquire up to 49.9% of Cinema stock, and that such a result would be contrary to the legislative history and policies of the H-S-R Act.

E. THE COMMISSION'S DENIAL OF HEUBLEIN'S REQUEST FOR PERMISSION TO ACQUIRE CINEMA'S STOCK SIMULTANEOUSLY WITH CINEMA'S ACQUISITION OF HEUBLEIN'S STOCK

18. On Thursday, March 4, 1982, the Bureau of Competition denied Heublein's request for early termination not because of any concern about the competitive effects of Heublein's acquisition of up to 49.9% of Cinema's stock, but because, in its view, Heublein had not demonstrated the existence of a "special business reason" in accordance with the Bureau's Formal Interpretation, dated April 10, 1979. The Bureau's position was that a "special business reason" was not shown by the fact that early termination was necessary so that Heublein

would be free to acquire up to 49.9% of Cinema's stock at the same time that Cinema would be free to acquire up to 49.9% of Heublein's stock. The Bureau believed it should to remain "neutral" with respect to contested acquisitions and believed that to grant early termination to Heublein in this case would be to favor Heublein and disfavor Cinema. . . .

F. CINEMA'S EFFORTS TO DETER HEUBLEIN'S ACQUISITION OF UP TO 49.9% OF CINEMA'S STOCK

20. On March 9, 1982, Cinema was reported to have announced that it intended to acquire up to three million shares of its own common stock. Wall Street Journal, March 9, 1982 at 52. It was reported that Cinema's acquisition of three million of its shares would increase the holdings of Cinema's chairman, vice chairman and their families to 47.5% of Cinema's then-outstanding shares. On March 12, 1982, Cinema was reported to have purchased on the open market 1,060,800 of its shares and increased its borrowing capacity from $160 million to $300 million. On that date, a share of Cinema's stock was reportedly priced on the open market at $42, the highest price of such stock in the previous fifty-two weeks. Wall Street Journal, dated March 12, 1982 at 46.

CONCLUSIONS OF LAW . . .

III. STANDARD FOR GRANTING A TEMPORARY RESTRAINING ORDER . . .

IV. IRREPARABLE HARM TO HEUBLEIN

4. As a Connecticut corporation, Heublein has the right to acquire and sell property and to invest corporate funds. . . .

5. If Heublein's right to invest is to be preserved, Heublein must be permitted to invest now. Already, as a result of the Commission's actions described above, nine days have elapsed since Cinema became free to acquire up to 49.9% of Heublein's stock, and during this time Heublein has been prohibited from acquiring a like amount of Cinema's stock. The favorable market opportunities which, absent the Commission's action, would have been available to Heublein during that period, have been irretrievably lost. Moreover, Heublein cannot be compensated for such lost opportunities by money damages. Hence, Heublein has already been irreparably harmed as a result of the Commission's action and it has no adequate remedy at law.

6. In addition, as each day passes during which Heublein is prohibited from acquiring up to 49.9% of Cinema's stock, Heublein loses the favorable market opportunities which would be available to Heublein were it able immediately to acquire up to 49.9% of Cinema's stock. In addition, Cinema's purchases of its own stock, and other actions which Cinema, as a target company, may take to defeat Heublein's effort to purchase Cinema's stock, are further evidence of the likelihood that Heublein will be irreparably harmed unless it is immediately permitted to consummate its proposed acquisition of Cinema's stock. . . .

V.   THE BALANCE OF HARDSHIPS TIPS DECIDEDLY IN HEUBLEIN'S FAVOR

8. The balance of hardships in this case decidedly favors issuance of a temporary restraining order to Heublein.

9. Neither defendants nor the public interest will be harmed if Heublein is permitted to acquire up to 49.9% of Cinema's stock, because defendants have determined to allow consummation of that acquisition.

10. Since neither the defendants nor the public interest will be harmed by issuance of the requested temporary restraining order and Heublein will be irreparably harmed absent such relief, the balance of hardships tips decidedly in favor of Heublein.

VI.   HEUBLEIN IS LIKELY TO SUCCEED ON THE MERITS OF THIS ACTION

A.   HEUBLEIN IS LIKELY TO SUCCEED IN SHOWING THAT THE COMMISSION EXCEEDED ITS STATUTORY JURISDICTION AND AUTHORITY IN DENYING HEUBLEIN'S REQUEST FOR EARLY TERMINATION OF THE H-S-R WAITING PERIOD

11. Sections 702 and 704 of the Administrative Procedure Act, 5 U.S.C. ss 701 et seq. provide for judicial review of the Commission's denial of Heublein's early termination request.

12. Under §706(2)(C) of the APA, agency action must be set aside if it exceeds the agency's statutory jurisdiction or authority. . . .

13. The Commission's denial of Heublein's early termination request exceeded the Commission's jurisdiction and authority for each of several reasons. First, the H-S-R Act is intended to permit the antitrust enforcement agencies to evaluate the competitive effects of a transaction and the purpose of the H-S-R waiting period is to provide those agencies sufficient time, in advance of an acquisition, to conduct that analysis. But Heublein was denied early termination on a ground unrelated to competitive considerations. Hence, the Commission's denial of Heublein's request was contrary to the H-S-R Act's purpose and, therefore, beyond its jurisdiction and authority and serves no governmental purpose under the Act.

14. Second, Heublein was denied early termination because the Commission believed that Heublein's request was governed by the standards set forth in the Bureau of Competition's Formal Interpretation, dated April 10, 1979. That Formal Interpretation states that an early termination will not be granted unless the requesting party demonstrates a "special business reason" justifying early termination. However, neither the H-S-R Act nor its legislative history justifies a requirement that a "special business reason" be shown in order to obtain an early termination. If, as here, the Commission has determined well prior to the expiration of the waiting period that the particular transaction will not likely lessen competition and if, as here, Heublein has presented a lawful business reason for early termination, it is beyond the Commission's authority not to grant early termination on the ground that a "special business reason" has not been shown.

15. Third, Heublein's request was denied not because of any concern about the competitive effects of Heublein's acquisition of Cinema's stock, but because the Commission believed that it must remain "neutral" with respect to contested acquisitions and that to grant early termination to Heublein would be to favor Heublein and disfavor Cinema. This rationale is wrong because if the Commission intends to remain "neutral" with respect to the Heublein-Cinema acquisitions, it should grant Heublein early termination to permit Heublein to acquire Cinema's stock at the same time as Cinema is acquiring Heublein's stock. . . .

17. For these reasons, Heublein is likely to succeed in establishing that the Commission's denial of Heublein's early termination request exceeded its jurisdiction and authority and must, therefore, be set aside.

B. HEUBLEIN IS LIKELY TO SUCCEED IN SHOWING THAT THE COMMISSION WAS ARBITRARY, CAPRICIOUS AND ABUSED ITS DISCRETION IN DENYING HEUBLEIN'S REQUEST FOR EARLY TERMINATION OF THE H-S-R WAITING PERIOD

18. Section 706(2)(A) of the APA provides that on review of agency action:

> The reviewing court shall — (2) hold unlawful and set aside agency action, findings and conclusions found to be —
> (A) arbitrary, capricious, an abuse of discretion, or otherwise not in accordance with law. . . .

In reviewing agency action under this standard, the court must determine whether the agency's decision was based on a consideration of relevant factors and whether it is consistent with the overall policy of the governing Act.

19. For several reasons, Heublein is likely to succeed in establishing that the Commission's denial of Heublein's early termination request was arbitrary, capricious and an abuse of discretion. First, the H-S-R Act is intended to permit the antitrust enforcement agencies to evaluate the competitive effects of a transaction and to provide those agencies sufficient time to conduct that analysis. Heublein, however, was denied early termination on a ground unrelated to competitive considerations. Second, there appears to be no rational basis for the Bureau's requirement that a "special business reason" be shown in order to justify an early termination. Third, the Commission has granted a large number of early termination requests including many involving acquisitions among large companies. Fourth, there appears to be no rational basis for the Bureau's position that it must remain "neutral" with respect to contested acquisitions and that to grant early termination to Heublein would be to favor Heublein and disfavor Cinema. If the Commission intends to remain "neutral" with respect to the Heublein-Cinema acquisitions, it should grant Heublein early termination to permit Heublein to acquire Cinema's stock at the same time as Cinema is acquiring Heublein's stock. Finally, the Commission has applied its policy prohibiting early terminations in contested acquisitions in a discriminatory fashion. "In this instance, to maintain a neutral posture, it is incumbent upon the

Commission to grant an early termination, because to deny the same places it is an active posture against the petitioner corporation, Heublein."

20. For all of these reasons, Heublein will likely succeed in showing that Heublein's early termination request was arbitrary, capricious and an abuse of discretion.

Appendices

Diagrams of Deal Structures to Be Analyzed

DIAGRAM 1
Traditional Form of Stock for Stock Direct (Statutory) Merger

• BEFORE Transaction •

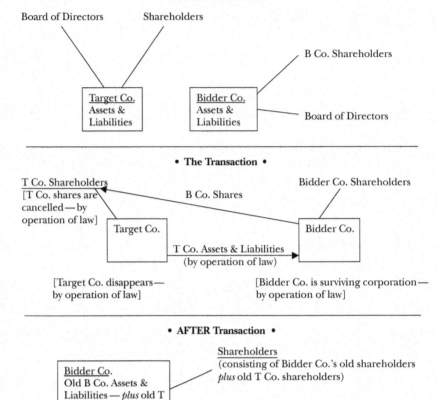

• The Transaction •

• AFTER Transaction •

DIAGRAM 2
Stock for Cash Merger
(Cash Out Merger)

• **BEFORE Transaction** •

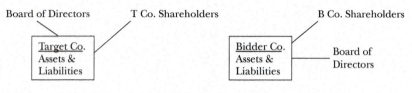

• **The Transaction** •

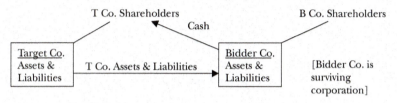

[Target Co. disappears—extinguished by operation of law]

• **AFTER Transaction** •

Old B Co. Shareholders

[Old Target Co. shareholders
hold cash—no stock]

Bidder Co.
Old B Co. Assets &
Liabilities — *plus* old T
Co. Assets & Liabilities

DIAGRAM 3
Short Form Merger

• **BEFORE Transaction** •

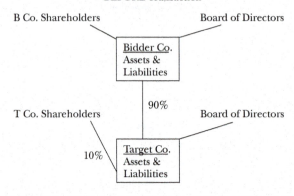

B Co. Shareholders   Board of Directors

<u>Bidder Co</u>.
Assets &
Liabilities

90%

T Co. Shareholders   Board of Directors

10%   <u>Target Co</u>.
Assets &
Liabilities

• **The Transaction** •

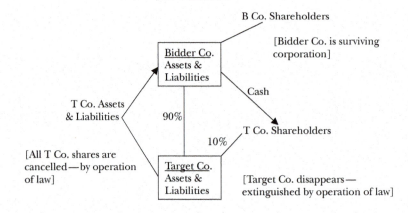

B Co. Shareholders

[Bidder Co. is surviving
corporation]

<u>Bidder Co</u>.
Assets &
Liabilities

Cash

T Co. Assets
& Liabilities

90%

T Co. Shareholders

10%

[All T Co. shares are
cancelled—by operation
of law]

<u>Target Co</u>.
Assets &
Liabilities

[Target Co. disappears—
extinguished by operation of law]

• **AFTER Transaction** •

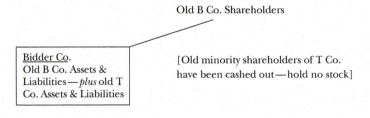

Old B Co. Shareholders

Bidder Co.
Old B Co. Assets &
Liabilities—*plus* old T
Co. Assets & Liabilities

[Old minority shareholders of T Co.
have been cashed out—hold no stock]

DIAGRAM 4
Traditional Form of Asset Purchase:
Sale of Substantially All of Target Co. Assets for Cash, Followed by
Dissolution of Target Co.

• BEFORE Transaction •

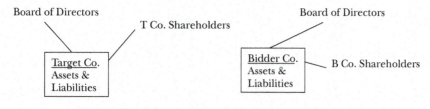

• FIRST Step: Sale of Target Co. Assets to Bidder Co. •

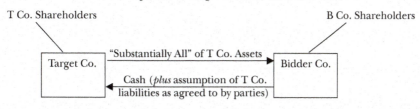

• AFTER Sale of Substantially All of Target Co. Assets •

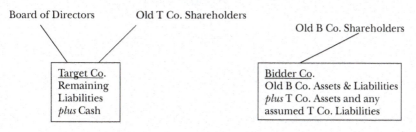

• SECOND Step: Dissolution of Target Co. •

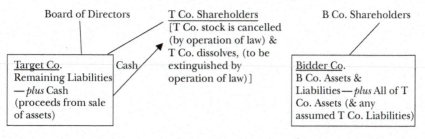

• AFTER Second-Step Dissolution •

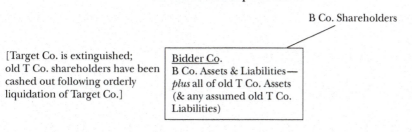

DIAGRAM 5
Asset Acquisition for Stock

• BEFORE Transaction •

Board of Directors   T Co. Shareholders   Board of Directors

B Co. Shareholders

Target Co.
Assets &
Liabilities

Bidder Co.
Assets &
Liabilities

• The Transaction •

T Co. Shareholders   B Co. Shareholders

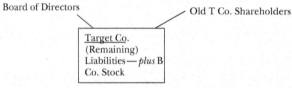

Target Co. ◄── B Co. Stock ─── Bidder Co.

T Co. Assets
(*plus* assumption of T Co.
Liabilities as agreed to by parties)

• AFTER Transaction •

Old T Co. Shareholders   Old B Co. Shareholders

Target Co.
Remaining Liabilities
— *plus* B Co. Stock

Bidder Co.
Old B Co. Assets &
Liabilities — *plus* all of old
T Co. Assets & any
assumed T Co. Liabilities

Step 2: Dissolution of Target Co.
• BEFORE Dissolution •

Board of Directors   Old T Co. Shareholders

Target Co.
(Remaining)
Liabilities — *plus* B
Co. Stock

• The Transaction •

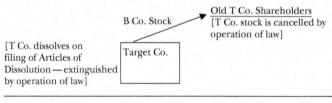

Old T Co. Shareholders
[T Co. stock is cancelled by
operation of law]

B Co. Stock

[T Co. dissolves on
filing of Articles of
Dissolution — extinguished
by operation of law]

Target Co.

• AFTER Dissolution •

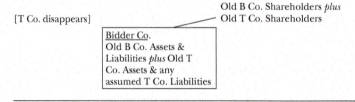

Old B Co. Shareholders *plus*
Old T Co. Shareholders

[T Co. disappears]

Bidder Co.
Old B Co. Assets &
Liabilities *plus* Old T
Co. Assets & any
assumed T Co. Liabilities

DIAGRAM 6
Traditional Form of Stock Purchase for Cash

• BEFORE Transaction •

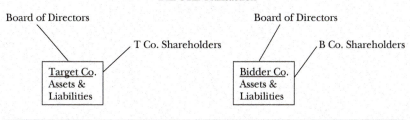

• The Transaction •

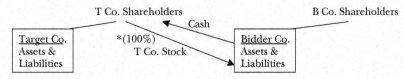

*It is possible (but often not likely) that all (100%) of Target Co. stock is exchanged for cash in this transaction.

• AFTER Transaction •

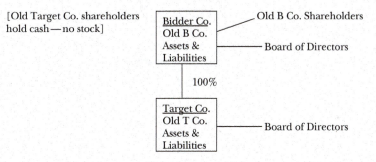

DIAGRAM 7
Stock for Stock Acquisition
(Stock Purchase for Stock — Stock Exchange Offer)

• BEFORE Transaction •

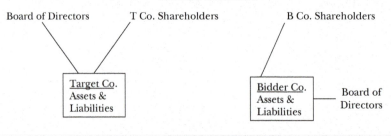

• The Transaction •

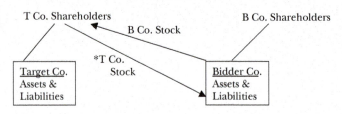

*This assumes that all (100%) of Target Co. Shareholders accept the offer and exchange their T Co. shares for B Co. stock.

• AFTER Transaction •

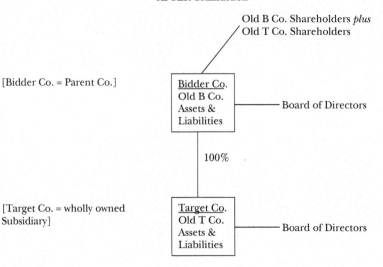

DIAGRAM 8
Forward Triangular Merger
(Using *Stock* as Merger Consideration)

• BEFORE Transaction •

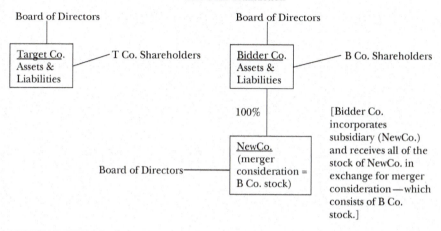

Board of Directors   Board of Directors

Target Co.   ——— T Co. Shareholders   Bidder Co.   ——— B Co. Shareholders
Assets &   Assets &
Liabilities   Liabilities

                                    100%

                                                 NewCo.   [Bidder Co.
                                                 (merger   incorporates
                  Board of Directors——   consideration = subsidiary (NewCo.)
                                                 B Co. stock)   and receives all of the
                                                                 stock of NewCo. in
                                                                 exchange for merger
                                                                 consideration—which
                                                                 consists of B Co.
                                                                 stock.]

• The Transaction •
(Target Co. merges into NewCo.)

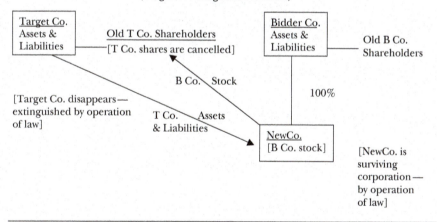

Target Co.   Bidder Co.
Assets &   Old T Co. Shareholders   Assets &   Old B Co.
Liabilities   [T Co. shares are cancelled]   Liabilities   Shareholders

                            B Co. Stock
                                                                    100%
[Target Co. disappears—
extinguished by operation   T Co. Assets
of law]   & Liabilities
                                                 NewCo.
                                                 [B Co. stock]   [NewCo. is
                                                                 surviving
                                                                 corporation—
                                                                 by operation
                                                                 of law]

• AFTER Transaction is Completed •

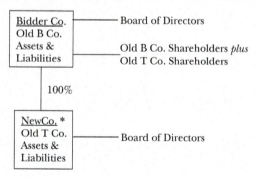

                  Bidder Co.   ——— Board of Directors
                  Old B Co.
                  Assets &   ——— Old B Co. Shareholders *plus*
                  Liabilities   Old T Co. Shareholders

                            100%

                  NewCo. *
                  Old T Co.   ——— Board of Directors
                  Assets &
                  Liabilities

*NewCo. may undertake the transaction costs associated with changing name to "Target Co.".

DIAGRAM 9
Forward Triangular Merger
(Using *Cash* as Merger Consideration)

• BEFORE Transaction •

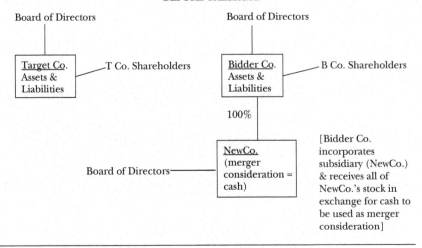

• The Transaction •
(Target Co. merges into NewCo.)

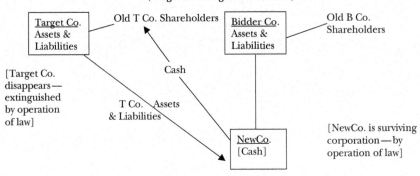

• AFTER Transaction Is Consummated •

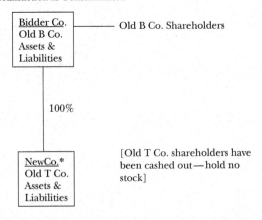

*NewCo. may undertake the transaction costs associated with changing name to "Target Co.".

DIAGRAM 10
Reverse Triangular Merger
(Using *Stock* as Merger Consideration)

• **BEFORE Transaction** •

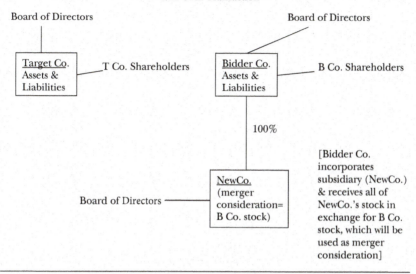

Board of Directors

Board of Directors

| Target Co. |
| Assets & |
| Liabilities |

— T Co. Shareholders

| Bidder Co. |
| Assets & |
| Liabilities |

— B Co. Shareholders

100%

| NewCo. |
| (merger |
| consideration= |
| B Co. stock) |

Board of Directors ————

[Bidder Co. incorporates subsidiary (NewCo.) & receives all of NewCo.'s stock in exchange for B Co. stock, which will be used as merger consideration]

• **In the Transaction** •
(NewCo. merges into Target Co.)

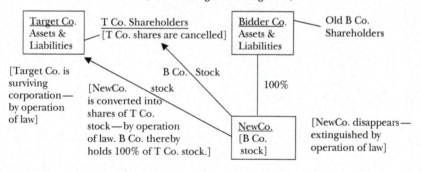

| Target Co. |
| Assets & |
| Liabilities |

T Co. Shareholders
[T Co. shares are cancelled]

| Bidder Co. |
| Assets & |
| Liabilities |

— Old B Co. Shareholders

[Target Co. is surviving corporation— by operation of law]

B Co. Stock

[NewCo. stock is converted into shares of T Co. stock—by operation of law. B Co. thereby holds 100% of T Co. stock.]

100%

| NewCo. |
| [B Co. |
| stock] |

[NewCo. disappears— extinguished by operation of law]

• **AFTER the Transaction** •

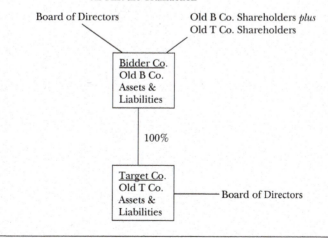

Board of Directors

Old B Co. Shareholders *plus*
Old T Co. Shareholders

| Bidder Co. |
| Old B Co. |
| Assets & |
| Liabilities |

100%

| Target Co. |
| Old T Co. |
| Assets & |
| Liabilities |

———— Board of Directors

DIAGRAM 11
Reverse Triangular Merger
(Using *Cash* as Merger Consideration)

• **BEFORE Transaction** •

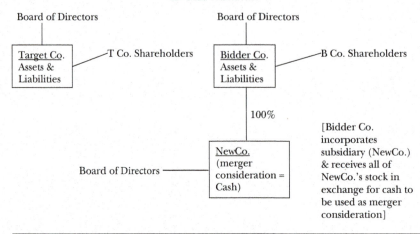

Board of Directors

Target Co.
Assets &
Liabilities
——T Co. Shareholders

Board of Directors

Bidder Co.
Assets &
Liabilities
——B Co. Shareholders

100%

NewCo.
(merger
consideration =
Cash)

Board of Directors ————

[Bidder Co.
incorporates
subsidiary (NewCo.)
& receives all of
NewCo.'s stock in
exchange for cash to
be used as merger
consideration]

• **In the Transaction** •
(NewCo. merges into Target Co.)

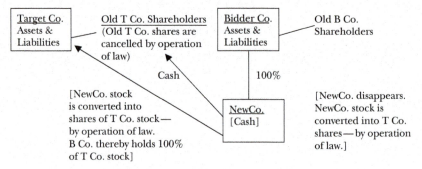

Target Co.
Assets &
Liabilities

Old T Co. Shareholders
(Old T Co. shares are
cancelled by operation
of law)

Bidder Co.
Assets &
Liabilities

Old B Co.
Shareholders

Cash

100%

NewCo.
[Cash]

[NewCo. stock
is converted into
shares of T Co. stock—
by operation of law.
B Co. thereby holds 100%
of T Co. stock]

[NewCo. disappears.
NewCo. stock is
converted into T Co.
shares—by operation
of law.]

• **AFTER the Transaction** •

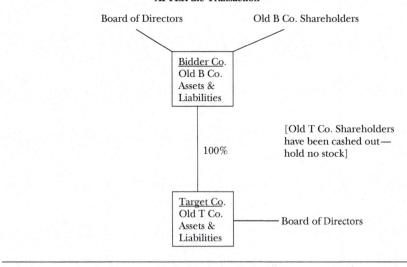

Board of Directors

Old B Co. Shareholders

Bidder Co.
Old B Co.
Assets &
Liabilities

100%

[Old T Co. Shareholders
have been cashed out—
hold no stock]

Target Co.
Old T Co.
Assets &
Liabilities
——— Board of Directors

DIAGRAM 12
TWO STEP TRANSACTION:
Stock Purchase, Followed by Squeeze Out/Cash Out Merger
(Using *Either* a Reverse *or* a Forward Triangular Merger)

STEP ONE: Stock Purchase
• BEFORE Stock Purchase •

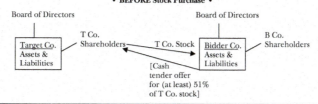

• AFTER Stock Purchase •

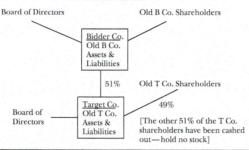

STEP TWO: Squeeze Out (Cash Out) Merger
(Using *Reverse* Triangular Merger)
• BEFORE Transaction •

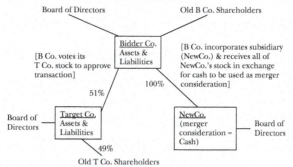

• In the Transaction •

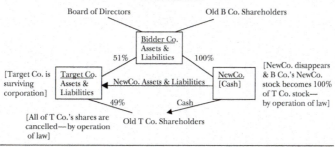

(continued)

DIAGRAM 12
Continued

• AFTER the Squeeze Out Merger •
(Using *Reverse* Triangular Merger)

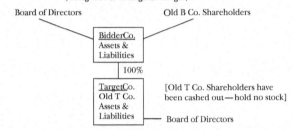

Board of Directors   Old B Co. Shareholders

BidderCo.
Assets &
Liabilities

100%

TargetCo.
Old T Co.
Assets &
Liabilities

[Old T Co. Shareholders have
been cashed out—hold no stock]

Board of Directors

ALTERNATIVE SECOND STEP: Squeeze Out (Cash Out) Merger
(Using *Forward* Triangular Merger)
• BEFORE the Transaction •

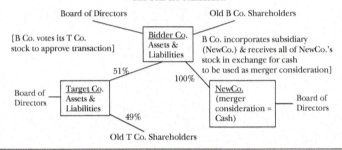

Board of Directors   Old B Co. Shareholders

[B Co. votes its T Co.
stock to approve transaction]

Bidder Co.
Assets &
Liabilities

B Co. incorporates subsidiary
(NewCo.) & receives all of NewCo.'s
stock in exchange for cash
to be used as merger consideration]

51%   100%

Board of
Directors

Target Co.
Assets &
Liabilities

NewCo.
(merger
consideration =
Cash)

Board of
Directors

49%

Old T Co. Shareholders

• In the Transaction •

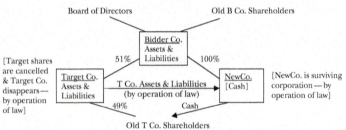

Board of Directors   Old B Co. Shareholders

Bidder Co.
Assets &
Liabilities

[Target shares
are cancelled
& Target Co.
disappears—
by operation
of law]

51%   100%

Target Co.
Assets &
Liabilities

T Co. Assets & Liabilities
(by operation of law)

NewCo.
[Cash]

[NewCo. is surviving
corporation—by
operation of law]

49%   Cash

Old T Co. Shareholders

• AFTER the Squeeze Out Merger •
(Using *Forward* Triangular Merger)

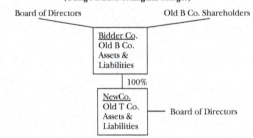

Board of Directors   Old B Co. Shareholders

Bidder Co.
Old B Co.
Assets &
Liabilities

100%

NewCo.
Old T Co.
Assets &
Liabilities

Board of Directors

[Old T Co. Shareholders have been cashed out—hold no stock]

AT&T–DirecTV Merger Agreement

AGREEMENT AND PLAN OF MERGER

among

DIRECTV,
AT&T INC.

and

STEAM MERGER INC.
Dated as of May 18, 2014

NOTE: This Merger Agreement has been revised for teaching purposes. As originally proposed, the deal between AT&T and DirecTV was structured as a forward triangular merger, using a wholly-owned Delaware LLC as the acquisition subsidiary, which was formed for the sole purpose of completing the proposed acquisition transaction. At closing, the LLC, named "Steam Merger Sub LLC" in the original agreement, was to be renamed "DirecTV." I modified the agreement to refer to the acquisition subsidiary as a wholly-owned Delaware corporation (named Steam Merger Sub, Inc.) of the parent, AT&T, and changed the deal structure to a reverse triangular merger, leaving DirecTV as a wholly-owned subsidiary of AT&T at closing.

TABLE OF CONTENTS

ARTICLE VII
CONDITIONS

ARTICLE VIII
TERMINATION

ARTICLE IX
MISCELLANEOUS AND GENERAL

EXHIBIT
EXHIBIT A—EMPLOYEE MATTERS AGREEMENT

INDEX OF DEFINED TERMS
[omitted]

AGREEMENT AND PLAN OF MERGER

AGREEMENT AND PLAN OF MERGER (hereinafter referred to as this "Agreement"), dated as of May 18, 2014, among DIRECTV, a Delaware corporation (the "Company"), AT&T Inc., a Delaware corporation ("Parent"), and Steam Merger Sub, Inc. a Delaware corporation and a wholly owned Subsidiary of Parent ("Merger Sub").

RECITALS

WHEREAS, the Board of Directors of the Company, by resolutions duly adopted, has approved the merger of the Company with Merger Sub (the "Merger") in which the Company will be the surviving entity, upon the terms and subject to the conditions set forth in this Agreement and adopted, approved and declared advisable this Agreement, and has resolved to recommend to its stockholders the adoption of this Agreement;

WHEREAS, the Board of Directors of Parent, by resolutions duly adopted, has approved the Merger and the issuance of shares of common stock, par value $1.00 per share, of Parent (the "Parent Common Stock") pursuant to the Merger upon the terms and subject to the conditions set forth in this Agreement and adopted and approved this Agreement;

WHEREAS, the Board of Directors of Merger Sub, by resolutions duly adopted, has determined it is advisable and in the best interest of Merger Sub to enter into the Merger Agreement;

WHEREAS, for U.S. federal income tax purposes, the parties hereto intend that the Merger shall qualify as a reorganization within the meaning of the Internal Revenue Code of 1986, as amended (the "Code"), and the regulations promulgated thereunder and intend for this Agreement to constitute a "plan of reorganization" within the meaning of the Code; and

WHEREAS, the Company, Parent and Merger Sub desire to make certain representations, warranties, covenants and agreements in connection with this Agreement.

NOW, THEREFORE, in consideration of the premises, and of the representations, warranties, covenants and agreements contained herein, the parties hereto agree as follows:

ARTICLE I
THE MERGER; CLOSING; EFFECTIVE TIME

1.1 The Merger. Upon the terms and subject to the conditions set forth in this Agreement, at the Effective Time, Merger Sub shall be merged with and into the Company. The Company shall be the surviving company in the Merger (sometimes hereinafter referred to as the "Surviving Company"), and the separate corporate existence of Merger Sub shall cease. The Merger shall have the effects specified in the Delaware General Corporation Law, as amended (the "DGCL").

1.2   <u>Closing</u>.   The closing of the Merger (the "Closing") shall take place (a) at the offices of Sullivan & Cromwell LLP, 125 Broad Street, New York, New York 10004 at 9:00 a.m. local time on the first business day following the day on which the last to be satisfied or waived of the conditions set forth in ARTICLE VII (other than those conditions that by their nature are to be satisfied at the Closing, but subject to the satisfaction or waiver of those conditions) shall have been satisfied or waived in accordance with this Agreement, or (b) at such other place and time and/or on such other date as the Company and Parent may otherwise agree in writing (the date on which the Closing occurs, the "Closing Date"). For purposes of this Agreement, the term "business day" shall mean any day other than a Saturday or Sunday or a day on which banks are required or authorized to close in the City of New York.

1.3   <u>Effective Time</u>.   Immediately following the Closing, the Company and Parent will cause a Certificate of Merger with respect to the Merger (the "Delaware Certificate of Merger") to be executed, acknowledged and filed with the Secretary of State of the State of Delaware as provided in the DGCL. The Merger shall become effective at the time when the Delaware Certificate of Merger has been duly filed with the Secretary of State of the State of Delaware or at such later time as may be agreed upon by the parties hereto in writing and set forth in the Delaware Certificate of Merger in accordance with the DGCL (the "Effective Time").

ARTICLE II
ORGANIZATIONAL DOCUMENTS OF THE SURVIVING COMPANY

2.1   <u>The Certificate of Incorporation</u>.   The certificate of incorporation of the Company, as in effect immediately prior to the Effective Time, shall be the certificate of incorporation of the Surviving Company until thereafter changed or amended as provided therein or by applicable law.

2.2   <u>Effects of the Merger</u>.   At the Effective Time, all the property, rights, privileges power and franchises of the Company and Merger Sub shall be vested in the Surviving Company, and all debts, liabilities and duties of the Company and Merger Sub shall become the debts, liabilities and duties of the Surviving Company.

ARTICLE III
OFFICERS AND DIRECTORS

3.1   <u>Officers and Directors</u>.   From and after the Effective Time, until successors are duly elected or appointed and qualified in accordance with applicable law, (i) the directors of Merger Sub at the Effective Time shall be the directors of the Surviving Company and (ii) the officers of the Company at the Effective Time shall be the officers of the Surviving Company.

ARTICLE IV
EFFECT OF THE MERGER ON CAPITAL STOCK;
EXCHANGE

4.1. <u>Effect on Capital Stock</u>. At the Effective Time, as a result of the Merger and without any action on the part of the holder of any capital stock of the Company:

(a) <u>Merger Consideration</u>. Each share of Common Stock, par value $0.01 per share, of the Company (the "<u>Common Stock,</u>" and each a "<u>Share</u>" and collectively, the "<u>Shares</u>") issued and outstanding immediately prior to the Effective Time (other than (i) Shares owned by Parent or the Company, not held on behalf of third parties and (ii) Shares that are owned by stockholders ("<u>Dissenting Stockholders</u>") who have perfected and not withdrawn a demand for appraisal rights pursuant to Section 262 of the DGCL (each such Share referred to in clauses (i) and (ii) above, an "<u>Excluded Share</u>" and, collectively, "<u>Excluded Shares</u>")) shall be converted into the right to receive, and become exchangeable for a number of validly issued, fully paid and non-assessable shares of Parent Common Stock equal to the Exchange Ratio (the "<u>Stock Consideration</u>") *plus*$28.50 in cash (the "<u>Cash Consideration</u>" and, together with the Stock Consideration, the "<u>Merger Consideration</u>"). At the Effective Time, all the Shares (other than the Excluded Shares) shall cease to be outstanding, shall be cancelled and shall cease to exist, and (A) each certificate (a "<u>Certificate</u>") formerly representing any of the Shares (other than Excluded Shares) and (B) each uncertificated Share (an "<u>Uncertificated Share</u>") registered to a holder on the stock transfer books of the Company (other than Excluded Shares) shall thereafter represent only the right to receive the Merger Consideration, and the right, if any, to receive pursuant to Section 4.2(e) cash in lieu of fractional shares into which such Shares have been converted pursuant to this Section 4.1(a) and any distribution or dividend pursuant to Section 4.2(c), and each certificate formerly representing Shares owned by Dissenting Stockholders shall thereafter represent only the right to receive the payment of which reference is made in Section 4.3.

For purposes of this Agreement, "<u>Exchange Ratio</u>" shall mean the following (in each case rounded to three decimal places):

A) If the Average Parent Stock Price is an amount greater than $38.577, then the Exchange Ratio shall be 1.724;

B) If the Average Parent Stock Price is an amount greater than or equal to $34.903 but less than or equal to $38.577 then the Exchange Ratio shall be an amount equal to the quotient obtained by <u>dividing</u> (x) $66.50 by (y) the Average Parent Stock Price; or

C) If the Average Parent Stock Price is an amount less than $34.903, then the Exchange Ratio shall be 1.905.

For purposes of this Agreement, "<u>Average Parent Stock Price</u>" shall mean the average of the volume weighted averages of the trading prices of Parent Common Stock on the New York Stock Exchange (the "<u>NYSE</u>") (as reported by Bloomberg L.P. or, if not reported therein, in another authoritative source mutually selected by the parties) on each of the thirty consecutive Trading Days ending on (and including) the Trading Day that is three Trading Days prior to the date of the Effective Time.

For purposes of this Agreement, "<u>Trading Day</u>" shall mean a day on which shares of Parent Common Stock are traded on the NYSE.

(b) <u>Cancellation of Excluded Shares</u>. Subject to Section 4.3, each Excluded Share shall, by virtue of the Merger and without any action on the part of the holder thereof, cease to be outstanding, shall be cancelled and retired without payment of any consideration therefor and shall cease to exist.

(c) <u>Merger Sub</u>.   At the effective time, by virtue of the Merger and without any action on the part of the holder thereof, each share of common stock, par value $0.01 per share, of Merger Sub issued and outstanding immediately prior to the Effective Time shall be converted into one validly issued, fully paid and non-assessable share of common stock, par value $0.01 per share, of the Surviving Company in the Merger.

4.2   <u>Exchange of Certificates</u>.

(a) <u>Exchange Agent</u>.   At the Effective Time, Parent shall deposit, or cause to be deposited, with an exchange agent selected by Parent with the Company's prior approval, which shall not be unreasonably withheld or delayed (the "<u>Exchange Agent</u>"), for the benefit of the holders of Shares, (i) an aggregate number of shares of Parent Common Stock to be issued in uncertificated form or book-entry form and (ii) an aggregate amount of cash, in each case, comprising approximately the amounts required to be delivered pursuant to Section 4.1(a) in respect of Shares. In addition, Parent shall deposit, or cause to be deposited, with the Exchange Agent, as necessary from time to time after the Effective Time, any dividends or other distributions payable pursuant to Section 4.2(c) with respect to the Parent Common Stock with respect to Shares with a record and payment date after the Effective Time and prior to the surrender of such Shares and cash in lieu of any fractional shares payable pursuant to Section 4.2(e). All shares of Parent Common Stock and cash, together with the amount of any such cash dividends and distributions deposited with the Exchange Agent pursuant to this Section 4.2(a), shall hereinafter be referred to as the "<u>Exchange Fund</u>". The Exchange Agent shall invest the cash portion of the Exchange Fund as directed by Parent; . . .

(b) <u>Exchange Procedures</u>.   Promptly after the Effective Time (and in any event within four business days thereafter), Parent shall cause the Exchange Agent to mail to each holder of record of Shares (other than Excluded Shares) entitled to receive the Merger Consideration pursuant to Section 4.1(a)(A) a letter of transmittal in customary form advising such holder of the effectiveness of the Merger and the conversion of its Shares into the right to receive the Merger Consideration, and specifying that delivery shall be effected, and risk of loss and title to the Certificates shall pass, only upon delivery of the Certificates (or affidavits of loss in lieu of the Certificates as provided in Section 4.2(g)) to the Exchange Agent, and instructions for use in effecting the surrender of the Certificates (or affidavits of loss in lieu of the Certificates as provided in Section 4.2(g)) in exchange for the Merger Consideration to the Exchange Agent. Upon the surrender of a Certificate (or affidavit of loss in lieu thereof as provided in Section 4.2(g)) to the Exchange Agent in accordance with the terms of such transmittal materials, the holder of such Certificate shall be entitled to receive in exchange therefor (i) that number of whole shares of Parent Common Stock that such holder is entitled to receive pursuant to this ARTICLE IV in uncertificated form (or evidence of shares in book-entry form), and (ii) an amount in immediately available funds (or, if no wire transfer instructions are provided, a check, and in each case, after giving effect to any required Tax withholding provided in Section 4.2(h)) equal to (A) the cash amount that such holder is entitled to receive pursuant to Section 4.1(a) plus (B) any cash in lieu of fractional shares pursuant to Section 4.2(e) plus (C) any unpaid non-stock dividends and any other dividends or other distributions that such holder has the right to receive pursuant to Section 4.2(c), and the Certificate so surrendered shall forthwith be cancelled. No interest will be paid or accrued on any amount payable upon due surrender of the Certificates . . .

(c) <u>Distributions with Respect to Unexchanged Shares; . . .</u>   (i) All shares of Parent Common Stock to be issued pursuant to the Merger shall be deemed issued and outstanding as of the Effective Time and whenever a dividend or other distribution is declared by Parent in respect of the Parent Common Stock, the record date for which is after the Effective Time, that declaration shall include dividends or other distributions in respect of all shares issuable in the Merger . . .

(d) <u>Transfers.</u>   From and after the Effective Time, there shall be no transfers on the stock transfer books of the Company of the Shares that were outstanding immediately prior to the Effective Time.

(e) <u>Fractional Shares.</u> Notwithstanding any other provision of this Agreement, no fractional shares of Parent Common Stock will be issued and any holder of Shares entitled to receive a fractional share of Parent Common Stock but for this Section 4.2(e) shall be entitled to receive a cash payment in lieu thereof, which payment shall be calculated by the Exchange Agent and shall represent such holder's proportionate interest in a share of Parent Common Stock based on the Average Parent Stock Price.

(f) <u>Termination of Exchange Fund.</u> Any portion of the Exchange Fund (including the proceeds of any investments of the Exchange Fund and any Parent Common Stock) that remains unclaimed by the stockholders of the Company for 180 days after the Effective Time shall be delivered, at Parent's option, to Parent. Any holder of Shares (other than Excluded Shares) who has not theretofore complied with this ARTICLE IV shall thereafter look only to Parent for delivery of any shares of Parent Common Stock of such stockholder and payment of cash and any dividends and other distributions in respect of the Parent Common Stock to be issued or paid pursuant to the provisions of this ARTICLE IV (after giving effect to any required Tax withholdings as provided in Section 4.2(h)) upon due surrender of its Certificates (or affidavits of loss in lieu of the Certificates as provided in Section 4.2(g)), without any interest thereon. Notwithstanding the foregoing, none of the Surviving Company, Parent, the Exchange Agent or any other Person shall be liable to any former holder of Shares for any amount properly delivered to a public official pursuant to applicable abandoned property, escheat or similar Laws.

(g) <u>Lost, Stolen or Destroyed Certificates.</u>   In the event any Certificate shall have been lost, stolen or destroyed, upon the making of an affidavit of that fact by the Person claiming such Certificate to be lost, stolen or destroyed and, if required by Parent, the posting by such Person of a bond in customary amount and upon such terms as may be required by Parent as indemnity against any claim that may be made against it, the Exchange Agent or the Surviving Company with respect to such Certificate, the Exchange Agent will issue in exchange for such lost, stolen or destroyed Certificate the shares of Parent Common Stock and the cash and any dividends and other distributions in respect of the Parent Common Stock that would have been issuable or payable pursuant to the provisions of this ARTICLE IV (after giving effect to any required Tax withholdings as provided in Section 4.2(h)) had such lost, stolen or destroyed Certificate been surrendered.

(h) Withholding Rights.   Each of Parent and the Surviving Company shall be entitled to deduct and withhold from the consideration otherwise payable pursuant to this Agreement to any holder of Shares such amounts as it is required to deduct and withhold with respect to the making of such payment under the Code or any other applicable state, local or foreign Tax Law . . .

(i) Uncertificated Shares.   Promptly after the Effective Time, Parent shall cause the Exchange Agent to (i) mail to each holder of Uncertificated Shares (other than Excluded Shares) materials advising such holder of the effectiveness of the Merger and the conversion of their Shares into the right to receive the Merger Consideration and (ii) issue in registered form to each holder of Uncertificated Shares that number of whole shares of Parent Common Stock that such holder is entitled to receive in respect of each such Uncertificated Share pursuant to this ARTICLE IV, cash that such holder is entitled to receive in respect of its Shares pursuant to Section 4.1(a), cash pursuant to Section 4.2(e) in lieu of fractional shares in respect of each such Uncertificated Share and any dividends and other distributions in respect of the Parent Common Stock to be issued or paid pursuant to the provisions of this ARTICLE IV (after giving effect to any required Tax withholdings as provided in Section 4.2(h)), without interest thereon.

4.3 Dissenters' Rights.   No Dissenting Stockholder shall be entitled to receive shares of Parent Common Stock or cash or any dividends or other distributions pursuant to the provisions of this ARTICLE IV unless and until the holder thereof shall have failed to perfect or shall have effectively withdrawn or lost such holder's right to dissent from the Merger under the DGCL, and any Dissenting Stockholder shall be entitled to receive only the payment provided by Section 262 of the DGCL with respect to Shares owned by such Dissenting Stockholder. If any Person who otherwise would be deemed a Dissenting Stockholder shall have failed to properly perfect or shall have effectively withdrawn or lost the right to dissent with respect to any Shares, such Shares shall thereupon be treated as though such Shares had been converted into the shares of Parent Common Stock plus the cash amount that such Person is entitled to receive pursuant to Section 4.1(a). The Company shall give Parent (i) prompt written notice of any written demands for appraisal, attempted withdrawals of such demands, and any other instruments served pursuant to applicable Law received by the Company relating to stockholders' rights of appraisal, and (ii) the opportunity to direct all negotiations and proceedings with respect to demands for appraisal. The Company shall not, except with the prior written consent of Parent, voluntarily make any payment with respect to any demands for appraisal, offer to settle or settle any such demands or approve any withdrawal of any such demands.

4.4 Adjustments to Prevent Dilution.   In the event that the Company changes the number of Shares or securities convertible or exchangeable into or exercisable for any such Shares, or Parent changes the number of shares of Parent Common Stock, in each case issued and outstanding prior to the Effective Time as a result of a distribution, reclassification, stock split (including a reverse stock split), stock dividend or distribution, recapitalization, subdivision, or other similar transaction, the Merger Consideration shall be equitably adjusted to eliminate the effects of such event on the Merger Consideration.

4.5   Company Stock Based Plans.   (a) At the Effective Time, each outstanding option to purchase Shares (a "Company Option") under the Company Stock Plans, whether vested or unvested, shall be converted into an option to acquire a number of shares of Parent Common Stock equal to the product (rounded down to the nearest whole number) of (i) the number of Shares subject to the Company Option immediately prior to the Effective Time and (ii) the Option Exchange Ratio, at an exercise price per share (rounded up to the nearest whole cent) equal to the result obtained by dividing (A) the exercise price per Share of such Company Option immediately prior to the Effective Time by (B) the Option Exchange Ratio; provided that the exercise price and the number of shares of Parent Common Stock purchasable pursuant to the Company Options shall be determined in a manner consistent with the requirements of Section 409A of the Code. The "Option Exchange Ratio" shall mean a fraction (x) the numerator of which is the sum of the Cash Consideration and an amount equal to the product of (I) the Exchange Ratio and (II) the Average Parent Stock Price and (y) the denominator of which is the Average Parent Stock Price. Except as specifically provided above, following the Effective Time, each Company Option shall continue to be governed by the terms and conditions applicable to such Company Option immediately prior to the Effective Time, including all vesting conditions . . .

(f)   As soon as practicable after the Effective Time, Parent shall, if registration of the shares of Parent Common Stock issuable under a Company Stock Plan or other Company Plan is required under the Securities Act of 1933, as amended (the "Securities Act"), file with the Securities and Exchange Commission (the "SEC") a registration statement on Form S-3 or Form S-8, as the case may be (or any successor form), or another appropriate form with respect to such Parent Common Stock and shall use commercially reasonable efforts to have such registration statement declared effective as soon as practicable following such filing.

(g)   At or prior to the Effective Time, the Company, the Board of Directors of the Company and the compensation committee of the Board of Directors of the Company, as applicable, shall adopt any resolutions and take any actions which are necessary to effectuate the provisions of this Section 4.5. Parent shall take all actions as are reasonably necessary for the assumption of the Company Stock Plans pursuant to this Section 4.5 . . .

ARTICLE V
REPRESENTATIONS AND WARRANTIES

5.1   Representations and Warranties of the Company.   Except as set forth in the corresponding sections or subsections of the disclosure letter delivered to Parent by the Company at the time of entering into this Agreement (the "Company Disclosure Letter") or, to the extent the qualifying nature of such disclosure with respect to a specific representation and warranty is reasonably apparent therefrom, as set forth in the Company Reports filed on or after January 1, 2014 and prior to the date of this Agreement (excluding all disclosures in any "Risk Factors" section and any disclosures included in any such Company Reports that are cautionary, predictive or forward looking in nature), the Company hereby represents and warrants to Parent and Merger Sub as of the date of this Agreement and as of the Closing that:

(a)   Organization, Good Standing and Qualification. Each of the Company and its Subsidiaries is a legal entity duly organized, validly existing and in good standing under the Laws of its respective jurisdiction of organization and has all requisite corporate or similar power and authority to own, lease and operate its properties and assets and to carry on its business as presently conducted and is qualified to do business and is in good standing as a foreign legal entity in each jurisdiction where the ownership, leasing or operation of its assets or properties or conduct of its business requires such qualification, except where the failure to be so organized, qualified or in good standing, or to have such power or authority, would not, individually or in the aggregate, reasonably be likely to have a Company Material Adverse Effect . . .

As used in this Agreement, . . . the term . . . (iv) "Company Material Adverse Effect" means (A) an effect that would prevent, materially delay or materially impair the ability of the Company to consummate the Merger, or (B) a material adverse effect on the financial condition, properties, assets, liabilities, business or results of operations of the Company and its Subsidiaries, taken as a whole, excluding any such effect resulting from or arising in connection with (1) changes in the financial or securities markets or general economic or political conditions in the U.S. or any foreign jurisdiction in which the Company or any of its Subsidiaries or the JV Entity operates, including any changes in currency exchange rates, interest rates, monetary policy or inflation, (2) any acts of war, sabotage, civil disobedience or terrorism or natural disasters (including hurricanes, tornadoes, floods or earthquakes), (3) any failure by the Company or any of its Subsidiaries to meet any internal or published budgets, projections, forecasts or predictions in respect of financial performance for any period, (4) a decline in the price of the Shares on the NASDAQ Stock Market, Inc. (the "NASDAQ"), provided that the exception clauses (3) and (4) shall not prevent or otherwise affect a determination that any change, effect, circumstance or development underlying such decline has resulted in, or contributed to, a Company Material Adverse Effect, (5) changes in Law, (6) changes in U.S. generally accepted accounting principles ("GAAP") (or authoritative interpretation of GAAP) or (7) the taking of any specific action expressly required by, or the failure to take any specific action expressly prohibited by, the Agreement; provided, however, that the changes, effects, circumstances or developments set forth in the foregoing clauses (1), (2), and (5) shall be taken into account in determining whether a "Company Material Adverse Effect" has occurred to the extent such changes, effects, circumstances or developments have a disproportionate adverse effect on the Company and its Subsidiaries, taken as a whole, relative to all other participants in the multi-channel video programming distribution industry, but, in such event, only the incremental disproportionate impact of such changes, effects, circumstances or developments shall be taken into account in determining whether a "Company Material Adverse Effect" has occurred, . . . and (vi) the term "Knowledge of the Company" means the actual knowledge of the individuals identified on Section 5.1(a)(iv) of the Company Disclosure Letter. The representations and warranties made in Section 5.1(a), 5.1(b)(iii)(B), 5.1(d), 5.1(f), 5.1(g), the first sentence of 5.1(k) and 5.1(o), shall to the extent made with respect to the Subsidiaries of the Company also be deemed made with respect to the JV Entity, but only to the Knowledge of the Company.

(b)   Capital Structure.   (i) The authorized capital stock of the Company consists of (A) 3,950,000,000 Shares and (B) 50,000,000 shares of preferred stock, par value $0.01 per share (the "Preferred Stock"). As of the close of business on May 16, 2014, 502,224,444 shares of the Common Stock were issued and outstanding and no other shares of the Common Stock or shares of the Preferred Stock were issued and outstanding on such date. All of the outstanding Shares have been duly authorized and validly issued and are fully paid and nonassessable. The Company has no Shares, shares of Preferred Stock or other shares of capital stock reserved for or subject to issuance, except that, as of the date of this Agreement, there are an aggregate of 48,529,270 Shares reserved for issuance upon exercise of Company Options under the Company Stock Plans . . .

(c)   Corporate Authority; Approval and Fairness.   The Company has all requisite corporate power and authority and has taken all corporate action necessary in order to execute, deliver and perform its obligations under this Agreement and to consummate the Merger, subject only to adoption of this Agreement by the holders of a majority of the outstanding Shares entitled to vote on such matter at a meeting duly called and held for such purpose (the "Company Requisite Vote"). This Agreement has been duly executed and delivered by the Company and constitutes a valid and binding agreement of the Company, enforceable against the Company in accordance with its terms, subject to bankruptcy, insolvency, fraudulent transfer, reorganization, moratorium and similar Laws of general applicability relating to or affecting creditors' rights and to general equity principles (the "Bankruptcy and Equity Exception"). As of the date of this Agreement and subject to Section 6.2, the Board of Directors of the Company has (i) (A) unanimously determined that the Merger is fair to, and in the best interests of, the Company and its stockholders, (B) approved the Merger and the other transactions contemplated hereby, (C) adopted, approved and declared advisable this Agreement, and (D) resolved to recommend the adoption of this Agreement to the holders of Shares (the "Company Recommendation"), (ii) received the opinions of its financial advisors, Goldman, Sachs & Co. and Merrill Lynch, Pierce, Fenner & Smith Incorporated, dated as of the date of this Agreement, to the effect that, based upon and subject to the various qualifications, assumptions and limitations set forth in such opinions, the Merger Consideration to be received by the holders of the Shares in the Merger is fair to such holders from a financial point of view, as of the date of such opinion, and (iii) directed that this Agreement be submitted to the holders of Shares for their adoption. The Board of Directors of the Company has taken all action so that Parent will not be an "interested stockholder" or prohibited from entering into or consummating a "business combination" with the Company (in each case, as such term is used in Section 203 of the DGCL) as a result of the execution of this Agreement or the consummation of the transactions in the manner contemplated hereby.

(d) <u>Governmental Filings; No Violations</u>. (i) Other than the necessary filings, notices, reports, consents, registrations, approvals, permits, expirations of waiting periods or authorizations (A) pursuant to Section 1.3, (B) required under the HSR Act, or the foreign competition laws set forth on Section 5.1(d)(i)(B) of the Company Disclosure Letter (the "<u>Foreign Competition Laws</u>"), . . (C) to comply with state securities or "blue-sky" Laws, (D) with or to the Federal Communications Commission ("<u>FCC</u>") pursuant to the Communications Act of 1934, as amended (the "<u>Communications Act</u>"), or applicable rules and regulations promulgated thereunder (together with the Communications Act, the "<u>Communications Laws</u>"), (E) with or to the local and state public utility commissions or similar local and state regulatory bodies (each, a "<u>PUC</u>") and the local and state Governmental Entities and other entities identified in Section 5.1(d)(i)(E) of the Company Disclosure Letter pursuant to applicable local and state Laws regulating the telecommunications and satellite delivered video and audio businesses or services ("<u>Utilities Laws</u>") and (F) with or to the foreign and transnational regulatory bodies (each, a "<u>Foreign Regulator</u>"), . . . no filings, notices and/or reports are required to be made by the Company or its Subsidiaries with, nor are any consents, registrations, approvals, permits, expirations of waiting periods or authorizations required to be obtained by the Company or its Subsidiaries . . .

(ii) The execution, delivery and performance of this Agreement by the Company do not, and the consummation by the Company of the Merger and the other transactions contemplated hereby will not, constitute or result in (A) a breach or violation of, or a default under, the Company's Third Amended and Restated Certificate of Incorporation, effective as of August 27, 2012 (the "<u>Company Charter</u>") or Amended and Restated By-Laws, effective as of August 27, 2012 (the "<u>Company Bylaws</u>") or the comparable governing instruments of any of the Specified Subsidiaries, . . . For purposes of this agreement, Specified Subsidiaries shall mean DirecTV Holdings, LLC, DirecTV Financing Co., and any direct or indirect non-wholly owned subsidiary of the company.

(e) <u>Company Reports; Financial Statements</u>. (i) The Company has filed or furnished, as applicable, on a timely basis, all forms, statements, certifications, reports and documents required to be filed or furnished by it with or to the SEC pursuant to the Exchange Act or the Securities Act since December 31, 2012 (the "<u>Applicable Date</u>") (the forms, statements, reports and documents filed with or furnished to the SEC since the Applicable Date and those filed with or furnished to the SEC subsequent to the date of this Agreement, in each case as amended, the "<u>Company Reports</u>") . . . As of their respective dates (or, if amended prior to the date of this Agreement, as of the date of such amendment), the Company Reports did not, and any Company Reports filed with or furnished to the SEC subsequent to the date of this Agreement will not, contain any untrue statement of a material fact or omit to state a material fact required to be stated therein or necessary to make the statements made therein, in light of the circumstances in which they were made, not misleading.

(ii) The Company is in compliance in all material respects with the applicable listing and corporate governance rules and regulations of the NASDAQ . . .

(iii) The Company maintains disclosure controls and procedures required by Rule 13a-15 or 15d-15 under the Exchange Act . . .

(f) <u>Absence of Certain Changes</u>. Since December 31, 2013 and through the date of this Agreement, (i) there has not been any change, effect, circumstance or development which has had or would, individually or in the aggregate, reasonably be likely to have a Company Material Adverse Effect; (ii) the Company and its Subsidiaries have conducted their respective businesses in the ordinary course of such businesses consistent with past practice in all material respects; (iii) the Company and its Subsidiaries have not declared, set aside or paid any dividend or distribution payable in cash, stock or property in respect of any capital stock, . . . ; (iv) the Company and its Subsidiaries have not incurred any indebtedness for borrowed money or guaranteed such indebtedness of another Person, or issued or sold any debt securities or warrants or other rights to acquire any debt security of the Company or any of its Subsidiaries; (v) the Company and its Subsidiaries have not . . . disposed of any of the Company's or its Subsidiaries' property or assets . . . with fair market values in excess of $25,000,000 individually or $50,000,000 in the aggregate (other than with respect to sales of inventory in the ordinary course of business consistent with past practice); (vi) the Company and its Subsidiaries have not made any loan, advance or capital contribution to, or investment in, any Person (other than the Company or any direct or indirect wholly owned Subsidiary of the Company); (vii) the Company and its Subsidiaries have not acquired any business, whether by merger, consolidation, purchase of property or assets or otherwise; (viii) other than in the ordinary course of business and consistent with past practice, there has not been any increase in the compensation payable or to become payable to the Company's and its Subsidiaries' officers; and (ix) the Company and its Subsidiaries have not made any material change with respect to accounting policies or procedures.

(g) <u>Litigation and Liabilities</u>. There are no civil, criminal or administrative actions, suits, claims, hearings, arbitrations, investigations or other proceedings, pending or, to the Knowledge of the Company, threatened against the Company or any of its Subsidiaries, except for those that would not, individually or in the aggregate, reasonably be likely to have a Company Material Adverse Effect . . .

(h) <u>Employee Benefits</u> . . .

(i) <u>Labor Matters</u>. As of the date of this Agreement, neither the Company nor any of its Subsidiaries is a party to or otherwise bound by work rules or a collective bargaining agreement or other similar Contract with a labor union or labor organization, nor is the Company or any of its Subsidiaries the subject of any proceeding asserting that the Company or any of its Subsidiaries has committed an unfair labor practice or is seeking to compel the Company to bargain with any labor union or labor organization nor is there pending or, to the Knowledge of the Company, threatened, nor has there been since January 1, 2009 and prior to the date of this Agreement, any labor strike, walkout, work stoppage, slow-down or lockout involving the Company or any of its Subsidiaries . . .

(j) <u>Company Satellite Systems</u>. (i) Set forth on Section 5.1(j) of the Company Disclosure Letter is a true and complete list, as of the date of this Agreement, of each satellite (A) owned by the Company or any of its Subsidiaries, whether or not in orbit, (B) on which the Company or any of its Subsidiaries now leases or has the right to lease capacity or (C) in production which is or will be owned by the Company or any of its Subsidiaries or with respect to which the Company or any of its Subsidiaries has or will have a right to use any capacity (each, a "<u>Company Satellite</u>"), listing each Company Satellite by its owner, current and any other authorized orbital location, and, if the Company Satellite is in production, the anticipated launch date and expected lifetime . . .

(k)   <u>Compliance with Laws, Licenses</u>.   (i) The businesses of each of the Company and its Subsidiaries since January 1, 2010 have not been, and are not being, conducted in violation of any applicable federal, state, local, foreign or transnational law, statute or ordinance, common law, or any rule, regulation, standard, judgment, determination, order, writ, decree, injunction, arbitration award, license, authorization, agency requirement, treaty or permit of any Governmental Entity (collectively, "<u>Laws</u>"), except for such violations that would not, individually or in the aggregate, reasonably be likely to have a Company Material Adverse Effect. To the Knowledge of the Company, no investigation or review by any Governmental Entity with respect to the Company or any of its Subsidiaries is pending or, as of the date of this Agreement, threatened, nor has any Governmental Entity indicated an intention to conduct the same, except for such investigations or reviews the outcome of which would not, individually or in the aggregate, reasonably be likely to have a Company Material Adverse Effect. Except as would not reasonably be likely to have, individually or in the aggregate, a Company Material Adverse Effect, the Company and its Subsidiaries possess each permit, license, certification, approval, registration, consent, authorization, franchise, concession, variance, exemption and order issued or granted by a Governmental Entity (collectively, "<u>Licenses</u>") necessary to conduct their respective businesses . . .

(iv)   (A) The Company, its Subsidiaries and, to the Knowledge of the Company, their respective owners, officers, directors, employees and agents are in compliance with and since January 1, 2010 have complied in all material respects with: (A) the provisions of the U.S. Foreign Corrupt Practices Act of 1977, as amended (15 U.S.C. § 78dd-1, et seq.) ("<u>FCPA</u>"), as if its foreign payments provisions were fully applicable to the Company, its Subsidiaries and such owners, officers, directors, employees, and agents, and (B) the provisions of all anti-bribery, anti-corruption and anti-money laundering laws of each jurisdiction in which the Company and its Subsidiaries operate or have operated and in which any agent thereof is conducting or has conducted business involving the Company . . .

(l)   <u>Certain Contracts</u>.

(i)   Section 5.1(l) of the Company Disclosure Letter sets forth a list as of the date of this Agreement of each Contract to which either the Company or any of its Subsidiaries is a party or bound which (A) provides that any of them (or, after the Effective Time, Parent or its Affiliates) will not compete with any other Person, or which grant "most favored nation" status that, after the Effective Time, would restrict Parent or its Affiliates, (B) purports to limit in any material respect either the type of business in which the Company or its Affiliates (or, after the Effective Time, Parent or its Affiliates) may engage or the manner or locations in which any of them may so engage in any business or could reasonably be expected to require the disposition of any material assets or line of business of the Company or its Affiliates (or, after the Effective Time, individually or in the aggregate, any material assets or line of business of Parent or its Affiliates), (C) requires the Company or its Affiliates (or, after the Effective Time, Parent or its Affiliates) to deal exclusively with any Person or group of related Persons, (D) grants the Company or any of its Subsidiaries rights to any programming content or products, including retransmission consent agreements with broadcast television stations, content agreements with cable networks, video programming networks, motion picture studios and other rights holders or other agreements to secure programming content, in each case, which represented more than $1 billion of the Company's and its Subsidiaries' aggregate programming costs in fiscal year 2013, (E) provides for the construction, purchase, sale, launch, operation or maintenance of satellites, (F) provides for the lease, sale or purchase of transponders located upon satellites, (G) provides for the acquisition of residential set-top box equipment or conditional access technology, (H) is required to be filed by the Company as a "material contract" pursuant to Item 601(b)(10) of Regulation S-K under the Securities Act, (I) contains a put, call or similar right pursuant to which the Company or any of its Subsidiaries would be required to purchase or sell, as applicable, any equity interests of any Person or assets at a purchase price which would reasonably be expected to exceed, or the fair market value of the equity interests or assets of which would be reasonably likely to exceed, $10 million, or (J) was entered into with Affiliates of the Company or any of its Subsidiaries (other than the Company and its Subsidiaries) that is not a Company Plan and was entered into other than on arms'-length terms (such Contracts required to be listed pursuant to clauses (A)-(J) above, the "Material Contracts"). A true and complete copy of each Material Contract, as amended as of the date of this Agreement, including all attachments, schedules and exhibits thereto, has been made available to Parent prior to the date of this Agreement. Each of the Material Contracts, and each Contract entered into after the date hereof that would have been a Material Contract if entered into prior to the date hereof ("Additional Contract") is (or if entered into after the date hereof, will be) valid and binding on the Company or its Subsidiaries, as the case may be and, to the Knowledge of the Company, each other party thereto, and is in full force and effect, except for such failures to be valid and binding or to be in full force and effect as would not, individually or in the aggregate, reasonably be likely to have a Company Material Adverse Effect. Neither the Company nor any of its Subsidiaries nor, to the Knowledge of the Company, any other party is in breach of or in default under any Material Contract or Additional Contract, and no event has occurred that, with the lapse of time or the giving of notice or both, would constitute a default thereunder by the Company or any of its Subsidiaries, in each case, except for such breaches and defaults as are not, individually or in the aggregate, reasonably likely to have a Company Material Adverse Effect. The Company is not a party to or bound by any Contracts other than this Agreement.

(ii) The execution, delivery and performance of this Agreement by the Company do not, and the consummation by the Company of the Merger and the other transactions contemplated hereby will not, constitute or result in with or without the lapse of time or the giving of notice or both, a breach or violation of, a default or termination or modification (or right of termination or modification) under, payment of additional fees under, the creation or acceleration of any obligations under, or the creation of a Lien on any of the assets of the Company or any of its Subsidiaries pursuant to, a Contract that the Company is party to or bound by, except for any such breach, violation, default, termination, modification, payment, acceleration or creation that would not, individually or in the aggregate, be material to the Company and its Subsidiaries, taken as a whole.

(m)   Takeover Statutes.   Except for Section 203 of the DGCL, in respect of which the Board of Directors of the Company has taken the action described in Section 5.1(c), no "fair price", "moratorium", "control share acquisition" or other similar anti-takeover statute or regulation (each, a "Takeover Statute") or any anti-takeover provision in the Company Charter or Company Bylaws is applicable to the Company, the Common Stock, the Merger or the other trans-actions contemplated by this Agreement.

(n)   Environmental Matters . . .

(o)   Taxes . . .

(p)   Intellectual Property.   (i) Section 5.1(p)(i) of the Company Disclosure Letter sets forth, as of the date of this Agreement, a true and com-plete list of all material registered Intellectual Property ("Registered IP") and material unregistered Trademarks owned by the Company or its Subsidiaries, indicating for each registered item the registration or application number, the record owner, the date filed or issued and the applicable filing jurisdiction . . .

(q)   Insurance . . .

(r)   Brokers and Finders.   The Company has not employed any broker or finder or incurred any liability for any brokerage fees, commissions or find-ers' fees in connection with the Merger or the other transactions contemplated in this Agreement, except that the Company has employed Goldman, Sachs & Co. and Merrill Lynch, Pierce, Fenner & Smith Incorporated as the Company's financial advisors, the financial arrangements with which have been disclosed in writing to Parent prior to the date of this Agreement.

(s)   No Other Representations and Warranties.   Except for the repre-sentations and warranties of the Company contained in this Section 5.1, the Company is not making and has not made, and no other Person is making or has made on behalf of the Company, any express or implied representation or warranty in connection with this Agreement or the transactions contemplated hereby.

5.2   Representations and Warranties of Parent and Merger Sub.   Except as set forth in the corresponding sections or subsections of the disclosure letter delivered to the Company by Parent at the time of entering into this Agreement (the "Parent Disclosure Letter") or, to the extent the qualifying nature of such disclosure with respect to a specific representation and warranty is reasonably apparent therefrom, as set forth in all forms, statements, certifications, reports and documents filed or furnished by Parent with or to the SEC pursuant to the Exchange Act or the Securities Act on or after January 1, 2014 and prior to the date of this Agreement (excluding all disclosures in any "Risk Factors" sec-tion and any disclosures included in any such forms, statements, certifications, reports and documents that are cautionary, predictive or forward looking in nature), Parent and Merger Sub hereby represent and warrant to the Company as of the date of this Agreement and as of the Closing that:

(a) <u>Organization, Good Standing and Qualification</u>. Each of Parent and Merger Sub is a legal entity duly organized, validly existing and in good standing under the Laws of its respective jurisdiction of organization and has all requisite corporate power and authority to own, lease and operate its properties and assets and to carry on its business as presently conducted and is qualified to do business and is in good standing as a foreign legal entity in each jurisdiction where the ownership, leasing or operation of its assets or properties or conduct of its business requires such qualification, except where the failure to be so organized, qualified or in good standing, or to have such power or authority, would not, individually or in the aggregate, reasonably be likely to have a Parent Material Adverse Effect. Prior to the date of this Agreement, Parent has made available to the Company complete and correct copies of the certificates of incorporation and bylaws of Parent and the certificate of incorporation and bylaws of Merger Sub, in each case as amended to and in effect on the date of this Agreement . . .

(b) <u>Capital Structure</u>. (i) As of the date of this Agreement, the authorized capital stock of Parent consists of (A) 14,000,000,000 shares of Parent Common Stock, of which 5,190,509,146 shares of Parent Common Stock were issued and outstanding as of the close of business on May 15, 2014, and (B) 10,000,000 shares of preferred stock, par value $1.00 per share (the "<u>Parent Preferred Stock</u>"), of which no shares of Parent Preferred Stock are issued and outstanding as of the date of this Agreement and no other shares of Parent Common Stock or shares of Parent Preferred Stock were issued and outstanding on such date. All of the outstanding shares of Parent Common Stock and Parent Preferred Stock have been duly authorized and validly issued and are fully paid and nonassessable. Section 5.2(b)(i) of the Parent Disclosure Letter contains a correct and complete list as of May 15, 2014 of (x) the outstanding number of options to purchase Parent Common Stock (each, a "<u>Parent Option</u>") pursuant to certain of Parent's compensation and benefit plans (such compensation and benefit plans, the "<u>Parent Stock Plans</u>") and (y) the outstanding number of rights to receive Parent Common Stock (pursuant to deferred shares, performance shares and restricted stock units) under the Parent Stock Plans (each a "<u>Parent Common Stock Unit</u>"). From May 15, 2014 to the execution of this Agreement, Parent has not issued any Parent Common Stock except pursuant to the exercise of Parent Options and the settlement of Parent Common Stock Units outstanding on May 15, 2014 in accordance with their terms and, since May 15, 2014 to the execution of this Agreement, Parent has not issued any Parent Options or Parent Common Stock Units. As of the date of this Agreement, there are no preemptive or other outstanding rights, options, warrants, conversion rights, stock appreciation rights, redemption rights, repurchase rights, agreements, arrangements, calls, commitments or rights of any kind that obligate Parent or any of its Subsidiaries to issue or sell any shares of capital stock or other equity securities of Parent or any securities or obligations convertible or exchangeable into or exercisable for, or giving any Person a right to subscribe for or acquire from Parent or any of its Subsidiaries, any equity securities of Parent, and no securities or obligations of Parent or any of its Subsidiaries evidencing such rights are authorized, issued or outstanding. Parent does not have outstanding any bonds, debentures, notes or other obligations the holders of which have the right to vote (or convertible into or exercisable for securities having the right to vote) with the stockholders of Parent on any matter.

(ii)   The authorized capital stock of Merger Sub consists of 1,000 shares of common stock, par value $0.01 per share, all of which are validly issued and outstanding. All of the issued and outstanding capital stock of Merger Sub is, and at the Effective Time will be, owned by Parent, and there are (A) no other shares of capital stock or other voting securities of Merger Sub, (B) no securities of Merger Sub convertible into or exchangeable for shares of capital stock or other voting securities of Merger Sub and (C) no options or other rights to acquire from Merger Sub, and no obligations of Merger Sub to issue, any capital stock voting securities or securities convertible into or exchangeable for capital stock or other voting securities of Merger Sub. Merger Sub has not conducted any business prior to the date of this Agreement and has no, and prior to the Effective Time will have no, assets, liabilities or obligations of any nature other than those incident to its formation and pursuant to this Agreement and the Merger and the other transactions contemplated by this Agreement. Merger Sub has no subsidiaries.

(c)   <u>Corporate Authority; Approval</u>.   Parent and Merger Sub each have all requisite corporate power and authority and each has taken all corporate action necessary in order to execute, deliver and perform its obligations under this Agreement and to consummate the Merger. This Agreement has been duly executed and delivered by Parent and Merger Sub and constitutes a valid and binding agreement of Parent and Merger Sub, enforceable against each of Parent and Merger Sub in accordance with its terms, . . . The shares of Parent Common Stock comprising the Stock Consideration have been duly authorized and, when issued pursuant to this Agreement, will be validly issued, fully paid and nonassessable, and no stockholder of Parent will have any preemptive right of subscription or purchase in respect thereof. No approval by the stockholders of Parent is required in order for Parent to execute, deliver and perform its obligations under this Agreement or to consummate the transactions contemplated hereby on the terms and subject to the conditions of this Agreement.

(d)   <u>Governmental Filings; No Violations</u>.   (i) Other than the necessary filings, notices, reports, consents, registrations, approvals, permits, expirations of waiting periods or authorizations (A) pursuant to Section 1.3, (B) required under the HSR Act, Foreign Competition Laws, the Exchange Act and the Securities Act, (C) to comply with state securities or "blue-sky" Laws, (D) with or to the FCC pursuant to the Communications Laws, (E) with or to the PUCs and the local and state Governmental Entities and other entities identified in Section 5.2(d)(i)(E) of the Parent Disclosure Letter pursuant to applicable local and state Utilities Laws and (F) with or to the Foreign Regulators and the foreign and transnational Governmental Entities and other entities identified in Section 5.2(d)(i)(F) of the Parent Disclosure Letter, no filings, notices and/or reports are required to be made by Parent or Merger Sub with, nor are any consents, registrations, approvals, permits, expirations of waiting periods or authorizations required to be obtained by Parent or Merger Sub . . .

(ii)   The execution, delivery and performance of this Agreement by Parent and Merger Sub do not, and the consummation by Parent and Merger Sub of the Merger and the other transactions contemplated hereby will not, constitute or result in (A) a breach or violation of, or a default under, the certificate of incorporation or bylaws of Parent or the certificate of incorporation or bylaws of Merger Sub, (B) with or without the lapse of time or the giving of notice or both, a breach or violation of, a default or termination or modification (or right of termination or modification) under, payment of additional fees under, the creation or acceleration of any obligations under, or the creation of a Lien on any of the assets of Parent or any of its Subsidiaries pursuant to any Contract binding upon Parent or any of its Subsidiaries, or, assuming (solely with respect to performance of this Agreement and consummation of the Merger and the other transactions contemplated hereby) the filings, notices, reports, consents, registrations, approvals, permits, expirations of waiting periods and authorizations referred to in this Section 5.2(d) are made or obtained, under any Law to which Parent or any of its Subsidiaries is subject or (C) any change in the rights or obligations under any Contracts to which Parent or any of its Subsidiaries is a party, except, in the case of clauses (B) and (C) above, for any such breach, violation, default, termination, payment, acceleration, creation or change that would not, individually or in the aggregate, reasonably be likely to have a Parent Material Adverse Effect.

(e)   Parent Reports; Financial Statements.   (i) Parent has filed or furnished, as applicable, on a timely basis, all forms, statements, certifications, reports and documents required to be filed or furnished by it with or to the SEC pursuant to the Exchange Act or the Securities Act since the Applicable Date (the forms, statements, reports and documents filed with or furnished to the SEC since the Applicable Date and those filed with or furnished to the SEC subsequent to the date of this Agreement, in each case as amended, the "Parent Reports"). Each of the Parent Reports, at the time of its filing or being furnished, complied or, if not yet filed or furnished, will comply in all material respects with the applicable requirements of the Securities Act, the Exchange Act and the Sarbanes-Oxley Act, and any rules and regulations promulgated thereunder applicable to the Parent Reports. As of their respective dates (or, if amended prior to the date of this Agreement, as of the date of such amendment), the Parent Reports did not, and any Parent Reports filed with or furnished to the SEC subsequent to the date of this Agreement will not, contain any untrue statement of a material fact or omit to state a material fact required to be stated therein or necessary to make the statements made therein, in light of the circumstances in which they were made, not misleading.

(ii)   Parent is in compliance in all material respects with the applicable listing and corporate governance rules and regulations of the NYSE . . .

(f)   Absence of Certain Changes.   Since December 31, 2013 and through the date of this Agreement, (i) there has not been any change, effect, circumstance or development which has had or would, individually or in the aggregate, reasonably be likely to have a Parent Material Adverse Effect; (ii) Parent and its Subsidiaries have conducted their respective businesses in the ordinary course of such businesses consistent with past practice in all material respects; and (iii) except for normal quarterly cash dividends in an amount equal to $0.46 per share of Parent Common Stock, Parent has not declared, set aside or paid any dividend or distribution payable in cash, stock or property in respect of any capital stock.

(g)   Litigation and Liabilities . . .

(h)   Employee Benefits. All contributions required to be made under each Parent Pension Plan, as of the date of this Agreement, have been timely made and all obligations in respect of each Parent Pension Plan have been properly accrued and reflected in the most recent consolidated balance sheet filed or incorporated by reference in the Parent Reports prior to the date of this Agreement . . .

(i)   Compliance with Laws, Licenses. The businesses of each of Parent and its Subsidiaries since January 1, 2010 have not been, and are not being, conducted in violation of any applicable Law, except for such violations that would not, individually or in the aggregate, reasonably be likely to have a Parent Material Adverse Effect. To the Knowledge of Parent, as of the date herof, no investigation or review by any Governmental Entity with respect to Parent or any of its Subsidiaries is pending or threatened, nor has any Governmental Entity indicated an intention to conduct the same, except for such investigations or reviews the outcome of which would not, individually or in the aggregate, reasonably be likely to have a Parent Material Adverse Effect.

(j)   Takeover Statutes.   No Takeover Statute or any anti-takeover provision in Parent's restated certificate of incorporation or bylaws is, or at the Effective Time will be, applicable to the Parent Common Stock, the Merger or the other transactions contemplated by this Agreement.

(k)   Brokers and Finders.   Parent has not employed any broker or finder or incurred any liability for any brokerage fees, commissions or finders' fees in connection with the Merger or the other transactions contemplated in this Agreement except that Parent has employed Lazard Frères & Co. LLC as its financial advisor.

(l)   Reorganization.   Parent has not taken or agreed to take any action, and is not aware of any facts or circumstances, in each case, that would prevent or impede, or would reasonably be expected to prevent or impede, the Merger from qualifying as a reorganization within the meaning of Section 368(a) of the Code.

(m)   Available Funds.   Parent and Merger Sub have available to them, or as of the Effective Time will have available to them, all funds necessary for the payment to the Exchange Agent of the Merger Consideration.

(n)   No Other Representations and Warranties.   Except for the representations and warranties of Parent and Merger Sub contained in this Section 5.2, Parent and Merger Sub are not making and have not made, and no other Person is making or has made on behalf of Parent or Merger Sub, any express or implied representation or warranty in connection with this Agreement or the transactions contemplated hereby.

ARTICLE VI
COVENANTS

6.1   Interim Operations.   (a) The Company covenants and agrees as to itself and its Subsidiaries that, from and after the execution of this Agreement and prior to the Effective Time (unless Parent shall otherwise approve in writing, which approval shall not be unreasonably withheld, conditioned or delayed, and except as otherwise expressly disclosed in Section 6.1(a) of the Company

Disclosure Letter), the business of the Company and its Subsidiaries shall be conducted in the ordinary course of business consistent with past practice and each of the Company and its Subsidiaries shall, subject to compliance with the specific matters set forth below, use reasonable best efforts to preserve its business organization intact and maintain the existing relations and goodwill with Governmental Entities, customers, suppliers, content providers, distributors, licensors, creditors, lessors, employees and business associates and keep available the services of the Company and its Subsidiaries' present employees and agents. Without limiting the generality of, and in furtherance of, the foregoing, the Company covenants and agrees as to itself and its Subsidiaries that, from and after the date of this Agreement and prior to the Effective Time, except (A) as Parent may approve in writing (such approval not to be unreasonably withheld, conditioned or delayed), (B) as expressly disclosed in Section 6.1(a) or (d) of the Company Disclosure Letter or (C) as expressly provided for in the Employee Matters Agreement, the Company shall not and will not permit its Subsidiaries to:

(i)   (A) amend its certificate of incorporation or bylaws (or comparable governing documents), (B) split, combine, subdivide or reclassify its outstanding shares of capital stock, (C) declare, set aside or pay any dividend or distribution payable in cash, stock or property (or any combination thereof) in respect of any shares of its capital stock (except for any dividends or distributions paid by Sky Brasil Servicios Ltda. or a direct or indirect wholly owned Subsidiary of the Company to its stockholders or unitholders on a *pro rata* basis in the ordinary course of business consistent with past practice), (D) enter into any agreement with respect to the voting of its capital stock, or (E) purchase, repurchase, redeem or otherwise acquire any shares of its capital stock or any securities convertible or exchangeable into or exercisable for any shares of its capital stock;

(ii)   merge or consolidate with any other Person, except for any such transactions among wholly owned Subsidiaries of the Company, or restructure, reorganize or completely or partially liquidate or otherwise enter into any agreements or arrangements imposing material changes or restrictions on its assets, operations or business;

(iii)   knowingly take or omit to take any action if such action or failure to act would be reasonably likely to prevent or impede the Merger from qualifying as a "reorganization" within the meaning of Section 368(a) of the Code;

(iv)   (A) establish, adopt, amend or terminate any Company Plan or amend the terms of any outstanding equity-based awards, (B) grant or provide any severance or termination payments or benefits to any director, officer, employee or other service provider of the Company or any of its Subsidiaries, except to comply with applicable Law or as expressly required by the provisions of the Company Plans as in effect on the date hereof or the provisions of this Agreement, (C) increase the compensation, bonus or pension, welfare, severance or other benefits of or pay any bonus to any director, officer or employee of the Company or any of its Subsidiaries, (D) take any action to accelerate the vesting or payment, or fund or in any other way secure the payment, of compensation or benefits under any Company Plan (including any equity-based awards), except to the extent expressly required by any such Company Plan or provided in this Agreement, (E) change any actuarial or other assumptions used to calculate funding obligations with respect to any Company Plan or to change the manner in which contributions to such plans are made or the basis on which such contributions are determined, except as may be required by GAAP or to comply with applicable Law, or (F) forgive any loans to directors, officers or employees of the Company or any of its Subsidiaries;

(v)   incur any indebtedness for borrowed money or guarantee such indebtedness of another Person, or issue or sell any debt securities or warrants or other rights to acquire any debt security of the Company or any of its Subsidiaries, except for (A) indebtedness for borrowed money incurred in the ordinary course of business consistent with past practice not to exceed $25,000,000 in the aggregate on terms substantially consistent with or more beneficial to the Company and its Subsidiaries, taken as a whole, than existing indebtedness for borrowed money . . . ;

(vi)   make or commit to any capital expenditures other than in the ordinary course of business consistent with past practice and in the aggregate in any event not in excess of (A) in 2014, 110% of the aggregate amounts reflected in the Company's capital expenditure budget set forth in Section 6.1(a)(vi)(A) of the Company Disclosure Letter (the "2014 CapEx Budget") and (B) in 2015, the sum of (1) the remainder (if a positive number) of (x) 100% of the 2014 CapEx Budget minus (y) the actual amount the Company made or committed to pursuant to the preceding clause (A) plus (2) 110% of the Company's 2015 capital expenditure budget set forth in Section 6.1(a)(vi)(B) of the Company Disclosure Letter; provided that the Company's timing of such capital expenditures in 2015 shall be consistent with past practice;

(vii)   other than transfers among and between wholly owned Subsidiaries of the Company, transfer, lease, license, sell, assign, let lapse, abandon, cancel, mortgage, pledge, place a Lien (other than Permitted Liens) upon or otherwise dispose of any of their respective properties or assets (including capital stock of any of its Subsidiaries) with a fair market value in excess of $50,000,000 individually or $100,000,000 in the aggregate (except with respect to Intellectual Property that is material to the respective businesses of the Company or its Subsidiaries, which shall not be included in this exception) or that are otherwise material other than ordinary course sales of customer premises equipment, or, with respect to Intellectual Property, non-exclusive license grants, in each case, made in the ordinary course of business consistent with past practice;

(viii)   issue, deliver, sell, grant, transfer, or encumber, or authorize the issuance, delivery, sale, grant, transfer on encumbrance of, any shares of its capital stock or any securities convertible or exchangeable into or exercisable for, or any options, warrants or other rights to acquire, any such shares . . . ;

(ix)   other than acquisitions of inventory or assets in the ordinary course of business consistent with past practice and making or committing to any capital expenditures in compliance with Section 6.1(a)(vi), spend in excess of $50,000,000 individually or $200,000,000 in the aggregate to acquire any business or to acquire assets or other property, whether by merger, consolidation, purchase of property or assets or otherwise (valuing any non-cash consideration at its fair market value as of the date of the agreement for such acquisition); provided that neither the Company nor any of its Subsidiaries shall make any acquisition that would, or would reasonably be likely to prevent, delay or impair the Company's ability to consummate the transactions contemplated by this Agreement;

(x)   make any material change with respect to its accounting policies or procedures, except as required by changes in GAAP or by applicable Law;

(xi)   except as required by applicable Law, (A) make any Tax election that is material to the Company and its Subsidiaries, taken as a whole, . . . ;

(xii)   (A) (1)enter into any new line of business other than any line of business that is reasonably ancillary to and a reasonably foreseeable extension of any line of business as of the date of this Agreement, . . . ;

(xiii)   file or apply for any License outside of the ordinary course of business consistent with past practice;

(xiv)   other than in the ordinary course of business consistent with past practice in an aggregate amount not to exceed $100,000,000, make any loans, advances or capital contributions to, or investments in, any Person . . . ;

(xv)   enter into any Contract pursuant to which the Company or any of its Subsidiaries agrees to provide any wireless, wireline or Internet services to any Person (other than Parent or its Subsidiaries) as an agent or reseller if such Contract is not terminable by the Company or one of its Subsidiaries on 60 days' or less notice without penalty;

(xvi)   other than in the ordinary course of business, (a) amend or modify in any material respect or terminate (excluding terminations upon expiration of the term thereof in accordance with the terms thereof) any Material Contract . . . ;

(xvii)   settle any action, suit, case, litigation, claim, hearing, arbitration, investigation or other proceedings before or threatened to be brought before a Governmental Entity;

(xviii)   assign, transfer, forfeit, cancel, fail to renew, or fail to extend or defend any Communications License that is material to the Company and its Subsidiaries;

(xix)   enter into any collective bargaining agreement, unless required by applicable Law;

(xx)   enter into any Contract that obligates or purports to obligate any existing or future non-controlled Affiliate of the Company (including any parent entity) to grant licenses to any Intellectual Property; or

(xxi)   agree, resolve or commit to do any of the foregoing.

(b)   Parent covenants and agrees, from and after the execution of this Agreement and prior to the Effective Time (unless the Company shall otherwise approve in writing, which approval will not be unreasonably withheld, conditioned or delayed and except as otherwise expressly contemplated by this Agreement or expressly disclosed in Section 6.1(b) of the Parent Disclosure Letter):

(i)   Parent shall not (A) amend Parent's certificate of incorporation or bylaws in any manner that would prohibit or hinder, impede or delay in any material respect the Merger or the consummation of the other transactions contemplated hereby or have a material and adverse impact on the value of the Parent Common Stock; provided that any amendment to its certificate of incorporation to increase the authorized number of shares of any class or series of the capital stock of Parent shall in no way be restricted by the foregoing, or (B) declare, set aside or pay any dividend or distribution payable in cash, stock or property in respect of any capital stock, other than regular quarterly cash dividends on the Parent Common Stock as described on Section 6.1(b)(i) of the Parent Disclosure Letter and other than dividends or distributions with a record date after the Effective Time;

(ii)   Parent shall not, and shall not permit any of its Subsidiaries to, acquire another business that, at the time such action is taken, to the Knowledge of Parent, would be likely to prevent the Closing;

(iii)   Parent shall not knowingly take or omit to take any action if such action or failure to act would be reasonably likely to prevent or impede the Merger from qualifying as a "reorganization" within the meaning of Section 368(a) of the Code; or

(iv)   Parent shall not agree, resolve, or commit to do any of the foregoing . . . ;

6.2   <u>Acquisition Proposals</u>.

(a)   <u>No Solicitation or Negotiation</u>.   The Company agrees that, except as expressly permitted by this Section 6.2, neither it nor any of its Subsidiaries nor any of its or its Subsidiaries' officers and directors shall, and it shall use its reasonable best efforts to cause its and its Subsidiaries' employees, investment bankers, attorneys, accountants and other advisors, agents and representatives (a Person's directors, officers, employees, investment bankers, attorneys, accountants and other advisors, agents and representatives hereinafter referred to as its "<u>Representatives</u>") not to, directly or indirectly:

(i)   initiate, solicit, knowingly encourage or otherwise knowingly facilitate any inquiries or the making of any proposal or offer that constitutes, or would reasonably be expected to lead to, any Acquisition Proposal;

(ii)   engage or participate in any discussions or negotiations with any Person regarding any Acquisition Proposal; or

(iii)   provide any non-public information or data to any Person in connection with, or otherwise knowingly facilitate, any Acquisition Proposal or attempt to make an Acquisition Proposal.

The Company shall, and the Company shall cause its Subsidiaries and use its reasonable best efforts to cause its Representatives to, immediately cease and cause to be terminated any discussions and negotiations with any Person conducted heretofore with respect to any Acquisition Proposal, or proposal that could be reasonably likely to lead to an Acquisition Proposal. The Company will promptly inform the individuals and entities referred to in the preceding sentence of the obligations undertaken in this Section 6.2. The Company will promptly request from each Person that has executed a confidentiality agreement in connection with its consideration of making an Acquisition Proposal to return or destroy (as provided in the terms of such confidentiality agreement) all confidential information concerning the Company or any of its Subsidiaries and promptly terminate all physical and electronic data access previously granted to such Person.

(b)   <u>Fiduciary Exception to No Solicitation Provision</u>. Notwithstanding anything to the contrary in Section 6.2(a), prior to the time, but not after, the Company Requisite Vote is obtained, the Company may, in response to an unsolicited, bona fide written Acquisition Proposal after the date of this Agreement, (i) provide access to non-public information regarding the Company or any of its Subsidiaries to the Person who made such Acquisition Proposal, providing for the acquisition of all or substantially all of the assets (on a consolidated basis) or total voting power or economic interests of the equity securities of the Company, so long as, in the case of a transaction which is not all cash, the holders of the Company's equity securities (including Shares) would not receive in the aggregate more than 65% of the total voting power of the equity securities of the issuer that is issuing securities in the transaction or 70% of the economic value of the issuer that is issuing securities in the transaction, in each case as measured based on the securities of such issuer outstanding at the time of the making of such Acquisition Proposal and giving effect to all securities and other consideration proposed to be issued by such issuer in such transaction, provided that such information has previously been, or is substantially concurrently, made available to Parent and that, prior to furnishing any such non-public information, the Company receives from the Person making such Acquisition Proposal an executed confidentiality agreement with terms at least as restrictive in all material respects on such Person as the Confidentiality Agreement (as defined in Section 9.7) (it being understood that such confidentiality agreement need not, at the Company's discretion, prohibit the making or amending of an Acquisition Proposal); and (ii) engage or participate in any discussions or negotiations with any such Person regarding such Acquisition Proposal if, and only if, prior to taking any action described in clause (i) or (ii) above, the Board of Directors of the Company determines in good faith after consultation with outside legal counsel that such Acquisition Proposal either constitutes a Superior Proposal or could be reasonably likely to result in a Superior Proposal.

(c)   Notice. The Company shall promptly (and, in any event, within 24 hours) notify Parent if (i) any written or other bona fide inquiries, proposals or offers with respect to an Acquisition Proposal are received by, (ii) any non-public information is requested in connection with any Acquisition Proposal from, or (iii) any discussions or negotiation with respect to an Acquisition Proposal are sought to be initiated or continued with, it, its Subsidiaries or any of their respective Representatives, indicating, in connection with such notice, the name of such Person and the material terms and conditions of any proposals or offers (including, if applicable, copies of any written requests, proposals or offers, including proposed agreements) and thereafter shall keep Parent informed, on a current basis, of the status and terms of any such proposals or offers (including any amendments thereto) and the status of any such discussions or negotiations, including any change in the Company's intentions as previously notified.

(d)   Definitions.   For purposes of this Agreement:

"Acquisition Proposal"   means (i) any proposal or offer from any Person or group of Persons, other than Parent and its Subsidiaries, with respect to a merger, joint venture, partnership, consolidation, dissolution, liquidation, tender offer, recapitalization, reorganization, spin-off, extraordinary dividend, share exchange, business combination or similar transaction involving the Company or any of its Subsidiaries which is structured to permit such Person or group of Persons to, directly or indirectly, acquire beneficial ownership of 15% or more of the Company's consolidated total assets or any class of the Company's equity interests and (ii) any acquisition by any Person or group of Persons (other than Parent and its Subsidiaries) resulting in, or proposal or offer, which if consummated would result in, any Person or group of Persons (other than Parent and its Subsidiaries) obtaining control (through Contract or otherwise) over or becoming the beneficial owner of, directly or indirectly, in one or a series of related transactions, 15% or more of the total voting power of any class of equity securities of the Company, or 15% or more of the consolidated total assets (including equity securities of its Subsidiaries) of the Company, in each case other than the transactions contemplated by this Agreement.

"Superior Proposal" means an unsolicited bona fide Acquisition Proposal involving the acquisition by a Person or a group of Persons, other than Parent and its Subsidiaries, of all or substantially all of the assets (on a consolidated basis) or total voting power of the equity securities of the Company (in each case measured based on the participation of the existing stockholders of the Company in the successor Person of the Company (which may be the Company)), so long as, in the case of a transaction which is not all cash, the holders of the Company's equity securities (including Shares) would not receive in the aggregate more than 65% of the total voting power of the equity securities of the issuer that is issuing securities in the transaction or 70% of the economic value of the issuer that is issuing securities and other consideration in the transaction, in each case as measured based on the securities of such issuer outstanding at the time of the making of such Acquisition Proposal and giving effect to all securities proposed to be issued by such issuer in such transaction, that its Board of Directors has determined in its good faith judgment is reasonably likely to be consummated and, if consummated, would result in a transaction more favorable to the Company's stockholders from a financial point of view than the transaction contemplated by this Agreement (after taking into account any revisions to the terms of the transaction contemplated by this Agreement pursuant to Section 6.2(f) of this Agreement).

(e) No Change in Recommendation or Alternative Acquisition Agreement. Except as provided in Section 6.2(f), the Board of Directors of the Company and each committee of the Board of Directors shall not (i) withhold, withdraw, qualify or modify (or publicly propose or resolve to withhold, withdraw, qualify or modify), in a manner adverse to Parent, the Company Recommendation (it being understood that publicly taking a neutral position or no position with respect to an Acquisition Proposal at any time beyond ten business days after the first public announcement of such Acquisition Proposal by the Company or by the party which made the Acquisition Proposal shall be considered a modification adverse to Parent) or make or authorize the making of any statement (oral or written) that has the substantive effect of such a withdrawal, qualification or modification; (ii) cause or permit the Company or any of its Subsidiaries to enter into any letter of intent, memorandum of understanding, agreement in principle, acquisition agreement, merger agreement, option agreement, joint venture agreement, partnership agreement, lease agreement or other agreement (other than a confidentiality agreement referred to in Section 6.2(b) entered into in compliance with Section 6.2(b)) (an "Alternative Acquisition Agreement") relating to any Acquisition Proposal; or (iii) approve or recommend, or propose to enter into an Acquisition Proposal or an Alternative Acquisition Agreement.

(f) Fiduciary Exception to Change in Recommendation Provision. Notwithstanding anything to the contrary set forth in this Agreement, prior to the time, but not after, the Company Requisite Vote is obtained, (x) the

Board of Directors of the Company may withhold, withdraw, qualify or modify the Company Recommendation or approve, recommend or otherwise declare advisable any Superior Proposal made after the date of this Agreement that did not result from a material breach of this Agreement, if the Board of Directors of the Company determines in good faith, after consultation with outside counsel and a financial advisor of nationally recognized reputation, that the failure to take such action would be inconsistent with its fiduciary duties under applicable Law (a "Change in Recommendation", it being understood that a customary "stop, look and listen" disclosure in compliance with Rule 14d-9(f) of the 1934 Act shall not, in and of itself, constitute a Change in Recommendation) and/or (y) the Company may terminate this Agreement in accordance with Section 8.3(b) and concurrent with such termination cause the Company to enter into an Alternative Acquisition Agreement providing for a Superior Proposal that did not result from a material breach of this Agreement (a "Superior Proposal Termination"); provided that in no event shall the Company take, or agree or resolve to take, any action other than in compliance with this Section 6.2; provided further that no Change in Recommendation and/or Superior Proposal Termination may be made until after at least five business days (or such shorter time period if the Company Stockholders Meeting is held within such five business day period) following Parent's receipt of written notice from the Company advising that the Company's Board of Directors intends to take such action and the basis therefor, including all information required to be provided under Section 6.2(c) and in the case of a Change in Recommendation not related to a Superior Proposal, all material information related thereto. After providing such notice and prior to effecting such Change in Recommendation and/or Superior Proposal Termination, (i) the Company shall, during such five business day period (or such shorter time period if the Company Stockholders Meeting is held within such five business day period), negotiate in good faith with Parent and its Representatives with respect to any revisions to the terms of the transaction contemplated by the Agreement proposed by Parent, and (ii) in determining whether to make a Change in Recommendation and/or effect a Superior Proposal Termination, the Board of Directors of the Company shall take into account any changes to the terms of this Agreement proposed by Parent and any other information provided by Parent in response to such notice during such five business day period (or such shorter time period if the Company Stockholders Meeting is held within such five business day period). Any amendment to the financial terms or other material terms of any Acquisition Proposal will be deemed to be a new Acquisition Proposal for purposes of this Section 6.2(f), including with respect to the notice period referred to in this Section 6.2(f), except that the five business day period (or such shorter time period if the Company Stockholders Meeting is held within such five business day period) shall be three business days (or such shorter time period if the Company Stockholders Meeting is held within such three business day period) for such purposes.

   (g)   Limits on Release of Standstill and Confidentiality.   From the date of this Agreement until the Effective Time, the Company shall not terminate, amend, modify or waive any provision of any confidentiality, "standstill" or similar agreement to which the Company or any of its Subsidiaries is a party and shall enforce, to the fullest extent permitted under applicable Law, the provisions of any such agreement, including by seeking injunctions to prevent any breaches of such agreements and to enforce specifically the terms and provisions thereof. Notwithstanding anything to the contrary contained in this Agreement, the Company shall be permitted to fail to enforce any provision of any confidentiality, "standstill" or similar obligation of any Person if the Board of Directors of the Company determines in good faith, after consultation with its outside legal counsel, that the failure to take such action is necessary in order for the directors to comply with their fiduciary duties under applicable Law; provided, that the Company promptly advises Parent that it is taking such action and the identity of the party or parties with respect to which it is taking such action; provided further that the foregoing shall not restrict the Company from permitting a Person to orally request the waiver of a "standstill" or similar obligation to the extent necessary to comply with fiduciary duties under applicable Law.

(h) <u>Certain Permitted Disclosure</u>. Nothing contained in this Section 6.2 shall be deemed to prohibit the Company from complying with its disclosure obligations under applicable U.S. federal or state Law with regard to an Acquisition Proposal; <u>provided</u> that, if such disclosure has the effect or substantive effect of withholding, withdrawing, qualifying or modifying the Company Recommendation, such disclosure shall be deemed to be a Change in Recommendation and Parent shall have the right to terminate this Agreement as set forth in Section 8.4(b).

6.3 <u>Information Supplied</u>. (a) The Company shall promptly prepare and file with the SEC the Prospectus/Proxy Statement, and Parent shall prepare and file with the SEC the Registration Statement on Form S-4 to be filed with the SEC by Parent in connection with the issuance of shares of Parent Common Stock in the Merger (including the proxy statement and prospectus (the "<u>Prospectus/Proxy Statement</u>") constituting a part thereof, the "<u>S-4 Registration Statement</u>") as promptly as practicable. Parent and the Company each shall use its reasonable best efforts to have the S-4 Registration Statement declared effective under the Securities Act as promptly as practicable after such filing, and promptly thereafter mail the Prospectus/Proxy Statement to the stockholders of the Company. The Company and Parent shall also use their respective reasonable best efforts to satisfy prior to the effective date of the S-4 Registration Statement all necessary state securities Law or "blue sky" notice requirements in connection with the Merger and to consummate the other transactions contemplated by this Agreement and will pay all expenses incident thereto.

(b) No filing of, or amendment or supplement to, the S-4 Registration Statement will be made by Parent, and no filing of, or amendment or supplement to, the Prospectus/Proxy Statement will be made by the Company or Parent, in each case without providing the other party a reasonable opportunity to review and comment thereon. Each of the Company and Parent shall furnish all information concerning such Person and its Affiliates to the other, and provide such other assistance, as may be reasonably requested by such other party to be included therein and shall otherwise reasonably assist and cooperate with the other in the preparation of the Prospectus/Proxy Statement, the S-4 Registration Statement and the resolution of any comments to either received from the SEC . . .

6.4   <u>Stockholders Meeting</u>.   (a) The Company will use, in accordance with applicable Law and the Company Charter and Company Bylaws, its reasonable best efforts to convene and hold a meeting of holders of Shares to consider and vote upon the adoption of this Agreement (the "<u>Company Stockholders Meeting</u>") not more than 45 days after the date the S-4 Registration Statement is declared effective. Subject to the provisions of Section 6.2, the Company's Board of Directors shall recommend in the Prospectus/Proxy Statement and at the Company Stockholders Meeting that the holders of Shares adopt this Agreement and shall use its reasonable best efforts to obtain and solicit such adoption. Notwithstanding the foregoing, if on a date preceding the date on which or the date on which the Company Stockholders Meeting is scheduled, the Company reasonably believes that (i) it will not receive proxies representing the Company Requisite Vote, whether or not a quorum is present, or (ii) it will not have enough Shares represented to constitute a quorum necessary to conduct the business of the Company Stockholders Meeting, the Company may postpone or adjourn, or make one or more successive postponements or adjournments of, the Company Stockholders Meeting as long as the date of the Company Stockholders Meeting is not postponed or adjourned more than an aggregate of 15 calendar days in connection with any postponements or adjournments in reliance on the preceding sentence. In the event that during the five business days prior to the date that the Company Stockholders Meeting is then scheduled to be held, the Company delivers a notice of an intent to make a Change in Recommendation and/or Superior Proposal Termination (including in connection with an amendment pursuant to the last sentence of Section 6.2(f)), Parent may direct the Company to postpone the Company Stockholders Meeting for up to five business days and the Company shall promptly, and in any event no later than the next business day, postpone the Company Stockholders Meeting in accordance with Parent's direction.

(b)   Notwithstanding any Change in Recommendation, the Company shall nonetheless submit this Agreement to the holders of Shares for adoption at the Company Stockholders Meeting unless this Agreement is terminated in accordance with Article VIII prior to the Company Stockholders Meeting. Without the prior written consent of Parent, the adoption of this Agreement shall be the only matter (other than matters of procedure and matters required by Law to be voted on by the Company's stockholders in connection with the approval of this Agreement and the transactions contemplated hereby) that the Company shall propose to be acted on by the stockholders of the Company at the Company Stockholders Meeting.

6.5   <u>Filings; Other Actions; Notification</u>.

(a)   <u>Cooperation</u>.   The Company and Parent shall, subject to Section 6.2, cooperate with each other and use, and shall cause their respective Subsidiaries to, use their respective reasonable best efforts to take or cause to be taken all actions, and do or cause to be done all things, necessary, proper or advisable on its part under this Agreement and applicable Laws to consummate and make effective the Merger and the other transactions contemplated by this Agreement as promptly as reasonably practicable (it being understood that nothing contained in this Agreement shall require Parent to obtain any consents, registrations, approvals, permits, expirations of waiting periods or authorizations prior to the Termination Date), including preparing and filing as promptly as reasonably practicable all documentation to effect all necessary notices, reports and other filings (including by filing no later than 20 calendar days after the date of this Agreement all applications required to be filed with the FCC and the notification and report form required under the HSR Act; <u>provided</u> that the failure to file within such 20-day period shall not constitute a breach of this Agreement) and to obtain as promptly as reasonably practicable all consents, registrations, approvals, permits, expirations of waiting periods and authorizations necessary or advisable to be obtained from any third party and/or any Governmental Entity in order to consummate the Merger or any of the other transactions contemplated by this Agreement . . . Except as provided in the immediately preceding sentence, nothing in this Agreement shall require, or be construed to require, (i) Parent or any of its Subsidiaries to take or refrain from taking any action (including any divestiture, holding separate any business or assets or other similar action) or to agree to any restriction or condition with respect to any assets, operations, business or the conduct of business of Parent or any of its Subsidiaries and (ii) Parent, the Company or any of their respective Subsidiaries to take or refrain from taking any action (including any divestiture, holding separate any business or assets or other similar action) or to agree to any restriction or condition with respect to any assets, operations, business or the conduct of business of the Company and its Subsidiaries, if, in the case of this clause (ii), any such action, failure to act, restriction, condition or agreement, individually or in the aggregate, would reasonably be likely to have a Company Material Adverse Effect (read without regard to the exceptions set forth therein and without giving effect to clause (A) thereof) (except as provided in the immediately preceding sentence, the occurrence of any of the matters specified in clause (i) or clause (ii) above shall constitute a "<u>Regulatory Material Adverse Effect</u>"). In addition, in measuring whether a Regulatory Material Adverse Effect has occurred, the expected loss of any reasonably expected synergies (both cost and revenue) relating to any restriction or condition shall be taken into account as if the Company had an adverse effect to its financial condition and results of operations equal to the expected amount of applicable synergies affected by any such restriction or condition. The Company and its Subsidiaries shall not agree to any actions, restrictions or conditions with respect to obtaining any consents, registrations, approvals, permits, expirations of waiting periods or authorizations in connection with the Merger and the other transactions contemplated by this Agreement without the prior written consent of Parent (which, subject to this Section 6.5(a) may be withheld in Parent's sole discretion). Subject to applicable Laws relating to the exchange of information, Parent and the Company shall have the right to review in advance, and to the extent practicable each will consult the other on, all of the information relating to Parent or the Company, as the case may be, and any of their respective Subsidiaries, that appears in any filing made with, or written materials submitted to, any third party and/or any Governmental Entity in connection with the Merger and the other transactions contemplated by this Agreement. To the extent permitted by applicable Law, each party shall provide the other with copies of all correspondence between it (or its advisors) and any Governmental Entity relating to the Merger and the other transactions contemplated by this Agreement and, to the extent reasonably practicable, all telephone calls and meetings with a Governmental Entity regarding the transactions contemplated by this Agreement shall include representatives of Parent and the Company. In exercising the foregoing rights, the Company and Parent each shall act reasonably and as promptly as reasonably practicable.

(b) Information.   The Company and Parent each shall, upon request by the other, promptly furnish the other with all information concerning itself, its Subsidiaries, directors, officers and stockholders and such other matters as may be reasonably necessary or advisable in connection with the Prospectus/Proxy Statement, the S-4 Registration Statement and any other statement, filing, notice or application made by or on behalf of Parent, the Company or any of their respective Subsidiaries to any third party and/or any Governmental Entity in connection with the Merger and the other transactions contemplated by this Agreement.

(c) Status.   The Company and Parent each shall keep the other reasonably apprised of the status of matters relating to completion of the transactions contemplated hereby, including promptly furnishing the other with copies of notice or other communications received by the Company or Parent, as the case may be, or any of their respective Subsidiaries from any third party and/or any Governmental Entity with respect to the Merger and the other transactions contemplated by this Agreement.

6.6 Access; Consultation.   (a) Upon reasonable notice, and except as may otherwise be required by applicable Law, the Company shall, and shall cause its Subsidiaries to, afford Parent's Representatives reasonable access, during normal business hours during the period prior to the Effective Time, to the Company's employees, properties, assets, books, records and contracts and, during such period, the Company and Parent shall, and shall cause their respective Subsidiaries to, (x) in the case of Parent, furnish promptly to the Company information regarding the matters set forth in Section 6.6(a) of the Parent Disclosure Letter as may reasonably be requested and (y) in the case of the Company, furnish promptly to Parent all information concerning its or any of their respective Subsidiaries' capital stock, business and personnel as may reasonably be requested; provided that no investigation pursuant to this Section 6.6 shall affect or be deemed to modify any representation or warranty made by the Company or Parent; . . . All information exchanged pursuant to this Section 6.6 shall be subject to the Confidentiality Agreement. To the extent that any of the information or material furnished pursuant to this Section 6.6 or otherwise in accordance with the terms of this Agreement may include material subject to the attorney-client privilege, work product doctrine or any other applicable privilege concerning pending or threatened legal proceedings or governmental investigations, the parties understand and agree that they have a commonality of interest with respect to such matters and it is their desire, intention and mutual understanding that the sharing of such material is not intended to, and shall not, waive or diminish in any way the confidentiality of such material or its continued protection under the attorney-client privilege, work product doctrine or other applicable privilege. All such information that is entitled to protection under the attorney-client privilege, work product doctrine or other applicable privilege shall remain entitled to such protection under these privileges, this Agreement, and under the joint defense doctrine.

(b) Each of the Company and Parent shall give prompt notice to one another of any change, effect, circumstance or development that is reasonably likely to result in a Company Material Adverse Effect or Parent Material Adverse Effect (as applicable), of any failure of any condition to Parent's or the Company's obligations to effect the Merger (as applicable) or of any other change, effect, circumstance or development which would cause or constitute a breach of any of the representations, warranties or covenants of the Company or Parent (as applicable) contained herein . . .

6.7   Stock Exchange Listing, De-listing and De-registration.   Parent shall use its reasonable best efforts to cause the shares of Parent Common Stock to be issued in the Merger to be approved for listing on the NYSE, subject to official notice of issuance, prior to the Effective Time. The Company shall take all actions necessary to permit the Shares to be de-listed from the NASDAQ and de-registered under the Exchange Act as soon as possible following the Effective Time.

6.8   Publicity.   The initial press release with respect to the Merger and the other transactions contemplated hereby shall be a joint press release and thereafter the Company and Parent shall consult with each other prior to issuing any press releases or otherwise making public announcements with respect to the Merger and the other transactions contemplated by this Agreement and prior to making any filings with any third party and/or any Governmental Entity (including any national securities exchange) with respect thereto, except (i) as may be required by applicable Law or by obligations pursuant to any listing agreement with or rules of any national securities exchange or NASDAQ (ii) any consultation that would not be reasonably practicable as a result of requirements of applicable Law or (iii) with respect to any Change in Recommendation made in accordance with this Agreement or Parent's response thereto.

6.9   Employee Benefits.   (a) Upon or promptly following the execution of this Agreement, Parent and the Company shall enter into an employee matters agreement substantially in the form of Exhibit A attached hereto (the "Employee Matters Agreement") and the Surviving Company shall be bound by such Employee Matters Agreement following the Effective Time.

(b)   Prior to making any written or material oral communications to the directors, officers or employees of the Company or any of its Subsidiaries pertaining to compensation or benefit matters related to the transactions contemplated by this Agreement, the Company shall provide Parent with a copy of the intended communication, and Parent shall have a reasonable period of time to review and comment on the communication . . .

6.10   Expenses.   Except as otherwise provided in Sections 6.16 and 8.5(b), whether or not the Merger is consummated, all costs and expenses incurred in connection with this Agreement and the Merger and the other transactions contemplated by this Agreement shall be paid by the party incurring such expense, except that expenses incurred in connection with the filing fee for the S-4 Registration Statement and printing and mailing the Prospectus/ Proxy Statement and the S-4 Registration Statement shall be shared equally by Parent and the Company.

6.11   Indemnification; Directors' and Officers' Insurance.   (a) From and after the Effective Time, Parent shall, and shall cause the Surviving Company to, indemnify and hold harmless each present and former director and officer of the Company (when acting in such capacity) and those individuals set forth on Section 0 of the Company Disclosure Letter serving at the request of the Company or any of its Subsidiaries as a director (or equivalent position) of a specified Person (when acting in such capacity) (the "Indemnified Parties"), against any costs or expenses (including reasonable attorneys' fees), judgments, fines, losses, claims, damages or liabilities incurred in connection with any claim, action, suit, proceeding or investigation, whether civil, criminal, administrative or investigative, arising out of matters existing or occurring at or prior to the Effective Time, whether asserted or claimed prior to, at or after the Effective Time, to the fullest extent that the Company would have been permitted under Delaware Law, any applicable indemnification agreement to which such Person is a party (a form of which is an exhibit to the Company's annual report on Form 10-K for the fiscal year ended December 31, 2011, 2012 or 2013), the Company Charter or Company Bylaws in effect on the date of this Agreement to indemnify such Person (and Parent and the Surviving Company shall also advance expenses as incurred to the fullest extent permitted under applicable Law; provided that the Person to whom expenses are advanced shall provide an undertaking to repay such advances if it is ultimately determined that such Person is not entitled to indemnification). Parent shall ensure that the organizational documents of the Surviving Company shall, for a period of six years from and after the Effective Time, contain provisions no less favorable with respect to indemnification, advancement of expenses and exculpation of present and former directors, officers, employees and agents of the Company and its Subsidiaries than are presently set forth in the Company Charter and Company Bylaws. Any right of indemnification of an Indemnified Party pursuant to this Section 6.11 shall not be amended, repealed or otherwise modified at any time in a manner that would adversely affect the rights of such Indemnified Party as provided herein.

(b) Prior to the Effective Time, the Company shall and, if the Company is unable to, Parent shall cause the Surviving Company as of the Effective Time to obtain and fully pay for "tail" insurance policies with a claims period of at least six years from and after the Effective Time from an insurance carrier with the same or better credit rating as the Company's current insurance carrier with respect to directors' and officers' liability insurance and fiduciary liability insurance (collectively, "D&O Insurance") with benefits and levels of coverage at least as favorable as the Company's existing policies with respect to matters existing or occurring at or prior to the Effective Time (including in connection with this Agreement or the transactions or actions contemplated hereby); provided, however, that in no event shall the Company expend for such policies in an amount with a premium amount in excess of 300% of the annual premiums currently paid by the Company for such insurance . . .

(c) If Parent or any of its successors or assigns (i) shall consolidate with or merge into any other corporation or entity and shall not be the continuing or surviving corporation or entity of such consolidation or merger or (ii) shall transfer all or substantially all of its properties and assets to any individual, corporation or other entity, then and in each such case proper provisions shall be made so that the successors and assigns of Parent shall assume all of the obligations set forth in this Section 6.11.

(d)   The provisions of this Section 6.11 are intended to be for the benefit of, and shall be enforceable by, each of the Indemnified Parties, their heirs and their representatives.

6.12   <u>Regulatory Compliance</u>.

(a)   The Company agrees, and shall cause its Subsidiaries to, use its reasonable best efforts to (i) cure no later than the Effective Time any material violations and defaults by any of them under any applicable Communications Laws, . . . (ii) comply in all material respects with the terms of the FCC Licenses and the FAA Rules and the Foreign Licenses and (iii) file or cause to be filed with the FCC and the Foreign Regulators all reports and other filings required to be filed under applicable rules and regulations of the FCC and the Foreign Regulatory Laws.

(b)   During the period from the date of this Agreement to the Closing, the Company and its Subsidiaries shall (i) take all actions reasonably necessary to maintain and preserve the Communications Licenses and (ii) refrain from taking any action that would give the FCC or any other Governmental Entity with jurisdiction over the Company or any of its Subsidiaries reasonable grounds to institute proceedings for the suspension, revocation or adverse modification of any Communications License.

6.13   <u>Takeover Statute</u>.   If any Takeover Statute is or may become applicable to the Merger or the other transactions contemplated by this Agreement, the Company and its Board of Directors shall grant such approvals and take such actions as are necessary so that such transactions may be consummated as promptly as practicable on the terms contemplated by this Agreement and otherwise use reasonable best efforts to act to eliminate or minimize the effects of such statute or regulation on such transactions.

6.14   <u>Control of the Company's or Parent's Operations</u>.   Nothing contained in this Agreement shall give Parent or the Company, directly or indirectly, rights to control or direct the operations of the other prior to the Effective Time. Prior to the Effective Time, each of Parent and the Company shall exercise, consistent with the terms and conditions of this Agreement, complete control and supervision of its operations.

6.15   <u>Section 16(b)</u>.   The Board of Directors of the Company and Parent shall, prior to the Effective Time, take all such actions as may be necessary or appropriate to cause the transactions contemplated by this Agreement and any other dispositions of equity securities of the Company (including derivative securities) or acquisitions of Parent Common Stock (including derivative securities) in connection with the transactions contemplated by this Agreement by each individual who is a director or executive officer of the Company to be exempt under Rule 16b-3 promulgated under the Exchange Act.

6.16   <u>Financing</u>.

(a)   Upon the written request of Parent, the Company and its Subsidiaries shall execute and deliver, or shall use reasonable best efforts to cause to be executed and delivered, at the Closing, one or more supplemental indentures, legal opinions, officers certificates or other documents or instruments required for the due assumption of, and succession to, DIRECTV Holdings LLC's ("<u>DIRECTV Finance</u>") outstanding debt, guarantees, securities and other similar agreements to the extent required by the terms of such debt, guarantees, securities or other agreements (and any debt, guarantees, securities or other agreements entered into by the Company or its Subsidiaries in connection therewith) and the Company and its Subsidiaries shall provide all assistance reasonably required by Parent in connection with obtaining the execution of such instruments by the other parties required to execute such instruments. Parent and Merger Sub acknowledge and agree that the provisions of this Section 6.16(a) shall not create any independent conditions to Closing.

(b) The Company shall, and shall cause each of its Subsidiaries to, use its commercially reasonable efforts to commence, as promptly as reasonably practicable, at Parent's expense, after the receipt of a written request from Parent to do so, tender or exchange offers, and any related consent solicitations with respect to, any or all of the outstanding notes, debentures or other debt securities of DIRECTV Finance on such terms and conditions as specified and reasonably requested by Parent and in compliance with all applicable terms and conditions of the applicable indenture (the "Debt Offers"); provided that (i) Parent shall have provided the Company with the offer to purchase, related letter of transmittal, and other related documents (collectively, the "Offer Documents") and (ii) the closing of the Debt Offers shall be conditioned on the Closing. The Company shall, and shall cause its Subsidiaries to, use respective reasonable best efforts to and to cause their respective representatives to, provide cooperation reasonably requested by Parent in connection with the Debt Offers, and in connection with any tender or exchange offers commenced by Parent, and any related consent solicitations with respect to, any existing indebtedness of DIRECTV Finance. Parent shall only request the Company and its Subsidiaries to conduct any Debt Offer in compliance in all material respects with the applicable rules and regulations of the SEC, including Rule 14e-1 under the Exchange Act and the applicable indenture or other Contract. Parent shall ensure that at the Effective Time, the Surviving Company shall have all funds necessary to pay any consideration required to be paid in connection with the Debt Offers on the Closing Date. Parent and Merger Sub acknowledge and agree that the provisions of this Section 6.16(b) shall not create any independent conditions to Closing.

(c) If requested by Parent in writing, the Company and its Subsidiaries shall take any actions requested by Parent that are reasonably necessary for the payoff, satisfaction, discharge and/or defeasance of any existing indebtedness of DIRECTV Finance, and shall payoff, redeem or satisfy, discharge and/or defease, as applicable, such indebtedness in accordance with the indenture, credit agreement, or other Contract governing such indebtedness (the "Debt Payoffs"), including taking any action reasonably necessary to obtain a payoff letter in connection therewith; provided that any such action described above shall not be required unless it can be conditioned on the occurrence of the Closing, and, it being understood that at Closing, Parent shall deposit, or cause to be deposited, with the appropriate trustee, agent or other recipient, cash or cash equivalents sufficient to actually effect such payoff, redemption, satisfaction, discharge and/or defeasance. The Company shall, and shall cause its applicable Subsidiaries to, use their respective reasonable best efforts to and to cause their respective representatives to, provide cooperation reasonably requested by Parent in connection with any Debt Payoff. Parent and Merger Sub acknowledge and agree that the provisions of this Section 6.16(c) shall not create any independent conditions to Closing.

(d)   In the event that the Company commences a Debt Offer, the Company covenants and agrees that, promptly following any related consent solicitation expiration date, assuming the requisite consents are received, each of the Company and its Subsidiaries as is necessary shall (and shall use their reasonable best efforts to cause the applicable trustee or agent to) execute a supplemental indenture or amendment to the applicable indenture or other Contract governing such indebtedness, which shall implement the amendments described in the Offer Documents, subject to the terms and conditions of this Agreement (including the conditions to the Debt Offers) and the applicable indenture or other Contract; provided, however, that in no event shall the Company, any of its Subsidiaries or any of their respective officers, directors or other representatives, have any obligation to authorize, adopt or execute any supplemental indenture or other agreement that would become effective prior to the Closing. Subject to the terms and conditions of the Debt Offer, concurrently with the Closing, Parent shall cause the Surviving Company to accept for payment and thereafter promptly pay for, any indebtedness that has been validly tendered pursuant to and in accordance with the Debt Offers and not properly withdrawn using funds provided by Parent.

(e)   Parent shall prepare all necessary and appropriate documentation in connection with any Debt Offers or Debt Payoffs, including the Offer Documents, as applicable and the Company shall have a reasonable opportunity to review and comment upon such documents. The parties hereto shall, and shall cause their respective Subsidiaries to, reasonably cooperate with each other in the preparation of any Offer Documents or other appropriate documents. The Company shall, to the extent requested, keep Parent reasonably informed regarding the status, results and timing of the Debt Offers. If, at any time prior to the completion of the Debt Offers, the Company or any of its Subsidiaries, on the one hand, or Parent or any of its Subsidiaries, on the other hand, discovers any information that should be set forth in an amendment or supplement to the Offer Documents, so that the Offer Documents shall not contain any untrue statement of a material fact or omit to state any material fact required to be stated therein or necessary in order to make the statements therein, in light of circumstances under which they are made, not misleading, such party that discovers such information shall use commercially reasonable efforts to promptly notify the other party, and an appropriate amendment or supplement prepared by Parent describing such information shall be disseminated by or on behalf of the Company or its Subsidiaries to the holders of the applicable indebtedness of the Company. Notwithstanding anything to the contrary in this Section 6.16(e), the Company shall, and shall cause its Subsidiaries to, comply with the requirements of Rule 14e-1 under the Exchange Act and any other Law to the extent applicable in connection with the Debt Offers or Debt Payoffs and such compliance will not be deemed a breach hereof.

(f)   In connection with any Debt Offer and any Debt Payoff, Parent may select one or more dealer managers, information agents, depositaries and other agents, in each case as shall be reasonably acceptable to the Company, to provide assistance in connection therewith and the Company shall, and shall cause its Subsidiaries to, enter into customary agreements with such parties so selected; provided, that neither the Company nor any of its Subsidiaries shall be required to indemnify, defend or hold harmless, or pay the fees or reimburse the costs and expenses of, any such party, which indemnification, fee and reimbursement obligations shall be borne by Parent pursuant to separate agreements with such parties to which neither the Company nor any of its Subsidiaries shall be a party or have any obligations under.

(g)   From and after the date of this Agreement, and through the earlier of the Closing and the date on which this Agreement is terminated in accordance with Article VIII, the Company shall, and the Company shall cause each of its Subsidiaries and use reasonable best efforts to cause its and their representatives (including their auditors) to, use its respective reasonable best efforts to provide all customary cooperation (including providing reasonably available financial and other information regarding the Company and its Subsidiaries for use in marketing and offering documents and to enable Parent to prepare pro forma financial statements) as reasonably requested by Parent to assist Parent in the arrangement of any bank debt financing or any capital markets debt financing for the purposes of financing the payment of the Cash Consideration, any repayment or refinancing of debt contemplated by this Agreement or required in connection with the Merger and the other transactions contemplated by this Agreement and any other amounts required to be paid in connection with the consummation of the Merger; provided, however, that no obligation of the Company or any of its Subsidiaries under such bank debt financing or any capital markets debt financing shall be effective prior to the Closing.

(h)   Parent shall indemnify and hold harmless the Company and each of its Subsidiaries and their respective Representatives from and against any and all liabilities, losses, damages, claims, costs, expenses (including reasonable attorney's fees) interest, awards, judgments and penalties suffered or incurred in connection with any and all of the matters contemplated by this Section 6.16 (other than arising from fraud or intentional misrepresentation on the part of the Company or its Subsidiaries), whether or not the Merger is consummated or this Agreement is terminated. Parent shall, promptly upon request by the Company, reimburse the Company for all reasonable out-of-pocket costs (including reasonable attorneys' fees) incurred by the Company or its Subsidiaries in connection with this Section 6.16, whether or not the Merger is consummated or this Agreement is terminated.

(i)   The Company agrees that, from and after January 1, 2015 and prior to the Effective Time, the Company and each of its Subsidiaries shall not file any prospectus supplement or registration statement or consummate any offering of securities that requires registration under the Securities Act or that includes any actual or contingent commitment to register such securities under the Securities Act in the future.

6.17   Approval by Merger Sub.   Immediately following the execution and delivery of this Agreement by the parties hereto, Parent, as sole shareholder of Merger Sub, shall adopt this Agreement and approve the Merger, in accordance with Delaware Law, by written consent.

ARTICLE VII
CONDITIONS

7.1   Conditions to Each Party's Obligation to Effect the Merger.   The respective obligation of each party to effect the Merger is subject to the satisfaction or waiver at or prior to the Closing of each of the following conditions:

(a) <u>Stockholder Consent</u>.   This Agreement shall have been duly adopted by holders of Shares constituting the Company Requisite Vote.

(b) <u>NYSE Listing</u>.   The shares of Parent Common Stock issuable to the Company stockholders pursuant to the Merger shall have been authorized for listing on the NYSE upon official notice of issuance.

(c) <u>Governmental Consents</u>. (i) The waiting period applicable to the consummation of the Merger under the HSR Act shall have expired or been earlier terminated and (ii) all Governmental Consents required to be obtained from the FCC for the consummation of the Merger shall have been obtained and be in full force and effect. For purposes of this Agreement, the term "<u>Governmental Consents</u>" shall mean all notices, reports and other filings required to be made prior to the Effective Time by the Company or Parent or any of their respective Subsidiaries with, and all consents, registrations, approvals, permits, expirations of waiting periods and authorizations required to be obtained prior to the Effective Time by the Company or Parent or any of their respective Subsidiaries from, any Governmental Entity in connection with the execution and delivery of this Agreement and the consummation of the Merger and the other transactions contemplated hereby.

(d) <u>Litigation</u>.   No Governmental Entity of competent jurisdiction shall have enacted, issued, promulgated, enforced or entered any Law (whether temporary, preliminary or permanent) that is in effect and restrains, enjoins or otherwise prohibits consummation of the Merger or the other transactions contemplated by this Agreement (collectively, an "<u>Order</u>").

(e) <u>S-4</u>.   The S-4 Registration Statement shall have become effective under the Securities Act. No stop order suspending the effectiveness of the S-4 Registration Statement shall have been issued, and no proceedings for that purpose shall have been initiated or be threatened, by the SEC.

7.2 <u>Conditions to Obligations of Parent and Merger Sub</u>.   The obligations of Parent and Merger Sub to effect the Merger are also subject to the satisfaction or waiver by Parent at or prior to the Effective Time of the following conditions:

(a) <u>Representations and Warranties</u>. (i) The representations and warranties of the Company set forth in Section 5.1(b)(i) (Capital Structure) shall be true and correct, subject only to de minimis inaccuracies (A) on the date of this Agreement and (B) at the Closing (in each case except to the extent that any such representation and warranty speaks as of a particular date, in which case such representation and warranty shall be true and correct as of such earlier date), (ii) the representations and warranties of the Company set forth in (x) Section 5.1(l)(ii) (Certain Contracts) shall be true and correct and (y) the last sentence of Section 5.1(l)(i) (Certain Contracts) and Section 5.1(m) (Takeover Statutes) shall be true and correct in all material respects (in the case of this clause (y), without regard to any materiality qualifiers specified therein), in each case, (A) on the date of this Agreement and (B) at the Closing (in each case except to the extent that such representation and warranty speaks as of a particular date, in which case such representation and warranty shall be true and correct as of such earlier date); and (iii) the other representations and warranties of the Company set forth in Section 5.1 shall be true and correct (A) on the date of this Agreement and (B) at the Closing (in each case except to the extent that any such representation and warranty speaks as of a particular date, in which case such representation and warranty shall be true and correct as of such earlier date); <u>provided</u> that notwithstanding anything herein to the contrary, the condition set forth in this Section 7.2(a)(iii) shall be deemed to have been satisfied even if any representations and warranties of the Company are not so true and correct unless the failure of such representations and warranties of the Company to be so true and correct (read for purposes of this Section 7.2(a)(iii) without any materiality, Company Material Adverse Effect or similar qualification), individually or in the aggregate, has had or would reasonably be likely to have a Company Material Adverse Effect; and (iv) Parent shall have received at the Closing a certificate signed on behalf of the Company by the Chief Executive Officer or Chief Financial Officer of the Company to the effect that the condition set forth in this Section 7.2(a) has been satisfied.

(b) <u>Performance of Obligations of the Company</u>. The Company shall have performed in all material respects all obligations required to be performed by it under this Agreement at or prior to the Closing, and Parent shall have received a certificate signed on behalf of the Company by an executive officer of the Company to such effect.

(c) <u>Governmental Consents</u>. (i) All Governmental Consents required to be obtained from any PUC for the consummation of the Merger set forth in Section 7.2(c) of the Parent Disclosure Letter and any Governmental Consents from foreign Governmental Entities set forth on Section 7.2(c) of the Company Disclosure Letter shall have been obtained and be in full force and effect (the foregoing together with the Governmental Consents described in Sections 7.1(c)(i) and 7.1(c)(ii), being the "<u>Required Governmental Consents</u>") . . .

(d) <u>No Company Material Adverse Effect</u>. After the date of this Agreement, there shall not have occurred any change, effect, circumstance or development that, individually or in the aggregate, has resulted, or would reasonably be likely to result, in a Company Material Adverse Effect.

(e) <u>Tax Opinion</u>. Parent shall have received an opinion of Sullivan & Cromwell LLP, on the basis of representations and warranties set forth or referred to in such opinion, dated as of the Closing Date, to the effect that the Merger will qualify as a reorganization within the meaning of Section 368(a) of the Code. In rendering such opinion, such counsel shall be entitled to rely upon representations of officers of the Company and Parent contained in the certificates provided by the Company and Parent in accordance with Section 6.1(c) (with such changes as are necessary, in the opinion of such counsel, to reflect any change in applicable Law, regulation or official interpretation thereof occurring between the date hereof and the Closing Date).

7.3 <u>Conditions to Obligation of the Company</u>. The obligation of the Company to effect the Merger is also subject to the satisfaction or waiver by the Company at or prior to the Effective Time of the following conditions:

(a) <u>Representations and Warranties</u>. (i) The representations and warranties of Parent set forth in Section 5.2(b)(i) (Capital Structure) shall be true and correct in all material respects (A) on the date of this Agreement and (B) at the Closing (in each case except to the extent that any such representation and warranty speaks as of a particular date, in which case such representation and warranty shall be true and correct as of such earlier date); (ii) the other representations and warranties of Parent and Merger Sub set forth in Section 5.2 shall be true and correct in all respects (A) on the date of this Agreement and (B) at the Closing (in each case except to the extent that any such representation and warranty speaks as of a particular date, in which case such representation and warranty shall be true and correct as of such earlier date); provided that notwithstanding anything herein to the contrary, the condition set forth in this Section 7.3(a)(ii) shall be deemed to have been satisfied even if any representations and warranties of Parent and Merger Sub are not so true and correct unless the failure of such representations and warranties of Parent and Merger Sub to be so true and correct (read for purposes of this Section 7.3(a)(ii) without any materiality, Parent Material Adverse Effect or similar qualification), individually or in the aggregate, has had or would reasonably be likely to have a Parent Material Adverse Effect; and (iii) the Company shall have received at the Closing a certificate signed on behalf of Parent and Merger Sub by executive officers of Parent and Merger Sub to the effect that the condition set forth in this Section 7.3(a) has been satisfied.

(b)   <u>Performance of Obligations of Parent and Merger Sub</u>.   Each of Parent and Merger Sub shall have performed in all material respects all obligations required to be performed by it under this Agreement at or prior to the Closing, and the Company shall have received a certificate signed on behalf of Parent and Merger Sub by executive officers of Parent and Merger Sub to such effect.

(c)   <u>Tax Opinion</u>.   The Company shall have received an opinion of Weil, Gotshal & Manges LLP, on the basis of representations and warranties set forth or referred to in such opinion, dated as of the Closing Date, to the effect that the Merger will qualify as a reorganization within the meaning of Section 368(a) of the Code. In rendering such opinion, such counsel shall be entitled to rely upon representations of officers of the Company and Parent contained in the certificates provided by the Company and Parent in accordance with Section 6.1(c) (with such changes as are necessary, in the opinion of such counsel, to reflect any change in applicable Law, regulation or official interpretation thereof occurring between the date hereof and the Closing Date).

(d)   <u>No Parent Material Adverse Effect</u>.   After the date of this Agreement, there shall not have occurred any change, effect, circumstance or development that, individually or in the aggregate, has resulted, or would reasonably be likely to result, in a Parent Material Adverse Effect.

ARTICLE VIII
TERMINATION

8.1   <u>Termination by Mutual Consent</u>.   This Agreement may be terminated and the Merger may be abandoned at any time prior to the Effective Time, whether before or after the adoption of this Agreement by the stockholders of the Company referred to in Section 7.1(a), by mutual written consent of the Company and Parent, by action of their respective Boards of Directors.

8.2   <u>Termination by Either Parent or the Company</u>.   This Agreement may be terminated and the Merger may be abandoned at any time prior to the Effective Time by action of the Board of Directors of either Parent or the

Company if (a) the Merger shall not have been consummated by May 18, 2015 (as it may be extended below, the "Termination Date"), whether such date is before or after the date of adoption of this Agreement by the stockholders of the Company referred to in Section 7.1(a); provided that, (i) if either the Company or Parent determines that additional time is necessary in connection with obtaining a Required Governmental Consent from the FCC or any PUC listed in Section 7.2(c) of the Parent Disclosure Letter and foreign Governmental Entities listed in Section 7.2(c) of the Company Disclosure Letter or in connection with the expiration of the waiting period pursuant to the HSR Act, the Termination Date may be extended by either Parent or the Company from time to time by written notice to the other up to a date not beyond August 17, 2015 and (ii) if the Termination Date has been extended to August 17, 2015, the Termination Date may be extended further by the mutual written agreement of Parent and the Company from time to time up to a date not beyond November 13, 2015, which date or dates pursuant to clauses (i) or (ii) of this Section 8.2, as extended from time to time, shall thereafter be deemed to be the Termination Date, (b) the adoption of this Agreement by the stockholders of the Company referred to in Section 7.1(a) shall not have occurred at a meeting duly convened therefor or at any adjournment or postponement thereof at which a vote upon the adoption of this Agreement was taken, (c) any Order permanently restraining, enjoining or otherwise prohibiting consummation of the Merger shall become final and non-appealable, whether before or after the adoption of this Agreement by the stockholders of the Company referred to in Section 7.1(a), provided that the right to terminate this Agreement pursuant to this Section 8.2 shall not be available to any party that has breached in any material respect its obligations under this Agreement in any manner that shall have proximately contributed to the failure of the Merger to be consummated, or (d) the FCC adopts a hearing designation order in respect of the transactions contemplated by this Agreement.

8.3 Termination by the Company. This Agreement may be terminated and the Merger may be abandoned (a) at any time prior to the Effective Time, whether before or after the adoption of this Agreement by the stockholders of the Company referred to in Section 7.1(a), by action of the Board of Directors of the Company if there has been a breach of any representation, warranty, covenant or agreement made by Parent or Merger Sub in this Agreement, or any such representation and warranty shall have become untrue after the date of this Agreement, such that Section 7.3(a) or 7.3(b) would not be satisfied and such breach or failure to be true is not curable or, if curable, is not cured by the 30th day following notice to Parent from the Company of such breach or failure; provided, that the Company shall not have the right to terminate the Agreement pursuant to this Section 8.3 if the Company is then in material breach of any of its representations, warranties, covenants or agreements under this Agreement or (b) at any time prior to the Company Requisite Vote being obtained, (i) if the Board of Directors of the Company authorizes the Company, subject to complying with the terms of Section 6.2, to enter into an Alternative Acquisition Agreement with respect to a Superior Proposal that did not result from a material breach of this Agreement, (ii) concurrently with the termination of this Agreement the Company, subject to complying with the terms of Section 6.2, enters into an Alternative Acquisition Agreement providing for a

Superior Proposal that did not result from a material breach of this Agreement and (iii) prior to or concurrently with such termination, the Company pays to Parent in immediately available funds any fees required to be paid pursuant to Section 8.5(b), subject to and in accordance with Section 8.5(b).

8.4   Termination by Parent.   This Agreement may be terminated and the Merger may be abandoned at any time prior to the Effective Time by action of the Board of Directors of Parent if (a) the Board of Directors of the Company shall have made a Change in Recommendation prior to the adoption of this Agreement by the stockholders of the Company referred to in Section 7.1(a), or (b) whether before or after the adoption of this Agreement by the stockholders of the Company referred to in Section 7.1(a), there has been a breach of any representation, warranty, covenant or agreement made by the Company in this Agreement, or any such representation and warranty shall have become untrue after the date of this Agreement, such that Section 7.2(a) or 7.2(b) would not be satisfied and such breach or failure to be true is not curable or, if curable, is not cured by the 30th day following notice to the Company of such breach or failure; provided, that Parent shall not have the right to terminate the Agreement pursuant to this Section 8.4(b) if Parent is then in material breach of any of its representations, warranties, covenants or agreements under this Agreement.

8.5   Effect of Termination and Abandonment.   (a) In the event of termination of this Agreement and the abandonment of the Merger pursuant to this ARTICLE VIII, this Agreement (other than as set forth in this Section 8.5 and in Section 9.1) shall become void and of no effect with no liability on the part of any party hereto (or of any of its Representatives); provided that no such termination shall relieve any party hereto from any liability for damages to any other party resulting from any prior willful breach of this Agreement or from any obligation to pay, if applicable, the Termination Fee pursuant to Section 8.5(a).

(b)   If this Agreement is terminated (i) by Parent pursuant to Section 8.4(a) (Change in Recommendation) or (ii) by the Company pursuant to either (x) Section 8.2(b) (Stockholder Vote) at a time when Parent had the right to terminate pursuant to Section 8.4(a) (Change in Recommendation) or (y) Section 8.3(b) (Termination for Superior Proposal), then the Company shall, within two business days after such termination in the case of clause (i) or concurrently with such termination in the case of clause (ii) be obligated to pay Parent a fee equal to $1,445,000,000 (the "Termination Fee"). In addition, if (i) this Agreement is terminated (A) by Parent or the Company pursuant to Section 8.2(a) (Termination Date) or 8.2(b) (Stockholder Vote) or (B) by Parent pursuant to Section 8.4(b) (Company Breach), (ii) prior to such termination referred to in clause (i), but after the date of this Agreement, a bona fide Acquisition Proposal shall have been made to the Company or any of its Subsidiaries or shall have been made directly to the Company's stockholders generally or any Person shall have publicly announced an intention (whether or not conditional) to make a bona fide Acquisition Proposal with respect to the Company (a "Company Acquisition Proposal"); and (iii) within 12 months after the date of a termination in either of the cases referred to in clauses (i)(A) and (i)(B) of this Section 8.5(b), the Company consummates a Company Acquisition Proposal or enters into an agreement contemplating a Company Acquisition Proposal, then the Company shall be obligated to pay the Termination Fee concurrently with such entry or consummation; provided that solely for purposes of this Section 8.5(b)(iii), the term "Acquisition Proposal" shall have the meaning assigned to such term in Section 6.2(d), except that the references to "15% or more" shall be deemed to be references to "50% or more". The Company acknowledges that the agreements contained in this Section 8.5(a) are an integral part of the transactions contemplated by this Agreement, and that, without these agreements, Parent and Merger Sub would not enter into this Agreement; accordingly, if the Company fails to pay promptly the amount due pursuant to this Section 8.5(a), and, in order to obtain such payment, Parent or Merger Sub commences a suit which results in a judgment against the Company for the fee set forth in this Section 8.5(a), the Company shall pay to Parent or Merger Sub its costs and expenses (including attorneys' fees) in connection with such suit, together with interest on the amount of the fee at the prime rate of Citibank N.A. in effect on the date such payment should have been made. At the time the Termination Fee is paid by the Company, the Company shall concurrently give to Parent wire instructions in the event of a refund of the Termination Fee.

(c)   In the event that a Termination Fee is paid pursuant to clause (i) of the first sentence of Section 8.5(b), Parent shall have the right, exercisable by written notice to the Company within one business day after the receipt of payment of such Termination Fee, to refund such Termination Fee to the Company, and in that event that the Company actually receives a full refund of the entire Termination Fee within two business days after the delivery of such notice, the Company, Parent and Merger Sub shall be entitled to all remedies available as contemplated by Section 8.5(a). In the event that a Termination Fee is paid pursuant to clause (ii) of the first sentence of Section 8.5(b) or the second sentence of Section 8.5(b), Parent shall have the right, exercisable by written notice to the Company within two business days after the receipt of such Termination Fee, to refund such Termination Fee to the Company, and in the event that the Company actually receives a full refund of the entire Termination Fee within two business days after the delivery of such notice, the Company, Parent and Merger Sub shall be entitled to all remedies available as contemplated by Section 8.5(a). If, after receiving the Termination Fee, Parent fails to exercise its right to refund the Termination Fee in accordance with the time periods provided for in this Section 8.5(c), Parent shall be deemed to have irrevocably waived such right and the Company shall have no further liability to Parent or Merger Sub, and Parent and Merger Sub shall have no further liabilities to the Company, under this Agreement except as set forth in Section 9.1. The parties agree that in no event shall the Company be required to pay the Termination Fee on more than one occasion.

ARTICLE IX
MISCELLANEOUS AND GENERAL

9.1 Survival. This ARTICLE IX and the agreements of the Company, Parent and Merger Sub contained in Article IV and Section 6.11 (Indemnification; Directors' and Officers' Insurance) shall survive the consummation of the Merger. This ARTICLE IX (other than Section 9.2 (Modification or Amendment), Section 9.3 (Waiver) and Section 9.12

(Assignment)) and the agreements of the Company, Parent and Merger Sub contained in Section 6.10 (Expenses), Section 6.16(h) (Financing Indemnification), Section 8.5 (Effect of Termination and Abandonment) and the Confidentiality Agreement (as defined in Section 9.7) shall survive the termination of this Agreement. All other representations, warranties, covenants and agreements in this Agreement and in any certificate or other writing delivered pursuant hereto shall not survive the consummation of the Merger or the termination of this Agreement. This Section 9.1 shall not limit any covenant or agreement of the parties which by its terms contemplates performance after the Effective Time.

9.2   Modification or Amendment.   Subject to the provisions of applicable Law (including Section 251(d) of the DGCL), at any time prior to the Effective Time, this Agreement (including any Schedule hereto) may be amended, modified or supplemented in writing by the parties hereto, by action of the board of directors of the respective parties.

9.3   Waiver.   (a) Any provision of this Agreement may be waived prior to the Effective Time if, and only if, such waiver is in writing and signed by the party against whom the waiver is to be effective.

(b)   No failure or delay by any party in exercising any right, power or privilege hereunder shall operate as a waiver thereof nor shall any single or partial exercise thereof preclude any other or further exercise thereof or the exercise of any other right, power or privilege. Except as otherwise herein provided, the rights and remedies herein provided shall be cumulative and not exclusive of any rights or remedies provided by Law.

9.4   Counterparts; Effectiveness.   (a) This Agreement may be executed in any number of counterparts (including by facsimile or by attachment to electronic mail in portable document format (PDF)), each such counterpart being deemed to be an original instrument, and all such counterparts shall together constitute the same agreement, and shall become effective when one or more counterparts have been signed by each of the parties hereto and delivered to the other parties hereto.

9.5   Governing Law and Venue; Waiver of Jury Trial.   (a) THIS AGREEMENT SHALL BE DEEMED TO BE MADE IN AND IN ALL RESPECTS SHALL BE INTERPRETED, CONSTRUED AND GOVERNED BY AND IN ACCORDANCE WITH THE LAW OF THE STATE OF DELAWARE WITHOUT REGARD TO THE CONFLICT OF LAW PRINCIPLES THEREOF. The parties hereby irrevocably submit exclusively to the jurisdiction of the courts of the State of Delaware and the federal courts of the United States of America located in the State of Delaware, and hereby waive, and agree not to assert, as a defense in any action, suit or proceeding for the interpretation or enforcement hereof or of any such document, that it is not subject thereto or that such action, suit or proceeding may not be brought or is not maintainable in said courts or that the venue thereof may not be appropriate or that this Agreement or any such document may not be enforced in or by such courts, and the parties hereto irrevocably agree that all claims relating to such action, proceeding or transactions shall be heard and determined in such a state or federal court. The parties hereby consent to and grant any such court jurisdiction over the person of such parties and over the subject matter of such dispute and agree that mailing of process or other papers in connection with any such action or proceeding in the manner provided in Section 9.6 or in such other manner as may be permitted by Law, shall be valid and sufficient service thereof.

(b) EACH PARTY ACKNOWLEDGES AND AGREES THAT ANY CONTROVERSY WHICH MAY ARISE UNDER THIS AGREEMENT IS LIKELY TO INVOLVE COMPLICATED AND DIFFICULT ISSUES, AND THEREFORE EACH SUCH PARTY HEREBY IRREVOCABLY AND UNCONDITIONALLY WAIVES ANY RIGHT SUCH PARTY MAY HAVE TO A TRIAL BY JURY IN RESPECT OF ANY LITIGATION DIRECTLY OR INDIRECTLY ARISING OUT OF OR RELATING TO THIS AGREEMENT, OR THE TRANSACTIONS CONTEMPLATED BY THIS AGREEMENT. EACH PARTY CERTIFIES AND ACKNOWLEDGES THAT (i) NO REPRESENTATIVE, AGENT OR ATTORNEY OF ANY OTHER PARTY HAS REPRESENTED, EXPRESSLY OR OTHERWISE, THAT SUCH OTHER PARTY WOULD NOT, IN THE EVENT OF LITIGATION, SEEK TO ENFORCE THE FOREGOING WAIVER, (ii) EACH SUCH PARTY UNDERSTANDS AND HAS CONSIDERED THE IMPLICATIONS OF THIS WAIVER, (iii) EACH SUCH PARTY MAKES THIS WAIVER VOLUNTARILY, AND (iv) EACH SUCH PARTY HAS BEEN INDUCED TO ENTER INTO THIS AGREEMENT BY, AMONG OTHER THINGS, THE MUTUAL WAIVERS AND CERTIFICATIONS IN THIS SECTION 9.5.

9.6 <u>Notices</u>. Notices, requests, instructions or other documents to be given under this Agreement shall be in writing and shall be deemed given, (a) on the date sent by facsimile or e-mail of a PDF document (with confirmation of transmission) if sent during normal business hours of the recipient, and on the next business day if sent after normal business hours of the recipient, (b) when delivered, if delivered personally to the intended recipient, and (c) one business day later, if sent by overnight delivery via a national courier service (providing proof of delivery), and in each case, addressed to a party at the following address for such party:

if to Parent or Merger Sub

AT&T Inc.
One AT&T Plaza
208 South Akard Street, Suite 3702
Dallas, Texas 75202
Attention: D. Wayne Watts
Fax: (214) 746-2103
Email: wayne.watts@att.com

with copies to (which shall not constitute notice):

Sullivan & Cromwell LLP
125 Broad Street
New York, New York 10004
Attention: Joseph B. Frumkin
Fax: (212) 558-3588
Email: frumkinj@sullcrom.com
Sullivan & Cromwell LLP
1888 Century Park East, Suite 2100

Los Angeles, California 90067
Attention: Eric M. Krautheimer
Fax: (212) 558-3588
Email: krautheimere@sullcrom.com

if to the Company

DIRECTV
2260 E. Imperial Highway
El Segundo, CA 90245
Attention: Larry D. Hunter
            Executive Vice President and General Counsel
Fax: (310) 964-0834
Email: Larry.Hunter@directv.com

with copies to (which shall not constitute notice):

DIRECTV
2260 E. Imperial Highway
El Segundo, CA 90245
Attention: Patrick T. Doyle
            Executive Vice President and Chief Financial Officer
Fax: (310) 964-0835
Email: Patrick.Doyle@directv.com
Weil, Gotshal & Manges LLP
767 Fifth Avenue
New York, NY 10153
Attention: Frederick S. Green
            Michael E. Lubowitz
Fax: (212) 310-8007
Email: frederick.green@weil.com
       michael.lubowitz@weil.com

or to such other persons or addresses as may be designated in writing by the party to receive such notice as provided above.

9.7 <u>Entire Agreement</u>. This Agreement (including any exhibits hereto, the Company Disclosure Letter and the Parent Disclosure Letter), the Confidentiality Agreement, dated March 27, 2014, between the Company and Parent (the "<u>Confidentiality Agreement</u>") and the Employee Matters Agreement constitute the entire agreement, and supersede all other prior agreements, understandings, representations and warranties both written and oral, among the parties, with respect to the subject matter hereof.

9.8 <u>No Third Party Beneficiaries</u>. This Agreement is not intended to, and does not, confer upon any Person other than the parties hereto any rights or remedies hereunder, other than (a) as provided in Section 6.11 (Indemnification; Directors' and Officers' Insurance) and (b) the right of the Company's stockholders to receive the Merger Consideration after the Closing.

9.9 <u>Obligations of Parent and of the Company</u>. Whenever this Agreement requires a Subsidiary of Parent to take any action, such requirement shall be deemed to include an undertaking on the part of Parent to cause such Subsidiary to take such action. Whenever this Agreement requires a Subsidiary of the Company to take any action, such requirement shall be deemed to include an undertaking on the part of the Company to cause such Subsidiary to take such action and, after the Effective Time, on the part of the Surviving Company to cause such Subsidiary to take such action.

9.10 Severability. The provisions of this Agreement shall be deemed severable and the invalidity or unenforceability of any provision shall not affect the validity or enforceability of the other provisions hereof. If any provision of this Agreement, or the application thereof to any Person or any circumstance, is invalid or unenforceable, (a) a suitable and equitable provision negotiated in good faith by the parties hereto shall be substituted therefor in order to carry out, so far as may be valid and enforceable, the intent and purpose of such invalid or unenforceable provision and (b) the remainder of this Agreement and the application of such provision to other Persons or circumstances shall not, subject to clause (a) above, be affected by such invalidity or unenforceability, except as a result of such substitution, nor shall such invalidity or unenforceability affect the validity or enforceability of such provision, or the application thereof, in any other jurisdiction.

9.11 Interpretation. The table of contents and the Article, Section and paragraph headings or captions herein are for convenience of reference only, do not constitute part of this Agreement and shall not be deemed to limit or otherwise affect any of the provisions hereof. Where a reference in this Agreement is made to a Section or Exhibit, such reference shall be to a Section of or Exhibit to this Agreement unless otherwise indicated. Whenever the words "include", "includes" or "including" are used in this Agreement, they shall be deemed to be followed by the words "without limitation." The words "hereof", "herein" and "hereunder" and words of similar import when used in this Agreement shall refer to this Agreement as a whole and not to any particular provision of this Agreement. The word "or" when used in this Agreement is not exclusive. When a reference is made in this Agreement, the Company Disclosure Letter or Parent Disclosure Letter to information or documents being provided, delivered, made available or disclosed to Parent, such information or documents shall mean any information or documents provided in the "Project Star" virtual data room maintained by the Company or in a "clean room" maintained by the Company and made available to each of Parent and its Representatives to the extent set forth on Section 0 of the Parent Disclosure Letter, in each case, in writing (including electronically) to Parent or its Representatives, in each case, on or before May 16, 2014. All terms defined in this Agreement shall have the defined meanings when used in any certificate or other document made or delivered pursuant hereto unless otherwise defined therein. The definitions contained in this Agreement are applicable to the singular as well as the plural forms of such terms and to the masculine as well as to the feminine and neuter genders of such term. Any agreement, instrument or statute defined or referred to herein or in any agreement or instrument that is referred to herein means such agreement, instrument or statute as from time to time amended, modified or supplemented, including (in the case of agreements or instruments) by waiver or consent and (in the case of statutes) by succession of comparable successor statutes and references to all attachments thereto and instruments incorporated therein.

(a)   The parties have participated jointly in negotiating and drafting this Agreement. In the event that an ambiguity or a question of intent or interpretation arises, this Agreement shall be construed as if drafted jointly by the parties, and no presumption or burden of proof shall arise favoring or disfavoring any party by virtue of the authorship of any provision of this Agreement.

9.12   <u>Assignment</u>.   This Agreement shall not be assignable by operation of law or otherwise; <u>provided</u> that Parent may designate, prior to the Effective Time, by written notice to the Company, another wholly owned direct or indirect Subsidiary to be a party to the Merger in lieu of Merger Sub, in which event all references herein to Merger Sub shall be deemed references to such other Subsidiary (except with respect to representations and warranties made herein with respect to Merger Sub as of the date of this Agreement) and all representations and warranties made herein with respect to Merger Sub as of the date of this Agreement shall also be made with respect to such other Subsidiary as of the date of such designation; <u>provided</u> that such assignment shall not relieve Parent of its obligations hereunder or otherwise enlarge, alter or change any obligation of any other party hereto or due to Parent or such other Subsidiary. Any assignment in contravention of the preceding sentence shall be null and void.

9.13   <u>Specific Performance</u>.   The parties hereto acknowledge and agree that irreparable damage would occur and that the parties would not have any adequate remedy at law if any provision of this Agreement were not performed in accordance with its specific terms or were otherwise breached, and that monetary damages, even if available, would not be an adequate remedy therefor. It is accordingly agreed that the parties shall be entitled to an injunction or injunctions to prevent breaches of this Agreement and to enforce specifically the performance of the terms and provisions hereof in accordance with Section 9.5 of this Agreement, without proof of actual damages (and each party hereby waives any requirement for the security or posting of any bond in connection with such remedy), this being in addition to any other remedy to which they are entitled at law or in equity. The parties further agree not to assert that a remedy of specific enforcement is unenforceable, invalid, contrary to applicable Law or inequitable for any reason, and not to assert that a remedy of monetary damages would provide an adequate remedy for any such breach or that the Company or Parent otherwise have an adequate remedy at law.

IN WITNESS WHEREOF, this Agreement has been duly executed and delivered by the duly authorized officers of the parties hereto as of the date first written above.

DIRECTV

By: /s/ Patrick T. Doyle

Name: Patrick T. Doyle

Title: Executive Vice President and Chief Financial Officer

AT&T INC.

By: /s/ Rick L. Moore
                 Name: Rick L. Moore
                 Title: Senior Vice President—
                 Corporate Development

STEAM MERGER INC.

By: /s/ Rick L. Moore
                 Name: Rick L. Moore
                 Title: President

EXHIBIT A
EMPLOYEE MATTERS AGREEMENT

EMPLOYEE MATTERS AGREEMENT, dated as of May 18, 2014 (as the same may be amended from time to time, the "Agreement"), between DIRECTV, a Delaware corporation ("DIRECTV"), AT&T Inc., a Delaware corporation ("Parent"), and Steam Merger Sub Inc., a Delaware corporation and wholly-owned Subsidiary of Parent ("Merger Sub"), each a "Party," and collectively, the "Parties."

WHEREAS, the respective Boards of Directors of each of DIRECTV and Parent, by resolutions duly adopted, have approved the merger of DIRECTV with and into Merger Sub (the "Merger") upon the terms and subject to the conditions set forth in that certain Agreement and Plan of Merger (the "Merger Agreement") and DIRECTV has resolved to recommend to its stockholders the adoption of the Merger Agreement;

WHEREAS, the Board of Directors of Parent, by resolutions duly adopted, has approved the Merger and the issuance of shares of common stock, par value $1.00 per share, of Parent pursuant to the Merger upon the terms and subject to the conditions set forth in the Merger Agreement;

WHEREAS, Parent seeks to efficiently and effectively integrate the businesses and employees of DIRECTV as soon as practicable after the Merger in a manner which maximizes the value of the transaction to shareholders and employees, and minimizes negative employee relations as well as restraints on post-Merger flexibility;

WHEREAS, in connection with the Merger, the Parties are entering into this Agreement in order to address certain employee compensation and benefit matters and this Agreement shall be a part of the Merger Agreement (and, for the avoidance of doubt, subject to the provisions of Article IX thereof); and

WHEREAS, this Agreement shall become effective as of the date hereof.

NOW, THEREFORE, in consideration of the mutual covenants and provisions hereinafter contained, the Parties hereby agree as follows:

1. DEFINITIONS. All initially capitalized terms used herein shall have the meanings ascribed to such terms in the Merger Agreement unless the context indicates otherwise.

2. INTERIM OPERATIONS.

(a)   With respect to Company Employees who are not Senior Executives, from and after the execution of the Merger Agreement and prior to the Closing Date, DIRECTV will be permitted to make customary annual base salary, wage piece rate and/or commission increases including promotions and merit increases in the ordinary course of business and consistent with past practice not to exceed 4.0% per year in the aggregate; additionally, DIRECTV will be permitted to continue to hire additional employees in the ordinary course of business and consistent with past practice; provided, however, that DIRECTV may, subject to Parent Approval (with such approval not to be unreasonably withheld, conditioned or delayed), make customary annual base salary, wage and/or commission increases for Senior Executives in the ordinary course of business and consistent with past practice that are subject to the aggregate maximums set forth above. For the purposes of this Agreement, "Senior Executives" shall mean Company Employees with the title of Executive Vice President or above, and "Parent Approval" shall mean the approval of the Senior Executive Vice President of Human Resources of Parent.

(b)   From and after the execution of the Merger Agreement and prior to the Closing Date, DIRECTV may grant and pay annual bonuses to Company Employees in the ordinary course of business consistent with past practices, based on actual performance in accordance with the terms of existing Company Plans as of the date hereof. The 2015 target cash incentive awards (and any subsequent pre-Merger cash incentive awards) provided to employees under the DIRECTV Employee Cash Bonus Plan will be pro-rated based on completed months of service if involuntarily terminated without cause prior to the end of the performance period (for the avoidance of doubt, if the employee is entitled to a bonus for the current year under such plan, the employee will only receive one such bonus payment and will not receive a duplicate bonus payment because of a pro-rata provision in another Company plan covering annual cash bonuses).

(c)   From and after the execution of the Merger Agreement and prior to the Closing Date, DIRECTV may grant long-term equity awards to Company Employees in the ordinary course of business consistent with past practice, provided that (i) the annualized grant date value of such awards shall not exceed 105% of aggregate target equity awards granted in the twelve (12) months prior to the date hereof, including the grant value of any outstanding stock grant cancelations during the period, (ii) the grant date value of awards to each Senior Executive shall not exceed the grant date value of the long-term equity awards granted to such person in 2014 prior to the date hereof and (iii) no award granted pursuant to this provision shall vest or pay out on an accelerated basis solely as a result of the transactions contemplated by the Merger Agreement and the 2015-2017 RSU grants (and any subsequent pre-Merger RSU grants) will be pro-rated based on completed months of service if involuntarily terminated without cause prior to the end of the performance period (for the avoidance of doubt, the proration of any such award(s) will be in lieu of, and not in addition to, any treatment upon termination of employment that would otherwise apply to such grant(s) under other Company Plans).

(d) DIRECTV may establish a retention pool in accordance with the terms of the plan set forth on Section 5.1(h)(i) of the Company Disclosure Letter of the Merger Agreement.

3. EMPLOYEE MATTERS.

(a) Parent agrees that, through December 31 of the calendar year following the Effective Time (the "Continuation Period"), Company Employees will be provided with (i) salary, base compensation, annual short term cash incentive target opportunities, long term equity award target opportunities, and employee benefits (including pension, 401(k) and retiree medical benefits) that are substantially comparable in the aggregate to those currently provided by DIRECTV and its Subsidiaries to such employees as of the date hereof.

(b) Parent shall or shall cause Merger Sub to (i) for 24 months after the Effective Time, continue in effect in accordance with its terms, each of the DIRECTV Executive Severance Plan and the DIRECTV Chief Executive Officer Severance Plan, each as in effect as of the date hereof and (ii) during the Continuation Period, continue in effect in accordance with its terms, the DIRECTV Severance Plan as in effect as of the date hereof.

(c) Parent shall or shall cause Merger Sub to provide that no pre-existing conditions, exclusions or waiting periods shall apply to Company Employees under the benefit plans provided for those employees except to the extent such condition or exclusion was applicable to an individual Company Employee prior to the Closing Date. When administratively practicable, Parent will transition Company Employees to applicable health and welfare plans of Parent at the start of the new plan year. Otherwise, with respect to the plan year during which the Closing Date occurs, Parent shall provide each Company Employee with credit, or a cash payment (on a tax neutral basis) in lieu thereof, for deductibles and out-of-pocket requirements paid prior to the Closing Date in satisfying any applicable deductible or out-of-pocket requirements under any Parent plan in which such Company Employee is eligible to participate following the Closing Date.

(d) From and after the Closing Date, Parent shall or shall cause Merger Sub and any successors to, provide credit (without duplication) to Company Employees for their service recognized by DIRECTV and its Subsidiaries as of the Closing Date for purposes of eligibility, vesting (e.g. pension & 401(k)), continuous service, determination of service awards, vacation, paid time off, and severance entitlements and eligibility to retire under applicable Parent plans to the same extent and for the same purposes as such service was credited under the Company Plans, provided, that such service shall not be recognized to the extent that such recognition would result in a duplication of benefits for the same period of service, for purposes of any frozen or discontinued Parent plan

or any frozen or discontinued portion of a Parent plan or for purposes of benefit accrual under any defined benefit pension plan or retiree medical plan, and
provided further, that if "hire date" is used to determine the particular Parent
plan or benefit structure in which a Company Employee would participate, if
any, then "hire date," solely for such purposes, shall be the Closing Date.

(e)   To the extent permitted by applicable Law and the terms of the applicable plan, and subject to the continued maintenance of the qualified status
of each plan, Parent may take action necessary to merge the DIRECTV 401(k)
Savings Plan (including outstanding loan balances) into the Parent 401(k) plan,
subject to the consummation of the transactions contemplated by this Agreement
and to commence Company Employees participation in Parent's 401(k) plan
after the Effective Time.

4. ADDITIONAL MATTERS.

(a)   Notwithstanding the foregoing and except for managerial, super-
visory or other employees statutorily exempt from collective bargaining, with
respect to any Company Employee who becomes subject to a collective bargaining agreement after the Effective Time, all compensation and benefits treatment
(as well as all terms and conditions of employment) afforded to such Company
Employee shall be provided only in accordance with the applicable collective
bargaining agreement (and shall no longer be covered by this Agreement).

(b)   The provisions of this Agreement are solely for the benefit of the
parties to this Agreement, and neither any union nor any current or former
employee, nor any other individual associated therewith, is or shall be regarded
for any purpose as a third party beneficiary to this Agreement; furthermore no
provision of this Agreement shall give any third party any right to enforce the
provisions of this Agreement, or be deemed to confer upon any such individual or legal representative any rights under or with respect to any plan, program or arrangement described in or contemplated by this Agreement, and
each such individual or legal representative shall be entitled to look only to the
express terms of any such plan, program or arrangement for his or her rights
thereunder.

(c)   No provision of this Agreement is intended to, or does, (i) constitute
the establishment of, or an amendment to, any Company Plan or any employee
benefit plan of Parent, DIRECTV, or any of their Affiliates, or (ii) alter or limit
the ability of Parent or DIRECTV to amend, modify or terminate any Company
Plan or any other benefit plan, program, agreement or arrangement; provided
that with respect to clause (ii), any actual amendment, modification or termination of any Company Plan impacting the provisions of this Agreement will take
into account the undertakings set forth herein.

[SIGNATURE PAGE FOLLOWS]

IN WITNESS WHEREOF, the Parties hereto have executed this Agreement as of the date written above.

DIRECTV

By: _____

Title: _____

Date: _____

AT&T INC.

By: _____

Title: _____

Date: _____

Stock Purchase Agreement

[ESCROW]
[DEFERRED NOTES]
[SHAREHOLDER REPRESENTATIVE]

DRAFT ___/___/04

STOCK PURCHASE AGREEMENT

by and among

THE STOCKHOLDERS NAMED HEREIN

TREKKER MARKETING, INC.
A California Corporation

THE MANAGEMENT STOCKHOLDERS NAMED HEREIN

and

GALAXY INTERNATIONAL CORP.
or its Nominee

for

all of the outstanding capital stock of

TREKKER MARKETING, INC.
A California Corporation

dated as of

April ___, 2004

TABLE OF CONTENTS

GLOSSARY OF DEFINED TERMS

ARTICLE IX   INDEMNIFICATION; REMEDIES

ARTICLE X   REPRESENTATIVE

ARTICLE XI   MISCELLANEOUS

[EXHIBITS OMITTED]

GLOSSARY OF DEFINED TERMS

STOCK PURCHASE AGREEMENT (this **"Agreement"**), dated as of June___, 20___, by and among the Stockholders listed on <u>Annex I</u> attached hereto (collectively **"Stockholders"**), Trekker Marketing, Inc. (**"Company"**), and Galaxy International Corp., a Delaware corporation, or its Nominee (**"Buyer"**), and Stanley Rockledge and Fred Merlin in their capacity as Management Stockholders (**"Management Stockholders"**).

RECITALS:

1.   The Company and the Company Subsidiaries (as defined in Section 3.1(c) hereof) design, manufacture and market high-end proprietary branded skateboards, snowboards, surfboards, apparel and related accessories through specialty retailers and a network of distributors worldwide (the **"Business"**).

2.   The Stockholders own all of the issued outstanding shares of capital stock of the Company as described and identified on <u>Annex I</u> (the **"Shares"**).

3.   Pursuant to the Company's Stock Option Plan (**"Stock Option Plan"**), 1,200,000 common stock options (**"Stock Options"**) are outstanding as of the date hereof.

4.   The Board of Directors of the Company believes that it is in the best interest of the Company and the Stockholders to enter into a transaction for the sale of the Company and that it is in the best interest of the Stockholders to structure a sale of the Company as provided in this Agreement. In consideration for Buyer entering into this Agreement Buyer has required the Company to enter into this Agreement and to make various representations and warranties and agree to take certain actions.

5.   Stockholders desire to sell to Buyer, and Buyer desires to purchase from the Stockholders, all of the Shares. Company intends to cause the Stock Options to be cancelled in exchange for the consideration to be paid to holders of options by Buyer.

6.   The Stockholders have appointed the Representative (as defined in Section 10.1) hereof) to take such actions, and accept such deliveries as provided herein to be taken or accepted by Stockholders other than the representations, warranties and covenants made by the Stockholders.

NOW, THEREFORE, in consideration of the foregoing and the respective representations, warranties, covenants, agreements, undertakings and obligations set forth herein, and intending to be legally bound hereby, the parties agree as follows:

ARTICLE I
SALE AND PURCHASE OF SHARES

Section 1.1   Sale and Purchase of Shares.   Upon the terms and subject to the conditions set forth in this Agreement and on the basis of the representations, warranties, covenants, agreements, undertakings and obligations contained herein, at the Closing (as defined in Section 2.1 hereof), Stockholders hereby agree to sell to Buyer, and Buyer hereby agrees to purchase from Stockholders, the Shares, free and clear of any and all Liens (as defined in Section 3.2(b) hereof) and Company shall cancel the Stock Options, for the consideration specified in this Article I.

Section 1.2   *Purchase Price.*   The purchase price (the **"Purchase Price"**) for the Shares and Stock Options shall consist of the following:

(a) $30.0 million, subject to any adjustment pursuant to Section 1.5(b), payable in cash and in shares of Galaxy International Corp. (**"Galaxy"**) common stock (**"Galaxy Shares"**) as more fully described in Annex II (the **"Initial Purchase Price"**);

(b) $5.0 million evidenced by promissory notes payable in four semiannual equal cash payments, plus accrued interest, commencing April 1, 2005, bearing simple interest of 7.25% per annum from the Closing Date (the **"Deferred Notes"**); and

(c)   Up to an additional US $7.0 million of Earnout Payments (as defined in Annex II attached hereto).

Section 1.3   *Delivery of Shares and Purchase Price.*   At the Closing:

(a)   The Stockholders, as holders of all outstanding certificates representing the Shares, shall upon surrender of such certificates to Buyer, be entitled to receive their respective allocation of the Initial Purchase Price and Deferred Notes determined pursuant to Section 1.2 and as set forth in Annex II, less $___ (the **"Escrow Amount"**) to be deposited in the Escrow Account (as defined in Section 1.4(a)) pursuant to Section 1.4. The Escrow Amount shall be allocated among the Stockholders as set forth on Annex II.

(b)   The cash portion of the Initial Purchase Price and any subsequent cash payments to be made by Buyer shall be paid by wire transfer in immediately available funds to the accounts designated in writing three (3) business days prior to Closing by each Stockholder.

(c)   Any Galaxy Shares issued toward payment of the Purchase Price shall be subject to the execution of the Stock Issuance Agreement between the Stockholder receiving the Galaxy Shares and Galaxy International Corp. in the form attached hereto as Exhibit 1.3(c) (**"Stock Issuance Agreement"**).

(d)   The Deferred Notes issued toward payment of the Purchase Price shall be in the form attached hereto as Exhibit 1.3(d).

(e)   None of the Purchase Price shall be delivered until the certificates or affidavits of lost shares and assignment, as applicable, representing 100% of the Shares have been surrendered by all of the Stockholders, provided that Buyer in its sole and absolute discretion may waive this provision.

(f)   Each issued and outstanding Option issued under the Company's Stock Option Plan shall be cancelled and converted into the right to receive the cash consideration set forth on Annex II.

Section 1.4   *Escrow.*

(a)   On the Closing Date, Buyer, Company and the Stockholders shall enter into an escrow agreement in the form attached hereto as Exhibit 1.4(a) (the **"Escrow Agreement"**) with a bank or a licensed escrow agent (the **"Escrow Agent"**), and Buyer, on behalf of the **Stockholders**, shall deposit into an interest bearing account in escrow (**"Escrow Account"**), pursuant to the Escrow

Agreement, the Escrow Amount. The Escrow Amount will stand as security for, but not as a limitation on, any and all claims for Damages (as defined in Section 9.2 hereof) (the **"Claims"**) and breached prior to or on the periods set forth in the Escrow Agreement (the **"Determination Period"**). The Escrow Amount shall also be available to Buyer for any Purchase Price adjustments due Buyer under Section 1.5. From time to time, the Escrow Agent will pay to the Buyer such amounts as may be required by the Escrow Agreement. On the fifteenth (15th) day following the expiration of the Determination Period, the Escrow Agent shall pay to the Stockholders, on a pro rata basis on their ownership percentages, the excess of (i) any Escrow Amount which has not already been paid to Buyer in respect of Claims over (ii) the aggregate amount of all Claims then pending. Claims made by Buyer against the Escrow Amount may be made at any time prior to the expiration of the Determination Period.

(b)   It is understood that the provisions of this Section 1.4 in no way limit the amount and timing of any claims made by the Buyer against the Company, Management Stockholders or Stockholders under this Agreement.

(c)   Buyer and the Stockholders will each pay one-half of the Escrow Agent's fees. Interest earned on the Escrow Amount shall be distributed pro rata in the same proportion that the principal is distributed to the parties under the Escrow Agreement.

Section 1.5   *Determination of Shareholders Equity.*

(a)   Definition of Shareholders Equity. The term **"Shareholders Equity"** shall mean the dollar amount by which the net book value of the assets of Company exceeds the net book value of the liabilities of Company, as reflected in the Closing Balance Sheet (as defined in Section 1.5(b)).

(b)   Closing Balance Sheet. A balance sheet of Company prepared as of the Closing Date (**"Closing Balance Sheet"**) and certified by Buyer's independent accountants (**"Buyer's Accountants"**) shall be prepared as follows:

(i)   Within forty-five (45) days after the Closing Date, Buyer (with the assistance of the Company and the Stockholders) shall deliver to the Stockholders an unaudited balance sheet of Company as of the Closing Date, prepared in accordance with GAAP (as defined in Section 3.3(b) hereof) from the books and records of Company, on a basis consistent with the generally accepted accounting principles theretofore followed by Company in the preparation of the Balance Sheet (as defined in Section 3.6(a) hereof) and in accordance with this Section 1.5(b), and fairly presenting the financial position of Company as of the Closing Date. The balance sheet shall be accompanied by detailed schedules of the assets and liabilities and by a report of Buyer's Accountants (1) setting forth the amount of Shareholder Equity (as defined above) reflected in the balance sheet, and (2) stating that the examination of the balance sheet has been prepared in accordance with GAAP, on a basis consistent with the accounting principles theretofore followed by Company.

(ii)   Within thirty (30) days following the delivery of the balance sheet referred to in (i) above, the Stockholders' Representative or its independent accountants (**"Stockholders Accountants"**) may object to any of the information contained in said balance sheet or accompanying schedules which could affect the necessity or amount of any payment by Buyer or Company pursuant to Section 1.5(d) hereof. Any such objection shall be made in writing, shall state the particular objection(s) and the basis therefor, and shall state the Stockholder's determination of the amount of the Shareholders Equity.

(iii)   In the event of a dispute or disagreement relating to the balance sheet or schedules which Buyer and Stockholders' Representative are unable to resolve within thirty (30) days following Buyer's receipt of Stockholders' Representative objection, either party may elect to have all such disputes or disagreements resolved by _____ (the **"Third Accounting Firm"**). Each party will furnish to the Third Accounting Firm such work papers and other documents and information as the Third Accounting Firm may request and are available to that party and will be afforded the opportunity to present to the Third Accounting Firm any material relating to the determination and to discuss the determination with the Third Party Accounting Firm. The Third Accounting Firm shall make a resolution of the disputed items of the balance sheet of Company as of the Closing Date and re-calculate the Shareholders Equity in order to reflect the resolution of such disputed items, which shall be final and binding for purposes of this Section 1.5. The Third Accounting Firm shall be instructed to use every reasonable effort to perform its services within fifteen (15) days of submission of the balance sheet to it and, in any case, as soon as practicable after such submission. The fees and expenses for the services of the Third Accounting Firm shall be shared equally by Buyer and Stockholders.

(iv)   Buyer and Stockholders agree that they will, and agree to cause their respective independent accountants to, cooperate and assist in the preparation of the Closing Balance Sheet and the calculation of Shareholders Equity and in the conduct of the audits and reviews referred to in this Section 1.5, including making available to the extent reasonably required books, records, work papers and personnel.

(c)   Adjustment of Final Cash Purchase Price. On or before the fifth business day following the final determination of the Closing Balance Sheet pursuant to this Section 1.5 (such date being hereinafter referred to as the **"Settlement Date"**), either (i) Buyer shall be paid from the Escrow Account the amount, if any, by which Shareholders Equity as reflected on the Balance Sheet (as defined in Section 3.6(a) hereof) exceeds Shareholders Equity as reflected on the Closing Balance Sheet, together with interest on the amount being paid from the Closing Date to the date of the payment at a rate per annum equal to seven percent (7%); or (ii) Buyer shall pay to the Stockholders pro rata according to their respective ownership of Common Stock as set forth in Annex I the amount, if any, by which Shareholders Equity as reflected on the Closing Balance Sheet, exceeds Shareholders Equity as reflected on the Balance Sheet, together with interest on the amount being paid from the Closing Date to the date of payment at a rate per annum equal to seven percent (7%) per annum.

ARTICLE II
THE CLOSING

Section 2.1 *Closing.*   The closing (the **"Closing"**) of the sale and purchase of the Shares (the **"Stock Purchase"**) and the other transactions provided for herein shall take place at the offices of Bigar, Strong & Wise, a professional corporation, at 5000 Wilshire Blvd., Los Angeles, California, at 10:00 A.M. (Los Angeles time) on the fifth (5th) business day following satisfaction or, if permissible, waiver of the conditions set forth in Article VII of this Agreement (excluding those conditions which by their nature are to be satisfied as a part of the Closing) or at such other place, time or date as the parties hereto may agree (the time and date of the Closing being herein referred to as the **"Closing Date"**).

Section 2.2   Deliveries by Stockholders to Buyer.   On the Closing Date, Stockholders (or the Stockholders' Representative and Company, as applicable) shall deliver, or cause to be delivered, to Buyer the following:

(a)   an original certificate or certificates evidencing all of the Shares, duly endorsed in blank or accompanied by stock powers duly executed in blank, in proper form for transfer, or affidavits of lost shares and assignment, as applicable;

(b)   the certificates, opinions, agreements and other documents and instruments to be delivered pursuant to Section 7.1 hereof;

(c)   a long-form "good standing" certificate for the Company and each Company Subsidiary (as defined in Section 3.1(e) hereof, and a copy of the Articles of Incorporation or Certificate of Incorporation and all amendments thereto (or equivalent document) of the Company and each Company Subsidiary, in each case certified by the Secretary of State of the jurisdiction of incorporation, each dated as of a date within five days prior to the Closing Date and certification to the good standing of such entities and listing all documents on file;

(d)   the Stock Issuance Agreements;

(e)   the Subordinated Note Agreement (as defined in Section 7.1(k) hereof);

(f)   the Stockholder Releases (as defined in Section 7.1(o)); and

(g)   such other closing documents as Stockholders' Representative, Company and Buyer shall reasonably agree.

Section 2.3   Deliveries by Buyer to Stockholders.   On the Closing Date, Buyer shall deliver, or cause to be delivered, to the Stockholders the following:

(a)   cash in immediately available funds and certificates representing the Galaxy Shares that comprise the Initial Purchase Price in accordance with Annex II (which shall be distributed by the Stockholders' Representative);

(b)   the Deferred Notes in accordance with Annex II;

(c)   the certificates, opinions, agreements and other documents and instruments to be delivered pursuant to Section 7.2 hereof; and

(d)   such other closing documents as Stockholders' Representative, Company and Buyer shall reasonably agree.

Section 2.4   Deliveries by Buyer to Escrow Account.   On the Closing Date, Buyer shall deliver, or cause to be delivered, to the Escrow Account the Escrow Amount in accordance with Section 1.3(a) hereof.

Section 2.5   Conversion of the Options; Other Securities.

(a) On the Closing Date, each Option shall be exercised in full, and if not exercised shall be terminated as of the Closing Date (including the Options issued under the Company's Stock Option Plan).

(b)   The Company shall promptly take all actions necessary to ensure that following the Closing Date no holder of the Options or rights pursuant to, nor any participant in, the Stock Option Plan or any other plan, programs or arrangement providing for the issuance or grant of any interest in respect of the capital stock of the Company and any Subsidiary of the Company will have any right thereunder to acquire equity securities, or any right to payment in respect of the equity securities, of the Company, or any subsidiary of the Company.

ARTICLE III
REPRESENTATIONS AND WARRANTIES OF COMPANY AND MANAGEMENT STOCKHOLDERS

Company and the Management Stockholders hereby represent and warrant to Buyer that the statements contained in this Article III are correct and complete as of the date of this Agreement and will be correct and complete as of the Closing Date (as though made then and as though the Closing Date were substituted for the date of this Agreement), except (i) as set forth in the Company's disclosure schedule accompanying this Agreement as the same may be modified or amended in accordance with Section 6.10 hereof (the **"Disclosure Schedule")**, or (ii) to the extent that such representations and warranties are expressly made as of a specified date.

Section 3.1   Organization and Good Standing; Company Subsidiaries.

(a)   Each of Company and each Company Subsidiary (as defined in Section 3.1(c)) is a corporation duly organized, validly existing and in good standing under the laws of their respective jurisdiction of incorporation, with full power and authority to conduct its business as it is now being conducted, to own or use the properties or assets that it purports to own or use, and to perform all of its respective obligations under all Applicable Contracts (as defined in Section 3.5(c) hereof). The Company and each Company Subsidiary is duly qualified or licensed to do business as a foreign corporation and is in good standing as a foreign corporation in each jurisdiction in which either the ownership or use of the properties owned or used by it, or the nature of the activities conducted by it, requires such licensing, qualification or good standing.

(b)   Company has made available or delivered to Buyer a true, complete and correct copy of the Company's and each Company Subsidiary's Certificate of Incorporation, and Articles of Incorporation and By-laws, each as amended to date (collectively, the **"Company's Organizational Documents")**. Neither the Company nor any Company Subsidiary are in violation of any of the provisions of the Company's Organizational Documents and, to the Knowledge (as defined in Section 11(b) hereof) of the Company, no condition exists that could reasonably be expected to constitute or result in such a violation. The Company's Organizational Documents so delivered are in full force and effect.

(c)   Schedule 3.1 (c) of the Disclosure Schedule sets forth a true, complete and correct list of all Subsidiaries (as defined below) of the Company (each hereinafter referred to individually as a **"Company Subsidiary"** and collectively as the **"Company Subsidiaries")**. For purposes of this Agreement, the term **"Subsidiary"** shall mean with respect to any Person (as defined in

Section 3.2(c) hereof), any corporation or other entity of which such Person has, directly or indirectly, ownership of securities or other interests having the power to elect a majority of such corporation's Board of Directors (or similar governing body), or otherwise having the power to direct the business and policies of that corporation. Schedule 3.1(c) of the Disclosure Schedule states, with respect to the Company each jurisdiction in which it is qualified to do business, and with respect to each Company Subsidiary, its jurisdiction of incorporation or organization, its authorized capital stock, its outstanding and issued shares of such capital stock, the percentage of each class of its capital stock owned by the Company and any other Persons and jurisdictions in which it is qualified to do business.

(d)   The minute books of the Company and each Company Subsidiary are up to date and contain accurate and complete records of all meetings held of and corporate action taken by the stockholders, and the Board of Directors.

Section 3.2   Capitalization.

(a)   The authorized capital stock of the Company consists solely of (i) 40,000,000 shares of Common Stock, $.001 par value (**"Common Stock"**), of which 12,000,000 shares of Common Stock are issued and outstanding, (ii) 11,000,000 shares of Series A Preferred Stock, $.001 par value, (**"Series A Preferred Stock"**), of which 1,000,000 shares of Series A Preferred Stock are issued and outstanding, (iii) 5,000,000 shares of Series B Preferred Stock, $.001 par value, (**"Series B Preferred Stock"**) of which 4,000,000 shares of Series B Preferred Stock are issued and outstanding. The Company's Common Stock, Series A Preferred Stock and Series B Preferred Stock is collectively referred to as **"Company Stock."** All of the issued and outstanding shares of Company Stock and the capital stock of each Company Subsidiary have been duly authorized and are validly issued, fully paid and nonassessable. All of the issued and outstanding shares of Company Stock have been issued in compliance with state and federal securities laws. Schedule 3.2(a) of the Disclosure Schedule sets forth a true and complete list of the holders of record shares of Company Stock and the number of such shares owned of record and beneficially by each such holder. Schedule 3.2(a) of the Disclosure Schedule sets forth a true and complete list of the Options, outstanding as of the date hereof, including the name of each holder thereof, the number of shares of Company Stock subject to each such Option, the per share exercise price for each such Option, the grant date of each such Option and whether each such Option was intended at the time of issuance to be an incentive stock option or a non-qualified stock option.

(b)   The Company is and shall be on the Closing Date the sole record and beneficial holder of all the issued and outstanding shares of capital stock of each Company Subsidiary, free and clear of all Liens. For purposes of this Agreement, the term **"Liens"** shall mean any charges, claims, community property interests, conditions, conditional sale or other title retention agreements, covenants, easements, encumbrances, equitable interests, exceptions, liens, mortgages, options, pledges, rights of first refusal, building use restrictions, rights of way, security interests, servitudes, statutory liens, variances, or restrictions of any kind, including any restrictions on use, voting, transfer, alienation, receipt of income, or exercise of any other attribute of ownership.

(c)   Except as set forth in <u>Schedule 3.2(c)</u> of the Disclosure Schedule and the Options listed on <u>Annex I</u>, there are no shares of capital stock or other securities of the Company or any Company Subsidiary (i) reserved for issuance or (ii) subject to preemptive rights or any outstanding subscriptions, options, warrants, calls, rights, convertible securities or other agreements or other instruments outstanding or in effect giving any Person the right to acquire any shares of capital stock or other securities of the Company or any Company Subsidiary or any commitments of any character relating to the issued or unissued capital stock or other securities of the Company or any Company Subsidiary. The Company does not have outstanding any bonds, debentures, notes or other obligations the holders of which have the right to vote (or convertible into or exercisable for securities having the right to vote) with the stockholders of the Company on any matter. For purposes of this Agreement, the term **"Person"** shall mean any individual, corporation (including any non-profit corporation), general or limited partnership, limited liability company, Governmental Entity (as defined in Section 3.4 hereof), joint venture, estate trust, association, organization or other entity of any kind or nature.

Section 3.3   Authority.   Company has the full legal right, requisite corporate power and authority and has taken all corporate action necessary in order to execute, deliver and perform fully, its obligations under this Agreement and to consummate the transactions contemplated herein. The execution and delivery of this Agreement by the Company and the consummation by the Company of the transactions contemplated herein have been duly authorized and approved by the Board of Directors of the Company and no other corporate proceeding with respect to the Company is necessary to authorize this Agreement or the transactions contemplated herein. This Agreement has been duly executed and delivered by Company and constitutes a valid and binding agreement of Company, enforceable against Company in accordance with its terms, except as such enforceability may be limited by general principles of bankruptcy, insolvency, reorganization and moratorium and other similar laws relating to creditor's rights (the **"Bankruptcy Exceptions"**).

Section 3.4   Governmental Filings and Consents.   Except as set forth in <u>Schedule 3.4</u> of the Disclosure Schedule, no notices, reports, submissions or other filings are required to be made by, and no consents, registrations, approvals, declarations, permits, expiration of any applicable waiting periods or authorizations are required to be obtained by, (collectively, **"Consents"**) the Company or any Company Subsidiary from, any foreign, federal, state, local, municipal, county or other governmental, quasi-governmental, administrative or regulatory authority, body, agency, court, tribunal, commission or other similar entity (including any branch, department or official thereof) (**"Governmental Entity"**), in connection with the execution or delivery of this Agreement by Company, the performance by Company of its obligations hereunder or the consummation by Company of the transactions contemplated herein.

Section 3.5   No Violations.   Assuming the obtaining of the Consents set forth in <u>Schedule 3.4</u> and <u>Schedule 3.5</u> of the Disclosure Schedule, the execution and delivery of this Agreement by Company does not, and the performance and consummation by Company of any of the transactions contemplated herein will not, with respect to the Company and each Company Subsidiary, directly or indirectly (with or without the giving of notice or the lapse of time or both);

(a)   contravene, conflict with, or constitute or result in a breach or violation of, or a default under any provision of the Company's Organizational Documents;

(b)   contravene, conflict with, or constitute or result in a breach or violation of, or a default under, or the acceleration of, or the triggering of any payment or other obligations pursuant to any existing Benefit Plan (as defined in Section 3.10(a) hereof) or any grant or award made under any Benefit Plan;

(c)   contravene, conflict with, or constitute or result in a breach or violation of, or a default under, or the cancellation, modification or termination of, or the acceleration of, or the creation of a Lien on any properties or assets owned or used by the Company or any Company Subsidiary pursuant to, or require the making of any filing or the obtaining of any Consent under, any provision of any agreement, license, lease, understanding, contract, loan, note, mortgage, indenture, promise, undertaking or other commitment or obligation (whether written or oral and express or implied) (a **"Contract"**), under which the Company or any Company Subsidiary is or may become bound or is or may become subject to any obligation or Liability (as defined in Section 3.23 hereof) or by which any of their respective assets owned or used are or may become bound (an **"Applicable Contract"**), in each case other than as set forth in Schedule 3.5 of the Disclosure Schedule;

(d)   contravene, conflict with, or constitute or result in a breach or violation of, any securities laws of any state, or any other federal, state, local, municipal, foreign, international, multinational, or other constitution, law, rule, standard, requirement, administrative ruling, order, ordinance, principle of common law, legal doctrine, code, regulation, statute, treaty or process (**"Law"**) or any award, decision, injunction, judgment, decree, settlement, order, process, or ruling, (whether temporary, preliminary or permanent) entered, issued, made or rendered by any court, administrative agency, arbitrator, Governmental Entity or other tribunal of competent jurisdiction (**"Order"**) or give any Governmental Entity or any other Person the right to challenge any of the transactions contemplated herein or to exercise any remedy or obtain any relief under, any Law or any Order to which the Company or any Company Subsidiary, or any of the assets owned or used by the Company or any Company Subsidiary, are subject; or

(e)   contravene, conflict with, or constitute or result in a breach or violation of, or a default under, any provision of, or give any Governmental Entity the right to revoke, withdraw, suspend, cancel, terminate or modify, any approval, franchise, certificate of authority, order, consent, judgment, decree, license, permit, waiver or other authorization issued, granted, given or otherwise made available by or under the authority of any Governmental Entity or pursuant to any Law (**"Governmental Authorization"**) that is held by the Company or any Company Subsidiary or that otherwise relates to the Business or any of the assets owned or used by the Company or any Company Subsidiary.

Section 3.6   Financial Statements.   (a)   The Company has previously furnished to Buyer the following financial statements (collectively, the **"Financial**

Statements"): (i) audited consolidated balance sheet of the Company and each Company Subsidiary as at December 31, 2002 and December 31, 2001, and the audited consolidated statements of income, changes in stockholders' equity and cash flow for each of the fiscal years then ended, together with the report thereon of Ernst & Young, independent certified public accountants, (ii) audited consolidated balance sheet of the Company and each Company Subsidiary as at December 31, 2003 (including the notes thereto, the **"Balance Sheet"**), and the related audited consolidated statements of income, changes in stockholders' equity and cash flow for the fiscal year then ended, together with the report thereon of Ernst & Young, independent certified public accountants, and (iii) an unaudited consolidated balance sheet of the Company and each Company Subsidiary as at March 31, 2004 (the **"Interim Balance Sheet"**) and the related unaudited consolidated statements of income, changes in stockholders' equity and cash flow for the three months then ended, including in each case the notes thereto.

(b)   The Financial Statements and notes fairly present, the financial condition and the results of operations, changes in stockholders' equity and cash flow of the Company and the Company Subsidiaries as at the respective dates of and for the periods referred to in such Financial Statements, and have been in accordance with United States generally accepted accounting principles (**"GAAP"**) applied on a consistent basis during the periods presented, subject in the case of unaudited financial statements, to normal recurring year-end adjustments (which adjustments shall not in any event result in a Material Adverse Effect) and absence of footnotes. No financial statements of any Person other than the Company and the Company Subsidiaries are required by GAAP to be included in the consolidated financial statements of the Company.

(c)   The Financial Statements were compiled from and are in accordance with the books and records of the Company and each Company Subsidiary, as the case may be. The books and records (including the books of account and other records) of the Company and each Company Subsidiary, all of which have been made available to Buyer, are true, complete and correct, have been maintained in accordance with sound business practices and accurately present and reflect in all material respects all of the transactions and actions therein described. At the Closing, all of those books and records shall be in the possession of the Company and each Company Subsidiary.

Section 3.7   Absence of Certain Changes and Events.   Except as set forth in Schedule 3.7 of the Disclosure Schedule, since the date of the Balance Sheet, the Company and each Company Subsidiary has conducted the Business only in, and has not engaged in any transaction other than according to, the ordinary and usual course of such business in a manner consistent with its past practice (**"Ordinary Course of Business"**), and there has not been any:

(a)   change in the business, operations, properties, prospects, assets, or condition of the Company or any Company Subsidiary that is reasonably likely to have a Material Adverse Effect (as defined in Section 11.1(a) hereof) on the Company:

(b)   (i) material increase in salary, bonus or other compensation (other than compensation increases in the Ordinary Course of Business of any employee, director or consultant of the Company or any Company Subsidiary;

or (ii) increase in benefits, material waivers or variations for the benefit of any such employee, director or consultant, material amendments, or payments or grants of awards that were not required, under any Benefit Plan), or adoption or execution of any new Benefit Plan;

(c)   (i) damage to or destruction or loss of any material asset or property of the Company or any Company Subsidiary, whether or not covered by insurance;

(d)   payment of, accrual or commitment for, capital expenditures in excess of $25,000 individually or $100,000 in the aggregate;

(e)   (i) making of any loans or advances to any Person (other than intercompany receivables extensions of credit to customers in the Ordinary Course of Business); or (ii) payment, discharge or satisfaction of Liabilities reflected or reserved against in the Financial Statements or subsequently incurred in the Ordinary Course of Business;

(f)   (i) change in the authorized or issued capital stock of the Company or any Company Subsidiary; (ii) grant of any stock option, warrant, or other right to purchase shares of capital stock of the Company or any Company Subsidiary; (iii) issuance of any security convertible into the capital stock of the Company or any Company Subsidiary; (iv) grant of any registration rights in respect of the capital stock of the Company or any Company Subsidiary; (v) reclassification, combination, split, subdivision, purchase, redemption, retirement, issuance, sale, or any other acquisition or disposition, directly or indirectly, by the Company or any Company Subsidiary of any shares of the capital stock of the Company or any Company Subsidiary; (vi) any amendment of any material term of any outstanding security of the Company or any Company Subsidiary; (vii) declaration, setting aside or payment of any dividend (whether in cash, securities or other property) or other distribution or payment in respect of the shares of the capital stock of the Company or any Company Subsidiary, except in respect of satisfaction of intercompany payables and receivables; or (viii) sale or pledge of any stock or other equity interests owned by the Company in the Company Subsidiaries;

(g)   sale of any material asset or property of the Company or a Company Subsidiary;

(h)   material change in accounting methods used by the Company; or

(i)   agreement (whether written or oral and express or implied) by the Company or any Company Subsidiary to do any of the foregoing.

Section 3.8   Actions; Orders.

(a)   Except as set forth in Schedule 3.8 of the Disclosure Schedule, there are no civil, criminal, administrative, investigative, quasi-judicial or informal actions, audits, demands, suits, claims, arbitrations, hearings, litigations, disputes, investigations or other proceedings of any kind or nature in any federal, state, local or foreign jurisdiction or before any arbitrator at law, in equity or otherwise (**"Actions"**) filed, commenced, pending or, to the Knowledge of the Company, or Management Stockholders, Threatened (as defined in Section 11.1(c) hereof), against the Company or any Company Subsidiary or any of their respective assets.

(b)   Except as set forth in Schedule 3.8(b) of the Disclosure Schedule, neither the Company nor any Company Subsidiary or any of the assets owned or used by the Company or Company Subsidiary is subject to any Order.

(c) None of the matters set forth in Schedule 3.8 (a) or (b) of the Disclosure Schedule are reasonably expected to result in a Material Adverse Effect on the Company. To the Knowledge of the Company or the Managing Stockholders, no Action or Order has been Threatened and no event has occurred or circumstance exists that is reasonably likely to give rise to or serve as a basis for the commencement of any such Action or the issuance of any such Order of the nature described in Section 3.8(a) or 3.8(b). Company has delivered or made available to Buyer copies of all pleadings, correspondence and other documents relating to each Action and Order listed in Schedule 3.8(a) or 3.8(b) of the Disclosure Schedule.

Section 3.9   Taxes.

(a)   Except as set forth in Schedule 3.9(a) of the Disclosure Schedule, (i) all Tax Returns (defined in Section 3.9(j) hereof) that are or were required to be filed by or with respect to the Company and each Company Subsidiary, either separately or as a member of an affiliated, combined, consolidated or unitary group of corporations, have been filed on a timely basis (taking into account all extensions of due dates) in accordance with applicable Law, (ii) all Tax Returns referred to in clause (i) are true complete and correct in all material respects, (iii) all Taxes (defined in Section 3.9(j) due for the periods covered by such Tax Returns, including any Taxes payable pursuant to any assessment made by the Internal Revenue Service or other relevant taxing authority in respect of such periods, have been paid in full, and (iv) all estimated Taxes required to be paid in respect of the Company and each Company Subsidiary have been paid in full when due in accordance with applicable Law. Company has delivered or made available to Buyer true and correct copies of all Tax Returns filed by the Company, each Company Subsidiary, and any affiliated, combined, consolidated or unitary group of which the Company or any Company Subsidiary is or was a member (insofar as such Tax Returns relate to the Company or any Company Subsidiary).

(b)   Except as set forth in Schedule 3.9(b) of the Disclosure Schedule, (i) the Tax Returns referred to in Section 3.9(a) have been examined by the Internal Revenue Service or the appropriate state, local or foreign taxing authority, or the period for assessment of the Taxes in respect of which such Tax Returns were filed has expired under the applicable statute of limitations (after giving effect to all extensions and waivers), (ii) all deficiencies asserted or assessments made as a result of such examinations have been paid in full, and no issues that were raised by the Internal Revenue Service or other relevant taxing authority, in connection with any such examination are currently pending, and (iii) none of Seller nor the Company nor any Company Subsidiary has given or been requested to give a waiver or extension (or is or could be subject to a waiver or extension given by any other Person) of any statute of limitations relating to the payment of Taxes of the Company or any Company Subsidiary or for which the Company or any Company Subsidiary is or is reasonably likely to be liable.

(c)   Except as set forth in Schedule 3.9(c) of the Disclosure Schedule, the charges, accruals and reserves with respect to Taxes provided in the Balance Sheet and the Interim Balance Sheet are adequate (determined in accordance with GAAP on a basis consistent with that of the preceding period) to cover the aggregate liability of the Company and each Company Subsidiary for Taxes in respect of all Pre-Closing Tax Periods (defined in Section 3.9(j)) for which Tax Returns have not yet been filed or for which Taxes are not yet due and payable.

(d)   There is no Tax sharing agreement, contract or intercompany account system in existence that would require any payment by the Company or any Company Subsidiary after the date of this Agreement. Neither the Company nor any Company Subsidiary has any liability for indemnification of third parties with respect to Taxes or any liability for Taxes as a transferee.

(e)   The Company is not a "foreign person" within the meaning of Section 1445 of the Code.

(f)   Neither the Company nor any Company Subsidiary is a party to any agreement, contract, arrangement or plan that has resulted or would result, separately or in the aggregate, in the payment of any "excess parachute payment" within the meaning of Section 280G of the Code.

(g)   There are no Liens for Taxes (other than Liens for current Taxes not yet due and payable) upon the assets of the Company or any Company Subsidiary. There is no basis for the assertion of any claim for Taxes which, if adversely determined, would or is reasonably likely to result in the imposition of any Lien on the assets of the Company for any Company Subsidiary or otherwise adversely affect Buyer, the Company or any Company Subsidiary or their use of such assets.

(h)   All Taxes that the Company or any Company Subsidiary is or was required by Law to withhold or collect have been duly withheld or collected and, to the extent required by applicable Law, have been paid to the proper Governmental Entity or other Person.

(i)   Company has provided or made available to Buyer copies of all record retention agreements currently in effect between the Company or any Company Subsidiary and any taxing authority.

(j)   For purposes of this Agreement, the following terms shall have the following meanings:

"Code" means the Internal Revenue Code of 1986, as amended.

"Pre-Closing Tax Period" means any taxable year or period that ends on or before the Closing Date and, with respect to any taxable year or period beginning before and ending after the Closing Date, the portion of such taxable year or period ending on and including the Closing Date.

"Tax" means any Federal, state, local or foreign income, gross receipts, license, severance, occupation, capital gains, premium, environmental, customs, duties, profits, disability, registration, alternative or add on minimum, estimated, withholding, payroll, employment, unemployment, insurance, social security (or similar), excise, production, sales, use, value-added, occupancy, franchise, real property, personal property, business and occupation, mercantile, windfall profits, capital stock, stamp, transfer, workmen's compensation or other tax, of any kind whatsoever, including any interest, penalties, additions, assessments or deferred liability with respect thereto, and any interest in respect of such penalties, additions, assessments or deferred liability, whether or not disputed.

"Tax Return" means any return, report, notice, form, declaration, claim for refund, estimate, election, or information statement or other document relating to any Tax, including any Schedule or attachment thereto, and any amendment thereof.

Section 3.10   Employee Benefits: ERISA.

(a)   <u>Schedule 3.10(a)</u> of the Disclosure Schedule sets forth a true, complete and correct list of, each profit-sharing, pension, severance, thrift, savings, incentive change of control, employment, retirement, bonus, deferred compensation, group life and health insurance other employee benefit plan, agreement, arrangement or commitment, which is maintained, contributed to or required to be contributed to by the Company or any Company Subsidiary on behalf of any current or former employee, director or consultant of the Company or any Company Subsidiary (all of which are hereinafter referred to as the **"Benefit Plans"**). <u>Schedule 3.10(a)</u> identifies each of the Benefit Plans which constitutes an "employee benefit plan" as defined in Section 3(3) of the Employee Retirement Income Security Act of 1974, as amended (**"ERISA"**). Neither the Company nor any Company Subsidiary has any formal commitment, or intention communicated to employees, to create any additional Benefit Plan or modify or change any existing Benefit Plan.

(b)   With respect to each of the Benefit Plans, the Company has delivered to Buyer true, complete and correct copies of each of the following documents, if applicable: (i) the plan document (including all amendments thereto); (ii) trust documents and insurance contracts; (iii) the annual report for the last two years (iv) the actuarial report for the last two years; (v) the most recent summary plan description, together with each summary of material modifications; (vi) the most recent determination letter received from the Internal Revenue Service; (vii) the most recent nondiscrimination tests performed under ERISA and the Code (including 401(k) and 401(m) tests).

(c)   Each Benefit Plan has been operated and administered in accordance with its terms and with applicable law including, but not limited to, ERISA and the Code, and all notices filings and disclosures required by ERISA or the Code have been timely made. Each Benefit Plan which is an "employee pension benefit plan" within the meaning of Section 3(2) of ERISA (a **"Pension Plan"**) and which is intended to be qualified under Section 401 (a) of the Code has received a favorable determination letter from the Internal Revenue Service for "TRA" (as defined in Rev. Proc. 93-39), or will file for such a determination letter prior to the expiration of the remedial amendment period for such Benefit Plan and, to the Knowledge of the Company or Management Stockholders, there are no circumstances that are reasonably likely to result in revocation of any such favorable determination letter. There is no pending or, to the Knowledge of the Company, Threatened litigation relating to any of the Benefit Plans. None of the Company or any Company Subsidiary has engaged in a transaction with respect to any Benefit Plan that, assuming the taxable period of such transaction expired as of the date hereof, could subject the Company or any Company Subsidiary or any Benefit Plan to a Tax or penalty imposed by ERISA. No action has been taken with respect to any of the Benefit Plans to either terminate any of such Benefit Plans or to cause distributions, other than in the Ordinary Course of Business to participants under such Benefit Plans.

(d)   None of the Pension Plans is a "multiemployer plan" (within the meaning of Section 4001(a)(3) of ERISA) and neither the Company nor any Company Subsidiary (or any current ERISA Affiliate) has contributed to or had any obligation to contribute to a multiemployer plan during the six-year period immediately preceding the date hereof. Neither the Company nor any

Company Subsidiary has formerly contributed to, or had an obligation to contribute to a multi-employer plan.

(e) All contributions required to be made under the terms of any Benefit Plan have been timely made when due. No Pension Plan has an "accumulated funding deficiency" (whether or not waived) within the meaning of Section 412 of the Code or Section 302 of ERISA and none of the Company, any Company Subsidiary or any ERISA Affiliate has an outstanding funding waiver.

(f) The consummation of the transactions contemplated by this Agreement will not (or will not upon termination of employment within a fixed period of time following such consummation) (i) entitle any employee, director or consultant to severance pay, unemployment compensation or any other payment or (ii) accelerate the time of payment or vesting or increase the amount of payment with respect to any compensation due to any employee, director or consultant.

Section 3.11   Labor Matters; Employees.   Except as set forth in <u>Schedule 3.11</u> of the Disclosure Schedule:

(a)   The Company and each Company Subsidiary has not been a party to, and is not bound by, any collective bargaining agreement or other labor Contract nor is any collective bargaining agreement or other labor Contract currently being negotiated, nor, to the Knowledge of the Company or Management Stockholders, are there any activities or proceedings of any labor union or labor organization to organize any of the employees of the Company or any Company Subsidiary Threatened.

(b)   There has not been, there is not presently pending or existing and, to the Knowledge of the Company or Management Stockholders, there is not threatened and there has not occurred any event or circumstance that is reasonably likely to provide the basis for, any strike, slowdown, picketing, work stoppage, labor difficulty, labor arbitration or other proceeding in respect of the grievance of any employee, application or complaint filed by an employee or union with the National Labor Relations Board or any comparable Governmental Entity and none of the employment policies or practices of the Company or a Company Subsidiary is currently being audited or investigated by any federal, state or local government agency.

(c)   There is no labor strike, dispute, claim, charge, lawsuit, proceeding, labor slowdown or stoppage pending or Threatened against or involving the Company or any Company Subsidiary.

(d)   To Knowledge of Company and Management Stockholders no key employee of the Company or any Company Subsidiary, intends to terminate his or her employment following the Closing. Since December 31, 2003, neither the Company nor any Company Subsidiary has experienced any difficulties in obtaining any qualified personnel necessary for the operations of its business. The Company is not a party to any employment Contract with any individual or employee. There is not pending or existing or to the Knowledge of the Company, any Action Threatened against or affecting the Company or any Company Subsidiary relating to the alleged violation of any Law pertaining to labor relations or employment matters. To the Knowledge of the Company no event has occurred or circumstances exist that could provide the basis for such Action. The Company and each Company Subsidiary has complied in all respects with all Laws relating to employment, equal employment opportunity, nondiscrimination, immigration ages, hours, benefits, collective bargaining, the payment of social security and similar taxes, occupational safety and health. The Company is not subject to any settlement or consent decree with any present or former employee, employee representative or any Governmental Entity relating to claims of discrimination or other claims in respect to employment practices and policies; and no Governmental Entity has issued a judgment, order, decree or finding with respect to the labor and employment practices (including practices relating to discrimination) of the Company or any Company Subsidiary. Since December 31, 2001 the Company has not incurred any liability or obligation under the Worker Adjustment and Retraining Notification Act or similar state laws; and neither Company nor any Company Subsidiary has laid off more than ten percent (10%) of its employees at any single site of employment in any ninety (90) day period during the twelve (12) month period ending at the Closing Date.

(e)   The Company is in compliance in all respects with the provisions of the Americans with Disabilities Act.

(f)   The consummation of the transactions contemplated by this Agreement will not (or will not upon termination of employment within a fixed period of time following such consummation) (i) entitle any employee, director or consultant to severance pay, unemployment compensation or any other payment or (ii) accelerate the time of payment or vesting or increase the amount of payment with respect to any compensation due to any employee, director or consultant.

Section 3.12   *Compliance with Laws; Governmental Authorizations; etc.*

(a)   Except as set forth in <u>Schedule 13.12(a)</u> of the Disclosure Schedule, the Company and each Company Subsidiary is in compliance in all material respects with all applicable Laws.

(b)   Except as set forth in <u>Schedule 3.12(b)</u> of the Disclosure Schedule, the Company and each Company Subsidiary hold and maintain in full force and effect all Governmental Authorizations required to conduct the Business in the manner and in all such jurisdictions as it is currently conducted and to permit the Company and the Company Subsidiaries to own and use their respective properties and assets in the manner in which they currently own and use such assets.

(i)   The Company and each Company Subsidiary is, and at all times has been, in full in compliance with all of the terms and requirements of each such Governmental Authorization;

(ii)   no event has occurred or circumstance exists that is reasonably likely to (with or without the giving of notice or the lapse of time or both) (A) constitute or result, directly or indirectly, in a violation of, or a failure to comply with, any term or requirement of any such Governmental Authorization, or (B) result, directly or indirectly, in the revocation, withdrawal, suspension, cancellation, or termination of, or any modification to, any such Governmental Authorization;

(iii)   neither the Company nor any Company Subsidiary has received, at any time since December 31, 2001 any notice or other communication from any Governmental Entity or any other Person regarding (A) any actual, alleged, possible or potential violation of, or failure to comply with, any term or requirement of any Governmental Authorization or Law, or (B) any actual, proposed, possible, or potential revocation, withdrawal, suspension, cancellation, termination of, or modification to any Governmental Authorization or Law;

(iv)   all applications required to have been filed for the renewal of each such Governmental Authorization have been duly filed on a timely basis with the appropriate Governmental Entity, and all other filings required to have been made with respect to each such Governmental Authorizations have been duly made on a timely basis with the appropriate Governmental Entity.

Section 3.13 Title to Properties. The Company and each Company Subsidiary has good and marketable title to all real and personal properties and assets owned by the Company or such Company Subsidiary, free and clear of any Lien, except for (i) liens for Taxes not yet due and payable or for Taxes that the taxpayer is contesting in good faith through appropriate proceedings, (ii) purchase money liens and liens securing rental payments under capital lease arrangements, and (iii) other minor imperfections of title that do not have any material impact with respect to the ownership or use of the applicable property (**"Permitted Exceptions"**). All properties held under lease by the Company or any Company Subsidiary are held under valid, subsisting and enforceable leases.

Section 3.14   Real and Personal Property.
(a)   Real Property. Neither the Company nor any Company Subsidiary owns or hold any interest in real property other than as set forth in Schedule 3.14(a) to the Disclosure Schedule (the **"Real Property"**). Except as set forth on such schedule, the Company and each Company Subsidiary, as applicable, has good and marketable title to all Real Property and none of the Real Property is subject to any Lien, except for Permitted Exceptions.

(b)   Personal Property. Except as set forth on Schedule 3.14(b) of the Disclosure Schedule and except for inventory, supplies and other personal property disposed of or consumed, and accounts receivable collected or written off, and cash utilized, all in the Ordinary Course of Business consistent with past practice, the Company and each Subsidiary, as applicable owns all of its inventory, equipment and other personal property (both tangible and intangible) reflected on the Balance Sheet free and clear of any Liens, except for Permitted Exceptions. All of the assets presently owned by the Company and its subsidiaries are sufficient to operate the Business as currently conducted.

(c)   Condition of Properties. Except as set forth on Schedule 13.14(c) of the Disclosure Schedule, the tangible personal property owned or leased by the Company and each Company Subsidiary, as applicable, is structurally sound, free of defects and deficiencies and in good operating condition and repair, (ordinary wear and tear excepted).

(d)   Compliance. The continued ownership, operation, use and occupancy of the Real Property and the improvements thereto, and the continued use and occupancy of the leasehold estates the subject of the Real Property Leases (as defined in Section 3.15 hereof) as currently operated, used and occupied will not violate any zoning, building, health, flood control, fire or other law, ordinance, order or regulation or any restrictive covenant. There are no violations of any Law affecting any portion of the Real Property or the leasehold estates and no written notice of any such violation has been issued by any Governmental Entity.

Section 3.15   Real Property Leases; Options.   Schedule 3.15 to the Disclosure Schedule sets forth a list by common address and description of lease parties (i) all leases and subleases under which the Company and each Company Subsidiary is lessor or lessee or sublessor or sublessee of any real property, together with all amendments, supplements, nondisturbance agreements, brokerage and commission agreements and other agreements pertaining thereto (**"Real Property Leases"**); (ii) all material options held by the Company and each Company Subsidiary or contractual obligations on the part of the Company and each Company Subsidiary to purchase or acquire any interest in real property; and (iii) all options granted by the Company and each Company Subsidiary or contractual obligations on the part of the Company and each Company Subsidiary to sell or dispose of any material interest in real property. Copies of all Real Property Leases and such options and contractual obligations have been delivered to Buyer. The Company and each Company Subsidiary has not assigned any Real Property Leases or any such options or obligations. There are no disputes, oral agreements or forbearance programs in effect as to any Real Property Lease; all facilities leased under the Real Property Leases (including alternations constructed by the Company and each Company Subsidiary and shelving installed by the Company and each Company Subsidiary) have received all approvals of Governmental Entities (including licenses and permits) required in connection with the operation thereof; and all facilities leased under the Real Property Leases are supplied with utilities and other services necessary for the operation of said facilities. There are no Liens on the interest of the Company and each Company Subsidiary in the Real Property Leases except for Permitted Exceptions. The Real Property Leases and options and contractual obligations listed on Schedule 3.15 to the Disclosure Schedule are in full force and effect (subject to Bankruptcy Exceptions) and constitute binding obligations of the Company and each Company Subsidiary, as applicable, and (x) there are no defaults thereunder by the Company or the applicable Company Subsidiary and (y) no event has occurred that with notice, lapse of time or both would constitute a default by the Company or the applicable Company Subsidiary, as applicable, or, to the Knowledge of the Company and the Management Shareholders, by any other party thereto.

Section 3.16   Intellectual Property Rights.
(a)   For purposes of this Agreement, the following terms shall have the following meanings:
"Intellectual Property" means (whether international or United States) (a) all trademarks, service marks, trade dress, logos, trade names, and corporate names (whether registered or unregistered), together with all translations, adaptations, derivations, and combinations thereof and including all goodwill associated therewith, and all applications, registrations, and renewals in connection therewith (**"Marks"**), (b) all copyrightable works, all copyrights (whether or registered or unregistered), and all applications, registrations, and renewals in connection therewith (**"Copyrights"**), (c) all mask works and all applications, registrations, and renewals in connection therewith, (d) all trade secrets and

confidential business information (including ideas, research and development, know-how, formulas, compositions, manufacturing and production processes and techniques, technical data, designs, drawings, specifications, customer and supplier lists, pricing and cost information, and business and marketing plans and proposals), (e) all computer software (including data and related documentation), all inventions (whether patentable or unpatentable and whether or not reduced to practice), all improvements thereto, (f) all URL's and domain names, and (g) all patents, patent applications, and patent disclosures, together with all reissuances, continuations, continuations-in-part, revisions, extensions, and reexaminations thereof (**"Patents"**), (h) all other proprietary rights relating to the foregoing, and (i) all copies and tangible embodiments thereof (in whatever form or medium).

"Company Intellectual Property" shall mean any Intellectual Property that is owned by or licensed to the Company or any Company Subsidiary (other than mass marketed software licensed to the Company or any Company subsidiary) or used thereby (collectively, the "Intellectual Property").

"Company Registered Intellectual Property" means Company Intellectual Property consisting of (i) Patents, (ii) registered Marks, and (iii) registered Copyrights, (and in each case applications for registration), and (iv) any other Company Intellectual and Property that is the subject of an application, certificate, filing, registration or other document issued by, filed with, or recorded by any Governmental Entity.

(b)   Schedule 3.16(b) of the Disclosure Schedule lists the Company Registered Intellectual Property. Each item of Registered Intellectual Property registered with a Governmental Entity is valid and subsisting; all necessary registration, maintenance and renewal fees currently due in connection with such Registered Intellectual Property have been made and all necessary documents, recordations and certificates in connection with such Registered Intellectual Property have been filed with the relevant patent, copyrights, trademark authorities in the United States or foreign jurisdictions, as the case may be, for the purpose of maintaining such Company Registration Intellectual Property.

(c)   The Company owns and has good and marketable title to, or has the right to use pursuant to a written license, sublicense, agreement or other permission, exclusive right and title to each item of Company Intellectual Property free and clear of any Lien (excluding non-exclusive licenses and related restrictions granted in the Ordinary Course of Business). Except as stated on Schedule 3.16(c) of the Disclosure Schedule, there are no pending proceedings or adverse claims made or, to the Knowledge of the Company or Management Stockholders, Threatened against the Company or any Company Subsidiary with respect to Company Intellectual Property; and there has been no litigation commenced or Threatened in writing within the past five (5) years with respect to Company Registered Intellectual Property or the rights of the Company or a Company Subsidiary therein. The Company Intellectual Property or the use thereof by the Company or a Company Subsidiary does not conflict with or infringe any Intellectual Property of any other Person (**"Third Party Intellectual Property"**), (ii) such Third Party Intellectual Property or its use by others or any other conduct of a third party does not conflict with or infringe upon any Company Registered Intellectual Property or its use by the Company or any Company Subsidiary.

(d) To the Knowledge of the Company and Management Stockholders, none of the Company's or any Company Subsidiary's key employees is in violation of any term of any employment contract, patent disclosure agreement, confidential agreement or any other Contract relating to the relationship of any such employee with the Company or any Company Subsidiary or any other party the result of which has had or is reasonably likely to have a Material Adverse Effect.

Section 3.17 *Inventory.* The inventory of the Company and each Company Subsidiary consists of raw materials and supplies, manufactured and purchased parts, goods on order and in process, and finished goods, all of which is merchantable and fit for the purpose for which it was procured or manufactured (including all inventory, that is reflected on the Interim Balance Sheet) is of such qualify and quantity as to be saleable and useable by the Company and Companies subsidiaries in the Ordinary Course of Business, and none of the inventory is slow moving and obsolete (including without limitation, inventory of a type which has not had substantial sales during the past 12 months), damaged or defective, except as accounted for in the reserve for inventory writedown reflected in the Interim Balance Sheet as adjusted for the passage of time through the Closing Date in accordance with the past custom and practice of the Company.

Section 3.18 *Accounts Receivable.* Except as set forth in <u>Schedule 3.18</u> of the Disclosure Schedule, all accounts receivable of the Company and each Company Subsidiary presented in the Balance Sheet and the Interim Balance Sheet and those arising since the date thereof are (a) reflected properly on their respective books and records, (b) are valid and genuine, (c) arise out of bona fide performance of services or transactions, (d) are not subject to setoffs, defenses or counterclaims, (e) are current and collectable, and will be collected in accordance with their terms at their recorded amounts (except as set forth as reserves on the Interim Balance Sheet.

Section 3.19 *Contracts; No Default.*
(a) Except as set forth in <u>Schedule 3.19(a)</u> of the Disclosure Schedule, neither the Company nor any Company Subsidiary is a party to or bound by any Contract (excluding in each case policies of insurance issued in the Ordinary Course of Business):
(i) evidencing indebtedness for borrowed money or pursuant to which the Company or any Company Subsidiary has guaranteed (including guarantees by way of acting as surety, co-signer, endorser, co-maker, indemnitor or otherwise) any obligation of any other Person;
(ii) prohibiting or limiting the ability of the Company or any Company Subsidiary (A) to engage in any line of business, (B) to compete with any Person, (C) to carry on or expand the nature or geographical scope of the Business anywhere in the world or (D) to disclose any confidential information in the possession of the Company or any Company Subsidiary (and not otherwise generally available to the public) that is reasonably likely to have a Material Adverse Effect on the Company or any Company Subsidiary in the conduct of the Business which relates to the use of an item of Intellectual Property;

(iii) pursuant to which it (A) leases or licenses from or to any other Person any tangible personal property providing for lease payments in excess of $10,000 per annum or (B) purchases or sells materials, supplies, equipment or services outside the Ordinary Course of Business;

(iv) which is a partnership agreement, joint venture agreement, profit sharing or other Contract (however named);

(v) providing for the acquisition or disposition after the date of this Agreement of any portion of the Business or assets of the Company or any Company Subsidiary other than in the Ordinary Course of Business;

(vi) providing for team rider agreements, or sponsorship agreements;

(vii) provides for a distribution or seller representative agreement or arrangement;

(viii) pursuant to which the Company or a Company Subsidiary has the right to use an item of Third Party Intellectual Property;

(ix) pursuant to which the Company or a Company Subsidiary has granted a Person to use an item of Company Intellectual Property;

(x) involving a payment after the date hereof of an amount of money in excess of $10,000 and continuing (including mandatory renewals or extensions which do not require the consent of the Company or any Company Subsidiary) more than one year from its date and not made in the Ordinary Course of Business;

(xi) a mortgage, pledge, security agreement, deed of trust or other document granting a Lien over any real or personal asset or property owned by the Company or any Company Subsidiary.

Company has delivered or made available to Buyer a true, complete and correct copy of each Contracts identified or required to be identified in Schedule 3.19(a) of the Disclosure Schedule and each such Contract is in full force and effect and is valid and enforceable in accordance with its terms.

(b) Except as set forth in Schedule 3.19(b) of the Disclosure Schedule,

(i) the Company and each Company Subsidiary is in substantial compliance with all applicable material terms and requirements of each Contract identified or required to be identified in Schedule 3.19(a) of the Disclosure Schedule;

(ii) to the knowledge of the Company and the Management Stockholders, each other Person that has or had any obligation or Liability under any Contract identified or required to be identified in Schedule 3.19(a) of the Disclosure Schedule is in substantial compliance with all applicable terms and requirements of each such Contract;

(iii) no event has occurred or circumstance exists (presently or as a result of the change in control of Company by this Agreement) that is reasonably likely to (with or without the giving of notice or the lapse of time or both) contravene, conflict with, or result in a violation or breach of, or give the Company or any Company Subsidiary or other Person the right to declare a default or exercise any remedy under, or to accelerate the maturity or performance of, or to cancel, terminate, or modify, any Contract identified or required to be identified in Schedule 3.19(a) of the Disclosure Schedule.

Section 3.20   Environmental Matters.

(a)   Except as set forth in <u>Schedule 3.20</u> of the Disclosure Schedule,

(i)   the Company and each Company Subsidiary has conducted the Business in full compliance with all applicable Environmental Laws (as defined in Section 3.20(b) hereof), including having all permits, licenses and other approvals and Governmental Authorizations necessary or appropriate for the Business under any Environmental Law;

(ii)   neither the Company nor any Company Subsidiary has, in connection with the Business, disposed of or released any Hazardous Substances (as defined in Section 3.18(c) hereof) or hazardous wastes on any properties presently or formerly owned, operated or used by the Company or any Company Subsidiary (including soil, groundwater or surface water on, under or emanating from the properties, and buildings thereon) (the **"Properties"**) in violation of applicable Environmental Law;

(iii)   the Company and each Company Subsidiary has not received any notices, demand letter, claim, notice of violation noncompliance letter or request for information from any Governmental Entity or any third party indicating that the Company or any Company Subsidiary may be in violation of, or liable under, any Environmental Law;

(iv)   there are no Actions pending or Threatened against the Company or any Company Subsidiary with respect to the Company, any Company Subsidiary or the Properties relating to any violation or alleged violation of or liability under any Environmental Law;

(v)   no reports or notifications have been filed, or are required to be filed, by the Company or any Company Subsidiary concerning the release of any Hazardous Substance or the threatened or actual violation of any Environmental Law on or at the Properties;

(vi)   no Hazardous Substance or any waste has been disposed of, transferred released or transported from any of the Properties during the time such property was owned or leased or operated by the Company or any Company Subsidiary, other than as permitted by, and would not be expected to result in Liability under, applicable Environmental Law;

(vii)   there have been no environmental investigations, studies, audits, tests, reviews or other analyses conducted by, in the possession of, or otherwise available to the Company or any Company Subsidiary relating to the Company, any Company Subsidiary or the Properties which have not been delivered to Buyer prior to the date hereto; and

(viii)   the Company and each Company Subsidiary has not incurred, and none of the Properties are subject to, any Liabilities (fixed or contingent) including those relating to any Action or Order, arising under any Environmental Law.

(b)   **"Environmental Law"** means (i) any Law or Governmental Authorization, (x) relating to the protection, preservation or restoration of the environment (including air, water vapor, surface water, groundwater, drinking water supply, surface land, subsurface land, structures or any natural resource), or to human health or safety, or (y) the exposure to, or the use, storage, recycling, treatment, generation, transportation, processing, handling, labeling, production, release or disposal of Hazardous Substances, in each case as amended and as now or hereafter in effect. The term Environmental Law includes, without limitation, the federal Comprehensive Environmental Response Compensation and Liability Act of 1980, the Superfund Amendments and Reauthorization Act, the Federal Water Pollution Control Act of 1972, the federal Clean Air Act, the federal Clean Water Act, the federal Resource Conservation and Recovery Act of 1976 (including the Hazardous and Solid Waste Amendments thereto), the federal Solid Waste Disposal and the federal Toxic Substance Control Act, the Federal Insecticide, Fungicide and Rodenticide Act, the Federal Occupational Safety and Health Act of 1970 and any similar state or local law, each as amended and as now or hereafter in effect, and (ii) any common law or equitable doctrine (including, without, limitation, injunctive relief and tort doctrines such as negligence, nuisance, trespass and strict liability) that may impose Liability or obligations for injuries or damages due to, or threatened as a result of, the presence of or exposure to any Hazardous Substance.

(c) **"Hazardous Substance"** means any substance presently or hereafter listed, defined, designated or classified, as hazardous, toxic, radioactive or dangerous, or otherwise regulated, under any Environmental Law, whether by type or by quantity, including any substance containing any such substance as a component. Hazardous Substance includes, without limitation, any carcinogen, mutagen, teratogen, waste, pollutant, contaminant, hazardous substance, toxic substance, hazardous waste, special waste, industrial substance or petroleum or any derivative or by-product thereof, radon, radioactive material, asbestos, asbestos containing material, urea formaldehyde insulation, lead and polychlorinated biphenyl.

Section 3.21 Insurance.

(a) Schedule 3.21(a) of the Disclosure Schedule sets forth a true, complete and correct list of all insurance policies or binders of fire, liability, workmen's compensation, motor vehicle, directors' and officers' liability, property, casualty, life and other forms of insurance owned, held by, or applied for, or the premiums for which are paid by the Company or any Company Subsidiary. Company and each Company Subsidiary has delivered or made available to Buyer (i) true, complete and correct copies of such policies and binders and all pending applications for any such policies or binders and (ii) any statement by the auditors of the Financial Statements with regard to the adequacy of the coverage or of the reserves for claims. Notwithstanding anything to the contrary contained herein, the assets of the Company and the Company Subsidiaries shall include any proceeds of any such policy and any benefits thereunder, and any claims by the Company or any Company Subsidiary in respect thereof, to the extent arising out of any such casualty to any asset of the Company or any Company Subsidiary occurring after the date hereof and prior to the Closing, and no such proceeds shall be divided, distributed or otherwise paid out of said Company or any Company Subsidiary.

(b) Except as set forth in Schedule 3.21(b) of the Disclosure Schedule, (i) the Company and each Company Subsidiary maintains insurance coverage for the Business that is customary and consistent with past practice, (ii) the Company and each Company Subsidiary is, and since December 31, 1998 has been, covered on an uninterrupted basis by valid and effective insurance policies or binders which are in the aggregate reasonable in scope and amount in light of the risks attendant to the business in which the Company or any Company Subsidiary is or has been engaged, (iii) all such policies or binders are in full force and effect, no notice of cancellation, termination, revocation or limitation that any insurance policy is no longer in full force or effect or that the issuer of any policy is not willing or able to perform its obligations thereunder, has been received with respect to any such policy and all premiums due and payable thereon have been paid in full on a timely basis; and will continue in full force and effect through and following the Closing, (iv) there are no pending or, to the Knowledge of the Company Threatened, material claims against such insurance by the Company or any Company Subsidiary as to which the insurers have denied liability, and (iv) there exist no material claims under such insurance policies or binders that have not been properly and timely submitted by the Company or any Company Subsidiary to its insurers.

Section 3.22 *Brokers and Finders.* Except as set forth in <u>Schedule 3.22</u> of the Disclosure Schedule, no agent, brokers investment banker, intermediary, finder, Person or firm acting on behalf of the Company or any Company Subsidiary or which has been retained by or is authorized to act on behalf of the Company or any Company Subsidiary is or would be entitled to any broker's or finder's fee or any other commission or similar fee, directly or indirectly, from any of the parties hereto in connection with the execution of this Agreement or upon consummation of the transactions contemplated herein.

Section 3.23 *No Undisclosed Liabilities.* Except as set forth in <u>Schedule 3.23</u> of the Disclosure Schedule, since the Date of the Interim Balance Sheet, neither the Company nor any Company Subsidiary has incurred any Liabilities other than Liabilities for performance under contracts or agreements to which the Company or any Company Subsidiary is a party, (ii) Liabilities which are reflected or reserved against in the Closing Balance Sheet, or (iii) Liabilities incurred in the Ordinary Course of Business. For purposes of this Agreement, the term **"Liability"** shall mean any indebtedness, debt, liability, commitment, guaranty, claim, loss, deficiency, cost, expense, obligation, liability or obligation of any kind, character or nature whatsoever, whether known or unknown, choate or inchoate, secured or unsecured, matured or unmatured, accrued, fixed, absolute, contingent or otherwise, and whether due or to become due.

Section 3.24 *Bank Accounts.* <u>Schedule 3.24</u> of the Disclosure Schedule hereto sets forth a list of the bank names, locations and account numbers of all bank and safe deposit box accounts of the Company and each Company Subsidiary including any custodial accounts for securities owned by the Company or any Company Subsidiary and the names of all persons authorized to draw thereon or to have access thereto.

Section 3.25 *Intercompany Accounts.* <u>Schedule 3.25</u> of the Disclosure Schedule contains a complete list of all intercompany account balances as of the date of the Balance Sheet the Company and each Company Subsidiary.

Section 3.26 *Suppliers and Customers.* <u>Schedule 3.26</u> of the Disclosure Schedule sets forth a list of (a) the ten largest suppliers of materials or services to the Company by value during the twelve (12) month period ended December 31, 2003 (**"Major Suppliers"**) and (b) the ten largest wholesale customers of Products (as defined in Section 3.27 hereof) or services of the Company by value during the twelve (12) month period ended December 31, 2003 (the **"Major Customers"**). Except as set forth on <u>Schedule 3.26</u> of the Disclosure Schedule, no Major Supplier or Major Customer of the Company has during the last twelve (12) months decreased materially or, to the Knowledge of the Company (or Management Stockholders), Threatened to decrease or limit materially its purchase of products, provision of services or supplies to the Company. To the Knowledge of the Company and the Management Stockholders there is no termination, cancellation or limitation of, or any material modification or change in, the business relationships of the Company with any Major Supplier or Major Customer. To the Knowledge of the Company and Management Stockholders, there will not be any such change in relations with Major Suppliers or Major Customers of the Company or triggering of any right of termination, cancellation or penalty or other payment in connection with or as a result of transactions contemplated by this Agreement which would or could reasonably be expected to have a Material Adverse Effect.

   Section 3.27   Products; Business.   Except as set forth on <u>Schedule 3.27</u> of the Disclosure Schedule, during the most recent three (3) years, there are and will be no Actions or Orders by any Governmental Entity stating that any product manufactured, sold, designed, distributed or marketed by the Company (**"Products"**) is defective or unsafe or fails to meet any standards promulgated by any Governmental Entity. Except as set forth on <u>Schedule 3.27</u> of the Disclosure Schedule, there is no (a) duty to recall any product or a duty to warn customers of a defect in any Product, (b) latent or overt design, manufacturing or other defect in any Product or (c) Liability for warranty claims or returns with respect to any Product. None of the Products has been subject to recall. All Products sold by the Company or a Company Subsidiary comply in all material respects with all industry and trade association standards applicable to such Products, including, without limitation, consumer product, manufacturing, labeling, quality, purity and safety laws of the United States and each state in which the Company or a Company Subsidiary sells its Products and each other jurisdiction in which the Company sells its Products. <u>Schedule 3.27</u> of the Disclosure Schedule sets forth a complete and correct list of all Products currently manufactured or sold by the Company or a Company Subsidiary or manufactured or sold by the Company or a Company Subsidiary in the past twelve (12) months, or for which the Company is currently engaged in planning or product development.

   Section 3.28   Promotions.   <u>Schedule 3.31</u> of the Disclosure Schedule contains a complete and accurate description of the Company's material accounting policies with respect to discounts, allowances, rebates, bill-backs, price concessions, advertising fund payments, bonuses, incentives, trade deals, slotting fees, any other trade promotion program, or extended payment terms (collectively, **"Promotions"**).

   Section 3.29 Sales Representatives.   <u>Schedule 3.31</u> of the Disclosure Schedule sets forth a complete and correct list of each sales representative, agent, broker, distributor or other Person who has received commissions or other consideration in respect of the sale of any Product of the Company at any time from March 1, 2003. Schedule 3.31 also sets forth with respect to each such Person (a) the amount of sales generated during such time period, (b) the time period during which such sales were generated, and an indication of whether such Person is still affiliated with the Company as of the date hereof, (c) the commission rate and any other consideration paid or payable with respect to such sales, and (d) any geographic territory or customer with respect to which such Person held exclusive rights. Except as set forth on Schedule 3.31 of the Disclosure Schedule, no Person listed on Schedule 3.31 of the Disclosure Schedule was an employee of the Company during the period in which such Person generated the sales listed on Schedule 3.31 of the Disclosure Schedule. Except as set forth on Schedule 3.31 of the Disclosure Schedule, any domestic commitment in effect on the date hereof between any person listed on Schedule 3.31 of the Disclosure Schedule and the Company is terminable by the Company upon no more than 60 days notice, without any additional obligation to the Company, except for commissions or payments earned but not yet paid through the date of any such termination. Except as set forth on Schedule 3.31 of the Disclosure Schedule, any international commitment in effect on the date hereof between any Person listed on Schedule 3.31 of the Disclosure Schedule and the Company is terminable by the Company upon no more than 180 days notice, without any additional obligation to the Company, except for commissions or payments earned but not yet paid through the date of any such termination.

Section 3.30   Foreign Corrupt Practices Act.   Neither the Company nor any officer or employee has at any time made or committed to make any payments for illegal political contributions or made any bribes, kickback payments or other illegal payments. The Company has not made, offered or agreed to offer anything of value to any governmental official, political party or candidate for governmental office (or any person that the Company knows or has reason to know, will offer anything of value to any governmental official, political party or candidate for political office), such that the Company or its subsidiaries have violated the Foreign Corrupt Practices Act of 1987, as amended from time to time, and all applicable rules and regulations promulgated thereunder. There is not now nor has there ever been any employment by the Company of any governmental or political official in any country while such official was in office.

Section 3.31   Related Party Transactions.   Except as set forth in Schedule 3.31 of the Disclosure Schedule or the Financial Statements: (a) no Related Party (as defined in Section 11.1 (d) hereof) has, and no Related party has at any time since December 31, 2001 had, any direct or indirect interest of any nature in any asset used in or otherwise relating to the business of any of the Company or the Company Subsidiaries; (b) no Related Party is indebted to the Company or the Company Subsidiaries; (c) since December 31, 2001, no Related party has entered into, or has had any direct or indirect financial interest in, any Applicable Contract, or any of the transaction or business dealing of any nature involving any of the Company or the Company Subsidiaries; (d) no Related Party is competing, or has at any time since December 31, 2001 competed, directly or indirectly, with any of the Company or the Company Subsidiaries in any market served by any of the Company or the Company Subsidiaries; (e) no Related Party has any claim or right against any of the Company or the Company Subsidiaries for borrowed money or money owed for past services (other than normal compensation and reimbursement); and (f) no event has occurred, and no condition or circumstance exists, that might (with or without notice or lapse of time) give rise to or serve as a basis for any claim or right in favor of any Related Party against the Company or the Company Subsidiaries.

Section 3.32   Disclosure.   No representation or warranty by the Company or Management Stockholders herein, the Disclosure Schedule, or any certificate or annex furnished or to be furnished by any of them pursuant to this Agreement or in connection with the transactions contemplated herein, contains or will contain any untrue statement of a material fact, or omits, or will omit to state a material fact necessary to make the statements contained herein or therein, in light of the circumstances in which they were made, not misleading.

ARTICLE IV
REPRESENTATIONS AND WARRANTIES OF BUYER

Buyer hereby represents and warrants to Company and Stockholders that the statements contained in this Article IV are correct and complete as of the date of this Agreement and will be correct and complete as of the Closing Date (as though made then and as though the Closing Date were substituted for the date of this Agreement), except as set forth in the Buyer's disclosure schedule accompanying this Agreement (the **"Buyer Disclosure Schedule"**):

Section 4.1   Organization and Good Standing.   Buyer is a corporation duly organized, validly existing and in good standing under the laws of its jurisdiction of incorporation.

Section 4.2   Corporate Authority.   Buyer has the full corporate power and authority and has taken all corporate action necessary in order to execute, deliver and perform fully, its obligations under this Agreement and to consummate the transactions contemplated herein. The execution and delivery of this Agreement by the Buyer and the consummation by the Buyer of the transactions contemplated herein have been duly authorized and approved by the Board of Directors of the Buyer and no other corporate proceeding with respect to the Buyer is necessary to authorize this Agreement or the transactions contemplated herein. This Agreement has been duly executed and delivered by Buyer and constitutes a valid and binding agreement of Buyer, enforceable against Buyer in accordance with its terms, except for the Bankruptcy Exception.

Section 4.3   Governmental Filings and Consents; No Violations.
(a)   No Consents are required to be obtained by Buyer from any Governmental Entity in connection with the execution or delivery of this Agreement by Buyer, the performance by Buyer of its obligations hereunder or the consummation by Buyer of the transactions contemplated herein.

(b)   The execution and delivery of this Agreement by Buyer does not, and the performance and consummation by Buyer of any of the transactions contemplated herein will not, with respect to Buyer, directly or indirectly (with or without the giving of notice or the lapse of time or both):

(i)   contravene, conflict with, or constitute or result in a breach or violation of, or a default under any provision of the charter documents, Certificate of Incorporation or By-laws (or equivalent documents) of Buyer;

(ii)   require Buyer to make any filing with or obtain any Consent from any Person under any Contract binding upon Buyer; or

(iii)   contravene, conflict with, or constitute or result in a breach or violation of, any Law or Order to which Buyer, or any of the assets owned or used by Buyer, are subject.

Section 4.4   Securities Act.   Buyer is acquiring the Shares for its own account and not with a view to their distribution within the meaning of Section 2(11) of the Securities Act of 1933, as amended (the **"Securities Act"**) in any manner that would be in violation of the Securities Act.

Section 4.5   Brokers and Finders.   No agent, broker, investment banker, intermediary, finder, Person or firm acting on behalf of Buyer or which has been retained by or is authorized to act on behalf of Buyer is or would be entitled to any broker's or finder's fee or any other commission or similar fee, directly or indirectly, from any of the parties hereto in connection with the execution of this Agreement or upon consummation of the transactions contemplated herein.

Section 4.6   Galaxy Shares.   Galaxy Shares to be issued as part of the Purchase Price shall be upon satisfaction of the conditions of this Agreement validly issued, fully paid and non-assessible common shares of Galaxy International Corp. Based on the representations made by the recipients of the Galaxy Shares made in the Stock Issuance Agreement, the Galaxy Shares will be issued in compliance with the securities laws of the United States.

ARTICLE V
REPRESENTATIONS AND WARRANTIES OF STOCKHOLDERS

Each Stockholder hereby represents and warrants severally for themselves and not jointly with any other Stockholder to Buyer that the statements contained in this Article V are correct and complete as of the date of this Agreement and will be correct and complete as of the Closing Date (as though made then and as though the Closing Date were substituted for the date of this Agreement), except as set forth in the Stockholders' disclosure schedule accompanying this Agreement (the **"Stockholders Disclosure Schedule"**):

Section 5.1   Title to Shares.   Such Stockholder has good and valid title to and is the record and beneficial owner of the Shares listed for such Stockholder in Annex I free and clear of all Liens with full right, power and authority to enter into this Agreement and to sell, assign, transfer and deliver to Buyer the Shares to be transferred by such Stockholder to the Buyer, and upon delivery of and payment for the Shares, the Buyer will acquire valid right and title to the Shares to be transferred by the Stockholder to the Buyer.

Section 5.2   Authority.   Such Stockholder has the absolute and unrestricted right, power and authority or capacity to enter into and perform such Stockholder's obligations under this Agreement and to consummate the transactions contemplated herein. The respective spouses of such Stockholders have the absolute and unrestricted right, power and capacity to execute and deliver and to perform their obligations under the spousal consents being executed by them. Said spousal consents constitute their legal, valid and binding obligations, enforceable against them in accordance with their terms. If applicable, the execution and delivery of this Agreement by such Stockholder and the consummation by such Stockholder of the transactions contemplated herein have been duly authorized and approved by the Board of Directors (or similar governing body) of such Stockholder and no other corporate proceeding with respect to the Buyer is necessary to authorize this Agreement or the transactions contemplated herein.

Section 5.3   Enforceability.   This Agreement has been duly executed and delivered by such Stockholder and constitutes a valid and binding agreement of such Stockholder, enforceable against such Stockholder in accordance with its terms, subject to general equitable principles and to Bankruptcy Exceptions.

Section 5.4   Governmental Filings and Consents; No Violations.
    (a)   No filings are required to be made by such Stockholder with, nor are any Consents required to be obtained by such Stockholder from, any Governmental Entity, in connection with the execution or delivery of this Agreement by such Stockholder, the performance by such Stockholder of its obligations hereunder or the consummation by such Stockholder of the transactions contemplated herein.
    (b)   The execution and delivery of this Agreement by such Stockholder does not, and the performance and consummation by such Stockholder of any of the transactions contemplated herein will not, with respect to such Stockholder, directly or indirectly (with or without the giving of notice or the lapse of time or both):
        (i)   contravene, conflict with, or constitute or result in a breach or violation of, or a default under any provision of the charter documents or Bylaws (or equivalent documents) of such Stockholder;
        (ii)   require such Stockholder to make any filing with or obtain any Consent from any Person under any Contract binding upon such Stockholder; or
        (iii)   contravene, conflict with, or constitute or result in a breach or violation of, any Law or Order to which such Stockholder is subject.

Section 5.5   Other Contracts.   No Stockholder is a party to: (i) any Contract under which any of the Company or Stockholders is or may become obligated to sell or otherwise issue any shares of his or its capital stock, or any other securities or interest; (ii) any Contract that may give rise to or provide a basis for the assertion of a claim by any Person to the effect that such person is entitled to repurchase, acquire or receive or reacquire any shares of capital stock, partnership interest, or other securities or interest of any of the Company (whether from the Company or the Stockholders); or (iii) any other Contract relating to the Shares, the voting of, or any other rights associated with, the Shares or any other shares of capital stock, partnership interest, or other securities or interest of any Company, including any buy-sell agreements, voting agreements, proxies, rights of first refusal, tag along rights, bring along rights, shareholder agreements, repurchase agreements, co-sale agreements, stock transfer agreements or similar Contracts.

Section 5.6 Brokers and Finders. No agent, broker, investment banker, intermediary, finder, Person or firm acting on behalf of Buyer or which has been retained by or is authorized to act on behalf of Stockholder is or would be entitled to any broker's or finder's fee or any other commission or similar fee, directly or indirectly, from any of the parties hereto in connection with the execution of this Agreement or upon consummation of the transactions contemplated herein.

Section 5.7 Stockholder Claims Against Company or a Company Subsidiary. Such Stockholder has no claims outstanding that would result in a Liability against the Company or a Company Subsidiary, and no facts exists which could reasonably be likely to result in such a claim by such Stockholder against the Company or a Company Subsidiary.

Section 5.8 Brokers and Finders. No agent, broker, investment banker, intermediary, finder, Person or firm acting on behalf of Buyer or which has been retained by or is authorized to act on behalf of such Stockholder is or would be entitled to any broker's or finder's fee or any other commission or similar fee, directly or indirectly, from any of the parties hereto in connection with the execution of this Agreement or upon consummation of the transactions contemplated herein.

Section 5.9 Stockholder Claims Against Company or a Company Subsidiary. Stockholder has no claims outstanding that would result in a Liability against the Company or a Company Subsidiary, and no facts exist which could reasonably be likely to result in such a claim by the Stockholder against the Company or a Company Subsidiary.

ARTICLE VI
COVENANTS

Section 6.1 Conduct of Business by Company. During the period from the date of this Agreement and continuing until the earlier of the termination of this Agreement pursuant to its terms or the Closing Date, Company shall, and covenants and agrees to cause each Company Subsidiary to use commercially reasonable efforts to carry on its business, in the Ordinary Course of Business, in substantially the same manner as heretofore conducted and in compliance with all applicable laws and regulations, pay its debts and taxes when due subject to good faith disputes over such debts or taxes, pay or perform other material obligations when due, and use its commercially reasonable efforts consistent with past practices and policies to (i) preserve intact its present business organization, (ii) keep available the services of its present officers and employees and (iii) preserve its relationships with customers, suppliers, manufactures, distributors, licensors, licensees, and others with which it has business dealings. In addition, Company will promptly notify Buyer of any material event involving its business or operations or the business or operations of the Company Subsidiary.

In addition, except as expressly permitted by the terms of this Agreement or as set forth in Schedule 6.1 of the Disclosure Schedule, without the prior written consent of Buyer (with [_____] acknowledged as the point person who can authorize such actions), during the period from the date of this Agreement and continuing until the earlier of the termination of this Agreement pursuant to its terms or the Closing Date, Company shall not, and covenants and agrees to cause each Company Subsidiary not to do any of the following:

(a)   Waive any stock repurchase rights, accelerate, amend or change the period of exercisability of options or restricted stock, or reprice options granted under any employee, consultant, director or other stock plans or authorize cash payments in exchange for any options granted under any of such plans;

(b)   Grant any severance or termination pay to any officer or employee except pursuant to written agreements outstanding, or policies existing, on the date hereof and as previously disclosed in writing or made available to Buyer, or adopt any new severance plan;

(c)   Transfer or license to any person or entity or otherwise extend, amend or modify any rights to Intellectual Property, or enter into grants to transfer or license to any person future patent rights other than extensions, amendments, modifications, transfers or licenses in the Ordinary Course of Business in connection with the sale of commercially available Company Products through the Company's standard distribution channels consistent with past practices, provided that in no event shall Company license on an exclusive basis or sell any Intellectual Property;

(d)   Declare, set aside or pay any dividends on or make any other distributions (whether in cash, stock, equity securities or property) in respect of any capital stock or split, combine or reclassify any capital stock or issue or authorize the issuance of any other securities in respect of, in lieu of or in substitution for any capital stock;

(e)   Purchase, redeem or otherwise acquire, directly or indirectly, any shares of capital stock of Company or any Company Subsidiary;

(f)   Issue, deliver, sell, authorize, pledge or otherwise encumber or propose any of the foregoing with respect to, any shares of capital stock or any securities convertible into shares of capital stock, or subscriptions, rights, warrants or options to acquire any shares of capital stock or any securities convertible into shares of capital stock, or enter into other agreements or commitments of any character obligating it to issue any such shares or convertible securities, other than the issuance, delivery and/or sale of shares of Company Common Stock pursuant to the exercise of stock options outstanding as of the date of this Agreement;

(g)   Cause, permit or propose any amendments to the Company's Organizational Documents;

(h) Acquire or agree to acquire by merging or consolidating with, or by purchasing any equity interest in or a portion of the assets of, or by any other manner, any business or any corporation, partnership, association or other business organization or division thereof, or otherwise acquire or agree to acquire any assets, other than in the Ordinary Course of Business or enter into any joint ventures, strategic partnerships or alliances;

(i) Sell, lease, license, encumber or otherwise dispose of any properties or assets except (A) sales of inventory in the Ordinary Course of Business, and (B) for the sale, lease or disposition (other than through licensing) of property or assets which are not material, individually or in the aggregate, to the Company and the Company Subsidiaries;

(j) Incur any indebtedness for borrowed money or guarantee any such indebtedness of another person (other than borrowings under the Company's existing credit facility), issue or sell any debt securities or options, warrants, calls or other rights to acquire any debt securities of Company, enter into any "keep well" or other agreement to maintain any financial statement condition or enter into any arrangement having the economic effect of any of the foregoing other than in connection with the financing of ordinary course trade payables in the Ordinary Course of Business;

(k) Except as required under applicable Law or in the Ordinary Course of Business, adopt or amend any employee benefit plan, policy or arrangement, any employee stock purchase or employee stock option plan, or enter into any employment contract or collective bargaining agreement (other than offer letters and letter agreements entered into in the Ordinary Course of Business with employees who are terminable "at will"), pay any special bonus or special remuneration to any director or employee, or increase the salaries or wage rates or fringe benefits (including rights to severance or indemnification) of its directors, officers, employees or consultants;

(l) (i) Pay, discharge, settle or satisfy any claims, liabilities or obligations (absolute, accrued, asserted or unasserted, contingent or otherwise), or litigation (whether or not commenced prior to the date of this Agreement) other than the payment, discharge, settlement or satisfaction, in the Ordinary Course of Business, or (ii) waive the benefits of, agree to modify in any manner, terminate, release any person from or fail to enforce any confidentiality or similar agreement to which Company or any Company Subsidiary is a party or of which Company or any Company Subsidiary is a beneficiary;

(m) Make, or incur any obligation to make, any individual or series of related payments outside of the Ordinary Course of Business other than payments to legal, accounting, and other professional service advisors and other expenses in connection with the negotiation and closing of the transactions contemplated hereby;

(n) Except in the Ordinary Course of Business, modify, amend or terminate any material contract or agreement to which Company or any Company Subsidiary is a party or waive, delay the exercise of, release or assign any material rights or claims thereunder;

(o) Except in the Ordinary Course of Business, enter into or materially modify any contracts, agreements, or obligations relating to the distribution, sale, license, sponsorship or marketing by third parties of Company's Products or products licensed by Company;

(p)   Revalue any of its assets or, except as required by GAAP, make any change in accounting methods, principles or practices;

(q)   Incur or enter into any agreement, contract or commitment in excess of $50,000 individually, except in the Ordinary Course of Business;

(r)   Make any tax election or settle or compromise any material income tax liability; or

(s)   Agree in writing or otherwise to take any of the actions described in Section 6.1 (a) through (r) above.

Section 6.2   *Acquisition Proposals.*

(a)   The Company agrees that it shall not, and shall cause each Company Subsidiary and each of its and their respective directors officers, employees, agents, consultants, advisors or other representatives of such Person, including legal counsel, accountants and financial advisors (collectively, **"Representatives"**) not to, directly or indirectly, solicit, initiate, encourage, or otherwise facilitate, any inquiries or the making of any proposals or offers from, discuss or negotiate with, provide any confidential information or data to, or consider the merits of any unsolicited inquiries, proposals or offers from, any Person (other than Buyer) relating to any transaction involving the sale of the Company, Business or assets (other than in the Ordinary Course of Business) of the Company or any Company Subsidiary, or any of its capital stock, or any merger, consolidation, business combination, or similar transaction involving the Company or any Company Subsidiary (any such inquiry, proposal or offer being hereinafter referred to as an **"Acquisition Proposal"**).

(b)   The Company shall, and shall cause each Company Subsidiary and each of their respective Representatives to, immediately cease and cause to be terminated any existing activities, discussions or negotiations with any parties conducted heretofore with respect to any of the foregoing. Company shall promptly notify Buyer if any such inquiries, proposals or offers are received by, any such information is requested from, or any such negotiations or discussions are sought to be initiated or continued with or about the Company and shall promptly request each Person which has heretofore executed a confidentiality agreement in connection with its consideration of acquiring the Company or any Company Subsidiary or the Business or assets (other than in the Ordinary Course of Business) of the Company to return all confidential information heretofore furnished to such person by or on behalf of the Company or any Company Subsidiary.

Section 6.3   *Access.*   Between the date of this Agreement and the Closing Date, Company shall, and shall cause the Company Subsidiaries and each of their respective Representatives to, (i) afford Buyer and its Representatives full access, upon prior notice, at all reasonable times during normal business hours and in a manner so as not to interfere with the normal business operations of Company and each Company Subsidiary, to the Company's and each Company Subsidiary's personnel, premises, properties, Contracts, books and records, and other documents and data, (ii) furnish Buyer and its Representatives with copies of all such Contracts, books and records, and other existing documents and data as Buyer may reasonably request, (iii) furnish Buyer and its Representatives with such additional financial, operating, and other data and information as Buyer

may reasonably request and (iv) otherwise cooperate with the investigation by Buyer and its Representatives of the Company and each Company Subsidiary and shall authorize the Company's independent certified public accountants to permit Buyer and its independent certified public accountants to examine all accounting records and working papers pertaining to the Financial Statements (subject to appropriate indemnifications). No investigation pursuant to this Section 6.3 shall affect or be deemed to modify any representation or warranty made by Company, the Management Stockholders or Stockholders. All requests for information made pursuant to this Section 6.3 shall be directed to an executive officer of the Company or such other persons as may be designated by Seller.

Section 6.4 Required Approvals. Each party to this Agreement hereby agrees to cooperate with each other party and use its commercially reasonable efforts to promptly prepare and file all necessary filings and other documents and to obtain as promptly as practicable all necessary Consents of all third parties and Governmental Entities necessary or advisable to consummate the transactions contemplated herein. Each party shall have the right to review in advance and to the extent practicable each will consult the other on, in each case subject to applicable Laws relating to the exchange of information, all the information relating to Buyer, or the Company or any Company Subsidiary, as the case may be, that appear in any filing made with, or other written materials submitted to, any third party or Governmental Entity in connection with the transactions contemplated in this Agreement. In exercising the foregoing right, each of Buyer and Company shall act reasonably and as promptly as practicable. Buyer and Company agree that they will keep the other apprised of the status of matters relating to completion of the transactions contemplated herein, including promptly furnishing the other with copies of notice or other communications received by Buyer or the Company or any Company Subsidiary, as the case may be, from any third party or Governmental Entity with respect to the transactions contemplated herein.

Section 6.5 Commercially Reasonable Best Efforts. Between the date of this Agreement and the Closing Date, each of the parties hereto shall use their respective commercially reasonable best efforts to cause the conditions in Sections 7.1 and 7.2 to be satisfied.

Section 6.6 Publicity. The initial press release announcing the transactions contemplated herein shall be released jointly after consultation between the Buyer and the Company and the parties hereto shall consult with each other prior to issuing any press releases or otherwise making public announcements with respect to the transactions contemplated herein and prior to making any filings with any Governmental Entity, except as may be required by Law. Any press release or announcement shall conform to New York Stock Exchange Rules and Delaware Corporate laws.

Section 6.7 Confidentiality.
(a)   Each of Buyer and the Stockholders, after the Closing Date, Buyer, Company and Stockholders shall maintain in confidence, and shall cause its Representatives to maintain in confidence, and not use to the detriment of any

other party hereto any written, oral or other information relating to another party (including, without limitation, information about processes, procedures, techniques, know-how, financial or sales and marketing matters, and other similar proprietary and confidential information). Notwithstanding the foregoing a party shall be free to discuss (i) any such information that is or becomes generally available to the public other than as a result of disclosure by any other Party or any of its Representatives, (ii) any such information that is required to be disclosed to a Governmental Entity of competent jurisdiction or (iii) any such information that was or becomes available on a non-confidential basis and from a source (other than a party to this Agreement or any Representative of such party) that is not bound by a confidentiality obligation to the Buyer Company, any Company Subsidiary or any Stockholder as applicable, or (iv) such information if it is necessary or appropriate in making any filing or obtaining any Consent required for the consummation of the transactions contemplated herein, and each party shall instruct its respective Representatives having access to such information of such obligation of confidentiality and such party shall be legally responsible for any violation or breach of the foregoing obligations of confidentiality. If for any reason this Agreement is terminated, or the transactions contemplated herein are abandoned, the provisions of this Section 6.7 shall remain in full force and effect and Buyer, Company and Stockholders, as applicable, shall return to the appropriate party, or at such party's option, destroy all copies of material containing confidential or proprietary information disclosed to such party. The redelivery or destruction of such material shall not relieve a party of its obligations regarding confidentiality.

Section 6.8   Expenses.   Except as otherwise expressly provided in Section 8.2, whether or not the transactions contemplated herein are consummated, all costs and expenses incurred in connection with this Agreement and the transactions contemplated herein shall be paid by the party incurring such expense. In the event of termination of this Agreement, the obligation of each party to pay its own expenses will be subject to any rights of such party arising from a breach of this Agreement by another party. Stockholders shall be liable for all stock transfer taxes arising from the sale of the Shares.

Section 6.9   Further Assurances.   At any time and from time to time after the Closing Date, the parties hereto agree to (a) furnish upon request to each other such further assurances, information documents, instruments of transfer or assignment, files and books and records, (b) promptly execute, acknowledge, and deliver any such further assurances, documents, instruments of transfer or assignment, files and books and records, and (c) subject to the provisions of this Section 6.9 hereof, do all such further acts and things, all as such other party may reasonably request for the purpose of carrying out the intent of this Agreement and the documents referred to herein.

Section 6.10   Notification.   Between the date of this Agreement and the Closing Date, Company and the Management Stockholders shall promptly notify Buyer in writing if the Company or Management Stockholders becomes aware of any fact or condition that causes or constitutes a breach of any of Company's or the Management Stockholder's representations and warranties as of the date of this Agreement, or if the Company or the Management Stockholders becomes aware of the occurrence after the date of this Agreement of any fact or condition that could (except as expressly contemplated herein) cause or constitute a breach of any such representation or warranty had such representation or warranty been made as of the time of occurrence or discovery of such fact or condition. Should any such fact or condition require any change in the Disclosure Schedule if the Disclosure Schedule were dated the date of the occurrence or discovery of any such fact or condition, Company and the Management Stockholder shall promptly deliver to Buyer a supplement to the Disclosure Schedule specifying such change. During the same period, Company shall promptly notify Buyer of the occurrence of any breach of any covenant, agreement, undertaking or obligation of Company in this Article VI or of the occurrence of any event that may make the satisfaction of the conditions in Section 7.1 not reasonably likely. No supplement to the Disclosure Schedule or notification to Buyer made pursuant to the requirements of this Section 6.10 shall have any effect for the purpose of determining the satisfaction of the conditions in Section 7.1 or for the purpose of determining the right of Buyer to claim or obtain indemnification or set off from the Stockholders under Article IX.

Section 6.11 *[Alternative Notification].*
(a) Between the date of this Agreement and the Closing Date, Company and the Management Stockholders shall promptly notify Buyer in writing if the Company or Management Stockholders becomes aware of any fact or condition (i) not disclosed in this Agreement or the Disclosure Schedule which existed on or prior to the date of this Agreement and whose existence causes or constitutes a breach of any of Company's representations and warranties as of the date of this Agreement, or (ii) not disclosed in this Agreement or the Disclosure Schedule which did not come into existence until after the date of this Agreement, or, in the case of a representation or warranty by its terms qualified by a reference to Knowledge, become required to be disclosed until after the date of this Agreement, that would, were it not for the provisions of this Schedule 6.10 cause or constitute a breach of Company's representations or warranties had such representations or warranties been made as of the time of occurrence or discovery of such fact or condition. If any such fact or condition in (i) or (ii) would have required any change in the Disclosure Schedule if the Disclosure Schedule were dated the date of the occurrence or discovery of any such fact or condition, Company and the Management Stockholder shall promptly deliver to Buyer a supplement to the Disclosure Schedule specifying such change. During the same period, Company shall promptly notify Buyer of the occurrence of any breach of any covenant, agreement, undertaking or obligation of Company in this Article VI or of the occurrence of any event that may make the satisfaction of the conditions in Section 7.1 not reasonably likely.
(b) No supplement to the Disclosure Schedule or notification to Buyer made pursuant to Section 6.10(a)(i) of this Section 6.10 shall have any effect for the purpose of determining the satisfaction of the conditions in Section 7.1 or for the purpose of determining the right of Buyer to claim or obtain indemnification or set off from the Stockholders under Article IX. Any supplement to the Disclosure Schedule provided in accordance with Section 6.10(a)(ii) shall,

unless the Buyer has the right to terminate this Agreement pursuant to Section 8.1(b) below by the reason of the existence of a fact or condition required to be disclosed pursuant to Section 6.10(a)(ii), and actually exercises such right within five (5) business days of being notified of the Disclosure Schedule supplement, be deemed to have amended the Disclosure Schedule and to have qualified the representations and warranties contained in Article III and to have cured any misrepresentations or breach of warranty that otherwise might have existed by reason of the existence of such fact or condition.

ARTICLE VII
CONDITIONS TO CLOSING

Section 7.1   Conditions to Obligations of Buyer.   The obligation of Buyer to consummate the transactions contemplated by this Agreement and to take the other actions to be taken by Buyer at the Closing is subject to the satisfaction, at or prior to the Closing, of each of the following conditions (any of which may be waived in whole or in part by Buyer):

(a)   <u>Representations and Warranties.</u>   All of the representations and warranties of the Stockholders and the Managing Stockholders and the Company set forth in this Agreement shall be true and correct (considered individually and collectively) in all material respects as of the date of this Agreement and as of the Closing Date, with the same effect as though such representations and warranties had been made on and as of the Closing Date, without giving effect to any supplement to the Disclosure Schedule (delivered to Buyer in accordance with Section 6.10 hereof), except (i) that such representations and warranties that are made as of a specific date need only be true in all material respects as of such date, (ii) each of the representation and warranties in Section 3.2, 3.6, 5.1, 5.3 and 5.4 shall be true and correct in all respects, and (iii) any representation and warranty qualified by "material" or "Material Adverse Effect" shall be true and correct in all respects.

(b)   <u>Covenants.</u>   All of the covenants, agreements, undertakings and obligations that Company or Stockholders are required to perform or to comply with pursuant to this Agreement at or prior to the Closing, shall have been duly performed.

(c)   <u>Officer's Certificate.</u>   Company shall have delivered to Buyer a certificate dated as of the Closing Date and signed by a senior executive officer or officers of Company, representing that the conditions referred to in Sections 7.1(a) and 7.1(b) have been satisfied and the changes set forth in 7.1(i) have not occurred; provided, however, that such senior executive officer or officers shall have no personal liability on account of the delivery of such certificate.

(d)   <u>Secretary's Certificate.</u>   Buyer shall have received copies of the resolutions of the Board of Directors (or other similar governing body) of the Company, authorizing the execution, delivery and performance of this Agreement. Buyer also shall have received a certificates of the secretary or assistant secretary of the Company, dated as of the Closing Date, to the effect that such resolutions were duly adopted and are in full force and effect, that each officer of the Company who executed and delivered this Agreement and any other document delivered in connection with the consummation of the transactions contemplated by this Agreement was at the respective times of such execution and delivery and is now duly elected or appointed, qualified and acting as such officer, and that the signature of each such officer appearing on such document is his or her genuine signature.

(e) No Action or Order. No Action or Order shall be issued or pending which (i) involves a challenge to or seeks to or does prohibit, prevent, restrain, restrict, delay, make illegal or otherwise interfere with the consummation of any of the transactions contemplated herein, (ii) seeks or imposes damages in connection with the consummation of any of the transactions contemplated herein, (iii) questions the validity or legality of any of the transactions contemplated herein or (iv) seeks to impose conditions upon the ownership or operations of the Company or any Company Subsidiary or the operations of the Buyer reasonably deemed unduly burdensome by Buyer.

(f) Receipt of Shares. Buyer shall have received from the Stockholders an original certificate or certificates evidencing 100% of the Shares, duly endorsed in blank or accompanied by stock powers duly executed in blank in proper form for transfer or affidavits of lost shares and assignments, as applicable. There shall not have been made or Threatened by any Person any claim asserting that such Person (i) is the holder or the beneficial owner of, or has the right to acquire or to obtain beneficial ownership of, any stock of, or any other voting, equity, or ownership interest in, the Company or any Company Subsidiary, or (ii) is entitled to all or any portion of the Purchase Price payable for the Shares.

(g) Consents. Each of the Consents set forth in Schedule 3.4 and Schedule 3.5 of the Disclosure Schedule and or otherwise required for consummation of the transactions contemplated by this Agreement shall have been obtained and must be in full force and effect provided, however, that such Consents (i) shall not contain one or more terms or conditions that individually or in the aggregate in Buyer's reasonable judgement could be expected to have a Material Adverse Effect, or (ii) materially and adversely impair the economic benefits of the transaction contemplated by this Agreement to Buyer.

(h) Opinion of Counsel. Buyer shall have received an opinion, dated as of the Closing Date, of Klever & Sharp, counsel for the Company, as to the matters referred to in Exhibit 6.1(h) attached hereto.

(i) No Material Adverse Effect. There shall not have occurred any change in the business, operations, properties, prospects, assets, or condition of the Company or any Company Subsidiary since the date of the Interim Balance Sheet that is reasonably likely to constitute a Material Adverse Effect on the Company and the Company Subsidiaries (taken as a whole), and no event has occurred or circumstance exists that is reasonably likely to result in such a Material Adverse Effect.

(j) Stock Options. (i) Buyer shall have received evidence of the cancellation of each outstanding Option issued by the Company pursuant to its Stock Option Plan, and (ii) Buyer shall have received evidence of the repayment of each loan made by the Company to an option holder for the exercise price of an option under the Company's Stock Option Plan.

(k) Subordinated Notes. Company shall have entered into an agreement with each holder of its issued and outstanding subordinated notes (the **"Subordinated Notes"**) in the form attached hereto as Exhibit 7.1(k) (**"Subordinated Note Agreement"**).

(l)   Financing.   Buyer shall have obtained financing for transactions contemplated herein on terms it believes, in its sole discretion, are reasonable to Buyer [, provided, that a placement of ordinary shares of Galaxy at up to a [____]% discount average closing price during the preceding ____ day period, shall be deemed reasonable]. **[Galaxy to Consider.]**

(m)   Escrow Agreement.   The Company and Stockholders shall have executed and delivered the Escrow Agreement.

(n)   Employment Contracts.   Each of the Employment Agreements shall have been executed and delivered.

(o)   Stockholder Releases.   Buyer shall have received the Stockholder Releases for each Stockholder in the form attached hereto as Exhibit 7.1(o) (the **"Stockholder Releases"**).

(p)   Noncompete Agreements.   Each of the Noncompete Agreements shall have been executed and delivered.

(q)   Execution of Closing Documents.   Each of the Closing documents described in Section 2.2 hereof shall have been executed and delivered by each of the named parties (other than Buyer).

(r)   Other Documentation.   Buyer shall have received such other documents, certificates, opinions or statements as Buyer may reasonably request.

Section 7.2   Conditions to Obligations of Stockholders and Company.   The obligation of the Stockholders and the Company to consummate the transaction contemplated by this Agreement and to take the other actions to be taken by the Stockholders and the Company at the Closing is subject to the satisfaction, at or prior to the Closing, of each of the following conditions (any of which may be waived in whole or in part by the Stockholders' Representative or the Company):

(a)   Representations and Warranties.   All of the representations and warranties of Buyer set forth in this Agreement, shall be true and correct (considered individually and collectively) in all material respects as of the date of this Agreement and as of the Closing Date, with the same effect as though such representations and warranties had been made on and as of the Closing Date, without giving effect to any supplement to the Disclosure Scheduled (delivered to Company in accordance with Section 6.10 hereof), except (i) that such representations and warranties that are made as of a specific date need only be true in all material respects as of such date, and (ii) any representation and warranty qualified by "material" or "Material Adverse Effect" shall be true and correct in all respects.

(b)   Covenants.   All of the covenants, agreements, undertakings and obligations that Buyer is required to perform or to comply with pursuant to this Agreement at or prior to the Closing, shall have been duly performed.

(c)   Officer's Certificate.   Buyer shall have delivered to Company and the Stockholders' Representative a certificate, dated as of the Closing Date and signed by a senior executive officer or officers of Buyer, representing that the conditions referred to in Sections 7.2(a) and 7.2(b) have been satisfied; provided, however, that such senior executive officer or officers shall have no personal liability on account of the delivery of such certificate.

(d) <u>Secretary's Certificate</u>. Company and the Stockholders' Representative shall have received copies of the resolutions of the Board of Directors (or other similar governing body) of Buyer authorizing the execution, delivery and performance of this Agreement. Company and the Stockholders' Representative also shall have received a certificate of the secretary or assistant secretary of Buyer dated as of the Closing Date, to the effect that such resolutions were duly adopted and are in full force and effect, that each officer of the Buyer who executed and delivered this Agreement and any other document delivered in connection with the consummation of the transactions contemplated by this Agreement was at the respective times of such execution and delivery and is now duly elected or appointed, qualified and acting as such officer, and that the signature of each such officer appearing on such document is his genuine signature.

(e) <u>No Action or Order</u>. No Action or Order shall be issued or pending which (i) involves a challenge to or seeks to or does prohibit, prevent, restrain, restrict, delay, make illegal or otherwise interfere with the consummation of any of the transactions contemplated herein, (ii) seeks or imposes damages in connection with the consummation of any of the transactions contemplated herein, or (iii) questions the validity or legality of any of the transactions contemplated herein.

(f) <u>Payment of Initial Purchase Price and Escrow Amount</u>. Stockholders shall have received from Buyer the Initial Purchase Price as provided in Section 1.2 and <u>Annex II</u>, including as applicable, the Galaxy Shares and Deferred Notes.

(g) <u>Opinion of Counsel</u>. Seller shall have received an opinion, dated as of the Closing Date, of Bigar, Strong & Wise, a professional corporation.

(h) <u>Escrow Agreement</u>. Buyer shall have executed and delivered the Escrow Agreement.

(i) <u>Execution of Closing Documents</u>. Each of the Closing documents described in Section 2.2 hereof shall have been executed and delivered by Buyer.

(j) <u>Other Documentation</u>. Company and the Stockholders' Representative shall have received such other documents, certificates, opinions or statements as Company or the Stockholders' Representative may reasonably request.

ARTICLE VIII
TERMINATION

Section 8.1 Termination.
Notwithstanding anything in this Agreement to the contrary, this Agreement and the transactions contemplated herein may, by written notice given at any time prior to the Closing, be terminated:

(a) by mutual written consent of Buyer, Company, and the Stockholders' Representative;

(b) by the Buyer, if a material breach of a representation or warranty or any other provision of this Agreement has been committed by any of the Stockholders or the Company and such breach has not been waived or cured within five (5) business days after written notice; or by Company or Stockholders' Representative if a material breach of a representation or warranty or any other provision of this Agreement has been committed by the Buyer and such breach has not been waived or cured within five (5) business days after written notice; provided, however, that termination pursuant to this Section 8.1(b) shall not relieve the breaching party of liability for such breach or otherwise;

(c)   by Buyer, if any of the conditions set forth in Section 7.1 has not been satisfied as of_____, 2004 or if satisfaction of such a condition is or becomes impossible (other than through the failure of Buyer to fully comply with its obligations hereunder) and Buyer has not waived such condition on or before _____, 2004; or

(d)   by Buyer if the Company or its Board of Directors shall have recommended to the Stockholders an Acquisition Proposal (as defined in Section 6.2 hereof).

(e)   by Company and Stockholders' Representative if any of the conditions set forth in Section 7.2 has not been satisfied as of_____, 2004 or if satisfaction of such a condition is or becomes impossible (other than through the failure of Company or the Stockholders to fully comply with their obligations hereunder) and Company and Stockholders' Representative have not waived such condition on or before_____, 2004.

Section 8.2   *Effect of Termination.*   Termination of this Agreement pursuant to Section 8.1 shall not in any way terminate, limit or restrict the rights and remedies of any party hereto against any party which has related, breached or failed to satisfy any of the representations, warranties, covenants or other provisions of this Agreement prior to termination hereof; provided, however, that (i) Company shall within five (5) business days after termination of this Agreement by Buyer pursuant to Sections 8.1(b), (c) or (d) shall pay Buyer a fee of $500,000 in cash by wire transfer and (ii) Buyer shall within five (5) days after termination of this Agreement by Company and Stockholders' Representative pursuant to Section 8.1(b) or (e) pay the Company an amount equal to its reasonable expenses not to exceed $ _____.

ARTICLE IX
INDEMNIFICATION; REMEDIES

Section 9.1   *Survival.*   Notwithstanding (a) any investigation or examination conducted with respect to, or any knowledge acquired (or capable of being acquired) about the accuracy or inaccuracy of or compliance with, any representation, warranty, covenant, agreement, undertaking or obligation made by or on behalf of the parties hereto, (b) the waiver of any condition based on the accuracy of any representation or warranty, or on the performance of or compliance with any covenant, agreement, undertaking or obligation, or (c) the Closing hereunder;

(i)   All of the representations and warranties of the parties contained in this Agreement, the Disclosure Schedule, the supplements to the Disclosure Schedule (delivered to Buyer in accordance with Section 6.10), and any other certificate or document delivered pursuant to this Agreement shall survive the Closing until 36 months after the Closing Date, except for the representations and warranties contained in (A) Section 3.2 (Capitalization) and

Section 5.1 (Title to Shares), each of which shall survive the execution and delivery of this Agreement and the Closing indefinitely, and (B) Section 3.20 (Environmental Matters), Section 3.9 (Taxes) and Section 3.10 (Employee Benefits; ERISA) which shall survive the execution and delivery of this Agreement and the Closing until the expiration of all relevant statutes of limitations (including any extensions);

(ii) All of the covenants, agreements, undertakings and obligations of the parties contained in this Agreement, the Disclosure Schedule, the supplements to the Disclosure Schedule (delivered to Buyer in accordance with Section 6.10 hereof), and any other certificate or document delivered pursuant to this Agreement shall survive until fully performed or fulfilled, unless non-compliance with such covenants, agreements, undertakings or obligations is waived in writing by the party or parties entitled to such performance.

No claim for indemnification, reimbursement or any other remedy pursuant to Sections 9.2 or 9.3 hereof may be brought with respect to breaches of representations or warranties contained herein after the applicable expiration date set forth in this Section 9.1; provided, however, that if, prior to such applicable date, a party hereto shall have notified the other party hereto in writing of a claim for indemnification under this Article IX (whether or not formal legal action shall have been commenced based upon such claim), such claim shall continue to be subject to indemnification in accordance with this Article IX notwithstanding such expiration date.

Section 9.2 Indemnification and Reimbursement by Stockholders. Subject to Section 1.4, Section 9.4 and Section 9.6 hereof, Stockholders shall indemnify and hold harmless and defend Buyer and its respective successors, assigns, stockholders, subsidiaries, controlling persons, affiliates, officers and directors and the Representatives of each of them (collectively, the **"Buyer Indemnified Persons"**) from and against, and shall reimburse the Buyer Indemnified Persons for, any and all losses, Liabilities, Actions, deficiencies, diminution of value, expenses (including costs of investigation and defense and reasonable attorneys' and accountants' fees and expenses), or damages (excluding punitive damages consequential damages and lost profits) of any kind or nature whatsoever, whether or not involving a third-party claim (collectively, **"Damages"**), incurred thereby or caused thereto, directly or indirectly, based on, arising out of, resulting from relating to, or in connection with:

(a) any breach of or inaccuracy in any representation or warranty made by the Company or the Management Stockholders in Article III of this Agreement, without giving effect to any supplement to the Disclosure Schedule, the Disclosure Schedule, the supplements to the Disclosure Schedule (delivered to Buyer in accordance with Section 6.10 hereof).

(b) any breach or violation of or failure to fully perform any covenant, agreement, undertaking or obligation of the Company (to the extent to be performed prior to Closing), set forth in this Agreement.

(c) any breach of or inaccuracy in any representation or warranty made by the Stockholders in Article V of this Agreement (without giving effect to any supplement to the Disclosure Schedule), the Disclosure Schedule, the supplements to the Disclosure Schedule (delivered to Buyer in accordance with Section 6.10 hereof).

(d)   any breach or violation of or failure to fully perform any covenant, agreement, undertaking or obligation of Stockholders (to the extent to be performed prior to Closing) set forth in this Agreement.

(e)   Any Taxes arising out of or in connection with the transaction contemplated by this Agreement.

For purposes of this Article IX and for purposes of determining whether Buyer is entitled to indemnification from Stockholders pursuant to this Section 9.2 hereof, any breach of or inaccuracy in any representation or warranty of Company or Stockholders shall be determined without regard to any materiality qualifications set forth in such representation or warranty, and all references to the terms "material," "materially," "materiality," "Material Adverse Effect" or any similar terms shall be ignored for purposes of determining whether such representation or warranty was true and correct when made.

The matters set forth in Sections 9.2(a) and (b) are joint obligations of the Stockholders. This means that with respect to each indemnification claim thereunder, each Stockholder shall be responsible for a pro rata share of any Damages a Buyer Indemnified Person may suffer based on his, her or its respective holding of Common Stock as set forth in Annex I. Each Stockholder's liability shall be limited to his, her or its respective proportion of the overall limit on indemnification claims set forth in Section 9.4(b) hereof.

The matters set forth in Sections 9.2(c) and (d) are individual and several obligations of each Stockholder. This means that with respect to each indemnification claim thereunder, the particular Stockholder shall be solely responsible for any Damages a Buyer Indemnified Person may suffer. Buyer acknowledges and agrees that no Stockholder shall be liable for any breach of a representation, warranty, covenant or agreement of any other Stockholder.

The matters set forth in Section 9.2(e) shall be joint and several obligations of the Stockholders.

Section 9.3   Indemnification and Reimbursement by Buyer.   Buyer shall indemnify and hold harmless and defend Stockholders from and against, and shall reimburse Stockholders for, any and all Damages incurred thereby or caused thereto, directly or indirectly, based on, arising out of, resulting from, relating to, or in connection with:

(a)   any breach of or inaccuracy in any representation or warranty made by Buyer in this Agreement, the Buyer Disclosure Schedule or any other certificate or document delivered by, or on behalf of, Buyer pursuant to this Agreement, or

(b)   any breach or violation of or failure to fully perform any covenant, agreement, undertaking or obligation of Buyer set forth in this Agreement.

For purposes of this Article IX and for purposes of determining whether Stockholders is entitled to indemnification from Buyer pursuant to Section 9.3(a) or Section 9.3(b) hereof, any breach of or inaccuracy in any representation or warranty of Buyer shall be determined without regard to any materiality qualifications set forth in such representation or warranty, and all references to the terms "material," "materially," "materiality," "Material Adverse Effect" or any similar terms shall be ignored for purposes of determining whether such representation or warranty was true and correct when made.

Section 9.4 *Limitations on Amount — Stockholders.*

(a) The Stockholders shall not be liable for Damages arising in connection with its indemnification obligations under Section 9.2 hereof until the amount of such Damages exceeds $[_____] in the aggregate. If the aggregate amount of such Damages exceeds $[_____], the Stockholders shall be liable for all such Damages including the first $1.00 thereof.

(b) Notwithstanding anything to the contrary contained herein, except for Damages based on, arising out of, resulting from, or relating to any breach of the representations and warranties contained in Section 3.2 (Capitalization), Section 3.9 (Taxes) Section 3.20 (Environmental Matters), Section 3.22 (Brokers and Finders), Section 5.1 (Title to Shares), or resulting from Section 9.2(e), Stockholders shall have no liability for Damages under this Article IX in excess of [$_____]. Notwithstanding any other provision of this Agreement, for purposes of any indemnification liability with respect to Damages based on, arising out of, resulting from, or relating to any breach of the representations and warranties contained in Section 3.2 (Capitalization), Section 3.9 (Taxes), Section 3.20 (Environmental Matters), Section 3.22 (Brokers and Finders), Section 5.1 (Title to Shares), or resulting from Section 9.2(e), there shall be no limit on the amount of Damages for which Stockholders shall be liable.

(c) The limitations set forth in this Section 9.4 will not apply to any breach of any of the representations and warranties of which Stockholders had knowledge at any time prior to the date on which such representation and warranty is made or any intentional or willful breach by Stockholders or Company of any covenant, agreement, undertaking or obligation, and shall be liable for all Damages with respect to such breach or breaches.

Section 9.5 *Limitations on Amount — Buyer.*

(a) Buyer shall not be liable for Damages arising in connection with its indemnification obligations under Section 9.3 hereof until the amount of such Damages exceeds $[_____] in the aggregate. If the aggregate amount of such Damages exceeds $[_____], Buyer shall be liable for all such Damages including the first $1.00 thereof.

(b) The limitations set forth in this Section 9.5 will not apply to any breach of any of Buyer's representations and warranties of which Buyer had knowledge at any time prior to the date on which such representation and warranty is made or any intentional breach by Buyer of any covenant, agreement, undertaking or obligation, and Buyer shall be liable for all Damages with respect to such breach or breaches.

Section 9.6 *Other Limitations.*

(a) The Stockholders' indemnification obligations to the Buyer Indemnified Persons in respect of Damages for which indemnification is provided under this Agreement (**"Stockholder Indemnified Damages"**) will be reduced by any amounts actually received by or on behalf of the Buyer Indemnified Persons from third parties (net of deductible amounts, costs and expenses (including reasonable legal fees and expenses) incurred by such Buyer Indemnified Persons in connection with seeking to collect and collecting such amounts), in respect to such Stockholder Indemnified Damages (such amounts are referred to herein as **"Indemnity Reduction Amounts"**). If any Buyer

Indemnified Persons receives any Indemnity Reduction Amounts in respect of Stockholder Indemnified Damages after the full amount of such Stockholder Indemnified Damages has been set off against the Deferred Notes or disclosure from the Escrow Account pursuant to Section 9.6 hereof, then either the amount of such set off will be reduced (and the underlying debt obligation shall be revised) by an amount equal to the Indemnity Reduction Amount, or Buyer shall refund the Escrow Account with the amount of the Indemnity Reduction Amount. No insurer or other third party who would otherwise be obligated to pay any claim shall be relieved of the responsibility with respect to such claim or, solely by virtue of the indemnification provisions hereof, have any subrogation rights with respect to such claim. The parties agree that the indemnification provisions hereof shall not confirm any benefit upon an insurer or any other third party which such insurer or other third party would not be entitled to receive in the absence of indemnification provisions. Buyer will, or will cause each Buyer Indemnified Person to, use its reasonable best efforts to pursue any claims or rights it may have against all third parties which would reduce the amount of Stockholder Indemnified Damages.

(b)   The parties hereto acknowledge and agree that the foregoing indemnification provisions in this Article IX shall be the sole and exclusive remedy of an Indemnified Party (as defined in Section 9.7(a) hereof) with respect to the transactions contemplated by this Agreement and any and all claims for any breach or liability arising under, or in connection with, this Agreement or any of the agreements ancillary hereto, or otherwise relating to the subject matter of this Agreement and the transactions contemplated hereby and thereby shall be treated solely in accordance with, and limited by, the indemnification provisions set forth in this Article IX, provided, however, that, nothing contained in Article IX shall in any way limit, impair, modify or otherwise effect the rights of an Indemnified Party (including rights available under the Securities Exchange Act of 1934, as amended or the Securities Act of 1933, as amended) nor shall there be any limitation of liability of any Indemnified Party (as defined in Section 9.7 (a) hereof) to bring any claim, demand, suit or cause of action otherwise available to an Indemnified Person based upon an allegation or allegations that the Company or an Indemnified Party had an intent to defraud or made a willful, intentions or reckless misrepresentations or willful omission of a material fact in connection with this Agreement and the transactions contemplated hereby.

Section 9.7   *Notice and Payment of Claims; Set Off.*

(a)   <u>Notice</u>. The party entitled to indemnification pursuant to this Article IX (the **"Indemnified Party"**) shall notify the party liable for indemnification pursuant to this Article IX (the **"Indemnifying Party"**) within a reasonable period of time after becoming aware of, and shall provide to the Indemnifying Party as soon as practicable thereafter all information and documentation necessary to support and verify, any Damages that the Indemnified Party shall have determined to have given or may give rise to a claim for indemnification hereunder. Notwithstanding the foregoing, the failure to so notify the Indemnifying Party shall not relieve the Indemnifying Party of any Liability that it may have not any Indemnified Party, except to the extent that the Indemnifying Party demonstrates that it is prejudiced by the Indemnified Party's failure to give such notice.

(b) <u>Payment; Set Off</u>. The Indemnifying Party shall satisfy its obligations hereunder within five (5) days after receipt of a notice of a claim. Any amount not paid to the Indemnified Party by such date shall bear interest at a rate equal to ten percent (10%) per annum from the date due until the date paid. Buyer agrees and acknowledges that before it may demand payment for Damages under this Article IX it must seek reimbursement from the following, and in the following priority: FIRST up to an aggregate of $_____ for all claims under this Article IX, by reducing the principal amount (and any accrued interest to date) pro rata according to each Stockholder's respective obligation set forth in Section 9.4(a) and (b), which shall affect the timing and amounts required under the Deferred Notes in the same manner as if Buyer had made a permitted prepayment without premium or penalty thereunder, and SECOND, by submitting a claim to the Escrow Agent for reimbursement from the Escrow Account in accordance with the terms of the Escrow Agreement.

Section 9.8 Procedure for Indemnification—Third Party Claims.

(a) Upon receipt by an Indemnified Party of notice of the commencement of any Action by a third party (a **"Third Party Claim"**) against it, such Indemnified Party shall, if a claim is to be made against an Indemnifying Party under this Article IX, give notice to (and in any event within five (5) business days) the Indemnifying Party of the commencement of such Third Party Claim as soon as practicable, but the failure to so notify the Indemnifying Party shall not relieve the Indemnifying Party of any Liability that it may have to any Indemnified Party, except to the extent that the Indemnifying Party demonstrates that the defense of such Third Party Claim is prejudiced by the Indemnified Party's failure to give such notice.

(b) If a Third Party Claim is brought against an Indemnified Party and it gives proper notice to the Indemnifying Party of the commencement of such Third Party Claim, the Indemnifying Party will be entitled to participate in such Third Party Claim (unless (i) the Indemnifying Party is also a party to such Third Party Claim and the Indemnified Party determines in good faith that joint representation would be inappropriate or (ii) the Indemnifying Party fails to provide reasonable assurance to the Indemnified Party of its financial capacity to defend such Third Party Claim and provide indemnification with respect to such Third Party Claim) and, to the extent that it elects to assume the defense of such Third Party Claim with counsel satisfactory to the Indemnified Party and provides notice to the Indemnified Party of its election to assume the defense of such Third Party Claim, the Indemnifying Party shall not, as long as it diligently conducts such defense, be liable to the Indemnified Party under this Article IX for any fees of other counsel or any other expenses with respect to the defense of such Third Party Claim, in each case subsequently incurred by the Indemnified Party in connection with the defense of such Third Party Claim, other than reasonable costs of investigation.

If the Indemnifying Party assumes the defense of a Third Party Claim, (i) it shall be conclusively established for purposes of this Agreement that the claims made in such Third Party Claim are within the scope of and subject to indemnification; (ii) no compromise, discharge or settlement of, or admission of Liability in connection with, such claims may be effected by the Indemnifying

Party without the Indemnified Party's written consent (which consent shall not be unreasonably withheld or delayed) unless (A) there is no finding or admission of any violation of Law or any violation of the rights of any Person and no effect on any other claims that may be made against the Indemnified Party, and (B) the sole relief provided is monetary damages that are paid in full by the Indemnifying Party; (iii) the Indemnifying Party shall have no Liability with respect to any compromise or settlement of such claims effected without its written consent; and (iv) the Indemnified Party shall cooperate in all reasonable respects with the Indemnifying Party in connection with such defense, and shall have the right to participate in such defense, with counsel selected by it. If proper notice is given to an Indemnifying Party of the commencement of any Third Party Claim and the Indemnifying Party does not, within ten (10) days after the Indemnified Party's notice is given, give notice to the Indemnified Party of its election to assume the defense of such Third Party Claim, the Indemnifying Party shall be bound by any determination made in such Third Party Claim or any compromise or settlement effected by the Indemnified Party.

(c) Notwithstanding the foregoing, if an Indemnified Party determines in good faith that there is a reasonable probability that a Third Party Claim may adversely affect it or its directors, officers, subsidiaries, controlling persons or affiliates other than as a result of monetary damages for which it could be entitled to indemnification under this Agreement, the Indemnified Party may, by notice to the Indemnifying Party, assume the exclusive right to defend, compromise, or settle such Third Party Claim.

Section 9.9   Company Representations and Warranties.   Anything contained herein to the contrary notwithstanding, the representations and warranties of the Company contained in this Agreement (including, without limitation, the Disclosure Schedule and any supplements thereto pursuant to Section 6.10 hereof) (i) are being given by the Company on behalf of the Stockholders and for the purpose of binding the Stockholders to the terms and provisions of Article IX and the Escrow Agreement, and as an inducement to Buyer to enter into this Agreement (and the Company acknowledges that Buyer have expressly relied thereon) and (ii) are solely for the benefit of the Indemnified Persons and each of them. Accordingly, no third party (including, without limitation, the Stockholders or anyone acting on behalf of any thereof) other than the Indemnified Persons, and each of them, shall be a third party or other beneficiary of such representations and warranties and no such third party shall have any rights of contribution against the Company or any Company Subsidiary with respect to such representations or warranties or any matter subject to or resulting in indemnification by such third party under Article IX or otherwise.

Section 9.10   Tax Indemnification.
(a)   Stockholders and Deferred Optionholders shall indemnify the Buyer and hold it harmless from and against Taxes of the Company and each Company Subsidiary for all Pre-Closing Tax Periods, but only to the extent that such Taxes are in excess of the amount, if any, reserved for such Taxes (excluding any reserve for deferred Taxes established to reflect timing differences between book and Tax income) on the face of the Final Closing Balance Sheet. Stockholders and Deferred Optionholders shall reimburse Buyer for any Taxes

of the Company and each Company Subsidiary which are the responsibility of Stockholders and Deferred Optionholders pursuant to this Section 9.9 within fifteen (15) business days after payment of such Taxes by Buyer or the Company or a Company Subsidiary.

(b)   In the case of any taxable period that includes but does not end on the Closing Date, the amount of any Taxes for such period shall be determined based on an interim closing of the books as of the close of business on the Closing Date (and for such purposes, the Taxable period of any partnership or other pass-through entity in which the Company or a Company Subsidiary holds a beneficial interest shall be deemed to terminate at such time).

(c)   Buyer shall prepare and file or cause to be prepared and filed all Tax Returns for the Company and each Company Subsidiary which are filed after the Closing Date. Buyer shall permit Stockholders' Representative to review and comment on each such Tax Return described in the preceding sentence prior to filing and shall make such revisions to such Tax Returns as are reasonably requested by Stockholders' Representative.

(d)   Any Tax refunds that are received by Buyer or the Company or a Company Subsidiary, and any amounts credited against Tax to which the Company or a Company Subsidiary becomes entitled, that relate to PreClosing Tax Periods shall be for the account of Stockholders, and Buyer shall pay over to Stockholders any such refunds or the amount of any such credits within fifteen (15) days after receipt or entitlement thereto. In addition, to the extent that a claim for refund or a proceeding results in a payment or credit against Tax by a taxing authority to Buyer or the Company or a Company Subsidiary of any amount accrued on the Final Closing Balance Sheet, Buyer shall pay such amount to Stockholders within fifteen (15) days after receipt or entitlement thereto.

(e)   Buyer, the Company, each Company Subsidiary, and Stockholders shall cooperate fully, as and to the extent reasonably requested by the other party, in connection with the filing of Tax Returns pursuant to this Section 9.9 and any audit, litigation, or other proceeding with respect to Taxes. Such cooperation shall include the retention and (upon the other party's request) the provision of records and information which are reasonably relevant to any such audit, litigation, or other proceeding and making employees available on a mutually convenient basis to provide additional information and explanation of any material provided hereunder. The Company, each Company Subsidiary, and Stockholders agree (A) to retain all books and records with respect to Tax matters pertinent to the Company or a Company Subsidiary relating to any Pre-Closing Tax Period until the expiration of the statute of limitations (and, to the extent notified by Buyer or Stockholders' Representative, any extensions thereof) of the respective taxable periods and to abide by all record retention agreements entered into with any taxing authority, and (B) to give the other party reasonable written notice prior to transferring, destroying, or discarding any such books and records and, if the other party so requests, Buyer, the Company, a Company Subsidiary, or Stockholders, as the case may be, shall allow the other party to take possession of such books and records.

(f)   Buyer and Stockholders agree, upon request, to use their commercially reasonable efforts to obtain any certificate or other document from any Governmental Entity or any other Person as may be necessary to mitigate, reduce, or eliminate any Tax that could be imposed (including, but not limited to, with respect to the transactions contemplated by this Agreement).

ARTICLE X
REPRESENTATIVE

Section 10.1 Appointment. The Stockholders hereby irrevocably make, constitute and appoint [_____] as their agent and representative (the **"Stockholders' Representative"**) for all purposes under this Agreement. In the event of the death, resignation or incapacity of the Stockholders' Representative, the Stockholders shall promptly designate another individual to act as their representative under this Agreement so that at all time there will be a Stockholders Representative with the authority provided in this Article X. Such successor Stockholders' Representative shall be designated by the Stockholders by an instrument in writing signed by the Stockholders (or their successors in interest) holding a "required interest" of the Shares, and such appointment shall become effective as to the successor Stockholders Representative when such instrument shall have been delivered to him or her and a copy thereof delivered to the Buyer and Company. For purposes of this Agreement, **"a required interest"** of the Shares or Stockholders means the holders of [_____] percent (_____%) of the Company's Common Stock on as converted and fully diluted basis.

Section   10.2 Authorization. Stockholders   hereby   authorize   the Stockholders' Representative, on their behalf and in their name to:

(a)   receive all notice or documents given or to be given to the Stockholders pursuant hereto or in connection herewith and to receive and accept service of legal process in connection with any suit or proceeding arising under this Agreement. The Stockholders' Representative shall promptly forward a copy of such notice of process to each Stockholder.

(b)   deliver at the Closing the certificates for the Shares or affidavits of lost shares and assignment, as applicable, in exchange for their respective portion of the Purchase Price, including the Galaxy Shares and Deferred Notes;

(c)   deliver to Buyer at the Closing all certificates and documents to be delivered to Buyer by the Stockholders pursuant to this Agreement, together with any other certificates and documents executed by the Stockholders and deposited with the Stockholders' Representative for such purpose;

(d)   [act as disbursement agent for distribution of the Purchase Price (including the Galaxy shares and Deferred Notes) to the Stockholders in accordance with Annex II];

(e)   engage counsel, and such accountants and other advisors for the Stockholders and incur such other expenses on behalf of the Stockholders in connection with this Agreement and the transactions contemplated hereby as the Stockholders' Representative may deem appropriate;

(f) take such action on behalf of the Stockholders as the Stockholders' Representative may deem appropriate in respect of:

(i)   waiving any inaccuracies in the representations or warranties of Buyer contained in this Agreement or in any document delivered by Buyer pursuant hereto;

(ii)   waiving the fulfillment of any of the conditions precedent to the Stockholders' obligations hereunder; or terminating this Agreement if Buyer fails to satisfy its obligations under Section 7.2 hereof;

(iii)   taking such other action as the Stockholders' Representative is authorized to take under this Agreement or on written instructions executed by a required interest of Stockholders;

(iv)   receiving all documents or certificates or notices and making all determinations on behalf of the Stockholders required under this Agreement;

(v)   all such other matters as the Stockholders' Stockholders' Representative may deem necessary or appropriate to consummate this Agreement and the transactions contemplated hereby;

(vi)   negotiating, representing or entering into settlements and compromises of any disputes arising in connection with this Agreement and the transactions contemplated hereby; and

(vii)   taking all such action as may be necessary after the date hereof to carry out any of the transactions contemplated by this Agreement.

Section 10.3   Irrevocable Appointment.   The appointment of the Stockholders' Representative hereunder is irrevocable and any action taken by the Stockholders' Representative pursuant to the authority granted in this Article X shall be effective and absolutely binding on each Stockholders notwithstanding any contrary action of, or direction from, an Stockholder, except for actions taken by the Stockholders' Representative which are in bad faith or grossly negligent. The death or incapacity of a Stockholder shall not terminate the prior authority and agency of the Stockholders' Representative.

Section 10.4   Exculpation and Indemnification.

(a)   In performing any of his, her or its duties as Stockholders' Representative under this Agreement, the Stockholders' Representative shall not incur any Liability to any Person, except for Liability caused by the Stockholders' Representative's gross or willful misconduct. Accordingly, the Stockholders' Representative shall not incur any such Liability for (i) any action that is taken or omitted in good faith regarding any questions relating to the duties and responsibilities of the Stockholders' Representative under this Agreement, or (ii) any action taken or omitted to be taken in reliance upon any instrument that the Stockholders' Representative shall in good faith believe to be genuine, to have been signed or delivered by a proper Person and to conform with the provisions of this Agreement.

(b)   The Stockholders, jointly and severally, shall indemnify, defend and hold harmless the Stockholders' Representative against, from and in respect of any Liability arising out of or resulting from the performance of his or her or its duties hereunder or in connection with this Agreement (except for Liabilities arising from the gross negligence or willful misconduct of the Stockholders' Representative). Neither the Buyer nor the Company shall be liable to the Stockholders for dealing with the Stockholders' Representative in good faith (other than as a result of the gross negligence or willful misconduct of Company or Buyer).

Section 10.5   Actions of Stockholders.   Whenever this Agreement requires the Stockholders to take any action, such requirement shall be deemed to involve an undertaking by the Stockholders to cause the Stockholders' Representative to take such action on their behalf.

ARTICLE XI
MISCELLANEOUS

Section 11.1   Certain Definitions.

(a)   As used herein, the term **"Material Adverse Effect"** means with respect to the Company (i) any occurrence, condition, or effect that individually or in the aggregate is or reasonably likely to be materially adverse to (ii) the assets, properties, business, operations, prospects, results of operations, or conditions (financial or otherwise) of the Company and the Company Subsidiaries, taken as a whole.

(b)   When references are made in this agreement of information being **"to the Knowledge of the Company"** or similar language it shall be deemed to have "knowledge" of a particular fact or other matter if: (a) such individual is actually aware of such fact or other matter; or (b) a prudent individual could be expected to discover or otherwise become aware of such fact or other matter in the course of conducting a reasonable investigation concerning the existence of such fact or other matter.

(c)   When reference is made to **"Threatened"** such term shall be deemed to mean any demand or statement that has been made (orally or in writing) or any notice has been given that would lead a prudent Person to conclude that such a claim, event Action or Order is likely to be asserted, commenced, or taken in the future.

(d)   As used in this Agreement **"Related Party"** means (i) each of the Stockholders; (ii) each individual who is, or who has at any time since December 28, 1999 has been, an officer or any of the Company or any Company Subsidiary; (iii) each spouse, parent, child or sibling of each of the individuals referred to in clauses "(i)" and "(i)" hereof; and (iv) any Person entity (other than the Company or Company Subsidiaries) in which any one of the individuals referred to in clauses "(i)", "(ii)" and "(iii)" above hereof (or in which more than one of such individuals collectively hold), beneficially or otherwise, a material voting, proprietary or equity interest.

Section 11.2   Assignment; Successors; No Third Party Rights.   No party may assign any of its rights under this Agreement (including by merger or other operation of law) without the prior written consent of the other parties hereto (which may not be unreasonably withheld or delayed), and any purported assignment without such consent shall be void, except that Stockholders and Buyer hereby agree that Buyer may assign all of its rights and obligations under this Agreement to a wholly-owned direct or indirect subsidiary of Buyer (in any or all of which cases Buyer nonetheless shall remain responsible for the performance of its obligation hereunder). Upon Buyer's sale, disposition or other transfer, in whole or in part, of the Business or assets or properties of the Company or any Company Subsidiary, Stockholders and Company hereby agree that Buyer may assign, in whole or in part, any of Buyer's indemnification and set-off rights related thereto set forth in Article IX hereof, without the consent of the Company or Stockholders. Subject to the foregoing, this Agreement and all of the provisions hereof shall apply to, be binding upon, and inure to the benefit of the parties hereto and their successors and permitted assigns and the parties indemnified pursuant to Article IX. This Agreement and all of its provisions and conditions are for the sole and exclusive benefit of the parties to this Agreement and their successors and permitted assigns and nothing in this Agreement, express or implied, is intended to confer upon any Person other than the parties hereto any rights or remedies of any nature whatsoever under or by reason of this Agreement or any provision of this Agreement, provided however, that the Stockholders' Representative shall be a third party beneficiary to the provisions of Article X.

Section 11.3   Entire Agreement.   This Agreement, including the Disclosure Schedule, Buyer Disclosure Schedule, Annex I and Annex II, and Exhibits hereto and the other agreements and written understandings referred to herein or otherwise entered into by the parties hereto on the date hereof, constitute the entire agreement and understanding and supersede all other prior covenants, agreements, undertakings, obligations, promises, arrangements, communications, representations and warranties, whether oral or written, by any party hereto or by any director, officer, employee, agent, or Representative of any party hereto, other than [Confidentiality Agreement].

Section 11.4   Amendment or Modification.   This Agreement may be amended or modified only by written instrument signed by the Buyer, the Company and the Stockholders' Representative all of the parties hereto.

Section 11.5   Notices.   All notices, requests, instructions, claims, demands, consents and other communications required or permitted to be given hereunder shall be in writing and shall be deemed to have been duly given on the date delivered by hand or by courier service such as Federal Express, or by other messenger (or, if delivery is refused, upon presentment) or if by facsimile transmission upon receipt of confirmation, or upon delivery by registered or certified mail (return receipt requested), postage prepaid, to the parties at the following addresses:

   (a)   If to Buyer:

       Galaxy International Corp.
       100 Melbourne Ave
       Brooklyn, New York 10001
       Tel: 212-222-2222
       Facsimile: 212-222-2223
       Attn: Michael Sherman
             Chief Financial Officer

  with copy to:

       Bigar, Strong & Wise
       5000 Wilshire Blvd.
       Los Angeles, California 90017

Tel: (213) 789-4321
Facsimile: (213) 789-1234
Attn: Mark A. Bigar

(b)   If to Company:

Trekker Marketing, Inc.
333 Surfside Road
San Diego, California 90001
Tel: (619) 222-9876
Facsimile: (619) 222-6789
Attn: Frank Merlin
Chief Executive Officer

with copy to:

Klever & Coolidge
100 Hollywood Blvd.
Los Angeles, California 90002
Tel: (213) 678-7654
Facsimile: (213) 678-4567
Attn: Julie Hartbreaker

(c)   If to Stockholder:

[Stockholders Representative]

_____
_____
_____
_____

with a copy to:

_____
_____
_____
_____

Section 11.6   Actions of the Company and the Company Subsidiaries.   Whenever this Agreement requires the Company or any Company Subsidiary to take any action, such requirement shall be deemed to involve, with respect to actions to be taken to or prior to the Closing, an undertaking on the part of Management Stockholders and Stockholders to cause the Company or any Company Subsidiary to take such action.

Section 11.7   Descriptive Headings; Construction.   The descriptive headings herein are inserted for convenience of reference only and are not intended to be part of, or to affect the meaning, construction or interpretation of, this Agreement. Unless otherwise expressly provided, the word "including" does not limit the preceding words or terms.

Section 11.8 Counterparts. For the convenience of the parties hereto, this Agreement may be executed in any number of counterparts, each such counterpart being deemed to be an original instrument, and all such counterparts shall together constitute the same agreement.

Section 11.9 Governing Law; Contest to Jurisdiction. THIS AGREEMENT SHALL BE CONSTRUED IN ACCORDANCE WITH THE LAWS OF THE STATE OF CALIFORNIA WITHOUT GIVING EFFECT TO ANY CHOICE OR CONFLICT OF LAW PROVISIONS OR RULES THAT COULD CAUSE THE APPLICATION OF THE LAWS OF ANY JURISDICTION OTHER THAN THE STATE OF CALIFORNIA. THE PARTIES HERETO EXPRESSLY CONSENT AND AGREE THAT ANY DISPUTE, CONTROVERSY, LEGAL ACTION OR OTHER PROCEEDING THAT ARISES UNDER, RESULTS FROM, CONCERNS OR RELATES TO THIS AGREEMENT MAY BE BROUGHT IN THE FEDERAL AND STATE COURTS IN AND OF THE STATE OF CALIFORNIA AND ACKNOWLEDGE THAT THEY WILL ACCEPT SERVICE OF PROCESS BY REGISTERED OR CERTIFIED MAIL OR THE EQUIVALENT DIRECTED TO THEIR LAST KNOWN ADDRESS AS DETERMINED BY THE OTHER PARTY IN ACCORDANCE WITH THIS AGREEMENT OR BY WHATEVER OTHER MEANS ARE PERMITTED BY SUCH COURTS. THE PARTIES HERETO HEREBY ACKNOWLEDGE THAT SAID COURTS HAVE JURISDICTION OVER ANY SUCH DISPUTE OR CONTROVERSY, AND THAT THEY HEREBY WAIVE ANY OBJECTION TO PERSONAL JURISDICTION OR VENUE IN THESE COURTS OR THAT SUCH COURTS ARE AN INCONVENIENT FORUM.

Section 11.10 Exercise of Rights and Remedies. Except as otherwise provided herein, no delay of or omission in the exercise of any right, power or remedy accruing to any party as a result of any breach or default by any other party under this Agreement shall impair any such right, power or remedy, nor shall it be construed as a waiver of or acquiescence in any such breach or default, or of any similar breach or default occurring later; nor shall any waiver of any single breach or default be deemed a waiver of any other breach or default occurring before or after that waiver.

Section 11.11 Reformation and Severability. In case any provision of this Agreement shall be invalid, illegal or unenforceable, it shall, to the extent possible, be modified in such manner as to be valid, legal and enforceable but so as to most nearly retain the intent of the parties, and if such modification is not possible, such provision shall be severed from this Agreement, and in either case the validity, legality and enforceability of the remaining provisions of this Agreement shall not in any way be affected or impaired thereby.

Section 11.12 Specific Performance; Other Rights and Remedies. Each party recognizes and agrees that in the event the other party or parties should refuse to perform any of its or their obligations under this Agreement, the remedy at law would be inadequate and agrees that for breach of such provisions, each party shall, in addition to such other remedies as may be available to it at law or in equity, be entitled to injunctive relief and to enforce its rights by an action for specific performance to the extent permitted by applicable law. Each party hereby waives any requirement for security or the posting of any bond or other surety in connection with any temporary or permanent award of injunctive, mandatory or other equitable relief.

   Section 11.13   Stockholder Parties.   [In the event that not all of the Stock-holders execute this Agreement and become a party thereto, then this Agreement shall nevertheless be binding on only those Stockholders who become a party hereto, provided that such executing Stockholders constitute or own at least ninety percent (90%) of each of the Common Stock, Series A Preferred Stock and Series B Preferred Stock. In addition, the Buyer, the Company and the executing Stockholders agree to amend this Agreement as may be reasonably necessary to reflect that not all of the Shares are being sold and that not all of the Stockholders are a party to the Agreement.]

IN WITNESS WHEREOF, the parties hereto have caused this Stock Purchaser Agreement to be executed by their officers duly authorized, if applicable as of the date first written above.

TREKKER MARKETING, INC.

By: _____
Name: Fred Merlin
Title: Chief Executive Officer

GALAXY INTERNATIONAL Corp.

By: _____
Name: Robert Halfacre
Title: Chief Executive Officer

By: _____
Name: [————————————————]
Title: Secretary

MANAGEMENT STOCKHOLDERS[1]

_____
Stanley Rockledge

_____
Fred Merlin

STOCKHOLDERS:

SWIFT ROHN CAPITAL LLC

By: _____
Name:
Title:

YORK LIFE FUND III, LLC

By: _____

FRED MERLIN

_____

---

1. Please revise stockholder names to reflect stock ledger which we believe is in your possession.

STANLEY ROCKLEDGE

———————————————————————————————

RANDY MOSES

———————————————————————————————

JAMES KILJOY

———————————————————————————————

MELVIN KIRKPATRICK

———————————————————————————————

CHARLES TEALEAF

———————————————————————————————

LAWRENCE BROAD

———————————————————————————————

ROBERT ALLSTOCK

———————————————————————————————

STOCKHOLDERS' REPRESENTATIVE:

[————————————————————————————]

By: _____
Name:
Title:

ANNEX I

TO THAT CERTAIN
STOCK PURCHASE AGREEMENT
DATED AS OF APRIL _____, 2004
BY AND AMONG
THE STOCKHOLDERS NAMED THEREIN
THE MANAGEMENT STOCKHOLDERS NAMED THEREIN
TREKKER MARKETING, INC.
AND
GALAXY INTERNATIONAL CORP.

STOCK HOLDERS

NAME AND ADDRESS	SHARES OF COMMON STOCK	SHARES OF SERIES A PREFERRED STOCK	SHARES OF SERIES B PREFERRED STOCK	OPTIONS	PERCENTAGE OWNERSHIP OF COMMON STOCK

ANNEX II

TO THAT CERTAIN
STOCK PURCHASE AGREEMENT
AND COMPANY
DATED AS OF APRIL _____, 2004
BY AND AMONG THE STOCKHOLDERS NAMED THEREIN
THE MANAGEMENT STOCKHOLDERS NAMED THEREIN
TREKKER MARKETING, INC.
AND GALAXY INTERNATIONAL CORP.

Aggregate consideration to be paid to the Stockholders:[2]

Cash—$____, including $___ of such amount to be held by the Escrow Agent pursuant to the Escrow Agreement pursuant to Section 1.4 hereof for the purchase of Common Stock and Preferred Stock and for the cancellation of Stock Options.

Galaxy Shares— [____] shares of Galaxy Shares ($[___] in value)[3] for the purchase of a portion of the Shares. The issuance of the Galaxy Shares shall be subject to execution by the recipient of a Stock Issuance Agreement.

Deferred Notes—$5.0 million principal amount for the purchase of a portion of the Shares.

Aggregate consideration to be allocated among the Stockholders and holders of Options as follows:

[Add Chart]

(a)   Earnout. Buyer will pay the Stockholders an earnout as set forth below (**"Earnout Payments"**):

(i)   For the year ended December 31, 2004, $1.75 million if the Company's EBITDA (as defined below) equals $8 million and rising at a linear rate to $3.5 million if EBITDA equals or exceeds $10.5 million; and

(ii)   For the year ended December 31, 2005, $1.75 million if the Company's EBITDA equals $9 million and rising at a linear rate to $3.5 million of EBITDA equals or exceeds $11.5 million.

(b)   The Earnout Payments, if any, shall be allocated 57.14% equally among [NAMES OF SENIOR MANAGEMENT] (collectively **"Senior Management"**), and 42.86% among the Stockholders (other than Senior Management) pro rata in relationship to their ownership of Shares.

For purposes of this *Annex II* **"EBITDA"** shall mean the earnings before interest, taxes, depreciation and amortization of the Company before calculation

---

2.   Subject to upward or downward adjustment to the extent that the Shareholders' Equity of the Company on the Closing Date as calculated in accordance with GAAP and on a basis consistent with past practices as set forth on Section 1.5 hereof.

3.   Determined by reference to the weighted average price per share of Galaxy Shares for the six (6) months ending on the date this Agreement is executed less 10% for the Earnout Payments. The payments at closing are to be valued at the same price granted by Galaxy in stock sales made immediately prior to closing to fund this transaction.

of the Earnout (as defined below) if any, based in accordance with upon GAAP and on a basis consistent with past practice.

(c)   <u>General</u>. In calculating EBITDA, actual reported results of the Company:

(i)   Shall neither be reduced by Buyer corporate allocations, except for direct services provided by the Company at cost (not to exceed the cost of the same services performed on an out-sourced basis);

(ii)   Shall be reduced by the interest expense associated with any capital that Buyer or any affiliate will be required to infuse into the Company in order for the Company to reach its targeted EBITDA objectives at an assumed interest rate of 10%;

(iii)   Assumes operating expenses will include total lease costs if leases do not meet the criteria for a capital lease or will include appropriate depreciation and interest expenses related to lease equipment if such leases do not meet the criteria for a capital lease;

(iv)   Shall be reduced by the costs (if any) of additional administrative staff which the Company and Buyer determine shall be necessary to meet reporting and administrative requirements of the Company while relieving the Company management and other personnel from certain administrative duties to allow them to focus more of their efforts on business development; and

(v)   Shall be reduced by profit-sharing contributions, increases in compensation packages paid to the Company's Senior Management under employment agreements that might be put in place as a result of this transaction other than the agreements required in this Agreement.

(vi) Shall not be reduced by any Damages for which the Buyer recovered in accordance with Article IX, however, to the extent any Damages are not reimbursed in accordance with Article IX then actual results shall be reduced by such amount.

(vii)   [other Adjustments to be discussed]

The Buyer agrees that subsequent to the Closing Date and until the expiration of the time period related to the Earnout Payments, it shall maintain the separate corporate existence of the Company as a wholly-owned direct or indirect subsidiary of Buyer and shall maintain separate books of account in order to calculate the Earnout Payments.

The Company and Buyer shall use all reasonable efforts to prepare financial statements necessary for calculation of the Earnout Payments as soon as practicable and in any event within thirty (30) days following expiration of the applicable 12-month period. After calculation of the Earnout, if any, the Company shall provide the Stockholders' Representative with copies of all workpapers and other relevant documents to verify the calculation of such Earnout Payments, if any. In addition, Company will provide the Stockholders' Representative with annual financial statements of the Company. In the event of any dispute or controversy concerning the calculation of the Earnout Payments, the parties to the Agreement shall use their reasonable best efforts to resolve the matter to the reasonable satisfaction of the parties within sixty (60) days following such calculation of the Earnout Payments. Any dispute or controversy with respect to the Earnout Payments that is not resolved within such sixty-day period shall be settled exclusively by arbitration, conducted before a panel of three arbitrators in Los Angeles, California, in accordance with the rules of the American Arbitration Association then in effect. The arbitrators shall not have the authority to add to, detract from, or modify any provision of this Agreement nor to award punitive damages. A decision by a majority of the arbitration panel shall be final and binding, and judgment may be entered on the arbitrators' award in any court having jurisdiction. The costs of any arbitration proceeding shall be borne by the party or parties not prevailing in such arbitration as determined by the arbitrators.

Payment of the Earnout Payments, if any, will be made within sixty (60) days following preparation of the financial statements described above, if applicable, or promptly upon the determination by the arbitrators. Any amounts paid pursuant to the shall be paid in cash to the Stockholders pro rata in the same proportion as their ownership of Shares (other than Senior Management) and in Galaxy Shares to Senior Management (valued for this purpose based on the volume weighted average per shares of Galaxy Shares for the six (6) months ending prior to the date on which the Company's audited financial statements are issued, less 10%). Any issuance of Galaxy Shares will be subject to the execution of a Stock Issuance Agreement.

Letter of Intent

February 1, 2004

Mr. Fred Merlin
Chief Executive Officer
Trekker Marketing, Inc.
333 Surfside Road
San Diego, CA 90001

Dear Fred:

Introduction

We are writing to you following the discussions between Galaxy International Corporation ("Galaxy") and J.B. Hubble and yourself regarding Trekker Marketing, Inc. ("Trekker").

This letter confirms the interest of Galaxy in acquiring Trekker, and reflects our understanding of the key issues of the non-binding proposal as discussed by us in our teleconference of February 1, 2004.

Non-binding Proposal

The terms of Galaxy's non-binding proposal to acquire Trekker are:

Galaxy or its nominee will acquire 100% of the issued capital of Trekker, comprised of common and preference shares and outstanding options for $42 million, of which $30 million will be payable on completion, and $5 million will be payable in four semi-annual equal payments commencing in the second quarter of calendar 2005, bearing simple interest of 7% per year. Galaxy to have the right to prepay at any time and from time to time part or all of the deferred consideration without penalty. Specified Trekker Senior Management will be required to accept Galaxy shares in respect of their common and preference share holdings in Trekker.

In addition there may be up to $7 million of contingent payments, of which up to $3 million will be paid to the fully diluted Common Stock owners of Trekker and up to $4 million to specified Trekker Senior Management as specified by Galaxy. These contingent payments would be based on the hurdles proposed by Galaxy:

(i)   In the year to December 31, 2005, Trekker must achieve EBITDA of $8 million to trigger a payment of $1.75 million, rising at a linear rate to $3.5 million on achieving EBITDA of $10.5 million.

(ii)   In the year to December 31, 2006, Trekker must achieve EBITDA of $9 million to trigger a payment of $1.75 million, rising at a linear rate to $3.5 million on achieving EBITDA of $11.5 million;

Of this $7 million contingent payment the up to $3.0 million payment to the Common stock owners would be paid in cash and the up to $4.0 million payment to Trekker Senior Management would be satisfied by the issuance of Galaxy shares of that value. The Galaxy shares would be valued at a 10% discount to the volume weighted average price of Galaxy shares over the six-month period prior to the signing of the accounts in respect of the year which is the subject of the additional consideration. All shares issued would be subject to three-month escrow;

(iii)   An additional $1.0 million will be paid to specific Trekker Senior Management in respect of four year Service Agreements and Non-Compete Agreements. The payment would be made with cash paid in four annual equal installments on 4/05, 4/06, 4/07, and 4/08. These payments are of a capital nature as are all other payments referred to in this letter proposal save for interest payments and Galaxy will require the purchase agreement to be structured to reflect that fact;

(iv)   Settlement amount to be adjusted for rise and fall in balance sheet items between December 31, 2003 accounts and completion; and,

(v)   Trekker's existing subordinated notes to be rescheduled as follows: principal repayments to cease at the effective date of the completion of the acquisition of Trekker ("Effective Date"); 50% of the remaining principal to be repaid on July 1, 2005; 25% to be repaid July 1, 2006; and, the residual 25% to be repaid July 1, 2007. The coupon of the existing notes will be reduced to 7.0% and interest in arrears on the outstanding balance will be paid monthly to noteholders. Galaxy to have the right of early repayment of part of any or all of the notes at any time or from time to time without penalty. Trekker's payment obligations to noteholders will be guaranteed by Galaxy. Galaxy will need to review the other terms of the notes and may seek additional amendments to those terms.

Financing

Galaxy proposes to finance the cash component of any acquisition of Trekker from a combination of three sources. These are, first, the existing cash resources of Galaxy; second, borrowings by Galaxy; and, third, the proceeds of a placement of common shares in Galaxy to be completed if Galaxy is successful in acquiring Trekker. The mix of these forms of financing is yet to be determined by Galaxy.

Timing

Galaxy is in a position to complete the acquisition of Trekker once agreement is reached and due diligence is satisfactorily completed. Under Delaware law, the proposed acquisition does not require Galaxy shareholder approval.

Any placement of ordinary shares by Galaxy necessary to fund a part of the proposed acquisition consideration of Trekker does not require approval of Galaxy shareholders.

Galaxy requires exclusive rights for 60 days to negotiate with Trekker and its shareholders during the due diligence period.

Conditions Precedent

This preliminary proposal is subject to the following conditions precedent:

1. Approval of the Galaxy Board of Directors to the final terms of any transaction to acquire Trekker;

2. The entering into by selected members of the management team of Trekker of employment contracts and non compete contracts to the satisfaction of Galaxy;

3. The entering into by members of the Trekker sponsored riding team of satisfactory sponsorship contracts and/or non compete contracts to the satisfaction of Galaxy;

4. The assets of Trekker to be acquired by Galaxy are to include the Dud and Druids brands currently owned by Mirage, Inc. It is understood that Trekker owns or will own, inter alia, the businesses or entities: Dwarf; Mirage; and Green Hat;

5. The satisfactory completion by Galaxy of a due diligence review of Trekker including the financial and other information concerning Trekker; and,

6. The completion by Galaxy of any new placement of ordinary shares in Galaxy necessary in order to fund the completion of the proposed acquisition of Trekker.

Level of Review

This non-binding proposal to acquire Trekker has received review from the senior executive team of Galaxy. The Board of Directors of Galaxy will be required to review and approve the terms of any definitive proposal by Galaxy to acquire Trekker.

Conclusion

We look forward to welcoming Trekker to the Galaxy International, Corp., and we are very excited about working with Trekker management to grow Trekker and Galaxy over the long term to be the world's premier skate-board equipment and apparel company.

Yours sincerely,
For and on behalf of Galaxy International, Corp.

Robert Halfacre   Date: _____
Chief Executive Officer

Agreed and Accepted:
For and on behalf of Trekker Marketing, Inc.

Fred Merlin   Date: _____
Chief Executive Officer

Due Diligence Checklist

What follows is an itemized outline of certain of the documents and materials we would initially like to review concerning the business of the Company (the "Business"). All references to the Company apply to any members of the affiliated group of companies having as its ultimate parent Company. To the extent any requested documents are available as part of filings made by the Company with the SEC, in lieu of providing the document you may reference the applicable filing.

A. CORPORATE MATTERS

1. A corporate structure chart depicting the various entities within the Company conducting the Business, and the ownership and relationship of those entities.
2. A list of jurisdictions in which the Business is being conducted indicating the entity conducting the Business in each jurisdiction.
3. A list of any governmental (federal, state, or local) approvals, permits, certificates, registrations, concessions, exemptions, etc., required for the Company to conduct the Business in every jurisdiction in which the Business is conducted.
4. Audited and/or unaudited financial statements for the last 3 years, and current budgets and projections for each Company engaged in any aspect of the Business.
5. Independent accountants' management letters on internal controls and contingent liabilities (if any) for the last 3 years for each financial statement provided in response to item A.6.
6. Agreements relating to the ownership and control of each Company involved in the Business (if any), including all shareholder agreements, voting trusts and voting agreements, proxies, transfer restriction agreements, registration agreements, stock purchase rights (including the Company's current rights plan) and warrants.

7. Agreements to which the Company is a party relating to any completed or proposed business acquisitions, mergers, sales or purchases of substantial assets, equity financings, reorganizations and other material transactions outside of the ordinary course of business for each Company involved in the Business with in the last 3 years.

8. Agreements relating to ownership of or investments in any business or enterprise, including investments in joint ventures and minority equity investments.

B. MATERIAL CONTRACTS

1. Descriptions of arrangements between each Company involved in the Business and the 50 largest customers and 50 largest suppliers of the Company.

2. All sales distribution agreements, sales representative agreements, franchise agreements and advertising agreements involving each Company related to the Business.

3. All service contracts with customers of each Company in the Business (or if all such contracts are substantially similar, the form of such contract and a list of persons or entities party to such an agreement).

4. Agreements of each Company in the Business for research and/or design and development.

5. Any agreement which prohibits each Company in the Business from freely engaging in any business anywhere in the world.

6. Any tax sharing or tax indemnification agreements involving each Company involved in the Business.

C. LABOR

1. Employment agreements with any officer, individual employee or other person on a full-time or consulting basis.

2. Non-disclosure agreements and non-compete agreements binding any present or former employees.

3. Management, consulting or advisory agreements with any third party.

4. Collective bargaining agreements with any labor union.

5. Files relating to any outstanding orders, decrees or judgments and files with respect to pending or threatened labor disputes (including strikes, grievances and arbitration proceedings).

D. EMPLOYEE BENEFITS

1. Bonus, pension, profit sharing, retirement and other forms of deferred compensation plans together with all actuarial reports and last agreements, evidence of any qualification under the Internal Revenue Code and ERISA (or similar Canadian or other foreign statues and regulations), correspondence with respect to such qualification and the last

three annual reports on Form 5500 (or the Canadian equivalent), severance plans, employee handbooks or pamphlets.

2. Stock purchase plans, stock option plans, health and welfare, insurance and other employee benefits plans.

3. Agreements with any person or organization affiliated with the Company providing for the payment of any cash or other compensation upon the change in control of the Company or any of its subsidiaries or prohibiting competition or the disclosure of secrets or confidential information.

E.   LITIGATION

1. Copies of all counsel letters received by the Company in response to audit inquiries for the past 5 years.

2. List of, and files concerning, any pending or threatened litigation, any material claims settled or adjudicated within the past 5 years, and any past or current investigations or proceedings (pending or threatened) by any third party or governmental agencies (including environmental, tax, employee safety matters and EEOC (or pay-equity or other similar Canadian) matters).

3. Information regarding any material contingent liabilities and material unasserted claims and information regarding any unasserted violation of any employee safety and environmental laws and any asserted or unasserted pollution clean up liability.

F.   REAL ESTATE

1. Description of any real estate owned by the Company and copies of related deeds, surveys, title insurance policies, title opinions, certificates of occupancy, easements, condemnation orders, zoning variances and recent appraisals.

2. Copies of all leases whereby the Company leases (as lessee or lessor) any real estate, facility or office space.

G.   PERSONAL PROPERTY

1. Copies of all leases, whereby the Company leases (as lessee or lessor) any machinery, vehicles or other equipment (both operating and capitalized) with annual payments in excess of $ _____.

H.   INTELLECTUAL PROPERTY

1. List of registered and unregistered proprietary rights (patents, trademarks, service marks, trade names, corporate names, copyrights, and applications therefore) of the Company.

2. Agreements and files relating to proprietary rights (patents, trademarks, service marks trade names, corporate names, copyrights, etc.) of the Company, including registrations and royalty agreements and licenses held or granted with respect thereto (including without limitation foreign manufacturing and/or technology licenses), and any pending or threatened infringement actions by or against the Company related to such rights.

3. Agreements and files to any other proprietary rights of the Company.

I.   INSURANCE MATTERS

1. Summary description of insurance coverage, including but not limited to the name of the insurer, insured party, insurance agent, policyholder and period and scope of coverage (including whether the coverage is claims made or occurrence or other basis and a description of the method of calculation of deductibles and ceilings); copies of policies and agreements.

2. Information on claims history, methods of reserving for uninsured portion of claims and methods of self insurance.

J.   ENVIRONMENTAL

1. A list of facilities or other properties formerly owned, leased or operated by the Company and reports of environmental audits or site assessments in the possession of the Company, including any Phase I or Phase II assessments or asbestos surveys, relating to any such facilities or properties;

2. Copies of environmental permits for facilities or properties currently owned or operated by Company;

3. Copies of all environmental notices of violations, complaints, consent decrees, and other documents indicating noncompliance with environmental laws or regulations or guidelines, received by the Company from local, state, provincial or federal governmental authorities, together with documentation indicating how such situations were resolved;

4. Copies of any private party complaints, claims, lawsuits or other documents relating to potential environmental liability of the Company or any of its subsidiaries to private parties;

5. Listing of underground storage tanks currently or previously present at the properties and facilities listed in response to Item 1, copies of permits, licenses or registrations relating to such tanks, and documentation of underground storage tank removals and any corrective action or remedial work; documentation of "sign-offs," "no further action letters," "clean closure letters" and information submitted to or received from regulatory agencies regarding underground storage tank matters;

6. Description of any release of hazardous substances or petroleum known by the Company to have occurred at the properties and facilities listed

in response to Item 1; descriptions of any corrective or remedial action relating to any such releases;

7. Copies of any information request, PRP notices, "106 orders," or other notices received by the Company pursuant to CERCLA or similar state or Canadian federal or provincial laws relating to liability for hazardous substance releases at offsite facilities or facilities described in response to Item 1, together with material correspondence and documents (including any relating to the Company's share of liability) with respect to any such matters; and

8. Copies of any written analyses conducted by the Company or any outside consultant relating to future environmental activities (e.g., upgrades to equipment, improvements in practices, etc.) of the Company for which expenditure of more than $_____ is certain or reasonably anticipated within the next five years and an estimate of the costs of such activities.

K.   FINANCIAL STATEMENTS

1. All audited financial statements for the Company for the most recent five (5) years and fiscal year and unaudited financial statements for each fiscal quarter since the most recent audited statement.

2. Any notes from conferences with accountants or financial officer for the Company to review information provided pursuant to Item L.l and accounting problems.

3. Auditors' reports to management and attorneys' letters to auditors of the Company applicable to each period covered by the audited financial statements provided.

L.   TAXES

1. Federal, state and local income tax returns for the five most recent fiscal years of the Company.

2. Property and other tax returns, reports and forms, if any, for the five most recent fiscal years.

3. List of audits or examination of returns, reports or forms described pursuant to Items M.1 and M.2 and of all deficiencies, proposed and assessed as a result of such examinations, if any; evidence of satisfaction of same.

M.   FINANCIAL AGREEMENTS

1. Indentures and loan agreements, to which the Company is a party if any.

2. Guarantee agreements to which the Company is a party.

3. Credit agreements for the Company including lines of credit and a description of banking relationships.

N.   INSURANCE

1.   List and description of all insurance policies.

O.   REGISTRATION, FILINGS, LICENSES AND PERMITS

1.   Copies of all filings of the Company with the Securities and Exchange Commission (including registration orders).
2.   Copies of all state Blue Sky filings.
3.   Copies of all filings with the National Association of Securities Dealers (including CRD Report).
4.   Copies of all other government licenses or permits.
5.   Copies of government licenses or permits of employees or agents.
6.   Copies of any documents relating to or investigations or audit of the Company, agency governmental agency or authority.

P.   LIENS AND ENCUMBRANCES

1.   List and description of all material liens (including tax liens), charges, security interests, pledges, easements, covenants, agreements, restrictions and encumbrances.
2.   All decrees, awards, orders or judgments applicable to the business or operations of the Company, with out limitation, any relating to wages, hours and working conditions, advertising and sale of services, trade regulation, license, patent or copyright infringement, and antitrust.

Closing Checklist

ACQUISITION OF TREKKER MARKETING, INC.
BY
GALAXY INTERNATIONAL CORPORATION
JUNE _____, 2004

I. PRINCIPAL AGREEMENTS AND RELATED DOCUMENTS

1. Stock Purchase Agreement by and among the Stockholders named therein, Trekker Marketing, Inc. and Galaxy International Corporation, or its Nominee for all of the outstanding capital stock of Trekker Marketing, Inc. dated as of April _____ 2004, including Annex I and the following Schedules and Exhibits attached thereto ("Stock Purchase Agreement"):

   a. Schedule 1.2(a)   Purchase Price
   b. Schedule 1.3   Delivery of Shares and Purchase Price
   c. Schedule 9.2(f)   Indemnification and Reimbursement by Stockholders and Optionholders
   d. Exhibit 1.3(c)   Form of Stock Issuance Agreement
   e. Exhibit 1.3(g)   Form of Deferred Note
   f. Exhibit 2.3(g)   Form of Guaranty
   g. Exhibit 7.1(k)   Form of Subordinated Note Exchange Agreement and Subordinated Note
   h. Exhibit 7.1(n)   Form of Employment Agreement
   i. Exhibit 7.1(o)   Form of Stockholder Release
   j. Exhibit 7.1(p)   Form of Non-Competition Agreement

2. Trekker Marketing, Inc. Disclosure Schedules to the Stock Purchase Agreement
3. Stockholders Disclosure Schedules to the Stock Purchase Agreement

4. Stockholders' Representative Request and Authorization dated as of _ _____, 2004 authorizing the execution and delivery of Amendment Number One to the Stock Purchase Agreement.

5. Stock Issuance Agreement by and between Galaxy International Corporation and Stanley Rockledge dated as of June _____, 2004, including Investor Certification attached thereto as Exhibit A.

6. Stock Issuance Agreement by and between Galaxy International Corporation and Fred Merlin dated as of June _____, 2004, including Investor Certification attached thereto as Exhibit A.

7. Stock Issuance Agreement by and between Galaxy International Corporation and Randy Moses dated as of June _____, 2004, including Investor Certification attached thereto as Exhibit A.

8. Stock Issuance Agreement by and between Galaxy International Corporation and Charles Tealeaf dated as of June _____, 2004, including Investor Certification attached thereto as Exhibit A.

9. Copy of Galaxy International Corporation-Annual Report for the year ended December 31, 2003, and the Quarterly Report filed on March _____, 2004, delivered to each of the Stockholders who were party to the Stock Issuance Agreement pursuant to paragraph 6 thereof.

10. Amended and Restated Employment Agreement dated as of June _____, 2004 by and among Trekker Marketing, Inc., Galaxy International Corporation and Fred Merlin with Exhibits attached thereto, including Trade Secret and Confidentiality Agreement and Invention Agreement.

11. Employment Agreement dated as of June _____, 2004 by and among Dwindle, Inc., Trekker Marketing, Inc., Galaxy International Corporation and Randy Moses with Exhibits attached thereto, including Trade Secret and Confidentiality Agreement and Invention Agreement.

12. Employment Agreement dated as of June _____, 2004 by and among Trekker Marketing, Inc., Galaxy International Corporation and Melvin Kirkpatrick with Exhibits attached thereto, including Trade Secret and Confidentiality Agreement and Invention Agreement.

13. General Release dated as of July _____, 2004 from each Stockholder of Trekker Marketing, Inc. to and in favor of, and for the benefit of Trekker Marketing, Inc. and Galaxy International Corporation.

14. Spousal Consents of Stockholders of Trekker Marketing, Inc.

15. NonCompetition Agreement dated as of June _____, 2004 by and among Trekker Marketing, Inc., Galaxy International Corporation, and its nominee and Fred Merlin.

16. NonCompetition Agreement dated as of June _____, 2004 by and among Trekker Marketing, Inc., Galaxy International Corporation, and its nominee and Randy Moses.

17. NonCompetition Agreement dated as of June _____, 2004 by and among Trekker Marketing, Inc., Galaxy International Corporation, and its nominee and Stanley Rockledge.

18. Consulting Agreement dated as of June _____, 2004 by and among Trekker Marketing, Inc. and Stanley Rockledge.

II.   **Documents Delivered by Trekker Marketing, Inc. and Its Shareholders**

1.   Termination of Stockholders Agreement dated as of June _____, 2004 executed by all the Stockholders of Trekker Marketing Inc.

2.   Termination of Amended and Restated Management Agreement dated as of June _____, 2004 by and among Swift Rohn, L.L.C. and Trekker Marketing, Inc.

3.   Trekker Marketing, Inc. Officer's Certificate dated as of July _____, 2004 delivered in accordance with Section 7.1(c) of the Stock Purchase Agreement.

4.   Trekker Marketing Inc. Secretary's Certificate dated as of July _____, 2004 delivered in accordance with Section 7.1(f) of the Stock Purchase Agreement, including Exhibit A attached thereto.

5.   Trekker Marketing, Inc. Written Consent in Lieu of Meeting of the majority holders of Common Stock, Series A Preferred Stock and Series B Preferred Stock dated June _____, 2004 approving the Stock Purchase Agreement and related transactions and copy of the notice dated June _____, 2004 to remaining shareholders pursuant to Section 603(b) of the California Corporations Code as to action taken by majority holders.

6.   Consent to Assignment Agreement dated as of June _____, 2004 by and between Trekker Marketing, Inc. and Lois Merlin Trust for the lease premises located at 333 Surfside Road, San Diego, California.

7.   Officer's Certificate for Trekker Marketing, Inc. dated as of June _____, 2004 as to the repayment of all option loans pursuant to Section 7(j)(ii) of the Stock Purchase Agreement.

8.   Letter dated June _____, 2004 from Trekker Marketing, Inc. and acknowledged and agreed to by each of Option Holders of Trekker Marketing, Inc. as to the cancellation of their stock options under the terms of the Stock Purchase Agreement.

9.   Copies of the stock certificates representing 100% of the capital stock of Trekker, including stock powers executed by the stockholders transferring the shares to Galaxy International Corp. on _____, 2004 under the terms of the Stock Purchase Agreement.

10.   Letter dated July _____, 2004 from Trekker Marketing, Inc. to Galaxy International Corp. waiving the requirement of the receipt of an opinion of counsel as a condition to the transfer or assignment of the shares of Common Stock, Series A Preferred Stock and Series B Preferred Stock.

11.   Wire Transfer Instructions for cash portion of Initial Purchase Price pursuant to Section 1.3(d) of the Stock Purchase Agreement dated June _____, 2004.

III.   Documents Delivered by Galaxy International Corporation

1.   Evidence of notification of issuance of shares of common stock of Galaxy International Corporation to Charles Tealeaf, Randy Moses, Melvin Kirkpatrick, Merlin Family Trust, and Stanley Rockledge.
2.   Copies of the Deferred Notes issued on June _____, 2004 to the following Stockholders in the amounts indicated:

     [List Omitted]

3.   Copies of the Deferred Notes issued on June _____, 2004 to the following Option Holders in the amounts indicated:

     [List Omitted]

4.   Guaranty of Galaxy International Corporation to each of the holders of the Deferred Notes dated June _____, 2004.
5.   Galaxy International Corporation Officer's Certificate dated of June _____, 2004 delivered, in accordance with Section 7.2(c) of the Stock Purchase Agreement.
6.   Galaxy International Corporation Secretary's Certificate dated as of June _____, 2004 delivered in accordance with Section 7.2(d) of the Stock Purchase Agreement, including Exhibit A attached thereto.

IV.   Corporate Documents Delivered by Trekker Marketing, Inc. and Its Subsidiaries

1.   Trekker Marketing, Inc. certified Articles of Incorporation and Good Standing, Certificate both issued by the California Secretary of State on June _____, 2004 and Tax Status Letter issued by the California Franchise Tax Board on June _____, 2004.
2.   El Segundo Rat, Inc. certified Articles of Incorporation and Good Standing Certificate both issued by the California Secretary of State on June _____, 2004 and Tax Status letter issued by the California Franchise Tax Board on June _____, 2004.
3.   Skateboard World Industries, Inc. certified Articles of Incorporation and Good Standing Certificate both issued by the California Secretary of State on June _____, 2004 and Tax Status Letter issued by the California Franchise Tax Board on June _____, 2004.
4.   Trekker Asia Limited Memorandum of Articles of Association and Certificate of Continuing Registration issued by the Register of Companies of Hong Kong on June _____, 2004.
5.   Resignations of J.B. Hubble, Stanley Rockledge, Fred Merlin, Andrew Norton and Linda Swine as Directors of Trekker Marketing, Inc. effective as of June _____, 2004.
6.   Resignations of Fred Merlin, Stanley Rockledge, Linda Swine, J.B. Hubble and Andrew Norton as Directors of El Segando Hat, Inc. effective as of June _____, 2004.
7.   Resignations of Fred Merlin and Stanley Rockledge as Directors of Skateboard World Industries, Inc. effective as of June _____, 2004.

V. LEGAL OPINIONS

1. Opinion letter of Klever & Coolidge dated June _____, 2004, including Trekker Marketing, Inc Support Certificate, with exhibits attached thereto.
2. Opinion letter of Bigar, Strong & Wise, P.C., dated June _____, 2004.

VI. DOCUMENTS DELIVERED IN CONNECTION WITH THE SUBORDINATED NOTE EXCHANGE AGREEMENT

1. Subordinated Note Exchange Agreement dated as of June _____, 2004 by and among the Note Holders named therein and Trekker Marketing, Inc.
2. Consent and Amendment No. 1 to the Loan. Guaranty and Security Agreement dated as of June _____, 2004 by and among Comenca Bank-California, Trekker Marketing, Inc. and its subsidiaries named therein.
3. Amendment No. 1 to Intercreditor and Subordination Agreement dated as of July 2, 2002 by and among Trekker Marketing, Inc. and its subsidiaries named therein, Comerica Bank-California and the holders of the Subordinated Notes.
4. Wire Transfer instructions for Sub Note Holders payout of $XX pursuant to Section 1.3(e) of the Stock Purchase Agreement.
5. Copies of the "canceled" Senior Subordinated Notes issued to the following individuals in the amounts indicated:

[List Omitted]

6. Guaranty of Galaxy International Corporation to each of the holders of the Subordinated Notes dated June _____, 2004.

VII. SECURITIES FILINGS OF GALAXY INTERNATIONAL CORPORATION AND GALAXY INTERNATIONAL CORP.

1. Form D—Notice of Sale of Securities Pursuant to Regulation D, Section 4(6) and or the Uniform Limited Offering Exemption filed by Galaxy International Corporation with the Securities and Exchange Commission and the California Commissioner of Corporations on June _____, 2004 in connection with the issuance of the Common Stock.

Fairness Opinions

- Goldman Sachs Fairness Opinion—Annex B to AT&T/DirecTV Proxy Statement/Prospectus
- Bank of America/Merrill Lynch Fairness Opinion—Annex C to AT&T/DirecTV Proxy Statement/Prospectus

Goldman Sachs Fairness Opinion

GOLDMAN SACHS

May 18, 2014

Board of Directors
DIRECTV
2230 E. Imperial Hwy.
El Segundo, CA 90245

Ladies and Gentlemen:

You have requested our opinion as to the fairness from a financial point of view to the holders (other than AT&T Inc. ("AT&T") and its affiliates) of the outstanding shares of common stock, par value $0.01 per share (the "Shares"), of DIRECTV (the "Company") of the Consideration (as defined below) to be paid to such holders pursuant to the Agreement and Plan of Merger, dated as of May 18, 2014 (the "Agreement"), by and among the Company, AT&T, and Steam Merger Sub LLC, a wholly owned subsidiary of AT&T ("Merger Sub"). Pursuant to the Agreement, the Company will be merged with and into Merger Sub and each outstanding Share (not owned by AT&T or the Company or subject to a demand for appraisal) will be converted into $28.50 in cash (the "Cash Consideration") and that number of shares (or fraction thereof) of common stock, par value $1.00 per share ("AT&T Common Stock"), of AT&T equal to (a) 1.724 if the Average Parent Stock Price (as defined in the Agreement) is greater than $38.577, (b) the quotient obtained by dividing $66.50 by the Average Parent Stock Price if the Average Parent Stock Price is greater than or equal to $34.903 but less than or equal to $38.577 or (c) 1.905 if the Average Parent Stock Price is less than 34.903 (the "Stock Consideration"; together with the Cash Consideration, the "Consideration").

Goldman, Sachs & Co. and its affiliates are engaged in advisory, underwriting and financing, principal investing, sales and trading, research, investment management and other financial and non-financial activities and services for various persons and entities. Goldman, Sachs & Co. and its affiliates and employees, and funds or other entities they manage or in which they invest or have other economic interests or with which they co-invest, may at any time purchase, sell, hold or vote long or short positions and investments in securities, derivatives, loans, commodities, currencies, credit default swaps and other financial instruments of the Company, AT&T, any of their respective affiliates and third parties, or any currency or commodity that may be involved in the transaction contemplated by the Agreement (the "Transaction"). We have acted as financial advisor of the Company in connection with, and have participated in certain of the negotiations leading to, the Transaction. We expect to receive fees for our services in connection with the Transaction, the principal portion of which is contingent upon consummation of the Transaction, and the Company has agreed to reimburse certain of our expenses arising, and indemnify us against certain liabilities that may arise, out of our engagement. We have provided certain financial advisory and/or underwriting services to the Company and/or its affiliates from time to time for which our Investment Banking Division has received, and may receive, compensation, including having acted as co-manager with respect to a public offering of the Company's 4.375% Senior Notes due September 2029 (aggregate principal amount $1,200,000,000) in September 2012; as joint bookrunner with respect to a public offering of the Company's 1.750% Senior Notes due January 2018 (aggregate principal amount $750,000,000) in January 2013; as co-manager with respect to a public offering of the Company's 5.200% Senior Notes due November 2033 (aggregate principal amount $562,000,000) in November 2013; as joint bookrunner with respect to a public offering of the Company's 4.450% Senior Notes due April 2024 (aggregate principal amount $1,250,000,000) in March 2014; and currently acting as dealer for the Company's commercial paper program. We also provided certain financial advisory and/or underwriting services to AT&T and/or its affiliates from time to time for which our Investment Banking Division has received, and may receive, compensation, including having acted as joint bookrunner with respect to a public offering of AT&T's 0.8% Global Notes, 1.4% Global Notes and 2.625% Global Notes due December 2015, December 2017 and December 2022, respectively (aggregate principal amount $4,000,000,000) in December 2012; as joint bookrunner with respect to a public offering of AT&T's 2.3% Global Notes, 3.9% Global Notes and Floating Rate Global Notes due March 2019, and March 2024 and March 2019 respectively (aggregate principal amount $2,500,000,000) in March 2014; and currently acting as dealer for AT&T's commercial paper program. We may also in the future provide financial advisory and/or underwriting services to the Company, AT&T and their respective affiliates for which our Investment Banking Division may receive compensation.

In connection with this opinion, we have reviewed, among other things, the Agreement; annual reports to stockholders and Annual Reports on Form 10-K of the Company and AT&T for the five fiscal years ended December 31, 2013; certain interim reports to stockholders and Quarterly Reports on Form 10-Q of the Company and AT&T; certain other communications from the Company and AT&T to their respective stockholders; certain publicity available research analyst reports for the Company and AT&T; a publicly available research analyst report for AT&T, as adjusted by the management of the Company, certain internal financial analyses and forecasts for the Company prepared by the management of the Company, in each case, as approved for our use by the Company (collectively, the "Forecasts"), and certain cost savings and operating synergies projected by the management of the Company to result from the Transaction, as approved for our use by the Company (the "Synergies"). We have also held discussions with members of the senior managements of the Company and AT&T regarding their assessment of the strategic rationale for, and the potential benefits of, the Transaction and the past and current business operations, financial condition and future prospects of AT&T and with members of the senior management of the Company regarding their assessment of the past and current business operations, financial condition and financial condition and future prospects of the Company; reviewed the reported price and trading activity for the Shares and shares of AT&T Common Stock; compared certain financial and stock market information for the Company and AT&T with similar information for certain other companies the securities of which are publicly traded; reviewed the financial terms of certain recent business combinations in the pay TV industry and in other industries; and performed such other studies and analyses, and considered such other factors, as we deemed appropriate.

For purposes of rendering this opinion, we have, with your consent, relied upon and assumed the accuracy and completeness of all of the financial, legal, regulatory, tax, accounting and other information provided to, discussed with or reviewed by, us, without assuming any responsibility for independent verification thereof. In that regard, we have assumed with your consent that the Forecasts, and the Synergies, have been reasonably prepared on a basis reflecting the best currently available estimates and judgments of the management of the Company. We have not made an independent evaluation or appraisal of the assets and liabilities (including and contingent, derivative or other off-balance-sheet assets and liabilities) of the Company or AT&T or any of their respective subsidiaries and we have not been furnished with any such evaluation or appraisal. We have assumed that all governmental, regulatory or other consents and approvals necessary for the consummation of the Transaction will be obtained without any adverse effect on the Company or AT&T or on the expected benefits of the Transaction in any way meaningful to our analysis. We have assumed that the Transaction will be consummated on the terms set forth in the Agreement, without the waiver or modification of any term or condition the effect of which would be in any way meaningful to our analysis.

Our opinion does not address the underlying business decision of the Company to engage in the Transaction, or the relative merits of the Transaction as compared to any strategic alternatives that may be available to the Company; nor does it address any legal, regulatory, tax or accounting matters. We were not requested to solicit, and did not solicit, interest from other parties with respect to an acquisition of, or other business combination with, the Company or any other alternative transaction. This opinion addresses only the fairness from a financial point of view to the holders (other than AT&T and its affiliates) of Shares, as of the date hereof, of the Consideration to be paid to such holders pursuant to the Agreement. We do not express any view on, and our opinion does not address, any other term or aspect of the Agreement or Transaction or any term or aspect of any other agreement or instrument contemplated by the Agreement or entered into or amended in connection with the Transaction, including, the fairness of the Transaction to, or any consideration received in connection therewith by, the holders of any other class of securities, creditors, or other constituencies of the Company; nor as to the fairness of the amount or nature of any compensation to be paid or payable to any of the officers, directors or employees of Company, or class of such persons, in connection with the Transaction, whether relative to the Consideration to be paid to the holders (other than AT&T and its affiliates) of Shares pursuant to the Agreement or otherwise. We are not expressing any opinion as to the prices at which shares of AT&T Common Stock will trade at any time or as to the impact of the Transaction on the solvency or viability of the Company or AT&T or the ability of the Company or AT&T to pay their respective obligations when they come due. Our opinion is necessarily based on economic, monetary, market and other conditions as in effect on, and the information made available to us as of, the date hereof and we assume no responsibility for updating, revising or reaffirming this opinion based on circumstances, developments or events occurring after the date hereof. Our advisory services and the opinion expressed herein are provided for the information and assistance of the Board of Directors of the Company in connection with its consideration of the Transaction and such opinion does not constitute a recommendation as to how any holder of Shares should vote with respect to such Transaction or any other matter. This opinion has been approved by a fairness committee of Goldman, Sachs & Co.

Based upon and subject to the foregoing, it is our opinion that, as of the date hereof, the Consideration to be paid to the holders (other than AT&T and its affiliates) of Shares pursuant to the Agreement is fair from a financial point of view to such holders.

Very truly yours,

/s/ Goldman, Sachs & Co.

(GOLDMAN, SACHS & CO.)

Bank of America/Merrill Lynch Fairness Opinion

BOFA/MERRILL LYNCH

Bank of America
Merrill Lynch

GLOBAL CORPORATE &
INVESTMENT BANKING

Merrill Lynch, Pierce, Fenner & Smith Incorporated

May 18, 2014

The Board of Directors
DirecTV
2260 East Imperial Highway
El Segundo, CA 90245

Members of the Board of Directors:

We understand that DirecTV ("DirecTV") proposes to enter into an Agreement and Plan of Merger, dated as of May 18, 2014 (the "Agreement"), among DirecTV, AT&T ("AT&T") and Steam Merger Sub LLC, a wholly owned subsidiary of AT&T ("Merger Sub"), pursuant to which, among other things, DirecTV will merge with and into Merger Sub (the "Merger") and each outstanding share of the common stock, par value $0.01 per share, of DirecTV ("DirecTV Common Stock"), other than shares of DirecTV Common Stock owned by (a) AT&T or DirecTV, not held on behalf of third parties, and (b) Dissenting Stockholders (as defined in the Agreement), will be converted into the right to receive (i) $28.50 in cash (the "Cash Consideration") and (ii) a number of shares (such number of shares, the "Stock Consideration" and, together with the Cash Consideration, the "Consideration") of the common stock, par value $1.00 per share, of AT&T ("AT&T Common Stock") equal to the Exchange Ratio (as determined below). The "Exchange Ratio" means the following (in each case rounded to three decimal places): (a) 1.724, if the Average Parent Stock Price (as defined below) is greater than $38.577; (b) an amount equal to the quotient obtained by dividing $66.50 by the Average Parent Stock Price, if the Average Parent Stock Price is greater than or equal to $34.903 but less than or equal to $38.577 or (c) 1.905, if the Average Parent Stock Price is an amount less than $34.903. "Average Parent Stock Price" means the average of the volume weighted averages of the trading prices of AT&T Common Stock on the New York Stock Exchange on each of the thirty (30) consecutive trading days ending on (and including) the trading day that is three (3) trading days prior to the date of the effective time of the Merger. The terms and conditions of the Merger are more fully set forth in the Agreement.

You have requested our opinion as to the fairness, from a financial point of view, to the holders of DirecTV Common Stock of the Consideration to be received by such holders in the Merger.

In connection with this opinion, we have, among other things:

1. reviewed certain publicly available business and financial information relating to DirecTV and AT&T;
2. reviewed certain internal financial and operating information with respect to the business, operations and prospects of DirecTV furnished to or discussed with us by the management of DirecTV, including certain financial forecasts relating to DirecTV prepared by the management of DirecTV (such forecasts, the "DirecTV Forecasts");
3. reviewed certain publicly available financial forecasts relating to AT&T (the "AT&T Public Forecasts") and discussed with the management of DirecTV its assessments as to the future financial results reflected in the AT&T Public Forecasts;
4. reviewed certain estimates as to the amount and timing of cost savings and revenue enhancements (collectively, the "Synergies") anticipated by the management of DirecTV to result from the Merger;
5. discussed the past and current business, operations, financial condition and prospects of DirecTV with members of senior management of DirecTV to result from the Merger;
6. reviewed the potential pro forma financial impact of the Merger on the future financial performance of AT&T, including the potential effect on AT&T's estimated earnings per share, free cash flow, balance sheet, and dividend coverage ratios;
7. reviewed the trading histories for DirecTV Common Stock and AT&T Common Stock and a comparison of such trading histories with each other and with the trading histories of other companies we deemed relevant;
8. compared certain financial and stock market information of DirecTV and AT&T with similar information of other companies we deemed relevant;
9. compared certain financial terms of the Merger to financial terms, to the extent publicly available, of other transactions we deemed relevant;
10. reviewed the relative financial contributions of DirecTV and AT&T to the future financial performance of the combined company on a pro forma basis;
11. reviewed the Agreement; and
12. performed such other analyses and studies and considered such other information and factors as we deemed appropriate.

In arriving at our opinion, we have assumed and relied upon, without independent verification, the accuracy and completeness of the financial and other information and data publicly available or provided to or otherwise reviewed by or discussed with us and have relied upon the assurances of the management of DirecTV that they are not aware of any facts or circumstances that would make such information or data inaccurate or misleading in any material respect. With respect to the DirecTV Forecasts and the Synergies, we have been advised by DirecTV, and have assumed, that they have been reasonably prepared on bases reflecting the best currently available estimates and good faith judgments of the management of DirecTV as to the future financial performance of DirecTV and other matters covered thereby. As you are aware, although we requested financial forecasts relating to AT&T prepared by the management of AT&T, we have not been provided with, and we did not have access to, any such financial forecasts prepared by the management of AT&T. Accordingly, we have been advised by AT&T and have assumed, with the consent of DirecTV, that the AT&T Public Forecasts are a reasonable basis upon which to evaluate the future financial performance of AT&T and, based on the assessments of the management of DirecTV as to the likelihood of AT&T achieving the future financial results reflected in the AT&T Public Forecasts, we have, at the direction of DirecTV, used the AT&T Public Forecasts in performing our analyses. Further, in reviewing the potential pro forma financial impact of the Merger on the future financial performance of AT&T, we have relied on the purchase accounting assumptions given to us by DirecTV. We have not made or been provided with any independent evaluation or appraisal of the assets or liabilities (contingent or otherwise) of DirecTV or AT&T, nor have we made any physical inspection of the properties or assets of DirecTV or AT&T. We have not evaluated the solvency or fair value of DirecTV or AT&T under any state, federal or other laws relating to bankruptcy, insolvency or similar matters. We have assumed, at the direction of DirecTV, that the Merger will be consummated in accordance with its terms, without waiver, modification or amendment of any material term, condition or agreement and that, in the course of obtaining the necessary governmental, regulatory and other approvals, consents, releases and waivers for the Merger, no delay, limitation, restriction or condition, including any divestiture requirements or amendments or modifications, will be imposed that would have an adverse effect on DirecTV, AT&T or the contemplated benefits of the Merger.

We express no view or opinion as to any terms or other aspects of the Merger (other than the Consideration to the extent expressly specified herein), including, without limitation, the form or structure of the Merger. Our opinion is limited to the fairness, from a financial point of view, of the Consideration to be received by holders of DirecTV Common Stock and no opinion or view is expressed with respect to any consideration received in connection with the Merger by the holders of any class of securities, creditors or other constituencies of any party. In addition, no opinion or view is expressed with respect to the fairness (financial or otherwise) of the amount, nature or any other aspect of any compensation to any of the officers, directors or employees of any party to the Merger, or class of such persons, relative to the Consideration. Furthermore, no opinion or view is expressed as to the relative merits of the Merger in comparison to other strategies or transactions that might be available to DirecTV or in which DirecTV might engage or as to the underlying business decision of DirecTV to proceed with or effect the Merger. We are not expressing any opinion as to what the value of AT&T Common Stock actually will be when issued or the prices at which DirecTV Common Stock or AT&T Common Stock will trade at any time, including following announcement or consummation of the Merger. In addition, we express no opinion or recommendation as to how any stockholder should vote or act in connection with the Merger or any related matter.

We have acted as financial advisor to DirecTV in connection with the Merger and will receive a fee for our services, a portion of which is payable upon the execution of the Agreement and a significant portion of which is contingent upon consummation of the Merger. In addition, DirecTV has agreed to reimburse certain of our expenses and indemnify us against certain liabilities arising out of our engagement.

We and our affiliates comprise a full service securities firm and commercial bank engaged in securities, commodities and derivatives trading, foreign exchange and other brokerage activities, and principal investing as well as providing investment, corporate and private banking, asset and investment management, financing and financial advisory services and other commercial services and products to a wide range of companies, governments and individuals. In the ordinary course of our businesses, we and our affiliates may invest on a principal basis or on behalf of customers or manage funds that invest, make or hold long or short positions, finance positions or trade or otherwise effect transactions in equity, debt or other securities or financial instruments (including derivatives, bank loans or other obligations) of DirecTV, AT&T and certain of their respective affiliates.

We and our affiliates in the past have provided, currently are providing, and in the future may provide, investment banking, commercial banking and other financial services to DirecTV and certain of its affiliates and have received or in the future may receive compensation for the rendering of these services, including (i) having acted as a manager or book runner on various debt offerings of DirecTV, (ii) having acted or acting as documentation agent, arranger, and book runner for, and a lender under, certain credit facilities and lines of credit of DirecTV and certain of its affiliates, (iii) having provided or providing certain derivatives and foreign exchange trading services to DirecTV and (iv) having provided or providing certain treasury and management services and products to DirecTV.

In addition, we and our affiliates in the past have provided, currently are providing, and in the future may provide, investment banking, commercial banking and other financial services to AT&T and certain of its affiliates and have received or in the future may receive compensation for the rendering of these services, including (i) having acted as a book runner on various debt offerings of AT&T, (ii) having acted as financial advisor to AT&T in connection with a divestiture transaction, (iii) having acted as a dealer manager for an exchange offer by AT&T, (iv) having acted or acting as documentation agent, arranger, and book runner for, and a lender under, certain credit facilities, lines of credit and leasing facilities of AT&T and certain of its affiliates, (v) having provided or providing certain derivatives and foreign exchange trading services to AT&T and (vi) having provided or providing certain treasure and management services and products to AT&T.

It is understood that this letter is for the benefit and use of the Board of Directors of DirecTV (in its capacity as such) in connection with and for purposes of its evaluation of the Merger.

Our opinion is necessarily based on financial, economic, monetary, market and other conditions and circumstances as in effect on, and the information made available to us as of, the date hereof. It should be understood that subsequent developments may affect this opinion, and we do not have any obligation to update, revise, or reaffirm this opinion. The issuance of this opinion was approved by our Americas Fairness Opinion Review Committee.

Based upon and subject to the foregoing, including the various assumptions and limitations set forth herein, we are of the opinion on the date hereof that the Consideration to be received in the Merger by Holders of DirecTV Common Stock is fair, from a financial point of view, to such holders.

Very truly yours,
/s/ Merrill Lynch, Pierce, Fenner & Smith Incorporated

MERRILL LYNCH PIERCE FENNER & SMITH INCORPORATED

Table of Cases

Principal cases are indicated by italics.

Index